U.S. Ast. Exp. Chili. Plate I.

P. S. Duval & Co's Steam lith. Press, Phil^a.

SANTA LUCIA.

33d Congress, 1st Session. } HOUSE OF REPRESENTATIVES. { Ex. Doc. No. 121.

THE

U. S. NAVAL ASTRONOMICAL EXPEDITION

TO

THE SOUTHERN HEMISPHERE,

DURING

THE YEARS 1849–'50–'51–'52.

Lieut. J. M. GILLISS, Superintendent.

Lieut. Archibald MacRae,
Acting Master S. L. Phelps,
Captain's Clerk E. R. Smith, } *Assistants.*

VOLUME I.

CHILE:

ITS GEOGRAPHY, CLIMATE, EARTHQUAKES, GOVERNMENT, SOCIAL CONDITION, MINERAL AND AGRICULTURAL RESOURCES, COMMERCE, &c., &c.

BY LIEUT. J. M. GILLISS, A. M.,

MEMBER OF THE AMERICAN PHILOSOPHICAL SOCIETY, THE ACADEMIES FOR PROMOTION OF THE NATURAL SCIENCES AT PHILADELPHIA, LEIPSIG, DANZIG, AND MARBURG (IN HESSE); HONORARY MEMBER OF THE FACULTY OF MATHEMATICAL AND PHYSICAL SCIENCES OF THE UNIVERSITY OF CHILE AND THE HISTORICAL SOCIETY OF MARYLAND; CORRESPONDING MEMBER OF THE ROYAL GEOGRAPHICAL SOCIETY, BERLIN, ASTRONOMICAL SOCIETY, LEIPSIG, HISTORICAL SOCIETY, NEW YORK, &C., &C., &C.

WASHINGTON:
A. O. P. NICHOLSON, PRINTER.
MDCCCLV.

IN THE SENATE OF THE UNITED STATES, *August* 2, 1854.

Resolved, That there be printed and bound five thousand extra copies of the Report and one thousand extra copies of the Observations of the United States Naval Astronomical Expedition to Chile: two hundred and fifty copies of the Report and one hundred copies of the Observations for the use of the Secretary of the Navy; one hundred copies of each for the Superintendent of the Expedition; and the remainder for the use of the Senate.

Attest:

ASBURY DICKINS, *Secretary*.

ASTRONOMICAL EXPEDITION.

MESSAGE

FROM

THE PRESIDENT OF THE UNITED STATES,

TRANSMITTING

The First Part of the Results of the United States Naval Astronomical Expedition.

JULY 13, 1854.—Laid upon the table, and ordered to be printed.

JULY 25, 1854.—*Ordered,* That 6,000 copies of the Report and 2,000 copies of the Observations be printed; 500 copies of each for the use of the Secretary of the Navy, and 250 copies of each for the Superintendent of the Expedition.

To the House of Representatives:

I transmit herewith the enclosed communication from the Secretary of the Navy, respecting the Observations of Lieutenant James M. Gilliss, of the United States Navy, and the accompanying documents.

FRANKLIN PIERCE.

WASHINGTON, *July* 12, 1854.

NAVY DEPARTMENT, *July* 10, 1854.

SIR: Under a clause of the act making appropriations for the naval service, approved August 3, 1848, directing the Secretary of the Navy "to expend five thousand dollars, or so much thereof as may be necessary, in causing the observations to be made which have been recently recommended to him by the American Philosophical Society and the Academy of Arts and Sciences," I have the honor to state that Lieutenant James M. Gilliss, of the Navy, was appointed to make the observations authorized; for which purpose he proceeded to Santiago, in Chile, accompanied by assistants, and prepared with the necessary instruments and facilities to accomplish the wishes of Congress. In furtherance of this object, Lieutenant Gilliss has sent to the Department the first part of the results of his work, accompanied by a letter addressed to the Secretary of the Navy, under date of July 8, 1854, which I respectfully place before you for such further disposition as to you may seem proper.

With the highest respect, I have the honor to be, sir, your obedient servant,

J. C. DOBBIN.

To the PRESIDENT.

U. S. N. Astronomical Expedition,
Washington, *July* 8, 1854.

Sir: I have the honor to lay before you the first part of the results of the U. S. N. Astronomical Expedition directed by Congress, August 3, 1848. The other volumes will be presented as rapidly as the computations can be completed.

Should Congress be pleased to direct the printing of the Report and Observations, as the latter can only be arranged for quarto pages, I would most respectfully suggest the propriety of printing the volumes of a uniform size. To secure faithful copies of the maps and illustrations, it is particularly desirable that the Department have supervisory control over their execution; and I beg leave to suggest that such recommendation be made to the honorable House of Representatives, where the Expedition was originated.

Respectfully submitted.

J. M. GILLISS, *Superintendent.*

Hon. J. C. Dobbin,
Secretary of the Navy.

PREFATORY.

The information embraced in the following pages was obtained in occasional intervals of leisure during nearly three years occupied in prosecuting the observations for which Congress more immediately instructed the honorable Secretary of the Navy to send an Astronomical Expedition to the southern hemisphere. Charged by the Department with the conduct of that honorable enterprise, I was also directed to furnish any other information of a useful character which there might be opportunities to obtain.

At that period the young republic of Chile was daily becoming of greater consequence to our people. Those who had encountered the long and dreary voyage round Cape Horn passed on their way north, or to the islands of the Pacific, with exalted ideas of its fertility and wealth, and pleasant remembrances of Talcahuano or Valparaiso; the thousands who left the eastern shores of the United States for the auriferous region of the West by more expeditious routes, looked to it for the larger supplies of bread and fruits; the merchant saw in it a rapidly growing market for his ship-loads of domestic manufactures; and the statesman greeted cordially the nation every day giving stronger proofs of its ability for self-government.

Within the preceding quarter of a century Chile has advanced far more rapidly than any other nation of Spanish America in intelligence, good order, agricultural and mineral wealth, and commercial importance. But all, or very nearly all, the volumes of information we possess of it were written before the era of progress, and tell what Chile was, not what it *is*. Nor do they enlighten us on many subjects deeply interesting to the cultivated reader. Indeed, notwithstanding the munificent and most laudable efforts of the government of that country to the present time, even its best informed citizens have few reliable data concerning the geography or statistics of any other department or province than the one in which they reside. At the cost of the national treasury, both its political and natural histories have been elaborately written, and the latter superbly illustrated;* and in course of time, an account of its geography, ethnography, and statistics will probably follow. Until then, the present volume may supply some deficiencies. But I beg it may be remembered that no pretensions are made to elegance of literary composition; and if the most trustworthy information which other duties permitted me to obtain is detailed comprehensibly, it is all that it was expected to accomplish.

J. M. G.

U. S. N. Astronomical Expedition,
Washington, July, 1854.

* Historia Fisica y Politica de Chile segun documentos adquiridos en esta republica. Publicada bajo los auspicios del Supremo Gobierno por Claudio Gay.

CONTENTS.

SECTION I.—DESCRIPTIVE.

CHAPTER I.

DESCRIPTIVE GEOGRAPHY.

CHAPTER II.

POLITICAL DIVISIONS AND DISTRIBUTION OF INDUSTRIAL RESOURCES.

CHAPTER III.

THE CLIMATE.

CHAPTER IV.

EARTHQUAKES.

CHAPTER V.

THE GOVERNMENT.

CHAPTER VI.

SOCIETY.

CHAPTER VII.

THE CHURCH AND ITS CEREMONIES.

CHAPTER VIII.

SANTIAGO.

CHAPTER IX.

VALPARAISO.

CHAPTER X.

A VISIT TO THE PROVINCES OF ATACAMA AND COQUIMBO.

CHAPTER XI.

MINERAL SPRINGS.

CHAPTER XII.

THE PRESIDENTIAL ELECTION IN 1851.

CHAPTER XIII.

EVENTS SUCCEEDING THE ELECTION.

CHAPTER XIV.

A VISIT TO THE COUNTRY.

CHAPTER XV.

A VISIT TO THE SOUTHWARD.

SECTION II.—NARRATIVE.

CHAPTER I.

NEW YORK TO PANAMA.

CHAPTER II.

THE CITY OF PANAMA.

CHAPTER III.

FROM PANAMA TO LIMA.

CHAPTER IV.

LIMA.

CHAPTER V.

FROM LIMA TO VALPARAISO.

CHAPTER VI.

FIRST EXPERIENCES IN CHILE.

CHAPTER VII.

EXPERIENCES CONTINUED.

CHAPTER VIII.

A VISIT TO THE CACHAPUAL.

CHAPTER IX.

PUNISHMENT OF CRIMINALS.

CHAPTER X.

THE NATIONAL HOLIDAYS.

CHAPTER XI.

POLITICAL TROUBLES.

CHAPTER XII.

A BRIEF ACCOUNT OF OUR WORK.

APPENDIX A.

OBSERVATIONS OF EARTHQUAKES, &c.

APPENDIX B.

METEOROLOGICAL OBSERVATIONS IN ATACAMA.

APPENDIX C.

METEOROLOGICAL OBSERVATIONS BETWEEN THE UNITED STATES AND CHILE.

CORRIGENDA.

Page 17, line 18, for las Incas, read los Incas.
" 23, " 24, " annales, " anales.
" 30, bottom line, inlets, " islets.
" 92, line 8, for ten, " six (part of the edition.)
" 254, " 33, word "on" omitted.
" 261, " 30, " estimaing, read estimating.
" 296, " 25, " southward, " northward.
" 307, " 45, " dele "previously."
" 350, " 13, " on, read or.
" 364, heading of chapter, for PERRALES, read PERALES.
" 459, " 48, "a" left out in "that."
" 460, bottom line, "t" left out in first word.

LIST OF ILLUSTRATIONS.

OVERSIZE FOLDOUT

(LARGER THAN 11X17)

UNABLE TO SCAN

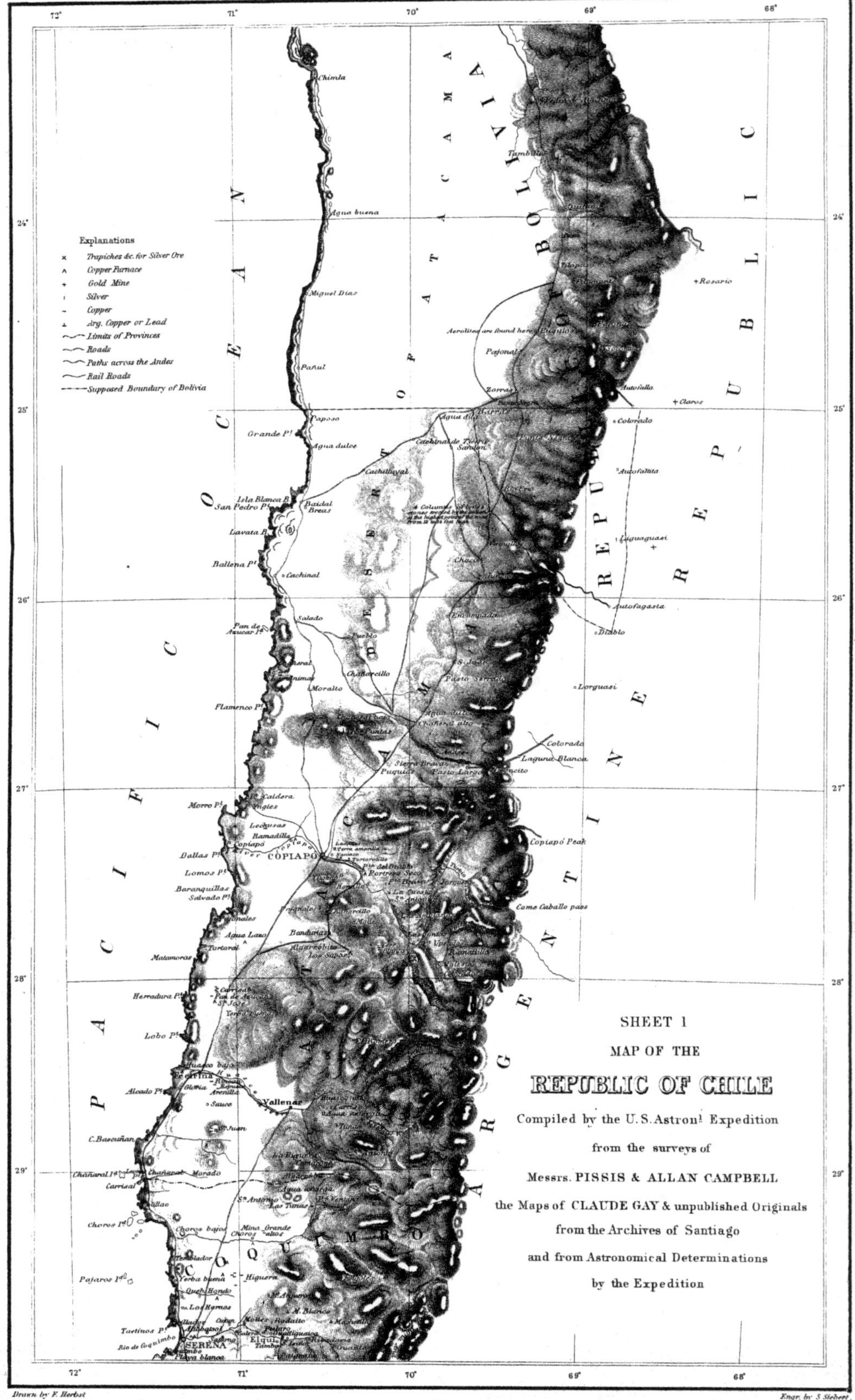

SHEET 1
MAP OF THE
REPUBLIC OF CHILE
Compiled by the U.S. Astron[l] Expedition
from the surveys of
Messrs. PISSIS & ALLAN CAMPBELL
the Maps of CLAUDE GAY & unpublished Originals
from the Archives of Santiago
and from Astronomical Determinations
by the Expedition
Explanations
Trapiches &c. for Silver Ore
Copper Furnace
Gold Mine
Silver
Copper
Arg. Copper or Lead
Limits of Provinces
Roads
Paths across the Andes
Rail Roads
Supposed Boundary of Bolivia
PACIFIC OCEAN
DESERT OF ATACAMA
REPUBLIC OF BOLIVIA
ARGENTINE REPUBLIC
COQUIMBO
COPIAPO
Vallenar
SERENA
Copiapó Peak
Come Caballo pass
Drawn by F. Herbst
Engr. by S. Siebert

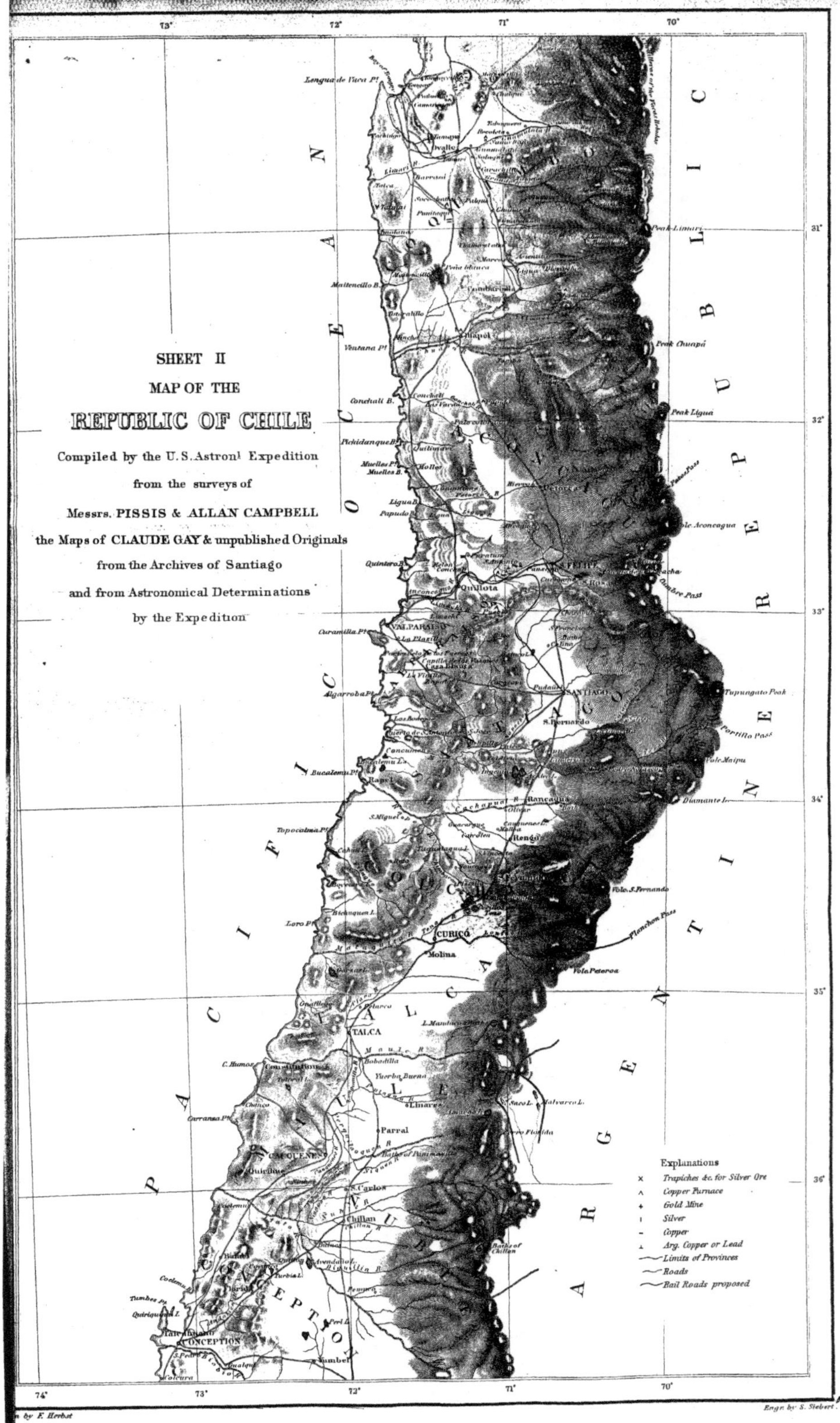
SHEET II
MAP OF THE
REPUBLIC OF CHILE
Compiled by the U.S. Astron[l] Expedition
from the surveys of
Messrs. PISSIS & ALLAN CAMPBELL
the Maps of CLAUDE GAY & unpublished Originals
from the Archives of Santiago
and from Astronomical Determinations
by the Expedition
PACIFIC OCEAN
ARGENTINE REPUBLIC
73°
72°
71°
70°
74°
31°
32°
33°
34°
35°
36°
Lengua de Vaca Pt.
Ovalle
Peak Limari
Maitencillo B.
Illapel
Peak Chuapá
Ventana Pt.
Conchali B.
Peak Ligua
Pichidanque B.
Muelles Pt.
Muelles B.
Ligua B.
Papudo B.
Quintero B.
Quillota
Cumbre Pass
Curaumilla Pt.
VALPARAISO
Algarroba Pt.
SANTIAGO
S. Bernardo
Tupungato Peak
Portillo Pass
Volc. Maipu
Bucalemu Pt.
Diamante L.
Rancagua
Topocalma Pt.
Rengo
Volc. S. Fernando
Loro Pt.
Planchon Pass
CURICÓ
Molina
Volc. Peteroa
TALCA
C. Humos
Constitucion
Yerba Buena
Linares
Curranza Pt.
Parral
Baths of Chillan
CAUQUENES
S. Carlos
Chillan
Tumbes Pt.
CONCEPTION
Yumbel
Explanations
× Trapiches &c. for Silver Ore
^ Copper Furnace
+ Gold Mine
ı Silver
- Copper
⊥ Arg. Copper or Lead
Limits of Provinces
Roads
Rail Roads proposed
n by F. Herbst
Engr. by S. Siebert.

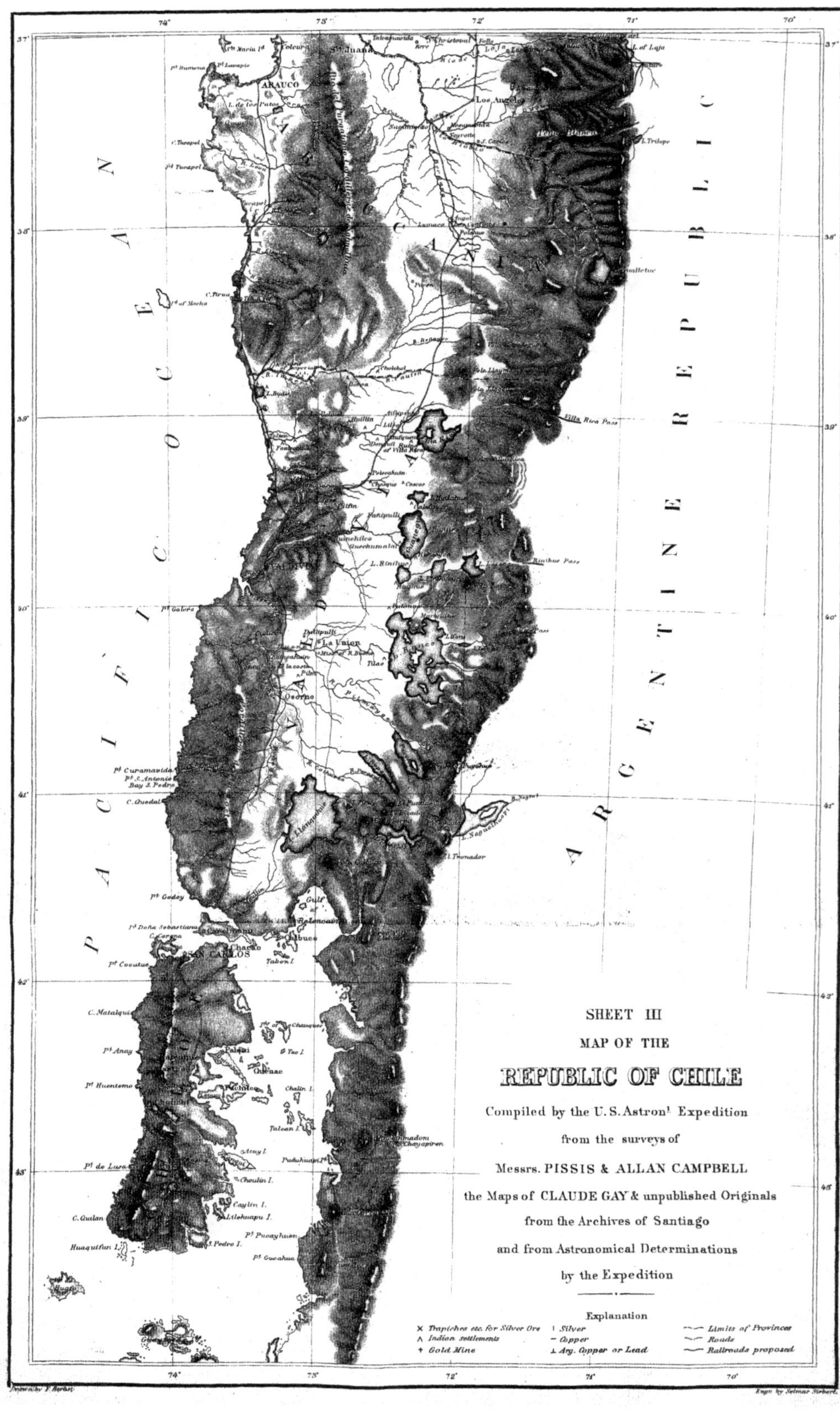

SHEET III
MAP OF THE
REPUBLIC OF CHILE
Compiled by the U.S. Astron[l] Expedition
from the surveys of
Messrs. PISSIS & ALLAN CAMPBELL
the Maps of CLAUDE GAY & unpublished Originals
from the Archives of Santiago
and from Astronomical Determinations
by the Expedition
Explanation
× Trapiches etc. for Silver Ore
∧ Indian settlements
+ Gold Mine
| Silver
– Copper
⊥ Arg. Copper or Lead
Limits of Provinces
Roads
Railroads proposed
PACIFIC OCEAN
ARGENTINE REPUBLIC
ARAUCO
Los Angeles
Osorno
La Union
SAN CARLOS
Villa Rica Pass
Riñihue Pass
Gulf of Relencavi
74°
73°
72°
71°
70°
37°
38°
39°
40°
41°
42°
43°
Engd. by Selmar Siebert

CHILE.

CHAPTER I.

DESCRIPTIVE GEOGRAPHY.

INVASION OF CHILE; ITS LIMITS; ORIGIN OF THE NAME.—MOUNTAINS; VOLCANOES: ANTUCO AND ITS NEW CRATER; LLAYMA; LLOGOL.—MOUNTAIN PASSES: THE CUMBRE; THE PORTILLO; COME-CAVALLO; LAGUNA AND DOÑA ANA; LA DEHESA; LOS PATOS; EL PLANCHON; ANTUCO.—TABLE SHOWING THE HEIGHTS, LATITUDES, AND LONGITUDES OF THE PRINCIPAL SUMMITS.—LAKES; LLANQUIHUE; RUPANCO; PUYCHUE; RÁNCO; HUITAHUE; GUANEGUE; RINIHUE; PIREHUECO; LAJARA; VILLARICA; GUALLETUE; LAJA; AMARGO; TOTORAL; MAULE; MONDACA; LAS GARZAS; TAGUATAGUA; CAUQUENES; ACULEO; INCA; THE LAKES OF COQUIMBO AND ATACAMA.—RIVERS: ORIGIN OF NEARLY ALL THE CHILE STREAMS: THE BUENO; VALDIVIA, OR CALLE-CALLE; TOLTEN; IMPERIAL; BIOBIO; ITATA; ÑUBLE; MAULE; MATAQUITO; RAPEL; MAYPU; ACONCAGUA; CHUAPA; LIMARI; COQUIMBO; HUASCO; COPIAPO.—BAYS AND HARBORS: VALPARAISO; TALCAHUANO; COQUIMBO; HERRADURA; HUASCO; COPIAPO AND CALDERA; PORT YNGLES; CONSTITUCION; VALDIVIA; ANCUD; PORT FAMINE.—ISLANDS: CHILÓE AND THE SURROUNDING ISLANDS; MOCHA; SANTA MARIA; QUIRIQUINA; JUAN FERNANDEZ; SANTA CLARA; MAS-AFUERA; PAJAROS.

With an arid desert on its northern frontier—successive ranges of mountains, whose summits are covered by everlasting snows, on the east; Cape Horn, with its appalling storms of ice and sleet, to the south; and the vast unexplored Pacific ocean washing its western shore,—the holy fathers, who accompanied Pedro de Valdivia to the Chilean territory in 1540, may well have regarded themselves at "*la fin de la Christiandad.*" No terrestrial obstacles, however, were of sufficient magnitude to overcome the thirst for gold and conquest which enticed so many sons of Spain from their homes during the sixteenth century; and the desert of Atacama, with scarcely a drop of water or a particle of sustenance for man or beast in many hundred miles, was traversed by a handful of Spaniards, with a few Peruvian allies, confident in their success against the host which had virtually expelled Almagro but a year or two previously. Valdivia, meeting with little resistance from the natives in the northern portion of the country, only halted in his march to leave a dozen men, with a few allies, in the valley of Coquimbo river; and there, in the vicinity of Serena, was established the first colony of his new possession. The main body, numbering one hundred and forty of his own countrymen and the Peruvians, pushed on toward the plain in which lies the present city of Santiago; neither the ornaments of the natives about Copiapó, nor Coquimbo, being sufficiently rich to gratify their avarice.

In the body of the commission conferred by Valdivia on Pasteñe, in 1544, the territory of *Nueva Estremadura*, as the country was then called, was only recognised to consist of the "valley of Posicion, which, in the Indian tongue, is called Copayapo; the valley of Coquimbo, Chile, and Mapocho; and provinces of Promaocaes, Rabeo, and Quiriquino, with the island of Quiriquina, now ruled by the chief Leochengo,"—that is to say, from the desert of Atacama to the parallel of Concepcion. Indeed, even a part of this territory was still in possession of unsubdued Indians. During the preceding four years, his sway over the natives of the northern and central provinces had been acknowledged. To the south dwelt the Promaucanos and Araucanos, over whom neither the Inca Yupanqui nor Almagro had been able to obtain decided advantage by attacks on the land side; and the tenor of his orders to Pasteñe renders it certain that his conduct was instigated by military tact and necessity, as well as "for the better service of his Majesty, whose subjects will be gratified with knowledge that there are lands to repay their labors, of which I have taken possession." He then goes on directing him to proceed from the port of Valparaiso to the Straits of Magellan, making examination of the coast and ports; to land with armed men, and take possession whenever he may consider it expedient; to bring back with him a cargo of provisions and live stock; and to render, at his return, an accurate account of his doings.

After sailing to the southward thirteen days, finding himself beyond 41° south latitude, Pasteñe bore up for the coast, and landed at a port which he baptized "San Pedro," as well in compliment to the governor as to the name of the ship that bore them. This was to the northward of Chilóe, and would coincide nearly with Puerto Estaguillas of the maps, though M. Gay has actually marked on his map of the province of Valdivia, published under the auspices of the Chilean government, a small creek and indentation of the coast, "*Ensenada y rio de San Pedro.*" A subsequent attempt was made to penetrate southward, as well by land as by sea, and the parties did succeed in seeing one of the islands composing the Chonos archipelago; but the claim of Chile to the territory as far as Magellan is based on the instructions to Pasteñe. As the Portuguese were the only nation to dispute the right—and they suffered their title to be lost by non-occupation—a penal colony was established by the republic within the straits, and the jurisdiction of Chile has thus been perfected. Apparently, without regard to the varying distance of the Andes—a natural boundary known to exist at the time of the invasion—the eastern limits of Chile were fixed at one hundred leagues from the coast. But the spirit which had instigated the foray from Peru was not less restless in the breasts of Pizarro's lieutenants, than when they braved the privations of Atacama; and though constantly harassed by attacks from the most warlike race they had ever encountered in America, yet, in the twenty years that followed, the Andes had been repeatedly traversed by small armed bands, and all the country, as far east as the sixty-third meridian from Greenwich, had been formally added to Valdivia's government. True, there were controversies and contests, on territory far within this limit, between subordinates of President Gasca, who had succeeded the Pizarros, and Francisco de Villagra, who was under the authority of Valdivia; but before the close of 1560, the provinces from Tucuman to Cuyo, inclusive, and west of the Rio Dulce, had acknowledged immediate allegiance to the last. The last added were the first lopped off from the new confederation. Almost incessant wars with the Araucanos during the next two centuries permitted few succors to be sent to colonies offering so little in recompense as did those to the eastward of the Andes; and so completely do they appear to have been lost sight of, that even the epochs at which they severally separated are not noted by the historian of Chile.* Mendoza was last. Its people having expressed a preference for the Argentine republic about the time that Chile accomplished its independence of the mother country, no obstacle was interposed; and the eastern boundary, which until then was at the foot of the Andes, on the Argentine side, was withdrawn to the crests of the highest range. Long before this, however, the name Chile—which, at the time of Valdivia, belonged properly but to the basin in which lies Santiago—had been applied to the entire territory. The derivation of the name is in dispute. Some assert that it was given by the Peruvians, in whose language *Tchi-li* signifies "snow;" whilst others believe that the aboriginal tribes so called it because of the constantly-repeated cry, resembling *Chi-li*, uttered by a species of thrush, the Trille (*Agelaius thilius*), though the former derivation seems most probable.

Thus, when the republic took its place among the nations of the earth, Chile consisted but of

* Sir Woodbine Parish says, that San Luis, San Juan, and Mendoza were added to the vice-royalty of Buenos Ayres in 1776.

the narrow strip of land lying between the highest peaks of the Andes and the Pacific, and the twenty-fourth and fifty-sixth degrees of south latitude. Its length, from north to south, is, therefore, 1,900 geographical miles, though the coast line is considerably greater, owing to its numerous indentations. As the ocean approaches and recedes from the mountains unequally at various parts of its length, the breadth is by no means uniform. In latitude 24°, the eastern boundary line is only eighty miles from the Pacific; in 34°, it is ninety-seven miles; in 44°, about one hundred and thirty miles to the outer line of Chilóe; and near 56°, it terminates in Cape Horn. These distances are by no means given as absolute measures, except in the parallel of 34°, but as the nearest approximations to truth from all trustworthy data now attainable. Assuming seventy-seven miles as a mean breadth for the whole, it embraces 146,300 square miles of territory—not half that (378,000) assigned by Abbé Molina, although he made the 45° its southern boundary. Even of this there is only a small portion cultivable. The great Andine chain, which stretches almost continuously from one frozen ocean to the other, probably attains its maximum elevation in Chile; and, with branches spreading in every direction along its line for more than a thousand miles, to the skirts of the ocean itself, it occupies quite two thirds of the republic.

North of the thirty-third parallel, the entire space from the Argentine boundary to the Pacific is occupied by mountainous ranges that lie in all imaginable directions. These have but narrow intermediate valleys or basins between them rarely traversed by a single rivulet. The longest, though at the same time the narrowest valleys, and which are scarcely more than ravines, are those through which flow the melted snow-waters. These streams, coming from great elevations, bring with them masses of stones and sand, to be distributed along uneven beds; and it is only where they approximate to the level of the ocean, and the action of the tides has assisted in forming comparatively flat spaces a mile or two in width, that subsequent geological changes have rendered the valleys arable. In all this region the productions of the soil do not supply the necessities of one half of its limited population.

Beginning in the extreme north, the principal chain of the Andes rises higher and higher to latitude 35°, from whence southward the declension of its prominent points is not less uniform. In Central Chile, it is composed of two lofty and several lower ranges of mountains, enclosing lakes whose frigid waters teem with animal life, in the midst of longitudinal valleys often of exquisite beauty and fertility; black gorges and chasms, with roaring torrents, beside which the nervous stand tremblingly; oases, with trickling rivulets, to charm the lover of sylvan beauty; deserts, on which, for many continuous leagues, nature has never vouchsafed a leaf of verdure; and black and broken masses of rock towering to mid-heaven, on which the snow has rested since the convulsion that raised them above the line of perpetual congelation. The absence of forest trees; the brilliancy of the snow-mantle, rendered more remarkable by blackened, radiant lines that tempests denude on the giant's shoulders; and the extraordinary sharpness of every outline under this wonderful atmosphere,—are the characteristics which most fix the attention.

North and south of this district the number of ranges vary, there being no less than five near the parallel of Talca. From their bases, in the great Chilean valley, to the pampas of Buenos Ayres, the distance is about one hundred and twenty miles. Their general direction coincides with a meridian of longitude; though of the minor lines, some have N.W., and others N.N.E. inclinations; whilst lateral spurs occupy nearly every point of the compass.

Aconcagua and Tupungato, the culminating points in all the known Andine chain, unless Parinacota and Sahama, in Peru, rival them, lie in a line nearly N.N.W. and S.S.E. from each other, the latter being to the southward. From Aconcagua northward the main chain continues in the same general direction, throwing off an infinity of lines towards the coast—one unbroken range extending westward, and terminating on the sea just beyond the right bank of the river Quillota. Ten miles north of Tupungato originates the Dehesa range, a broad and elevated chain extending in a northwest line as far as the intersection of the meridian of Santiago with the 33° of latitude. Thence, bending to the south, it is divided into two nearly parallel chains, the most easterly of which traverses the republic in a constantly descending line, and terminates on the Pacific, opposite the north end of the island of Chilóe. This, known as the *central* chain, is only interrupted where broken through by rivers. The other branch, parting from it at Cerro de Chapa, in latitude 33° 05′, longitude 70° 56′ W., first has a direction W.S.W.; then, throwing off spurs into the province of Valparaiso, proceeds irregularly in a south course; and is lost as a distinct chain not far from the mouth of the Maule. This is the *coast* range proper, though the central range is very often called *la Cordillera de la costa* also. The greatest elevations of the coast range are in the province of Santiago, yet it rarely attains more than half the height of the loftier portion of the central chain. Besides these continuous ranges, there are multitudes of isolated hills through the length of the valley enclosed between the Andes and central chain, as well as on river margins and terraces near the coast. Among the latter, none is so well known as the Campana de Quillota, visible from the bay of Valparaiso. The great diversity in the forms of these eminences, their geognosy and botany, contribute much to diversify and make interesting the scenery of Chile.

Very little reliable information has ever been obtained of the cordilleras either north or south of the central provinces. Bleak, precipitous, and barren sides deter all other natives than professional mine-hunters from encountering the almost unendurable privations inevitably attending their exploration, and these men have intelligence only of metallic veins. The few scientific individuals who have taken a day or two from other occupations whilst in this out-of-the-way quarter of the globe, have only traversed the beaten passes of the Portillo and Cumbre, not unfrequently deducing general theories from knowledge of individual localities. In the course of a trigonometrical survey for the government, Señor Pissis has explored from latitude 32° 20′ to latitude 34°, as far east as the culminating ridge, and he has kindly furnished me with a small copy of his map. Except of the several passes into the Argentine territory, and a few places of noted interest visited by Professor Domeyko, very little is known beyond those parallels. There will be other occasions to refer to the journeys of the latter gentleman; here, I need only allude to one other fact relating to the mountains.

On all the maps hitherto published, there will be found distributed along the Andes of Chile a line of volcanoes, which the geographical student naturally infers are in constant activity, or that, like Ætna and Vesuvius, during their intervals of comparative repose, smoke is seen to issue from them. Two of these so-called volcanoes—Aconcagua and Maypu—are in sight from the vicinity of Santiago, and neither of them gave the least evidence that combustion was going on within it during the three years terminating September, 1852. In the absence of actual information, even in Chile it was believed, until very recently, that Chillan—or, as it is more generally named, Antuco—near the 36th parallel, and Osorno, in 40° 09′, were incessant in their emissions of flame and lava. This is not strictly so. Osorno was visited by Captain Muñoz in 1850, under an order from the government, and Dr. Philippi has more recently been there. Neither of them saw anything more than an occasional puff of smoke; so that there has probably been no great eruption of it since that witnessed by Dr. Darwin just prior to the earthquake which destroyed Concepcion, in 1835. Antuco has been burning from November, 1852, as was witnessed by E. R. Smith, Esq. Mr. Smith reached the village of Antuco, a collection of ranchos near the foot of the Andes, on the 8th of January, 1853; from thence the flames from the new craters could be seen plainly at night, and explosions were heard similar in sound to the reports of distant cannon. The eruption had been going on since the close of the preceding November, though so little interest appeared to be felt in the matter, that no one at the village could give him the precise date. He started for the volcano on the following day, under escort of a *Capitan de amigos*—a sort of Indian agent—the vicinity of the Pehuenches of the pampas rendering such companionship essential. Ascending a fine, romantic valley for five hours, with Antuco in full view, he arrived at the Castillo de Vallenar, formerly a military station, and the scene of many a desperate struggle with the fierce Pehuenches and wilder bandits of Pinchiera, now but a dilapidated pile of bricks. After breakfast at the house of a guide, the party entered the gorges of the mountains, with fine forest trees, crystal streams, and wild scenery on every side. An hour's ride brought them to a rough granitic ridge, some three hundred feet high, from the top of which the view was magnificent: in front, Antuco, black and desolate; to the southward, Sierra Belluda, a lofty, rugged, and Alpine pile, white with eternal snows, down whose sides innumerable cascades dashed headlong to the valleys; to the north, a lower though picturesque range of mountains; and at their feet the river Laja, here a small but romantic stream foaming through a deep gorge, its volume augmented at short intervals by torrents that fall over nearly vertical cliffs. At the foot of this ridge they entered upon volcanic scoriæ, volcanic sand, ashes, and other evidences of former explosions. Over this they travelled for about three hours, to a massive stream of hardened lava, the outpouring of some previous eruption. Beyond it, there is a belt of vegetation, with grass and wild strawberries; and a little further on, another though a smaller stream of scoriaceous lava. Ascending the cone of an extinct crater, perhaps three hundred feet high, the new crater was immediately before, and the lake of La Laja below them, to the eastward. Here they intended to have passed the night, in full view of the burning mass; but a sudden storm of rain drove them again to the trees for shelter. From thence they witnessed the glare, but heard no explosions during the night; and early on the following morning ascended a hill, from which there was a better view than was permitted from that to which the rain had driven them.

Mr. Smith says, that Antuco is a regular cone, with sides inclined at an angle of 45°. It is covered with snow perpetually for about one third of the distance from its apex downwards; and showers of sand and ashes, thrown out at intervals, keep it blackened. Though perceptible at no great distance, the light and smoke from its summit are incessant, and have been witnessed from time immemorial. This last eruption formed two small craters, about two thirds of the height of the mountain up the northern side; and the current of descending lava has dammed up the outlet of the lake by a solid wall more than 250 yards wide and 15 yards thick. This is black as the volcano itself, and, with the other analogous masses in the vicinity, presents a grand, almost terrible, scene of desolation. In the midst of snow-peaked mountains, without a tree on its margin, or a fowl on its surface, the lake seemed lifeless; indeed, the whole locality was apparently marked for the display of nature's wildest phenomena—a gloomy and inhospitable region, whose silence is rarely broken except by the thunders of the volcanos, the violence of storms, or the whoops of wandering Pehuenches.

The eruption had nearly ceased when they arrived. There were occasional small descending streams like molten iron, but no violent outbursts. At the same time there was heard a noise resembling the rolling of a cart-load, or, rather, of a hundred cart-loads, of iron over a rough road, broken masses of rock being evidently jostling one another in a war for supremacy within the bowels of the earth.

Between Antuco and El Descabezado, a new volcano burst out on the 26th November, 1847. For several days this filled the air with the odor of burning sulphur, and its smoke was visible from Talca during more than a year. The cone then thrown up is about 300 feet high, though, from being within the cordilleras, it is not visible from the plain. Its discharges of smoke had ceased entirely in April, 1852; and as every eminence in the range from that called Copiapó, in latitude 27° S., to Antuco, had been seen within the year then terminating, there was conclusive evidence that no active volcano existed within those summits.

Between Antuco and Villarica there are two other volcanos, which were active at the close of 1852: Llayma, near the head-waters of the river Imperial, and Llogol, within a few leagues of it. The natives mention a third in the same vicinity, which they call Changid; but there was no smoke seen to issue from it at the date above mentioned. Natives often mistake summer lightning over the Andes for volcanic fires, more especially after an earthquake—a phenomenon they have been taught to associate with the former. At such times the mind unconsciously seeks and clings to the marvellous in natural causes and effects, and imaginings are often given to the press at home, to be converted into historic facts by those abroad.

The passes of the Andes best known and most frequently travelled across are those of the Cumbre and Uspallata, to the northeast, and the Piuquenes and Portillo ridges, to the southeast of Santiago. The former is not so elevated, and the route to Mendoza is probably 50 miles longer than by the latter; but the *casuchas* (huts) for refuge, in case of snow-storms, and a greater number of localities where scanty pasturage may be had, induce nearly all travellers to prefer it; indeed, so great is the danger of a storm between the two ranges to be crossed on the Portillo route, that, except for about two months of the summer, merchandise is never risked over it. By the Cumbre pass the journey may be made from Santiago to Mendoza in six days, the muleteers making every provision for the mountains prior to their departure from Santa Rosa de los Andes. It is said to have been known to and constantly travelled by Peruvians, who came to Aconcagua for supplies of grain, after Yupanqui annexed this portion of Chile to his dominions; and the *arrieros* (muleteers) have many traditions and local names which might be received in confirmation of the assertion. Lieut. MacRae crossed it twice in prosecution of his magnetical investigations, and his narrative gives full account of it. He found two roads, traversable at different periods, according to the condition of the snow; one, and that generally crossed, 12,488 feet above the sea; the other, 12,656 feet.

Except those whom necessity compels to make the journey, and the semi-mensual *courier* with the mail, few attempt to cross the Andes earlier than October or later than May. Arrieros can be found ready to accompany you at all times; but between these months they will demand triple prices for the use of their mules, and the risk of precipices and starvation amid the snow is fearful.

The road to the Portillo pass winds up the valley of the river Maypu as far as its junction with the Yeso, one of its principal affluents, and thence along the north bank of the latter torrent through a basin-like valley with beds of pure gypsum, estimated at some 2,000 feet in thickness. The river and valley take their name from these strata, though Mr. Pissis calls it the valley of "Los Piuquenes" (*Bernicla melanoptera*). As far as this, the road is a constant ascent, but good. Here begins the tiresome zig-zag climbing of the great cordillera, over strata of porphyries, sandstones, conglomerates, and calcareous clay-slates, not unfrequently intermixed with gypsum and marine fossils. Few ever reach its summit—13,189 feet* above the sea—without experiencing difficulty of respiration; and the poor mules, scarcely less than the masters whom they are serving. In Chile this sensation is called "*puna*;" in Peru, "*veta*," "*soroche*," and "*mareo*," indifferently by natives and creoles; its causes, in their ignorance of the true one, being attributed to exhalations from metallic veins abounding in the Andes. At times it is attended with a feeling of excessive lassitude and weariness, vertigo, temporary blindness, and nausea, not unfrequently accompanied by bleeding from the nostrils and ears. All are not subject to its influence, and there are evidently particular conditions of the system when attacks are most liable. Onions and garlic are recommended by the arrieros as specifics, though Dr. Darwin found nothing so effectual as the pleasure derived from the discovery of fossil shells at this great height. Terrible winds prevailing in the cordilleras, heat, and reflection of sunlight from the snow, are other sources of painful affliction. Every traveller complains bitterly of these annoyances. These tempests usually continue from 9 or 10 A. M., until late in the afternoon; and so drying are they, that the skin cracks and bleeds; and moisture is so rapidly absorbed from deceased animals, that even the intestines do not rot. When Lieut. MacRae reached the Cumbre, at 10½ A. M., the violence of the wind was such as almost to overturn both himself and mule; and on his arrival at Mendoza, after eight days in the mountains, his face and hands were so disfigured by scabs that he would scarcely have been recognised by acquaintances.

* See Lieutenant MacRae's narrative.

From the summit of the Piuquenes there is a descent of about 3,000 feet to a valley fifteen miles in extent, lying between it and the Portillo range, the latter having its origin at Tupungato, and extending into the Argentine territory in a south by west direction. The river Tunuyan has its source near the head of this basin, and flows nearly through its centre. As no animals are sufficiently fresh to attempt crossing both summits and the plain in one day, it is necessary to pass a night here; and this is the locality where most danger is to be apprehended from snow-storms. They are accompanied with violent thunder and lightning, rendered more terrific by the rarity of the atmosphere and deafening echoes of the surrounding rocks. Except during the winter months, they rarely occur by day; and it is only when the sun has gone, and the wind has ceased at night, that the arriero apprehends accumulating clouds; even then, until the thunder startles him, he sleeps tranquilly. Should a storm occur, unless the animals have been sufficiently rested to recommence their journey, (as there is scarcely any place of refuge,) the danger of burial alive is imminent. Nor does it terminate here; so intricate is the path, that there is scarcely less risk of wandering astray in the darkness, and of falling into one of the mighty chasms, or into no less perilous snow-banks, from whose depths none ever escape. As these great beds evaporate and thaw under the more moderate temperature and drying winds of summer, they leave solid columns and pinnacles of ice, many of them so closely resembling draped human figures, immovable in the desolation, that they have been called "*Los Penitentes*" (the penitents). Colossal as they are, in comparison with the bare and barren cones of granite around, they are as pigmies; and in this region, where every object is so unlike all previous experience, it would require little effort of imagination to regard them as monuments of Divine wrath, like Lot's wife, punished for crime. When Dr. Darwin crossed—in March, 1835—a frozen horse stood on one of these ice-columns as on a pedestal, its hind legs in the air. No doubt it had fallen headlong when the snow around that spot was nearly level, and had been left in this position by subsequent evaporation. In summer, when the basin is covered with pasturage, cattle are sometimes driven from the Chile side, where it becomes exhausted much earlier; and herds of guanacos are occasionally seen browsing along its borders, the condor, from his pinnacled eyrie or circling flight, impatiently watching for the feasts these visits seldom fail to afford him.

The ascent to the Portillo from the valley of the Tunuyan is even more toilsome and wearying than that up the Piuquenes ridge. The narrow path lies amid immense conical hills of reddish granite, overlaid by quartz and conglomerates of pebbles and shells, sometimes within a foot of vertical precipices, and at others beneath overhanging masses of rock, apparently ready to tumble from their balance under the slightest effort. Here Tupungato, with its glacier peak, first comes in sight; and when, after climbing 14,475 feet (measurement of Lieut. MacRae) above the ocean, the Portillo itself is reached, the ocean-like pampas of Buenos Ayres may be overlooked through its contracted aperture. From this narrow cleft or door in the ridge, just wide enough for a loaded mule to pass, comes the name "*portillo*"—a little door.

Prof. Domeyko is the only scientific traveller known to me who has penetrated to the crest of the Andes by any other of the passes. A geological account of his journey to "Come Cavallo" (literally *eat horse*) pass, in the province of Atacama, and "Laguna" (*lake*) pass, in the province of Coquimbo, may be found in the *Annales des Mines*, vol. ix, 1846. These journeys, and others, to different elevations in the Andean chain, south of Santiago, made subsequently, were frequent subjects of conversation; and the information respecting them has been wholly obtained from him.

Come Cavallo Pass.—Leaving the city of Copiapó, the road leads up the valley of the river of the same name as far as the confluence of the Jorquera, Pulido, and Manflas, which, from my determinations of the geographical position of Copiapó, and the bearings and distances thence of Prof. Domeyko, will be near latitude 27° 56′ south, and longitude 69° 50′ west. The elevation of this confluence is somewhat less than 4,000 feet, and it is below this only that the river takes the name Copiapó. A more detailed notice of the valley, or rather ravine, as far as Punta del Diablo, about one half the distance to these rivers, will be found in the narrative of a journey to the mines of Chañarcillo. There it will be seen that only the geologist and mineralogist find objects of interest. Reflected heat from utterly barren rocks on both sides of a long narrow gorge; scarcely water to quench the thirst, after hours of travel over broken and stony paths; probably not one representative from all the animal kingdom to show that man is not the only creature tempted to visit scenes nature has so desolated—these are some of the characteristics not easily forgotten.

As one ascends the valley towards the confluence of the rivers, the supply of water increases, and the soil permits occasional patches to be brought under cultivation through its aid; indeed, "*Potrero grande*," between the village of San Antonio and the junction, has become famous in this region for its fruits and vegetables. The mind ever seeks objects of comparison; and the few standards belonging to the vegetable kingdom nature has vouchsafed in many thousand square leagues of northern Chile, have doubtless their influence to enhance the charms and products of Potrero grande; so that, when the lover of verdure arrives there, worn out by days and weeks of travel amid sterility, as his vision may not have rested on a leaf or stalk in all that time, he hails the sight of fig-trees in full bearing as would the patient, long stricken by fever, a stream of cool and limpid water.

From the confluence of the rivers there are two paths towards the cordilleras—one by the Jorquera, the other by the Pulido. That by the Jorquera is the longer, though it possesses attractions making it of sufficient interest for one to encounter the additional fatigue, viz: a ravine, whose strata contain an abundance of marine fossils, and, a little further up stream, the ruins of an Indian village, probably built when the Peruvians were masters of the country. One house, at the southern end of the village, was much larger than the others, the fragments of its walls proving that it must have contained several rooms. Besides this, there are the walls of some thirty others, from 8 to 10 feet in diameter, and about 2 feet thick. There is no cement to any of them. As somewhat similar settlements are found at several places in the Andes, between Copiapó and San José, it is somewhat surprising that Indians should have chosen such inhospitable heights for their homes, whilst there was a more genial temperature and less aridity below. The most numerous fossils are pectens, lying in calcareous strata, among layers of porphyry, breccia, and stratified porphyry. South of the Pulido, and on the same meridian as this, there is another deposite of marine fossils even more interesting, from the greater variety of shells exposed to sight, pectenites and terebratulæ being very abundant.

In the valley of the Pulido, at an elevation of 10,000 feet, there are ruins of another Indian village, called Pircas, now occupied only as a preventive station against contrabandists. Freshly fallen snow was found here early in March, and the warmly-clad guard were shivering over fires in a locality once occupied by half-naked Indians. Somewhat higher up, a depression in the mountains called "Portezuelo Pulido"* would indicate that here was the highway; but, in reality, the road leads northward into the valley of El Pan, on the river Jorquera, where the night is usually passed in a natural cavern of the red porphyritic breccia. This cave affords mountain travellers a commodious shelter from storms, and there, also, they lie by during the violence of noon-day winds, the guides invariably telling each one that, after 11 o'clock, it is often impossible to move; therefore they must start up the final ascent by early dawn, although the distance from the cave to the dividing line is only two hours.

In this final stage of the journey, short as it is, one has full opportunity to examine the last lines of stratified formation, which, as they approximate the granites composing the most elevated ridge of the Andes, exhibit evidences of the violent revolutions and terrific shocks that they have experienced; as if the force which thrust these enormous granite masses from the bosom of the earth, had actually concentrated its energy for the very crest of the mountains. Among the rocks which enter into the composition of this up-borne formation, the

* *Portezuelo* is a depression in chains of hills or mountains, always selected for roads passing from one side to the other.

breccias and brecciated porphyries predominate. Their surfaces are at times black as coal, at others of a deep crimson, again of an ashy-gray, and not unfrequently are striped in lines of every imaginable shade. Though there are places where the inclination is in a contrary direction, the general dip is to the west. However, such are the characters of the rocks, there is so great a variety and so many modifications of species, that one must acknowledge nature has brought together, at this last pinnacle of the system, a specimen from almost every class composing the secondary formation of the western slope of the Andes. At this immediate point, the summit is composed of a rounded mass, entirely without vegetation, covered with feldspathic and quartzose detritus, forming gentle slopes marked by moderate ravines. Though snow was seen on the south sides of cones somewhat higher than the *portezuelo*, and even in the deep ravines much lower down, none was found in the pass 14,522 feet above the sea in the latter days of March.

There is a striking contrast in the configuration and colors of the two sides of the Andes, as seen from the summit here. To the west there is a complete reversal of the primary formation; escarpments overturned, stratifications distorted and interrupted, and, indeed, no two mountains of the same constituents, form, or shade. On the other hand, eastward we see gentle declivities, with beds of nearly horizontal and rarely interrupted rocks, whose extremities form lines almost parallel with the horizon; few tints, vegetable or mineral, to shade the picture, and only a small number of conical and isolated summits, distant from the line of the crest, by which the monotony is partially relieved. There is a conical peak to the northward, some eight or ten leagues, which is apparently much higher, and the guides say that it is perpetually covered with snow; but those in the immediate vicinity of the pass do not rise more than 300 or 400 feet above it. All beyond is *terra incognita*, except to the professional mine hunter or smuggler.

LAGUNA and DOÑA ANA Passes, in the province of Coquimbo.—The first portion of the road to these passes is through the valley of the river Coquimbo, where, from the number of its affluents, there is a much greater supply of water, and a broader space of alluvial soil, to render it more cheerful than the barren rocks of Atacama. Within the first nine leagues, the river is increased by a stream from the northeast through *quebrada* Santa Gracia, near whose source are the rich silver mines of Arqueros, more rare for their combination with quicksilver in a pure state. At a short distance from the left bank are some of the most productive copper mines. The valley now makes a short turn to the northeast, and then, resuming its original direction to the E.S.E., it continues in the same general line by the windings of the river more than thirty leagues farther. Midway this distance it becomes quite a plain, on which the villages of Elqui, Tambo, San Isidro, and Diaguita, principally occupied by persons engaged in mining operations, are, amid vegetation and fruit-trees of great luxuriance, reminding one of the most fertile portions of the republic. Fifty miles in a straight line from the ocean, though more than twice that distance in its serpentine course, the Coquimbo loses its name; its main and northern branch, whose origin is more than a degree of longitude farther to the east, being first called the *Laguna*, and afterward the *Turbio*, until the union with the *Claro*, a small limpid stream from the southeast. The contrast of the colors in the two streams is very striking, and the whole vicinity, from the fossil pectens, nautili, and terebratulæ, and extensive mineral veins and vegetable products, that claim attention on every hand, is more than ordinarily interesting. Above the junction of the Claro, the valley has again a northerly direction for five leagues; and thence from the silver mines of Chapilca, on the right bank, the course is east as far as Guanta, a little triangular valley at the distance of eight miles. This valley, at the confluence of Malpaso creek with the Turbio, is surrounded on all sides by enormous vertical rocks, giving the most out-of-place aspect to the cluster of fruit-trees in its midst. Although more than 3,900 feet above the sea, its climate is so precocious that the second crop of figs matures before the first ripens at Coquimbo. From Guanta across the Andes, there are two roads: one by the valley of the Turbio and Laguna, which is the shorter of the two, and the other by the ravines of the Guanta and Malpaso, more to the north. The former is only practicable during a few months of summer, and it is some 700 feet higher than the Malpaso route; moreover, it is exceedingly rough, and requires frequent fording of the river, so that travellers usually give preference to the latter. But there are many objects to repay the scientific man for encountering these hardships: warm mineral baths, in a wild-looking ravine, with milky torrents of water tumbling through it; a lake more than 1,100 yards long, and 600 broad, surrounded by nearly vertical cliffs of stratified porphyry, a thousand feet high; its surface covered with aquatic birds and plants, although at an elevation of 10,500 feet; and cascades tumbling from rock to rock of the momentarily ascending gorge.

Half a league above the lake, the river supplying it is divided into three branches, and after following the middle one for a long day's journey, one reaches the foot of the immediate dividing line of waters between the two great oceans. Here, at an elevation of 13,300 feet, in the ravines and on the southern slopes, screened from the violent winds prevailing by day, as at all the other passes named, snow remains all the year. These winds are distressing in an atmosphere so rarified. As the sun declines they cease, and the temperature is comparatively pleasant so long as it continues calm; but towards daylight there commences a frigid easterly breeze, which mountaineers call *el terral*, and the cold becomes extremely severe. The *terral* usually ceases at sunrise, and from this time until between 9 and 10 o'clock there is a perfect calm. These are the hours during which travellers endeavor to climb their last stage, and make such descent on the opposite side, that the high walls of its ravines may afford them shelter. Here it is easily done, the ascent to overcome being only about 2,000 feet, and the elevation of the pass above the ocean 14,920—rather more than both of the others, though the summit does not command a picture so interesting as either of them. A few peaks in the vicinity, perhaps 1,500 feet higher than the *portezuelo*, preserving a little more snow, narrow strips of verdure along thread-like rivulets on the west side, and an atmosphere of exquisite transparency—these are all the objects worthy of mention, for even the geology offers no departure from the general law of formations. Cattle are sometimes brought this way from the Argentine provinces, and even the long and desolate journey does not wholly prevent traffic with San Juan, on the opposite side of the Paramillo range.

Mr. Miers mentions* a pass called La Dehesa, immediately up the valley of the Mapocho from Santiago, to the vicinity of its source north of Tupungato, and thence, after crossing the ridge, through a valley of the same name as far as the juncture of the river with the Mendoza, near *Punta de las Vacas*. Beyond this, the Cumbre and Uspallata road is followed. We never heard of any such pass, and from the great elevation of the ridge between the Cumbre and Uspallata it would seem impracticable. But there is no doubt that persons in search of mines repeatedly traverse the Andes at points far from the usual lines of travel, and it is quite probable some such may have crossed here notwithstanding the lofty line. Such a road would be far shorter than those generally known, and as the distance in an air-line from Santiago to Mendoza is less than 100 miles, who shall contradict the story current in the former city—that in the earlier days of the church, a worthy priest constantly performed mass in *both* cities every week?

Another route more frequently travelled, if not much better known to the world, is from San Felipe up the valley of the river Putaendo, and across the main ridge north of Aconcagua peak. This is called the pass of Los Patos (the ducks). Descending the Andes the road strikes the head-waters of the San Juan, and, following through its valley, terminates at a town of the same name. It has the advantage of abundant water and pasturage, which are inducements for drovers of cattle, to whom time is no great object; but the disadvantages of no

* Travels in Chile and La Plata, by John Miers: London, 1826.

less than five elevations to overcome between the northern provinces of Buenos Ayres and Chile, and a greater distance than that through Mendoza, of course prevent ordinary traffic.

Except *vaqueros* (cow-herds) and predatory Indians, few cross the Andes south of the river Maule. Those residing in the southern provinces, whom business compels to undertake the journey, make Santiago or San Felipe their starting point. There are no resources within or beyond the mountains south of Luxan, and the voyager must start provided with every necessity, unless a few dry sticks at occasional places, with which to boil a kettle for himself, or a handful or two of pasturage as often, though scarcely more nutritious, for his mule, may be excepted from his list of indispensables. Should the Indians of the pampas ever become civilized, or the white man can so inspire them with fear of retribution as to prevent murder solely for the bright buttons or coat he may wear, there are two places even now well known, which must become the great thoroughfares to the Atlantic and its tributaries. These are the passes by the PLANCHON and ANTUCO. There is no sort of doubt that the pampas will afford ample supplies of water, pasturage, and game, to all who journey towards Buenos Ayres, Montevideo, or the mouth of Rio Negro, for many centuries to come; and when commerce justifies it, the distances, elevations to overcome, and character of the country, all designate these as the highways on which money should be expended.

Curicó, in the province of Colchagua, is usually the origin or terminus of journeys by the Planchon, the road crossing the great longitudinal valley in the vicinity of Rio Colorado, and through most abundant vegetation. Cultivation is left at the base of the first range of mountains—2,500 feet above the sea, though the traveller immediately enters amid native forest-trees of luxuriant growth and deep colors. Indeed, the citizens of Northern Chile, shortly after crossing the Rio Claro, stop amazed before a wall of vegetation nearly vertical for more than a thousand feet in height. This side of the hill is formed of different rocks, dispersed in alternate layers—some solid and durable, others soft and decomposing by the action of air and moisture. The latter furnish material for the roots and sustenance of the trees, whilst the former support their weight. The upper branches of the most vigorous Robles (*Fagus obliqua*) rise to the level of the first strata, from whose border spring the trunks of others intermixed with Canelos (*Drymis chilensis*), twined with an infinity of creeping plants and parasites. In the same manner follow others to the very summit of the hill, so that the departure of the leafy wall from a vertical plane is almost insensible to an eye at its base. So dense is the foliage, that at a short distance one is not able to distinguish trees separately, nor can the vision penetrate to the interior of the wood; here and there a ray of light, pushing its way from above, illumines a pile of rocky basaltic-looking crags, now dark as slate, now white as Kaolin—all the rest is obscure.

The road continues up the Claro nearly to its head-waters in the valley of *Los Leones;* but before entering this, the robust forest vegetation ceases, at an elevation of 4,200 feet. Here there is a division. One branch of the road continues a southeasterly direction, along the western base of Descabezado, and by which was the travel prior to the formation of the new crater near Cerro Azul, in 1847, and the other turns to the north and passes by the baths of Mondaca. In less than two hours after leaving the last trees, by the latter road, Professor Domeyko found himself on the Cuesta de las Animas, in the midst of perpetual snow. Although his elevation was less than 7,500 feet, its color and compactness assured him of the fact, and his guides corroborated it; but he attributes its preservation here not to the height of the hill, more than to the circumstance that immense rocks keep it constantly in shade during the hottest hours of the day. On the high table-land beyond the Cuesta, he found a small and nearly circular lake of clear water, which, from the scorias and other volcanic rocks bounding it, evidently occupies the crater of an extinct volcano. From the summit of Las Animas the Planchon becomes visible, its snow-covered ridge bursting through blackened rocks. In vain does the pen attempt to describe the beauty of the contrast between the broad translucent masses of ice, almost like glass, and the asphaltic color of the mountain range, of which it forms part. Apparently it is close at hand, but, in reality, the Lontue and more than a league of territory intervene between us. From here, too, in a narrow valley whose bottom is some 3,500 feet below us, we descry the lake of Mondaca, a canopy of vapor overhanging its greenish-yellow and waveless surface. The road continues along its south shore through elliptic valleys, or rather basins, of different elevations, enclosed by porphyritic columnar rocks, and clothed with pasturage. These prisms, in some places not more than eight or ten inches in diameter, have from three to five faces, as equal and symmetrical as though cut by art. Thousands of them are grouped together—sometimes erect, at others curved, while again others spring from a common centre. From the loftiest series of these grim pillars, partially covered with snow, gush an infinity of tiny rivulets tending to one common stream below, whose limpid waters foam wildly over a bed composed of material—breccia of obsidian—whose formation is yet a mystery to the geologist, and thence flow on to the lake.

Four or five leagues above the Laguna the road turns from its stream more to the southeast, passes over a hill of nearly the same height as Cerro de Cruces, and subsequently a lofty table plain covered with fragments of stone and destitute of vegetation. Here we perceive, for the first time, the Descabezado, with its two cones, united by a plain of perpetual snow more extensive than that of the Planchon, the bed of snow resting on an antique mass of lava, perceptibly, even at this distance, rugged and broken. Both these mountains form points in the plane of greatest elevation of the Andes, but they are not in the line of hills dividing the waters of the two oceans. The latter is found beyond Cerro del Medio, which is also volcanic, snow-covered, and three or four leagues farther east. From the now extinct craters, and the snow of Cerro del Medio, originates quite a stream, whose course is first northwardly through Valle Grande, and eventually (Prof. Domeyko says) unites with one from Lake Mondaca, the union of the two forming the Lontue. But in another place he asserts that, "the Lontue does not originate in Lake Mondaca, although people say it does;" and as he neither made a circuit of the lake nor traced the stream of the Valle Grande, there is very reasonable ground for doubting whether there is any such break here in the continuity of the great chain. Crossing the valley, we attain the final range of elevations and ascend to Puerta del Yeso, as the immediate pass is called, by a tolerably good mountain road which is entirely free from snow during all the summer months. The height above the ocean is only 6,600 feet, scarcely half that of any of the northern passes. The eastern slope, with its gentle declivities, fertile valleys, and broad pampas—a stream of water flowing away to the northeastward, and herds of cattle that have been driven from haciendas in the province of Talca for the rich grasses that bound its margin—all these are spread before us; but, as at the north, there is great monotony in the forms of the hills, in the colors of the rocks, even in the verdure itself; and we greatly miss the luxuriant trees that adorn the western slopes of the Andes in this latitude. I could not find any one who had travelled farther than to the Valle del Yeso, but was told that there is a continuation of the road, through the country of the Pehuenches to Mendoza.

Pass of Antuco.—It is admitted that this is more easy of access than any of the known passes. Instead of following the direction of streams to near their sources, and then climbing rugged ranges, often at great inclinations, as is done at all the others, the path proceeds from the junction of the Laja and Biobio, on the great plain, immediately up and along the ridge of a spur of the Andes, and the ascent is so gentle that a cart may travel the whole distance over it. By order of the colonial government, such a journey actually was made nearly half a century ago, the engineer reporting, at his return, that a carriage road could be made at small expense. The elevation above the sea to be overcome is only 6,500 feet; there are no steep acclivities, and almost all the rocky formation is covered with a stratum of earth. If such a road was made, the distance between Buenos Ayres and Concepcion would be shortened at least one third, and passengers from the north of Chile, embarking for the latter port in a steamer, might proceed to the shores of the Atlantic through a country beautiful in scenery and abounding in the necessities of life, and in half the time that they now occupy in a voyage round Cape

Horn. But the Indian tribes are warlike and merciless, and those who must travel either brave sea-sickness with the storms and snows of the Cape, or take the Uspallata route, rather than encounter the children of the pampas on their homesteads—spectres, armed only with lances and slung-balls, who "rush like the whirlwind, destroy, and are gone," and whose territory, to this day, remains absolutely "terra incognita."

Table showing the Heights of some of the principal Mountains and Mountain Passes in Chile above sea-level.

Name.	Chain to which it belongs.	Latitude.	Longitude.	Height in feet.	Height of perpetual snow.	Remarks.
		° ′	° ′			
Portezuelo Come Caballo	Andes	27 36	69 20	14,521	14,784	
Cordillera de Doña Ana	Do	29 51	69 52	13,431		Fossil shells abound.
Portezuelo Doña Ana	Do			14,849		
Cordillera de la Laguna	Do	30 30	69 23	15,575		Snow sometimes remains all summer.
Aconcagua	Do	32 38	69 57	22,301		
Campana de Quillota	Cordilleras	32 57	71 06	6,053		
Cumbre Pass		32 49	70 07	12,488 12,656		Observations of Lieut. MacRae.
Joncal	Andes	33 05	69 48	20,368		
San Francisco	Do	33 12	70 12	16,998		
Cerro Amarillo	Cordilleras	33 18	70 54	7,316		
Cerro del Plomo	Andes	33 19	70 07	17,825		
Tupungato	Do	33 22	69 51	22,450	11,480	
Cuesta Prado	Cordilleras	33 25	70 50	6,083		
La Vinilla	Do	33 26	71 14	5,357		
Portillo, East Pass	Andes	33 35	69 46	14,315		Observations of Lieut. MacRae.
Portillo de los Piuquenes	Do			13,362		
San José	Do	33 42	69 51	18,150		
San Pedro Nolasco	Do	33 46	70 15	10,952		
Horcon de Piedra	Cordilleras			7,313		
Aculeo	Do	33 55	70 50	4,888		A mine of argentiferous lead.
Cerros de Alhue	Do	33 59	70 54	7,332		
Cruz de Piedra	Andes	34 12	70 03	17,126		
Maypu	Do	34 17	69 43	17,664		
Descabezado	Do	35 00	71 03	13,100	8,455	
Cerro Coligual	Cordilleras	36 50	72 15	807		
Volcano of Antuco	Andes	37 07	71 02	9,245	6,594	
Volcano of Llayma	Do	38 50	72 03	Not known		Active volcano, 1852.
Volcano of Villarica	Do	39 14	71 57	16,000?		Active volcano, 1852.
Cuesta Paragudehue	Cordilleras	40 02	73 15	511		
Volcano of Osorno	Andes	41 09	72 36	7,550	4,800	
Volcano Minchinmadom	Do	42 48	72 31	8,000		
El Corcovado	Do	43 12	72 50	7,510		
Yanteles	Do	43 29	72 48	8,030		

The descent of the limit of perpetual snow through 10,000 feet, in a little more than 800 miles, is a fact which cannot fail to arrest the attention of the physical geographer, affording, as it does, conclusive proof of rapid decrease in the mean temperature, and increase in the quantity of water which falls in the form of snow.

If other evidence than the natural configuration which has been indicated were necessary to prove that the whole of Chile has been raised from the ocean within a period geologists regard very modern, the marine fossils found on the great cordilleras, the multitude of recent shells that now lie hundreds of feet above their native element, retaining their natural colors, and almost intact though exposed to the constant action of heat and dew, whilst the adjoining ocean contains living members of the same family, and the alluvial strata of the valleys and shelves bounding the rivers, would be ample proofs to convince the most skeptical. That the great central plain was once the bed of an ocean-gulf, similar to the Californian, in which the tides ebbed and flowed, and the islands of Chilóe and the Chonos Archipelago were shoals, or, at most, islets, there cannot be the least doubt. Time after time the great continent sank to the darkened depths of ocean, burying animals and forests beneath layers of detritus; tide-waves subsequently rolled over its surface, which each time at its emergence exhibited a new stratum of entombed creatures, ineffaceably marking the lapse of another era. As it finally rose from the mass of waters, and heats of summer dissolved the snows deposited on summits that subterranean fires had forced far upward into space, the inequalities partially caused by this volcanic action were filled from the trickling streams; and this, perhaps, was the origin of most of the fresh-water lakes.

The most extensive lakes are those at the immediate base of the Andes, in the province of Valdivia. They occupy a very considerable portion of the country from latitude 39° to latitude 41° 30′. As the region of country in which they lie is almost entirely uninhabited, and innumerable varieties of climbing plants so entangle the forests that the utmost difficulty attends their penetration, very little is known of any others of them than Llanquihue, Llauquihue or Rupanco, and Todos los Santos. These have been reconnoitred by Capt. Muñoz, of the Chilean navy, and subsequently by Dr. Philippi, a German naturalist of distinction.

Llanquihue, at the foot of Osorno and Calbuco, is the largest. It is nearly of a triangular form, thirty miles long from north to south, and twenty-two broad from northeast to southwest. The southwest extremity is distant only three leagues from the gulf of Reloncavi, into which its surplus waters are discharged through the river Maullin. Capt. Muñoz states, in a report to the government, that at the origin of the Maullin the lake is 183.7 feet above the level of the Pacific.

Todos los Santos or Esmeralda lies immediately east of Llanquihue, and on the opposite side of Osorno. It is surrounded by volcanic mountains, whose rapid streams feed it from nearly every side. The greatest length from E.N.E. to W.S.W. is eighteen miles; and its breadth, at the western extremity, is about one third that amount. It also has an outlet into the gulf of Reloncavi. There is a little island in the western half of the lake.

Twelve miles further north is Llauquihue or Rupanco, a long and narrow body of water, in which originates the Rahue, one of the tributaries of Rio Bueno. Its length from W.N.W. to E.S.E. is twenty-four miles, and breadth scarcely more than four miles.

According to a sketch by Dr. Philippi, a very narrow strip of land intervenes between the Rupanco and Puychue, the next lake to the north. He makes Puychue twenty-five miles long, six miles wide, and rather lozenge-shaped, lying nearly parallel with Rupanco, a small island diversifying its eastern extremity. On the map of M. Gay, published in 1846, the body of the lake lies in a direction from N.E. by N. to S.W. by S., in which line it is eleven miles long: its eastern shore is crescent-shaped, and the northern like the base of a pear. In the same year, (1846,) Capt. Philippi, of the Chilean engineers, who had been a good deal in the province of Valdivia, and had been designated by government to encourage emigration from Germany, published another map of the province, at Cassel. On it Puychue is quite an oval, though the dimensions vary very slightly; but in extenuation of the discrepancy, there is a note inserted along the western and northern shores, informing you that there are "swamps, virgin forests, with various kinds of trees, and many canes, impenetrable because of the vines." To the S.E. of the lake, on this map, is Volcano Puychue, which on that of M. Gay is converted into Copigue peak. The Pilmayquen, another tributary of the Bueno, has its source in this lake.

In the same general N.N.E. line as the others, and from ten to twelve miles north of the last, is Ranco, considerably the largest and most irrregular body of water in Chile. There is a difference between the authors quoted, respecting its dimensions, and scarcely less as to its configuration and the number of islands diversifying its surface. M. Gay's information is perhaps the most reliable, and he makes its length, in a N.W. by N. direction, thirty-two miles—breadth, eighteen miles. It is supplied by many streams from the cordilleras, and in its turn furnishes Rio Bueno. If the information is to be depended on, some of the tributaries of the Rio Negro approach within a mile or two of this lake, and the mountain-ridge dividing the waters of the Atlantic and Pacific is scarcely more than a chain of hills. There are several pretty islands within Ranco, and four settlements of friendly Indians on its different borders, the whole territory within which lie these large lakes being entirely in control of independent tribes. Along the north shore is one of the paths from Valdivia into the Argentine territory.

Immediately east of Valdivia, M. Gay has placed on his map Huitahue, Guanegue, Rinihue, Pirihueco, and Lajara, five lakes forming a right angle, of which the angular point is to the west, with Rinihue in the centre. They extend from latitude 39° 24′ to latitude 39° 52′; and are united by channels, forming a continuous chain, from which the surplus water discharged by Guanegue is one of the principal supplies of the river Valdivia. Each leg of the right angle is about twenty-five miles long. There are seven settlements of Indians on the borders of the three western, and a path across the Andes, along the southern shore. South of Lajara, in latitude 39° 55′, longitude 71° 12′ W., is a volcano of the same name.

Capt. Philippi has but three lakes on his map. These lie in a N.N.E. and S.S.W. line between latitude 39° 10′ and 39° 47′, and are called Calafquen, Huanchue or Panguipulli, and Rinihue. He agrees with M. Gay in connecting them by small streams, with an outlet supplying the Valdivia, or, as he here names it, the Ciruelas, the Indian appellation being Calle-calle. In latitude 39° 42′, longitude 71° 43′, just north of the east extremity of the Rinihue, which he makes a long narrow body of water, is a volcano of the same name; and east of Huanchue the volcano of Panguipulli, latitude 39° 38′, longitude 71° 35′ W. These are grave geographical discrepancies between officers of the same government, and we are not likely to learn the truth until the survey of M. Pissis is extended over this province. In this instance, I have preferred following the authority of M. Gay in compiling our map, and offer in extenuation of these differences the experience of Dr. Darwin, when endeavoring to penetrate the country a little farther south. "The forest was so impenetrable, that no one who has not beheld it can imagine so entangled a mass of dying and dead trunks. I am sure that often, for ten minutes together, our feet never touched the ground, and we were frequently ten or fifteen feet above it, so that the seamen, as a joke, called out the soundings. In the lower part of the mountain, noble trees of the Winter's bark and laurel, like the sassafras, with fragrant leaves, and others, the names of which I do not know, were matted together by a trailing bamboo, or cane. Here we were more like fishes struggling in a net than any other animals."

Villarica—or, as it was formerly called, Llauquen—whose main body is to the south of latitude 39° (M. Gay)—covers more than one hundred square miles. Valdivia gave it the new name, from the quantity of gold discovered in the vicinity, and founded a city on its S.W. shore; though, as the Indians twice destroyed it within a short time after the Spaniards made their settlements, it is probable the so-called city never embraced above a dozen houses. It has an outlet to the sea through the river Tolten, a small island near the centre, and the volcano of the same name on its S.E. shore. In the very heart of the Indian territory, as is Villarica, with the ruins of its city to remind the children of the soil how gallantly their forefathers struggled to retain independence, it has remained even more unknown than the others.

Quite close to the seacoast there are several smaller collections of salt water, sometimes consisting of natural depressions in the surface, communicating with the sea through short canals; and at others, of basins, into which sea-water is only driven during the storms of winter. In the latter cases they are native salt-works, from which the Indians of the vicinity collect all their supplies. Beyond this, they are of little interest.

The two largest lakes in the province of Concepcion, and the only ones requiring mention, are Gualletue, in latitude 38° 14′, at the base of the cordilleras, and Laja, in latitude 37° 05′, near the foot of the volcano of Antuco. Gualletue covers about fifty square miles within the Andes, deriving its supply from melting snows. La Laja is the most picturesque of all. It lies at the base of Antuco, by whose immense black cone, and the snowy peaks of Cerro Belluda, it is overshadowed. The form is nearly that of a crescent, with cusps, nearly five miles apart, clasping the foot of Antuco. It is 4,600 feet above the level of the ocean, is about 300 yards across in the broadest part, and is supplied by snow-water not only from the overhanging mountains, but also from all the basin to the eastward, as far as the dividing line of waters. The foam of its surplus water tumbling over a cliff at a short distance, is in fine contrast with the surrounding masses of blackened lava and scoriæ.*

As we proceed northerly, the number and volumes of the lakes diminish, until we find that no such bodies of water exist except those on lofty elevations of the Andes. There are but two which merit attention in the province of Maule. Amargo—or, as it is sometimes called, Hermoso—being in the very midst of the great mountain chains near latitude 35° 40′, is one of those just referred to. It is about three leagues in circumference, of great depth, and, to this time, has no known outlet. One of its names would indicate that its water is bitter; but such is not the case, and it is a constant resort of herdsmen frequenting the cordilleras for pasturage.

Totoral, formed by the waters that descend from the Cerros de Namé during winter, is some fifteen miles from the coast, and near the northern part of the province. It is only about a mile long, with an outlet by the Arenales creek, one of the tributaries of the river Cauquenes. M. Gay has inserted on his map of the province lakes at the source of the Maule and Achihueno. From this authority, the former covers more than 50 square miles, and the latter is many times the size of Totoral. But mention of them is neither made in the carefully prepared report to the Statistical Office, which was published in 1845, nor by Prof. Domeyko, who made a geological tour in the cordilleras of the vicinity of the Descabezado, near which the Maule originates. For this reason they have been omitted from the accompanying map.

Mondaca lies in a valley of the same name to the N.W. of Descabezado, and 3,700 feet above the ocean. There seems but little doubt that its origin is due to the earthquakes attending the eruption of Peteroa, in December, 1760, when the mountain formed for itself a new crater, and filled the neighboring valleys with lava and ashes so as to obstruct, and in some cases dam up, the mountain streams. No writer alludes to its dimensions. Its reddish-yellow waters are almost surrounded by barren and broken hills, piles of shingle, pumice, and other volcanic rocks. At the eastern extremity only, where the noisy torrent that supplies it tumbles through a ravine, are there symptoms of vegetation. Mineral springs, elsewhere mentioned, are found on its southern shore. This lake is not on the map of M. Gay, and it may be his Laguna del Maule.

Of Las Garzas, lying in a basin of the hills near the N.W. corner of the province of Talca, the only information is that afforded by the map of M. Gay; its latitude is 34° 54′ S., and longitude 72° 05′ W.

Taguatagua, a former lake in the province of Colchagua, and four leagues N.W. of San Fernando, was the most extensive and best known south of the river Cachapual. Its site still is more than ordinarily interesting to the geologist, and therefore a brief notice is given of what it was. The lake occupied a basin just at the western base of the Central cordilleras, whose distance from the sea is about 60 miles, and elevation above it not less than 1,400 feet. On the western side, the rim of the basin is lower than the opposite hills, one natural gorge or depression being not more than 40 feet above the surface of the lake. Advantage was taken of this a few years ago to cut a drain and lead off the water, by which means 8,000 acres of the most productive land was obtained. At that time the lake was of an oval form, nine miles in circuit, the water increasing in depth regularly to the centre, where bottom was found at twenty-five feet. Then, it had an outlet into the Cachapual from its southeastern extremity, through which there was a constant stream; and as there were neither rains in summer, nor melting snows on the adjacent hills, to counterbalance this loss and that by evaporation, it was

*A letter from Chile, since the above was written, informs me that the lava of a recent eruption had dammed up the outlet. Who can say how much destruction will be caused when the accumulating volume bursts its barriers?

reasonably inferred that the deficiency was supplied by springs at the bottom. The water was quite clear, abounded with fine fish, and aquatic birds of many varieties, whose nests were to be found on islands which floated on its surface. These last appear to have been formed by the matting together of multitudes of dead plants, which subsequently floated, and on whose surface others took root as soil was formed by natural decay, until even trees of medium size found foothold. The thickness of the sustaining mass was from four to six feet, of which the greater portion was submerged.* When a strong wind arose, it was no little curious to witness what one supposed to be terra firma, with its trees and browsing cattle, perhaps, go floating to the other side of the lake. Fossil shells are found in numbers on the Cerro de Borbollon, which bounds the eastern shore; and in cutting the drain mentioned, the bones of two Mastodons were disinterred at a distance of two hundred yards within the original margin of the water, and twenty feet below its surface. Part of a femur, a broken lower jaw, and other teeth, were presented to me by Richard Price, Esq., an intelligent English gentleman long resident in Chile. They have been minutely figured and described in an accompanying report from Dr. Wyman, and it is not a little remarkable that these relics, accidentally obtained from within a few feet of each other, should completely sustain the assertion of Cuvier, that two species of this huge animal formerly existed in South America. On the neighboring Cerro de las Incas exist the remains of a rude temple or fortress, erected by the Promaucaes, the tribe whose continued hostility drove Almagro from the country.

Cauquenes, a smaller though similar deposite of water, in the same province, is within the hacienda of the Requinua, three or four leagues to the eastward of the high road to the south, and about an equal distance south of the river Cachapual. It is not more than a mile in length, and is the probable source of the river Claro, a tributary of the Cachapual, if not also of the Cauquenes. The authority for this, and other information respecting it, is given in Chapter XV. Like Taguatagua, great numbers of fish and birds may be obtained from it.

Cahuil, Boyecura, and Bichuquen, in the western part of the province, are called lakes by M. Gay; but they are, more properly, estuaries.

Almost every traveller who has felt sufficient interest to make the journey from its port to the capital of Chile, has been tempted to extend his ride as far as Aculeo, a picturesque lake, 13 leagues to the S.S.W. of Santiago, and within the Central cordilleras. It is in the form of an hour-glass, extending six miles from east to west, and four across the broadest portions, from north to south, though scarcely more than half a mile between the promontories which give it its peculiar shape. From the disintegrated materials constantly washing down the sides of the mountains that surround it, the level of its water is gradually rising. During the winter, and until summer evaporations reduce it below the outlet, the surplus flows by a short stream to the Angostura, a tributary of the Maypu. Further account of it will be found in Chapter XIV.

The other deposites of water, in the province of Santiago, are the salt lakes of Bucalemu, to the westward of Aculeo, and separated from the sea only by sand-hills; Batuco, of considerable superficial extent in winter, though often a mere marsh in summer, between the Colina and Chacabuco creeks; and in the Andes, the small lakes in which the Mapocho and Yeso originate. The last, called Piuquenes, from the number of these birds (*Bernicla melanoptera*) that frequent it, is at an elevation of 8,500 feet above the sea-level.

Aconcagua has but one lake, and that is situated in a lofty spot of the Andes, so distant from the usually travelled road to Mendoza, that few persons are willing to add to the hardships of their journey by a visit to it. The Laguna del Inca is in latitude 32° 50′, longitude 69° 42′, within a dike of oval form, nearly surrounded by lofty and precipitous declivities, about 8,000 feet above the ocean. It is nearly two miles in its greatest diameter, and apparently of such great depth that the arrieros declare it has no bottom. Mr. Peter Schmidtmeyer,

* Annales des Sciences Naturelles, Tom. xxviii.

who crossed the Andes in 1820–'21, says of it: "On my return over the cordillera, we slept at nearly three miles from the lake; I walked to it, and found it about as much in circumference; it appeared very deep, and to have been the crater of a volcano, like a *solfatara,* as the mountains are tinged with yellow, and this color is concentrated in many of the rocks detached from them. With some trees and a habitation, this lake would form a very picturesque object; but the only thing seen growing about it is a little grass of brownish hue, and it is a very cold spot. I observed among the rocks near it the prettiest flower that I have ever seen in the Andes, and which reminded me of the Alps." Mr. Miers states, that it is constantly supplied from numerous small cataracts and streams derived from the melting snows; and as it has no apparent outlet, there is little doubt its surplus water escapes through the bottom, to appear again at a spot within the mountains lower down, and which, from the number of perpetual springs in a small locality, is called Ojos de Agua.

Of the Lagunas del Toro and Carisso, mountain collections, alimenting branches of the river Chuapa, the only information obtained is that contained on the published map of M. Gay, which has been adopted on the map accompanying, except for their latitudes and longitudes.

In the province of Coquimbo, as yet, but one has been mentioned by travellers, and to this no name is assigned. Adopting the position on a MS. map of Prof. Domeyko, it is situated at an elevation of 10,400 feet above the level of the ocean, in latitude 30° 24′, longitude 69° 44′. It consists of the waters of three considerable torrents, which descend through as many ravines of the loftier Andes, collected in a reservoir here, after dividing into many rivulets on a beach extending nearly two miles above the basin. The walls of this last are nearly vertical rocks, more than a thousand feet high, having a narrow pathway only along the southwestern shore, and a natural dyke to the northwest, with a narrow aperture through which the water escapes. Its length is near two thirds of a mile, and its breadth rather more than half that amount. As may be inferred from the number of aquatic plants covering one third of the surface, its water is very shallow. As in summer the supply by the river for irrigating the fields on its banks is notably deficient during many years, and the aperture in the natural dyke is only about fifty yards across, Prof. Domeyko suggested that it would be easy to increase the elevation of the latter so as to retain a larger quantity for such seasons of necessity; but no steps have been taken to carry his useful proposition into effect.

On his map of Atacama M. Gay introduces at the headwaters of the Rio de los Naturales—one of the branches of the Huasco—two small lakes, and *cateadores* (professional mine-hunters) have brought crystals and concretions of salt from a lake in the vicinity of Cerro de Azufre, besides vague information of salt lakes near the coast in the great desert to the north. None of them, however, can be of such considerable extent as would justify a journey of the geographical student solely for their examination.

Critical examination of their margins shows that the water-courses were once deep streams, susceptible of being navigated by vessels of the largest class. Indeed, the fact is demonstrable by geologists, that they were inlets or arms of the sea, into which melted snows and overflowing lakes in the mountains first discharged their waters. Then, as the continent rose higher and higher, winding brooks, accumulating in volume with each succeeding age, became the torrents that we now see them. From time to time sliding glaciers undermine rocks, and earthquakes dam up channels, until the heaped-up body of water bears everything before it, not unfrequently, on its swollen tide, transporting boulders of many tons weight to localities far away from analogous rocks. At these epochs, fields are submerged by the destroying element; the course of the river is changed; and when an affrighted populace return to the sites of former homes, it is only to weep over garden spots irrecoverably buried beneath gravel and sand deposited by the deluge. One such scene occurred on the Cachapual only a few years since, painfully proving how rapidly beds of shingle may be formed, and forcibly exhibiting the abrading powers of water. Even on ordinary occasions, the noise of stones striking together beneath the surface, as they are borne along by the current, comes most audibly to the ear above the rushing sound of the stream over its rocky bed. How fearful, then, the spectacle during such storms as constantly occur in winter,* when this vast sloping water-shed, saturated by continuous rains, pours all that descends upon it into the narrow ravines! Every one along which I have travelled—the Copiapó, Mapocho, Maypu, Cachapual, and Maule—has its high-bounding terraces, at irregular distances, in whose vertical cliffs the running streams have left unmistakable marks, sometimes more elevated than beds of fossil vegetation forming a part of them. That some of these changes have taken place recently, there seems little reason to doubt; for Molina tells us the Maule was navigable for half its length at his day (1787) by ships-of-the-line, and there still lived, in 1850, a native of Coquimbo, whose memory extended to the time when the sea beat against the terrace on which Serena now stands. Now, the base of the terrace is 25 feet above the ocean, and quite a mile from it, and the Maule has not six feet of water at five miles from its mouth.

In the narrative of Dr. Von Tschudi, (American translation,) Chapter XI, he says: "I have in my last chapter observed, that the Cordillera is the point of partition between the waters of the Pacific and Atlantic oceans. All the waters of the eastern declivity of the Cordillera—all those which have their sources on the level heights and on the western declivity of the Andes—flow from them in the direction of the east, and work their way through the eastern mountain chain. Throughout the whole of South America there is not a single instance of the Cordillera being intersected by a river; a fact the more remarkable, because in southern Peru and Bolivia the coast-chain is lower than the Andes. This interesting phenomenon, though it has deeply engaged the attention of geologists, has not yet been satisfactorily explained. I concur in the view taken by Mr. Darwin, who observes that it would be too rash to assign to the eastern chain of Bolivia and central Chile a later origin than the western chain, (near the Pacific,) but that the circumstance of the rivers of a lower mountain chain having forced their way through a higher chain, seems, without this supposition, to be enigmatical. Mr. Darwin is of opinion that the phenomenon is assignable to a periodical and gradual elevation of the second mountain line (the Andes); for a chain of islets would at first appear, and as these were lifted up, the tides would be always wearing deeper and broader channels between them."

On a preceding page he has very clearly defined what he means by the *Andes* and the *Cordilleras*, so that we cannot possibly mistake the ranges of mountains mentioned at any time; and it is to be regretted that all writers have not taken like pains to avoid confusion. But in the Spanish language, "*cordillera*" means "a chain of mountains;" and one may say "*cordillera de la costa*" with the same propriety as "*cordillera de los Andes.*" However, when Creoles speak of "*la cordillera,*" they mean invariably the Andes.

Circumstances prevented Dr. Von Tschudi, when *en route* for Peru, from seeing much beyond the range of hills bounding the bay of Valparaiso; and the opinion of Dr. Darwin respecting the rivers of central Chile, quoted by him, may have been formed when the latter gentleman passed the Portillo line. It is evident he regarded this line as the main chain of the Andes, and was not aware that Aconcagua, Tupungato, and San José, all above 18,000 feet high, belonging to the same ridge, were to the westward of that which more recent examination proves to be only a spur from the actual dividing line of waters. True, he was within twenty miles of Tupungato, in an air-line; but till that time it had been considered about 15,000 feet high, and only a mountain traveller can tell how many disappointments attend views of distant objects.

It has already been stated that Chile, north of 33°, is a series of mountains, extending from the ocean to the Andes, without any continuous chain which could properly come within the definition of *cordillera*, as meant by Dr. Von Tschudi; but the Coquimbo, whose waters do continue to the Pacific, has its origin near the highest range of the Andes, eastward of the 70° of longitude, and thence works its way. From Chacabuco, south, we have seen that the

* Five inches of rain fell at Santiago during twenty-four hours ending July 24, 1851, and more than three inches on the day following.

Andes are composed of separate ranges of mountains, three being sometimes distinctly visible between the plain and the highest range. Though there are anomalous portions, and, in some places, complete reversals of the geological structure usually found, geologists are satisfied that all these ranges belong to one epoch. These are separated from the central chain (the *cordilleras* of Dr. Von Tschudi) by a plain with an average breadth of fifteen to eighteen miles, sometimes expanded to thirty-five or thirty-eight, and at others narrowed to a few hundred yards. But the Andes and central chain never unite, and in every instance where they approximate to each other there is an interruption of the general declination of the plain from E.N.E. to W.S.W., and through every one of these *angosturas* (narrow gorges) there is a stream flowing from the southward and eastward. Its strata prove that the Central cordillera is older than the Andes, and the continuity of its line is quite as seldom interrupted. Westward of this, and south of the Rapel, the topography of the country is much the same as it is north of Chacabuco—successions of hills, with small intervening valleys, extending to the coast.

Now, I shall show that every river of consequence in Chile has its source not far from the highest summits of the Andes, traverses the intermediate plain in an average direction west by south, penetrates the Central cordilleras, and discharges its waters in the Pacific. Some few tributaries are exceptions to the law, and in one instance, (the Biobio,) they somewhat influence the course of the main stream after junction; but it originates in the Andes, and otherwise fulfils the rule. Commencing at the south, as we did with the lakes, on account of their greater volume, the Bueno is the first stream of any note. It is, however, necessary to apprize the reader that all the geographical information from the provinces of Valdivia and Concepcion, not excepting that published "by authority," must be received with many grains of allowance.

The Bueno has its source in Lake Ranco, in latitude 40° 16′, longitude 72° 28′, and after winding nearly west, through a very serpentine course, for about thirty miles, is joined by the Pilmayquen, flowing from the E.S.E., and which originates in Lake Puychue. The united waters of the two follow the direction of the main stream, without its contortions, twelve miles further. Here the Rahue, to which the excess of water in Lake Llanquihue has given birth, and its tributary, the Coihueco, springing from the base of Osorno, after flowing northwest nearly a hundred miles, falls into the Bueno just at the line of hills into which the Central cordilleras have degenerated. The distance from the junction of the Rahue to the ocean is above twenty miles, through nearly all of which the Bueno is navigable; and as rains in this section of the republic are not only frequent, but are also heavy at all seasons, the river is never low, as is often the case with those at the north.

The Valdivia, or Calle-calle, originates in Lake Huanchue, or, as M. Gay writes it, Guanegue. Its principal affluents from the southeast, the Colileufu and Quinchilco, have not the volume of the Rahue or Pilmayquen. These streams fall into it near longitude 72° 40′ west, and the course of the river, which from its source had been west by south, becomes more southerly. Fifteen miles from the ocean it is joined by the Cruces, an affluent of equal size, draining the valley to the northeast and west of the Andes; and the two are thence navigable to the estuary at its mouth, where ships may lie in greater security than in any other harbor on the whole coast. There is abundance of water for quite large vessels as far as the town of Valdivia, situated on the south bank, and near the confluence of the two rivers. Boats ascend as far as San José, 12 leagues further, with no greater difficulty than is encountered on the Maule; and there is no doubt, that under the management of the German colonists who have recently settled in the vicinity, the fertile lands of this province will soon attract more commerce. A number of islands and forests of evergreens on the banks add much to the beauty of this stream.

The Tolten, principally alimented by the surplus water from Lake Villarica, after crossing the Indian territory, empties into the sea in latitude 39° 07′. Except the portion near the coast, and in the immediate vicinity of the high road, very little is known respecting it; for, although the Indians raise cattle, cultivate fields, and dwell in houses far better than many of the lower class of Chilenos possess, their antipathy to all of Spanish descent is unmitigated, and the white man is not permitted to come among them. Travellers who pass between Concepcion and Valdivia state that the plains on its banks, at five leagues from the mouth, are highly fertile and exceedingly beautiful. Here its breadth does not exceed 150 yards, though the depth is sufficient for steamboat navigation, if a bar existing across its exposed mouth, and the Indians, would permit the entrance of such vessels to the heart of their country. Mr. Miers says there is no obstruction to the entrance of ships of the largest class.

The Imperial drains nearly all the sub-Andine valley between latitude 38° 06′ and the Tolten; but, though many parties of Spaniards have visited its banks, they have been too constantly harassed by the Araucanians to think of geography, and even less is known of it than of the latter. The Cauten, a tributary from the loftier Andes, joins the united volume of the north and northeast streams in latitude 38° 48′, whence the whole volume flows, in a serpentine course, due west to the ocean. Several smaller streams empty into it between the confluence of the Cauten and the Pacific, at the junction of one of which, Las Damas, the early invaders founded the city of Imperial. Many a desperate encounter occurred in its vicinity; time after time was it burned, and now scarce a vestige remains. Here, at four leagues from the sea, there is water enough quite close to the shore for vessels of considerable tonnage. The breadth of the river is more than four hundred yards, and it has a scarcely perceptible current; indeed, the tide is said to ebb and flow more than twenty miles higher. Eight miles below, it divides into two branches, one, and the broader, continuing in a southwest direction; the other, a deeper though narrow current, turning to the northwest, empties into the sea amid scarped rocks. As the prevailing wind on the coast blows directly into the mouth of the larger volume, the sea heaps a bar of sand across it. All the country in the vicinity of the roads is described as fertile, and capable of producing wheat, vegetables, and fruits in profusion.

The Biobio is, beyond question, the great river of Chile. No less than two considerable lakes, which receive the melted snows of very extensive basins within the Andes, and also a large number of tributaries draining western ravines of the same chain and more than 600 square miles of the eastern slope of the Central cordilleras, unite to form it. At their junction, the Laja, Duqueco, and Bergara, its three principal affluents, have each a breadth of from 400 to 500 yards, with an average depth exceeding a foot. Of the three, the first is best known, its cascade having made it quite notable. Its origin is in a lake of the same name, at the foot of the volcano of Antuco, this lake receiving a part of its waters from the cordilleras of Pichachen, eight miles further east, although Antuco, Sierra Belluda, and a range to the northward, form the culminating points of the Andes. Within the Andes, the Laja flows in a deep ravine, which it has worn through beds of sand and volcanic conglomerates; but on arriving near the centre of the plain, its stream is almost at the level of the latter, the immediate bed being also composed of like materials. The falls are at sixteen miles to the southeast of Yumbel, and not far from half-way across the great plain. No less than six different strata are visible in the gorge between the superficial bed and the base of the fall, their faces forming a vertical escarpment some sixty feet high, by 1,200 to 1,300 feet wide. Though on a much smaller scale, the water pours in a double fall, not unlike Niagara. Prof. Domeyko says that the vapor of water which moistens and separates the porous and friable underlying strata, is here producing an analogous effect to that of the waters of Niagara, which wear away the schists under the calcareous strata there; and the falls of the Laja are receding towards the Andes, precisely as those of Niagara are approaching Lake Erie. The volcano of Antuco, with its smoke and flame, and the Sierra Belluda, with its glaciers and banks of snow, add no little to the charm of the panoramic view; but apart from the fact that the picture is probably the most enchanting in all Chile, the spot is more than ordinarily interesting to the student of geology. On the southern branch of the same river, there are also two fine cataracts, highly attractive in themselves, though scarcely comparable with the more imposing one just mentioned. Below the falls the two streams again unite, and have worn a deep and narrow channel in the solid rock, through which the volume rushes with great fury.

Originating on the slope dividing the waters of the Atlantic and Pacific, which is here to the westward of the Sierra Belluda, the Duqueco, after a west by south course of sixty miles, falls into the main stream not far from the western limit of the plain. The Bergara is the most southern tributary, its source being in latitude 38° 18′. Together with its affluents, it drains the plain between the Central cordilleras and the Biobio, joining the latter at Nacimiento, a small settlement in latitude 37° 26′, and about two leagues below the mouth of the Duqueco. The Biobio commences in an outlet of Lake Gualletue, from whence its course, as far as the valley of Santa Barbara—forty miles—is nearly northwest. Across the plain, to the confluence of the Bergara, its direction is more westerly, and thence the three united streams proceed, in a north by west route, seven leagues further, to the Laja. From the last point to the ocean—forty miles—the general direction is W.N.W., through an extremely fertile country—all its ravines, most of the hills, and a portion of the level fields between them being covered with fine timber. For two thirds of this distance the river, now more than a mile in width, flows majestically through the Central and Western cordilleras, in this latitude diminished to hills, none of which attain a greater elevation than 1,000 feet. From their rolling and diversified surface, large quantities of grain, wine, and timber are exported to the northern provinces; and were not the people of the district still apprehensive of the terrible aboriginal tribes—their neighbors to the south—it would inevitably become the most valuable part of the republic. That which seems most remarkable in the vegetation of this country, is the fact that forests do not exist either on the eastern slopes of the Central cordillera or the great plain; whilst the whole sub-Andine belt, as well as the entire region west of the first-named divisional line, is covered with grand Araucarias, Robles, Alerces, and Laurels, of various kinds, growing to the very surface of the water. At Concepcion the Biobio is a noble stream, nearly two miles wide, with abundant water for shipping, and it is navigable by boats as high up as Nacimiento; but, unfortunately, on account of the sand-banks across its mouth, and a heavy southwest swell very generally setting into it, it is not accessible from the ocean, except by small craft. To compensate for this somewhat, the Bay of Talcahuano is close by to the northward, and government has recently caused a survey to be made for a canal between the bay and river. The task was confided to Mr. Allan Campbell, a highly scientific and experienced engineer, whose report shows that such communication is practicable, and may be made at comparatively small cost.

The Itata has its origin in the lower Andes, nearly 2,000 feet above the Pacific, and not far from the thirty-seventh parallel. This is the branch that preserves the name to its source, though the Ñuble, its principal affluent, has really greater extent and volume. Above the junction of the latter stream, several torrents from the mountains discharge their waters into it, and impart velocity to its otherwise sluggish current. A part of these are heated mineral waters issuing from a district several leagues in extent, between latitude 36° 15′ and 36° 27′, longitude 71° and 71° 10′. From its head to the confluence of the Ñuble, by the winding of the river, the distance in a northwest direction is thirty leagues. The Ñuble is formed within the Andes at an elevation of 6,000 feet, partly by the copious streams of hot mineral water known as the sulphur baths of Chillan, and partly from the melting snows, whose summer line is scarce a thousand feet above them. As has just been stated, there is a large heated tract in this vicinity, some of the rocks being of such temperature that they scorch shoes or clothing remaining on them a few minutes, and for leagues around the air is poisoned by villanous emissions from *fumarolas* in many parts of it. The ridge which separates these waters from one of the sources of the Neüquen, a tributary of the Rio Negro, is about four leagues further east. From its western shed several small torrents descend to the Ñuble, from whose origin to the junction of the Itata the distance is thirty-five leagues, and thence to the ocean, in latitude 36°, thirteen leagues further. A number of smaller tributaries from the southward tend to swell its volume, though only one of any consequence empties into it from the north; and it is worthy of remark that whilst there is a regular decline of the plain from Chacabuco to the Chonos Archipelago, the principal tributaries of all the large rivers are from the southward. In its general extent, the Itata is regarded by those who know it as a wider and deeper river than the Maule, with less current than the latter, though interrupted by frequent ledges of rocks. Mr. Miers says that its banks are rocky and precipitous, preventing the use of its waters for irrigation—a natural obstacle of some consequence, as in this latitude there are times when agriculture would derive much benefit from such contribution. A bar across its mouth excludes vessels of all classes, and there is no shelter near, where they could safely embark the abundant products of the fertile country on its banks. Early writers speak of all these rivers as navigable; and it may be, that the gradual rising of the land and recession of the ocean, caused by continued earthquakes—facts now indisputably established—have reduced the depth of water to what it is at the present epoch; but unless we suppose a diminution in the volume from the Andes, an explanation seems more properly to be sought in the sand and shingle brought down by the rivers and deposited where the currents and swell of the ocean are in equilibrium.

In a statistical account of the province of Maule, made to the supreme government in 1845, the commissioners say: "The river *Maule*, which is the largest of all that water this province, has its origin among the mountains Descabezado and Campanario, situated at the centre of the cordilleras of the Andes. Thence it flows in a direction from east to west, until it discharges itself in the ocean, traversing consequently the widest part of the republic here, which is about forty leagues." They make no allusion to a lake there, nor is one of any extent mentioned in a detailed account of every visible object from the table-land at the base of the Descabezado given in the "Annales de la Universidad de Chile," by Professor Domeyko. He says: "At 3, P. M., we reached the upper plateau (*meseta*) of the Descabezado, which, at a spot where the bases of the greater and lesser Descabezados rest, is covered with perpetual snows, and from whence a *small* lake is seen at a little distance, as smooth and quiet as though it was in the most retired and sheltered valley of the world." This can scarcely be the ten square leagues of water here located by M. Gay, and it is to be regretted that his map of this vicinity is less satisfactory than those of even more southern districts.

The Descabezado, one of the summits in the fourth range counted from the plain, is still some miles to the southward of the dividing line of waters, from which, to the junction of the Loncomilla at the eastern base of the Western cordilleras, the Maule has few tributaries, and flows in a serpentine line with a resultant direction west by south. At the same time, here, as well as at many other points of the Andes, the hills separating the waters from those that fall to the Atlantic are invariably less elevated than the line which would connect the great cones or peaks. Deriving its supply in summer wholly from melting snows, the stream is deeper and more rapid during the earliest warm days, when the sun's heat is first powerful in the lower and sheltered ravines. After January the volume gradually diminishes; and even where it crosses the great plain, although the bed sometimes occupied is more than a mile wide, the rapidity of its current alone renders the Maule a river of note. There it is composed of several streams spread over the extent mentioned, with islands of shingle and sand occupying at least three fourths of the space between them. Its main volume does not exceed forty yards in width, with an average depth of two feet; and probably three fourths of all the water at this season passes through this channel. According to a MS. map in the archives at Santiago, its frequent distribution into several streams continues almost to the base of the Andes.

The Loncomilla, after gathering nearly all the water from the Andes and plain north of the Ñuble and the Western cordilleras, falls into the Maule six leagues south of Talca. Its three principal sources are the Perquilaoquen, the Longaví, and the Achihueno. The first of these has its origin within the Andes, near Cerro Florido, receiving many mountain brooks in its descent to the plain, and after a most circuitous course of twenty-six leagues unites with the

Longaví, the two being subsequently called Loncomilla. The Longaví and Achihueno also rise within the Andes, one to the north and the other to the south of the Cerro Nevado. Though neither of so great volume nor so long as the Perquilaoquen, they are much more rapid. Only the lower half of the Loncomilla was visited by me. Generally, that has steep rocky or alluvial banks, separated from fifty to one hundred yards according to the locality, and which, in the same manner, vary in height from fifteen to forty feet. Its length is only twenty miles, through ten of which it is navigable even in the dry season by launches carrying forty tons. For these ten miles it runs through and parallel with the mountains composing the Western cordilleras, its water clear, and current scarcely exceeding two miles per hour. As might be inferred from its sluggishness, there is very little shingle or sand, and its bed partakes much of the rocky character of its banks.

After draining the plain to the north and northeast, through nearly seventy miles, the Claro empties into the Maule twelve miles below the Loncomilla. This, also, is a stream of clear water from forty to fifty yards wide in the wet season and early summer, when it is navigable as high up as Talca; but which between January and June, at a league from its mouth, is only a brook, never exceeding twenty yards wide nor two feet deep.

Between the junction of the Claro and Loncomilla, the Maule may be said to enter the Western cordilleras; the first-named stream having washed the base of these mountains during the last forty miles of its course. From thence to the ocean, a distance of near eighty miles by the windings of the stream, the mountains on both sides are broken ranges of hills, never less than 200 nor more than 1,000 feet high. In some places they slope to the water; in others, terminate in short and narrow terraces or plateaus twenty feet above its level; and, except where occasional strata of rocks crop out, the whole is covered with forest-trees and plants in great luxuriance and variety. Until quite near to its mouth, the river apparently increases very little in width, its mean breadth from the Claro to within three leagues of the ocean not exceeding one hundred yards. Below the Claro, islands and deposites of shingle become much less frequent. The river bed, however, is by no means a uniformly inclined plane, but in places is obstructed by strata of rocks or accumulations of rolled stones, over which the rapidity of the current is much increased. If we consider the elevation of Talca (derived from six barometrical observations on four different days) to be the same as that of the mouth of the Loncomilla, (and it cannot differ very greatly,) the average fall of the Maule will be nearly eight feet per mile.* As more detailed information is given in Chapter XV, it need only be added here, that the river is navigable, at all seasons, by vessels of 300 tons to Constitucion, a secure port within its mouth, and by boats drawing eighteen inches water as high as half way up the Loncomilla.

This is the most northern of the rivers of Chile which is useful, except for irrigation or drainage; and the others will be briefly mentioned. Having their sources at greater elevations, and crossing portions of the plain more above the sea-level as we advance, whilst the distance from their sources to the ocean is not increased proportionately, they partake more and more of the nature of torrents loaded with detritus, whose places of deposite are constantly changing, and whose momentum no boat could resist. West of the ranges of mountains bounding the plain, there are ferries across all of them south of Santiago; and very near the sea, boat navigation would be practicable if there were suitable anchorages in the vicinity to render such mode of transport useful. But there is only one indifferent shelter for vessels between Constitucion and Valparaiso, and the products of the adjoining provinces must find their way to market through one or the other of these ports. Of all, the water from the Andes is divided into two or more streams spread over beds of shingle and silt, sometimes more than a mile

* On a map, in his notices of "*Araucania y sus habitantes*," published by Professor Domeyko in 1846, the height of Talca is 374 feet; and in the "Annales des Mines" for 1848, he says only 311 feet. The number of observations from which the results are derived is not mentioned; but he used the same barometer as myself, and the extreme differences of my observations were only 0.201 inch, or less than 200 feet.

wide. This, from its nature, cannot be permanent. Every freshet changes the channels, and thus a great obstacle is interposed to the erection of any but extensive and costly bridges to preserve communication between the north and south—improvements which the scarcity of suitable materials and the revenue of a young country scarcely authorize it to undertake. Only one such bridge has as yet been erected—that across the Maypu—at six leagues from the capital, and where a natural configuration of the shores favored the undertaking. Consequently, there are often days when travel to the south is wholly interrupted by streams ordinarily having only the volume of brooks, and even the highway between Santiago and Valparaiso becomes impassable.

The Mataquito, formed by the union of the Lontue and Teno, empties into the ocean in latitude 34° 48′. Its longest tributary—the Lontue—takes its rise about the centre of the Andes, and near Cerro del Medio, a snow-covered mountain, midway between a line joining the Planchon, Cerro Azul, and Cerro Nevado of Chillan, and the point occupied by the Descabezado. Cerro del Medio is on the dividing line of waters here, two leagues to the eastward of that which would pass over the crests mentioned. Passing through valley Grande, the stream descends almost parallel to the sources supplying Lake Mondaca, with whose surplus water it unites to the westward, and the two form the principal volume of the Lontue. Two leagues westward of Curicó, and near the western limit of the plain, the Teno, a much smaller stream from the northeast, unites with it, the two being called, from thence to the ocean, the Mataquito. Where the last penetrates the Central cordilleras their height exceeds 1,000 feet, with hills to the north and south of more than treble that altitude. In comparison with the rivers mentioned, the course of the Mataquito is quite straight, and conforms to the resultant of the two inclinations of the plain. From the source of the Lontue, by the windings to the sea, the distance exceeds forty leagues. Some years ago it was proposed to open a canal between this river and the Maule, so as to throw its whole volume into the latter stream, in the hope that its channel might be deepened and the bar across its mouth be broken down. But wiser counsels prevailed, and whenever journeying to Talca, one still crosses its principal arm over a lasso bridge.

The Rapel is formed from the waters of the Tinguiririca and Cachapual, both streams of considerable volume, whose sources are at very great elevations. Those of the former stream have their origin in the melting snows about the extinct volcano of San Fernando, and flow nearly west to the vicinity of the town of that name, where, after penetrating a range of hills belonging to the Central cordilleras, the stream is deflected to the northward and unites with the Cachapual. This last takes its rise on the eastern slope of the Cruz de Piedra (stone cross) group, a part of the culminating line of the Andes, here more than 17,000 feet high. Descending rapidly through a transversal ravine whose direction is somewhat north of west, and which terminates at the foot of the mountains, it thence turns northwest as far as Rancagua; next southwest by west, to a point formed by a prolongation of the central chain; and, having divided the latter, passes to the ocean in a nearly northwest line. Its origin is about latitude 34° 30′, longitude 69° 44′; its mouth, latitude 33° 53′, longitude 71° 51′; between which points its sinuosities measure 155 miles, with an average fall during the last hundred rather exceeding twenty-six feet per mile. At its entrance on the plain of Rancagua it divides into two principal arms, enclosing an island above the village of Peumo, which is above thirty miles in length. This is entirely composed of alluvium, and is noted for its fertility, as indeed is every part of both provinces irrigated by these streams.

The Maypu originates at an elevation of more than 11,000 feet above the Pacific in a portezuelo or depression between the extinct volcano of the same name and the Cruz de Piedra range. Popular opinion located its source in Lake Diamante, which occupies the bottom of a vast basin just to the eastward of the portezuelo, through whose volcanic strata the waters were supposed to filter; but by a series of levels Señor Pissis ascertained that the surface of the lake is actually seventy-five feet below the Maypu springs. For the first sixty miles the stream rushes through an exceedingly narrow and deep defile between two ranges of mountains, whose general direction is N. 28° W., and to which its course across the plain and through the central chain is nearly perpendicular. The thirty miles next the sea are in a line inclined a few degrees to the north of west. Its mouth is in latitude 33° 39′, longitude 71° 41′. Estimating its length at 150 miles, its mean fall is one foot in about seventy-three ; of which it descends 1 for 35 during thirty miles, 1 for 28 in the next 25, 1 for 174 through the following fifty, and 1 for 390 from thence to the sea. A bar extends across its mouth, which is nearly two miles from the land and parallel with the coast. Three miles north is San Antonio cove, a small place affording indifferent shelter to a few coasters and fishermen; the former finding occasional freights of produce from the estates on the lower part of the river.

Its principal tributaries are the Colorado and Mapocho. The former, whose name is derived from the reddish color of its always muddy waters, is alimented by snows from some of the loftiest mountains in America, four of the summits that overshadow its basin ranging from 17,000 to 22,000 feet in height. Scarcely forty miles in length, its whole course is within the Andes, along whose rocky defiles it rushes, urged by a momentum attained by falling one foot in every twenty-four of its *trajet*. The Mapocho also falls into it on the north shore. This is a clear stream, which proves the lower origin of most of its small affluents. It drains the ravines to the northward of the Colorado, enters the plain just to the eastward of Santiago, and crosses it in a nearly east and west line, as far as the Central cordilleras, along which it flows southwest until its junction with the Maypu. As its supply in very dry seasons is often small, and additional fields brought under cultivation required an additional supply, a canal cut from the Maypu along the very base of the Andes constantly pours a large stream into it just above the city of Santiago. The whole plain to the westward can be irrigated at will from this canal. Notwithstanding this addition to its volume, such is the nature of its bed, the extraordinary dryness of the air, and consequent consumption by the porous soil of the vicinity, that the small remaining rivulet not unfrequently disappears in the shingle a league west from the capital. It again appears, however, where the harder sub-strata, a mile or two nearer the Central cordilleras, force it above the surface. Its length is about seventy miles, and elevation of the headwaters above the junction with the Maypu, 12,000 feet.

The headwaters of the Quillota, or Aconcagua, are to be found in the basin, nearly enclosed between the Chacabuco ridge, which starts from Tupungato in a northwest direction, and the Cumbre ridge, which unites two of the Andean giants—Tupungato and Aconcagua. The most commonly travelled road from Mendoza passes near the banks of the principal stream for more than fifty miles, and travellers speak of it as a wild brook that is generally fordable early in the morning, and until the sun is high enough to dissolve the snows rapidly. It has but two tributaries of any note, the Colorado and Putaendo, both of which flow from the more immediate vicinity of the peak of Aconcagua. Although all the water produced by the melting snow on the western side of the main chain, and its more immediate lateral ramifications between the two great summits named, must pass into the valley of Aconcagua through one of these channels, yet, in the vicinity of the capital of the province, the stream is very little greater than the Mapocho, say fifty yards wide and two and a half feet deep in the centre. Its course is most serpentine and irregular; but, originating at an elevation of 10,500 feet in latitude 33° 05′, longitude 69° 51′, after winding 140 miles, it empties into the ocean in latitude 32° 55′, longitude 71° 20′. From the fact that they are more extensively subdivided, the valleys of Aconcagua and Quillota, watered by it, are the best cultivated and most productive in Chile. Valparaiso looks almost wholly to the valley of Quillota for its supplies of vegetables and fruits in their seasons.

The Chuapa, the Limari, the Coquimbo, the Huasco, and the Copiapó, small streams of melted snow-water that tumble through craggy defiles of the higher Andes with gradually swelling volumes, until they reach an atmosphere so parched that evaporation almost equals the supplies, are all mere brooks when they have descended to levels where man can render them useful. Over the tract they cross, between latitude 27° and 31½°, the scanty products of the soil grown under their influence are of value almost proportionate to the seemingly inexhaustible mineral wealth buried within the rocks of that district, as though nature would preserve in equilibrium man's reward for the sweat of his brow. Higher and higher within the cordilleras, wherever a plateau can be found with a ribband of water over it, there the husbandman creeps, and we may find him cultivating figs, peaches, and melons, nearly 4,000 feet above the ocean, and wheat some 3,500 feet higher. At 10,800 feet in these parallels, the water is found frozen every morning at sunrise; and though it never rains at that altitude, snow-storms commence before the close of autumn. There, only a few herbaceous plants are found.

The region crossed by these streams varies greatly from the country further south in its topographical features. It is far more broken and rugged, the quebradas are deeper and more numerous, isolated and groups of hills more frequent; even the candelabra-like Cereus has ceased; and though there do exist plains, often of many square leagues in extent, the surfaces of the streams are usually so far below their levels as to keep them hopelessly barren. One such plain, more than a hundred miles long and ten miles wide, exists between Vallenar and Copiapó, at a distance of seven or eight leagues from the sea. Across the southern extremity the Huasco river flows; but the level of its water is nearly fifty yards below the plain, and the rivulet can only be used in irrigating a plateau some 250 yards wide on each side of it. No doubt exists that the plateau was once the bed of a noble river. Now, water can only be obtained at two places on the whole plain; and so small is the quantity, that a traveller with a dozen animals will not leave a drop for those who may come after him on the same day. As it rarely rains more than once in two or three years, vegetation lies dormant, and then pasturage is not to be found; the animals that pass over it being from fifty to sixty hours without other food than nibblings from the posts to which they are tied at night. If the volume of the Copiapó, the Huasco, or the Coquimbo, could be augmented to equal even that of the Mapocho, the mining proprietors would cheerfully pay a million dollars.

For the geographical position, courses, and lengths of the several streams north of latitude 32°, reference is given to the map; though it must not be inferred either that they are laid down with great accuracy, or that their volumes are proportionate to the space on the map occupied by the lines indicating them. Not a drop of water reaches the ocean through the old bed of the Copiapó, and no one would suppose that the brooklet he steps across at Huasco is the *river* of that name on the map. None but professional mine-hunters have ever explored them all, and their chorography is not always very reliable. Prof. Domeyko made journeys to the sources of the Copiapó and Coquimbo, and from his MS. map the relative courses and distances have been laid down, after locating the mouths in the latitudes given in the Appendix to the second volume of the "*Voyages of the Adventure and Beagle.*"

BAYS AND HARBORS.

Were the eastern coast of the Pacific subject to such storms as constantly sweep over the corresponding shores of the Atlantic, if not actually diminished to a large extent, its present limited foreign trade would certainly be restricted to a smaller number of ports. Its proverbial tranquillity, however, authorizes vessels to anchor in roadsteads that are wholly open to the almost unvarying swell rolling across its broad expanse. Between the equator and Chilóe, anchorages entirely protected from the sea or gales are very rarely to be found; nor were the most secure of the few which nature has afforded always chosen by the settlers of the country as ports to the capitals and other cities they founded. They looked upon the sea only as a highway over which they must necessarily transport luxuries desired from home, or convey treasures they intended to amass in America; nor could they consider a harbor of any other utility than as a place where ships sometimes came for these purposes, or to land them succors. Whether five or five hundred miles from the sea, cities could only be founded where most of their treasures were to be the most speedily garnered, or the exigencies of conquest and control made necessary. Thither flocked colonists, soldiers, and priests; and there commerce and territorial wealth centred and accumulated. Moreover, their experience with the buccaneers was by no means a pleasant one. Cities on the coast were too accessible to men like Dampier, Morgan, *et id genus omne;* and on this account, if no other, they would have found it expedient to place their wealth at such distance from the ocean as would give them time to prepare for the reception of freebooters. Thus we find that every city of importance in South America, with one exception, is at a distance from the port through which it communicates with the world abroad; and there, also, until within very recent periods, were their principal custom-houses. A few officers, and a store or two at the ports, nominally prevented smuggling, and afforded temporary shelter to the goods which bad weather or want of conveyance delayed in despatching to the capital; but in those days contraband and *douceurs* were scarcely regarded criminal acts, and merchants and officers seemed to make common cause to prevent government from collecting a sum larger than a regard for outward appearances rendered indispensable. Scarcely any *employé* was too elevated to be bribed, and smuggling was carried on in the face of day, facilitated by the very fact alluded to at the commencement of the paragraph—the tranquillity of the Pacific.

At that epoch, Spain permitted commerce with her colonies only to national vessels, or others under licenses; none ever purchased who did not intend to repay themselves by fraud. Even vessels distressed for provisions, or damaged by stress of weather, were prohibited from entering the ports of her colonies; and when forced in by necessity, they were often refused assistance, or if assistance was granted as a favor, no other intercourse was permitted between the crews and the people on shore. Under these circumstances, towns built at the ports often remained mere villages; and Chile, being but a dependency of Peru, was traded with only from the great *dépôt* at the "City of the Kings." Even Valparaiso, the *entrepôt* for all the agricultural products supplied to the coasts of Bolivia and Peru, remained an insignificant town, inhabited principally by agents whose employers resided at Santiago, until the first quarter of the present century had passed. As late as 1820 not even good blacksmiths were to be found at Valparaiso, and those who built houses there were obliged to resort to the capital for such iron-work as they needed; nor is it yet fifteen years since government transferred the principal custom-house from the centre of the republic to the seashore. From that moment a new impetus was given commercial life at the port; merchants deserted the capital, property rapidly increased in value, new streets were opened, more elegant and commodious houses arose in every direction; and now, beyond dispute, Valparaiso is the greatest city bathed by the waters of the Pacific.

Of its port, in latitude 33° 2′, every writer on Chile has more or less to say; and the accurate plan of it given in Maps and Plans, No. 6, renders unnecessary here more than a few words. It is a semi-circular bay, nearly two miles wide across the mouth, which is wholly open to winds from the northward, and whose bottom also seems to partake of the hemispherical form, as deep water extends to within quite a short distance of the shores on all sides. These last rise rapidly to lofty encircling hills and precipices, broken by deep ravines filled with stunted though evergreen vegetation. As southwest winds prevail by day during the greater portion of the year, and the holding-ground is good, it offers a secure anchorage, and danger is to be apprehended only in the northerly gales occurring in winter months. It has usually been regarded safer for vessels to lie on the southwest side of the bay, when it is possible to get there; and in summer, the closer in-shore the better for the rapidity of discharging cargoes. This is also the most advantageous berth in winter; because, when the northers commence, the steepness of the bottom prevents ships from dragging far, and the undertow, or reaction of the surf from the rocks, greatly relieves the strain on their cables. But, in this place, as many vessels seek it, there is danger of their dragging down on each other, and, in the heavy sea that sets in, these collisions are fatal as the rocks. Sometimes northers pass over without doing much damage; at others, their effects are most disastrous, and all badly found or ill-placed vessels are driven ashore, or upon others, which they not unfrequently involve in their own destruction. At such times, too, vessels have been known to go down at their anchors, the gale and sea rendering it impossible for those on shore to send them the least assistance. During the violence of these storms—*temporales*, as they are called—the pressure of the atmosphere varies very little (rarely more than three tenths of an inch of the barometer) from its normal condition, but heavy showers of rain are frequent. In such a gale, occurring July, 1851, several valuable vessels, and even one of the British mail steamers, were lost, though the latter was evidently owing to mismanagement by the officers who remained on board. Then the bay was crowded with ships from every part of the world, numbers of which, *en route* for California, had come in only for refreshments; and the sight from the overhanging hills, though painfully appalling, was grand and majestic beyond description. Latterly it has been suggested that one or two powerful steam-tugs, retained in the bay through the winter, would be able to afford material aid to vessels so distressed. Government would do well to make this provision, since there is no doubt that, under the confidence which such auxiliaries would inspire, commerce would increase, and the outlay be repaid. In summer they might be employed to transport the mail or freight to and from the southern ports, and tow vessels into harbor.

Ships only find difficulty in entering when the southwest winds outside are so strong as to prevent their carrying sufficient sail to work up to the anchorage within the bay. There is abundant depth of water for vessels of the largest size quite close in-shore, and no dangers within any distance to which a prudent commander would approach, so that he may beat fearlessly to any unoccupied anchorage that suits him. The strong southerly winds never last more than a few hours; but as the squalls from the hills are often more violent than those in the offing, it is often better to await their moderation outside.

The never ceasing swell of the ocean, and great depth of water in the more secure parts of the bay, have hitherto prevented the erection of wharves for loading and discharging cargoes; and these operations are accomplished by means of launches, to and from which all packages are carried through the surf on men's shoulders. How they manage to handle parcels of such great dimensions and weight, as are many of the shipments, with the sea rushing between their legs, seems most extraordinary; yet accidents are quite as rare as at cities where every facility of machinery and smooth water is afforded.

Next in importance to Valparaiso on account of its commerce, but more extensive, better protected, and the natural port of a far more productive portion of the country, is the bay of Concepcion, or, as it is sometimes called, Talcahuano, in latitude 36° 42′. It is six miles long and four miles wide, with anchorage ground everywhere, abundant space, and all well sheltered. At the northwest extremity, protecting a portion of the entrance, is the island of Quiriquina, nearly three miles in length and one mile broad in its widest part, leaving a channel above half a mile across between it and the promontory that forms the western boundary of the bay. The main channel, which is quite two miles broad, lies to the eastward of the island. There the tide flows with less rapidity, and vessels usually prefer it, though with ordinary prudence the western approach is perfectly safe at all times. If without plans of the bay, and the wind is unfavorable for proceeding to the port of Talcahuano, in the southwest corner, on account of two or three shoals not far from its principal anchorage, vessels often come to under the southeast extremity of the island. Captain Beechy, R. N., also reported that a rock or rocky shoal, having only 15 feet water on it, existed in the southeast part of the bay, but the boats of H. B. M. surveying ship Beagle failed, in 1835, (after the great earthquake,) to find less than nine fathoms water about the place indicated.

The town of Talcahuano, containing with its suburbs about 4,000 inhabitants, bears the same relation to Concepcion, which is nine miles distant, that Valparaiso does to Santiago. Formerly the city of Concepcion—or, as it was often called from the Araucanian settlement on which Valdivia founded it, Penco—was on the southeastern shore and near to the mouth of the little river Andalien; but repeated destruction by earthquakes, and their consequent sea-waves that rolled into the bay, finally drove its inhabitants to a somewhat more elevated site on the banks of the Biobio. Beyond a doubt the bay of Concepcion offers greater commercial advantages than any harbor in the South Pacific. Besides being sufficiently extensive to accommodate all the transporters of goods the entire nation can ever require, it has neither obstacles nor danger to prevent access by the most ordinarily intelligent masters, is amply protected from storms, is within a temperate and salubrious climate, and is the natural outlet to a country of unsurpassed fertility, from which may be obtained valuable mineral as well as agricultural products. At one time many believed that these great local advantages would build up Concepcion, at the expense of Santiago, or, in fact, that the former must inevitably become the capital of the new republic. And such would have been the case with an enterprising commercial population; but this result is no longer possible; too much influence, priestly as well as pecuniary, has been concentrated at Santiago, ever to permit such translation. Had it not been that the Indians hemmed them in on all sides, and no settlement was safe from their raids much beyond musket-range of the town, poor agriculturists as they were, the people of Concepcion would have offered such amounts of produce for export as would have created a far more extensive city than now exists. Indians, earthquakes, and neglect of its interests by the Central government, have prevented its wealth and resources from being fully developed. The former, like all of their origin elsewhere, are disappearing under the vices and diseases sown by the white race; and already so much of the land about the Biobio has been brought under cultivation, that, within a few years, foreigners have erected extensive mills for grinding the large quantities of wheat grown. Most of the flour has latterly found its way abroad—to California and Peru; though a large portion, together with nearly all the wine and other products of the soil, are still sent to Valparaiso and other northern ports. The largest number of vessels known to enter the bay of Concepcion, in any one year, was during 1850. Of all nations the number was 363, of native 104, of American 198. A very large proportion of the last were *en route* for California, and stopped here for refreshments; and others, whaling ships, called for the same purpose. The total number of vessels which entered the port during the four years ending with 1851, and their tonnage, are shown in the subjoined table.

Nation.	1848.		1849.		1850.		1851.	
	Vessels.	Tonnage.	Vessels.	Tonnage.	Vessels.	Tonnage.	Vessels.	Tonnage.
Chilean	113	18,639	90	16,422	104	19,169	88	16,495
American . . .	70	22,908	135	42,598	198	59,921	106	36,227
English	8	2,115	7	2,309	26	8,401	23	5,459
Peruvian . . .	13	3,170	10	2,550	12	2,696	9	1,908
Other nations . .	8	2,460	13	3,816	23	7,526	9	2,723
	212	49,293	255	67,695	363	97,713	235	62,811

During the latter half of 1851, whilst the port was under blockade, and the province in rebellion against the government, only six American vessels entered.

Under Spanish rule, the bay of Concepcion was well protected by fortifications which the immediate vicinity of their warlike neighbors compelled them to preserve in order; but according to the last report (1851) from the Minister of War, in my possession, the two forts were in very bad repair, and needed new batteries. Only eleven guns were then mounted.

From the number of vessels frequenting it, its capacity, and security, Coquimbo bay, in latitude 29° 56′, next claims attention. Its form and dimensions are those of a quadrant of a circle with a semi-diameter of about two and a half miles. On the west, south, and east, it is well sheltered. To the north it is open; yet as there are never tempestuous winds from this last direction, the anchorage is regarded as perfectly secure at all seasons, the only losses of vessels being through gross carelessness. Usually the winds are from the south and west, which causes a current to the northward, between the rocky promontory bounding the western side and the Pajaros Niños, two rocky inlets to the northwest of it. If it fall calm whilst a vessel is attempting to enter through this channel, she is in great danger of being swept against the almost vertical face of the rocks. When the islets are passed, there are no other obstructions; and as four fathoms of water will be found within one cable's length of the seaward shore, and twice that space on the landward side of the harbor, a ship may work into the anchorage in all security. Along the latter, the surf breaks quite constantly, and sometimes with considerable violence; though at the anchoring ground, under the promontory, as the prevalent winds are off the lands, the swell is scarcely felt. Here the weather is almost uniformly fine; the atmosphere is clear for many successive months of the year, and the temperature charming. Foreigners have generally been led to believe the town of Serena, which is rather more than two leagues distant, owes its name to this delightful atmospheric condition; but, in fact, the city was christened, in 1549, *San Bartolomê de la Serena*, in honor of the birthplace of Valdivia, when none professing the Christian faith knew whether its skies were clear or cloudy.

So tranquil is the sea at the little town of Coquimbo, that wharves to facilitate the loading of ships may be built safely and advantageously. Then, if the proposed railroad to Serena be extended up the valley of the river to the vicinity of the copper mines, the trade of the port must greatly increase. Ores and bar-copper form the principal exports. There are some hides and a few Chinchilla skins; but the province is too poorly supplied with water to afford agricultural products, and, indeed, is at times dependent on the South for a portion of its own wants. Water may be had in abundance, though neither of very good quality, nor to be obtained without considerable trouble. Fine fish, both vertebrated and testaceous, may be had at very low prices, and crustacea abound among the rocks.

Separated from Coquimbo bay by a terrace of sand and fossil shells, one mile in width, is Port Herradura, a small and almost land-locked harbor, shaped, as its Spanish name imports, like a horse-shoe. Its entrance is not more than three cable-lengths across, which is further narrowed by a rock under water off the northern point. Within, the harbor is about three fourths of a mile in diameter, with deep water until close in with the southern and eastern shores. On the west side it is steep to the very rocks. With a leading wind vessels may enter easily, and in the southwest angle they will find perfect shelter from all winds, and water so smooth that they may carry on repairs with the utmost security. Here, an English company under the direction of Robert E. Allison, Esq., has an extensive smelting establishment for copper ores, at which a large proportion of the workmen are Europeans. Availing himself of two masses of rock called Whale islands, Mr. A. is forming a wharf near the works, alongside which vessels may load and discharge their cargoes. A few fishermen and his workmen are the only settlers here.

Herradura is not a port of entry, and vessels must obtain permission to enter from the custom-house at Coquimbo. In the two ports, the number of vessels and their tonnage, since 1848, have been as follows:

Nation.	1848.		1849.		1850.		1851.	
	Vessels.	Tonnage.	Vessels.	Tonnage.	Vessels.	Tonnage.	Vessels.	Tonnage.
Chilean	75	10,647	63	9,562	63	11,014	37	6,386
English	65	30,876	119	58,139	135	60,969	101	42,777
American . . .	7	4,074	11	5,094	15	6,011	11	4,345
French	4	950	4	1,228	6	1,725		
Hamburg . . .	2	518			2	385	2	504
Other nations . .	3	798	2	713	6	1,565	3	1,512
	156	47,863	199	74,736	227	81,669	154	55,524

Other information respecting these harbors will be found in Chapter X, giving an account of a visit to the provinces of Atacama and Coquimbo.

Huasco, a port of entry, though scarcely more than an open roadstead, in latitude 28° 27′, is resorted to by vessels for copper and copper ores, and coasting vessels carrying food and other necessaries for the mining population of this portion of the province. Owing to very deep water outside, its anchorage is close in with the shore and wholly exposed to northerly winds. These bring in a heavy swell, when vessels are obliged to rely wholly on their cables and anchors for safety, as it would be next to impossible to clear the rocky island, lying seaward, in anything like a blow. Fortunately, severe northers rarely occur here. When the surf will permit boats to approach the beach, good water may be had from the little river just to the northward of the village; but there is no other refreshment for vessels. Except where the solitary rivulet gives animation to the borders of the channel which conducts it to the sea, the surrounding country is most barren and miserable. Yet so long as the mines continue to yield, so long will vessels continue to resort there, even the British mail steamers stopping regularly for the silver freight, although the distances from Coquimbo and Caldera are such as inevitably cause their arrival in the night. Recently, one was totally lost in the attempt to go in. Counting them, the average number of foreign arrivals during the last four years has been 43, measuring 23,248 tons; of national vessels 34, tonnage 4,859; vessels under the English flag 36, tonnage 20,746. Only 13 American vessels, or about 3 per year, entered at the Custom House within the same period.

Until the completion of the railroad between Caldera and the capital of the province of Atacama, the port of the latter was at the village of Copiapó, a wretched open and dangerous roadstead, difficult to enter because of numerous rocks about it, and unsafe to lie in from bad holding-ground and the sudden swell that frequently sets toward the shore. Why it should have been chosen when there were two safe harbors within 20 miles, neither of which is more distant from the capital, it is impossible to understand. Of course, such a place was unfitted for the terminus of a railroad, and the engineers having selected Caldera bay, in latitude 27° 03′, government transferred its Custom House and officers to that locality during the year 1851.

This is a fine bay of nearly square form, quite a mile across, with neither external nor internal dangers, and deep water. Though open to northwest winds, these are extremely rare and never very violent, and under all circumstances the anchoring ground in the northeast angle is a safe one. Since the completion of the railway, the company have erected a long pier in the southeast quarter, which serves as an excellent breakwater as well as for discharging and loading ships. This is the most thorough engineering work yet executed in Chile, and reflects great credit on the gentleman who planned and executed it in a region so destitute of resources.

Copper and silver ores from the mines toward the Andes are the only exports. Except that distilled from sea-water and sold by the railroad company, even good water is not attainable. That from the wells is so completely impregnated with lime and salts, that only the wretched fishermen who dwell on like inhospitable parts of the coast can ever drink it. Notwithstanding the enormous prices of every article of food, the town laid out soon after the work commenced is gaining rapidly; and in less than three years after the engineers landed on the hopelessly barren shores of the bay, the road and mole were completed, and more than 2,000 people were housed, though there never had been more than 300 or 400 inhabitants at the old village of Copiapó. At the last accounts, Caldera was thriving even more surprisingly. The road afforded facilities for transporting ores previously worthless because of the cost of freight to the sea, furnaces were in course of erection for smelting, new and handsome houses were being built, and many ships came with coal and goods to exchange for copper and silver ores. Even a cargo of Yankee ice had found ready purchasers, and government had given one of our countrymen the exclusive privilege of selling this product of Massachusetts.

During four years ending with 1851, the trade of this collection district, which embraces the minor ports of Chañeral de las Animas, latitude 26° 24′; Paposo, latitude 25° 02′; and Barranquillas, latitude 27° 31′, as well as Caldera, was carried on in 355 vessels, measuring 114,768 tons. Of these, 208 arrivals were of national vessels, 130 English vessels, (including semi-monthly steamers,) and 4 American vessels. At the minor ports, vessels only call when they know that a load of copper ore is ready; and as the transportation from the mine is on the back of mules, the process of collecting a ship-load is tedious, and several years probably elapse between their visits.

Southwest of Caldera, and separated from it by a rocky peninsula a mile wide across the sandy neck connecting it with the main land, is Port Yngles. Its entrance is open to the northwest, and only four cable-lengths across, after which it widens into a bay a mile broad, of nearly the same length, and having two or three coves secure against all winds. The water is very deep, clear, and smooth; but the bottom is hard and stony, and in consequence is not so good holding-ground as that of Caldera. Nevertheless, the facilities it offers for building wharves, and the less swell than in the former port, would have secured its selection as a terminus for the road, but that the distance must have been increased two miles, or a heavy grade constructed at the verv outset. There are no settlers on this bay, and I do not know of any vessel that has visited it legally since H. B. M. surveying ship Beagle.

So much is elsewhere said of the harbor within the mouth of the Maule—Constitucion—that little remains to be told except for strictly professional men. Its latitude is 35° 19′, and the approach to it rendered unmistakable by the *Piedra Iglesia* (church rock,) which lies a mile to the southward. If the wind be fresh, or was so on the day preceding, the breakers across the bar, or certainly on its southern extremity, will clearly designate one of the dangers to be cared for, and one must patiently wait the tardy movements of the harbor pilot. In fine weather a ship may anchor temporarily two to three miles northwest of the Piedra Iglesia, though it is better to remain under weigh and keep to the southward of the port. Boats may land on the outer beach under Cerro Mutün, or, as it is called in the sailing directions of Captain Fitzroy, *Maule Head;* but there is always delay and no little risk in attempting it, for the surf is constantly high and always treacherous, and the beach of sand is so mixed with broken shells that it is too soft and steep for even a whale-boat to be hauled up without danger. Yet, with a little enterprise, how great a place in Chile this might have been! As long ago as 1835, Captain Fitzroy said of it: "To land here was perplexing enough, for a heavy surf broke on the bar of the river, and nearly as much along the shore; but with some risk and difficulty we effected our purpose in two light whale-boats, which could be hauled up directly they touched the beach. Nearly all the population of a thriving village, called Constitucion, came down to meet us (on the 21st) and assist in hauling our boats up the steep though yielding sand, where, for our comfort, they told us a whale-boat's crew had been drowned not long previously in attempting to land. From a height overlooking the river, village, and neighborhood, we enjoyed a very pleasing view so long as we turned away from the bar of the river, and the surf. A rich country and a fine river are pleasing things at all times, but the difficult approach to Constitucion mars half its beauty. Only the smallest craft can cross the bar; it is dangerous for boats to land on the outer beach, and difficult for them to profit by the few opportunities which occur of passing the bar without risk."

"Notwithstanding these local disadvantages, Constitucion may thrive wonderfully hereafter, by the help of small steamers; for she has a most productive country around her, abounding in internal as well as external wealth, and a navigable river at command. Besides this, in 1805 a very practicable passage was discovered through the Andes, about seventy leagues south of Mendoza, not far from the latitude of the river Maule, almost entirely level, and fit for wagons—the only pass of such a description between the Isthmus of Darien and Patagonia."

It was only when the harbor of Valdivia, in latitude 39° 53′, had been thoroughly surveyed, that navigators learned how small a portion of its extended waters were suited for vessels above the size of coasters. Previously it had been pronounced by several—and one of them no less

5

a person than that paladin of modern sailors, Lord Cochran—the finest harbor in the Pacific. At the entrance, the distance between Morro de Gonzales, on the south shore, and Molino point, northeast of it, is two and three-quarter miles. Both eminences are high and covered with wood, as are all the hills of the vicinity. From mid-channel there, to the narrowest part of the harbor in a southeast direction, the distance is two miles and a quarter; all that portion of the bay being without hidden dangers, except close in with Molino point, though considerably exposed to the action of the wind and sea. Just beyond this an extensive sand-bank, of late years dry at low water, is formed by the silt brought down in the water of the river, whose form and dimensions are subject to constant vicissitudes. Here the basin assumes a totally different form, suddenly widening to twice its dimensions at the narrows, and then dividing into two river-like inlets, one of which extends in a south by east direction three and a half miles, and the other toward the southeast more than five miles. Midway between the sand-bank and the point of the promontory separating the inlets is Manzera island, half a mile in length and 300 feet high, its northern point being in a line with, and distant from, the south shore of the river more than three fourths of a mile. No vessel drawing more than twelve feet water should attempt to enter the latter, and under all circumstances it is safest to have the local pilot's advice. The best anchorage for large vessels has been found in the little cove immediately west of the bank, and where the shore is quite steep, and the water so deep and smooth that they may be hove down in all security so close that a good long plank will reach the land. Lord Cochran hove down and repaired the frigate O'Higgins here, after his gallant capture of all the fortifications in 1820. There also is the best watering-place; and provisions may be had in abundance and at moderate rates from the town, eight miles distant.

At one time Valdivia was regarded as almost impregnable. The fortresses which were commenced by the Dutch squadron under Hendrick Brower, in 1643, were added to and strengthened when recovered by the Spaniards, until nine separate batteries had been erected on opposite shores of the harbor. Their 118 guns of all calibres (when Lord Cochran attacked it) were so mounted as to rake the entrance and channel from several points at the same time. Fifteen years later the forts were almost in ruins, and the guns so nearly disabled that they could hardly fire a salute without danger. Only four are now garrisoned, and these mount but 22 guns, of which 6 form a mountain battery constantly in demand against the neighboring Indian tribes.

From 1848 to 1851, both inclusive, there entered the port 121 national and 45 foreign vessels; the former measuring 28,799 tons, and the latter 12,180. Of the foreign vessels, 8 were under the American flag and registered 2,192 tons; though from the Custom House returns they scarcely appear to have had trade sufficient to pay port dues, the total invoices of goods landed amounting only to $587. Within this district is also Rio Bueno, across whose bar very small crafts can pass.

The last revenue district whose port remains to be specially described, embraces not only the island of Chilóe, with its multitude of good harbors and safe coves, but also San Miguel, a harbor in latitude 50° 17′, on the eastern shore of Madre island, and which is spoken of as a convenient anchorage. The name of this district and its most frequented port is Ancud, or, as it was called by its founders, San Carlos. It is situated at the northern extremity of Chilóe, in latitude 41° 51′. Formerly Castro, about midway of the eastern shore of the island, was the capital of the province, and there the annual ships from Peru landed their treasures. San Carlos is a broad and open bay, more than ten miles across, whose southwest termination is a land-locked inlet or harbor, quite four miles in length by an average width of one mile. Unlike most of the other ports that have been mentioned, it has several shoals and obstacles for the navigator to avoid, whose risks are no little increased by strong tides. Once anchored in Port San Carlos, as the inlet is called, a ship may lie in all security. However, to facilitate loading and discharging, the usual berth is much nearer to the town, situated on a little promontory at the bottom of the bay; but this is greatly more exposed during the prevalent northerly and westerly winds; and as the bottom is both shoal and rocky, and a heavy swell immediately sets in, the anchorage is very unsafe.

When the island was under the rule of Spain, the port was in a good state of defence. There were two fortifications on points of Lacuy peninsula, northwest of the town, which commanded both entrance and anchorage; several batteries on the town side, and one on Corona point, the northern extremity of the island. Most of these were long since suffered to fall into decay, and now only two, mounting in all fourteen pieces of artillery, remain guarded; even these can scarcely be considered in serviceable order. What its commerce was under the laws of the mother country, may be judged of very fairly from Byron's narrative of the loss of the Wager. He says: "They have what they call an annual ship from Lima, as they never expect more than one in the year; though sometimes it happens that two have come, and at other times they have been two or three years without any. When this happens they are greatly distressed, as this ship brings them baize, cloth, linens, hats, ribbons, tobacco, sugar, brandy, and wine; but this latter article is chiefly for the use of the churches: matte, an herb from Paraguay, used all over South America instead of tea, is also a necessary article. This ship's cargo is chiefly consigned to the Jesuits, who have more Indians employed for them than all the rest of the inhabitants together, and, of course, engross almost the whole trade. There is no money current in this island. If any person wants a few yards of linen, a little sugar, tobacco, or any other thing, brought from Peru, he gives so many cedar planks, hams, or punchos (ponchos) in exchange. Some time after we had been here a snow arrived in the harbor from Lima, which occasioned great joy amongst the inhabitants, as they had no ship the year before, from the alarm Lord Anson had given upon the coast. This was not the annual vessel, but one of those that I mentioned before which came unexpectedly. The captain of her was an old man, well known upon the island, who had traded here once in two or three years for more than thirty years past. He had a remarkably large head, and therefore was commonly known by a nick-name they had given him of Cabuço (Cabeza) de Toro, or Bull Head. He had not been here a week before he came to the governor and told him, with a most melancholy countenance, that he had not slept a wink since he came into the harbor, as the governor was pleased to allow these English prisoners liberty to walk about, instead of confining them, and that he expected every moment they would board his vessel and carry her away; this he said when he had above thirty hands aboard. The governor assured him he would be answerable for us, and that he might sleep in quiet; though at the same time he could not help laughing at the man, as all the people in the town did. These assurances did not satisfy the captain; he used the utmost despatch in disposing of his cargo, and put to sea again, not thinking himself safe till he had lost sight of the island." Great must have been the terror inspired by Lord Anson's squadron, of which poor Byron's vessel formed one.

Its safe harbor and abundant supplies of the provisions most needed by ships, made it a favorite resort for whalers in the South Pacific; and as soon as relief from the Spanish incubus permitted the port to be thrown open, the number of vessels calling for refreshments rapidly increased. The coasting trade, too, has augmented in far greater ratio than either the population of the island or that of the entire country. An exhibit of the last four years is given in the following table:

Nation.	1848.		1849.		1850.		1851.	
	Vessels.	Tonnage.	Vessels.	Tonnage.	Vessels.	Tonnage.	Vessels.	Tonnage.
Chilean	47	9,678	41	10,149	46	12,899	65	16,831
American . . .	14	4,146	4	1,614	17	5,212	17	5,794
Other nations . .	8	2,364	15	4,976	15	4,438	7	1,099
	69	16,188	60	16,739	78	22,549	89	23,724

Of the foreign vessels during the above period, fourteen were English, thirteen French, and ten Peruvians.

These are the ports resorted to by foreign vessels most generally; nor are they permitted to enter others without first anchoring at one of them and obtaining permission to do so. Except for an occasional load of copper sometimes conveyed to points of the coast north of Valparaiso, or perhaps coal from the Colcura or Coronel mines, south of Talcahuano, there is nothing to attract them elsewhere, and no shelters in stress of weather. Vessels coming through the Straits of Magellan have sometimes found it necessary to stop for wood* and water, or by adverse winds, at Port Bulnes, a good harbor within the first narrows; but it has no trade whatever, and hitherto the convict colonists have not been able to cultivate a sufficient supply for their own wants.

Most disastrous have proved the two attempts to form settlements here. First, the King of Spain despatched a numerous fleet, under the command of Sarmiento, in 1582, who founded a city with all the pomp and solemnities practised on like occasions by his nation at that era, giving to it the name of San Felipe, in honor of his royal master. Four hundred men and women were embarked for this colony; though it is probable that a portion of them never reached the locality, as we have authentic record of only three fourths of that number having landed on the shores which had played so treacherous a part when that most energetic and faithful officer and seaman had first passed to the eastward through the straits. Of these, only two survived, one of whom was picked up by Cavendish, who called the place Port Famine, in allusion to the fate of the emigrants, nearly all of whom had died from starvation; and the last survivor was taken off in 1589 by Andrew Mericke, though he did not live to cross the Atlantic. And subsequently, when the young republic of Chile found Juan Fernandez an impracticable penal settlement, the prisoners were transferred to Port Famine, to which the name of Port Bulnes was given in honor of their then President. Inducements were offered other citizens to emigrate there, and at the close of 1849 the population comprised 378 persons, of whom 194 were men, 88 married women, and the remainder children. Owing to the fostering care of the government, their condition was reported to be most prosperous; sheep, hogs, and black cattle had been introduced, which multiplied well; and the prospects were that wheat, potatoes, and certain vegetables, could be cultivated advantageously: but there was not a soul willing to remain beyond the term of condemnation or service for which he had stipulated. Hoping to make them more contented, and to advance the growth of the colony more rapidly, a new governor was sent out, with enlarged powers, in February, 1851; but, instead of attaining the desired objects, the prisoners and a part of his own guard mutinied during the revolutionary struggle of the same year, barbarously murdered him and the priest, and made their escape in two vessels lying in the harbor, of which they took possession forcibly. A part of the criminals were retaken and executed, and another governor sent there in 1852, of whom my last intelligence (May, 1853) was, that himself and six companions had been made prisoners by the Patagonians and carried to the interior of the country six months previously. Large sums had been offered for their ransom, and it was still hoped that they would be liberated.

ISLANDS.

Of the thousand islands which line the western coast of Patagonia, we have little intelligence. The region is too wild and rugged, and the soil too cold and moist, to encourage the settlement of civilized human beings; and the few wretched Indians who wander from place to place along their inhospitable shores are driven to exist on a scanty supply of seals and fish snatched from the ocean. Excepting the unfortunate colony in the Straits of Magellan, Chilóe

* There are also veins of coal more than five feet thick in the vicinity, but they have never been worked for want of intelligent miners.

and the smaller islands between it and the main land, as far south as Caylin, are the most austral settlements acknowledging Christian rule.*

Chilóe, or the "*ysla grande*," as it is designated by the natives in contradistinction to the numerous lesser islands about it, is the most northern of the series extending from Cape Horn to the southern extremity of Chile proper. It lies between the parallels of 41° 46′ and 43° 26′, and the western meridians 73° 23′ and 74° 27′, and is separated from the continent to the eastward by the Corcovado and Ancud gulfs, whose average breadth is about thirty miles. The strait or narrows of Chacao, between the northern end of the island and the main land, is only two miles wide. The western and southern shores are tolerably unbroken in the direction of their lines; the eastern and northern are deeply indented, so that the mean breadth of the island probably will not exceed 38 miles. This gives an area of 3,800 square miles, whose average elevation above the sea is more than 500 feet. None of the hills rise higher than 2,600 feet; and except in small cleared tracts about the towns, nearly all the land is covered with dense forests. These embrace Robles, Alerce, Mañu, Avellana, Muermo, and other varieties of useful woods, of which large quantities are exported. From the numberless rivers interlacing them, the forests render the country almost untraversable except along the road from San Carlos to Castro, and in their immediate vicinity. On this account, and as most of the inhabitants live within a short distance of the eastern shore, very little is known of the interior of the country. On the western side there is a lake 12 miles long, which communicates with the sea; several smaller ones on the southern half of the island; and many short streams flowing from the central ridge in both directions.

During six years' experience of Padre Agüeros, (*Descripcion Historial de la Provincia y Archipielago de Chilóe*,) ice had never been known even in the small streams, and frost or snow was very rare. Rains, however, are continual during many months of the year, and are known to fall without ceasing during an entire lunation, accompanied by violent winds from the north and west. Nor can the weather be depended on when it is fine even in summer; for in the month of January he often experienced as heavy storms of wind and rain as during the winter months, and good weather lasted only so long as the wind prevailed from the south. Capt. King was led to believe that the longitudinal range of hills traversing the island, by arresting a portion of the wind and rain from the Pacific, very sensibly modified the climate of the eastern side and the islands in the Gulf of Ancud, these enjoying much finer weather than was to be experienced about San Carlos. The inhabitants also say that their climate is undergoing change, and rains are not so frequent as formerly. They attribute it to the gradual clearing of the land and disappearance of the forests. Yet, cloudy and damp as writers have made it, fine crops of wheat, barley, and potatoes, are raised every year. This archipelago is one of the native localities of the potato, whose cultivation here, as elsewhere, has transformed a watery and insipid tuber into one of the most valuable esculents known. Horses, cattle, and swine, propagate rapidly and contribute to the commerce of the island, whilst its coasts abound with fish, oysters, and other shell-fish, which enter largely into the consumption of its inhabitants.

Chilóe was first seen by the party under Don G. H. de Mendoza, who, in 1558, started from Valdivia to discover the Straits of Magellan, at that time supposed to be the only opening between the north and south seas. Alonzo de Ercilla, the since famous epic poet, and one of his companions, tells us of a supposed broad lake, with many beautiful inhabited islands, from among which a gondola came to them, impelled by twelve oars. The Indian rowers leaped to the shore, and saluted the Spaniards humbly and reverently, evidently regarding them as

* When the Intendente or Governor of the province visited Castro for the purpose of taking a census of the population, a family of Indians waited upon him to render an account of their property; who, upon being asked whence they came, replied, "*Del fin de la Christiandad.*" The name being new to the Intendente, it was explained to him that they belonged to Caylin, which was more generally known by the above name, because there existed no Christian population beyond, or to the southward of that island.—*Narrative of the Surveying Voyages of H. B M. Ships Adventure and Beagle, vol. i.*

"Hombres ó Dioses rusticos, nacidos
En estas sacras bosques y montañas."

Learning from them that the apparent lake was but a gulf, communicating with the sea through a narrow though dangerous channel, himself and ten other adventurous spirits resolved to visit the land on the opposite side; and there, on a wild spot, half a mile farther from the shore than the wanderings of his companions, the bark of a tree served as a tablet for the first inscription in Chilóe. At that time the Chonos tribe inhabiting it were extremely numerous; but shortly afterward, the Spaniards founded Castro, and a portion of their number was soon destroyed by labors in the mines discovered on the island. A raging epidemic carried off nearly one third of the remainder; multitudes fled in terror from the pestilence and tyranny; and, at the present day, there are scarcely any remnants of the tribe on their ancient homestead. The majority of the actual population belong to the Huilli-che tribe, whose ancestors were brought from the adjoining continent by the Spaniards; next them are creoles of mixed descent; and lastly are foreigners, who are neither born on the island nor of Chilóe parentage. Their total numbers in 1832 were 22,540 souls; and in 1844, 24,498—an increase of less than one per cent. per annum during the twelve years. In 1848 there were 537 males and 538 females born, of whom 168 were illegitimate; and 317 males and 327 females died, showing a much greater ratio of increase. In the same year there were 240 marriages.

All writers, from the time of Padre Ovalle, in the first third of the 17th century, to the officers of the British surveying ships, in 1835, speak in high terms of the amiability and hospitality of the Chilotes; traits which their countrymen at Santiago, who have more recently visited the island, take great pleasure in mentioning. They are not, however, an industrious race, owing partially to the fact that nature has dealt so beneficently by them. Subsistence may be obtained with very little labor; and thus the lower orders are contented with their supplies of shell-fish, and pigs and poultry—the latter being attainable with almost as little trouble. As late as the visit of the Beagle, ground was prepared for cultivation in a most primitive manner. Even the old Roman plough in use by their countrymen on the continent had been introduced to small extent, and most of the people continued to break up their fields by means of two sticks of hard wood. These are made from six to eight feet long, much larger at one end than the other, and tapering to points at the smaller extremities. One is held near the middle with each hand, and, being pointed obliquely to the ground, they are forced forward by pressure of the abdomen and chest, until ten or twelve inches under the surface. A boy or other assistant then places near the ground, and beneath them, a third stick, or piece of wood. The latter serves as a fulcrum for the levers, whose longer ends being forced down, the soil is raised up. Whilst the ploughman shifts his poles to a spot in advance, his companion breaks up the clods; and the rich, sandy loam, with this little preparation, affords quite excellent crops. Capt. King says: "Rude as this process is, the operation is rapidly performed; and I have seen a field ploughed in this way, that would not do much discredit to an expert ploughman with a European plough." The vicinity of Castro and Dalcahue, on the eastern side of the island, and the archipelago in the Gulf of Ancud, have most land under cultivation. These afford the greater proportion of the provisions needed by ships that call at San Carlos, as well as a large contribution for its own consumption, and surplus for coasting-trade. Multitudes of canoes, or piraguas, are employed in transporting the various commodities to the capital, whose people become no little excited if a continued northerly wind greatly delays their customary supplies. These piraguas—some of them as much as forty feet in length—are constructed of planks literally sewed together with flexible vines, and caulked with Alerce bark and moss. They are sharp at both ends, like whale-boats; and, to preserve their forms and resist the pressure of water, have ribs to which the planks are secured with tree-nails. No metal is used in any part of their construction; even the anchors, or grapnels, being pieces of strong wood, crossed, and loaded with stone. For a sail, the ponchos of the eight or ten men who compose the crew are temporarily sewed together and hoisted, by means of a lasso, on a rude mast—the crazy bark tottering along before the breeze, almost miraculously delivering its timid mariners in safety at their ports. Few of them, it is alleged, have learned to swim; and when danger impends, instead of endeavoring to extricate their boat, they throw themselves on their knees, beat their breasts, and invoke their patron saint, to whom they make vows of candles or penance. Yet they sometimes make voyages as far as Concepcion.

The principal islands between Chilóe and the continent are San Pedro, Lilehuapu, Caylin, Tanqui, Lemuy, Quehuy, Chelin, Quinchao, Chaulinec, Apiao, Chalin, Nayahiu, Talcan, Cahuach, Meulin, Los Chauques, Caucahue, Tabon, Calbuco, and Puruqui; of which Quinchao, Lemuy, and Tanqui are the largest, most populous, and productive. Nearly all named are settled, and many of them have excellent harbors. Besides these there are numerous smaller islands, in all eighty-two, which are resorted to by the natives for their marine products. To the southward is the Guaytecas group, the northern cluster of the Chonos archipelago; from which to Staten land, east of Cape Horn, the chain of islands is continuous. Some of the Guaytecas group are nearly twenty miles long. They are frequently visited by sealing and otter-hunting parties from Chilóe; who have one of the best harbors on the coast at Port Low, at the northern island. Water, wood, and fish, both testaceous and vertebrated, may be had there in abundance.

Westward of the Guaytecas, and somewhat nearer to the *ysla grande*, is Huafo—called by Narborough, (*Sir John Narborough's Journal*,) in 1670, "No-man's-land." It is about twelve miles long, eight miles broad, and was inhabited by Huy-huen-ches until the Spaniards transported its people, nominally to prevent their giving aid and information to the buccaneers, though, in reality, the working of their mines had no little influence.

Chilóe and its archipelago are the only islands of intrinsic value to the State.* The others are all of much less extent than those of the archipelago; and, with one exception, are either so nearly desolate, or so unsafe as places of refuge for ships, as to be worthless to organized society. First in order of these is Mocha, under the 74th meridian, in latitude 38° 23′—a lofty island, seven miles in length by three in breadth. Previous to the seventeenth century it was inhabited by Araucanians, under whose care domestic animals multiplied with great rapidity; and its 800 people (or 3,000, as mentioned by Ovalle) being removed to the main land in 1685 by Quiroga, the island was, at one time, almost overrun by them. Subsequently, ships seeking whales and seals among the Pacific islands hunted down great numbers of them, and now only a few stray horses and pigs are to be found. There is no doubt that its soil and climate would permit sustenance to quite a large industrious population, though no effort has been made to re-populate it. During the great earthquake of February, 1835, the island was uplifted about two feet; and the shock was so strong that the people accidentally there taking seals could not stand on their feet.

Santa Maria, a comparatively low island, of the same length as the last, with an arm-shaped sand-spit extending to the E.S.E. from near its centre, is in latitude 37° 03′, and distant from the main land but a few leagues. It has a cliffy coast, and many dangerous, outlying rocks and shoals, which require more than ordinary care on the part of the navigator who approaches it. In the year 1712 Frézier† found the island low and nearly a plain, and about three quarters of a league in length, from north to south. Southwest of it there was a little island, but it no longer exists separately, and a rock at some distance to the W.N.W.; one dangerous bank to the N.E., and another, near half a league in extent, on the N.W. side. The anchorages were to the north and south of a point on the eastern shore, though, as there was but little water, few vessels resorted to them. Now, both hydrographical and topographical features are greatly

*The name Chilóe is derived from Chil-hue, which signifies a district or province of Chile, and was given to it by the tribe which emigrated from the main land, prior to the arrival of the Spaniards, under the influence of a desire to preserve the memory of their father-land. According to Molina, all the natives—subjugated as well as free—call their country Chile-mapu, the land of Chile; and its language, Chili-dugu—the language of Chile. Why it has been transformed into Chilóe, instead of Chilue, no one knows.

†Relation du Voyage de la Mer du Sud aux côtes du Chily et du Perou: Paris, 1716.

changed; but since that period there have been three violent earthquakes, at each of which the city of Concepcion, at a distance of 30 miles, has been almost totally destroyed. If analogous and only equal effects were produced during those of 1730 and 1751 to those of 1835, the present dimensions and form of the island are at once accounted for. That single subterranean phenomenon raised the entire surrounding bed of the ocean an average of nine feet; so that where there was a depth of 30 feet of water in 1834, the officers of the Beagle could find only 21 feet in the following year. Two months after the earthquake, Capt. Fitzroy took many measures in places on the island, where no mistake could possibly be made respecting the amount of its elevation. On large steep-sided rocks, where vertical measures could be correctly taken, beds of dead muscles were found ten feet above the recent high-water-mark. A few inches only above what was then the spring tide high-water mark were putrid shell-fish and sea-weed, which evidently had not been wetted since the upheaval of the land. One foot lower than the highest bed of muscles, chitons and limpets were adhering to the rock where they had grown; and two feet lower than the same, muscles, chitons and limpets were abundant. Before the earthquake an extensive rocky flat around the northern portion of the island was covered by the sea, only a few projecting rocks showing themselves above water. After it, the whole surface was exposed for many square acres, and the stench arising from the dead shell-fish, with which it was covered, was abominable. The result of his measurements proved that the southern extreme of the island had been raised eight feet, the central portion nine, and the northern portion upwards of ten feet.

Close as it is to Arauco, whose people, jealous of their liberties, have it ever in sight, it has been the scene of more than one struggle with Europeans. Within our own century, Benavides, a notorious renegade chief, seized more than one American vessel which had gone there to take seals and replenish their stocks of provisions. A brief outline of these piratical acts and other audacious events in the career of this freebooter is given in Capt. Basil Hall's "*Extracts from a Journal written on the coasts of Chile, Peru, and Mexico,*" Chapter XXIII. The island is inhabited, and its people are able to furnish abundant supplies of vegetables. Wood and good water may also be had, though very little else.

Quiriquina, three miles long and one mile broad, lies in the mouth of Concepcion bay; its direction being N.N.E. and S.S.W. The outline is undulating, and elevation much less than that of the continent on either side of it. A recent geological examination by M. Crosnier developed a stratum of coal or lignite, of bad quality, where it crops out near the N.W. extremity; and, from its analogical structure to portions of the neighboring land, he was led to believe that extensive beds exist below the surface strata. The entire soil is composed of a reddish detritus, exhibiting in many places strata of fossil-shells, similar to those mixed with the sands of its beach; proving that it must have undergone at least two submersions before it was definitively elevated above the surface of the bay. From what we have seen of earthquake agency and effects on the neighboring island of Santa Maria, such a result cannot be regarded as very extraordinary. There is a very good anchorage for vessels near its S.E. extremity.

Perhaps no portion of our globe, of like dimensions, has ever been invested with interest for so great a number as has the island of Juan Fernandez. Even in after life, when "sober second thought" would teach us that Crusoe and his humble servitor had not even the exile of Selkirk as their basis, memory refuses to part with its juvenile heroes, and we live on repeating Defoe's narrative to our children, sincere in our early sympathies in behalf of those whom his life-like portraits had seduced to belief in their reality. Yet, why this island should have been fixed upon by the world as the scene of poor Robinson's trials and resignation is not comprehensible, unless by association with the narrative of Selkirk, in Capt. Woodes Rogers's "*Cruising Voyage round the World,* 1708-11, *with an Account of Alexander Selkirk's living four years on an island:* 8vo., 1712;" which had been printed, as the title shows, but a short time previously. The island of Defoe's narrative would undoubtedly be in the north Atlantic, and not in the south Pacific ocean.

Instead of one, there are two principal and several smaller islands composing the group under this name. They were discovered in 1563 by Juan Fernandez, a Spanish navigator, who gave his name to them, and subsequently endeavored to obtain a patent from the Viceroy of Peru for the purpose of colonizing them. Though it is also called by the Chilenos *mas-á-tierra*, (nearest the land,) the largest and nearest to the continent is that which is commonly known by the discoverer's name. Its length from E.N.E. to W.S.W., measured through the centre, is 13½, and its greatest breadth less than 4 miles, the form being somewhat that of a crescent, with its cusps to the southward. The latitude of Cumberland or San Juan Bautista bay, as English and Spaniards have differently named it, a tolerably good anchorage on the N.E. side, and the only one at the island, is 33° 38′; its longitude, 78° 53′; and its distance from the coast 360 miles.

The approach to it is described as most remarkable and picturesque—a mountain resembling in form a blacksmith's anvil, and hence called "El Yunque," rising 3,000 feet above a shore formed by an abrupt wall of dark-colored, bare rock eight or nine hundred feet in height. As is all the more elevated portion of the island, El Yunque is wooded nearly to its summit; but there are grassy and fertile plains of considerable extent, with beautiful ravines watered by streams which originate in the mountains and come tumbling towards the sea. Such is the northern aspect. The southern forms a marked contrast, being comparatively flat and low, and nearly barren; and the sea-fowl about Santa Clara, off its southern extremity, and the surf along its beach, adding to, rather than detracting from, the desolation of the scene.

The first attempt to populate the island was by the discoverer, who brought several families and a few domestic animals with him from Peru; but they soon found their isolated residence irksome where gold was not to be had, and returned to the continent, leaving behind only goats and the germs of future fruits. Afterwards it became a resort for pirates and buccaneers, who found there abundant refreshments for debilitated crews; and it is very sure that without such supplies at command, these rovers could not have prosecuted their depredations on the eastern shores of the Pacific in the manner they did. Some have thought that the animals and edible plants were introduced by the buccaneers for their own benefit; as it is well known that the Viceroy caused a great many dogs to be landed from Peru and Chile, for the purpose of hunting down and exterminating them, in order to prevent the island from affording so much assistance to the freebooters. The names of Sharpe, Hawkins, Dampier, and Watlin, inspired terror from Chilóe to Acapulco; and Juan Fernandez—too near the track of ships homeward, as well as outward bound, yet too distant from the main land for reliable protection—must, if possible, be deprived of those supplies which rendered it so attractive and valuable to these daring men. It is now certain that seals and sea-lions are the only indigenous animals; but goats, being unmolested during many years, had multiplied rapidly, and literally overran the island, affording all the fresh meat that could be desired. Unfortunately, the scheme of the Viceroy proved ineffectual; for the dogs only drove the goats to crags and eminences where they could not follow, and have since been compelled to hunt seals or starve. To the present day, numbers of goats may be seen browsing about the cliffs or bounding from crag to crag on the loftier portions of the island; but if, by chance, one meets a troop of the dogs ranging the low grounds, they flee, terrified at the sight of man.

Subsequent to the marauding adventurers, Juan Fernandez was visited by Anson and Ulloa, officers whose attainments placed them among the highest of their respective nations, whilst they insured a more enviable fame for posterity. The former—tempest-tossed, his squadron broken up, more than half his crew annihilated by scurvy, and scarcely enough of the remainder in health to manage his ship—was only too happy to find any place of refuge where the bloated and tottering creatures around him could be restored to health and vigor, and his ship somewhat prepared for the warlike service on which he had been despatched. During the three months that he remained at the island in 1741, an accurate topographical survey was made, and a most faithful account of its topography, climate, productions, &c., is given in the narrative compiled by his secretary, Rev. Richard Walter: "*Lord Anson's Voyage around the World,* 1740 *to* 1744, *compiled by R. Walter: London,* 1748." The squadron had long been expected on the coast; and the Ulloas, then engaged with the French academicians, La Condamine, Bouguer, and Godin, in measuring an arc of a meridian across the equator, were recalled by the Viceroy of Peru for the purpose of placing the coast in a state of defence. This completed, as far as practicable, they were placed in command of two fine frigates, with orders to search for the English navigator, something of whose disasters had reached the vice-regal court at Lima. When they reached Juan Fernandez, however, Anson had departed, and they soon returned to Callao and their scientific labors, in their account of which, this cruise to the island forms an interesting episode. Shortly afterwards, the island was garrisoned by the Spanish government, and a fort erected for the protection of the harbor; but the fort was destroyed by an earthquake the year following, (1751,) when the sea rose to a great height, overwhelmed nearly all the dwellings which had been erected, and drowned a large number of the colonists. Though the fort was soon and more securely rebuilt, the settlement was abandoned after a few years, and no farther attempt was made to people the island until 1819, when the Chile government made it a place of exile for state prisoners. Four years later its only inhabitants were three or four herdsmen; and although a large number of prisoners, together with a governor and guards, have since been sent to it, a mutiny among the latter left the governor without a charge, and the great earthquake of 1835 so destroyed the buildings that government has never attempted their restoration. At this last shock, the island was so violently shaken that the trees beat against each other, and a volcano burst through the sea about a mile distant from the land, where the ocean was more than 300 feet deep, from which water and smoke were thrown up during the greater part of the day. Great waves swept the shores of the island; and after the sea had retired, old anchors and other evidences of ships that had visited the bay, were laid bare several times. A particular description of the phenomena may be found in Sutcliffe's "*Account of the Earthquake that occurred on the Island of Juan Fernandez and Talcahuano,* 1835: 8vo., *London,* 1839." Sutcliffe was then governor of the island.

Under the auspices of a Chilean company, another effort has been made to render the island useful. In 1851 this company rented it from government for a specific term of years, with the intention of cultivating vegetables and fruits for the northern mining districts; and to carry out their plan, they held out inducements to emigrants and afforded them facilities for agriculture. For the latter, its agreeable temperature and abundant rains eminently fit it during the season when vegetation on the neighboring continent would perish but for artificial irrigation and fertile soil. Though there are probably not more than 100 acres of level land, its valleys abound in streams and are exceedingly productive—apples, peaches, figs, grapes, quinces, cherries, and strawberries, together with all the varieties of vegetables, being well flavored and attaining large sizes. Among the most interesting and valuable indigenous plants, none of which have yet been found on the continent, are Azara fernàndesiana, Berberis corymbosa, Colletia spartioides, two varieties of Eugenia, seven varieties of Rea, Zanthaxilon mayen, and a Santalum, which last, according to the account of Capt. King, R. N., is a true Pterocarpus. No mention is made of the last, however, in the Botany of Chile by M. Claude Gay. In addition to the wild goats and dogs, already mentioned, there are also horses and asses, birds of several varieties in the forests, and almost incredible numbers of fish and lobsters, of excellent quality, in the sea surrounding it. Quite a large quantity of dried codfish is annually taken to the Valparaiso market. In short, for vessels requiring only refreshments prior to or after the long voyage round Cape Horn, and a moderately smooth harbor in which to refit, there is no place in their track offering so many facilities as this Eden of the east Pacific.

Santa Clara or Goat island lies a mile to the southward of the west extremity of Juan Fernandez. It is a mile and three quarters long, one mile broad, and is in undisturbed possession of goats and birds.

Mas-á-fuera (the most distant or outermost) is about ninety-two miles to the westward of

Juan Fernandez, in latitude 33° 49′, longitude 80° 53′. Though smaller, it is quite as lofty as the latter island, and, like it, is covered with trees, through avenues in which, rivulets of water may be seen pouring to the sea. There is a sort of bank on the north side; but it is so steep, and the water is so deep over it, that there is no safe anchorage for vessels, and no attempt has been made to colonize it. Padre Guzman says there are multitudes of wild goats upon it.

Los Pajaros, or Tres Coquimbanas desiertas, are low rocky islets, lying about 12 miles from the coast, in latitude 29° 34′, of which the northernmost is much the smallest. As their names import, they are deserts, resorted to only by sea-fowl. To the northward there are two or three others, of still less extent, but they are of no value whatever: these are the Choros, three islands in latitude 29° 16′, of which the longest is two miles long; and Chañeral, an island of nearly similar size, in latitude 29° 01′. There was an American sealing schooner lost here a few years ago, from a norther coming on whilst she was at anchor in the bay on its north side.

CHAPTER II.

POLITICAL DIVISIONS, AND DISTRIBUTION OF INDUSTRIAL RESOURCES.

PROVINCE OF ATACAMA: ITS BOUNDARIES, TOWNS, MINERAL WEALTH, AND BALANCE OF TRADE.—PROVINCE OF COQUIMBO: ITS BOUNDARIES, TOWNS, SOIL, ROADS, PRODUCTS, AND TRADE.—PROVINCE OF ACONCAGUA: ITS BOUNDARIES, TOWNS, SOIL, AND PRODUCTS, MINES, AND TRADE.—PROVINCE OF SANTIAGO: ITS BOUNDARIES, TOWNS, FERTILITY OF SOIL, AGRICULTURAL AND MINERAL WEALTH, AND PROPOSED RAILROAD.—PROVINCE OF VALPARAISO: ITS BOUNDARIES, TOWNS, THE VALLEY OF QUILLOTA AND LAVADEROS.—PROVINCE OF COLCHAGUA: ITS BOUNDARIES, EXTENT, DEPARTMENTS, TOWNS, AGRICULTURE, CATTLE, AND REVENUE.—PROVINCE OF TALCA: ITS BOUNDARIES, DEPARTMENTS, TOWNS, AGRICULTURAL SURPLUS, AND MINERALS.—PROVINCE OF MAULE: ITS BOUNDARIES, EXTENT, TOWNS, AGRICULTURE, STATISTICS, CATTLE, MINERALS, AND MANUFACTURES.—PROVINCE OF ÑUBLE: ITS BOUNDARIES, TOWNS, BATHS OF CHILLAN, AGRICULTURE, CATTLE, MINES.—PROVINCE OF CONCEPCION: ITS BOUNDARIES, TOWNS, FERTILITY, AGRICULTURAL PRODUCTS, WINES, TIMBER, MINES, COAL, FLOUR MILLS.—PROVINCE OF ARAUCANIA: ITS LIMITS, THE PEOPLE, PHYSICAL DIVISIONS OF THE PROVINCE, SKETCH OF THE NATURAL FEATURES ALONG THE TWO ROADS THAT TRAVERSE THE COUNTRY, PHYSIOLOGICAL DESCRIPTION OF THE INHABITANTS, THEIR DWELLINGS, AGRICULTURE, AND PROBABLE MINERAL WEALTH.—PROVINCE OF VALDIVIA: ITS BOUNDARIES, TOWNS, SMALL AMOUNT OF CULTIVATED LAND, GERMAN COLONISTS, AGRICULTURAL PRODUCTS, MINES, FORESTS, AND COMMERCE.—PROVINCE OF CHILÓE: ITS BOUNDARIES, TOWNS, CHONOS ARCHIPELAGO, FORESTS, CULTIVATION, APPLE ORCHARDS, SHELL-FISH, MINES, MANUFACTURES, AND COMMERCE.—STATISTICS OF POPULATION AND MORTALITY FOR EACH DEPARTMENT OF THE REPUBLIC.

The territory of the republic is separated into thirteen principal portions, styled Provinces. These are divided into Departments, the departments into Sub-delegations, and the sub-delegations into Districts; each having its appropriate ruler, whose commission is held, either directly or by delegated authority, at the sole will of the President. Several of the provinces have been created subsequent to the organic law at the declaration of independence, and one of them so lately as July, 1852.

ATACAMA.—This, the most northern, erected into a separate province in 1843, originally formed part of the province of Coquimbo. It is bounded on the north by Bolivia, south by the department of La Serena, in the province of Coquimbo, east by an imaginary line passing through the culminating points of the Andes, and west by the Pacific ocean. Elsewhere it has been said that Chile claims to the 24th parallel of latitude. In the instructions from Capt. Fitzroy, R. N., to one of his officers about to leave on detached service, he says: "Remember that Paposo is the northernmost inhabited place over which the government of Chile has authority;" and by the observations of that officer, Paposo was found to be in latitude 25° 02′ 30″. Native writers on geography, speaking of the boundaries, say: "On the north by the desert of Atacama,"—a broad tract several degrees in width; so that where Bolivia begins and Chile terminates, is yet to be decided. I have copied a boundary line, as far as it is laid down, from a MS. map in my possession, compiled from data furnished by Don Bartolomé Navarete.

Atacama comprises three departments—Copiapó, Vallenar, and Freirina—divided into 25 sub-delegations, and 82 districts. Each department has a capital city of the same name, to which is usually prefixed that of a titular saint. Copiapó—or, as it was christened, San Francisco de la Selva—is also the capital of the province, and, by consequence, the residence of the Intendente. Besides these interior towns, Caldera and Huasco are its commercial ports; and there are villages, with more than 1,000 inhabitants each, at the Chañarcillo and Tres Puntas mines, and smaller assemblages in other mineral districts. Coasting vessels and others, which obtain license at Huasco or Copiapó, are also permitted to visit at Chañeral, Peña Blanca, Herradura, and Pajonales, in the former district, and at Chañeral de las Animas, Paposo, Flamenco, and Baranquillos, in the latter; all of them villages numbering from 50 to 500 souls each. Commerce with the Argentine republic is permitted through the custom station at Rio del Transito ó Naturales, which is between Vallenar and the Andes. Such statistics relating to the population of this and the other provinces as it has been possible to obtain, will be found in a table at the end of the chapter.

As its soil, except on very narrow bands along the Copiapó and Huasco rivulets, is utterly barren, the whole industrial resources of the inhabitants are in the mines, with which its hills abound. But from want of fuel to reduce the ores, and because of the expense of transportation across regions destitute of water or grass for their animals, they are prevented from deriving full advantage from even this source of wealth. Notwithstanding these obstacles, however, the prosperity of the province has latterly made rapid advancement, and the impetus given its trade by the success of the railroad between Caldera and Copiapó has already roused its citizens to other enterprises. Extensions of the same road are under contract to Chañarcillo and Tres Puntas, that will pass near copper mines whose ores, though rich in metal, it has never been possible to transport lucratively. More than this, as there is a very eligible pass near the headwaters of the Copiapó river, towards which there will be transportation by rail for about 90 miles, it is expected that the commerce with Salta and Tucuman, which is now carried on through Cobija in Bolivia, will be transferred to Caldera, and the communication with those Argentine provinces be greatly increased. During 1850 there were shipped from Atacama to foreign ports products to the value of $1,443,642, and to domestic ports to the value of $5,175,231; almost all of which—silver and copper—forwarded to Valparaiso only in obedience to the laws of trade, was immediately sent abroad. The silver uniformly goes to England. In the same period the value of the imports was $2,457,501; of which the foreign goods naturalized—for there were no direct arrivals—were estimated at $804,876, leaving a balance in favor of the province amounting to $2,717,730.

Coquimbo.—This province is limited, on the north, by Atacama; its southern boundary is the river Chuapa; and the eastern and western are as those of the preceding great division. La Serena, Illapel, Combarbala, Ovalle, and Elqui, are its departments, which are divided into 58 sub-delegations, and these again into 227 districts. La Serena, a prettily situated town on the south bank of the Coquimbo river, and within a mile of the sea, is the capital of the province. Each department has its capital of the same name; besides which, the principal towns are Coquimbo, La Compania, San Isidro, Tambo, and Guanta, on or near the Coquimbo river; Barrasa, Guamalata, Sotaqui, Antileu, Rapel, and Carreu, on the Limari and its branches; Huantelauque, Pupido, Mincha, Canela, and Chuapa, on the river of the latter name; and there are intermediate villages about Punitaque, Tamaya, Andacollo, and other mining stations. Its ports for coasting-trade are at Tongoi and Totorallillo; and for the collection of duties on cattle and goods brought from the Argentine provinces there is a custom-house at Calderon, near the base of the Andes.

Mountain streams are more frequent than in Atacama, and, as their supplies last longer, a much greater quantity of land is under cultivation; yet there is not sufficient to supply food for the numbers whom its mineral wealth attracts. After the valley of the Coquimbo, the vicinity of the Chuapa is the most productive agricultural district; not that the latter region is destitute of mineral wealth, but that the roads over which mining products must be transported to market are so long and defective that ores will scarcely repay cost, and there is no superabundance of wood for smelting purposes. Like every other in Chile, this valley is nearly level, broad, and, wherever water can be applied to it, very fertile; but above the straight line of the uppermost irrigating trench, all is as bare and brown as is the highway. Dr. Darwin was surprised to observe how the seeds of grass and other plants seemed to accommodate themselves, as if by acquired habit, to the quantities of rain which fell in different parts of

Chile. One shower far northward in Atacama produced as great an effect on the vegetation as two in the parallel of Huasco, and three or four about Illapel; and a winter at Valparaiso so dry as greatly to injure the pasture, would produce the most unusual abundance at Huasco, only 275 miles farther north. Nor is it a less interesting fact for pomologists, that in all parts of northern Chile, fruit-trees produce more abundantly at a considerable height than in the lower country. This circumstance has been remarked by more than one traveller in the mountainous region; and the size and flavor of the dried figs, peaches, and grapes, from Huasco and Guanta, have surprised all in our own country who have had the opportunity to see them.

Communication between the extremities of the province is kept up over two principal roads—or, rather, two bridle-paths—one quite near to the coast, the other through the departmental capitals. There are, also, innumerable similar tracks, leading from them to the several mining districts. Wheeled vehicles can be used only in the immediate vicinities of the larger towns, and for a few miles along the valley of the Coquimbo river. Since our departure from Chile, one railroad has been projected between La Serena and the port eight miles distant, and another between Tongoy and the copper mines of Tamaya, in the vicinity of Ovalle. As may be inferred, these mines are exceedingly productive; and, fortunately, they are in the possession of gentlemen fully resolved to profit by the experience of their countrymen in Atacama. A road is also needed from La Serena as far up the valley as Elqui, and then Coquimbo would rival Atacama in wealth, though one mostly produces silver, and the other only copper. I am not prepared to say that such a road could be constructed without a great outlay, but am fully assured it would prove a valuable investment. Another measure of great public utility is the erection of a dam across the outlet of the lake, near the headwaters of the Coquimbo river, by which the supply to the valley could be regulated. For want of such provision, the haciendas suffer very greatly during years when there has been but a light fall of snow on the Andes.

As a portion of the domestic trade is carried on by land, and does not enter the custom-house statistics, it is not possible to ascertain the actual agricultural deficiency. Taking the year 1850, when the crops were a fair average, as a standard, provisions were brought by sea to the value of $433,503, and from the Argentine provinces to the value of $22,840, of which three fourths of the latter sum was for black cattle. In the same year, similar domestic provisions were exported to the value of $47,872. Adopting the last census as correct, its 85,000 people will have required, for the subsistence of each individual, food which cost $4.75, besides the introductions from Aconcagua by land.

Aconcagua.—The northern limit of this province is the river Chuapa; its southern is partially the range of mountains which, springing from the peak of Tupungato, near the 33d parallel, leaves the main chain of the Andes in a northwest direction, then, after crossing the head of the great longitudinal valley, bends to the southward and forms the Central and Coast ranges, and partially by the Cuesta Blanquillo, a northern spur of the same range, which separates it from the province of Valparaiso. Its eastern and western boundaries are, respectively, the Andes and the Pacific. The range from the Andes, in its original direction, is called the Cuesta de Chacabuco, subsequently the Cuesta de la Dormida. It was at the former mountains that the first great battle was fought between the royalists and patriots, whose eventual results liberated the country from the crown of Spain; and the Cuesta de Chacabuco has thus become holy ground to the nation. Within this province is the peak of Aconcagua, the loftiest summit (22,300 feet) now known on the American continent.

Its departments—San Felipe, Andes, Ligua, Petorca, and Putaendo—are divided into 41 sub-delegations and 242 districts. Its capital, the city of San Felipe, one of the largest and most prosperous interior towns of Chile, is situated near the junction of the main stream of the Aconcagua with the Putaendo, one of its tributaries. San Felipe is laid out like the other large towns; has its public square, paved and lighted streets, alameda, is well watered, and has many large and commodious houses. Santa Rosa de los Andes—or, as it is sometimes called, Villa Nueva—the chief city of the department of the Andes, lies on the margin of the southern bank of the river, and 15 miles to the southeast of San Felipe. Its extent and appearance in 1825 were not greatly dissimilar to the latter city, each then having a population of about 5,000 souls. But Santa Rosa has stood still during the progress of its neighbor, whose dimensions and numbers have nearly doubled. Santa Rosa is the frontier customs station, in Aconcagua, for goods to and from the Argentine republic, and travellers usually make their final arrangements here for the passage of the Andes. Putaendo, in the valley watered by the river of the same name, is about 10 miles to the northward; its population, including the suburbs, not far from 5,000. Petorca is in the valley of, and near the headwaters of the Longotoma, one of the streams whose combined waters form the Ligua. In 1847 its population numbered 2,400. La Ligua is still smaller. It is on the southern bank, and about 10 miles from the mouth of a stream of the same name; its people, as well as those of Petorca, relying as much on mining as on agricultural labors for their support. Besides these towns, there are villages named Coquimbito, Llaillay, San Roque, Panxegua, Curimon, Puente de la Viscacha, Melon, and Purutum, on or near the Aconcagua; Molles, Quilimari, Conchali, and Guantelaque, near the coast; and Lunaula, Pupido, Hierro, Alicagua, and Longotoma, more in the interior. The southern half of the province is much the most densely settled, this moiety having a better supply of water for agricultural purposes, and a shorter distance to market for the produce of its mines. It has no port of entry, though coasting and other vessels call at Papudo, Pichidanque, Conchali, and Zapallar, where they deliver small quantities of goods, and receive copper and agricultural products. None of these are very safe anchorages, nor is there one in all the province. They are embraced in the Valparaiso collection district, from which license must be obtained before visiting them—a formality not followed by all mariners, as is known, to the cost of the revenue.

The face of the country is thoroughly broken, several ranges of mountains from the great cordilleras dividing into minuter ramifications, that spread over by far the larger proportion of the province. Yet, even among these there are many small ravines and basins favorably situated for cultivation, and the valley of Aconcagua and Quillota, as it is called nearer the sea, is justly famed for its fertility and fruitfulness by every stranger who visits it. The length of the valley in which San Felipe is situated is about 15 miles, its breadth 13; that of Putaendo, north of, but communicating with it, somewhat smaller. All of this valuable portion is parcelled out in possessions of small extent, which are separated by enclosures of adobes; and it is said that, by this system, the land here will yield about one third more than an equal space of ground elsewhere in the republic. Further north there are other less extensive, though scarcely less productive, plains. All the fruits, vegetables, and cereals cultivated in any part of Chile thrive well here and lower down the valley: even the cherimoya, an exquisite tropical fruit, attains considerable perfection. Its white strawberries and grapes have great reputation at Santiago, and the aguardiente, distilled from the juice of the latter, is preferred to that of any other province. Olives also yield well, and there is wanting but a little more enterprise and industry to obtain an immense produce from this small district. As its ample fields afford adequate supplies of alfalfa, a most nutritious pasturage with which to fatten cattle, very large numbers are raised. The part of the province most used for breeding and rearing them lies between the valleys and central ridge of the cordilleras, whose ravines and table-heights afford very good natural pasturage from the time that the snow disappears. Some of these tables and other similar tracts near the coast are sown with wheat or barley, dependent on rains to sustain and mature them before the dry season is fully commenced. Such crops, called "*de roule*," are never so good as those of artificially irrigated fields.

Gold, in small quantities, is found at several "*lavaderos*" (washing places). Argentiferous copper in many mines, and varieties of exceedingly rich copper ores, have been discovered about the hills of San Lorenzo, San Antonio, Catemo, and Jajuel; all of which are wrought productively. From most of these mines specimens are now in the collection brought home by the Astronomical Expedition, as is mentioned in the report of Dr. Smith. There are no published statistics to show what amounts of agricultural or mineral products are obtained, but it is well known that there is a large surplus of both above the provincial consumption. For the same reason, there are neither means of ascertaining its domestic trade nor its consumption of foreign goods, except of those which pass through the custom-house at Santa Rosa. From its returns, the imports from the Argentine provinces in 1850 amounted to $229,003, of which the sum of $44,453 was in silver piña and bars; $24,145 in copper; $7,300 in gold dust; $25,166 for (3,353) black cattle, yearlings, &c.; $16,474 for (2,884) horses, mules, and asses; $38,793 for common soap; $19,592 for tallow; and $13,939 for raisins. Of course, the larger proportion of all these articles were consumed elsewhere. Neither native nor foreign naturalized goods were exported in return. The railroad commenced between Santiago and Valparaiso will, when completed, pass across the southwestern corner of the province, and within about 22 miles of San Felipe. If this distance be also laid with iron, the choice of markets and reduced costs of transportation must greatly increase the receipts for Aconcagua products; and as the engineer found nearly smooth ground on which to build such branch road, the less than a million of dollars it is estimated to cost will readily be subscribed.

Santiago.—The limits of this province are the culminating line of the Andes, which separate it from the Argentine republic, on the east; to the north, the dividing ridge between the waters which fall into the Mapocho from those whose outlet is the Aconcagua; to the west, the Zapata chain and ocean; and to the south, the river Cachapual. Thus, it lies between 32° 54′ and 34° 26′ latitude, and 69° 36′ and 71° 48′ west longitude. From Algarroba point to Tupungato, its greatest length is 132 miles, and its breadth, perpendicular to the direction of the line indicated, about 116 miles. Its superficial extent is 14,923 square miles, divided into two natural regions, of which the relative proportions are as 10 to 14. One, and the smaller, generally unsuited for cultivation, is occupied by the Andes; the other, nearly all of which is arable, is composed of plains and wooded hills, that never attain the region of perpetual snow.

Its departments are Santiago, Melipilla, Rancagua, and Victoria, divided into 46 sub-delegations and 235 districts. Santiago, the metropolitan city, is minutely described in a subsequent chapter; from which a proper estimate may be formed of the mode of laying out, building, adorning, and government of every town in the republic, one pattern having served for all Chile, if not for all Spanish America. Rancagua is also given account of in another place. Melipilla, a well-built town of some pretensions to wealth and style, is situated near the north bank of the Maypu, 18 leagues W.S.W. from Santiago, and 10 leagues from the sea. Together with the suburbs it contains rather more than 8,000 souls. Much of the produce from Colchagua and the southern part of Santiago, destined for Valparaiso, passes through this town; and as it is in the midst of a most fruitful district, enterprise alone is wanting to render it prosperous. Ponchos, some coarse woollens, and blankets, are manufactured in the town, and pottery ware of a superior kind in the vicinity. San Bernardo, a town of 2,500 people, lies 4 leagues (Spanish) S.S.W. from the capital, and on both sides of one of the great high roads. It also is regularly laid out, with its public square, municipal buildings, and alameda; but the citizens, instead of erecting their houses close to each other, or seeking sites on the public square or alameda, have spread their town over the largest space. Many of their dwellings have large ornamental flower-gardens on the road, and some few of them all the elegance of the best-finished residences at Santiago; from which place families come in summer, and find here all the "*abandon*" permissible in country life, whilst they preserve some of the conveniences of their town homes. Two or three small flour-mills, with machinery driven by water brought in a canal from the Maypu, are the only manufacturing establishments brought to my attention. It has no special facilities for trade or agriculture, and is so near a powerful controlling market at Santiago, that it can never be of much greater extent.

The other towns are—Curacavi, between the Zapata and Prado ranges, on the road from Valparaiso; Polpaico, Lampa, and Renca, on the Quillota road; Chacabuco and Colina, on the San Felipe road; Peñaflor, Talagante, San Francisco del Monte, Paico, and Concumen, on

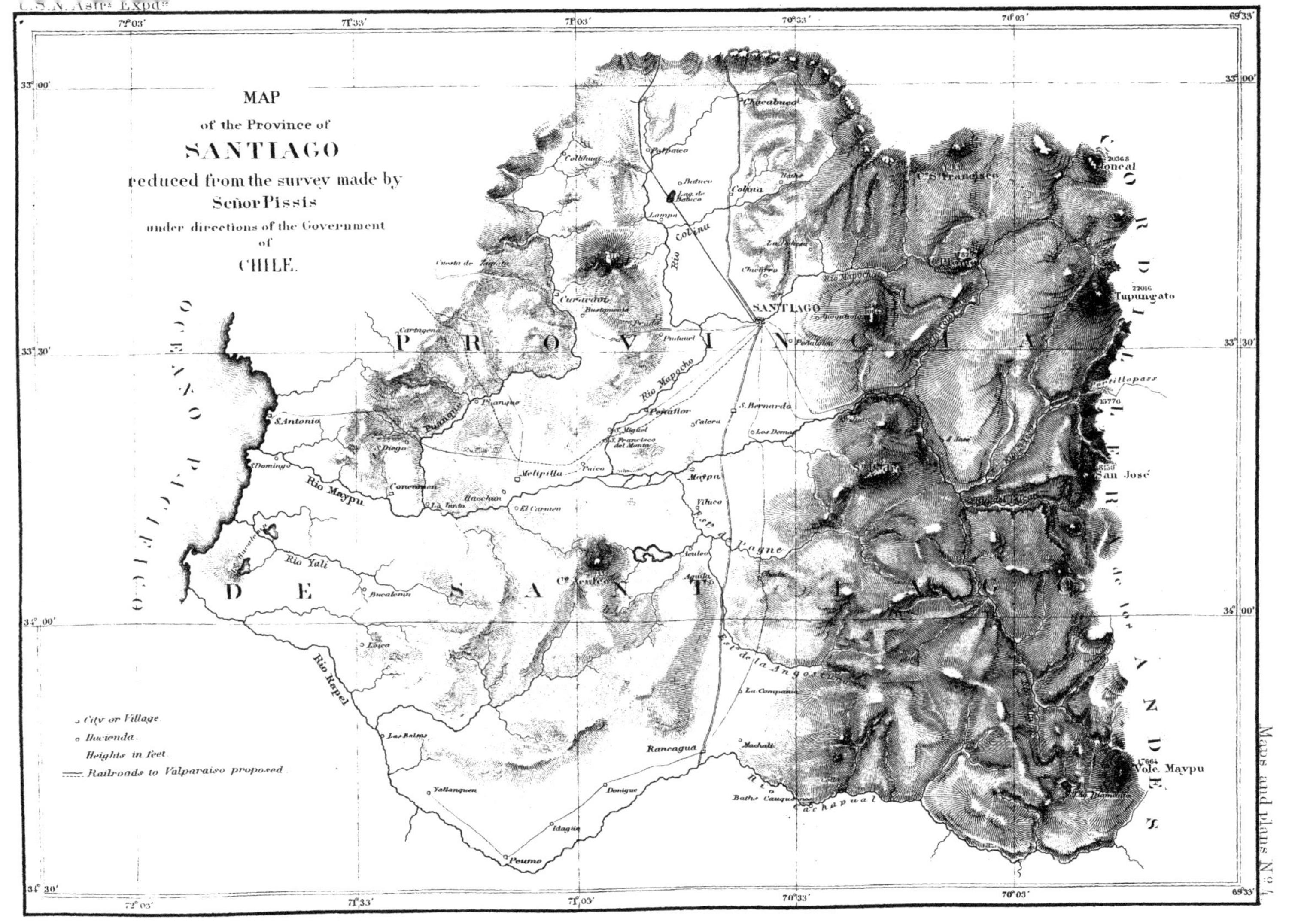
MAP
of the Province of
SANTIAGO
reduced from the survey made by
Señor Pissis
under directions of the Government
of
CHILE.
OCEANO PACIFICO
PROVINCIA DE SANTIAGO
CORDILLERA de los ANDES
SANTIAGO
Tupungato
San José
Vole. Maypu
Chacabuco
Colina
Lampa
Rio Colina
Rio Mapocho
Rio Maypu
Rio Yali
Rio Repel
Rio Cachapual
S. Antonio
S. Domingo
Melipilla
El Carmen
Rancagua
Peumo
Idagua
Donigue
Yallanquen
Las Raisas
La Compania
Machali
S. Bernardo
Peñaflor
Calera
Maypu
Paico
Lo Prado
Las Docas
Cuesta de Zapata
Cuesta de Lagne
Est. de la Angostura
Baths Cauquenes
Portillo pass
Coltihua
Polpaico
Batuco
Lag. de Batuco
Chicureo
Curacabí
Bustamente
Pudahuel
Puangue
Cartagena
Los Domas
Vilueo
Aculeo
Aguila
Concepcion
Bucalemu
Loica
Ilocalemu
Alhué
Tiltil
C. S. Francisco
Plomo
20368
Joncal
22016
15770
17664
33° 00'
33° 30'
34° 00'
34° 30'
72° 03'
71° 33'
71° 03'
70° 33'
70° 03'
69° 33'
City or Village
Hacienda
Heights in feet
Railroads to Valparaiso proposed

the route through Melipilla, from San Antonio de las Bodegas to the capital; and Maypu, Algüe, and Peumo, in the southwestern quarter of the province. San Antonio, the only roadstead frequented by coasting vessels, is about three miles to the north of the Maypu. From thence the agricultural products of the maritime portion are shipped to Valparaiso, to which customs district it belongs. The quantity of wheat shipped in 1850 was 243,000 bushels. Its inhabitants are mostly fishermen, who send daily supplies to Melipilla and Santiago, and offer at the metropolitan market fish which had been taken from the sea on the preceding morning. Strange as it may appear, they are in much better condition when they arrive during the summer, than in the colder weather of winter—warm, dry air being a better preservative from decay than that which is cool, but moist.

Until a canal to conduct water from the Maypu to the Mapocho was cut along the base of the Andes, cultivation in the central districts of the province was limited to the immediate vicinity of the streams. Nor was the full value of the canal appreciated until quite recently. Apparently large tracts of land were composed only of sand and shingle, on which it is waste of time to spend labor or seed; but as the Maypu water was found to deposite mineral sediments rapidly, and these were just the fertilizers needed in this porous soil, these unpromising fields have been cleared of the larger stones little by little, and now there is scarcely an unoccupied level space between the two rivers. A desert has literally been made to bloom and blossom here, though to the northward of the Mapocho there is still scarcity of water, without the prospect of augmenting the supply until the climate shall change, or each proprietor provides an artesian well, capable of furnishing it for his fields. Nevertheless, the little valleys about the Colina and Lampa yield more than three-fold the quantity consumed by their populations; and with such modes of cultivation as are followed in the United States, they would produce ten-fold. Here it was (at Colina) that one of our countrymen reaped at three harvests more than two hundred fold from one sowing of rye. Cultivation *de roule* is also practised to some extent, and there are fields of wheat and barley on the sides of the Andes quite 3,000 feet above the sea. Olives, oranges, lemons, figs, grapes, and all the fruits of temperate zones, grow well; though from the extreme dryness of the air in summer, the skin of apples and peaches often cracks, and the fruit has little juiciness. But the quantities of every class are enormous; and could the people only be induced to give some little attention to the trees or vines by judicious selection of varieties, or even occasional pruning of those they have, there is no country in the world which would produce more perfect specimens.

The ravines and mountain sides, of which each large estate owns a portion, serve for rearing herds of neat cattle, horses, and sheep; for whose care there are special men to drive the flocks to new localities, as fast as the herbage and pasture grounds they range become denuded. Some haciendas possess as many as 20,000 head of neat cattle, from the increase of which, at least one fourth may be annually disposed of; and "charqui," (sun-dried beef), hides, grease and tallow, form large items in the home and extra-provincial trade.

Nor is Santiago destitute of mineral wealth. Gold, silver, lead, copper, cobalt, zinc and iron, gypsum, alabaster, kaolin, salt, marble, sulphate of barytes, and sulphate of alumina, are all to be found in different localities, and some of them in large quantities. If we are to believe the earlier writers, the quantity of gold attainable here at one period must have formed one of the reasons influencing Valdivia to its selection for his residence. Garcilaso de la Vega says, that the vassals of Valdivia paid an annual tribute of more than a hundred thousand dollars. Another writer states that "fifteen Indians were able to extract daily from 400 to 600 ducats;" and there remain evidences on the haciendas of Payen, the Cerros Amarillos, and Aculeo, and the whole chain extending from Algüe to the village of Peumo, which prove them to have been wrought extensively for this coveted metal. Only one mine—that of la Leona, near Rancagua—is now in operation. Mining for silver ore was found profitable only at three or four localities; all but three of which have been discontinued either by reason of lawsuits, or from want of means to prosecute the works further. The mines of San Pedro Nolasco, at

10,900 feet above the sea, on the south bank of the Maypu, and of San Lorenzo, also within the Andes, but on the opposite side of the same river, are now the only ones wrought to much profit. Lead has scarcely ever been thought worth taking care of, though abundantly found in all the silver veins, and largely with those of copper. At the present day, this last metal occupies the first rank among the mineral products of the province, the most valuable mines being near good supplies of fuel for smelting. Unfortunately, there are no printed statistics from which to learn either the yield of the mines or of the haciendas, and we can only roughly infer the aggregate amounts from the fact that in 1851, about 28,000 tons of surplus passed into Valparaiso from this province. The railroad between the capital and its port, which has already been referred to, will pass along the valley of the Aconcagua river as far as Llaillay; thence, for rather more than eleven miles, rises 118¾ feet per mile to a tunnel through the central range of the cordilleras; after which there is quite a rapid descent into the great valley. This grand work of 110 miles in length was estimated to cost $7,500,000, and to be completed within five years from its commencement, October 1, 1852. An extension of their surveys southerly from the capital, satisfied the engineers that there were few countries in the world which presented such unrivalled facilities for the construction of a railroad as this portion of Chile. The only impediments they found to work of the cheapest kind were, the rivers that intersect the plain; and to them it seemed inevitable that the construction of a road between Valparaiso and Santiago must be followed by its extension towards Talca and Concepcion. Santiago has already some of the great flour-mills; here, too, are the only manufactories of any note, and the residences of nearly all the wealthy miners and farmers; and should these predictions be realized—of which there is scarcely a doubt—as the road will pass through the most fertile and populous districts of the country, the metropolitan city will become, within a quarter of a century, the centre of commercial as it now is of political importance.

Valparaiso.—On the north, east, and south, Valparaiso is separated from the provinces of Aconcagua and Santiago by portions of the central ranges of the cordilleras named in indicating their boundaries. On the west is the ocean. Its length from north to south is about 52 miles, and its breadth, between the Cerro de la Viscacha and Punta Coronilla, is 45. Making allowances for irregularities of outline, the superficial area is about 2,300 square miles; of which more than two thirds is useless, because of its mountainous character and want of water for irrigation. Its departments are Valparaiso, Quillota, and Casa-blanca, which are divided into 19 sub-delegations and 111 districts. Valparaiso, the provincial capital, having the control, and being the recipient of, nearly all the foreign commerce of the country, a special chapter is devoted to an account of it. Quillota, the next in importance—a city of nearly 10,000 inhabitants—is near the south bank of the river Aconcagua—or, as it is here called, the Quillota—and 30 miles northeast of Valparaiso. The beautiful valley in which it lies is very broad and quite flat, with huge bare mountains on either side, and the famous Campana or Bell mountain in the background. Abundance of water for irrigation is obtained from the river flowing through its midst; and, as the land is distributed among many proprietors, the view of the cultivated fields from a hill to the southward of the town is one of remarkable artificial luxuriance. First are fine ever-green forest-trees in the mountain ravines; then green open lawns, separated by small valleys with rivulets, cottages on the hill-sides, fields of corn and grain; and, lastly, little square gardens, crowded with fruit-trees and every variety of vegetable, having in their midst the white walls and steeples of a town, wandering more than two miles farther away. Valdivia having sent a colony here about three years after the foundation of Santiago, this is, of course, one of the oldest settled districts of Chile. Casa-blanca, the other departmental capital, is 27 miles southeast from Valparaiso, in the midst of a narrow valley, watered by a small stream of the same name. Its elevation above the sea is 790 feet; that of Quillota, 405. Situated on the high road to Santiago, its increase has been along the thoroughfare rather than by concentration, and its plaza to this day is adorned only by the mud-walls of surrounding gardens. Large quantities of fruits, vegetables, and poultry are sent daily from this vicinity to the Valparaiso market; and the traveller who stops at its best "*fonda*" will have no reason to complain either of the quality of the fare called for, or of the charge made for it. As the town is mentioned more than once in the subsequent narrative, there remains only to add, that most of the houses along its principal street are shops, having for sale such articles as are most sought by the constant stream of cartmen and muleteers from Santiago and Melipilla, on their way to the port. Its population is rather less than 2,000 souls. Besides these cities, the villages are Concon, Tavalonga, San Pedro, and Limache, in the department of Quillota; Viña la Mar and la Plazilla, in that of Valparaiso; and las Dichas and Vinilla, in Casa-blanca. None of them are scarcely more than small assemblages of very common houses, whose proprietors are mainly supported by the sale of provisions and drink to the public carriers.

The province of Valparaiso is almost entirely indebted to the valleys of the Quillota, Limache, and Casa-blanca, not only for all that it has of agricultural wealth, but also for the vegetables and fruits consumed by its entire population, nearly one half of which is concentrated within the city of the same name. In the first of these valleys, especially, there is a succession of luxuriant orchards, vineyards, gardens, meadows, and fields of grain, from the ocean to the province of Aconcagua, nearly 2,000 feet above it—a soil that yields from 40 to 60 for one, and a climate more equable, yet charming, than the sun and mountains have elsewhere power to effect. Here the cherimoya, the date, and the lucuma attain perfection, rivalling the growth of native localities; and nectarines, olives, oranges, grapes, and strawberries, a size and profusion almost incredible; whilst cereals and esculents, alike of the temperate or torrid zone, amply repay the husbandman for their culture. So great was the surplus in 1850, that we may safely estimate one third of all that passed over the road between Quillota and Valparaiso as the product of this little valley. From the toll returns, this amounted to 3,520 loaded carts and 200,606 loaded mules, or about 43,500 tons, of which the proportion afforded by Quillota was 14,500 tons; the other two-thirds consisted of merchandise to and from Valparaiso, Aconcagua, and the Argentine Republic. Genial as is its climate, and fruitful as is its soil, these were not the attractions which led Valdivia to attempt its colonization. The great gold deposite of the time was in the valley of Quillota! Frézier says: "The vale of Quillota did so abound in gold, that Gen. Valdivia thought fit to erect a fort there, for the security of the settlement, and to curb the Indians he employed to get the gold. But they possessed themselves of it by a very ingenious stratagem. One of them, on an appointed day, carried thither a pot-full of gold dust to excite the curiosity and covetousness of the garrison soldiers. In short, they all soon gathered about that little treasure; and, whilst they were busy contending about their private interest to divide the same, an ambuscade of Indians, concealed and armed with arrows, rushed in upon them and found them defenceless. The victors then destroyed the fort, which has never been rebuilt since, and they have given over searching for gold there." I do not find any authentic account of a fort built there; but Valdivia certainly did cause a brigantine to be constructed at the mouth of the Aconcagua, which appears to have been completed and in charge of a dozen men, who fell a sacrifice to their cupidity in the manner stated by Frézier. In nine months he had obtained from the mines of Margamargo, situated just to the southward of the Aconcagua, and eight or nine miles from the sea, more than $75,000 in gold. Since Frézier's time (1712) much gold has been obtained from lavaderos, not only in this, but also in other districts of the province; and though the value of the more precious metal obtained at these deposites is now inconsiderable, there are many mines which annually send quite a large quantity of pure copper to the Valparaiso market.

Colchagua.—This province, next in importance to Santiago in population, and superior to it in agricultural resources, is separated from it by the rivers Cachapual and Rapel; from the Argentine republic by the crests of the Andes; from the province of Talca by the rivers Lontue and Mataquito; and its western boundary is the sea. Its superficial extent is about 3,900 square miles; and although there are some very lofty ranges of mountains, and the bases of the numerous different chains occupy about two thirds of its territory, so ample is the supply of water, and so rapid the fall of the Cachapual, Tinguiririca, and Lontue, that considerably more than one third is under cultivation.

It is divided into three departments—San Fernando, Caupolican, and Curicó—of which the first and last have capitals of the same name; that of the second is called Rengo. These departments are subdivided into 32 sub-delegations, which comprise 128 districts. San Fernando city, with a population of 12,000 souls, is very badly located between the Tinguiririca river and Antinero creek, and below the level of their waters during winter floods. Its houses are, generally, at some distance from each other, each having a garden enclosed with rude mud walls, which gives an unpleasant aspect to the city. Some of the streets have been paved, but the buildings have been spread over so much ground that the funds of the municipal exchequer have not generally warranted such luxury. Rengo, though legally a city, in 1848 was only a village, with 48 taxed houses. It is near the south bank of one of the three Rio Claros in this province, and though not so much exposed as San Fernando, is also liable to winter inundations. It has only one very tortuous street, along which in 1852 there were more than three times the number of houses stated above. The exteriors of some of these were handsomely finished, though, like San Fernando, the town was spread over much ground. Usually its long street is filled with carts or herds of animals, either passing through or halting for a time whilst their proprietors have a little traffic at the straggling shops. Curicó is by far the neatest, and, apparently, it is the most thriving town in the province. It is compactly built on the fork between the Lontue and Teno, and is supplied with water from a small tributary stream to the former. The streets are paved from the plaza to the eastern boundaries, and it has a very pretty alameda, as well as most attractive suburban promenades. All three of these cities are mentioned more at length in the chapter detailing "A visit to the southward." In the department of Caupolican, the other towns containing more than 3,000 inhabitants are Huacargüe, Zuñiga, Pencagüe, Chanquagüe, Requinua; Olivar, Coinco, Tunca, Pichidegüa, and Rastrojos, have each more than 2,000; and there are ten others having a greater number than 1,000. In the department of San Fernando, Manantiales, Estrella, and Navidad have each more than 2,000 people; and there are fourteen other towns exceeding 1,000. In the department of Curicó, Las Palmas has 4,815; Lolol 3,008; Bichuquen 3,271; Auquinco, Ranguili, Medano, San Pedro Alcantara, and Los Negros, above 2,000 each; and there are twenty-eight others exceeding 1,000 souls for every settlement. Its ports are Topocalma, San Antonio de Bichuquen, Llico, and Tuman, which are occasionally visited by small coasters, though none of them are safe, nor are the last two recognised by government as habilitated anchorages. The first two belong to the Valparaiso collection district. Llico is at the mouth of the Mataquito. Tuman is sheltered from the southerly winds, and communicates with the interior of the province by a good carriage-road, an advantage not possessed by Llico. It has been made known to the government that the entrance to Lake Bichuquen could be rendered navigable by vessels for an expense of $6,000, and a secure harbor be thus obtained; but no steps have been taken to carry the recommendations of the Intendente into effect. This, and the repairs of nearly all the roads, are objects of incalculable consequence to the interests of the "haciendados." Otherwise, they must continue to transport their surplus commodities by carts or mules to Santiago or Valparaiso—distances of 40 and 50 leagues respectively from San Fernando. Should their estates lie elsewhere than on the great highway, the bodies of water deposited by rains in winter, and overflows from the irrigating canals, are so great, that most of the lateral roads are rendered intransitable, and produce is kept from market. Indeed, there is a part of the principal thoroughfare in no better condition.

Agriculture and the raising of cattle are the only industrial resources of the people. Though having the same base as that of its neighbor on the north, the soil of Colchagua generally has been rendered more fertile by the greater amount of detritus left by more abundant artificial irrigation. Rain also is more frequent and copious, and disintegration of the cordillera slopes has not only formed soil for the roots of forest-trees quite low, but these retain moisture which permits cultivation on a much larger proportion of surface than in Santiago. Even between the central range and the coast there are extensive arable plains. All the great staples of the country—wheat, barley, corn, beans, potatoes, hemp, flax—grow luxuriantly and yield largely, as do also the vineyard and orchard plants.

As excellent pasturage may be obtained within the ravines of the cordilleras all the year, cattle-raising is considered more lucrative than crops of wheat, &c., although there are few years when there are not great numbers lost by disease. The most fatal epidemic to which they are subject is called "*la picada.*" It usually attacks them in summer, when they are fattest, and so poisons the whole system that every man or beast touching the skin, after death of the animal, becomes infected. Very few cattle recover, unless the disease is immediately discovered, and many herdsmen formerly fell victims to it; but a successful mode of treating the human patient has of late been ascertained, and it is no longer held in such dread. Some years 14,000 or 15,000 animals die, the mortality among them being sometimes attributed to the very heavy rains of winter, at others to the want of rain, and consequent loss of pasturage, and again at others to *la picada;* which last is alleged to have been introduced from the Buenos Ayres pampas. It has been estimated that the annual average loss by disease and birds (*Condors*) and beasts (*Pumas*) of prey, will amount to at least $100,000. There are no published statistics of the products of Colchagua; but the best informed persons state that more than one half are sent elsewhere for consumption. Its known mineral resources are comparatively insignificant. A gold mine, called Yaquil, near the former Lake Taguatagua, was worked by an American for several years, and it is said that there are rich copper mines in the vicinity of Curicó. No doubt much copper and gold remain in its mountains, awaiting the enterprise and energy of man to develop them. In 1850 the revenue of the province amounted to $73,058, and its expenses to $69,679.

TALCA.—Talca, originally a department of Colchagua—erected into a province in 1833—has the Lontue and Mataquito for its northern, the Maule for its southern, and the crests of the Andes and the Pacific respectively for its eastern and western limits. Its superficial area is about 2,200 square miles, divided into the departments of Lontue and Talca, which comprise 19 sub-delegations and 96 districts. The provincial capital, having the same name, and Molina, the chief city of the department of Lontue, are elsewhere described; and to that account ("A Visit to the Southward") reference is also made for other details of the resources and trade of the province. No city in the republic exhibits evidences of rapid and substantial growth equal to Talca; which, but for the blunder of locating it in the middle of the plain, instead of at the mouth of the Rio Claro, must have attained far greater importance than it now possesses. Pelanco, Lircay, Colin, Corcolen, Pencahüe, are the other towns, nearly all of which are in the southwestern quarter of the province, where the character of the soil and the greater abundance of water have concentrated three fourths of the total population. Within widely spread precincts, as is mentioned of Colin, some of these towns contain more than 5,000 inhabitants. Its traffic with other provinces is mostly carried on through Constitucion, a port of entry at the mouth of the river Maule.

West of the Central cordilleras, though generally hilly, there is a greater extent of level and cultivated surface than in any similar district of the more northern provinces. Several rivulets water it, and it abounds with timber of good size and quality for every species of construction. Northward from Talca, quite a large tract is overlaid by a volcanic stratum, on which the superficial soil is so thin that productive cultivation must for ever be prevented. The *tufa* is as often at as below the surface, is generally from two to three feet thick, and lies nearly parallel with it; whilst the country is at the same time so undulating that artificial irrigation could not be adopted, unless at very great cost. Wheat is sown wherever there is sufficient surface soil, the proprietors hoping for rain to nourish and mature the plants. Here the plain is from ten to twelve Spanish leagues wide, bounded on one side by a lofty range with evergreen forests at its base, and perpetual snows at its crests, and on the other by a low chain of hills, barren to the vision as the sands of Zahara. Far up the slopes of the eastern range, and deep within its valleys, does the husbandman spread his fields; whilst his herds of sheep, oxen, and horses roam never-failing pastures yet farther within the Andes. If, by chance, the summer affords no rains, and the near grazing-grounds are exhausted, the flocks are driven to sequestered glens beyond the first range, where they are sure of an abundant supply. From its surplus of grain, charqui, tallow, cheese, wine, aguardiente, and wool, most of the haciendados derive handsome revenues. The expense of conveying grain to the distant northern markets, attended as it is with so many charges on a long land-carriage, amounts to so large a proportion of its value, that cattle-raising has become of more importance in the province. This kind of farming scarcely encourages the growth of population; and as the small return for cereals is no incentive to extend their cultivation, and the inducement of higher wages in Colchagua or Concepcion tempts many laborers born here to leave their homes, the average annual increase during the last twenty-five years has not exceeded 500 souls. This impediment to prosperity and the true agricultural interests of Talca must continue until navigation of the Maule is facilitated by steam, or a railroad be completed to the north; then the haciendados may extend their operations, as its fine soil and climate justifies. Other individuals, of humble rank, now manufacture "ponchos," coarse woollens, and blankets, all of which have fame in the northern markets for the closeness of their texture and durability of colors. Many of the blankets are elaborately embroidered in colors, and form handsome as well as ornamental bed-coverings. There are two flour-mills in operation, both of which are at the city of Talca.

Its mineral wealth, so far as known, is not great. Gold and copper are found; but the ores of the first are mixed with so much rubbish, and those of the second are so distant from market, that mining them pays a very small profit. The mines of Chivato and Chuchuncho are both mentioned in the chapter before referred to, and Mr. Miers *heard* of many very valuable ones in the cordilleras to the eastward of Talca; but the accounts of their extent and richness are undoubtedly exaggerated, as is proved by the fact that nothing could be ascertained respecting their products. Molina gives a marvellous account of "a little hill to the northeast of Talca (which) consists almost entirely of amethysts. Some are enclosed in a gray quartz, which serves them for a matrix, and others isolated among the sand. They are more perfect, both in color and hardness, in proportion to their depth; and were those who search for them to dig deeper, they would, most probably, discover them in the highest state of perfection. A short time before I left Chile, I saw some that were of a beautiful violet, and would cut glass repeatedly without injuring their points. Among them were a few of as fine a water as the diamond, and perhaps they may serve as precursors to that most valuable gem. They are so abundant, that in some of the crevices of the rocks, those of a fine purple may be discovered at almost every step." If such a deposite ever existed, it was long ago exhausted; but it is to be apprehended that Molina's information on this as well as many other points of natural history was derived from visitors to his monastery who were not always the most intelligent or reliable.

MAULE.—The province of Maule (formerly called Cauquenes), erected in 1826, from a part of Concepcion, has for its northern boundary the river Maule. Its southern is the provinces of Ñuble and Concepcion, from which it is separated by the rivers Perquilaoquen and Itata; by the former from its source to the central range of the cordilleras, and by the latter from the same chain to the ocean. The Andes and central chain from the Perquilaoquen southward form its eastern, and the Pacific its western limit. There are portions of the province from latitude 35° 12′ to latitude 36° 10′, and from longitude 71° to longitude 72° 48′. From the best estimates made by a commission specially appointed, in 1843, to collect provincial statistics, it appears that the departments composing it embrace 750 square leagues of territory. These are named Cauquenes, Constitucion, Linares, Parral, and Itata; which are separated into 30 sub-delegations, comprising 129 districts. In the first department there are two towns, Cauquenes and Chanco. Cauquenes, the provincial capital, made a city in 1826, was founded in 1742. It is situated on the slope of a hill, between a river of the same name and Tutuben creek, not more than four or five squares distant from either. From these and wells a supply of drinking-water is derived. Its 150 taxable houses are built on seven streets, running north and south, and six others which cross them at right-angles. There is a plaza on the eastern side of the city, a public promenade, two churches, and seven schools. Of the last, one is supported by the city government, one by the Franciscan convent, and the others by individuals. Only 80 males and 45 females were in attendance—just one for each 28 inhabitants. Population, 3,500.

The village of Chanco, W.N.W. from Cauquenes, and near the ocean, is a small and miserable place, composed of 30 or 40 wretched houses, built mostly of straw and without order. For a long period the sea has been steadily wearing away the small intervening strip of land; and in a few years more the waves will probably overwhelm it, should not its people remove to a locality where there is something else than barren sands. Its actual population scarcely exceeds 200 souls, for whom and the country children of the vicinity there were five schools, though only 47 boys and 6 girls were in attendance. Formerly, Chanco cheese was quite famous along the coast as far as Peru.

Constitucion is fully mentioned in the "Visit to the Southward." The town of Linares was founded in 1793, on the plain between the rivers Longaví and Maule. Its streets are rather wider than usual, but are not paved; indeed, it was laid out for a more magnificent city than the wealth of its 2,500 inhabitants have yet permitted them to make it. No less than twelve streets cross its plaza; and the alameda, which is above 200 feet wide, is planted with four rows of trees for nearly a third of a mile, and terminated by public squares. In all, the town comprises 80 squares, about 300 houses—some of the latter very well built, a handsome church, a smaller chapel, and a large market-house. 96 boys were in attendance at its only public school. The village of Yerbas-Buenas, in the same department, owes its origin to a chapel, erected there many years ago. It contains only about 20 houses and 250 inhabitants, of whom 35 boys and 6 girls were distributed among four public teachers.

Parral, also on the great plain and midway between the Longaví and Perquilaoquen, was founded in 1795, under the title of Reina Luisa. Although near much swampy ground, it is reputed to be very healthy. The great highway from north to south passes through it; and from this origin, perhaps, most of its streets in that direction are tortuous. It has about 100 houses supplied with water from the Longaví, through a canal cut by the municipal board, at an expense of $8,000. The population is 2,200, for whom there is one church and six schools, the latter attended by 106 boys and 31 girls. There is no other town in the department.

Quirihue, departmental capital of Itata, is situated half a league west of Cerro Coiquen, from which the percolation of water is such as to keep the town very little better than a swamp. Including ranchos of the suburbs, there may be 300 houses—built on four longitudinal and six transversal streets, an incomplete parish church, and a market-house, in which last is also the school for primary instruction. There is one other school in the town, supported by individuals, and the two have 87 male pupils. Population of Quirihue, 1,500.

The ports of the province are Constitucion and Curinape—the latter an open bay, midway between the mouths of the Itata and Maule, where very small craft sometimes take off timber and other products; but physical obstacles will forever prevent it being rendered fully available for the wants of even this small district.

In 1843 the total number of schools in all the departments was 56. They were attended by 871 male and 172 female scholars; and among the entire population, numbering 119,428 souls, there were only 7,353 males and 3,141 females who could read and write. The ratio of distribution of the population was found to be 292 for each square league in the department of Cauquenes, 239 in that of Constitucion, 220 in Itata, 102 in Linares, and only 76 in Parral; 55,550 were less than fifteen, and 2,141 more that seventy years of age; 547 cripples, 175 blind, 158 lunatics, 54 paralytics, 81 deaf-mutes.

Of the 750 square leagues embraced within its limits, mountains and forests occupy one half. Another portion is barren, and there remain 260 leagues arable. As we advance southerly, spring rains are more frequent, and summer showers not uncommon; the supply of water from the mountains is greater, and the soil and air preserve their humidity far into the latter season. Therefore, there is little or no risk in planting anywhere on the plain, although the surfaces of the streams are so much below its general level as to render artificial irrigation difficult. Only 10,000 acres, or the seventy-fifth part of the arable land, is thus watered. As a rule, the soil of the Andes and central range is composed of vegetable mould, well suited to cultivation; and as there are springs of water in all directions, many small tracts have been cleared of their forests and are planted in vines and wheat. Higher, natural pasturages abound; and there the herdsmen take up their residences until driven down by the rains and snows of winter. The plain is composed of the same materials as farther north—deposited in the great flood through the antique gulf, and overlaid with small portions of mineral and vegetable sediments, whose productive qualities have not been fully developed for want of proper implements, enterprise, and industry. However, from the fact that it does not receive the annual mineral deposite under artificial irrigation, it is probable that Maule is not so productive as the more central provinces. So many obstacles to agriculture present themselves, that the territory actually under cultivation in 1842 amounted to only fourteen leagues square. Some of these difficulties are stated by the commissioners to be: "The vicinity of other agricultural provinces;" "the cost of transportation to Constitucion, at one extremity of the province, or to Tomé, in the province of Concepcion, even farther away, and over worse roads;" and "the want of capital." The result of their investigations showed that the mean yield of wheat was 13½ fold, barley 24½, corn 41, beans 13½, and potatoes 15; proving quite conclusively how much the provinces from Aconcagua to Talca owe to mineral manure.

In order to arrive at the true condition of the agriculture of any country, it is necessary to know the exact quantity of its products. In Chile, one would suppose this attainable readily and with great approximation to accuracy, from the returns of the "*diezmo*" (tithe) and "*catastro*" (land tax), both of which are based on the annual products of each estate. But the commissioners say: "The diezmo is commonly paid with so few conscientious scruples (*religiosidad*), that from its returns the crops harvested do not amount to more than one fortieth of the products known to have been consumed. The catastro is so arranged and distributed as to serve still less than the diezmo for reliable data; and individual investigations, even if made by persons interested in the results, are often rendered nugatory by arousing suspicion among the laborers and ignorant." The least fallible mode then, and that which was adopted by them, was based on knowledge of the habits of the population, the products entering into trade, either extracted or introduced, and the number of souls. They assumed, as the average consumption of each individual—

2¾ fanegas wheat,	¾ fanega peas,	½ fanega beans,
¾ do. corn,	½ do. barley,	46 cabbages;
	¾ do. potatoes,	

and supposing one fifth of the crop to have been reserved for seed and lost, there should have been harvested for food—

344,848 fanegas of wheat,	62,800 fanegas of peas,	31,350 fanegas of beans,
93,849 do. corn,	31,350 do. barley,	5,642,868 cabbages;
	93,849 do. potatoes,	

instead of which, the returns only show—

260,807 fanegas of wheat,	15,438 fanegas of peas,	12,380 fanegas of beans,
15,438 do. corn,	18,056 do. barley,	1,909,000 cabbages.
	15,382 do. potatoes,	

From these last numbers at least one sixth part should be deducted as having been grown in the department of San Carlos, then forming part of the province, but now belonging to that of Ñuble, and which has, consequently, been omitted in all that has previously been said. As a consequence, there must have been famine in the province without introducing all these articles of universal food to amounts equal to twice the product of the soil. But the commissioners well knew that they were deceived; for large quantities of each were actually sent beyond the province for sale, and the mean price of wheat remained at 43 cents per bushel. At the same period a fat ox was worth only $18,and a sheep could be bought for five eighths of a dollar. Here the vine thrives well without artificial irrigation, and, as it will grow with less attention or care than almost anything else, it is a favorite crop. The estimated number of plants was about 8,000,000, of which each hundred afforded 30 gallons of grape-juice. Part is made into a red wine called "mosto," part boiled to make "chicha," and the remainder is distilled for aguardiente. Olives and oranges are also grown to some extent; and from the department of Cauquenes, bordering the Maule, large quantities of valuable forest-timber are sent annually to market. The exportation of this last native product will, with time, become more valuable.

The abundance and excellence of its natural pasturages perhaps renders this more suitable for rearing and grazing cattle than either of the other provinces. By the census of 1842 it possessed 108,361 neat cattle, 46,336 horses and mules, 410,306 sheep and goats, and 7,167 swine. 20,939 of the first were sold out of the province, in the same year. Notwithstanding the great mortality that frequently occurs among them during winter, it is known that the numbers of all are rapidly increasing; and it is probable there were quite twice as many at the close of 1852 as at the census ten years previously. In November, 1850, the Intendente reported to the Minister of the Interior that the unavoidable mortality during the winter just terminated had amounted to 10,043 neat cattle, 4,815 horses and mules, 139,535 sheep and goats, and 317 hogs, most of which great loss was attributed to diseases originating from excessive rains. The destruction by Pumas, Condors, and Eagles is about one quarter of one per centum among the larger, and two per centum among lesser animals.

Its mineral resources have not obtained for it great fame. "Lavaderos" and mines of gold, the richest of which are in the litoral departments, are the only ones known to be in operation. A silver mine, within the Andes, was denounced some fifty years ago, and two others within fifteen years; but they were soon abandoned. Copper has never been offered in market, though there can be no doubt of its abundant existence in and near the coast range. The total ascertained product of the mines and lavaderos is less than $10,000 per annum, unless the one discovered in 1851 prove more valuable. Very glowing accounts were sent from it to the Intendente, and two or three hundred people crowded to the spot immediately; but it failed to create interest beyond its own provincial precincts.

The only established manufactories or mills are those for flour, built near streams along the central line of travel of the plain, at Constitucion and at Curinape. One, sufficiently extensive to grind half the wheat grown in the province, has recently been erected on the Loncomilla, about ten miles from its mouth. But on examining the goods exposed for sale, quite large proportions of the ponchos, blankets, church carpets or rugs, and coarser cloths, are found to be of domestic manufacture; showing that the poorer classes of women are not idle beside their spinning-wheels and hand-looms. Their ponchos and church mats are greatly esteemed at the north, and numbers are sent to Santiago for sale. It is estimated that the product of these and other wrought articles amounts to at least $230,000 annually. How stands the balance of its trade account cannot be accurately ascertained from the published statistics, because goods for the province of Talca also pass through the custom-house at Constitucion. It was definitely ascertained, however, that the exportation of agricultural produce in 1842 amounted to $383,662, divided as follows: Cattle, $209,394; wheat, $64,375; sheep, $24,602; cheese, $23,310; skins and hides, $10,982; aguardiente, $10,635; wool, $8,575; timber, $8,221; wine, $6,572, &c., &c. No one in Chile doubts that Maule is rapidly accumulating wealth.

Ñuble.—Ñuble was created a province in 1848 from a part of the territory of the old divisions—

Maule and Concepcion. Its northern boundary is the Perquilaoquen, its eastern the Andes, and its southern and western the river Itata and the central range of the cordilleras, as far as the point where the last are met by the stream first named. Five eighths of its superficial extent, or about 1,550 square miles, is occupied by the greater chains of mountains and their elevated ramifications. It has two departments—San Carlos and Chillan, which are divided into 20 sub-delegations, and these into 105 districts.

The city of San Carlos, founded in 1801, is very well situated on Nabotavo creek, eight or ten miles to the north of the river Ñuble, from which a canal supplies all the water needed for irrigation and domestic purposes. Including ranchos, there are some 300 houses built on seven longitudinal and an equal number of cross-streets, a plaza at their centre, one church, one public and two private schools attended by 92 male and 18 female pupils, and an alameda. In 1843, its population was 4,250.

Old Chillan, near a river of the same name, was destroyed by an earthquake in 1751; and, as it had often been subject to inundations, it was finally built in its present position—five miles to the south of the Ñuble. But, as late as 1850, the new town was near being totally destroyed by a flood that occurred in July; and numbers of its people were rescued on horseback from the river, then rushing through its streets. Since then, a canal has been dug to carry in another direction the waters of the creek from which so much injury is received; and for further security a strong dike has been built above the city. Although the Indians of the southern and mountainous districts harassed its citizens to a very late period, and revolting troops have more than once been billeted on them, it has grown with much rapidity, and the number of taxable houses entitles it to rank fourth among the cities of the republic. In 1848, these amounted to 650. More recently, it was occupied by belligerents for many weeks—first by the revolutionary and next by government troops, each of which consumed and carried off all accessible provisions. Yet such is the fertility of the surrounding country that no calamity seems great enough to drive people away from the location; and "*los dos Chillanes*," as they are called, now contain from ten to twelve thousand inhabitants. The Jesuits made this the seat of one of their missions, and established a college here for the education of Indian youths; since their departure neither Indians nor Creoles have had much time so devoted to them, though of late years it has been rather from indisposition on the part of the people than from negligence by government to provide schools. Of the entire population of the province, amounting to 89,955 in 1843, there were not 400 attending school, and only one school for each 1,200 of the children under fifteen years of age. At the same time the number of boys attending school in the department of San Carlos was one out of each 32, and of girls one from each 148! Only one in ten were able to read and write. Two schools for gratuitous instruction to women were opened at Chillan in 1850; and so many pupils offered themselves, that government found it necessary to aid the municipal fund by establishing a second at the old town.

The other towns are Bulnes, ten miles S.S.W. of, and nearly as populous as Chillan—the provincial capital—Remuco, and Pueblo de las Minas; the last, as its name imports, a mining village, in whose rude houses some four or five thousand people are assembled. It lies ten leagues east of Chillan, within the first hills at the base of the Andes, and was commenced about fifteen years ago. That which gives it a character perhaps different from every other settlement in the world, is the rare fact that mines of gold have never before been discovered in lands suitable for cultivation, where neither the riches of the first are sufficient to excite the avarice of man and cause him to despise agriculture, nor the fertility of the last so great as to stifle desires for mining. Here, in the midst of excavations and ravines, where groups are washing gold, and surrounded by heaps of attle, one may find wheat stubble, piles of recently harvested and unthreshed grain, yokes of oxen, and habitations totally unlike the ranchos of miners. In all directions the population is in a state of ferment. Loud shouts on the threshing fields are responded to by deadened subterranean blasts; the cry of the herdsmen on the neighboring mountains, by the clamors of clusters of gamesters. The tradesman only, ever calculating his gains, remains in his shop, silent and unmoved as he quickens the circulation of the gold, whose scarcely washed particles serve instead of money for exchanges.

The province does not reach to the sea; and, as it has no port, its products are sent to Talcahuano, or Tomé, on the opposite side of the bay, where they find a market, or are shipped to the north.

Within the Andes, and to the E.S.E. from Chillan, there are the great sulphur baths of the country, and the extraordinary deposits of that mineral may one day prove lucrative among other commercial resources of the province. In its vicinity, and all about the region of the baths, innumerable *fumarolas* render the air almost intolerable.

In the statistics of the province of Maule, there are many data relating to its then department—San Carlos; but of the department of Chillan, forming the other half of Ñuble, nothing authentic has yet been published by the government which will serve as an index to its industrial resources. Both departments, however, are extremely well watered, very fertile, and well adapted to the cultivation of cereals, vines, most fruits, and to the rearing of cattle; though incursions of the Indians have somewhat impeded agricultural prosperity. As these warlike neighbors have of late years yielded measurably to the influences of civilization, and have themselves become settled and agriculturists to a limited extent, their marauding forays are no longer held in such dread, and unoccupied lands are rapidly filling up. But the disposition to accumulate real estate to which this comparative security has given rise, has also had an unfavorable effect by exhausting the means with which these new possessions, or parts of them, might have been brought under culture, and thus large tracts still remain to be redeemed from a state of nature. The same reasons have operated to still greater extent in preventing the increased rearing of cattle. These are the objects most coveted by the aboriginal hordes, who collected and drove off every animal from slightly protected districts; often murdering every male whom they encountered, and forcing the women into captivity to form part of their seraglios. Applying the laws of increase established by experience to the statistics of San Carlos, for 1843, viz: 20 per cent. per annum for neat cattle, 15 per cent. for horses, 60 per cent. for sheep, 120 per cent. for goats, and 600 per cent. for swine; and assuming Chillan to have had an equal number of these animals at that time, if one third the annual augmentation remain to multiply the stocks, at the commencement of 1850 the numbers in the province will have been 33,931 neat cattle, 17,714 horses and mules, 220,769 sheep, 21,023 goats, and 778,000 swine. Except in the last, which was trebly in excess, these numbers coincide very nearly with an estimate given me by one of the largest land-holders. Notwithstanding the obstacles mentioned, and the super-added one of difficult transport, quantities of surplus grain, cattle, wool, and wines, are annually sent out of the province.

Its principal gold mines have already been alluded to. These were at first only *lavaderos*. Subsequently, as the earth was excavated to be washed, mines were detected, and the working of these has gradually afforded increased profits. In August, 1850, the Intendente reported to government respecting one of them, that each day's labor produced a greater quantity of the precious metal than the preceding one. On the first day after striking the vein, only $34 could be obtained, and then by the aid of quicksilver; at the end of nine days, it had augmented to $150; and before the close of the month, the average of each hide-bag of ore, measuring something more than half a bushel, afforded $75, without the use of mercury. There were also several lavaderos and one gold mine in operation in the department of San Carlos, but their products did not amount to much. All these mines need machinery and competent directors to develop their full value.

CONCEPCION.—The province of Concepcion, created by the law of division of the republic, has recently been deprived of the larger portion of its territory, and now consists of the tract lying between the rivers Itata and Biobio, the crests of the Andes and the Pacific. Its greatest extent from S.E. to N.W. is 130 miles, and its average breadth 45; so that its superficial area is 5,850 square miles. The departments are Concepcion, Talcahuano, Coelemu,

Puchacai, Rere, and Laja, divided into 43 sub-delegations, and 212 districts. Its capital, the city of Concepcion, is situated in the valley of "la Mocha," on the northern bank of the Biobio, and three leagues distant from the sea. The city of this name founded in 1550, by Valdivia, was at the port of Penco; but that rebuilt after its destruction by the Araucanos having been overwhelmed by the sea during extraordinary earthquakes on two subsequent occasions, its people removed to the present site in February, 1764. Misfortune still pursued them. The great earthquake which occurred in 1835 again totally destroyed their city, and to this day they have not wholly made good their losses. After the last calamity, many desired to remove the site to a new position on a rising ground about two miles on the Talcahuano side of Concepcion, which has several and great advantages; but many had been impoverished, others were reluctant to change, and thus all who could obtain means eventually rebuilt on their old homesteads. Instead of contributing liberally to relieve its municipal board from expenses for improvements, government has actually deprived them of the taxes collected within their own limits; and though one may see many handsome dwellings, there are but few of the streets paved, and all its leading thoroughfares are in bad condition. It is the residence of a bishop, and the seat of one of the collegiate institutions of the republic; has several schools, both municipal and private, three or four charitable institutions, and one little newspaper. The cathedral and other public buildings on the plaza are commodious, if not very elegant specimens of architecture.

It is thought by all of Saxon blood who have visited Concepcion, that there is not in the world a situation more advantageous for the prosperity of a commercial city than the one to which the unsuccessful party wished to remove after the earthquake of 1835. It is centrally placed between the great and navigable river Biobio, the port of San Vicente, and the sheltered and commodious bay of Talcahuano, and in the midst of one of the finest countries of the globe. With a large extent of level and fertile land on every side, good potable water at a very small depth, and the blessing of an unexceptionable climate, the new city has failed to overshadow the opulence of Santiago only from the jealousy of some of the wealthy miners of the north, and the want of that fostering care which it had a right to expect from the government. It has now a population of 10,500 souls.

Talcahuano, the port of Concepcion and chief town of the department of the same name, is on the S.W. side of the bay. What the earthquake of 1835 left standing, the huge following waves of the sea utterly demolished, bearing away on its troubled surface alike the contents of warehouses and dwellings. Since then, the town has again been rebuilt, and in a somewhat more secure and better manner, though the proximity of Concepcion will always prevent its becoming much more than a place of business. Its population is about 5,000, who are well provided with the means of mental and religious instruction. Penco—the pride of its founders and first cradle of Christianity in southern Chile—still lies in ruins, a few fishermen only inhabiting huts amid the fallen walls of temples and fortifications. The other towns are Tomé, Rafael, Coelemu, and Ranquil, in the department of Coelemu; Florida, Coyarco, Quellon, and Gualqui, in Puchacai; Yumbel, Rere, (famous in times past for its golden bell,) Tucapel, and Talcamavida, in Rere; and Los Angeles, Santa Fé, Mesamavida, San Carlos, Santa Barbara, and Antuco, in La Laja. Many of these last were, and are, mere military posts, located near Indian districts for the purpose of keeping them in check; the others, rather straggling villages, oftener built of wood or canes, than of more permanent and substantial materials. Most of them are famous for the combats on their sites, rather than from present prosperity or local attractions. Penco, Lirquen, and Tomé, on the eastern side of its bay, and Colcura, on the coast between Concepcion and Arauco, are ports frequented by coasting vessels. From its exposure to westerly winds and sea, Colcura is a very unsafe anchorage. They all belong to the customs district of Talcahuano.

The intermediate plain separating the Andes and Central cordilleras, which at Santiago is 1,850 feet above the level of the sea, is here only about 250 feet; and although there still are elevations of the great chain far above the line of perpetual congelation, in the central range there is scarcely a hill 1,000 feet high. Admirably intersected by rivers, no less than beneficially irrigated by nature, the broad valley is covered with vegetable mould, fertile in the highest degree, whilst the slopes of its mountains afford excellent exposures for vineyards or abundant pasturage for animals. Under Spanish rule quite large portions of its domain were as well cultivated as those of any other part of Chile. Then, each proprietor either lived on his estate or in the neighboring best protected town; but subsequent years of war carried devastation nearly everywhere: first, in the struggle for liberty; next, in the contests between Chilenos and Aborigines; finally, in the fratricidal conflicts from which, unfortunately, the nation has not been wholly exempt, and more than one of which has originated in this very province. Sometimes one party have been masters of the country, sometimes the other; but it mattered not to the peacefully-inclined haciendados which was successful, as both consumed or took away their grain and cattle, and they were fortunate if life and dwellings were spared with which to begin the world anew. Of late years, however, additional security has been given to life and property. The unsubdued Araucanians are permanently beyond the Biobio; and though nomadic tribes living on the opposite side have made occasional raids on the western slope of the Andes, and a large body of revolted troops were for months in the northern part of the province, the influences of peace, the markets opened to their products by the discovered wealth of California, the increased riches of Atacama, and the examples set by foreigners who have settled among them, have had wonderful effect towards the extension of agriculture and general provincial prosperity. In 1850 the Intendente estimated its wheat crop at 395,000 bushels, there being still 84,000 of the previous year's growth in the hands of producers, and a large quantity in the mills about Concepcion. This estimate was probably derived from the diezmo or catastro returns; which, as was shown respecting the province of Maule, are data that serve only to mislead, as the exports will conclusively establish. But wheat is only one of many lucrative crops: corn, beans, peas, potatoes, hemp, barley, vegetables of every description, fruits, wine, cattle, sheep, and timber, all yield remunerative returns. When properly made, the wine called *mosto* is very little, if at all, inferior to Burgundy. Then, there are literally forests of apple-trees growing without culture, from whose fruit large quantities of chicha are made; and the *Araucaria imbricata*, with which the slopes of the Andes abound, yields the "*piñon*," a nut so similar in taste and farinaceous properties to the chestnut, that it is no less prized by the ladies of Santiago, than by the Araucanians and Pehuen-ches. To the former they are delicacies—to the latter, bread. Valuable, also, are the beds of wild strawberries, and an indigenous tuber from which a fine quality of arrow-root is prepared. In short, Concepcion has soil and climate capable of supplying all the wants of the entire population of Chile.

Nor do its industrial resources end here. Gold, copper, and coal exist abundantly, and need but enterprise and mining intelligence for their proper development to make the mines contribute largely to provincial wealth. The positions and extent of some of them are given in the chapter (A Visit to Atacama and Coquimbo) which details the general mineral distribution of the country, and no further allusion need be made here to this source of revenue than by a quotation from Frézier and a statement of their produce shipped in 1850.

Frézier says: "La Concepcion is seated in a country abounding in all things, not only to supply the necessities of life, but also containing infinite wealth. All about the city there is gold found, especially 12 leagues to the eastward at a place called 'Estancia del Rey,' the King's Station, where by washing they get those bits of gold which the Spaniards call *pepitas*—that is, grains; there have been some found weighing eight or ten marks, (a mark is eight ounces,) and extraordinarily fine. Formerly much was got about Angol, which is 24 leagues off; and, if the country were inhabited by a laborious people, it might be had in a thousand parts, where they are satisfied there are good washing places—that is, lands whence it is taken by only washing, as shall be observed hereafter.

"If they penetrate as far as the long ridge of mountains called *La Cordillera*, there is an infinite number of mines of all sorts of metals and minerals; and, among the rest, are two mountains that are only 12 leagues from the *Pampas de Paraguay*, and 100 leagues from La Concepcion. In one of them they have discovered mines of pure copper—so singular, that there have been found in them grains or lumps of above a hundred quintals weight (note that a quintal is a hundred weight). The *Indians* call one of those mountains *Payen*—that is, copper; and Don John Melendez, who made the discovery, called it *S. Joseph*. He drew thence one piece of 40 quintals weight, of which he was, during my stay at *La Concepcion*, making six field-pieces, all six-pounders.

"There are stones which are partly copper quite formed, and partly imperfect copper; for which reason they say in that place that the earth there breeds—that is, that copper is there daily formed. In that mountain there is also *lapis lazuli*.

"The other mountain adjoining, by the Spaniards called *Cerro de Santa Ines*, or *St. Agnes'* Hill, is remarkable for its great plenty of load-stone, which composes almost the whole body of it.

"In the next neighboring mountains, inhabited by the *Puel-ches*, there are mines of sulphur and salt. At *Talcahuano*, at *Irequin*, and in the very city, there are excellent coal-pits without digging above a foot or two. The inhabitants do not know how to make their advantage of it. They were much surprised to see us dig up earth to make fire when we laid in provision for our forge."

Timber in great abundance and of many excellent kinds may be had from the shores of the ocean to a height on the Andes of about 3,000 feet. The only tracts which are not covered are the eastern slope of the central range and the intermediate plain. Much of it is trimmed and floated in rafts to market on the waters of the Biobio. Yet, with all these forests at their doors, the want of proper saw-mills keeps up a demand for boards, and several thousand dollars' worth are annually introduced from the United States. Their herds of cattle are not so numerous as further north. The tribes east and south of them seem to have set value only on their women and cattle; both of which were constantly stolen, whilst the proprietors remained contemptuously disregarded, so long as no personal resistance was attempted. During 1850, the principal staples of the province exported and their values were as follows:

COASTWISE.		TO FOREIGN PORTS.	
Flour	$994,552	Flour	$910,093
Bar copper	97,214	Wheat	96,356
Wine	62,677	Bar copper	100,431
Timber	50,097	Wool	69,018
Chaños	34,752	Timber	24,837
Sole-leather	26,515	Salt beef	9,103
Coal	9,710	Potatoes	7,873
Aguardiente	7,601	Barley	7,354
Barley	3,773	Beans	5,116
Other products	57,123	Coal	6,540
		Other products	5,802
Total coastwise	$1,344,014	Total foreign	$1,242,523

In the same period its imports were: Directly from foreign countries, to the value of $130,998; of foreign naturalized goods (from Valparaiso,) $648,999; and of domestic produce, $77,606—of which last $28,395 was for regulus, and $32,093 for copper ores. These make a total expenditure of $857,603, against an export of $2,586,537; leaving a balance of nearly one and three-quarter millions of dollars in its favor. There is no doubt, however, that a large part of the great staples were received from extra-provincial territory, and had to be paid for from the great apparent surplus.

Its important mills are for grinding wheat. They are principally in the vicinity of Concepcion; and have been erected mainly by American enterprise, and directed by American operatives. Seventeen establishments under various proprietors were in operation within 30 miles of the city. Ponchos, some of which are of superior quality, are made by hand-looms; the very fine ones occupying nearly a year in their manufacture. These often sell for as much as $40 to $60, and some few as high as $100. When it is known that the supply of good wool at very low rates is ample—that water-power is unlimited, and that the forests abound with dye-stuffs, many of whose colors are indestructible, we can only wonder why woollen factories have not been established on a large scale. One or two enterprising and intelligent capitalists would easily make Concepcion the greatest city of South America. The objects of primary importance to them would be: 1st. The erection of saw-mills. These would enable them to build houses of lumber, the only material proper in that region of terrific earthquakes—to say nothing of the unceasing demand for it along the coast. 2d. Manufactories for woollen goods. 3d. A ship canal between the Biobio and Bay of Talcahuano, by which vessels might load and unload at the city, and a channel be opened for heavy rafts and other produce from the great plain to the ocean. And, 4th. Proper miners and machinery for the coal deposites. These completed, agriculture would, of necessity, receive impetus; and in course of time a road will be made across the Andes near the volcano of Antuco, where a pass has been traversed by carriages, and from whence it may readily be continued to the city of Buenos Ayres. There they have no water-power for factories—few fields for cereals; whilst from the foot of the Andes, on the eastern side, to the waters of the Atlantic, nature has made a gradual and unbroken slope, across which a road could be constructed at trifling cost for the transportation of the superabundant products of Concepcion.

Araucania.—In 1852 Congress erected the territory lying between the Biobio and the Imperial, the crests of the Andes and the Pacific, into a new province under the title of Araucania, and authorized the President to direct the usual departments and subdivisions, and appoint appropriate officers. What has been done subsequently is not known, though it is not likely that the laws of civilized life will be acknowledged in the larger portion of this territory for many years to come. A nation which maintained its independence against the powers of Spain and its descendants during three centuries—a veritable *imperium in imperio*—is not likely to recognise much virtue in the *dictum* of a few dozen legislators, presented only through the columns of a newspaper.

The territory thus set apart embraces a superficial area of not less than 11,000 square miles; nearly all of it, away from the coast, as completely unknown as the interior of Africa. Travellers may pass over the road from Concepcion to Valdivia, perhaps, without other molestation than the loss of their horses; but the Indian preserves the same jealous watchfulness for his liberties, and, looking with equal suspicion on all the white race, the only individuals who are permitted to penetrate to the plain are the peddlers, who occasionally bring packs with toys and finery. Unfortunately, these are neither geographers nor political economists; and all we have learned with certainty is, that Araucania is a country in no respect inferior to the province of Concepcion; that its people are, measurably, an agricultural and pastoral race, who live in far greater comfort than the laborers on the haciendas of central Chile; that many of them have herds of cattle to barter for the trinkets, bridles, and other commodities of the peddlers; that they do not aggregate in towns or villages, but each has his tract of land for cultivation and pasturage in the vicinity of one of the many streams; and that they are polygamists, and their wives manufacture ponchos and coarse woollen cloth to greater extent than the wants of their families demand. The art of weaving was known to them before the visit of Europeans; and in the fineness of thread, evenness of weaving, durability and brilliancy of colors, and elegance of patterns, they far excel their more civilized neighbors. Though their agricultural staples are, in general, the same as those grown in Concepcion, a greater proportion of Indian corn, beans, and barley, are raised for their own consumption; orchards of apple and pear trees supplying them with fruits with which to prepare chicha, a drink they are passionately fond of, as, indeed, they are of all intoxicating beverages. The *Araucaria imbricata* furnishes them with piñones, and, in their season, the fields are covered with wild strawberries.

Ercilla, the warrior poet—

" Tomando ora la spada, ora la pluma"—

with nothing to write on but small scraps of waste paper, and sometimes only leather, struggling at the same time against enemies and surrounding circumstances, has left sketches of topography whose fidelity would have done honor to the 19th century. A keen observer of human nature, kind and compassionate to a fault, the pages of the knightly historian contain some few geographical outlines, many that are topographical, more from which we may infer the moral traits of the people; but most of them are glowing details of combats with a race whose great energy and physical strength enabled them so often to defeat the iron-clad warriors of Spain. After him Molina is the writer whose avocations and opportunities best qualified him to give truthful accounts of Chile, and whose volumes have been received as text-books by geographical and ethnographical students. But, unless great degeneration has occurred since the date of his account, the world has been led to entertain most erroneous impressions respecting the degree of civilization and culture of these people. Such statements were the more unpardonable from him, because the order to which he belonged had long had opportunities to study the Araucanians through its missionaries, and the Society at Santiago must have been in possession of many reliable reports from them. What he gave the public has scarcely more fact for its foundation than the so-called historical novels of the present day. Most of the recent writers on Chile have adopted his statements, and thus, from many apparently different sources, we have only one story. However, in 1822, a body of troops was sent from Valdivia to chastise some of the interior tribes and compel them to give up certain Spanish refugees, who continued to excite them to acts of hostility against the patriots. Dr. Leighton, an Englishman, attended them as surgeon, and a part of his journal during the expedition was afterwards published by Mr. Miers. He had opportunities to see many of their dwellings, and to examine the condition of agriculture, their moral and physical qualities, and there is a tone of candor in his narrative which carries conviction with it. Twenty-three years later, Professor Domeyko made a journey as far south as Valdivia, following the coast-road referred to, and his subsequently published* information we are bound to give credence to. Though he writes more of the moral condition of the people, and a mode of ameliorating it, than of their political geography, or the distribution of industrial resources among them, there are many interesting facts stated, from which one may form very approximate estimates of both. What follows is derived from the writings of these two gentlemen.

The three principal physical divisions remarked from Chacabuco southward also extend through the Indian territory, the only modifications produced being occasioned in the vegetable kingdom by the frequency of rains. A multitude of streams originate in the Coast range, amid dense forests, and flow directly to the sea; some of them, wide rivers at their mouths, though of little depth or current. Many others, whose sources are in the same chain, fall along the eastern slope, and spread their waters over the intermediate plain, until they unite with others which originate in the lakes or summits of the more elevated Andes. To the present time, neither their number, their ramifications, nor their names, are known; and all we have learned with certainty is, that before they penetrate the Western cordilleras they are united in three great rivers—the Biobio, the Cauten or Imperial, and the Tolten—all of which would be navigable for some distance but for the bars across their mouths. The two forest belts traversing the length of this province are very luxuriant. Among their trees, the roble (*Fagus obliqua*) is the most abundant. This frequently attains a height of 80 feet, through one half of which its stout, straight trunk is without branches. Its constant and, in many

* Araucania y sus habitantes. Recuerdos de un viaje hecho en las provincias meridionales de Chile en las meses de Enero y Febrero de 1845. Por Ignacio Domeyko. Santiago, 1846.

respects, similar companion, is the hard and heavy Raulé, (*F. procera.* Pœppig.) Both of them are often half concealed amid an infinity of creeping and climbing parasites. There are also laurels, including the *L. peumo;* myrtles; the elegant luma, (*Escallonia thyrsoidea,*) whose fragrance loads the air in the valleys of the rivers, and whose white-cupped flowers and rosy bark are in exquisite contrast with the green of its narrow leaves; the avellano (*Quadria petero-phylla*, R. P.); the canelo (*Drymis chilensis*); and that most beautiful of all climbing plants, the copigue, (*Lapageria rosea,*) so remarkable for its velvety, yet wax-like, coral-colored bells. The Araucaria, on the higher portions of the coast range and the most elevated of the sub-Andine belt, here attains its greatest size and perfection, its trunk being often more than a hundred feet in height, almost as regular and upright as the mast of a ship. The outline of its foliage is a hemisphere, with the convex surface downward. There are many places in these forests where trees and shrubs are so enlaced and intertwined as to be wholly impenetrable. This is more particularly the case with the forest along the western chain; and thus a natural barrier is formed which cuts off communication, except along certain established roads.

Natural transversal highways are the valleys of the Imperial and Tolten—broad ravines, cultivated to a great extent, and enclosing numerous populations. It was on the first of these streams, and near the junction of the Damas, that the Spaniards founded the city of Imperial, now, and for more than two centuries past, a pile of ruins, scarcely recognisable amid the forest. Another road extends from Arauco to Santa Juana, a small village on the south bank of the Biobio, nine leagues above Concepcion; and a fourth from Tucapel, across the celebrated pine tract, to Los Angeles. There are two longitudinal roads—one across the intermediate plain, the other along the coast, and generally within a moderate distance of the sea. Leaving San Pedro, a small village opposite the city of Concepcion, the latter passes through Colcura, a town of nearly 2,000 inhabitants, whose support is derived from the coal mines of the vicinity, and one or two large flour-mills erected here. The surrounding country traversed by it is tolerably well cultivated. Passing the Altos de Villagran, (Mariguenu,) memorable for the disastrous defeat of the Spanish army under Valdivia's immediate successor, the fort of Arauco is reached after a journey of 10 leagues from Concepcion. Formerly the entire Christian population sheltered itself within and under the walls of Arauco; but they now amount to nearly 4,000 souls, who have fraternized with the semi-civilized natives, and fearlessly live at a distance. From Arauco to Tucapel Viejo—sixteen leagues—there are two roads at unequal distances from the coast; though the greater portion of each is over cultivated prairie lands, and among habitations owned by those recognising Christianity. Many of these lands are occupied by Araucanians; and others belong to the natives, but are rented by Christians. It is not known how numerous is the mixed population actually existing between Arauco and the river Leubú; but as the province of Concepcion extended to this river until the law of 1852, and most of it is under control, the Leubú may be regarded as the true northern frontier of the independent Indians.

Along the inner of the two last roads, and which is the most direct and best, there is scarcely a dwelling; but there are many Indian and Christian families near the hills of Quiapo, and about others leading from it to the mouth of the Leubú. Just beyond Tucapel the road crosses a high table-land, where a missionary station has recently been established, not far from the ruins of Cañete, one of the seven cities, and a dilapidated fortress, now in the midst of a wheat-field. On this plain, now cultivated and occupied by many Indian dwellings, tradition informs us that Valdivia was taken and perished.* A little further on is the plain of Taulen, occupying nearly the whole space between the rivers Leubú and Paycavi, from the coast range to the ocean, and which is covered with dense pasturage. As the inhabitants have not a sufficient number of cattle to consume all the grass, and it is regarded beneficial to do so, the dry pasture is annually burned off during the month of February. Wherever the vision is

* One tradition is, that they poured melted gold into his mouth, bidding him drink to his fill of the metal he so much thirsted for.

9

directed, it encounters the dwellings of Indians, no two of them being together. The best information respecting the people inhabiting the country west of the mountains, from the Leubú to the Cudico assigning the number of fighting-men at from 600 to .800, the total population would be from 5,000 to 6,000 souls.

Immediately beyond the Cudico, a broad spur from the coast range extends to the very shores of the sea. The river Tirua originates near its centre, and there are some fifteen or twenty families living about the sort of bay formed at its wide mouth. After ascending the highest part of the ridge, at seven or eight leagues from the sea, the road bends southward again, and begins its descent through forests difficult of transit, miry sloughs and trunks of fallen trees not unfrequently breaking down the strength of the horse more rapidly than the patience of the traveller. But emerging from this upon the basin of the Imperial, a sight is presented him which has no equal in all Araucania. Two chains of hills, extending from the eastward, far as the eye can reach, towards the sea, exhibit habitations over their declivities, sheltered by enclosures, with grain-fields, orchards, or pasture-grounds. Through a broad and meadow-like valley between them flows the placid Imperial, well confined within its slightly sinuous banks. Up the stream, and sepultured in its ruins, now more than two and a half centuries old, lies unfortunate Imperial; and to the southwest, but somewhat more distant, (five or six leagues,) the great Pacific beats against a few isolated rocks at the river's mouth. There is no aspect of savage or barbarian life here—well-built and spacious houses, a laboring population, extensive and well cultivated fields, fine horses and fat herds, are all testimonials of prosperity and a thrifty people.

There is so little current in the river that the tide flows to many leagues above its mouth, and good canoes may be found to speed the traveller on his way. On the opposite shore, the road passes over four or five leagues of pasture-land to the seashore and banks of the Budi or Colem, a stream which exhibits the same picture of a provident agricultural people as does the Imperial. How many Indians inhabit these two districts is unknown. Protected by the transversal spur near the Tirua, as well as by the longitudinal range to the eastward, as there are no anchorages on the coast which will permit these Indians to be approached by sea, they have remained wholly without contact with the Spaniards since the destruction of Imperial, and to this day resist alike the efforts of the government to make a treaty with them, and the solicitations of missionaries to be allowed a residence among them. It is believed that they are not less numerous than those last mentioned. To the eastward of them are the Boroanos, who have been remarked for their fair hair and complexion; to the south their neighbors are the Toltenos.

To the banks of the Tolten there are five or six leagues of straight beach, overlooked by a low and sloping table-land of silicious formation, similar to that in which the Talcahuano and Colcura coal mines have been found. Most of these lands are sandy and arid, and there are no inhabitants near the coast between the Budi and the Tolten. The natural history of the latter stream, its fields and pasturage, are the same as those of the Imperial. Between the Tolten and Queule, seven or eight leagues of a tolerably open country, the natives are more docile, the houses are nearer together, and altogether they appear a poorer and much more humble race. Here, it may be said, is the true southern frontier of Araucania, between which and Valdivia there is a forest so dense that travel through it is greatly impeded, and dangerous for cattle in winter; nevertheless many herds are constantly being driven to be sold in the markets of Concepcion.

The interior road through the intermediate plain is much less known, but is reputed to be more monotonous, though not less interesting from local causes, its fertility and agricultural wealth. Beyond the Biobio are the plains of Angol, with the ruins of its city; and a little further south, the fields of Lumaco and the site of Puren, now possessed by one of the most powerful caciques, whose title to command has been won by prowess and his lance—not obtained by heritage. Surrounding his tribe, there are others not less warlike and relentless;

among whom, that under control of Paynemal numbers at least five hundred warriors. He is said to be owner of many horses and very large herds of cattle. Bordering his tribe are the restless and turbulent Cholchols and the Boroanos. The latter call themselves *Uin-gues*,* a name they also apply to Europeans, though they seem to have no traditional genealogy to throw light on the subject. Southwest of these are the Maquegüas; and beyond them, again, the Villaricas, whose mineral wealth was concealed at the approach of the Spaniards, and on whose lands remain intact the ruins of a city—meet fate for the avaricious presumption of its sponsors. Finally, we meet with the Pelecauhuin and Petrusquen tribes, both of whom are under the influence of the missionaries and the commissariat of the garrisons in Valdivia. There can be no doubt that these last people are descendants of the Cuncos and Huilli-ches, who responded to the calls of the Araucanians, bore an active part in the destruction of the seven cities, effectively resisted the rebuilding of Osorno, and no later than the close of the last century put to death the missionaries on the Rio Bueno. Now, however, much as such estrangement subjects them to enmity, hatred, and persecution, they can no longer be induced to take part with their old allies.

Ercilla describes the Araucanians—

——— 'robustos, desbarbados,
Bien formados los cuerpas y crecidos:
Espaldas grandes, pechos levantados,
Recios miembros, de nervios bien formidas;
Ajiles, desenvueltos, alentados.
Animasos, valientes, atrevidos,
Duros en el trabajo, sufridores
De frios mortales, hambres y calores.'

which, freely rendered, is—"robust, though beardless; large, well-formed bodies; broad shoulders and high chests; pliant muscles and strong limbs; agile, patient, and daring; avengers, brave and bold; persevering in labor; and sufferers to extremity of mortal cold, hunger, and heat."

Prof. Domeyko says they are of a tawny and cleaner though less ruddy color than the other native Americans, and have oval faces, with large or middle-sized sprightly eyes; narrow, arched eyebrows; generally broader and more prominent noses than those at the north; projecting lower lips, but well-formed mouths; in short, the physiognomy assimilates them with the Caucasian rather than the Mongolian race. Their hair is extremely black, thick, coarse, and straight; and the predominant expression of their features, haughtiness, self-possession, imperturbability. Ordinarily, the title of cacique is by heritage, and among them there are many with features and color wholly European—characteristics readily explained by the numbers of Spanish women who were carried off during the wars, and became valued prizes in the chief's seraglio. The native women are generally short, with oval faces and low foreheads. Their eyes have an expression of timidity and tenderness, and their voices are extremely sweet and plaintive, indicative of misfortune and slavery. They talk half singingly, prolonging the final syllables with a sigh, and high, sharp intonation. Their motions are somewhat crouching, and their dresses conceal all the person but the feet and arms. The hair is divided into two neat plaits, entwined with a multitude of glass beads, and then wound about their low foreheads in imitation of the head-dresses or turbans of Asiatic women. Strings of beads or little bells to hang about the neck and breast, with a large breastpin of silver, and bead bracelets, are the ornaments most grateful to their taste. When young, many of them are quite handsome; but from the fact that they are bought from their parents, and are treated with scarcely more deference than cattle, they are utterly destitute of domestic affection, and when captured during war, have been known to leave their children almost without a tear, and ride off

* Pronounced Win-ges, in which one may trace analogy to "Yen-gees," used by the tribes of Massachusetts bay.

behind their new masters in sprightly conversation with them. At the same time, they would suffer death rather than betray the place of concealment of their husbands.

Dr. Leighton's portrait of the men is less flattering. He considered them below the common stature; of a dark complexion; round and full-faced, with small, keen, black eyes; very little forehead, the hairy scalp, in many cases, almost reaching the eye-brows; flat-nosed, with wide nostrils; large mouths, their teeth white and regular, with the exception of the superior dentes canini, which are, in general, very large and long; they have no beard; their bodies are large, their limbs muscular, and their legs, besides being disproportionately short, are very much bowed. In general, they go bareheaded, with their long black hair flowing loosely over their shoulders; though many tie it in a knot on the crown of the head, all having the head encircled by a band. A cacique who came to Santiago during our residence being thought, by those who had had opportunities to judge, a fair type of the race, a daguerreotype was taken of him by Mr. Smith, and the portrait opposite is copied from it.

Their residences are small estates, as distinct and independent of each other as though the capitals of separate nations. Some of them have well constructed wood or reed-plastered houses, above 60 feet long and 25 feet wide. Usually, these have but one entrance, and a single aperture through the roof for the escape of smoke. Adjoining are their orchards and fields of wheat, barley, maize, peas, potatoes, flax, and cabbages, all enclosed and well cultivated; and as the dwellings are, generally, near a river or creek, we perceive on its banks broad and flowery meadows, over which graze their herds of horses, oxen, and sheep. Some of the caciques of the interior are known to possess more than four hundred horses, and still more extensive herds of neat cattle. Those on the coast are not so wealthy; but the latter have the advantage of fisheries, and, in many places, boil down sea-water to make salt for sale—means of subsistence denied to the first. For breaking up the ground, they make use of the common plough of Chile. Artificial irrigation is not needed, and consequently is unknown. It may be added, that they carve platters, trays, and spoons, of wood, with much dexterity; and make vessels of earthenware similar in form and dimensions to those found in the graves of the Indians of Peru and Bolivia. A few smiths are not unskilled in manufacturing spurs, bridle-bits, and other parts of horse-trappings; and the women spend much time in weaving, as has been said.

It is more than probable that great mineral wealth exists, which will be developed as soon as the German colonists in the adjoining province find it indispensable to spread their homes over these lands. It is well known that there were valuable deposites of gold in the vicinity of Puren, and Villarica is said to have obtained its name from the richness of the mines thereabout; but the natives are reputed to have destroyed all external traces of their existence; and, if tradition has preserved knowledge of the localities of these mines, it has also preserved memory of the centuries of war and tyranny to which the seductive metal betrayed them, and the secret of such treasures remains hidden in their own bosoms.

From what has been said, the actual present and possible future resources of Araucania may be inferred. Were a good road made between Valdivia and Concepcion, so as to facilitate intercourse between those cities, it would be greatly beneficial to the trade of each. The tribes along the route, who now look surlily at every passer, and often rob him, even when protected by a *Capitan de Indios,* (a sort of Indian agent,) would soon become familiarized with white men, and their natural dispositions for agriculture would be fostered with the opportunities to dispose of their produce. Under the influence of such intercourse, the next generation would probably witness the warriors abandoning the few customs which now distinguish them from their half-brothers of the north, and this most fertile and beautiful province might then take its place among the wealthiest of the republic.

Valdivia.—The province of Valdivia, created by the law of division of the territory, has for its limits the river Cauten, or Imperial, on the north, the Caramavida from the ocean to its head-waters, and thence a line in an E.S.E. direction to a point on Lake Llanquihue, in

Painted by J.M. Stanley from a Dag.e P.S.Duval & Co. steam lith. press. Phil.a

ARAUCANIAN CHIEF

latitude 41° 06′ S.* on the south, the Andes and Pacific, respectively, on the east and west. Its three departments—Valdivia, Osorno, and Union—embrace a superficial area of 12,000 square miles. These are divided into 14 sub-delegations and 48 districts, a large number of which are in possession of subdued but not conquered aborigines.

The city of Valdivia, founded by the invader of the south, in 1551, stands on a point of land of the southern bank, and about eight miles from the mouth of the river of the same name, called by the aborigines Calle-calle. Several times destroyed by them and a power more irresistible—the earthquakes—once in possession of the Dutch, and at another time regarded by government as a sort of penal colony, its prosperity has been retarded, in spite of many natural advantages; and it is yet scarcely more than a village, amid apple-orchards, most of whose houses are of boards. Many of its best houses, and a large stone church, were overthrown by the earthquake of November, 1837; but a large and more elegant edifice, to replace the latter, was in course of erection, on the plaza, in 1851. Its *Liceo literario*—the provincial college—numbers among its professors a very able German naturalist, who preferred remaining near the body of his own countrymen to a more lucrative post in the "Instituto Nacional," at Santiago. As yet, the population is small, and little thought is given by the mass to the education of their children.

On the island of Manzera, and about the mouth of the river, there are one or two settlements, principally of half-breeds, and villages at Arique, ten miles above Valdivia, on the same river, and at Cruces and San José, on the Cruces river. Each village, with its suburban agriculturists, numbers from 1,000 to 1,300 souls. Though thirty miles from the sea, boats ascend to San José, and canoes descend from a like distance above it, at all seasons. The current is not stronger than that of the Maule; but forests prevent the use of drag-ropes to ascend, as on that stream. Cruces was formerly defended by a fort; but the latter is now in ruins, and only one of its old iron guns remains. In the departments of Union and Osorno there are settlements of the same name, which are dignified with the title of cities. That at the latter place has only been permitted by the Indians within the last five and twenty years; and, in fact, neither of them is more than a straggling village. La Union is on the great plain, five miles to the northward of Rio Bueno, and Osorno is at the junction of the Damas and Rahue, an affluent of the first-named water-course. The native tribes of the province having been found more tractable than their countrymen on the north, the missionaries have many stations among them, and numbers receive annual presents from government for their good behavior. Besides the custom-house at Valdivia, coasting trade is permitted with the Rio Bueno, which is navigable for about twelve leagues; but a bar across its mouth excludes all except small craft.

Excepting the more elevated portion of the Andes and an occasional swampy tract, all the remainder of the land in this province may be rendered useful to the economy of man. But the long resistance of the aboriginal possessors to the white race, many of whom would have become agriculturists, has greatly prevented the increase of population beyond the range of a musket-ball from the forts; and their own aversion to more labor than will produce supplies for themselves, has almost confined cultivation to the borders of streams within the intermediate plain. Beyond it there is very little cleared land, and for thirty miles from Valdivia there is one almost continuous forest. In many parts the undergrowth of creepers, vines, and reeds is so dense, that they can only be passed by circuitous routes. Yet, nearly all the trees are useful, and would readily command purchasers if conveyed to market, whilst the land would be left ready for farming purposes. In consequence of the abundance of rain that falls, and the virgin fertility of the soil, the extensive tract that lies between the Calle-calle and Cruces rivers is

* The *Repertorio Nacional* (official) says: "On the south by Rio Negro." But this cannot form a *southern* boundary. Both Major Philippi and M. Gay, who visited that region, and have published maps under the auspices of government, found only a short river of that name, which emptied into the Rahue, after a nearly north course. As this boundary would throw half of the department of Osorno into the province of Chilóe, I have preferred to adopt the boundary indicated on the maps of those gentlemen.

perhaps more peculiarly adapted to agricultural improvement than even those of the central provinces; and still this great body of land is almost untouched by the hand of the husbandman. Here it is that government has been urged to locate the colonists who come from Germany, in accordance with inducements and promises by its agent. Should it be done, there will be interposed between the Creoles and their warlike neighbors a hardy and temperate race, whose industrious and frugal example will do more towards breaking down the jealous pride, warlike propensities, and exclusivism of the Araucanians, than a regiment of missionaries armed with crosses, or twice that number of soldiers in all the panoply of war. At present, the larger cultivated fields are parts of the plain in the departments of Union and Osorno, which are also the most populated portions of the province. Many of these tracts belong to Indians, who acknowledge Chilean authority, and are nominally Christians; though they neither attend mass voluntarily, nor willingly conform to the Christian law of marriage. Dr. Darwin found them good-sized men, with prominent cheek-bones, resembling the great American family, to which they belong, though with physiognomy slightly different from any tribe he had previously seen. Their expression was generally grave, and even austere, and possessed much character. Those he met on the road had none of that humble politeness he had witnessed in the Chilöe tribes, and were neither inclined to respond to his salutations, nor to acknowledge favors received—a deportment which might be construed into honest bluntness, or fierce determination. They cultivate mostly wheat, beans, and potatoes, and have herds of horses and cattle, but are not as wealthy as the independent tribes. With them, as in every part of the globe where the white and red men come in contact, drunkenness and disease have followed, and, as a distinct race, they are rapidly disappearing.

Flax, barley, peas, and grapes are also cultivated; the juice of the latter being made into chicha, wine, and aguardiente. But the great crop for chicha is apples, of which an amazing quantity are grown, and there is probably no part of the world where the trees thrive better or with less trouble. Nor is the manufacture of chicha the only use to which this fruit is applied. By one process they extract a white and finely-flavored spirit from the refuse pulp; by another, a sweet syrup, or, as they call it, honey; and their children and pigs seem almost to live in the orchards when the fruit is ripening. Though not so numerous in proportion as in the more populous districts, their herds of cattle are rendered more valuable. Few of the cows of the north give milk; here the greater abundance of nutritious pasturage all the year increases the lacteal secretion: larger numbers are kept for dairy purposes, and cheese forms one of their principal articles of domestic export.

Although there are frequent reports of the discovery of mines, Dr. Philippi had not found any traces of auriferous deposites in the partial examination which he made of the coast range near Valdivia. Iron pyrites abounded, and coal or rather lignite formations are frequent. He had found one on the road between Valdivia and Osorno, of which the stratum was of great extent and thickness, and there are two or three others in the same department near the mission of San Juan. That the more precious metals abounded during the middle of the sixteenth century, we have ample historical evidence; and present ignorance of the mines from which they were drawn is to be attributed solely to the jealous care with which the natives have concealed them.

The forests of Valdivia have hitherto proved its greatest source of wealth. Here the Araucaria disappears, and the Alerce, a sort of cypress, takes its place. In some parts of the Andine woods, they are said to attain diameters of 7 to 10 feet, five feet above the ground, and grow 80 or 90 feet without a branch, above which the summit rises 50 feet more. The tree has short, stout branches, with leaves of a bluish-green color, like those of the pine, but which are only half an inch in length and one twentieth of an inch wide. The color of its wood is a darker red than the heart of cedar, and becomes nearly the color of slate after exposure to the weather. Like cedar and cypress, it is somewhat odorous, and as its grain is remarkably straight, with the aid of iron wedges the natives are able to split it into thin planks. These, some four feet long, six inches broad, and half an inch thick, are made into bundles, and find ready markets throughout Chile, as well as at nearly every port on the west coast of South America. As the wood does not shrink or warp, it is used for partitions, weather-boarding, shingling, casks, and almost universally for the ceilings of rooms, mortar being objectionable for the last purpose in earthquake countries. Here, also, is found, in the greatest profusion, the Coligue—a cane resembling the bamboo of Brazil. It grows in clusters, and ornaments the banks of some of the streams in a very pretty manner, often attaining a height of more than 20 feet. Being durable, light, flexible, and very strong, they are used as supports for the tiles in roofing houses; and it is of these that the Indians make their long, tapering, and terrible lances. The other trees and plants are much the same as in the province of Concepcion.

During the year 1850 its commerce with domestic ports consisted of the following articles, of which the home valuation is also given:

EXPORTS.		IMPORTS.	
Lumber	$71,535	Aguardiente	$13,024
Cheese	20,480	Manufactures	7,934
Flour	2,768	Flour	7,756
Charqui	2,728	Aji (red pepper)	4,784
Hides	2,110	Wine	3,505
Aguardiente	1,578	Beans	1,064
Fire-wood	1,130	Madeira nuts	630
Wheat	980	Grasa	374
Grasa	817	Dried figs	316
Wine	717	Tallow	156
Potatoes	298	Other products	976
Hams	150		
Other products	906		

To foreign ports it sent, in the same period, to the value of $2,379, receiving to the value of $6,892; of which sum $6,190 was in common salt, and $270 in iron cut-nails. The foreign naturalized goods brought from Valparaiso amounted to $31,816, leaving a balance in its favor of nearly $30,000.

CHILÓE—This province, created by the law of division of the territory, is composed of the island of the same name, the Chonos archipelago, and the continent from the southern boundary of Valdivia to Cape Horn. Chile claims jurisdiction over all Patagonia and Tierra del Fuego, with the intermediate Straits of Magellan;* so that, according to the above official

* The author has recently forwarded to me a copy of a pamphlet written at the request of the Minister of the Interior of Chile, in which is set forth the "*Titulas de la República de Chile á la soberania y dominio de la estremidad austral del continente Americano*"—(Titles of the republic of Chile to the sovereignty and dominion of the southern extremity of the American continent.) His arguments in answer to a preceding publication in Buenos Ayres are supported by documents, and appear to be conclusive. Assuming as a principle that "las nuevas repúblicas tienen por limites las mismas que corresponden á las antiguas demarcaciones coloniales de que se formaron, salvo las modificaciones que la guerra de la independencia hizo esperimentar á algunas de las mencionadas demarcaciones"—(the new republics have as limits those corresponding with the colonial demarcations, from which they were formed, except as modified in some instances by the war of independence); he concludes as follows: "La república de Chile puede presentar titulas de la misma especie de las que ostenta la república Argentina; pero ésta no puede, como lo hace Chile, apoyar sus pretensiones en leyes claras, precisas y terminantes, que realmente marcan las divisiones territoriales. Siempre que el monarca español se ha propuesto deslindar sus provincias ultra-marinas? á quien le ha asignado la Patagonia, el estrecho de Magellanes y Tierra del Fuego? A Chile, en todas ocasiones desde la conquista hasta la independencia. * * * Nuestra soberania sobre ese territorio es pues indisputable; y pierda cuidado Señor Anjelis (the author of the pamphlet insisting on the right of Buenos Ayres)—Chile, si en esta cuestion debiera oirse la voz del cañon con preferencia á la voz de la justicia, sabria hacer respetar por la fuerza una propiedad cuya posesion le garantiza la lei."—(The republic of Chile may present claims (titles) of the same character as those of which the Argentine republic boasts; but the latter cannot, as Chile does, support its pretensions on plain laws, precise and definite, which really mark territorial divisions. Whenever the Spanish monarch proposed to delineate his ultra-marine provinces, to whom has he assigned Patagonia, the Straits of Magellan, and Tierra del Fuego? To Chile, on all occasions, from the conquest to the independence! Our sovereignty over

delineation, this province embraces an extent of territory many times greater than all the rest of the republic.

Its departments are Ancud, Carelmapu, Chacao, Calbuco, Dalcahue, Quinchao, Quenac, Castro, Lemui, and Conchi, which comprise 24 sub-delegations and 110 districts. We have reliable accounts of the island from Hon. John Byron, Padre P. G. de Agüeros, Pœppig, Capts. King and Fitzroy, R. N., and Dr. Darwin, with others of a less definite nature, from whose volumes most of the information which follows has been obtained.

San Carlos, the provincial capital—or Ancud, as it has been called since the Spanish troops were defeated, in 1826, by the Chileans, under Gen. Fréire—is built on two rising grounds and an intermediate valley near the bottom of a bay of the same name, at the north end of the island. A rivulet runs through the little ravine, and at its mouth there is a mole, under which boats and piraguas frequenting the port find protection. The houses generally are of wood, small, and have been built with little knowledge of comfort. Its plaza is on a flat piece of ground at the summit of the southern hill, and commands an extensive view. On the north side there is a strong and well built storehouse of stone; opposite to it is the cathedral, also of stone; on the side next the sea is the residence of the Intendente and offices; and the fourth side is taken up by inferior-looking dwellings. Some in better taste and of more substantial character have been erected within a few years, equally creditable for strength and convenience; though, as good wood is so abundant and cheap, it is still the principal material used. Damp as is the climate, and unpainted as is most of the weather-boarding, the habit of charring the ends of timbers before they are inserted into the ground, renders them quite durable; and such is the nature of most of the outside wood, that there are many houses in good repair, which are nearly a hundred years old. The bishop of Chilóe, whose residence is here, has spiritual jurisdiction over the province of Valdivia also. There is a school, at the expense of government, for instruction in nautical science, a normal school for teachers, one for instruction in drawing, cosmography, &c., and fourteen primary schools in different parts of the province, all paid from the public treasury. In 1848 the population of Ancud amounted to 3,865.

On a steep hill near the bottom of the island-locked bay, and eastern side of the "*ysla grande*," is Castro, next in size to Ancud. It is styled a *city*, but consists only of about 250 ordinary wooden houses, on two or three short streets, and two churches. One of the latter, built by the Jesuits more than a hundred years ago, is fast decaying, though supported on all sides by props. The principal church stands in the middle of the plaza, and has a picturesque and venerable appearance; but the former, as well as the streets, are coated with grass, and their aspect is most forlorn and desolate. Government supports a model and two primary schools here. Byron speaks most gratefully of the considerate hospitality extended to himself and the two half-starved companions who reached Castro with him from the desolate shores of Patagonia. Its intercourse with the world, as late as 1835, may be judged of by the fact that a boat-party, from H. B. M.'s ship Beagle, were unable to purchase a pound of sugar or an ordinary knife, nor was there any one in the town possessed of a clock or watch. An old man, who was supposed to have a good idea of time, was employed to strike the church-bell by guess. Yet, among the islands of the vicinity, money was scarcely of any value, and tobacco, indigo, capsicum, old clothes, and powder, were greatly more cared for, the last being for church celebrations. A stick of tobacco, of the value of three cents, purchased two fowls; and cotton handkerchiefs which had cost a dollar and a half, were exchanged for three sheep and a large bunch of onions. This is still the most populous department of the province.

Chacao, near the northeast extremity of the island, and where the Intendente resided at the

this territory, then, is indisputable; and rest assured, Señor Anjelis! that Chile, if on this question the voice of cannon is to be heard rather than that of justice, by force, will know how to cause to be respected a property which is guarantied to her by law)—This would be very well, but the 1st Article of the Constitution proclaims to the world: "*The territory of Chile extends from the desert of Atacama to Cape Horn, and from the cordilleras of the Andes to the Pacific ocean, comprising the archipelago of Chilóe, all the adjacent islands, and those of Juan Fernandez.*"

time of Byron's visit, (1742,) is only a hamlet. Remains of a town, such as lines of streets and the ruins of a church, are visible; but there are now only a few straggling cottages and a chapel in ruins. It is said, on the spot, that the former church of Chacao was burned by the old Spaniards, to oblige the natives to quit the place and go to San Carlos, which was designated for the capital as early as 1566. There are also small settlements at Dalcahue, Conchi, and Vilinco, on the same island; at Calbuco, Palqui, Quenac, and Puchilco, on islands of the archipelago; and at Carelmapu, on the main land. Their inhabitants have at least three parts in four Indian blood. The district of Cucao is the only inhabited part of the western coast of Chilóe. It contains about fifty Indian families, who are scattered along four or five miles of the shore, but who, whilst having plenty to eat, and tolerably good clothes of their own manufacture to wear, have no commerce, except in a little seal-oil. Ancud is the port of entry; San Miguel and Bulnes, in the Straits of Magellan, are also open to coasting trade. There are four distinct classes of inhabitants on Chilóe and the adjacent islands—the aboriginal Huyhuen-che, or Chonos; the Huilli-che, who came from southern Chile; the foreigners, who were neither born on the island nor of Chilote parents; and the Creoles. Of these four, in consequence of disease and emigration, the Chonos form but a small number, and the principal population belong to the Huilli-che tribe, a tame and docile race when compared with the former, whose spirit of independence has shown itself in their emigration. Capt. Fitzroy says of the Huilli-ches, that they are "nominally Christians, but painfully ignorant of pure Christianity." That they should be extremely superstitious, is not at all to be wondered at; for theirs is a confused demi-religion, in which a medley of ideas concerning the Virgin Mary, saints, images, and witches, is found far more often than any clear reference to our Saviour or the Almighty. Those who reside upon the coast are scarcely superior to the uncivilized savages further south. They live principally upon shell-fish, and what little they are enabled to procure by the sale of a few pigs, or poultry, which they rear on the scanty store of potatoes and wheat that remains after their new crop comes to maturity. One roof shelters a whole family. Father and mother, sons and daughters, dogs and pigs, all live and sleep in their only room; in the middle of which a fire is made, whence the smoke escapes by numerous apertures in the roof and sides of the dwelling. The foreigners, who are few in number, of course, resemble their own countrymen as to morals and habits, and the Creoles are quite ready to adopt their ideas. Their warm-hearted kindness and hospitality towards strangers is conspicuous, even among the descendants of Spaniards in South America. The language in common use is Spanish, the original Indian tongue being almost forgotten; but it is supposed to have been the same as that spoken by the Indians of Madre de Dios—Molu-che. Hervas, in his work on languages, says that they now speak a language of which the words are Spanish, but all the inflections, syntax, and idioms, are Chilean.

A very large proportion of the island is covered with dense forests of robles, tiquis, mañus, muermos, maytens, &c., all of those named being valuable woods. Even where paths exist through them, they are scarcely passable from the soft and swampy nature of the soil. In these shaded highways, where the sun never penetrates the evergreen foliage, it is absolutely necessary that the whole road should be made of logs of wood. These are squared and placed beside each other, and are longitudinally fastened down by transverse poles, pegged on each side, into the earth. Without this, neither man nor beast would be able to pass from settlement to settlement. In most countries, forests can be removed without difficulty by the aid of fire; but from the damp nature of the climate, and the character of the trees, it is necessary that they be first cut down; and thus natives complain greatly of the want of land. The islands of Quinchao and Lemui are almost entirely cultivated, and both are populous. These, together with the vicinity of Castro and a smaller space round Ancud, and on some of the other islands, are the most fertile and productive portions of the province. The soil is a rich, sandy loam, of a dark-red color; and though rarely, if ever, manured, produces fair average crops of wheat, barley, flax, and potatoes. Wheat is sown in April, and cut in the same month of the following year; but from the humidity of the atmosphere, particularly at that season, (the commencement of winter,) it is frequently reaped before it is quite ripe, and is almost always gathered in wet. By moving it about, and keeping it thinly strewed in granaries, it dries rapidly, though, of necessity, some portion becomes mildewed. The mode of threshing and winnowing is the same that is practised in other parts of Chile.

According to the returns made to the Intendente, the harvest of 1850 yielded 163,170 bushels of wheat, 15,650 of barley, 1,580 of flaxseed, and 940,700 of potatoes. This last esculent is planted from September to November, and is ready for gathering in May following. Large quantities are sold to whale-ships and others that frequent Ancud, and of which no account is given in the custom-house statistics. Except of potatoes, the returns are smaller than they were twenty-two years previously—conclusive inferential evidence that there has been little augmentation of the population, or progress in clearing land. There is neither wine nor spirit made to any extent in the province; but chicha is manufactured from apples in large quantities. Here, as in Valdivia, the apple-trees are very numerous, and the Chilotes have a marvellous short way of making an orchard. At the lower part of almost every branch, small, conical, brown, and wrinkled points project. These are always ready to change into roots, as may sometimes be seen when any mud has been accidentally splashed against the tree. A branch as thick as a man's thigh is chosen in the early spring, and is cut off just beneath these points. All the smaller branches are lopped off, and it is then placed about two feet deep in the ground. During the ensuing summer, the stump throws out long shoots, and sometimes even bears fruit. Dr. Darwin was shown one which had produced as many as twenty-three apples, though this was thought very unusual; and another was pointed out to him, which in the third season was changed into a well-wooded tree, loaded with fruit. The only good indigenous fruits are the strawberry, which grows abundantly on several of the islands, and the chupon, a sort of bromelia (?) that may be found on the main land also, as far north as the river Maule.

Owing to the scarcity and indifference of the pasturage and the excess of rainy weather, horned cattle and sheep do not multiply more rapidly than the home consumption demands. Swine thrive amazingly on the wild potatoes and other indigenous roots; and the hams of Chilóe are acknowledged luxuries on every part of the coast.

Allusion has been made to the quantities of excellent fish, both vertebrated and molluscous, with which the sea and creeks abound. In summer, smelt, mullet, a kind of bass, and several other varieties, are taken by placing very simple weirs across creeks, leaving a passage in the middle, which is left open during the flood, and closed when the tide begins to ebb. Some of these weirs are rough stone walls, on a small scale; others are wattled, like hurdles; and as the water falls, the number of fish kept back by them is really surprising. The shell-fish most esteemed are two varieties of choros (*Mytilus*), oysters, picos (*Balanus psittacus*), and piures (*Pyura*, Molina). Choros are often found seven or eight inches long. Of these the fish is nearly as large as a goose's egg, and when baked in a hole in the earth, which has been heated properly, they are very juicy and of delightful flavor. In size, as well as taste, the oyster rather resembles the European than the North American. They are occasionally sent as presents to friends at Valparaiso, by whom they are highly esteemed. The pico is a barnacle, often four or five inches long, and has much the flavor of the crab. Not only by the inhabitants of this archipelago, but also by those of Concepcion and Caldera, in whose bays it is found, it is preferred over all other shell-fish. The piure, which Molina considered a genus allied to *Ascidia*, as an edible is still less inviting to the eye than the generality of that family. Its body is about the size and shape of a small pear, an inch in diameter, shut up in a firm glutinous case of various shapes, one of which often contains eight or ten distinct bodies, separated from each other by a strong membraneous substance. They are found attached to rocks or stones under water, and are eaten boiled or roasted in their shells, having, when fresh, a flavor not unlike that of the lobster. Occasionally they also are dried and sent to the Valparaiso market.

At Chilóe, the piure is said to be a remedy for barrenness; and Capt. King narrates that "to such extent has this idea prevailed, that a Chilote woman eating this dish literally says, if asked what she is doing, that 'she is making children.' One would not, however, suppose, from the number of children which are seen crowding round the door, that the Chilotes had any necessity for such food." Yet, if the statement of the population by Agüeros be correct, the rate of increase has only been 80 per cent. during the last 65 years, and in the last 16 years it was but 0.64 per cent. per annum.

During the last quarter of the sixteenth century, and the first quarter of the seventeenth, several gold mines were worked on the "ysla grande;" but they were only productive so long as there was a numerous native population, over whom barbarous task-masters could exercise cruelties unquestioned, and they were abandoned prior to 1633. Neither silver nor copper ores have been found. Lignite exists abundantly in the vicinity of Ancud, as well as on the island of Lemui; but wood is too abundant in the forests to make coal valuable at present. Indeed, but for these forests, without a change of character the Chilotes would at once become bankrupts. Where so little personal exertion is necessary to provide subsistence, it is not greatly to be wondered at that the lower classes remain indolent; and we may, perhaps, find a reason for the remarkable want of industry here, in the apparently inexhaustible abundance of fish, the facility with which they may be taken, and their consequent cheapness. Since the island became subject to the Chilean government, continuous efforts have been made to improve the condition of the people. But apathy is a national characteristic, inherited from the aboriginal mother—a consequent to her vassalage and an almost changeless temperature. If the most energetic at the capital confess to this predominant trait, how much more deeply fixed shall we expect to find it in unadulterated blood—a race, physically no less than morally, trampled under foot during three centuries, and from whom even yet there are constant and cruel extortions to preserve the memory of the past?

Manufactories, properly so called, are yet to be erected. Coarse woollen cloth of a very durable quality, ponchos, bordillos, (a smaller kind of poncho,) common and embroidered blankets, and carpets (small square rugs) for church, are made with hand-looms to supply the home demand—no more; and the wheat and barley are ground within the province. Cables, hawsers, and a sort of rope, needed for the piraguas, are made of a plant they call *quilineja*, which is supposed to be the root of a species of callixene. The material of the sail has already been mentioned.

During 1850 the trade of the province consisted in the following articles, whose values are annexed:

DOMESTIC IMPORTS.	
Rum and spirits	$46,259
Flour	28,883
Tallow candles	12,192
Wheat	8,260
Wine	7,550
Red pepper	6,130
Charqui	3,212
Barley	2,245
Beans	2,139
Biscuit	1,895
Soap	1,839
Dried fruits	1,683
Grasa	1,223
Other articles	13,541
Foreign naturalized goods	68,911
FOREIGN IMPORTS.	
Common salt	5,000
Other articles	1,400
Total imports	$212,362

DOMESTIC EXPORTS.	
Timber and lumber	$234,659
Sole-leather	2,922
Hams	1,480
Cheese	833
Potatoes	546
Fire-wood	527
Hides	508
Red pepper	319
Brooms	245
Other articles	924
FOREIGN EXPORTS.	
Timber and lumber	41,994
Hams	3,867
Potatoes	1,525
Joiners' work (doors)	1,475
Fire-wood	147
Flour	140
Other articles	325
Total exports	$292,436

The foreign trade was wholly with California and Peru.

Statistics of the Population and Mortality for 1848.

Provinces.	Departments.	Population.	Marriages.	Births.			Deaths.		Totals.		Ratio births to population.	Ratio deaths to population.
				Male.	Female.	Illegitimate.	Male.	Female.	Births.	Deaths.		
											1 *for*	1 *for*
ATACAMA	Copiapó, (*a*)	11,898	50	210	219	179	125	108	429	243	27.7	49.0
	Freirina, (*b*)	4,883	37	66	66	35	36	21	132	57	37.0	85.7
	Vallenar	8,384	47	99	103	85	64	49	202	103	41.5	81.4
COQUIMBO	Serena	23,612	153	514	440	334	140	105	954	245	23.7	96.4
	Elqui	9,307	54	84	137	86	30	71	221	101	42.1	92.1
	Combarbala	8,411	133	320	295	197	47	42	615	89	13.7	94.5
	Illapel	17,640	97	282	264	163	91	117	546	212	32.3	83.2
	Ovalle	26,379	250	669	671	435	206	208	1,340	414	19.7	63.7
ACONCAGUA	San Felipe	19,973	174	567	540	339	206	208	1,107	414	18.0	48.2
	Andes	22,111	172	543	478	355	160	148	1,021	308	21.6	71.8
	Ligua	10,587	90	232	249	90	55	36	481	91	22.0	116.3
	Petorca	23,612	296	689	529	320	179	176	1,268	355	18.6	66.5
	Putaendo	15,401	172	361	339	355	186	165	700	351	22.0	43.9
SANTIAGO	Santiago, (*c*)	95,795	1,113	2,794	3,096	1,190	1,925	2,013	5,890	3,638	16.3	26.3
	Melipilla	23,958	165	393	386	141	282	280	779	562	30.8	42.6
	Rancagua, (*d*)	66,859	417	1,166	1,050	409	785	761	2,216	1,546	30.2	43.9
	Victoria, (*e*)	20,822	179	350	323	79	189	130	673	329	30.9	63.3
VALPARAISO	Valparaiso	30,826	267	1,105	1,070	675	682	512	2,085	1,177	14.8	26.2
	Casablanca	12,714	34	119	100	42	59	63	219	122	58.0	104.2
	Quillota	32,422	337	996	865	364	421	410	1,858	830	17.4	39.1
COLCHAGUA	San Fernando	66,000	381	1,279	1,082	424	483	526	2,431	1,009	27.1	65.4
	Caupolican, (*f*)	47,341	377	1,142	1,314	440	661	563	2,756	1,224	17.2	38.7
	Curicó, (*g*)	59,732	362	1,082	1,053	344	630	663	2,125	393	28.1	144.4
TALCA	Talca, (*h*)	60,847	410	1,008	1,064	381	781	855	2,072	1,636	29.3	37.2
	Lontue	10,534	113	324	307	91	84	69	631	153	16.9	68.9
MAULE	Cauquenes	45,554	373	655	607	335	506	521	1,262	1,027	36.1	43.4
	Constitucion	5,011	44	161	167	43	74	64	328	138	15.3	36.3
	Itata	24,583	258	534	512	145	301	333	1,046	634	23.5	38.8
	Linares	27,753	238	782	548	292	228	229	1,366	457	20.3	60.8
	Parral	15,428	125	191	287	53	71	68	478	139	32.3	111.0
ÑUBLE	Chillan	62,841	357	580	547	243	364	341	1,157	705	54.3	89.1
	San Carlos	27,114	114	264	264	94	136	140	528	276	51.3	98.2
CONCEPCION	Concepcion	10,393	76	240	210	137	241	171	441	412	23.6	25.2
	Coelemu	20,410	210	515	506	153	207	232	1,021	439	20.0	46.5
	Laja	17,682	117	453	377	88	94	61	830	155	21.3	114.1
	Puchacai	21,007	79	252	244	82	83	70	496	153	42.3	137.3
	Rere	22,090	115	540	506	363	154	160	1,046	314	21.1	70.4
	Talcahuano	4,101	34	110	91	71	80	75	201	155	20.4	26.5
ARAUCANIA	Lautaro	13,843	115	470	458	239	95	139	928	251	14.9	55.1
VALDIVIA	Valdivia	7,059	19	68	61	35	42	31	129	73	54.7	96.7
	Osorno	9,256	28	75	62	16	25	22	137	47	67.5	197.0
	Union	6,783	16	59	48	21	12	12	107	24	63.4	282.3
CHILÓE	Ancud	5,269	72	117	139	50	56	64	256	117	20.6	45.0
	Calbuco	7,477	72	214	184	47	38	58	398	96	18.8	77.9
	Carelmapu	2,014	19	20	22	6	16	15	42	31	48.0	65.0
	Castro	8,579	68	138	121	43	73	71	259	144	33.1	59.6
	Chacao	2,331	25	51	44	20	36	33	95	69	24.6	33.8
	Conchi	4,231	42	145	156	34	119	107	301	226	14.1	18.7
	Dalcahue	4,089	33	86	78	21	33	52	164	85	24.9	48.1
	Lemui	5,191	59	87	74	11	66	36	161	102	32.2	50.9
	Quenac	2,921	11	34	46	11	14	13	80	27	36.5	108.2
	Quinchao	6,774	67	71	84	29	83	68	155	151	43.7	44.8
	Totals	1,119,802	8,666	22,306	22,483	10,235	11,856	11,485	44,789	23,341	25.0	48.0

(*a*) No returns from 9 districts.
(*b*) No returns from 4 districts.
(*c*) No returns from 33 districts.
(*d*) No returns from 25 districts.
(*e*) No returns from 16 districts.
(*f*) No returns from 10 districts.
(*g*) No returns from 19 districts.
(*h*) No returns from 15 districts.

It is conceded, by the best informed, that the returns gave at least ten per cent. less than the actual population at the time of the census; and if, for those provinces from some of whose districts no returns were made, we assume an average for such districts, it will be necessary further to increase the province of Atacama 3,760, Santiago 66,121, Colchagua 65,137, and Talca 11,638, making a gross aggregate of 1,393,125 souls.

The census of 1832 gave, for that year, 1,010,336; the editor of the "Repertorio Chileno," in which it is published, remarking, that as the people could not be convinced that the object of their enumeration was not for the imposition of a new tax or to levy recruits, quite ten per cent. absented themselves on the visits of the commissioners, and therefore this proportion should be added to their returns. Adopting his conclusion, the population in 1832 was 1,111,370 souls ; since which time, according to the census of 1848, the annual increase has been 17,610. But, by the ratios derived from the census last referred to, the number of births at the close of 1832 should have been 44,455, and of deaths 23,154 ; leaving the yearly augmentation 21,301—very nearly what it was sixteen years later! These are the only general statistics of population. Subsequent returns have been made of individual provinces, and provincial bills of mortality are published quite regularly.

The statistics do not include the tribes of independent Indians, whose numbers are unknown, but have been estimated at from 20,000 to 25,000 souls.*

* A census was completed after writing the above. In publishing the results (October 21, 1854), the "*Mercurio*" of Valparaiso states that minute scrutiny of the details in the Statistical Office may possibly alter the following numbers slightly:

Province.	Population.	Province.	Population.
Atacama	50,783	Maule	156,470
Coquimbo	110,718	Ñuble	100,397
Aconcagua	111,137	Concepcion . . .	109,753
Valparaiso	117,257	Araucania	43,167
Santiago	270,415	Valdivia	28,239
Colchagua	191,999	Chilóe	61,586
Talca	80,219	Magellan colony . .	3,381
		Aggregate . . .	1,435,521

CHAPTER III.

THE CLIMATE.

DOES CLIMATE INFLUENCE THE MORAL AND PHYSICAL ENERGIES OF MAN?—PROBABLE CHANGE IN CHILE AS AGRICULTURE IS MORE GENERALLY EXTENDED.—WINTER AT SANTIAGO; ZODIACAL LIGHT.—WINTER AT VALPARAISO.—WINTER NORTH OF LATITUDE 33°; EXTRAORDINARY DRYNESS AND TRANSPARENCY OF THE AIR.—WINTER AT VALDIVIA; AT THE ISLAND OF CHILÓE.—SPRING AT SANTIAGO; THUNDER-STORMS; AURORA AUSTRALIS; PROGRESS OF VEGETATION; PRESSURE, TEMPERATURE, AND MOISTURE AT SANTIAGO DURING THE SUMMER; RADIATION; HAIL-STORM; PERIODICAL WINDS; CLEAR ATMOSPHERE.—SUMMER ON THE COAST: AT COQUIMBO: AT CONCEPCION: AT VALDIVIA: AT CHILÓE.—AUTUMN AT SANTIAGO; INDIAN SUMMER; METEORS; SUNBEAMS; RED SNOW.

Every traveller who has made a sojourn in Chile unaffectedly lauds its climate, no matter what the period of the year at which his visit was made. Sufficiently to the south of the equator to mark perceptibly changes of the seasons, the Pacific and giant Andes combine to prevent extremes to which similar parallels of the north Atlantic coast are subject; and there is a genial uniformity, most grateful to the corporal frame, throughout the year. Whether such uniformity is best for the development and progress of mankind, eminently deserves the attention of the physiologist, instigated, as he is, to the inquiry, by the fact that the enterprising and energetic nations of the globe are those who inhabit climates subject to frequent and extreme vicissitudes. Is not the mind, like the body, more inert in summer: its perceptions more vivid and quick, when the frosts of winter demand vigorous bodily exertion to heat the blood? If so, how can we expect great energy of character, or brilliant acquirements, from those who are born and dwell in climates that never experience such changes? That such a temperature will sap the energies of man, there is ample evidence among Americans and Europeans who reside long in Chile; men who went there with all the industry, activity, and perseverance characterizing their races, yet who now differ little from native residents. Active as the members of our small party were compelled to be, and exposed, as we often were, to the severest cold ever known at Santiago, three years' residence made a sensible impression even on us; and another like period would probably have gone far towards imbuing us with the national trait—apathy.

It is proposed to give, in this place, only such outlines of each season as will interest the general reader, referring the meteorologist, for detailed instrumental results, to the volume ot observations and notes specially devoted to the subject. But, as to the south of the equator, their winter is our summer, our spring their autumn; to follow our order, requires commencement at the middle, rather than with the beginning of the calendar year—with June or July, the first winter months, instead of December and January, the beginning of ours. June, July, and August, then, are the winter months of the southern hemisphere, and the season of rains, when every one complains of wet and cold, and when, from the structure of their houses, and improvidence, disease is rife among the poor. Near the equator, the coast, sheltered by the Andes, is not subject to rain-storms; but Chile, beyond the torrid zone, forms no exception to the general rule.

Santiago, of which I shall speak the most extendedly, is on a plain, 2,000 feet above the ocean, from which it is sixty miles distant in an air-line. The plain, bounded on the east by the Andes, and on the west by the cordilleras of the coast, commences at the base of a spur, which, 30 miles to the northward, joins the two mountain chains, and extends almost uninterruptedly to the sea, 500 miles distant, in a southerly direction. Its width is variable, but nowhere exceeds 40 miles. Geographically, the city is five degrees beyond the tropic of Capricorn, and not far from the centre of the republic.

Thirty years ago, rain was never expected until the early part of May, nor a continuance of showers before the middle of June. From the latter epoch, until the close of August, there were often five to eight successive days when rain fell heavily during many hours; and an inch for each hour was no extraordinary deposit. But at the time of our arrival, and subsequently, the change in their climate was the subject of common conversation; and the fact that rain fell during nearly every month of our residence, was good evidence in support of the popular belief. A register, which had been kept through twenty-seven years, showed that the average number of hours, per year, during which rain had fallen in the city, between 1824 and 1850, was 215½, or nine entire days. These were distributed as follows:

	h. m.		h. m.		h. m.		h. m.
June	56 33	September	16 20	December	1 42	March	1 36
July	48 11	October	11 45	January	2 00*	April	11 31
August	29 58	November	2 02	February	0 18	May	34 22

The most remarkable years were 1832 and 1843, in the former of which the precipitation was only during ninety-nine and a half hours; and in the latter, during three hundred and ninety hours, distributed through every month of the year. Señor Reyes, by whom the register was kept, had no instrument for measuring the quantity of water; and, unfortunately, he has omitted all other data than those from which the preceding results are compiled. When his register was commenced, the immediate plain to the southward of the city was little better than a desert. Some three or four garden-spots, and a few dwarf Acacia cavenias, offered the only green spots away from the banks of the river; and the S.W. wind, which swept across it, came loaded with heat reflected from the arid surface. Till then, there was no mode of irrigating most of the tract; and it was long after the canal was cut to convey water from the Maypu, along the base of the Andes, to the Mapocho, before its value was properly estimated. Contemporaneously, a few slips of Lombardy poplar were introduced from Mendoza; ten thousand minor rivulets were led from the canal across the valley; in every direction the land was gradually brought under cultivation; poplars and vineyards rose as by magic on every part of it; and now, wherever the eye turns, there are groves of trees and verdant fields. These give out a part of the moisture introduced for their fructification; and clouds by day, and rains out of season, in following a law of nature, must increase with their multiplication.

So long as the wind continues from the south, no precipitation of moisture takes place. If it comes from the east of south, the sky remains clear, and frosts are probable; but within an hour or two after, it changes to north or N.W., the temperature rises, a dense sheet of vapor is seen pouring over the coast range into the valley, and rain soon follows. When the earth has become saturated after successive days of storm, one may often observe the formation of clouds, and their precipitation in rain, within ten minutes of each other. As the vapor from the sea comes into the valley, it meets a warmer air near the surface, expands, rises, and is lost to sight. It is still moving in the same direction, however; and on encountering the cold current from the Andes, condensation ensues so rapidly that in less time than it has occupied to write of it the fleecy nebula we saw originate a mile to the N.W. is sprinkling its waters over us. At a moderate elevation on the mountains, the rain-storms are converted into snows; and snow is often seen falling there whilst the valley is enjoying good weather. Occasionally the latter has been known to fall in the city, though it never remains more than a few hours on the ground. The amount of water deposited during some of these *temporales* (as they are called) is quite surprising—as much as fifteen inches having fallen in June of 1850. During the same months of 1851 and 1852 the quantities were respectively two and a half and ten and a quarter inches. Our observations furnish results only for two completed years—1850 and 1851; during which the quantities measured by the gauge amounted to 56.032 inches in the former, and 39.238

* A result produced by forty hours of rain, in 1837.

inches in the latter year. During these months, rain was never accompanied by thunder and lightning, nor were the winds ever very violent, although it is the period when the greatest inequalities occur in the atmospheric pressure. In the same latitude of the northern hemisphere, fluctuations of the barometric column through an inch and a half are not extraordinary; but at Santiago it was never half so much in the three years of observation; indeed, the whole oscillation was from 27.817 to 28.506 inches, or rather less than seven tenths. Of course, one would not expect storms of wind with so uniform a pressure, and the only instance remembered when a moderate gale occurred was during a *temporal* on the 24th July, 1851. At Valparaiso, the violence of the wind caused the loss of several vessels, though the only damage at the capital was the prostration of a few evergreen trees covered with dense foliage, and the blowing over of a little observatory erected for an instrument lent to the government students. I was in Valparaiso at the time, and quote from the account Lieut. MacRae wrote me:

"We had quite a fright this morning. Our old friend, the sergeant, who lives at the Castle, came down with news that the instrument in the lower house was broken; and having forgotten, at the moment, the little telescope in the Castle yard, I supposed it was the meridian circle. On repairing to the spot, we found that the wind had partially capsized the little building, and that the polar-axis had broken off the weather-boarding, though the instrument remained uninjured. As the wind continued blowing violently, we commenced dismounting it; but Mr. Phelps's strong back saved all trouble, as he picked up the whole affair—stand and all—and carried it into the room of the Castle, where our boxes were originally stored. I think it probable that one of the *discipulos* (students) neglected to hook the braces; for, although the wind blew stronger than I have ever felt it here, I do not think it would have turned the house over had they been secure. This has been the first sailor-work we have had to do since our arrival in Santiago—shortening sail on an observatory; and it was done in a manner that startled Mr. ——, the *discipulo*, whom we sent for."

And well it might. The stand, counterpoises, and telescope, must weigh well nigh 400 pounds—no trifle to shoulder in a gale of wind, and march off with the greater half of it towering above one's head. The wind at the time was from N.W., and the barometer about three tenths of an inch below its mean elevation, as it was at Valparaiso also.

Much as the winter is complained of by natives, and unpleasant as it is to all, when compared with other seasons, it must not be inferred that these months are wholly without cheerful days. Sometimes weeks occur in succession when not a drop of rain falls; there are no clouds to obscure the sky, the temperature is charming, and the sun lends additional glory to the snow-mantle of the cordilleras. A long line of cumuli, perhaps, hangs half-way up the mountain-slopes; but there is not a speck to interfere with vision of the crests limiting the horizon in every direction, and the blue of the heavens seems even darker than in summer. On nights succeeding such days, the planets and stars are extraordinarily brilliant, and exact admiration from every one. The inexperienced supposed we should find these the most favorable for observations; but it was almost always far otherwise, owing to the rapidly varying temperature of a nearly saturated atmosphere. Towards daylight, and more especially of the August mornings, when the bed of snow is deep and low on the Andes, the roofs become covered with white frosts; and, in exposed places of the fields, or along the ravine through which the river flows, a skim of ice may sometimes be found on little puddles of water. Yet, as the mean temperature of the season is 49°.6, and its mean minimum temperature (42°.7) is nearly eleven degrees above the freezing-point, it is not considered necessary to protect many of the greenhouse plants; and the Floripondia, (*Datura arborea*), Calla Ethiopica, and Heliotrope, load the air of the gardens with their fragrance.

These are the months when the zodiacal light is brightest, and its perfectly formed pyramid is most distinctly traceable in the evening twilight. In no other part of the world have I ever remarked it so well. It is a pyramidal, or rather a lenticular body of light, which appears in the plane of the sun's equator, and is consequently inclined to the horizon after sunset, before the vernal, and before sunrise after the autumnal equinox. The light, neither as ruddy as the glow of the sky after sunset, nor as silvery as rays heralding the moon, is usually so faint that few remark it, unless attention be directed to it; then, every one wonders why it has so long escaped his attention. It is brightest about the horizon, and fades gradually as it recedes; so that it is rarely definable at a greater altitude than 40°. The base of the cone or pyramid was never more than 15°, and generally much less in diameter when its outline became discernible, its apparent breadth depending wholly on the diaphaneity of the atmosphere at the time. It was seen as early as July 6, and is once noted in our journal "*very bright*" as late as September 6, its place in the heavens and inclination to the horizon changing as the sun gradually advanced from his northern limit towards us.* No variations in the intensity or undulatory motion of the light, such as Humboldt mentions having witnessed in the tropical regions of South America, were ever seen by me in Chile; but only a mild radiance, whose brightness sensibly increased as the twilight faded, and more slowly disappeared an hour later; and by 8 o'clock in the early days of September, (corresponding with our March), it was no longer perceptible to eyes that had been so greatly taxed. Whether this beautiful phenomenon consists of a ring of nebulous matter, revolving freely in space between the orbits of Mars and Venus, or is the outermost stratum of the solar atmosphere, is a question yet to be decided by physicists.

By the middle of July the almond-trees, wild violets, hyacinths, ranunculuses, and several other varieties of plants, are in flower; and before the close of the month, the Acacia cavenia fills the air with the perfume of its feather-like florets. The rains seem to have roused the frogs from their torpor, too, and every little pond resounds with their croakings, whilst the vineyards and olive-groves are rendered gay by the birds gathering harvests of insects. Peaches, plums, cherries, the Acacia lophantha, a number of indigenous amaryllidæ and anemones, and a fumaria, flower in August; cherries ordinarily before any of the others named.

The nearer we approach to the ocean, the more the influence of that great moderator and equalizer of terrestrial climates is felt. In the deep ravines between it and the longitudinal valley, some moisture is preserved during the period of drought; and there one may find shrubbery and plants at all seasons. But it is not until after the rains of winter commence that their sides, and the basins on which they open, are fully covered with verdure. A greater prevalence of fogs, and more frequent and heavier dews near the sea, afford moisture to plants by absorption through their leaves; and there one may always perceive vegetation and flowers. A difference exists, however, between hills having an ocean or an Andean aspect, the latter being almost barren. There, too, the *temporales* occur with greater frequency and violence, and the atmosphere is more hazy and opaque at almost all times. If it become clear, so that distant objects can be seen distinctly, and the barometer falls ever so little, the ships in the bay of Valparaiso are warned to prepare for a norther. During its continuance the wind blows in gusts from north to N.W. by N.; the barometer sometimes falls as much as half an inch, whilst the thermometer rises from 4° to 8°, and showers of rain are both frequent and heavy. These storms have been known to continue three days, after which pleasant weather succeeds for several weeks. There are years when the wind has not sufficient violence to effect injury, and others in which each winter month has one or two storms; but northers never prevail, within the definition of the word monsoon. Easterly winds bring cold and fogs over the coast. These latter are usually dispelled by the southerly winds, (proper monsoons,) which blow from 9 or 10 A. M. until 4 or 5 P. M. As the monsoons rarely have the same violence in winter as in summer, there is no climate more charming than that of Valparaiso on the bright days of the former season. According to observations at 8 A. M., noon, and 4 P. M., made at the Exchange during a number of years, barometric oscillations in time and amplitude are subject to precisely the same laws as at Santiago. From a mean of the thermometric observations, the

* Thus, when visible in the northern hemisphere in the morning, it is an evening phenomenon to the other half of the globe.

winter temperature for those hours is 60°.4; and as it has been found that the results of records at 8 A. M., noon, and 4 P. M. exceed the true mean temperature 6°.5, one may well appreciate what its inhabitants enjoy. Commander Wilkes found the mean temperature of May, 1839, 55°.2, and the range of the thermometer from 46° to 65°. It has been supposed that the cold current of water from the vicinity of the Antarctic circle, that has been traced as far as the coast of Peru, and which, from its discoverer, has been named Humboldt current, has some influence in modifying the climate of maritime Chile; but there are too few observations to prove that its eastern limit is much within the island of Juan Fernandez on this parallel. The temperature of the water found by the United States Exploring Expedition was 56°, from which degree of heat Commander Wilkes had reason to believe that it varied very little throughout the year.

As we proceed northward from Santiago, the humidity of the climate varies more rapidly than a mere difference of latitude seems able to explain. Beyond the spur uniting the two chains of mountains, there are no extensive plains or valleys except the transversal depressions through which flow the mountain streams; and within one geographical degree of the capital the number and duration of the rain-storms is diminished quite one half. In the parallel of 30°, even on the coast, there are rarely more than five or six moderate showers, and sometimes not more than two, though night-dews at this season are heavy and constant much further north. Deposits of snow on the Andes are frequent, and from the melting of these the inhabitants anticipate benefits scarcely inferior to those which winter rains afford. This snow-water brings a current of cold air through the ravines with it, and fogs are frequent over the mouths of the streams where the contact of the cold with the warmer and moister atmosphere of the ocean takes place.

No register of meteorological phenomena has been regularly kept except at La Serena, in latitude 29° 54′; and even this embraces only pressure and temperature, except a hygrometric remark on the occasion of an earthquake. Situated at the margin of the sea, the climate of La Serena is sensibly modified by it; its mean winter temperature (54°.8) being more than 5° greater than that of Santiago, whilst the mean of the extremes between 8 and 9 A. M., and 9 and 10 P. M., is only 17°.4. Taking the decrease of temperature with elevation found by Humboldt and Boussingault at 1° for each 330 feet, the difference of level of the two cities will account for 5°.5, leaving 0°.3 only to be explained by the 3° 32′ of geographical latitude and the difference of their topographical locations. Though less extensive than at Santiago, the barometric oscillations are greater than at any other season. Its mean diurnal tide is only 0.010 of an inch. No violent winds occur. The southerly monsoon prevails, though it is not uniformly attended by clear skies. When it changes to north or N.W., clouds and precipitation of moisture usually follow.

In latitude 27° we are almost at the northern limit of the rain zone, and there the risk of injury from rain is so small that the larger number of houses are roofed with canes externally, plastered only with mud. If three slight sprinkles occur during the year, the country is regarded very fortunate, and the sandy surfaces of terraces and ravines are soon clad with verdure and flowers. But it is rare to have two entire cloudy days following each other, and at mid-winter the prevailing westerly wind most annoyingly drives the dust of this region before it. There are no instrumental data to refer to, except during a few days of July in 1851. On the coast, I found a low barometric pressure, small diurnal tide, and extreme oscillations, with predominant though light winds from the northward. On one occasion, when the barometer had been 0.250 of an inch below its normal elevation for three days with a partially overcast sky, a sudden change of the wind from W.N.W to S.W. was almost instantly followed by rain, though half an hour previously the temperature of the air and of evaporation differed by 4°.8. The mean of these differences during five days was 4°.38; mean temperature during the same period, 56°.6; highest at any hour, 66°; and lowest at midnight, 50°.5.

Fifty miles inland the hygrometric condition of the atmosphere is wonderfully different. There, whilst the mean temperature of evaporation was 51°.3, that of the air was 61°.2, and the difference between them was sometimes so great as 18°. They approximated more closely at midnight than at any other of the observation hours, being then at an average of less than 4° apart. Here, then, one would anticipate clear weather, and cloudless skies do predominate. We are beyond even this distinction between winter and summer, nor are we surprised to find that some of the deciduous trees at times neglect to shake off their summer livery. Twenty miles yet nearer to the Andes, and at an elevation of 3,700 feet, the degree of dryness, electrical tension, and transparency of the atmosphere, are still more remarkable, and its temperature more uniform. The wood of boxes which had withstood the dry summer atmosphere of Santiago during two seasons was here warped and split; and it is not unusual for strangers who pass several hours of the day in the sun to find the nostrils, eyelids, and lips crack under the powerful influences of evaporation and reflected heat. In this vicinity it was that a party of us saw the cusps of Venus in the morning twilight with our unassisted eyes, and I never tired with looking on the countless brilliant orbs which seemed to have descended half-way from infinity. Away from the mountain rivulets, there is no indigenous vegetation except a few dwarf cacti; and it is only when a chance shower once in two or three years sprinkles the surface for an hour or so, that Nature proves how many plants and seeds she has guarded dormantly for the occasion.

That the number of rainy days in winter and the constant humidity of the climate increase with the latitude, are evidenced by the character and distribution of vegetation, which has already been stated; and, if we credit all that is said, the ratio of increase is not less rapid proceeding southerly than is the diminution in the direction of the tropic. Yet the testimony hitherto—mostly the experience of navigators during a few days, or of native travellers who returned to the capital with disheartened recollections after no longer sojourn—has been too limited to warrant proper conclusions. Even now we have no meteorological record for any portion of the country between Santiago and Valdivia, differing in latitude 383 miles; and it was not until we had left Chile that some instrumental data and carefully recorded facts respecting the latter place were published in the "*Anales de la Universidad.*" The journal referred to was kept by Mr. Anwandter, and extends from April 1, 1851, to March 31, 1852. It embraces thermometric observations and notes on the direction of the wind; the state of sky, whether clear or cloudy; and the number of days when rain fell. As there were no records during the night, Dr. Philippi, to whom they were given for discussion, undertook a semi-hourly series for one day to determine the diurnal march of the temperature, and from these ascertained that a mean between observations taken at 6 A. M. and 6 P. M. exceeded the true mean temperature 0°.55; but between 6 A. M. and 7 P. M. observations, it fell short about 2°.02.

Valdivia, it will be remembered, is in latitude 39° 49′, on the north bank of the river of the same name, nine or ten miles from the sea, and therefore much under its influence.

Applying corrections in accordance with the above indications, the mean temperature of winter was found to be 46°.8; the lowest at 6 A. M., 34°.3; the highest observed, 61°.8; and the mean difference between observations at 6 A. M. and the warmest hour of the day, 5°.85. As in every part of the world, the minimum heat occurs a short time before sunrise, but the maximum here has a different hour for each season—that of winter approximating to noon. This very moderate temperature is attributed partially to a predominant N.E. wind, and it is only during clear nights, when radiation proceeds rapidly, that frosts occur. Gales are very rare, only one having been noted in June, one in July, and two in August. After the winds from N.E., those from east are most frequent, then those from west; and there were only two days out of the ninety-two when it blew from south. There were 23 clear, 15 cloudy, and 54 rainy days; snow falling on three of the last, though it melted immediately in the city, and only continued a few days on the cordilleras of the coast. Hail, also, is infrequent, and rarely causes injury.

Of Chilóe, 3° farther to the south, Padre Agüeros (*Descripcion Historial de las Provincias y Archipielago de Chilóe*, Chap. XI) says of the winter: "At the latter season the temperature is low, but the frosts are by no means so severe as in Europe. I have never seen ice even in the small streams, nor does snow lie any length of time on the ground. Greater cold is experienced in Chilóe than in Santiago or Concepcion; but we must remember that it is nearer to the pole and the rigorous climate of Cape Horn.

"That which renders the winter, as well as some months of the other seasons, most disagreeable, are the continual rains, with violent storms from the north, N.W., and west. It frequently occurs that rain falls for an entire lunation without ceasing, accompanied by hurricanes so furious that no one within the house is secure, and the largest trees are torn up by the roots.

"Although the winter months, and a considerable part of the other seasons, are very disagreeable, owing to the severity of the winds and exceeding quantity of rain, it cannot be denied that the climate is healthy." Agüeros resided six years on the island, and published his volume in 1791.

In the narrative of the *Voyages of the Adventure and Beagle*, Vol. I, it is stated: "Capt. Fitzroy arrived there in July, during the latter part of which, and the month of August, the weather was very wet, with some heavy gales from the N.W.; but, in his meteorological journal for those months, there is no record of the thermometer falling below 38°, and it is recorded to have fallen to that degree only on one occasion, the general height being from 45° to 50°." From the same volume the mean pressure of the barometer at 9 A. M. during twenty-two days of July, 1829, was 29.927 inches, and the temperature of the air 46°.9. Five years later the island was revisited by the same officer, from whose published journal I find that the mean pressure at noon during fifteen days of June and July, 1834, was 29.723 inches (reduced to 32°); the range of the barometer from 29.37 to 30.31 inches; the mean temperature at the same hour 48°.6, and range from 40° to 53°. At the time the barometer was so low it was raining heavily, with a light air from the eastward; when highest, the wind was from S.E., light breezes, with cumulous clouds. Altogether, Chilóe is not so bad as it has been reputed, and its temperature is nearly 20° higher than that of Boston harbor.

It would be interesting to trace the climate of these several enumerated districts through each of the seasons, but from some of them proper data are wanting; and therefore, with brief reference to the characteristics of spring and autumn at Santiago, most that remains to be said will refer to the summer. If the winter at Coquimbo and Atacama is so dry and cloudless, what must be their climates at mid-summer?

The diurnal tide of the atmosphere—always small at the capital—not unfrequently has its hours of maxima and minima reversed, in spring, by the amount of the extraordinary fluctuations, and thus the means show greater pressure near 9 P. M. than near 9 A. M. If we take a mean of the observations at the several hours as indicator of the oscillations, the extreme vertical displacement, one day with another, amounts to .0085 of the whole atmosphere, the limits of the barometer (reduced to 32°) being from 28.069 to 28.104 inches. On the other hand, the range of the temperature is very great, extending through more than 40° between the warmest and coldest hours of the days during the season, though the mean difference is only 20°.1, and the temperature of spring is 59°. At the surface of the plain the thermometer never fell so low as the freezing-point, although there were frequent deposits of snow at small elevations above us on the Andes. Nor are the differences between the temperature of the air and that of evaporation less remarkable: 15° was a common difference at the warmest hours of the day; 24° was occasionally observed, and the mean was 6°.8. Yet rains were not infrequent during the spring months, and September has uniformly been considered the most cloudy month of the year.

Three of the four thunder-storms we witnessed were in spring, two taking place within five days of each other, in November, 1850, and the third in September, 1851. These are very rare phenomena on the plain, and produce terror scarcely inferior to earthquakes. The first one (November 25) was attended by very high barometer, unusual southerly wind, and heavy cumulous clouds, and was followed by a copious fall of rain during eight hours. That of the

30th of the same month continued about three quarters of an hour. It commenced two or three miles to the S.E. of the city, striking one house and killing a woman as it passed over us, and expended itself to the northward. No such event as a thunderbolt at Santiago had ever been chronicled in its annals. This storm, also, was accompanied by rain, though the fall was quite moderate, and the atmosphere cleared away much as it does after electrical discharges on summer afternoons in the United States. The third occurred after midnight, continued more than an hour, and was more violent than the preceding. Terror was added to its ringing peals of thunder by their reverberating echoes from and among the Andes; and when it struck near the same place as the preceding bolt, the neighbors considered their vicinity the special *locale* of Divine wrath. There were no forewarning instrumental indications; the barometer was about its usual height, the temperature moderate all the preceding day and evening, and a rainbow at sunset rather promised clear weather than a night-storm. Lightning—most unusual in that direction—had been seen to the N.W. on the preceding evening, over the coast range, and this was followed by light showers of rain, a heavy fall taking place after the thunder-storm.

Summer lightning—that form of electrical explosion in which, without audible thunder, or any indication of storm, the whole cloud is illuminated at the same instant and continues visible for some seconds—is a frequent phenomenon of the spring evenings. It is usually seen over the higher Andes to the E.N.E., but sometimes extends as far south as the summits in the direction of San Josè, flashing almost continuously for more than an hour at a time. Travellers have crossed the elevated passes of the mountains at these times without witnessing the phenomenon, and only learned on arrival at Santiago how brilliant had been the displays seen in directions of the road they must have occupied at the same moment. So bright and incessant were the corruscations after one of the great earthquakes, that many persons on the coast believed the old volcanoes to the eastward had re-opened, and a statement to this effect was made in the Valparaiso papers. Whilst all previous experience on the coast and plain seemed to prove them exempt from thunder and lightning, storms of that kind were quite common within the greater cordilleras; and few crossed the Andes without being witnesses to these battles of the elements during some portion of their journey.

One other phenomenon, regarded by physicists of the present day as scarcely less intimately allied with electricity than with disturbance of magnetic equilibrium, remains to be mentioned in connection with the spring months. I refer to the Aurora Australis, of which (or some closely-resembling light) there was one display during our residence in Chile, viz: shortly after midnight of the 21–22d November, 1851. After several days of clear weather, for forty-eight hours previous the sky had been completely overcast; and though the clouds partially broke away three hours before the aurora, by midnight they had rolled back again dense as ever. There was nothing unusual in either pressure or temperature, and only a more moist atmosphere than is customary in November. Without wholly passing away, soon after midnight the mass of clouds lying in strata to the southward broke into cumuli, and a luminous bank was perceived below the Southern Cross, then bearing S.S.E. At first it was supposed to be only a portion of the Milky Way; but, whilst looking attentively, bands or streamers of light passed through interstices of the clouds to altitudes of nearly 40°. These faded, brightened, and changed inclination, locality, and color, not less remarkably than I had often observed during auroral displays in the northern hemisphere, and I could but think this an analogous phenomenon. At 1 A. M. it had wholly ceased, and a little while after, the sky was again entirely obscured by clouds. Occurrencé of the aurora during the continuance of clouds is contrary to an hypothesis recently advanced (before the American Association for the Promotion of Science); but, unless we suppose a volcano to have burst out in the Andes, and burned actively only during the half hour, there is no other mode of expaining the phenomenon mentioned.

Vegetation makes rapid strides in this season. Pear and apple trees flower within the first fifteen days of September, and the fig-tree and Lombardy poplar are in full leaf before its close. Lilacs, fleurs de lis, gladiolus, (*byzantinus*,) pinks, and a host of other garden flowers, unfold their wondrous petals; and from the plants that bloomed in early September, ripe strawberries may be gathered before the middle of November. In this last month the olive-trees flower, and maize is in tassel; and towards its close not only are the grain-fields golden-hued in the sunlight, but natural pasturage and herbs on the hill-sides, no longer receiving supplies of moisture, have been scorched under the same powerful influence. After this, verdure remains only in the deeply shaded ravines, in the vicinity of streams, or where the soil is artificially irrigated; and all the surrounding hills look dark and denuded, the giant Quisco, (*Cereus* Q.), with its black, branching arms, as projected against the sky,* corroborating the impression that no vegetation has withstood such heat and drought.

From an examination of hourly observations, made on the 21st day of each month, it appears that the barometer not only stands about 0.08 inch lower in summer than in winter, but also its oscillations are more uniform, and the hours of maxima and minima fall later in the day. Like facts are shown in the means of the tri-hourly observations; and we find that the greater maximum takes place nearer to 10 than to 9 o'clock; the afternoon minimum invariably after 4 o'clock. In this season the average pressure is 28.042 inches, and its mean daily range 0.040 of an inch. These are the months when the aqueous atmosphere is most disturbed; when the temperature of evaporation, which, at an hour or two after sunrise, may be within 2° or 3° that of the air, between 3 and 4 P. M. has been known to descend more than 27° below it, and preserves an average difference of 11°.33. The range of temperature, also, is extreme. The highest ever known was 90°.3; the mean, at the hottest hour, 79°.8, and of the coldest hour 58°.7; though it was once so low as 47°.5. With the thermometer at 80° in the warmest part of the day, one would suppose the heat oppressive; and so it is, when the person is exposed to the direct rays of the sun. But even then, evaporation is so rapid, that perspiration is carried off as fast as formed, and the sensations of the body are wholly unlike those experienced under the same temperature in an atmosphere loaded with moisture. Out of the sun, it is never too warm for cloth clothing; and during the first month (November) that we passed at Santiago, I often walked rapidly to the summit of Santa Lucia with a cloth coat buttoned, yet failed in producing sensible moisture on the skin—a climatic condition no little trying to those suffering with disordered nerves.

It has been shown, by the table of Señor Reyes, that rain was scarcely to be expected during these months; and when by chance any fell, the quantity was so small that the atmosphere of the valley immediately returned to its normal dry state. The probable progress of agriculture in modifying the climate was also alluded to; and, as testimony in support of it, nine rains occurred in the nine summer months, on one of which an inch and a third of water fell in less than five hours. By covering the ground with umbrageous vegetation, both the radiated and absorbed heat are diminished—results producing lower and more equable temperature in summer, whilst irrigating channels and watered fields, by exposing increased surface for evaporation, augment the volume of vapor and probabilities of precipitation. An accession of clouds from the same sources also diminishes the radiant heat during winter nights, and the temperature is thus prevented from falling very low. Were the sky clear at the latter season, as in summer, Santiago, under the joint influences of radiation and perpetual snow within twenty miles, would possess a most rigorous climate. As evidence of the power of radiation in this atmosphere, on the authority of the Director of the *Escuela de Artes y Oficios*, Prof. Domeyko publishes as follows: "On the 11th March, 1849, they were building a high chimney at the school named; and when the masons came down from their work at night, they left on top of the chimney, overlooking all the neighboring edifices, a wooden trough containing water of little depth, exposed to the action of a perfectly clear and calm sky. What was the surprise of the workmen, when they returned on the following morning to conclude their job, to find about an inch of ice in the trough! At daylight that morning the thermometer stood at 56°.5, the barometer at 28.146 inches; and the phenomenon was the more notable, because, when calm, the temperature of water may fall 2° or 3° below the freezing-point before ice forms."*

The formation of masses of ice in the atmosphere belongs rather to electrical phenomena, and would more properly have followed notice of the thunder-storms of the Andes, so common in summer. There was only one during the three years, viz: on the 13th January, 1852. It commenced suddenly about 4 P. M., after a day moderately overcast by masses of cumuli and a low temperature, (68° at 3 P. M.) and *was unaccompanied by lightning*. The stones were truncated cones and pyramids, with spherical bases, as though they had formed portions of spheres perhaps an inch in diameter. Their bases were of a milky yet translucent ice, whilst the upper halves were softer, whiter, and more opaque. The storm lasted about ten minutes, though the sky remained clouded over until after 7 P. M., and occasional drops of rain fell all the afternoon. Two miles west of the observatory there was a violent squall of wind, but no hail; and on the *distant* summits of the Andes a large body of snow, or hail, was deposited. At night the thermometer fell below 50°, the barometer remaining nearly 0.15 inch above its mean height—a very great variation from its normal elevation, in a country where the fluctuations are so small.

Ordinarily, the air is calm from about sunrise until between 9 and 10 o'clock A. M., at which time a wind commences from the S.W. This increases in strength till 2 or 3 P. M., and then moderates as gradually to sunset, when it is again calm. Its violence on the plain was rarely more than what, in nautical parlance, is called "a fresh breeze;" but on the elevated summits of the Andes, over which it also extends, it is usually excessive. Lieut. MacRae wrote me that it was so strong when he arrived at the pass of the Cumbre, between Santiago and Mendoza, that, as early as 10½ A. M. it almost overturned both mule and rider; and arrieros declare they have seen small stones blown away by it. Deep ravines debouching on the plain near Santiago, and many hills near it, cause so many deflections as to render it impossible to determine the true direction of this wind by estimation; nor will it be practicable to do so, except by placing a register anemometer half-way across the plain. Our guides were, the direction that smoke was moved, or, failing this, the plane in which some of the lofty and pliant poplars were inclined. From these we found that the current varied in its direction from W.S.W. to S.S.W., and when strongest was most generally from S.W. These winds are attended with a clear atmosphere, and the only clouds to be seen are formed within the valleys of the rivers, at elevations of 5,000 to 10,000 feet above the plain, and which continue ascending until they rest in heavy cumulous masses over the elevated range. Vapor is rarely condensed immediately over the valley during the day, but a line not unfrequently collects at night half-way up the near chain, and remains there until dispelled by the heat of the day. With night the entire mass above the Andes disperses, though not until after a display of lambent sheets of lightning, sometimes continuing beyond midnight. Whenever similar corruscations were seen over the central range to the N.W., as was the case on two or three occasions, they were invariably followed by rain.

After sunset "*el terral*," or, as it is called in the south, "*el puelche*," a land breeze, commences. This, first perceptible on the coast, recedes slowly towards the Andes, where it is scarcely felt until near morning, thus proving itself a true wind of aspiration. Its apparent direction is modified at Santiago by causes analogous to those influencing the "*travesia*," as the day wind is named; and we find it one night from N.E.; the next, perhaps, or even at a subsequent hour of the same night, from S.E. It is never more than "a light breeze," and ceases entirely throughout its range by sunrise.

Late in the season a sort of dry fog, resembling thin smoke, deprives the atmosphere by day of something of its transparency, though the nights are all that the astronomical observer can desire. Then the Andes, whose crests are not less than 18 miles distant in an air-line, look almost within stone-throw, and the stars rise over them with a steadiness and brilliancy known

* Anales de la Universidad de Chile, Junio, 1851.

in our climate only at mid-heaven. The observer will appreciate me when he is told that I have made very fair micrometrical measurements of Venus when the planet was not more than 3° above the eastern horizon, and its crescent was more than once seen with the naked eye. At times, the atmosphere was steady as the earth itself; and the colors of close double stars not greater than the twelfth magnitude were satisfactorily distinguished, though the magnifying power was 235, and the telescope fully illuminated for other observations. Such a climate places a small telescope on equality in optical capacity with a much larger one in a moist atmosphere, and there were opportunities to distinguish small objects with our 6½-inch achromatic, which could only be seen with difficulty with the 20-inch reflector of Sir John Herschel at the Cape of Good Hope. Adopting Maskelyne's ratio between reflectors and achromatics (8:5), the illuminating powers being as the squares of the diameters, our 6½ inches at Santiago was quite equal to 12½ inches at the Cape. Early in December, wheat and barley are harvested. After the strawberry, figs and cherries are the next to ripen, the former being somewhat forced by puncturing them with an oiled needle. By Christmas day, melons, apricots, early nectarines, and one or two other fruits, are brought to market—some of them ripe, but more partially green, in which state nearly all fruits and vegetables are gathered. Garden flowers are in their perfection; dahlias, tuberoses, carnations, diamelos, (*Jasminum sambac*) jasmines, and a host of others, enable the ladies to exercise freely their graceful and refined custom of sending charming bouquets to friends on their Saint's day. But the hill-sides and uncultivated plain are completely denuded and desolate; the south wind drives clouds of dust from their surfaces, and the traveller avoids as much as possible the heat of the day, making his journeys before 9 A. M., or after 4 P. M.

On the coast the heat is moderated by the ocean. There, the thermometer never rises as high by day, nor falls so low at night, as between the great mountain chains. In three years the temperature at the Exchange of Valparaiso, at 8 A. M., was not lower than 62°, nor higher at 4 P. M. than 78°, and the mean of all the observations was 70°.8. Owing, however, to the imperfect exposure of the instrument, these records can scarcely be regarded as true indices of out-door temperature. Moreover, each district of country has its local peculiarities; so that there is no general law by which observations made at a particular hour can be reduced to the mean temperature of that place upon the application of the correction found for any other station. Obtaining a correction for stations with whose latitude and chorography there is least contrast, the average temperature from the Valparaiso observations will not be far from 6°.5 in excess of true summer heat, or nearly 5° below that of Santiago. If it has the advantage of a lower temperature, the southerly winds quite counterbalance it by their greater violence, and the annoyance of clouds of fine sand which they whirl from hills in the rear of the town. Sometimes they are so furious as to prevent vessels from reaching an anchorage in the bay. Though it is well known that they are equally constant at a little distance from the land from Chilöe to Lima, and draw more from the westward outside of the islands of Juan Fernandez, their entire limits have never been satisfactorily ascertained. North of Valparaiso, and within a few leagues of the land, they are feebler by day, and the land breeze replaces them at night. Even in summer, fogs over the land are not uncommon.

Coquimbo also enjoys at this season a cooler and more agreeable atmosphere than Santiago. The mean of the observations at the selected hours are there in excess of the mean for the day 3°.2, which, applied to Señor Troncoso's results, shows a summer temperature of only 63°.6. During the seasons of 1849 and 1850, the range of the thermometer between 8 and 9 A. M. and 9 and 10 P. M. did not exceed 16°.8; the barometer quite steady, and the atmosphere often cloudy. This last fact is obtained from his notices of earthquakes, which, omitting April and November, are more frequent than during any other months; and it is greatly to be regretted that there is no diurnal record from which to decide whether the clouds that accompany or almost immediately follow these subterranean disturbances have been only coincidences.

From daily observations at Concepcion during the summer of 1850, the temperature at 3 P. M.

was found to be 73°.5; that of evaporation at the same hour, 61°.3. At sunrise during seventeen days of February, 49°.2; sunset, 66°; and that of the wet thermometer for the same epochs, respectively, 47°.8 and 58°.2. On the 29th November preceding, Mr. Theodore Philippi, by whom the journal was kept,* tried the temperature of water in seventeen different wells, and found the thermometer range from 55°.4 to 61°.7. Selecting those where the water came nearest to the level of the earth, the lowest temperature was found in a well only nine feet deep, and at a small superficial spring. On the 7th December the temperature of the well continued the same; but by the 31st January it had risen to 57°.2, and on the 28th February was 57°. From these results he deduces that the mean temperature of Concepcion will be between 55°.4 and 57°.2. There was neither storm, hail, nor earthquake from the commencement of September to the close of February, nor did any rain fall during the last month. Poeppig † mentions an interesting fact respecting the influence of the easterly winds here. He says that when they blow in spring, they depress the thermometer in a short time from 12° to 15°; but towards the end of February, they raise it almost as much. The first he attributes to the deep snow with which the Andes are covered at that season, and the second to the high temperature to which the air upon the sandy plains of the Pampas of the Argentine republic is raised during the summer months; but neither of the three Philippis who have resided several years in the south notices the fact. It is supposed that its climate has been undergoing a gradual change ever since active destruction of the forest-trees of the vicinity commenced, and to this decrease of mean heat is attributed injury to the peach-trees during some years past. Trees of the same kind introduced from abroad, flourishing somewhat later, had proved less liable to blight. It had also been remarked that there was a great difference in the time of maturing of fruits at Tomé, on the coast, and Concepcion—less than six leagues distant in a south direction.

At Valdivia the summer temperature is 60°; the lowest observed at 6 A. M., 41°; the highest (in January), 96°.2; and the mean difference between the 6 A. M. and maximum temperatures, 18°. There are, however, great differences from day to day; and the coldness of some of the nights may be judged of from the fact that there are localities of small extent where the leaves of potatoes, beans, and other plants, are occasionally frosted. From the same cause, almond-trees rarely mature their fruit, and there is a difference of more than two months in the times of flowering of similar plants here and at Santiago. The prevailing winds are from west; after that, they are most common from S.E. and S.W.—never from north, and only once from west. Rain fell on twenty-eight of the ninety-one days, and twelve others were cloudy. In all the year there were one hundred and fifty-six rainy and seventy cloudy days. In Washington the annual average number of the former is ninety. Grouping the winds with the rainy days, it is found that those which blow from any point of the compass between N.E. and N.W. are essentially rain winds; those from south to east, dry winds. In winter and spring the greatest number of rains are with N.E. winds; in summer, with west; and in autumn, from the N.W. At a little distance off the coast, northerly and N.W. winds are invariably accompanied by damp, disagreeable, and unsettled weather. When a change takes place, it is usually to the S.W., and thence to the southward; sometimes in a violent squall, accompanied by rain, thunder, and lightning; at other times it draws gradually round, and as a steady southerly wind approaches, the sky becomes clear and the weather healthily pleasant. Though usually a prelude to a clearing-up storm, lightning is always a sign of more immediate bad weather.

The only barometrical observations known to have been published are those of Capt. Fitzroy, which were made in the harbor at noon from the 9th to the 22d February, 1835. On one day, (20th, when the earthquake destroyed Concepcion,) there were two other records, viz: at 6 A. M. and 6 P. M. The instrument was suspended at the level of the sea: its range, during thirteen days, was from 29.85 to 30.10 inches; and the fall recorded between 6 A. M. and 6 P. M.,

* Anales de la Universidad, Marzo de 1850.

† Poeppig. Reise in Chile, Peru, und auf dem Amazonenstrome in 1827–'32.

from 29.99 to 29.92 inches. The mean of all the noon observations is 29.973 inches, and both extremes of pressure occur with northerly winds.

At San Carlos, (Ancud,) from January 18th to February 4th, 1835, the barometer at noon was never lower than 29.95 inches, nor higher than 30.03 inches; mean, reduced to 32° Fahrenheit, 29.917 inches. There was a due proportion of fair weather, though moderate winds prevailed from the northward and westward, and there were only three days when it blew from S.W. The thermometric variation at the same hour was from 50° to 68°—the former temperature with a wind from S.W., and the latter with one from W.S.W. The mean at noon, 57°.3. Such temperature scarcely confirms the experience of Agüeros, who says: "Chilóe has its four seasons, but does not enjoy the benefit of those changes as do other parts of Chile; for there is neither that abundance of fruit, nor are its fields adorned with so many and such beautiful flowers and useful medicinal plants. The summer is the most pleasant season; for though, in the month of January, it is excessively hot from 10 in the morning until 3 in the afternoon, there is a sea-breeze during those hours, called '*virazon*,' which refreshes the air. At this time the day is from seventeen to eighteen hours long, and conversely in winter. * * * The weather, when it is fine, cannot be depended on for any length of time; for, in the month of January I have frequently seen rains as copious and gales as violent as in the winter. During the summer months, southerly winds are more prevalent; and while they last, the weather is fine and clear, and the air particularly dry." Capt. King found the first half of December, 1829, tempestuous and wet; but it proved scarcely one-third as bad as he had experienced at St. Martin's Cove, near Cape Horn. During the preceding month the range of temperature had been from 42° to 68°.5, and the mean at 9 A. M. 53°.5. At Hobarton, (Van Dieman's land,) which does not differ much in latitude, the temperature of November, at 9 A. M., exceeds the mean annual heat 6°.65; that of February, at noon, is 7°.89 greater; and supposing these corrections approximate, the mean temperature of the northern extremity of Chilóe will not vary greatly from 48°.

Autumn in the province of Santiago is not less charming than the other seasons of this so favored region—a country in whose soil and climate vegetation typical of the torrid and temperate zones, side by side, thrive equally. The native palm and pine of Araucania—the cherimoya of tropical America and the medlar of Japan—the magnolia of Florida and the olive of Asia, may all be found within the compass of a garden, not less luxuriant in their proportions and ever-verdant foliage than under the climes of their origin.

All through March, and the larger half of April, unexceptionable fine weather lasts, though the atmosphere is less transparent by day than during the other seasons, and copious dews at night show its increasing relative humidity. About the close of the former month, or in the first half of the latter, there are usually from ten to fifteen days when it assumes that peculiar appearance between smoke and dry fog which is so notable at the "Indian summer" of North America. During its continuance there is scarcely any wind; and, as the temperature after noon rises to summer heat, with its fresh southerly breeze, the air is more enervating than at the latter season. Here the resemblance between the two hemispheres ceases. Unlike the North American "Indian summer," of which, its continuity once broken, there is no return until the following year, the Chilean "verano de San Juan"* is often interrupted by a renewal of the periodic winds with greater force, or by clouds; and after a day or two, there succeeds another interval when the air is tranquil and smoky.

Even the moderate daily breezes from the S.W. lose their strength in autumn, and *el terral* is frequently replaced by one from the Western cordilleras, though the direction of the daily surface current is rarely doubtful. The mean atmospheric pressure is 28.065 inches, and the extreme of its mean daily fluctuations 0.039 inch; its periods of maxima and minima conform-

* St. John's summer. So named in the Argentine republic, though St. John's day is June 24th. I never heard a Chileno designate it

ing to those of spring and summer during the first two months, but through May as often reversed as in winter. Between the coldest and warmest hours of the day there is an average difference of 20°; and between the extreme heat of the first and the cold of the last month, the thermometer ranges through 50°, though the difference of their mean temperature is only 10°, and that of the season 59°.4, differing very slightly from that of the whole year. The hygrometric condition of the atmosphere changes more rapidly: the mean height of a wet thermometer at 3 P. M. during March being 16° below its temperature; and in May, at the same hour, only 8°.5. The average difference at all the observation hours in the former month is 10°.1, and in the latter 4°.3; even the very last figures proving that there is still a less amount of aqueous vapor in the atmosphere than during the driest months at Washington. These would tell the reader that the rainy season was not fully commenced, had he not been prepared for the fact by the compilation from the tables of Señor Reyes. Our three years give a somewhat different result, showing an increase in the average daily time during which rain falls in May, from 1*h.* 7*m.* to 1*h.* 42*m.*, and the deposit of water 6.9 inches.

Every effort is made to harvest the crops of beans, capsicums, potatoes, and other vegetables, for winter use, before the rains commence; and as the grapes are ready for the vintage between the 10th and 20th of April, this is the busiest season of the agriculturist. It is also the period of the year when morning fogs are the most frequent; when the halos that almost nightly encircle the moon are most opaque, and the meteors brightest; when clouds above the Andes are in densest masses, and storms of rain, snow, and lightning are phenomena of daily occurrence among their heights. On one occasion a meteor exploded, in the direction of the greater Magellanic cloud, with a noise so audible as to command attention; and another, which was very brilliant, was witnessed by Lieut. MacRae and myself, *ascending* from the S.E. quarter of the heavens in a nearly vertical direction.

More particularly during our last year, and in the months of May and June, there were beams of light visible on many mornings, radiating from a point of the heavens opposite the sun. Sometimes they were so broad, well defined, and distinct, as to give the intervening shadows the appearance of black streamers on a rose-colored ground. The dark spaces were usually blacker to the south than to the north of the zenith, across which many of them could be traced almost to the eastern horizon. The effect was greatly heightened when there were banks of cumuli about the mountains, for these were often brilliantly lighted up, as one witnesses at a tropical sunset. Occasionally the phenomenon was visible on both sides at once; and then it was a most beautiful sight to watch one point of radiance descend as the other gradually rose to the summit of the Andes. In twenty minutes to half an hour the presence of the sun would obliterate every trace of it.

Another phenomenon, which attracted my attention soon after reaching Chile, was the red color assumed by the snow-crests as the sun approached the western horizon. The change of color began as soon as the plain had fallen under the shadow of the Western cordilleras, and increased in depth until the direct light of the sun had entirely left the peaks. Above the shadow of the cordilleras, as it crept up the Andes, there were violet and purple hues, according to their distance from the illuminated portion; and not only these, but also the red, were of greater intensity at the close of spring and in winter, when the sun was farthest north, and there had been recent deposits from the clouds. At such times the view was certainly very exquisite; and if there were radiant beams of light and shade over the Andes at the same time, as was quite frequently the case, it was a picture to which no words can render justice. To my vision the color of the snow at such times was more of a vermillion than of a red or rose color, but the assistants could only recognise it a rosy pink, even with prepared water-colors before us; another example that all eyes were never alike sensitive to colors. The *Protococus nivalis*, mentioned by arctic voyagers, has been found also on patches of perpetual snow of the Andes; but this shows the red color only when accidentally crushed, or a rapid thaw has taken place, and we must look to the atmosphere, rather than to such groups of atomic plants, for explanation of the phenomenon.

Bright as are its skies, soft as are its breezes, and charming to the corporal frame as is a temperature without the fierce heats of summer or rigorous frosts of winter, one would expect to find its people enjoying the glorious aggregations of eternal snow-crests and ever-verdant valleys to a green old age. But, in truth, Chile can scarcely be regarded as a country favorable to longevity ; and we have already seen that, under the most favorable interpretation of its census returns, the population has only increased three per cent. during the last six years. What influence to effect such a result have the appetites and diet of its people ; the possibly semi-stagnant atmosphere of deep valleys, where there are neither electrical phenomena nor strong winds for its frequent renovation ; or habits induced by the apathetic disposition engendered in a climate with so few vicissitudes,—are questions not yet solved by their physiologists. We look abroad and wonder to see so few who have attained "three score years and ten ;" and they tell us that phthisis pulmonalis, hypertrophy of the heart and liver, and epidemic dysentery, sweep off numbers in their prime, leaving scarcely one in a thousand to attain such age, whilst multitudes are cut off to whom life is only at its dawn.

CHAPTER IV.

EARTHQUAKES.

SENSATIONS WHICH THEY PRODUCE.—BRIEF ACCOUNTS OF THE EARTHQUAKES OF 1570, 1647, 1657, 1688, 1722, 1730, 1751, 1783, 1819, 1822, 1829, 1835, 1837, 1849.—OUR MODE OF OBSERVING SHOCKS.—THE EARTHQUAKE OF DECEMBER 6, 1850; THAT OF APRIL 2, 1851.—SUCCEEDING LESSER AGITATIONS, MAY 26, 1851.—SEVERAL TREMORS OF ESPECIAL INTEREST.—LOCAL AND METEOROLOGICAL INFLUENCES.—VOLCANIC THEORY OF EARTHQUAKES.—DYNAMICS.—PERMANENT EFFECTS.—OTHER ATTRIBUTED RESULTS.—CONCLUDING REFLECTIONS.

Of all terrestrial phenomena in Chile, there is not one so thrilling to the stranger from the temperate zones of the northern hemisphere as that which deprives him of confidence in the immobility of the earth. "From our earliest childhood we are accustomed to contrast the mobility of water with the immobility of the earth; all the evidences of our senses have confirmed this belief; and when suddenly the ground itself shakes beneath us, a natural force of which we had no previous experience presents itself as a strange and mysterious agency. A single instant annihilates the illusion of our whole previous life; we feel the imagined repose of nature vanish, and that we are ourselves transported into a realm of unknown destructive forces. Every sound affects us; our attention is strained to catch even the faintest movement of the air; we no longer trust the ground beneath our feet."*

Nor does time ever reconcile him to the recurrence of the convulsions. Every return forces the impression more powerfully on his mind, and with each he recognises his helplessness more painfully. From the lightning and tempest, from the floods of rivers, and, measurably, from stormy billows of the ocean, art has enabled him to interpose safeguards; but the accumulation of that internal agent, the growth of whose pent-up power no mortal eye can watch, no human knowledge neutralize or control, discloses not its hidden laboratories—baffles all efforts to foretell its completed volume; and when least he anticipates it, the elastic crust of the earth, no longer resisting the pressure, is heaving and undulating as the waves of a troubled sea. Sometimes there are no warnings of impending danger, and, in the twinkling of an eye, cities lie level with the plain, their inhabitants buried beneath the ruins; though, most generally, one of the sound-waves travels more rapidly than the great earth-wave, and there are some few seconds during which one may rush from the danger of crashing walls. With this all knowledge ceases; the heavy, unmistakable subterranean rumble has bidden you fly; the violence or duration of the earth-storm is known only to God.

Natives of South America have two words by which they designate the phenomenon—*temblores* and *terremotos*. The former are only partial agitations of the surface, confined to very limited districts, and rarely, or never, producing serious damage; the latter consist of violent upliftings or horizontal oscillations, extending many hundred miles, when the destruction of life and buildings is proportionate to the distance of the localities from the origin of the disrupting force. Objects have been so moved during terremotos as to induce the belief that there is sometimes circular or vorticose disturbance of the surface; but it is by no means certain that such displacements may not be accounted for in another manner. The longer one remains in a region subject to them, the more promptly he follows the custom of the country, and flies at the sound of danger, unfitted, in most instances, for studying either the motions, or other physical facts of interest, during the brief instant allowed him. From the frequency of their

* Kosmos, Vol. I.

occurrence in Chile, it was supposed we might collect much information that would aid to dispel doubts on several points. Clever men had asserted that the pressure of the atmosphere was least; that earthquakes were of electrical origin; that there were emanations from the earth, rendering it sterile, and generating diseases often wholly new; that extraordinary meteoric phenomena accompanied them; that, for hours in advance, the atmosphere was of a sultry closeness, almost insupportable; that they are intimately connected with volcanoes; that they permanently elevate and depress districts of much extent; and a multitude of other terrestrial consequences of great interest to mankind. How far this has been done will be seen in the sequel, for which it seems proper to prepare the reader by a succinct notice of the well-authenticated attendant phenomena of preceding recorded terremotos in Chile, as a partial apology for contributing so little to his information. In Appendix A will be found specified each tremor and shock that occurred at Santiago and Serena from November 1, 1849, to September, 1852, a period of nearly three years, with such brief facts as it was possible to note. Of old earthquakes:

1570.

The first shock mentioned by the historians of the country occurred on the 8th February, 1570, destroying Concepcion, the then most promising and flourishing city of the infant colony. A frightful roaring noise which preceded enabled most of the inhabitants to escape from their dwellings, and an instant afterwards the earth sank, so that the ocean flowed over the sites of their homes; and to this day a part of old Penco remains beneath the waves. For five months subsequently the earth continued agitated, and the sea unquiet; and the whole kingdom experienced the subterranean thunders which threatened to rend its surface into fragments. The courses of rivers were changed, fields inundated, even the mountains menaced a new deluge, and no part escaped some injury. On the authority of Padre Miguel Olivares,* it is stated that more than 2,000 persons perished. The cathedral of Santiago was among the ruins.

1647.

Don José Carvallo† says, that the earthquake of this year, though most destructive at Santiago, was felt throughout all South America. It gave no warning, but in an instant levelled the city with the ground. This was on the 13th May, at 10½ P. M.; and the extent of the loss may be estimated, when that of the churches, according to the Bishop, was more than $300,000. Several MS. accounts of it are still in existence, a part of which have been printed by two authors; but they so abound with the religious superstition of the time, that few of the data tending to illustrate the phenomena can be received. One of the most elaborate is a letter from Bishop Villaroel to the President of the Council of the Indies, which bears date 9th June following. He says he was not able to verify the direction of the centre of disturbance, though from some of the effects, and the fact that the noise was as great about Valdivia and Concepcion, it was to the southward. The shock lasted, with terrific noise, from seven to eight minutes; and though the moon was high, the air was so filled with dense clouds of dust that the scene was one of horror, and the boldest thought the day of judgment at hand. It was affirmed that the noise was heard from the summit of the Andes, fifteen leagues distant. Cracks were opened in the earth across the plaza; and those of the roads, to a distance of ten or twelve leagues from the sea, threw out sand and foul-smelling water. There were seventy shocks within twenty-three days, and destruction was spread on the plain from the vicinity of the river Maule to the Chuapa. A heavy storm of rain and snow followed the great shock; and all the bake-ovens having been destroyed, the houseless people endured great suffering. Six hundred is the smallest number at which the dead were estimated; the *Real Audiencia* reported to the King one thousand. A letter from the *Oidores* bears date July 12, 1648, more than a year

* Historia de Chile, MS. † Historia de Chile, MS.

after the event; and by that time we may suppose they were able to speak of it with calmness and impartiality. Within that period there had been more than three hundred tremors, and desolation was spread throughout this part of Chile in consequence of exposure, and diseases incident thereto. The Indians had suffered very little. Their ranchos were built of straw or boards, which yielded to the passing convulsion. When the Spaniards commenced the erection of massive temples and dwellings on the territory from which they had been expelled, these children of nature warned them of the consequences, telling them it was labor lost, for the *nuyun* would come and bury them;* and twice had thus their prophecy been fulfilled. At the mouth of the Chuapa the subterranean noise lasted three quarters of an hour, and the surface shook with such violence that those who were near believed a dissolution of the elements at hand. The inhabitants of Cuyo, on the opposite side of the Andes, assert, that after the violence of the shock had passed, for half an hour the noise was so terrific that they thought the very mountains torn from their bases and warring against each other. Immense rocks were thrown from lofty elevations; the highways were blocked up and changed; the springs dried, so that they yielded no water for a long time; and a flood ensued in the rivers of Colchagua, which rose to near the height of the trees upon their banks, sweeping away 60,000 head of cattle. So extraordinary was the agitation of the sea in all the ports along the coast, that the fishermen fled to the hills for safety. On the same day the waves rolled so furiously against a sea-wall in the port of Callao, 1,500 miles distant, as to destroy a portion of it. *It was supposed* that the shock was felt at Cuzco, in Peru, at the same hour. About 6 P. M. on the 16th June following, a ball of fire issued from a black cloud obscuring a part of the heavens, and, bursting in the air like a rocket, returned to the cloud, where it remained, much resembling a comet. This was seen as far south as Concepcion, then estimated to be 80 leagues distant; but the noise at its explosion was not much greater than that of a musket. In another letter to the same august personage, the officers of the Treasury intimate a connexion between volcanoes and earthquakes, the latter occurring when the former burst into activity; but no one mentions that either of the neighboring summits exhibited signs of fire before or after.

1657.

At 8 P. M. on the 15th March, nearly all Concepcion was again overthrown. But it was not alone the excessive vibration of the earth which afflicted the unfortunate Penquistas: after that ceased, the sea retired many leagues from the old shore-line; and two hours later,† returning with impetuosity to the beach, swept everything before it, with the reflux bearing men, cattle, and household effects upon its billows. Such as succeeded in gaining the hills remained there until danger had ceased, listening to the shrieks of those whom the waters buffeted, or who were buried beneath walls; nor was it until daylight that the horrors of the scene were fully appreciated. Another statement is, that the shock occurred between 8 and 9 in the morning; and though the sea sent its waves over the town three times, only four persons perished. A venerable man had sent a warning to the inhabitants that the town would be destroyed by an earthquake that very morning, and in consequence they made timely escape.‡

1688.

A part of Santiago was destroyed shortly after 1 P. M., July 12. The people were already suffering under terrors of Hollandese pirates, small-pox, and famine; and the earthquake filled to the brim their cup of wretchedness.

* Gay. Historia Fisica y Politica de Chile. Tom. II.

† Eyzaguirre. Historia Eclesiastica, Politica, y Literaria de Chile. 1850. Tom. I.

‡ P. C. Figueroa Historia de Chile, MS.

1722.

The shock of May 24th of this year was less violent than the preceding, though sufficiently so to injure much property.

1730.

Probably the most extended in its destructive effects yet experienced was that which took place between 1 and 2 A. M., 8th July, when ruin extended from Concepcion to Coquimbo. Eyzaguirre says that the citizens of Concepcion were warned at 8 P. M. by awful subterranean noises, and had barely escaped from their houses when the whole town came to the ground with a crash. A few minutes afterwards, and before they had recovered from their consternation and terror, the sea retired several hundred yards, and, as though it had gone to gather strength, a momentary pause was followed by a wave no less appalling in its appearance than its effects. About one hundred persons lost their lives. Though M. Gay publishes at length, in a supplementary volume, the letter from which the succeeding information is derived, the date of the earthquake given in his history is July 2d, at 2 A. M. At Santiago the towers of several churches were thrown down, and two women killed. Serena, Valparaiso, and all the fortifications on the Indian frontier, were destroyed; and at Valparaiso, as at Concepcion, the sea swept away what the oscillations had overturned. According to the report from the Bishop of Santiago to the King, just referred to, there were three violent shocks on the same day, 8th—9th July, within twelve hours. The first was between 1 and 2 A. M., the second at 4¾, and the third between noon and 1 P. M. During the second, which was the most severe, the churches and houses were injured, the air was filled with clouds of dust, and it was almost impossible to stand. So many shocks occurred in the ensuing two months, that no one could preserve account of them; indeed, there were portions of the time when the agitation was incessant. To add to their miseries, rain followed soon after the great shock, and continued for thirty hours, the citizens still under too great panic to enter their tottering dwellings.

1751.

Quite a sharp shock on the preceding evening, and another of no great violence some ten minutes before the fatal catastrophe, had prepared the people of Concepcion for the convulsion of May 24th. Carvallo says May 25th, and Eyzaguirre has it March! Most of the citizens were asleep when they were roused by the warning tremor, and scarcely were they clear of their chambers when a roaring noise, lasting six minutes, was accompanied by three shocks, each more severe than that which preceded it. Temples, dwellings, people, all were prostrated; and for some minutes many were unable to flee to the hills, to avoid the feared sea-wave. Had it followed immediately, a moiety of the population must have been drowned; but more than half an hour elapsed before the water receded from the bay of Talcahuano. Then the basin was emptied (dry, one writer says*) with great rapidity; and seven minutes later, wave after wave rolled inward in awful majesty. The front seemed a very wall of water, higher than the mainmast of a ship which had been left on bare sands, where seven fathoms water had flowed a little while before. Three times in that terrible night could they hear the roar of its advancing billows, the earth throbbing from moment to moment and each repetition adding to the terrors of the half-clad people. All human feelings seemed paralyzed under the influence of the panic: parents thought neither of children nor of their partners in life; and even priests gave not absolution to the terrified wretches around them, who supposed the day of final retribution had come. With morning came knowledge of the destitution in which they had been left: houses, furniture, clothing, all had been borne away by the treacherous sea; and the multitude stood in their slight garments, shivering in the cold of an autumn storm. All

* Gay. Historia de Chile. Documentos, Tom. II.

that day, the sea continued ebbing and flowing excessively, though not as during the night; and the ship was whirled about her anchors with such frequency, that the crew were four days in clearing her cables. Owing to their timely escape from the town, only 25 or 30 persons lost their lives out of the entire population. Fatal as had proved the site of old Penco, yet owing to the opposition of the Bishop, several years passed before it was abandoned, and Concepcion rebuilt where the city now stands.

Chillan also was prostrated by the shocks; and the bed of the river having been dammed by them, a flood ensued, which destroyed the little left uninjured. Great was the destruction at Santiago and the intermediate towns. Not yet wholly recovered from the effects of the last earthquake, the churches and most of the more solid buildings of the capital were split from their eaves to their foundations; and it is said that the great bell suspended in a tower of the Cathedral was thrown to the very centre of the plaza. Juan Fernandez, too, was included in the disturbed region; the fortifications, garrison, and habitations of the colonists, were shaken in pieces; and the governor, his wife, and thirty-eight others, were hurried to a watery grave by waves similar to those at Concepcion.

Molina says that the course of this earthquake was from south to north, and that one of the premonitory shocks, about a quarter of an hour before the fatal one, was accompanied by a ball of fire that precipitated itself from the Andes into the sea. The great shocks began about midnight, and continued four or five minutes each. Just before, the sky was perfectly clear in every direction; but immediately after its commencement, it became covered with black clouds, that poured down continual rain for the space of eight days; at the end of which, there was a recurrence of slight tremors during a month, with intervals between each of fifteen or twenty minutes.

1783.

The shock of 17th April, of this year, though causing considerable damage in Santiago, probably would not have been noted by Gay, but for the flood which occurred in the river Mapocho in June following, and before the citizens had been able to repair injuries.

1819.

Molina says that the provinces of Atacama and Coquimbo have never suffered from earthquakes. This is incorrect. The city of Copiapó was visited by them about once in every twenty-three years, viz: in 1773, 1796, and 1819 (1818*). On this last occasion not a single house was left standing. After some minor shocks, that destroyed the church of La Merced, the principal one, which overthrew the town, took place on the 11th April, 1819, between 8 and 9 in the morning. It was preceded by a noise like distant thunder; and its effects must have been more destructive, had not the inhabitants had time to quit their houses.† Many slabs of copper, which had been covered with sand by advances of the sea, were afterward dug out again.

1822.

That of November 19, 1822, has been minutely described by Miers, and other writers on Chile, from whose volumes I shall extract all physical concomitants pertaining to the phenomenon, and quote at length the official account, which is not found in any English author known to me. There were two violent shocks, that lasted from two to three minutes, destroyed a large portion of Valparaiso, Quillota, Mellipilla, and Casablanca, and did much injury at Santiago and other intermediate towns. The commission left in charge of the government at Santiago, in writing to the supreme director, O'Higgins, casually at Valparaiso, say: "On

* Peter Schmidtmeyer: Travels into Chile over the Andes.

† Encyclopædia Britannica. Art. Chile.

Tuesday, 19th inst., at 10*h.* 50*m.* P. M., after three or four hours of overpowering heat and extreme rarefaction of the air, a horrid noise announced, and preceded by some seconds, an earthquake, the like of which Chile has not experienced since 1730. Its explosion was manifested by two powerful concussions, which lasted from two and a half to three minutes; the second—longer than the first—continuing some twenty seconds. Total ruin of the city was apprehended; consternation was general; but, happily, there have been no other misfortunes than a few persons wounded by the falling of tiles or fragments from broken edifices. According to the most general opinion, the action of the earthquake was a trepidation from N.E. to S.W., as is manifested by the direction of fallen objects, furniture, &c. The earth was in motion all night, and much injury was done to property. On the 20th, at 3*h.* 8*m.* A. M., there was a slight tremor without sensible noise; and thirty-four minutes afterwards a meteor passed across the sky in the same line as the earthquake, that is from N.E. to S.W. Its train was so bright, that, for four seconds, the light was equal to that of advanced dawn. Citizens, generally, deserted their houses; some flying to the country, others taking refuge in their gardens or patios, where they continued to sleep under light shelter during the week that the agitations were most frequent and violent."*

General O'Higgins† says the shock occurred at Valparaiso at "ten and three quarters," a time for that city on which all writers agree, say 10*h.* 45*m.* As the difference of longitude is 3*m.* 56*s.*, on the supposition that the instant of shock was correctly observed and the time properly determined, the centre of disturbance must have been equidistant from the capital and its port. At the latter, the houses were nearly all unroofed; many were entirely thrown to the ground, while the thick adobe walls that remained erect were split in all directions. The tower of La Merced church, 60 feet high before the shock, was one of the most remarkable ruins. Its walls, six feet thick, and well built of brick and mortar as high as the belfry, were shivered into large blocks and thrown to the ground. The walls at both ends of the church fell to the north, whilst its longitudinal walls in the same direction, although much damaged, remained, supporting the ridge-roof of timber. The covering of the roof was entirely shaken off, and the whole body of rafters inclined considerably towards the north—every house in Valparaiso, not thrown down, leaning in the same direction. On each side of La Merced there were a number of square buttresses, of solid brick-work, six feet square, which stood at a small distance from the walls. Those on the western side were all thrown down; as were, also, all but two on the eastern side, which last had been twisted in a northeasterly direction, each presenting an angle to the wall. At Quintero, and other places to the northward, the same twisting to the N.E. was observed; the destruction, in all cases, being in proportion to the solidity of the walls, and inversely as the solidity of the formation. Many people were wounded and bruised, though only about 150 lost their lives. During the shock a sea-wave rolled in, nearly twelve feet high; nor did the surface of the bay reach its accustomed level or quietude for several days.

Mr. Miers was at Concon, 11 miles N.N.E. from Valparaiso. There the first oscillation was very sudden and violent, the earth heaving up and down in a manner hardly conceivable, cracking timbers, and throwing down everything loose. The great shock continued about two minutes; then there was a lull of three minutes, when the agitation returned violently for another minute, completing the destruction. With the last, there was a loud rumbling noise like the distant echo of thunder in a mountainous country; and the heaving of the ground seemed not of horizontal oscillations only, but also of violent uplifting concussions, as if repeated explosions were exerting their force upon the roof of a hollow cavern under foot, threatening to burst open the ground. There was nothing remarkable in the appearance or state of the atmosphere; the moon and stars shone with their usual resplendence. Severe shocks continued during three quarters of an hour, with intervals between, seldom exceeding five minutes. The

* Gaceta Ministerial de Chile, Tom. III, No. 64. † Ibid.

ground of the vicinity afforded numerous instances of the convulsions it had undergone. Clefts above a foot wide presented themselves at the distance of every few yards, and in several places the surface had sunk two feet below its previous level. On many spots there were hillocks of sand and mud, which had been forced through the fissures, and looked like miniature volcanoes. Some of these had again sunk, leaving in their places muddy pools; and at other points there were little lakes formed by the overflow of the sea, or by collapse of the banks of the streams, by which the old channels had been filled up and the current forced in a new direction.

Rain, never before known in the month of November, descended upon them on the night of the 27th, whilst yet the majority were bivouacked on the hills. Had it not ceased by morning, not only would it have destroyed all their property, but famine and disease must have followed, to complete their wretchedness. Mr. Miers says (though he evidently did not see it) that the meteor seen in the southward about half-past 2 o'clock on the morning after the shock, was nearly as large as the moon; that it left a long train of light behind; and that, though it visibly exploded, there was no noise distinguishable, nor were any stones known to fall from it.

The violence of the shock was greater at San Felipe than at Santiago; at the latter city than at Rancagua; and in the province of Colchagua it was extremely slight. It was, however, felt from Copiapó to Valdivia—certainly as far east as Mendoza, and some even say at Cordova, in longitude 64°. From the fact that the inland towns, though severely shaken and much damaged, were not overthrown like Valparaiso and those of its more immediate vicinity, it was argued that the centre of the shock was out at sea, somewhat to the southward of the latter city. Remarkable as was its extent, it appears to have left no less extraordinary evidences of its force; for all the line of coast, fifty miles in extent about Valparaiso, was raised nearly three feet above its former level.* One writer† states, that on the day preceding the first shocks, myriads of dead and dying fish were seen covering the water near Valparaiso and San Antonio. In the Journal of Science, Vol. XVII, it is said: "At the moment the shock was felt, two volcanoes in the neighborhood of Valdivia (where the earthquake was pretty sharp) burst out suddenly with great noise, illuminated the heavens and the surrounding country for a few seconds, and as suddenly subsided into their quiescent state." And the writer of the article "Chile" in the Encyclopædia Britannica, informs us that the volcano of Maypu had frequent eruptions after it. For several succeeding weeks the number of tremors was unusually great, and for months the inhabitants never went to their beds with confidence.

1829.

In the "*Report of the British Association for the Advancement of Science*" for 1851, Mr. Bollaert comments as follows on a letter from Valparaiso, giving him some account of the earthquake of April 2d of that year: "I was also in that of 1829, being (then) in Santiago. The commotion commenced on Saturday, 26th of September, at twenty minutes past 2 P. M. The principal undulation appeared to come from S.E. The great shock was 1½ minutes' duration. Half an hour afterwards there was a shower of rain, and another slight shower at half-past 4 P. M. The weather, however, before the earthquake, was rather inclined for rain. During the night of the 26th there were slight shocks; also some on the following days, Sunday and Monday. On Friday, October 1, at half-past 12 there was another shock, as well as at half-past 1. I went out into the street and found the inhabitants looking at two volcanoes that had broken out—one in the Dehesa, behind the first range of the cordilleras; the other in the mountains of Maypu (which last was observed to be in activity just after the earthquake of the 26th), the smoke rising majestically."‡

* Messrs. Graham and Miers assert this; but the fact is denied by Cuming, a conchologist then also at Valparaiso: Geological Trans., Vol. V, second series.

† Schmidtmeyer.

‡ After writing the foregoing, I addressed a letter to an intelligent friend at Santiago, from whose reply the following extracts are made:

"1st. No one remembers having either seen or heard of any eruption of any volcano in Chile coincident with the earthquake

1835.

So many accounts* of the great earthquake which took place on the 20th February, 1835, have already been published, that repetition of all the details here would be supererogation.

It is *reported*, that the mercurial column of a barometer fell four or five tenths of an inch between the 17th and 18th, though it rose to its normal height before the 20th; but as such a depression here is invariably attended by a gale and much rain, and it is known that the weather had been fair, great doubt hangs over the observations. When flocks of sea-birds were seen flying towards the interior an hour or two before the shock, although it was a cloudless summer morning, the weather-wise regarded it as ominous of an approaching storm. At forty minutes past 11 o'clock the tremor commenced without noise, its violence gradually increasing during the first half minute, yet not so much as to cause general alarm. Meanwhile the rumble was heard, and at the end of that time the convulsive motion became so strong that the whole population fled to open places for safety. Before a minute had elapsed, the awful motion so increased that people could scarcely stand; and in thirty seconds more, an overpowering shock caused universal destruction. Concepcion was a fourth time in ruins—its people shrieking under the agony of terror and bodily injury; the very ground on which they were prostrated gaping wide with every throb, and the atmosphere almost irrespirable with dust. From the first tremor to the termination of the great shock was two and a half minutes, during the longer portion of which time none were able to stand unsupported, even animals spreading out their legs to avoid overthrow, and birds taking to the wing. Nor were these brute creatures less terrified than man, as they evinced by excessive trembling and moans or wild screams.

It was the general opinion that the undulations had come from the southwest. All the walls thrown down had, without exception, fallen to the N.E.; those which presented their ends to the point whence the waves came, if not broken and scattered, were fearfully fractured. The fissures in the ground generally, though not uniformly, extended in a S.E. and N.W. direction, corresponding with the lines of undulation or principal flexure. When most excessive, besides the waving or undulatory, there were also felt vertical, horizontal, and circular motions. The cathedral walls exhibited each of these kinds of motion. They were of good brick and mortar, four feet thick, and supported by stout buttresses. That fronting the N.E. was thrown to the ground, part of the angular blocks into which its masonry was broken having been rolled to a distance in the plaza; the side-walls, standing N.E. and S.W., remained erect though broken;

of 1822. The only event noted was a fall of the barometer greater than had ever been known before or since. There was rain three days afterward. *I* attribute the fall of the barometer to the actual loss of mercury which was thrown out of its cistern during the shock, but Don Domingo Reyes assures me it was a true depression. At Valparaiso the sea fell remarkably.

"2d. What the traveller whom you cite asserts respecting the smoke that he saw thrown out on the Dehesa and Maypu mountains, at the time of the earthquake of 1829, is wholly untrue.

"3d. I have not yet been able to learn anything of the condition of the volcanoes to the north of Talca.

"4th. The volcano of Maypu, also called San José, is in activity; and, especially during summer evenings, may be seen ejecting smoke. This is attested by Don Juan de Dios Corréa, who perceives it from his hacienda, the Compania; by Don Domingo Reyes, and various other persons whom I have asked."

With great deference for the opinion of these gentlemen, it may be suggested that the smoke supposed to be seen is only cloud formed by rapidly rising warm air from the valley just after the influence of the sun on the mountain tops ceases, and the light is probably that of summer lightning. It will be seen further on that similar phenomena over the same peak were pointed out to me after the earthquake of December 6, 1850, but which were unquestionably of the nature just indicated.

* See the admirably graphic narratives of Capt. Fitzroy and Mr. Chas. Darwin: Surveying Voyages of the Adventure and Beagle, Vols. II and III;

Journal Royal Geographical Society, Vol. VI;

Transactions Geological Society, London, Vol. V, second series;

Alison: Geological Transactions, 1835;

Caldcleugh: Philosophical Transactions, 1836;

M. Coste: Comptes Rendus, 1838;

Padre Guzman: El Chileno Instruido en su Pais, Vol. II;

Sutcliffe: Account of the Earthquake that occurred on the Island of Juan Fernandez and Talcahuano: London, 1839 whilst the buttresses (at right angles to the latter) were in many cases wrenched off and hurled to the ground, and one stood on its foundation entirely separated from the wall. Some square ornaments on the coping of the same walls were moved into a diagonal position, and an angular stone pinnacle was turned half round without leaving its base. The formation of the site occupied by Concepcion is alluvial; northward and eastward are irregular and rocky tertiary hills, from the foot of which the loose alluvial earth was parted by the great shock, and cracks were left, varying from an inch to a foot in width.

For many hours the earth was tremulous—considerable shocks occurring at short intervals, harassing and alarming; nor was the surface ever long quiet during the three days following the great shock. Between that and the 4th March, more than three hundred other shocks were counted. Most though not all of them were preceded by subterranean noises, compared by some to the rumbling of distant thunder; by others, to the discharges of many pieces of artillery far away; and sometimes, though not often, the sound was unaccompanied by perceptible motion. These sounds were always first distinguished in the southwest quarter, and usually preceded the shocks two or three seconds.

Simultaneously with the beginning of the convulsion, the water rose about a foot in the river at Concepcion, and in the bay of Talcahuano, without first retiring, swelled up to high-water mark; but the great sea-waves came not for a long time afterward. Like Concepcion, Talcahuano was in ruins; and from the summit of the island of Quiriquina a mass of rock, estimated at more than 25,000 tons, had been hurled to the waters at its feet. Capt. Fitzroy learned that the first great wave was "about half an hour after." The governor of the department reports "*a las doce y media*" (at half-past 12); and as, by his account, the town had been shaken down at twenty minutes past 11, an hour and ten minutes had elapsed. First, the sea retired nearly a mile, leaving in the mud vessels that had anchored in from four to six fathoms water. A few minutes after, the first great wave approached in an unbroken wall of water, thirty feet high, between the island of Quiriquina and the western shore of the bay. It broke over everything within that distance of tide-level; dashed the ships along like boats; bore one from the stocks, where it was nearly ready for launching, 200 yards inland; removed 24-pounder cannon some yards, and overturned them; and finally rushed back with such a torrent, that everything movable not buried under the ruins was carried out to sea. The inhabitants occupied the heights back of the town, not less appalled at this display of resistless power than despondent at the ruin it caused them. Ships were again left aground in the bay until half-past 1 P. M., at which time a second wave was seen rolling through the same channel, with more impetuosity than the first, whirling them about each other as they floated, and was only less destructive in its effects because there was less left to destroy. Twenty minutes later, a third came onward. But this was crested—foaming like the breakers across a dangerous bar during a storm; and as it swept tumultuously along the shores bearing everything irresistibly before it, the roaring noise was horrible. Quickly retiring, the sea was seen covered with the wreck of houses, furniture, and goods of every character, from the shattered magazines. Apparent exhaustion followed these efforts, for there were no more great waves, though for some hours the sea rose and fell two or three times each hour, and both earth and water trembled. Eastward of the island of Quiriquina, where the volume was not compressed within a narrow channel, the wave was neither so elevated nor so rapid as that which passed between it and the peninsula. Several days elapsed before the tide rose to within five feet of the usual marks; and as late as the middle of April there was still a difference of two feet, indicating an elevation of the coast to that amount—a fact substantiated by beds of dead muscles and limpets. At the same time the island of Santa Maria, 40 miles distant in a S.W. direction, and the southern shore of the neighboring bay of Arauco, were more affected. The former was upheaved an average of nine feet, its north end having been raised two feet more than the south point, whilst the main land S.E. of it was only left six feet above its previous height.

At the time of the ruin, and until after the great waves ceased, the water of the bay was quite black, and, from the bubbles of air or gas that escaped, was apparently boiling in every direction. It also exhaled a sulphurous smell, and destroyed shoals of fish, whose dead carcasses added to the variety of floating objects. Whilst the waves were coming in, two explosions were seen: one, a column of dark smoke, like a tower, outside the island of Quiriquina; the other resembled a huge jet of aqueous vapor, thrown up in the bay of San Vincente, which is separated from that of Talcahuano by a narrow isthmus. At the disappearance of the latter, a whirlpool marked the spot, as though a cavity had been opened, into which the sea was pouring. At one place in Talcahuano, and several near Concepcion, the ground swelled like large bubbles, and then bursting, discharged quantities of black and fœtid water.

Two days after these calamities, and while yet their only shelters were rudely constructed huts, arbors, or tents, a violent rain-storm came, completing the ruin of the little property they had rescued from the ocean or fallen walls, and to jeopardise their very means of subsistence by destruction of the grain and flour, now wholly exposed to the weather.

At Colcura, midway between Talcahuano and Arauco, as well as at the mouth of the river Tubul, six great waves were counted. Some of these, at the first-named village, reached objects 70 feet above high-water mark.

Los Angeles, on the great plain,and 66 miles S.E. from Concepcion, was almost destroyed at the same instant. There were two violent shocks within three minutes, during the whole of which time the earth was in motion. The island of Mocha was so shaken that people were unable to stand. In a boat, lying east and west on the rocks, water ran from one end to the other, as though alternately lifted and put down; but there was no washing from side to side. The sea broke higher than it had ever been known to do during heavy gales, and the island was found to have been permanently elevated about two feet.

"At Valdivia the shock began gently, increased gradually during two minutes, was at its strongest (at 11*h.* 40*m.*) about one minute, and then diminished. The motion was undulating and regular, like waves rolling from west to east, but strong; it lasted nearly ten minutes. * * * Some thought the motion was from S.W. to N.E.; but Mr. Darwin, and a person with him, thought the reverse. The river swelled or rose at the same time, and quickly fell to its former height. In the port, the sea swelled suddenly upon the shore to high-water mark, though it was then nearly the time of low water, and quickly fell again."* There were many shocks during the afternoon, though none of them were preceded or accompanied by noise.

Chilóe, yet more distant, seems to have been more violently moved, though no great injury resulted from it. There, a premonitory tremor was felt twenty minutes before the great shock, or rather the succession of shocks, extending through six to eight minutes without noise. The motion was undulating from N.E. to S.W., and forest-trees waved nearly to the ground in those directions. The ebb and swell of the sea was observed here also, though its volume was not greater than at Valdivia. "At the moment of the shock, Osorno threw up a thick volume of dark-blue smoke; and directly that passed, a large crater was seen forming on the S.S.E. side of the mountain: it boiled up lava, and threw up burning stones to some height; but the smoke soon hid the mountain. When seen a few days afterwards, it showed very little smoke by day; but by night the new crater, as well as the old one on its truncated summit, shone with a steady light. This volcano appears to have remained in activity throughout the year. The action of Minchinmadom was similar to that of Osorno. Two curling pillars of white smoke had been observed all the morning; but, during the shock, numerous small chimneys seemed to be smoking within the great crater, and lava was thrown out of a small one just above the lower verge of the snow. Eight days afterwards this little crater was extinct; but at night five small red flames were seen in a line equidistant from each other, like those in the streets of a village. By the 1st of March its activity was much diminished; but on the 26th there was a smart earthquake, and at night the five fires were again seen. A

* Journal Royal Geographical Society, Vol. VI.

fortnight afterwards the tops of fifteen conical hills could be seen within the wall of the great crater; and at night nine steady fires, of which seven were in a line and two straggling."* No flame or smoke was observed on the Corcovado, 23 miles south; though Dr. Darwin thinks there is abundant evidence to believe that the volcanic chain, as far as Yanteles—150 miles from Osorno—was affected not only at the moment of the great shock, but remained in very unusual activity during many subsequent months. Mr. Caldcleugh states† that two volcanoes were observed in the Andes, near Talca, a few days after the 20th February, both near the lake of Mondaca; that another new vent was observed on the right bank, and near the head of the Maule; and that Peteroa, Maypu, and Aconcagua had been for some months in activity. Capt. Fitzroy says, that the accounts of the neighboring volcanoes, before and after the earthquake, were so various and indistinct, that he could not ascertain the truth.

There is no information from any point further south than Chilóe; but we have seen that the violence of the disturbance was less at each increase of distance from the vicinity of Concepcion. East of it—at Yumbel—scarcely a house remained on its foundations, and those which were not prostrated were in too dangerous a condition for occupation. The time at Florida, also, was reported 11½ A. M. There, the earth opened in many places, and a little mountain sank to such depth that it left precipitous banks round its former site. From Chillan the only physical facts of interest related are—that the noise and shock seemed to come from the south, the latter following the former with the rapidity of lightning; that the sensation was as though the earth floated on moving billows, each instant more violently disturbed by a wave greater than the undulating mass; that it lasted about three minutes, and destroyed buildings almost as completely as at Concepcion; and that the rain-storm which followed was preceded by a whirlwind and hail, the former of sufficient power to elevate objects of much weight. Cauquenes, the Intendente says, was shaken down at 11¼, and some of its people killed. Talca did not suffer so greatly. The earth began to move slowly, and without noise, at twenty minutes past 11; and the great shocks followed, as at Concepcion, only much less violently. The more substantial houses of brick and mortar were thrown down, including the churches and prison. Constitucion was also numbered among the doomed cities. As at Talca, the first tremor was noiseless, and excessively slow; but the violent oscillation did not continue a minute. Many fissures opened and discharged water, and great sea-waves rolled in, twelve feet in height. The first came an hour and a half after the shock, and did not recede for half an hour. Fifty minutes later the greatest wave rolled in, tore two schooners from their anchors, and transported them among the bushes, more than a hundred yards from the old river banks.‡ Nine waves were counted, and for forty-eight hours lesser rollers came forward. The governor, pilot, and others, thought the land had settled about two feet; as the banks of the river appeared that much lower, and there was certainly two feet more water on the bar. Capt. Fitzroy was certain that no elevation had taken place, but regarded the sinking of the banks doubtful, and thought the reflux of the sea might readily wash away two feet of the loose sands of the bar.

Towards the north the injuries were less and less. Curicó lost the towers of its churches; Rancagua had a few walls broken. Santiago vibrated for two whole minutes, hurrying its people to open places, and causing many a thought for distant fellow-countrymen who, the length of the shock told them, were surely in jeopardy. At Valparaiso the sea was observed to advance and recede rapidly, though without violence: Coquimbo, Huasco, Copiapó, all felt it (according to newspaper accounts) at nearly the same instant, and even Mendozinos observed a gentle undulation. From the sea we have information only from two points, viz: a barque bound to Valparaiso, which at the time was in latitude 35½°, longitude 74½°, and therefore nearly on the line between Concepcion and Juan Fernandez; and the second is from that island. The speed

* Transactions Geological Society, Vol. V, second series.

† Philosophical Transactions, 1836.

‡ Padre Guzman, Vol. II; and El Araucano, No. 234.

of the vessel was suddenly diminished from seven knots per hour to one knot: the sea was greatly agitated, apparently lifting her up twenty feet, and the master thought her dragging over a sand-bank. At Juan Fernandez the sea rose without warning to the level of the little bay on the N.E. side, and, during its rapid recession a few minutes later, a tremendous noise was heard, and a column of white smoke burst from it about a mile from Bacalao Point. At the same instant, the shock was felt. Two hundred yards of the bay was left bare by the reflux; and with the second rush, the water reached 15 feet above its usual level, carrying every thing before it. All through the night, bursts of flame illuminating the whole island rose from the spot where the smoke had been seen to issue; but when it was sounded a month later, 69 fathoms of water covered it.

Considering the great violence of this earthquake and the extent of territory disturbed, the loss of life was comparatively small, in all not exceeding 200 persons. It is also worthy of remark, that while all the buildings on alluvial soil within a certain distance of Concepcion were destroyed, three houses on rock foundation in Talcahuano, and the villages of Gualqui and Rere within that distance, but on the granite of the Coast cordilleras, remained uninjured.* Nor did Antuco, at the very foot of the volcano of that name, suffer harm.

1837.

The governor of Valdivia, in an official report to the Intendente, dated 7th November of this year, says that the earthquake of that morning, beyond all question, was the most severe ever known. It began at five minutes past 8 o'clock, and for ten minutes the motion of the earth was so violent that one could only stand with great difficulty. From that time until 9½, strong shocks occurred every few moments; and tremors, gradually diminishing in force, continued throughout the day. Both churches and all the public offices were thrown down; and if the other buildings did not share the same fate, it was because they are constructed of wood and yielded to flexure more readily.†

This was the last great earthquake prior to our arrival in the country. Tremors in one province or another were of daily occurrence, and are duly chronicled in the local papers of the period; but they had no general interest, and no facts are recorded with them likely to benefit the geologist. Nor do I propose to specify in this place the multitude observed in the ensuing three years, but only such as exhibited peculiarities, or merit notice by the extent of the disturbed district. In Appendix A will be found all, of which records were made both by Señor Troncosa at La Serena, and ourselves at Santiago.

1849.

At La Serena, the month of November, 1849, was particularly marked. There were tremors on the 8th, 12th, 13th, 14th, 16th; five on the 18th, six on the 19th, four on the 20th, one on the 21st, one on the 23d, five between the 24th and 26th, one on the 27th, two on the 28th, and one on the 30th: in all, thirty-one shocks during less than the same number of days. That which took place at 6*h*. 12*m*. A. M. (M. T. Santiago) on the 18th, was by far the most violent, and the earth was in motion for 84 seconds. The line of oscillation, indicated by the swinging of a barometer suspended at two inches from the wall, was from N.W. to S.E. The barometer would have been broken had it not been held, though no injury was done to houses. At the port, a sea-wave 16 feet higher than tide-level followed immediately after the shock, greatly injuring the copper-smelting furnaces and other property on the beach. A short, terrifying noise preceded it. The same shock was felt sensibly at Santiago and Valparaiso, rousing the inmates of a hotel in the former city where we were staying, and starting them, as

* Similar consequences were observed during the great Catania and Jamaica earthquakes in 1693 and 1694. Phil. Trans., Vols. XVII and XVIII.

† Araucano. December 8, 1837

well as the occupants of the ground floor, to the patio and street—the female portion in dresses which might be permissible at a "*bal costumé*," though they certainly were not "*à la mode*" in the highways of a capital. No one observed the direction of the undulation at Santiago: there was much noise, and my iron bedstead struck quite violently against the walls during more than a minute. It was not noticed to the southward, nor was any earthquake mentioned between the 1st September and close of December.

In a little while our perceptions were quickened, and we were able to detect the customary premonitory noise as well as the oldest native; yet we needed something more reliable than corporeal pulsations—something that would watch whilst we slept, for none can say when the earth will be rended. Finding that the instrument brought for the purpose could not be made sufficiently sensitive to record the many slight shocks frequently occurring, another was made by suspending with a fine silver wire a ball of lead weighing about two pounds. From the point of suspension to a plate of glass resting on a board placed horizontally on the earth, and touched by a needle inserted in the ball, was 9 feet 10 inches. Under the glass was placed a paper, engraved with the points of the compass and concentric circles, the latter having radii increasing a quarter of an inch from the centre outward. This was adjusted so that the points of the paper coincided with the corresponding points of the horizon, and the centre fell precisely under the point of the needle. Black sand was then sifted over the glass uniformly, and the instrument was ready; any motion of the earth must leave a trace in the sand easy to be transferred by means of the engraved paper. Perfectly glazed paper firmly secured to a smooth surface would have obviated the necessity for interposing a plate of glass, and a longer pendulum would have been better; but we had no apartment where such an instrument could be put up, and the satisfactory action of even this was much interfered with by mice and insects. Besides the arrangement for self-register of the line of oscillation and comparative disturbance, each member of the party noted the time of the subterranean noise, with the beginning and end of the tremor, and estimated the direction from which they came; and one went to the barometer, as well to preserve it from injury as to ascertain the fluctuation of the mercurial column.

Before these arrangements were completed, a favorable opportunity was afforded, on the afternoon of the 22d December, 1849, to observe one from the summit of Santa Lucia. The approach of the earth-wave could be unmistakably calculated by the increasing violence of the rumbling noise, and no doubt was left that the line of motion was from W.S.W. Several seconds had elapsed, when there was a quick, slight tremor. An interval of repose succeeded, which was followed by a more violent and longer shock, the duration of the two being precisely six seconds. It was felt at Valparaiso, but not at Coquimbo or Talca.

DECEMBER 6, 1850.

I was sleeping profoundly, and disturbed. With the first glimmerings of consciousness there was associated an impression of heavily laden carts passing over the newly made pavement in front of the house, separated from the chamber only four or five feet; but even in the brief second or two that lingered whilst reason was resuming its sway, the deep, rumbling noise was combined with a short, quick rocking of the bed, a vibratory trembling of the walls, and such a creaking of the ceiling, as left no doubt respecting the disturbant of my morning slumbers. Seizing the watch overhead, and springing to the floor, the earth was felt in excessive agitation; its quick throbbings starting every object in contact with it, and by degrees communicating an oscillating motion to walls and roofs. The water of the ewer on the wash-stand was tossed into a pyramidal form three or four inches high, and dashed out on either side in such quantity that its surface was finally more than an inch below the rim. The doors of the chamber, though bolted above and locked, had been thrown wide open. Articles suspended against the walls were beating them with rapid blows: windows rattled, as we sometimes hear in a railway-train: tiles on the opposite houses were in motion like the short, quick billows of a rapid current across which a breeze blows freshly; and the street was filled with a terror-stricken populace. To sally out in such a dress *as did my neighbors*, would have been more shocking still; and as it was next to impossible that the phenomenon would not have ceased long before the very first garment could have been adjusted—even were there not aversion to perform any act hurriedly—during the forty mortal seconds that elapsed, I watched round me with all the reflection at command. Thus I stood in the middle of the floor, trying to feel if there was any undulation, and in what direction it was progressing, not knowing how soon the earth might open and suddenly admit me to a sight of her great laboratory; and striving to estimate the number of inches through which the walls were swaying, uncertain how early they would spread a little wider than usual, and permit the ceiling to catch me like a rat under a dead-fall.

Whilst dreamy scenes of other lands cling about the brain, thus suddenly to find our emblem of stability trembling and throbbing under foot—quivering in its convulsions, and with deep-toned mutterings filling the air and stunning the ear—is no less astounding than terrific. When so roused, one cannot readily appreciate the passing event; the mental and physical faculties are not synchronous in action, and judgment remains partially dormant long after the mechanism of the body has been called into play. One may be self-possessed to a degree, absolutely regardless of personal danger, resolved to study the grand terrestrial phenomenon with the keenest appreciation intelligence will permit; but, until reason resumes her throne, instinct prompts, and the body ordinarily accomplishes flight to places of comparative safety, at least to spots where walls and roofs cannot add to the dangers. We had not experienced any earthquake that continued more than a few seconds: the present one lasted thirty-five after my foot touched the floor, and fifty-five from the commencement, as was observed by one of the assistants.

Up to 2 A. M. the atmosphere had been clear, and the pressure of the barometer about its mean. At 6 o'clock the sky was partially overcast with light, fleecy clouds, and the air calm, indeed somewhat stagnant. The preliminary rumble was heard by Lieut. MacRae about forty minutes afterwards; and, as customary, he went to a chronometer always in his room. This was instantly followed by a slight shock, of scarcely three seconds' duration. In less than five seconds more, and while the rumble of the first was still audible, the second shock commenced, continued increasing in violence for more than half a minute, and then slowly subsided. Those who were in the open air by the end of the first shock, say that the line along which it travelled was from N.W. to S.E., as was also shown by the major axis of the ellipse described by our pendulum. To all, the motion was evidently vertical, rather a succession of rapid pulsations of almost sufficient power to lift one off his feet, than undulatory to any extent. Oscillation by such a power as was seemingly in action beneath us, would have levelled Santiago with the plain.*

Walls standing east and west opened at their junctions with the ceilings, so as to permit the falling of things from above; those occupying north and south directions were cracked nearly from the ground-line upward. Many of the former, of two stories height, and surmounted by balustrades with heavy ornaments of masonry—as the old palace, and mint—threw the ornaments to the north and south, whilst others of a like elevation and structure in the latter direction, retained them in place. Portions of masonry fell within the cathedral and other churches, starting early worshippers—priests and all—from mass; tiles rattled from the house-roofs in all the streets; and nearly every dwelling with a ceiling of plaster had it shaken down. All the town-clocks, and most of those in private houses, were stopped; that of the observatory, whose heavy mercurial pendulum swung N.W. and S.E., had its error changed two seconds, showing acceleration of its vibrations during the disturbance.

Where so much was falling, and instinct drives every one, for self-preservation, without the reach of walls even before they are fully threatened by danger, one would anticipate casualties

* Mr. Phelps likens the motion to that of a railroad car off the track, bumping over the sleepers.

to individuals; but only two were mortally injured. The streets, at such times, present curious scenes. Matrons and maidens, fathers and beaux, children and nurses, all in the costumes of repose in this instance, with the bright light of a summer morning to betray their scanty apparel. Nearly all are on their knees, beating their breasts, and invoking the intercession of *Maria Santissima;* others, with a child under each arm, fly wildly towards the church, or the residence of a mother, their solitary garment streaming in the air; some cling to husbands or children, and piteously shriek their terror; very few—like Jacob Faithful—take things coolly, and after quietly making themselves presentable for so general an assemblage, are ready to wrap dressing-gown or blanket about the shoulders of wife or sister, when the restoration of stability and quiet brings consciousness to the latter.

A gentleman, who had been riding on the plain to the south of the city, had dismounted, and was standing with a companion, watching the efforts of an old Guaso to force a nearly broken-down horse to the top of his speed. This had been going on for some time, when the old man suddenly slid to his knees in the dust, and so continued as long as the earthquake lasted. At first my friend could not comprehend what was the matter; but, as the first deep rumble and tremor came beneath his feet, himself and companion exchanged but a look and the word—*temblor*. He says, that he had read of the *crust* of the earth, and of the boiling state of the materials at its centre, but until that instant had never given a thought as to how *thin* the shell might be! As the shocks increased in rapidity and violence, with the awful rumbling precisely under him, he was almost certain that it was but pie-crust thick after all, and was irresistibly impelled to stand on tip-toe, lest the whole foot should break through, and he go—he knew not whither. Previously the horses of himself and his companion fought whenever they approached; but during its violence they crept close to each other, and were evidently much terrified.

Certain lines of the surface were greatly more affected than others. The houses to the eastward of the city had their windows broken by the violence of the vertical concussions; those on the belt passing through the western squares experienced greater damage than others about the line in which Santa Lucia is placed, whilst an intermediate tract was excessively disturbed, and furniture overthrown and glass destroyed in large quantities. Objects, as books or bottles, placed on east and west shelves, were often thrown six feet horizontally from the vertical plane in which they stood. On estates near the cordilleras, and more particularly at those much embayed by hills, the noise, aided by masses of rock which came thundering down their sides, was terrific. The cattle flocked to the dwellings with moans of fear and distress, those that were secured spreading out their fore feet to avoid being overthrown.

It was felt from Coquimbo to Talca, 310 miles distant from each other in a straight line; but there being contradictory accounts from Mendoza, the eastern limit of the disturbance is not so well known, and the farthest point in that direction from which there is reliable information is San Pedro Nolasco. There, it was quite severe; the miners witnessing the dislodgment of many masses of stone, and their subsequent descent to the valley. At Valparaiso, 64 English miles W.N.W., there was but a slight tremor; and the reports from Curacavi and Casablanca showed that its main strength had been exerted under the immediate plain on which Santiago lies. Shortly after 8 o'clock there were two other shocks, though so slight as not to have been noticed very generally; and before the close of the month our journal records five more. For forty hours after the great shock, and at each of the others, cloudy weather ensued; a state of the atmosphere almost unknown at this season of the year. Our pendulum left no trace, because of displacement of the sand by the concussions; but we found it vibrating through more than an inch.

For some time afterwards we were regarded as little better than wizards. It was known that the new instrument had been put up only two days before the shock; and, arguing from the length of time since the last preceding one, and the consequent accumulation of the disturbing agent, an acquaintance was told, "The next earthquake will probably be severe." When the surmise so soon proved a reality, notwithstanding positive assurance that we could have no foreknowledge of terrestrial or meteorological events, even intimate friends were skeptical. Certain it was, that season at Santiago had proved unlike any in the memory of man. Rains in December! thunder-storms, and deaths by lightning in the heart of the city! clouds on more than half the nights! all were associated with our presence; and the populace firmly believed that we not only officially announced the coming earth-storm to government, but specially prepared for its observation.

MARCH 24, 1851.

After the severe shock of December, there were a number (twelve) minor ones, of interest only to keep us reminded of the great laboratory beneath, and of man's helplessness. Some weeks had elapsed without one of these memory-joggers, when, to sharpen our recollections, quite an old-fashioned shake occurred soon after midnight of the 24th March. I had just extinguished the night lamp, when the first unmistakable rumble reached me. Wide awake, not even wrapped up for the night, and desirous to note everything presented during the phenomenon, my motions were by no means slow; and, thanks to that universal blessing—lucifer matches—I do not think four seconds had elapsed before I was on foot, in a dressing gown, the lamp re-lighted, and my watch in hand. It is wonderful what celerity is imparted to one's motions at such times, and with what "hot haste" even apathetic Chilenos, yet half sleeping, hurry to the patios or streets. Quick as I had been, however, the street-doors of all our neighbors had been flung open, and their exclamations could be heard. Slowly and uniformly the noise approached from the northward, increasing in violence as it drew nearer; until, at the end of seven seconds, it was perfectly awful. At this time there was a very gentle and slow though unmistakable undulation, and all was over; even the roar seeming to die away of a sudden. The mail of next day brought intelligence that a similar shock had been experienced at Valparaiso; where, also, the origin of the earth-wave was supposed to have been to the northward.

APRIL 2.

For several days previously the sky had been unusually overcast, the barometer fluctuating as it does during winter rain-storms. Not far from 9 o'clock, on the night of the 1st, there was a vivid, quick flash of lightning to the N.N.E., so intense in brightness as to illuminate within the observatory, where I had been at work some hours. I was startled by the sudden brilliancy, and listened for close-following thunder, but no sound came; neither was the flash repeated, nor was there the smallest speck of cloud even about the horizon in that direction.* Coming down the hill, about midnight, my left eye was found to be injured by over-exertion; and the pain which soon followed brought on nervous restlessness that kept me awake several hours. Sleep, long courted, came so profoundly at last, that when nature, in wrath, was shaking the city on its foundations, and a startled population fled with cries of terror, though roused by the incipient shock, nearly half its violence had passed before full consciousness returned. Habit brought me instantly to the floor, watch in hand, and in such a position that I could embrace, at a glance, the roofs across the street, a little mirror directly in front, and the wash-stand diagonally to the right. But reason was torpid. Though there was a consciousness of excessive oscillation of the floor, and most infernal subterranean roarings; a recognition that the pictures of the paper on the opposite wall were waving from side to side across the mirror; a conviction that the roofs and tiles of the houses in front were "dancing like mad;"

* Many of the most intelligent persons in Chile regard earthquakes as due wholly to electrical agency; and as we have no right to reject popular belief until every phase of the phenomenon is satisfactorily explicable without such influence, it is proper that the occurrence of such remarkable lightning—so short a time before the shock, and in the direction from which it came—should not be omitted. For the same reason Humboldt mentions (*Rélation Historique.* Liv. IV., Chap. 10) "two strong shocks simultaneously with a clap of thunder."

and knowledge that the affrighted people were invoking the mercy of their God in the utmost distress, and the rattle of windows and doors was making no small addition to the uproar, still several seconds must have elapsed before I could realize the actual magnitude of the storm agitating the crust of our abiding-place. Nevertheless, experience having taught that the phenomenon is of little continuance, there was sufficient rationality to prevent my leaving the room; and I stood with senses gradually returning, thinking each vibration would be the last. But I watched and watched the dial of the monitor in my hand, and, instead of subsidence, there came accessions to the force of the moving power with each beat of its balance-wheel, till the walls on either side were swaying to and fro, the plank ceiling screeching overhead, and finally the doors flew open, exhibiting the opposite room filled with a cloud of dust, and its floor covered with broken adobes, which had fallen between the ceiling and walls. Half a minute had now elapsed, each second of which seemed at least a day; and in the fiercest violence, as the creaking of the ceiling was too ominous to disregard longer, I found myself creeping for shelter beneath the lintel of the door. Of a sudden the wall swayed away from the roof, showing the blue sky above, and a mass of rubbish fell, blinding and almost stifling me; so that it became necessary to take refuge under the lintel of the outside door, where fresh air might be obtained. As the tiles were falling in a shower from the roofs, escape to the patio was more hazardous than to remain under the doorway; for one had better risk being partially buried than have his head split with one of these heavy pieces of earthenware.

The motion had now became fearful, and the roar of the pent up vapor, as it moved heavily along, most awful; yet every little while there would reach me the clear ringing laugh of one of the assistants—inspired by the efforts of a companion to attain a place of greater apparent safety—marked contrasts of expressed human sensations in this terrestrial convulsion. I was not conscious of fear at any instant, nor was it possible to make the mind realize that the house might fall, although the walls were breaking all round, and at every few seconds the sky was visible through their crevices; but there was a sensation of dread—a feeling of absolute insignificance in the presence of a power that shook the Andes as willows in the breeze. I was humbled to the dust. Afterwards I learned, that among the mass in the streets there was but one thought, one desire—*flight*. But where fly to? The massive stone arches of the sanctuary had been broken, their key-stones had partially fallen, and the priests had been driven from the altars by masses of masonry precipitated around them; the hills were shaking huge rocks from crests where they had slumbered since the dawn of nature, their trains marked by streams of fire; in the streets tiles were falling in showers mid clouds of dust; and on the open plain, in addition to that most unearthly and distressing noise and the moaning of cattle in their brute terror, the trees were waving from side to side under the influence of that same unseen but omnipotent agent.

Preceded some seconds by the usual rumbling noise, the first shook commenced at 6*h*. 48*m*. 10*s*. A. M., and for eighteen seconds continued with nearly uniform violence, equal to, and in the kind of motion not altogether unlike that of December 6th. This started the tiles and walls, though it broke nothing, a fact which may perhaps be accounted for by the greater rapidity with which the atoms at the surface of the earth were disturbed on the last occasion; for, if one may judge from bodily sensations, the shaking was certainly as great as in December, though the effects were much less. The most excessive displacements were between 6*h*. 48*m*. 28*s*. and 6*h*. 48*m*. 53*s*; and at 6*h*. 49*m*. 38*s*. terminated an earthquake unparalleled in central Chile since 1822. Less than one minute and a half: a brief period of one's life when marked only by events of ordinary transpiration—but an age when one stands on a world convulsed. Beginning at 6*h*. 48*m*. 28*s*., the oscillations, then quite distinct, rapid, and abrupt, were of such magnitude that one involuntarily sought support; and though this actually lasted only twenty-five seconds, the time seemed endless, when measured by the multitude of thoughts crowded into it. Liquids were tossed to the north and south; and at the end, the surface of the mercury in a cup with vertical sides was left 1.4 inch below the rim. A barometer suspended on a north and south wall was thrown down, and all objects not summarily shaken off were moved by successive jolts to the north or south; generally in the latter direction. Every wall in the house was broken, some of them so that day-light shone through; others were thrown permanently out of the vertical, and scarcely a tile remained in place on the roof. Our pendulum was still gyrating when we could venture into the room where it was kept. Unfortunately the board supporting the glass for the register had not been secured to the ground, and was transferred during the severe agitations nine tenths of an inch W. by N., as well as thrown out of the horizontal plane. Thus it gave broken instead of closed curves precisely as represented here, which are traced from the original sheet.

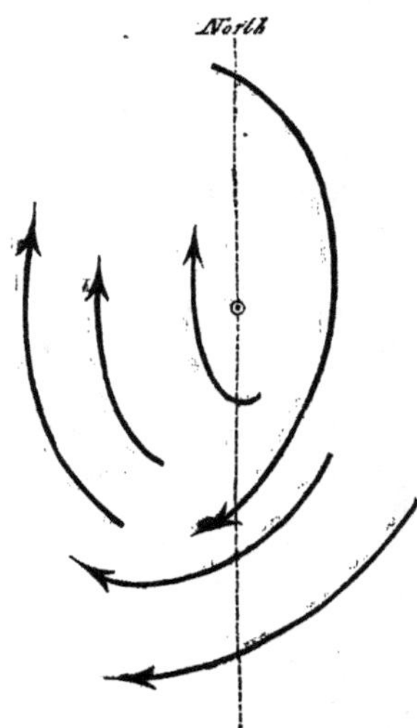

But the direction of the moving power admitted of no doubt, the point of the pendulum having passed along a line very nearly S. by W., and then described nearly elliptic curves, the major axis of one of which probably exceeded 4 inches. Observations of this character would be of high interest, could they be obtained in numbers; but local causes, as the geological formation, orology, &c., influence both direction and apparent violence to such extent that isolated observations are of little absolute value.

We suffered on Santa Lucia too. Whilst we were dressing, our servant had been despatched immediately that the great shock ceased, to learn the condition of the instruments. Following a few minutes later, the rocky mass was found broken across from east to west between the observatories and castle, and a crevice remained, which, at the surface, was nearly an inch wide. A glance showed the instruments uninjured, but one of the piers supporting the meridian circle (the western) had been greatly disturbed. These piers are composed of three blocks each, forming massive obelisks 6½ feet high above the floor, and 2 feet square at the base, secured to each other and to the base of porphyry *in situ* with hydraulic cement. The joint nearest the floor of the west pier was opened; the blocks, no doubt, rocked, and the whole pier was shifted to the south, until it formed an angle of 5′ with the eastern pier. Our clock had not been stopped, or rather we found the pendulum oscillating; but observations proved that it had been retarded eleven and a half seconds! Every other pendulum clock in Santiago had come to a stand.

The streets were filled with an excited and still greatly alarmed multitude, wandering from place to place in examination of the ruins of walls and turrets, and the masses of tiles and rubbish that occupied a portion of every thoroughfare.

Where the tiles had not fallen, the roofs looked as though ploughs had upturned them; and men were at work in all directions pulling down the tottering ones. With every brief interval a new shock came, and one can scarcely conceive the terror and consternation with which many rushed from their doors at these times, or the despondent anxiety settled on the countenances of all. The injury throughout the city was very severe, and the loss of walls, roofs, glass, and furniture, extensive. On the plaza the cathedral suffered most seriously; all its arches north and south were sprung, and the key-stones settled an inch or two; the tie-beams securing the outer and longitudinal arches in the same direction were drawn almost out of the walls, and masonry had fallen in piles. It was found necessary to close it forthwith. The central dome of the old palace and its western parapets were so broken that they were immediately pulled down to prevent further injury. Examination of these fractures showed that bricks had given way in many cases when mortar would not; and adobe walls had more tenacity than burned bricks, yielding to the flexure of the foundation without entire prostration. In every instance where objects could fall freely, they had gone off to the northward; though if not precipitated at the first shock, they generally jolted in the opposite direction. East and west of the line of motion through the plaza, much less damage was done, a fact also peculiar in the December earthquake.

The loss of life was small. Three persons only were ascertained to have been killed, and some thirty or more wounded. Of the fatal cases—all women—two deaths had been caused by the fall of the cornice in the church of San Francisco, as the congregation rushed out; and the third was a poor girl who proved a victim to a custom of the country. In conformity with this custom, she could not be left alone, in an open house, whilst her mother attended early mass, and had been locked in the second story. When the earthquake came, she leaped in terror from the balcony, and the mother returned to find her a corpse.

There was a striking peculiarity about this great shock. Like a tense chord rudely struck, its vibration was perceptible for two hours without intermission; and its subsidence was so gradual as to leave one almost in doubt when it actually ceased. In addition to this, a somewhat similar vibration from 6*h.* 30*m.* to 8*h.* 30*m.* P. M., and a multitude of "slight tremors," we have the recorded times of eighteen sharp earthquakes before midnight. Two of the last, following at an interval of two seconds, appeared the effect of sudden and distinct explosions, without noise or tremor, unlike every motion we had felt, and Lieut. MacRae, in his surprise, writes them down "two distinct and sharp thumps underneath." The first of these occurred at 7*h.* 33*m.* 36*s.*, the other just two seconds later. The most severe subsequent shock during the day was at 11*h.* 34*m.* 36*s.*, which lasted seven seconds. By this time most of the populace had lost something of their apprehensions, and, having the magnitude of their sins brought thus pressingly to mind, had again flocked to the churches in numbers. As this was the season of lent, when the churchman expects to accomplish so much by compliance with prescribed ordinances, it is not difficult to believe that many would be reminded of their short-comings at mass, vespers, and confession, by such visitants as the morning had brought us. But there were few whose faith in the altar persuaded them to abide at its feet during the shock—none willing to return for the completion of devotions when the shock had passed; and the streets were again filled at a most unusual hour.

Most deplorable intelligence was soon brought from the neighboring villages and *haciendas*. Lampa and Renca, lying to the northwest, were reported in ruins; their inhabitants in the streets, and the dwelling-houses and dividing walls of adobes on the estates lamentably destroyed. By night there were travellers from Curacavi, a town of 5,000 people on the Valparaiso road, and beyond the first range of mountains. Among them was Mr. Campbell, the engineer of the Copiapó and Caldera railroad, who had passed through it about two hours after the earthquake. In many parts of the town he saw numbers of houses whose roofs had fallen in; and scarcely one remained which could be regarded safe so long as the agitation continued. At the first great shock a portion of the church steeple had been flung to N.N.E.; other portions fell by degrees, crushing the roof and wholly destroying the building; but these latter had been prostrated in every direction. At one of the inns the earth had opened in a nearly east and west line, entirely across the court-yard; and the water of its well was rendered turbid for several hours. The same thing occurred with a number of the wells at Valparaiso. At Casablanca—still farther west—the destruction was even greater, no walls having escaped unbroken, no matter what their direction; indeed it was said, that the only safe house remaining was the inn. This was, undoubtedly, exaggeration, fright in the first hours having driven many to arbors and tents, which they were willing enough to abandon after a day or two. There were accounts, too, that the earth had opened in a great many places near the line of the road, particularly some three or four leagues west of Santiago, and also that water had been seen to issue from the crevices in considerable quantities; but subsequent investigation brought to light only one person, to the westward, who had actually seen water ejected, and this was near Viña la Mar, close to the sea-shore. It was also well attested, that the high bank of the Angostura (a little stream emptying into the Maypu) had opened, and a black and slimy substance oozed out. Unfortunately, when searched for some five days afterwards, a heavy rain had intervened and obliterated all traces.

As no intelligence from Valparaiso reached us before the arrival of the mail, next morning, the omen was regarded as most favorable. Yet it did not prevent the assembling of an immense crowd about the post-office at the hour when the letters were expected, and anxious impatience could only be gratified by one of the clerks reading aloud from the first paper obtained. This stated, that all the walls of houses in the Almendral had been shaken to their bases; many roofs wholly destroyed; the tiles of others flung into the streets; full five hundred houses were uninhabitable, and more than that number of people without any shelter whatever; and in short the residents remembered no such earthquake since 1822. Even those whose houses had not been seriously injured in many cases took refuge on board ships; others fled to the hills, and others again erected tents and wooden shanties in the plazas. The hotels, principally occupied by strangers, were deserted at once, the occupants taking to the water forthwith. It was especially remarkable, that the houses built on the sandy foundation of the Almendral were far more injured than those on the narrow rocky ledge of the port. Though the injuries had been greatest to those whose walls stood in a N.E. and S.W. line, no direction had proved a safeguard; and, as at Casablanca, every one in the Almendral had been broken.

Judging by a line in which a cross was thrown from the steeple of La Matriz church, and the place at which part of a marble fountain in the Plaza Victoria was left, the direction of the earth-wave must have been from N.E. by N. to S.W. by S., the cross having been thrown nearly 20 feet from the body of the edifice in the former direction, and the vase of the fountain jolted on its pedestal two inches towards the latter point.* No lives were lost, nor were any serious wounds received, the hour of the day and long interval of warning having given people a chance to escape to the streets and patios. The family of one friend in the Almendral had been in agonizing tribulation. At the first tremor, the door of their chamber was permanently secured by the sinking of the ceiling; and they found themselves wholly unable to escape to the rescue of their children, occupying an apartment on the opposite side of the patio. Cries from the nurse told them that the door of her room was similarly beyond her power to force; and the thought passed through their minds that they would be buried without again embracing their darlings. But a moment after, the iron railings barring all windows fell with a crash from the nursery, and the mother had the intense joy to hear the woman escape with her treasures. Then her husband and self lay down, not ready perhaps—and certainly not willing—but expecting and resigned to die, now that their children were safe.

Of eighteen shocks recorded at Santiago before midnight of the 2d, some occurred whilst the assistants were at work on Santa Lucia, and of these they distinctly recognised the warning noise to the N.E., in one instance, full fifteen seconds before the earth under foot was in motion. Most of them were slight: some lasted only a second or two; others continued nearly

* Personally verified.

a quarter of a minute; and others again were followed at very brief intervals, as one or two seconds, by other tremors. Some were preceded and accompanied by a rumbling noise, others were wholly in silence, and there was more than one instance of noise without the least perceptible disturbance.

On the following day I started for the purpose of examining the line of destruction in a southerly direction, and soon found that the effects diminished as the plain widened. Even at the Maypu, 16 miles south of the city, had not attention been previously occupied, one would not specially have noticed crevices in the walls. Though the toll-receiver assured me he had seen large masses of earth thrown down from the vertical banks, on the south side of the stream, its bridge, with high abutments and supporting piers, was wholly uninjured. No crevices could be found in the banks near the bridge.

On a line west of the latter, where the Maypu passes through the Central cordilleras, the latter make a sudden bend eastward; and the Andes—at a nearly opposite point—curving to the westward, the two chains closely approach each other at a pass twenty miles south of the stream, called the Estero de Payne. Indeed, the two chains of mountains, here about 2,000 feet above the plain, are separated by a gorge of the same level as the plain, whose average width is not more than 100 yards. Thus, from the Cuesta de Chacabuco to the Angostura, except where the Maypu passes through the central range, there is a continuous though irregular elliptic plain, whose diameters will not vary greatly from 55 and 25 miles. The widest part of the basin or plain is where the Maypu crosses it in latitude 33° 42′, and here the high road to the south seemed to be near the eastern line of injurious disturbance. Subsequently, we learned by a traveller from Mendoza that a very slight though long tremor had been felt at *7h. 10m.*, in that city, on the morning of the 2d.

Proceeding toward the Angostura, from the Maypu, every quarter of a mile exhibited increase in the extent of the injury done; and within a league of it, the destruction was excessive. Not only had houses, walls, and division lines been more completely destroyed than about the capital, but losses had been more universal. Neither dimension nor material of wall had saved it; those of adobe, 30 inches thick and extending round two sides of a parallelogram 125 feet each way, were perhaps broken rather more frequently than short partitions, though not so much so as masonry. In one case the back wall of an old store-house was lifted bodily to the north and set down two inches from its former foundation; whilst a short piece at right angles to it, forming a sort of abutment to its eastern end, was shaken down piecemeal. The wall stood nearly east and west, was of adobes eighteen inches thick, some 80 feet long and 9 feet high. Nothing but the roof, itself partially sustained by the stakes of an outer corridor, prevented the whole from going over. In the parlors to the mansion of this *hacienda*, things were thrown in all directions: lamps, chairs, books, fell in every possible line, almost inducing belief that the increasing resistance offered to the onward movement of the explosive agent by the rapidly approaching mountains, had converted rectilineal into gyratory motion. These objects fell in the several directions at different periods.

At the time of the shock, the proprietor was in the fields giving orders for the work of the day. Turning at the first rumble that reached his ear in the direction of the mansion, where his wife and children were, he put spurs to his horse, which had not yet become frightened. But an instant after, the poor brute suddenly stopped and spread out its feet, giving expression to the utmost terror by deep-breathed snorts and starting eyes, nor could any punishment make it move until the phenomenon had ceased. Apart from thoughts of his loved ones, this was a trying interval to my friend. Alone, and all nature convulsed! The earth heaved and trembled till foot-hold was not secure, its profoundly vaulted caverns pealing thunders stunning to the ears; the atmosphere was serene and balmy without a stirring breath, yet trees around were waving and bending half way to the very soil as in a storm; flocks of birds in rapid flight screamed their sympathy; and herds of cattle came tearing down the mountain sides, pursued by great boulders of granite, mid clouds of dust and sparks of fire.

Along the line of the road beyond the Angostura, there were scarcely any visible effects; and although the inhabitants of Rancagua say that the shock was extremely severe, there were only a few small crevices in the higher walls. If not exhausted to the northward of the gorge, the strength of the earth-storm had evidently passed to the westward of it, a supposition to which neither examination nor inquiry lent their support. The mountains *had* arrested the progress of the great earth-wave, and the re-action of its generating power was plainly exhibited on the alluvial stratum of the deep terrestrial bay.

Travellers from as far south as Talca stated that the shock had been quite moderate at that city, and none had given it a thought beyond the Cachapual, except for its unusual length. Nearly all of them, however, as did those north of the Angostura, believed that its origin had been to the southward. Whilst at Rancagua, a violent rain-storm commenced on the morning of the 5th, preceded by excessive thunder and lightning. This was a widely extended storm, reaching from latitude 33° to latitude 40°.

As nothing further was to be gained in a southerly direction, I returned to Santiago, and two days afterwards crossed the axis of the earth-wave in the direction of Valparaiso, though without obtaining many new facts to relate. The disturbance had certainly been greater at Curacavi and Casablanca than at the capital and port, much property having been so injured that it was necessary to tear it down. Repairs were out of the question, for the walls were no longer stable. One crack in the earth, west of Casablanca, at the surface, was still nearly three inches wide, and about 200 yards long. Its general direction was W.N.W. and E.S.E. The same fact was observed on the Almendral as had been remarked near the Angostura; objects were thrown from tables and shelves in every imaginable direction, as though each vibration was from a different quarter. No special agitation was observed at the surface of the sea, nor did any great wave follow to wash away prostrate buildings, of which some forty were level with the ground. One of the papers stated that a lead line thrown overboard at the time from the U S. frigate Raritan, was so buried in the sand that it could only be extracted with great difficulty; but this, like many of the wonderful stories told of earthquakes, should probably be received "*cum grano salis;*" else we must conclude that the ships, being unable to heave them up, probably left their anchors in the bay when about to sail. There was no indication whatever that the shores of the bay had been raised either by the great shock or the multitude of smaller ones continuing throughout the succeeding fortnight. I examined the rock shores closely during several tides, but could find no unprotected memento.

Mr. R. Budge, F. R. G. S., considers* the motion to have been westward, because water in basins, jugs, &c., spilt over the east side; clocks whose pendulums vibrated east and west stopped, while those beating north and south did not; walls standing east and west were cracked in every way—particularly lengthways, and vessels at sea felt it at an hour corresponding to the difference of longitude. He supposes the phenomenon to have been subject to instantaneous cessations, and says that it turned round things on their base instead of throwing them down at an angle of 20°, showing a circular motion for at least an instant. I shall have something to say presently respecting the two vessels which felt the shock at sea. He goes on to remark: "I have experienced at this place (Valparaiso) three ruinous earthquakes—that of 1822, which I passed in the house until the back fell, that of 1829, and the present. On the last occasion the barometer and thermometer indicated nothing, nor was there the least warning of any description; but, as invariably occurs after a heavy shock, we had, on the third day after, a shower of twelve hours' rain, for which I had already prepared, aware of its being the consequence, happen whatever season it may. I conceive also that I have felt less relaxed than before it. I cannot understand all these things, unless electricity be the agent; while the atmosphere must be affected in some way to shower down rain at seasons when, under ordinary circumstances, it does not fall. * * * * On that occasion (1822) the sea in the bay of Valparaiso retired considera-

* Report of British Association, 1851.

bly, and was several days in reaching its former level; while on this, no such thing was observed."

Only two vessels bound to Valparaiso felt the shock. One was forty miles southwest of the port, and the other a like distance to the northwest, and therefore they were some fifty-seven miles apart. Until he learned, after anchoring, that an earthquake had occurred on the morning of the 2d, the master of the former was fully persuaded he had passed over a reef of rocks; the other felt no shock whatever, though at the time designated the crew had heard explosions like distant discharges of heavy artillery. San Antonio, near the mouth of the Maule, and Talcahuano, both experienced a tremor; Melipilla, between San Antonio and the capital, felt it severely. There was a violent shake at Quillota, also, and San Felipe de Aconcagua suffered some injury. Even the Copiapó papers mention a "*temblor*" on the morning of the 2d; but nothing special was remarked, and it passed as one of those occurring almost daily.

Efforts to obtain reliable data for determining the velocity of earth-waves meet with little encouragement among those with whom "*mañana*" (to-morrow) is proverbial, and who have not yet learned that a few minutes are worthy of appreciation. Moreover, people generally are too much alarmed when the shock comes. *Eternity* occupies more of their thoughts than *time;* and had they self-possession to record the instants, probably no two time-keepers in the city agree within several minutes. Of the great shock one Talca paper says, "this morning a quarter before seven;" the other, "at twenty minutes past six in the morning." Even in Valparaiso, where government has placed a clock visible to nearly all the town, the papers differ two minutes, though the custom-house clock was stopped by the shock at 6*h*. 42*m*. But here are the Santiago mean times at which the greatest shock was felt at each place, with its bearing and distance from the capital.

Name of city.	Time.	From Santiago.	Distance.
	h. m. s.	°	*Miles.*
Talca	6 25 00 6 45 00	S. 21 W.	112
Santiago	6 48 40.5		.
Valparaiso	6 44 55.5 6 45 55.5	N. 67 W.	64
Quillota	6 48 49.5	N. 62 W.	64½
San Félipe	6 44 12	N. 16 W.	45
Mendoza	7 03 18	N. 73 E.	105

No possible supposition will reconcile them.

For days—it may be said weeks—after, the whole district of country disturbed by the principal shocks was visited by tremors. At Santiago the times of four were noted on the 3d; only one on the 4th; two or three on the 5th; and so on up to the 20th; indeed, for several months their occurrence was more frequent than during the same period of the preceding year. Having passed from the afternoon of the 6th at Aguila, the hacienda of a friend within the deep bay of the mountains, there were opportunities to experience some of them in the open fields. Of two or three it may not be uninteresting to quote the brief memoranda.

APRIL 7.

There was a shock at 1*h*. 51*m*. P. M., which lasted twenty-three seconds, and was quite strong. It was preceded, *nearly twenty seconds*, by a rumbling noise that approached from the northward, and the earth had a very perceptible rocking motion. At Santiago it continued only two seconds!

APRIL 9.

From about 9*h*. 00*m*. until 9*h*. 17*m*. A. M., there were smart shocks, some of them very prolonged and without noise. They were uniformly from the northward, as I sometimes verified by an echo from the hills near the Angostura. Besides the number referred to, in the interval there were five others during the day.

APRIL 11.

Just before 10 A. M. (9*h*. 57*m*.) there was a very loud subterranean noise, but not the least sensible motion.

APRIL 13.

At 3*h*. 41*m*. P. M., there was a very terrific and long continued noise, its duration being thirty-two seconds; but on horseback there was no motion experienced by either of the three composing our party. We were unanimous that it came from the north, even before the echo returned, as it did on this occasion also. Birds of all descriptions were startled and flew away to the south; the parrots screeching most discordantly. The same long and profound noise was heard at the mansion, three quarters of a mile to the west; but there it was accompanied by much motion. Our horses were standing beside a stream when the noise was first heard, nor did they move a limb until after it had died away; but we did not perceive the least tremor. At Santiago it was noted at 3*h*. 41*m*. 40*s*. P. M., "a smart shock which lasted seven seconds;" and afterwards (3*h*. 41*m*. 53*s*.), "a pretty severe shock which lasted five seconds."

APRIL 14.

The noise and shock were simultaneous at 11*h*. 37*m*. P. M.

There having been few of the roofs repaired, when the rain-storm came, three days after the great shock, the damage to furniture, goods, and wall-paper of houses was very great. If to this we add the loss of grain not yet put under cover, and the injury to charqui, we may safely put down the loss in the provinces of Santiago and Valparaiso at $2,000,000. None of the extinct volcanoes bordering the disturbed district (or elsewhere in Chile) were opened by the convulsion. Señor Pissis, an engineer in employ of government, saw something resembling smoke at the summit of Aconcagua, on the 2d; but he thought it might have been light vapory cloud, formed by the meeting of the moist current ascending the western slope with the cold air at those great heights, which is so constantly seen about the elevations of the Andes. The clouds which thus form soon fall by increased density, are dissipated, and re-ascend to be again condensed; and this is going on from ten or eleven o'clock in the morning until late in the afternoon. This suspicion of Señor Pissis was the only one heard of. Tupungato, San José, and Peteroa were perfectly quiet.

APRIL 25.

Earthquake shock commenced at 3*h*. 28*m*. 12*s*. P. M., was most violent at 3*h*. 28*m*. 22*s*., and ended at 3*h*. 28*m*. 42*s*. Though long, it was not severe; nor would it have attracted notice during the first ten seconds, but for the rattling of the doors, and the very audible rumbling sound that accompanied it, like a cart, coming from the eastward. The same shock was recorded by me at Valparaiso at 3*h*. 14*m*. 15*s*., or 3*h*. 18*m*. 11*s*. Santiago time; and it is probable that an error of 10*m*. was committed by myself or the assistant at Santiago. It was cloudy at the time, and rained next day.

MAY 26.

At 0*h*. 14*m*. 10*s*. P. M. there was a very moderate earthquake, which lasted nearly ten seconds. The wave was extremely long, and consequently its motion slow; for which reason the phenomenon escaped the attention of a large number of the population. All the city clocks were stopped by it. We learned, subsequently, that it had been very severe at the north; Copiapó and Huasco having suffered extremely from its effects. One Copiapó paper says it occurred there "about a quarter past 1 P. M.;" the other is more specific, and fixes the epoch at 1*h*. 20*m*. A number of houses were thrown down, many unroofed, and large quantities of property destroyed. Similar destruction was experienced in the mining districts, each about 50 miles distant—one to the S.E., the other to the N.W. From the fact that the injuries were greater at the former than at the latter, and also because of the estimated motion of the strong horizontal shocks, many supposed that the origin of the disturbance was to the southward. Others believed that it was in the Andes, or to the east. A great noise accompanied the vibration, which lasted nearly two minutes. It was said that a crevice, fifty yards long and eight inches wide, was opened within the city, from which water issued; but when I visited Copiapó, five weeks later, the account proved, like ten thousand other earthquake prodigies, wholly fabulous. The injury to property was not so great as at Santiago and Valparaiso, April 2; though its better preservation was evidently attributable to less elevated walls and lighter roofs. Between the time of the great shock and midnight of the 27th, more than one hundred tremors were counted; and, on the 31st, the Editor of *El Pueblo* says: "We have arrived at the sixth day of the earth-storm, and still the shocks cease not. Last night and this morning we have had at least six; two or three of which were of some duration and violence."

At Caldera the duration of the shock was much the same as at Copiapó, but it was not thought so violent. Afterwards, the sea ebbed and flowed in waves at intervals of seven to ten minutes, until darkness prevented its being longer observed. The height of the wave never appeared more than four feet; and when lowest, the receding volume bared the bay two feet below the lowest tide-mark.* It was estimated by W. W. Evans, Esq., resident engineer of the railroad, that 2,000,000 cubic feet of water passed through the entrance of the bay twice in every seven to ten minutes.

At Huasco, the shock was felt at 1*h*. 07*m*. P. M., when the church and many houses were irreparably injured. Shortly afterwards the sea retired from the beach with incredible velocity, until about 150 yards were left bare. Some of the vessels dragged their anchors, and one parted its cable in the rush. Of a sudden, a wave, more than ten feet higher than the highest tides, rolled to shore, inundated the custom-house, and washed out the goods deposited in its patio. This phenomenon was observed half a league out at sea, repeating itself many times and at short intervals.

An official letter to the Minister of the Interior, from the governor of Freirina, (three or four leagues east of Huasco,) says, that the earthquake occurred there *about* a quarter past 1 P. M., that it was more severe than the oldest persons remembered for above fifty years, and that the duration of its greatest violence was more than a minute. Some houses were prostrated, and many walls broken; but no mention is made of the supposed direction from which the disturbance came. Up to the hour of writing—at the close of the second day—the phenomenon was repeated at short intervals.

The governor says, it took place in Vallenar (thirty miles in an air-line E.S.E. from Freirina) at 1*h*. 42*m*., that the total duration of the oscillation was three minutes, and that of the greatest violence fifteen seconds. Every house was much deteriorated, and some wholly ruined. Shocks were repeated at intervals during the remainder of the day and night.

At Serena its duration was a minute and a half, and it was so sharp that all the inhabitants took to the streets, though no injury to property resulted. It occurred at 1*h*. 17*m*. P. M., and

* The rise and fall of the tide here is 5 feet.

came from the north, or is so stated to have done by the Intendente. Señor Troncoso was absent. This was the last great shock during our stay in Chile. For further details of it, and also of the April earthquakes, the reader may consult Appendix A.

There were, however, two or three lesser tremors, which merit attention. The first of these was on the night of November 15th, 1851, whilst I was looking with the equatorial telescope at the moon, whose apparent motion from north to south was through quite four minutes of arc. I was unable to detect the least diagonal displacement, other than the tremor inseparable from such disturbance of the base of the instrument. It lasted seven seconds. Owing to a strong wind blowing in at the door of the observatory, the direction of the rumbling noise accompanying it was not distinguishable. Perhaps a similar sight—the vision of terrestrial convulsion under a magnifying power of 235 times—may never occur again in all my life.

MAY 31, 1852.

There was a slight shock about 11*h*. 30*m*. A. M., which was felt at Valparaiso at the *same time.*

JULY 5.

The earth was agitated from 0*h*. 41*m*. 03*s*. to 0*h*. 41*m*. 38*s*. P. M. Its motion was apparently to the southward, in the direction of the longer axis of Santa Lucia, though the meridian circle oscillated tremblingly in the transverse direction through more than a quarter of an inch. The bottle of mercury kept for nadir determinations was shaken so uniformly that it would not serve as a guide to the origin of the disturbing force. The agitation of the surface of the mercury was rather due to a succession of rapid impulses than a series of waves of much amplitude.

AUGUST 12.

A line of telegraph (magneto-electric) having been erected between Santiago and Valparaiso, the operating director very kindly consented to adopt an earthquake signal. This signal was to be struck at the commencement of a tremor at either end of the line, and the time, noted at the other end, between the receipt of the signal and arrival of the shock, was to be immediately compared by Mr. Mouat's (astronomical) or the observatory clock on Santa Lucia. This was the first we had had an opportunity to observe, and it was more than commonly severe. With an intermission of two seconds, the earth continued in motion from 11*h*. 58*m*. 32*s*. until 11*h*. 59*m*. 10*s*. A. M.; the second shock having been longest and sharpest. The noise was heard to the N.W. But that which was of most interest was the fact established by the telegraph—*two cities*, 64 *miles apart, had been shaken at precisely the same instant*—when the signal was struck in Valparaiso, the finger of the operator was on the key at Santiago for the same purpose.

Accurate record of most of the tremors that occurred from November, 1849, to September, 1852, are believed to have been kept only at Santiago and Serena; though it is well known that shocks are even more frequent in the province of Atacama than Coquimbo; and that as one travels southward they are less and less common, until at Valdivia months pass without one to startle the population. No doubt some at night escaped observers at both specified places; but when we recollect that the two are only 220 miles apart, it is a matter of surprise that of the 218 enumerated in Appendix A, only those of November 13 and 18, 1849, and December 6, 1850, were recognised at each of them. Stronger evidence of the limited districts to which the phenomenon is usually confined could not be adduced. Examination of this Appendix develops other facts also. First: That the province of Coquimbo is more liable to disturbance than that of Santiago, in the proportion of 139 to 69, these numbers of tremors having been observed during twenty-eight corresponding months; and it is proper to remark, had not Señor Troncoso been absent from Serena on the 26th May, 1852, the disproportion would doubtless have been greater. Second: They prove that there are no permanent centres of disturbance, the apparent direction of the vibrations varying at each occurrence. Third: A large proportion of these tremors are neither undulations nor vibrations, but rather rapid vertical displacements of the crust of the earth; almost, if not absolutely, simultaneous over the whole disturbed district. Our sensations caused suspicion of the fact, the shivering of our pendulum without oscillation supported the belief, the instrument of Señor Troncoso afforded direct evidence, and the telegraph confirmed it on two occasions. The instrument alluded to consisted of an inverted pendulum within a closed glass globe from which the air had been exhausted. The pendulum is a spiral made of steel wire sensible to very slight disturbances, and he frequently remarks, "the spring is opened as far as the top of the globe will permit, but the pendulum has no lateral motion." A very experienced English gentleman wrote to me on this subject from the mining districts of Atacama: "Shocks are sometimes horizontal, sometimes vertical; but the former appear to me the more dangerous. A few days ago, we had quite a strong horizontal shake that did much damage, though a vertical shock two days after, which to our senses was of the same force, caused very little injury. At the same time the latter was so strong as to throw the water out of tumblers and jars." Fourth: So far as conclusions may be drawn from observations during thirty-five consecutive months at one place, and twenty-eight months at the other, the season of the year has influence. The numbers in each season, with the average monthly number of shocks at each city, are embodied in the subjoined table: April at Santiago, and November at Serena, embracing the extraordinary disturbances of 1849 and 1851.

Earthquakes at Santiago and Serena.

Month.	Season.	Santiago.		Serena.	
		Quarterly.	Monthly.	Quarterly.	Monthly.
September	Spring	22	4⅓	45	2½
October			1		5
November			2⅓		15
December	Summer	29	4⅓	26	8
January			3⅓		6⅔
February			2		2⅔
March	Autumn	50	1⅔	30	5⅓
April			13⅔		2⅔
May			1⅓		4
June	Winter	26	4	21	4
July			2⅓		3
August			2⅓		4

Humboldt thinks we have no right to reject belief in "the influence of particular seasons, the vernal and autumnal equinox, the setting in of tropical rains after long-continued drought, and the change of monsoons, solely because we do not at present understand the causal connection which may exist between meteorological and subterranean phenomena."* Popular belief even yet associates them with peculiar meteorological conditions: many assert that the barometer is low, the thermometer high, the atmosphere calm and oppressive, and that the color of the sky changes just before the shock. The tables bear directly on all these questions; and whilst instrumental data, with other recorded evidence extracted from our meteorological journal, show that neither the pressure, the temperature, nor the hygrometric condition of the air *have*

* Kosmos, Vol. I.

influence, the preponderance of shocks during autumn is particularly observable. Nor is this peculiar to the tremors alone; for of the fifteen great earthquakes since 1570 which have been mentioned, two were in February, one in March, three in April, three in May, two in July, one in September, one in November, and one in December; or, distributed in seasons, there were seven in autumn, three in summer, and two each during spring and winter.

But because the earth does not evolve heat or moisture to produce sensible effect on the atmosphere, and thus announce the agitation shortly to occur, it by no means follows that the aerial strata in contact with it are not disturbed at such agitation, and that an extraordinary meteorological state does not ensue, explicable only as a consequence of the earthquake. Ordinarily rain falls in central Chile twice in nine years, between the close of October and commencement of April; yet there has been but one great earthquake not soon followed by a rain-storm, and, on that occasion, clouds and vapors (altogether unusual in December) wholly obscured the sun for days. Deluges of rain, with excessive lightning, followed also the Catania, Lisbon, and Calabria earthquakes.

The occurrence of luminous meteors about the times of the shocks seems pretty well authenticated in Chile, as well as elsewhere. They were seen before the Catania earthquake of 1693.* During the remarkable one in New England, 29th October, 1727, persons of credit affirm that they perceived flashes of light before the shock;† at Lisbon they were perceptible on the sides of the near hills at the third shock;‡ in Calabria, during the commotion; and in Chile, sometimes before, though most generally after it. We are, therefore, authorized to infer that unusual electrical disturbance is, at least, a consequence of the phenomenon. That it is the cause, has been argued by more than one philosopher, more especially at the period when our illustrious countryman established the identity of lightning and electricity. In an account of the earthquakes which occurred in England in 1750, published by Dr. Stukely in the Philosophical Transactions for that year, after referring to a discourse on electricity by Franklin, he goes on to argue that, "on the same principle, if a non-electric cloud discharges its contents on any part of the earth when it is in a highly electrified state, an earthquake must, of necessity, ensue." This theory of its origin serves him to explain why shocks are simultaneous over such extended tracts, and also why they are most violent in rocky countries. A like hypothesis is suggested by Dr. Donati, the professor of botany at Turin. Others, as Dr. Martin Lister,§ regarded the material cause of thunder and lightning and earthquakes as the same, viz: "the inflammable breath of the pyrites; the difference is, that one is fired in the air, the other under-ground;" and when we remember that there are no electrical displays in the atmosphere west of the Andes, we need not be surprised that many in Chile and Peru, notwithstanding the mass of testimony in favor of volcanic origin, continue to believe that equilibrium is thus restored.

Buffon's supposition, that they were attributable to the falling in of caverns existing in the interior of the globe, is pronounced, by geologists,‖ only admissible under one of two conditions: such cavities must either have been formed at the original cooling of the earth, and, therefore, would not be likely to sink at the present day; or they could only have been created by subsequent convulsion, implying, in itself, volcanic agency. Their connection with volcanoes is shown by multitudes of isolated facts, that might be quoted from many writers; though only Humboldt and Darwin have enumerated series of events tending to establish it. The former selects the earthquakes of 1811–'12, the latter that of February, 1835; prior to recapitulating which, from their writings, three or four individual instances may be mentioned, of more than ordinary interest because of the magnitude of their consequences.

On the 29th September, 1759, after eighty days of earthquakes and subterranean thunders, the volcano of Jorullo (Mexico) burst out, increasing the height of its crater nearly 1,700 feet, and elevating 24 to 30 square miles several feet above the surrounding plain. Vesuvius exhi-

* Philosophical Transactions, Vol. XVII. † Ibid., Vol. XXXIX. ‡ Ibid., Vol. XLIX. § Ibid., Vol. XIV.

‖ Daubeny: On volcanoes. Second edition, 1844.

bited a very uncommon appearance, in the column of smoke proceeding from it during the Lisbon earthquake; Stromboli, for the first time in the memory of man, was quiet in 1783; and the closing of the vent in Pasto was followed by the earthquake of Riobamba, in which 40,000 persons perished.* Humboldt's series† commences with the formation of a new island in the Azores, at a spot where 40 fathoms water existed previously. In February, 1811, a volcano, accompanied by violent earthquakes, burst from the sea near the west end of St. Michael's, and in June following, after raging several days, and ejecting cinders and stones, the crater appeared above the surface. Two days after, it was 150 feet high, and ultimately it rose to more than 300, with a diameter of nearly 600 yards. From May, of the same year, until April, 1812, severe earthquake shocks were felt at St. Vincent and most of the smaller West India islands in the vicinity of that usually very active volcano. The Mississippi valley earthquakes were in December, 1811, and through the winter of 1812. One occurred at Caraccas, also, in December; the city was destroyed in March, and the earth continued shaking until the 5th of April. Finally, on the 30th April, 1812, the volcano of St. Vincent broke out, with an explosion so terrific that the shock was felt on the Apuré, more than 200 miles distant, and subterranean noises were heard at Caraccas at the same time.

Mr. Darwin's series is as follows: There was a dreadful earthquake at Sabionday, near Pasto, (latitude 1° 15′ N.,) on the 20th January, 1834. Eighty persons perished, and the town of Santiago (Peru) was swallowed up. Sixty bad shocks threw down two thirds of Santa Martha, about the 22d of May; and there was a violent shake at Jamaica on the 7th September. On the 20th January, 1835, the volcanoes of Osorno, Aconcagua, and Conseguina were in eruption, and the last continued in activity during the ensuing two months. February 12th a very strong earthquake was felt at sea, off the coast of Guyana; and eight days afterwards submarine explosions, off Juan Fernandez and Talcahuano, accompanied the destruction of Concepcion. The coast of Chile was then permanently elevated; and volcanoes were in continued eruption, for some months subsequently, along the whole length of the Andes. November 11th there was another severe earthquake at Concepcion, Osorno and Corcovado being in violent action; and on the 5th of December Osorno fell in with a grand explosion.‡

The disengagement of water, smoke, ashes, sulphurous vapors, and even flames, at times, when earthquakes occur in regions where volcanoes do not exist, must be regarded as additional proofs of the connexion of the phenomena; and the frequency and now recognised universality of tremors, has been supposed to point to the deep-seated molten strata as their origin. At one time, those tremors which manifested themselves in alluvial formations apparently very remote from igneous action, and kept the earth in vibration for months successively, as France in 1808, the United States in 1811–'13, and Asiatic Turkey in 1822, remained as exceptions seemingly inexplicable. But, as the vibrations ceased in every case with the bursting out of a volcano, and there was "scarcely room to doubt that every active volcano is in immediate communication with the whole melted matter in the interior,"§ the identity of the forces seems apparent; and it is now generally admitted that elastic fluids, subjected to enormous pressure in the interior of the earth, are not only quite sufficient to account for these harmless tremblings, but also for those terrific explosions which devastate kingdoms.

Although it is probable that the surface of the earth is almost always shaking at some point, fortunately for mankind terrific explosions are rare. Moreover, experience has shown that most of them are submarine, and so far from the habitations of man that their effects are greatly modified before reaching him. That such was the case with all the great earthquakes felt in Chile, except that of April 2, 1851, is evident from one concomitant, as we shall perceive in the explanation given of them.

* Daubeny: On volcanoes. Second edition, 1844.

† Personal Narrative, Vol. IX.

‡ Geological Transactions, Vol. V, second series.

§ Edinburgh New Philosophical Journal, 1838.

The origin and phenomena of earthquakes were treated of by Rev. John Mitchell, A. M.,* as far back as 1760; and he appears to have been the first to appreciate and advocate the wave motion of the earth at such times. He conceives the impulse given by the sudden production or condensation of aqueous vapor, under the agency of volcanic heat beneath the bed of the ocean, and that the motion of the earth is due to a wave propagated along its surface from a point where it was produced by this impulse. On the supposition that the crust, filled with cavities and fissures, floats on molten matter, he goes on to say: "As a small quantity of vapor, almost instantly generated at some considerable depth below the surface of the earth, will produce a vibratory motion, so a very large quantity (whether it be generated almost instantly or in any small portion of time) will produce a wave-like motion. The manner in which this wave-like motion will be propagated may in some measure be represented by the following experiment. Suppose a large cloth or carpet, spread on the floor, to be raised at one edge, and then suddenly brought down again to the floor, the air under it, being by this means propelled, will pass along till it escapes at the opposite side, raising the cloth in a wave all the way as it goes. In like manner a large quantity of vapor may be conceived to raise the earth in a wave as it passes along between the strata, which it may easily separate in a horizontal direction, there being little or no cohesion between one stratum and another. The part of the earth that is first raised, being bent from its natural form, will endeavor to restore itself by its elasticity; and the parts next to it, beginning to have their weight supported by the vapor which will insinuate itself under them, will be raised in their turn, till it either finds some vent, or is again condensed by the cold into water,† and by that means prevented from proceeding any further." Recognising the sea-waves following earthquakes as due to the undulations given to the ocean water at the point directly over that at which the primary terrestrial wave originates, he suggests the determination of the centre of disturbance by observations of the direction and times at which several waves reach different stations.

In 1846 Mr. Mallet, then president of the Geological Society of Ireland, collated the mass of facts furnished in narratives of earthquakes, and educed from them a theory of motions more consonant with the known laws of mechanics. A paper "On the Dynamics of Earthquakes," replete with interest, may be found in volume XXI of *Transactions of the Royal Irish Academy*, directions for scientific inquiry in the *Admiralty Manual* of 1849, and several subsequent investigations and elaborations of the same subject by him in the *Reports of the British Association*. In one of the last-mentioned volumes—viz: that for 1847—there is also a detailed report on the "Geological theories of elevation and earthquakes," by Wm. Hopkins, Esq., in the second section of which he discusses, with much detail, the vibratory motions of the earth's crust produced by subterranean forces.

Mallet conceives that Mitchell wholly mistook the nature of the earthquake, the mechanism advanced by the latter to account for the origin of the wave and its propagation through the floating crust being inconsistent with the conditions essential to that order of wave which the ascertained phenomena of earthquakes show to be the true one. He divides the phenomena into two classes, viz: those which properly belong to the transit of the wave or waves through the solid or watery crust of the earth, the air, &c., and those which are only the *effects* of this transit. Both must be kept distinct from co-existent forces, as volcanic eruption, permanent elevation and depression of land, which form no true part of the earthquake, however clearly they may be connected with originating its impulse. Of whatever nature that impulse, the phenomena that present themselves will differ according as its origin is inland or under the sea. If inland, we have, first, *the great earth-wave*, or true shock, a real roll or undulation of the surface, which travels with immense velocity outwards in every direction from the centre of impulse, and is finally spent and lost in the ocean; second, the *forced sea-wave*, carried into deep water on the back of the earth-wave. If the beach be very sloping and the water still,

* Philosophical Transactions, Vol. LI. † See also Prof. Bischoff, Edinburgh new Phil. Jour., Vol. XXVI

the former wave should have the same elevation as the latter; but such fluid ridge would scarcely be generated at the base of precipitous cliffs with deep water. If the centre of impulse "be at small depth below the surface, the shock will be felt principally horizontally; but if the origin be profound, the shock, which is propagated from it in every direction in spherical shells, will be felt more or less vertically; and in this case, also, we *may* be able to notice two distinct waves, a greater and a less, following each other almost instantaneously—the first due to the originating normal wave, the second to the wave vibrating at right angles to it." He estimates the amplitude of the earth-wave at several miles, and its velocity of translation at thirty miles per minute, so that it often takes ten or twenty seconds to pass a given point. During its passage a continuous tremor is often felt, which arises from secondary waves upon its surface, like the small curling waves on the surface of the ocean swell. When strata are fractured, or masses of matter blown away, at volcanic vents, then, and then only, (he says,) at the moment of shock, or nearly coincident with it, we hear *the sound-wave through the earth*, and, at an interval after this, *the sound-wave through the air*.

This does not accord accurately with many previously observed facts, nor with our experience. When Riobamba (Ecuador, latitude 1½° S.) was destroyed in February, 1797, there was no noise; and the detonation at Quito and Ibana, heard more than a quarter of an hour after the catastrophe, was inaudible at Tacunga and Hambato, both nearer the centre of explosion.* Nor did the least tremor occur, either in the deep mines or on the surface, during the subterranean thunders of Guanaxuata in 1785. These lasted for above a month; and for some days were "as if there were storm-clouds under the feet of the inhabitants, in which slow rolling thunder alternated with short thunder-claps."† It is only considered necessary to mention these extreme prior instances—one an awful convulsion without audible noise, the other an excessive noise without tremor, because analogous cases, though of far less violence, constantly occur in our observations. Subterranean noise, however, is a most general concomitant, its intensity and tone varying with every repetition of the phenomenon, though never to such a degree as by possibility to be mistaken for any other. When the crust of the earth is about to be agitated at any place, there is previously heard a sound resembling the roll of a muffled drum, faint at first, but rapidly louder, and then dying away in the distance beyond us. After an interval varying from one to ten or more seconds, the earth moves slightly, and is still—the violence of this shock being inversely as the time during which the earth-wave was coming after the sound-wave was detected. Within ten seconds another and more severe shock almost invariably follows, and frequently without farther rumbling noise, sometimes slow and wave-like, at others quick and vibratory; and quite often the motion is such as would result from rapid vertical concussions.

In the report of Mr. Hopkins, the mathematical laws which govern the propagation of vibrations through fluid and solid masses are ably discussed, and simple instructions and formulæ are given by which the centre of disturbance may be determined. But these formulæ are of necessity based on the supposition of perfect homogeneousness in the strata of the agitated district—a geological condition that varies in Chile with every step, and renders the application of his arguments practically impossible. That extensive tracts are disturbed simultaneously, and that the centres of impulse are not permanent, have already been referred to as sustained by the observations; and there remain to be pointed out the obstacles to satisfactory conclusions of either the geographical position or depth below the surface of the impelling agent.

The great longitudinal plain, or, more properly speaking, the series of basins on which most of the cities of Chile are built, are also diversified by isolated hills of stratified porphyry, sometimes rising to a height of 1,500 feet. Immediately bounding their west sides is a range of porphyritic mountains. From thence to the ocean, more than sixty miles, there are chains of granite, with narrow intermediate valleys and smaller basins; and their eastern border is

* Humboldt: Cosmos. † Ibid.

walled up by the great Andes, whose innumerable ramifications, rising far above the line of perpetual snow, yet belong to an epoch subsequent to that of the western ranges. Whether thrown up at one continuous impulse, or the result of successive upheavals, geologists are not yet agreed, and perhaps a fact to be mentioned presently may not be wholly without interest in this connexion. The immediate surface of the plain of Santiago inclines in two directions—from the Andes towards the sea, and from north to south. It consists of alluvial detritus, which, wherever penetrated, shows that water once flowed from north to south; and, as the porphyritic masses rise with moderate inclination on each side, we may infer that the depth of the deposit is not very great.

If originated in either of these homogeneous formations, the earth-wave will move uniformly in every direction from the centre of impulse, and arrive simultaneously at equidistant points; but the moment it encounters a stratum of different density, a portion is reflected, and another portion refracted, so that the times and directions at which it will reach each locality will vary with the density or refractive indices of the several media through which it has to pass. Where it passes from a formation of high elasticity to one of low elasticity, or *vice versa*, it will be partly reflected, and a wave sent back will produce a shock in the opposite direction; and it will be partly refracted, that is to say, its course onwards will be changed, and shocks will be felt upwards, downwards, and to the right and left of the original line of transit. But as the velocity of transit is probably the same as that of sound through the same media, and the surface of the comparatively narrow basin of low elasticity rests on strata of highly elastic rock, if the centre of impulse be deep seated, the contents of the basin will be constrained to vibrate as one system with its walls—the Andes and Western cordilleras. Thus, on the supposition that the origin is profound, until the thickness and composition of the strata composing the solid crust west of the Andes be determined, it appears a hopeless task to attempt locating the centre of even a violent earthquake. Taking that of 2d April, 1851, as the best example in point, the lines of transit determined with reasonable accuracy at Santiago and Valparaiso, if projected without reference to different media, meet in latitude 31°, longitude 69° 50′—a spot within the Andes. But we know that San Felipe, Santa Rosa, and Quillota, all lying nearer to this spot, were scarcely disturbed; whilst, if the violence of the shock be in proportion to the distance from the centre of impulse, that centre must have been nearer Casablanca and Curacavi than either of the cities named. That this was not deep-seated, seems indicated by the effects observed at the southern extremity of the basin, where the onward course of the vibration was almost wholly arrested by the two mountain chains, and the reflected shock was far more destructive than the normal vibration had been two or three leagues further to the north. Such may also have been the occasion of the ruin at Casablanca and Curacavi, which lie in small alluvial basins west of the mountain range that bounds the plain—the former at an elevation of 803 and the latter 633 feet above the ocean. Even more unsatisfactory was the previous 6th of December earthquake, whose line of transit was N.W. and S.E.; yet Quillota, 64½ miles distant, in precisely that direction, experienced only a tremor.

It has been mentioned that all the violent earthquakes of which we have reliable accounts, before that of April, 1851, were submarine, as could be shown from one concomitant—the great sea-wave which followed them. In accordance with Mr. Mallet's views, which are fully borne out by observation, when the original impulse comes from beneath the bed of the deep ocean, six sorts of waves are formed and propagated. *First.* One or several successively, through the land—the true earthquake shock or shocks. *Second.* The forced sea-wave, which is formed as soon as the true shock or undulation of the bottom of the sea gets into shallow water, forcing up an aqueous ridge directly above itself, which it brings to shore, and causes the slight disturbance of the margin of the sea often remarked at the moment of the shock. *Third.* Coincident with and answering to every shock, one or more sound-waves through the earth. *Fourth.* A sound-wave through the sea, which arrives after that through the earth. *Fifth.* A sound-wave through the air. When there is more than one impulse, or a single one extending along a considerable line of operation, passing away from the observer, the sound-waves will be rumbling noises, and may be more or less confounded from the different velocities with which they are transmitted through the several media. When no fractures or explosions occur, sound-waves may be wholly wanting. If the amount and peculiar character of the disturbance at the centre of impulse be such as by partial disturbances to set in motion waves of sound through the earth or sea, before any sufficient impulse has been given to propagate a sensible shock, the rumbling noises may precede the actual shock considerably. So also when the centre of impulse is beneath highly elastic crystalline rock, overlaid by soft rock and alluvion, the sound-wave through the earth, passing first horizontally and then vertically through the small distance to the surface occupied by the less elastic materials, will reach the ear quicker than if it passed first vertically and then horizontally. But as the earth-wave *must* pursue the latter course, the sound-wave and a slight vertical shock will be first sensible, and the principal waves some time after. This is precisely what occurs, not only during extraordinary earthquakes, but also at most of the tremors observable in Chile. *Sixth.* Some time after the shock, the great sea-wave rolls in to land. The impulse given to the bed of the sea originated this and each of the other waves simultaneously; but the great earth-wave moves with a velocity dependent upon a function of the elasticity of the crust of the earth, whilst that of the sea-wave depends upon a function of the depth of the sea; and thus the former immediately leaves the latter pursuing its slow career. Should the depth of the sea be uniform, the wave is propagated with uniform velocity in all directions; but where the depth decreases, not only will the initial annulus* change form, but the velocity of propagation will decrease, and as the wave advances toward the beach, its front slope becomes short and steep, the rear first long and gentle, then more and more depressed about its centre, until finally it separates into two or more smaller waves. These lose their equilibrium on arriving where the depth of water below the mean surface is less than their altitude, and, toppling over, fall in breakers on the shore. Consequently, where deep water continues close to the land, the great sea-wave comes in as a long, wide and unbroken swell, one such wave arriving for every earth-wave generated. But before it reaches the coast, the water retires to some distance from the ordinary shore-line, and then, after an instant's pause, the great wave rolls with fury upon the devoted land. Within bays like Talcahuano, Coquimbo, and Caldera, where the water continues deep only to the mouths, the momentum of such waves is overwhelming. Valparaiso, with deep water less than half a mile off the land, would only have a swell proportionate to the height of the impulse. The sea will then again retreat and a second and a third or more waves *of oscillation* succeed—the number dependent on the form and slope of the beach. As with the earth-wave, it by no means follows that the sea-wave will reach an observer with the same direction of motion as it set out. Such result can only occur when there is uniform depth of water between the origin and nearest point of the coast; at every change of depth, or deviation of the coast line from a tangent to the advancing curve, the direction will be distorted.

All the coast of Chile, Valparaiso excepted, has suffered excessively under the effects of these waves at every great earthquake recorded by historians until that of April, 1851. We should, therefore, have a right to believe them submarine, even without the corroborative testimony of approximate direction; and the absence of oceanic disturbance, on the last occasion referred to, is the best proof of its inland origin. That earthquakes of oceanic origin should be excessive, is readily comprehensible. Only a violent effort of the internal forces can overcome the enormous pressure in deep water. The heterogeneous formations of the coast, uneven in surface and broken by fissures, presents many weak districts which readily yield to slight accumulation of the disturbing agent. Apparently two such seats of disturbance exist near the coast of Chile—one near the latitude of Concepcion, the other near that of Copiapó, 600 miles to the

* The height of the crest at formation of the wave will be nearly in proportion to the reciprocal of the square root through which it has diverged.—*British Ass. Rep.*, 1847.

north. And it is worthy of remark, that the first continuously active volcano (Antuco) is on the same parallel with, and within 120 miles of the former city. Thence, southward, Ketredegui, Llayma, Llogoll, Villa Rica, Osorno, &c., succeed in rapid succession, which, serving as so many safety-valves to the great internal cauldron, probably diminish the number of earthquakes as we go south. North of Antuco the evidence of activity of any volcano, during the last quarter of a century, except the new crater near Talca, formed in 1847, and the solfataras eastward of Chillan, is by no means conclusive. Mr. Darwin says* that the volcanoes along the whole length of the cordilleras of Chile were in eruption, and so continued for some months, subsequent to the earthquake of February, 1835—quoting Mr. Caldcleugh, Dr. Gillies, and Mr. Byerbach as authorities, all of whom, except the last, had their knowledge second-hand. Within six weeks of the earthquake, he crossed the Andes by two passes, and must have seen Maypu, San José, Tupungato, and Aconcagua—four of these so-called volcanoes; and had he witnessed smoke or flame from either, so important a fact would have found place in his most instructive and charming narrative. Captain Fitzroy, R. N., writing at the same epoch, explicitly remarks:† "As to the state of the neighboring volcanoes, so various and indistinct were the accounts of their action after and before the earthquake, that as yet I have no means of ascertaining the truth;" and we have the evidence of Professor Domeyko,‡ that no active volcano exists from Copiapó to beyond Santiago. Therefore, in the absence of further testimony, I would suggest that the supposed volcanic flames or smoke during earthquakes, within the period mentioned, may have been only electrical displays, not unusual over the Andes in summer, and which were rather more brilliant than common on these occasions. Not only do three persons in five believe them volcanic lights, but editors of journals, whom we expect to comprehend something of natural phenomena, gravely publish paragraphs telling of the new eruptions. This was the case at the December earthquake.

The absence of such vents in the northern and central parts of the republic may explain the greater frequency of tremors there, and those concussive or pulsatory movements and vibrations, similar to successive fracturing of their rock strata immediately beneath. Belief that the crust of the earth is but a shell, and the origin of disturbance quite near to the surface, seems almost a necessary consequence, else the crust must be immeasurably broken by fissures, and the activity of internal combustion enormous. To the geologist, the loss of a few hundreds or thousands of lives, or the annihilation of man's choicest creations, are effects of internal combustion, unimportant in comparison with a continent uplifted or depressed, even though these mutations extend through more than the "three score years and ten" allotted to him. Numerous instances of instantaneous elevation and subsidence of great magnitude which occurred during earthquakes, might be quoted from the authors already referred to, as well as other analogous changes, more gradual, though scarcely less evidently attributable to the same agent. Indeed geologists acknowledge that nothing—not even the wind that blows—is more unstable than the level of the earth's crust; and such quotations would swell the chapter unnecessarily. We need not go out of Chile for illustrations: the sinking of a part of old Penco in 1570, and the upheaval of the island of Mocha and the adjacent coast in 1835, are examples of one class; the myriads of fresh-colored and unbroken marine shells that lie on the sands of Atacama hundreds of feet above the sea, and the geology of the Andes themselves, many designate as examples of the other. And this brings me to the fact alluded to as possibly bearing on the question of the elevation of the Andes; and our astronomical instruments have served geology, a *rôle* certainly not contemplated at their construction.

Santa Lucia, one of the isolated hills on the inclined basin of Santiago, is an oval porphyritic mass, whose columnar strata, resembling basalt, lie at every inclination from the vertical, *toward the west*, to horizontal. The side next the Andes slopes at an angle of about 45°, and is slightly covered with decomposed rock, on which there is scanty verdure during a few months,

* Transactions Geological Society, Vol. V, second series.

† Journal Geog Society, Vol. VI.

‡ Annales des Mines, Tom. IX.

and its western face is precipitous and nearly vertical, almost without a foothold for vegetation. Our observatories occupied a platform made by breaking down the rock near the northern limit of the crest, and 175 feet above the running water at the base of the hill. A foundation for the meridian-circle piers was obtained by levelling one of the strata *in situ*, and to this their bases were secured with hydraulic cement. Composed of three blocks, each pier formed an obelisk eight feet high, two feet square at bottom, and one foot at top. Shortly after mounting the instrument, its eastern pivot was found to be rising slowly though constantly, and at last an error accumulated that was inconveniently great. At first this was attributed to unequal shrinking of the cement between the three joints of each pier, and to the plaster used in securing the several adjuncts; but time brought no change, and within the following ten months the support under that pivot was lowered 49″.3, or an average of very nearly 5″ per month. Then followed the succession of earthquakes in April, during which changes of adjustment were frequent, though the records do not tell to what extent the screws were altered. However, it is very sure that the eastern extremity of the axis was never *elevated* by the screw. During most of the winter, and until August, the axis remained quite steady. In the latter month a motion equal to 5½″ took place in the opposite direction; but from the commencement of spring, and until the close of the following autumn, the same uplifting of the east pier ensued, so uniform in its monthly amount that the change of error from this cause could be calculated within a second or two. In seven months the support was, of necessity, lowered 45″ more, making 1′ 34″ in twenty-two months; and then, during the remainder of our sojourn, as throughout the preceding winter, the axis fluctuated about a horizontal line, with a tendency upward of its western pivot.

The two piers are from the same quarry of red porphyry, similar in form and dimensions, based on the same rock; in fact there is no reason apparent why one should change more than the other. How is this elevation of the eastern pier to be accounted for? Do the Andes still rise, as might a hinge, of which the coast line formed the axis, or is it only that Santa Lucia is tilting over to the westward? And if so, why do the rains of winter interrupt the progressive elevation? No satisfactory responses to these questions have yet offered themselves, and the facts are presented, as perhaps connected with geology and earthquakes. I cannot believe that any elevation so rapid as these measures indicate is going on; for the length of the axis of the meridian-circle being forty inches, its eastern pivot was moved nearly two hundredths (.0182) of an inch (1′ 34″) in twenty-two months; or, on the supposition that the basin of Santiago changed at a uniform angle, the base of the Andes rose sixty feet more than the cordilleras to the west—an amount too great to have escaped detection, even by the eye alone. Moreover, the westerly inclination apparently continues as it was thirty years ago, although it is well known that nearly half an inch of silt is annually deposited in artificial irrigation of the cultivated estates, and that the drainage from east to west is very great during the excessive rains of winter. One might infer that the two sides of the basin would have approximated to a level from these causes, even unaided by washings from the Western cordilleras.

Other effects yet more disastrous than the loss of edifices and property have been attributed to earthquakes by more that one writer. Public health is alleged to be affected; whole districts, previously fruitful, have become hopelessly sterile, and certain classes of trees wither and die of the poison which is imparted to the soil during the convulsion. With regard to the first of these, too little is known of the normal sanitary conditions of the several countries prior to great earthquakes to warrant inference that subsequent endemics were due to them. It is certain that there were more than the usual number of fatal diseases after the earthquake of 1822; and some of the physicians of Santiago* consider that the virulence of several epidemics—as dysentery, erysipelas, and aneurism—has increased since that epoch. That much sickness should immediately follow, is readily explicable from the influence of exposure whilst half clad. Terror, and

* Anales de la Universidad, 1849 and 1850.

consequent derangement of the digestive organs during days and weeks of excitement, will produce nervous disorders; but we need further evidence to establish as truth, that characteristic changes in the diseases named are solely attributable to this cause. Nor are the reasons for the supposed effects on soil and horticulture much better based. Certain tracts in Peru, permanently elevated or otherwise distorted by earthquakes, have been deprived of their supplies of water, preventing the irrigation essential to cultivation in that rainless region; and the oranges, figs, peaches, and latterly the grapes in Chile have become diseased, deteriorating and dying out gradually from north to south of the republic, as we find elsewhere in America and Europe. Formerly, the vicinity of Melipilla was famed for its oranges; now, scarcely a tree remains; and the *peste*, as it is called, is making rapid work with trees as far north as Quillota.

In conclusion, I may repeat, there are no phenomena which affect one so powerfully as earthquakes. The frequency of their repetition, instead of familiarizing the mind and diminishing apprehension, produces an effect precisely the reverse; and a stranger, who is, perhaps, charmed to experience the novelty, falls rapidly into the custom of the country, and flies from the danger of toppling walls with the earliest rumble of the subterranean storm. How keenly sensitive the ears become to the faintest vibration of this unmistakable sound is credible only to those who live in earthquake countries. When even a loud knock at the door had proved inaudible amid the boisterous mirth of a party seated about the centre-table of a parlor, I have known one of the number suddenly exclaim—*temblor!* And so it was; the shock occurring before all had escaped to the open patio. Others have a different faculty sharpened. Visiting at the house of a friend one evening, a guest sprang from her seat, uttering the same ominous word, and fled from the parlor. As at such times none wait to judge for themselves; all followed her, though neither sound nor motion became perceptible to us until some seconds after. Subsequently, she assured us that she could always detect a slight tremor through the earth before the rumbling noise preceding the shock felt by most persons, and thus could warn her family. So timid do many become that they never sleep with closed doors, as these are apt to become jammed at the first shock, and escape becomes impossible. An anecdote is told of a German, who saved the lives of himself and companions by a similar precaution. They had sat down to play at cards, on the night of the earthquake in November, 1822, and, from his previous experience, he rose to open their door, positively refusing to remain in a room where it was closed. The shock commenced before he regained his seat, and the house they occupied was shaken to the ground. Had their door jammed at that shock, they must have been buried beneath the ruins.

Sad and terrible as are the realities, the most marvellous exaggerations are perpetrated in nearly all oral and many written accounts of earthquakes. In the terror inspired by the exhibition of an unseen, mysterious, yet overwhelming power, credulity clothes creatures of the imagination with reality, and when time has obtained for such data a respect due only to facts, the inquirer after truth finds difficulty in determining which is fact, which is fiction. Something of this may be appreciated by comparing the accounts (in the Appendix) which the several newspapers gave of the April and May earthquakes with that of the preceding pages. Let us be thankful to an all-wise and all-powerful Creator, that he has exempted our land from similar dread convulsions, one of which, no greater than that of December 6, 1851, would raze the proudest city of our country to its foundations.

CHAPTER V.

THE GOVERNMENT.

CITIZENSHIP.—DEPUTIES AND SENATORS.—CONGRESS.—CHAMBER OF DEPUTIES.—SENATE.—CONSERVATIVE COMMISSION.—THE PRESIDENT.—CABINET MINISTERS.—COUNCIL OF STATE.—PROVINCIAL GOVERNMENT.—THE ADMINISTRATION OF JUSTICE.—TRIBUNALS, AND JUDGES OF COURTS.—RECEIPTS AND EXPENDITURES.—PUBLIC DEBT.

To be entitled to the rights of citizenship in Chile, one must have been born within the republic, or of Chilean parents temporarily residing in a foreign country. Strangers desiring to become citizens may obtain letters of naturalization by special act of Congress; otherwise they are required to declare their intentions before the municipality in which they reside, and undergo a probation of ten years, unless married and their families reside in the country, in which case six years' residence entitles them to naturalization. If married with a Chilena, the period is farther reduced to three years.

Freedom of suffrage extends to every male citizen, twenty-five years of age, who can read and write, and possesses real estate of a certain value (fixed by each province once in ten years), or who has a trade or employment, the income or usufruct of which is equal to the annual rent of such real estate. The limitation is now $200 per annum. These requisites being fulfilled, his name must be registered in the archives of the municipality to which he belongs at least three months before an election, and a certificate of qualification be taken out. His rights are suspended when he becomes a domestic servant, when physically or morally incapacitated from exercising free will, if a long-standing debtor to the treasury, and if under arrest for a crime involving infamous punishment. They are forfeited when he becomes naturalized elsewhere; when he remains abroad more than ten years without permission from the President; when he accepts foreign service, distinction, or pension, without especial authority from Congress; when guilty of fraudulent bankruptcy; and when condemned to infamous punishment. Besides the freeholders and artisans who possess the requisite income, all who are enrolled as members of the national guard are entitled to the right of suffrage.

So far as the property and intellectual qualifications are concerned, the law is a dead letter, or at least is openly violated at every election; and thus, whilst there is nominal republicanism, and a ballot-box through which public sentiment may be expressed, the result of every election is so perfectly well known in advance at Santiago, that preparations are made for it in all confidence. In the country there are neither small property-holders, nor moderate-sized estates, unless the summer residences of a few wealthy citizens may be so regarded. These, the miners, and the *haciendados*, who own thousands of acres, alone possess property outside the limits of the cities. As for reading and writing, it may be safely asserted that not more than one in five of the *inquilinos* or *peons* on the estates are able to tell one letter from another. To them the will of the proprietor is paramount; and as he furnishes them fictitiously with the property qualification, they, of course, deposit the ticket he supplies. The few who can read or write are without newspapers or books; even the Bible is prohibited to them. Knowing nothing of politics, or of the candidate or candidates, if by chance there be opposition to those chosen by government, and, if possible, caring less, compliance with what is desired brings with it neither sacrifice of principle nor bitterness of feeling. There can be no doubt that all candidates, even the presidential aspirant, was under control of the haciendados and miners a few years ago; but the law which gave a vote to each member of the national guard, and continued the appointment of officers in his hands, will, for a while, weaken their power over him.

Legislative power is confined to a Chamber of Deputies, and Senate. The former is composed of fifty-six members, one of whom is chosen for each 20,000 of the population, or a fraction of that number not less than 10,000; and the latter consists of twenty individuals. Deputies are chosen for three, senators for nine years—one third of the latter vacating their seats with each new Congress. Deputies are elected by direct vote. They must be entitled to the right of suffrage, and possess an income of at least $500. No one can be elected to such post who was not born in Chile, unless his naturalization took place six years before the election. This law gave rise to a somewhat interesting discussion in the Chamber, respecting the right of a deputy to a seat, he having been born in England whilst his father was in that country in a diplomatic capacity. It was eventually decided in his favor. Substitutes are chosen at the same time as the deputies, and these are summoned in case of disability or continued absence of the latter. On the same day, a number of electors equal to three times the number of deputies to which the province may be entitled, are balloted for; and these, subsequently uniting in college, elect the senators—to which post none can be commissioned under 36 years of age, or who do not possess an annual income of at least $2,000. The fact that candidates hold other commissions of honor and profit under the government is not a disqualification, nor do they resign such commissions on assuming seats in the legislature. Only those members of either house who reside without the capital receive compensation; and, as nearly all of both houses are citizens of Santiago, the government is at no great expense on account of its legislators. In reality, there were but fifty-three deputies during the session of 1851, the Minister of War and Marine (also a colonel in the army) being representative for two provinces, the collector of customs at Valparaiso for two others, and a third government *employé* for a like number. Fifty of these resided at Santiago; seventeen of whom, and ten of the twenty senators, held offices of profit under government. Nearly all the remainder were wealthy haciendados, or miners, and one a priest. Those who are paid for legislative services, receive three dollars per diem and their travelling expenses; but, as will probably have been inferred, there are many deputies and substitutes who have never seen the provinces they represent, government having forwarded their names to its officers prior to the election, and caused the ballots to be cast accordingly. Where the intendentes, governors of departments, all the civil employés under them, and every officer of the national guard, hold office at the sole will of the President, and wealthy landholders have a common interest in being on good terms with him, it is not difficult to perceive how such results are brought about. The members of both houses are nominally inviolable for their opinions and votes; nor can they be arrested from the day of their election, unless "*flagrante delicto.*" Every protection is also given them in the initiation of charges.

Each house has the right to decide respecting the seats of its members. The Chamber of Deputies only can accuse; the Senate only has authority to try offences against the state. Their sessions are limited to the period between the 1st of June and 31st of August of each year; but, for extraordinary purposes, with consent of the Council of State, the President may convene them at any time. There was no year of our residence without its extraordinary session; the subjects on which legislation was needed being specified in the precept which summoned the members. No other matter can be acted on at these times. Jointly, the two houses have power to levy taxes, contract debts, and appropriate funds; to control the annual expenses of the administration, and military and naval forces; to fix the weight and value of money; to approve or reject a declaration of war proposed by the President, or his resignation of office: they may confer on him extraordinary powers; create new provinces, or departments; establish or suppress offices; permit the national troops to leave, or foreign troops to enter the republic; and permit portions of the regular army to be quartered in the city when Congress is in session. Laws respecting taxes must originate in the lower house; such as refer to changes of the constitution, only in the Senate. Those passed by both houses, if disapproved by the President, must be returned by him to the body with which it originated within fifteen days, or, if so many do not remain of the session, then within the first six days after Congress shall again assemble. If not returned as prescribed, it becomes a law of the land. Should a law passed by Congress be rejected by the President, a majority of two thirds may re-enact it at any time within the period for which they were elected; and in such case it becomes a law, his veto to the contrary notwithstanding. Both bodies are required to close their sessions at the same time, the lower house having authority to remain, after the Senate has adjourned, only when sitting as a presenting jury; and the Senate, after the Chamber of Deputies has closed its labors, only when exercising judicial functions, or when assembled to count the votes for President or for members of their own body.

An oblong room in the old university building is occupied by the lower branch of the legislature. It is probably sixty feet long by half that breadth, has a high ceiling, three or four small grated windows in its north wall, and a door at each extremity. The walls are covered with painted paper, ornamented with medallions and panels in fresco. On a raised platform at the western extremity there is a table for the president of the body, as also for the secretaries and ministers of state, when they attend the sessions. Back of the president's chair there is a drapery of crimson velvet; and from beams ornamentally carved, which tie the north and south walls together near the ceiling, two or three cut-glass chandeliers are suspended. On the same level as the platform, and ranged opposite each other on the north and south sides of the room, are the seats of the deputies. Between them is the space allotted to the audience, from whom they are separated by balustrades, supporting boards placed at regular intervals, to serve as desks, though the only use to which it was our fortune to see them applied was the support of hats and canes. Writing, and the luxurious appliances to that end, deemed essential by North American legislators, are thought of little moment by republican law-makers of the South. Altogether, the room is tasteful, and its occupants—nearly every individual of whom, at the session of 1850, was in the prime of life—were properly grave and dignified.

Once seen, there is nothing to induce repetition of a stranger's visit. It is as unlike an assemblage of Anglo-Saxons met to discuss the affairs of the nation as possible; for there is no eloquence, no animation—indeed scarcely more life among the speakers than a moderate Quaker meeting offers. They never rise to address the Chamber; but a debater, turning to the president, says, in his ordinary conversational tone, "*Pido la palabra*" (equivalent to "Mr. President;" literally, "I ask the word"), and continues to harangue in the same quiet tone, without gesture, until his "*He dicho*" ("I have said") notifies you that he will drop back to apathy again. It is to be regretted that the like grave and dignified deportment is not usually observed by the auditors, and that the Chamber does not promptly enforce respect, by the punishment of deliberate contempt, too frequently shown by partisans. When the audience is pleased with the opinions of speakers, or takes an opposite view of public policy from them, cries of "*viva,*" "*à bajo,*" "*muera,*" (hurrah for—down with—death to), coupled with the name of the speaker or measure, are sometimes heard; nor is applause or loud whistling very rare. Such conduct in a little room the portion of which allotted to visitors is incapable of containing one hundred persons, is no less annoying to the deputies than disgraceful to the persons guilty of it.

For the first time in the annals of government, at the session commencing June, 1850, there was not only a decided opposition, but the two parties were accurately divided, and it was a matter of interest to know how the Chamber would organize. It must not be inferred that members originally opposed to government had been elected: indeed, from what has been said, it will have been seen that such could not have been the fact; nor had more than one solitary case ever occurred; and this was so remarkable a result, that it gave rise to many congratulatory editorials in the liberal or democratic paper then published at Valparaiso. The dissension and division of the Chamber originated in the removal of a portion of the ministers only a month or two before Congress met, the friends of the ejected cabinet officers taking ground against the President. Unlike the struggle for supremacy which had taken place in nearly the same parallel of north latitude only six months before, in order that the duties of legislation might proceed, a compromise was at once made, and the officers chosen. But rumors soon became current that each party was making an effort to win one from the opposite side, and, after the choice of a ministerial President, the audience watched with no little interest, from day to day, for some vote, or expression of opinion, to indicate the success which no one doubted. Although the administration soon obtained a majority, the session was spun out in talk, or, at least, without acting on many of the measures recommended by the President, there being still a sufficient number in opposition to stave off a[illegible]on somewhat. Meanwhile, there was a socialist club, (of whose doings at Santiago, and in the neighboring province of Aconcagua, an account is given in the sequel,) which furnished nominal excuse for strong measures; and within two months from the time that Congress adjourned by limitation, both provinces were placed under martial law, and seven of the strongest deputies in the opposition party were sent out of the way. One, a colonel of artillery, was despatched to examine localities suitable for military defences; a second, the collector of customs at Valparaiso, was sent to investigate custom-house affairs at Valdivia; the third, a clerk in one of the ministerial bureaus, was pronounced in delicate health, and leave granted him to travel in Atacama for its restoration; and the others, not being in government employ and thus controllable, were directly banished. These being absent, Congress was convened in extraordinary session just before the state of siege expired, and all the measures of the administration were briefly and satisfactorily passed.

The Senate occupy a room in the old consulado, similar in arrangement, and very like in size, to the hall of the deputies. Its walls being windowless, during the day it is lighted only through the doors and a handsomely stained window in the ceiling. As the sessions of this body are always at night, and the temperature at that period is grateful even in summer, there is ample ventilation, and the absence of other windows is of no consequence. The furniture of the room is richer than that of the hall of the deputies; and, from the greater age and graver appearance of its individual members, the aspect of the assembled body is more imposing. But, as in the co-ordinate branch, there is no forensic display, and no stranger cares to be a frequent visitor.

Ordinarily, the sessions of the two chambers are held on alternate days—perhaps to accommodate the ministers, who must be present, to answer questions or to defend measures; perhaps, because they are so little loquacious, that if the sessions were daily, they would soon meet only to adjourn again. Neither house often passes more than two or three hours at a time in session; and even during these brief periods, the Senate invariably takes a recess of fifteen or twenty minutes, in order that its members may have a smoke in the ante-room.

On the day before the close of the ordinary session, seven members are elected from its number by the Senate, to compose the *conservative commission*, whose functions continue until the next regular meeting. Their duties are to watch that the constitution and laws be observed; to make to the President such representations on the subject as they may deem proper, and to refuse their sanction or consent to such of his contemplated acts as are not provided for by fundamental law.

These guards and checks by the legislature, theoretically leave little power in the hands of the Executive; practically its working is quite different. In accordance with the letter of the Constitution, the President must have been born within the republic, and be at least thirty years of age at the time of his election. The term for which he is chosen is five years; and, as there is no prohibition to the contrary, he may be re-elected for any following periods of like length, provided five years have elapsed between the second and third terms. To the present time, the nation has followed the example of the United States, and will not extend the period of office beyond two terms. As with us, the President is chosen by electors, who are selected by direct vote of the people. On the 25th day of June, of the year in which the presidency expires, three electors are appointed for each representative to which the department is entitled, and on the 25th of the following month the electors of each province assemble at its capital to cast their votes. One copy of the vote of each college is filed in the municipal archives of the provincial capital, and another is sent to the Senate, which body is required to preserve the seals unbroken until the 30th of August. On that day the members of the two chambers meet in the hall of the Senate to examine the votes, and he who has received a majority of all is proclaimed elected for the next term. If there be no majority for either of the candidates, Congress then proceeds to elect one of the two who had received the greatest number of votes. On the 18th of September following, the inauguration takes place, with ceremonies which are elsewhere described.

The Chief Magistrate is declared to be the supreme head of the nation, and his authority extends to everything which has for its object the preservation of public order within the republic, as well as its external security. He is required to take part in forming laws, and to give his sanction to or disapprove them; to attend carefully to the administration of justice and the ministerial deportment of judges. He may prorogue ordinary sessions of Congress for fifty days, and, by consent of the Council of State, may at any time call an extra session. With the approbation of the Council, he proposes such laws to Congress as he deems necessary, and has the privilege of returning any act to which he objects either wholly rejected, or with such modifications as meet his views. He can appoint and remove at will his cabinet ministers, diplomatic and consular agents, intendentes and other officers of the provinces, and the officers of the national guard; but, whilst giving him power to nominate all other officers, the Senate or Council of State have a voice in their appointment; and, once confirmed, their removal can only be effected by trial for malfeasance and conviction. In other respects his powers are analogous to those intrusted by the Constitution of the United States to their President—he of Chile also being required to present to the Congress an annual report on the condition of affairs both foreign and domestic.

Should he assume personal command of the army, or become incompetent, by illness or other grave cause, to fulfil the duties of his office, they are to be executed by the Minister of the Interior, whose title then becomes Vice-President. At other times no such officer is known. If the President die or resign during the term for which he was elected, or there be other cause which will absolutely prevent his resuming the duties of office, the Vice-President is required to order a new election within ten days after the casualty occurs. If there be no Minister of the Interior, then the oldest minister takes the office, and, failing one of them, the oldest Councillor of State, unless he should be an ecclesiastic. During the term for which he is elected, the President is inviolable; but in the year succeeding his term, and in that year only, he may be arraigned for any act of his administration.

No specific number of ministers have been provided for by the constitution. At present there are four, viz: foreign and internal relations; finance (*hacienda*); war and marine; religion and public instruction. The first named is highest in rank, and at the head of the cabinet officers. No one can be appointed to these posts unless he has been born in Chile; is in possession of all the rights of citizenship, and has an income of at least $500 a year. They are directly responsible to Congress for every order of the President that they countersign, and no order or document from him is legal without such signature. Immediately at the assembling of Congress, each one is required to furnish a statement of the affairs under his department, together with estimates of all expenditures proposed to be made in the coming year. Any senator or deputy may, at the same time, be a cabinet minister. At the commencement of 1850 the whole body were members of the Chamber of Deputies; nor is it unusual for one person to hold several offices. One gentleman was at the same time lieutenant general, vice-admiral and commandant general of marine, intendente of Valparaiso, and senator; and another was senator, rector of the university, commissioner plenipotentiary to form a treaty with the United States minister, and confidential clerk in the Foreign Office! Ministers, whether members of Congress or not, have a right to take part in the debates at will. Being responsible to the Congress, the Chamber of Deputies may cause their arrest for treason, subornation, malversation of the public funds, infraction of the constitution or laws, or for compromising the honor or security of the country. Having made their charges, two deputies are appointed prosecutors of the trial before the Senate. No cabinet minister can leave the country until six months shall have expired after the termination of his office as such: within that period he is liable for every official act.

Not satisfied to rely on the judgment of the President and his cabinet, controlled as they are by the conservative commission, the framers of the Constitution have provided an advisory board for him, called the Council of State. This comprises the four ministers, two members of the supreme court, a titled ecclesiastic, a general of the army or navy, the chief of a treasury bureau, two persons who have previously served as cabinet or foreign ministers, and two who have been intendentes, governors, or members of municipal boards—in all thirteen persons. They are required to advise him on all matters in which he may consider their opinion necessary; to nominate proper persons in case of vacancies among the judges, bishops, or other church dignitaries; to ask the removal, for cause, of a cabinet minister or others; to settle all differences between contractors and the government; to examine and pass upon all public estimates, and all laws, as well those to which the President proposes to ask the sanction of Congress, as those passed by that body and sent to him for final action. Without their consent the President can neither recommend nor approve. They are appointed and removed at his sole will; but for the advice they may give him they are liable to arrest and trial, in the same manner as ministers. In council, the Chief Magistrate presides.

Four colonels of the army attend his excellency as aides-de-camp, whenever he needs their services; and a squadron of lancers generally escort him. On all public occasions, whether on horseback or in the national coach, he wears the insignia of office—a band or scarf over the shoulder, embracing the three national colors, and a cocked hat, adorned with plumes of the same tints—red, white, and blue. At such times his body-guard follow close after. There is also constantly a guard at the palace door, some of whom serve as orderlies for the conveyance of letters and despatches from the ministers through the city; and one of the aids occupies the ante-room to the President's private apartments. As the door at which the guard is stationed is the common entrance to various offices embraced within the extensive building, the presence of troops may be regarded as ornamental rather than useful; for none are obstructed or questioned at entrance.

General Manuel Bulnes, who was at the head of the nation from 1841 to 1851, performed the crowning act that entitled him to this distinction by his countrymen at the battle of Yungai, in Peru, just two years before his election. He is a tall, corpulent man, with a broad and expressive face, very decidedly more Hibernian in cast than Spanish. Though light, curling hair, a florid complexion, and jovial expression when in company with strangers, add their testimony to such apparent origin, he is, nevertheless, a very thorough Chileno. As an Executive, he proved prompt and efficient, avoiding no duty, fearing no responsibility. During his administration, and more particularly in the latter part of it, many measures were brought forward of the utmost consequence to the advancement of the country, among which may be mentioned railroads from Santiago to Valparaiso, and from Caldera to Copiapó; the erection of bridges across the Maypu, Cachapual, and Biobio; the abolition of the monopoly of steam navigation; and the reduction of postage on letters. Having served two terms, he was succeeded, on the 18th of September, 1851, by Don Manuel Montt, the first civilian ever elevated to that office—a gentleman who had served with distinction as rector of the national institute, as cabinet minister, and as a judge of the supreme court.

These are the officers charged with the administration of national affairs. For more direct supervision and control, the republic is divided into provinces, each province into departments, the departments into sub-delegations, and the sub-delegations into districts. Supreme control of the province is confided to an *Intendente*, who is the immediate agent of the President, and is appointed or removed by him at will. His commission can only be made for three years, but may be renewed indefinitely. He also exercises the functions of Governor over the department in which he immediately resides, and nominates to the President suitable persons to serve as governors for the other departments. Theoretically, the system of responsibility is perfect, every officer having the selection of the immediate subordinates on whom he is to rely for the execution of his duty. The Intendente must be native-born, or have obtained letters of naturalization at least six years before his appointment. He is responsible for the preservation of public order; the security of life and property; the prompt administration of justice; the legal collection and disbursement of the public funds; the public establishments of education, charity, or others; the administrative conduct of every functionary serving the public within his province; and, finally, for the punctual observance of the Constitution and of legal commands emanating from the supreme executive power. His services are compensated with reasonable liberality.

Any one entitled to citizenship may be appointed Governor, Sub-delegate, or Inspector. These are regarded as honorary offices, for which no salary is provided, and which no one can decline under a heavy penalty, unless he is more than sixty years of age, or already holds some employment with which such duties are incompatible. And thus most of these posts are filled by junior officers of the army, whose lineal rank is not prejudiced thereby. The Governor is charged to pay the most careful attention that all the duties of a certain class exacted of the Intendente be executed in his own department. He may arrest and imprison any one apparently culpable (except members of Congress, who can only be seized *flagrante delicto*), provided he file a charge with the proper judge within forty-eight hours. He may direct a judge to examine any one accused, or prepare an indictment to try him, and require the judges to furnish him from time to time with the state of every pending cause. For disrespect to himself, or disturbance of the peace, he may impose fines not exceeding twenty-five dollars, or, in defect of payment, imprison the offender for forty-eight hours. Especially intrusted with the preservation of order, if he apprehend disturbance, he may close any place of public amusement or entertainment, can at any time refuse permission for public spectacles or for the exercise of ambulant professions, and may punish police functionaries who wilfully or negligently disobey orders relative to this important matter, to the extent of one month's imprisonment. These are some of the arbitrary powers confided: a specification of all the duties demanded and privileges accorded him fills ten large octavo pages of the "*Lei del Rêjimen Interior,*" together with references to half as many more of the same book, embraced in the prescription for the Intendente.

Municipal affairs are intrusted to a board composed of *Alcaldes* and *Regidores*, elected by the people, and presided over by the Governor, who is also authorized to preside at the corporate meetings in any town within his department. These officers are required to have especial regard to a sanitary police, and the promotion of education, agriculture, industry, and trade. There will be occasion to show the distribution of their duties more particularly when treating of the municipality of Santiago.

Judicial power is administered by primary courts, three courts of appeal, and a supreme court. The courts of appeal hold their sessions at Concepcion, Santiago, and La Serena. No one can be tried by an *ex post facto* law, nor by any specially-constituted tribunal. Except in cases *flagrante delicto*, no arrest can be executed the order for which does not emanate from proper authority, and which must be named to the accused at the time; but in the excepted cases, any one is authorized to make arrests for the purpose of conveying the criminal before the appropriate judge. At entrance of the accused into prison, the keeper is directed to record the warrant of arrest on his book, or, if no such warrant has been issued, he must then present the individual to the proper judge within twenty-four hours; and a prisoner may require that a copy of the order for his incarceration be sent to this magistrate at any instant. In criminal causes the accused is not obliged to give evidence against himself; nor are his descendants, husband or wife, or relatives, to the third degree of consanguinity and second of affinity inclusive, obliged to serve as prosecuting witnesses. Such at least is the verbal guaranty of the Constitution, though nearly every trial proves that its working is somewhat different. The following instance, that occurred within a few weeks of the time when this was penned, is a case in point, and shows the course of law:

A travelling peddler was overtaken on the banks of the Cachapual by three miscreants, who, after binding him hand and foot, proceeded to divide his stock in trade, and make free with his edibles and wine more leisurely. This accomplished to their satisfaction, the question arose how to dispose of his unimportant person—one party being in favor of sticking a knife into him; another for tying a stone about his neck, and tossing him into the river like a blind kitten; the third was of opinion that it would be safest to bury him alive, for the stain of blood would be sure to betray them, or the body might be washed on shore, and in some manner bear evidence of their guilt; whilst, if buried, there was an end of the matter. Pleasant discussion this to the poor creature who sat by, listening. Finally, after dark, it was concluded to secure a big stone to him, and then hold him under water until dead—a measure they proceeded to execute with the utmost coolness and barbarity. Fortunately, as they trampled the body under water, the rapid current of the river whirled it from under foot before life was wholly extinct; and by one of those providential results occurring in the existence of every man, the peddler was freed from the stone at the same instant, and thrown on the shores of a little island rather more than a hundred yards down the stream. There was a ferryman residing there, to whose rancho he proceeded as soon as sufficiently recovered from the ill treatment of man and water; but as the former had often to deal with desperate characters, he had become suspicious, and would not readily grant admission to his castle at such hours. Convinced, however, by the appearance of the half-drowned peddler, that his story was at least partially true, a place of concealment was found at last; for the trio had freely spoken of their intended journey, and it was rightly judged they would soon arrive at the island. Fearing that their victim might have escaped, for the purpose of satisfying their doubts in this locality, it was determined to state that one of their number had been accidentally drowned. Completely deceived by the feigned condolences of the old ferryman, and his assurances that no corpse had as yet been washed ashore, they passed the night very quietly at his hut. Bright and early in the morning, and before they were stirring, the peddler was assisted on his way to the next town through which they were to pass, made his complaint before the judge, and, when the highwaymen made their appearance a little later, they were immediately taken into custody. Meanwhile, it had been arranged, that in case no acknowledgment could be obtained, the intended victim should be produced as evidence, under such circumstances as would startle them into a confession; and to this end he was directed to hold himself ready in an adjoining room, dripping with water, as though just from the river. And such was the course of the investigation. They were no less indignant than grieved that poor and innocent men like themselves should be charged with a murder so barbarous; and even when the judge stated he would produce the peddler, they were so confident that his body still lay beneath the waters of the Cachapual, they persisted in entreaties that his honor would not teaze humble and well-meaning men like themselves. Finding they would not acknowledge the crime, the door between the two rooms was thrown open, and there stood the peddler before them, bruised and dripping with water, as had been agreed on—evidence so sudden and unexpected, though threatened, that terror brought immediate confession.

There was sufficient evidence in the testimony of the accuser, corroborated by circumstantial proofs of occurrences at the rancho of the ferryman, and the identity of the goods found on the persons of the robbers, to have convicted these men, so that no actual injury was done them by pressing a confession of the crime. But the principle involved is the same in all cases, and, as far as could be ascertained, a similar course of examination is always followed. Therefore, in a country where so many others of the old Spanish customs continue, it is well that the torture has been prohibited.

No person can be tried twice for the same offence, and, consequently, when a cause is once decided, it cannot be again brought before a court. In criminal convictions, however, there is a final appeal from the judgment of the supreme court to the Council of State, and there are constant recommendations by the former for modifications of the sentences awarded by it under the existing laws. Indeed, for certain crimes, there are no instances where the penalties of the law are ever exacted, and it is difficult to understand why such punishments should still be threatened by the statute-book. One or two cases will be cited from the official law journal of the same epoch as the last, premising that, next to suits for the recovery of money, those which are the most numerous are for assault with knives, and rape. By law, the penalty for the last crime is death; but, in the report of every case read, the sentence runs somewhat as follows:

"*Against C. Ogalde, for rape.* Santiago, June 5, 1850. Seeing that the criminal, Carmen Ogalde, confesses having committed a rape, with force and violence, on the person of Carmen* Carthagena, a child of seven years, whom he surprised on a public highway; in accordance with the disposition of the law, 3ª tit. 20, part 7ª, he is condemned to the customary penalty of death, with costs. Appealed from.

"Supreme Court, Santiago, July 27, 1850. The sentence appealed from is confirmed; but, taking into consideration that the law on which it is based is not now in use, because of its excessive rigor, its execution is suspended, whilst it is presented to the President of the republic; this tribunal believing that it would be equitable to commute the punishment proposed, for six years of hard labor in the house of correction, with the understanding that, if the prisoner does not conduct himself well, he shall be sent to the general presidio (penal colony) to complete the sentence, which shall be counted from the fifth of April last."

The next case is not less remarkable, and shows how little regard is paid to the plain terms of the law.

"*Against Don Ambrosio Maria. Ramirez, for seduction.* Don Ambrose Maria. Ramirez was accused by Don Joseph Miranda of having seduced and committed rape on the person of his god-daughter, Doña ———, an orphan, of eighteen years, living in his house and treated with all the attention of a truly adopted child—Ramirez having accidentally met her whilst a guest in the house. The criminal denies the charge, but confesses that, before the event, he had asked the young lady if she loved him; that on the night of 31st January last she was surprised in his room; and, latterly, in a letter to his brother, he has acknowledged that he slept with Doña ———, committing certain frailties with her; which confessions import a legal conviction of the crime of seduction, with violation of confidence, there being no evidence to show that the said letter was written under the influence of bodily fear or threatened violence, as Ramirez alleges. The assertion of the accused, that he was provoked to the act by Doña ——— herself, is also rejected, although he proves this, by her reply to the interrogatory of f. 22; for the law, 1ª tit. 19, part 7ª, does not excuse the crime, although it be shown that it was by consent of the woman; because it supposes that the flattery of virtuous women with vain promises is a dangerous power towards making them badly use their persons. Rape has always been punished in Chile in accordance with the law laid down in Chap. I of the decrees of Gregory IX. Inasmuch as the penalty of confiscation expressed in the 3d law, 20th tit. part 7th, is abolished by the political constitution, and, in the present case, the criminal has not only committed the offence, but has abused the hospitality and confidence of the girl's adopted father, the penalty should be inflicted on him which is explicitly cited in law 2d tit. 29, lib. 12, Nov. Recap., to wit: that of death, and this sentence is imposed on said Ambrose Maria. Ramirez, with costs. Appealed from.

"Santiago, August 7, 1850. The sentence appealed from is confirmed; but, taking into consideration that the punishment imposed is excessively rigorous, and that the law which decrees it is not now in use, execution of the sentence will be suspended in the interim, until it is presented to the President of the republic that this tribunal believes it would be conformable with equity to commute it for eight years' imprisonment in the public jail, unless Don Ambrose Maria. Ramirez will either marry Doña ——— or pay her damages to the amount of two thousand dollars."

* Carmen, Jesus, and one or two other names, are given to both sexes.

The number of individuals and courts empowered to decide litigated cases of different characters may be judged of from the following synoptical table:

Table showing the Tribunals and Judges according to the constitutional division of the Republic.

Division		Tribunals and Judges
1st. Each district		The Inspector.
2d. Each sub-delegation		The Sub-delegate.
3d. Each department		1. The Alcalde. 2. Censors of the press. 3. The Governor. 4. Market Masters.
4th. Each province		1. Primary Judge, civil cases. 2. Primary Judge, criminal cases. 3. Law Officer of Treasury. 4. Commercial Deputy. 5. Custom-house court. 6. Public roads. 7. Military Judges. 8. Commercial court. 9. The Intendente.
5th. The republic	Everywhere	*With ordinary jurisdiction.* 1. The Supreme Court. *With administrative jurisdiction.* 2. The Tribunal of Accounts. 3. The Supreme Exchequer. 4. The Council of State. *With political jurisdiction.* 5. Congress. 6. The Senate. 7. The Chamber of Deputies. 8. The President. *With international jurisdiction.* 9. The Mixed Commission.
	In the greater portion	*With ordinary civil jurisdiction.* 1. The Courts of Appeal. *With ecclesiastical jurisdiction.* 2. The Ecclesiastical Judges.
6th. The republic		1. Arbitrators. 2. Practical Judges. 3. Family Council. 4. Juries.

Many of these, it will be seen, have no corresponding tribunals in the United States. First in order are the censors of the press. These actually consist of two bodies, over both of which the primary criminal judge presides. The first comprises nine jurymen, to whom is presented the printed matter complained of. Should a majority of them decide that there is cause for indictment, the accusation is made, and a second jury of three find whether the publication is blasphemous, immoral, seditious, or injurious—penalty or acquittal being awarded in proportion to the degree of turpitude. Juries are drawn by lot from a list of sixty names, prepared annually—those of ecclesiastics, advocates, notaries, and government officers, being excluded. The judge only may sit in both bodies: from the decision there is no appeal.

The custom-house court, composed of the primary civil judge, the collector of the customs at the place, and the commercial judge, is empowered to decide irrevocably on matters of confiscation for violation of revenue laws, to an amount not exceeding $300.

The consulado, or commercial court, comprises a prior, first and second consuls, three subpriors or consuls, an assessor, and a notary. They have cognizance of all disputes arising out of mercantile transactions of every kind, bankruptcy, and shipwreck. They may decide verbally, and without appeal, all questions where the amount involved does not exceed $600. Whatever the sum at stake in the suit, the sentence pronounced is invariably to be executed, whether appeal be filed or not; but in case of appeal, or other admissible recourse to annul sentence, the party in whose favor it has been given must furnish bond, with proper security, that he will fulfil the decision of the higher court.

There are ecclesiastical courts in each of the five dioceses. They have cognizance of all church benefices, chapels, divorces, nullity and illegality of marriages, nullity of (religious) profession, heresy, simony, and, in general, everything relating to spiritual affairs. The vicars general, or others to whom the bishop may delegate authority, are judges in these courts, for the exercise of whose functions, or execution of whose mandates, the secular authority is bound to render all necessary aid.

The mixed commission owes its establishment to the seventh article of a treaty relative to the slave trade, made in 1839 with England. Each of the high contracting parties names a judge and an arbiter, and a secretary or actuary is added by the government of the country where the court is in session. As might be inferred, this is an eventual tribunal, whose jurisdiction refers wholly to contingent causes.

The family council: When the parents of a male of eighteen, or of a female sixteen years of age refuse assent to marriage, the aggrieved may appeal to the Intendente, or Governor, who is required to summon five of the nearest relatives of the applicant, and preside at their deliberations, though without the right of discussion. The relatives examine into the causes of resistance or dissent to the marriage by the parent, and may confirm or annul it; but this appeal made, the judgment rendered cannot be departed from.

Judges are appointed during good behavior, except those who decide matters relating to trade, or the ordinary magistrates, who have specified terms of service; but even the latter cannot be removed during the periods for which they were appointed, unless legally convicted of crime or malversation. They are held personally accountable for bribery, neglectful observance of the laws governing the cause under trial, prevarication, or distorted administration of justice. Neither Congress nor the President may exercise judicial functions, advocate pending causes, or revive decided suits in any case. Nevertheless, as president of the Council of State, the Chief Magistrate of the nation necessarily intervenes in the administration of justice, conceding pardons and mitigations of sentence to criminals not convicted of offences against the State, appointing the judges of many of the tribunals, and watching over the ministerial conduct of these guardians of the law.

Slavery is prohibited, and all who tread the territory are free. Even traffic in slaves is forbidden the Chileno; nor is a stranger engaged in it permitted to reside in Chile. The domicil and epistolatory correspondence are inviolable, unless, in execution of law by competent authority, it become necessary to make examination. Personal service or contribution to the State or local authorities can only be exacted under specific laws—it being prohibited to every officer of the State to demand or receive them under any pretext whatever. No armed body may deliberate, demand aid, or make requisitions, except by the sanction of and through the civil authorities; and every concession obtained of the President, the Senate, or Chamber of Deputies by an armed force or mob, is illegal, and of no effect. No magistrate, person, or body of men, may, under any pretext, assume other powers than are conferred by law; and he who arrogates to represent the people is guilty of sedition. These are some of the rights and privileges guarantied; but when any portion of the republic is declared under martial law, either by the President with sanction of the Council of State, or by Congress, the constitution is suspended in the district specified. During the period, which must be stated in the edict, the only punishments that can be inflicted legally are imprisonment or translation from one part of the republic to another—the penal colony at Magellan, Juan Fernandez, or Atacama.

Regarding education as of paramount importance, the framers of the constitution of 1833 pledge Congress to prepare a general plan for national education, to appoint a superintendent charged with inspecting the modes of instruction, and to instruct the minister under whose control the subject is placed to render an annual account of its progress and all matters pertaining to it throughout the republic. And liberally has Congress voted money, year after year, to carry out the noble purpose, offering instruction, "without money and without price," to all who offer, whether at the primary school or the highest collegiate institution of the land.

Passing from administrative and judicial officers to subordinate agents of the government, it need only be stated, that the annual expenditure for those in its employ on the first of January, 1851, was:

For salaries and expenses of Congress	$9,857 09
Intercourse with foreign nations	56,456 84
Department of the interior	512,004 48
Administration of justice	206,559 22
Expenses of public worship	195,583 41
Expenses of education	249,626 15
Salaries and expenses of the treasury department	914,551 54
Interest and liquidation of internal debt	72,167 85
Interest on foreign debt	514,319 15
Salary and expenses of war department and army	925,171 95
Salaries and expenses of national militia	159,241 06
Salaries and expenses of the navy	264,927 97
Total expenses in 1850	$4,080,466 71

To meet which there was in the treasury, on the first of January of that year, $2,620,562 78, and there was received during the year—

From duties on imports	$2,627,442 47
Sale of monopolies*	718,777 01
From tithes	363,552 80
From excise duties	71,542 50
From tax on land	118,365 01
From patent privileges	47,087 00
From stamped paper	73,270 25
From profits of the mint	155,169 47
From post-offices	61,521 93
From tolls on roads and bridges	46,491 87
From auctioneers	4,050 00
From casual sources	47,044 31
Total receipts in 1850	4,334,314 62

The public debt of Chile, most of which was contracted during the revolution, amounted, on the first of August, 1851, to $9,155,975; on which the interest has regularly been paid for many years. This sum consists of 7,611 sterling bonds for £100 each, bearing six per cent. interest, and 6,961 similar bonds bearing 3 per cent. interest, all of which were negotiated in England. The original loan, obtained in 1822, was one million pounds sterling, at an interest

* Tobacco and playing-cards.

of six per cent.; but payment of interest having been withheld for a long time, a compromise was effected with the creditors in 1842, by which the debt was settled at $8,452,700, divided into stocks of two rates; and a sinking fund was to be created, from which Chile was to redeem its obligations at the current prices. Of the Anglo-Chilean loan, a million and a half of dollars was yielded to Peru, to aid in its struggles for republican government; and on this no interest has been paid. In 1852, Congress authorized President Montt to hypothecate both debt and interest in favor of the railroad between Santiago and Valparaiso. Punctual in the fulfilment of its own obligations even amid civil war, Chile deservedly stands well on 'Change, and its bonds (6's) are constantly quoted above their par value.

The internal debt ($1,869,975) has been incurred at various times, and the rates of interest paid are from three to ten per cent.—twelve per cent. being the common and legal rate in mercantile transactions. There is a sinking fund in operation for the liquidation of this obligation also; and, as the revenues exceed the current expenses already, it is reasonable to suppose that the means at disposal for this purpose will increase in rapid ratio with the grand improvements in intercommunication commenced under the auspices of the late President. Few nations have shown such broad and liberal views, such meritoriously emulous desire to command the admiration of contemporaries. Presenting to mankind the spectacle of stable and systematic government, unsurpassed climate and soil, a profitable market for foreign and domestic products, protection to all industrial pursuits, more than regal patronage to science and art, but two further acts of its legislature seem necessary to advance the moral and physical wealth and population in unprecedented ratios. These are: abolition of tithe laws and the exclusive church; both of which, as at present administered, are demoralizing and suicidal to a degree appreciable only by those who long to see Chile occupy the rank among nations to which numbers, culture, liberal institutions, and wealth would entitle her.

CHAPTER VI.

SOCIETY.

INTRODUCTION OF STRANGERS.—VISITS.—DRESS.—EVENING TERTULIAS.—GOSSIP.—NONE MOLEST LADIES IN THE STREET AFTER NIGHT.—COURTSHIPS.—FORCED MARRIAGES.—A MARRIAGE.—BIRTHS.—A CHRISTENING.—SOCIAL EDUCATION OF CHILDREN.—GIRLS.—BOYS.—NATIONAL CHARACTERISTICS.—DEATH.—A FUNERAL.—VISITS OF CONDOLENCE.

Though letters of introduction are not absolutely indispensable to obtain for one access to the first circles of society, still, as in every other country, they greatly facilitate the intercourse of a stranger at the capital, whether he come from abroad or from one of the provinces. If he has no letters, there is a degree of form observed in his presentation, even among most intimate friends; no one presuming to introduce a chance acquaintance without first ascertaining whether it will be agreeable, and asking that an hour be named for his reception. On arrival, one is welcomed by the host, in the courtly style of his ancestors, who "celebrates greatly acquaintance with you," and, when about to make your *congé*, after a reasonable time, you are assured that "the house, and all it contains, are wholly at your service." Very pretty phrases these in that sonorous language, and, though one may surmise them really meaningless, they are very pleasant to hear.

If the stranger has neither letters nor acquaintances, and awaits courtesy from the male residents, it is probable he will lead a solitary life at Santiago, for this virtue is yet in its infancy among them. Indeed, gentlemen rarely make more than one or two visits to strangers who do bring letters to them, but consider their obligations fulfilled when these ceremonious calls have been made, and the new comer has been presented at the *tertulia* of his wife and daughters. Their habits and dispositions make them averse to intercourse with foreigners generally, of whom they are undoubtedly jealous, as well because of the superior education, intelligence, and energy of the latter, as on account of the preference which their countrywomen exhibit for their society. Of course, there are many individuals not to be numbered with these—gentlemen who appreciate the customs of the Old World, and seek opportunities to exercise kindness and hospitality to those whose position or deportment indicate them as entitled to such attentions. It is a source of regret, however, for one to confess, that nearly every member of this class has passed years abroad, either in travel or at school. Whether the custom has arisen from the indifference shown by their husbands and relations towards strangers, or other causes, cannot be very readily ascertained; but there are many ladies in the highest circles who endeavor to make amends for this want of attention by sending their own cards as soon as it is ascertained that the new comer is worthy to mix in their society. It is also quite customary for a husband to leave the wife's card, with his own, at the first visit of ceremony, thus showing a desire to have you become acquainted with his family.

From 2 o'clock until 4½ P. M. of Sunday is the most fashionable period for visits. Every one is prepared to receive company at that time, and, though the proprietress may not contemplate going beyond the square in which she resides, the carriage, which cumbers its house all the rest of the week, must be dragged out on these occasions. In the cool hours of other evenings during the week, she will probably ramble over half the town on foot; but it is fashionable to appear in the *calesa* on Sunday, and out it must come, even though one borrow a driver from a neighbor. Visits of ceremony and compliment are common among acquaintances, and permissible by strangers, at the hour of *oracion* also, that is, just at dusk; whilst those intended to be sociable are at 9 or 10 o'clock P. M., according as the season may be summer or winter. In the latter case, the party will not separate before midnight, and, if specially invited, perhaps not until after daylight. To insure its baptism, a child must have as one of its names that of some saint, and, on the anniversary of the day which the church calendar assigns to the canonized individual, friends call to felicitate the "namesakes" of the holy one. A failure to call, or at least to send a card, on these occasions, is considered a special slight. The actual birthday anniversary is never remembered. Those more intimate send presents of flowers, ornamental pastilles, or other pretty fancy articles prepared and sold by the nuns; and the family assemble to dine and pass the evening together. No greater proof of their regard and confidence can be shown than an invitation to make one of this family circle.

As the parlors have windows facing the front patio, a light seen through them is all the evidence one needs that the mistress of the mansion is at home. True, there is a man-servant in the lodge under the archway at the street door, of whom inquiry might be made; but he is rather a guard to the castle than its Mercury, and one takes no notice of him. The door of the saloon will most probably be found open, except during the winter months, and, as it is not customary to knock or to ask for the family, the visitor enters, places his hat in the most convenient corner, and proceeds to salute the hostess about the centre-table or sofa. Only one or two "would-be exquisites," who returned to Chile subsequent to our arrival, annoyed themselves by nursing their hats, and none but servants or "*gringos*," like ourselves, ever announced their coming by a knock; presence in the saloon was quite sufficient evidence that the ladies were ready to receive you, and needed no warning. Be it summer or winter—a matron or a maiden that you visit; no matter how costly the material of her dress, how exquisite the taste of its colors or the beauty of its adaptation to the person—you will find every female with a shawl about her. Nor are they laid aside except when dancing, and these are the only times when their really beautiful forms can be seen. Muffled in these parlor abominations, one sees neither bust, nor arms, nor even hands: whether it was because I had forgotten the appearance of taper fingers, or fancied, from their eternal concealment, that Santiaguinas must possess ungraceful ones, cannot now be decided; but, if one must pronounce on the few that were accidentally visible, it is feared many could not be selected as models for sculptors. The very general absence of fire-places would be a sufficient apology for the costume during the cool and damp nights of winter, or if it was intended as a modest effort to conceal "a very interesting condition" at times. But neither of these apologies is available, for they persevere in its use even when complaining of intolerable heat in summer; and there are few who will hesitate to talk to you of her *embarazo*—not immodestly, with boastfulness, or levity, but simply as one of the events of life that may explain the tooth-ache or other ill under which she may be suffering. Indeed, if the shawl were evidence of such "interesting condition," we should number within the category every female in Santiago above twelve years old.

Whether for the parlor, the ball-room, or the street, all Chilenas dress with taste; the unmarried plainly, those who have quitted that estate often with costliness and elegance—a *passion* for diamonds and fine jewels belonging to all the daughters of Eve. Formerly, there existed only costumes copied from their Spanish ancestors or those modelled after their fatherland, modified by peculiarities of their climate. Now, French *modistes* have invaded the land, and have almost wholly expelled national characteristics, substituting Parisian styles in their stead. Even the custom of covering the head with a black-lace mantilla only, kept up in old Spain to the present day, and to which the ladies are probably indebted for such beautiful hair, has almost become extinct at Santiago, and the promenades are now filled with those disfigurers of the human face—French bonnets. The black church-dress, with its long, gracefully worn *manto,* are all that is national remaining; the priests having done at least one praiseworthy act in the prohibition of bonnets and fancy dresses at mass. The manto is of fine black wool or silk-cloth, bordered with lace or fringe. It fits close over the hair, and is pinned under the chin so as to leave the forehead and a narrow braid of hair exposed on each side of the face. One corner is thrown in a *negligé* manner across the left shoulder, whilst the remainder, fitting quite closely to the person, falls nearly to the ground. A more appropriate costume for the place—a more becoming dress, one better calculated to show graceful carriage to advantage or lend a charm to even a plain face—cannot easily be devised. But let us return to the parlor.

Should you have gone early, and the lady of the house be still occupied with domestic concerns, her parlor lamps unlighted, no embarrassment is evinced, no ill-at-ease manner or apology, no calling of servants (and bells are unknown); but she quietly lights the lamp in the adjoining saloon herself, and invites you off to it. By ten o'clock the *habitués* of the house —those who pass night after night there—will have assembled, and the tea-tray will be brought in, the Chinese beverage having so far superseded the use of maté as to banish it from the parlor. Very few visits will serve to make the hostess and her daughters acquainted with the tastes of a guest, and a cup of tea is prepared for each one accordingly. In intercourse frank and cordial as exists at these *tertulias*, one quickly falls into the habit of occupying a particular seat at the centre-table. By this time, too, you will be addressed by the surname only; and though the more frigid rules of your country seem to make the prefix of "doña" or "señorita" on your part essential, it is impossible not to be gratified with the degree of familiar and affectionate interest which is exhibited in their mode of addressing each other. A matron elsewhere regards herself as slighted if called "*miss,*" and will correct you at once; not so here—the grandmother is still "*señorita,*" if there be not intimacy enough to warrant the use of her christian name, the diminutive in this case being a term of compliment or affection.

Sprightly and pleasant conversation, with good instrumental or vocal music, are, very generally, the entertainments offered you. Possessing fine natural abilities, with no inconsiderable share of energy and enterprise, there are few ladies whose dispositions have not led them to cultivate their colloquial powers, and one cannot fail to contrast them with their apathetic and generally ill instructed countrymen. Of the better class, a majority speak French, and speak it well too; the necessity for this language being greater than any other foreign idiom, because of the number of professional men and artisans of that nation. Knowledge of music is equally common, and there are many fair musicians whose attainments are of high character. Yet the nation is not musical. The airs and ballads of the mass are "sing-songs" of the very rudest character, destitute of harmony or melody, and tiresomely monotonous. Among the *elite* the music of Bellini seemed to have few admirers, or at best would draw but a listless audience to the opera-house, when one of Verdi's soulless comic effusions would fill the edifice night after night. It must also be remembered that boxes are paid for by the season, whether occupied or not; and it was not a little annoying, when Santa Lucia occasionally permitted such enjoyment, to find oneself near a bevy of ladies who persisted in laughing and talking when Pantanelli might be in the midst of "*Casta Diva*" or some other inspiration of the great master. At home, however, a lady will promptly comply with one's solicitation for music, and sing or play as long as you continue to desire it. There is no affectation in her deportment, no plea of hoarseness or headache, intended to be cured by flattery and importunity; and even if the piano chance to be out of tune, she will touch the key to show that the false note is not her fault: the request is deemed to have been made in sincerity, and she is pleased in being able to gratify you.

Towards midnight the husband will come home. Perhaps he may pass to his own apartments without entering the saloon; perhaps salute the guests of his wife and daughters, light a cigarito, and retire; or he may remain, to assist in their entertainment during the last half hour or so. But custom does not require it. He is known to be pleased that his wife's parlors are filled, and is rarely thought of. He has a circle of friends, whom he visits all the year round, where he plays *malillo* at a *medio* a game, or perhaps one less innocent; and, as a longer silence than usual seems to call for it, smokes, every half hour, one of those little packets of paper and tobacco, well contented that his family are enjoying themselves with their circle at home. Except the church, no place is sacred from the fumes of the cigarito: the parlor, the dinner-table between the different courses, the promenade, are alike infested; and if one is known to smoke the weed at any time, he is really importuned to follow the custom incessantly. It is presumed that the ladies have become "used to it," as eels are said to do about skinning; for it is difficult to conceive that the odor of burning tobacco is originally grateful to the olfactories of any one. Erstwhile they, too, were accused of indulging in the vice, and of especially favoring gallants by the presentation of a cigar which their own sweet lips had touched in lighting; but as no such distinguished compliment ever was paid to ourselves, we are envious enough to believe the charge wholly scandalous. So universal is the custom among the "lords of creation," that it is rare to find a parlor without its silver *brasito*, containing a burning coal; and the three principal promenades are frequented by boys provided with fire, which they offer to passers-by, in expectation of a *mediocito* in return.

Like an overgrown country village through which there are few travellers, and but occasional intercourse with the rest of the world, it is quite natural that Santiago should become a very hot-bed of gossip, if not of scandal. If a stranger of note arrive, there being but one direction to come from, it is known through the city by nightfall. Should he, in his ignorance of the habits of the nation, make a remark respecting any one, it is repeated through every coterie; and in this case, contrary to the proverb respecting the "rolling stone," so much moss is gathered that, before the end of the week, his originally innocent language may come back to him in a shape causing the deepest mortification or regret. At times, intelligence of the most trivial character is transmitted with a degree of celerity absolutely surprising, and it seems impossible for any act or conversation wholly to escape the argus-eyed and inquisitive public. With such a propensity to gossip, few families wholly elude slanderous remarks; and, in justice to all, one must discredit at least three fourths of the reports circulated. These rumors, or *presumed* events, are not generally talked of with malicious motive, or from ill-will toward the person, but from a desire to tell news; indeed, amiability is quite a decided characteristic with the most inveterate gossips among them. But, as might be anticipated, the predilection has disunited no small number of families, whose individuals, with bitterness at heart, are courteous and affable when by chance they meet in the house of another, though nothing would tempt them to darken each other's doors. Sincerity and affection are what they are most wanting in; virtues in which they cannot become eminent until a different system of domestic education has been administered to at least two generations.

If ladies are out visiting, unless some one of the young men is sufficiently an admirer to offer such courtesy, they come home at all hours unattended by gentlemen. Although there may be half a dozen beaux in the saloon they have left, they are rarely accompanied except by a servant; so that, if a gentleman and lady are met in the street together even after midnight, it would be safe to wager, nine times in ten, that they are not husband and wife. Yet, insults to ladies in the streets are exceedingly rare, and it is a source of the deepest mortification to acknowledge that Anglo-Saxons have been the most (in)famous in this respect. One to whom special reference was made by citizens, was a countryman of our own in Santiago some years since; another, equally notorious, an Englishman more recently a resident, both occupying positions which should have warranted ladies to regard them as protectors. Yet, if not guilty of rude language, there is an evident want of courtesy towards them in the street, on the part of their countrymen; men who claim to be gentlemen retaining their places on the narrow sidewalk, or, as often as not, taking the inside, unless the promenader happen to be an acquaintance. At the same time, if a male friend to whom he is desirous of showing marked civility approach, he will turn out from the instant of recognition to give him the inside; and a complimentary contest often occurs in the middle of the street, on these occasions, each one striving to make the other pass inside. In order to carry out an excess of attentive civility at such times, gentlemen often cross to the opposite wall rather than be outdone in their fancied courtesy.

In all countries where the Catholic religion is exclusive, the customs of society prohibit unmarried ladies from receiving the visits of gentlemen, or from being in their company unless attended by one of the parents, a brother, or married female friend; and Chile is not an exception to the rule. Whence its origin? No one can believe that the unmarried girl has inclinations or propensities which compel the mother to exercise this want of confidence, unless prepared to charge home to the mother such education of the child; and therefore that such is the condition of society in Catholic countries, reflects most vitally on the honor of their men or upon the tenets of their creed. Has Protestantism the effect to render the women of a country tolerating it more chaste, or are the men more honorable by nature? Which is it? One or the other, or both, it must be; for the confessional, that terrible engine of power, (and debasement, too, perhaps,) sways an irresistible moral influence. It cannot claim even negative absolution from the charge of interference, since none can deny that, through the mother, the confessor rules supremely over every family.

In the most important event of woman's life—marriage—she not only has neither right of election nor time to overcome prejudices, but is frequently forced to marry a man whom she has directly told: "I hate you; for God's sake don't marry me;" and that without having ever exchanged a word with him, unless in the presence of a parent. Yet, she is beautiful and has excited his passions, or is wealthy and has aroused his cupidity; and what cares he for her aversion? In one case, the honey-moon will scarcely have passed before he will be spending the evenings at his old haunts, leaving her to make her own circle; in the other, her fortune may enable him to live in a style long coveted; or, what may be still worse, it may afford him opportunity to gratify a passion for gaming. Though each was somewhat remarkable in its way, two marriages of a different kind occurred very shortly after our arrival. The first was between a young couple remarkable for their personal beauty and standing in the social scale. He was penniless; herself wealthy. They had accidentally met some four or five years previously; and though neither of them was then grown, they were "smitten at first sight." Excluded from the house of the father, every opportunity was availed of to visit her at the church door, on her way to mass, and at the balls of the philharmonic club, when they entered society. At the church he could touch her fingers, when offering holy water; and at the ball-room the dance permitted a few words of conversation. As he was known to have squandered every farthing left by his father at cards, as soon as her parents suspected what was going on, she was scolded, watched, and every possible effort made to prevent even visual intercourse. But he seemed ubiquitous; whenever she appeared in public, he was just so far off as to keep up her excitement and interest, following in all her walks. Wearied by his persecution and her obstinate liking for him, her parents at last confined her to her own apartments, hoping to destroy the predilection. Her health failing, a journey to Valparaiso became necessary, as the only probable place where the admirer could be avoided. Vain hope! on the subsequent day he was found promenading in front of the house they had taken, and within twenty-four hours had succeeded in obtaining a room on the opposite side of the narrow street, so narrow that he might whisper to his dulcinea from the balcony without being intelligible to the passers-by below; and of course he could watch every movement, so long as her windows were open. As their house overlooked the bay, the mother closed the front windows, retreating to the sea-rooms. Alas, poor lady! she "reckoned without her host." All the next day his boat was idling beneath their northern balcony; and as soon as night came, a serenade was improvised, to add yet more to the romance. Mother and daughter forthwith returned to Santiago; his importunity and her unfailing constancy had carried the day. Their marriage was consented to, for the daughter was dearly loved; but with the consent was coupled the condition that she was dowerless, and henceforth and for ever her paternal home would know her no more. A relative was despatched to the wooer with these items of intelligence, and a notice that he might claim his bride at the earliest moment. This was scarcely looked for: he was not prepared to act so suddenly; and, alleging want of income to support a wife at that time, he promised to marry her as soon as he should receive an appointment which had been promised to him from the government. And it so resulted; though not before friends, who were strenuous in efforts to obtain the office for him, had very generally joined in their belief that his love was based on her probable wealth, and the poor girl would soon be made to feel the difference between a rich bride and a poor one. Luckily for her, a reconciliation with the family took place a few months afterwards.

In the customs of matrimonial management at Santiago, though totally unlike the first, the other case was scarcely less remarkable. Visiting at the house of an acquaintance a month or two after our arrival, my attention was called by the mother to her eldest daughter—a tall, robust, and blooming girl, with hair *en papillotte* about a face half Iberian and half Hibernian, who was just entering the room; the mother closing her remark by adding: "*Y todavía no es muger;*" from which only one inference was to be drawn. Returning from a short visit to Valparaiso three or four months later, one of the first items of social intelligence related to me was, that a marriage was to take place immediately between a most esteemed gentleman and this very young lady; the story being somewhat as follows: The moment she *was* a woman, her mother, anxious to have her settled and out of the way of the nine or ten younger daughters already around, to say nothing of a like number whom she yet expected to place in the circle, at once projected a match with her own husband's brother,* an older man than her "liege-lord," and one in every way distasteful to the daughter. As the young lady had had neither opportunity to make conquests for herself, nor even time to attract visitors to the house, he was probably the only person who was immediately available. Matters were supposed to be drawing to a close, and the wedding was to have taken place within a day or two, when the gentleman previously alluded to called to make an early visit to the family. Finding the young lady in the parlor, sad and in tears, instead of sending for the mother as custom required him to do, he took a seat beside her to inquire into the cause of her grief and offer sympathy. Lamentations most bitter, at the cruel marriage the family were forcing her into, came thick and fast to the only listener who had approached her since the hated alliance had been made known to her. Whilst she poured out her troubles, his mind was not less active; and she had scarcely ceased when he asked: "Would you rather marry me than your uncle?" According to the account, this startling and unexpected question flashed a ray of light and hope into the darkened chamber of her soul, which increased to full illumination before the close of the day; and ere the week expired they were man and wife—herself scarce fourteen, he not many days short of fifty years of age! Nevertheless, as things are in Chile, he will certainly make her a good husband, for all the disparity.

The only marriage at which I had the privilege to assist was quite a private affair, and perhaps may scarcely serve as a proper example by which to judge of the ceremony. Presenting myself at the house of the mother of the bride punctually at the designated hour, I found that the centre-table had been removed from the principal saloon; its piano placed across one end, so as to occupy the least space; and the room, ornamented with vases of superb natural flowers, very brightly lighted. This room was filled with ladies, or rather, as is usual at gatherings, they were seated around three of its sides; from fifteen to twenty gentlemen occupying the other parlor. They were all either immediate connexions of the family, or intimate fellow-countrymen of the groom; one other gentleman besides myself being the only exceptions. *He* had acted as groomsman when the *mother* of the bride was first married. Neither the bridesmaid, (heaven save the mark!) the groomsman, nor the clergyman had yet arrived. The (intended) bride, arrayed in white, and wearing a single camelia in her hair, occupied one corner of the sofa, half muffled in a fur cape, as it was winter—a son, some eight years old, being presumptive evidence that she was "out of her teens." The groom in prospective, whom every one had set down as on the wrong side of thirty-eight, walked among his friends calm as a summer morning, a white vest only designating him as in party costume. Nor was the bride much more excited by the coming ceremony, if one could judge by the steadiness of her voice. The rest of the

* Marriages within these degrees of consanguinity are not uncommon. They require a dispensation from the archbishop; but dollars will readily obtain that. We might almost as well marry our sisters at once.

company wore dresses of such colors as suited their tastes, not even the young ladies appearing in white; and there was among them a staid undisturbed serenity, as though marriages were attended by them at least every day of their lives. Doña ———, the mother, was the only fluttered person present, or apparently so; herself a little fairy of a woman, scarce four and a half feet high, here and there and everywhere in a minute, and nervous as an aspen leaf.

Not expecting to find the bride in the parlor, I had seated myself in a corner by one of the elderly ladies, and was chatting quietly for some minutes, when the former hailed to know if it was my deliberate intention to pass her without notice all the evening, after having been specially invited to see herself and ———. Half an hour later the priest came, though, to my great disappointment, he had on no "regimentals," but only the long black robe or sutan usually worn by secular clergy. Yet another half hour beyond the appointed time the bridesmaid (*padrina*) came; and when Doña ——— had almost flurried herself into a fever, the groom's attendant (*padrino*) made his appearance. As soon as the last had been presented to a brother of the groom and myself, Doña ——— said to the priest, "As soon as it pleases you, these young folks will be married." The groom stepped across the room from his circle of friends, offering an arm to the bride, who laid aside her furs for the moment. A like service was performed by his attendant for her maid. The clergyman advanced toward the quartette, and we all rose to our feet. It may not be amiss to mention here that the bridesmaid was her own grandmother, and the groomsman the father of seven or eight children! Think of that, now! An old lady with a score of great-grandchildren bearing a torch at the altar of Hymen! Yet the custom requires that married persons be selected for these offices, and the "*padrinos*" are expected to make presents to the new couple.

There was the delay of a minute in getting into proper place, and taking each other by the appropriate hand, after which the priest asked each: "Do you love this woman (man), and are you willing to take her (him) as your wife (husband)? Do you know any impediment why you should not marry her (him)?" And the questions being satisfactorily answered, he made the sign of the cross before them, pronounced them man and wife, and the ceremony was over. "Not one minute by Shrewsbury clock!" Not altogether over, either; for though there was no exhortation or prayers, there were embraces and congratulations, beginning with the newly married couple themselves, and extended by them to all with whom such intimacy was warranted. I had a squeeze from each—the bride holding out her arms as I went up, telling me I was a friend esteemed no less by herself than by her mother and father. There were no tears, except a few drops by Doña ———, nor kisses by any of the parties. Indeed I never remember to have witnessed any given in Chile except by parents to very little children. Five minutes afterwards all the younger folks were engaged in a quadrille, in which the bride and groom led off the first set. At 10 o'clock we went in to tea—the bridesmaid falling to my charge, as I was seated beside her when it was announced; and half an hour afterwards the gentlemen were left to discuss alone the superabundance of confectionery, ices, hams, wines, and flowers, with which the tables were literally crowded. Escorting the old lady back to the parlor, I availed myself of the bustle to take *French leave*.

The first month is usually passed in the house of the bride's mother, where all to whom the family have given "*parte*"—that is, a formal notice of the marriage—go to make congratulatory visits. But as soon as they have a house of their own, it is more than probable that the couple will have distinct apartments—the custom of occupying separate chambers having its advocates among the ladies also. Almost invariably on the birth of a child, it is given in charge to a nurse, few mothers being willing to encounter the trouble of rearing their own offspring, alleging as a reason for turning it off, that in the climate of their country their constitutions will not bear it. Nevertheless they are far more robust and healthy in appearance than the men. In about a year another nurse is needed; and so they go on, numbering in one case as many as twenty-seven children—a degree of fecundity rivalled only by the soil on which they live. Calling to visit a friend one evening, I learned that within the twenty-four hours his wife had added another "responsibility" to the half dozen already possessed by them, and that the young stranger was to be taken to the cathedral for baptism as soon as the *padrinos* (sponsors) came. Although it might cost me an hour or two—and time was precious just then—as there was no impropriety, and I wanted to witness the ceremony, I concluded to join the party. The carriage of the padrinos drove to the door in a little while, and they came in preceded by a servant with a silver waiter filled with ornamental pastilles, for distribution to those who attended the christening or wished "long life" to the padrinos. These are the customary offerings—some of the pastilles having pendants of gold or jewels, if the padrinos are very opulent.

Doña ———, the padrina, with the nurse and child, went in her close carriage—her husband and myself in his gig—the father remaining at home. The gig having broken down with us in the plaza, some minutes elapsed before the horse could be properly secured, so that the carriage arrived first, and we found madam, with a priest from the convent of La Merced, another from the cathedral, and a rabble of boys, who had obtained an inkling of what was going on, awaiting us at a side entrance. The Mercedario soon slipped on his embroidered robes in the vestuary, and we proceeded towards the church door in the following order: Imprimis, a dirty-faced, shock-headed boy, carrying a wax candle ornamented with tinsel flowers, and a box containing the cruet of oil, salt, and one or two towels, which certainly had not just come from the hands of the laundress; next, the two priests; one under a robe of cream-colored silk, embroidered with every imaginable figure—a short, fat, good-natured, lazy fellow; the other in his long black sutan only—short, lean, ceremonious, but lazy too; third, the padrinos—he, tall and stout—she, short and thick, the mother of fourteen children, and (as he told me when we walked back half an hour later) likely to be the mother of fourteen more; and fourth, the nurse, with the youthful candidate for honors, enveloped in a long, heavily embroidered, white silk shawl or other contrivance. These were the essentials; your humble servant and half a score of rowdy boys, who jingled the bells and other things about the cathedral, were accessories, following closely in the rear.

Arrived at the door, the padrinos were directed to hold each a part of the child and of the wax candle—the latter until then in possession of the page. There, prompted by the cathedral priest as to the proper portions of the ritual, our Mercedario friend blundered through a jargon of Latin words, without having inspired the slightest thought of solemnity on the part of any one concerned, unless it might have been the god-mother or myself. Although audibly told two or three times that the name of the infant was "José Santiago," he sometimes said "José Santiago," sometimes "Santiago José," sometimes only one of them, and at others, again, stopped to ask the name. A most oblivious memory the worthy padre seemed to have, and its effect was such as to render the ceremony no little ludicrous. The ritual at the church door—concluded by marking the sign of the cross with a finger moistened with spittle, inserting a pinch of salt into the little fellow's mouth, and anointing him on the back of the head—may have occupied ten minutes, perhaps, when we proceeded, in the same order as before, to one of the chapels, on whose altar half a dozen wax candles had been lighted. Here the padrinos, again jointly holding the child, were required to promise certain religious offices in his behalf; and this satisfactorily agreed to, the robe of the officiating priest was changed for another as like to it, in my eyes, as another pea. The child was then anointed with the sign of the cross on the forehead; and finally, master José Santiago having been asked *three* times whether *he* wished to be baptized, and the sponsors answering affirmatively for him each time, water was dripped across the back, or rather the top, of his head, "in the name of the Father, and of the Son, and of the Holy Ghost." So persecuted had the little fellow been, I am very sure that he would have answered "yes" also could he have talked, on the same principle that girls are said to do who take lovers to get rid of them; but it *did* seem to me the questions would have been more appropriate at the commencement. As we were about to leave the altar, the priest belonging to the cathedral suggested an ave or two, and we all dropped to our knees, each one invoking a blessing, it is to be hoped, on the neophyte, though there was apparently very little feeling or sincerity in the audible portion. The baby was a plump, round-faced specimen of humanity, with a full head of black hair, and bore the glare of light in his eyes, spitting on, salting, and greasing, without a whimper; and if he did make very wry faces at the salt, it must be recollected he had had scarcely six and thirty hours of experience in this outer world, and wasn't used to it. By this time most of the boys, among whom it is customary to scatter small coins on these occasions, had stolen in from the various offices of the edifice, and the padrinos were beset on all sides—a rabble following until the carriage protected us from their importunities, and we had got beyond the precincts of the cathedral.

It is difficult to believe that this ritual of the church is always performed with the same indifference—indeed levity would be a more appropriate expression; for there was not, as has been said, the least approximation to reverence from the beginning to the end of it. That the act they were performing would save an immortal soul from perdition—that it was the primary event of life to prepare for eternity, as every church inculcates—seemed not for a moment to dwell on their minds. It was but the execution of a mandate unquestioningly obeyed by those immediately responsible, and for whose performance fees and presents reward the others. Though both are increased in accordance with the opulence or generosity of the padrinos, the minimum fee is an *escudito* ($2.15) Chile currency, and the presents are usually of wax-candles or fine linen handkerchiefs.

Were not mortality so great among children, the country would soon become densely populated; but the habits of the nurses are vicious, and they have little attachment for the infants committed to their charge; so, what with neglect and bad treatment combined, whilst the number of births in the republic during the year 1848 amounted to 46,216, the deaths of those under seven years of age who received religious burial were 11,962. The number of those whose parents have not the fees for the priest, and whose bodies are unceremoniously tossed over the walls of the cemeteries if near cities, or are put into holes if in the country, will be quite as many more, and these never enter the statistical tables.

Gotten rid of at the birth—reared by a servant—sent out of the house to school, or rather placed at a boarding-school within the city, from which they can only visit their homes once during the month—it is not to be expected that as strong affection can grow up between the mother and her child as if the latter had drawn its nourishment from her breast, and had subsequently been the object of her daily attentions. If the daughter live at home, from the time she attains ten years of age, the mother must daily accompany her to and from school, or she must be sent with a well-tried servant in a close carriage. Even brothers are not always trusted with this responsibility. Thus, there early arises a want of confidence between mother and daughter, which the confessional probably widens just at the period when the latter most needs a counsellor. There never has been intimate intercourse between them; in distress the child has never sought advice from the being who, of all others, should ever have shown her sympathy; and when a licentious priest at her first confession asks questions suggestive of thoughts no pure-minded girl should entertain, instead of listening to the narrative of her life and administering counsel only, what does she do under the mental conflict? She flies for consolation to a companion or relative. The mother, who should have been regarded as her only true and tender friend, has never treated her familiarly, and she dare not appeal to her. This is the beginning of estrangement, if not of actual distrust, and which, going on from day to day, is not observed only because of its too frequent occurrence. "Look at ——," said a friend to me one day, when we were talking on this subject. "You know that she is quite a *beata*,* and has acknowledged to you that she cares not to read the Bible, nor to inquire for herself respecting the truth of divine revelation, preferring to follow precisely as directed by her confessor. You know how amiable, how kind-hearted, and how very intelligent and indulgent is her mother;

* Bigot is the nearest actual signification of the word.

but have you ever witnessed the least evidence of affection between them?" I was obliged to acknowledge that no such feeling had ever been betrayed before me. I say *obliged;* for the individuals were among the friends most regarded, and it was a painful truth to acknowledge. Arrived at maturity, the young lady enters society, usually sprightly, intelligent, and well educated; yet there has been no opportunity to try her powers, and constant *surveillance* has at last deprived her of the confidence in herself essential to graceful address, if it has not rendered her unpleasantly silent and retiring. If one of the opposite sex approach, he rarely says more than "How pretty you are this evening!" "How very elegant is your dress!" with one or two other equally sapient remarks; and having made an engagement for a dance, should that amusement be going on, he moves off to talk with his more affable and agreeable companions, twist his moustache, and smoke another cigarito.

Let us look at the characteristics of the latter sex for a moment, for they require no very prolonged examination. Originally the basis of education imparted is good; unfortunately, it is almost wholly theoretical. The means of communicating experimental knowledge, so necessary to enlist the mind in its subsequent prosecution, have not hitherto existed to any considerable extent; and it is only very recently that there have been men in Chile competent to teach the elementary branches of physical science. Even yet much is wanting to place the schools on a level with those of Europe or North America; and thus, for want of proper apparatus and tutors, a young man takes his leave of school just when he has received an amount of information which would elsewhere make him feel the necessity of study. There are neither engineers, chemists, machinists, nor architects by profession. Neither is there any pursuit a young man can follow which renders further application to books necessary, except in preparation for the practice of law or medicine; and when it is stated that the whole number of licentiates for both these professions from 1843 to 1849 was only 143, an estimate may be formed of the demand for mental application. Therefore, with the college they also take leave of books, become clerks in the houses of merchants or retailers, and the knowledge which was at first but superficial is soon forgotten. Others enter the convents, adding to the drones of the population; a small number obtain places under government, and a few embark in mining, though not, as do the Californians, with their own hands, for personal labor is considered degrading. Want of occupation, encouraged by the climate, soon confirms a habit of indolence where there is no mental energy to shake it off; and in a brief while the youth who might have become a man of ability and enterprise falls irreclaimably into idleness and listlessness. Societies for the promotion of science, literature, the professions or arts, so beneficial in the dissemination of knowledge, and so productive of laudable emulation in the world of letters, have no existence here; and the rendezvous of the young men becomes, instead, the tailor's shop, where the fashions are discussed, and the public promenade or parlor, where they can display ultra fine dresses. Conversation with young ladies is not general, as has just been remarked. If they attempt it with any not of their own sex, it is with the mothers, thus voluntarily avoiding intercourse which could not fail in leading to mental improvement, and preparing for more rational domestic life. Neglected by those whom she knows to be inferior in mental as in moral worth, yet whom Nature has assigned as her companions through life—bitterly sensible that she will scarcely be permitted the privilege of selection among them, but must take as a husband him whom her parents consider most suitable—the girl soon thinks with indifference and apathy of the abilities of the beaux surrounding her, and learns to value them by the contents of their coffers rather than by their characters or talents.

There are very life-like pictures drawn of both sexes in a little work (*Repertorio Chileno*) published at Santiago, in 1835. Of the men the author says: "They are indolent to excess, and, whilst possessing moral courage to undertake anything, have neither the resolution to continue nor the constancy to complete it—more especially if there are others who direct or take part in it. It is this pernicious and culpable indolence which domineers over and, in a great measure, keeps down public and religious spirit; they themselves confessing to *apathy*." The gentler sex is deservedly spoken of in a more lenient manner. "They are good wives, and, though it cannot be said that they love passionately or are very jealous, they are faithful in the care of their children, and more constant and persevering than men in all they undertake. They possess something of the indolence characterizing the men, though not to so great a degree; for, charged with the direction of domestic affairs, they not only exhibit discretion, but, at times, are precipitate in terminating whatever is to be done. A prudent economy being exercised as far as is possible, what they possess is rather taken care of than expended ostentatiously. Under certain circumstances, their love of luxury is excessive; and in this men participate equally. Yet, if it be a crime, as we cannot doubt, the habits of both will improve in this respect when they shall have learned the eternal truth, None should aspire to more than they can fulfil."

Ordinarily, such is life in Chile—calm, monotonous, without thought for the future or to benefit mankind; almost passionless, save when civil war or the gambling table stirs up the hideous sentiments of our nature. To woman such a vegetable sort of existence seems propitious, and she becomes robust, and lives to an average age beyond that of her sex in the northern hemisphere, whilst man shrivels and passes away at an age scarce beyond the prime. I must not be understood as saying that this inactivity, this apathy, alone produces the different effects on the two sexes, but simply as stating, as a general rule in connexion with it, that men die at much earlier ages than women; and, with brief reference to the ceremony which closes one's career on the surface of the earth, the chapter will terminate.

The death of General ——— occurred during the excitement attending the civil war in 1851, and his remains were accompanied to the grave by persons of the highest rank of both parties, as well as by all the foreigners of note. He had ever been a warm friend to the latter during life, remembering that the divine precept of "good will to all men" would tend to the advancement of his country; and, to this end, he constantly manifested the utmost interest in their wants and comforts. Scarcely an hour had elapsed, after sending to his residence a package of letters given me in the United States, before he came to see me; and from that time both himself and family were unremitting in attentions, inspiring my esteem and respect. Returning from a walk with a lady on the evening of his death, she stopped to visit the family, and, assuring me that it was a custom of the country, to which I, as a friend, would be expected to conform, I also went to the parlor, where relatives awaited visitors. Only one of the four sons was present—he who had been the constant attendant during the last illness of his father. The others were in a room where gentlemen only were received. But it appeared strange that any one should intrude on a family in the very hour of direst affliction.

Usually the corpse is sent to the chapel of the cemetery between midnight and daylight, and the male friends follow at 6 or 7 o'clock in the morning, to attend the masses and deposit it in the tomb. Nor is there any variation of the rule, except by special permission from the Intendente, in cases of distinguished persons, like the present. On this occasion the body remained at the house till morning, from which it was taken in a handsome funeral-car, drawn by relatives and other gentlemen. His sons and immediate relatives followed on foot, and the military cadets escorted it as a guard of honor. In advance were all the civil troops of Santiago, with their bands playing sprightly marches; and an immense concourse of carriages brought up the rear. The streets through which the procession moved were thronged to an excess we had never seen equalled; and where there were so many prancing horses, so few skilful drivers, and no kind of order observed in the march, it is miraculous how accidents were avoided. Indeed, each coachman appeared desirous to outstrip his predecessor, and there were thus sometimes two and sometimes three lines of vehicles in the narrow streets, crossing and recrossing each other in shocking confusion.

A halt was made for some minutes in front of one of the churches on the opposite side of the river, where prayers for the soul of the deceased were said at an altar put up temporarily by some of the priests from *La Merced.* Most of the followers knelt in the road beside their carriages during this service. The body was received at the entrance to the cemetery by the bishop of Chilóe (temporarily visiting Santiago) himself, and the priests of La Merced, chanting as they preceded it to the chapel. His sons and near relatives bore the coffin on their shoulders, the accompanying crowd ranging themselves on either side, and following as the corpse passed them. The civic troops were drawn up on one side, and the *Guardia del Orden* (a battalion of young gentlemen formed at the revolutionary epoch) occupied the east half of the open space—the two firing alternate volleys during the progress of the masses within the building. At conclusion of this salute, the coffin was deposited in the house specially appropriated for the purpose, until the family vault was ready; and finally there were eulogistic discourses, whose delivery occupied until nearly noon. The great crowd kept me at such a distance that I only heard the concluding words of the first speaker's address, and these were pronounced in a tone and with an energy that made no little stir among those around me. Turning his face to the mass without the building, he exclaimed, "*Pueblo, F***** es muerto, y la libertad con el!*" (Citizens, F. is dead, and liberty with him!)—a sentiment few dared publicly express, and sufficiently significant, under the triumph which the government was believed to have obtained a few days previously on the field of Loncomilla. At the gate the sons and two nearest relatives took leave of the parting crowd, thanking each one individually for his attention to the memory of their parent.

Ladies never attend funerals. Their duties cease with the departure of their relative's body from the house on the night following the death. Nor are they seen when male friends assemble early next morning, prior to the interment. As soon as the latter arrive at the *panteon* with the priests who are to say the masses, a brief service is first recited over the body, lying in an ante-room to the chapel. The mass succeeds; and as each one said is supposed to help the soul on its journey through purgatory, to say nothing of the ostentation which may be displayed even in this particular, sometimes three priests, at as many altars, within ten feet of each other, are performing the same service at the same time. On one occasion, when I was present, after three masses had been said in this manner, a fourth priest began another, just as we left the chapel with the body, and it is quite probable others succeeded him; but we were dismissed at the front door, and did not again enter the building.

Within ten days, all friends are expected to make the survivors a visit of *pesame*—condolence it can scarcely be called, for the visitors rarely have much sympathy in such ceremony. Day after day the mourners await these calls by their acquaintances, usually in the far corner of a semi-obscure room, where individuals or objects are hardly distinguishable; and if one does not stumble over a table, he is quite as likely to address any one else as the lady of the house. On such occasions, you best show appreciation of their misfortune by appearing in as deep a suit of black as the family themselves would wear; by exhibiting in your countenance a proper degree of sadness; and by speaking only of the deceased or his survivors. Formerly, chairs were never moved from their regular lines round the walls. The first visitor who came took the seat by the mourner, those succeeding occupying the next vacant ones, in unbroken order. Conversation respecting the defunct was carried on only by those near the survivor, the others remaining solemnly silent, shifting one seat nearer the corner of the room as the first-comers departed, until their turn came to make a eulogy. Curious must it have appeared to see a score of persons shift their seats every few moments, as one of their number departed! Though one widow did cause the heart of her husband to be extracted, for preservation in a crystal vase, and another directed the teeth of her departed "lord" to be set as a bracelet, now, in accordance with the more recent rules of society, a sister or other near relative is deputed to receive these visits for them.

CHAPTER VII.

THE CHURCH AND ITS CEREMONIES.

EXCLUSIVELY CATHOLIC.—INTERFERENCE OF THE ARCHBISHOP IN MARRIAGES WITH PROTESTANTS.—HE CLAIMS SPIRITUAL JURISDICTION OVER FOREIGN LEGATIONS.—PASSING OF THE HOST THROUGH THE STREETS.—BIGOTRY AND INTOLERANCE INSEPARABLE AMONG ALL SECTS.—METROPOLITAN ORGANIZATION.—CHURCH REVENUES.—PARISHES — CONVENT OF AUGUSTIN NUNS.—OTHER NUNNERIES.—MONASTERIES.—THE DOMINICANS.—FRANCISCANS.—RECOLETA FRANCISCANS.—FRANCISCAN HERMITS.—MERCEDARIOS (WHITE FRIARS).—SACRED HEART.—CEREMONIES ON ASH WEDNESDAY.—DEATH OF A DEAN OF THE CATHEDRAL.—EXEQUIES OF DON ———.—INCIDENTS OF HOLY WEEK.—PALM SUNDAY.—HOLY THURSDAY.—GOOD FRIDAY.—SATURDAY —EASTER SUNDAY.—QUASIMODO (SUNDAY AFTER EASTER).—ANNIVERSARY OF THE EARTHQUAKE OF 1647.—CORPUS CHRISTI.—ASSUMPTION DAY.—SANTA EUSEBIA.—ANNIVERSARY OF THE NATIVITY OF THE VIRGIN.—OUR LADY OF MERCY.—OUR LADY OF THE ROSARY.—OUR LADY OF CARMEN.

The fifth article of the Constitution, sworn and promulgated on the 25th of May, 1833, is in these words:

"ARTICLE 5. La religion de la Republica de Chile es la Catolica Apostolica Romana, con esclusion del ejercicio publico de qualquiera otra." (The religion of the Republic of Chile is the Apostolic Roman Catholic, to the exclusion of the public exercise of every other.)

Acting on the blind policy which dictated the foregoing article of its fundamental law, it was not until the numbers of Protestants at Valparaiso became too powerful to be prudently disregarded any longer, that they were permitted to occupy a chapel in which they might worship GOD as had been taught them by their fathers, or to possess a piece of ground in which to deposit the remains of mortality. Even these boons, however, were not openly conceded. They were indebted to the liberal sentiments of the sterling patriot then President, General Friere, for authority to make a new reading of the Constitution; and were told they should have his protection so long as their church and worship were without the *external* evidences which the words "public exercise" seemed to imply. So intolerant was the church in those days, that burial in consecrated ground was refused the crew of a national ship of war, because they were foreigners, and, *primâ facie*, heretics. But the President, recognising them as citizens of the republic from the moment that they embarked in its service, felt bound to provide a place where dogs and condors would not desecrate their bodies, and directed that they should be interred within the fortress at Valparaiso. It thus became a naval cemetery, in which other strangers also found a final resting-place. The ground which Protestants were subsequently allowed to obtain at the port has obviated further necessity for its use; but at Santiago three foreigners have been deposited within the castle walls of Santa Lucia, and, for many years to come, there the remains of any others must rest whose misfortune it may be to die without the pale of the apostolic Roman Catholic church.*

The privileges thus winked at were the earliest movements toward breaking down overbearing intolerance; an intolerance which not only shut out young men from domestic life, except through its exclusive portals, but which forced them, bareheaded, to their knees whenever the bell gave warning that the "host" was elevated in church, or a part of the same imaginary body of our Saviour was being conveyed to a sick person through the street they chanced to be

* Under date June 14th, 1853, a distinguished fellow-countryman wrote me from Santiago: "A party were recently stoned while engaged at midnight in burying a Protestant in the fort on Santa Lucia; and I have just been informed by the American Consul for Talcahuano, among other such-like acts, that the local authorities of that place refused permission to bury the dead body of an infant, the son of the captain of an American vessel, and that the body was taken to sea."

passing along. Yet to this day there exists a law on the statute-book, which declares that all marriages on Chilean territory not performed in *the* church are illegal, and of no effect; and the children born of such wedlock illegitimate and incapacitated from inheriting property, except such portion of the father's estate as is guarantied to all natural children.

It is still fresh in the minds of many what heart-burning and bitter words marked the marriage of a Chargé d'Affaires from the United States, only a few years back; nor is it doubted that his controversy with the archbishop expedited the demand for passports and his return home. Why he should have condescended to communicate with any one but the Minister of Foreign Affairs, or have permitted any priest to deliver letters to a member of his family against his wishes, may appear somewhat extraordinary in a national representative; but it was probably one of those occurrences in diplomacy unpardonable in the code of Talleyrand—*a blunder*—discovered only when too late. It is understood that the marriage had been prohibited by the archbishop on two grounds: first, because the Catholic church does not permit re-marriage by divorced persons during the life of a previous husband or wife, as the case may be; and, secondly, because the Chargé was a heretic. These causes of interdiction were made known to the lady. Herself and a sister were unprotected orphans of good family, though poor; and the offer was too tempting to refuse, even though the ban of the church might be expected to attend its acceptance. Fortunately for the lovers, the presence of an American ship of war at the port afforded opportunity for the Commodore and a *suite* of officers, including the chaplain, to visit Santiago; and, for the purpose of giving to the wedding as much of an official character as possible, the foreign diplomatic corps assisted, and the ceremony was performed under the "stars and stripes," with all honors due to the occasion. One would have supposed that the very reverend prelate would suffer the matter to drop after this; yet such was not the case; his persecutions of the lady seemed just to begin, and his letters tell her, almost in so many words, that she is living in concubinage. As well to show something of the temper of the head of the church, as because it advances a doctrine fraught with interest to bachelor diplomats who may hereafter represent their countries in Chile, one or two paragraphs are quoted from a letter written to the lady, of which a labored defence was subsequently submitted to Congress by the Minister of Foreign Affairs.

"I cannot doubt, because it is public and notorious, that you have proceeded to celebrate without the presence of the curate, and contrary to the will of the church, a *soi-disant* (pretendido) marriage with a gentleman of distinct religion; and, although this proceeding gains for you the love of a fellow-being, and gives you possession of earthly goods, neither can accompany you beyond the tomb, that point where your soul casts upon itself immense responsibilities in the presence of our Saviour. 1st. You have proceeded to perform a matrimonial act with one who is without the pale of the Catholic church. 2d. You performed it knowingly, notwithstanding a direct impediment that annuls the marriage; and which is, without the presence of your curate and two witnesses. 3d. You have consented to associate in divine ceremonies with Protestants, by permitting a minister of that sect to celebrate this *soi-disant* marriage.

"In the first place, if the church regards matrimony with persons of different creeds as prejudicial, even when these pledge themselves to educate their children in the Catholic religion, and previously solicit a dispensation, how will it regard a violation of its prohibitions, the contempt of its laws, and abandonment of the sacred interests of innocent offspring? Will the acquisition of earthly goods sanctify this outrage upon the church, and calm the upbraidings of conscience? Will God bless a union associated with such transgressions? If you do not experience sorrows in this life, your apprehensions should be the greater; but it cannot be that the Saviour will reward your past good deeds with transitory happiness, and reserve the scourge of justice for eternity.

"In the second place, you have given your hand in matrimony, despite an inseparable impediment; and for this act, in the eyes of religion, you are not married. Chapter I, concerning the reforms of matrimony, by the Holy Council of Trent, expressly declares all marriages null and void which may be contracted, after promulgation of said Council, without the presence of the curate and two witnesses; and, as such promulgation has been made in Chile, and yours, who are a Chilena, was effected in the territory of this diocess, without the required formality, it follows that it labors under immediate nullity. In vain will it be told you that the gentleman whom you look upon as your spouse was the diplomatic agent of the United States; and that, in conformity with the laws of nations, his residence enjoys the privilege of being considered a part of the North American territory. These privileges extend only to temporal matters, and not to those of religion. The power of legislating in matters touching religion has been received by the Catholic church from its divine founder, and it is a point of Catholic faith that its laws and discipline may not be altered by any other authority than that of the church. Therefore, when nations accord privileges to the residences of diplomatic agents, they concede temporal prerogatives only, and do not change the religious conditions of the places in which those dwellings may be situated. To Catholics, the Council of Trent has as much force within the houses of diplomatic ministers in Chile, as it has beyond them. Men cannot make perfect, by their determinations, that which the church annuls. I refer to that which touches the jurisdiction of conscience; and though by North American law you may be reputed the legitimate wife of the Chargé d'Affaires, and enjoy the civil rights of a wife, in the presence of God you are not. You live in prohibited union, and multiply the number of your sins every time you avail yourself of the privileges of a spouse. * * * * * *

"The third injury which you have done to your soul has been communication with Protestants in religious acts of their sects. I am assured you consented that a Protestant minister should come here to perform the matrimonial service which you celebrated with the Chargé d'Affaires of the United States; and as the rite of matrimony is an act of religion, you held communication in divine things, as theologians explain them, with those of a strange creed. The church highly reproves this species of communication; because he who renders to God the tribute of a worship that he knows to be false, sacrilegiously mocks at Divinity, and participates in foreign impiety. The sacred canons impose the heaviest pains of excommunication on the person who has committed it, and it is your misfortune to have rendered yourself liable to the gravest and most fatal punishment a Catholic can suffer. Though it may overwhelm your sensitive heart, I must not conceal from you whatever may hang over it. The public manner in which you have acted, the open contempt with which you have treated your pastor, the incorporation in a Protestant act of religion performed by a minister of that sect, and, finally, the air of ostentation with which it has all been done, induce the most vehement suspicions that you have apostatized from your religion; because it would be very difficult to believe you can have remained a Catholic after such cold-blooded proceedings."

I did not think to follow the Right Reverend prelate so far, and must also apologize to him should I have misconstrued his letter published in a "*Memorio sobre las incidencias ocurridas en el matrimonio del* ———, *encargado de negocios de los Estados Unidos de America con Doña* ———, *ciudadena Chilena, en que se justifica la conducta del gobierno. Presentado al Congreso Nacional*, 1849." There should have been added to the title-page, "*Por Manuel Camilo Vial, Ministro de Relaciones Esteriores*," whose name appears at the end of one hundred and three octavo pages of defence.

Thus, a foreigner brought up in the Protestant faith is tacitly obliged to abjure that faith at marriage in Chile, consent that his wife shall follow the little better than image worship into which the service of the church has degenerated, and his children also be brought up under its discipline; or, if she so far overcome the prejudices of education and church prohibitions as to consent to marriage with him by a Protestant clergyman, must make up his mind to have her encounter persecution not unlikely to end in separation from him.

At Valparaiso, as has been said, the presence of so many foreigners has secured to them something of toleration. Formerly the passage of the priest through a street conveying the host, with pomp of military guards, and bells, and lights, (even during the day,) and the custom of kneeling uncovered during its elevation in church, was the occasion of daily difficulties between foreign unbelieving sailors and faithful natives. Finally, the government found it necessary to prohibit these outward demonstrations at the port; but they still continue at the capital and elsewhere in the republic, and the few outside barbarians whom business has attracted elsewhere have deemed it wiser to follow the custom, so far as pride will permit, rather than risk collision with peons and *rotos*, who are the most bigoted and likely to resent fancied insult to their religion. On the morning of the Sunday following my arrival, as I issued from the court-yard of the post-office, a superb carriage drawn by a pair of handsome horses was entering the plaza, preceded and followed by an armed soldier or two, and a number of other persons, part of whom carried lanterns mounted on short poles, and the rest had bells. As the populace were kneeling upon the sidewalks of the street through which the procession had just come, and the crowd between the carriage and myself were humbling themselves in like manner as it approached them, I took it for granted that the very rotund and comfortable-looking gentleman in clerical robes, whom I could perceive occupying a back seat, was none other than the archbishop, to whom, as the head of the church, I meant to make such salute in passing as would be rendered to the most distinguished in North America. This appeared not to suit the kneeling crowd, each one of whom gave the tails of my coat a tug as I passed, and not a few scowled their blackest, because I neither knelt nor removed my hat to "*el majestad*," as the consecrated wafer is called. The cortége continued to advance, jingling bells, the postillion constantly repeating "*Santo, santo, santo, Dios de los ejercitos; llenos estan los cielos de la majestad de vuestra gloria!*" (Holy, holy, holy, Lord of hosts! the heavens and the earth are full of the majesty of thy glory); to which the lamp-bearers and bell-ringers responded, "*Gloria al Padre, y al Hijo, y al Espiritu santo!*" (Glory to the Father, and to the Son, and to the Holy Ghost!); but it was "Greek" to me, and I continued on my way ignorantly. Passing the carriage-door I very politely raised my hat, bowing, as I supposed, to the highest dignitary of the church. But the salute was not returned, except by a stare expressive of astonishment and indignation, so that I concluded the old gentleman was not very courteous. When the hotel was reached, the landlord explained the object of the procession to me, and advised the propriety of turning into a side-street whenever a carriage conveying "the host" should be perceived, else refusal to conform to the custom of the country might one day subject me to personal outrage. So sacredly do the entire population guard the observance of this form, that all the inmates of a parlor will kneel as the *Viatico* passes in front of the house; and there is no doubt that they would drop to their knees and beat their breasts in like case, at the moment the tinkle of the bell first struck their ears, even though whirling round in a waltz. On one occasion, when in a garden full a hundred yards from the road, the lady who was showing me her beautiful flowers all at once stopped, and saying, "I pray you will pardon me whilst I follow the customs of my country," herself and daughter bowed their knees and repeated a prayer for the soul of a departing mortal to whom the sacred wafer was passing. They had detected the tinkle of the bells and the solemn monotony of the cries long before I could have possibly noticed them; indeed it is quite probable that my ears would not have remarked either at such distance, had not their acts called attention to the sounds.

If reason be allowed to rule, the ceremony as practised here is the veriest mockery of a religious ordinance. Leaving the question of transubstantiation to be discussed by theologians, and admitting the propriety of such pomps, if the Catholic side of the argument be true, there are circumstances connected with the administration of this sacrament which strongly tend to bring it into disrepute. No sooner is it known that a wealthy person is dangerously ill, than a priest, and sometimes two or three, appears at his house to administer counsel. There they remain to the last, earnestly striving to obtain legacies; failing in which, they make extortionate demands for the cast-off garments of some reputed holy friar, which are greatly prized for shrouds. Whilst there is a shadow of apology for it, and even after the corpse has been removed to its sepulchre, they remain at the dwelling. On the other hand, if the invalid has the misfortune to be poor, their memories sometimes need jogging more than once to convince them that a soul awaits the indispensable safe-guiding passport to eternity; and when at last one does go, the stay of the holy father is sometimes so short that I have more than once doubted whether his fingers had not been used to expedite the passage of the wafer down the sick man's throat. This is more especially notable on the day called "*Quasimodo*," when high dignitaries of the church visit the sick in carriages driven and served by gentlemen of the city; bands of music, troops of cavalry, and a motley crowd attending them with rockets and fire-works of various descriptions. Nor is the administration of this sacrament in church attended with solemnity, or accompanied by a word of spiritual counsel. The communicant comes to the altar-railing of a side chapel where a priest attends with a box of consecrated wafers. Kneeling in a vacant spot, he receives one in his mouth from the fingers of the priest, and at once departs to make room for another communicant. At the same time, mass is being said before the principal altar, and people come and go from all parts of the church without intermission. If it be the veritable body of Christ they are dispensing,—a belief they perseveringly endeavor to force on others by humbling them before it on *all* occasions,—it is undoubtedly treated with little reverence even by themselves. But the success and influence of their teachings are constantly exhibited, some even among persons of the better class being unable to control sentiments of indignation whenever there is an imagined disrespect shown to their observances.

For a long while I was a tolerably regular attendant on Sunday mornings at the cathedral; not from faith in the doctrines there practised, as will have been perceived, but from habit, and the devout feelings the music of its choir never failed to arouse. No doubt it was proper that I should outwardly conform to the ceremonies of the church; but as it was not possible to comprehend them, or to know the proper times at which to kneel or cross myself, I remained seated behind a high-backed bench that almost entirely concealed me from the congregation. My deportment was of course most grave and respectful; and when the congregation began beating their breasts at the elevation of the host, my head was invariably bowed beneath the front bench. After attending without molestation through more than a year, one morning an old gentleman, immediately in front, felt bound to speak in behalf of the offended dignity of his church. I was seated, as usual, with my head bowed low, more than ordinarily saddened by the plaintive anthem, when he turned full toward me, demanding in a most violent tone, as he shook his clenched fist, "How dare you sit there whilst we kneel?" Of course every one near me looked surprised, not less than myself; yet it was neither the time nor place for reply, and I could but endeavor to smile blandly on the asthmatic worshipper. Thinking that he might desire to read me a lecture after mass on church behavior, and being nothing averse to offer in return one on courtesy to strangers, I moved to the farther end of the bench, in order that proximity as he passed out should prevent forgetfulness of my existence; but he could not afford to waste more breath on a heretic, and was content to express his indignation and pity by looks.

It is impossible for bigotry and intolerance to exist apart, or for them to exist at all where the mind is highly cultivated. None know this better than the potentates of the Apostolic Roman Catholic church, whose policy it has ever been to present themselves as instructors, not—as they would have you infer—for the purpose of breaking down these barriers, but the more certainly to obtain control of education, for the purpose of instilling tenets that will inevitably perpetuate their sway, and to bound the extent of knowledge, for the same great end. This being understood, their hostility to Protestant modes of instruction is not to be wondered at. They would yet have us all believe the earth remains motionless in space, as mental progress undoubtedly would do, did they universally control mankind. And thus in Chile, wherever there are half a dozen men, women, or children brought together in a school, the hospital, or the almshouse, some one of the clergy secures an office as chaplain over them.

Pius IV sent the first bishop to Santiago in 1563, twenty-two years after the foundation of the city. In 1574 another was despatched to Concepcion: and the jurisdiction of the first was limited between the desert of Atacama and the river Maule; that of the latter to extend to all the territory south of the Maule. In 1836 the government determined to create two new sees; and having nominated individuals as bishops of Serena and Ancud, one was confirmed by the Pope in 1843; the other not until five years afterward. Meantime, having been urged by the Metropolitan Diocess, Gregory XVI erected Santiago into an archbishopric in 1841; and the seat is now occupied by a native of the city, who was consecrated in 1848 by a bull of Pius IX. When vacancies occur in these high offices, three persons are nominated by the Council of State, one of whom the President selects, and submits his name to the Senate for confirmation. If confirmed by that body, it is then sent to the Pope for final ratification. Besides the extraordinary powers especially delegated to the bishops of America in the early days of the church on this continent, the archbishop has the control of all benefices, and is the superior of all the monasteries and religious orders whatsoever within the republic.

In addition to the archbishop, the metropolitan establishment comprises: a secretary and two clerks to his reverence; an ecclesiastical council, composed of one dean, an arch-dean, a chanter, a teacher of ecclesiastical science, and treasurer; six canons; three prebends and three sub-prebends; an ecclesiastical court, consisting of a judge and vicar-general; an associate-fiscal and a notary; a conciliary college, with a rector and vice-rector; eight chaplains in the choir, and eight acolytes.

Under a former system there was collected, exclusively for the support of the church, a tenth of all the produce of the country; but this has been abolished, and the government, though continuing the tax, apportions such incomes as they think proper to the maintenance of the metropolitan and suffragan bishops, and those curacies which do not obtain in fees a given sum. To these ends, including also repairs of the cathedrals and other churches, the appropriations, by Congress, for 1850 amounted to $195,600; of which $62,800 was for the metropolitan establishment alone. Inmates of the convents and monasteries are supported from the income of their property, in all cases more than ample. With a view to ameliorate the moral condition of the people, growing out of their poverty and the refusal of curates to perform marriage, baptismal, or burial services without the fixed stipend, a proposition was made in Congress that the whole system of fees should be abolished, and parochial churches as well as missionaries be paid from the public treasury. So long as an exclusive church exists, it is greatly to be regretted that the proposal should have failed through the influence of the church itself. But it was a result to have been anticipated; because it is scarcely probable that government would have assigned salaries large enough to gratify the propensities of some of the vicious curates. These now manage to accumulate property, and live discreditably by forcing payment from the poor *guasos* of $12 for marriage, $2 for baptism, and $4 for interment, without which the souls of the latter will inevitably descend to the place of torture. However, there were in Congress some who really desired reformation in the church, but who at the same time opposed the measure, on the ground that if the parochial duties were shamefully attended to, even under the stimulant "no work no pay," they would be infinitely more so when payment should be made certain, whether the parishioners were attended to or not. During the discussion in the Chamber, a late Minister of Worship and Public Instruction said: "I have never hesitated to state that the parochial service is badly administered, and fear not to repeat it, because the fact is public and notorious. Whenever the occasion offers, I write it without regarding who may think ill of me. Every time that I have made a journey, I have personally witnessed the neglect of the parishes. The churches of nearly every curacy were in worse condition than the most miserable ranchos; uncleanliness was notable in the furniture destined for worship; and even cloths serving to cover the altars were unwashed. I am aware that exaggerated criticisms have been made; that the curates, if not wicked, are said to be so; and that their private conduct is the subject of espionage, without the right for such act—for I dispute the right of any one to pry into their private affairs. My strictures are animated by no mean passions. Curates by their mission should occupy themselves mainly with what belongs to their religion. I have seen for myself that they do not attend to it, and this is sufficient for me to augur ill of the zeal with which they fulfil their other obligations." All of the ex-minister's fellow-countrymen have not been equally scrupulous; and there are few who do not know that a large number of the curates have found it necessary to console themselves with families in the country, and to pass an occasional evening with a neighbor playing *monte*. Nor are these facts unknown to the archbishop, one of his own metropolitan establishment (to use his own words in the letter quoted) "publicly and notoriously" participating in these prohibitions; so much so, that when we talked about it one day, he confessed: "They are nearly all like me, *except* that they have not my candor to acknowledge it." He *was* a liberal man, having given evidence of such sentiment by urging liberty of worship on the Chamber, when one of its members some years previously. He considered a multitude of sects one of the safeguards of piety; each kept watch over the rest.

The city is divided into six parishes, viz: Cathedral, Santa Ana, Estampa, San Michael, San Lazaro, and San Isidro; besides which, there are churches belonging to the convents numbering fifteen more. Within the diocess, and exclusive of the conventual clergy, there are 232 ordained priests. Although some of the monastic orders are vowed to poverty, most of them own sufficient property to live in comfort. Since the departure of the Jesuits, and the partition of their property, the Augustina sisterhood and Dominican friars may be considered the two wealthiest communities; and the latter, it will be remembered, was originally a mendicant order. The former possess some of the most valuable real estate within Santiago; on which, from a part of its proceeds, while we were in Chile, a new building was erected for their better accommodation. As the convents are barred to all of the male sex, (and, indeed, to the female also,) except the archbishop, the doctor, and to the new President for a single visit, I took occasion to examine the arrangements of their intended domicil before they moved into it. The apartments open on long corridors which communicate with extensive chambers for the use of the abbess, and in bad weather afford them places for exercise. Each nun has a small sitting-room, a dormitory, and a servant's room, with conveniences for cooking, washing, and stowage of household necessities; a stream of water passing through the premises of every one. The luxuriously disposed keep a servant, who is free to return to the world when tired of cloistral labor, but is not at liberty to go back and forth each day. For the supply of their necessities, a sort of market is held daily in a court of their property specially provided, and hither are brought for sale provisions and materials and such articles as their industry embraces. Neither purchaser nor seller sees the other; but the commodity offered is placed within one of the recesses of a turnstile filling an aperture of the wall, and if accepted its value is returned in the same manner. Many of the nuns are skilled in needle-work, and in making ornamental pastilles, fancy toys of earthenware, and confectionery of various kinds; in the sale of which they employ servants outside. In 1850, the convent numbered 75 nuns and 176 seculars.

Besides San Augustina, there are two convents dedicated to Santa Clara, two Carmelites, one to Santa Rosa, one Capuchin, and one of the Sacred Heart; embracing in all 252 nuns, 325 seculars, and 31 servants, or a total of 859 women, withdrawn from the purposes of society, their accumulating wealth absolutely locked up. Recently, government made a large appropriation to import from France Sisters of Charity, the archbishop probably preferring a foreign article to one of home materials.

Of monks there are seven foundations, viz: Dominicans, Recoleta Dominicans, Franciscans, Recoleta Franciscans, Franciscan Hermits, Mercedarios, (White Friars,) and Sacred Heart. The convents contain 529 inmates. The Dominicans were the first who obtained foothold as an order. They are by far the most *recherchés* in their dress, have features of more refinement, indicating a better origin than either of the others, and are reputed to be by far the most intelligent. They came to Chile in 1552. Their library contains above six thousand volumes. Next year the Franciscans followed, and for a while occupied a portion of Santa Lucia, where my orisons were so long made. According to the narrative of one of their number, (Padre Guzman, author of "*El Chileno instruido en la historia topographica, civil y politica de su pais*,") there have since been many among them distinguished for an incredible amount of learning, and more than one in whose behalf wonderful miracles were performed. The order have obtained a library of works, principally ecclesiastical, nearly as extensive as the Dominican, and there are one or two who avail themselves of its antiquated treasures; but the majority are ignorant, and their dress and habits, under their vows, render their personal appearance far from inviting. They have also a crucifix which is carried in procession on the 13th of May, the anniversary of the great earthquake of 1647, its crown of thorns having fallen, during the convulsion, from the brow to the neck of the image of the Saviour, from which position it has since been impossible to replace it. Many believe that the earth trembles at every renewed attempt to do so.

Six priests of the order of Our Lady of Mercy came with Valdivia in 1541. These continued with the army in all the campaigns against the Indians, contenting themselves with a small chapel and a house for succor at the capital, until they found that the other two orders were greatly superior in numbers and power to themselves. One of their number was then despatched to Peru for recruits; and returning in 1566, a monastery was founded for their use. In addition to the living and breathing laborers for their cause, the reverend father also brought with him a precious image of Mary of Mercy, which was placed over the great altar; and that benign lady has rendered to her faithful devotees "extraordinary prodigies and indubitable miracles." The dress of the order is entirely white, whence they are sometimes called the White Friars.

Under their own and legitimate name, the Jesuits established a portion of their society at Santiago in 1594. In a little while they became the oracles of society, and absolute masters of every conscience and heart among the laity in Chile, as their brethren had done in Spain. Nor did this condition of things arouse less jealousy here among their natural enemies, the Dominicans, than the power of the greater order had done among the same foundation in the mother country. Under the royal edict banishing them from all Spanish dominions, those of Chile were driven out in August, 1767; at which time more than four hundred, exclusive of the sick, were embarked from Valparaiso and Talcahuano, of whom sixty perished with one of the vessels. When the order for their dismissal arrived, they possessed thirteen schools in operation, six other houses for residence and schools commenced, a convent for novices, two boarding-schools, a seminary for instruction to the Indians at Chillan, six houses for penance, and fifteen missionary stations. The number of their possessions throughout the country was almost incredible; and money alone would have given them colossal power, even had they not obtained the moral influence stated above. Under the ban, their property of every kind was seized by the Crown, each individual being allowed only his wardrobe and breviary.* One by one, members have subsequently wandered along the west coast of South America, and already the order has again a foothold in Chile.

After the Jesuits, the Franciscan hermits came in 1595, the Recoleto Franciscans in 1663, Recoleto Dominicans in 1751, and the order of the Sacred Heart in 1838. The Recoletos live more secluded than other members of the same family; but there is no hour of the day or night when one may not encounter friars in the streets. As there are occasional opportunities to mention them in the body of the narrative, no other allusion will be made here; and it is also far more agreeable for me to exhibit the probable influences of the church on the progress and morals of society by brief accounts of a portion of its public ceremonies.

ASH WEDNESDAY.—The streets are nearly deserted this morning, unusual numbers of the better classes attending at mass, and the rabble still sleeping under the effects of indulgence permitted on the last day of the carnival. To-day commences the forty days' fast, and the season of self-mortification which the church imposes. As an initiatory act, each person suffers a cross to be marked on the forehead by the priest, with the warning, "dust thou art, and unto dust shalt thou return," as he traces the sacred emblem with ashes and water. Three fourths of those met in the street in the morning were females returning from church, bearing to their homes this evidence of their humility. Most of them were of the poorer class; but among them

*"All Chile mourned their loss." *Historia Eclesiastica, politica, y literaria de Chile, por José J. V. Eyzaguirre, Presbitero:* Valparaiso, 1850.

there was not one individual of the male sex so distinguished. Nothing is more impressive to the stranger's mind than to find himself in a crowded thoroughfare in which the multitude reverentially fall to their knees and uncover themselves at the first stroke of the cathedral bell. Spite the dictates of judgment, pronouncing such public pageant idle, if not a mockery of religion, the upturned faces of a silent multitude, and the death-like stillness which that single vibration has imposed on all within its sound, forces a feeling of solemnity on the mind. The rapid strokes of a smaller bell have warned the instructed; and the *guaso* on his dashing steed, the *carretero* with his huge packed ox-cart, the man of business, and the modest *donzella*, alike acknowledge the power of the priest, by humbling themselves in the public highway when the host is elevated at the cathedral, or as they encounter it in possession of the curate, on his way to comfort the dying sinner. A second stroke is given after an interval of a minute; and with the third, at a like lapse of time, the crowd rise crossing themselves, and hurry on their several occupations. This occurs every morning about 9½ o'clock. So powerful is the impression, that laborers amid the crags of Santa Lucia never fail to bend their knees and uncover themselves on these occasions, or to the passing *viatico*, though more than a quarter of a mile distant.

A circumstance connected with this ceremony, narrated by a gentleman who had formerly represented his country in Bolivia, is repeated here as illustrative only. He states that the name of Christ was enrolled among the Alguazils of Chuquisaca, the capital of that country, in the following manner.

Formerly, under old Spanish law, the Alguazils were entitled to a body-guard of five or six men whenever they moved from place to place. The location of the city being ill suited for carriages, the host was ordinarily conveyed by a priest on foot, attended only by one acolyte, or servant of the church. That the body of our Lord should be so conveyed, whilst the Alguazils were honored with a guard, was sore mortification to a devout millionnaire; and as the title and privileges were purchasable, he bequeathed some $20,000 to obtain a similar rank for the Saviour. Now, therefore, the incarnated wafer is attended by the proper guard. How true the blasphemous story may be, there is no means of ascertaining at such a distance; but it was corroborated by the "hearsay" evidence of a second traveller to the centre of America. There is no doubt that San Antonio long bore the rank of Colonel on the Brazilian records; and what is more, the church of that name regularly drew his salary!

The sudden death of the dean of the cathedral gave occasion to one of the pompous displays to which the church seems prone, since no possible opportunity is omitted to influence the mass. On Sunday, the anniversary of the Dominicans, the old gentleman was to have borne an important part in their ceremonies by singing, chanting, or something else, in the procession to come off from their church to the great plaza and back. But on the appointed morning he was found to have been summoned to that great concourse from which none have ever returned to tell of its pomp. In the silent watches of the night, and when none were present to offer relief or consolation, apoplexy had taken off his immortal spirit. The intended procession was therefore deferred, and two or three other pageants substituted. First, the body, decorated in official robes, and in a semi-erect position, was placed in the most appropriate room of his dwelling. A corps of friars were summoned for chants. Lighted candles were placed round the bier, and the doors thrown open to the public. As is customary with almost every event that transpires, intelligence of it was conveyed through the city within a brief space, and the street was kept crowded by a throng pressing to obtain sight of the corpse. This continued during two days—other friars taking the place of those tired down by chanting. On the third day, when most of the people had seen it, and interest began to flag, a gorgeous catafalque was prepared, and the body, preceded by a crowd bearing candles, was conveyed to the front of the altar of the Dominican church. Although in a reclining position, the wafer and chalice were placed in his hands, as if about to partake of the communion. The nave of the building was filled with friars and priests, a portion of whom chanted incessantly—the others, perhaps, reflecting on the uncertainties of life, and the necessity of obtaining as many of its comforts as possible during the years left to them. A rumor having spread by the human telegraph that the door would be closed at 8 o'clock, every one who had not followed to the church in procession crowded to see the display, and the edifice was densely thronged until the last instant—the odor of garlic and paper cigaritos from so many unwashed peons being altogether unlike the "gales from Araby."

On the following morning a grand procession came off from Santo Domingo to the cathedral, within which, as a token of especial regard, the body was to obtain its final resting-place. Absence from town prevented my seeing this part of the exhibition; but the assistants told me the features of the corpse looked to have been tampered with, and there remained an idiotic or unearthly leer most painful to behold. Arriving at the cathedral door, the clergy and municipal board contended for precedence—each claiming the right. Whether supported by the rights of law or the moral force of virtue, none ever successfully resist the demands of the priesthood here, as they might well have known, and, to avoid the scandal of public contention, the city fathers withdrew. Nor is it on public occasions, or respecting public events, that the clergy wield such power. Each household is controlled by them, and no husband or father has the authority over his family possessed by the confessor. In fact, it is not unfrequently the case that the views and opinions of the father are wholly disregarded, if at variance with those of the spiritual adviser; and thus heart-burnings, bickerings, estrangement, and immorality creep in.

The individual whose decease has been the subject of these paragraphs, appears to have been an exception among the multitude; and his memory will be cherished for the many acts of benevolence and kindness adorning a long life of usefulness, that rendered his name "familiar as household words." No dismembered family, no betrayed woman, no half score of *nieces*, were left to curse him; but the intelligent, the poor, and the afflicted lamented a companion and friend departed. Few possessed his powers of self-denial, or would have thought they had a right to decline the exalted positions which had been tendered to him, viz: the bishopric of Coquimbo on one occasion, and the archbishopric of the republic on another. Yet he evidently preferred the more useful and humble sphere indicated by the course of his divine Master before popes and bishops were known on the earth.

Ceremonies in honor of Don ———. "The board of directors of the Asylum del Salvador, having determined to celebrate exequies in memory of the beneficent founder of that institution of mercy, Don ———, we make known to you that they will take place at the chapel of the Asylum on Monday next, 19th instant, at 9 A. M. We hope that you will favor us with your presence. May God preserve you," &c.

Not willing to omit rendering homage to the manes of a gentleman who had devoted a portion of his life to ameliorating the condition of his kind, or to slight an invitation so prettily worded, (in the original,) it was not difficult to reach the chapel named at a reasonable hour. Even to dinner one need not haste in Chile; an hour later than the time named will be quite early enough in almost all cases. On the present occasion, however, it was eleven o'clock when I reached the chapel.

It is a small though tasteful building, belonging to the house of refuge in Yungai, and adjoins the normal school of agriculture. Its only windows are in the western end above the altar, and these were covered with drapery of black cambric. The main door of entrance and side-walls were also draped in black. Above the altar was an effigy of the deceased, (he had been interred for weeks,) with his sword and its scabbard crossed over the lower portion of the body, and the insignia of merit which a grateful country had awarded for important services. On either side was a large vase, from which poured a flame of burning spirit, blue and mystic; whilst about the altar, and around a table covered with a black velvet pall that occupied the body of the church, there were long wax tapers. A large silver urn stood on the table.

Before the altar eight priests were engaged in the ceremonies, of which a dirge formed the longer part. In this they were assisted by a choir of male voices, all cultivated artists; and the music, though appropriately solemn, was effective and pleasant. The mass and dirge occupied two hours. At their conclusion a eulogistic discourse on the deceased was pronounced, the mind of the orator being so excessively florid that his auditors had many occasions to suspect his memory equally oblivious. The services concluded with a discordant and disagreeable chant by the priests, a dozen who had come as guests aiding the officials. There were only invited guests present. These, to the number of a hundred perhaps, embraced many of the first men in Santiago; and though the doorway was crowded with the straw-hat gentry, they were considerate enough to keep their odors beyond the influence of the incense burned around the altar. A darkened edifice, with funereal drapings lighted only by tapers and the pale-blue unearthly flames of the vases, with the solemn melody of the priests and singers, as beneath this spectral gleam they passed from side to side or knelt in obedience to the rubric, were well calculated to render the ceremonies and scene imposing. I could not but think the object and its results far more likely to awaken virtuous energies, to arouse philanthropic spirit, and to draw man nearer to his Creator, than many of the incomprehensible pageants so often witnessed.

Most of those whose attendance at the obsequies had been solicited were fellow-laborers with Don ——— in his works of philanthropy, and were known to be willing promoters of every object having in view the advancement of their country. Believing, perhaps, that whilst their feelings were under the influence of the eulogy, and themselves more earnestly desirous to merit like commendation from successors, a new object of public utility could be brought forward with greater probability of success, a second note, accompanying the invitation, solicited our attendance, on conclusion of the exequies, at the normal school of agriculture; the object being to form a society to encourage agriculture and horticulture in Chile. The enthusiastic and energetic director of the normal school had provided a superb *déjeuner à la fourchette*, embracing every imaginable luxury from the *pâté de foie gras* and preserved *bécassines* of France to the less palatable but more substantial *cazuela* of the country, with fish, fowls, hams, pastry, and fruits, to be washed down with wines in variety *ad libitum*. Ample justice was done to the comestibles set out, and ample gratification afterwards experienced by those who for the first time examined the extensive preparations to educate a corps of agriculturists scientifically, not less than by others who marked the rapid progress a few months had enabled the enterprising chief to make. And thus, when he came to sketch out a plan for the society, his propositions were adopted *nem. con.*: everybody wrote his name; and in this manner has commenced the first botanical organization of the republic.

Palm Sunday.—There are processions in the morning by the friars of each order. As I passed down the street for my morning's walk, those of La Merced, with long wands of the cocoa palm in their hands, followed by the crowd which had been packed within the church, and a larger concourse from the street, were just coming out of the north door. Their cowls and loose-flowing robes are not ungraceful, and the color is a decided recommendation. Those of the provincial and priests were covered with richly embroidered garments, in shape and ornaments strongly resembling the pictures one sees of Chinese mandarins. The whole body, priests and laity, chanted as they moved bareheaded to the western door; and there a ceremony was performed which the crowd prevented me from seeing. A cloud of incense ascending above the sea of heads was all that could be discerned, until I followed them inside to the high mass.

Near the door was a table jointly occupied by a priest and a layman, engaged in the sale of indulgences and pardons; whilst a juvenile member of the fraternity perambulated the body of the church, with a plate to receive oblations in one hand, a string of amulets for sale to the peons over one arm, and a piece of the white material of which their dress is made for the faithful to kiss in the unemployed hand. The white cloth may have been a veritable relic from the petticoat of our Lady of Mercy herself, since none failed to kiss it when presented; though there were neither offerings nor purchases in my presence. A sharp glance was cast towards me as the young monk passed, and I fancied a twinkle from the corner of his eye, almost saying:

My pearls are not for swine like you. The confessionals were all occupied by priests, with a kneeling penitent on each side, one awaiting the conclusion of the other's *peccavi;* though service was performing at the altar, and the nave and aisles were densely packed by the crowd. A part of the ceremony consists in blessing the palm-branches, which the congregation afterwards struggle to obtain and religiously preserve at their dwellings as preventives against a multitude of human misfortunes. There is no other special ceremonial until,

Holy Thursday.—Every day, and all the day, churches are open, and multitudes who are careless during the rest of the year become outwardly devout in the intervening days of Lent; but there is too little difference apparent to be specially remarked by a stranger. On this day the furor of the church-goers seems, if possible, to attain its maximum. Crowds pass uncovered, and in long lines, from church to church, repeating aves; and he or she who makes the greatest number of *estaciones*—as a visit to each church is called—performs the greatest expiation. Five or six *estaciones* are generally considered sufficient, and these can be accomplished without walking more than half a mile; but there are very great sinners whose consciences are scarcely appeased until they have made twice that number. All the churches are brilliantly lighted until late at night; and they, as well as the streets leading to them, are so thronged by the penitent populace that it is difficult to thread one's way. It seeming to have been ascertained here, as well as at the charitable fairs of our more calculating land, that grace of person and manner have rare influence to loose the purse-strings, ladies are stationed with salvers beside each church door, to solicit alms in aid of missionaries among the Indians.

During this and the following day, the "*Cucuruchos*"—a sort of Odd-Fellows—may be met rapidly walking the streets, aiding by their costume to render the scene a solemn masquerade. Their dress is a closely-fitting domino of black cambric, crossed by bands of white over the shoulders and back; a long, conical, black hat (whence the name, most probably); a black mask, and a cane—a style of dress which certainly renders them remarkable objects in public highways, and well calculated to inspire terror among children, to whom they are held out as threats, if not to secure the veneration to which their more dignified name, "Brothers of St. Sepulchre," might entitle them. The object of their association is charitable. Each member pays a real monthly for the purpose of securing medical and spiritual attendance (masses) and proper burial at the close of his earthly career. They also seek alms, carrying a little box from house to house. These are the only two days when they are publicly known as "*Cucuruchos.*"

Good Friday.—All secular employments are interrupted on Wednesday at noon, nor is any wheeled vehicle or horse permitted in the streets after seven o'clock in the morning of the three following days. Indeed, in the thoroughfares there is scarcely any evidence of life on this day until towards ten o'clock, at which hour the cathedral becomes the great centre of attraction.

On the Good Friday of 1850, the archbishop was received at the door of the cathedral by its officials, and, preceded by them, passed through the nave to the altar in the ordinary purple robes of his rank. The whole vast edifice was literally packed with a living multitude. A silver ewer and water, for the ablution of hands, presented to his Reverence, commences the rites; repeated changes of vestments subsequently occupy much time, and, from the attention given them, evidently constituting an important feature of the ceremonies. Luckily for the unbelievers present, this could not be done without the accompaniment of music, and those to whom the sight of the gorgeous robes produced pleasure had two senses gratified at once. Both vocal and instrumental music were of a high order, well executed, plaintive, and melancholy throughout. A basso from the Italian opera company and a tenor from the priesthood were the two principal voices; but when all the choristers united in chanting the solemn *miserere,* many a humid eye told of the hearts throbbing under its influence for the sufferings of "the meek-eyed Saviour." One must be well acquainted with the forms of the Roman church to be able to describe, or even to name, the ceremonies on this occasion; indeed, the fact that there is a special master of ceremonies, who, from time to time, indicates the rite and form to be observed in turn, as directed by the volume in his hand, is quite proof that they are neither thoroughly understood nor remembered by the actors themselves in this serious drama.

After a sermon, comprising a salutatory discourse to the cross adorning the altar—invoked as an animate object capable of inflicting good or evil, rather than as the emblem of faith—and a brief detail of events during the early career of the Redeemer, a venerable looking cross was reverentially laid at foot of the platform on which the high altar stands. Commencing with the highest in rank, one by one the clergy prostrated themselves before the relic, kneeling at two different places in the nave before placing their lips upon it. Next, the archbishop removed the host from the altar with much solemnity, conveying it through the nave and aisles under a canopy of silver lace. He was preceded by a priest, who bore the insignia of his office—a golden crozier—and a procession numbering hundreds of clergy and laity, carrying wax candles. The congregation continued kneeling as the procession passed through their midst, beating their breasts in concert with the noise of a rattle called "*matraca*" and the solemn dirge chanted by the priests during their march. Even bells are prohibited after Thursday, and the matraca alone is used. Returning to the front of the altar, the consecrated wafer was consumed amid a cloud of incense; and this, with additional music, ended the four hours' ceremonies of the morning.

At night there was a torchlight procession from the church of San Francisco, in the cañada, to the plaza, the clergy, including the archbishop and monks, the cucuruchos, and others specially devout among the laity, taking part in it. They had images of the crucified Saviour, of all the evangelists, many angels, Judas, the cock that witnessed against Peter, and his Satanic Majesty himself, all as large as life. To accommodate a crowd of youthful singers, pupils of the National Conservatory of Music, who were to greet the procession on its arrival, a stage surmounted by a huge cross had been erected in the plaza. These juvenile musicians had been some time in training for the occasion; and, in the stillness of the night, their voices penetrated even to my distant scene of labor, on Santa Lucia. To a near spectator it was probably a rare sight; but from the hill, though aided by a strong moon and the light of a thousand torches, there could only be distinguished a towering illuminated cross amid a dense, dark sea of human forms. In the following year I was at Valparaiso, too busy with the mail for the United States to think of church ceremonies; and in 1852 in one of the provincial towns, of whose celebrations an account is given in its proper place.

Saturday.—A heavy rain during the very early morning imparted a bright and cheerful look to the dusty verdure surrounding the city, and vigorous freshness to the air. Higher in the atmosphere the congealed moisture had fallen unchanged, and many a peak of the nearer cordilleras, which, from its bleak sterility, had looked, oh, so hot! for two or three months, had been clad with its winter mantle. Apparently above, and at the very base of the eastern chain, floated huge piles of cumuli, through whose interstices the sun poured a flood of golden light over the city; the sky to the north and west being, at the same time, of that intense blue which only the depths of ocean can rival.

Service at the cathedral commenced by a procession of the priests through the aisles and nave. Though but the day following the crucifixion, or *second* day, the church could not longer postpone celebrating the resurrection of the Saviour. The altar was shrouded in darkness, the multitude of tapers in the chandeliers near it being unlighted, and, though the edifice never possesses the glare of our Protestant buildings without these adjuncts, there was now only a sombre and mystic light, well suited to a mourning community. Had there been no parade of presenting, on silver salvers, the half hundred or more articles composing the archbishop's robes for different parts of the ritual, and two or three fancifully dressed priests to assist in putting them on and taking them off every little while, and the stillness of the cathedral had only been broken by the low and wailing strain of the organ, devotional feelings would have germinated even in the soul of a heretic. But, with such constant changes of costume, the dancing round of priests in their white "josey" gowns, the lighting, extinguishing, and shifting of candles from side to side before the altar, and the incessant bobbing up and down of some one or other of the crowd of priests and acolytes, if not in time, at least to the accompaniment of first-rate quadrille music, the show was quite equal to a melodrama, and I could only wish it had been possible to behold it somewhat nearer. Some such scene as this must have been witnessed by Sidney Smith to cause him to define the Roman Catholic religion as "posture and imposture, flexions and genuflexions, bowing to the right, courtesying to the left, and an immense amount of man-millinery." Perhaps, after all, the distance of my position lent enchantment.

All at once the black veil which concealed the altar and its ornaments was drawn aside, displaying it brilliantly illuminated. "Christ risen!" pealed from the choir and organ; the bells throughout the city, which had been so long silent, were started to merry chimes; and the artillery of Santa Lucia poured out its thunders in the national ecclesiastical rejoicing. At egress from the church, when the services were completed—half an hour later—the apparent incubus which had been hanging over Santiago was gone; shops were opened, displaying gaudy goods to the moving multitudes let loose by the sound of the bells; loaded carretas from the port already occupied the plaza, tabooed to them during so many days; and the thousand and one peddlers, with their equally numerous varieties of goods, were again rendering the thoroughfares a nuisance by their cries.

Easter Sunday.—Were not so much time occupied in robing, unrobing, and re-robing the archbishop, high mass at the cathedral would be an attractive ceremony even to the uninitiated. The arrangements for his toilet occupy full one half of the time; and with this senseless drawback the service becomes irksome, especially when one is obliged to stand amid a crowd of unwashed and unsavory peons, whilst the seats are filled with scores of priestlings, many of whom have not yet entered their 'teens. To add to the annoyances, half a dozen fleas or so—the unfaithful wretches!—desert their lawful masters for strangers; and so closely is one pressed in the crowd, that a finger cannot be raised to attempt arresting their frolicsome gambols, induced at finding so fair a field to race over as the middle of one's back.

At one time I began to think the archbishop would be so loaded down by robes that he would not be able to walk, and mentally congratulated him on the change of temperature, which would give him ability to support the heat of such a mass without much suffering. There was most excellent music by the choir and organ; quite an impressive sermon; and, at the conclusion, a pastoral letter of moderate length—exceptionable only for the sentiments of intolerance with which it terminated. From the dignity and rank of the officiating priests, and intrinsically, the service—as one of the highest known to the church—was an interesting one. An old gentleman, to whom a portion of the ritual was assigned, began reading from the missal at a place appropriated to another occasion, and it was some minutes before the master of ceremonies could set him right, having made somewhat unholy haste to do so from the vicinity of the altar. In other lands, it is to be feared that such a *scene* would have brought smiles and titters to the countenances of more than one of the congregation, but there was no such exhibition here; and I could but think it a pity to mortify the venerable prelate by such interruption; for, even ***had*** his aged voice been audible, all pages of the book are alike unintelligible to the multitude.

It is alleged as one reason for anticipating the resurrection, and celebrating it on Saturday, that the number of prayers and lessons could not be gotten through with in reasonable time on a single day. Yet it is quite certain, as has already been said, that more than one half of the whole time of yesterday and to-day was consumed in displaying the archbishop's wardrobe, either on the salvers or on his person; music only, and that often selections from operas, accompanying the exhibitions. If this be a part of the *religion*, nothing more can be said; if not, they had better read more prayers in a language understood by the audience, and practise fewer theatrical shiftings.

Sunday after Easter.—By sunset of the preceding day, the ringing of church-bells and firing of rockets at the same places, heralded the advent of another fiesta—*Quasimodo*—the day on which is celebrated "Christ visiting the sick." Such an uproar was kept up throughout the night, that it was not an easy matter to sleep.

Nominally at daylight, but really not until after a reasonably early breakfast, in imitation of their divine Master, the curates of the churches begin their missions of mercy. Unlike "the man of many sorrows," however, some of them ride in luxuriously cushioned carriages, driven and attended by gentlemen of the best blood in Santiago, and are escorted by troops of cavalry and a military band. In the archbishop's cortége there were two other and unoccupied carriages, also with gentlemen drivers and footmen, some few mounted guasos, and, of course, a great crowd of peons and boys. Attending them were venders of rockets and fireworks of various descriptions, who reaped an excellent harvest; and the incessant explosions of pyrotechnics overhead, rendered the pompous parade as unlike a religious festival as possible.

Opposite our residence there lived a lady too old to attend church, before whose door the carriage stopped whilst the sacrament was taken within and administered to her. The delay was entirely too brief for spiritual counsel, and it may well be doubted whether the priest remained long enough to see her swallow the wafer; but she is well endowed with worldly goods which she cannot possibly enjoy much longer, and the holy honor of a visit by his reverence on this occasion may secure a rich legacy to the church. Bred to the law, his Right Reverence knows well the human heart; and when called on to write testamentary documents—as he frequently is—he fails not to secure provision for mother church. In a recent instance of the kind, to which one of our countrymen was a subscribing witness, his Reverence had managed to secure a legacy of $100,000 for spiritual purposes.

MAY 13.—On this day the great earthquake of 1647 is commemorated by a procession from San Augustin. In this the members of the legal profession unite, as a body, with the clergy. Its origin may be traced in the following extract from an account of the earthquake, given by the then bishop of Santiago—Gaspar de Villarroel (himself an Augustin)—to the president of the Supreme Council of the Indies:

"During sixty years they had been building a sumptuous temple, of brick and mortar, for San Agustin. It had three naves, of which the principal one was finished; the arches were partially raised, and to its final completion they had commenced covering it in. In the nave of the Evangelist, covered with heavy materials, service was celebrated. It all fell; and that which did not fall is in worse condition than that which did, because the thousand openings of so great a building will only serve to fill the pious with horror and fear. These fathers have a most revered crucifix, miraculously made, it having been done about forty years ago by a most pious monk, who was neither joiner nor carver. It was against the then partition wall, which closed an arch so easy to fall that it did not need the earthquake; yet, though the whole nave was prostrated, the image remained erect on its cross, without even injury to the canopy. They found it with the crown of thorns about the throat, as though to intimate that so severe a sentence moved him to compassion; and because it remains, we promise ourselves his great mercy. The population being moved by their ancient devotion, and this recent miracle, we brought it in procession to the plaza; the bishop and religious persons coming barefoot, with great lamentations, many tears, and universal groans."*

Padre Olivares, who wrote a history of Chile, the MS. of which is in possession of Presbyter Eyzaguirre, adds to this: "And though attempts were afterwards made to replace it, no matter how great the force used, they could not accomplish it, and it remains in that position to the present time, much venerated by the people." The bishop immediately afterward instituted a fraternity under the name of *Brothers of Jesus, Mary, and San Nicholas of Penitence;* and in memory of the day, at the hour of the earthquake they were to make an annual procession through all the public streets. Driven from their offices by the general ruin, the royal auditors and municipal board assembled in the open air, passing an order binding themselves and successors to participate in the ceremony, with red candles in their hands, and that all their officers should confess and commune on that anniversary. All the citizens were entreated to fol-

* Villarroel: Gobierno Eclesiastico Pacifico.

low their example in each respect. The interest was kept up, for at a later period the Captains General regularly assisted in the ovation.

Rain having fallen a day or two previously, the celebration (of 1850) was postponed by the archbishop to the following Thursday; some of his own countrymen having the malice to say that he was not willing to tramp through the mud with new slippers on. Towards 5 P. M. a number of civilians, with lighted torches, sallied from the doors of San Augustin in two lines, separated from each other about ten feet. Neither the president, the cabildo as a body, nor any of the eminent members of the legal profession were among them; the majority being hangers-on of the notary offices and boys. Following them was a nearly life-size image of an unknown saint (to me) mounted on a platform, borne on the shoulders of ten or twelve men. The friars of La Merced, Santo Domingo, and San Augustin, two and two, came next, and each of these also bore lighted candles. Immediately in the rear of the Franciscans came the image of the "Christ of agony," mounted and borne like the preceding; next were the clergy of the cathedral and parish churches, chanting a hymn whose refrain was, *Ora pro nobis;* and then an image of the Virgin, dressed with all imaginary finery, and perched on a fancifully decorated stand. Close to this platform came the archbishop, one priest carrying his train, and another perfuming the air in front with clouds of incense. A military band followed his right reverence, who were in turn defended by a battalion of the National Guard, and the rear of the procession was brought up by the mounted grenadiers. At intervals along the line, boys scattered flowers in the path of the devout crowd, from waiters piled high with these gems of nature. Nor must I omit to mention that the vulgar and inquisitive crowd, with which the streets and plaza were thronged, was thrust aside by stalwart pioneers with their huge battle-axes. Whether the soldiers in their gay uniforms are humble volunteers, desirous to return thanks in this manner for the great mercy shown to their ancestors, or are brought out to swell the parade and pomp of the church, was not asked. The show was pretty, even brilliant; but there was not an enthusiastic word among the populace—scarcely evidence of life, their countenances expressing neither pleasure nor animation.

Corpus Christi.—This festival originated in the year 1230, from the vision of a Westphalian nun, who alleges that while looking at the full moon she saw a broken place or gap in its limb, of which Heaven miraculously revealed to her this explanation: That the moon symbolized the Christian church, and the imperfect portion of its disk typified the want of a special festival, in which the consecrated host should be adored as the actual body of Christ. On the strength of this vision, such a festival was actually ordained by Pope Urban IV. Thursday of the week after Pentecost was appointed for its celebration, and an absolution of from forty to one hundred days was promised to the penitents who should participate in it. In 1850, it was due on the 31st of May; but as there had been rain at Santiago on the preceding day, the archbishop directed that the parade should be postponed until the following Thursday. This is quite customary with all festivals which occur during unpropitious weather.

On the morning of the 6th of June, therefore, altars were erected at each corner of the main plaza, with extravagantly dressed saints on top; plenty of tinsel ornaments; a dozen or two of wax candles to each; a missal on either side; and a carpet in front, for the archbishop to kneel upon when halting, during the perambulation of the clergy. On another occasion, priests in their robes were substituted for two of the saints. Each had an open Bible in his hand, and a foot on the breast of a prostrate image, one labelled "Luther"—the other "Calvin."

By 4 o'clock the regular troops and national guard had collected, and formed in double lines round the plaza, with sufficient space between them for the procession to pass. A mass of spectators crowded every other spot of ground, and each balcony and window overlooking the scene of display had also its occupants. Next year, however, standing in balconies or windows above the level of the street was prohibited. None were allowed to *look down* on the body of Christ as it passed, and the crowd were peremptorily driven from these portions of their own domicils. Elbowing my way into the cathedral with difficulty, it was found crowded, and a pompous ceremony going on, like those of Holy Week, or, if unlike them, too little so for appreciation by the unlettered, since, in addition to the ordinary amount of robing and unrobing, and pantomimic motions, I could only detect that now both choirs were firing away at each other. The little old instruments in the west end had a choir mainly of boys, and the new and deep-toned organ over the eastern door a choir of matured singers.

At the termination of the ceremonies within the church, the head of the procession, composed of between one and two hundred boy-priests, with lighted candles, marched into the square. These were followed by the archbishop, bareheaded, but protected by a canopy of embroidered silver, borne by four gentlemen of the city, and surrounded by all the officials of the cathedral. All were chanting as they came into the open square, the appearance of his Reverence being the signal for the special guard at the door to uncover themselves, present arms, and fall to their knees; and for the artillerists on Santa Lucia to fire a national salute. As soon as the whole body of the clergy was fairly out, those who bore the golden crozier and cross of the archbishop took up their position in front of him, and a military band fell into his rear, striking up a pleasant air. The guard of honor rose, and the procession moved on to the different altars, between kneeling and bareheaded lines of troops with presented arms. The sea of heads filling the plaza was also uncovered, and the crowds prostrated themselves whenever the sacred emblem, borne by his Reverence in a golden vessel, approached them. Until within two years, it had been customary at this festival for the troops to prostrate the national flag for the clergy to walk over, as is still done (I have heard) in Spain and Bolivia; but, to the credit of the officer then in command, the desecration was resisted, and, though it created no little anger, the government sustained him. To appease the church, however, it was ordered that the "silken flags should feed the moth" on every succeeding anniversary.

A prayer or two, or other devotional exercise, occupying three or four minutes, was recited at each altar. The first one where the procession halted was surmounted by an image of the Virgin Mary, about two thirds the size of life, holding by the hand a waxen doll representing the infant Jesus. Both were dressed extravagantly, seeming to inspire little either of veneration or respect from the surrounding lookers on, except by outward form, and at the moment when the consecrated wafer was in their vicinity. It was impossible to detect what was said or sung by the clergy; but, from the language and conduct of the rabble, composing a large proportion of the assemblage, an unfavorable impression was drawn, which was fully confirmed when the band struck up an air from "*La Fille du Régiment,*" and most effectually drowned the voices of the priests.

Quite enough had been seen by the time the procession reached the second altar, and it was a relief to escape into the free air of a side street. Yet the mortifying reflection of the tyranny to which the human mind is subjected still pursued me, and flight to Santa Lucia, instead of obliterating, served but to enforce it; for the castle below the Observatories was uttering another hallelujah with its iron lips, as the pageant passed into the cathedral again.

Assumption Day.—The day on which the church celebrates the miraculous ascent of the Virgin, body and soul, into Heaven. A presumptuous assumption, too, it would seem, since there is no scriptural warrant for its basis; though for all that, like many others of the *traditions* handed down by the fathers, it is none the less religiously believed. Whether Catholic or Protestant, it is greatly to be apprehended that the church has assumed many more things than were ever contemplated by the humble Nazarene, each striving, regardless of reason, to enslave the outward senses. Should reason dare rebel against their dicta, heresy, apostacy, infidelity, or atheism, are the certain harsh epithets by which arguments are characterized; and the unwise searcher for truth finds no peace but by blind submission to the incomprehensible dogmas of an interested clergy, however far-fetched the tenets themselves, or how unlike in precept or practice their expounders. Were the eleventh commandment acknowledged in good faith by mankind, it embraces an essential without which true piety cannot exist, viz: absolute toleration; and yet the sectarians, who are willing to "do unto others as ye would that they should do unto you," and thus recognise those of other creeds as endeavoring to pursue the path to eternal happiness, are like "fabled visits of the angels." The Catholic church on one hand, with its door so broad that tottering children, inebriate greybeards, and dissolute priests, staggering under the spoils of the gambling-table or cock-pit, may enter without the risk of striking its side-posts, pronounces the doom of everlasting punishment on all who do not avail themselves of it, and absolutely refuses them the rite of sepulture within its so-called consecrated depositories of mortality. On the other, the ranting Methodist, with a torrent of verbiage breathing of the fires of hell, the thrilling tortures of the accursed amid flames of sulphur, and other gross appeals to the fears of the timid, boldly denounces the followers of the Pope as idolaters, beyond the pale of salvation. Here are the extremes. One adheres to the rites, ceremonies, and autocratic government, perhaps essential ere the light of education was so generally diffused: the other is almost destitute of fixed rule, and to a fault democratic in discipline. Which is right?

The Virgin being (apparently) of more consequence in the Catholic religion than is the Saviour, any event connected with her, however assumed, merits especial observance, and the day is kept as a holyday. All secular employment is prohibited, the cathedral and churches are opened for high mass in the morning, and the theatres have extra performances at night. In the cathedral a life-size image of Mary was displayed on one side of the altar, amid drapery which, at a little distance, was no bad representation of clouds. As might be inferred, the figure was extravagantly dressed, the skill of a French *modiste* having been exercised in arranging a toilette selected in accordance with the taste of the lower classes—cheap finery. In the vicinity, the whole aisle was filled with kneeling suppliants, to whom she was the centre of attraction. The archbishop officiated at mass; but the services presented nothing differing from those before spoken of.

At night the hills were adorned with multitudes of lighted candles, it is said in payment of vows, or as propitiatory offerings to Santa Eusebia, whom the faithful believe has power to grant whatever earthly good one may desire. Many legends are told of the origin of placing the lights on surrounding eminences. One, and that in which most agree, is as follows:

A child, diseased with loathsome sores from the crown of its head to the soles of its feet, being deemed incurable, was placed by its parents, with a portion of bread and water, on a neighboring eminence, and there left to shift for itself or die. Returning to bury its remains at the expiration of a year, to their surprise the parents found their child seemingly alive and healed; but the moment they spoke a dove flew from its mouth, and their offspring disappeared. Whether it ascended bodily among the angels, or was converted into vapor, the legend says not. A moment afterwards the dove alighted on a rock near them, and on the surface wrote an inscription with its bill, directing them, as a penance for their sinful desertion, to burn a specified number of candles on the spot every year, in honor of Santa Eusebia. On their way homeward the distressed couple narrated their adventure to an incredulous friend whom they met, who flatly refused belief in the power of Santa Eusebia to work miracles, and asserted that ocular proof alone would convince him. Sustained in their faith by the special demonstration just witnessed, they persevered with their doubting companion until he petulantly exclaimed, "Well, I would as soon believe that I shall find an ounce ($17.25) on my table, as what you say about Santa Eusebia." Impious man! the door of his rancho was scarcely opened to receive them, as they passed by, when a golden coin of that value was discovered on the table! So runs the story; and the power of her ladyship to grant small favors is no more doubted, even by many of the highest class, than we doubt that the sun will rise on any following day. As an instance in point, the following anecdote may be told of a personal friend:

During the forenoon her house-servant had displaced the key of the *despensa*, or pantry, and it could not be found in any direction. Guests were expected at dinner; the hour approached; without the key not even the china could be obtained, and the mistress also joined in the search. Their efforts being fruitless, in her distress under the reprimands occasioned by the *contretemps*, the maid vowed a dozen candles to be burned on Santa Lucia if the saint would restore the missing instrument. No sooner promised than responded to, for on returning to the dining-room there lay the crooked thing on the centre of the table; and both vow that it was neither there when they left the room, a few minutes previously, nor had any one but themselves had access to it. The mistress assured me of *her* firm belief in the interposition of the saint on this occasion, and, of course, the maid would not dare doubt.

Many of them being in colored lanterns, the effect of the lights is very pretty on a dark ground; and it is probably as innocent a method in which to spend money as any other, whilst it gives encouragement to one branch of domestic industry, candle-making. It was maliciously said that these light-manufacturers encouraged belief in the miraculous deeds of the saint to serve their own ends. The illuminations continued from Assumption day until late in September, Santa Lucia often presenting a brilliant spectacle from the multitudes of lights arranged in crosses, triumphal arches, or other fancy forms, not unfrequently intermingled with vari-colored lanterns. As the mania continued spreading, so that even the summits of San Christoval and Renca were not too lofty for the display of these votive offerings, the church took exception, and the populace was notified that within its holy walls or their own dwellings were the proper places for such pious exhibitions. This caused a falling off, but not entire cessation, until a positive prohibition was issued. Government suspected the socialist club as in some manner connected with the new religious fervor, apprehending that in the out-of-the-way crags and precipices other matters than "good will to men" were the subjects of discussion, and the placing of candles in fulfilment of vows mere pretexts for gatherings boding no good to the peace and prosperity of Santiago. A guard was therefore sent to the castle and sentries were posted along the paths leading to the summit of the hill, whilst the archbishop at last put the seal of condemnation on the display altogether. Previous to 1850, Santa Eusebia had very few votaries in Santiago; after that time I never saw a propitiatory candle publicly burned.

September 8.—Anniversary of the Nativity of the Virgin.—All named Mercedes celebrate this as their day instead of the actual anniversaries of their births, and in preference to the 24th, which is the regular day of *Nuestra Señora de las Mercedes.* In 1850 it came on Sunday, and, as each lady deemed it especially desirable to attend mass on that day, the great number who are thus called renders morning service at the cathedral and the church erected to her ladyship no little attractive to the beaux and undevout. The archbishop was not present at the cathedral, and, though his second in command officiated, the ceremonies remained as little like devotion as ever. Of the music it is not necessary to say anything more; it is always good, and may be listened to much to the satisfaction and moral edification of all rightly inclined. After the mass, the usual procession of feast-days came off, through the nave, the aisles, and around the church. It consisted of a number of men and youths, wearing silk capes of different colors and with lighted candles in their hands, and the dean with the consecrated wafer in a golden vessel resembling an image of the sun. He was surrounded by the clergy of the episcopal establishment; four gentlemen carried a silken canopy over his head, and boys scattered flowers in the path of the coming procession.

The church possesses hundreds of the capes worn, and during mass servants go round with armfuls, silently offering one to each *genteelly dressed* male whom they may catch upon his knees. If he nod his head, the cape is tied over his shoulders, and this symbol authorizes another set of servants to supply him with a wax candle. The salvers borne by the boys were piled high with the earliest offerings of spring, and it seemed desecration to trample so many of nature's exquisite productions under the feet of a crowd of rude and portly male bipeds. I can yield something to woman, and would not be hyper-critical when seeing flowers spread for any men whose countenances indicated devotion and self-sacrifice for the benefit of their kind; but to witness them crushed as sand under feet of the people who compose the processions at Santiago, not excepting the clergy and friars (who are the fattest and most corpulent of all), makes me regret that such things as religious pageants exist.

Nuestra Señora de las Mercedes: Our Lady of Mercies.—In other countries annual festivals interrupted from any cause are irrecoverable; here, however, such is not the case: the importance of constant appeals to the outward senses of the multitude is never to be lost sight of; and if the weather prohibit parade out of doors, the church authorities defer it to a more propitious season. Tuesday, the 24th, was the legitimate anniversary, but on that day the flood-gates of heaven were opened, and the rain descended in such torrents as to keep every one at home; the procession was, therefore, postponed to the 29th. The festival was heralded by a *novena*, or nine-days' service, at the church; not uninterruptedly, for that would have altered the proportions of the plump-looking friars, and made them more like every-day working-men, but by preachings and exhortations just after twilight in the evenings, and confessions and masses at all hours of the period named. So great were the numbers attending night-service, that the streets in front of the church-doors were also filled by women. The church had been partially decorated with flags some days previously, and at sunrise of the 29th no less than thirty national banners of different sizes were flying from its front and turrets. There was also between the towers a large star made of paper, of the three national colors, which was illuminated by night, adding much to the effect. Nor was the scene inside less flaunting or showy. The procession, in the afternoon, is stated to have been extremely pretty, but not unlike that of the following Sunday, under charge of the Dominicans.

Nuestra Señora del Rosario: Our Lady of the Rosary.—The multitude of silver and tinsel ornaments decorating the altars of Santo Domingo was extraordinary, and the quantity of natural flowers arranged in vases, wreaths, and festoons, not less striking. From each of the longitudinal arches there was suspended a flag of one of the civilized nations of the earth—that of Spain occupying the post of honor, if the column next the high altar can be so regarded; the "stars and stripes" not far from the central arch. At vespers, on the preceding evening, all the side altars, as well as the body of the church, were lighted up, curiosity attracting an immense crowd to witness it. A larger number might be accommodated were there seats, as in Protestant edifices; but under present arrangements, each female must not only leave space for new-comers to pass between herself and neighbors, but also take care that they do not encroach within the space intended to allow change of position to her feet. There seems no fixed period for them to remain either at mass or vespers, some leaving immediately after the priest consumes the host, the majority just before the sermon—even those who stay through the discourse being engaged in paters and aves with their rosaries rather than with the oration. High-backed benches are placed along the columns forming the nave, and across its base, for the accommodation of the men; but our sex does not often form a very numerous part of the congregation.

There was much chanting from a body of friars stationed in the nave, no small amount of whispered admiration among the dark-eyed dames and maidens occupying their humble seats around, and any amount of pressing and squeezing by the gaping, odorous gentry, whose uncombed locks are ever thrust under one's nose in such places. At the termination of the ceremonies inside, the bells of both towers were set in motion, a band stationed in one turret struck up a gay tune, and the air of the plazuela before the church literally teemed with fireworks of various descriptions, fizzing and exploding to a degree that rendered the confusion of bell, and military band, and human voices, "worse confounded."

The procession came off at 5 o'clock of the afternoon, and was composed of a body of the devout bearing torches; next came the Dominican friars, preceded by an image of San Pio V, under a canopy borne on men's shoulders; Santo Domingo, a similar paste and pasteboard image, followed immediately after; two or three orders of monks succeeded; and then the archbishop, with his golden cross, surrounded by his suite. A military band followed his reverence, and Our Lady of the Rosary, flanked by parts of a company of lancers, brought up the rear. All the canopies were more or less composed of silver, and ornamented with flowers in wreaths and bouquets, as well of silver as natural products. That, however, under which the last image of the procession was moved was by far the most costly. All the dresses were of the richest silks and velvets—strings of diamonds and pearls, borrowed from many a fair dame's casket for the occasion, adding to the brilliancy of her ladyship. The most attractive object, however, was a representation of the infant Saviour, in robes and ornaments still more luxurious, borne on her left arm—her right hand displaying at the same time the insignia of a Chilean general. Although the procession moved only from the church to the plaza, thence round three of its sides, and back again, through another street, much time was consumed. The platforms, saints, and canopies were very weighty, and each moment added a shower of natural flowers to their load from the balconies beneath which they passed, so that the bearers were obliged to pause for rest quite frequently.

Nuestra Señora del Carmen, *patrona jurada del ejercito:* Our Lady of Carmel, sworn patroness of the army.—The church of San Augustin was decorated with flags and flowers, as those of La Merced and Santo Domingo had been, the variety and profusion of nature's exquisite productions effectively captivating one's sight. A grand mass was performed in the morning, at which as many of the civic troops attended as the edifice would contain, after their arms had been stacked in the plazuela, under charge of a guard. How many the officers managed to pack, it is difficult to say; for, finding that it would not be easy to retreat at will, and that the squeaking tones of the little old organ offered no recompense for a stand of two or three hours among the copper-colored citizens composing the *Guardia Nacional,* whilst they poured in at one door, I escaped through another. A procession was made in the afternoon, composed of the highest military chieftains, monks and priests *ad libitum,* the order of St. Sepulchre, representations of several saints, male and female, and Our Lady of Carmel, under canopies and on thrones and platforms, as mentioned on the day of the Rosaries, and finally, as then, the archbishop, with his ever-attendant suite and insignia. Most of the ornaments about the canopies and thrones were rich and gorgeous to a degree—embossed silver flowers eclipsing in brilliancy, if not in beauty, the natural creations in whose midst they were placed. The toilet of Our Lady of Carmel particularly, and those of the female images generally, though most costly and profuse in ornaments, scarcely concealed so much of their persons as *danseuses* of the French school have considered it politic to cover in presence of an audience. Daylight as it was, each member of the procession carried a long wax taper. From the difficulty with which the porters supported the cumbrous stages, though cheered by the inspiriting sound of military music, the column necessarily moved slowly. To render anew their vows of subservience, the civic battalions were drawn up in two lines, extending from the door of the church along the street leading to the great plaza, and around its four sides, with a space between the lines just wide enough for the cortége to pass. All the remainder of the plaza, the balconies which commanded a view of it, and the thoroughfares leading into it, were filled by the populace, embracing every class of society, whose murmurs of delight were scarcely drowned in the fizzing and cracking noise of the fireworks which welcomed the advent of the pageant. What reverence or faith in the result of this propitiatory display was exhibited in the countenances of the lookers-on, may be told in one word—none!

PLAN of the CITY of SANTIAGO

Lat. 33°26′ S. Long 70°38′ W.

References.

1 Presidents Palace.
2 Barracks of the Grenadiers.
3 Monastery of S[t] Augustin.
4 San Augustin.
5 Chamber of Deputies.
6 Nunnery of S[ta] Clara.
7 Convent of la Merced.
8 Recoleta Dominica.
9 Church of la Estampa.
10 Nunnery of Carmen Bajo.
11 Recoleta Francisca.
12 Barracks.
13 Nunnery de S[ta] Rosa.
14 Church de S[ta] Anna.
15 Seminary.
16 Nunnery de la Victoria.
17 " " " las Capuchinas.
18 Church of St. Domingo.
19 Prison. Comandant of Army Barracks.
" Firemen Barracks of Vigilantes.
20 Cathedral.
21 Church of la Compania. Museum.
" University.
22 Consulate.
23 Senate Chamber.
24 Barracks of the Artillery.
25 Military Academy.
26 Alms House.
27 Nunnery of Carmen Alto.
28 National Institute. Church of S[t] Diego.
29 Women's Hospital.
30 Church of S[t] Miguel.
31 School of the Augustin Monks.
32 Nunnery of S[ta] Rosa.
33 School of the French Nuns.
34 School of the Mechanic Arts.
35 Church of San Francisco.
36 Men's Hospital.
37 Church of S[t] Lazaro.
38 " " " Isidro.
39 Chapel of la Vitilla.
40 U.S.N. Observatories.
41,42 Markets.
43 Cemetery.

Scale $\frac{1}{30.000}$

From survey by officers of the Academia Militar Santiago

Drawn by M. C. Gritzner C.E.

CHAPTER VIII.

SANTIAGO.

From the summit of the *Cuesta de Prado* the eye embraces a verdant basin lying N.N.E. and S.S.W., wholly closed in on all sides by the Andes and Central cordilleras, except through one narrow gorge or outlet at the south. Its length will vary little from sixty miles, and its average breadth is more than one third of that space; although there are places where spurs, thrown off like abutments to the two chains, diminish materially at such points the width between the basin walls. The bottom of the basin, a plain rising gently to the eastward from near the base of the western boundary, is traversed in its southern half by the Maypu. Across the centre comes the Mapocho; and still nearer to us, along the base of the hill we occupy, flows the Lampa—tributaries of the first-named, whose courses are distinctly traceable. At two thirds the distance across the oval, and on both sides of the Mapocho, lies Santiago, scarcely perceptible at so great a distance by reason of its structure, the multitude of poplars within and around it, and the lofty back-ground of the Andes, which apparently cast a dark shadow over the city; but the eye is soon able to detect amid the dark foliage a white wall, and occasionally the turret of a church.

The approach from the westward is not of the most interesting character—an arid, uncultivable, and dusty waste, a mile or two broad, with wretched hovels inhabited by a slovenly and unwashed population, heralding suburban streets in many places deep in mire from negligence of the acequias. For a mile on either side of the road there are cabins of unplastered adobes, with loosely-thatched roofs; the absence of chimneys, open walls, and roofs plainly indicating the geniality of the climate and the improvident nature of their occupants. Diversifying these, there are rows of Lombardy poplars; patches of flowers in gardens, matted together in wild luxuriance; here and there earthen ovens for baking bread, resembling in form the bee-hives of the old spelling-book; and rude arbors, with tables, displaying their loaves for sale. A little farther on, streets paved with rolled pebble-stones, and more compactly built and whitewashed houses, and mounted policemen at each corner, indicate that you are within the city founded in 1541 by Pedro Valdivia. Should your arrival be during the business hours of the day, or rather if it be during that portion of the day elsewhere devoted to business, the impression is more striking. Its long streets are almost deserted. There is no life, no activity, none of the bustle usually belonging to a capital large or small, nor evidences of trade except rude signs painted on the walls in orthography which will scarcely be regarded by others as an improvement on the Castilian, although sanctioned by so learned a body as the University of Chile. Unless it be a chain-gang repairing a street under surveillance of armed guards, a guaso, or the water-carriers hurrying homeward, from the western limits to the base of Santa Lucia there are few to greet the stranger ; the stores are all closed, and even the plaza is vacant.

The city covers nearly seven square miles of ground, its longer axis being from W.N.W. to E.S.E., whilst the direction of the streets and fall of water is nearly from east to west. The acclivity is moderate and uniform from the west to the E.S.E. quarter, where a mass of compact sienite resembling basaltic organization rises suddenly, and whose crest was for so long a time the *locale* of our nightly labors. The horizontal dimensions of this hill, Santa Lucia, may be judged of from the plan of the city. Its west side is the most precipitous and rugged, and the summit is only attainable by rudely terraced walks on the more inclined faces next the Andes. From the running water at its base to the pinnacle is some two hundred feet, though the principal observatory was only about 175 feet above the water. From thence, excepting a narrow belt to the southward interrupted by the rocks, we commanded a view in all directions. To the westward the vision is bounded by the undulating line of the Central cordillera, most cerulean in its hue in this lucid atmosphere. To the right, its junction with the giant chain is perceptible, as observed from the Cuesta de Prado; whilst to the left, the hills wind away to the southward until their separate outlines are no longer distinguishable. Limiting the view to the northwest and north, two other isolated hills that spring abruptly from the plain attract attention. These are Renca, a long, irregular, yet gracefully formed mass in the former direction, and Cerro Blanco, a conical granitic eminence quite close at hand, in the latter. Near by, also, and a little to the east of north, a spur of the Andes terminates in the sugar-loaf of San Cristoval, enclosing between two bases a deeply embayed and picturesque valley, through which the Mapocho flows. Turning our eyes on the hills to the southward, thirty miles or more away, and then following the chains up, every altitude and color rewards the sight—from the contrast of the golden hues of the ripened cereals with the dark verdure of the olive groves and vineyards about the bases, to the blackened slopes, grisly sides, and snow-crested summits in the distance to the northeast. How magnificently they stand out against the sky ! how sharp and distinct they tower mass over mass into the blue depths of space !

Groves of trees in clusters or in long winding lines, whitened dwellings here and there amid fields of grain, and a tortuous streamlet between low banks, compose the scenery of the placidly embayed glen to the northeast, and, with slight exception, characterize the appearance of the valley without and surrounding the city. How softened its tints in the early morning and evening, or how golden the sunbeams reflected from the cordilleras, when lies Santiago in the shadows, a painter's pencil alone can tell.

At our feet lies the city, with its right-angled streets, low and tile-roofed houses—quaint in style, though not wholly without ornament or architectural pretension. A universal love for flowers and shrubbery has caused the introduction of plants within almost every enclosure, and oranges, acacias, myrtles, pines from New Holland, magnolias from North America, here a graceful Araucaria, there a native palm, rise above the walls and relieve the sameness necessarily consequent to houses built almost without exception of the same material and in the same style. But that which earliest arrests the sight are long lines of poplars shading a broad avenue extending from east to west nearly through its midst. Noisy streamlets of snow-water from the mountains gush beside their roots and throw cool vapors around ; and neatly cut benches, at equal intervals, invite to the enjoyment of this public walk. Next, an open, unshaded square (plaza), with a marble fountain at its centre ; half a score or so of smaller ones, alike without verdure, in different parts of the city ; a handsome arched bridge, and, nearer by, one of humbler pretensions across the Mapocho ; a strong wall with a terraced walk guarding its winding waters within and above the city ; and a multitude of ungraceful church and convent turrets,—these are all that claim the attention from our elevated eyrie. Nor are there many changes in the panorama in a climate where almost every plant that is duly irrigated becomes an evergreen.

Early morning brings a crowd of peons from the country with panniers and baskets of fowls, fruits, or vegetables; bakers and milkwomen, with huge trunk-like receptacles slung one on each side of a mule, or stout tin cans similarly arranged; droves of water-venders distributing to families their daily supplies from the turbid fountains; men atop of dark-green moving piles, that prove to be horses enveloped to their nostrils in bundles of alfalfa (a variety of lucerne); a drove of pack-mules or a train of carts just entering from the port; and the streets are like a hive,—the voices of all the thousand venders ascending Santa Lucia and rendering it a very Bedlam. Every material and variety of food or clothing may be bought in the streets; the peddlers scream out their wares at the top of their voices, and many of them are accompanied by one or more boys who carry the baskets and echo the song.

At noon, silence and solitude reign, the sun driving almost every one within doors. To us he sends a glare of reflected light, from the white walls and shadowless streets, with currents of heated air that imparts undulation to every object—no little painful to the eyes. Perhaps straggling peons may be seen about the heaps of melons or other fruits for sale in the smaller plazas, devouring the cool and juicy pulp of a water-melon, or hugging the walls as they pass on errands; or a *guaso,* detained by pleasures of the chicha cup, with brain stimulated and money gone, dashes over the stony pavement, a long bridle-rein or lasso whirling about his head, and poncho streaming in the wind as he thrashes his horse onward; but the contrast to the morning is very great.

With the decline of the sun the streets again become populated, and at twilight those in which the shops are situated are thronged with a sauntering multitude. But there is a brief intermediate time when the grander cordilleras claim attention, viz: the period commencing when the city first falls under the shadow of the western range, and ending when the sun's last rays leave the snow-crests. We must watch the mellowing tints as the shadow creeps upward; be an eyewitness of its change from gold to vermillion, then violet, and its final purple, followed by "a glory" of radiant beams streaming upward from a point opposite that at which the day-god disappeared, to confess how inadequate are human acquisitions to portray the impressions nature vouchsafes to the retina. Darkness creeps over the earth; one by one the stars come forth, until the firmament glitters with its myriads of gems "trembling with excess of light;" and the peaks of the Andes, now black, seem to have been brought almost within our grasp. Yet the outlines of the glen and valley are not wholly obliterated, and the lights scattered over their surfaces present no dissimilar counterpart to the view overhead. Within the city, long lines of lanterns mark the course of the streets and bridges; and the clusters about the plaza show that the peddlers are illuminating their wares; whilst the hum of voices and the roll of carriage-wheels afford tokens of a busy mass. Later, when the convent bells have long tolled midnight, and the moon has risen high in the heavens, silence again reigns, save when broken by the shrill whistle or cries of the *serenos.* To me, this was the most charming period. There is light enough to illumine very near objects, and even the masses of snow; to exhibit the deeper indentations of the mountains, and to soften their harsher outlines; whilst its reflection from the rapid stream below, as it flows murmuringly westward, adds a charm to the scene which day does not unfold.

"——— In the sky
A thousand stars are beaming bright,
And low-voiced waters, rippling by,
Are gleaming in the silvery light."

Many an hour has been passed under the soothing influence of its ripple, the world of Santiago wrapt in slumber.

But the most exquisite views of the cordillera of the Andes are just before sunset, after days of rain, in the latter part of autumn. With the first shower from heaven, vegetation, which has lain dormant on the mountains and hill-sides since December, springs forth as though by magic; and in the briefest space the slopes and curves, that have been parched and desolate since that period, are clothed in the brightest verdure. After one of these continued storms the elevated ranges display only masses of snow; a little lower the black and grayish rocks occasionally peep out; and lower still, where the heat of the valley has been felt, there are lines of white and gray, green and black, intermingled as in mosaic work. As the power of the sun is felt, low, dense, lead-colored clouds overhang the valley. A little above them, or apparently so to us, there are long lines of feathery cumuli, like wreaths, floating midway to the summits of the Andes, whose loftiest peaks shine glittering in the sunlight. At times the clouds hang so low over the valley, that the sunbeams to us only illuminate the lower portion of the mountains, first dazzlingly, then changing to softer tints—orange, rose color, and violet. Anon comes the shadow of the Central chain above the feathery wreaths, casting on the snow an intensely black image, that perceptibly creeps upward as you look at it; and, at the same time, a portion of the lower cumuli, expanding under the increasing warmth derived from the sun and earth, change their colors to the darkest azure, and float away. It is after these rains, too, that all impurities appear to have been washed out of the atmosphere, and the stars seem to move in mid-space, twinkling and glittering with wonderful brilliancy.

The city is divided into *quadras* (squares), somewhat less than 420 feet each way, with a stream of water, answering the purposes of a sewer, through every one. Its streets are generally paved, and most of them have sidewalks five or six feet wide; but as the immediate outskirts are not so improved, and the rule has been to make the centre lower than the sides of the streets, the condition of the thoroughfares leading out of Santiago during the wet season is disgraceful in the extreme. Why it should be suffered, while the land inclines so rapidly, and there is usually a stream for artificial irrigation on each side, is comprehensible only on the assumption that, like the Chinese, they make no innovations on the customs of their forefathers. This, and the wretched ranchos on each side, whose squalid denizens squat in the sun against their mud-splashed walls, surrounded by troops of yelping curs, is scarcely calculated to impress an arriving stranger favorably.

Ten minutes' sharp driving through miry sloughs if winter, or clouds of dust if summer, will carry one over the paved portion of any street from its limit to the great plaza, very near which is the only hotel having any pretensions to style or convenience: comfort, in our sense, is out of the question in any South American public house. There are two or three eating-houses where lodgings may be obtained, not far from the same locality; but the limited number of travellers through a city on the outskirts of civilization, and the habits of the people themselves, have not yet created the necessity for an Astor House, Mivart's, or Hôtel des Princes; so that the most commodious hotel in Santiago only possesses some thirty small and untidy rooms, in the second story of a very stylish-looking house one square distant from the plaza. When it is known that the fear of earthquakes has very generally caused the *alto* (second story) to be avoided by the family to whom it belongs, and that this prejudice usually excludes aspirants to fashion from their occupation, a proper estimate may be formed of the position "mine inn" holds in the world of elegance.

As in all Spanish America on the western slope of the Andes, earthquakes suggested the propriety of low houses; whilst the scarcity of timber, of suitable clay for handsome bricks, and of fuel, even were the clay accessible, have compelled the use of *adobes*.* There is good stone for building, in abundance; but the mechanics are behind the age in its manipulation—blasting, transporting, and dressing—and a cart-load of roughly broken bits quarried from Santa Lucia for foundations, will cost at least double the sum that would be asked in the United States, although in the latter case it might have been brought a hundred miles by rail-car. Consequently, there

* Clay with an admixture of straw, formed in a mould, and dried in the sun. They are eighteen inches long, nine inches wide, and three inches thick.

is only one private residence, and two or three churches, in all the city, that are built of stone —a sort of granite; a dozen, perhaps, of hard-burnt brick; and all the others of adobes, plastered over and whitewashed. Until recently, private residences never exceeded a single story in height, but consisted of suites of rooms built around open *patios* (courts) that extended in series back of each other to one half the depth of the square. Experience having measurably dissipated the fear of destruction by earthquakes, of late years it has become fashionable to add a second story to the range of rooms on the street; and although adobes allow but little range for the exercise of architectural fancy, and the universal custom of guarding all windows externally with iron bars still gives to edifices something of a prison look, yet the town is gradually acquiring a more European aspect. Many of the bars are fancifully wrought, with scrolls in the centre containing the initials of the owner's name, and, when gilded or painted in lively colors, are rather pretty. Most of the rooms on the street are occupied by mechanics, as residences or workshops, the proprietor rarely retaining more than the one he uses as a carriage-house. The streets immediately leading out of th plaza are exceptions, shopkeepers taking the place of artisans; and their goods displayed under a blaze of lamps by night, renders these thoroughfares very gay. Moreover, as it is not considered the best road to fortune to devote oneself to a single class of merchandise, the attractiveness is increased by the variety of wares exhibited.

A doorway high and wide enough for a mail-coach to pass through, admits you within the first patio of a residence. Around it, and also the interior ones, there is either a corridor supported by columns, or the eaves project far enough beyond the walls to shelter one from the sun or rain. A Norfolk-island pine, a magnolia grandiflora, or other fine evergreen, occupies its centre, and vines or clusters of plants adorn the columns. The second patio, however, is more generally devoted to flowers. Fronting the entrance are the parlors; dormitories, and perhaps a small room used as a library, occupying the remaining sides of the first patio. The inner patios furnish space for dining-rooms, family dormitories, and domestic purposes. Few proprietors have as yet ventured on the extravagance of cut-stone pavements, though none fail to pave the patios with pebbles from the Mapocho, sometimes incorporating in the doorway or near the centre, a crest or date, formed of the extremities of the leg-bones of mules and asses. A stream of water, distributed from broad canals in the upper part of the town, flows through the inner patio, and, though turbid, is useful in carrying off slops and dirt. By the time it reaches the lower part of the city, much has been accumulated; and it may well be conceived that its odor in summer is not as pleasant to those who live there as would be that of a red apple. These *acequias* (as they are called) are attended with one equally annoying inconvenience to those who live, like ourselves, near Santa Lucia: they bring a vast deal of sand from the river, which constantly chokes them by its deposition. Careless and unclean as the habits of the lower classes are known to be, and essential as it is to comfort and health to preserve a rapid flow, although the city supplies offal-carts gratis that call daily at each house, the police regulations to prevent extraneous matter being thrown into them are wholly disregarded, and the contents of the drains must be brought through the house from time to time, the odorous heap often lying for days before the front door. Thus, what was intended as a benefit has become a nuisance; and the day will arrive when the practice in Lima—open acequias in the middle of the streets—must be substituted for the closed ones within the premises.

With thick walls, high ceilings, and few windows, there is a degree of comfort within the better class of houses which is rarely met with at home in the extremes of temperature to which the climate of the northern hemisphere is subject. As the floors are of square tiles laid directly on the earth, one would expect to find them damp and chilly during the three months in which rains prevail; and that such is not the case, is no doubt attributable to the porous nature of the soil the city stands upon, and the rapid drainage of the plain. Besides our little observatories, there was only one of the houses we visited that had plank floors; and that was erected by an opulent and hospitable fellow-countryman for his own use. The only wood on the plain surrounding the city suitable for carpenters' work is poplar. All other kinds must, therefore, be carted either directly from the southern provinces or from Valparaiso. In the latter case, as the pine of the United States is held in great repute, a large portion of it has been brought round Cape Horn. Raw material is thus sold at extravagant rates; and so small is the number of good or even tolerable mechanics, that their charges for labor are scarcely less exorbitant. It may safely be said that the carpenters obtain for their labor at least four times the amount paid to similar artisans in North America; their wages being double, whilst the amount of work accomplished in a day is not more than one half. On these accounts, it would be true economy to have all the wood-work of houses prepared in the United States or Europe and shipped to Valparaiso.

If the floors are not of boards, the ceilings are; a style of finish probably originating in the impossibility of preserving them whole where earthquakes are so frequent, and the difficulty in obtaining proper plasterers. The walls, being only smooth-plastered with mud, are covered with ornamental paper in every apartment, causing the greatest possible contrast between the appearance of a dwelling in progress and when finished. In passing through their saloons, one misses the elasticity of the floors and the cheerful look of fire-places; but the carpets are soft and yielding, the climate is benignant, and as it is customary to retain the cloak if the weather be cool, habit soon reconciles one to the change. With a lantern in the door-way, another in the porter's room under its arch, others in the corridor, and a blaze of light from the parlor windows, there is an external air of cheerfulness which intercourse with the inmates fully realizes. Wealth and good taste, the latter almost universally characterizing refined women, have been specially combined here to furnish many houses in elegant style, the dominant fashions being those of France, whose mechanical productions, as well as *personnel*, are more numerously represented than those of any other foreign nation.

At the close of 1850 there was quite a furor for house-building. The April earthquake had seriously injured many dwellings, and there were piles of rubbish from those torn down in every street. By intercourse with the world their proprietors had learned to appreciate more commodious arrangements, and the new dwellings were a marked improvement on the old. No less than three immense structures were going on at the same time on different sides of the plaza; so that when the carts came in from Valparaiso in the morning, it was almost impossible to pass amid the heaps of materials. Wherever one turned, evidence was encountered that opulent citizens were determined their capital should no longer be reproachfully compared with its port, but they would build it up with attractions which would call back the merchants, when the telegraph and railroad shall facilitate their intercourse.

In order to control the valley, and at the same time to have a secure retreat in case of being pressed hard by the Indians, Valdivia selected the vicinity of Santa Lucia for his residence. The house still stands, in a street a little to the east of the hill, and in nearly the same condition as he left it three centuries ago—differing from those now constructed only in the thickness of its walls and ruder work on the iron grating of its single high-placed window. Time has done little to mar its exterior; its carved lintel and door-way are perfect; and it is only when we compare the present occupants with the members of the vice-regal court who once inhabited it, that the deterioration is made appreciable. At the approach of the national anniversary of 1850 it was proposed to lay the corner-stone of a monumental chapel on the spot, but something intervened to prevent it then; and it is not improbable that the civil war which subsequently raged will have created other necessities for the public funds.

The Cathedral.—Though begun more than a hundred years ago, unlike most works commenced by the church, the cathedral remains incomplete to the present day. Its front, rather more than a hundred feet broad, is intended to be a copy of that of St. John de Lateran, at Rome; and even in its unfinished state it has an imposing appearance. Through its whole length of 350 feet, it is divided by two heavy colonnades supporting longitudinal and transverse arches, on which rests the framing of a semi-cylindrical roof. For additional strength, the colonnades and outer walls are tied together with broad, perforated beams of wood, ornamentally carved and gilded, and the walls are externally supported by strong abutments. Ash-colored granite, quarried from Cerro Blanco, has been used in its construction throughout. Like all other churches in South America, its windows are few in number, and near the roof; so that when all the doors are closed, the light from without, aided by a multitude of candles in glass chandeliers about its high altar, scarcely penetrates its gloomy recesses. There are no less than sixteen altars in its side aisles; though their grotesquely wreathed columns and arches, in most cases, are neither well executed, rich, nor in good taste. Much more that is favorable may be said of the principal altar, placed about two thirds of the distance from the main entrance, and also of the pulpits and reading-desks. What we most remark is, the inferior and unartistic execution of a majority of the pictures adorning(?) its walls, whilst those of the adjoining vestries, as well as the carvings of the wardrobes and furniture, are so creditable. The cathedral is reputed rich in relics and ornaments, to which it became heir at the expulsion of the Jesuits.

The high altar occupies the centre of a platform elevated from the floor, well carpeted, and furnished with carved seats. Within an open temple, perhaps twelve feet square, and whose hemispherical dome is sustained by groups of columns at its corners, there is one smaller and of circular form. This also is open. Within it is a massive vase of carved and burnished silver, with a fluted and gilded Corinthian shaft supporting a plated globe. The base of the column is surrounded by wax lights. In front is the officiating desk, and at a little distance off, on the south side, there is a canopy of crimson and gold over the archbishop's seat. Two pulpits face each other near the extremity of the platform; one being for papal and archiepiscopal letters, and the other for the priest who "holds forth" to the congregation. In the rear and on the same level is the choir, semi-elliptic in form, and furnished with richly carved mahogany. In a surrounding gallery, intended for choristers, there are two small organs, still used at the ordinary service of mass, but a much more costly and finer instrument of English structure was put up in a specially built loft-room after we arrived. Of a calm morning this fine instrument may easily be heard across the plaza. Leaving out the boys, who but mar the melody of the parts assigned for female voices, there are many fine singers in the choir, and the music amply recompenses for attendance through service during the numberless festivities.

Along the massive colonnade within the nave there are rows of carved high-backed benches for the use of the male part of the congregation. Ladies, as in all other churches here, are compelled to occupy the floor. On this they spread small carpet-rugs brought by themselves or servants—seats, one would think, not only comfortless from the cold brick floor, but prejudicial to health also. Yet they seem to fancy the position, with their feet coiled under them—at least they not unfrequently resort to it elsewhere. Nor are they permitted to wear gay-colored dresses or bonnets of any kind. A dress of black with a flowing *manto* of the same color, the latter enveloping the head and thrown over the shoulders as men do their cloaks, is almost the only costume; and a graceful one it is, bringing out every charm of the face and person. In illness some make vows to wear garments and *mantos* of white or blue—colors of the Mercedarios (White Friars) and Franciscans—but they are few in number; and when the morning service ceases, a stranger for the first time in Santiago might well think himself in a city of nuns.

The other churches of most note for their size are those belonging to the ex-Jesuits, the Dominicans, the Mercedarios, the Augustins, and the Franciscans—all convents, of which the second, third, and last have recently been entirely renovated within. That of the ex-Jesuits, La Compania, is lighted through stained glass in the roof, and windows surrounding a cupola nearly above its high altar. Its altars and paintings are in good taste, extremely neat, and by far the best in the city. San Augustin is also well finished and chaste within; but none of the buildings would be selected as models of architectural taste, and in their very rudeness they differ too little from each other, or in the general style of their altars, to attract special attention. It must not be lost sight of, however, that all these churches were erected at a period long gone by, when Chile was the "*ultima thule*" of civilization, to which artists of merit never dreamed of wandering ; that they were to be built on a soil constantly shaken by subterranean convulsions, and in the midst of a community comparatively small in number, who had not the wealthy mines of Peru from which to draw their pious oblations. Besides those named, there are San Diego, San Isidro, San Miguel, Santa Ana, San Pablo, San Salvador, San Lazaro, Recoleta Dominica, Recoleto Francisco, Estampa, Santa Clara, and Carmelita two each, Augustina, Capuchina, and Santa Rosa—in all twenty churches and chapels. That belonging to the Claras, near the southern extremity of Santa Lucia, has been lately refitted, and is a gem of a chapel, with its elaborate carvings of silver and wood, its altar decorated with freshly cut flowers, and its floor covered with costly carpeting. Even the iron grating, beyond which its holy sisterhood pass not, save by sight and thought *perhaps*, has been covered with gilding—if possible, to rob it of its gloom. But who shall tell how many a darkened heart throbs within the golden prison?

The order of La Merced came to Chile with Valdivia ; but as they continued with the troops and among the Indians, no permanent establishment was made by them until after both the Dominicans and Franciscans had obtained a footing. The former order came in 1552, and the latter during the following year. The church and monastery occupy three fourths of a square near the western base of Santa Lucia, from whose summit one looks into their long corridors. These surround a garden planted with oriental-looking but native palms, that tower above trees and shrubbery of every hue, under whose grateful shade the monks saunter in white and flowing robes. If the color of the garment worn be emblematic of the purity of the life they lead, even a Protestant may breathe a prayer from this elevated oratory that they may ere long awaken from apparent indolence and apathy to a knowledge of what man may and should do for his fellow. Their cells possess no great amount of luxury ; and however charming may be this "*dolce far niente*," there would be few to prove its ease were it a life of seclusion. Rare is the hour of the day when some one of the order may not be encountered in the streets.

The monastery of the Dominicans is in a street of the same name, two squares from the plaza ; and that of the Recoleto Dominican (a secluded branch of the order), on the north side of the river. Both have good libraries, that of the latter being rich in MSS. and only second in extent to the national library, their members at the same time being reputed the most devoût and learned of any resident order. Nor is it possible to avoid perceiving that the former are men from a higher class of society than the others, proved as it is by their features, carriage, and deportment. The order is extremely wealthy.

Next to the Dominicans in opulence are the Augustin nuns. The erection of a new building for their accommodation afforded an opportunity to enter precincts over which the foot of man, except the physician, the archbishop, and the *newly* inaugurated President at one visit, never will pass when once they come within it. Each cell comprises a parlor fifteen feet square opening on a long corridor, a dormitory within, a servant's room, and one yet smaller for stores, with closets and a fire-place for cooking, arranged on the sides of a little court through which passes a stream of water. Thirty or forty of these cells face each other on opposite sides of a quadrangle some twenty yards wide ; those for the abbess being in the rear and more commodious. Adopting communism in one respect, yet providing for lives of entire seclusion at the same time, seems a contradiction. But thus the gentle sex live : telling their beads, chatting with servants who occasionally go into the outer world, and listening to every stroke of the porter's bell to learn whether some friend calls to tell *her* of events in the kingdom of Mammon.

Before passing to buildings of other characters, though there is nothing of note in their construction, it may be proper to mention the "*Casas de Ejercicios*," a sort of temporary convent erected for spiritual penance, to say nothing of the clever rents reverend proprietors receive for their use. There are three or four of these—some for males, others for females ; a part for the better off in the world, and others for the humbler classes. They are large edifices, divided into multitudes of small unfurnished rooms, each establishment having several presiding clergymen. Notices are posted on the church doors of the days when each routine of services will begin, and

P. S. Duval & Co's Steam lith. Press Phil^a

P. S. Duval & Co's Steam lith. Press Philad!

sinners who feel especially called on, flock there during Lent to punish the flesh and receive pious exhortations. Such furniture as they have the conscience to gratify themselves with is conveyed from their own houses, where they leave husband or wife, parents or children, to manage as best can be done whilst they pass nine days in *ejercicios* (penances). Many come out lean and wan, their bodies lacerated with self-inflicted castigation—no doubt richly merited for deserting their families on such an errand, if for no other reason. There is, moreover, a large unfinished church, which was commenced by the order of San Juan de Dios, adjoining the hospital of that name; but the government having displaced the monks from the charge of the hospital, their resources failed, their numbers gradually diminished, and the order no longer exists in Chile.

The Mint, not far from the centre of the city, is by far the most extensive and imposing in appearance of any of its edifices. The style is Doric. Its centre is of three stories, ornamented with eight columns projecting two thirds of their diameter from the face of the walls. The remainder of the building is of two stories only, with pilasters between each window, which support a well-constructed cornice surmounted by a balustrade. To each of the windows, which are placed twenty feet apart, there is a light iron balcony. The external ranges of rooms are crossed by others at right angles, enclosing courts from forty to fifty feet square, some of which have basins and fountains of water at their centres. The *mint*, properly so called, is a separate edifice of the same order of architecture, crossing the entire space within the second range of courts. Until recently the operations of coining were exceedingly slow, its machinery being of the most primitive description, and worked by mules. Within a year or two, however, a steam-engine and coining apparatus have been imported from France, which were in progress of putting together when we left Santiago.

A part of the eastern half is occupied by the President, whose large and commodious rooms have been handsomely furnished in modern style at the expense of the government. In other portions, the several ministers of state and their clerks are accommodated with offices, and a guard stationed constantly at the door have temporary quarters on either side of the main entrance; indeed every portion of its more than 400 feet square seems to have occupants. *La Moneda* (the Mint) was erected by the Spanish government towards the close of the last century, at a cost of nearly a million of dollars, little thinking how soon the flag of an independent nation would float above its portals. A fountain in the middle of the narrow plazuela in front, and a low range of barracks facing it, are scarcely in keeping with its magnitude and elegance.

There are no buildings so pleasant to the sight as the range on the north side of the plaza, known as *El Palacio* (the Palace), from a part having been occupied by the several chiefs of the nation as a residence. At the same time, more than two thirds of it were devoted to other purposes. It is composed of three edifices of different dimensions; yet, as the style of architecture is preserved and they are united, the façade is a harmonious whole. Of the three, that in the centre has been the most elaborately finished; and did it stand alone, it would be regarded with admiration in any part of the world. Reference to the plate, however, will show that the Spaniards of the past century profited by the example of their Moorish neighbors, and, in their national edifices of America, have left monuments of their liberal and cultivated judgment. The eastern portion is a prison, the central is devoted to municipal offices, and the western, formerly occupied by the governors and presidents, is now used by the fire brigade for their engines and quarters.

On the plazuela of *La Campania* there are two other buildings erected by the Spanish government, one intended as a custom-house, the other for the commercial tribunal (*consulado*), a court for the decision of suits and disputes in matters of trade. Each of these occupies nearly half the front of a square, and their architecture is similar to that of the eastern portion of *El Palacio* without its central tower. Neither the university building, the three theatres, nor the cockpit—for which there is a large establishment near Santa Lucia—merit particular attention; the other public buildings will be referred to in connexion with their uses. Two on the plaza belonging to individuals rival, if they do not exceed, in size, all except the Mint. That on the south side, the "Portal," is completed; the other, on the east, is in the course of construction; but neither of them will add to the reputation for taste of the architects or the proprietors.

There are several markets in the city, the principal one near the main thoroughfare over the Mapocho. Within a square enclosed by rows of one-story houses there are covered ranges of open stalls and benches, at which one may find in its season not only every production of the earth, air, and water of the country, but also groups of peddlers with articles of haberdashery, combs, soaps, cutlery, and common pottery in all its various forms; and as few of the poorer class have any other than earthenware utensils, the last is no unimportant item in their domestic economy. On the street sides, the houses enclosing the quadrangle are occupied as stores for the sale of grain, beans, clothing, &c.; a long, low shed on the west front is filled with *ponchos*, *pellons* (skins dressed with the wool on), and all appurtenances for horses; and another street next the river is crowded with awnings, beneath which sit women with baskets of shoes, from the coarse, high-heeled, quaint-looking brogan worn by *peons*, to the delicate gaiter-boots for ladies. Here are the carts and mules, with their loads, from or for the country—a crowded spot, from which one is happy to escape through a door leading among the butchers. If we take into account the numbers of black cattle and sheep raised and the unsurpassed pasturage for fattening them, meats are neither fat, well prepared, nor cheap. The butchers seem not to comprehend slaughtering, but leave the greater part of the blood in all meat, afterwards cutting beef into graceless junks wholly destitute of fat. No effort is made to improve the breeds of sheep or hogs, and rare are the occasions that fat or tender mutton or tempting pork may be found. What most surprises a stranger is the quantity of grease exhibited for sale. This is preserved in the cleaned stomachs of cattle, into which it is poured in a liquid state, and the marketing is not complete without a huge lump with which to season the cookery. Wild ducks in great variety, fine partridges, a native pigeon one third larger than the North American bird, doves (*Columba auriculata*), and parrots (*Psittacus cyanalysios*), are the birds most numerous and cheapest, there being an abundant supply from April to October. Some years the pigeons do not appear in this part of the republic, and during others they may be purchased three and four for a real. The flesh of Guanacos—the only edible native animals common in the province of Santiago—is never brought to market; though the meat is excellent, and they may be readily taken when snow drives them from the higher parts of the Andes. The young are often caught and brought to the city for sale as pets. As they are very common, and never can be broken of the habit of throwing acrid saliva towards the nearest person whenever they are excited, few care to be plagued with them. Moreover, the young are extremely difficult to raise; four in my possession that were in charge of native servants having died in spite of the utmost care and attention. Fish, two or three kinds of muscles (*mytilus*), crabs, and sea-eggs (*Echinus albus*), are brought by night from San Antonio, near the mouth of the Maypu, and from the fresh-water lakes and streams; and, though conveyed from thirty to eighty miles on mules in the summer months, they have been pronounced generally better than the same varieties purchased at Valparaiso. If such be the fact, it must be owing to the difference in the hygrometric condition of the atmosphere at the two places.

Of vegetables, fruits, and flowers, the supply is extensive, and prices moderate; but from the indolence of the gardeners, and their unwillingness to adopt modes of cultivation followed elsewhere, or because of the difference of temperature between day and night, there are few of the vegetable productions common to the northern hemisphere which attain equal perfection here. Indeed, it is quite safe to assert that little more is done in market-gardens than to put the seed into the ground after moderately scratching its surface, clean it of weeds once or twice, and turn water on it as often. And yet with this little care, with all the fertilizing agents of the city emptied into the river, with a bit of stick for a plough, a bunch of brush for a harrow or rake, no spades, and the rudest kind of hoe, finer cabbages, cauliflowers, peas, beans, pumpkins, melons, and onions cannot be produced anywhere. Asparagus, celery, beets, and other roots requiring the soil to be prepared to some depth, and maize, are only indifferent in quality. In the case of the last, the inequality of day and night temperatures has, most probably, much influence. Asparagus, which they begin to cut as early as August (corresponding with our February), is not cultivated at all, but grows wild in all the vineyards. Sweet potatoes, for which there is great partiality, are brought from Peru by the steamers, and are retailed at very high prices. All efforts to grow them in this province have heretofore proved unsuccessful. From the sea, too, several marine vegetables are brought; and one of them, a species of kelp, is largely consumed by the poorer classes. It is dried before being brought to market, and, when well disguised with condiments, finds plenty among those of better condition who pronounce it *muy rico* (very delicious).

The strawberry is the earliest fruit that ripens. There are three varieties, the first of which—of a light scarlet color—makes its appearance about the beginning of November. This variety is not unfrequently an inch and a half in diameter, and may be found wild throughout the southern provinces. Next in maturing is a bluish-white kind that is occasionally tinged with red, its dark crimson seeds forming a marked contrast to the usual color. This is called the "Aconcagua," of which province it is a native, and where it attains even a greater size than the preceding. The third is an elongated scarlet berry much smaller in size, indigenous in Valdivia and Concepcion. Neither of them has the fragrance or sweetness of the wild Virginia fruit, though they preserve enough of both, in combination with their enviable dimensions, to carry away the palm from the native North American berry. Raspberries are never seen for sale. A few are cultivated in private gardens, from which they are sent as presents to friends on gala days. Currants and gooseberries are not more abundant. Figs succeed strawberries. Of these there are two crops in the year: the "*Breva*" of spring, which is large, sweet, and luscious; and the "*Higo,*" six months later, a small and comparatively dry fruit. Cherries, plums, apricots, nectarines, peaches, pears, quinces, apples, pomegranates, and grapes, succeed each other rapidly. All thrive well and yield remarkably, wanting only in juice and flavor; which in part, no doubt, arises from want of proper attention. But the fruits consumed in the greatest numbers and quantities are melons, of which, during the season, there are not less than fifty large cart-loads brought into the city daily. Both watermelons and muskmelons are of fine quality, and the latter attains a great size. Cherimoyas grown in the valley of Quillota, the gardens of the valleys south of Coquimbo, and in a few warm exposures about Santiago, are not unfrequent; but they will not bear comparison with the Peruvian fruit either in size or lusciousness. Oranges, lemons, and citrons, may be found in every garden. All the trees near Melipilla, producing a very fine variety of oranges, were destroyed by an insect a few years ago, and the only tolerable ones are now brought from Quillota. Of the indigenous fruits, the Lucuma (*L. ovata*), Maqui (*Aristotelia m.*), Coigui (*Dolichos funarius* of Molina), Peumo (*P. alba rubro*), Piñon (*P. araucaria*), Chupon (*Bromelia sphacelata*), Coco (*Jubæ spectabilis* or *Molina*), and Avellano (*Corylus a.*), are the only ones experimentally known. The Copigue (*Lapageria rosea*) is said to produce a fruit of a sweet and very pleasant taste; and there are doubtless many others useful or agreeable to the natives.

Molina states that there are five species of Lucuma, and many varieties. Three are known to me, including a small uncultivated species, found near Valparaiso. The other two are edible, and considerable attention is given to the care of them in the valley of Coquimbo and Quillota, where the trees often attain a height of forty or fifty feet. Its fruit is oval, from two to three inches in diameter, with a dark-green skin, and dry, sweet, and insipid pulp. It begins to ripen in June. There is a difference in the sizes and colors of the two edible species, though both have the same general form and flavor. The "maqui" is a small, black-skinned, oval berry, not larger than a grain of coffee, with a sweet and not unpleasant taste. There is also a white, but much scarcer, variety. Decoctions of fresh maqui leaves are used as gargles, in cases of sore throat, cleansing ulcers, &c.; and cataplasms on the loins are considered beneficial in allaying fever. When dried and powdered, the leaves are also applied to wounds. Its deep-yellow colored flowers open in October, and the fruit matures in December. The Coigui, or Coiguil, grows on a ligneous vine, found among the trees in the ravines, at considerable elevations above the plain. It climbs from tree to tree, adding grace to the scene by its purple flowers and contracted leaves. The fruit is a leguminous pod, containing an unctuous saccharine substance quite agreeable to the palate. In size and form, the Peumo is similar to the kernel of the acorn, and covered with a reddish, or rather with a rose-colored, pellicle. Though its taste resembles that of brown soap more than anything else immediately recollected, when boiled, the enveloping skin is very much liked by the natives. The Araucanian pine is not indigenous north of the province of Concepcion; and its pyramidal-shaped nut is brought, in considerable quantities, from the cordilleras in the Indian territory, where it is most luxuriant. The nuts—an inch long, one third that diameter at their larger extremity, and covered with a yellowish-red skin—are contained in oval cones, from six to seven inches long. Though somewhat drier, when boiled, they have much of the sweetness and mealy character of the boiled chestnut, and, consequently, are greatly sought after by the ladies. The Indians make use of them as bread, for which they are an excellent substitute. The Chupon is not known north of the river Maule. Dr. Darwin found it growing extensively on the island of Chilöe, and it was brought to me from the ravines near Constitucion; but no one in Santiago had knowledge of it. The fruit, resembling, in size, form, and appearance, an artichoke, is packed with the seed-vessels, containing a sweet, aromatic, and pleasant pulp. It ripens in March and April, on the Maule. The plant has been called by M. Gay, *Bromelia sphacelata;* its vulgar name evidently comes from *chupar*, to suck. Except in gardens, I have never seen the coco-palm within the Central cordilleras. In the glens about Valparaiso, plants are numerous; and on the coast west of Rancagua an estate has been named from the millions of these trees growing upon it. Some few may be found in the province of Maule, in native locations; but there are none in the northern provinces, unless transplanted. It is said that the tree does not bear until it is a hundred years old; then each one produces annually from two to four immense sheaths, or pods, which burst as the fruit begins to ripen, exposing clusters comprising near a bushel of miniature cocoa-nuts. In every respect does this nut—the size of a small walnut—resemble its tropical prototype. It is ripe in February, and finds a market in Peru, as well as at home. A sirup, or molasses, much esteemed, is obtained by boiling the sap of the tree, multitudes of which are annually destroyed for the purpose. The Avellano, a genus of the family *Amentaceæ*, is called by Molina "*Gevuina avellano.*" It is a native of moist localities, and, like others of its kind in the northern hemisphere, spreads itself into a shrubby bush. The nut has the flavor of the filbert, and is somewhat larger; but its shell is shaped more like that of the hickory-nut. The Copigue, like the chupon, is confined to the southern provinces, where it climbs among the trees, in moist ground. Its flowers are of every shade from white to dark coral-color, by their hues and velvety forms contrasting most exquisitely with the leaves. Its fruit ripens in May. Only one could be obtained during a visit to Talca in April, 1851; it was an oblong, of a yellow color, more than half an inch in diameter, and filled with a pleasant, sweet pulp. The plant seems to thrive best about Concepcion, from which locality numbers are brought to the northern provinces, to be cultivated for the beauty of their flowers; but they are delicate, and badly bear transplanting, so that scarcely one in twenty thrives after its removal. The Araucanian pine, the cocoa-palm, the avellano, and copigue, with many other interesting specimens, have been successfully introduced into the United States by the Astronomical Expedition, and will undoubtedly grow in our southern States.

Arising in part, probably, from irrigation, during seasons when they receive no water in native localities, most of the indigenous flowers are difficult of cultivation in gardens, as are the copigues; and, though many of the bulbous tribe found on the cordilleras possess rich colors, are showy, and some of them fragrant, few persons are willing to transplant them a second time. As I have too often found when trying to remove them with a bit of stick, their roots are invariably buried so deep in the earth that the moisture is not entirely evaporated from them in summer. By a little attention, not only might these be domesticated and improved, but the Calandrina splendens, Boisduvalia tocornalii, Loxodon chilensis, Eucryphia pinnatifolia, Malva belloa, Hexaptera jussiæi, the Fuchsias, and Tropœolums, all found in the central provinces, would be elegant additions to any collection. However, the taste is rather for imported flowers, and the gardens of several wealthy gentlemen in the neighborhood contain many most costly and choice specimens. Camellias, magnolias (grandiflora), fuchsias (exotic), and azaleas, thrive almost without any care, except irrigation; and their anemones, ranunculæ, pinks, and several varieties of foreign bulbs, cannot be surpassed anywhere. Cape jasmins, roses, dahlias, tulips, and hyacinths, do not flourish so well as in the northern hemisphere. As a very large number of inter-tropical plants grow in the open air here, the market is well supplied throughout the year; and, though not arranged with the taste a skilled bouquet-maker would exhibit, for a very insignificant expenditure one may obtain many varieties of beautiful flowers. Forbidding as were the precincts, from their odors and dirt, and the dogs and fleas certain to be encountered, their flowers were attractions not easily resisted.

The street next west of the market leads to a substantial bridge, of masonry, erected over the river about the year 1775. Including the abutments, it is more than 650 feet long, wide enough to allow footways and the passage of two carts abreast, and is supported, at some thirty feet above the stream, on eleven most solidly built arches. As one of the arches will deliver more water than ordinarily descends from the Andes, Padre Guzman says, that at the sight of so extensive a structure over so diminutive a stream, more than one has been tempted to suggest that "the city ought either to sell the bridge, or buy a river for it." There are times, however, when it is neither too great nor too firm for the volume of water which comes roaring through the ravines. On one side, at regular intervals, there are small semi-circular turrets, like watch-towers without the parapet wall, and between them stone benches, for the convenience of pedestrians. The turrets contain bread, fruits, and confectionery, for sale; but they are not tempting. Three squares farther to the east, up stream, there is a bridge of wood, resting on brick piers. This is intended for foot-passengers only.

Beginning at the lower part of the city and bounding the south bank between it and the river, there is a solid brick wall, four or five feet thick, with a parapet three feet high next the stream. The wall is paved on top with small pebbles. This also was a work of the Spaniards, intended to prevent overflow of the city, during freshets in the river; hence its name, *Tajamar*—breakwater. At intervals of three or four squares there are openings in the walls, with sloping embankments and flanking masonry, to allow of the passage of horses or vehicles, and there are flights of steps at convenient places by which pedestrians may ascend. A row of majestic poplars above the densely populated part of the city renders the Tajamar a favorite resort of promenaders, when rain has rendered the *Cañada* muddy. The latter, which has already been alluded to, extends through the heart of the city from east to west, and is one of the most beautiful walks in the world. The Andes and Central cordillera only limit the vision beyond its many parallel rows of poplars; and its shade and refreshing coolness, from evaporation of the water in its irrigating streams, renders it a favorite resort in the evening. A bronze fountain and a *jet d'eau* ornament it near the Mint.

The National Institute.—For more than a quarter of a century after the invasion of Chile, the followers of Valdivia had too much occupation in combating their Indian neighbors, to devote thought to education; a subject which, if not actually disdained, they at least regarded as rather the province of priests than of knights. Nor was it until the arrival of the Jesuits, in 1593, that any step of consequence was taken for the general instruction of children. In a "History of the Church in Chile" by Señor Eyzaguirre, published in 1850, he says: "All the schools of Santiago proceeded to the Compania on Friday evenings, carrying their crosses and banners before them; and there a padre was designated to instruct them in the rudiments of religion, making them repeat, by classes, the questions and replies of the cathechism, and concluding by explanation of the doctrinal points, suited to their capacities. In this manner, and until they could establish one of their own, they taught the children of other schools. Up to that epoch, knowledge in primary schools had been obtained by payment to the masters or preceptors; but the Jesuits opened the doors of their establishment for gratuitous instruction, and thus broke down the formidable barrier opposing enlightenment of the poor." During nearly a century and a half that followed, the only schools were those under charge of the several convents, in which the course of instruction was far too limited to develop the abilities of their pupils; and hence youths who might have been trained to habits of study in after life, of a necessity acquired those of indolence, of which one result is the desire for employments consonant with a lethargic disposition, rather than occupations requiring intellectual exertion—a labor that would inevitably have led to improvement of themselves and their race. Even to the present day, with all the encouragement given by government in the way of high salaries to professors of the National Institute and provincial colleges, and the exorbitant sums expended by parents to the same end, the standard of education is far below that of Europe or the United States. But to proceed with a brief history.

The two principal colleges or seminaries were known as "*Colĕgio Azul,*" and "*Colĕgio Carolino,*" or sometimes "*Colĕgio Colorado;*" the former under charge of the Jesuits till their expulsion, and the latter since 1619 belonging to the Dominicans. At the solicitation of the municipality, the University of *San Felipe,* intended as a counterpart to that at Salamanca, was authorized by the King of Spain in 1738, the city agreeing, to endow professorships from its surplus revenue. These were to consist of ten: Medicine, 1; Theology, Canonical and Ecclesiastical Law, 3; Maestro de Sentencias, 1; Mathematics, 1; National and Civil Law, 2; Arts and Languages, 2. From some delay, the cause of which is not now known, the institution was not organized until twenty years afterwards. Padre Guzman, however, says the charter was only received in 1747, and that it went into operation three years later, or in 1750. It cannot be ascertained, with any degree of precision, what number of pupils availed themselves of either the new University or the *Colĕgio Carolino,* which had survived as late as 1810. Then the latter institution, teaching Latin, theology, philosophy, and international law, numbered only sixteen in all its classes! To so low an ebb had the tide of knowledge fallen, that when an academy for instruction in *mathematics* and *drawing* was opened, its proprietor was actually arraigned before the courts as "the author of dangerous innovations!" Up to this period the education of females was cruelly neglected, and, if attended to at all, never extended beyond reading and writing to an extremely limited number.

The National Institute—a child of the University that sprang into existence at the close of the revolution of 1810, and was intended, by the dissemination of knowledge, to strengthen more effectively the bonds of the new republic—died with the liberty that gave it birth, and before its fair proportions were fully developed. In order to bring it into operation more rapidly, the pupils of the principal schools were united in a common establishment, and the professors of the University were directed to continue the same course of instruction in the new institution or to resign. Its inauguration took place in 1813, amid the firing of cannon, orations, and masses, at which the principal officers of government and a large concourse of citizens attended. Of the fourteen professorships then endowed, there were for Religion and church matters, 5; Laws of Nations and Political Economy, 1; Experimental Physics, 1; Chemistry, 1; Geography and Military Science, 1; Pure Mathematics, 1; Drawing, 1; Logic, Metaphysics, and Moral Philosophy, 1; Latin, 2. Eight of the professors were clergymen. A fair creation to have been so short-lived!

During the reconquest, the *Colĕgio Colorado* was the only school of importance continued. But the patriots had scarcely achieved independence again before they commenced reorganizing the Institute; and in 1819 its classes, numbering about thirty youths taken from that seminary, recommenced with a modification in the professorships previously existing. This number rapidly increased, and the apparent desire for education thus expressed could not but have been gratifying to the most enlightened men of the country. Yet the government seems not to have been satisfied with either the matter taught, or the manner in which it was taught; for on the appointment of a new rector in 1825, the decree naming him says: "The Institute being the hope of the nation, the government not only desires to see adopted in it the best methods of instruction, but also expects that its pupils from tender age will be very especially inspired with sentiments of morality and decorum, cleanliness, propriety, habits of order, and all other qualities which good education and manners require, more particularly among those destined to occupy offices and commissions under it. Until now, this part of their education has been greatly neglected, or has been under the charge of persons who, whilst possessing sufficient zeal and the best intentions, either from the education they themselves have received, or because they do not mix with the world, have not been able to estimate what is due to it." Subsequent to this reproof, the institution has slowly but steadily and surely advanced in usefulness, elevating the standard of education, and, as the numbers of students increased, drawing its rules more stringently. At present it numbers 900 pupils, of whom 260 are *interns*, or live wholly within the precincts, and the remainder are day-scholars.

The old building in the rear of the cathedral being both small and unsuited to the accommodation of so many, a new one has recently been erected south of the Cañada, which was opened for use after our arrival in Chile. It is an extensive quadrangular block, two stories high, with wide corridors surrounding its open courts, intended for communication between the several rooms, and for exercise. There are gymnastic schools in three of the courts; and all of them are planted with young trees of foreign growth, which in time will greatly conduce to their comfort during summer. The recitation rooms are of good size, and airy; its dormitories commodious, well ventilated, and neatly kept; and, indeed, all the arrangements for personal wants are quite satisfactory.

To conduct the establishment there is a rector, a vice-rector, thirty-six professors and tutors, a treasurer, and a chaplain. These receive their appointments from government at the recommendation of the Council of the University; and for their pay, as well as for any deficiency in the funds caused by an excess of expenditure over the receipts, an annual appropriation is made by Congress. Pupils are admissible between the ages of nine and fifteen years; or above that age when offering as *interns*, if they produce certificates of good conduct and studious habits from the school previously attended. Instruction is free to all; the *interns*, only, being subject to a charge of $150 per annum for their board. Sixty of these are at the cost of the government, who nominally select for the benefices poor youths whose fathers have rendered services entitling them to such mark of a nation's gratitude, or those who propose dedicating themselves entirely to the country. Among the latter the most eligible are: 1st, those who propose becoming teachers of normal schools; 2d, those who embrace the study of medical, natural, or mathematical science; and 3d, *externs* who have been most distinguished in their classes, and whom the rector thus proposes to reward. Those living within the Institute building are divided into three sections, each of which has its own enclosures; and no communication is allowed with the others, except when permitted to make visits on holidays. They are required to rise at 6 A. M., and, after a cup of chocolate or tea, attend mass. With short intervals for recreation, they attend classes from that time until breakfast, at 11 o'clock. An hour and a half is allowed between breakfast and dinner, at 5 P. M.; and after vespers all are required to retire at half-past nine, a tutor sleeping in each dormitory for the preservation of order. Besides six weeks' vacation during summer, all the feast days of the church, the national anniversaries in September, and the saints' days of the rector and vice-rector, are holidays. Moreover, they are excused from study during the last three days of Holy Week, and the three days preceding Ascension, in order that they may prepare themselves for confession and communion. Corporal punishment is not permitted; but offences designated in the statutes, and separated into three classes, are dealt with according to their gravity, by tasks, privation of holidays, incarceration in solitary cells, and diet of bread and water. Among the gravest offences specified are not retiring at the appointed hour, leaving the Institute without permission, and neglect to confess at the appointed times; among the lightest are uncleanliness and disrespect to their companions!

The classes taught are Latin, Greek, English, French, arithmetic, algebra, right-angled trigonometry, geography, cosmography, drawing, history, rhetoric, and moral philosophy; religion, music, and the elements of physics; chemistry, mineralogy, and natural history. If the pupil enter without previous instruction, the course occupies six years. Subsequently he may study law, medicine, surgery, and the natural sciences, for which from three to four years more are necessary; but he is not permitted to enter the latter classes without previous examination in all the others. Examinations are held at the close of the collegiate year, and are strictly impartial, it being permissible and customary for invited guests to propound questions on the subject under consideration as long as they may be so disposed, so that the pupil can have no previous intimation of replies to learn by rote. Degrees are conferred only by the University.

Connected with the National Institute, and under the immediate direction of the Minister of Public Instruction, is a normal school. Twenty-eight young men, all *interns*, are prepared here as tutors for primary education in the provinces. The course of study occupies three years, vaccination being one of the subjects in which they are instructed. Notwithstanding government offers the best education "without money and without price," there are a number of boarding and day schools, under the direction of convents and individuals, which are well patronized. Besides these, there are thirty-five primary institutions at the cost of the municipality. The last, as also most of the day-schools for the humbler classes, are ordinarily held in rooms miserably lighted and ventilated, of whose vicinity one becomes aware at the distance of a hundred yards by the loud voices of all the children conning their lessons at the same time. These rooms are shamefully close, unhealthy places, into which air and light in many cases only find entrance through small apertures or windows in the upper part of the door; and they are quite Bedlams from the mode of memorizing just mentioned. But that which is most painful is the sight of boys from eight to ten years of age clad as monks—miniature monks, priests in embryo; and though contrary to law, many of them receive the tonsure when they have scarce entered their teens. Few who enter convent schools ever adopt any other pursuit than that of the idle class among whom they are brought up.

All of these establishments, as well as every other in the republic which has science or education for its object, are under the control of the University—the old University of San Felipe, reorganized in 1842. The corporation consists of a rector, a vice-rector, and five faculties, with their corresponding secretaries, to wit: philosophy and humanities, physical and mathematical sciences, medicine, law, political science, and theology. The President of the republic and the Minister of Public Instruction are *ex officio* patron and vice-patron. These, with the rector, vice-rector, two councillors named by government, the deans of the faculties, and the secretary-general, form a council for the transaction of business. They have entire control of every thing relating to instruction, not only in the public but also in private institutions; nor can any new school be opened without their sanction. Twice a year returns must be made to the council of the number of pupils, the branches taught and text-books, the hours of instruction, the emoluments received—in short, of every circumstance bearing on education. More than this, a member is deputed to make personal inspection of every school, and report to the board in writing. They and their secretary are paid from the public treasury. One of the members is called on annually to deliver a discourse on some subject connected with the history of the country. This, together with the scientific and literary papers read before called meetings of the different faculties, is published in a monthly bulletin of their proceedings, entitled "Anales de la Universidad de Chile." Each faculty is composed of thirty members elected by itself, and confirmed by the patron and vice-patron. It is also authorized to appoint honorary and corresponding members, whose diplomas, however, must be recommended by the council before they can be submitted for the approbation of the patron. The faculty of mathematical and physical sciences having been pleased to elect me an honorary member immediately after I arrived in Chile, it was gratifying to have an opportunity to attend its meetings and become personally acquainted with its members. Their meetings are held at night in a large and well constructed two-story edifice in the rear of the cathedral, formerly used as a part of the National Institute.

An academy was established in 1842 for the formation of officers destined to serve in the regular army and navy. At present it contains sixty cadets at the expense of the State, of whom forty are intended as commissioned and twenty as non-commissioned officers. As supernumeraries are permitted, the number actually benefiting by the most thorough system of education yet known in Chile is quite double that expressed in the statute. Cadets must be between twelve and twenty years of age; supernumeraries, who are at liberty to withdraw at any time, but who also may become cadets as vacancies occur, enter at any age over ten years. The allowance to a cadet is $14, and that to a corporal, as the others are ranked at admission, $8 per month; which sums are wholly devoted to their maintenance. Supernumeraries are required to pay $120 annually; for which sum they are furnished and taught in every respect as the cadets, to whose discipline they are required to conform. The director of the academy is General J. S. Aldunate, than whom a more gallant soldier, a truer patriot, or a more honorable or amiable man, it would be difficult to obtain for a post of such trust. Ardently devoted to the service, in which he gained high distinction in struggles against the royalist forces, his whole thoughts and energies are devoted to the creation of corps of officers who may be relied on in times of doubt and danger—men who will not be open to the purchase of every faction able to collect a few thousand dollars, but who will ever be found on the side of law, order, and the legitimately constituted authorities of the nation. Having been authorized so recently, the school has scarcely had opportunity to prove how beneficial will certainly be its results; but, to their credit be it said, in the recent anarchical struggles, the few cadets who have graduated have proved themselves worthy of their instructors. Indeed, when the revolt broke out, on the 20th of April, every individual in the academy was earnest in his desire to aid in its suppression, although some of the little fellows could not have held a musket horizontally had their lives depended on the result. Yet many of these, the General told me, wept bitter tears of mortification when their older companions were about marching to the President's without them, and he eventually took them along.

The vice-director is a sergeant-major; and there are thirteen professors, who give instruction in religion and sacred history, ancient history, Spanish grammar, arithmetic, algebra, elementary and descriptive geometry and spherical trigonometry, cosmography and uranography as applied to navigation, the French and English languages, drawing, infantry and artillery tactics, field fortification, and gymnastic and sword exercises. Between five and six o'clock in the morning and eight and nine at night, according to the season, they are allowed three hours for meals and recreation, the remainder of the time being devoted to study, recitations, or exercises. Provided there are no misdemeanors, they are allowed to visit relatives on one Sunday in each month, and during certain other holidays. The course of study occupies five years; after which they are incorporated into the army or navy, according as their inclinations have developed themselves, and they have been consequently prepared. Their uniform is a dark-green frock with metal buttons, military cap, sword, and white pantaloons, without which no one is permitted to leave the academy. An old Jesuit convent three squares southeast of Santa Lucia has been fitted for their accommodation; its broad *patio* forming a fine parade-ground, and its long corridors ample space for exercise and study. The building is sufficiently extensive to afford wholesome quarters for four times their number; yet, in every part of it there is the utmost cleanliness and order—nothing luxurious or elegant, but everything frugal, simple, and comfortable. In every respect the institution reflects credit on its able director and the government.

Under the patronage of the State also, there are schools for instruction in the mechanic arts (*artes y oficios*), agriculture, painting, and music; in all of which the majority of the pupils are maintained wholly at its expense. In the first named, a portion of the day is given to intellectual instruction; and during the remainder the young men are employed in various workshops belonging to the establishment, as carpenters, blacksmiths, founders, &c. The school is in Yungai, where a large building has been erected especially for the purpose; and a steam-engine imported from France serves to drive the machinery, and as a model for instruction at the same time. Unfortunately, on account of its complicated construction, the engine is not perfectly adapted to the circumstances, and it would be economy of mental labor to substitute a simpler one. There are forty pupils, who, at the termination of their apprenticeship, are required to direct personally for six years a workshop of the trade they have learned, in such province as the government may elect. Backward as the mechanics are in the knowledge of the commonest arts, no more valuable school could have been instituted; and the citizens of Chile may of right anticipate adequate returns from such expenditure of the public funds in better and cheaper products of labor.

The *Quinta Normal*, as the Agricultural School is called, is also in Yungai, and has in view not less interesting and important results. About one hundred and twenty-five acres of land have been enclosed and laid off for practical instruction, and the buildings are already erected for officers and pupils of the institution. The number of the latter is limited to thirty, twelve of whom, selected according to the same rules as those of the gratuitous pupils at the National Institute, are at the expense of government. The other eighteen are required to pay $100 per annum, which is expended in their maintenance and clothing used whilst at labor. No one is received whose age is under fifteen years or over twenty years; and the course occupies four years, during which they are taught grammar, geography, arithmetic, practical geometry, drawing, religion, agronomy, practical agriculture, and rural economy—the last three subjects embracing every branch that can be of use to an agriculturist in the widest sense. All the pupils are *interns*. The school was only organized in 1850, and its beneficial effects are not yet visible; though I believe that government has found it necessary to meet all the expenses, no paying pupils having offered themselves. Another of its objects, however, has already been accomplished to some extent—viz: the foundation of a nursery of native and foreign useful and ornamental plants, to be sold at equitable prices. With the climate and soil of Central Chile, almost every vegetable product thrives luxuriantly; and there is little doubt that industry, united to the practical information to be gained in the *Quinta Normal*, will enable its graduates to render this one of the garden-spots of the world.

The schools of Painting and Music are in a part of the old University building, near Santa Lucia. For the former there have been imported a number of plaster statues and busts, and engravings of different portions of the human frame, which are conveniently arranged in a tolerably well lighted room. These are to serve as models. There is neither a fixed number of pupils nor a period assigned in which the studies are to be completed; and the only distinctions are amateurs, who are under no rule except such as good manners require, and those who obtain permission from the Minister of Public Instruction to become enrolled pupils, in consideration of which they may twice a year compete for the rewards government holds out to the most proficient. The latter are, by law, required to be present at least two hours every day; and if absent for fifteen consecutive days, they forfeit their right to compete for the premium. They are divided, for instruction, into three classes: 1st. Elemental drawing from engravings, subdivided into three sections—rudiments and heads, extremities, and full-length figures. 2d. Imitation of relievo or statuary, arranged in the same number of sections as the preceding. 3d. Drawings from the living model and imitation of costumes. These complete the series required for historical composition (say the regulations), though the pupil should have followed a complete course of literature, or at least of rhetoric, and another of philosophy, in order to comprehend and express the passions that are developed in parts of the compositions. The five orders of architecture and landscape painting should also be understood, in order to draw the back-ground of pictures. The director is an Italian, who receives a handsome salary; for which, in addition to instruction, he contracts to paint two historical pictures for the national gallery every year. Those completed under the agreement are probably imaginary portraits of heroes in American history—Columbus, Valdivia, Ercilla, &c.; as no originals are known to be in Chile, and that of Columbus certainly has no resemblance to portraits of the same individual elsewhere. A single full-length figure is considered a historical painting. Though it has now been in operation three years, landscape painting has not yet been taught in the school. Surrounded as is the city with scenery of rare beauty, the omission would appear most extraordinary, did not the products of the director's brush tempt one to infer that he cares not to risk his fame with the earth or its own products. At the time of my visit to the academy there were only ten or twelve students present, one of whom was a young Araucanian, who had been brought from the Indian territory when a child and educated by a charitable lady of the capital. He was regarded as among the most proficient of the pupils.

The musical conservatory is of more recent origin. It embraces a school for instruction in vocal and instrumental music, and an academy. In the former 150 pupils are gratuitously taught. The course of instruction occupies three evenings in the week for five years; after which, graduates are obliged to assist another five years at such national and civic celebrations as government may direct. Attendants on this school are exonerated from military service; and if arrested for civil misdemeanor, the director of the school is expected to interest himself in behalf of the accused, and testify to his or her character. Considerable advance has been made in vocal instruction already, and the public exhibitions of proficiency at the national festivities of the last two years have not only been creditable to the children, but they lead one to hope that a musical taste may be created in the nation. The academy is composed of professional artists and amateurs of both sexes whom the president may be pleased to appoint as members. To them is especially assigned the cultivation and advancement of musical science through the study of the classical compositions of the great masters. They are required to give concerts of sacred music every Sunday during Lent, and of dramatic music once a fortnight in the winter months. The proceeds are applied to charitable objects.

The national library is contained in some of the larger rooms on the eastern quadrangle of the old National Institute. Its volumes fill two of these rooms, and a third serves for the office of the assistant librarian and for visitors; for whose use while consulting the books there are chairs and convenient tables. In the latter room, also, there are a few periodicals and newspapers, and a number of valuable MSS. relating to the history of Chile—classes of matter that attract more readers than any others. In ecclesiastical history and literature the library is particularly rich, the books formerly belonging to the Jesuits forming part of its wealth. The total number of volumes exceeds 21,000, distributed as follows:

Mathematical and Physical sciences	2,530
Geography, Natural History, and Travels	1,478
Arts, Political Economy, Commerce, and Industry	682
Theology in all its branches	5,206
Laws and Politics	1,571
Rhetoric, Literature, and Languages	3,975
History, Biography, and Miscellaneous	3,514
Periodicals and other native works	487
Manuscripts	81
Not classified	794

These books are accessible to the public from 10 A. M. to 1 P. M. every day except holidays, and two hours later on Mondays and Thursdays. No one is permitted to remove a volume from the building under any pretext, though every facility is afforded to make extracts or otherwise benefit by the information to be obtained in the library. Unfortunately, too little provision is made for extending its usefulness. The whole sum appropriated in 1850 for the support of the librarians and purchase of books was only $2,000, a sum not greater than might well be expended in current publications alone. Thus, there being few additions to the shelves except by donations, the literature and science treated of here are of the past age. In a separate building there is a law library containing 1,700 volumes, as accessible to the public as the preceding.

At the time of our arrival there were three newspapers printed at the capital, two at Valparaiso, and one at each of the cities Copiapó, Serena, Talca, and Concepcion. Of those at Santiago "El Araucano" is the official organ, and rarely publishes aught but decrees, regulations, or other matters emanating from the ministers. During the close of General Bulnes's term, and the revolutionary struggle following the accession of Mr. Montt, there were occasional editorials in defence of the administration; but even these were subsequently omitted, and the "Araucano" was of interest only for reports of the proceedings in Congress, and an occasional statistical table. The other journals were "La Tribuna" and "El Progreso;" the former in the pay of government also, and the latter decidedly in opposition to it. It cannot be said that either of them was conducted with much spirit. The latter, together with an irregular quarto sheet, commenced, in 1850, to advocate the cause of "Los Egualitarios" (Socialists), and indeed all others opposed to the precise measures of the government, were suppressed, under the dictatorial powers with which Congress invested the President in September, 1851. At the advent of Mr. Montt, without changing hands or doctrines, the "Tribuna" was re-baptized "La Civilizacion;" but the nation or Santiaguinos seemed scarcely ready for such a change, and the newly made literary infant, like the majority of the human race given birth to here, expired within the year. "El Telegrafo" was to rise from its grave at the completion of electro-magnetic communication between Valparaiso and the capital; but, from the fact that it had not been issued as late as September 1, 1852, it is probable that the proposition met with little favor, and that the "Araucano" has remained alone in its glory. There is a "Gaceta de los Tribunales," printed weekly, and devoted to judicial decisions exclusively; the "Revista Catolica," a monthly periodical, advocating intolerance to the satisfaction of the devout; and a little paper started for musical and dramatical criticism: all with very limited circulation. It may be inferred from this, that a taste for the reading of current events is not very general; and one may perhaps justly infer that there is a like indifference to more serious literature.

Above the library is the cabinet of natural history. The origin of this museum is mainly due to M. Claudius Gay, a French gentleman, who went to Chile nearly twenty years since, and, not having succeeded as he desired, commenced collecting native animals and plants, most of which were forwarded to the galleries at Paris. Having subsequently made an agreement with the Minister of Public Instruction, he undertook a systematic examination of the native products, with a view to an authentic natural and political history of the republic. Beginning his multifarious and arduous task in 1833, the first volume of the civil history was published in 1844, and in the following year the first volume of descriptive botany. Since then other volumes—four of political history, eight of botany, eight of zoölogy, and two of documents—have been distributed, accompanied by 350 elegantly engraved and colored folio plates, illustrative of the natural history, antiquities, scenery, and customs of the country. The work is still going on, M. Gay having been in Paris to superintend the engravers and printers for the last six or seven years. The plates, coloring, and general execution of the work are in the highest degree interesting and honorable; and if the text prove equally satisfactory to the mass of readers devoted to those branches, the little republic of Chile will have accomplished more for the enlightenment of mankind than nine tenths of the older and wealthier states of the world.

The specimens collected by M. Gay were forwarded to the capital from time to time, himself subsequently preparing them for exhibition; and now, the ornithological and botanical departments, if not complete, are certainly so far advanced towards perfection that the inquisitive student will have little to learn hereafter from other collectors. They are arranged in a long room, in well constructed cases, affording full opportunity for minute examination, and are *nominally* open to the public on Thursdays. When proper application is made, the cabinet is accessible to strangers every day. Limited as is the country to a small number of families both in the animal and vegetable kingdoms, it has not been difficult to obtain good specimens of every member belonging to some of them; and it is only to be regretted that the more valuable ones should not have fallen into the hands of more skilful taxidermists.

Among the most conspicuous of the mammalia are the Hüemul* (M. Gay writes *Guamul*), (*Cervus chilensis*), Guanaco (*Camelus g.*), Leon (*Felis concolor*), and Chingue (*Mephitis chilensis*); and among the feathered tribe the condor, swan, herons, flamingos, and ducks. The first named of each class, being national emblems, are of interest; and the Hüemul particularly so, from the doubts respecting its existence, created by the extraordinary classification of it by Molina as "*Equus bisculus.*" It is more than probable that his ideas of it were obtained from the Indians, else an animal so unmistakably deer-formed could never have been classed among horses; though this is by no means the only instance in which the Abbé was at fault. Unfortunately, in later times, when its existence was placed beyond doubt, and the Congress adopted its figure as a part of the national escutcheon, heralds thought more of appearance in their picture than of observing nature, and by following the Abbé's description have done no little towards perpetuating an absurdity. Yet more—in addition to the long tail and cloven hoofs of the Abbé's fancy, they have capped the animal with a crown, and this on the shield of a new republic!

It is not so graceful an animal as most others of its class. The length of a full-grown specimen, excluding the tail, is rather more than three feet and a half, and its height something above two feet. It is short in proportion to its altitude, and *bunchy*, though strongly and actively built. The head is rather oval than elongated; its eyes moderately large, and liquid; ears long, and erect; tail short. Males are said to have short, bifurcated horns, not possessed by the other sex, to which both of the specimens that I saw belonged. Its long and soft hair is of a brownish fawn-color, profusely sprinkled with yellow; its breast and belly of a somewhat lighter hue than the rest of the body; and the lower part of the legs and under portion of the tail are quite white. As may be inferred from the fact that mammalogists entertained doubts of its existence until within twenty years, the animal is very seldom seen—more rarely by those capable of describing it. Its only haunts, M. Gay says, are the most rugged portions of the Andes, between the provinces of Colchagua and Concepcion; and so timid is it, that it can be approached by the hunter only on rare occasions, and with the utmost difficulty. One perfect specimen is to be found in the cabinet, a second was sent to Europe by M. Gay, and a third living animal was in Quillota when we left Chile. The skins are by no means rare.

Some notice of the condor will be found in the chapter giving an account of country life, and the ornithologist is referred to the able report of Professor Cassin on the collection of birds brought home at my own expense.

There are not wanting varieties of shells, recent and fossil; parts of a fossil mastodon, of which animal two skeletons were found in draining Lake Tagua-tagua, a few years since; insects; reptiles; earthenware antiquities, most probably the handiwork of Peruvians during their ingressions into the country; and a few weapons of the Araucanians. But the institution greatly needs an enlightened and energetic naturalist for its scientific arrangement, as well as its increase, towards which government no doubt would cheerfully and liberally contribute.

Another room contains a valuable mineralogical cabinet, which has been arranged under the direction of Professor Domeyko. Many of the specimens from native mines are of rare beauty and value, some of them crystals of silver ores, not found in any other mines of the world. In gold, copper, lead, iron, cobalt, and sulphur, the collection is also quite complete, and of much interest to the mineralogist. No country, perhaps, offers in so small a compass as does Chile so many and such rich specimens of mineral ores.

In an adjoining room, and carefully preserved in cases with glass doors, are the flags and other trophies captured in battle; in all cases sad emblems of human suffering and violated rights, and whose exhibition by any nation is one of the relics of barbaric chivalry scarcely consonant with an enlightened age.

An edifice which bears the name of University is within a square or two west of Santa Lucia.

* It is also written Güemul.

It covers one fourth of a square, is only of one story in height, and is of the plainest possible appearance, as it is thrown back from the line of the street on its north front, where there is a little open plaza between it and the houses on the opposite side. One of its rooms is used as a hall for the representatives of the nation; others, for their clerks and offices. Opposite the representatives' hall is the school of painting, already mentioned; and within the court, in the rear of these, is the principal theatre—the doors of the three scarce twenty feet apart. The theatre is quite large enough to accommodate the regular play-goers, though one cannot say that very great regard was had to their accommodation by those who planned it: being an oblong, with a semi-circular extremity facing the proscenium, very few can either see or hear. The floors of its three ranges of boxes are without inclination, and without seats, each lessee conveying the chairs he chooses to provide. These it is customary to arrange in two lines, facing each other; and thus one row of persons in each of the side boxes sit with their backs to the stage, either taxing the imagination for a picture of the scene, or twisting their heads half off in efforts to peep between the shoulders of those who are between them and the actors. There is a much better contrived house in the Calle del Puente, not far from the cathedral; but, among other unfortunate oversights, it was built over an *acequia*, whose odors occasionally proved more powerful than the attractions of the performers, and it was never used during our stay, except by travelling jugglers, and the like. A third theatre was commenced, in 1850, on the south side of the Cañada, and its company, at first representing comedies appreciable rather by the mob, soon obtained a popularity which drew many of the better classes to witness their performances. But the population of Santiago are not generally theatre-goers. Their love of change could not be gratified by any histrionic company in the world; and they are too apathetic to encounter the trouble of frequenting the opera-house to hear a repetition of even Bellini's music, or witness a second time the plays of Calderon or Lope. Hence, except during the September holidays, even the little Teatro de la Universidad is never filled. Sundays especially, and feast-days generally, are those on which these only places of diversion are best attended—the Thursday evening performances never having half as large audiences as the houses will accommodate.

The Portal, an ungraceful building opposite the palace, and before referred to, deserves farther mention, from the multitudes who frequent it. Its front is an arched colonnade, extending the entire length of the plaza, separated from which, by an arcade, is a continuous line of two-story edifices. The lower rooms of these are occupied as shops, and the upper as dwellings, accessible by stair-ways at each end and a gallery of wood above the shop doors. The windows that properly belonged to the shops have been converted into triangular stalls, scarcely large enough for a man to turn round within the upright cases. These are in great demand by small retailers, as are also the wooden shanties built round the base of every column of the arcade. The shanties take off four or five feet each way from the walk within the colonnade, yet leave space sufficient to offer an attractive scene at candle-light, when the ladies flock to it. Encouraged by a French architect in the employ of the government, and by the avidity with which every place was grasped at in this vicinity, the late President purchased about a third of the ground within the square, pulled down the old houses occupying it, and erected covered arcades, with entrances from two other streets, similar to the Parisian *passages*—a blow at the prosperity and popularity of the Portal probably not anticipated by its proprietor, when selling a right of way through it. Including the grounds, the cost of this could not have been much short of half a million of dollars. A somewhat similar building, of equal dimensions, is in progress on the west side of the plaza; but its architectural style, thus far developed, is scarcely better than that of the Portal.

At the centre of the plaza there is an octagonal basin, 30 or 35 feet in diameter and about three feet deep, resting upon a platform elevated a step above the level of the surrounding earth. Water for the supply of that part of the city is taken out of the Mapocho more than a mile above, from whence it is led in earthen pipes. As might be supposed, from what was said respecting deposites in "acequias," these are constantly becoming deranged. The sides and bottom of the octagonal basin are made of blocks of red porphyry. From its centre rises an oblong marble pedestal, with panelled sides sculptured in alto-relievo, representing on the first side a medallion image of General O'Higgins, surrounded by warlike implements; on the second, the entry of General San Martin into Lima; on the third, the battle of Maypu; and on the fourth, the taking of the frigate Esmeralda by Admiral Blanco. On its corners are crocodiles, from whose mouths flows the water supplying the basin; and above are life-size figures of Liberty striking chains off an Indian girl, typical of the genius of Chile. The Indian figure is somewhat recumbent, with a quiver of arrows at her back, plumes of feathers on her head, and chains on her arms. That of Liberty has a stout club, with which she appears rather to have thumped her *protégée* over the head than to have contributed to her deliverance from bondage. As a work of art, it is by no means creditable; but as evincing a disposition on the part of an infant nation to ornament its capital whilst endeavoring to perpetuate the memory of the most prominent events in its revolutionary history, it is worthy of all commendation.

Two bronzed superposed basins on ornamented pedestals, forming directories for a *jet d'eau*, and which formerly occupied this plaza, have been removed to a reservoir prepared for them in the Cañada, as has already been mentioned. These are the only attempts at ornamental fountains, though there are a sufficient number of stone basins for water to place a supply within a moderate distance of each square. Good water is found within 30 to 50 feet of the surface in every part of the city; but very few wells have been dug, and, consequently, the family supply is brought by *aguadores* (water-carriers), for about a dollar per month; or six cents for the mule-load, if one buys only a small quantity. A mule carries two kegs, containing from ten to twelve gallons each, between which the *aguador* seats himself; and all day long one hears his "*aguatiro*," or simply "*tiro*," above the thousand cries that render the streets such nuisances at certain hours. To save the trouble of removal, though filled from the top, the kegs also have apertures at the bottom, through which the water is drawn off. As it not unfrequently happens that the lower stopper drops out while the animal jogs along, the *aguador* must then empty the other to restore equilibrium, or risk being capsized—events causing no little mirth among the passing boys and peons.

Above the junction of the Maypu canal the water of the Mapocho is comparatively clear, and it is said to be not only much softer but also more wholesome. It is, therefore, a subject of surprise that the necessities of so large a population have not induced the government to attempt its introduction through iron pipes, which would enable each housekeeper to provide a hydrant. Now, the water is taken from the river just above the city, and conveyed in badly-burnt earthen tubes, which are constantly out of order. No city has better command of water than Santiago, or is more favorably located for its distribution; and who knows but that we might see more clean faces if it were more freely accessible? Though quite turbid, and containing ingredients by no means healthy,* the poorer classes drink it as it comes from the fountains; those able to afford it have filterers, made of the conglomerate of shells found in such quantities on the coast from Coquimbo northward. Dripping from the filterers in the dry atmosphere of summer, it cools to a temperature that renders the use of ice wholly unnecessary. Properly speaking, ice is not known, except occasional thin pellicles that form on little pools in the most exposed situations, and melt again by ten o'clock in the morning; but snow, mixed with hail, is to be had in abundance. This is brought into town daily from the hacienda of the Dehesa, four leagues distant; and, considering that it is a monopoly for which the municipality receives $15,000 per annum, it is sold at very moderate prices. Two parcels, of about fifty pounds each, enveloped in straw and enclosed between frames of hide net-work, are loaded on a mule; and trains of these bring the supply from the Andes a day's journey beyond the depository at the Dehesa. From the latter place it is conveyed to the city in carts. The privilege to sell it, like that of almost every other source of revenue to either the general or municipal governments, is

* Some say that the goitre was not known until the Maypu emptied a part of its muddy stream into the Mapocho; others assert that it came with the poplars from Mendoza.

disposed of to the highest bidder at auction. But as the successful competitor never reveals his profits, and takes especial care to conceal the quantity that has been consumed, or what he receives in tolls or tithes from the landed proprietors, there are few persons willing to risk the uncertainty. Ices are called for at all seasons, and by all classes—from the *peon* about the market at early light, to the *rotos* (loafers) and street loungers at midnight. The favorites are water-ices flavored with cinnamon, coffee, or chocolate, though almost every imaginable condiment is used; and they may be had day and night, not only in the confectioners' and pastry-shops and market-houses, but also from dozens of itinerant venders. Not to like *dulces* and *helados* (confectionery and ices) at all hours, is an evidence of want of taste at Santiago which only a Goth will acknowledge. Sunday is *the* day for the *dulceros* (venders of confectionery). Then, children are at home from school; all journeymen, as well as many servants, have been paid off; it is a holiday (not a *holy* day)—all facts of which confectioners are aware; and, in consequence, they let loose troops of peddlers on the city, to tempt the nation on one of its weakest sides with the stale cake and candy accumulated during the week.

Besides the jail at the northeast corner of the *Plaza de la Independencia*, there is a penitentiary on the plain beyond the southern suburbs. Its walls enclose near ten acres of ground. Within, the cells are built in radial lines, with intermediate open courts between them of a triangular form. This arrangement facilitates inspection, and will one day afford places for workshops. Two hundred and fifty cells have been completed on about one half of the enclosed area. They are of brick, with arched roofs of the same material, and extremely small. Each has a little opening at the bottom of an iron door which may be closed with a slide, and one of like size above the door—the only mediums of light and ventilation. An alley three feet wide, with a gutter in the middle, separates each pair of the radial lines. There is a water-closet to each.

A large number having been sent to the colony at Magellan only a short time previously, there were but about 350 state prisoners at the time of our visit in October, 1851. A few were in solitary confinement; others in cells with as many as three companions; many of them in these little dens heavily loaded with chains. All were either idle or performing voluntary labor, and in discomfort the most painful to witness. None seemed to have water for ablution; many were scarcely half clad. Beds were equally rare; indeed, the best were but pallets, a few skins, or perhaps a poncho spread on the bare, unclean brick floor. Their food, of the coarsest and commonest kind, is served to them in dirty tin pots, the discipline seeming to embrace neither cleanliness nor the preservation of health. A like aggregation of vice and misery to that which sent Howard on his mission of humanity may yet be found in Chile. Instead of compelling convicts to work and earn something towards their maintenance, affording occupation to their minds whilst forcing them into habits of industry in the acquisition of a useful trade, the months and years of captivity are passed in idleness and indolence, each hour more strongly confirming vices whose exhibition had already brought upon them the penalties of the law. What but manifold crimes can result from such a system? Of the prisoners, few had attained middle age; a still smaller number were old men: nearly all were young and active—just at that period of life when associations and habits take the strongest hold; and it was distressing to think of the career to which they are hereafter condemned by the present course of treatment. Among them were several officers of the Chacabuco regiment, who had taken part in the revolt of the 13th of September. Their cells were of the same dimensions as the rest, though a little whitewash had imparted an air of cleanliness which other criminals less fortunate in means did not possess. They had the freedom of the narrow alley. Formerly, as there were no cells, (it was only in 1847 that any part of the penitentiary was completed,) when night came, the prisoners were huddled into cages and locked up. A part of these vehicles yet remain in the penitentiary yard. They are about 12 feet long, 4½ feet high, mounted on wheels, and in no respect differ from those constructed for the safe-keeping of wild beasts. When to be employed on the public works, they are still conveyed from one place to another in these cages.

The benevolent friends whom I accompanied had provided a heavy purse of silver change, bundles of clothing, and a basket of tobacco, for distribution (there being no prohibition against smoking), and they found but one who actually declined their bounty. He, poor fellow! had been seized in the conveyance of ammunition to Aconcagua last year, and condemned as though taken in actual revolt. With a spirit of generosity rivalling that of the fair almoner, he entreated her to give to others really in need; for himself, he had no wants—a self-denial which may be appreciated when it is known that the only food furnished by government is bread, boiled beans, and water; and that neither clothes nor bedding are supplied. He had known better days, and the keeper told us that his health had been greatly impaired since he entered the prison. It might be supposed that the arrival of such a visiter amid a mass of human beings suffering great want and hardships, as do the majority who are without charitable friends to succor them, would be hailed as that of an angel; but the truth must be acknowledged: though words of thanks were spoken and the blessings of God and the Virgin invoked upon her, the instances when they appeared to come in tones of the heart were exceedingly rare; the same stereotyped expressions came from all—mere lip service. It made my heart ache to learn that there were so many of my kind from whom the sentiment of true gratitude was so distant. Not one was omitted. Some of those who had been accidently overlooked clamorously made known their presence, and almost demanded as a right a share equal to that received by their fellows. Even the officers received the delicately offered gifts, the painful expressions of their countenances telling of the privations to which they were subjected, and contradicting their disclaimer of want.

The management of the institution is confided to a superintendent, who is a minister (judge) of the court of appeals, a chaplain, a physician, and stewards, with a military guard and their officers. The chaplain receives $500, the medical officer $300, and the other employés, exclusive of the military, about $2,500 per annum in the aggregate. The duty of the superintendent is of a supervisory rather than of an executive character; and he who is charged with the cure of souls, being better paid, probably attends better than the mere curer of the body;* the guard only being surely called upon to watch this castle of crime and idleness.

For the year 1850 Congress made the following appropriations: "Maintenance of prisoners and the troops that guard them, repairs of tools, and other expenses, $16,000," of which $14,090 was spent; and "for clothing of the criminals, $600," not one farthing of which was thus applied! At the same time, there were no less than 346 convicts; so that if we make a reasonable deduction for the diet of the numerous guard, for the high prices of all repairs in Chile, and other expenses, each prisoner will have been an expense to the treasury of nearly $40. Of the convicts there were condemned:

For cattle stealing	94	Counterfeiting money	5
Other robberies	100	Bigamy	3
Desertion	72	Rape	3
Murder and homicide	33	Bestiality	2
Assault and wounding	21	Other crimes and vagrancy	13

Among them, 178 had conducted themselves commendably during the year, 58 passably well, 76 dubiously, and 28 viciously.

At the same time, there were 488 convicts at the colony of Magellan; 90 of whom had been added during the year, principally because of participation in the revolutionary difficulties. Many years ago the island of Juan Fernandez served as the Botany Bay of the republic, and more recently Port Famine; but both proving objectionable, a change has been made to its present location at Punta Arenas. Its governor† is an officer of the navy, for the support of whom in preserving order there are two companies of troops especially enlisted for the service; government holding out as inducements free passage to their families and bounty lands after

* During our visit one of the prisoners was seized with violent convulsions; and though there was probability of a fatal result, no one appeared to think of sending into town for the Doctor, whose regular *semi-weekly* visit had been made on the preceding day.

† Since murdered by the prisoners, and replaced by Major Philippi.

arrival; and to encourage the emigration of foreigners, the governor is not only authorized to admit them on equal privileges with citizens, but is required to afford them such protection and assistance as may be necessary. From the report of the Minister of Marine for that year, the colony was in a most prosperous and attractive condition: the convicts had a primary school for instruction, and an abundance of tools for various trades and agriculture, with a supply of seeds; there were a hospital and medicines for the sick, and all were furnished with bedding and clothes. Shortly afterwards they revolted, murdered the governor and chaplain most inhumanly, and, capturing vessels in transit, nearly all escaped. A part were retaken and executed at Valparaiso in 1852, and the colony re-established with more powerful guards for its preservation.

Respecting the penitentiary during the same period, the Minister of Justice tells Congress: "The penitentiary, whose cells will be completed in the early part of next year, has not failed to be an object of careful attention to government. The workshops established last year afford prisoners constant and lucrative labor, at the same time that it is notably known their physical and moral condition has been greatly improved by the regimen. Having, as a stimulant for improvement in the branches of industry then established, not only the advantage of occupation to alleviate and distract their minds, but also an interest in the acquirement of a respectable and lucrative trade, in the gains of whose product they participate, it is not surprising that the improvement of the convicts corresponds with what may be expected from such powerful incentives in favor of industrial progress.

"I can assure the legislature that products of iron, carpentry, and shoemaking, are so elaborated in the penitentiary as to leave nothing to desire when compared with the best finished work of the most accredited free laborers. Nevertheless, there is wanted in the establishment a well regulated accounting office, in whose books will be posted the first cost of materials used in work, the product of the sales, and the quota to be subsequently rendered with that just exactitude indispensable in favor of the institution, as well as those who have elaborated them. For this object, one of such vital importance, the three thousand dollars granted in the estimate will not be sufficient to pay the officers of the institution; and I find myself under the necessity of recommending Congress to give its early attention to a message from his Excellency the President of the Republic, in which he asks that the office of treasurer of the penitentiary be created, and a proper salary be assigned to him.

"All the partial improvements adopted in the discipline of the penitentiary up to the present time will be fully carried out, as soon as store-houses, barracks for the guard, and a residence for the director shall have been completed. The government desires to begin these works of absolute necessity, and is preparing to carry them into effect at the earliest period.

"Nor has it neglected to charge a gentleman of known probity and zeal to visit the best regulated prisons of North America, instruct himself in the discipline of each, and make such notes of their divers rules and the mode of maintaining them, that when he returns to the country he may submit for examination of government the documents gathered, in order that, selecting the mode of discipline most suitable, it may be adopted in the fullest extent, and under the superintendence of a person who has acquired information on the subject necessary to conduct it to the advantage that is desirable."

As the actual state of the prison and prisoners three months after the date of the report was so greatly at variance with his statement, as has been shown, it is to be apprehended that, like too many other documents, it was prepared by subordinates who should have carried out more closely the instructions of government. It is not intended to be asserted that there was no work going on, because there was a small party of blacksmiths employed in one of the triangular courts, three or four shoemakers each at work in his cell, a plaiter of bridles with fine fibres of hide, and a maker of finger-rings from horse-hair; but more than eight tenths were absolutely without occupation. Nor is the information obtained in the United States likely to be rendered useful very soon, as the gentleman to whom its collection was assigned was appointed Intendente of Coquimbo almost immediately on his return to Chile.

Females convicted of crime are sent either to the *Casa de Correccion* (House of Correction) or to the colony at Punta Arenas. The building temporarily serving for the former is a comparatively large establishment, in the *Calle de las Augustinas*, which has been fitted for their accommodation until one shall be properly built by government. Here also they send women of the town, unruly children, and others who may be reformed by separation from evil disposed associates, and forced labor. Parents and employers, too, are permitted to confine offspring or servants, whenever they can show necessity for moral reformation in the person for whom they make application—a dangerous power, whose abuse, combined with the habits of the inmates, has probably suggested to the poor the nickname of "*Casa de Corrupcion.*" The inmates are employed in various manufactures, which yield nearly sufficient to pay all expenses, including the rent of the premises. There is also an appropriation for it by Congress. The number of those confined in March, 1852, were:

Married men	2	Unmarried men and youths	62
Married women	33	Unmarried women and girls	119

Though provision is made by regulation for a separation of the sexes, according to popular belief great immorality still exists; and it is scarcely to be wondered at when we remember that the class associated there scarcely consider it a sin thus to indulge their passions, and the guards themselves are among the first to set the example.

A part of an old convent formerly belonging to the Jesuits, and in front of the Military Academy, has been converted into a dwelling for mendicants, who, by municipal law, are not allowed *in the streets*. Nor is one often annoyed by them there. In one respect the institution is well arranged, married and single having each their distinct portions of the building. But it is far too small; and in one court even the corridors were literally crowded with human beings, many of whom, wan and emaciated, were lying on pallets. Whole families, whom indolence or disease, or both, had reduced to poverty, were there, living in idleness and (of course) uncleanliness; a few only employing themselves on trifling articles of handicraft, which they are afterwards permitted to sell in the streets. There appears to be no want of food or clothing, as at the penitentiary; and the more than 300 paupers are really far more comfortable than their unfortunate countrymen in that establishment.

The alms-house derives its principal support from donations and legacies left by charitable individuals, many of whom also bequeath portions of their wealth to be periodically distributed by surviving relatives; and thus on certain days one may find multitudes of the "lame, and halt, and blind" patiently awaiting their customary pittances in the courts of the persons made the dispensers of these charities. On these days not only are the occupants of the alms-house allowed to come out, but many others avail themselves of the occasion to beg from house to house "*una limosnita por el amor de Dios*" (a little alms for the love of God). During one of the nights of Holy Week, when the multitudes are making their "*estaciones*" (visit to a church for prayer) at the different churches, the poor prisoners are permitted to leave the jail under charge of armed sentinels. Placing themselves in the great thoroughfares, as the crowds pass by they piteously implore a *mediocito* ($6\frac{1}{4}$ cents), and clank their chains in the hope to inspire more compassion whilst they attract your attention by the sound. Churches too have their beggars; most of them sleek, well-fed friars, who pass from house to house with a tawdrily dressed doll in a sort of child's baby-house, ornamented with tinsel and artificial flowers, a picture of some saint, or a bit of cloth. Not unfrequently they offer a part of their own garment to be kissed, as they do whatever may be trusted to them, and receive alms in return. A part of them travel on horseback, and others with servants to transport their show-boxes; though the greater number go on foot and alone. These make their visits with a regularity no little annoying to the stranger. One of them who was a frequent comer to our house during the first five or six months after we were settled, but who, by some good luck on my part, had never seen me, at last followed me into the room as I returned from a walk one morning. Having seen him gambling with a peon in a by-street only a few days previously, my mind was at once made up. Pretending to believe that the box he carried had been sent from one of the nunneries for sale, before he had time to say a word, half a dollar was offered for it, with a remark that one of my little daughters would be pleased with so pretty a baby-house. The look of indignation and hatred with which my really liberal proposition was received, was sufficient warranty that our door would never by darkened by him again.

There is another class of beggars more persevering, and with whom a stranger finds it far more difficult to deal unscathed. Whilst writing one Sunday morning the servant announced three ladies, who followed immediately behind her. They were evidently just from mass, as their church dresses and carpet-rugs over their arms established. The eldest stated that they were neighbors, who had long desired to become acquainted with me, but had been prevented by various causes, and then presented me to her two daughters, who were somewhere about twenty years of age. Knowing that it was not an unusual custom for the lady of a house to send her card to strangers arriving at the capital, if its male head or her husband should be absent, their civility was duly acknowledged, and nothing more was thought of the visit until it became time to repay it. As I did not possess sufficient "modest assurance" at the time to ask either their names or residence, it became necessary to inquire of friends, and thus describe the persons as well as tell of their visit. They were unanimous in the opinion that it was a scheme to obtain money, as it proved; and no small amount of wit and laughter were indulged in at my expense and that of my lady visitors. A few days afterwards a little grandson came with a handsome bouquet; bringing also a message that I was not punctual in returning calls, but was a poor neighbor. Having excused myself under the plea that their house could not be found, only a day or two passed before he came again,—this time with a basket of early nectarines, and an offer to show me the way. But the warning of my friends made me ungallant enough to allege occupation which prevented my going with him. When my little son arrived from home, the grandmother came alone to felicitate me on his safe journey, and pressingly offered to take charge of the repairs of his wardrobe. Both attentions were received with as cold courtesy as it was proper to exhibit in one's own parlor to a well dressed and lady-like woman, even though her motives were strongly suspicious. Several weeks elapsed before anything further was seen of my visitors, except in passing along the street. At last, tired of waiting to see me in their own house, the trio came again, the elder daughter saying, with a pretty smile, it was to ask a favor. They had concluded to sell their "*quinta*" on the "*Tajamar,*" but the house needed repairs which would cost three doubloons—a sum not at their immediate command. To dispose of it in its then condition would be a loss to them of many hundred dollars; and as they knew of a purchaser ready, they took the liberty of asking me to *lend* them the former sum for a week or two. Luckily it was Sunday, and I had not so much money in the house, thus escaping "for the nonce." But at a later period, when the old lady found that her manœuvres were suspected, if not actually understood, and came to borrow two dollars to pay a doctor whom she felt bound to consult (she told me) for one of her daughters, the excuse could not be made, and I considered myself fortunate to get off so cheaply. The persecution, however, did not end here. Within a week another came, desiring conversation for a single minute with Don Santiago (as they called me), a servant girl attending her, conformably to the customs of society. And in this so-called minute was narrated—how she was a stranger from Quillota, who had come to nurse a sick mother, actually destitute of necessities; how her own husband had gone to my country (California), leaving her a very small sum, and two years had passed without her hearing from him; how a friend had told her that I was sympathetic and generous to the unfortunate; and how sorry she would be if I considered her importunate. Though convinced from the first that she was an emissary of the old lady, what could I reply under the circumstances? Absolutely nothing not of a conciliatory nature; but notice was given to the portress, the moment she was out of hearing, that when ladies called thereafter for Don Santiago, he would be "not at home."

For want of a lunatic asylum, the insane also are brought to the alms-house, unless their violence compels close confinement; in which case relatives alone are the guardians. Fortunately for Chile, the number of these is small, and their malady of a harmless nature; yet it is discreditable to the nation that it has not at least one institution whose especial object is the care of those from whom the light of reason has departed. Walking along the Cañada one day, a room was pointed out to me in which an insane gentleman had been confined fifteen years. His malady was of so violent a character that none dared approach him, and death only relieved him from his den of filth and misery. Latterly, patients have been sent to the hospital at Lima, where some provision has been made for them, though its arrangements are far, very far, behind the age. So great an objection is felt to having persons thus afflicted among them, that when a deranged Italian came from Copiapó to Valparaiso in 1850, although his malady was of a perfectly harmless nature, the Intendente attempted to *force* the British mail steamer to take him away again. Being without means to pay his passage, it was refused him. Then the other passengers protested against his coming on board with them, and the agent positively denied him passage, causing him to be sent on shore in the ship's boat after the Intendente had sent him on board with money to pay all charges. For these acts the agent was arrested and tried by the criminal court for disrespect towards the constituted civil authority of the province.*

An institution of a somewhat similar character to that last named, is the "*Christian Society for the Relief of Deserving Poor,*" under the patronage of the ecclesiastical and secular cabildos. They have a house of refuge and grounds of considerable extent in Yungai, which they call the "*Asilia del Salvador.*" Only widows and their families are admitted. Any one desiring this privilege must produce certificates of poverty and moral deportment from at least two well known persons in their parish. There is a chapel belonging to the establishment.

The hospital of "*San Juan de Dios*" for males was founded by Valdivia, who not only provided the funds then necessary, but amongst his earliest acts also wrote out rules for its government. When monks of the order bearing this name came to the country in the early part of the seventeenth century, the hospital was confided to their care; the sick of both sexes, as well as the monks, dwelling under the same roof. The building at present occupied was erected nearly two centuries later, and principally from funds arising from lotteries authorized to this end. It is a large and extremely good looking edifice on the south side of the Cañada, with a garden and fountain of water in its principal *patio*, adding to the attractiveness without. Wide and cleanly corridors, furnished with benches, surround three sides of the *patio*, affording comfortable places of resort for invalids, and the location of the establishment in the widest and most airy portion of the city cannot fail to be wholesome. In one respect, however, the building is not properly constructed. There are windows only on one side of some of its long wards, and the sills of these are high above the floor, (ten feet). Opposite there are two or three doors, by which patients near them must either be subjected to cross-draughts or stagnated air. The ward for surgical cases is in the second story, fronting the Cañada, and is somewhat better ventilated; but the fact that so large a proportion die of those who undergo operations at all serious in their character, is worthy of the most serious consideration. Is such a result attributable to diseased blood existing widely in the race, to imperfect ventilation, or to improper treatment? One of the largest wards is in the form of a cross, with a little altar at the intersection of the arms, where the sick may have an opportunity to witness mass; their beds being in alcoves along the walls. Its plan is admirable for the convenience of the attending nurses, though by no means so to the medical officers; nor is it promotive of cleanliness. Unfortunately, it is even worse ventilated than most of the others, the air being extremely offensive at all times. The hospital is capable of accommodating six hundred patients, with ample room and far greater comforts than most artisans possess in their own houses, ventilation not excepted. Its upholstery for beds and bedding, and its washing and culinary departments, are on an equally

*An asylum for the insane has since been established at Santiago.

liberal scale. Besides these preparations for civilians, there are apartments for the military sick also, and an anatomical saloon for the use of medical students.

From the time that the establishment passed under the charge of the monks, its funds rapidly increased; partially through their influence, and partly through other bequests. Then the sick of the better classes were often removed to it, and the ghostly nurses were not unskilled in attending to their own interests, as well as to the bodily and spiritual welfare of their patients. They are adepts in testamentary documents; and there is no doubt that whilst making the latter ready for a better world, their exhortations added many a rich legacy to the possessions of these spiritual amanuenses. At present the institution owns estates, houses, and funds valued at more than $250,000; which, together with those of the hospital San Francisco de Borja, the foundling hospital, and cemetery, are under the control of a special board organized by government. The property yields an average income of nine per cent. per annum; but, unfortunately, all of those who have portions of the funds on interest are not punctual in their payments, and its actual usefulness is somewhat crippled. One individual of this character was openly spoken of as having been in possession of $45,000 for five years without paying a farthing; his political position preventing that recourse to law from which an humbler citizen would not have been exempted. As the establishment also receives a portion of the *diezmo* (tithes), its annual income is not less than $46,000, of which $16,000 is paid to the medical attendants and servants.

On an average, six hundred patients per month were received during the year 1850; among whom the most prevalent diseases were distributed in the following numbers:

Hospital of San Juan de Dios—1850.

	Entered.	Venereal diseases.	Dysentery.	Simple fevers.	Hepatitis.	Rheumatism.	Small pox.	Consumption.	Pneumonia.	Pleuritis.	Hypertrophy of the heart.	Contusions.	Wounds.	Bronchitis.	Deaths.
January	810	120	142	107	46	19	19	13	51	29	28	30	32	10	117
February	597	118	75	73	44	14	17	10	24	26	21	21	27	9	71
March	414	108	68	54	43	21	7	18	17	15	17	18	28	6	87
April	581	108	79	47	50	24	22	13	24	18	12	17	25	13	89
May	593	128	73	55	40	15	65	18	15	13	13	20	29	8	103
June	570	159	81	57	38	16	42	20	10	15	9	14	21	11	109
July	609	117	118	61	50	23	43	25	12	11	21	10	23	6	115
August	635	135	81	78	35	23	29	23	18	12	15	22	23	9	94
September	547	144	71	64	42	26	18	11	14	8	16	26	32	18	94
October	605	150	95	53	44	13	22	22	29	20	23	12	17	26	87
November	594	181	82	48	32	11	14	24	28	16	24	17	21	19	109
December	677	202	72	94	94	14	6	17	34	4	20	18	18	12	82
Average	603	139	86	66	46	18	25	18	23	16	18	19	25	12	96

Returns have been made regularly for a series of years. These have recently been rescued from oblivion by the Statistical Office, by whose permission all the valuable information they contain has been condensed into the following tables. The new administrador of San Juan de Dios introduced a more specific classification of the diseases in 1850, as is seen above; and which, if systematically followed, cannot fail to be of much interest to students of medical statistics. The returns from 1846 to 1849 were either incomplete or wholly missing at the time of obtaining the extracts subjoined:

Hospital of San Juan de Dios.

	1840.								1841.							
		DIED OF—								DIED OF—						
	Entered.	Fevers.	Diseases of chest.	Small pox.	Dysentery.	Venereal.	Dropsy.	Various and unknown.	Entered.	Fevers.	Diseases of chest.	Small pox.	Dysentery.	Venereal.	Dropsy.	Various and unknown.
January . . .	662	21	24	57	35	18	7	6	604	11	17	22	31	5	3	14
February . . .	665	26	16	61	28	7	8	10	482	12	20	20	16	9	3	11
March . . .	652	12	16	49	15	7	8	3	447	18	15	12	27	4	4	9
April	546	27	12	53	25	8	6	6	437	11	17	28	16	14	3	6
May	668	34	20	79	31	13	7	9	485	18	16	32	26	14	4	3
June	592	20	13	70	28	14	1	5	500	15	24	49	18	1	3	3
July	532	20	18	60	23	17	9	4	450	16	16	32	13	17	4	7
August . . .	499	17	25	36	28	19	11	5	484	10	15	18	10	20	10	4
September . .	431	19	21	22	25	13	7	5	455	18	17	17	11	12	5	1
October . . .	528	21	24	19	10	9	1	6	515	14	21	13	12	16	3	3
November . .	536	26	14	15	14	11	3	4	449	18	18	6	18	8	1	6
December . .	610	21	13	38	18	11	5	7	524	14	28	9	17	13	4	4

	1842.								1843.							
		DIED OF—								DIED OF—						
	Entered.	Fevers.	Diseases of chest.	Small pox.	Dysentery.	Venereal.	Dropsy.	Various and unknown.	Entered.	Fevers.	Diseases of chest.	Small pox.	Dysentery.	Venereal.	Dropsy.	Not named.
January . . .	535	19	32	2	28	12	3	8	616	23	14		27	14	4	9
February . . .	484	20	12	8	26	10	4	6	573	20	27	1	18	16	2	10
March . . .	588	27	10	10	16	12	8	5	546	9	22	6	18	10	12	13
April	457	17	19	10	14	14	7	2	489	10	19	1	25	14	4	3
May	448	11	11	8	21	5	3	7	480	6	26	6	18	16	3	5
June	473	7	17	14	25	6	6	12	486	7	20		20	14	5	3
July	493	16	20	15	28	8	7	6	574	4	37	1	18	14	5	4
August . . .	457	10	25	5	11	13	6	6	592	14	27	2	24	12	6	7
September . .	524	22	14	6	19	13	2	1	545	8	38	1	14	29	7	3
October . . .	570	27	29	6	20	14	6	9	531	15	24	1	18	21	5	6
November . .	588	10	34	3	17	14	6	4	595	14	41		14	17	5	8
December . .	584	20	18	1	18	8	4	10	610	12	22	2	22	8	4	8

	1844.								1845.							
		DIED OF—								DIED OF—						
	Entered.	Fevers.	Diseases of chest.	Small pox.	Dysentery.	Venereal.	Dropsy.	Not named.	Entered.	Fevers.	Diseases of chest.	Small pox.	Dysentery.	Venereal.	Dropsy.	Not named.
January . . .	631	18	30	1	25	17	5	7	749	6	43	13	31	20	6	5
February . . .	541	5	29		26	12	2	8	590	12	14	6	16	9		6
March . . .	571	3	23		16	14	5	4	655	5	23	10	20	18	3	12
April	521	4	37	1	27	10	3	6	699	8	31	13	22	14	4	9
May	591	4	30	4	20	12	7	8	671	6	34	20	21	19	2	6
June	537	5	25	2	30	5	1	4	601	3	36	12	27	15	1	7
July	586	5	23	3	16	10	4	8	591	7	23	6	24	14	6	6
August . . .	619	14	26	5	20	8	1	5	613	8	27	2	29	14	5	2
September . .	574	4	28	6	21	10	2	7	585	10	33	2	17	10.	1	3
October . . .	682	7	38	2	20	15	5	8	657	8	36	3	23	17	4	4
November . .	685	10	28	3	17	12	12	4	645	13	26	4	22	17	3	1
December . .	742	14	18	8	21	20	9	2	701	10	33	1	31	7	6	7

Ratio of Mortality in the several years.

Year		
1840	1 out of each	4.30
1841	do.	5.22
1842	do.	5.93
1843	do.	6.37
1844	do.	7.33
1845	do.	7.01
1850	do.	6.25
Average	do.	6.06

A proper estimate of the influence of season on diseases can scarcely be formed from registers imperfectly kept during so short a time; yet even these hospital reports are not without interest, as showing the predominant diseases and the comparative mortality among the patients. Confirmatory evidence of the most prevalent diseases is contained in the following remarks, for which I must express obligation to the head of the medical faculty:

"The most frequent diseases are hypertrophy, hepatitis, and dysentery. The last is at times complicated with a hepatic condition, and at others is caused solely by inflammation of the larger intestines. In the winter season a catarrhal influenza is the most predominant; though bronchitis, pneumonia, and pleuritis are very frequent. The treatment of the last which is most employed is anti-phlogistic; and it is more or less active, according to the constitution of the patient and the character of the disease.

"In summer, ordinary or gastric fevers, dysentery, and hepatitis are the most common. At times fevers assume an ataxical or adynamical, though rarely a typhoidal character, true typhus being rarely seen among us.

"From time to time there are infirmities which may be considered endemic or epidemic. Santiago being in a valley, its somewhat stationary atmosphere favors the development of epidemic disorders. In 1829 scarlet fever was an epidemic that caused great loss of life throughout the republic. It began like the catarrhal influenza known as '*la grippe*.' In 1842 the '*grippe*' manifested itself in an epidemic manner; and last August (1851) there was another visitation by the same disease.

"But within the last few years the disease which has become most frequent is tuberculous phthisis, attacking every class of society, though its ravages are greatest among the poor. Its most general causes are want, intemperance, and atmospheric changes."

A fever not unfrequent during summer, and called by the natives "*chevalongo*," from all accounts is very decidedly typhoid. The name is of Indian origin, equivalent to "hair of the head," and seems to have been adopted from the fact that those who have the misfortune to be attacked by it invariably lose this adornment of the cranium, if so lucky as to retain life. Nor is anything said by the medical gentleman, in his note to me, of blindness and goitre,—both diseases prevailing to a notable extent, and more particularly among the poor. In alpine countries, where the latter disease is most prevalent, it is usually attributed to snow-water, though instances are not wanting which afford reason to believe it hereditary; and, as has been already alluded to, there is a class in Chile who attribute it to the influence of the poplar-trees. If it be the water, it is certain that filtration will not wholly deprive it of influence on constitutions predisposed to the disease; many cases being known to me where the sufferers have never partaken of water not thus freed from its turbid particles. Blindness is equally common. It has been mentioned that alms are distributed by certain wealthy families at stated periods, and on these occasions nearly a hundred of the poor blind have been counted returning to their homes just after receiving their charitable pittances. Many are inmates of the alms-house, permitted to come out under guidance of other mendicants, whilst others are comparatively well clad. A medical man, after examination only, could designate the different diseases of the eyes among this multitude, and assign the true cause to each; though it is not at all improbable that most of them would be traced to the whitewashed walls in a climate which in summer is as dry as an oven, venereal diseases, and uncleanliness. A paper stating that the disease just named is one of the principal causes of mortality, was read before the faculty of medical science, and published in the "*Anales de la Universidad*" in August, 1850. After speaking at length on the constitutions of the present generation, the author goes on to say:

"Looking round the whole horizon, we do not find a single spot that casts the germs of epidemic miasma towards our blue sky; nor can we find on the soil any of the venomous reptiles infesting other countries, and in whose presence their people are stupefied. Yet, in the midst of this bountiful land we perceive death cutting down the tender plants of the generation, and striking off the young branches of the genealogical tree, whose sap vivifies the trunk, leaving only the dried limbs in whose veins flow the poisons that afflict society. In my view these poisons are, first, syphilis; second, immorality; third, improper rearing; and fourth, want. These combined are the causes operating to produce the evils spoken of.

"Syphilis, or venereal disease. This is the prime mover of the revolution effected in the human species—the infernal contagion transmitted to our generation. I will not stop to show how this mortal poison penetrates all the tissues of the body, how it combines with the fluids, nor how it is communicated from parent to child. It is only necessary for me to prove that it engenders scrofula, and that such a constitution is a misfortune for the individual as well as society. * * * That the mortality of the country is due to it I cannot doubt, after seeing the innumerable children who have been brought to the charity hospital suffering with scrofulous syphilis. * * * * * * *

"It is not difficult to estimate the character of people who possess lymphatic temperaments. Their natural or acquired debility makes them reserved in thought, unstable in determinations, inconstant in affection—in a word, they are passive from timidity, and tolerant for want of energy. Our generation is moving in this direction, towards that condition when good and evil are alike matters of indifference; old age, the picture of this temperament, is an irrefragable proof of this indolence. But having already gone over one half the fatal journey in which generations lose in stability in proportion as they advance, they must be treated more leniently, more especially the delinquent condemned to suffer without pity. His incipient timidity cannot withstand the rigorous chastisement applied to him, and he prefers dying rather than submit to the absolute privation of vital elements—light and heat. I speak now of the penitentiary of the capital, where most of the prisoners live unoccupied, sleep in wet and narrow dungeons, and rapidly hasten death by the inhalation of an atmosphere insufficient for respiration. The greater portion of those who come from the penitentiary to the hospital die from the effects of this treatment. The Chileno is too docile to be subjected to such harsh trials—trials that result in augmenting a depravity whose origin was physical want, and which terminates by confirming its moral necessity. Occupation in forced labor would be the best punishment to correct the misled heart, and strengthen bodies enervated by vice. * *

"Negligence, or mismanagement, is the third predisposing cause of mortality, or rather it is the efficient one. The period of lactation is the most dangerous in childhood, because of the practice of mothers to render the food given more palatable, and thus digestive organs not yet perfected are unable to elaborate it. But it commonly occurs that necessity rather than choice compels this evil, so many mothers having a scarcity of milk. Nevertheless, this mal-practice is very general, even among the better classes of society, and appears to have originated in the vulgar belief that *the child may break its gall* if its inquietude is not acceded to. Experience, which has so often shown the falsity of the popular prejudice, seems not to have been sufficient to do away with it among parents. * * * * * *

"The fourth and last cause of mortality in Chile is want; not want resulting from actual deficiency of food—it being admitted that no one dies of hunger here—but from despair produced by idleness. Elsewhere I have said inactivity is the germ of all vice, and I now repeat it to sustain that want does not operate so powerfully on the authors as on their offspring, whom it would be greatly better to place in the hands of some charitable person than to leave in the power of parents whose examples only encourage immorality. Whilst the head of the family gambles or squanders his scanty earnings, and the mother, nourishing the child with food poisonous at its age, follows the example of the husband and prostitutes herself from want, the infant receives its death by instalments. Indeed, the greater number of the offspring among the lower orders being natural children, it is not possible for them to live under the indifference with which they are regarded; and it would seem that the authors of their lives are public executioners, rather than parents—their only bond of union being the brute feeling of sensuality. I repeat it, it appears that their exclusive object was the gratification of lust—unhappily not the creation of a new being. Under these circumstances the child passes nearly all of its life crying from cold and hunger. Seeking instinctively to satisfy its necessities, it finds only dry breasts whose milk has been expressed at the eyes in sorrow for a profligate husband; and the matricide is gratified to see the testimony of impure love gradually dwindle away. Whichever way we look, the child is a victim of want; and it would be far better to convey it to the asylum of public charity than to leave it with such unnatural parents."

Though the truth of the above may be easily substantiated by any one who will take proper measures to inquire, this is a state of things whose exposition might be regarded as very ungracious in a stranger. The writer might have added, very appropriately, that the disease whose ravages are considered the most extensive in sapping vitality is spread to no small extent by the almost universal custom existing among the better classes of employing wet-nurses for their children. Of necessity these women are taken from among the poor, whose ideas of chastity Dr. Mackenna has sufficiently expatiated upon in the article just quoted. Their own illegitimate offspring are either neglected and die, or are put aside, and they themselves, diseased in many instances, impart the seeds of infirmity with their contaminated milk to the children of their employers. The spread of this disease is frightful.

Another writer, whose paper also is printed in the Annals of the University (for 1849), considers that the earthquake of 1822 has had no little influence on the sanitary condition of the country. Some of his views are quoted, not so much from faith in his deductions as to exhibit opinions entertained by one of the medical profession at Santiago, which were considered of sufficient importance for publication by the faculty of medical science.

"The vivid impressions which the war of independence had left on the minds of many, the sorrow caused in numerous families by irreparable losses, and the terror created at the time by certain measures of the government, were causes more than sufficient to modify the health of the mass and profoundly affect its *morale*. Add to these the great earthquake and a hundred and fifty lesser ones that succeeded in the course of two months, and it is easy to estimate at what point the physical revolution would arrive under the influence of such great, unexpected, and repeated impressions, and which ignorance and equivocal zeal would carry to the most absurd exaggeration. From that fatal epoch those nervous disorders began to develop themselves which, increased by a thousand other causes, have since infested our cities. Dysentery, which to that period was of a mild character and by no means common, assumed a putrid form, became endemic, and at times an epidemic—more particularly at Valparaiso and the capital. Finally, to the causes mentioned is also due the formidable increase of that scourge of Santiago, every day assuming more colossal proportions, aneurism.

"The pernicious influence of the earthquake was not wholly limited to the changes mentioned. Forty-eight hours after the terrible shock, there began to appear in the women's hospital, then under my charge, a change in the patients, as well in medical as surgical cases. Violent fevers, preceded by prolonged agues and followed by delirium, were observed; in various surgical cases where only trifling ulcers had previously existed, in twelve hours after the fever, erysipelas spots came out, invariably commencing where the skin was broken, and extending from thence over the whole body. This made its course with incredible rapidity, terminating ordinarily in gangrene, the precursor of death. If caustic was applied, the first erysipelas spots appeared there: if an operation, however slight, was performed, erysipelas invaded the wound. Nor was this destructive disease alone confined to the hospitals: it spread itself over the city with great speed; and in a little while the 'black erysipelas,' as it was called, had attacked multitudes. Sixty-seven ladies of rank, among the highest of society, were victims to the terrible scourge. The first symptoms of the infection were experienced immediately after their *accouchements*, and in a few days they were carried to the grave, their tender offspring generally following. Among the latter the disease first manifested itself at the wound made by separating the umbilical cord; and in females, also at the punctures usually made in the ears. One of the phenomena that called my attention at the time, and in which I was incidentally occupied, was the following. It is known that we are happily exempt from hydrophobia or rabia, as a common disease; and though it is sometimes spontaneously exhibited among dogs, during the excessive heats of the dog-days, or after hard and continued frosts in winter, it is rare among other animals; nor is the disease accompanied by the same frightful symptoms, or attended by the same results, as in Europe. According to the vulgar idea, a dog which becomes rabid, or turns mad, in Chile, bites indiscriminately animals and persons; but neither the wounds nor the bitten exhibit anything extraordinary, and they are perfectly cured in a little while. At the epoch of the earthquake, however, a Frenchman was bitten in the finger by a pig he was killing. Twenty-four hours afterward, symptoms of erysipelas appeared on the wound; three days later it gangrened, and the patient exhibited more furious symptoms of rabia than had ever been witnessed in my practice. As other professors saw the case—the only one that I have known in the country in thirty-one years of experience—I cannot believe myself deceived. The unfortunate man died on the seventh day. Neither the quantities of water with which the city was washed, nor the most extensive sanitary measures suggested, proved sufficient to modify the epidemic (which was not transmitted by contact), until it ceased of itself with the trembling of the earth."

There is yet another prolific source of disease, to which neither refers. With all ages and all classes there is a passion for confectionery, sweetmeats, and ices. These, together with the large quantities of grease consumed in nearly every dish prepared for the table, and maté drunk almost scalding hot, produce disorders of the stomach resulting in fevers, indigestion (cholera morbus), destruction of the teeth, and headaches *ad libitum*. So prevalent are toothaches and headaches, that one rarely walks a square without meeting some one with a handkerchief about the jaws, or bits of plaster on the temples. The latter are considered infallible cures for headaches; and even infants in arms are often seen with little round patches on the sides of their heads, the mother inferring from its cries, when she is thus suffering, that it is similarly afflicted. These *emplastitos* are only a little sugar and soap, on a bit of cotton cloth; but faith in their virtue is co-extensive with the nation.

Before proceeding to speak of the mortality among all classes resulting from the various diseases alluded to, let us return for a moment to one or two other public institutions. *San Francisco de Borja*, a hospital for women, is established in an old convent, on the south side of the Cañada, used by the novitiates of the Jesuits before the expulsion of the order. It has eight wards, capable of accommodating 500 patients; but it is not as well arranged, nor is it even as well ventilated, as San Juan de Dios. The dispensary, conveniences for preparing beds, cooking, washing, &c., are very much in the same style; and the funds for its support, amounting to about $160,000, are invested in a similar manner. When I visited it in July, 1852, there were many small pox cases, between which and the other wards the barriers were criminally slight: good luck, rather than good management, prevented its communication throughout the establishment. Monthly returns have been made for a series of years, all the information contained in which is embraced in the following tables:

Hospital San Francisco de Borja.

		1840.							1841.					
		DIED OF—							DIED OF—					
	Entered.	Violent fevers.	Diseases of chest.	Small pox.	Dysentery.	Venereal.	Dropsy.	Entered.	Violent fevers.	Diseases of chest.	Small pox.	Dysentery.	Venereal.	Unknown and not specified.
January	236	25	7	19	7	19	3	302	25	5	17	14	8	9
February	296	21	12	22	17		2	245	10	3	11	17	9	11
March	298	27	3	45	13	10	6	273	20	28	6	2	12	12
April	232	19	1	52	14	14	7	248	7	11	19	14	2	6
May	286	31	2	48	18	12	4	273	16	18	20	12	3	25
June	297	30	7	41	13	17	7	236	7	2	23	16	1	35
July	292	25	7	51	18	16	5	238	6	2	12	7	1	34
August	298	17	10	45	24	20	5	244	7	1	9	12		42
September	219	14	8	35	18	13	2	233	5	3	5	10		34
October	225	22	4	10	6	16	4	232	10	2	2	8	3	38
November	252	24	5	10	12	10	3	243	10	2		9		26
December	286	25	11	12	15	13	4	295	18	1		6	1	38
Average	268	23.3	6.4	32.5	14.6	14.5	4.3	255	11.7	6.5	10.3	10.6	3.3	25.8

		1842.							1843.*						1844.			
		DIED OF—							DIED OF—						DIED OF—			
	Entered.	Violent fevers.	Diseases of chest.	Small pox.	Dysentery.	Venereal.	Unknown and not specified.	Entered.	Violent fevers.	Small pox.	Dysentery.	Venereal.	Unknown and not specified.	Entered.	Violent fevers.	Small pox.	Dysentery.	Unknown and not specified.
January	287	16	1		21	1	38							354	19		9	36
February	261	18	9	1	19	2	29	276	6		8	1	37	328	9		13	56
March	317	11	3	3	19	1	38	307	9		23	1	38	328	10	1	19	46
April	291	18	1	1	15		25	266	15	1	24		36	303	11	1	18	36
May	241	33	1	3	12	1	24	284	5		16		32	305	14		32	24
June	203	6	6	2	19	2	20	265	3	2	12		32	259	5	2	16	29
July	227	9	3	2	12	3	25	267	10	2	17		28	309	6	7	20	46
August	240	7		2	5	4	37	297	11	3	11		41	324	7	2	12	36
September	274	12	4		13	4	39	299	9	2	8		49	330	15	7	15	33
October	317	11	2	1	16	1	54	293	11	2	11		44	388	12	6	20	42
November	302	8		2	7	2	41	378	16	1	12		59	440		14	12	50
December	182	20			9	2	39	335	14		9		55	419	14	5	14	50
Average	262	14.1	2·5	1.4	13 9	1.9	34.1	297	9.9	1.2	13.7		41.0	341	11.1	3.7	16.7	40.3

* The return for January was not found, and *diseases of the chest* and *venereal* were omitted from March of this year until June, 1847.

		1845.					1846.					1847.					
		DIED OF—					DIED OF—					DIED OF—					
	Entered.	Violent fevers.	Small pox.	Dysentery.	Unknown and not specified.	Entered.	Violent fevers.	Small pox.	Dysentery.	Unknown and not specified.	Entered.	Violent fevers.	Small pox.	Diseases of chest.	Venereal.	Dysentery.	Not known or specified.
January	422	8	7	16	41	450	10	2	16	49	434	9	7			28	21
February	421	11	5	7	35	378	13		20	42	334	8	6			14	26
March	381	6	6	17	40	531	10	5	40	49	436	2	6			14	24
April	372	6	11	16	50	417	16	8	40	35	381	12	40			12	10
May	339	6	13	8	40	431	7	10	30	51	346	8	6			18	40
June	321	10	7	10	47	354	13	11	33	34	338	16	11	6		4	14
July	338	5	7	3	48	416	14	15	35	43	415	20	10	9	13	16	
August	434	15	7	18	54	403	18	10	28	11	391	23	10	9	13	18	
September	404	14	5	18	50	369	15	10	30	33	446	20	29	18	10	24	
October	403	12	6	22	52	469	10	8	30	37	431	19	9	9	12	15	
November	391	10	4	23	45	431	11	9	28	39	474	20	13	9	13	16	
December	445	29	3	28	54	412	9	6	32	28	481	24	12	10	14	18	
Average	389	11.0	6.7	15.5	46.3	422	12.2	7.8	30.2	37.6	409	15.1	13.2	10.0	12 5	16.4	22.5

Ratio of Mortality in the several years.

1840	1 out of each	2.80
1841	do	4.56
1842	do	3.85
1843	do	4.51
1844	do	4.75
1845	do	4.89
1846	do	4.81
1847	do	4.56
Average	do	4.34

During these eight years, one hundred out of each four hundred and thirty-four who entered the hospital died of their diseases—a ratio of mortality much greater than at the hospital of San Juan de Dios, the proportions there having been one hundred in every six hundred and six. The cause of this great difference between two institutions on the same street is well worthy of investigation by the medical men of Chile, more especially as they have for encouragement in the task another fact developed in these tables, viz: a constant decrease in the ratio of mortality in both hospitals.

A foundling hospital (*Casa de Expositos*), or rather, an establishment where any one may leave an infant in open daylight as well as in the darkness, to be brought up at the expense of the public, was founded about the middle of the last century. The building is in the lower part of the *Calle de las Augustinas,* but externally presents nothing to attract attention. At the time it was instituted, it was perhaps intended, in good faith, for the benefit of poor orphans and those whose unnatural parents had literally thrown them on the charity of the world. But the obstacles interposed to marriages of the poor by curates in many of the parishes, the example of certain members of the monastic orders, and even some of the secular clergy themselves, and the passions of a people taught to believe that no crime is remembered by their Maker after confession to the priest, have all combined to bring about a state of morals which has actually converted the *Casa de Expositos* into an institution for the encouragement of vice. Not only may the mother (or other) take her child to a revolving box fitted into the wall, and turn it within the asylum, tapping a farewell knock to call the porters as its face is perhaps for ever removed from her sight, but she may also avail herself of the same institution to *lie in,* and be known only to the "*partera*" who assists her. Thus, a universal style in the dresses of females which enables them to conceal pregnancy, knowledge that they may give birth to a child unknown to acquaintances, and the facility with which infants may afterwards be disposed of, are all so many barriers broken down from before the strongholds of morality. There is no novelty in an event occurring three times in every two days, and no one thinks to inquire whose is the little stranger turned within the wall; a nurse is provided for it, and there ends gossip or thought of its origin. Its own mother may perhaps pass from the turn-stile to the door, and, offering herself as a nurse, receive her child again; but now she obtains pay for the nourishment which nature had actually provided.

The building being wholly inadequate to accommodate the nearly 700 in its charge, who of necessity are accompanied by their nurses, very few are retained on the premises. Nearly all are, therefore, given to women from the country, who are supposed to have at their control sustenance suitable for infants, or to others in the city who have, or pretend to have, lost their own children; and in the latter case, there is no doubt many poor mothers are included, as has just been intimated. To prove themselves entitled to the salary allowed by the hospital, they are required to present the children on pay-day; but who, after the lapse of a month, could recognise an infant perhaps not six hours old when brought to the house, and which had been taken away within even a shorter time thereafter? On the 1st of January, 1850, there were 629 children at the expense of the establishment, and its operations during the two following years are shown in the subjoined table:

Casa de Expositos.

	1850.						1851.					
	ENTERED.		RECLAIMED OR SENT OUT.		DIED.		ENTERED.		RECLAIMED OR SENT OUT.		DIED.	
	Boys.	Girls.	Boys.	Girls.	Boys.	Girls.	Boys.	Girls.	Boys.	Girls.	Boys.	Girls.
January . . .	20	21	5	7	19	16	25	24	9	12	10	16
February . . .	18	19	11	10	12	7	25	14	12	10	14	15
March	17	11	11	12	15	7	13	16	8	10	10	17
April	13	20	16	14	10	8	17	15	9	7	14	9
May	17	14	5	11	12	8	23	23	10	8	8	5
June	24	20	6	4	8	9	23	17	8	8	13	9
July	18	22	12	18	7	5	17	22	9	8	15	10
August	36	21	10	13	6	8	22	26	13	16	15	10
September . .	26	10	8	10	8	9	28	24	14	18	9	7
October . . .	31	25	8	12	6	4	36	19	8	5	4	4
November . . .	26	31	12	14	13	10	26	30	9	2	12	11
December . . .	26	20	13	10	11	14	22	24	13	12	12	11
Total . . .	272	234	117	135	127	105	277	254	122	116	136	124

This would leave 684 in charge of the institution on the 1st of January, 1852. But—520 children annually abandoned by parents in a city of less than 90,000 inhabitants, or about one for every two marriages, and one out of every ten births!

The institution owns a large estate, yielding it $16,000 per annum; receives $1,000 from the *diezmo* (tithes); and has other funds, the interest of which increases its income to about $24,000; nearly all of which is paid at the rate of $2.50 per month to nurses, who are scattered through the city and adjoining country. Until there is a reformation, not only in the mode of paying curates, but also in the practices of them and others, it is to be apprehended that there will be no diminution in the number employed.

As guardians of the public health, there is a medical faculty for the examination of all candidates who propose to practise in Chile, whether graduates of other recognised institutions or not; and another board, whose duty it is to vaccinate gratuitously all who may offer. Some of the latter may be found in every province. The former sometimes make decisions far from palatable to strangers coming with the intention to become residents of Santiago. When they bring diplomas, and possess such knowledge of the language as enables them to answer readily, if they have tact to fall into the ideas and prejudices of the country, the examination is very trivial. But if the parchments of their early manhood have been forgotten in the long years of creditable service, even ten years of experience as a surgeon in her British Majesty's navy is not sufficient guaranty that the applicant has been regularly instructed, and he must submit to the whole trial. Such a case actually occurred during our residence; and one of the very ablest physicians who ever came to the capital was refused permission to practise until he should send to Europe for his musty sheepskins.

Manufactures.—In works of this nature Santiago does not occupy the position to which its raw materials and wealth entitle it, or its necessities actually demand. Foreigners arriving here have, from time to time, been granted exclusive privileges to establish within the republic manufactories of cloth, cotton fabrics, sugar refining, biscuit, glass-ware, paper, and many other articles of less immediate use, their privileges extending from two to ten years. Yet, to the present day the extraordinary advantages thus secured to them have not been availed of, and there is not one in operation. It must not be supposed that any of the applicants for patents proposed to conduct operations according to plans of their own invention, for such was not the case. The fact that no such machinery or method is in use in Chile has heretofore been sufficient warrant for the government to hold out, as inducement for its introduction, special protection to all who are willing to embark in objects of public utility. Were there more enterprise, such a system would create oppressive monopolies in a few years. No patent office proper exists. Any one who desires an exclusive right submits his plans or propositions to the Minister of the Interior, by whom they are referred to a commission of three persons, whose report for or against its usefulness or practicability generally decides the matter.

In the manufacture of silver, native workmen confine their ingenuity almost exclusively to ornaments for churches, an occasional maté-cup or bombilla, table-spoons, spurs, and other parts of the equipments for horsemen. As their whole workshop comprises but an anvil, a block of wood, a hammer, and a few bits of pointed steel, their models are neither prettily formed nor delicately executed; indeed they appear to possess little ingenuity or originality. Abundantly as the mines of Atacama yield, and wealthy as are very many families, silver ware for household purposes is far less common than with even the middle classes of North America. Those who possess services of silver rarely exhibit them; forks and spoons of so precious a metal offering temptations that few of their servants can easily resist. As those made in the country are only of the plainest and rudest description, the family desiring such luxuries, instead of endeavoring to raise the standard of skill by encouraging their own countrymen, import the manufactures of Paris. Two or three foreign jewellers, whose charges for everything are from 200 to 300 per cent. higher than the rates they would ever have received at home, are the only workers in gold.

Though the larger number of copper utensils for domestic purposes are brought from the province of Coquimbo, where the material is more abundant, they are also manufactured here to some extent. Pans and kettles for boiling water, and *braseros*, are the most common; each being composed of a single disk of copper, cast in an earthen mould, and subsequently hammered into the required form. If needed, handles and feet are riveted on afterwards. In order that the metal may the more easily be reduced to the proper form and thickness, the cake is heated from time to time over a common portable furnace. With no guides but the hands and eyes, and no implements but brass anvils, and hammers with long heads, to be used when the vessel becomes deep, it is not surprising that the sides of these articles should be rough and unequal. The earthenware moulds—which may be repeatedly used—the bellows for the little smelting-furnace, the hammers, in short everything is precisely as it was more than a quarter of a century ago. There are four such native establishments in the city, and two others which are under control of foreigners, who manufacture boilers and other parts of distilling apparatus on a more extensive scale. Of the first-named shops, the produce varies in price from 37½ to 56¼ cents per pound, according to the size and workmanship of the article. Latterly a brass-founder has also come to try his fortune at the capital; and from the signs of activity and sounds about his little establishment, he is driving a very good business. But the workers in metal who find the most constant though probably the least lucrative employment, are the blacksmiths, whose shops, both of natives and foreigners, are to be found in all parts of the city. Ornamental bars for all the windows, bedsteads, cradles, and carriage, cart, and horse trappings, in streets like these, give certain and incessant occupation, apart from the many other demands for their services. As an art requiring rather strength and industry than capacity or skill, native workmen soon rival strangers; and thus, by competition, their wares are sold at very equitable prices.

Machinery for a cloth factory was brought out from France by a company which had secured an exclusive privilege, and it may very shortly commence work; though some who took part in the adventure are no little doubtful of the result. Coarse, unfulled cloths, called *bayetas*, and used for ponchos, trousers of men, and under-garments of women, are woven with hand-looms, owned by poor individuals—a rancho being its usual *locale,* and an old woman the operative. They also weave blankets. Though substantially made and warm, these are neither so fine nor so tastefully wrought as those brought from the southern provinces; a remark which applies to all their woollen fabrics.

Ordinary qualities of leather are made at a number of tanneries in various parts of the suburbs. As the oak (*Quercus*) is not found in Chile, they use instead the bark of the Lingue (*Laurus l.*), Peumo (*Laurus p.*), and Panque (*Gunnera scabra*), which is ground, or rather is crushed, in a mill similar to those for pulverizing metallic ores, and is described in connexion with the mineral products of Atacama. From neglect in the vats, the leather is very often burned, and is extremely worthless. France supplies the finer qualities, and raw hide is substituted for many purposes to which the tanned article is applied elsewhere.

From the color of the garments worn by the lower classes and the appearances of their faces, one would infer that not only soap but even water was difficult to be obtained. Yet the number of those constantly occupied in making common varieties of the former, and in moulding candles of tallow, probably exceeds all other trades except those of shoemakers and journeymen tailors. To the present day, toilet soaps and stearine candles are either beyond their knowledge or facilities to manufacture.

If we omit the workers in iron, leather, and cloth, whoever learns a mechanic art may in a few years accumulate independence if he pursues his vocation industriously; the instances not being rare of foreign artisans, who have come to Chile within twenty years as shipwrights, joiners, and house-carpenters, that are now worth more than $50,000 each. Such is the spirit of emulation in society, and so exorbitant the prices demanded for furniture fashionable in style, that many prefer sending to France and paying high duties rather than purchase home-made goods. True, very little wood suitable for cabinet-work has, as yet, been brought to the country; and though carvers are beginning to imitate well, their products want the graceful finish which their brother-chips abroad are able to give.

The Intendente of the province is *ex officio* Mayor of the city; and he is not only charged with the preservation of public order and personal security, but, as the immediate representative of the President, it is made his duty to watch over the prompt and proper administration of justice, the legal collection and expenditure of public funds, the public schools and charitable institutions, to admonish or remove certain judges in special cases, to act as a judge in others, and even to interfere with the curates of the churches who neglect their duty or oppress their parishioners. *So says the law;* but in fact, except so far as regards the preservation of public order, an Intendente is only an instrument of the Minister of the Interior, or central government, for whose sanction he is obliged to refer every contemplated act of his administration.

Holding office wholly by the will of the President, as has been elsewhere stated, he is, of course, ready to carry out the views of the government or resign.

A municipal council called *cabildo*, to represent the interests of the people, is elected by them every three years, or rather is selected by the Minister of the Interior and Intendente, and voted for by the people accordingly. This is literally the fact. The Intendente presides at their meetings, and has the power to veto. Their duties nominally are: to fix the tax on householders for lighting the streets and police, on cattle killed for consumption in the city, and one or two other minor objects of direct taxation; to provide sanitary regulations; to direct public improvements and ornaments; supervise primary education, the hospitals, prisons, repairs of streets, &c. But the rates of taxation must be sent to the Minister for revision; they cannot establish even a primary school without the sanction of the Minister of Public Instruction, nor spend a condor ($10) in the most essential repair or improvement without the same high authority; and, in short, as far as any actual power intrusted to them is concerned, the body appears wholly superfluous. This is one of the subjects of complaint by the southern towns, who like not to see the revenues derived from their pockets taken for the adornment of the capital, whilst their own streets and neighboring roads so greatly need repairs. There are no taxes on personal or real estate, nor will property-holders listen for an instant to the propriety of changing the system by which the poor pay the great burden, as will readily be seen in the following exhibition of the receipts and expenditures during 1850:

RECEIPTS.	
Balance from 1849	$1,018
Tax for serenos, and lighting streets	47,775
Tax on animals slaughtered, and skins	30,167
Rent of market-houses	19,825
For privilege to sell snow	15,150
Rent of theatre	1,8[illegible]5
Tax on ball-alleys	2,520
Tax on cock-pits	2,200
Rent of pasturage, San José	1,820
Horses taken up and unclaimed	1,345
Tax on auctioneers	1,341
Ground-rents	1,060
Fires	747
Product of house of correction, &c.	423
Interest received from debts	39
Loan	4,000
Extraordinary receipts	3,389
Total	$134,714

EXPENDITURES.	
Police	$63,717
Prisons	18,551
Officers of Cabildo	5,124
Public schools	8,360
Salaries to persons not regularly employed	2,374
Lighting the streets	16,075
Loans to individuals	150
To watchmen and lamplighters	1,909
Ground-rents	2,349
Charities and insolvencies	1,897
Ordinary expenses	9,365
Extraordinary expenses	1,500
Unforeseen expenses	2,050
Total	$133,421

The privilege to sell snow, as also the contracts for lighting the streets and furnishing prisoners with provisions, is disposed of to the most favorable bidder at auction. It is not an extraordinary occurrence, however, that the competitor who comes with a note of recommendation to the treasurer presiding at the auction, succeeds in obtaining the contract he desires. Fortunately these collusions are now far less common, the spirit of the age tending towards greater integrity in public transactions.

From what has been said respecting the actual powers of the Cabildo and Intendente, we scarcely wonder that the streets remain in such a filthy condition during several months of the year, or that the most important works of public necessity should be so far behind the age in economy, utility, and convenience. One scarcely sees any repairs of a public nature, except those made by manacled prisoners from the public jail, under charge of police and armed soldiers, in such numbers that the latter alone might easily accomplish the task in less time than is usually occupied. It shocks one to pass along the street where these chain-gangs are at work. In the coldest weather of the climate, there are often thirty or more poor outcasts limping under the weight of iron they carry, many of them more than half naked, yet forced to work at street paving. Nearly all beg from every passer-by, whilst the dozen or two soldiers with fixed bayonets, and mounted supervisors, distributed along the street, lounge against the walls and enjoy their cigaritos as they chat with passing friends. Narrow thoroughfares, the materials of which the houses are erected, their method of paving on a layer of earth instead of sand, concave instead of convex streets, the great weight of the immense carts for conveyance of goods, and the habits of the people, all combine to keep the capital in a state by no means admirable. As there were very trifling if any improvements at all during the three years, I am satisfied that it is only saved from an annual pestilence by the extraordinary dryness of its climate in summer. There is no want of laws nor of police officers to see that they are properly executed ; and perhaps, were there a smaller number of each, it is not impossible both would be more efficacious.

The police consists of two bodies—*Vijilantes,* who have charge by day, and *Serenos,* who compose the night-guard. The former are invariably mounted when on duty. Of the latter only a part are furnished with horses, though all are armed alike with sabres, and have uniforms not mistakable in the darkest night. The Vijilantes go to their post at daylight, and are authorized to arrest, on the spot, any one violating the peace or public decency : cleanliness and good order must be preserved on their beats. There is at least one at the intersection of every two streets ; and it is not unusual to find two or three lounging under the shadow of one of the corners, gossiping with those who come to purchase from the second-rate grocery and liquor shop, to which corner rooms are usually appropriated. Unfortunately, they have not been much accustomed either to cleanliness or public decency, and they are scarcely competent judges of the violation of either. If a disturbance occur, the parties are summarily arrested, and the Vijilante, calling a relief to his post by a whistle, takes the prisoners to the police station to make his charges. As they are not permitted to leave their beats without protection, if one of the corporals or a supernumerary do not chance to be passing along, the call is sounded from corner to corner until it reaches the *Vijilancia,* when the proper force at once repairs to the seat of the disorder. Should resistance be made to a Vijilante in the execution of his duty, he may claim aid of all passers-by, and it is a criminal offence to refuse that assistance when he demands "*favor á la lei*" (aid the law). Thus an escape is almost impossible ; and consequently, disorders in the streets by day are of very rare occurrence.

At night-fall the Serenos are marched to the relief of the Vijilantes. Each of these also has his special beat, and he is instructed not to leave it under any pretext before his whistle shall have brought a relief. Including those who are mounted, they are more numerous than the Vijilantes. If required, he must accompany and protect any person to the extremity of his beat, and pass him or her under the care of the neighboring Sereno; or he may be sent to summon a physician or priest at the instance of any housekeeper, forwarding the message through his colleagues if the official reside beyond his district. It is their duty to examine whether the street-doors are properly secured; and as the wholesale stores are usually closed before sunset, the first act is an inspection of all the locks. The shops are generally kept open until ten o'clock; and if one prove to be improperly secured notice must be sent to the proprietor. From time to time they call the hour, accompanying it with a notice of the condition of the weather. When we first arrived, the cry was nominally at intervals of a quarter of an hour, but really every five minutes ; and it was annoying after being late at work to have one bawling under the window at such intervals, "*las dos han dado y seréno*" (past two o'clock and a starlight night); some of them extending it into a song that continued almost until the moment for its repetition. Subsequently the rule was changed to every half hour, and finally to once each hour, the cry being repeated without intermission during his walk from one end of the beat to the other. Notwithstanding the apparent security which their numbers should afford, and the castle-like construction of the houses, robberies are by no means unfrequent; thieves introducing themselves through the acequias or the inner patios, which often adjoin houses occupied by suspicious persons, and during stolen interviews of servants. Indeed, want of chastity and theft are such common vices among the lower orders, that it is extremely rare to obtain servants whose characters are free from both charges. And thus, the order of the Intendente diminishing the frequency of the Sereno's cry, though permitting quiet, has not tended to public security. Prior to this, as they called the hour, so they were incessant in perambulating the beat, and were really watchmen; now, an hour of interval tempts them to sit down when the streets are still towards morning, and sleep almost inevitably ensues. Many a time have those at the foot of Santa Lucia been startled in their slumbers when the light of my lantern was turned full on their eyes.

To arm the police with such weapons, and, in a manner, constitute them judges in their districts, is to place more confidence in their integrity and self-control than can properly be trusted with such a race as is the lower class of Chilenos. Subsequent to the revolutionary attempt, in 1851, their number was increased to about 800, many of whom were mere boys, scarcely tall enough to keep their sabres from clanking along the ground. As might have been anticipated, the boys were not inclined to depreciate their own importance, but, on the contrary, by arrogant interference, more than once created instead of quelling disturbance, using their arms on half-drunken and defenceless peons for the most trivial offences. Were the force a small one, or the people naturally pugnacious, there might be apology for placing swords in the hands of the police; but neither is the case, and the existence of 800 men so armed is at once a proof of disregard for the feelings of the weak, and of fear of those whom wealth renders powerful.

By the official census of 1830, the population included within the eight wards, or districts, of the city was 67,777 souls. The enumeration made in 1844 was imperfect; but, if the divisions of the city remain as before, there seems to have been a decrease in at least half the wards, without proportionate increase in the others. Allowing the number in the omitted district to have been the same as in 1830, the population falls short of what it was at that time 1,500 souls. Yet the statistical periodicals of the latter epoch speak of Santiago as containing more than 80,000 people. There has been no subsequent census, but general opinion, at the present day, has assigned above 90,000 souls to the capital; and a comparison of the plans of the city inhabited in 1830 and 1852, fully justifies belief in such proportionate increase. At no time can a correct census be made; the poor imagine that the officers make inquiries for the purpose of enlistments or taxation, and they are even more averse to telling the truth than the marshals have found some of our own countrymen.

If one asks a Santiaguino what proportion of his townsmen belong to the white and what to the mixed races, he will tell you all, or very nearly all of them, are white—an opinion which has been repeated by more than one writer who never saw Santiago. But if a light copper complexion, oval faces, low foreheads, close eyes, prominent cheek-bones, coarse and straight black hair, and short, robust figures, are at all evidences of Indian ancestry, I cannot think that there are more than one sixth who are really of pure Spanish or Caucasian origin. Even among those now wealthy and in the most responsible positions, there are not a few whose features retain very decided traces of their Indian mothers. Of pure Indian blood there are none to be seen, except when occasionally brought to the city for a few days by returning missionaries. The docile Mapochos, the former lords of the soil, like many of the tribes that inhabited the Atlantic States of North America, have wholly disappeared from the earth. Their blood only flows mingled with that of Iberians. There was a small colony of them still remaining on the banks of the Maypu, and near Mellipilla, until within a few years past; but the settlement probably does not now contain one individual of unadulterated blood.

It formed no part of the policy of the adventurers who, in the sixteenth century, left Spain for America to burden themselves with women; nor were they often men of delicate or refined tastes. The Indian girls were painted to them with a thousand charms; whilst to have brought one of their own countrywomen would, in most cases, have required the sanction of the church, and have been attended with expenses not easily met. Although no party or body of men dared trust their souls without a ghostly protector within hail, and many of them were accompanied by several of these tonsured celibates, the latter were probably too earnestly engaged in efforts to propagate Christianity among the natives to give much attention to a Moslem habit into which their special congregations were falling day by day. Moreover, each additional indulgence desired brought additional lumps of gold into the lap of the church—valuable reasons why too close attention should not be given to the persons whom their enterprising parishioners should choose as companions. Some were married, beyond a doubt, though not many. The offspring of these first emigrants—half white, half Indian—have transmitted their principal characteristics unchanged to the present day. There are shades, certainly, and these, from the further admixture of European with the half-blood, are very generally lighter than darker in color; but they are not common, the larger proportion of the population possessing just the shade and the other marked traits enumerated. If below the medium height of their European progenitors, and apparently wanting in muscular development, many of them are actually capable of physical exertions that would startle a stronger-built man. The "*cargador*,"* who never practises to strengthen himself, and, it may be, sits idle for two or three days, waiting as many jobs, will not hesitate to shoulder from 300 to 400 pounds, when such a package offers, and walk off with it half a mile or so. Having on one occasion a box ready to send to Valparaiso, I asked the cargador who brought me a small parcel just at the time to send me a cart, that it might be taken to the warehouse of an acquaintance constantly sending to the port. Among other heavy objects, it contained at least 300 pounds of ores and fossils, and weighed in all perhaps 400 pounds. He was a man of the form just mentioned, short, fleshy, robust, without marked muscles; and though it took two other men to assist in lifting it to the back of his neck, he carried it half a mile without a halt, well earning the price a cart would have charged, and cheerfully was it paid. Another departure from the anatomical structure of their European ancestors is rendered more observable by the manner in which women wear their hair, viz: A marked flatness of the posterior portions of the parietal and occipital bones, with a corresponding elevation in the upper part of the former. This is so very general that a gracefully-formed head is rarely seen.

Of a right, those who can trace their origin to Spain are no little proud of the "*sangre azul;*" and patriots as they were, and republicans as they claim to be, they would like well to be called by the titles belonging to their families before the revolution. These may be a sixteenth of the population; the other portion of the white inhabitants consists of French, Argentines, Germans, English, and Italians. The United States is represented by its minister and his secretary—two gentlemen who have been above twenty years in the country—and perhaps half a dozen mechanics. Therefore, when my own party came away, one half the American society in Santiago was lost. Of negroes there are very few. I do not remember to have seen twenty embracing all ages; and of their descendants with mingled blood there is apparently a smaller number. There are no such admixtures as are to be found at Lima, where slavery is still in existence.

The great mass of the population are day-laborers, and peddlers of one article or another; and the dress of the class is neither picturesque, neat, nor clean. A coarse cotton shirt, white wide-legged trousers of the same material, but which scarcely descend to the ankles, a pair of high-heeled shoes that compel the wearer to walk tip-toe fashion, a conical and ribbonless straw hat with narrow brim slouched about the ears, and a poncho of coarse woollen material, is the universal costume. The color of the poncho, or the shape and material of the hat, are the only variable articles of the wardrobe. The former, which at different times serves them for jacket, cloak, blanket, towel, and even basket, is a bit of cloth with a slit in the centre to pass the head through, and is long and wide enough to fall to the hips and elbows. They are of all colors; though bright red and green or yellow stripes, on each side and through the centre, seem essential to meet their taste. It is a most convenient article of equestrian costume, and is universally worn as a protection from dust, whilst its flowing folds act as a sort of fan to keep one cool. Those for ladies are usually of white Vicuña wool, or other light material. The

* These are the public carriers, carts being rarely used in the city unless the number of parcels would make it more economical to the owner.

native made are by far the most valuable, being literally wrought by the hand, of good wool, well twisted, and capable of turning rain. Some of them, composed wholly of the finest Alpaca or Vicuña wool, are valued at more than a hundred dollars; though one quite as handsome, and almost as serviceable, may be purchased for a fourth of that sum. So closely have English manufacturers imitated the fabric, that only an experienced eye can detect the foreign article. Nearly the whole supply of the inferior qualities comes from that source. Peru and Ecuador furnish straw hats; though one very often meets with perfect cones of felt, from the apex of which hangs a bunch of vari-colored ribbons.

As there are few of the day-laborers or peddlers who know the luxury of either bedstead or bed other than a raw hide in a corner, none of them who hesitate to seat themselves anywhere in the shade, and but a small number who risk their complexions by contact with water more than once in a week, it may well be imagined that their cotton garments do not long preserve a snow-colored aspect, and that these specimens of humanity have not the most tidy appearance. On Sundays and other holidays they brighten up, and along the Tajamar one may find a score of barbers, with a bit of canvass stretched across poles to make a shade, surrounded by crowds of attending customers. Equipped in a clean shirt and trousers, under the waistband of which he has stored a water-melon and mug of water for breakfast, he is ready to spend the week's earnings at a "*chingana*," or with "*bolas*," or other variety of gambling; stuffing himself with fruit all day, if it is attainable, and drinking no little *chicha* during the same interval. Monday is spent in recovery from his debauch. These are the only enjoyments he knows. A *puchero*, (composed of meat and all manner of vegetables boiled together) or a dish of boiled beans and a small loaf of bread, form the varieties of his weekly diet. The women of the same class are not much more careful of their personal appearance; but, though apathy predominates, they are redeemed by an expression of native intelligence and kindness. As a rule, they comprehend more quickly than the men, and are superior to them in energy as they are more liberal in sentiment; traits found among the better classes of society with even greater frequency. Hanging down their backs in plaits—a custom no doubt transmitted from their Indian ancestors—their long black hair is their greatest ornament, though very coarse, and often unsmoothed for days. Except in the very hottest weather, wherever they are, in the street or over the wash-box, (for they have not yet accomplished the refinement of coopered tubs), some sort of shawl envelopes them, one corner being temporarily confined to the person by being thrown over the left shoulder. The shawl enables them to remove their arms from the sleeves of their gowns, and free the shoulders and breast from its confinement. The whole sex in Chile appear to have an aversion to corsets and tight dresses; and nothing is more common than for ladies to move about the house, not excepting the parlors, their inseparable shawls concealing dresses open at the back: a *locust* fashion, as one of my countrymen called it, which one is not anxious to see introduced into the social life of the northern hemisphere.

The class to which mechanics and the retail shopkeepers belong is infinitely removed from the preceding in habits and appearance. There is an inherent want of tidiness in their domestic life; but in public, fine dress is a passion with them, and a stranger would scarcely suspect that the man he meets in a fine broad-cloth cloak, escorting a woman arrayed in silks and jewelry, occupied no higher rank in the social scale than that of a tinman, carpenter, or shopman whose whole stock in trade of cotton cloths or haberdashery might be packed in a box five feet square. They will go to any lengths to obtain fine clothes and fine furniture, or to attend the theatre on holidays, yet constantly live in the utmost discomfort. This disposition is not confined to the humbler class; it pervades all society, and impoverished families of rank live on in their huge houses with fine mirrors, fine carpets, a box at the opera perhaps, and scarcely a servant to keep the house in order. Pride thus becomes a vice, though it would be the most innocent of all that are dominant did it not beget indolence, which the old adage tells us is "the root of all evil." And here we have full evidences of its truth. The records of San Juan de Dios, San Francisco de Borja, the Casa de Expositos, fully exhibit one ruling criminal passion; the arrest of 456 persons principally for theft in less than a month (May, 1852) is proof sufficient of another; and the want of veracity among the lower orders, and the love of gambling among all, are notorious. Notwithstanding the 800 policemen, at one time thefts were committed in the densest part of the town during broad daylight. Whole wardrobes, and even an iron chest, were taken out of houses not far from the plaza at noon-day! and shortly prior to these robberies, $20,000 in specie were stolen from a residence close to Santa Ana early in the evening, the robbers escaping detection. And about this same period (May, 1852) the papers actually narrated in good faith the *miraculous* recovery of stolen clothing through the intercession of a saint, to whom the poor woman losing them had made a pious propitiatory offering. On a certain evening she was led to an out-of-the-way house, where a priest, or one so clad, delivered the missing articles, and she went on her way rejoicing—another link added to the chain of superstition that bound her. Elsewhere his priestship might probably have found it difficult to acquit himself of the charge of receiving stolen goods.

Gambling as a national vice is spoken of more at large in another place. Were the laws impartially enforced, it might soon be eradicated to a great extent; but the guardians of public morals well know whom to interfere with: and thus, so long as it continues to be publicly known that it is carried on with impunity in the houses of certain wealthy persons every night of the year, so long will it continue to increase among the class to whom it is perhaps most pernicious. Nor can the church be wholly counted on for its support in suppressing the custom, no inconsiderable number of its members, aye, dignitaries too! being among the most inveterate card-players. This would not have been asserted, but from ocular proof of the fact on more than one occasion. Miners carry it to the greatest excess. Individuals have been known to lose more than $100,000 at a single sitting; and one of the most confirmed, whilst possessing habits the most parsimonious, has not hesitated to stake a thousand doubloons ($17,250) on a single game. Such losses, amounting in some cases to all their property, would in other parts of the world drive many a man to suicide. Not so the Chileno. He cries a little, perhaps; lives on his creditors or friends for a while; and it may be that a rich vein is struck in a hitherto worthless mine of which he owns a share, and he is set up again. To put a pistol ball through his head or a rope about his neck, for the purpose of cutting short unpleasant thoughts, never enters the mind of any one: they reach the Panteon quite soon enough without any agency of their own; and with this public cemetery I will close the chapter on Santiago.

The magniloquent tendency that converts children's schools into *colegios* (colleges) has made of the cemetery *el Panteon* (the Pantheon). It is about a mile and a half north of the plaza, and not far west of the base of Cerro-Blanco. About sixteen acres of ground, enclosed by moderately high walls, are divided by iron railings into lots denominated the "cloister of monuments," "cloister of families," and "cloister of the poor;" names which sufficiently indicate the wealth or vanity exhibited by surviving relatives when selecting a depository for their dead. Along the southern front there are apartments occupied by the chaplain in charge and the workmen, together with appropriate rooms for tools, &c. A pleasant corridor extends their whole length. Separated from these buildings, by an open court, is a small octagonal chapel, which is lighted through windows in its dome. It has three altars—one in the centre surmounted by a large cross, and one on the east and west sides respectively. Over the latter there are paintings representing the marriage of Joseph of Arimathea with Mary, and the descent from the cross; and around the walls are smaller ones, illustrating more than twenty scenes from the trial and crucifixion of the Saviour—all badly executed, if not feebly conceived. Just under the octagonal skylight are short Latin inscriptions, selected from the Bible, and referring to the last mortal hours of man. One small room in the rear of the central altar is furnished with a marble table, to support the coffin when brought from the city; and another beside it is used as a vestuary for the officiating clergy. There is a prettily laid out garden behind the chapel, planted with flowers, cypresses, and orange-trees; and not only the vicinity of the chapel, but also many parts of the two cloisters first named, are adorned with rows of cypress-trees. Immediately adjoining the garden there are lots for the several religious orders; and at the rear of the enclosure there is one hall for anatomical purposes, and another used as a temporary deposit. Owing to the scarcity of other suitable material, and of proper workmen, the greater portion of the graves are covered with slabs of red porphyry, found on San Cristóval; though there are many mausoleums of fine marble, both of costly execution and in good taste. One of the latter is surmounted by a nude figure of Grief executed in white marble, which, by order of the arch-bishop, has actually been covered with a petticoat of black cloth from the waist to the knees!

But there is a portion most painful to the sight—the space allotted to the unfortunate poor, whose remains are not unfrequently disinterred before entire decomposition, and cover its surface in every direction—a perfect Golgotha. In one hole, not four feet deep, lay the bodies of four coffinless children, side by side. Innocent creatures they were, and fair to look upon even in death. More care had been bestowed on their adornment for this temporary (I was about to say *final*) resting-place than had ever been given in life perhaps; but it made me heart-sick to see their upturned faces and little crossed hands exposed, amid skulls and bones of every age, to the broad glare of sunlight, whilst awaiting the arrival of others to occupy a part of their horrid tenement. There is a place still more shocking at another part of the enclosure—a deep pit into which the bodies of paupers are tossed, with quicklime, and left to decay. But it was quite sufficient to have it pointed out to me—there was no inclination to go nearer to it. No good excuse can be offered for this. The money received from the rich and middle classes, under the most moderate calculations, must pay for the land over and over again; and there are hundreds of acres on Cerro Blanco and San Cristóval, utterly unfit for cultivation, that would well serve as grave-yards for the poor.

According to the returns, 3,567 persons died in 1849, 3,187 in 1850, and 3,444 in 1851; or a mean of 3,400 per year. If only one third of them pay for sepulture at the lowest rate, during a single year it amounts to no less than $3,400, or $212.50 per acre; which is nearly if not quite the market value of the land.

The tariff established is: For a perpetual sepulchre, 7 feet long and 34 inches wide, $20. In this it is permitted to inter relatives to the fourth generation. For the privilege of erecting a mausoleum on the same site, $30 additional. For the privilege of removing a body to be placed in a private chapel or a church, when authority has been obtained to do so, $30. For the interment of a single body during one year, $3. For the conveyance of a corpse from the city, in a carriage of the first class, $12; second class, $8; third class, $3; fourth class, $1. The last is only the common ox-cart of the country. For interring a child (in the family vault) brought in a private carriage, $3. The poor, brought in the fourth-class carriages, pay nothing for sepulture.

Of course not, *poor* creatures; they speedily find their way down the pit. Now here is a monopoly of the very worst kind. All believe that their salvation depends on interment in this the only consecrated ground, and a corpse cannot even be conveyed to it for less than the profits of a whole month's labor.

Table showing the number of Marriages, Births, and Deaths in the city of Santiago from 1842 *to* 1851, *both inclusive.*

Months.	1842.			1843.			1844.			1845.			1846.		
	Marriages.	Births.	Deaths.	Marriages.	Births.	Deaths.	Marriages.	Births.	Deaths.	Marriages.	Births.	Deaths.	Marriages.	Births.	Deaths.
January . .	42	401	335	51	389	281	55	342	383	76	301	243	64	387	413
February . .	124	373	303	47	326	227	60	306	262	109	347	205	69	342	353
March . . .	113	397	345	95	338	193	85	320	240	76	316	239	53	440	379
April . . .	58	321	269	93	329	208	67	285	236	68	331	224	83	416	340
May	81	334	228	47	336	185	63	298	247	56	313	191	52	365	330
June . . .	53	312	180	55	339	234	44	312	221	50	333	213	57	378	280
July	72	334	189	60	473	212	33	330	227	45	360	228	53	429	278
August . . .	108	387	216	62	362	264	43	320	170	49	452	286	77	442	286
September . .	113	360	210	54	314	205	70	377	213	56	456	219	58	411	206
October . .	105	406	256	71	381	262	79	485	214	70	431	253	67	488	251
November . .	57	344	289	74	304	278	68	379	266	62	372	270	88	464	252
December . .	64	364	279	70	361	335	51	348	267	69	378	366	83	398	285
Totals . .	990	4,333	3,099	775	4,298	2,884	720	4,102	2,946	787	4,390	2,937	804	4,960	3,663

Table showing the number of Marriages, Births, and Deaths—Continued.

Months.	1847.			1848.			1849.			1850.			1851.			AVERAGE.		
	Marriages.	Births.	Deaths.	Marriages.	Births.	Deaths.	Marriages.	Births.	Deaths.	Marriages.	Births.	Deaths.	Marriages.	Births.	Deaths.	Marriages.	Births.	Deaths.
January . . .	79	357	279	80	436	309	60	341	445	69	549	379	84	423	354	66	393	342
February . .	63	332	244	81	380	293	55	352	314	95	374	234	74	453	263	78	358	270
March . . .	97	384	238	79	390	208	77	421	287	137	534	282	202	484	314	101	402	273
April	84	395	247	107	365	218	111	450	279	110	421	237	93	423	245	87	374	250
May	88	374	210	108	482	228	98	437	248	83	415	224	94	453	262	77	381	235
June	46	374	204	83	389	252	96	437	251	77	461	229	98	493	232	66	385	230
July	57	400	241	77	486	266	57	504	255	63	526	252	51	482	241	57	432	239
August . . .	77	501	298	67	492	240	85	517	278	50	436	234	62	509	390	68	442	266
September . .	79	484	214	64	472	285	67	496	254	65	492	259	65	526	265	69	439	236
October . . .	79	543	223	82	510	343	76	538	239	79	492	270	65	502	250	77	478	256
November . .	65	494	246	86	497	467	112	481	326	69	494	274	75	511	319	76	434	299
December . .	72	388	268	78	446	535	90	457	391	79	433	313	83	443	309	74	402	335
Totals . .	886	5,026	2,942	992	5,345	3,644	984	5,451	3,567	976	5,627	3,187	1,046	5,702	3,444	896	4,920	3,231

RECAPITULATION.

	1842.	1843.	1844.	1845.	1846.	1847.	1848.	1849.	1850.	1851.	Average.
Births — Male . .	2,179	2,204	2,091	2,219	2,518	2,443	2,522	2,707	2,907	2,944	2,473
Births — Female .	2,154	2,094	2,011	2,171	2,442	2,583	2,823	2,744	2,720	2,758	2,450
Births — Illegitimate			835			962	1,108	1,333	1,358	1,347	1,157
Children died — Male . .	2,367	2,215	1,190	2,166	2,749	1,157	1,316	1,415	1,138	1,262	1,246
Children died — Female .			1,072			930	1,373	982	960	1,088	1,067
Died over 70 years of age .	62	68	82	55	78	63	96	94	86	90	77
Total deaths — Male . .		1,501	1,511	1,430	1,771	1,531	1,768	1,710	1,658	1,760	1,627
Total deaths — Female .		1,383	1,435	1,507	1,892	1,411	1,876	1,857	1,529	1,684	1,619

The interments at the Panteon, for every month of the year 1850, arranged in the order of the several parishes of the city from which the bodies came, are published in the "Araucano." They include Ñuñoa, a district at least three miles off, which has not been comprised in the preceding table. In that parish the number of deaths that year were—men 12, women 7, children 70, total 89; and the total numbers of the "Araucano"—men 1,469, women 1,265, children 3,120, or 5,854 in all! I cannot pretend to account for the discrepancy, my table having been made by myself with all care, from the returns kindly furnished me in the Statistical Office. A friend, to whom I wrote on detecting the difference, says, in reply: "Señor T. accounts for the great difference in the mortality between your lists, made out in his office, and the publications of the 'Araucano,' by your taking the mortality of the city of Santiago, whilst the published tables comprise the province." But this is not the fact; the "Araucano" specifies seven parishes, including Yungai and Ñuñoa, the two hospitals, and 20 found dead. As has been said, mine include all except Ñuñoa.

CHAPTER IX.

VALPARAISO.

ORIGIN.—ITS NAME.—EXTENT.—GROWTH OF THE CITY.—PLAZAS.—PUBLIC BUILDINGS.—CHURCHES.—BONDED WAREHOUSES.—HOSPITALS AND ALMSHOUSE.—WANT OF AMUSEMENTS.—POPULATION.—TABLE OF MORTALITY DURING TEN YEARS.—TRADE WITH TOWNS ON THE COAST.—FOREIGN COMMERCE.—STATISTICS OF IMPORTS, EXPORTS, COASTING TRADE, AND REVENUE.—EXPENSES OF COLLECTING THE REVENUE.—TABLE SHOWING THE NUMBER OF THE FOREIGN VESSELS AND THE VALUE OF IMPORTS AND EXPORTS FROM 1844 TO 1851, BOTH YEARS INCLUSIVE.—HOW THE BALANCE OF TRADE IS LIQUIDATED.—PRODUCTS OF THE HACIENDAS.—PRODUCTS OF THE MINES.—TABLE SHOWING THE VALUE OF THE SEVERAL METALS EXPORTED FROM 1843 TO 1852.—GOLD SENT TO THE MINT DURING THE SAME PERIOD.—TABLE SHOWING THE PRINCIPAL EXPORTS AND THE VALUE OF EACH.—TABLE SHOWING THE PRINCIPAL IMPORTS CONSUMED, AND THE VALUE OF EACH.—POSSIBLE DECREASE OF TRADE.—PROJECTED RAILROAD TO SANTIAGO.—STORMS IN THE BAY.

Valparaiso first comes into notice in the history of Chile as the port at which succors arrived for Pedro Valdivia, in July, 1544, and to which the new governor made a visit in September following, to confer with his intended lieutenant by sea, Juan Bautiste Pasteñe, respecting a projected voyage of discovery along the coast as far as the Straits of Magellan. Tradition, repeated by most of the naval officers, (and there are few others who have published experimental knowledge of Chile), assigns to its settlement, or at least to the time of its baptism, an earlier year; the salt-encrusted mariners who first gazed on its ever verdant ravines, after passing months on weary waters, exclaiming in the exuberance of gratified vision, *Val Paraiso!* (Vale of Paradise). Nor is there a doubt that it was named as early as 1543, there being among the archives at Seville a letter from Valdivia to the Emperor Charles the Fifth, dated 4th September, 1545, informing his Majesty that "in the month of September, 1543, a ship belonging to Lucas Martinez Vegazo arrived at the port of Valparaiso." When the city began, no one knows. No mention is made of the time by Ovalle, in the narrative and history of Chile, published about the middle of the next century; nor have subsequent investigators found anything that would throw light upon the question, either in the archives of the municipality, some of whose earlier members would probably have felt interest in it and made examination, or among the documents of Valdivia. As a large portion of the lands once belonged to the Augustin monks, it was supposed that their MSS. might afford some clue; but a search made at my request has been equally unproductive of information.

According to Ulloa, it was still a borough of small extent in 1744. He says: "At first it was only a few store-houses, built by the merchants of Santiago for their wares, until they could be shipped for Callao, to which *Valparaiso* is the nearest port. Then, it had no other inhabitants than the clerks whom merchants sent there to take charge of and expedite the goods. By degrees, the merchants established themselves there, with their families; and to these were added others, wholly drawn by the conveniences for commerce; until at last, the borough is so much increased that it is actually of considerable extent and quite populated. Were it not for the bad disposal of its land, no doubt it would become much greater; but there is a mountain very close, and so near to the sea that the larger number of houses are either built on its declivity or in the ravines, the remainder being at but a little distance from the water. This (last) quarter is larger and more commodious, so far as land is concerned; but on account of weather it is more objectionable, it being extremely exposed to north winds in winter, and these place it in danger from waves which the sea rolls in to the very doors of the houses. Some of these last are of stone and lime, others of *adobes* (*briques crues*), and others of thatch only." And a little

PLAN of VALPARAISO 1851.

1 Custom House
2 Exchange
3 Intendencia
4 Plaza de la Municipalidad
5 Parish Church
6 Theatre
7 San Augustine monastery
8 Franciscan monastery and nunnery
9 Barracks of batallon N°1.
10 Hospital and almshouse
11 Monastery of la Merced
12 Bonded Warehouses

further on he states that "the President-Governor of Chile, Don José Manso, and Lieutenant General Don José Pizarro, were then in the city." A few years before, this "larger quarter," by which Ulloa means the *Almendral*, was sold for less than two thousand dollars, the sale including all the ground between the crests of the hills to the eastward and the district now called *El Puerto*. Two millions would not purchase the same property at the present date.

Confident in the superior charms of their own valley and city, and, very properly, unwilling to have them robbed of even a possible honor, Santiaguinos will tell you that the name of Valparaiso originated among the soldiers who came with Alonzo de Monroy in September, 1543, and were told by those who had participated in their fascinations, "*Va al Paraiso*" (Go to the Paradise), by which their lovelier locality was meant. And when one sees the formation of the land surrounding its semi-circular bay, its hills that bound the vision to limited distances, cut by heavy rains into radiated ridges with deep intervening ravines, mottled with stripes of rock and clay, left bare by the washings of these cloud-deposited streams, whilst the native vegetation is nearly all shrubby and diminutive, he is strongly tempted to espouse their opinions. True, there are a few coco-palms, but no other trees on the shores of the bay; and even these seem to have thriven best in deeply sheltered spots with northern exposures, so that multitudes may come to Valparaiso and depart without having seen a plant growing in localities apparently so discordant with the habits of its genus. On the other hand, if we suppose the succoring party from Peru to have been the first who cast anchor here, and who must have seen all the arid coast south of Guyaquil, coming, as they did, in the month when nature is robed in her richest livery and all the hill-sides are verdant, it is not unreasonable to suppose them fascinated by the sight of so much vegetation, and hence gave to it so poetic a name.

Entering the mouth of the bay, we find it 2½ miles wide in a line drawn from the high bluff on our right, and on which stands the light-house, to an equally elevated continuation of the same hill to the eastward. From this chord to the beach south of us is 1¼ miles. The bay is entirely open to wind and sea between N.N.E. and W.N.W. On the western side and around quite one half of the semicircular curve, the radiating ridges spoken of approach closely to the sea, generally leaving but a strip of land wide enough for a row or two of houses and contracted streets between their extremities and its waves. This portion, called El Puerto (the Port), has, beyond a doubt, been formed by detritus washed from the *quebradas* (ravines), aided by a gradual uprising of the coast under the action of earthquakes. Many foreign residents well remember when the ground now occupied by the line of houses next the bay was entirely covered by water. On the eastern side, a triangular plain of sand, comparatively quite extensive, has been heaped up by the same causes, and to which the struggles of the northers and the streams whose united waters flow through what is now called the *Calle de las Delicias*, have contributed no little. This is known as the Almendral, from a grove of almond trees planted in years past by its earliest foreign proprietors, the Augustin monks. With the necessities of a growing population the almond grove entirely disappeared, and a few venerable olives near the northern extremity alone remain to mark the taste of the first settlers.

Along the narrow band between the ridges and the surf, over the surface of the Almendral, upon artificial terraces of the sloping declivities within the *quebradas*, and even to the very tips of the ridges themselves—more than 200 feet above the sea—is built the city; parts of some houses having no other foundations than piles driven into the earth far below the level of the street, from which one enters on the opposite side. Drawing closer in, one fortification is seen perched over the town to the left of the light-house; another occupies an eminence near the eastern termination of our imaginary chord; and soon, the eye embraces details of the whole panorama. In the rear of a well built mole, crowded with people and surrounded by boats and launches filled with merchandise from a crowd of ships rolling on the swell of the sea, stands a handsome custom-house with its tower and clock. Steeples of many churches projected against a dark background, a castellated edifice with its tall flagstaff amid numbers of rudely constructed cabins on the tip of a bluff overhanging the custom-house, picturesque mansions embowered amid a profusion of evergreens along the steep face of *Cerro Allegre* across the ravine, the Panteon with its white walls and pretty chapel still farther to the left, and back of all—on eminences more than a thousand feet above the ocean, approachable by zigzag roads—charming residences whose balconies and open corridors command a prospect of all the world below, from the volcano of Aconcagua, a hundred miles off, to the tiny sail-boat in the harbor,—these are striking objects of the picture. Nearly all its buildings have been the work of less than a third of a century, the whole town having been comprised within "El Puerto" prior to 1819, at which epoch there were scarcely a dozen houses of all descriptions erected on the Almendral. Then its 5,000 people, the better class of whom were merely agents, had only humble houses in which to live, few schools for the education of their children, and were almost without protection for themselves or property. Robberies and assassinations were committed in broad daylight; nor was it safe to pass from the Port to the Almendral except in parties sufficiently strong to resist the attacks of a gang of desperadoes who frequented a cave at the extremity of the former, which sailors have christened *Cape Horn*. At that time, and indeed until within the last twelve years, the custom-house was at Santiago, and there resided all the foreign as well as the native merchants of capital.

Now things are changed. When allegiance to Spain was thrown off by the countries bordering on the South Pacific, their ports were of necessity thrown open to the commerce of other nations. Till then it had been carried on only in Spanish bottoms, or in such few others as intended by bribery and smuggling to recover the enormous fees paid for the privilege of trade; and thus, from its position and facilities, Valparaiso soon became an entrepôt for the whole coast. With its increasing receipts, foreign merchants deserted the capital for the port; old houses were torn down to make places for better; and the city spread rapidly over the Almendral, until not a site remains vacant, except the summits of the hills and parts of ravine slopes.

There is a marked difference, however, in the architecture of the two districts. As ships can approach nearer to the Port, it has become more emphatically the commercial part of the town; and constantly augmenting trade has rendered ground of such importance, that they not only encroach upon the sea for the foundations of houses day after day, but they build story on story, European fashion, notwithstanding the risk of earthquakes. The Almendral is more national; edifices of one story, with *patios*, being the most numerous. Measuring the Port along its two curved streets, from the custom-house stores on the west to the narrow and crooked pass at Cape Horn (*Cueva del Chivato*), just wide enough for a carriage-road between the vertical face of the rocky cliff and the sea, the distance is about half a mile. Its breadth has been told, and there is but to add that the sea still breaks over the road at Cape Horn during the storms of winter. The Almendral, beginning at Cape Horn, is nearly three times as long as the Port, and its breadth across the base of the triangle is about half a mile. In both districts the streets are narrow; those in the Port being the most contracted, and intolerable from the quantities of mud which the rains bring down from the *quebradas* during winter, and the clouds of dust drifted from the hills in the strong southwest winds that prevail throughout summer. Terrible are these sand-storms. Only during the nights of the latter season could one enjoy a walk in the streets; and then, so badly are they lighted and so contracted are their sidewalks, that they are sufficiently comfortless. It is probable, however, that the first of these defects will shortly be remedied, as it is intended to light the city with gas during the next summer. Another inconvenience from which families and shipping long suffered—the want of a good supply of water—has been obviated only recently. Formerly it was furnished by carriers, who brought it on mules either from the rivulet beyond the Almendral, or from natural deposits on the hills; but within a year basins have been built on the eminences back of the town, from which spring-water is conveyed to the houses and mole in iron pipes. Both these improvements are due to our enterprising countryman, Mr. William Wheelwright.

In addition to the open space before the custom-house, and which is of the same width as that building, there are two other *plazas*: one a few hundred yards to the westward, the *Plaza de la*

Municipalidad, near the *Matriz* church; and the other the *Plaza Victoria*, not far from the centre of the Almendral. The latter is ornamented with a handsome basin of white marble resting on a tastefully cut pedestal, and intended for a fountain; but, as may be inferred from the scarcity of the element spoken of, its destination has not yet been fulfilled. For the same reason, and because of some little vandalism perhaps, a row of orange trees planted in tubs around this square have all perished, and their branchless trunks are forlorn-looking remnants of arboriculture. The first-named plaza is much smaller. The two ravines that debouch on it keep it in wretched condition all winter, and the multitude that collect here to sell shoes and common furniture render it disagreeable at all times. Two of its sides are occupied by handsome buildings three and four stories high; the others by more ordinary edifices, from among which issue the narrow and winding streets leading to localities which sailors have called the *Fore-top*, *Main-top*, and *Mizen-top*.

The custom-house is of stuccoed brick and in excellent taste. As a perpendicular cliff forms parts of two of its sides, the other two faces only are visible. That towards the sea is about 250 feet long; the other, to the eastward, not quite so large. It is two stories high, surmounted by a parapet and tower, and ornamented with pilasters of the Tuscan order.

One side of the Plaza Victoria is occupied by a handsome theatre capable of containing from 1,800 to 2,000 persons; and an equally well-built though unfinished church faces it, the remaining sides having houses of no especial note. Besides the church just mentioned, the Augustins, Dominicans, Franciscans, and Mercedarios, have each convents and chapels; and the Jesuits, under the name of "Religiosos de Propaganda" and "Padres de la Congregacion de los Sagrados Corazones de Jesus y Maria," have also their chapels and houses for spiritual penance. By sufferance, the Protestants have been allowed to put up an unpretending building back of the residences on Cerro Alegre, where service is performed every Sabbath morning according to the rubric of the Church of England. Indeed, it may be considered an exclusively English church; for her Majesty Queen Victoria is the only sovereign prayed for, although American and German families are among its attendants and supporters. It is proper to add, however, that England and the English pay the lion's share; government by act of Parliament appropriating a sum for the support of churches abroad equal to that voluntarily subscribed by its citizens.

A free Protestant chapel has also been permitted. To this end a room near the custom-house is used, and it is more especially intended for those "who go down to the sea in ships." Its expenses are borne by voluntary subscriptions from residents and one of the American missionary societies. The Rev. David Trumbull, in charge of it, devotes a portion of his time to editing "The Neighbor,"* a paper printed in English, whose object is "not gain, but the diffusion of intelligence, correct opinions, and sound morality." Some years ago, there was an amount of bigotry and intolerant oppression here proportionate to that which still remains at Santiago. Even quiet sepulture was denied the unfortunate *heretics* who died thus far away from homes and kindred; it being regarded commendable to disinter bodies, and leave them on the surface of the ground, after committing upon them indecencies of every kind. Of course they were not in the ground deemed consecrated by Catholics, nor has it been many years since a cemetery has been publicly permitted. But, in spite of the wry faces of the priests, the influx of Protestant population has forced measurable toleration at last; and, in consequence, the larger number of the long-robed and broad-brimmed gentry have retreated to the capital, where hypocrisy and indolence meet neither opposition nor criticism. It was not agreeable to witness other and simpler forms of worship practised amid their more sensual and unintelligible ceremonies, and still less so to forego the pomp of conveying the host, attended by a military guard, a bare-headed crowd kneeling humbly in the streets as they passed. Yet, their spiritual flocks do not desert to the Protestant fold, a conversion having rarely, if ever, been made.

* Since discontinued.

Such is the force of education and the power of the confessional, that even wives who had braved the anathemas of the church by marrying Protestants, and whose native intelligence must assuredly have enabled them to appreciate a domestic life so unlike that of the mass of their countrywomen, after years of such association, have left husbands and children for the convents, or have moped and pined, rendering all in their own homes as unhappy as themselves.

To the westward of the port proper, there are a few rudely built tenements that serve as residences for employés and as store-houses of the national *arsenal.* Of this our own naval corps have a right to expect some account; but I am quite sure that all of the number whom duties have called to Valparaiso within a few years will unite with me in opinion, that "the least said is soonest mended." The whole ground occupied is a short belt not above sixty yards wide between the sea and the vertical face of the cliff. There is no enclosure, nor is it desirable to make one; because roads to the fortress on the eminence above, as well as to the extensive range of bonded warehouses constructing still farther west, and to *Playa Ancha*—a table-land just back of the light-house, which is the favorite resort of equestrians—all, of necessity, lead through it. Within a few years a small corvette, a little iron steamer, and a brig, have been built here under direction of a French constructor; and, according to reports from the officers appointed to inspect them from time to time, they were very creditably modelled. An engine for the steamer was ordered from New York, and the vessel was finally launched towards the middle of 1852; but it was regarded as extremely doubtful whether she would ever prove serviceable. Besides these vessels, the navy of Chile comprises the frigate *Chile*, now dismantled and used as a ponton; the steamer *Cazador*, of 140 horse power; and the transport *Infatigable;* all inferior vessels, of French construction, and more than half worn at the times of their purchase.

For the bonded warehouses in course of construction, the terrace has been increased in width by excavating the cliff and filling the bay with the rocks thus obtained, behind casements of timber previously secured. Subject as is the coast to convulsions of the most terrible nature, one can scarcely doubt that the ocean will one day again claim its own, and the crowded magazines that now cumber the margin of the bay, like Baiæ of old, will exist only as ruins beneath its ceaseless waters.

There is a charity hospital in the Almendral, divided for the accommodation of the two sexes, and generally containing 200 patients, which are as many as can be accommodated. All who apply are furnished with advice and medicines gratuitously, though numbers are necessarily turned off for want of room where they could be lodged. If a foreigner desires admission, he must produce a note from the consul of his nation—if a native, one from his last employer: no other formality is exacted than an examination to ascertain the infirmity of the applicant. Its annual income amounts to $15,000, all of which is expended in behalf of suffering humanity; and, as its returns prove, with more successful results than in kindred establishments at the capital. The last publications to which I have had access show that the mortality amongst those who entered was fifteen per cent.; and we have seen that the ratios of San Juan de Dios and San Francisco de Borja, at Santiago, were respectively sixteen and a half and twenty-three per cent. A part of the same establishment is appropriated to the poor. Besides this hospital, there are several belonging to individuals, intended for the accommodation of those who are able to pay from their own resources, or whose governments have authorized their consuls to provide for them in like cases of illness. And in this connexion, it may be proper to mention that permission has recently been granted by government to locate a convent for sisters of charity recently emigrated from France; who, should they prove as attentive and self-sacrificing as their order have done in North America, will merit more gratitude than the race to whose wants they will minister are capable of feeling.

There is no lack of hotels, such as they are, in Valparaiso, the principal difficulty being to instil our ideas of method and cleanliness into the minds of Chileno servants; and thus, however disposed a foreign proprietor may be to imitate similar public houses in his own country, his efforts are soon paralyzed by the habits and ignorance of those whom he is forced to employ. Most happily for us, there are no bounds to the hospitality of our countrymen residing here, and their doors are thrown open with such cordiality that the inconveniences of the hotels are rarely tested by Americans who spend even a week or two in Chile. Elsewhere, it is pleasant to be independent, knowing that the expenditure of a few dollars will command the services of mine host in all that one wants for bodily comfort, without trespassing too greatly on the kindness of a friend, or putting his family to inconvenience ; but here, without the importation of all the appurtenances, the wealth of the Indies would not obtain such comfort.

For so large a permanent population, and the considerable number of strangers in transit for California during the last four years, there are few places of public amusement, the theatre being almost the only one, and this is open but one half of the year. Two clubs, similar to those in England, have been established, subscribers having the privilege to introduce friends, temporary sojourners. In their rooms may be found billiard-tables, papers, and periodicals ; and at the saloon of the Exchange, an institution organized and sustained by the merchants, there are files of American and English newspapers. Shareholders have the right to introduce transient persons, and, by the rules of the boards of management, naval officers are granted this privilege without farther formality than a registry of their names at the doors. The state of transition in which native society is just now, neither European nor South American in customs, robs it of many of the attractions so glowingly depicted by earlier visitors ; and for want of more rational diversions, numbers of the younger part of the foreign population seek the billiard-tables and cafés. This is not likely to continue long, however. A more liberal education of both sexes among the natives is in progress ; occasional intermarriages and more frequent intercourse are almost inevitable consequences ; and we may reasonably anticipate changes of person as well as mind at no very distant date. As an evidence of the appreciation of Anglo-Saxonism, four or five schools devoted to instruction, through the medium of the English language, are well attended by native children of both sexes, many coming from Santiago, and a large proportion boarding in the families of their preceptors. Besides these schools there are five others, at which teachers are paid by parents, and fifteen free institutions at the expense of the municipality. Nine of the latter are for boys, six for girls, and in all the attendance and progress are creditable.

By the census published in 1850, the population is put down at 30,826, or about 9,000 *less* than it was rated at three years before, and only 6,000 more than it was ascertained to contain in 1835. Competent persons, however, consider that the number is very little short of 45,000 ; but if we take the ratio of mortality at 3.1 per cent., and assume the mean of the last three years in the subjoined table, we have only 35,100 souls, which is probably nearest to the truth. Of these, about one third are foreigners, different nations having representatives in numbers in the following order : France, Germany, England, United States. Natives of the better class are descendants of Spaniards, retaining all their characteristics of feature, with something of the energy of the early adventurers also, else they would soon be distanced in the commercial race instituted among them by foreigners. The lower orders are of the mixed Spanish and Indian blood, which has been so freqently reproduced that broad foreheads, prominent cheek-bones and aquiline noses, as distinctive marks, have wholly disappeared ; and they retain only the modified color of skin, coarse, straight, black hair, and the habits of indolence and improvidence belonging to their mothers. At least three fifths of the creoles belong to this class ; negroes or zambos, so common in Peru, are very rare. The mortality among all classes of the Catholic population during the last ten years, as returned by the administrador of the Panteon, has been as follows :

Table showing the number of Interments in the Catholic cemetery at Valparaiso, from the year 1841 *to* 1850, *inclusive.*

Month.	1841.	1842.	1843.	1844.	1845.	1846.			1847.			1848.			1849.			1850.			Mean last five years.		
						Men.	Women.	Children.	Men.	Women.	Children.	Men.	Women.	Children.	Men.	Women.	Children.	Men.	Women.	Children.	Men.	Women.	Children.
January . .	46	64	45	92	110	22	16	179	18	17	78	10	14	49	14	8	111	24	18	78	17.6	14.6	99
February . .	58	70	68	86	101	16	17	126	21	9	57	13	15	70	10	2	64	27	15	39	17.4	11.6	71.2
March . . .	48	65	65	92	97	17	10	113	15	15	48	14	9	70	16	8	58	29	20	43	18.2	12.4	66.4
April . . .	35	56	60	74	111	17	9	100	13	18	51	27	6	40	11	19	53	32	18	60	20	14.4	60.8
May . . .	41	45	58	74	95	13	19	86	19	5	59	13	17	64	8	15	33	28	20	62	16.2	15.2	60.8
June . . .	53	41	52	63	74	12	18	66	11	11	41	10	4	45	11	17	54	31	22	39	15	14.4	49
July . . .	34	50	52	84	102	17	11	58	16	8	47	17	16	43	17	16	43	23	23	55	18	14.8	45.2
August . . .	40	45	68	94	95	16	14	45	14	12	38	18	21	42	23	11	60	29	18	54	20	15.2	47.8
September . .	41	49	53	91	87	20	16	53	16	23	45	18	14	44	11	19	39	28	22	44	20.6	18.8	45
October . .	38	48	81	87	128	20	11	45	15	13	41	13	14	76	19	12	33	32	31	61	19.8	16.2	61.2
November . .	65	48	73	93	111	16	18	58	11	10	59	15	6	133	16	15	36	28	32	57	17.2	16.2	68.6
December . .	50	62	71	101	164	20	19	72	12	24	74	13	10	137	33	20	54	33	24	57	22.2	19.4	78.8
Total each class						206	178	1001	181	165	638	181	146	813	189	172	638	344	263	649	222.2	183.2	743.8
Total . . .	531	640	746	1031	1215	1385			984			1140			999			1256			1149.2		

The records of adults and infants (under seven years), if kept separately prior to 1846, are not now obtainable; and from the great fluctuations in the different subsequent years, when no epidemics are known to have occurred, as well as the extraordinary increase of mortality since 1841, it is to be apprehended that very great reliance cannot be placed upon the returns. One cannot but be surprised at the disproportion between the numbers of deaths among adults of the two sexes—a disproportion of no less than 20 per cent. But the same matter is referred to at greater length in the account of Santiago; and as like influences concur to produce analogous results here, it is unnecessary to pursue the subject farther.

With its want of back-ground, its deficiency of supplies, its bad harbor,—or, more properly speaking, its want of a harbor,—and its comparatively limited back population to furnish, it is surprising how Valparaiso has continued to prosper as an *entrepôt* for the coast, with such capacious harbors as Concepcion and Coquimbo at moderate distances on either side of it. True, the latter has not supplies for an extensive commercial marine; but it offers admirably secure anchorage at all seasons, ample facilities for constructing wharves, on which goods may be landed without the hazardous impediment of surf, almost always in the bay of its neighbor,* whilst the distance from ports at which provisions may be shipped is, at most, only two days' sail farther. On the opposite side, Concepcion, in addition to all these advantages, is the natural outlet of a district whose climate is unrivalled, and whose soil is capable of being made to yield almost any product, to an extent unknown among agriculturists of the northern hemisphere. Its herds of cattle and flocks of sheep multiply with like rapidity. Nor is it wanting in mineral wealth—gold, copper, and coal existing in more than one locality. Unless it be that the greater wealth concentrated at Santiago is paramount to all these advantages, a reason for this preference of Valparaiso is not obvious. Whatever it be, merchants actually force the greater number of consumers to pay all the extra charges for landing and reshipment of goods consumed by themselves. If we take the populations to be supplied directly and by subsequent land carriage from each of the three ports, as given in the "*Repertorio Nacional*" for 1850, they are:

* At Valparaiso, goods are deposited with the tackles of the ship into launches alongside, are thence conveyed as near to the beach as the depth of water will permit, and, however heavy the package, it must be taken through the surf on the shoulders of men. The only wharf for landing goods north of the Maule is at Caldera.

1st. Coquimbo, embracing the provinces of Atacama, Coquimbo, and part of Aconcagua, 134,226.

2d. Valparaiso, embracing part of Aconcagua, Valparaiso, Santiago, and Colchagua, 524,531.

3d. Concepcion, embracing Chilóe, Valdivia, Concepcion, Ñuble, Maule, and Talca, 452,233.

It is true that the most convenient roads for transportation from the ports to every part of the districts thus laid off do not terminate at the proposed ports of entry, and reshipment would, of necessity, be made from each to minor towns on the coast. But the necessity for this reshipment still exists, and the distances would be lessened, if the commerce were divided, as the demand indicates. Now let us see what were the actual imports and exports coastwise from these ports during the year 1850.

Home Consumption.

Ports.	Direct imports.	Direct exports.	COASTWISE IMPORTS.		COASTWISE EXPORTS.	
			Domestic.	Foreign.	Domestic.	Foreign.
Valparaiso	$11,110,844	$7,069,173	$6,824,948	$1,400	$1,844,130	$1,626,413
Coquimbo, including Copiapó and Guasco . . .	342,668	2,994,407	2,361,411	859,076	4,374,075	14,400
Concepcion, including Constitucion, Valdivia, and Ancud (Chilóe) . . .	147,456	1,319,295	304,404	780,337	2,142,588	None.

Thus Valparaiso, with less than half the population to supply through the most direct channels, engrossed $\frac{23}{24}$ of all the foreign importing trade, whilst the other ports have shipped directly one half the means to pay the debt so incurred, besides sending to it native produce equal in value to the remainder of the foreign obligation.

This, then, being Chile, commercially speaking, no more proper occasion can occur in which to exhibit its trade with other nations; and the following tables, compiled from the annual statistics, published under the direction of the Minister of Finance, will show its progress during the last eight years. Premising that the number of vessels of all descriptions which bore its flag on the 1st of January, 1852, was 209, more than half of them naturalized purchases—and of these quite one half within two years—the maritime movement is shown in the following table:

Number of Vessels arriving in all the ports of Chile, &c.

Years.	Ships of war.	Number of guns.	Foreign merchant vessels.	Tonnage.	Number of their crews.	Chile merchant vessels.
1844	58	1,470	1,487	374,028	35,133	1,429
1845	71	1,759	1,452	359,859	36,450	1,486
1846	38	911	1,523	388,557	26,029	1,529
1847	58	1,477	1,434	360,097	32,680	1,521
1848	64	2,066	1,397	343,456	34,468	1,523
1849	73	1,730	1,777	503,259	35,445	1,541
1850	63	1,206	*2,599	740,425	45,248	1,784
1851	76	1,467	†2,351	686,185	24,692	†899

* The increase is principally due to vessels en route for California, which touched for supplies.

† The ports of Coquimbo and Talcahuano (Concepcion) were closed to vessels during the civil war, from September to December; which will explain the falling off.

Value of Imports, Exports, Coasting Trade, and Revenue.

Years.	Value of imports and exports conveyed in foreign vessels.	Value of imports and exports conveyed in Chilean vessels.	Value of imports brought across the cordilleras.	Value of coasting trade in foreign but naturalized products.	Value of coasting trade in domestic products.	Revenue collected.	Foreign goods re-exported.
1844	$14,145,288	$489,755	$48,674	$2,046,864	$3,106,741	$1,763,954	$1,205,462
1845	15,837,784	837,827	30,676	2,129,270	3,441,877	1,788,396	1,978,342
1846	17,474,678	758,925	30,823	2,230,744	3,725,480	2,033,010	1,774,904
1847	17,824,036	554,252	152,646	2,306,920	3,747,006	2,103,066	1,420,751
1848	16,159,701	771,242	24,009	2,506,127	4,078,594	1,940,539	1,116,126
1849	20,203,457	981,475	141,355	2,186,572	1,235,697	2,323,679	1,179,227
1850	22,759,608	1,240,253	214,601	1,640,813	9,390,793	2,626,956	1,033,817
1851	28,031,363		214,239		4,356,618	2,724,718	2,480,037

The increase in the importations across the cordilleras in 1850 arose from the demand for dried fruits in the California market, to which the flour and other agricultural products of Chile were, for the first time, sent in extraordinary quantities. The statistics for 1851 do not distinguish between foreign and national vessels employed in commerce that year, nor the value of the coasting trade in naturalized products. Assuming the population of the country at one and a half millions, each individual will have consumed foreign importations in 1851 to the value of $17.03.

Expenses of Collecting the Revenue.

1844	$
1845	316,719
1846	
1847	353,050
1848	385,817
1849	388,106
1850	448,411
1851	

Of the goods imported, those paying ad valorem, specific, or other duties, are shown as follows:

	1844.	1845.	1846.	1847.	1848.	1849.	1850.	1851.
Free	$1,335,474	$2,010,036	$1,673,137	$1,384,978	$1,017,355	$1,744,603	$2,132,333	$4,935,814
Government monopoly	532,401	587,993	796,334	799,527	537,751	571,607	352,942	663,866
Specific duties	145,717	185,348	186,832	212,698	187,568	228,687	237,474	343,710
Ad valorem	6,583,082	6,321,387	7,492,833	7,671,646	6,858,683	8,177,943	9,065,444	9,941,582

Commerce of Chile with Foreign Nations.

	1844.			1845.			1846.			1847.			1848.			1849.			1850.			1851.		
	Number of vessels.	Imports.	Exports.	Number of vessels.	Imports.	Exports.	Number of vessels.	Imports.	Exports.	Number of vessels.	Imports.	Exports.	Number of vessels.	Imports.	Exports.	Number of vessels.	Imports.	Exports.	Number of vessels.	Imports.	Exports.	Number of vessels.	Imports.	Exports.
France and colonies	26	$985,815	$323,333	30	$799,787	$1,144,971	30	$830,035	$717,963	26	$1,122,089	$764,546	23	$831,650	$981,639	49	$1,079,942	$676,755	43	$1,342,733	$1,098,580	42	$1,705,929	$851,113
Belgium	3	29,271	3,388	4	11,975	7,333	2	27,049		6	130,543	20,612	4	112,153	85,570	5	222,190	27,495	11	166,837	27,295	11	195,372	2,495
Holland	1	348						53,719		1	4,949	615	2	30,750	200	6	57,971		22	347,025	72,783	19	402,059	65,739
Germany	25	631,155	135,852	20	735,981	477,141	19	862,585	459,500	17	918,021	424,673	13	668,765	290,404	22	846,448	677,798	44	976,069	883,604	28	1,089,853	469,155
Austria				1	5,282				44		7,786			188	350				2	574	822			1,426
England and colonies	65	3,210,676	3,135,935	125	3,219,523	3,168,753	125	3,465,546	3,830,705	104	3,486,728	3,905,950	132	3,157,791	3,871,581	156	4,431,075	4,275,359	202	4,169,160	4,129,201	215	4,319,864	4,643,290
Denmark	1	259	7,209	1	89	3,175	2		6,941	1	3,999	8,106		13,500	6,113		522	18,451	1	1,940	3,208			1,390
Sweden and Norway	4	9,573	1,559		3,992	318		3,860			1,225		5	11,941			49	606	2	11,941	731		5,081	2,194
Prussia																	121	920			215			1,016
Spain and colonies	8	329,557	38,381	13	273,066	38,091	2	243,300	1,535	3	372,000	14,309	6	111,768	10,265	8	151,129	2,241	18	114,909	155,720	2	145,510	74,582
Portugal		2,301			3,682			2,914			23,900			4,045			12,346			19,188	338	1	18,168	
Sardinia	5	51,533	28,542		47,585	51,883	2	27,414	30,452	2	36,088	6,668	1	49,356	2,528	1	98,872	33,830	4	59,811	33,694	3	74,410	21,309
Russia		4,278			1,297			994	2,714		729	5			546					607	204			5,360
China	1	215,196	459,141	4	172,208	297,328	2	288,455	159,725	3	199,985	101,221	1	130,537	160,248	2	226,772	64,597	4	236,223	207,938	2	229,348	42,547
United States	30	667,205	956,052	28	674,246	1,288,042	33	932,716	1,453,278	21	819,445	1,596,154	41	1,124,171	1,634,749	233	1,100,345	3,589,888	533	1,911,479	4,012,612	319	4,594,211	3,515,235
Mexico	30	153,057	1,455	16	257,233	7,544	21	203,242	7,203	15	84,181	29,937	20	68,466	28,963	16	128,053	4,407	42	113,041	384	39	23,837	7,532
Central America	17	166,571	98,839	13	77,682	87,086	15	95,751	92,324	17	74,220	32,608	14	121,494	21,479	17	118,834	13,407	2	121,737	75,676	38	42,241	103,513
Equador	1	176,658	24,648	2	65,069	80,416	12	129,444	29,404	13	107,019	21,698	16	150,638	30,338	11	140,620	44,508	9	213,859	42,671	8	120,732	42,774
Brazil	22	197,878	12,967	24	241,568	67,351	44	599,047	227,720	19	338,953	85,969	19	236,382	38,955	104	198,257	8,964	125	288,141	184,651	67	624,877	513,898
Peru	211	929,263	633,028	202	1,474,889	674,552	173	1,204,161	754,699	160	1,173,302	904,079	125	1,326,663	788,548	127	1,286,172	839,748	165	936,125	1,022,638	181	1,616,644	1,179,247
Bolivia	45	735,548	102,727	44	933,442	114,775	31	1,032,917	81,905	26	954,699	132,168	27	419,959	140,936	15	446,225	128,877	12	477,609	166,127	24	436,988	209,902
Paraguay					41,808			18,920			67,627			8,566										
Uruguay				9		50,476	9	85,174	135,893	4	12	258,192	6	1,878	177,257	11	1,478	69,907	16	49,565	96,358	12	10,352	61,215
Argentine Confederat'n	20	91,377	8,299	6	46,215	5,627		32,193	1,439	1	132,646	750	1	16,627	9,466	23	171,753	37,886	29	219,077	112,214	4	170,586	46,624
Polynesia	42	9,045	99,668	18	11,391	44,661	19	9,700	121,744	22	8,603	133,825	27	4,369	73,440	12	3,665	63,976	19	4,472	1,080	24	58,910	59,352
New Grenada	3	88		3	9,754		2		100	2	100				100	2		23,827	16	6,071	97,525	51		225,483
Totals		8,596,674	6,087,023		9,104,764	7,601,152		10,149,136	8,115,288		10,068,849	8,442,085		8,601,357	8,353,595		10,722,840	10,603,447		11,788,193	12,426,269		15,884,972	12,146,391

Only vessels are enumerated which arrive from the countries to which they belong. The trade with Austria, Prussia, Portugal, Russia, and Paraguay seems to have been entirely indirect. No less than 318 vessels from the United States came into the ports of the republic during the year 1850, either with cargoes or for refreshments, against 64 in the following year; 210 arrived from California the first and 255 the second year, whilst the numbers of all nations sailing for the same territory during the same periods were 640 and 241 respectively.

The ordinary rates of interest being from three fourths to one per cent. per month, and the peaceful condition of the country for ten to fifteen years offering security to foreign capitalists, it is reasonable to infer that shippers have allowed a large part of the gradually accumulating balances against Chile to remain invested there. There is another mode in which a part of the $11,000,000 may be explained away. The value of imports is not the cost at the place of shipment, and shown by the invoices, but that of appraisers at the port of entry; so that a merchant who brings goods into the market which have cost him $100, and for which sum only he is responsible to the foreign creditor, finds himself subjected to duties on a valuation of $130 to $150, his shipment entered at the custom-house books at that amount, and an *apparent* deficit of $30 to $50 thus created. Supposing only fourteen per cent. to have been added to the invoice prices, and the whole indebtedness disappears. However, most of the houses having large transactions only receive goods on commission, and of course are accountable to shippers for the market value of their consignments; their charges for sales, guaranty, &c., being seven and a half per cent. These firms have agents at many of the ports and interior towns on the western side of the continent, and their business is so profitable that partners are able to retire with handsome fortunes after twelve or fifteen years.

Being almost without factories of any description, Chile is dependent on foreign nations for every supply except food; and even of this its *yerba mate*, coffee, and sugar are all imported. Proportionally to its population, more of the last is consumed than in almost any other country; the quantity introduced in 1850 being 13,600,850 pounds, and 2,281 pounds of sweetmeats, or $9\frac{1}{7}$ pounds for every individual.* On the other hand, except with its immediate neighbor, Peru, its isolated position has prevented its agricultural products from being brought into trade; and it was only when the discoveries of gold in California hurried a living tide to the auriferous region that its cereals and dried fruits found a market proportioned to their abundance. Even within a very few years North American flour has had preference in the markets of Valparaiso and Lima; the mills of Chile being so far behind the age, that large quantities were annually imported at handsome profits to the shippers. At the same time good wheat could be purchased, in the provinces immediately south of Santiago, as low as six reals (a real is $12\frac{1}{2}$ cents) the fanega of two and a quarter bushels; and as late as the close of 1849 it would only command from seven to nine reals, according to quality. With wheat at such prices, the new and extensive mills introduced by Americans at Santiago and Concepcion, and which were wholly managed by American operatives, soon drove flour made by their fellow-countrymen at home from the Chilean and Peruvian markets. To send it from the eastern coast of the United States to California, it had to cross the equator twice, exposing it when in bulk, as ordinarily prepared, to almost certain loss by heat; and, on this account, Chile has not only the advantage of one transit, but is on an average sixty days nearer the market to be supplied. Early appreciating these facts, at the commencement of 1850 three wealthy speculators made a monopolizing arrangement with the millers at Santiago and Concepcion, which would enable them to control the California market,—one of them, an American just retired from office, writing such an account of the quantity, quality, and cost of wheat in Chile over his ex-official signature as would deter shippers in the United States from attempting competition. The unfairness of the statement, and its object, were so transparent to those who knew of his participation in the speculation—a fact perhaps forgotten in writing his letter for the press—that it was at once pointed out to the government at home. But the evil somewhat corrected itself in the course of a year, though not before each of the trio had netted above $30,000.

Finding that the eastern States of the great confederation were sending no flour to their infant sister on the Pacific, and that its price had risen enormously at home, the *haciendados* (farmers) as the original producers of the staple began to believe themselves entitled to at least a small portion of the wealth flowing into the coffers of millers and speculators; and, their demands growing

* 21,025 pounds of sweetmeats were exported during the same year.

even more rapidly than the advance in California, at the beginning of 1852 wheat could not be bought for less than twenty-four reals the fanega. Thinking the haciendados would be forced to sell—as they would have been almost anywhere else—millers were unwilling to buy in quantity on such terms, and they took very little more than met the immediate home consumption. But they were doomed to be disappointed. The producers, for the first time, saw a chance of making fortunes by their estates; and they were resolved to have their share of the Californian profits. There are several estates larger than some of the European principalities, and no small farmers, who are dependent on certain sales of products to obtain other supplies, as in the United States and Europe; indeed, in many cases proprietors are wholly unable to spend their annual incomes. Moreover, as the loss by insects or deterioration is very trifling, they can well afford to hold back a crop unless their own price is offered. For this reason, except the quantities demanded for the country, grain remained stored until, from the superabundant crop of 1851 in the United States, flour could not only be shipped to California again, but a cargo in search of a market was actually sold in Valparaiso at a very liberal advance.

The haciendados had made a blunder, and it may prove a most unfortunate one. They can cultivate wheat advantageously at from twelve to thirteen reals the fanega; but by forcing the price to more than double that sum, as they did at last, they induced North American millers to seek means to combat the heats of the equator. The success of the Yankee in whatever he undertakes has become proverbial; and by kiln-drying his flour, if he has not effectually excluded the product of Chile from the California market, his clipper-ships have rendered him a formidable competitor for its profits. One of the reasons alleged for the high prices which began in 1850 was the old song, "short crop;" but, from conversation with several haciendados who produce extensively, the fact that 53,251,300 pounds of flour and 7,306 fanegas of wheat were shipped to a market it had not been accustomed to supply, and my knowledge of a national characteristic which would prevent even new wheat-fields from being brought under cultivation, I give little credit to the plea. It is quite probable there was a scarcity at the close of 1850, and before the new crop was harvested; but it arose from the temptations to shipments, not from niggardliness of the soil, or from diseases of the plant. The total amounts of flour and wheat exported during the year were 64,359,600 pounds of the former, valued at $1,892,548, and 181,125 fanegas of the latter, worth $360,728. During the same period, the quantity of biscuit furnished vessels in the harbors for their own use and shipment abroad was 1,874,300 pounds, at a valuation of $74,952.

After wheat, the two agricultural products that have assisted most in paying national indebtedness are barley and beans; the former yielding for exportation 109,469 fanegas, equal to $216,388; and the latter 51,225 fanegas, equal to $136,737.

The product of the haciendas that has been the most universally received in part payment, is hides; the aggregate of which shipped in 1850 was 57,605, producing $143,395; and this is nearly the whole sum that the surface of the earth offers to nations beyond Cape Horn. Some 70,740 pounds of salted beef ($15,518) are also sold to shipping, and the horns and hoofs of cattle likewise go; but these are trifling matters. Of *charqui* (sun-dried beef) there were 89,075 pounds, suet and tallow 59,225, and tallow candles 65,500 pounds. Allowing each pound of charqui to represent three of undried beef, and that the number of hides exported represent two thirds of the actual number slaughtered, as each head of cattle will weigh about 600 pounds, we have for a minimum home consumption about 45,700,000 pounds of fresh beef.

With such multitudes of cattle as some of the haciendas possess, one would expect to find ample supplies of butter and cheese for exportation; yet such is so far from being the case, that, strange as it may appear, there are estates with many thousands of heads where there is not only no butter for family use, but sometimes not even milk. At the same time, there is no country where better wool could be produced at a less cost, or which has greater water-power at command than this, southward of the thirty-third parallel; yet, from absolute negligence in the care of sheep and subsequent mismanagement of the staple, its market value is scarcely half that of the best qualities of cotton in North America, and the amount shipped is very trifling in value. Want of enterprise and confidence in each other prevent the establishment of manufactories, and the country spends $850,000 annually for woollen goods which could be made quite as well at home from their own sacrificed material.

Wheat, flour, biscuit, barley, beans, cattle, and wool, form an aggregate value of $2,963,296, leaving $7,791,080 to be obtained from other sources. Fortunately, nature has (or *is creating*, as mineralogists may decide) a treasure within the earth apparently sufficient to liquidate the deficiency arising from the indisposition or indifference of its lords to profit by the advantages its surface offers; the silver mines of Atacama, and the copper deposits of Coquimbo and Aconcagua, being treasuries almost rivalling Californian productiveness and abundance. The values of the metals exported from these districts in 1850 were:

Gold.	Value.	Silver.	Value.	Copper.	Value.
Bars of gold	$35,343	Bar silver and plata piña	$3,914,148	Bar copper	$2,653,979
Cobalt	10,709	Unreduced ores	39,324	Regulus	333,534
		Wrought silver	3,816	Ores	90,211
		Relaves	2,061	Wrought	5,342
		Silver and copper	351	Sheet	5,050
Total	$46,052		$3,959,700		$3,088,116

Forming an aggregate of $7,093,868, which very nearly equals the deficiency. To these must be added $733,165 of coined gold and silver. But, during the same period there was imported $1,777,634 in gold and silver, either in bars or coined; leaving an excess of introduction equal to $1,044,469 clear gain, in addition to its export of minor produce. This year, however (1850), seems to be the only one in which the balance of trade has been in favor of Chile.

The yield of the mines constituting so important an item in payment for importations, it is clearly proper that their products should be exhibited for the same years as are embraced in the commercial tables.

Metals exported.

Year.	Bars of gold.	Plata piña and bar silver.	Ores not reducible by amalgamation.	Relaves.*	Wrought silver.	Cobalt.	Bar copper.	Regulus.	Copper ores.	Sheet copper.	Copper utensils.
1844	$116,367	$1,230,456	$3,507		$2,875	$87	$1,236,747	$437,352	$374,620	†$2,730	$7,175
1845	218,875	1,655,698	8,714	$4,110	37,040		1,313,687	330,531	267,533	†31,584	14,484
1846	217,984	1,773,949	2,803		2,590	416	1,778,525	345,504	378,796	†6,804	24,932
1847	301,415	1,798,083	9,628		19,292		1,899,253	298,667	166,485	†1,620	6,705
1848	296,440	2,239,644	22,520		13,957	4,654	2,081,547	275,804	175,290	†2,540	5,564
1849	263,070	3,215,572	3,938	480	4,023	23,058	2,445,768	204,160	118,492	†2,670	9,239
1850	35,343	3,914,148	39,675	2,061	3,816	10,709	2,653,979	333,534	90,211	5,050	5,342
1851	299,753	3,277,319	205,962	64,056	800	360	1,749,780	216,539	106,195	15,488	1,973
	$1,749,247	$19,104,869	$296,747	$70,707	$84,393	$39,284	$15,159,286	$2,442,091	$1,677,622	$68,486	$75,114

* *Relaves.* This is the residuum after amalgamation, which often contains a large per-centage of silver not extractable with mercury.
† Old copper.

The table does not embrace the gold sent to the mint to be coined; which was—

In 1844	$155,370	In 1848	$478,877
1845	401,908	1849	300,426
1846	517,882	1850	697,556
1847	736,359	1851	239,602

Making an aggregate of $3,527,980.

The great increase in the amount of bar silver exported in 1849 was due to the discovery of the rich mines at *Tres Puntas;* and the decrease in this metal, and partially of the bar copper also, in 1851, arose from the fact that mining operations, both in Atacama and Coquimbo, were greatly interrupted by the revolutionary condition of the country. Indeed, some of the mines were temporarily abandoned by all the laborers for two or three months. Of the copper ores, much more is smelted than formerly ; new processes having rendered the operation more economical, and vessels sailing from England with freights of light goods finding it convenient to fill partially with coals, in which the mineral districts are wholly deficient.

Table showing the principal Exports and their value.

Articles.	1844.	1845.	1846.	1847.	1848.	1849.	1850.	1851.
Wheat	$179,374	$136,389	$256,219	$356,376	$190,480	$315,190	$353,670	$228,750
Flour	352,109	207,741	320,371	480,391	472,833	*803,798	1,899,606	*1,544,215
Biscuit	79,864	87,519	62,372	160,053	106,832	114,007	74,952	120,199
Frangollo†	1,353	1,323	471	2,704	1,098	6,694	2,604	3,440
Barley	53,245	37,357	29,971	41,069	34,979	76,910	216,388	567,406
Beans	24,672	18,526	64,201	90,394	53,267	48,563	136,737	167,055
Peas	3,129	666	99	3,514	1,970	3,420	5,789	7,645
Corn	1,174	430	1,684	1,241	2,187	545	2,974	8,739
Bran	1,333	867	1,567	2,289	2,517	994	3,429	5,068
Potatoes	10,168	10,523	9,404	18,501	13,356	14,514	43,806	32,722
Alfalfa seed	23,719	19,488	18,746	8,988	1,375	195	888	18
Chicha, aguardiente, and wine	2,252	3,004	460	1,427	15,327	50,768	2,361	3,527
Red pepper	2,305	378	32	68	225	3,565	504	1,453
Nuts	29,728	25,055	9,569	33,178	43,745	55,152	40,039	78,425
Dried fruits	8,788	6,864	5,179	21,475	35,173	72,147	79,911	24,643
Live horned cattle	3,444	1,844	1,296	2,443	2,240	224	192	840
Sheep	1,656	1,142	253	685	371	252	2,079	648
Hogs	3,303	1,746	931	32,512	730	1,100	3,695	4,220
Horses and mules	3,245	3,000	2,008	5,519	1,010	4,908	4,302	4,066
Salt beef	28,803	29,159	15,371	43,829	39,075	26,230	16,960	21,839
Charqui	14,872	23,818	22,590	38,484	21,518	74,398	26,643	34,854
Butter	2,002	2,797	1,255	12,741	5,053	7,170	6,538	6,920
Cheese	10,327	14,603	6,530	18,543	7,256	18,156	11,746	7,551
Tallow‡	25,698	19,632	12,001	23,857	21,129	39,043	31,046	47,554
Horns, hoofs, &c.	5,935	3,448	1,300	7,105	2,840	2,158	4,361	6,098
Hides	104,689	135,825	101,715	117,029	144,195	165,942	143,395	99,795
Goat, sheep, and chinchilla skins	7,141	5,125	6,967	1,638	7,953	17,754	31,201	31,307
Wool	40,509	158,409	171,161	85,345	93,324	64,303	83,333	104,301
Soap	2,033	387	503	144	3,516	3,593	920	2,248
Hams	6,558	5,926	3,583	1,980	6,702	3,007	3,594	800
Assorted provisions	93,214	157,081	10,529	26,347	21,822	50,454	30,571	18,290
Dried fodder	3,252	1,298	703	3,939	1,965	1,054	1,585	8,632
Cords and rope	7,884	2,326	7,516	14,938	26,824	26,614	7,278	4,850
Rigging for ships	11,200	7,938	5,782	6,818	4,719	988	4,510	3,825
Planks and lumber	42,037	37,701	59,166	49,445	61,254	310,914	106,372	29,795
Coal	39,327	10,312	2,401	783	483	4,933	7,590	2,540
Guano	12,536	93,663	24,537	2,356	10,379	13,645	37,708	55,392
Miscellaneous	68,513	65,707	80,117	65,679	180,913	30,022	451,751	198,857
Total exports, including precious metals	$4,881,561	$5,623,181	$6,340,384	$7,021,334	$7,257,469	$9,424,220	$11,392,452	$9,666,354

* This includes flour made from roasted wheat—*harina tostada.*

† Wheat or corn toasted and broken.

‡ Includes grease and tallow candles.

Table showing the principal Imports consumed, and their value.

Articles.	1844.	1845.	1846.	1847.	1848.	1849.	1850.	1851.
Aguardiente*	$17,463	$26,509	$22,937	$21,436	$22,456	$29,199	$31,734	$37,279
Ale and porter	13,109	13,759	17,613	14,667	5,333	10,607	16,033	18,053
Alpacas							40,407	64,204
Baizes	196,171	179,317	162,690	213,576	188,606	243,870	218,917	195,133
Bark, Peruvian	417	263	630	3,778	11,793	1,438	959	1,552
Bedsteads, brass	13,556	16,598	10,570	13,572	9,112	13,490	7,095	17,785
Books, printed	49,818	84,797	52,971	70,333	67,019	22,334	26,320	35,490
Buttons, assorted	15,715	10,655	11,203	14,740	8,808	12,280	22,788	16,919
Calicoes	394,974	403,927	509,750	447,089	431,070	656,512	486,527	516,148
Candles, sperm and composition	6,316	9,735	20,222	10,897	8,575	8,781	18,366	35,039
Canvass	23,706	38,466	37,900	27,308	38,904	27,577	44,788	35,438
Cards, playing	3,760	14,970	8,094	2,908	153	9,847	3,802	4,781
Carpets, Brussels	16,404	10,435	21,202	23,532	16,226	21,405	34,368	28,719
Carpets, Kidderminster	20,057	25,180	21,589	31,564	35,381	29,455	37,512	23,084
Carriages	19,880	14,481	12,903	11,347	1,180	24,030	11,060	23,418
Casimeres	88,198	88,878	129,719	131,471	114,230	223,459	235,714	236,574
Chairs	34,118	23,630	31,779	26,627	23,515	35,846	32,656	29,873
Cloth	208,571	179,240	184,395	168,835	133,811	170,561	171,217	154,572
Clothing	19,920	2,384	16,089	26,068	20,037	43,629	18,406	19,477
Coal	5,200	15,925	41,310	68,356	119,273	346,500	253,246	236,473
Cocoa	6,206	5,201	21,389	13,948	8,051	7,395	32,412	6,145
Coffee	17,376	15,835	15,492	7,484	16,465	9,825	18,042	12,705
Copper, sheet	27,712	66,947	11,929	13,461	32,629	56,475	14,889	9,017
Cottons, cambric	8,578	11,929	4,430	3,722	6,465	10,683	10,138	11,012
checks	4,244	8,455	15,402	3,889	11,317	14,628	15,166	17,506
damask	800	531	128	280	244	881	4,248	15,920
and wool damask	8,932	6,333	11,183	8,107	6,608	6,080	12,261	20,123
drillings	16,823	11,659	13,841	29,891	14,975	26,445	43,276	28,693
handkerchiefs	61,448	89,692	109,795	111,780	76,737	102,950	92,559	66,542
laces	4,382	7,592	9,376	8,287	8,204	10,193	22,403	20,127
linings	4,675	8,511	12,749	22,278	15,030	24,466	22,339	24,801
colored	42,116	41,651	75,466	60,755	38,723	56,287	56,666	9,077
raw	13,337	7,592	9,816	1,383	111		464	509
shawls	40,560	33,405	56,514	47,880	32,422	75,289	82,323	56,257
and wool shawls	53,829	104,248	109,985	74,446	70,186	71,627	101,931	118,737
silk and wool	11,893	17,920	19,583	31,370	24,295	49,966	43,204	42,337
stockings	79,914	63,263	87,265	62,315	31,768	56,678	52,423	66,390
tapes	8,738	20,006	21,204	12,852	12,947	10,814	14,858	23,226
tickings	7,360	29,296	20,016	7,128	24,173	27,196	21,450	38,498
thread	48,173	50,309	51,509	46,040	42,262	59,511	67,025	47,638
unbleached	332,349	402,060	459,028	698,091	670,302	681,201	475,504	615,825
vestings	8,243	15,324	24,799	19,730	20,043	16,632	18,624	13,921
white	547,045	620,315	798,941	781,750	774,025	1,039,338	748,951	800,872
and wool	103,138	83,132	96,398	95,337	93,478	166,849	160,534	159,453
Crape shawls	85,963	66,178	120,146	80,575	52,870	102,849	120,281	98,273
Crash	13,121	7,251	9,350	10,474	2,846	3,089	3,047	1,117
Drugs and medicines	16,836	16,212	26,086	35,180	37,580	36,581	29,054	29,084
Earthenware	60,024	34,830	33,001	52,721	47,721	71,292	77,865	34,929
Fire-bricks	36,283	8,808	20,777	21,291	28,578	27,990	32,433	16,444
Flannel	11,509	9,036	6,090	9,097	5,684	3,162	3,957	3,893
Flat-irons	14,205	4,552	2,246	667	135	2,720	7,146	7,387
Gauzes	4,730	8,318	9,659	9,544	6,910	15,547	11,427	10,892
Glassware	29,578	33,241	34,144	36,932	16,635	44,425	64,199	60,221
Glass windows	10,664	13,650	7,265	14,198	19,067	9,154	15,963	7,975
Gloves, assorted	9,705	7,124	7,845	10,415	12,947	8,742	13,590	22,008
Gold, bar	72,890	42,458	33,328	36,184	21,969	68,781	895,725	3,378,134
Gold, doubloons	207,424	263,407	166,187	115,830	16,491	39,814	26,324	60,204
Gold and silver coin	4,000	3,574	16,793	493	653,587	896,388	717,400	850,908
Horned cattle				21,904	5,660	23,588	40,166	50,371
Horses				2,108	255	5,626	11,316	9,061
Horse-rugs						10,512	14,342	10,023
Household furniture	18,122	13,986	50,702	18,668	27,630	22,870	46,689	52,621
Indigo	134,086	88,768	74,406	50,542	97,306	62,101	72,016	14,071
Iron, assorted	113,728	134,528	38,405	26,281	65,982	77,335	130,737	85,802
Iron chains	7,620	11,720	1,540	5,666	7,462	9,642	41,450	29,852

* Distilled spirits of every kind except gin, which is included in "liquors."

Table showing the principal Imports consumed, &c.—Continued.

Articles.	1844.	1845.	1846.	1847.	1848.	1849.	1850.	1851.
Iron, miners' hammers		$3,643	$2,775	$7,935	$7,800	$9,338	$16,359	$4,379
nails	$68,929	22,982	28,125	21,161	13,584	14,759	54,511	56,813
sheet	4,4 6	11,892	9,120	11,206	8,931	11,530	26,689	1,467
shovels and spades	6,034	16,537	10,683	8,451	9,061	3,707	13,033	14,345
Jewellery	34,894	30,115	40,140	67,463	36,368	38,503	31,758	109,983
Knives and forks	13,572	11,412	8,733	12,412	9,517	18,435	24,500	21,153
Lastings	49,436	34,719	38,697	46,883	34,802	36,115	12,815	15,665
Leather, ordinary	17,558	2,937	708	1,157	1,347	802	83	2,890
morocco	15,945	12,389	13,210	13,594	3,788	7,009	8,361	15,641
calf skin	13,187	19,927	24,660	34,238	25,159	46,375	48,657	42,973
Linen	24,678	19,912	39,135	22,158	22,527	18,405	22,323	19,986
Linen drilling	23,928	24,017	33,509	30,569	28,191	25,357	15,536	18,630
Liquors, assorted	6,225	6,829	11,012	15,928	11,503	13,973	10,469	15,434
Machinery	3,850	583	23,195	54,343	20,114	14,969	4,000	39,150
Marble	7,768	8,033	2,325	6,637	7,390	12,366	5,665	6,332
Matches, phosphorus	5,428	8,258	4,137	12,804	8,540	8,610	40,785	27,958
Mate	56,351	50,701	164,220	95,014	71,525	161,968	96,993	127,174
Matting, Chinese	5,499	3,539	820	25,901	2,302	36	6,244	258
Mercery, assorted	171,678	95,060	79,829	76,036	103,635	140,761	186,121	220,918
Merchandise, various kinds	321,546	263,341	275,696	367,168	277,429	249,070	360,178	381,427
Merino cloth	83,564	58,119	55,818	62,765	82,627	113,929	135,085	115,891
Mousselaines	76,440	80,388	87,790	80,748	69,119	111,222	110,587	118,866
Molasses	13,453	32,312	22,328	12,530	29,903	11,233	14,777	17,658
Mules			637	3,854	4,216	10,399	7,843	11,936
Muskets and fowling-pieces	23,427	26,631	13,112	3,386	1,687	1,779	4,748	3,058
Nankeens or florentines	15,315	8,863	847	61				124
Oil, linseed	3,390	1,395	9,417	13,217	3,861	4,066	6,075	4,723
olive	10,511	15,757	23,625	23,923	15,343	9,754	45,693	36,281
whale	2,803	12,340.	13,962	9,623	6,776	18,371	32,208	13,756
Paints	23,831	20,245	18,500	32,189	35,521	17,465	19,905	13.547
Paper, cigarito	3,976	3,402	5,457	4,642	3,857	3,432	8,734	16,974
letter	4,788	5,528	4,985	2,620	4,757	12,305	16,715	13,940
foolscap and printing	41,103	40,542	38,400	27,576	33,103	77,094	74,105	86,448
wall	19,740	13,228	12,753	22,200	23,598	18,175	17,985	42,577
Perfumery, assorted	8,505	3,655	6,257	10,557	5,219	7,261	12,228	10,097
Pianos	29,769	49,707	37,386	38,414	37,568	43,728	23,680	25,390
Pickles	1,905	6,249	8,471	6,741	9,448	7,746	14,639	32,084
Platillas	6,070	4,906	13,684	5,666	10,699	3,118	3,024	1,183
Powder	24,889	24,447	20,006	9,103	18,340	30,038	35,586	29,797
Quicksilver	36,205	36,280	57,724	57,857	75,458	239,557	58,684	227,752
Raisins	3,716	3,120	3,473	11,871	1,174	16,119	14,689	10,905
Ribbons	4,995	41,741	52,881	52,595	39,750	39,094	45,606	58,826
Rice	46,344	94,594	47,960	31,658	25,765	70,840	56,693	68,218
Rigging, ship	15,501	11,768	10,384	13,595	10,087	13,474	11,207	11,861
Sacks, empty	3,929	2,360	6,120	4,248	2,621	8,720	946	20,982
Saddles	8,872	9,017	6,400	15,115	16,101	17,578	15,886	19,152
Salt, common	16,279	42,596	45,163	45,761	30,787	33,791	47,173	11,134
Sateen	33,063	21,495	37,442	20,241	23,447	12,078	19,642	7,125
Satin	42,025	49,740	53,838	33,467	26,421	23,910	23,617	14,722
Satin and silk shawls	96,217	81,046	80,679	47,023	23,245	82,250	60,664	36,020
Segars	23,142	27,432	26,268	37,868	40,818	39,500	47,651	79,539
Scissors, assorted	10,186	5,961	6,096	8,469	4,916	4,607	5,300	4,527
Shoes and boots	26,062	22,365	47,139	33,750	25,182	35,857	21,253	43,778
Shot	2,929	3,453	4,216	3,760	5,939	11,989	13,980	4,477
Silk, assorted	26,594	53,050	36,987	57,382	23,319	80,671	82,594	161,850
serge	32,963	20,780	24,155	8,922	8,819	11,006	21,444	17,348
sewing	14,796	21,220	34,788	43,119	27,133	28,353	23,296	45,964
shawls and handkerchiefs	256,505	142,874	207,856	179,983	107,725	159,948	322,517	162,567
Silver, dollars	943,439	1,527,504	1,314,525	1,042,140	145,434	95,421	72,772	44,580
bar and plata piña	7,216	1,020	6,239	2,466	9,010	12,408	61,856	23,479
Soap	20,588	38,822	32,867	67,800	15,269	73,227	69,224	66,427
Steel	13,493	14,020	12,903	13,838	2,813	11,712	17,350	21,149
Straw hats	149,428	65,211	112,294	115,656	160,322	154,846	220,459	179,036
Sugar, refined	47,557	51,809	164,338	215,671	318,909	95,423	400,969	663,129
crushed	356,035	393,989	729,809	578,271	368,403	226,490	336,634	800,141

Table showing the principal Imports consumed, &c.—Continued.

Articles.	1844.	1845.	1846.	1847.	1848.	1849.	1850.	1851.
Sugar, Peruvian loaf	$124,167	$75,718	$88,648	$101,034	$55,171	$36,586	$119,020	$60,522
chancaca	71,740	104,409	55,323	95,398	94,331	56,074	48,004	138,120
Tallow	4,474	120	3,115	9,690	9,260	9,187	20,294	3,544
Tea	25,157	26,882	18,910	20,352	31,816	31,873	21,912	49,675
Tin	9,360	3,302	8,363	2,966	124	2,550	13,684	13,928
Tobacco	528,050	473,023	788,104	796,619	537,598	561,760	337,240	659,085
Umbrellas and parasols	11,243	16,025	18,792	26,619	14,030	21,254	52,507	18,261
Velvets	33,865	33,010	33,904	35,270	31,344	25,794	24,977	47,177
Watches, gold and silver		3,256	1,881	4,914	4,272	4,603	10,267	25,795
Waiters, assorted	2,049	1,487	3,668	3,043	1,115	15,623	1,127	1,158
Wax	11,675	2,004	23,542	20,145	12,183	14,129	11,781	9,861
Wine, white	25,191	39,090	33,352	46,256	30,645	46,619	53,067	70,861
red	30,853	43,053	43,994	53,504	32,213	42,893	38,036	48,556
Wood, cabinet	17,426	2,434	8,734	3,542	8,207	20,174	38,146	23,708
building	20,624	50,707	26,803	72,508	95,733	44,659	195,151	52,372
Woollen goods	35,260	27,629	72,640	95,158	63,566	92,949	62,714	77,013
shawls	60,221	32,761	24,507	102,302	69,963	87,421	115,073	143,801

Every article is embraced in the preceding table whose value in any one of the years amounted to $10,000.

Possessing, as has been shown, nearly all the foreign trade of the country, its narrow streets present more of bustle and activity than any other city of Chile ; indeed, its transient population have brought with them the habits and industry of the northern hemisphere, and there is scarcely a remnant of native customs among the better classes.

Being the seat of government of the province, Valparaiso is immediately under the control of an Intendente, who exercises the functions of military and naval as well as of civil governor. Its municipal affairs are in charge of the Cabildo, which is composed of seven members elected by the people, but over whose acts the Intendente has a controlling vote ; neither of them, however, having the power to enact any law without the sanction of one of the Ministers of State, whose duty it may be to take cognizance of the subject to which such enactment pertains. The revenues collected under taxes imposed by them during the last ten years have been as follows :

In 1843	$55,081	In 1848	$92,586
1844	72,703	1849	93,570
1845	78,793	1850	99,447
1846	80,118	1851	125,591
1847	89,684	1852	128,650

The whole of which, except $12,000 in 1847, and $4,000 in 1843, was expended for local purposes. Such prosperity can scarcely be wondered at after the facts stated.

But it is scarcely probable that Valparaiso can much longer continue in such a prosperous career. Hitherto it has not only engrossed all the trade, but tolls have been paid to it for supplies by nearly every ship that doubled Cape Horn, and thus many hundred thousand dollars have annually been contributed for native commodities forced there from the coast. This continued with the fleets of vessels from the United States during the Californian fever in 1849–'50, and partially in 1851, when the construction of clippers commenced a change, and now the voyage direct to San Francisco is made in less average time than was formerly occupied in that to Valparaiso. It has already become as rare for ships to call, as it previously was for them to pass by. Moreover, the transit of the Isthmus of Panama is made with such celerity and facility that light, valuable goods, which first found storage in Chile and subsequent distribution along the western coast, have begun to take that route direct to their ultimate markets ; and the quantity will undoubtedly increase as soon as the railroad or canal is completed, and reasonable rates of freight are established. Nor can the southern provinces much longer defer demanding their rights. Did they comprise only the native population, they might be willing to follow the custom of their forefathers for another quarter of a century or so; but it is impossible that the colony of Germans near Valdivia should not rapidly increase in numbers and prosperity. Emigration swells their ranks every year. They have brought industry and energy to a virgin soil of unlimited fertility, in a climate unsurpassed for salubrity and amenity; and they would be unfaithful representatives of Saxonism did they not become sufficiently powerful, in a few years, to break down this anomaly in the course of trade.

To its superficial increase there are interposed enormous physical obstacles. Every foot of ground is already covered by buildings from the face of the cliffs to the sea; and, to obtain space for other warehouses, either the sea itself must be encroached on, and its billows braved, or families must submit to dwell on the hills, so as to devote all the lower part of the town to business pursuits. Within the last two years each of these measures has been partially resorted to, and even the name "Cape Horn" will soon be forgotten in the shadow of the lines of magazines erected between it and the waves that once laved its Cimmerian cave, whilst elegant villas above *Cerro Alegre* have added no little to the beauty of the landscape. The completion of the projected railroad to Santiago would probably obviate this difficulty somewhat, as well as preserve the prosperity of the port: for a part of the merchants would prefer a residence at the capital, if the journey could be made in four or five hours; and we have the experience of the world in proof that increased facilities of transportation multiply rapidly the amounts of traffic and travel. A consummation of the object is, therefore, of vital importance; one which commercial men of both cities should leave no effort untried to perfect, but unite as a body to break down individual aspirations opposing themselves to the general good. It is conclusively shown by the accomplished engineer who made the survey, that there is not only a practicable route over which a road may be built, under the direction of a competent engineer, in five years, and for less than $8,000,000, but, from the statistics of traffic and travel, it is quite certain the investment will prove a safe one. Encouraged by his report, a company was formed of which government became a shareholder to the amount of $2,000,000, and a commencement of the work was made with great formality on the 1st of October, 1852: but the obstacles to be overcome at the very outset were such as only a practical man could grapple with; and the task being too great for the person whom the company had charged with it, this part of the work was abandoned for ground better suited to his capacities. It is much to be apprehended, that the successful operation of the road from Caldera to Copiapó, by exciting the envy of commercial capitalists, may cause the failure of this great work; as its two or three controlling stockholders seem determined to monopolize all possible immediate profits without regard to ultimate costs. Of course the engineer who surveyed, located, and exhibited the feasibility of the road, had too much experience in details to countenance the contracts they wanted on their own terms, and his services have not been needed subsequently.

Open as it is to the north, the sea rolls in from an illimitable distance; and during the storms of winter it often breaks across the street at Cape Horn, its roar along the beach at such times drowning even the stirring noises of commercial life. I was present during one of them —the third *temporal* of the winter of 1851, having just returned from Caldera. These northers are generally accompanied with much rain, far more falling in the course of a very few hours than is ever known in the same parallel of North America. At such times there are parts of Valparaiso wholly impassable by pedestrians, as volumes of water and mud pour down the ravines, deluging the contiguous streets, and discoloring the sea for miles. Though its fall is quite slight in comparison, the barometer is a very sure indicator; and as soon as it descends to 29.80 inches, a signal is thrown out from the Exchange, "Prepare for bad weather." In the most severe of the three storms within as many weeks, it fell only to 29.63 inches—the lowest that had been known in many years. The steamer Peru and four other vessels were driven on the beach during its violence. Even by daylight it is distressing to watch the ships tossed and plunging over their anchors amid seething seas which the tempest has driven across an

31

ocean's expanse, a raging surf close at hand warning of almost certain death in case of accident to cables; but when darkness comes over the face of the deep, and a wild scud wraps the heavens in impenetrable obscurity, the solitary lights that mark the spots of those struggling to secure safety to their ships, and their earnest and anxious voices as they occasionally come to the ear in lulls of the gale, still more painfully enlist our sympathies. Amid the thunders of the storm perhaps the "minute gun at sea" brings its sad story to the ear, or from some dragging ship there flashes a blue light telling how close they deem themselves to destruction; and the watcher from Cerro Alegre turns away heartsick, remembering the saying, "Between us and you there is a great gulf; so that they which would pass from hence to you cannot, neither can they pass to us that would come from thence."

Unlike the storms of the North Atlantic, the temporales seem to be wholly local, unless the axis is perpendicular to the direction of the wind, and the storm travels directly off the coast. They are hardly ever felt at Coquimbo, Constitucion, or Santiago, three points north, south, and east of Valparaiso respectively; and the only evidence which Constitucion and Santiago have that a storm is prevailing is from the frequent and heavy showers they experience at the same time.

CHAPTER X.

A VISIT TO THE PROVINCES OF ATACAMA AND COQUIMBO.

DEPART FROM SANTIAGO AND EMBARK ON BOARD STEAMER BOLIVIA AT VALPARAISO.—LOSS OF STEAMER ECUADOR.—GAMBLING ON BOARD.—PORT OF COPIAPÓ.—ARRIVE AT CALDERA.—ANCIENT SKELETONS.—FLIES AND FLEAS.—PLUTONIC ROCKS.—MARINE FOSSILS.—ORIGIN OF THE RAILROAD.—LEAVE CALDERA FOR THE INTERIOR.—APPEARANCE OF THE COUNTRY.—STERILITY.—COPIAPÓ RIVER.—DUST.—DEAD ANIMALS BY THE ROAD.—THE CITY OF COPIAPÓ.—BUILDINGS ON THE PLAZA.—HOSPITALS.—SCHOOLS.—EDUCATION.—DWELLINGS.—PEOPLE; THEIR HOSPITALITY.—LEAVE FOR CHAÑARCILLO.—VILLAGE OF TOTORALILLO.—LA ANGOSTURA —WATER.—CUESTA DE CHAÑARCILLO.—APERTURES IN THE HILLS BY THE ROAD-SIDE.—EL BOLACO; VIEW FROM THE SUMMIT.—DESCENT OF A MINE.—MAGNETICAL OBSERVATIONS.—METEOROLOGY.—DISCOVERY OF THE MINES.—JUAN GODOI.—JUAN CALLEJAS.—FATE OF DISCOVERERS.—ADMINISTRATION OF MINES.—MINERS; THEIR STRENGTH; PILFERING; RECEIVERS OF STOLEN ORES; GAMBLING.—GEOLOGICAL DESCRIPTION OF EL BOLACO.—NUMBER OF MINES, AND THEIR PRODUCE.—PROCESS OF REDUCING ORES —ARQUERITE.—ORES REDUCED AT THE CERILLOS MILLS DURING 1850.—VALUE OF THE SILVER EXPORTED FROM THE PROVINCE FOR EACH YEAR, FROM 1830 TO 1851.—THE DISTRICT OF TRES PUNTAS.—PRICES OF THE PRINCIPAL ARTICLES CONSUMED AT THE MINES.—PROFESSIONAL MINE-HUNTERS.—DISCOVERIES IN 1850.—ABANDONE MINES RE-DENOUNCED IN THE SAME YEAR.—LAWSUITS.—THE MINING BOARD.—RETURN TO THE CITY OF COPIAPÓ —ITS GEOGRAPHICAL POSITION.—METEOROLOGY AND AN EARTHQUAKE.—START FOR CALDERA.—RAILROAD ACCIDENT.—METEOROLOGY AT CALDERA.—MUSICAL FISH.—RETURN TO VALPARAISO, AND FROM THENCE BACK TO COQUIMBO.—COQUIMBO BAY.—CUSTOM-HOUSE IMPOSITIONS AND FRAUDS.—HERRADURA BAY.—SERENA.—TOPOGRAPHICAL VIEW FROM THE TERRACE.—THE PEOPLE —EDUCATION.—OCCUPATIONS.—CLIMATE.—COMMERCE.—PRODUCTS.—IMPORTS AND EXPORTS IN 1850.—COPPER SMELTING.—GEOLOGY OF THE MINING PROVINCES, AND DISTRIBUTION OF METALS.—TOWNS OF THE DEPARTMENTS OF FREIRINA AND VALLENAR.—MINES OF CARRISO; AGUA-AMARGA; TUNAS; CAMERONES; ARQUEROS; ALGODONES.—MINES OF THE PROVINCE OF ACONCAGUA; IN THE PROVINCE OF SANTIAGO; IN THE SOUTHERN PROVINCES.—COAL MINES OF CONCEPCION.—ANALYSES OF THE COALS.—OTHER MINES IN CHILE —ENGLISH ATTEMPTS TO WORK THE MINES.—THEIR FAILURE.

Taking advantage of the cloudy weather ordinarily prevailing during the month of July, I left the capital about the close of June, 1851, for the purpose of making a series of magnetical determinations in the mining districts of Atacama and Coquimbo, and of looking on the wealth that nature has denied to the surface of the northern Chilean provinces. Signifying my intentions to the Minister of Foreign Affairs, he not only caused orders to be sent to the collectors of the customs to facilitate the embarcation and landing of the instruments at the several ports, but also forwarded letters of introduction and particular recommendation to the Intendentes of each province.

The season and appearance of the country were in marked contrast to the corresponding period of last year. Then the mountains were covered with snow very far down; the earth, saturated with moisture, had permitted the carts to cut up the roads so as to be almost impassable; and the air was damp and chill. Now—although a considerable amount of snow had already fallen—there was none visible at a less elevation than seven or eight thousand feet; there had only been a few genial showers over the valley—just enough to clothe the hills in their brightest verdure; and the atmosphere was as soft and balmy as an early June morning of the northern hemisphere.

Only two days were spent at the port; on the last of which an election was commenced for a President to serve during the next five years. As the warehouses of the merchants were closed and business was very generally suspended, there was much less bustle than is usual, and the day passed off very quietly. It must be acknowledged, however, that places of business were closed and the population left the streets; not from law or inclination, but because of apprehended difficulties at the polls. On the last day of the polling, although steamer day, and a morning when five times the usual amount of business is generally transacted, the authorities did not open even the custom-house; and the Intendente, surrounded by aids, galloped through the streets every hour, in order to be present at every spot as often as was possible in case of disorder. It was well known to the friends of the government, and to merchants generally, that troops and extra policemen were ready for instant service; but even this could not restore tranquillity to the more timid, to whom the idea of revolution brought all the horrors of a stormed town.

It was during these two or three pleasant days that the zodiacal light was first seen in Chile; and, as observed from the terrace of Cerro Alegre, its brilliancy was far greater than I ever saw it north of the equator.

Embarking with a crowd of other passengers on board the steamer Bolivia, within forty-eight hours we had nearly all separated again; part landing at Coquimbo, part at Copiapó, and the remainder at Caldera, a little town whose existence is due to the persevering industry and intelligence of Mr. Wm. Wheelwright. This gentleman embarked from Valparaiso on the day of my arrival, in a steamer formerly belonging to the mail line he had established under subsidy of the British government, but which had been sold on the arrival of new vessels for the line. An American gentleman had purchased this vessel (the *Ecuador*), and placed her on the route between Copiapó and Valparaiso,—if not in direct opposition to the mail line, at all events to take away a portion of the profits on the only valuable part of the coast of Chile. As we rounded the point at the southern entrance to the bay of Coquimbo on the following afternoon, the Ecuador was perceived, nearly submerged, just by the little mole, having struck on the rocks when attempting to go out on the night after her departure from Valparaiso. Fortunately there were few passengers on board; and as most of them had known something of nautical life, they retained sufficient presence of mind to insure the safety of their personal effects before the water became too deep in the hold. Notwithstanding there were several vessels at anchor in the bay, and the steamer was within a mile of the little town when she struck, the guns and other signals resorted to were wholly disregarded—not a soul came to render them assistance; and after nearly four hours of hard work, the crew and passengers succeeded in beaching the vessel just in time to prevent her going down in deep water. This accident added considerably to the number of our passengers; no little to the gratification of the "sportsmen" who were journeying to Copiapó with us, and whose "Monte" was displayed as soon as the cloth was removed after dinner. Unlike the descendants of Saxons, who find diversion and pleasure in books, or in conversation when thrown together, a propensity to gamble is almost universal with those of Spanish blood. More especially does it exist among the Copiapinos, some of whom wake up and find themselves famously wealthy after going to bed poor. The products of mines in Atacama almost make one believe the genii of Aladdin have still their favored mortals on the earth, one of them having yielded its proprietor within a single year more than half a million of dollars! Whether such extraordinary fortunes have created a new passion in men who in many cases were pennyless previously, or its accession but knocks the manacles from one whom poverty had held captive, it would be no easy matter to ascertain; we only know that some of the miners are notorious gamblers, and are not contented to make the short voyage from their coffers in Copiapó to Valparaiso, or back, without risking sums often of considerable magnitude.

There was scarcely an hour's detention at Coquimbo; and before night had fairly closed in, we were losing the few evidences of vegetable life visible on the seacoast of this portion of Chile. In the morning the sky was overcast, and the land—a scene of desolation—interesting only from the varied outlines of distant hills and ravines. As we were to stop but an hour at the port of Copiapó, and the rough swell one must encounter in landing is more than an equivalent for the brief period one is allowed to spend at a place so uninviting, few are disposed to avail themselves of the opportunity to try how firmly they *can* stand on terra firma. But remembering that there were strata of marine fossils in the sea-worn caves on each side of the village, one of which might be reached, the captain's offer of a seat in his boat was accepted, and I landed once more at the desolate-looking place. Had my considerate friend then left me, there was ample time to reach one of these interesting geological localities; and the gratification of a specimen or two, added to his good company to and from the beach, would have fully repaid the pull to the shore. But such was not destined to be the result. He had been unremittingly attentive and kind from the moment of embarking at Valparaiso,—courtesies he apparently considered essential here also; and therefore would play the guide on shore, as well as the agreeable host on board. Before we were fairly clear of the little town, earnest and repeated looks towards the steamer satisfied me that he considered us at the end of the walk it was possible to accomplish in the time he intended to remain in the port, and he was not a little pleased when it was proposed that we should return towards the ship. Nearly all of our passengers with their luggage had been landed meanwhile, $300,000 in silver bars shipped on board for England, and we left the harbor still early in the afternoon.

The next port at which we stopped was *Caldera*, in latitude 27° 04′ S. and some eight leagues to the northward of the last. Less than two years previously it was known only as a pretty little bay, of rather more than a mile in diameter, but whose only attraction for ships was an old well of brackish water. As it is easy of access, has good anchoring ground, is protected from winds, except between N. and W.N.W., and its waters contain an abundant supply of excellent fish, it is preferable to every one of the anchorages in the sterile region extending from Arica to Coquimbo. Its distance from the city of Copiapó being nearly the same, we may well be amazed that it was not selected as the port, instead of the dangerous and exposed roadstead which was chosen.

When Mr. Wheelwright first landed, at the period referred to, there was neither house nor hut of any description; a fisherman or two, dwelling under sea-worn rocks, being the only inhabitants of its barren sand-hills. Yet skeletons recently disinterred in cutting for the railroad, and not far from the beach, prove that there once existed a settlement here. Nor—if all parts of the body were duly proportioned—did the people belong to the small race now in Chile; the crania being of unusual size and thickness, and the femur bones of extraordinary length. Nearly all were found in an erect position, with implements of bone and copper buried beside them. Whether they were *Changos*, a class of Indian fishermen who dwelt along the coast at the time of its discovery, may be questioned; for these did not and do not congregate in numbers, and some thirty skeletons have been found here. On the other hand, it is suggested that the skulls were too perfect to have been buried more than half a century; though it is well known that nitre is an admirable preservative. This is proved by the mummies at Arica and Iquique, both towns on the coast of Peru; and the soil here also abounds with it. Of the only two skulls remaining at my arrival, the sagittal suture of one was entirely closed, and the teeth, though much worn, were still quite perfect; the other was porous and spongy, as if the system had been penetrated by venereal disease. They were in possession of the medical officer of the railroad company, who intended taking them to the United States. But what of the colony?—there remains not even a tradition respecting them!

Unprovided with a tent or other shelter, Mr. Wheelwright was forced to take refuge in one of the water-worn caves of a cliff, now some thirty feet above the bay. This would have been comfortable enough had it not been tenanted by myriads of fleas, who pounced on the invader of their dominions with the thirst of vampires. Nor was it in the cave only that the guide and himself were subjected to their attacks; even the sand was literally alive with them, and from each handful indiscriminately picked up an admirer of saltatory feats could behold multitudes springing in all directions. These were not the only nuisances. Flies in numbers, if possible, yet greater, disputed every mouthful and every breath of air, whilst they claimed each particle that evaporated from the hands and face, compelling constant efforts for their dislodgment. Looking abroad upon the dominions occupied only by these pests, there was not a shrub to relieve the monotony or to protect the eye from the glare of the sand; nothing but sand-hills, through which nature, in some terrific throe, had here and there thrust out blackened rocks, leaving them on end, apparently to serve as stumbling-blocks for man in his efforts to unravel the mysteries of creation. Scattered over the surface of the hills—here in isolated parcels, there in broad patches; sometimes in huge piles whose gross weight exceeds many hundred tons, and at others in delicate strata that extend for miles parallel with though beneath them—there are untold millions of dead shells embracing multitudes of varieties. In some places the aggregations are composed wholly of one genus, as though they eschewed other association, in others they are of every species inextricably mixed; here they are worn and broken into lime, there they are perfect as though just extracted from the ocean; and again, in other localities there are strata embracing every kind, united by hard concrete or indurated sand, tough almost as gneiss. In one stratum 200 feet above the water, and more than a mile from where the tide now flows, there are more than fifty tons of small white clam-shells in one mass, nearly all of them perfect and almost without the admixture of sand through their interstices. They are buried beneath a stratum of sand about one foot thick, and look for all the world like the piles of clean shells one finds in North America before the houses of oystermen. How *did* all these ship-loads of the sea's product so get together, and how *were* they raised so many hundred feet above the element from which they drew sustenance? The making of this world of ours has been a wonderful process—or perhaps it would be more appropriate to say, *is* a wonderful process; for the changes still progressing in the upheaval of the broadside of this whole continent are here almost daily perceptible. That all the land from the ocean to the city of Copiapó, and probably farther into the interior to an elevation of 2,000 feet, was buried under the waters of the Pacific within less than a thousand years, I have no more doubt than that my pen traces these lines. If the shells, which exposure to the action of a tropical sun and night dews has failed to decompose, are not sufficient proof, we may bring the testimony of their still thriving descendants from the waters of the coast, and the still existing indigenous trees found in a valley near the city where no water has flowed within the memory of man.

But to return to Mr. Wheelwright and the purpose of his visit to a locality which had been the scene of such gigantic changes, then only the residence of such pests.

At that time the mining interests had just been enhanced by the discovery of incalculable wealth in the silver veins at *Tres Puntas*, a chain of hills some sixty or seventy miles in a N.N.W. direction from the city of Copiapó. Even to the city every ounce of food for man and beast is conveyed from the southern provinces; and their freight from the sea renders prices so exorbitantly high, that California is as nothing in comparison. True, some little pasturage is raised along the riband-like rivulet, and a few fruits and vegetables of native growth occasionally gladden the palates of millionnaires; but in the district surrounding the newly discovered wealth, there is not a drop of running water or a blade of grass—scarcely even a shadow in which to obtain shelter from the heat of a midsummer sun reflected from sand. To render the new mines workable—that is, to bring the cost of labor and food to sums which would make them profitable—the charges for transportation must be reduced; in short, carriage by animals, that consume nearly everything they can carry in the journey forth and back, must be abolished. Hence the need of a railroad, whose iron teams need but a bite of the coal which English ships often bring as ballast when coming for loads of copper, and a sip of the water which the ocean could be made to yield. There being no native fuel on the spot with which to smelt, and the value of the ores near the sea being scarcely equal to the cost of extraction and transportation, up to that period the multitudes of rich copper veins more than ten leagues from the sea were scarcely more valuable than the rocks that enclosed them. A railroad would add millions to their wealth, and Wheelwright was the only man who could carry through such an undertaking. He had previously pointed out its value to the miners. In themselves or each other there was too little confidence for great public works or moneyed associations; and as, by the introduction of steamships along the coast to shorten the communication with the only market for the product of their mines, he had proved himself to the Copiapinos their most valuable friend, he was selected as the man to build the road. Some eleven gentlemen at once subscribed the million of dollars estimated as the cost of its construction, giving Mr. W. ample authority in all respects, and offering him a

P.S. Duval & Co's Steam lith. Press Phil^{a}

share whose value should be $50,000 if he would direct the work to completion. As at times the old port of Copiapó, besides being open to northerly winds, is difficult of access, and not a little dangerous from the reefs of rocks outside, it was unfit for the ocean terminus of the road, and hence the visit of reconnaissance to the neighboring ports. Though not until after warm opposition by those who held property at the old port, Caldera eventually bore off the palm.

Landing after night, it was not easy to gather an idea of the place; but the sound of English voices in many directions, and the quick, nervous movements of those who passed me between the wharf and the rooms of Mr. Wheelwright, were sufficient evidences that we were in an embryo settlement surely destined to reverse the order of things among the descendants of Spain, and to "go ahead." When morning came, the aspect of the colony was by no means charming. Two or three long rows of board buildings facing the bay and hastily put up, scores of rudely constructed ranchos, piles of lumber, coal, and iron rails, the skeleton of a large and better edifice intended as a custom-house, and a few tents,—these were results of the first year, with untiring industry, of the party brought from the United States to build the road. Six ships laden with locomotives, cars, and other materials for the company, were at anchor in the bay, and a large number of launches passed to and from the temporary mole with parts of the cargoes. To the eastward the track was visible, winding through a low swell in the ground, with working cars already rattling over it, piled with materials for the party above; and in another direction the mechanical engineers were busy in putting together some of the locomotives just landed. Activity and life were apparent even among some of the peons who had been brought here to do the heavy labor, and who had already profited by example.

A town had been laid out by government officers, and the custom-house commenced bade fair to be a large and handsome building, though at that time there were no others coming under the latter designation, all the rest being the one-story, unpainted, plank tenements before mentioned. Foreseeing its necessity and value, Mr. Wheelwright had erected a large house for his own use some months previously: but it was scarcely completed before it was burned to the ground; and as fire was communicated to the building occupied by the resident engineer a few weeks subsequently, there is every reason to believe that both fires were the work of incendiaries. That any of the buildings occupied by the engineers and subalterns escaped when the latter fire took place, was almost miraculous. They are of thin pine boards, on which rain had fallen only two or three times since their erection. The fire was at the dead of night, and the only water at command was that of the bay, more than a hundred yards distant. Most fortunately, the stifling smoke in his room roused the engineer; and his assistants promptly rallying to the scene of common threatened danger, the portions in flame were actually cut out with axes. Whether the incendiary was a native or one of the drunken and worthless foreigners constantly flocking hither, and whose idle and dissolute habits the company had refused to foster, none will be likely to know, though suspicion most naturally attached to the latter.

With the facilities offered by its bay, the convenience for landing goods possessed by a long mole which was at once projected and was then in progress, and the extensive and wealthy back mining district to supply, it was evident that Caldera, as the terminus of the railroad, must in a few years become a large town, in spite of its arid locality. What another year effected may be seen in the plate opposite—Caldera just two years after the American engineers landed there in 1850! If speculation had not already been quite so extravagant as at some of the paper towns of California, at least all of the most valuable town-lots had been taken at fair prices; and there wanted but the completion of the road to bring many of the Copiapinos here as permanent residents. As an offset to the loss inevitable from abandoning the old port, government gave a site in fee at Caldera to each former property-holder; and already they had begun to pull down and transport houses for re-erection. In July, 1851, its population numbered only 800 souls, one half of whom were in the employ of the company; and about 150 of the remainder were women. A year later, more than 2,000 had gathered within its precincts.

Twenty-four miles of the track being completed, early next morning Mr. Wheelwright and myself started for the city in a little hand-car. Almost at the instant of starting, one of the peons who was to have assisted in propelling the car, having been over-cautioned, or being perhaps over-careless, was caught on the crank, so injuring the machinery and disabling himself, by being thrown over it, that a new car and a mule were provided for us. The animal was intended to drag us three or four leagues—as far as the top of the rapidly ascending grade—after which "man-power" would be brought into action. The grade referred to is rather over than under sixty feet to the mile, yet almost wholly on the natural surface, the few embankments or cuttings in any part of it being of trifling amount. In the latter the shell strata mentioned have been brought to light. These follow the undulations of the surface with great regularity. Nor is it less interesting to observe how uniformly, in many places, the several layers have been deposited on each other; each species having, apparently, had its era and lain down to die, to be covered by one entirely distinct. Thus, there are places where clams and volutes, spirals and picos (*Balanas*), overlie each other, as though on the under genus alone could be their resting-place. Generally there is a superstratum of sand—a foot thick—covering these deposits; the immediate surface being sprinkled with small blanched snails, interspersed with occasional tufts of green; but of bushes or grass there are none, and the eye, having no objects of comparison, falls far short of the truth in appreciating distances across these inhospitable fields. This condition of things continues to full 500 feet above the ocean; the same strata of recent shells being visible in every cutting, if possible more distinctly separated with successive elevations. Specimens of all have been brought to the United States, of which an account is given in the report of Professor T. A. Conrad, Appendix H.

At ten or twelve miles from the port a well has been sunk, and water obtained at quite a moderate depth; though, to avoid the risk of a deficiency during continued years of drought, it has been considered prudent to enlarge its capacity by lateral chambers. As it was now noon, the laborers employed at it were taking their siesta, in holes cut in the sand and covered with bits of hide or old canvass, leaving apertures on one side through which to crawl. And these are the only dwellings used by any of the peons at work on the whole line of road! Beds or tables, seats or culinary utensils, they know not. The bare earth serves them for the three first, and a shell from the neighboring bank for the spoon with which to dip their boiled beans from a common iron pot. In a country producing nothing, not even a drop of water, where every article of consumption, as well as for the advance of the work, had to be conveyed from the starting point, it is most fortunate that a race could be found who are content to live so poorly provided. Otherwise, the cost for the maintenance of laborers alone must have much longer deterred any one from undertaking such a road. But the engineers have already brought near the day when the natives laying this track must be startled from their lethargy by the scream of the engines upon its rails, or the doom of certain starvation awaits them. Notwithstanding the obstacles to be overcome, an advance had been made equalling any achievement of a similar nature in the midst of populated and fruitful districts of other countries; and in a little more than a year they not only located and graded three fourths of the fifty-one miles, but had laid rails on quite half of it, expecting to complete the remainder in four months more. The total cost of the road, including station-houses, mole at Caldera, machine-shops, engines and cars, &c., was $1,300,000, and its receipts at the commencement of 1853 averaged more than $32,000 per month. Before completion it was ascertained that none of the water could be used without rapid destruction of the engines, and it became necessary to erect a distilling apparatus to obtain suitable supplies. But even this has been a gain, the profits on the distilled water sold more than paying for the entire quantity prepared. So gratified are the Copiapinos with the result, that they have already begun extensions of the road in the directions of Chañarcillo and Tres Puntas.

About the summits of the hills we traversed, all the surface pebbles and stones have a smooth and glossy appearance, which has been effected by sand driven along by the S.W. wind, constantly blowing up the old valley of the river. They are quite polished on the windward sides. These, and a few bulbous plants, were nearly all that attracted attention during 17 or 18 miles. Occasionally we passed small flocks of birds, in form similar to diminutive snipes; but they were timid little things, and ran to their burrows in the sand almost as soon as they saw us. Half a dozen medium-sized condors, too, stood near the drivers who were flaying it, awaiting their share of an unfortunate mule that had been run over, in the morning, by a loaded train. They were evidently without apprehension, and with the snipes were the only animate objects seen until we descended to the valley of the river.

Being covered with shrubbery between high bounding hills, here more than a mile and a half apart, the valley a little distance presented quite an attractive appearance. But as we drew near, the bushes were found low, dwarfish, of few varieties, and covered with dust. One naturally looked for the stream or rivulet whose moisture had been diffused to aid in their sustenance; but there is nothing of the kind now here, every drop of water coming from the melted snow of the Andes being consumed long before it reaches this part of its ancient channel. As a contrast, however, the eye early recognises seeming beds of snow or salt, extending for miles along the valley; though closer inspection proves them to be only incrustations of sulphate of soda with which the earth of the vicinity is permeated, and which have been left by evaporation. In some places, where a recent rain had evidently collected in little pools, the remaining crystals were very beautiful; but in this dry atmosphere the reflection of the sun from so white a surface is almost as painful as it would be from snow.

The engineers at the end of the line soon set out lunch for us; and our journey towards the city was resumed shortly after, in a carriage that had been sent ahead on the previous evening.

With the progress up the valley, the height of the hills on both sides rapidly increases; willow-like or osier bushes are more numerous, and the varieties of plants augment. Occasionally there are marks, quite twenty feet above the road, where water has washed the steep banks; and rocks, not less than the sand and gravel, exhibit evidences of a former running stream. On the eastern slopes of the spurs that jut from the bounding chains of the valley, sand lies in drifts, deposited by the same currents which polished the stones on the hills nearer the sea. Soon one begins to perceive houses—but such houses! Thatched or mud walls, with almost flat and mud-plastered roofs! Poor shelter these in rain-storms, one would think; and no doubt they would so prove: but, it must be recollected, it never rains in northern Chile except in winter, and winter—at least such winter as is occasionally experienced even in Florida —is never known here. If moderate showers fall on three days of the year, the land is considered to have been extraordinarily blessed, and a prosperous season ensues. They tell me that at such times even the sand-hills become like flower-gardens with an infinite variety of bulbous plants, which otherwise lie dormant until nature so wills. Strange as it may seem under this almost cloudless sky, at a few inches beneath the surface the sand is quite damp, though the only drops of water known for half a thousand years are from the miserly distributions of the heavens. Yet, an examination of the fleshy bulbs and tubers that one may dig from the ground at hundreds of feet above the river valley, may well inspire belief respecting the flowers in fruitful years. Without such seasons oftener than once in eight or ten years, denied the running streams which melting snows elsewhere afford for irrigation—except one slender brook, to be presently mentioned, and another near Huasco of scarcely greater capacity—the whole province is so sterile, it would of necessity be abandoned, but that nature has lavished other wealth upon it wherewith to pay liberally for all articles of consumption.

Within twelve miles of the city the road at last approaches the river; but what sort of stream does the reader picture to himself? one like the Delaware, or Thames, or Seine? The geographical student would be warranted in such belief on inspection of the old maps; and such a stream as either would be a source of wealth more valuable than all the riches of Tres Puntas. No, no; the river Copiapó is but a trench half filled with water, not a foot deep, and across which you may easily stride! A small estate called *Ramadillas*, near here, consumes nearly the whole of its supply, leaving but a thread or two, which subsequently collects to trickle along the descending valley. On this estate there is an indigenous evergreen willow, which at a little distance greatly resembles the poplar so universal in central Chile, though preferable to it from the quality mentioned.

Five or six miles more bring us among gardens enclosed by high mud walls, containing trees in full foliage; several among them deciduous in North America. In their dust-covered leaves they afford little pleasure to the sight; even the Floripondia, with its velvety leaf and graceful bell, being robbed of its charms by the impalpable powder pervading every particle of air. During N.W. winds, Washington is considered almost intolerable; here one encounters perpetually, by day, a parched air loaded with fine sand from the coastwise hills, which penetrates every crevice of the house, and in an hour or two deposits on the furniture a stratum in which you may legibly write. As the town is approached, other objects, even less agreeable, claim the attention from their increasing number, viz: carcasses of oxen and mules which have fallen, in their journeys from the port, famished for water and food, and have been deserted to die. There are neither condors, buzzards, nor other carrion-birds to consume them; and though each train of carts has its watch-dog, provisions here are too valuable to keep many such pets, and the bodies, skins and all, are left to dry up or decay. Perhaps other animals might experience a like fate did the arrieros lose time for this purpose, and hence they hurry to their journey's end. It is not extravagant to say there are dozens of carcasses within the last two leagues, and hundreds between the city and the mines at Chañarcillo.

Externally the suburbs of Copiapó exhibit no evidences of wealth. There are neither stylish equipages nor elegant country seats, to serve as indices of the millions some of its citizens possess. Lank, travel-worn mules, and burden-carts drawn by oxen, under the control of dust-begrimed drivers, slowly travelling over a winding road between adobe walls, were all that we saw. Wherever a house is visible, even at the threshold of the city, its squat appearance and mud-plastered roof is sure to make an unpleasant impression; nor is it certain to be externally whitewashed.

In 1851 Copiapó was about three fourths of a mile long, half a mile wide, and numbered above 9,000 people, of whom nearly two thirds were males. Its first street was irregular, lying nearly in the direction of the valley, from S.W. to N.E.; but as the population increased, and others became necessary, they were laid off parallel with each other, as far as possible preserving the same original line. These last are crossed by others at right angles; and, as is customary with Spanish founders, a public square has been left at the intended centre. On one side of the plaza a large church, with a Grecian front, has been erected; a style so unlike any ecclesiastical edifice in South America, that it may readily be believed the architect studied his art in North America. As the same architectural order has been preserved inside, one is tempted to doubt whether the *soi-disant* children of the true church do not sometimes question the propriety of worshipping within an edifice so heretically constructed. Apart from Anglo-Saxon taste, to say that it is the most chaste and commodious church in Chile is simple justice; and when the slabs of vari-colored marble, which have been imported from Italy, shall have been formed into a tesselated floor, one may visit it without fear of the fleas that specially congregate among the tiles of the others. Opposite the cathedral are barracks and public offices, forming a decent looking range of buildings of the usual style, and on which a preceding governor, during whose administration they were erected, deemed it proper to emblazon his name. The other two sides of the square are still occupied by rows of insignificant tenements; though, as a commencement has been made towards its adornment by planting rows of trees, these houses, as the tall, straight willows grow up, will no doubt give place to better ones. There are two other churches in the western part of the city, and one in what is called "*El pueblo Indio*" (Indian settlement), to the eastward, where there was quite an extensive village of the natives at the invasion by Almagro.

Not far from "El pueblo Indio" there is a large charity hospital, which was mainly erected by donations of individuals. A house of correction adjoins it. The hospital was only opened in 1850; and as it has been almost dependent for support, as it was for its foundation, on the philanthropy of the citizens, it has neither been completed in the manner originally contemplated by its beneficent authors, nor has it been able to succor all who have presented themselves. Its expenses are somewhat lessened by the employment of persons as nurses who have been sentenced to the house of correction. Only 35 patients can be accommodated, whose maintenance in 1850, including the pay of chaplain, stewards, doctor, surgeon, &c., amounted to $17,665.

There may also be enumerated among the public institutions a college for the education of young men, under the patronage of government. It is under the direction of French Jesuits, who occupy a convent belonging to the Merced church. Besides the income of the convent, amounting to $1,500, and a yearly stipend of $1,000 from the public treasury, each resident student pays them $207 for board. At this time there were 25 interns and only 11 day scholars. In addition to the duties imposed as an equivalent for the government subsidy, they are required by their contract with the Minister of Public Instruction to teach gratuitously a primary school of 30 scholars, should so many offer. A college for instruction in mineralogy and mineralogical chemistry is in course of organization, under the auspices of the Mining Board, and will shortly be in operation. But the number of those within the province who receive even rudimentary instruction is extremely limited, the best estimate fixing it at one in every 59. The whole number attending schools in 1850 was 885, of whom 725 were males and 160 females.

In a report recently made to the Minister of the Interior by the Intendente of the province, a most deplorable account is given of the ignorance of those surrounding him. He estimates the population of Atacama at 50,000 souls, of whom one half belonged to the department of Copiapó, though not more than a third of them were regarded as having permanent residences therein. The remaining two thirds were young men, strangers and natives, whose families live elsewhere in the republic. Although a country of great wealth, yet because of the extravagant prices at which everything is held, it presents few attractions for the translation of families; and, consequently, those who emigrate here, and who compose the majority of the population, are young bachelors, active tradesmen, robust journeymen, clever artisans, or hard-working miners—in short, people without domestic ties, or at least without such ties here, and who are, in fact, but a floating population. If the number of actual inhabitants be reduced to its true limits, that of the uneducated will not appear so great as at the first glance; yet the Intendente says: "It must be confessed that the condition of education is far from meeting public exigency, and many children live in the greatest ignorance and abandonment because of the wretchedness of their parents." Essentially industrial and active as they are, the people of Copiapó do not need so much a collegiate or scientific education as practical and rapid instruction for the masses. Here a disposition to labor predominates, because of its remunerative results; and few or none think of a civil or military career as at the capital, because they possess no attractions to men wholly preoccupied in lucrative speculations or personal occupations affording the highest pay.

In order to obviate the odium attendant on a condition of society so uninformed, a normal school for the preparation of teachers was commenced under the authority of the Intendente, and also a night school at which mechanics could attend gratuitously. Both were promising good results, though the provision for females remained neglected as before, and there were only two establishments in the whole city where they were admitted.

With one exception the houses are of a single story, and constructed much lower than those to the southward, because of the greater frequency of violent earthquakes. Scarcely a day in the year passes without one being felt. Like the dwellings at Santiago, they have two or three patios, and the arrangement of rooms is commodious, if not in accordance with European ideas of elegance. As it rarely rains, reeds laced to the rafters to form a roof are plastered with mud—a material much lighter than tiles, and which at the same time affords sufficient protection from water, whilst it diminishes the danger of destruction by earthquakes. There are probably not a dozen roofs of shingle, or other materials than those mentioned, in the whole place. Many of them being of great size, the rooms of those on the original street have very generally been rented for stores. In each of these may be found goods of almost every variety, as well as mining and agricultural implements. As there is very little mud at any time, and few suitable pebble-stones nearer than a mile and a half, only a street or two has been paved, nor has the municipal council given much thought to the necessity of sidewalks.

As to the people, they are a darker race than that in central Chile. This is attributable in part, perhaps, to heat reflected from the sand whilst journeying to and from the mines and port; though among the lower orders the depth of color is artificially increased, from the rare occasions when the external skin is brought into contact with water. The men are well formed and robust, taller than the majority of the same classes about Santiago, and retaining more of the aboriginal cast of feature. As much cannot be said of the women, who are decidedly homely and untidy, as well as wanting in that ease of carriage which even the lowest of the Santiaguinas possess. As my friends told me it was not very customary to visit ladies in their own houses, I went to the opera one evening, hoping to see something of the better classes, as well as of the style of Copiapó. If the samples present were an average, the city has little to boast of; and their musical taste will be estimated by the fact, that at the commencement of the last act of Bellini's *I Capuleti ed i Montecchi* (Rossi being the *prima donna*) there were just thirty persons in the house, of whom three were females, and two of these members of the operatic company!

There is only one inn for the accommodation of strangers, and no one would recommend this. Therefore, those who determine to visit Copiapó must be provided with such letters as will obtain them relief from its discomforts. My fellow-traveller had been left at the house of a friend who enjoys a most enviable reputation for intelligence, liberality of sentiment, wealth, and hospitality; and as a letter had been sent to me for him, Mr. Wheelwright urged that I should not even prove the privations of the hotel an hour, but stop there with the instruments and luggage at once. Such liberty was inexcusable in my estimation; and though earnestly hoping some of the letters with which friends had supplied me would facilitate a rescue before the next day passed, I started at once for the much decried *Fonda*. Succor, however, was nearer than anticipated; for the carriage had scarcely gone half a square before its driver was summoned to return, and the hospitalities of the mansion insisted on with a cordiality not less pleasant than acceptable. The friend who gave me the letter had also written to his relative by mail, and my arrival had been expected for some days.

On the third day after, I left Copiapó for the silver district of Chañarcillo, in company with a German friend long resident in Chile—one for whose assistance in the observations at the latter place, and instructive information during more than two years, I am under lasting obligations. On this occasion he took upon himself all the trouble of preparations for the journey, obtaining good mules and a careful arriero, as well as proper saddle-horses for our own use. Though the distance is only fifty miles, and their several packing cases formed a very light load for one animal, the cost of transportation of the magnetical instruments to the mines and back was thirty dollars—a sum which did not include the expenses of the arriero or animals. For freight of the same packages from Santiago to Valparaiso and back—a distance nearly double—the charge is very little more than one eighth, and one has nothing to do with the maintenance of animals, either biped or quadruped. We rode out of town by a road leading in a southeast direction up the course of the stream, and through a valley, or, more appropriately, through a ravine, which became perceptibly narrower every few hundred yards. So far as the meagre supply of water could be made available, there was verdure on either hand, and here and there attempts to cultivate trees and shrubbery; but the road itself, like that below Copiapó, is a mass of almost impalpable sand, ground up by constantly passing carts and mule trains. Within the first five or six leagues, three other ravines debouch on this; and the inclination of their beds, the rolled pebbles on the surface, and marks in the banks, warrant the belief that they were formerly occupied by streams, confluents of the Copiapó when it filled the valley from side to side more than half a mile across. But the directions from which they come, and the inclination of their beds, cause a doubt whether they could have been more than torrents from the Andes when rain fell more abundantly in past ages. The river here, at present, is scarcely larger than about Ramadillo; and to insure that every possible portion of land may be impartially moistened, it is led during alternate periods to opposite sides of the ravine. So valuable are its effects, that $4,000 was paid in the preceding year for the alfalfa (lucerne) which could be cut from a single quadra of ground.

As one follows the windings of the road from side to side of the narrow valley and encounters so many unmistakable marks of the action of water, it is impossible to doubt that the original stream once filled it to a depth navigable by vessels of considerable size. The erosions, too, are not in the vertical faces of earth and gravel cliffs only, but also in granite and porphyritic rocks that form projecting termini of hills abutting on the course of the ancient stream.

Eight leagues from Copiapó is the village of Totoralillo, a straggling and untidy place. It has a large establishment for the extraction of silver from the ores, and a small *Posada,* where we passed the night at a charge of six dollars for the feed of four horses and the right to contend with fleas in its comfortless beds. That the latter obtained more blood from our veins than the parsimonious allowance of dried fodder imparted to those of the animals, both Don Jorje and myself will make our 'davits to. The elevation of the village above the sea is rather less than 1,900 feet.

On the following morning, it was no privation to leave the tormentors in bed and start towards our destination an hour before daybreak; and had it been, the appearance of the heavens fully studded with stars would have amply compensated the loss. As dawn advanced, and the planet Venus rose over the crest of the hills to our left, the atmosphere was so transparent that we thought its crescent quite distinct; and this could scarcely have been an illusion, as both agreed in the direction of the line joining its cusps. When the stars faded, and increasing daylight enabled us to perceive the aridity of the soil, a few small and dwarfish shrubs high in the ravines, or an occasional venerable *Algarrobo* (*Prosopis siliquastrum*) in the midst of the valley, which had been spared by the wood-hunters, were the only green objects. There were no animals, and birds were both rare and diminutive.

Five or six miles above Totoralillo the road forks: that to the left continuing beside the stream to its head-waters and "*Come Cavallo*" pass; while the right-hand path, inclining more to the south, leads to Chañarcillo. Ascending a little knoll at the separation of the roads, we enter a ravine not more than a hundred yards across, with a more rapid ascent, and lying between more precipitous hills. Both sides of the road are strewn with immense masses of rock which earthquakes had tumbled from the cliffs above; and the ravines, perpendicular to the principal line, are partially filled with drift-sand, whose attrition has perceptibly worn off the western faces of the dark strata. One of the rocks thus hurled down at three or four leagues from Totoralillo has been named "*El Pabellon,*" from its resemblance to a tent. Its height will not differ greatly from ten feet, nor its base from ten feet square, the form being quite regular and perfect. Algarrobos are still met with at long intervals—sad tokens of departed fertility amid present desolation.

Above "El Pabellon" the inclination of the road is still more towards the coast, its general direction being west of south; and the constantly narrowing valley it winds along tells us, not less emphatically than the last, of the water that formerly flowed within it. Twelve leagues from Copiapó we reach "*La Angostura,*" two narrow gorges separated from each other by an elliptic basin, with a major axis of several hundred yards. The first gorge, or "Angostura" proper, is only wide enough for the passage of a single cart, and so tortuous that one cannot see half a bow-shot in advance. Rocks rise perpendicularly on either hand to many hundred feet, sometimes sloping away from, and at others overhanging the path, their apparently slight hold *in situ* rendering them fearful objects to pass beneath in a locality so visited by subterranean convulsions. An examination of the two sides shows them wonderfully parallel in many places, the cavities of one having its projecting counterpart on the opposite wall, and we irresistibly conclude that one of these convulsions has rent the hills asunder. How awful must have been the shock! With the associations inseparable from the scenes of the preceding December and April still fresh in memory, one could not help shuddering at finding himself on such a spot, irremediably enclosed in case of a like catastrophe. It is, beyond all question, the locality which exhibits terrestrial mutability more extraordinarily than any one I had ever visited. T e gradual uprising of a continent inch by inch, extending, as it does, through ages—the wearing away of mountain ranges by torrents originating in trickling drops from over-full lakes—both tell of *time* whose duration wearies the mind in its contemplation; but in the accomplishment of the event whose results we witness here, there was perhaps no time. In the twinkling of an eye, almost before thought could give birth to terror, the pent up storm burst forth, flung wide the massive rocks opposing its egress, and in a brief space the earth had again settled tremblingly to quietude.

The road to the mines formerly passed by a zigzag over the hill here; nor was it discovered that nature had provided a practicable one at the very base, until a short time ago. For fifteen years mule-trains had travelled over its steep ascent, hundreds of the poor animals falling victims to the toil. When found, even levelling was unnecessary, for this service had been performed by the stream whose waters had traversed the Angostura; and it was only requisite to blast a few rocks which subsequent earth-storms had cast into the narrow space, to make a perfect carriage road. At several places there are little handfuls of surface water, and the earth is quite moist all round them, though no attempt appears to have been made to excavate for a supply. This seems more extraordinary when one sees such numbers of mule carcasses literally strewing the road from the Angostura to the Cuesta de Chañarcillo, a range of hills separating waters originally flowing into the Copiapó from the affluents of the Guasco river. An abundant supply is found at the base and on the northwest side of the range just mentioned; and from the wells there dug, both the mule-trains and the nearer mines are furnished. When the neighborhood is blessed by a rain, a scanty stick-like pasturage suddenly springs up and matures with like celerity. This is carefully gathered by the people of the little Posada at the wells, and is doled out for the horses of travellers at prices exceeding that of equal weights of pure copper. As lumps of scoria still remain on the hill, and even in the *corral* of the Posada, a furnace must once have existed in the vicinity for smelting ores of this metal. No information respecting it could be obtained from the people.

At the base of the Cuesta, the northwest side, an aneroid barometer indicated an elevation of 4,412 feet above the ocean; where the road crosses the summit, 4,850 feet; and at the base, on the southeast side of the range, 4,597 feet. A new and winding road, more easy of ascent, was in course of construction, the old one being extremely precipitous and fatiguing. Several varieties of plants may be found near the summit, whose sustenance in the way of moisture must be entirely drawn from the dews at night, or fog-clouds that hang about it during the winter and spring months. Although there was a cold and driving wind in our faces, under whose influence even the horses became restive, it was impossible not to stop when we repassed it some days subsequently, for admiration of the tints enveloping the entire landscape from the far away snow-peaks of the Andes on our right to the strata of the immediate basins and ravines below us. If not already beneath our horizon, the sun must have been very near it, and was wholly obscured. Thus, most of the objects were seen at an angle oblique to the direction of his rays, and the hues were of the darkest yet sharpest characters. The snow-crests were of a rosy pink, the summits of the nearer hills bright orange, and each successive stratum between us and the bottom of the western valley of a gradually darker shade to the most decided violet.

From the base on the eastern side to "*El Bolaco,*" its southerly termination four leagues distant, there is a continual and rapid descent; and though the road lies through a ravine with somewhat similar characteristics as on the opposite side, the latter may have been but the channel for occasional rains whose water accumulated from the sides of bounding hills. I could not but be struck with the frequency of apertures in the banks and hills on both sides of the range, their numbers increasing, however, on the southern side of the cuesta. They were usually in the projecting shelves of rocks whose faces had been worn vertical for ten to twenty feet, were very irregular, and extended beyond my vision within the hill-sides. Many of them looked as though worn by the outward rushing of air. Can the explosive gas of earthquakes sometimes find exit through them?

El Bolaco, the name of the principal hill in this silver district, more commonly called "*Chañarcillo*," which is the name of the chain, is remarked as soon as a bend in the road permits it to be seen, from the contrast of its cream-colored or whitish-yellow surface with the dusky hue of all the neighboring eminences. It is partially separated from the range to which it belongs by a saddle or indentation perhaps 150 feet deep, and is quite steep on all sides, the multitudes of roads which lead to its many mines ascending by zigzag lines. The portion which contains nearly all the silver hitherto discovered here, may be a mile and a half in length at the base, by a mile in breadth—its longer line extending east and west. Where the road to the mine "*La Candelaria*" begins the ascent, on the N.W. side, the valley is 3,294 feet above the sea, and the mouth of the mine, on the very summit, 3,698 feet, or 900 feet lower than the *base* of the same range only twelve miles off. I am thus particular in stating the precise locality at which the first elevation was observed, because the ground in the valley next to the village of Juan Godoi is much lower. At the same time it is proper to state that all these determinations are in doubt 150 feet, owing to a change in the zero of the aneroid, occasioned by jolting so far on horseback.

Most uninviting is the aspect of the surface as one ascends. Patches of marly dolomite, for all the world like scoriæ recently released from the action of fire, and a multitude of dark apertures, each with its pile of darker rubbish before it, resembling the excavations of a huge ant-hill, are all that vary the monotony of its color. They tell me verdure does have a brief existence after Heaven pleases to grant a shower, but such boons are like fabled "visits of the angels;" and as one had not occurred for a year or two, there was no vegetation, and the assertion might very well have been doubted. Notwithstanding its absence, there is a beautiful prospect from the summit, embracing, through an opening between two hills, the sea on one side, a part of the Andes covered with snow in the opposite direction, a bright village at its foot, and the commencement of a plain dotted with hills far as the eye can reach. The sky was beautifully clear on the afternoon of our arrival, and we were permitted to see the sun as he sank beneath the ocean, gorgeously gilded by parting rays: nor was the view less lovely on another occasion, when the plain beneath us was obscured by a sea of clouds, through which the hill-tops projected as islands from the midst of waters. To us the sky was perfectly serene and clear, the early rays of the sun tinting the clouds most exquisitely.

We were kindly welcomed at "*La Candelaria*," one of the mines of which my hospitable host at Copiapó was the principal shareholder, and were soon ready to descend for a glimpse at its buried treasures. As most of the shafts are very steep, in order to go down with least inconvenience strangers ordinarily equip themselves in miners' costume—a leathern apron, or sort of petticoat, and hide sandals; but we selected "*La Guia*," which had been wrought more horizontally, and where, without these adjuncts, though tolerably stiff from the effects of a fifty miles' ride, quite reasonable progress could be made behind the torch-bearers who accompanied us over its jagged paths. In an atmosphere redolent with the smoke of gunpowder and the tallow torches of laborers, a novice wants all the assistance he can obtain from feet and hands and back, in the tortuous and nearly vertical holes through which he descends. Nor has his suffering ended when he returns to the light and air of heaven. A stiffness of the muscles, called by miners "*macurka*," usually follows next day, and even the slightest exertion of them is painful. Descending, in some places, beside the blackest abysses—climbing, in others, where one would have supposed only a goat could find foothold—winding, now in this direction, then to one opposite—warned every moment to lean to the left or to the right, to avoid the risk of falling into some of the numberless dark pits beside the lode—and startled, at intervals, by the explosion and reverberation of blasts in dozens of mines scattered through the hill—with no little satisfaction I reached the shaft from which they were extracting ore. Why stay long amid half naked men, toiling like so many Vulcans by torchlight in an unclean atmosphere, with huge hammers and bars, when one can leisurely examine the metals and crystals and strata by sunlight, and with the profile of the map before him? And so, after spending half an hour in witnessing the mode of breaking out the ores, and in looking at the walls from which some of the great wealth had been extracted and where some of the best crystals still remained, my amateur curiosity was fully satisfied, and there was no desire to brave the difficulties of any less accessible mine.

As there were only slight symptoms of the macurka next morning, the magnetical and other observations were commenced at once. Absolute knowledge of the meteorology was not to be expected from the brief period appointed for our stay; yet, as the changes observable during even a few days, in a locality so entirely unknown, are not without interest, a series was kept as regularly as other occupations would permit. These are given at length in Appendix B. Here it is only necessary to state that the mean height of the barometer, deduced from records at five equidistant periods between 9 A. M. and midnight, was 26.02 inches; the mean temperature of the air 61°.2; and that of the wet-bulb thermometer 45°.3. The extreme fluctuations were .105 inch in the pressure, and 14°.3 in the temperature of the atmosphere. Its deprivation of moisture is very great; and this, too, it must be remembered, was mid-winter, when there is more humidity than at any other period. Such was its effect, that the instrument boxes, which had withstood the summers of Santiago during two seasons, were nearly all opened by shrinkage or splitting of the boards. As would be expected, the electrical tension is high; a comb passed through the hair, or the hand brushed rapidly over cloth, being accompanied by sparks and audible noise, more particularly noticeable at night. Clouds, they told me, were most frequent in October, though rains, if any, occur only during the winter months; and when, by good fortune, there are two showers, the entire surface of the ground in the valley is covered with verdure and flowers to an extent known only in countries like this, where they lie dormant through several successive seasons. Hence, for animals as well as man, all the food must be brought from a distance, only a few goats being able to obtain partial subsistence in crevices or rocks inaccessible to less sure-footed creatures. Abstinent as they are of water, even they would perish but for the supply brought from wells at a distance of more than ten miles—for each cargo of which, consisting of sixteen gallons, the price is a dollar. This water, however, is only drunk by animals; nor is there any drinkable by man nearer than the wells on the other side of the Cuesta de Chañarcillo, and for whose sale a deposit is established midway. To these wells asses may go, and return to the mines on the same day.

On the night of July 6th the valley and the hill, to two thirds of its height below us, were enveloped in clouds; whilst over our heads the sky was almost blackly clear, the stars moving apparently in mid-space. Next morning we perceived that there had been a snow-storm on the Andes, which are distant, in a S.E. direction, 40 leagues by the travelled road. With such evaporation and temperature, the climate is charming even at mid-summer; and one needs only to protect his eyes from reflected light, to brave the direct rays of the sun without discomfort. But at such a period there is nothing to attract one out of doors; and were it not for the eternal booming of the blasts in its profound caverns, that come to the ear like discharges of heavy ordnance at a distance, the visitor at El Bolaco might readily imagine himself in the predicament of the poor wood-hunter one day in May, 1832—alone on its desolate summit. Even at this brief distance of time, there is some little difference in the accounts of the first discoverer of silver here. The best authenticated version is given by Señor Vallejos, and is somewhat as follows:

On the 18th of May, 1832, Juan Godoi, sole master and owner of a donkey or two, was enticed from his legitimate trade of wood-hunting to the more exciting occupation of Nimrod's disciples, by the sight of a browsing guanaco, and, with dogs in advance and lasso in hand, gave chase to the nimble-footed animal. In the pursuit fortune led him along the southern slope of El Bolaco, and there, thoroughly tired down, he rested on one of the loose stones half way to its steep summit, expecting no greater good luck than a return of the dogs to lead him to the captured animal, whose bounds he could no longer keep pace with. Possessing, as does nearly every resident of mineral regions, some knowledge of metallurgy, it was not long before he detected that his seat contained ore of the purest silver, in great quantities; and in the excitement of joyful surprise, guanaco, dogs, and donkeys too, would have been forgotten, but that the last afforded means to transport his treasures to Copiapó. The other story is, that Godoi was a goat-herd, and received intelligence of the existence of silver at this spot from his expiring mother.

Arrived with his specimens at the then straggling town, the discovery was imparted to Juan Callejas, an old friend and *cateador* (professional mine-hunter), who, during forty-odd years of privations, whilst examining the veins and strata of the province, had collected only the wealth of experience. When the formalities of denouncing (entering a *caveat* for) the mine had been completed, a title to one third of it was given to the friend and counsellor in fee; and the latter in like manner surrendered it to Don Miguel Gallo, a citizen of Copiapó, and one of the munificent patrons for whose many services Callejas owed a long debt of gratitude. The heirs of Señor Gallo are among the well known millionnaires of Chile; and it is said they still retain the original seat of Godoi found near the mouth of the mine, thence called *La Descubridora*.

When the little fortune which Godoi had picked from the surface was gone, his remaining two thirds interest was sold, and he withdrew from the cares of business to the enjoyment of the pleasures which his extensive riches would command. In the briefest time people discovered that Don Juan was a man of respectability, assuredly allied to many persons of distinction; facts which memory told him had never before been urged by the housekeepers who had bought *cargas* from the poor wood-hunter, and to whom they now rendered homage. Flattered, however, by their recognition, he could do no less than repay frequent and seemingly earnest demonstrations of regard, and prove his appreciation of the extreme anxiety displayed to gratify him. Thus, balls followed dinners, licentiousness succeeded balls, breakfasts came after the night orgies, and gambling filled the unappropriated hours of the day, until the lamp of extravagance, for want of the precious oil, gave symptoms of expiring. Alas! poor Godoi, thine was not the wonderful instrument of Alladin! As soon as the crowd perceived this state of things they took French leave, and Don Juan awoke one morning as poor as he was a few months before, and bitterly lamenting how unreal are dreams. Unfortunate hunter! ruined by a guanaco chase!—for not even a mule was left with which to resume the livelihood of wood-seeking, and drown the memory of hours spent in gluttony and vice. He was not destined to starve, however. When his poverty was made known to Señor Gallo, a share in the mine was generously given to him, from the sale of which $14,000 was realized, and a small *chacra* purchased near Coquimbo. There Godoi shortly afterwards died, leaving a bare subsistence for his family.*

More moderate in the gratification of his desires, old Callejas has wholly escaped such vicissitude. Satisfied by having enriched so generous a patron, a life of exemplary sobriety enables him to enjoy the gifts with which in turn he has been recompensed. The residence of his predilection is at the Descubridora, which he loves as the apple of his eye. His favorite rambles are in the *pique del agua* (water shaft), *fronton de Castillo* (the castle wall), *el fenomeno* (the phenomenon), *la paloma* (the pigeon); in short, among all those labyrinths of its dark caverns, the greater part of whose productive labors have been directed by himself. To him "La Descubridora" is a loved and beautiful daughter, spouse to an idolizing friend; each rich new shaft that is opened is an additional charm, hailed as would be the grandchild brought to his arms. Happy old man! to whom wilt thou impart thy philosophy?

Numbers of "Cateadores" were attracted to the vicinity by the noise of this discovery, and

* To perpetuate his name near the scene of a discovery which has since given so many millions to Chile, the little town which sprang up at the foot of the hill was called "Juan Godoi."

new veins have been found from time to time in different parts of the hill, until there are now 118 mines in operation. One of the most valuable was found by four laboring miners quite close to the Descubridora, and so near to it in point of time that the patent for it is said to have been pushed through the forms of office on the day before the issue of that for the discovery of Godoi. It was called *El Manto de los Bolados*, from the extraordinary number of nearly pure silver stones extracted from one hole in it within an incredibly short time. A single block cut out with chisels —for it could not be drilled and blasted—weighed more than 3,300 pounds ; the entire mass upwards of 6,000 pounds, yielding above $80,000. The value of the stones extracted from this locality, exclusive of what each squandered on his mistress, is known to have been not less than $700,000; yet though the same four men also found the rich *Bolaco*, not one of them has left a farthing with which to buy bread for housefuls of half-starved children. And the like may be said of nearly every discoverer of silver mines in Chile. The sudden acquisition of wealth leads to extravagance and riotous living before the mine is fairly in progress to meet consequent demands, and after a month or two the necessities of the debauchee can only be met by its sale. Thus, few mines in any of the mineral districts remain as heirlooms to the families of the finders ; and not one among all that have been found in El Bolaco, unless of those denounced within a year or two. "*Tres Puntas*," a district more recently rescued from obscurity, has still its original proprietors in many cases ; their swarthy, almost Indian complexion and rough hands betraying, in circles to which sudden wealth has given them access, their humble parentage and previously rough lives, as does also the stiffness of their manner and language.

The entrances to most of the mines on El Bolaco are enclosed by railings, within which the ores are deposited as they are brought up. On one or more sides of the enclosure are the residences for the *administrador* (superintendent), assayer, if there be one, and treasurer, together with apartments for one or more of the proprietors when they come to make a personal overhaul. Many of these houses, as at "*El Delirio*," "*La Descubridora*," "*La Candelaria*," and others, are commodious and well furnished, notwithstanding obstacles to obtaining supplies; and though the tables may not exhibit the profusion of fresh vegetables one may find at Santiago, they are abundantly supplied with all that should be desired by a reasonable man, even in the midst of vegetable life.

One is apt to believe that the life of a laboring miner is one of great hardship and privation, and in certain respects it is so. Toil beneath the surface of the ground, where the only air to enter the lungs is saturated with the smoke of gunpowder and burnt tallow, and where the light of day can never penetrate, is doubtless more painful than if the same muscles and nerves were similarly exerted under the blue vault of heaven; but beyond these discomforts, the miners at El Bolaco have neither hardships nor privations not encountered by their fellow-laborers above ground. None work more than eight hours per day, for which there is good pay and abundant food. True, if the mine is in "*buen beneficio*" (producing well), night brings no relaxation from toil ; but what matters day or night to those who delve in the very bowels of the earth? Who among them can say when comes the daylight? They are of two classes: *barreteros*—those who break out the ore; and *apires*—those who bring it to the surface, or, if the mine have one, to the mouth of a vertical shaft, whence it is lifted by a windlass. Within the past year or two, shafts of this kind have been cut to nearly all the old mines, the proprietors finding ventilation indispensable at the extremity of some of their lodes, even did they disregard the labor of conveying quantities of rubbish so far.

On an average, barreteros receive $25 and apires $12 per month, 20 ounces of fresh baked bread, 24 figs, 16 ounces of boiled beans, and 6 ounces of wheat, daily—an amount of food quite sufficient to maintain two men—their families being thus tacitly acknowledged. The wheat is either boiled with the beans, or is made into *mote*, by scalding in lye, to remove the husks. They are generally strong, athletic men, with broader shoulders, deeper chests, and more muscular limbs than those engaged in agricultural life. Yet, while they all seem to enjoy the very best health, one is rarely known to live more than fifty years. There are instances of miners seventy years of age, but these are extremely rare. Apires are young men whose powers are scarcely developed, their promotion to barreteros depending on the experience obtained and strength acquired by practice. Some of them will bring on their shoulders, from depths of 120 yards, hide sacks of ores or stone weighing from 250 to 375 pounds, and one has been known to bring no less than 425 pounds up the rugged shaft that distance. It is painful to witness one of these half-naked fellows issue from the mine under such a load. With features distorted, eyes starting, perspiration dripping from every tensely-strained muscle, as he comes staggering into the fresh air, a shrill, deep-drawn breath penetrates to your very marrow, and tells more forciby than all of the bodily exertion. But as you turn from the man to the treasures he throws down in the light of day, he will have dashed the trickling drops from his brow, drank copiously from a cask of water near by, and you just catch a glimpse of his head as he descends for another load, very probably humming a stanza from some ribald song. Besides being short-lived, it has also been remarked that they have fewer children than their countrymen engaged in other pursuits—a fact not traceable to infidelity or analogous causes, but more probably attributable to the influence of impure air on their systems and fatigue of the body when they come out from the mines at the expiration of their periods of labor. When taken sick, the worthless or indifferent are discharged at once, the faithful laborer only being retained in wages and food until able to resume work. Physicians or surgeons there are none, and the only knowledge of the healing art is what the *administradores* may pick up by experience, and is possessed by the *medicas* who may be found about every inhabited place. Should the vein they are working exhibit symptoms of failing, which their experience from boyhood soon enables them to perceive, many of them quit the mine at the end of their month for a more productive one, from which they may have opportunities to steal richer stones. These last are perquisites entering into their calculations to an almost incredible extent, since it is estimated that the amount of *cangalla* (stolen metal) is at least from three to four per cent. of all the ore broken out. Most of the *cangalleros* (buyers of stolen metal) reside at Juan Godoi and Huasco; and such has heretofore been the integrity observed by these two classes in their dealings with each other, as well as the pertinacious refusal of miners to take employment where they are submitted to such espionage as prevents pilfering, that it has been found indispensable to wink at both thieving and receiving. The cangalleros, on several of whom it is easy to place one's finger, gather wealth rapidly; the barretero or apire obtains only enough to drown his compunctions of conscience for an hour or two at most. Of course none but the very richest stones of the vein are stolen. These the barretero breaks out, and the apire may afterwards stop and assort, before the administrador sees them.

Of 1,750 laborers employed in this district, about one third are Argentines; the remainder Chilenos, with very few exceptions. From their better knowledge, English miners always find immediate occupation, at high wages, and some few have found their way here. Whether mining induces a disposition to gamble, is a question already suggested, and cannot properly be answered respecting a race who have inherited the passion so strongly as nine tenths of the Hispano-Americans; though when we hear of the extravagant sums almost daily risked by Copiapinos, and of the multitude of fines imposed on their humbler imitators at the mines, who incur the misfortune of detection in the same offence, it is reasonable to believe that the occupation does have such an influence. Whilst the wealthy in the city win and lose their thousands of ounces ($85,000 in one *known* case) at a single sitting, and the guardians of the law intentionally overlook it, the barretero or apire is instantly arraigned to appease its violated majesty. The *Subdelegado* stated, during a visit made to me, that more than one hundred had been convicted of gambling in the preceding month, and that it was almost the only crime of constant occurrence among the 4,500 people of all classes embraced within his district. At the same time, they are so obedient to the law, that three of the soldiers who form the police had arrested twenty persons in one group, and brought them before him unresistingly. As an offset to this vice, they possess the most disinterested generosity, and, should his punishment admit such substitute, will surrender the entire earnings of a month, or even a greater sum, if it can be obtained in advance, to secure a companion from prison.

Under the orders of the proprietor, the direction of the work is confided to an administrador, usually a man of experience, whose salary is in proportion to the extent and productiveness of the mine, and ranges from $800 to $3,000 per annum. Though few, if any, possess the least acquaintance with geology or theoretical mineralogy, they are men of great observation and practical knowledge. Should the mine have several shareholders, the duty of supervision and instruction is performed by each proprietor in turn. Besides the classes of operatives named, there are blacksmiths, water-carriers, and *mayordomos*—the general duty of the last being to see that the metal be not abstracted during the process of breaking up. Their pay is from $300 to $600 per year.

In the *Annales des Mines*, Vol. IX, Prof. Domeyko gives the following geological description of El Bolaco: "The whole hill of Chañarcillo is composed of calcareous rocks, more or less argillaceous, compact, or earthy; some dolomitic, others containing only traces of magnesia. Sandstone is not seen, nor schist, properly so called; neither are there conglomerates, nor rocks of crystalline structure. The entire mountain is formed in regular and nearly horizontal strata, slightly dipping to the west in concordant stratification. The aspect of the formation announces a period of tranquillity and continuity of acting causes.

"The argil of these rocks is composed of two distinct parts, of which one is white, and not acted on by acids; the other a hydro-silicate of alumina and iron, which may be acted on—the silicate being soluble in a solution of potassium. It is wholly to the very variable proportions of this argil that are due the different aspects of the rock—its compactness and fracture—and which, probably, more than anything else, influences the richness of the mines traversing it.

"The more or less blue color of the rocks is not due to bitumen, but to a silicate of the protoxide of iron, which they contain. When boiled with muriatic acid, they also leave a white residuum.

"I found no organic remains in any part of the mountain which contained metallic veins, although, as I have said, they have been found along the road to the eastward, and near to Molle, as well as along the northwest road, in the environs of Ingenio. Nevertheless, I am assured that an ammonite was found in a rock of the mine *Reventon Colorado* at many yards below the surface.

"It is about three hundred metres in a vertical line from the summit of the plateau to the bottom of the lowest worked mine on this mountain, and we can distinguish three parts or stages in this thickness of the formation. We commence with the uppermost.

"The plateau at the top is composed of a stratum whose thickness varies with the inequality of the surface, but which on the northeast side is from twenty-five to thirty metres. It is composed of marly dolomitic rock, containing more than two thirds of its weight of argil; its color a yellowish gray, and its fracture a plane covered with dendrites. The whole rock is found completely fissured, and often full of cavities and hollows produced by the fracturing. The surfaces of the fissures, as also those of the cavities, are covered with small bright crystals of spathic lime. The cavities are also found filled with angular fragments of the same rock, each fragment covered on all sides with the same crystalline crust perceptible on the walls of the cavities. On the eastern slope of the same plateau, a part of the stratum is so fractured that it resembles a succession of enormous angular blocks of the same rock, whose interstices are often filled with marly matter pulverulent as chalk, and mixed with small stones of the same stratum. The pulverulent material gave the following analysis:

Carbonate of lime	0.335
Carbonate of magnesia	0.052
Alumina and oxide of iron	0.101
Silica soluble in potassium	0.170
Argil not acted on	0.270
Water and loss	0.072 = 1.000

"Considerable masses of the chloro-bromide of silver are found in the crevices, hollows, and cavities in the rock of this stratum. In general, the external aspect of the rock, its innumerable crevices and dislocations, its cavities filled with broken pieces of the same, all denote that this portion of the hill has experienced *in situ* reiterated shocks posterior to its formation, and independently of the movement upheaving the rest. We will call this part of the hill the *plateau* stratum; miners are in the habit of designating the lower portions of the same formation by the name of *manto*.

"Below this stratum follow others of divers thicknesses, composing that part of the mountain called by the miners *mesa-piedra* (literally stone table), and which they consider entirely sterile, because the greater number of the veins traversing it become poor or entirely sterile. The rocks constituting this stage differ little in their composition from those above; they are generally more argillaceous and compact; their fractures following old fissures, so that it is difficult to obtain a new one. Moreover, the surfaces of fractures ordinarily present dendritic designs, and the rock exhales a strong argillaceous odor when breathed upon.

"A sample of rock from this *mesa-piedra* taken from the Valenciana, gave fifty-eight per centum of argil not acted on, and six per centum of similar substance affected by acids.

"The strata of this part of the mountain are more regular than those above, and have neither the clefts nor the cavities mentioned as belonging to the preceding. The entire stratum of the *mesa-piedra* is about one hundred metres thick.

"About one hundred and thirty metres below the surface of the plateau begin strata called by the miners *mantos pintadores*, or strata that enrich veins. The most common rock is a calcareous clay containing about forty per centum of residuum not acted on by acids and containing only traces of magnesia. Its color is a bluish-grey, spotted with yellow; its structure compact, and fracture conchoidal, splintering in some parts. In general it much resembles the calcareous rocks most widely spread in the muscle-chalk formation of Europe.

"The stage which comprises all these strata, or *mantos pintadores*, encloses the principal wealth of the Chañarcillo mines, and the true lines of the chloro-bromide silver ores. It descends to thirty or forty metres below the surface of the mine of San José, situated near the base of the mountain. The two spiral hills (*collines en limaçon*) are also in the same vicinity, and I think I am not much deceived in estimaing the thickness of this stage at one hundred and twenty metres, which is divided into strata of divers thicknesses, though always composed of the same rock. Indeed, this undergoes very slight modifications of structure and color, and its strata are ordinarily thick, though sometimes separated from one another by an extremely thin layer of yellowish argil.

"Beneath this stage, and about two hundred and forty metres below the surface of the plateau, a second *mesa-piedra* is reached similar to the one above, causing metals to disappear from the veins in the same manner as the other. It is composed of rocks which are harder, more argillaceous, and more compact than those of the preceding stage, and to me is apparently not less thick. Up to the present moment (1846) it has only been observed in the mine of San José; and consequently we cannot decide whether it renders all the veins in that part of the mountain sterile, or only those of the mine cited.

"In the last, at the bottom of the deepest excavations, we also find a porphyroidal rock similar to that seen on the road from Ingenio to Chañarcillo. This rock effervesces with acids; we perceive within it incomplete feldspathic crystals disseminated amid a greyish paste, and its crevices are spread over with a red argil. It is found to be composed of—

Carbonate of lime	0.076
Carbonate of magnesia	0.034
Part acted on by acids	0.316, holding 0.08 of silica soluble in potassium.
Part not acted on	0.572 = 0.998

"I should add that the argillaceous rocks, those containing a small proportion of carbonate of lime, sometimes have a schistoidal structure, as we see on the western slope of the mountain near *Bolaco Nuevo;* and secondly, that on the northwest side, towards the mountains touching

Chañarcillo, we meet layers of porphyritic rocks having the same external characteristics as the rocks on the road from Ingenio, and those we shall see more fully developed in the mountain of *Agua Amarga.*"

Of the one hundred and fifteen mines* discovered and actually worked in El Bolaco at the time of our visit, only eighteen much more than paid expenses, and but four yielded abundantly. These were La Descubridora, El Delirio, San Francisco, and San José. Work in the others is continued in expectation that a rich vein will again be struck, many hundred thousand dollars being annually spent, for which not one dollar is immediately received in return. But the miner never gives up hope in El Bolaco, and never abandons the mine there for which he has been so lucky as to secure a patent.

The longest horizontal shaft excavated so far, is about four hundred yards; the greatest depth attained in any mine, about two hundred yards. All the best veins have a direction nearly north and south, the most productive inclining to the east. If the inclination be to the westward of north, it is regarded as an unfavorable symptom, and is very discouraging, because all such have hitherto proved to contain very poor metal. Though the several mines contain almost every combination of silver, no other metals have been found in El Bolaco, as there has been at some of the hills in the province of Coquimbo. Of 10,488,088 pounds of ore extracted and conveyed to the amalgamating establishments during the year 1850, its cost to the miners delivered and reduced was $600,000; and the clear profit to them, $2,100,000. In addition to the sum spent at the fruitful mines and their products, it is estimated that $400,000 was paid to persons employed in excavations producing nothing. Sometimes there are veins situated between others yielding the richest ores, but which on working prove wholly valueless. One in particular, so favorably situated in this respect, and externally promising so well, caused the ruin of every one who persevered in its deceitful exploration.

The following table will show to what extent silver mining is carried on in the province, and what were some of its results during the year 1850.

Mining district.	Number of productive mines.	Number of sterile mines.	Greatest number worked during the year.	Number of persons employed.	Pounds of ore extracted.
Chañarcillo	18	97	116	1,760	10,488,088
Tres Puntas	36	17	74	629	3,098,817
San Antonio	7	7	14	99	476,275
Romero	5	17	22	188	475,567
San José de Garin	5	12	22	148	524,100
Sacramento	4	8	46	90	336,149
Totals	75	158	294	2,914	15,398,996

Of these two hundred and ninety-four silver mines, there were only two hundred and fifty-five worked at the close of the year; the remainder had been abandoned. The other mines in operation were as follows:

Department.	Number of copper mines.	Number of laborers.	Number of gold mines.	Number of laborers.
Copiapó	14	128	6	46
Freirina	60	605	5	38
Vallenar	10	133		
Totals	84	866	11	84

* This is the number given in the report of the Intendente. On the spot one hundred and eighteen were named to me, and the latter number is more probably correct for the date at which I write—1851.

When brought up from the mines, ores are deposited in the *canchas*, as the enclosed yards are called. All those which will amalgamate with quicksilver are broken in pieces of about half a cubic inch, and assorted in three piles of different qualities, according to their richness. So well versed in ores do the men employed in breaking them become, that they tell by the touch, rather than by weight, to which of the piles a stone properly belongs. The fracture of the richest ores is most asperous. Other ores, denominated *metales frios*, comprising sulphurets, arseniates, &c., from which the silver cannot be obtained by amalgamation, are left in pieces just large enough to be easily transported, and are sent out of the country for reduction. When broken, and the accumulated dust is expelled by winnowing, as they do chaff from wheat, by tossing it in the air, the share of each proprietor is carefully weighed, and disposed of in conformity with his directions. There is a large quantity of ore, however, of which no use has been made to the present time, because the proportion of silver it contains is too small to justify the expense of transportation and amalgamation. Where water is so scarce, even for the latter purpose, and mule-hire so extravagant, unless the ore will yield fifteen marks to the *cajon* ($150 for 6,400 pounds), it remains in a heap before the mouth of the mine. Of this character there are now lying at El Bolaco ores that are estimated to contain not less than $20,000,000. A railroad connecting with that from Caldera has been pronounced practicable, by following the bank of the stream until it turns the northeast flank of Chañarcillo, and thence down to El Bolaco; and this silver cannot lie in waste much longer.

For extraction of metal from the ores, there are eighteen establishments in the district of Copiapó—all of them the property of companies or individuals. There is strict accountability in each of them, which offers security to the miner, independently of the criterion which the analysis of his ores affords him. In seventeen mills the system of Cooper is followed; in the other the old mode of treading the amalgam until the silver and mercury are thoroughly incorporated, when the earthy portions are washed away, and only the combined metals are left. Both men and animals are sometimes weeks in treading the metallic *tortas* (cakes). Most of these establishments are within the city—the others at various points along the stream above it. The machinery and mode of operations are as follows:

A circular block of granite, about three feet in diameter and fifteen or sixteen inches thick, is secured to an upright revolving shaft. This stone revolves over the flat surface of another block of the same material, placed at the bottom of a strong wooden tub, partially filled with water, and into which the ores are thrown, in the condition in which they come from the mine. In the course of a few hours, according to the character of the ores, they may be ground between these two stones as fine as flour. Thence they are drawn into large vats or tanks, and the heavier portions having settled at the bottom, the clear water is drawn off. In a second apartment there are other tubs of wood, somewhat larger than those used in the grinding process. These have discs of iron at the bottom, with a single groove from the centre to an aperture on one side. To an axis revolving vertically within each tub there are four iron arms, bent into this form,

whose motion with the axis or shaft preserves a constant agitation of the semi-fluid mass poured in from the vats. A due portion of quicksilver being added, the two metals will have become united, and sink to the bottom in six or eight hours, leaving the earthy substances still in solution. The former is then drawn off into a cavity beneath the floor, and poured into leathern or buckskin bags, through whose pores the larger portion of the quicksilver rapidly filters, and a silver as soft as putty remains. This being put into moulds, and subjected to pressure, another portion of the mercury is forced out, and the remainder is finally driven off by evaporation. For this purpose the *piñas*, as the moulds of metal are called, are placed under iron bells, resting on vessels of water within a furnace, and subjected to great heat. When all the quicksilver has been expelled, the silver is quite porous, and may easily be indented with the finger-nail. In this condition it is the *plata piña** of commerce, though before exportation the metal has latterly and very generally been formed into solid bars, after melting in other furnaces.

The whole process occupies only from 24 to 36 hours, according to the durability and other characteristics of the ores. Very little of the quicksilver is lost. The portion driven off by fire is received under the iron bells, and condensed in the water; and that remaining with the ground ores, having found no silver with which it could amalgamate, is afterwards washed out when the earthy particles have all subsided, and the water has been drawn off. Some few years since, one of the establishments, being short, borrowed a quantity of quicksilver from a native, and poured the whole into tubs, with ores that had been brought from one of the mines in the province of Coquimbo. At the end of the process, *more* quicksilver was found than had been borrowed—a fact no little surprising, until it was demonstratively ascertained that the vein contained a combination of pure mercury and silver, amounting to 13½ per cent. of the former and 86½ per cent. of the latter metal. This metal has since been called *arquerite*, from "Arqueros," the name of the mine in Coquimbo where it was found.

Prof. Domeyko says of this mineral:† "Disseminated in masses, sometimes filiform and crystallized in regular octahedrons. Its color, silver-white; the lustre, structure, and other characteristics are the same as those of native silver, for which it was for a long time mistaken. Its specific gravity is 10.80. Under the blow-pipe it throws off sublimate of mercury; and, on the introduction of melted lead to it in a cupel, it throws off drops of silver, which remain at the edge of the cupel. Dissolved in nitric acid, the application of muriatic acid produces a white precipitate, which blackens very little under the action of light. It is found in great abundance in the silver mines of Arqueros, in Chile, which scarcely yield any other silver mineral. Its gangue is sulphate of barytes, arsenate of cobalt," &c.

The reader is referred also to the accompanying report, by Prof. J. Lawrence Smith, containing an analysis of the specimens brought home by the Astronomical Expedition.

The *relaves*, as the earthy substances are called, sometimes contain as much as fifty per cent. of sulphurets and arseniates of silver, and, when dried, were sold for export to England, there being no smelting furnaces for silver ores then completed in Chile. There was one erecting at the "*Delirio*" mine at the time of our visit, which was regarded to be as mad a scheme as the project of working this very mine was pronounced to be some few years ago; and a patent or exclusive privilege was subsequently granted to an English gentleman, who proposed the erection of other furnaces at Caldera and Coquimbo. Water and animals have hitherto served as motive powers for the very simple machinery of the amalgamating mills; but now that coal may be transported on the railway from Caldera at comparatively reasonable rates, proprietors are discussing the advantages of steam, and there is no doubt that the substitution will soon be made.

* *Pine-apple silver*, probably from the shape of the moulds into which it is passed from the leathern bags.

† Elementos de Mineralogia: Por Ignacio Domeyko. Serena. 1845.

The following table will afford some idea of the amount of work, the purity of the metals from different mines, and the cost of reduction. Capital letters following the names of mines are initials of the several mineral districts. All not marked are within the Chañarcillo (Bolaco) district.

Amalgamating establishment of Cerillos, 1850.

Names of mines.	Weight of the ores delivered.	Value of the silver produced.	Silver, per pound.	Costs of amalgamation.	Other charges.	Deduction in favor of the miner.
	Pounds.					
Manto de Ossa	29,750	$9,391 25	$0 31.57	$1,025 12	$183 00	$74 37
Valenciana	195,650	47,202 89	24.54	4,808 93	1,274 12	489 12
Retamo	51,996	173,519 30	3 41.16	7,339 00	189 12	139 00
Delirio	810,068	297,259 65	36.70	23,159 06	5,281 25	2,906 93
Siete Denuncios, G	13,860	3,031 59	21.87	378 44		
Manto de Ossa	1,072,050	72,311 50	6.75	12,623 25	7,515 69	2,026 12
Descubridora	553,039	149,186 25	26.96	14,544 31	4,551 37	1,384 50
Carpas	25,200	2,637 90	10.46	402 56	214 37	63 00
Santo Domingo	55,650	5,260 27	9.42	795 50	153 62	140 87
Rosario, 1°	2,275	279 14	12.27	40 87	17 87	5 69
San Antonio del Mar	5,600	586 56	10.48	94 93	46 75	14 00
Ave Maria, S	1,190	282 50	24.61	35 25		
Descubridora, S	10,500	1,073 81	10.19	167 62	88 00	26 25
Cobriza, S	75,250	1,719 14	2.29	384 87	602 25	188 12
Manto Peralta	18,200	708 60	3.89	162 56	110 50	45 50
Cuatro Amigos, R	5,600	194 62	3 59	64 87	36 00	
Sin Pleito, G	2,885	111 93	3.89	37 31		
Merceditas, T. P	691	241 87	35.01	26 87		
San Ramon	9,700	3,404 25	35.09	353 75	59 00	24 50
Guia de Carvallo	33,950	8,445 25	24.89	1,073 69		93 25
Specimens	Not stated.	253 68		14 12		

The charge for amalgamation is according to the *ley* or ratio of pure silver contained in the ore, as ascertained by the analysis. This is expressed by the number of *marks* of bar silver that a cajon will yield. A mark is eight ounces, which, in preparing the above table, I have valued at $9. The deduction in favor of the miner is not made at any other establishment, and its presumed object is to attract custom. No returns from them for other years were obtainable; and in their absence we can best judge of the increase of the mining interest from the returns of silver exported since 1830 from the Copiapó custom-house.

Year.	Value of silver exported.	Year.	Value of silver exported.
1830	$59,931	1841	$739,009
1831	53,373	1842	745,563
1832	294,609	1843	622,792
1833	847,343	1844	1,106,949
1834	745,140	1845	1,381,030
1835	761,406	1846	1,444,143
1836	154,839	1847	1,836,940
1837	526,042	1848	2,349,996
1838	572,539	1849	3,080,157
1839	933,897	1850	3,555,045
1840	173,240	1851	2,134,653

I could not learn any satisfactory reason for the great falling off in the exportations of 1836 and 1840; and we must attribute it to the variable success to which mining is subject. That of 1851 is attributable to the revolutionary condition of the country, and the temporary abandonment of many mines in consequence thereof. The rapid increase in 1849 is principally due to the discoveries at *Tres Puntas* in September of that year.

Besides the silver exported in 1850, there were also sent from the province:

	From Copiapó.	From Huasco.
Bar copper	$4,932 00	$169,720
Regulus		346,366
Copper ore	45,291 00	59,223
Sulphurets, &c., of silver	1,324,750 00	362,220
Refuse ores	134 00	
Gold	10 50	
Totals	$1,375,117 50	$937,529

Making an aggregate of $5,867,691, of which $2,659,021 was shipped from Copiapó to Valparaiso, and the remainder direct to foreign markets; equal proportions having followed like destinations from Huasco.

In 1849 the mineral district of *Tres Puntas* was found. It is within the desert of Atacama, and distant from the city of Copiapó, in a northwest direction, some seventy-five miles. A road known as the "*camino de los Incas,*" which proceeds to the north, in an almost arrow-like line, from the vicinity of the city, for the first time in that distance makes a detour round the base of these hills, and resumes its original direction on the opposite side. It would thus appear that the followers of "the children of the sun" never learned of the entombed wealth beside the path so strangely departed from, the stones marking which are elsewhere in an undeviating line over hill and valley. The summit of the hill is about 7,500 feet above the ocean. Within many leagues of the mines there is not a drop of water; yet so astonishing were the accounts of its riches, that professional mine-hunters immediately flocked to it from all parts of the province, and already it rivals Chañarcillo, both in the number of mines wrought and operatives. Most extraordinary are the accounts respecting veins found in some of its mines, the almost fabulous narrations of the early discoveries at Chañarcillo being cast into the shadow by the millions that it is said may be embraced in a glance in the "*Buena Esperanza.*" Only such fortune can compensate one for remaining in a country utterly arid, where even the air is so parched that the skin of the face and hands cracks during the first four or five days, and the nostrils, eyelids, and ears become painful to the touch. At first it was necessary to transport everything from Copiapó; though latterly provisions have been sent from the southern provinces to the little roadstead of Flamenco, about twenty-five leagues to the westward. Chañarcillo, also, derives a portion of its supplies through the port of Totoral, twelve leagues west of it, by the road across an equally desert plain. Yet the cost of every necessity can only be properly appreciated from a statement of the actual prices. In 1850 they were as follows:

Prices of Articles most consumed at the Mines.

Mineral districts.	Flour, per 200 pounds.	Meat, per 100 pounds.	Beans, per fanega.	Water, per gallon.	Barley, per fanega.	Dry clover, per 100 pounds.	Wheat straw, per 100 pounds.	Fire-wood, per 100 pounds.	Charcoal, per 100 pounds.	Coal, per 100 pounds.
Tres Puntas	$17 *a* 18	$20 00	$7 50	$0.6	$12 00	$6 00	$3 00	$1 50		$4 50
Chañarcillo	15 *a* 16	18 00	7 00	6	6 50	4 50	1 75	62½	$1 50	2 50
Romero	15 *a* 16	18 00	7 00	2½	9 00	6 00	62½	50		
San Antonio	15 *a* 16	18 00	7 00	1	7 50	1 50	75	62½		
Sacramento	15 50	18 00	7 00	2½	8 50	5 00	75	62½		
Garin	16 00	20 00	7 00	3	10 50	6 00	75	62½		

With such inevitable expenses, it is impossible to work many of the multitude of copper-mines found in almost every part of the province, those only which are near the coast repaying cost. Yet the cateadores are none the less busy, but continue to pass days and weeks examining and denouncing their discoveries in expectation that a day will come when they may sell or work to advantage. What privations this class of men undergo can only be estimated by one who visits a country that offers no resources to sustain or shelter life north of latitude 30°, and who sees them take leave of their fellow-men. Their whole equipment is a mule or two loaded with water and provisions, and they are uncertain whether they will obtain other reward for their toil than a scanty allowance of food from day to day. One of them told me he once found himself near the base of the Andes in the desert of Atacama, without a drop of water for either the animals or himself, when, after hunting nearly all day, he espied a green-looking spot high in a ravine, surely indicating a supply of the longed-for element. Reaching it after several hours of fatiguing travel, it proved as bitter as the waters of the sea of Sodom. Even his mules would not drink of it; nor did he succeed in finding a potable supply until late next day, when scarcely able to drag one foot after the other. His journey was also at midsummer, when there are no clouds to screen one from the sun's scorching rays, and the reflection from the sand and rocky hill-sides is really terrific. Think of passing weeks in such a country and climate, with saddle-cloths or sand for a bed, a saddle for a pillow, the sky as a cover, and a little charqui or cheese and hard bread, with water, the only food!

So far it has been ascertained that the metallic distributions in northern Chile are almost uniformly regular. Gold ores are found in the Andes; silver veins in the chains of hills next west; and copper most abundantly in the elevations nearer to the coast. The following returns were made to the Intendente for the year 1850:

Mines discovered and claimed.

Months.	Gold.	Silver.	Copper.	Quicksilver.	Cobalt.	Iron.	Coal.
January	1	25	1		1		
February		18					
March		89	3	1			
April	2	50	4				4
May		60	1			2	
June		51					
July	2	32	7				
August		50	10				1
September	1	49	7				
October		26	13				
November	3	31	8				
December	2	14	3				
Totals	11	495	57	1	1	2	5

In accordance with the *Ordenanzas de Mineria*, when a new mine is discovered, the finder must designate its location before the proper tribunal; specify the direction and inclination of the vein; excavate an aperture one and a half varas in diameter, by thirty varas deep, in the line of the vein; and then publish a notice of the same, stating the day and hour of his discovery. Should no other person establish priority of discovery within a reasonable time, he is entitled to a patent for a portion of ground embracing it, which shall be 200 varas long, with a breadth varying from 200 varas when the vein is perpendicular, to 112½ varas if its inclination is 45°. It is of no consequence whether the land on which the discovery is made be private property or not—the finder has the same rights; and should it be an entirely new district, he is further entitled to three contiguous lots, of which his vein may be embraced in the central one. Should there be more than one vein, he may claim a fee-simple title to a lot embracing each of them. The *Ordenanza* excludes foreigners from these privileges; but *custom* has abrogated law, and they now enjoy equal rights with natives.

Mines abandoned and re-denounced in 1850.

Months.	Gold.	Silver.	Copper.	Quicksilver.
January	2	21	6	1
February	2	15	8	
March	1	29	3	
April	1	31	11	
May		18	3	
June	1	30	1	1
July		18	7	
August		25	15	
September		9	8	
October	1	17	6	
November	1	15	6	
December		4	7	
Totals	9	232	81	2

Want of knowledge not only in scientific mining, but even of the simple processes of surveying, soon led to disappointments, losses, altercations, and lawsuits, as numberless, almost, as the mines at Chañarcillo, and many a lawyer came in for the lion's share of the profits. By law each mine is divided into twenty-four shares, or parts, called "*varas*," one or all of which may be assigned or transferred by its proprietor, like any other stock. Probably the earliest suit dates from the "*Colorada*" (red) mine, whose discoverer, one Peralta, generously went on distributing shares until apparent sterility brought thoughtless prodigality to a stop; though it is said that before the mine was abandoned he had actually given away many more shares than it represented. Shortly afterwards other claimants denounced the Colorada; and with the opening of a valuable vein, up sprung the recipients of Peralta's generosity, each of whom filed a suit for his share, endeavoring to show that the legal period had not transpired between the abandonment and re-denunciation, so that "La Colorada" has become celebrated in the legal annals of Copiapó. But this is not the only one on the docket. Nearly a hundred others were similarly locked up; and so universal had suits become, that the proprietor of a modern discovery finding his title unquestioned, named the mine "*Sin pleito*"—without a law-suit. If those now pending can be permanently adjusted, the numbers will undoubtedly diminish with the increase of intelligence necessarily to result from the school for special education in mining operations. The Mining Board, who direct all matters appertaining to the mining interest, could not have made a more useful or wiser application of a portion of their funds than in this establishment.

This board (*Junta de Mineria*) is chosen by the miners to represent them with the Intendente and general government, as well as to prescribe rules for their common welfare. For the purpose of perfecting such propositions as are assented to by the local or general government, a share of all metals confiscated for violations of law, and a tax of half a real on every mark of silver exported through the custom-house, are assigned them as revenue. With this they pay for the police of the several mining districts; the repairs of roads; a chaplain at El Bolaco; and a contribution to the city hospital. About $50,000 were thus received and expended in 1850; part of it being for the expenses of laborers from the southern provinces. Want of operatives in the mining districts made it necessary to offer a free passage and a bonus to every family that would come to Atacama for labor in the mines; and when it is remembered how indolent are the lower orders, how little they care for the morrow, and how impossible it is with their habits to save sufficient for such a journey, it will be justly inferred that this was the only mode to obtain them. The inducements held out by the *Junta* tempted no less than 1,500 to emigrate within twelve or fourteen months after their offer was generally made known.

For the reasons already stated, numerous as are the mines, and rich as are many of the copper ores in the province, very little had been done with them prior to 1851. That the railroad, by reducing the cost of transportation to one half, will bring coal to a price which will permit its use at the capital, or the ores be conveyed to the port at a fair profit, and thus force these mines into operation, I have not the least doubt. Huasco in this respect is much better located. Its mines are in many cases quite near, coal comes from England in ballast, and fifteen furnaces find constant employment. At the city of Copiapó there are but five furnaces, and their fires are supplied with wood of a very indifferent kind.

We returned to Copiapó on the morning of the 8th, having passed the preceding night at Totorallillo, and with pretty much the same fate as on the journey up; so that it was no trifling pleasure to enter again the commodious establishment of my hospitable host. To speak only of the hospitality of the Copiapinos would be to do great injustice to other traits of character not less appreciable, and I should violate my own impulses not to express gratitude for the unremitting kindness and civility of those whom it was my good fortune to meet. In their agreeable conversation, in offers of service, whether to aid in observations, to accompany me to interesting localities, or in presenting rare specimens of silver ores, they seemed never to tire in the four remaining days of the visit.

From circum-meridian observations of the sun and stars on opposite sides of the zenith, the latitude of the plaza is 27° 22′ 23″ south; and on the assumption that the chronometer had a uniform rate from the time of leaving Valparaiso until my return to it, its longitude is *4h. 41m. 52s.* 5 W. If a mean of all the barometric observations (27) be adopted as the true pressure, the elevation above the sea is 1,286 feet. The extreme fluctuation during the seven days through which the latter observations extend was 0.172 inch, or from 28.528 to 28.700 inches. The temperature at 3 P. M. of the same days was 69°.6, and at midnight 51°.3; the wet thermometer showing at the same hours, respectively, 55°.3 and 46°.5. A westerly wind commences early in the morning, and blows up the valley with increasing freshness until towards 3 P. M., when it gradually subsides; and the nights are almost always calm. There were only three occasions when the wind blew from any other direction, and I was assured that variable winds were quite as rare during other seasons of the year. At twenty of the twenty-seven observations there was a perfectly clear sky, an atmospheric condition existing for at least ten months of the twelve. On the 9th of July, at noon, the temperature of the water in a well of Don Diego Carvallo, near the plaza, was 67°.7; that of the air at the same time 74°.2. The depth of the well is fourteen feet. On the 11th, at *5h. 15m.* A. M., there was quite a severe earthquake. As near as it was possible to estimate the direction of the wave, it moved from north to south, and was unusually long. Some ten minutes later a second shock, of much less violence, followed. The latter was preceded through a long interval by a sound not unlike the rushing of wind through a forest, and was totally unlike any sound I had previously heard attending this phenomenon. The first shock was almost without noise. A third shock was felt at twenty-three minutes after noon of the same day, the oscillation continuing only a second or two. Neither of them was noticed at the cities to the southward.

Leaving the city at ten o'clock of July 13, in a carriage well cumbered with boxes of instruments, the end of the railroad was not reached until two hours after the time calculated upon; a delay which came near proving very serious to me. As the day train had gone down to Caldera, the engineers very promptly and courteously placed at my disposition a hand-car, with two peons to work it, cautioning me, at starting, that two trains were coming up with parts of their encampment, then in progress of transferment to a new station. As we had daylight, and they came slowly, it was an easy matter to see them in time for the removal of our little vehicle; but night closed in as we were descending the last steep grade some nine miles from the port, and just at the only spot on the road where there are cuttings of any extent. The peons having given the car an extra impetus to carry us down the plane without farther labor, and seated themselves in the bottom so as to offer the least possible resistance to the air, we were rattling down the grade at the rate of ten to twelve miles the hour, when suddenly I perceived a dark object in a curve of the road ahead. No intimation had been given me by the engineers of another expected *up-train*, and for a moment it was supposed to be only a shadow of the embankment which the moon threw across the track. When its true character was discerned, we were within less than two hundred yards of it. Unfortunately, the brake to our car had been so worn by the sand-drift, that, even when the whole weight of one of the peons was thrown upon it, its friction was merely nominal; and as one of them got a thrust in the eye and the other a thump over the head in the hurry of snatching at the whirling cranks, both were rendered *hors du combat* during the brief interval when their services might have been useful. When too late, I found it a heavy car loaded with iron rails, drawn by oxen. These—sensible brutes as they were—wheeled to the right and left of the track, so as to give us the full benefit of the projecting ends of the rails. Finding we must have a collision, nothing could be done but to try and break its effects as much as possible, and endeavor to save the chronometer. Yet, in spite of bracing my feet against the front, stiffening my knees, and holding on to the back with one arm, of a sudden I found my left eye in contact with the wood-work protecting the machinery, and more stars apparently dashing across the heavens than I witnessed in the memorable meteoric shower of 1833. Luckily, except this and the tearing away, by the projecting ends of the rails, of the framework mentioned, there was no damage done, and we reached Caldera in another half hour without farther difficulty. So much for my first experience as a *conductor;* and when I recollect how closely my scalp was to a removal even more expeditious than a Blackfoot would have effected, I am quite willing to yield all claims for such a post to other competitors.

During the five days intervening before the arrival of the steamer from the north, magnetical observations similar to those at the other stations were made, and a record kept of the meteorological changes. The mean height of the barometer was 29.983 inches, corresponding to a height of fifteen feet above the sea, which is probably from twelve to fifteen feet too little for the site of the instrument; but it must be stated that on the 16th of July it was subject to rapid changes, and was very considerably above its mean height. Its extreme range was from 29.846 to 30.176 inches; temperature of the air at noon 62°.5, and at midnight 56°.3; the wet thermometer at the same hours 58°.1 and 52°.8. Cloudy weather greatly predominated, with a moderate wind from N.N.W. Shortly after 9 A. M. of the 16th, and whilst the wind blew freshly from that direction, an almost equally strong breeze came suddenly from the S.W., and rain followed instantly. The northerly wind returned by noon, when the atmospheric pressure reached its maximum, and the air continued loaded with mist, though no farther deposition took place. There was a beautiful display of the zodiacal light on the evening of the same day, the apex of its pyramid extending between Jupiter and the constellation of Hydra et Crateres.

During the following summer—January to March, 1852—a submarine phenomenon attracted no little attention among the residents and visitors at Caldera, of which more than one account reached Santiago. One correspondent wrote me: "The night I stopped at Caldera I went at half-past eleven o'clock to hear the submarine music, and I confess it has astonished me. Though the position is neither graceful nor comfortable, on lying down in the boat and placing your ear upon the bottom, you hear it to perfection. I stuck to it for a long time, and was charmed indeed. It has now been pretty well ascertained that it comes from fish, which gather in great numbers on a quiet and retired spot of the bay; and as each one produces a single note, the most soft and charming harmony results, resembling the Æolian harp nearer than anything to which I can compare it. If we suppose the sounds to be produced by fish, that will also account for the different localities where they are heard. At my return to Caldera I will endeavor to obtain the name by which the fish is known there, if I should not succeed in obtaining a specimen for you." Another friend to whom I wrote on receiving the above tells me: "The idea of the music heard here being produced by fish never entered my brain until you wrote me about Mr. H. I am not fully prepared to oppose the Señoritas who pronounce it a syren, and among whom it has caused no little sensation. It is always near one place, and is never heard during the day. You must come down for a personal examination; because, though I shall send you a box containing some of the small fish caught in the bay, I have no intention to assert that *a* or *the* musical fish shall be among them." My friend sent fish according to promise, of which an account is given in the report from Mr. Charles Girard. One of them he has named "*Alosa musica,*" from this circumstance. When I wrote again, only four months later, these charming aquatic serenaders had shut up their orchestra, or gone elsewhere. Nothing had been heard from them since May. The only analogous case of which I have information is that of Mr. Taylor when at Bathcaloa, in Ceylon. On going to a lake near the fort at night, he was struck by a loud musical noise proceeding from the bottom of the water. The natives told him it was caused by "singing shells," or at least by some animal inhabiting shells. The sounds were like those of an accordeon or Æolian harp, with vibrating notes pitched at different keys. And it is said that there is a snail on the island of Corfu which occasionally emits a distinctly audible and not unmusical sound. It would be interesting to establish the fact that the syren of Caldera and the singing-shells of Ceylon, half way round the globe, are members of the same family.

Expectation of our monthly supply of letters contributed no little to the impatience with which we North Americans awaited the arrival of the steamer; though the Chilenos probably exhibited more restlessness than we did, when hour after hour passed by beyond the usual period of its coming. Nearly the whole party had tired with watching, and were about retiring for the night, when the lights of the New Grenada were descried by one more keen sighted than the rest; and when her anchor was dropped in the port, half an hour later, in their joy at starting towards the capital and home, even natives could not resist the "stirrup-cup" of our liberal and attentive hosts. At leaving Santiago my plan had been to complete all the observations in Atacama, and proceed to Coquimbo in one of the small steamers, in time to make the magnetical determinations prior to the arrival of this vessel. This was frustrated by the loss of the Ecuador; and as continued cloudy weather had prevented the completion of the experiments at Valparaiso, it was concluded that time would be saved by returning thither in this steamer, finishing the work during her stay, and coming back to Coquimbo on the 27th. Embarking after midnight, the steamer left the port about daylight, and without material incident reached her destination on the morning of the 21st. The loss of the steamer Peru, belonging to this line, during a gale at Valparaiso only a few weeks before, and the destruction of a great many launches at the same time, rendered it prudent to take in coals at Coquimbo, where we remained some hours, during which most of the passengers made a visit to La Serena. With favorable weather, it would have been easy to accomplish all desired work at Valparaiso; but a norther set in next morning, and nothing could be effected out of doors. This was the third storm during the winter, and though not so violent as that in which the Peru and many other vessels had been driven on shore, it was sufficiently powerful to cause the most lively apprehensions for the safety of the shipping in the bay. A continuane of cloudy weather prevented the completion of the observations before the 26th; on which day there were an unusually grêat number of cabin passengers, sixty soldiers on their way to reinforce the garrison in the suspicious province of Coquimbo, and many peons at the cost of the *Junta de Mineria.* I re-embarked for Coquimbo. Our cabin number was doubled; those who would have gone two weeks before having been disappointed, owing to the loss of the Peru.

The roads were in very bad condition, and the streams so swollen by the copious rains of the two or three days preceding, that the mail was behind time, and we were detained to await it until some hours past noon. When at last we did get out, the deck was crowded and uncomfortable enough, until a heavy swell drove three fourths of our passengers to such resting-places as they could obtain; but the detention had affected our arrival at Coquimbo correspondingly, and when we reached the anchorage towards 9 P. M. of the following evening, the vehicles belonging to Serena, usually awaiting passengers, had all gone.

Neither were there custom-house officers to dispute landing, public accommodations which a person accustomed to the decencies of life could creep into until morning, nor a carriage of any kind to be had for money. No one expressing a desire to know what my half dozen cases contained, they were at once taken from the mole to a store for safe-keeping; and a travelling friend on board, who had long resided here, went with me to try and obtain lodgings at the house of a native, who occasionally provides hungry travellers by sea with a dish of shore-prepared edibles. We found her obliging and quite willing to make up a bed in the only vacant room at her command; but alas! there had been heavy rains only the preceding day, and the mud-plastered roof of her old house had been washed through to its floor. It was thoroughly saturated; the sky overhead as seen through the vacant crevices was ominous of another sprinkle, and rheumatism would have been a sure reward to him who lodged a night within it. We next went to one of his tenants, who kept a dram-shop and billiard table. He was not less civil—offering a bed on a sofa in a little ante-room, and only asking the privilege of passage through it for himself, wife, and child, as there was no other access to their chamber. If preferred, he would make a pallet on the billiard table as soon as his customers had left for the night. Fortunately, relief from this dilemma was at hand; and the courteous hospitality of Mr. A., during four or five days of my visit in this vicinity, will always be pleasantly remembered.

Coquimbo bay, in latitude 29° 57′ south, is by far the best anchorage on the coast between Callao and Talcahuano; unless Puerto Yngles, near Caledra, be an exception. It is broad and capacious, easy of access at all times, and protected from the violence of the sea whenever the effect of distant winds might otherwise be thus felt. A line of the coast which would effectually prevent heavy swells from thence extends across its mouth to the north, if by chance the wind should ever blow violently from that quarter; and there are two or three rocky islets just to the westward of the entrance, aiding to diminish its effects from that direction. The western side is bounded by a high promontory of rocks, having a nearly vertical face on the seaward side, and a steep slope on that next to the bay. Over the latter, arborescent cacti and a few equally fleshy shrubs are scattered. These have found sufficient soil among disintegrated portions of the rocks. The southern and eastern shores are low beaches, rising by steps or terraces towards the interior, at this season of the year covered with verdure; the southern part of the promontory and a peninsula connecting it with the main land form the northern shore of Herradura bay, distant from Coquimbo bay about one mile. On the highest part of the table-formed peninsula is the residence of Mr. A., from which there is a fine view of both sheets of water. Good water for shipping may be had in abundance. A supply of fine fish is always at command; and when Heaven propitiously bestows three or four showers, a moderate supply of vegetables, fruit, and excellent meat may be obtained.

Coquimbo, a village of two or three scores of houses, is on the western side of the bay. It has only one street, portions of which have a sort of sidewalk; though uniformity of direction, level, or paving, has not been attempted. As there are rarely more than two or three moderate rains in any year, and its inhabitants are generally operatives, most of the houses are of slight materials, and have roofs of reeds, plastered with mud; but the quantity of copper obtained from the mines of the province having very greatly increased of late, a number of furnaces for smelting have been erected; more vessels have frequented the port in search of it; several very creditable-looking buildings are in course of construction; and Coquimbo may one day really claim to be a town. At present it is uninviting enough to a stranger; and its population of 800 souls, mainly dependent, as they are, on the visits of ships for constancy of employment, make their extortionate demands with airs which one soon tires of.

There are smelting establishments for copper ores at the two extremes of the town, the larger one having eight furnaces. Both seem carelessly conducted; want of order and tidiness, as well in the work as the workmen, being rendered more apparent perhaps by the contrast which is presented in the establishment at Herradura. In addition to these, a church, a custom-house, and a post-office are the only other buildings of a public nature. The last two occupy part of a private house near the little mole. When I landed, there was no officer to receive the letter with which the Minister of Finance had provided me respecting the instruments, and, as has been said, they were conveyed to a store unquestioned; indeed a cargo of contraband goods might have been disposed of with no greater cognizance of the revenue guardians. Eight days afterwards, when the letter had been left with the Intendente at Serena as of no further use, and I was about to re-embark them in broad daylight, some of the underlings were quite unwilling to permit it without inspection. Their demand was too absurd, even had I not evidence that a written order lay at the office to facilitate instead of detaining me; and as a compliance would have subjected me to an hour's work among a mob of dirty boatmen and peons, their right to have the cases opened was refused. There was some little detention by maintenance of the principle; but as soon as the facts were communicated to the chief, he reprimanded his subordinates for malicious interference. Formerly there was great venality at all the ports along the coast. An anecdote of this nature occurring at Coquimbo came freshly to mind at the time of my detention on the mole; though it was scarcely probable that any of the custom-house officers who had borne parts in it still held places under government. The story was told me by one of the parties most interested, now a man of great wealth, and was substantially as follows: After loading a ship with copper ores, it was intimated to him that a *douceur* to the officer who had superintended its weighing would expedite the clearance papers—a consummation devoutly wished; and it occurred to him that this needy guardian of the customs might make a *mistake* of a few hundred quintals in his return, if *the consideration* was sufficiently tempting. On this return, or rather on the document given to the collector at Serena, depended the amount of export duty to be paid. Eighteen doubloons ($310) changed hands; and an error was detected in the quantities of ores delivered on board, which abated the dues to the government $600. But the process did not end here. From the next in rank to whom the papers passed there came a like intimation with precisely similar results, and they were finally sent up to Serena for the signature of the chief prior to payment of the duties. Days elapsed, and still there was no clearance; nor would there probably have been any for weeks, had not his purse been lightened of other eighteen ounces on the same conditions as the other two. The chief had got wind of the good luck of his subs, and was unwilling to be slighted; and thus the treasury was robbed by three men of export dues amounting to near two thousand dollars! Such pilfering was then of every-day occurrence. At present there is more system, and the risk of detection is greater. Moreover, the standard of probity in public officers has been very considerably elevated, and such crimes are rendered less frequent.

On the morning after landing, the instruments were conveyed to Herradura bay, and the magnetical elements determined near the spot occupied by Capt. Fitzroy sixteen years before. At that time the declination of the magnet was 14° 30′ east, and on the 28th of July I found it to be 15° 41′, showing an annual variation of nearly 4½′. The inclination observed by him was* 34° 20′, and on the 29th July it was 32° 10′, being a yearly decrease of 8′. Of the climate I shall have occasion to say something when speaking of Serena presently, to which it is so near that the same remarks will apply.

As its name imports, the bay is in the form of a horse-shoe, rather more than a mile and three quarters in diameter, with an entrance of only one eighth of a mile open to the northwest winds. On both sides the shore is high and rocky, with many cacti and woody plants, presenting a picturesque appearance. At the southeast extremity a sand-beach, with a shelf above, like that of Coquimbo, slopes off into a continuation of the first terrace. On the south and west sides there is deep water and good anchoring ground. Here vessels are exposed to the wind and sea; and where the north shore might protect them against these, the ground is rocky and the water shallow. A profusion of shells washed up during every blow find their way to the beach. Some of them are very beautiful, though generally they are defaced by abrasion. Perfect specimens may be had from the rocks at every reflux of the tide. Among them few are more attractive than the *Chiton magnificus* and *C. chilensis*, both found in great numbers, though

* June 4, 1835.

adhering to the rocks with a force not easily overcome by one's hands. Scarcely less numerous is a *Cardium*, called by the natives "*Choro*," and the *Ostrea violacea*, which is also found in multitudes on the sand-hills of Caldera. This *choro*—for the same name is applied to two or three very distinct shells—is edible, and its shells are collected to be used in making lime.

Being within the region which counts with considerable certainty on three or four rains during the winter months, the land surrounding both bays was now covered with verdure; and many varieties of plants were already in flower, none of them making greater contrasts with the dark-green herbage and dusky rocks than the *Cassia flaccida*, with racemes of brilliant orange-colored flowers; a tree Heliotrope, with large and fragrant bunches white and purple-shaded; and the rose-colored berries of a parasite (Quintral?) which crowns many arms of the arborescent cacti. From the earth, too, there were Añeñucas, bending under loads of scarlet bells, springing in all directions; and the *Orejas del Diablo* (*Eupatorium foliosum*) crept along the surface, hiding, as it were, in angles of the rocks, with curiously formed purple cups, adorned with apparently frosted filaments: shape, color, *age* enough, signified in the silvery fibres, and ugliness to merit well its name of *Devil's ears*. But Coquimbanos say one should visit their valley towards the close of September and during October, when the natural pasturage has grown head high, and the earth is dotted more exquisitely with flowers of every form than the gardens display. Then, too, spring offers its first fruit—the strawberry; and the sun pours only a flood of genial light and heat on gems he has aided to perfect, bidding you forth to admire and wonder at them.

There is a fine prospect from the terrace on which stands the house of Mr. A. The formation, counted from the sea, may be properly regarded as the second table or terrace. It extends a mile back, and nearly parallel with the eastern shore of Coquimbo bay, and terminates seven miles to the north by a valley, through which flows the Coquimbo river. Back of this again, with a like difference of elevation and facial line, is a third. The height of the first table may be 70 feet, the second 125, and the third probably 180. Their composition is a conglomerate of shells. Hills of every form rise to heights of several thousand feet along the skirts of the last; and at a distance of more than a hundred miles, the Andes, at this time covered with snow very far down, fill up the back-ground. Distant as they are, the lines of every spur and ravine of the great cordilleras are as sharp as in an engraving. On the northern extremity of the second terrace, and embowered amid luxuriant trees, is *La Serena*, its white walls sparkling pleasantly in the distance. Two roads conduct to it from Coquimbo: one along the hard, sea-washed beach, over which the birlocheros will drive you at the rate of three leagues per hour; and the other, just far enough inland to avoid the waves in bad weather, and to cross one or two little streams sometimes swollen during the rains. The former is shorter, and greatly preferable, except on the rare occasions referred to. Seven miles from Coquimbo the road turns from the bay at right angles, and for a mile continues in a straight line over a level plain, to the foot of the eminence on which La Serena is built. On either side there are well watered gardens, bounded by rows of poplars and willows, which form an agreeable walk or drive. The ascent of the terrace to the city is quite abrupt; and is the first departure from a uniformly inclined plain between it and the sea. A very few years since a gentleman died here who recollected the time when the ocean washed the base of the hill, now at least twenty-five feet above its level. Unless from the appearance of one or two of its seven churches, one would scarcely infer that La Serena had been founded within less than half a century after Columbus first sailed from the shores of the Old World. Its streets are straight, after the fashion of all others built within modern times in Chile, its houses are of good size, and in all its thoroughfares there is scrupulous cleanliness, worthy of imitation.

According to the record, it was founded by Valdivia in 1544, three years after Santiago; but if we reflect that Don Pedro had only one hundred and fifty of his own countrymen, and some Peruvian Indians, when he arrived from Cuzco, we may well doubt whether he could have done much more than leave names for localities afterwards to be built upon. It is stated in the history of Chile, by M. Gay, that, becoming more and more convinced by experience that he must have additional men and arms to carry on his conquest, Valdivia, as a precautionary measure to their safe arrival, undertook to keep the road open between the colony at Santiago and Perų. To this end Capt. Bohan was despatched with ten men to found a village in the valley of Coquimbo, where evil-intentioned Indians were always in waiting to attack travellers; and as Valdivia had been born in a town of that name, in compliment to him the little settlement received the name of "La Serena." But it was not destined to be long-lived: four years afterwards the Indians massacred the Spaniards, and burnt it. Under the command of Don Francisco de Aguirre a new party, numbering from thirty to eighty men, according to different versions, was sent to the valley in July of 1549; and the present site—much nearer to the sea—was selected in preference to that of the old village. The new town was called "San Bartolomé de la Serena," its birth dating from the 26th of August of that year.

Exclusive of houses along the inland road, and which extend to a length of several squares beyond the limits proper, the circumference of the city may be two miles. Its population is not far from 9,000 souls. There is no difference in its plan from other Hispano-American towns: a plaza near the centre; narrow, right-angled streets, 150 yards apart; rudely constructed churches, with bells enough to make up in noise what is wanting in melody or architectural taste; and streams of water through each square,—such are the salient characteristics. One side of its plaza is partially occupied by a new cathedral in progress of erection, and whose architect, like that of the sister edifice at Copiapó, seems to have forgotten the rules so long followed, and will soon complete for the Coquimbanos a temple which will be commodious, and at the same time pleasing to the eye. The material used in its construction is a compact conglomerate of shells, cut in blocks of any desirable size, from one of the terraces a few miles distant. Drip-stones for filtering water, and the sidewalks of the streets, are also made of this material. The other sides of the square are occupied by public offices, a prison, a garrison for troops, and residences of the Intendente and others: none of them are buildings of especial note. No trees have been planted about the plaza, as at Copiapó, to render it a place of recreation; though in this respect the capital of Atacama is an exception. Such is the prejudice against shrubbery about the plazas, that it is rarely permitted to thrive; and rows planted by a benevolent citizen at Melipilla were in one night torn up by the vandals among its inhabitants. Yet no people more scrupulously provide public walks with trees than descendants of Spain; and it must be an insignificant settlement which has not its "*alameda,*" with seats on either side. That of La Serena extends along the inland road to the port.

On the inner table-land, back of the town, is the cemetery. It covers from fifteen to twenty acres, enclosed by high whitewashed walls; and is divided into sections, purchasable with privileges according to the wealth of families. The portion occupied by the remains of the wealthy is ornamented with fancy and costly ornaments, trees, and flowers, and is well worthy of a visit. Without the enclosure there is a charming panoramic view. Off to the west is the ocean, robbed of its undulations even by this short distance, and apparently but a counterpart to the dark vault above. A little closer is the tranquil bay, with its shipping and high bounding promontory; against whose wall is projected, sharply clear, the little village and the tall chimneys of the furnaces, with pencils of steamy smoke streaming straight towards heaven. Below is the bright, clean little town, with multitudes of gardens interspersed among its houses; and to our right a winding valley, threaded by a stream whose waters are soon lost in the sea. The valley may be a mile wide between the higher shelves that were formerly its river banks, and which are bounded by ranges of lofty and undulating hills that stretch away to the E.S.E. until the cordilleras arrest the vision. After the desolation of Atacama, its cultivated fields and trees, its omnipresent vegetation, its herds of cattle, and numbers of ploughmen with their teams of oxen, were all most grateful to the eye; and it was impossible to resist the inclination to return on a subsequent day for re-enjoyment of the prospect. Across the valley, and in the eastern skirts of a considerable village, also forming part of our picture, there is an establishment, for smelting copper from ores, on a scale even more extensive than either of those at the port. The same proprietor has also erected rolling mills, and has already furnished quite an amount of sheet copper to the Valparaiso market. Bad weather and want of time prevented a visit to them. Between La Serena and the village the river is but a rivulet thirty or forty feet wide, with an average depth of one foot, and a fall at this season of the year producing a current not exceeding two miles per hour. During summer all the water is consumed in cultivation before it can reach the bay. As there is no other stream in this part of the province, and never any rain between August and May following, the agricultural product to supply a large mining population is very greatly less than the demand; and, in consequence, their neighbors are called on to make up deficiencies. Flour comes from the central and southern provinces, through Valparaiso; the Argentine republic supplies beef and beasts of burden; and their own land is thus left free for vegetables and fruits.

A college for the education of young men has been founded under the auspices of government, and is apparently quite flourishing. It has five or six professors, and, including day scholars, nearly one hundred students. When under charge of Professor Domeyko, it contained a mineralogical cabinet for instruction in organic chemistry superior to any other in the republic; but since his removal to the capital, there is less earnest interest in the science, and the cabinet already exhibits the want of his watchful care. An old convent, formerly occupied by Jesuits, is used as the college building. There were six primary schools for boys, badly as well as irregularly attended at that time, and a single private school for girls, at which there were nearly seventy pupils under charge of one teacher! As she instructs, or at least *receives*, so many scholars, her reputation is proportionably great with the Coquimbanos—her ability with them being in direct ratio to the number of half ounces ($8.62) per month paid to her. That she could receive more girls than it would be possible to give lessons to, seemed not to enter the minds of those who talked with me. If the capital of the province has so little regard for education, what must we expect from the different departments? In all of them—five in number—the Intendente officially informed the Minister of Public Instruction, on the 17th March, 1851, there were 33 schools of every class, 1,416 male and 357 female pupils. The published census of these departments shows a population of 85,349 souls at the last enumeration; but if the increase in the others has been in proportion, according to the information which the Intendente gives us,* there should now be in the province of Coquimbo nearly 130,000 souls, or about one in seventy of its population receiving the benefit of instruction.

Unless a theatre, not open at that time, and a tolerably good hotel (for Chile), can be included in the number, there are no other public buildings than those mentioned; and if one may judge from the concourse constantly assembled, the hotel possesses greater attractions than any other single edifice in La Serena. If Santiago is silent and *triste* to a stranger, La Serena is doubly so—its 9,000 people seeming to have no occupation to call them out of doors; and the city looks as if, after being nicely built and thoroughly whitewashed, its population had departed with the brooms which had been used to sweep its streets so clean. There are a few tolerably gay-looking shops on some of the streets, and in passing one may perhaps see a lounging customer or two dawdling with the clerks or proprietors; but there are no other evidences of business or activity: indeed the only place where any collection of persons could be seen, was around the billiard and domino tables at the *fonda*. There, from 10 o'clock in the morning until midnight of every day (Sundays not excepted), the tables were occupied by players, and the walls lined with expectants, who puffed cigaritos whilst awaiting their turns. If one were to judge from the richness of dress and the jaunty manner in which cloaks are worn over the shoulder, it would be fair to estimate that at least nine tenths of the better class of men visited the fonda during the day; but dress is an especially fallacious standard—it being a universal rule to make the greatest possible display in public. Some purchase costly equipages, which they exhibit on the *Pampilla* near Santiago only on one day of the national holidays; others, whose purses are

* Anales de la Universidad, 1851.

not so well filled, content themselves perforce with fine garments with which to appear in the alamedas. Thus the very tinman to whom one sends a trifling utensil for repair, may be as elegantly dressed, and twirl his moustache as cosily between the whiffs of his cigarito, as the man in the veins of whose parents flowed the *sangre azul* of Castile, and who really never gives a thought to money, except when called on to count sums that have administered to his gratifications. Aware of this passion for display, and of the sacrifices which the mass will make to obtain finery for the annual festivals, several of the large commercial houses contrive to have ships arrive with French and China goods during the last weeks of August, well knowing that every article will command a higher price than at any other time. There was no doubt, however, that the frequenters of the fonda belonged to the "upper ten," and the hours they passed in playing or looking over the billiard tables and child's game of dominos argued little in favor of habits more industrious or intellectual.

Some allowance is to be made for people whose principal occupation is mining, and who really have little to do when in the city. Their mines being at a distance, and under charge of administradores, the only actual demands on their time are for an occasional visit of inspection, which, at most, occupies a few days of the month, and for a like number spent in despatching provisions, and disposing of the ores when mule-trains arrive with the latter at the port. Add to this the low standard of education until within a very recent period, and, by reason of it, the little subsequent disposition for literature, and we will understand how incorrigible habits of idleness seem to have fastened on a large part of the present generation. Nor has the climate been without its influence in producing such result. It is too uniform, too benignant. Man needs extremes to give energy to his thoughts, sudden changes to send the blood vigorously through his veins. Here the temperature is soft and genial from year's end to year's end, leaving one's pulsations as quiet as its vicissitudes. This is shown in the record kept during two years by Señor Troncosa, and published in the *Anales de la Universidad*, from which I have condensed it.

Mean and Extremes of Temperature and Pressure in 1849 *and* 1850.

	Barometer—1849.			Barometer—1850.			Temperature—1849.		Temperature—1850.	
	Mean.	Extremes.	Mean diurnal tide.	Mean.	Extremes.	Mean diurnal tide.	Mean.*	Extremes.	Mean.*	Extremes.
	Inches.			*Inches.*			°	°	°	°
January	29.887	.228	.039	29.840	.201	.021	69.9	9	67.3	15.8
February	29.873	.221	.024	29.854	.130	.007	66.8	16	67.4	16.8
March	29.900	.205	.031	29.867	.154	.019	62	7.9	65.7	15
April	29.947	.241	.035	29.949	.351	.034	57.8	10.6	62.8	11.7
May	29.915	.248	.022	29.973	.193	.039	57	12.2	56.7	14.4
June	29.919	.205	.016	29.994	.252	.020	56.7	16.2	55	21.3
July	29.953	.315	.004	29.963	.343	.004	53.4	16.2	54.5	16
August	29.999	.352	.000	30.044	.422	.017	53.4	18	55.8	16.8
September	29.975	.307	.012	29.970	.303	.024	56.8	17.8	56.7	14.4
October	29.975	.256	.012	29.973	.319	.035	59.7	18	59.2	15.8
November	29.945	.158	.027	29.919	.122	.012	62.4	16.4	62.3	15.3
December	29.885	.197	.016	29.863	.217	.031	64.7	16.4	64.8	15.3
Means	29.930	.244	.020	29.934	.251	.022	60.05	14.56	60.68	15.72

* According to the Santiago observations, these temperatures are 3°.2 above the true mean.

The observations were made between 8 and 9 A. M., 3 and 4 P. M., and 9 and 10 P. M., with instruments having French scales. I have converted the millimetres into corresponding English inches, and reduced the readings to 32° Fahrenheit, as well as transformed the centigrade readings into equivalents of Fahrenheit's scale; but no correction has been made to the barometric observations on account of elevation above the sea. On the supposition that the instrument is correct, the elevation deduced from the mean of the two years is 61 feet, coinciding with what has already been said of the height of the terrace of Coquimbo. The extremes of pressure and temperature were the greatest observed at any hour during the months opposite which they are placed. It will be seen that the diurnal atmospheric tide is extremely small, whilst the annual wave is of more than usual amplitude, and the thermometric changes are embraced within very small limits. It is to be regretted that the observations do not include occasional notices of winds and clouds—an omission perhaps to be accounted for by the slight variation to which the direction of the former is subject, and a generally serene sky overhead. S.S.W. winds, or perhaps it would be better to say breezes, prevail during the greater portion of the year; for it would scarcely be proper to designate them as "winds," except when northers reach so far. Often, when its more humble port is enjoying clear weather, the city is enveloped in clouds and mist—an atmospheric condition due to the current of cold air which descends the valley of the river with the snow-water, and meets with the warm, moist air from the sea. Nevertheless, the sky is so little obscured by clouds, that many persons suppose the name Serena was given to the city on this account. A like phenomenon of clouds and mist is observable near the mouth of every stream in Chile.

Agriculture being possible only along the borders of two or three little streams, as in Atacama, the only occupation for the mass of the population is mining; and therefore nearly all the vessels arriving at the port come for freights of copper, or to bring supplies of provisions. A fair example of its foreign trade is exhibited in the following table:

Imports at Coquimbo, and their value, in 1850.

From —	Value.	
England	$308,923	The imports from England were: coal, $246,408; iron and steel, $16,407; fire-bricks, $15,922; ale and porter, $3,080; assorted, $47,006.
France	487	
Argentine . . .	25,366	
Peru	10,010	
Ecuador	600	
Domestic ports .	662,996	
Totals . . .	$1,008,382	

The imports from the Argentine republic consisted almost exclusively of live cattle, and from Peru of salt and common straw hats. Coal, iron, steel, and fire-bricks bespeak at once their mining purposes; and it is not at all improbable that a part of the latter articles were purchased on board ships which consignees determined to load with copper, and did not first land them at Valparaiso. That city, it has already been shown, is the great market all must seek for their supplies, the foreign merchants managing to reap profits on original importations as well as on the mineral products offered in payment. Indeed, even the flour and other provisions of the south are made to render tribute to the monopolists of Valparaiso before distribution to the hungry at the north.

The exports during the same period are subjoined:

Exports from Coquimbo in the year 1850.

	England.	U. States.	France.	China.	Germany.	Peru.	Equador.	Domestic ports.
Bar copper	$708,748	$392,045	$173,815	$81,161	$19,517			
Wrought copper . . .						$12,253	$805	
Regulus	102,062	6,010						
Copper ores	11,928	17,480	600		40			
Silver ores	172							
Gold bars			6,625					
Dollars			530					
Cobalt ores	9,713							
Guano	513							
Goat skins	2,000	11,348						
Chinchilla skins	126	190						
Hides		1,300						
Wool		1,680						
Assorted	51	2,037				28		$201,744
Totals	$835,313	$432,085	$181,570	$81,161	$19,557	$12,281	$805	$201,744

No returns of the mines and their people have been made to the government, as from Atacama. There is no Junta de Mineria to which one might refer for definite information; and as every one mines "on his own hook," it is not easy to elicit data from such suspicious natures. Going from Coquimbo to Valparaiso, I was in company with one of the most extensive copper operators in all its branches residing in the province, and whose intelligence and frankness were quite charming until the subject of copper mines and smelting were introduced. Had he been a snail basking in the genial air of a summer morning, and rudely touched, he could not have drawn within himself more suddenly; nor did he cease to regard me with suspicion during the remainder of our voyage together. Whether competition was feared, and, like other rare instances one meets in the journey of life, he imagined himself wholly entitled to this branch of industry, regarding with enmity all who obtained a part of his fancied right, I know not, but am glad to say there were very "few of the same sort" about. This instance is alluded to only because there was no one whose extensive engagements were so well qualified to furnish the intelligence which every stranger would seek in this secluded part of the world.

The entire region of country from latitude 29½° to 31° S., and from longitude 72½° W. to the ocean, is one vast labyrinth of metallic veins. Gold, silver, mercury, copper, bismuth, tin, lead, arsenic, cobalt—in short, almost the whole mining vocabulary might be summoned to enumerate its varied products; sometimes a simple metal, at others in specimens each of which will combine half the range of the mineralogist. Such aggregations as the latter are yielded by the mine of "*el Altar*," and perhaps by others unknown to me. Copper, however, is the largest product of the Coquimbo mines, and the ores generally find their way to the smelting establishments on the bay or at Herradura. Where the arborescent cactus (*Cereus quisco*) is obtainable for fuel, some small amounts are reduced at the mines. Other portions are sent for smelting to Tongoy, a bay some thirty miles south of Coquimbo, or are shipped to one of the other establishments. Of those brought to Herradura, the average contains sixteen per cent. of metal. The furnaces here belong to an English company, who have a special privilege from the government, and are managed with all the skill and economy that modern science has brought to bear on metallurgy. Owning no mines, their ores are obtained from regular customers, who keep them constantly supplied at prices agreed upon according to the *ley*, or proportion of pure metal contained in the ore. If not already broken into bits of proper size for the furnace, the first step, after the arrival of a troop of mules with ores, is the selection of samples for analysis. To this end the whole is broken into bits of less than a cubic inch. When thoroughly intermixed, a handful of these is taken indiscriminately, beaten into powder, and divided into three parts. One is analyzed by the chemist of the establishment; another is given to the owner of the mine from which it came, that he may obtain an analysis elsewhere should he doubt the impartiality of the company's officer; and the third is jointly sealed for reference in case of dispute. The regular charge for analyzing a sample at La Serena is a quarter of an ounce ($4.31); and several of the young men instructed by Prof. Domeyko have determined to devote themselves entirely to this pursuit. Thrown into a reverberatory furnace, its heat soon converts the ores into a liquid mass, from which the slag is raked with iron bars, until there remains very little more than metallic copper and its combinations of sulphur, lead, and antimony. This is drawn off in open moulds beside the furnace; and, whilst still quite hot, the "pigs" are thrown into vats containing water, the absorption of which crumbles them, forming the powder called "regulus." The latter is afterwards passed to a second furnace, in which the sulphurous acid is expelled; and then to a third, where the copper is melted and cast into bars of about 200 pounds each. At the Herradura furnaces it undergoes a final process of refining, and in this condition contains as near an approximation to pure metal as is attainable by man. The establishment is conducted in a manner to reflect great credit on Mr. A., for whom the operatives and their families—principally Europeans—evince the strongest regard and respect.*

Since 1844, the amounts of copper, silver, gold, and cobalt produced in the province have been as follows:

	1844.	1845.	1846.	1847.	1848.	1849.	1850.	1851.
Gold bars		$2,630		$4,088			$6,625	
Silver bars . . .	$124,425	140,425	$167,240	39,610	$105,648		32,128	$8,932
Silver ores . . .							172	
Copper bars . . .	484,625	435,104	647,113	796,796	742,519	$1,026,349	1,379,864	646,134
Regulus	167,542	134,818	151,628	143,225	31,991	9,702	112,013	939
Wrought bars . .	3,043	13,765	21,425	9,406	7,324	2,063	86,393	32,682
Copper ores . . .	88,767	65,810	87,650	25,918	34,658	12,972	57,849	18,297
Cobalt ores . . .					914	12,454	9,713	288
Totals . . .	$768,402	$792,552	$1,075,056	$1,019,043	$923,054	$1,063,540	$1,684,757	$707,272

The mineral wealth of Chile being almost entirely derived from these two provinces, before taking leave of them it seems proper to make known such general facts, relating to all the mines of the country, as were derived from other sources than personal observation.

Geologically speaking, Chile may be divided into two ranges of mountains—the Andes and cordilleras of the coast—sub-divisible into three formations belonging to different epochs. North of Chacabuco (latitude 33°), as has been mentioned already, the entire country west of the Andes consists of low, rounded mountains, expanded valleys, plateaus covered with granite detritus, and occasional tertiary basins. To the south of it these multitudes of irregular hills are collected into a tolerably uniform chain, extending parallel with the line of the Andes, and separated from it by a long plain, which terminates only at the ocean in the province of Valdivia. Professor Domeyko says that the cordilleras of the coast consist of non-stratified granite or porphyritic masses, of which the principal rocks contain four elements, viz: quartz, felspar, mica, and amphibole. As one of these predominates, and the others diminish or disappear, we have diorite, sienite, granite proper, greenstone, &c. Moreover, each of them sometimes passes into its corresponding porphyry or homogenous mass, in which the constituting elements are no longer distinguishable. Hence the group comprises an immense number of different rocks,

* By a patent from government, this is the only establishment in Chile which can use lime as a flux. It is obtained here by burning the *choros* gathered, in any quantity, on the beach. A recent analysis in England showed that its refined metal contained 99.934 per cent. of pure copper.

the shades and modifications of which it would be both difficult and useless to describe. However, there is one variety which perhaps merits particular attention, as it appears often in the vicinity of metallic veins, and this is a green porphyry in white felspar (albite), which passes into eurite.

As far as the eastern slope of the cordilleras of the coast, the entire Pacific shore is composed of rocks belonging to this formation. Here begins a secondary stratified formation of an epoch anterior to the upheaval of the Andes, under which, and the tertiary strata of the Great Basin, the first dips, to burst out again in many places of the loftier ridge, of whose very summits it not unfrequently forms a considerable portion. As has been intimated, the characteristics of the rocks of the primary formation are a crystalline structure, and absence of stratification. Examining the different portions of the group attentively, we may divide them into two classes: First, masses of granite that form the lower part of the system, which we usually detect at the greatest distance from the centre of the Andes. Their essential element is orthose felspar, sometimes passing into gneiss or mica-schist. And, second, granitic and porphyritic masses, almost always containing albite and amphibole, in contact with the secondary stratified formation they have upraised.

The rocks embraced in class first are generally sterile, easy to decompose, and probably are but the debris of a primitive formation, or, to speak more definitively, of a formation anterior to the epoch of the secondary, and which preceded the elevation of the Andes. Class second, on the contrary, consists of proper rocks of sublevation, which contain immense numbers of metallic veins, often found near their contact with the very formation they dislodge. They are very rarely encountered close to the shore and level of the sea ; and, as might be inferred from the difference in structure of the mountains north and south of Chacabuco, their development varies with the two sections of country. In the province of Atacama this formation generally reaches within 20 to 25 miles of the sea, with an elevation above it of 1,500 feet; in the southern provinces it is not found within twice that distance, nor until a great altitude is attained, sometimes near the very summits of the Andes themselves. From the organic remains found in it, it probably belongs to the epoch of the Jurassic or cretaceous formation. Though poor in calcareous and arenaceous rocks, it abounds in porphyries, alternating with porphyritic schist, breccia, porphyritic tufa, and different compact, schistoidal, siliceous rocks of unknown nature.

In the north, where they appear at different altitudes, and often in the first line of escarpments of this formation, calcareous strata and compact fossiliferous rocks are quite frequent; but south of Chacabuco they are only found near the summits of the cordilleras, and beyond the valley of the Maypu they disappear entirely. Thus, in the latitude of Copiapó we find them at very varied elevations; in that of Coquimbo, not far from its base; and in the parallel of Santiago, only in the superior portion of the formation over the Portillo Pass. They seem not to form a distinct layer in the group, but merely to be subordinate to the stratified porphyry and compact schistose or breccoidal rocks principally constituting the chain of the Andes, and which belong to an epoch anterior to its elevation. This is the secondary formation. The tertiary, whose epoch is posterior to the sublevation, is composed of horizontal or slightly inclined strata, comprising the great longitudinal valley and a part of the small plains on the coast—old water-courses, which appear as so many terraces or steps above one another, attesting epochs in the slow and continued rising of the coast subsequent to the brusque upheaval of the Andes. Not that I suppose this great chain to have been elevated by the tension of the fluidified rock at any single epoch, but simply desire to indicate the distinctive effects or results of plutonic and aqueous forces. There is no doubt that Dr. Darwin's views have received the sanction of geologists, and he has shown that its structure can only be explained on the supposition that the rent strata composing its axis were repeatedly injected after intervals sufficiently long to allow the upper parts or wedges to become cool. That at least a portion of the chain has encountered both agents, and passed alternate eras above and beneath the ocean, is proved by silicified trees, from three to five feet in circumference, having been found at an elevation of 7,000 feet. An interesting account of them is given by Dr. Darwin, in the narrative of his journey over the Uspallata Pass.

Generally, veins of gold and copper are found in the formation of which a detailed account has been given; those of silver, argentiferous copper, sulpho-arseniates and sulpho-antimoniates of silver, in rocks of the secondary formation. Subdividing the former into *ancient* and *rocks of sublevation*, gold veins are found in the midst of the ancient granitic masses, and copper veins (non-argentiferous and without antimony or arsenic) among diorites, dioritic-porphyries, sienites, &c., composing the strata in the vicinity of the upheaved formation. Examining in like manner the distribution of silver, we find chlorides and native amalgams near the principal line of contact of the primary and secondary groups in the vicinity of the sea; arseniates and sulpho-arseniates, cupriferous and argentiferous, farther east; and argentiferous sulphurets of copper, sulphuret of lead, argentiferous blendes, and pyrites, still nearer to the Andes. When all of these silver ores are encountered in the same lode, they are arranged in nearly the same order, those first named being nearest to the surface. Quicksilver is found in both formations: sometimes associated with gold and copper, sometimes with silver. In the first case it appears only as a sulphuret or chloride, and in the second as native amalgam. This general law is exact only as applied to the principal mines of the country; such as are remarkable either for the abundance or richness of their ores, and whose veins have been called by miners *vetas reales* (royal or veritable veins). As they are invariably of considerable extent, the name is really due to them; and in this respect they differ from others called *guias* (literally, guides), which often depart from the law, and present to us inexplicable anomalies.

A review of the principal mines will properly commence with Atacama. The portion of Chile which lies north of the valley of Huasco is undoubtedly the richest in mineral products, but is more especially so in silver, whose veins have seduced most of the gold and copper miners from their old pursuits. At the close of 1842, the number of mines worked in the department of Copiapó—one of the three forming the province—were, 100 of silver, 4 of gold, and 40 of copper. Eight years afterwards the number had increased to 290 of the first, and 6 of the second; whilst the number of the last had diminished to 30. No wonder copper mines should be deserted, when ores yielding twenty-five per cent. of pure metal could be purchased in the city of Copiapó at $39 per ton of 2,240 pounds as late as 1851. Late and definite information as might be wished from the other two departments is not obtainable, the Intendente whose report has been referred to having been prevented from personally inspecting them by want of time and ill health. The account published by Prof. Domeyko in the *Annales des Mines*, Vol. IX, for 1846, is the latest I have seen; and from this are extracted such facts as relate to the mines south of 27½°, except the statistics embraced in the subjoined table, which is compiled from the Intendente's memoir:

District and name of mine.	Silver.	Gold.	Copper.	Operatives.	Amalgamating establishm'ts.	Grinding mills.	Amalgamating tanks.	Pounds of ores produced.
Department of Copiapó.								
Chañarcillo	118			1,730				10,488,088
Pajonales	6			34				
Bandurrias	8			43				
Algarobito	3			12				
Cerro Negro	1							
Tres Puntas	55			629				3,098,817
San Antonio	14			99				476,275
Punta Brava	3			18				
Palo Blanco	4			16				
Garin	17			148	18	28	156	
					with 388	operativ	es.	

TABLE—Continued.

District and name of mine.	Silver.	Gold.	Copper.	Operatives.	Amalgamating establishm'ts.	Grinding mills.	Amalgamating tanks.	Pounds of ores produced.
Department of Copiapó—Continued.								
Garin Viejo	2			11				
Sacramento	12			90				524,100
Altar	3			23				336,149
Granate	2			10				
Checo Grande	1			9				
Pampa Larga	8			71				
Checo Chico	1			7				
Chañarcillito	1			20				
Portezuelo Blanco	2			16				
Cerro del Plomo	2			34				
Pintadas	1							
Romero	22							
Brea	4							
Inca		6	2	64				
Department of Freirina.								
Salado			9	30				1,400,000
Animas			5	20				
Vetado			2	8				
Quebrada Seca			2	16				
Algarroba			1	7				
Lechusas			2	20				
Lirias			1	11				
Ojancos			1	12				
Punta del Cobre			4	32				
Checo			1	12				
Camino			2	7				
Carizalillo			1	2				
Santa Cruz			1	4				
Leoncito			1	2				
Labrar			4	68				
San Juan			23	197				
Morado			6	59				
Mollaca			4	23				
Almireses			1	7				
Carrisal			18	226				
Espujuelas		4		18				
Rincon		1		20				
Department of Vallenar.								
Agua Amarga	14			73				
Tunas	4			24				
Carriso	2			15				
Jarilla			6	85				
San Antonio			1	8	2	2		
Tabaco			1	5				
Camarones			1	24				
Zapallo			1	11				
Totals	310	11	101	4,130	20	30	156	16,323,429

Cerro Blanco, with its 15 mines and 150 operatives, is not included in the preceding list. It lies some thirty or forty miles by the road, to the E.S.E. of Chañarcillo; and is remarkable for the many minerals embraced in some of the lodes, no less than for the manner in which their nature and composition varies with their depth in the veins. They have been worked quite a number of years by some of the most skilful native proprietors. On the surface, one of them gave abundance of the chloride of silver. At a depth of less than two hundred feet, neither this nor native silver could be found, even in the superior part of the lode, but only grey copper antimoniates rich in silver. A little lower, it passed into grey copper and galena; and in less than six hundred feet from the surface, pyritous copper and ordinary pyrites had driven the miners in despair from their labors. But as these ores yielded from twenty-five to thirty per cent. of copper, they were valuable to one in less haste to be rich; and for a trifle an English gentleman became their proprietor prior to 1850, erecting furnaces on the spot, and sending the produce through Huasco. On the purchase money for all such sales the national treasury levies a duty of two per cent.; and the number of mines and shares that change owners annually is not a small one. Cateadores are usually without means to prosecute their labors of discovery, or work the mines they find; their necessities are urgent, and in many cases speculation in shares has all the excitement of gambling. Indeed it becomes a mania like that which excites the lottery gambler, to whom the stimulant is not less fascinating, notwithstanding the utter ruin in which it often involves so many around him. Limited knowledge of scientific mining renders success so doubtful, that shares are frequently sold in new mines for a few hundred dollars which as many thousands would not repurchase a year later. Two such examples occurred with one of my friends. During the year 1850 he sold a share in the *Buena Esperanza*, at Tres Puntas, for $13,000; and in December following gave $500 for a *vara* of the Salvadora, in the same district. In July, 1852, stock of the Buena Esperanza could not be bought at $50,000, and he wrote me that his net *monthly* profits from the Salvadora exceeded $2,000! He had been offered $47,000 for his share.

South of the valley of Huasco, and nearest to the coast, the mines of most consequence are those of San Juan and Higuera. These yield oxides and pyrites of copper to the amount of 4,500 tons annually. There are others not so valuable in the vicinity of Freirina, five leagues from the port of Huasco, and one or two unimportant gold veins on nearly the same meridian. For smelting or shipment, the ores are transported to the port in their crude state. But here, as to the north of the valley, the most interesting district to the geological miner lies nearer to the Andes. At fifteen leagues from the coast is Vallenar, the capital of the department of the same name, in the midst of an oval valley some 600 yards broad, and whose principal extent is from east to west. The valley lies 150 feet below the general level of the sandy plains on either side, limiting the usefulness of the Huasco, a limpid rivulet flowing through its midst, and confining cultivation to a small number of orchards and pasture-fields on its banks. Such is the climate, that fruits, and more especially the raisins, have great fame throughout the republic. The town contains about 3,500 inhabitants, who are almost entirely dependent on the product of the mines for support; and as those of Agua Amarga and Tunas, to which its prosperity was mainly due thirty years ago, have been nearly exhausted, Vallenar is on the decline. Huasco thus is likely to become the important town of this portion of the province. Freirina, at five leagues from the port, having been injured by attempts to irrigate the esplanade at the back of it, the greater portion of the houses have necessarily been abandoned, and the citizens have petitioned government to establish a new city adjoining the present site. As a new custom-house and a convenient wharf for landing goods and passengers have recently been completed, if water can be obtained, Huasco will thrive.

The silver mines of Carriso, remarkable for the great variety of minerals they contain, are six or eight leagues east of Vallenar. Ruby-blende of a bright red, and sometimes crystallized, is the most abundant. Native antimoniacal silver; sulphuret of silver; native arsenio-sulphuret of iron, often with cobalt, and rich in silver; pure native antimony; arsenic; pure arsenite of iron; grey argentiferous copper; blende; galena; purple copper and iron pyrites, are also found. The native arsenic is sometimes compact, heavy, and testaceous, in which case it scarcely contains any silver; and is sometimes black, scoriaceous, and light, and then we find in its pores metastatic dodecahedrons of ruby-blende, or rather of pure filiform silver. The gangue is carbonate of lime and argil, and in 1846 the mine had been worked to a depth of 1,000 feet, in an average direction of S. 20° E. A vein containing native gold has also been found in a part of the same hill.

On the line of contact of the granitic and stratified formations, three leagues S.E. of Carriso, is the isolated hill containing the silver mines of Agua Amarga. Its external aspect bears strong resemblance to El Bolaco, though it is more extensive. From N.W. to S.E. its length is about $4\frac{1}{3}$ miles, its elevation above the sea 4,750 feet, and over the surrounding plain 1,000 feet. Mineral veins crop out almost at its very summit. Four different stages or strata are notable in its structure above the granite forming its base: 1. A formation impregnated with carbonate of lime, resembling compact euritic or felspathic rocks. 2. Blackish-grey porphyry, with small crystals of felspar and amphibole. 3. Compact calcareous layers, more or less argillaceous. 4. A stratum of compact blackened porphyry, from six to eight feet thick, which caps the most elevated crest of its southern extremity. More than two hundred metallic veins have been found—a number exceeding those at Chañarcillo; but as they are nearly vertical, they have not so great a horizontal length as in that district. They vary from an inch to three feet in width, with a general direction north and south, though some few lie N.E. and S.W. Six of them had been famous in their day, yielding abundance of chloro-bromide ores; but at the time of Prof. Domeyko's visit more than 200 mines had been abandoned, a great number of the miners' houses were in ruins, and there remained only a few huts, with about twenty operatives, who found occupation principally as gleaners from the previously rejected ores. There was still one mine yielding chlorated ores lucratively. It was at the very foot of the hill; and though it had been worked to a depth of 120 feet, the granite formation had not been encountered—a fact which proves, Prof. Domeyko says, "that the granite wall rises at nearly a vertical angle, instead of forming a horizontal bed under the rocks cropping out at the base of the hill."

Less than a mile S.E. of the last are the mines of Cañas and Rincon de Tunas; and half a mile S.S.W. of the latter are those of Tunas, which, in their day, afforded as much metal, in proportion to their number, as those of Agua Amarga. Like it, nearly all the veins have been abandoned, and only four remain in operation. Their riches also existed near the surface, some $400,000, principally of native and ruby silver, associated with native arsenic and arsenio-sulphurets, having been extracted within the first fifty feet of the surface. Below that they became sterile.

One of the most valuable copper districts is Los Camerones, distant in a westerly direction from Agua Amarga about two miles. The vein, enclosed between dioritic rocks composed of white felspar and black amphibole, lies in a N.W. and S.E. direction, and crops out on the southern face of the hill for nearly half a mile. In this length it is often separated into two parts, the interstices being filled with rocks of the same character. It is observed that the products from the divided vein are of unequal richness, the ratio of per-centage increasing in one as it diminishes in the other lying in the same transverse plane, and that ores extracted at the junction of the two branches contain the most metal. Carbonates, silicates, and oxides, exist near the surface; pyritous and purple copper lower in the fissure. The gangues of the oxides are charged with ferriferous argils and micaceous iron. Those of the sulphurets are more quartzy, and also contain much tremolite. Having been opened at the close of the last century, this is one of the oldest-worked mines of the province. As many of the ores afforded quite fifty per cent., although the price of copper was scarcely one third as much as at the present day, and there was no market for it nearer than Lima or Buenos Ayres, its proprietor died wealthy. Since then it has been purchased by an English company, who annually extract about 1,200 tons of ores, containing an average of 15 to 20 per cent. of copper. Those which will yield more than 24 per cent. are shipped to England; 7 to 8 per cent. are rejected; and the remainder are smelted on the spot. For this purpose several reverberatory furnaces have been erected, and the arborescent cacti and branches of shrubs collected in the vicinity afford a scanty supply of fuel.

Of several other mines in the province which yield small quantities of gold from veins and washings, argentiferous and other copper ores, we only know the names and localities. These the map will afford the reader. Their poverty hitherto, and that of all nature surrounding them, will ever remain as obstacles to prevent extensive or very remunerative operations.

As will have been seen from its export trade, the province of Coquimbo ranks among the most productive copper districts of the world; and, were there suitable machinery and skilful mining engineers, the more precious metals would be obtained in amply remunerative quantities. The entire region embraced between the parallels of 30° and 31° south, and the 73d and 74th degrees of longitude, is literally crowded with veins of gold, silver, quicksilver, copper, and other most rare combinations of metals. Only one or two of them, at which remarkable minerals have been found, will even be named. The reader must refer to the map for the localities, and to the accompanying report of Prof. Smith for an account of the ores produced, and the characteristics of many others. It will be well to bear in mind, too, that as we progress southward, mines exist in a more hospitable region; water and fuel, the two primary necessities, become abundant; and with the first there are consequently increased alimentary resources.

The mines which merit more than a passing reference are those of Arqueros and Algodones—one situated to the north and the other to the south of the Coquimbo river. The former lie thirteen leagues N.E. of La Serena, and nearly at an equal distance from the coast, at the contact of the porphyritic and dioritic masses constituting the base of the littoral region with the secondary stratified formation. They were accidentally discovered, in 1825, by one of the wood-hunters of the province stumbling over rolled stones containing a large per-centage of native silver, and which were uselessly cumbering the bottom of a ravine. As might be supposed, a crowd went to the spot when his good luck became known; and it is said that $10,000 worth of silver was picked from the surface in ores of this nature. In a short time, not only the vein from which these stones came was discovered, but also two others, lying nearly parallel with it; since when their combined products have realized more than four millions of dollars. The hill is not far from a league in diameter. Says Prof. Domeyko:

"Starting from the Bay of Coquimbo for Arqueros, we leave the granite and sienite at the shores of the Pacific, and traverse the amphibolic porphyries and diorites, in which we perceive the copper mines of Brillador, the gold mines of Santa Gracia, and many veinules of gold and copper of little importance. It is only at a league from Arqueros that we observe the layers of the stratified formation strongly marked; and at that very locality we find the mines of Rodaito and Romero, containing metallic silver and chlorite ore.

"The layers which here compose the system of stratification are banks of conglomerates, tufa, and porphyritic breccia, alternating with thin compact schistous and sometimes calcareous beds. One of the last, entirely composed of shells,* is found between the mines of Rodaito and Arqueros, on the road leading to the latter.

"Now this system of stratified rocks of Romero and Rodaito rests on felspathic masses, deprived of amphibole, which form the most elevated plateau of the mountain of Arqueros. Arrived at its summit, which, according to the observations of M. Gay, is 4,800 feet above the level of the sea, and casting an eye over the surrounding country, we perceive the escarpments of the stratified formation extending from W. to S.E.; and, as they indicate the boundaries of the upraised formations, one would say that the felspathic mass which has pierced them, and encloses within it here the great riches of Arqueros, forms the centre of a local sublevation.

"As we turn from S.W. to N.E., the mass changes its aspect. At first it is a green material (pâte), containing lamellar white and reddish felspathic crystals, or rather compact amorphous parts of the same nature as the crystals. It often becomes reddish or bluish gray, without change of color in the crystals. Sometimes the crystals disappear, and the rock becomes brecciaform, composed of reddish and bluish portions. In short, the main body of the mountain,

* "These are bivalves very elongated, the species of which it has been impossible for me to determine. There has likewise been found in it a small gryphite, which I have also met with in the silver mines between Agua Amarga and Huasco."—*Annales des Mines, 3d series, Vol. XX.*

that which contains the richest mines of Arqueros, is only euritic rock, compact, gray, greenish, or reddish, and in which there are no traces of crystals.

"Whether compact, euritic, porphyritic, or breccia-form, in general all these rocks effervesce more or less with acids, and are impregnated with carbonate of lime, manganese, and iron. A specimen from the enclosing rocks of the richest vein gave twenty per cent. of these minerals.

"There is only a small number of mineral species in the felspathic mass I have just described. Above all, we remark the absence of quartz and mica accompanying auriferous deposits and amphibole, more extensively spread than any species in the system of the Andes, and which ordinarily is found with copper mines. The most abundant mineral—that which constitutes the gangue of the ores, and forms an infinity of veins, lines, and nuggets through the entire extent of the mountain—is sulphate of barytes, associated with spathic lime and carbonate of barytes. This substance also serves as a guide to miners in their search for ores. It is almost always crystalline and lamellar, but never crystallized or transparent. Fissures five to six feet broad are found filled with this mineral, in a nearly pure state, containing no traces of silver. When such traces are found, it often becomes compact and mixed with ferriferous, calcareous, or cobaltiferous portions."

There are two principal veins parallel with and distant from each other, about half the diameter of the hill. They crop out 120 feet below the summit, extend for a mile and a half along a northwest and southeast line, and descend almost vertically, having only a slight dip to the southwest. The richest of the two veins, and whose discovery was due to the silver stones found in the ravine, is from two to three feet wide, sometimes separated into several strings, none of which ever depart far from the general line of the principal fissure. Nearly all of the best ores have been obtained from within about 150 horizontal feet of the central portion, after the vein had been wrought to a depth of sixty feet. Silver disappeared entirely at the depth of 230 feet. Neither of the veins had been worked 300 vertical feet; and both Dr. Darwin and Prof. Domeyko describe them as in bad condition, owing to the want of proper machinery to keep them free from water, and loss of the richest ores by theft.

The principal and almost the only valuable ore, and that which renders the mines remarkable, is a hydrargyrite of silver, or natural amalgam, whose composition is atomic and constant. Prof. Domeyko thinks it has not been found in any mine of silver or mercury of the old or new continent. His analyses gave,

Silver	0.865
Mercury . . .	0.135 = 1.000

or two atoms of silver for thirteen of mercury; that of Prof. Smith will be found in Appendix D.

Below the arquerite, as this mineral has been called, small quantities of filiform silver have been found. Cobaltiferous sulphuret of silver is often obtained with the rich ores from the centre of the vein; arseniate of cobalt, as in nearly all the silver mines of Chile, is a constant companion; and multiple cupreous sulphurets are quite numerous near the lowest wrought portions of the fissure. Besides these, there have also been found greenish arseniate of nickel, galena, and iron pyrites.

In the secondary stratified porphyry of the same meridian as Arqueros, and about thirty miles south of it, is Los Algodones, a mine not less interesting to the mineralogist. The height of the hill in which it is contained is rather less than that of Agua Amarga, and the veins are near its summit. Their general direction is north 5° to 7° west, the dip very slightly to the east, and their thickness from two to three inches. The enclosing rock is porphyry: sometimes of a sombre violet-brown, spotted with many grey, green, and bluish shades; and sometimes of an ashy grey spotted with red. Occasionally it is found brecciaform; that is to say, the spots resemble the angular fragments of breccia. The structure of the walls is almost always earthy, and rarely compact; their felspar crystals very small and irregular, as in most of the stratified porphyries; and in the neighborhood of the fissure we find calcareous spar, disseminated in nodules, filets, and very irregular veins.

Through the first fifteen or sixteen feet to which the vein was explored, the only metals found were ioduret of silver and native silver, the latter in very small proportion and in extremely attenuated particles. The ioduret is in very narrow and wholly irregular filets, and is perfectly pure, having no admixture of iodine or chlorine. Its gangue consists partly of carbonate of lime, and partly of an extremely fine argil of a dark brick-red color. To this earthy substance the small amorphous particles and veinules of ioduret seem to have given preference. An analogous material also exists in the fissures at Arqueros, where Prof. Domeyko succeeded in detecting traces of this rare silver ore of a fine citron color. Specimens of considerable size and purity have since been found in the mines of Chañarcillo, and form part of the collection brought home by the expedition. An analysis and description by Prof. Smith will be found in the Appendix.

About a ton and a half of ore containing ioduret were extracted from Los Algodones above the level mentioned; and then, although the gangue remained the same, the product changed to greenish chloro-bromide ores, similar to those of Chañarcillo. In its turn, this also disappeared, and was succeeded by chlorite of silver, the ore in the last case becoming cupriferous and siliceous.

Six hundred feet from the preceding vein, and parallel with it, a second has been found; but it contains no ioduret, and only a cupreous mineral with sulphuret and chlorite of silver in a green silicated gangue, mixed with carbonate of lime.

Between the valley of the river Barrasá and that of the Aconcagua, the granite formation extends much farther to the eastward; "the stratified formation is pushed towards the cordilleras. The calcareous and siliceous rocks of Chañarcillo and Agua Amarga are entirely wanting; only fossiliferous strata near the line of separation and stratified porphyries preponderate."* Auriferous deposits have been found in a multitude of places in the granite section; and though the most valuable ore is farthest removed from the ocean, there are more veins and washings along the coast. Near Illapel, Petorca, and Andacollo, the deposits have been the most productive. Those near the contacts of granite and stratified rock have not unfrequently copper veins among them. Many of the ores from these, situated in the valley of Barrasá, are smelted on the spot, and the rest are sent to Tongoy, whence they are shipped to Coquimbo or Valparaiso.

Of the actual wealth of the mines in Aconcagua much less is known, and it is only by inference that we can arrive at an approximate result. Nature has interposed obstacles to their transportation, even when liberated from the worthless earthy portions. There is no stream in the province navigable by boats even for a short distance; the whole face of the country is broken by hills, across which there are only mule paths; and unless the mines be found in the vicinity of towns or supplies of fuel, none but the most valuable ores repay exploration. In times past the province was famed for its gold washings, of which those of La Ligua, on a hill just to the northward of Quillota, and of Catemo, twelve leagues nearer to the source of the river, were among the most noted. The gold, disseminated in minute particles through sienite, was extracted by amalgamation at establishments erected on the river, both at San Felipe and Quillota. Dr. Darwin mentions valuable copper mines at Jajuel, a ravine east of San Felipe, on the flank of the great cordilleras. Its ores were all sent to England to be smelted. Specimens have been brought from mines in the hill of San Lorenzo, and an account of them is given in Prof. Smith's report. As Valparaiso exported in copper and its ores to the value of $1,086,000 during the year 1850, and received from Atacama, Coquimbo, and the furnaces at Talcahuano, only the value of $205,000 within the same period, there being no mines known in the province of which it is the capital, it follows that Aconcagua, Santiago, and Colchagua have furnished about $881,000. It is most probable that the greater portion was brought from Aconcagua.

As far back as 1803, a committee appointed under the captain generalcy of Guzman reported

*Prof. Domeyko: Annales des Mines.

no less than 175 gold deposits in the same three provinces which supply Valparaiso with copper. They are entirely within and west of the cordilleras of the coast, commencing at Chacabuco, as we leave the valley of Aconcagua to pass into the tertiary plain which separates them from the Andes. At the present day the only mine worked is that of La Leona, on the eastern declivity of the hills of Alhue, and about four leagues from Rancagua. The direction of the principal lode varies very little from north and south, and the vein is remarkable for the variety of mineral substances associated with its gold, disseminated through quartz. Señor Pissis mentions other veins at a short distance from this mine; but the greater number are too poor in gold to pay the expense of working them. Molina has a good many "*cuentas de frayle*" (fish stories) in his book, though none more thoroughly imaginative than that respecting the "celebrated" mine of Peldehue, in the neighborhood of Santiago, which was suddenly inundated, the workmen, after vainly making every exertion to free it from water, being compelled to abandon it at a time when its daily yield was fifteen hundred pounds of gold, or just about $300,000 !

The present generation have uniformly found silver mining more lucrative than working auriferous deposits. Probably the first veins explored were those of San Pedro, on the Uspallata range. They were undoubtedly known to the Peruvians; yet if the statement of Mr. Miers be correct, that their yield is only two marks (at most $19) to the cajon (6,400 pounds) of ore, it is not easy to comprehend why any one has persisted in efforts to obtain a quantity of silver that would scarcely repay the cost of working. These mines, however, are now within the Argentine republic, and the reader is referred to the volumes of Mr. M. and Capt. Head for further information respecting them. In the province of Santiago, the only mines wrought at the present date are at San Lorenzo (not the one just mentioned) and San Pedro Nolasco, both far up the Maypu. But little had been obtained from the former until recently, when a new rich vein was struck, and its proprietor found himself able to command above $200,000 for a mine which, a year previously, he would have gladly sold for a tenth of the money. The friend who writes me about it at one time was part owner, and sold out to avoid further loss. He says: "The *alcance* (discovery of the vein) has made no little stir in this dull place—Santiago—some $12,000 having been taken out within a week." The ores are similar to those of San Pedro Nolasco, still farther within the cordilleras—native silver and sulphurets of the same metal in the superior, and grey copper and galena in the inferior portions of their veins. Both hills have an elevation of more than 6,000 feet above the Pacific.* East of Santiago, in the Dehesa range, there is another valuable vein; but the meshes of the law have been thrown around it, and the litigants will probably be compelled to transfer many a golden ounce to the pockets of its expounders, before they are again permitted to prosecute the excavation. No workmen were employed during the whole time we were in Chile. A new vein, containing native silver with malachite, was found on San Francisco just prior to our departure; it was at so great an elevation, however, that it was buried under snow immediately after discovery, and its value had not been proved.

Copper, zinc, cobalt, and iron, have also been found; the two first in quantity, the others to no considerable extent. The mine of the *Teniente*, at the head-waters of one of the tributaries of the Cachapual, is among the most productive in copper, and some of its beautiful carbonates have been brought to the United States among our specimens. Native copper is also found. The other mines in operation are in the *Quebrada de las Vegas*, near the source of the main stream, and on the hacienda "Del Carmen," a part of the cordillera of the coast, on the left bank of the Maypu. In the Quebrada de las Vegas, masses of native copper have been found weighing more than a hundred pounds. Sulphuret of zinc accompanies abundantly the argentiferous veins of San Pedro Nolasco. Cobalt is only found, forming part of a mineral composed of arsenical pyrites and arseniate of cobalt, in the Cerro del Volcan; but the ore has never proved to contain more than 20 per cent. Iron is apparently scarcer than any other metal. To the present time only two small ologistic veins are known to exist near the plain; and a

* San Pedro Nolasco, 10,900 feet.

hydrate has been found near the crest of the Andes. Neither of them would repay the expenses of working in any country—least of all in Chile, where fuel is so scarce. More than one *cateador* has reported discoveries of coal mines within a reasonable distance of Santiago; and I read a letter from an Englishman, stating that samples which he had brought from one such deposit had proved highly satisfactory to the blacksmith who had tried their qualities. But no mention of such mineral is made in the report of Señor Pissis to the government; and the fact that stone-coal is still carted from Valparaiso, casts doubt on the existence of this important commodity.

I am not aware that there are any mines in operation in the province of Colchagua except those of Yaquil or Jajuel, mentioned by Dr. Darwin, near Lake Taguatagua. Two lavaderos have been recently announced to the government by the Intendente, but it is probable that they will prove like most of the rest,—not worth the attenion of capitalists. Those of Chivato, in the province of Talca, and their products, are mentioned in the Narrative of a Visit to the Southward, Chapter XV. Maule is very little better off. One gold mine, thirty-six lavaderos, three silver veins, and one of copper, are all that have been registered within eighty years. Many of these have been exhausted or abandoned as unproductive, and the whole yield at the last return was less than $10,000 per annum. The efforts which were made by Valdivia and his immediate successors to reconquer and retain the extreme southern provinces, after his temporary success against the Araucanians, is the best evidence we could have of the mineral wealth abounding there. We know that the Spaniards of that day cared only for the precious metals, and thought little of the natives whom they destroyed in their efforts to accumulate wealth. As each new district was reduced to submission, it was apportioned by the leader and his subordinates with all the inhabitants, thousands of whom were sometimes given as the share of a single officer. Avarice was predominant, and the unlettered savage whose previous life had been one of liberty and ease approaching the "*dolce far niente*," found himself tasked beyond his corporeal powers to fill the coffers of a master who hesitated not to scourge or starve him to exertion. Imperial, Villarica, Concepcion, and Valdivia, rose into wealth and importance under this system with a rapidity almost rivalling the growth of North American towns at the present day, and solely because of the abundance of gold extracted from the mines and lavaderos in their vicinity. Indeed the soil was so productive, that each Indian was said to have been required to pay his master to the value of thirty or forty ducats each week—some say, each day.* Frezier, who visited Chile in 1714, tells us: "Concepcion is situated in a country abounding not only with all the necessaries of life, but with immense riches, particularly a place called King's Camp, about twelve leagues to the east, from whence are obtained, by washing, pieces of pure gold, called in the country *pepitas*, of from eight to ten marks (sixty-four to eighty ounces) in weight." And in another place he says: "I saw at Concepcion a piece of (copper), ore of forty quintals (four thousand pounds) weight, from which, when melted, were cast six field-pieces of six pounds calibre." Although the accounts of this writer and Molina must be received *cum grano salis*, we know that there was such abundance of gold received in Valdivia as authorized the erection of a mint for its coinage.

But the Indians who had at first willingly given their glittering grains to those whom they then regarded at least as demigods, were soon painfully made to know the importance of these earth products, and looked with amazement on the cupidity of their tyrannical masters. In the northern and central provinces the gentle aborigines had sunk under harsh usage, as dwindled the snows of their own mountains under summer heats. The climate and habits of the Araucanians and Cunchos had rendered them more hardy and warlike; and when extortion, cruelty, and oppression had driven them to rebel against such conquerors and masters, the torch of liberty, rekindled in the darkest hour of adversity by Lautaro, grew brighter and brighter, until the invader was driven from their soil, lighted by the flames of the cities he had erected under the shadows of their Andes. Gold—the accursed metal which had drawn these evils on them, which had caused the slaughter of their bravest chiefs, the violation of their wives

* Sanson's Geography: article CHILE.

and daughters, the pillage of their humble homesteads, the enslavement of themselves and brethren—was looked upon with execration; and from the moment that the Spaniards were driven from their territory, every effort was made to destroy all traces of mines and mining. In a region where vegetation grows rankly and rapidly this was no difficult task; and now but few of the auriferous deposits could be discovered from former evidences, even did the jealous native permit his ancient foe within the territory. If any gold mines are worked, the product must either find its way to the mint at Santiago by land, or be smuggled out of the country; as there is nothing in the custom-house returns of the last few years to show it, and the Valdivia mint has long since been disused. Talcahuano exports annually about $100,000 in bar copper—doubtless the products of the mines of Payen and other veins in that vicinity.

Within a few years some of the vaqueros near Chillan brought pepitas of considerable value from a pretty locality five or six leagues to the eastward of that town. Its fame attracted the indolent,—always ready to embrace any occupation by which a subsistence may be obtained with the least amount of labor,—and at the last accounts some three thousand people had collected there. Not that so many find constant or lucrative employment in gold mining; but that the soil of the district is fertile, and a portion of the population occupy themselves in agriculture, which is probably more profitable than gold mining or washing.

The first grains were found at the confluence of two small streams, one of which descends from the immediate hills to the eastward, and the other flows parallel with the Andes. Here the settlement was made, and has gradually extended eastwardly for about a league, excavation and sifting going on simultaneously, though the majority continue washing the sands. Unlike any other auriferous region now worked in Chile, the granite in which the gold is embedded is buried under a thick stratum of vegetable mould on which a dense forest is growing, and there are few willing to risk outlay for its removal in the uncertainty of recovering expenses. The grains of gold obtained are exchanged on the spot for the necessaries of life, and consequently fall into the hands of a few dealers; but in three years there was not sufficient collected at *Pueblo de las Minas*, as the place is called, to be worthy of a newspaper paragraph.

But there are other deposits of mineral in these provinces, which may one day become of far more consequence than the precious metals ever were in the seventeenth century. In the vicinity of Concepcion several mines of coal, or rather of lignite, have been found; and as every deposit of combustible material on the west coast of America is of the highest interest to commercial men in every part of the world, any facts relating to them may be useful.

The mine called "Talcahuano," which is the nearest to the city of the same name, crops out on the northwest side of a hill or promontory between the shore of the bay and the modern alluvial formation. The promontory is about fifty yards long, and as many in height. It contains two veins dipping to the west, irregular in their direction, and presenting, in some places, contortions and faults. Each vein is three feet thick, and they are separated by a stratum of sandstone five yards wide. "The combustible material which they yield has external characters of a coal of mediocre quality: one sees neither traces of ligneous structure nor impressions of vegetables, leaves, or spots. It is very bituminous, and burns with the odor characteristic of lignites. It does not agglomerate or change form by carbonization. The sandstone of the superior part of the hill is yellowish, with brown spots, and encloses very ochreous lumps and fragments of modern shells. It passes to sands of the same color, and in some places is found covered with broken shells of the same species and varieties as are daily thrown on the beach by the waves. The sandstone on which the inferior stratum of lignite rests, and which constitutes all the lower part of the formation, is micaceous, presenting in the fresh fractures small carbonized spots, and sometimes impressions of leaves and fragments of turrilites, which seem to belong to the species so common in all the tertiary formation of the coast of Chile."*

* Annales des Mines, Tome XIV. 1848.

Next in point of distance are the mines of Tierras Coloradas, situated on the river Andalien, and about half way between Talcahuano and Concepcion. These have produced the best coal, and their position is such that boats can be loaded from the mouth of the mine without inconvenience. The vein runs north and south; it dips to the west, and is above 120 yards long, 80 yards wide, and 2½ feet thick. Near the surface it was very indifferent, but has improved in quality as the lode became deeper. There is an analysis of these coals by M. L. Crosnier, in the "Annales des Mines" for 1851, which is as follows:

Mine.	Coke.	Ashes.	Volatile matter.	Calorific power.	
Lota, near Colcura	*5.23	*6.46	0.31	24.30	* There is an evident error in one of these two data. J. M. G.
Lotilla do	4.27	5.43	0.30	24.95	
Penco	3.99	3.13	0.83	21.01	
Collumo	3.70	5.99	0.31	22.46	
Andalien	4.96	4.89	0.15	22.65	
Magellan, No. 1	3.99	5.74	0.27	†4.312	† Anales de la Universidad de Chile, 1850. Pure carbon being = 7.815.
Do No. 2	3.28	5.85	0.87	3.680	
Do No. 3	2.98	5.62	1.40	3.450	

A comparative estimate of their merits may also be formed from the investigations of a commission appointed by the Minister of the Interior to report on specimens of apparently similar material brought from Port Bulnes, in the Straits of Magellan. They say: "The fossil coal of the Straits of Magellan, though inferior to the fossil coal of Concepcion, differs very little from the latter, and may be used in the same manner. Each three quintals, in the consumption by furnaces, is equivalent to at least two quintals of good English coals, and each six quintals to five quintals of the best Concepcion coal."* Specimens from the Magellan formation afforded thirty-nine per cent. of pure carbon. Samples of both are embraced in the collection brought home, as stated by Prof. Smith.

Two other veins, on the east side of the bay of Talcahuano, never having been productive, were abandoned several years ago. Those of Coronel and Colcura, a few leagues southward of the Biobio, and near the ocean, are even more extensive than those of Tierras Coloradas. The character of the formation, however, is the same. At Colcura the veins crop out quite close to the sea, beneath which they dip within a very short distance—a fact that will probably have great influence in their prosecution. Those of Coronel were found only a short time before we left Chile, and the papers claimed for their products a very high character. When a supply of foreign (English) coal has been scarce at Valparaiso, of necessity the mail steamers have used the Concepcion variety; but much complaint is made by the engineers of its want of power to generate steam rapidly, and of the quickness with which it destroys the fire-bars. Latterly, small quantities have been taken to the north for the use of the railroad company at Copiapó and the smelting furnaces, the average export during the last four years being about 500 tons. Aided by proper engines to free the mines from water, and facilitated by a railroad to Colcura, there is no doubt that the products of these strata would be a valuable contribution to the domestic economy of a country so poor in combustible material as is all Chile north of the Rapel.

The presence of similar veins has also been recognised in the province of Valdivia, and on the island of Chilóe; and Professor Domeyko informed me that in more than one place, during journeys along the secondary formation of the Andes, he had met with small deposits of an inferior quality. Among them the structure of the wood was still quite distinct, and they were not unfrequently accompanied by ligneous petrifactions.

* Anales de la Universidad de Chile, 1850. See also "Memoria que el Ministro de Estado en el Departamento De Marina, presenta al Congreso Nacional de 1850."

These are not the only mineral productions of this favored land. Cinnabar and other ores of quicksilver, tin, lead, graphite, manganese, magnetic and other iron, cobalt, antimony, arsenic, zinc, bismuth, sulphur, rock-salt, alum, gypsum, chalcedony, agates, jasper, asbestos, all exist in such quantities as will some day cause them to become articles of commerce.

About thirty years ago, the ancient fame of the South American mines presented to the European public a new field for the employment of a large amount of capital then idle, and more than one company was formed in England for the purpose of working them. Without reflecting that even the first-formed association had not yet had time for its agent to perfect a purchase, the announcement that bars of gold and silver from one of them had reached the London custom-house created such excitement, that all the mining stocks rose to prices almost rivalling those of Law's Bank, in France, a century before. Surveyors, agents, and miners were despatched in all haste to the scene of operation; some companies shipped machinery and implements without waiting to learn from their subordinates whether they had obtained a single vein; others gave most responsible and confidential appointments to fellow-countrymen who had resided some time in Chile, inferentially believing their knowledge of the country paramount, and forgetting that traders on the South American coast have sometimes considered it remunerative to leave their consciences at home. In most cases the latter saw opportunity to enrich themselves in a rapid manner, and in a brief time hesitated at nothing to procure the recall of those more recently from the fatherland, and whose integrity would interfere with their operations. Mr. Miers had previously gone out with every preparation for refining, rolling, and manufacturing copper, taking with him above 200 tons of machinery. Capt. Head, R. A., and Capt. Andrews, R. N., who had previously passed several years in South America, followed as agents of different companies, and all of them have given the public the results of their judgments. Mines were purchased in Buenos Ayres, Peru, and Chile; and had a moderate prudence been observed by the directors at home, and had the share-holders exercised a little more patience, it is more than probable that the results would have been widely different. As it was, almost the whole capitals, amounting to nearly £2,000,000, were sunk within a few years, there remaining little more than immovable masses of machinery cumbering the beach in several parts of Chile. There was neither vehicle nor road by which it could have been moved, even had the engineers reported necessity for it.

The explanations which these gentlemen have given of the causes of failure are widely variant. Climate, rarity of the air, modes of working, scarcity of necessaries, difficulties of transportation, and lastly the *poverty of the mines*, have all been brought forward, one of them having published all these as obstacles to the public, after having literally made but a galloping tour to some of the districts proposed to be worked. The endurance and enormous strength of the Chilean miners, the simple food on which they subsist, their low rates of wages, and the economical modes of reducing ores, strangely enough, are all admitted; but they, as well as the directors, seem to have taken for granted the superiority of Cornish miners; and the propriety of having only foreign administration appears never to have been thought of, except by Capt. Andrews. It is not surprising, then, that the panic created on the publication of Capt. Head's narrative, added to the premature and injudicious outlays of directors, created a crash; but time has shown, as has been exhibited in preceding statistics of this chapter, that there is almost unlimited wealth in silver and copper from Atacama to Santiago.

CHAPTER XI.

MINERAL SPRINGS.

APOQUINDO.—COLINA: TOPOGRAPHY OF THE BATHS; ANALYSIS OF THE WATERS; ACCOMMODATIONS FOR VISITORS; A NIGHT IN THE CABINS.—CAUQUENES: CELEBRATED FOR THE CURE OF CERTAIN DISEASES; BEAUTIFUL LOCATION.—PANIMAVILA: THE ONLY BATHS KNOWN AT THE LEVEL OF THE GREAT VALLEY; TEMPERATURE, ODOR, AND MINERAL INGREDIENTS OF THE WATER.—MONDACA: THEIR LOCALITY, TEMPERATURE, AND MINERAL CONSTITUENTS; NO ACCOMMODATIONS.—CATO.—CHILLAN.—SULPHUR BATHS IN A RAVINE OF THE ANDES; DWELLINGS; TEMPERATURE OF THE SPRINGS; WHOLE ATMOSPHERE IMPREGNATED WITH SULPHURETTED HYDROGEN; BOILING WATER BENEATH A SNOW-BANK.—DOÑA ANA: THE ONLY MINERAL SPRINGS RESORTED TO IN THE NORTHERN PART OF CHILE; THEIR LOFTY POSITION AMONG THE ANDES; TEMPERATURE OF WATER, ETC.—SOCO: SITUATED NEAR THE OCEAN; ALSO IN THE PROVINCE OF COQUIMBO.

APOQUINDO.

The mineral baths of Apoquindo are three leagues to the eastward of Santiago, and on the base of the first chain of the Andes. The road towards them follows the Mapocho during the first league after leaving the city, and then, at the junction of the Maypu canal, bends more to the right. It passes between the best cultivated *chacras* and prettiest *quintas* of the neighborhood. Between the canal and the fields immediately at the base of the mountains, owing to scarcity of water, there is a strip of less productive land; yet all the fields are made to yield something for the supply of the great market so near to them, and groves of olives and fruit-trees may be seen on either side.

The baths are on an estate belonging to the Dominican monks, the white towers of whose large convent and chapel, a mile or more to the northward, loom pleasantly amid green foliage. To the convent, as well as to the entrance of the enclosed field in which are the baths, the ascent is almost imperceptible; but for the last mile the ground rises more rapidly, and at the spot where the water issues from the earth one will have attained a height of 2,600 feet above the level of the sea, and some 750 feet above that of the plaza of Santiago. In fact the ascent of the Andes will have been begun. The surrounding hills are covered with shrubbery and an undergrowth of pasturage; in spring, sprinkled with gay-colored flowers, overlooked by numbers of the tall cacti (*Cereus quisco*) so often mentioned, and whose large cream-tinted flowers render them striking and beautiful objects. Here many of them are more than fifteen feet high, with trunks larger than the body of a man, from which a score of smaller arms project, giving them the appearance of huge candelabra. Their flowers have an elongated pear-shaped base, an inch and a half in its greatest diameter, crowned by a double row of lanceolate petals, arranged in the form of a bell four or five inches across the mouth. Within, the pistils and stamens are gracefully grouped and equally pretty.

The baths, six in number, are supplied from small springs near the mouth of a ravine, which becomes somewhat wider, and, because of the rise of the hills, apparently much deeper, as one proceeds eastward. Those on the north side of the ravine have been called, indiscriminately, "*Baños de litre,*" a tree of that species (*L. venenosa*) growing over them, and "*Agua de la sarna*" (itch-water), from its efficacy in curing that disease;* and those on the south side, "*Agua de la cañita*" (water from the little spout), a small tube being inserted to facilitate its collection as it issues from the rock. The latter is drank, and is probably more

* It is very generally believed that the *litre* will poison all who remain long beneath its shadow, although they may not touch its foliage. Would it not be curious if its atmosphere, and not the water, is the remedy for this cutaneous disorder?

limpid than the "*Agua de la sarna.*" Though extremely unpleasant to the palate, both are odorless and crystalline, nor is any odor perceptible at the bursting of the gas-bubbles constantly ascending in the "*Agua de la sarna.*" The lessee of the baths told me that there are great differences in the taste and temperature of the water under varied circumstances; that the taste in winter differed from that of summer, and that the waters from the *Cañita* are not only warmer at night than during the day, but are also at a higher temperature in rainy than in cloudy weather. And an anecdote may be recited of a fellow-countryman, showing how powerful is the influence of popular impressions. He was with me at the visit when the lessee told of differences of temperature, and received each statement as so many Gospel truths. During the visit, clouds had accumulated over the previously unobscured sky, and a slight shower of rain fell within three hours from the time we had left Santiago. Ten minutes later he assured me that the water was much warmer than when he had put his hand in it after our arrival; but, unfortunately, the *thermometer* told a different story. The temperature of the air *had* fallen nearly five degrees, and he had only been able to detect the difference between the temperature of the air and water at the two periods. There is no greater difference between the temperatures of the springs on the two sides of the ravine than would result from the fact that the "*Agua de la sarna*" bubbles through sand and remains in the bath; while the "*Agua de la cañita,*" on which the experiment can be made, is only a diminutive jet. In the early days of April the former showed 74°.5, the latter 74°.3; and in November following they varied less than half a degree—a difference which may be explicable by the graduation of the thermometers used on the two occasions. There was a striking similarity in the atmospheric temperature at both periods. The November experiment was made near noon, with the air at 57°.2; the November trial at 6 A. M., with the air at 57°.7.

Analyses of the waters have been made by Profs. Domeyko and J. Lawrence Smith. The former says of them: "It is neither acid nor alkaline; it exercises no action on vegetable colors, and saline matters appear only by boiling, part of these forming a pellicle on the surface and part sinking to the bottom. The air that escapes during ebullition barely discolors water of barytes, showing that it scarcely contains any traces of carbonic acid. There is no indication of sulphur either as sulphate or hydrosulphate, and the porportion of sulphate of lime is very small. But that which is most notable in the water of Apoquindo is, 1st, the great quantity of salts contained, and which reach to nearly a maximum containable by the most energetic mineral waters; 2d, its great proportion of chloride of calcium; and 3d, the almost entire absence of carbonates, or free carbonic acid. Its constituents are:

Chloride of calcium	2.165
Chloride of sodium	1.177
Chloride of magnesia	0.034
Sulphate of lime	0.052
Iron and alumina	0.020
Silica	0.035
Organic matter	a trace.
	3.843

Prof. J. Lawrence Smith's analysis will be found in Appendix D.

The physicians of Santiago have found these waters valuable in the glandular affections succeeding adenitis, and the rheumatic diseases that often follow; also in cases of cachexia and chronic affections of the kidneys and abdominal regions, that prevail to an extraordinary degree in the country, and result from the quality and quantity of food consumed.

Two rows of wretched and unblanched ranchos, numbering a dozen windowless rooms with earthen floors, are the only accommodations offered to the invalid who seeks health at the waters of Apoquindo; nor are the conveniences for bathing much more attractive. The baths are thirty or forty feet below, and fifty yards distant from the ranchos. They are mere holes in the ground, two feet deep, three feet wide, and five feet long, which have been scooped from the earth and rocks, and some of them rudely bricked up ; though to others, nothing more than the excavation has been attempted. In two or three the water bubbles through a sandy deposit ; the others are filled by miniature streams through crevices in the euritic porphyry forming the base of the hills on both sides of the ravine. Divisions between bathers and the outer world are made in the same careless and comfortless style as everything else. The baths are merely enclosed with screens of reeds and brush-wood, loosely covered with like material, each visitor hanging a cloth over the doorway through which he enters. Unfortunately, the property is in bad hands for the proper development of its value ; and even natives are unable to encounter inconveniences forced on those whose want of health would recommend a sojourn there. Therefore, most Santiaguinos who avail themselves of the water either cause it to be brought to town or ride to the baths, and return immediately to their homes. Although the supply of water is limited, its undoubted medicinal value, its proximity to the city, an abundance of land for dwellings and a promenade which might soon be covered with fine trees, its healthy position, and the beautiful view that it commands, in any other country would long since have caused it to be improved and made a fashionable resort.

As a small rivulet flows down the ravine and between the baths, its source was sought under the impression that there might be some difference of temperature or other physical variation higher up, but the stream proved to be sweet and not mineral water. The ascent of its bed is not much more rapid than that of the majority of streams in Chile, though the hills continue to rise on either side ; and in a walk of a few hundred yards, one is within a deep quebrada filled with water-worn boulders and rocks, from amid which vegetation grows luxuriantly, but where the direct rays of the sun never penetrate except at midsummer.

COLINA.

These baths are on the hacienda of Peldegue, also the property of the Dominicans, and twenty-five miles to the southward of the city. At a greater distance than three leagues from Santiago in this direction, there has hitherto been very little water for the purposes of artificial irrigation, so that the vegetation of the plain east of the road is confined to dwarf acacias (*A. cavenia*) and herbage whose roots can resist the droughts of summer. The Colina river or rivulet affords a limited supply to the western side, and a recently cut canal will soon bring the rest under cultivation. Originating in the Andes near latitude 33° 05′ south, and longitude 70° 25′ west, the Colina flows S.W. by W. for thirty miles, and thence south for fifteen more, falling into the Mapocho at Pudagüel. One or two mountain rivulets increase its volume during the first part of its course ; but above their junction, and where the road to the baths crosses it, in the month of November it was only a brook, rapid and turbid as the Mapocho at Santiago, four or five yards wide and a foot deep. It is evident, however, from the space occupied by gravel, water-worn stones of considerable magnitude, and washings of the banks, that there are periods when the volume is more than one hundred yards broad ; but the growth of cacti and other plants shows that this cannot have been the case for several years.

The main road to San Felipe de Aconcagua winds along the base of precipitous spurs from the Andes, composed of rocks of the same porphyritic character as at Apoquindo, covered in some places with soil ; but in many others the masses are bare and columnar as are portions of Santa Lucia. To the eye the general width of the plain is as great as it is to the south of the city, with deep glens between the spurs of the Andes, partially cultivable by aid of rains and scanty supplies from natural springs. Overhung as they are by snow peaks, and dotted with groups of white dwellings among groves of trees and brighter colored fields of grain, some of these glens are exceedingly beautiful.

Leaving Santiago on horseback at 4 P. M., and riding leisurely, my companion and myself did not reach the river until twilight. As we were shut in by the hills, this deepened rapidly into obscurity. At some twelve miles from the city we had left the Aconcagua road to the west, and passing through a little *portezuelo*, entered a part of the valley which the water from the Colina has rendered highly productive. On the summit of an isolated and oval knoll at the intersection of the road and stream, there was a tall illuminated cross, which we supposed might be intended as a signal by the revolutionary party then agitating the country, until foot-travellers informed us that it was commemorative of a foul murder committed there some time previously, crossing themselves and whispering a prayer for the deceased as they told the story.

Darkness soon rendered the road doubtful. We had started under the belief that we had only six leagues to go, and after having travelled more than that distance, were not a little chagrined to learn that we were at least six miles from the end of our journey. No bribe we offered would tempt the peon to act as our guide, and we moved at a foot-pace towards the northeast, trusting to the sagacity of the horses to keep to the road. Close at hand, on the left, we skirted a chain of hills that rose so abruptly as to conceal more than half the heavens in that direction; on our right a high and rank growth of weeds separated us from the rushing water of the river, and before us a luminous cloud apparently rested against the wall of the Andes—a reflection of light, we hoped, from the heated vapor of the baths. Trusting as we were to the instinct of the animals, it was pleasant to see the lights of ranchos occasionally; for they were proofs that we had not passed the limits of human companionship in pursuing the undistinguishable road. When we had approached so near to the apparent cloud that a light near it could be perceived, instead of finding the path incline in its direction, the horses turned up a ravine to the left, and our dreams of rest were once more dispelled. There was no other path, and of necessity we continued on, each moment more and more shut in from even the twinkling light of stars, whilst climbing beside a brook that bounded from rock to rock beneath us. Once the horses stopped. The road passed from the west to the east face of the ravine across a narrow bridge, and they were terrified at the noise of the rushing water; but having gained confidence by soothing, they moved on up a zigzag path yet more precipitous. Evidently, in forming the road, the face of the cliff had been cut into; for we could touch its vertical wall with the hand, whilst on the other side there yawned a precipice dangerous enough to the sight at noonday, but whose terrors were no little augmented by darkness and the reverberations of falling waters. Greatly were we gratified when a sudden turn in the road brought us in presence of a number of lights so close at hand that our goal was reached in a few more minutes.

Whether it was that the sound of voices in a strange tongue within the precincts of the little settlement had roused the curiosity of its fair visitors, that they were desirous of tidings from friends at the capital from which they might reasonably suppose we had come, or that we were indebted to accident alone for a glimpse of their pretty faces, it cannot be said; but we had scarcely secured our horses in front of the room assigned us, before a bevy passed silently along the corridor, their black eyes brimming with curiosity and mirthful mischief. After inspecting us minutely without halting, as only girls can do, one whose appearance bespoke more experience than the rest good-naturedly said "Gringos,"* whereupon the whole party, herself excepted, immediately took to flight. It is bad enough to have one's nationality mistaken at any time; but at this particular period, when the interference of her Britannic Majesty's Chargé d'Affaires in their domestic quarrels had brought on all her subjects the odium of his fault, less than ever did one in Chile desire to be considered an Englishman. The gay-spirited Chilena was therefore promptly prayed to consider us, though from the frozen north, "Americans—not Gringos." What charms they might have added to our visit, there was no opportunity to test: we had not the assurance to seek an introduction at their cabins on the same evening, and until the hour of departure next day were too much occupied in rambles about the hills and baths.

Three narrow quebradas—one from N.W., another from S.E., and the intersecting one from

*The epithet *belongs* to the subjects of her Majesty Queen Victoria, although occasionally applied to other foreigners. Except in the diminutive—*Gringito*—or among intimate acquaintances, like *Godo*, (by which name patriots reproachfully designate natives of Spain), it is rarely used but offensively. Has it not, like *Yankee*, originated from the difficulty of pronouncing *English?*

N.E.—unite at an elevation of 3,020 feet above the ocean, and form, at their junction, a little tongue of inclined and rocky land perhaps two acres in extent. From one side of the tongue flow the waters that supply the baths of Colina. At as many distinct elevations within a hundred yards, there are four springs with different temperatures, and a fifth is found at a distance of three hundred yards farther down the ravine. All of them issue from rocks having the same characteristics as those at Apoquindo, and belonging to the same secondary stratification. Uniting below the tongue of land in a common stream, they form a considerable volume. This alternately flows and tumbles from rock to rock, forming innumerable miniature cascades in the steep ravine along whose side we had climbed, and finally empties into the Colina river near the base of the hills. Above the inclined platform the rocks rise precipitously some 800 or 1,000 feet, and thence more gently slope away to elevations on which, in sheltered places, the snow lies nearly all the year. The view of the heavens is thus cut off at an angle of 45° in all directions, except over the ravine by which the road ascends; and were it not for the influence of vegetation which has sprung from the soil, formed by disintegration of most of the slopes, the heats of summer would render the spot intolerable. At this season (the last month of spring) the ravines had lost none of their verdure or freshness; and only the pasturage on the steeper acclivities exhibited the short career to which the annual vegetation of such localities is subject in Chile, its golden hue forming a marked contrast with the evergreens of the glens.

The baths are mere excavations in the earth rudely bricked up, walled in with the same materials, and lightly covered with thatch, each bather, as at Apoquindo, supplying his own door. An analysis of the waters by Prof. Domeyko gives for each thousand parts by weight—

Chloride of sodium	0.1469
Chloride of magnesia	0.0092
Sulphate of soda	0.0780
Sulphate of lime	0.0196
Carbonate of lime	0.0670
Iron and a trace of alumina	0.0070
Silica	0.0160
	0.3137

That of Prof. Smith will be found in Appendix D.

Being perfectly limpid, without odor or gas whatever, and almost tasteless, every one drinks of the water without hesitation. If drunk in quantity, that of the spring lowest in the ravine, and called from its discoverer "*Agua de Grajales*," will produce vomiting; but the result of minute examination has not shown any constituent different from those called "*baño caliente*" and "*baño frio*" (warm and cold baths), and every other tepid water would have the same effect. The temperatures of the last two named were (November 14th) 89°.5 and 79°; that of the air at the same time 62°.5; and of evaporation 55°.2. Prof. Domeyko found the springs at the same temperatures in January and September of 1848, and he states that there is little or no variation throughout the year.

Did not daily experience prove the contrary, the almost total absence of organic substances would throw doubt on the medicinal properties attributed to the waters of Colina, and one would be induced to believe that change of scene, air, and diet, accomplishes more than the mineral constituents. Or is it that all their sanitary virtues are wholly due to the yet undeveloped gaseous substances which they hold in solution? They are recommended in most cutaneous diseases, chronic affections and debility of the digestive organs, and rheumatism.

Five or six rows of dwellings, with corridors in front, each row composed of a like number of quite comfortable apartments, occupy the narrow strip of land. At the intersection of the ravines, and well up on the promontory, there is a neat chapel, where mass is performed every morning; there being no lack of priests whom impaired health, or the pursuits of pleasure, bring annually to Colina. Though the fashionable season had not yet commenced, nearly all of the rooms were occupied, and quite an air of life reigned about the little colony. Only a scarcity of beaux prevented the younger portion of the señoritas from diversions which at other times are kept up during the greater part of every night. With snow on the mountains so near that it may be brought down in a few hours, as soon as the heat of the sun is gone, the temperature of the air becomes delightful; and with music, dancing, and ices, under the canopy of heaven, Colina is doubtless more attractive than the semi-deserted capital. Deeply shut in as it is, with heat radiating and reflected from rocks nowhere distant 100 yards, until the S.W. breeze commences in the morning the temperature is almost insupportable. All who can, avail themselves of the baths at these hours; and as some of the latter are large enough to accommodate half a dozen bathers at the same time, they frequently make a romp of it, and their shouts may be heard far up the hills. Breakfast follows near 11 o'clock; a gossip with neighbors, or half a dozen cigarritos, prepare one for the siesta; another bath for the dinner at 5 or 6 o'clock; and the evening winds up with music, conversation, or other diversion, with ices, mate, or tea, intervening. Our night was less charming.

My companion was too tired to resist the temptation of bed much beyond the time necessary for obtaining a cup of tea, prepared from a little package of stores a traveller always needs here; and I was left alone to enjoy "the weed" in the fresh night air. When I entered the chamber an hour later, he was unmistakably in the land of dreams, and there remained barely sufficient candle to afford light whilst I should prepare to follow the good example. But when one has reached the respectable age of two score years, of which nearly all the latter half has been pased in night-watching, the drowsy god is chary to grant the boon coveted; and though I was soon abed, it was only to lie awake and think how greatly we should enjoy the scenery next day. In a little while an occupant came to dispute the bed with me, and then another, and another, until there seemed to be hundreds of persecutors. Within an hour there was no square inch of my body which had not been punctured by the nimble enemy. What was to be done? Experience gained of the ascent of the cuesta was positively against an attempt to walk, lest the snarling and wolfish dogs occupying the corridor should refuse respect to the remains they might detect at the bottom of the quebrada, and one be cheated of the fame of a "crowner's 'quest." It was terribly dark; the corridor was broken by a short, steep flight of steps, somewhere near midway; the tallow dip was utterly burned out, and another could only be obtained from the mayordomo, who lived—Heaven knew where! In short, my position was without alternative, and quiet submission to the lot in which fate had cast me was all that could be hoped for until daylight would permit respite from the persecutors; but of all the nights yet passed in Chile this proved the most trying, there being no moment not employed in endeavors to capture one of the bloodsuckers whose proboscis was penetrating me. That at Rancagua, soon after the great earthquake, was long remembered; *this* marked a new era in discomfort. Nor could it have been anticipated, for the room was newly whitewashed and swept, and the bed apparently clean, the blankets—brought from another apartment after our arrival—being the only things which could have harbored so many fleas. My companion slept soundly, despite their attacks.

Deserting the field of battle early after daylight, a bath and breakfast sensibly mollified the exasperated feelings with which I was tempted to regard everything at Colina. And after ascertaining the temperatures of the several springs, and obtaining samples of the waters for analysis, a mule-path up the side of the northeast ravine enabled me to reach an elevation about 1,500 feet above the dwellings. From thence a prospect was obtained, not only of the glen through which we had ascended, but also of the great valley beyond; their cultivated fields and lines of trees; their multitudes of mountains and cliffs, infinite in varieties of form; the agitated waters of their little river, now glittering in sunlight, now lost in shade, as it wound near the bases of hills; the dark Central cordilleras, with their wavy and irregular outlines projected against the western sky; and the snow-peaks near Tupungato, one of the pinnacles of the continent,—all blending in one panoramic picture, with tints harmonizing as only nature can effect, and which the eye never wearies in looking upon. Two hours later we were *en route* for Santiago, where we arrived without incident—the memory of the landscape still pleasantly impressed.

CAUQUENES.

The baths which have obtained most celebrity for the cures effected in obstinate rheumatic and chronic affections following venereal disorders, and that have resisted every other remedy, are those of Cauquenes, in the department of Rancagua. They are from seven to eight leagues east of the town of that name, near the south bank of the river Cachapual, and on a sort of table-land high above the bed of the stream. From this spot a prospect is commanded even more romantic and beautiful than from the hill back of Colina just described. In the rear of the table-land, the hill-sides are covered with trees; farther back, snow is visible eternally; and in front, the river winds to the southwest, across a plain unsurpassed in fertility, and presenting all the loveliness of landscape this glorious valley has to boast of. The surrounding formation is a secondary stratified porphyry, and the immediate site of the baths a very modern conglomerate (pudding-stone), which may be traced in horizontal beds to the bottom of the valley.

Ranges of buildings, with corridors and an internal patio, Chile fashion, have been erected for the accommodation of visitors, though, instead of being managed as a hotel, each of the thirty parties who may find shelter under its roofs is obliged to seek elsewhere for every other necessity. A *bodegon* at hand can furnish most of the indispensable articles of food; and as a penance for the crime of omission to provide themselves before leaving home, visitors are contented, perhaps, to pay the two or three prices demanded. During summer—the season when they are most frequented—owing partially to radiated heat from the rocky back-ground of the narrow valley in which they are situated, the air is excessively dry, and the temperature by day very hot. There are four principal supplies of water, with temperatures ranging, in the month of April, from 79°.2 to 120°.5, and with constituents very closely analogous to those of Apoquindo. Two of them, called the "*Pelambre*" and "*Corrimiento*," evolve gas which is apparently azote. For a more minute account, the reader is referred to Chapter XV.

PANIMAVILA.

There are no other mineral waters of much repute until arriving south of latitude 35°, where those of Panimavila are situated—the only instance of mineral springs at the level of the valley throughout its extent. Their height above the ocean is less than 900 feet; and the geological situation being somewhat different from that of all the localities where mineral waters are found in Chile, they deservedly attract the naturalist's attention. The modern alluvial stratum constituting the surface portion of the Great Plain, forms a deep bay within the Andes nearly a league in diameter. This is almost surrounded by hills of secondary stratified porphyry, identical with the formation about the baths previously mentioned; but the springs here, instead of issuing from the midst of the porphyry, rise from alluvial and somewhat muddy ground almost in the centre of the bay. On this account the waters have an earthy odor. They soon separate into little streams that moisten the adjoining plain, but neither become turbid nor leave deposits or saline efflorescences. The water is of the same temperature—88°.4—in four or five different springs, is perfectly clear, emits no gas, though possessing the odor of mud, and is extremely disagreeable to the taste. Its principal mineral ingredients are chloride of sodium, sulphate of soda, and sulphate of lime, which, with other organic substances in smaller proportions, amount to 0.37 grain in 1,000 by weight. Being in the vicinity of Linares, which has a population of 3,000 souls, and only twelve leagues from Talca, where there are 15,000 people, its healthy and temperate climate renders it a favorite resort; and for a long period a greater number of convalescents have frequented Panimavila than any other watering-place in the republic. It has better accommodations for invalids than any of them.

MONDACA.

Not far from Talca, in an E.N.E. direction, and north from the Descabezado peak, on the southern shore of the lake of that name, are the baths of Mondaca—or rather, there are the mineral waters so called; for the only baths are a few holes scooped in the earth from time to time, and around which bathers as temporarily arrange a sort of screen with stones and brush-wood. In the midst of rugged mountains and utterly barren and desolate precipices, the lake slumbers tranquilly. At the farther end of its turbid waters, and in that direction only, are there symptoms of verdure. There the ground rises in terraces, over which the water of a little stream falls towards the lake in a pretty rapid, and partially diffuses itself over the surface, sustaining vegetable life.

The mineral waters issue from beneath granite rocks surrounded by gravel and coarse sand. They are 3,600 feet above the ocean; are clear; apparently emit no gas at their exit from the earth, yet have a slightly perceptible and disagreeable odor; and their temperatures range from 82°.5 to 111°.5, the heat being greater in newly made than in old excavations. Their principal organic matters are—

Chloride of sodium	0.496
Sulphate of soda	0.220
Carbonate of lime	0.207

—conforming them closely to the Colina waters.

Prof. Domeyko found a small hut of dried branches amid these holes and piles of stone; but they afforded protection neither from the morning frosts nor the fierce noonday heat. Quite a number of invalids occupied it. Their pallets were spread on the bare earth; yet, almost scorched as they were by the heat, and subjected to constant privation, they retained full confidence in the miraculous powers attributed to the water. But I must quote a paragraph published by him in the "*Anales de la Universidad*," respecting the condition in which he found the mineral baths of most consequence nearest the third city of Chile: "Seeing these people so weak and emaciated, exposed to every vicissitude of climate, in a region where no living soul is to be found, I cannot but admire the courage and faith of man, forced to struggle with the rigors of nature in pursuit of health, and am surprised that, at so short a distance from the capital of a populous province, and within four or five leagues of the finest forest in Chile, there has not been constructed at least one house for sheltering them, at a place so famous for its thermal waters. Invalids who come here remain only eight or nine days to drink the water; those most attacked by rheumatic pains, affections of the stomach, or cutaneous diseases, bathing also. At the end of that time, almost all of them, I am assured, are better, and return happily home, if one of the *temporales* that so frequently occur do not overtake them on the road."

CATO.

These springs are three in number. They are situated fifteen or twenty leagues to the south of Panimavila, in a location somewhat analogous, though the water issues from a coarse, sandy quartzose formation of an ashy-grey color. Their temperature is constant at 96°.8. They are perfectly colorless, have no odor, are unpleasant to the palate, and emit a gas which is probably pure azote. In two of them the gas-bubbles rise constantly; in the other only at intervals, as though impeded, but in this case they are much the largest. Their chief mineral constituents are sulphate of soda, chloride of sodium, and silica. The volume of water is considerably less than that at Colina. Prof. Domeyko says: "Persons worthy of confidence have assured me that these springs were entirely dried up by the great earthquake of 1835, and that it is only a year (in 1849) since they reappeared at the same place." M. Crosnier* states that the springs issue from green amygdaloidal porphyry, the water exhaling a very decided

* Annales des Mines, Vol. XIX, 4th series, page 219.

odor of sulphuretted hydrogen. Another was shown him at a little distance from the rest, whose temperature was only 59°.8; and this also, he was assured, very sensibly emitted the same odor in the morning.

CHILLAN.

The sulphur baths of Chillan are at the bottom of a ravine in the Andes, E.S.E. from the city after which they are named; not far from the head-waters of the river Ñuble, and nearly 500 miles from Santiago. Here, at an elevation of more than 6,000 feet, in the midst of capriciously broken hills and smoking solfataras of the desert cordillera, a citizen of Chillan —possessed of more enterprise than many of his countrymen on whose estates nature has mistakenly located fountains of alleviation—has erected a few rude houses, and provided accommodations for infirm guests, not far below the snow-line. Such has become the fame of these waters latterly, that visitors have come even from the remote capital—a journey of no trifling moment when we remember that at such times ox-carts are the usual vehicles of locomotion.

The dwellings are immediately at the baths. Five or six of the latter are supplied from springs whose temperatures range from 118°.4 to 140°. When it rises from the earth the water is perfectly diaphanous, and emits a strong odor of sulphuretted hydrogen; both of which properties are lost after a short exposure to the air, and a slight deposit of white sulphur succeeds. A residuum of the same character is observed on the bather, and the air of the whole ravine is so impregnated with the detestable gas, that its odor is a nuisance to all new comers. In the apertures through which the waters flow, the vapor accumulates a sublimated sulphur either in small concretions or delicate and fragile spiculæ. In a thousand grains of the water there exists nearly half a grain of mineral matter, consisting of carbonate of lime, sulphate of soda, carbonate of soda, and sulphate of sodium. Free carbonic acid and azote are also perceptibly present.

Three hundred feet lower in the same *quebrada* there are other sulphur springs in the midst of veritable fumarolas—that is, apertures from whence sulphurous acid, vapor of water, and sublimated sulphur, are thrown out. In one of these, nearly eighteen inches in diameter, there arises a stream of water at a temperature above 147°, and from its midst gas is evolved in such quantities that a large vessel may be filled with it in a few minutes. Prof. Domeyko found it colorless, clouding with a solution of barytes and an extinguisher of combustion—in short, a mixture of carbonic acid and azote. At a very few steps farther there is another spring, from which water at the temperature of 190° gushes in large bubbles. It is turbid, and emits a strong odor of sulphuretted hydrogen. The surrounding rock is hot enough to burn cloth left in contact with it some minutes. At the same spot there is heard the ebullition of another spring like that of a huge subterranean caldron; and the fumes of sulphuric acid thrown out deposit on the earth and rocks of the vicinity a yellow or reddish grey coating, similar to that produced on the surface of those near the solfatara of Cerro Azul. The whole locality is replete with interest.

There are other hot springs at the very foot of the ravine, below and above. One may not only find holes filled with water, apparently in eternal ebullition, but a part of the rocks are so hot that a little stream which pours over them is instantly converted into vapor, with a hissing noise, and from under foot comes a roar as of gigantic steam-boilers.* At one place there is a mountain of sulphur, and a little farther away one of snow, from whose eastern slope, and almost from beneath the snow itself, a stream of heated sulphur-water flows. Within a mile or two the latter tumbles into another that springs from the centre of the valley. This last is cold and crystalline, and the two flow off to mingle their discordant stream with the Ñuble. Thus, a locality whose proximity to the snow-line would render it almost if not quite uninhabitable by invalids with Chilean constitutions, is kept constantly at a charming tempera-

* Domeyko: Anales de la Universidad.

ture by nature's great subterranean furnace. The valley through which the streams flow from the baths takes its name—"*Aguas Calientes*" (warm waters)—from one of their qualities, and is one of the most beautiful in all Chile. Most sincere were the regrets that civil war should be raging at the only leisure period when the South could have been visited, and that the "Valle de las Aguas Calientes" did not become personally familiar.

The locality was subsequently visited by a most valued friend, from whose graphic description the following account is added: "We remained three days at Chillan, and then started for the baths, situated twenty-five leagues from the city, on the elevations of a cordillera called the 'Nevada de Chillan.' Our journey occupied two days, amid forests towering to the clouds, with occasional vistas, inspiring adoration of the Creator who had blessed our earth with so much loveliness. Part we accomplished in a birlocho, but the greater portion on horseback, there being some dangerous places for wheel-vehicles. Some persons, however, ascend to the very baths in their carriages.

"The baths are found at the foot of the snow-range, and at the very tenements we have enormous masses of the frozen substance. In every direction through the quebrada the vapors form little clouds; and sulphur, iron, and lime float liquidly around one. At the vapor baths there are springs where the waters boil as in a caldron. Quite close to them there is a cold ferruginous stream; and within less than a yard there is another orifice of warm water, besides many of various degrees of temperature. All these are led to the bathing-rooms through tubes of wood, and every one can temper the water to his liking. The houses are of boards and quite good, and at this time (January, 1855) are filled by visitors.

"Twelve leagues to the south, and at the same elevation as we now are, is the volcano of Antuco, which they inform me is in activity. The proprietor of the baths, who has visited the volcano, tells me that the mouth of the old crater closed in 1834, and that it is now burning through two others. Sometimes it burns with such violence that the cinders are thrown to a horizontal distance of four leagues."

DOÑA ANA.

The only mineral springs yet ascertained and resorted to in the northern portion of the republic are those of Doña Ana and Soco, both in the province of Coquimbo. Owing, however, to the difficulty of access and the sparseness of the population, neither of them has been much frequented. The former are in the midst of granite and stratified rocks, forming a part of the cordilleras, forty leagues east of Serena, and ten thousand feet above the sea. There are four or five principal and many lesser springs, with temperatures ranging from 78°.8 to 140°. They are all within a space of twelve or fifteen yards, and some of them, that differ quite 50° from each other, issue from apertures not more than three or four feet apart. They throw out carbonic acid, but no sulphuretted hydrogen; have a salt and bitter taste; are purgative; are considered to possess great medicinal virtues; and deposit a considerable quantity of deliquescent salts, that perhaps contribute to produce unusual dryness in the surrounding atmosphere. The principal mineral ingredients are chloride of sodium, chloride of calcium, and sulphate of soda. A torrent of turbid white water descends the ravine beside them, and unites with the river Turbio, ten or twelve miles farther down. When last visited, there was only one wretched rancho for the accommodation of invalids.

SOCO.

These baths are only four or five leagues from the ocean, and are the only mineral waters yet discovered in the granite formation of all Chile. However, very little more is known of them than that they are near Barrasá, on the river Limari, and are sometimes stopped at for a moment by travellers between Coquimbo and Valparaiso.

CHAPTER XII.

THE PRESIDENTIAL ELECTION, IN 1851.

PRELIMINARY MEASURES OF GOVERNMENT.—THE CANDIDATES.—DISORDER IN THE CHAMBER OF DEPUTIES.—QUALIFICATION OF VOTERS.—JUDGES OF THE ELECTION.—POLITICAL MEETINGS PROHIBITED.—ORGANIZATIONS FOR THE PURCHASE OF VOTES.—THE BALLOTTING.—PRICES PAID FOR VOTES.—INCIDENTS AT THE POLL.—THE OPPOSITION PARTY DISSATISFIED.—REGARDED THE MOST IMPARTIAL ELECTION WITHIN TWENTY YEARS.—FRAUDULENT QUALIFICATIONS.—NUMBER OF VOTES POLLED THROUGHOUT THE REPUBLIC.—THE RESULT.—FAILURE OF THE OPPOSITION DEPUTIES TO DEFEAT THE LAW.—CEREMONIES ON DECLARING AND INAUGURATING THE NEW PRESIDENT.

Prior to the day appointed for the meeting of Congress (June 1), rapid work was made with all those members against whom the least charge could be brought; and, under the powers exercised during the existence of martial law, four or five deputies, four prominent civilians belonging to the opposition party, and a part of the editors and contributors to the liberal papers, both at Valparaiso and Santiago, were banished. Meantime, as soon as the government could take decided measures, an order was sent to the south for all the regular troops to be put in motion towards Santiago. Gen. Cruz, the liberal candidate for the presidency, was, at the time, Intendente of Concepcion, and had quite a large portion of the standing army under his control, ready to back a popularity increasing rather too rapidly for the pleasure of the administration. Moreover, as it was possible he would not be willing to part with those whose muskets might be needed to sustain his own pretensions, in order to cripple him to the utmost in such case, it was currently believed that independent orders had been sent to each subordinate, directing him individually to repair to Santiago. If true—and there is little reason to doubt it—this was a breach of military courtesy and etiquette, to which no commander would quietly submit. Certain it is, within a few days many of the officers appeared at the capital; and the General, landing from a steamer at Valparaiso, also presented himself at head-quarters. But he was too old a soldier not to keep counsel, and the circles of gossips were for the time at fault.

On the 20th of May, just a month after the revolt, some sixty or seventy of the matrons of Santiago waited on Gen. Cruz in a body. They were arrayed in mourning. Their avowed object was to welcome a chief who they hoped would deliver their country from the despotism they considered prevailing, and free them from terrors consequent on the expatriation of fathers and husbands during the terms of martial law, to which they had, of late, been sō subject. These visitors were among the very first families of Chile. Besides this evidence of respect, whenever he appeared in public he was greeted by the mass with cheers; whilst the name of Señor Montt, the ministerial candidate, if heard at all, was only "damned with faint praise."

Congress met on the 1st of June, and as the substitutes of the banished members were generally in favor of the existing government, the ministerial candidates were elected as presiding officers at the first ballot. On the same day a paper was presented from one of the ablest of the expatriated deputies, asking that the decision by the conservative commission, which deprived him of his seat, might be revised by the Chamber to which he belonged. A discussion at once arose between the president and deputy presenting it, in which more than ordinary feeling was shown on both sides. The former affected to treat it as a common petition, to be referred—under the rule—to a standing committee, whose composition would, of course, conform to the wishes of government; and the latter claimed its consideration as a privileged question. In a little time affairs assumed a tone of such rancor that the audience, almost to a man espousing the side of the opposition, actually hissed and hooted down the ministers or their friends whenever an attempt was made by them to address the Chamber. Indeed the mob had complete control, and positively refused to quit the building; so that the president found it necessary, on several days, to adjourn the sittings. Perceiving that order could not be preserved in any other manner, each deputy received, for distribution, five tickets, without one of which no person was admitted; and as the tickets bore the signature of the distributors, each one of them would be responsible for those who entered with his sanction. There were no further disturbances. Subsequently, the opposition resorted to absenting themselves day after day, and thus want of the legal number prevented the transaction of business. Although nominally assembling on Mondays, Wednesdays, and Fridays of each week between June 1st and August 31st, yet for want of a quorum there were really only twenty instead of forty odd sessions.

The balloting for presidential electors took place on the 25th and 26th of June. Being absent from the capital, Lieut. MacRae prepared the following account of the occurrences there:

"For better comprehension of the events of this election, it is necessary to mention, in advance, what the law requires of voters, and its specifications of times and places of holding the polls. Shortly after every presidential election, the Cabildo appoints a commission charged with granting certificates of qualification to all citizens legally entitled thereto, and who shall establish such right in accordance with the public notice given. Every citizen who has never been convicted of a criminal offence, and whose income is $200 per annum, whether from real estate, trade, or other occupation, is entitled to a vote; and having proved these two facts to the satisfaction of the commission, a certificate to that effect is given, the number of which, together with the name and parish where the voter resides, is registered in a poll-book. A voter can exercise the privilege only in the parish of his residence. Service in the National Guard is regarded as equivalent to the income; and every member enrolled within the prescribed time becomes a voter. The number is further increased by haciendados and others, who agree with persons in their employ, on the day that they are to present themselves to the commissioner, for a nominal income of that amount, which contract is annulled before sunset, and the law thus evaded. Under these qualifications holders may vote for members of the Cabildo, of the Chamber of Deputies, and the presidential electors; after which it is necessary to renew them. When issued they are taken charge of by the commandants of batallions, haciendados, and employers, who keep them in charge until the day of the election, and do not give them up even then, unless quite sure they will be used only in favor of their own candidates.

"By law a member of the Cabildo, and two other persons to be appointed by that body, must preside at each poll; which is required to be kept open six hours of the 25th of June, and a like period of the following day. The additional judges of election are almost necessarily of the same political stamp as the appointing power, and in Santiago, of course, friends of the government, ten members of the twelve composing the Cabildo belonging to that party. From 144 names, twelve of which are thrown into a ballot-box by each member of the Cabildo, two are drawn for each of the six parishes of the city, and the individuals thus designated by lot are notified to attend. The parishes are La Catedral, Santa Ana, San Lazaro, San Isidro, Yungai, and Estampa. Santa Ana contains between 2,000 and 3,000 qualified voters—nearer to the latter than the former number—and is the most populous district. The polls were generally held in the corners of the *plazuelas* (little open squares), and no attempts were made to secure either free ingress or egress to voters; a neglect most probably intentional, as will be presently inferred.

"Public meetings, or rather meetings in public places, are forbidden by law; and after the disturbance at San Felipe, and the attempted revolution in April, the Intendente had also prohibited them in private houses. With friends of the ministry the order was only nominal; towards the opposition it was enforced to the letter; and, in consequence, the latter were unable to effect an organization or mature any system of operations. On the other hand, under the name of *tertulias,* their opponents held frequent political meetings in private houses, and adopted such a plan as, considering the character of the mass of voters, and the fact that every department of the government was ready to support them, must have insured the election against a much more powerful party.

"As near as could be learned, their organization was as follows: Head-quarters were established in the house of one of the leading men near the centre of the city, and there a bank was formed by subscription of all the wealthy men belonging to the ministerial party. Branch banks, drawing supplies from the central coffer, were instituted near each poll; about which last, three distinct classes of men were employed. The most numerous were the *apretadores* (pressers), whose business it was to jostle or intimidate from the polls as many opposition voters as possible, and facilitate the entrance or exit of their friends. A few intelligent men were stationed inside of the *apretadores*, to answer objections, challenge votes, and exchange checks with those whose votes had been purchased by their friends—a precaution necessary to prevent fraud by the vendor. Outside and circulating among the crowd was the third portion—the purchasers. These, on concluding a bargain, gave the vendor a check, with which and his vote he repaired to the polls, deposited his ballot, and received the counter-check from one of the 'intelligent' gentlemen standing near. This counter-check was an order on the local branch bank for the market value of the vote, regulated by the central institution, through intercourse constantly kept up by men on horseback, whom they called *vapores* (steamboats). Thus, when a steamer arrived from San Lazaro with intelligence that the opposition was very strong, and a majority of the voters were of that party, reinforcements of men and money were despatched there, the former having orders to hustle their opponents away from the ballot-box, and raise the price for votes one, two, or four dollars, as might be necessary. When another came from La Catedral with news that their friends carried everything before them, the *apretadores* were withdrawn, and a diminution ordered of the sum to be paid for votes. Although there was no actual great necessity for economizing, yet, under this system, no more money was expended than was essential to secure their objects, and uniformity of action was preserved in all the parishes. Their bank seemed inexhaustible.

"The opposition party abstained generally from voting at all; and from the fact that they made no efforts to carry the election after the first day, it was supposed that their bank had run out. That they were less willing to exercise corruption, must not be understood; they wanted but the leader and previous organization, and there were men among them who would have stopped at nothing. These perhaps relied on the chances of effecting their purposes by revolution, excusing themselves for such violent remedy on the ground that they were not allowed to vote; a charge which, if not strictly true, was not wholly without foundation, for it was certain that they had not equal chances with the ministerialists to approach the ballot-boxes.

"Some members of the latter party appear to have been especial favorites. A very intelligent gentleman of their number, in relating some of the occurrences of the election of which he had personal knowledge, mentioned one man in La Catedral who had voted seven times. He voted *right*, of course, and no objection was made; but when any *Cruzista* attempted the like, as they did once or twice, and was detected, he was immediately imprisoned. The poll was held in this parish at the entrance to the prison, and was presided over by gentlemen all of whom belonged to the ministerial party. For the preservation of order, as some said, in this central plaza (the usual *locale* of Spanish-American revolts)—to force the election, as others thought—two lines of soldiers guarded the immediate entrance to the ballot-box. On the arrival of a voter at the extremity of the lines, his certificate of qualification was held up to attract attention, and his intention to vote being announced, the president would direct the troops to open a line for him; but it was generally thought that this gentleman became both short-sighted and deaf whenever the applicant belonged to the liberal party.

"On one occasion the *rotos* (loafers) in the plaza got up quite an enthusiasm, vigorously hurrahing for Cruz. Imagining that they contemplated an attack on the ballot-box, the presiding judge ordered the troops to fire on them. Fortunately for humanity and the peace of the city, the soldiers understood their duties better, and the command was not obeyed. Other than this, there was little excitement apparent about the polls: few men were intoxicated; no fighting ensued; and there was but little of the noise or excitement to which we are are accustomed at elections in the United States. A leader occasionally threw a handful of small silver among the crowd, with a shout of 'Viva Montt' or 'Viva Cruz,' and the rabble would repeat the cry whilst scrambling for it; but interest expired as soon as all the money was picked up. Except in the vicinity of the polls, the city seemed deserted; nor were such crowds assembled there as might have been anticipated on a like occasion. Nearly all the police having been collected about the different polls in squads of thirty to forty each, even the customary sight of these in the streets was wanting, Dashing among the crowds with drawn sabres to arrest culprits, or to disperse numbers, they effectually prevented the realization of a free election.

"Though carried on to a scandalous extent, the purchase of votes was nevertheless managed quietly; and it would not have attracted attention, but that men were seen from time to time to enter neighboring houses with checks, and shortly after return counting money. In some of the parishes on the first day the market price was half a doubloon ($8.62); but there being no contest on the second, as has been stated, he was a lucky fellow who realized four reals.

"About 4 P. M. of the same day the polls were closed; and finding no further diversions in their vicinity, the masses instinctively flocked to the plaza as the centre of re-union and amusement. The first that came entered without obstruction; but mounted police were soon stationed at every entrance, and the majority were denied admittance. Meanwhile the crowd within, composed almost wholly of *rotos* and members of the opposition, collected about the door of 'El Progreso,' a liberal newspaper, and commenced depositing with leaders the certificates of qualification on which they had not been allowed to vote. Again the police interfered, preventing every one from entering the court who did not claim to have business with the post office, which was within the same enclosure. Though exercised gently, this obstruction prevented the larger number from depositing their real or fictitious papers; but that the party might not lose the benefit of this testimony as to the illegality of the election, a woman—wife or mistress to one of the slain in the revolt of April 20th—volunteered to receive the certificates, and succeeded in delivering them to their friends. As the rabble kept up their noise and excitement until after night-fall, they were finally driven out of the plaza with whips by squads of the mounted police.

"Taking advantage of the arrival of the daily mail next morning, the crowd re-assembled in front of the 'Progreso' office; and as they promised to become troublesome, the police charged among them as before. This time, instead of retreating from the plaza, the rabble took refuge on immense heaps of earth piled in front of two extensive buildings then in course of erection, and from there gave the police volleys of stones at every favorable opportunity. As it was almost impossible to charge up these hills, it was an hour or two before this dangerous pastime ended, and the rout of the mob closed the excitement of the election."

Although the same system seems to have been followed in every province, the election was regarded as the most fair that had ever been witnessed in Chile. An American gentleman of much observation, long resident in the country, remarked to me, "It is the very first I have known at which corporal punishment and imprisonment have not been resorted to." It is probable, however, that punishment was a sequel to it in more cases than the following.

When the time arrived for a renewal of the qualifications, the porter to the Astronomical Expedition was sent for by some one in whose employ he had served previously, and—under the system of nominal rates of income mentioned—was in a little while constituted a voter, as he had, no doubt, previously been before. But since the preceding election José had imbibed other notions, and, to the surprise of his disinterested patron, declined surrendering the certificate received, unwisely concluding that if he was entitled to obtain, he was also entitled to retain. This being more than the gentleman had bargained for, and a result which might cost his party half a doubloon or a vote against them, an altercation was forced and a scuffle ensued, terminating as all such affairs between rich and poor do—José was furnished with lodgings at the expense of the municipality.

Nor were qualifications prohibited by law issued to men of his class only; domestic servants, and inmates of the almshouse and hospital, were in some cases made recipients—the certificates remaining in possession of those who had instigated the fraud against the nation. A still worse feature in these cases was, the charge brought against certain members belonging to the ministerial party, that they had sold certificates of this class on the day preceding the election, intending to contest them when the spurious representatives should present themselves at the polls! And thus it may very safely be said, that the majority of persons interested in the election were either purchasers or sellers. Many haciendados, miners, and other legal voters, who controlled large bodies of men, were averse to both candidates, and kept aloof from the polls altogether. It was said in my presence to one of these gentlemen, "You know, Don ———, had but your finger been raised, every remaining vote would have been polled." Owing to the measures which allowed but the smallest number of ballots to be deposited, indifference to the success of either, and knowledge that the government would triumph, if necessary, by force, not one third of the legalized votes were cast. This is shown very plainly in the annexed table; and it must be recollected that every member of the National Guard is entitled to a vote.

Election for President in 1851.

Province.	Votes cast for Montt.	Votes cast for Cruz.	Population.	Enrolled national guard.
Chilóe			48,876	8,656
Valdivia			23,098	2,069
Concepcion			109,526	8,716
Ñuble	210	212	89,955	3,860
Maule	300	274	118,309	4,287
Talca	1,371	637	71,381	2,384
Colchagua	3,534	821	173,073	1,722
Santiago	7,211	1,654	207,434	12,024
Valparaiso	1,315	376	75,962	5,695
Aconcagua	1,054	217	91,674	5,574
Coquimbo			85,349	7,004
Atacama	375	1	25,165	4,250
Total	15,370	4,192	1,119,802	66,241

No returns of the number of votes in Chilóe, Valdivia, Concepcion, or Coquimbo, were published, nor were they made to the Minister of the Interior, so that I failed to obtain more than is given. Concepcion and Coquimbo were known to have given large majorities for Cruz; and if the other provinces voted in a like ratio to their population, the total number of votes did not exceed 25,700, of which Mr. Montt could not have had more than 20,000. He is therefore President of Chile by less than one fourth of the suffrages of his qualified countrymen. What became of the others—more than 40,000 voters?

It may appear strange that only one twentieth of the population, and in one province only one out of each hundred, should be enrolled in the National Guard; but this is owing to the fact that the masses live on estates where the haciendado has more control than the officers, and hence the government cares not to extend a privilege which may be used against its candidates.

The canvass being over, and the returns of the electoral colleges made, conformable to law, it was asserted that the opposition members of Congress would eventually defeat the election by absenting themselves in such numbers as would prevent legal scrutiny of the final returns on the 30th of August. This is the day specified by the Constitution, and, according to their interpretation, was the only one when the act could be consummated. Government, however, was not to be cheated of its candidate by any such North American manœuvre; and to this end, the Minister of the Interior presented a law, and got it passed, declaring that if anything should prevent the attendance of a quorum (three fourths) of the members on that day, then the scrutiny might be made subsequently. The Deputies, thus headed, assembled properly; but the Senate was in a predicament. A quorum of that body, when its number is complete, is fifteen. There was one death vacancy, several continued absent, and one was unexpectedly taken ill; so that only fourteen could be found in Santiago capable of attending. But as only one fourth of a senator was required to complete a quorum of the living members according to law, the two houses of Congress so interpreted the Constitution as to direct that the ballots be counted; and Mr. Montt was declared duly chosen President for the five years next ensuing September 18th.

To residents near the plaza the excitements of the day were not ended; and thousands were distressingly alarmed at a later hour by an incident really burlesque. An unfortunate ox, which had been liberated at the termination of a hard day's labor, was tempted from the shadow of his master's cart by the sweet odor of alfalfa, of which a mule-load was passing. Deftly did he follow the mule, and many a sweet mouthful was extracted from the moving stack, unconsciously approaching precincts where the law permits only men and dogs to be "at large." The serenos were absent from several corners at the time, and in the darkness he had approached, before detection, to within three or four squares of the plaza—a sudden blow from a lasso interrupting the pleasures of his repast. In the obscurity the sereno had failed in his aim, startling instead of capturing the estray; and a race incontinently ensued towards the centre of population, pursued and pursuer followed by rushing crowds, constantly increasing from all the lateral streets along which they passed. Not knowing the cause of the uproar consequent to so novel a spectacle, the lights on the plaza were extinguished, shops and dwellings were closed, and the more timid of those who lived at a distance rushed for their homes, fully believing and spreading intelligence that a revolution had broken out. Nor was tranquillity restored for some hours after the innocent bovine cause of mischief had been put in the pound, to remain until his master should come forward, "prove property, pay charges, and take him away."

At noon next day, amid the roars of a national salute fired on Santa Lucia, and the clangor of trumpets in the plaza, a *bando* was published to the troops and others assembled at the latter place, proclaiming Don Manuel Montt President elect of Chile. At the same instant he was attending a special mass of thanks in the cathedral adjoining. An hour later the same troops were drawn up in the Cañada, and the proclamation repeated there; but it fell on ears indifferent, and there was neither enthusiasm nor cheering on either occasion. The inauguration took place in the Senate chamber on the appointed day—members of the two Chambers, the diplomatic corps, and chief officials of government, being present. At this ceremony the retiring President also assists, laying down the insignia of office as the oath to support the Constitution and laws is administered to his successor by the presidents of the two Chambers.

CHAPTER XIII.

EVENTS SUCCEEDING THE ELECTION.

REVOLUTIONARY SYMPTOMS.—PROGRESS OF THE DISAFFECTION.—CONGRESS GIVES THE PRESIDENT EXTRAORDINARY POWERS.—REVOLT AT COQUIMBO AND CONCEPCION.—INTERFERENCE OF GREAT BRITAIN.—REPRISALS BY THE BRITISH, AND THEIR TREATY WITH THE INSURGENTS.—DEPARTURE OF GEN, BULNES FROM THE CAPITAL TO COMMAND ARMY OF THE SOUTH —REVOLTS AT SAN FELIPE AND SAN BERNARDO.—BATTLE OF PETORCA AND DEFEAT OF THE INSURGENTS.—SECOND INTERFERENCE OF THE BRITISH.—REVOLTS AT VALPARAISO AND CHAÑARCILLO.—STATE OF AFFAIRS AT SANTIAGO IN OCTOBER.—BANISHMENT OF LADIES.—THE ARMIES NEAR THE ÑUBLE.—MASSACRE OF ZUÑIGA AND HIS COMMAND BY THE ARAUCANIANS.—CONTEST AT LOS GUINDOS, NOVEMBER 19TH.—REPORT FROM GEN. BULNES.—LETTERS BETWEEN THE COMMANDERS-IN-CHIEF.—GEN. CRUZ CLAIMS THE VICTORY.—MONTONEROS.—BULNES IS OBLIGED TO RECROSS THE ÑUBLE.—AFFAIRS AT SERENA.—REVOLT AT TALCA.—FIRE AT SANTIAGO.—DEATH OF GEN. FREIRE.—FIRST NEWS OF THE BATTLE OF LONCOMILLA.—MINISTERIAL REJOICINGS.—BURIAL OF GEN. FREIRE.—FURTHER NEWS OF THE GREAT BATTLE.—PEACE AT THE SOUTH.—LETTER FROM GEN. CRUZ ANNOUNCING THE RESULT.—EVACUATION OF SERENA AND REVOLT AT COPIAPÓ.—CONFLICT AT LINDEROS AND SURRENDER OF THE INSURGENTS.—REVOLT AT THE PENAL COLONY IN THE STRAITS OF MAGELLAN.—CLOSE OF THE STRUGGLE.—ALLEGED CAUSES FOR THE INSURRECTION.—PROBABLE RESULTS HAD THE OPPOSITION PARTY TRIUMPHED.

Whilst the ministerialists were congratulating themselves on the success of their candidate, and making preparations to inaugurate him at the approaching national anniversary, with a degree of pomp previously unequalled, the members of the opposition were not idle. Though their acts were not quite so open to the world, there were not wanting some to assert publicly, "Mr. Montt will never assume the band of office." Rumors soon became rife that the 14th of September had been decided on for a revolutionary blow; and though, by its programme for the festivities and the erection of triumphal arches across the Cañada and many of the streets, the government continued its outward show of confidence, there were evident signs of apprehension.

The first tidings corroborating belief that the party beaten at the polls really meant to strike a more vital blow came from Valparaiso on the 5th of September. On that day a number of men were arrested in the manufacture of ball cartridges, intended for use in an attempt to take possession of the city on the following morning. On the 8th, news arrived from Concepcion that the Intendente (a general, also) had marched to the frontier with all the force under his command to preserve peace between two of the neighboring Indian tribes. As this province had been one of the two to give a decided majority for Gen. Cruz, his partisans were suspected of tampering with both regular and civic troops for the purpose of inciting them to march on the capital. Suspicion became fact; the alleged Indian difficulty was only a pretext of the Intendente to take officers and men away from the sophistry and money-bags of the liberals. Gen. Cruz, a much-beloved resident of Concepcion, had been its Intendente until very recently, and Gen. (then only colonel) Viel, its present chief, had been kept there some months on nominal duty—most probably to get him away from the regulars at Santiago, with whom he was too popular. The arrival of Cruz at the capital to remonstrate against the course pursued towards him subsequent to the revolt of April 20th, the adulation of influential gentlemen of his party, the cheers of the populace in public on more than one occasion, and the fact that he was a candidate for the Presidency in opposition to the government nominee, rendered it necessary to have in the province a military governor belonging to the ministerial side. After twenty odd years service as colonel, the merits of Viel became so suddenly apparent, that he was made general and Intendente at the same time—a sagacious and bold move to secure a valuable advocate, long a personal friend and partisan of Cruz.

On the morning of the 13th an express came from an estate within thirty leagues of Coquimbo, the rider having been so closely watched at many places that he only got through by subterfuge. He brought alarming news to government from a relative of the President. It was to the effect that the troops sent to preserve order in Coquimbo in July had revolted: they had shot the commandant of the civic force and one other officer who had resisted; imprisoned the Intendente; seized the custom-house, with its treasure; banished a part of the ministerial party; levied heavy contributions on others; and, finally, had created a provisional government. This had taken place on the day after the outbreak was to have been installed at Valparaiso. Many of the villages through which the rider passed were already in the possession of the disaffected; and, indeed, the whole northern part of the province might be regarded as in a revolutionary state. A few hours later in the day, by sanction of the Council of State, Santiago and the neighboring provinces were declared under martial law, and orders were issued for the Chacabuco battalion to take up its line of march next morning for Coquimbo.

To circulate such intelligence on the very day that a grand public ball was to be given would not only have subjected their own party to mortification, but anxiety for the fate of relatives and friends whose homes were near the seat of conflict would have deterred many from attending; and therefore few were informed of it beyond the palace. However, incidents were accumulating, and before the festivities were closed another was added to the national sources of regret. Instead of marching loyally to Valparaiso, about midnight the Chacabuco regiment revolted; imprisoned the colonel; placed at their head an officer who had risen from the ranks; and started for Aconcagua, with their whole equipment and the contents of the military chest. Both facts had to be told, and the ball hastily broke up—none knowing how soon the sounds of strife might be near their own domicils.

Prompt measures were indispensable. A confidential officer was forthwith despatched to the Intendente of Aconcagua, directing him to collect all trustworthy troops and march towards the capital. By avoiding the route the Chacabucos had taken, and riding with all speed, it was hoped he would be able to cross the hills for which the revolted regiment was named, and return with an opposing force by the time that it arrived there on the way north. Preparations were made to send other troops in pursuit; Congress was convoked, and requested to confer special powers on the President; and at earliest dawn a *bando* was published, declaring all the northern provinces except Atacama under martial law. By this time, too, portions of the artillery and lancers had gone, and the protective police remaining in the city were not only greatly increased in numbers, but each individual of them was furnished with an escopette in addition to his sabre. Later in the morning a part of *El Buin*, a new regiment, was also sent after their mutinous colleagues. This regiment was formed when the *Valdivias* were disbanded after the fight on the 20th of April; and as there was in fact little more than a change of name, many feared the Buins would array themselves under the banners of the Chacabucos as soon as they met. In such case, a military President was inevitable. It was believed that the regular troops almost to a man were opposed to Mr. Montt, and indeed to every civilian; and the fact that of five battalions the whole number of civic troops who obeyed the summons to the quartels was less than 200, whilst arguing little for the popularity of the government cause, was not much less indicative of the feeble opposition a mob would meet. No wonder, then, housekeepers were found preparing fire-arms; and the palace doors were besieged all day by a crowd anxious to obtain the earliest intelligence brought by the expresses. One who had been sent to the insurgent leader, with an offer of pardon if he would surrender, arrived while I was making a customary visit to the family of the President; and so great was the excitement that the crowd thronged even to their private apartments. The answer brought was, in effect, he would take his chance—"*seguir la suerte*"—rather than give up.

Before night Congress had conferred the extraordinary powers asked by the President.

When it is recollected how little power is given him by the Constitution, how much it grants the Council of State under the authority to declare martial law at will, and how representatives elsewhere regard what is due to their constituents, it is remarkable that only three deputies should have been found to oppose making him absolute Dictator. The law passed is in the following (translated) terms:

"The President of the republic during a period of one year is authorized to cause the arrest and removal of persons from one part of the republic to another; to fix the residence of any individual, and change it if he so considers necessary; to augment the standing army to such numbers as circumstances may require; to expend public funds without previously submitting estimates; and to displace public officers without the formalities prescribed in section 10 of the 82d article of the Constitution."

Towards morning the Chacabucos arrived at the ridge of that name, memorable as the scene of the first victory of the patriots under General San Martin over the Spanish forces. Instead of meeting welcoming friends from San Felipe, they were greeted by a summons to surrender from the confidential officer, who had succeeded in his mission and returned here with quite a force to back him. At the same moment, the pursuing troops from the capital were so close in the rear, that their bugles could be heard quite plainly. Traitors are cowards; and in this predicament the insurgent leader made his escape under the cover of darkness, when the serjeants, instigated by an ensign, without a blow arrested and delivered all the other officers to the government troops. A few hours later the leader also was captured; and before daylight of the 16th he was lodged in prison at the capital, the greater part of his troops for the moment dispersing. As this leader had been a known spy of the government, who was seen to issue from the President's quarters near midnight of the apparent revolt, many believed it only a feint to draw opposition leaders into acts which would authorize their arrest, and thus the new administration would come in with all the malcontents under lock and key.

But the news of this result—so gratifying to the mass of peaceable citizens—was not unalloyed. The revolutionary government at Coquimbo was hourly becoming stronger. It had above 2,000 men under arms; and had taken possession of a small steamer, on board which it shipped quite a large amount of treasure to the confederates at Concepcion, from which province not a word of information reached government until the middle of the festivities. When it did come, the news was much of the same character as that from Coquimbo, with the additional fact that the insurgents had appointed rulers *pro tempore* until answers should be received from Generals Cruz and Viel, to whom respectively they had tendered civil and military authority. They had obtained possession of all the arms, had seized a small steamer with money sent by government to pay troops, and had begun to drill men whose constant skirmishes with Indians on the frontier made adept pupils. They were overjoyed by the intelligence which the Coquimbo steamer brought them; and as General Cruz accepted the revolution, his name was all-powerful to raise both soldiers and money.

Meantime, it having been established to the satisfaction of the parties interested that the steamer Firefly had been forçibly taken from the port of Coquimbo, the British vice-admiral of the station declared that bay under blockade until restitution should be made, and the owners indemnified for damages. To this end, the war steamer Gorgon was sent to cruise in the mouth of the harbor. This was a deliberate interference in a domestic quarrel—a fact which the representatives of Chile and Great Britain knew well enough. But the officers of the former were in need of all the support attainable from every quarter; and if they did not directly solicit, as there is reason to infer, the following official notes show that they at least assented to the interference:

VALPARAISO, *September* 24, 1851.

SIR: The verbal communications which I had the honor to hold with his Excellency the

President of the Republic of Chile, with yourself, and Mr. Urmeneta (Minister of Finance), will have explained the delay in replying to your note of the 16th instant.

In the present state of affairs, it is my duty, and that of the commander-in-chief of the naval forces of her Majesty in the Pacific, to supervise the interests of her Majesty's subjects, and at the same time to afford to a government in amity with her Majesty the aid and assistance circumstances permit, without compromising the principle of neutrality.

The presence of her Britannic Majesty's steamer Gorgon prevented the premeditated capture of the mail steamer, and orders have been given to detain the Firefly, piratically taken at Coquimbo. Her Britannic Majesty's steam corvette Driver sailed for Talcahuano yesterday evening, as well for the protection of British interests as to take possession of the Firefly, if found at that port. Respecting the act of aggression upon the Firefly at Coquimbo, Vice-Admiral Moresby informs me that he is prepared to take more coercive measures against the persons in Coquimbo to whom is attributed the authority of ordering the capture of that vessel, as soon as the government of Chile expresses to me its need of means for the protection of foreign interests in that port; and in this opinion I wholly coincide, for those irregularly constituted authorities cannot be recognised by us, it being the government of Chile alone to whom we may apply for indemnification of the losses suffered in that illegal capture.

To avoid repetition of the insult to the English mail steamer, communication with her will only be permitted through the British ship of war stationed off the port of Coquimbo.

I avail myself of this occasion to renew to you, &c., &c.

J. H. SULLIVAN.

His Excellency Don Antonio Varas,
Minister of Foreign Relations.

Valparaiso, *October* 1, 1851.

The undersigned, Envoy Extraordinary and Minister Plenipotentiary of the United States of America near the government of Chile, has the honor to enclose to his Excellency Don Antonio Varas, Minister of State and Foreign Relations of Chile, a copy of a paper that has been placed for some days in the Exchange of this city, and which was inserted without comment in the "Mercurio" of the 29th ultimo—a periodical considered to be the organ of government.

The undersigned respectfully asks his Excellency the Minister of Foreign Relations to inform him whether the embargo or blockade of the port of Coquimbo, promulgated by the representatives of her Britannic Majesty by medium of that notice, is an act of hostility towards the government of Chile, or if said blockade has been instituted by the knowledge and consent of this government.

In asking this question, the undersigned is moved only by a desire to secure the interests of citizens of the United States.

The undersigned avails himself of this occasion to renew, &c., &c.

BALIE PEYTON.

His Excellency Don Antonio Varas, *&c., &c.*

Santiago, *October* 2, 1851.

The undersigned, Minister of State in the Department of Foreign Relations, has had the honor to receive yesterday's note which the Envoy Extraordinary and Minister Plenipotentiary of the United States of America near this government was pleased to direct to him, accompanied by a copy of an advertisement published in the "Mercurio" by the consul of her Britannic Majesty in Valparaiso, and posted in the Mercantile Exchange of that city, respecting the embargo or blockade of the port of Coquimbo, and requesting of the undersigned the nature and origin of that measure as a precautionary security towards American interests.

After making known to the President the communication of Mr. Peyton, the undersigned has been instructed by his Excellency to reply: That, on account of the revolution which broke out in the city of Serena on the 7th ultimo, in order to prevent the grave evils to be feared as consequences of excess, as well to the republic as to foreign commerce, and to stop the progress of the insurrection through maritime communication, the government ordered the closing of the ports in the province of Coquimbo. Persuaded, also, that the co-operation of the British forces in the execution of the measure would be of much importance, the government consented to the part taken by the British agents respecting the port of Coquimbo, after having communicated with the Chargé d'Affaires of H. B. M. concerning the prejudices already caused to British interests in Coquimbo by the insurrectionists, the necessity of preventing them in future, and the impossibility in which the government actually finds itself to afford those interests, at a point occupied only by factionists, the protection belonging to them.

In thus replying to the American envoy, the undersigned regrets that the actual circumstances of the administration should have caused him to forget the necessity of notifying his Excellency opportunely of what had occurred relative to the subject embraced in his note.

The undersigned will not close the present without adding, for the information of his Excellency, that the "Mercurio de Valparaiso" is not the organ of the government, as he mistakenly supposes.

The undersigned is gratified in repeating to Mr. Peyton, &c., &c.

ANTONIO VARAS.

To the Envoy Extraordinary and Minister Plenipotentiary
of the United States of America.

To blockade a port of a friendly nation with the armed vessels of the country against one of whose vessels wrong had been perpetrated in its waters, can be justified only as an ultimate mode of redress. For offences committed by its citizens, justice can be sought by the foreigner only at the hands of the government *de facto.* Disorders among its citizens should be quelled wholly by its own power, unless the party interposing be an ally both in war and peace. Insurrection may prove revolution, in which case the triumphant party become responsible for violation of neutral rights during the struggle.

On reaching Talcahuano, H. B. M. steamer Driver found that the Firefly had sailed; and the commander, instead of remaining "for the protection of British interests," returned to Valparaiso forthwith. By this arrival such information was obtained of the proceedings at the south as compelled the government to make every effort for the maintenance of its position. A large number of his rank and file having deserted, to preserve the remainder General Viel found himself under the necessity of retreating, instead of being able to march on the insurgents at Concepcion. Himself of French origin, a soldier of the revolution, and a liberalist all his life, he possibly remained faithful only because of the confidence reposed in him by government—not from want of sympathy with the Cruzistas.

Though official bulletins announced the loyal dispositions of surrounding provinces, and trivial advantages over detached parties near Coquimbo were published at the capital from day to day, and sometimes twice a day, yet the enlistment of new battalions in every province where a body of recruits could be trusted, and a constant despatch of arms and ammunition from Santiago, were direct contradictions to the repeatedly asserted belief expressed in the government paper that the insurrection would be quelled immediately. Of course, the opposition was not allowed a printing-press openly; nor were letters to them permitted to pass the post unopened. Indeed, the few known members belonging to it who dared remain within Santiago, clergymen not excepted, were forced to conceal themselves in the houses of friends. Yet they did manage to print brief notices; and when letters could no longer be trusted, confidential partisans were despatched with verbal communications. Overt acts were not needed to secure arrest and imprisonment; to speak openly, or to write in opposition to the government, was sufficient.

Early in October, the Firefly was retaken by a party of English sailors, who had been sent on board of the mail-steamer for protection of the monthly remittance of silver from Atacama, an amount of treasure which it was feared might prove too strong a temptation to the necessitous Coquimbanos. A convention of indemnification ensuing between the British consul at that place and the commander of the Gorgon on one part, and the "self-constituted authorities" on the other, there was no longer any pretext for continuing a blockade which at least one of the foreign diplomatic corps had shown a determination to disregard. No doubt commercial men were very sorry, as they were at any event favoring the rebels; for so long as the country continued unsettled, so long would business be paralyzed. Want of confidence throughout the land stopped trade, and their profits were cut off. With their dividends to guide their sentiments, they very sensibly urged the course that had been adopted by H. B. M. representatives; but, apart from them, and in a point of view strictly international, the act of interference was too unpopular, even with the majority of ministerialists, not to have been a source of regret to the chiefs who took part in it. Although made by subordinates on one side, and "those irregularly constituted authorities" on the other, there is no doubt that they were gratified at being relieved from the responsibility. For Coquimbo, the contracting parties were José Miguel Carrera, a relative of those who had borne so conspicuous a part in the earlier revolutionary scenes of Chile, and Colonel Arteaga, whose flight on the preceding 20th of April had lost to his party the victory which cost so many lives. Without military knowledge fitting him to lead, Carrera was known to be valiant and desperate, as all his predecessors of the name had been. On the other hand, Arteaga was undoubtedly an able tactician; but his previous career was not calculated to inspire confidence. From such a combination of leaders, the government had little cause for apprehension as to the final result in this quarter; nor did the opposition expect much from Coquimbo alone.

As fast as they could be collected, men, arms, and ammunition were despatched from the capital, to check the advance of the army mustering in the south. Even the Chacabucos were reassembled and marched away with the rest; and General Bulnes, appointed to the command, left Santiago early in October, the Minister of War following a few days after, to superintend the campaign in person. The former chose as members of his staff two ex-ministers, whose separation from his cabinet had been brought about by those who supported Mr. Montt as government candidate for the Presidency. With Bulnes and these gentlemen a large sum of money was forwarded.

Had the two regiments of regulars near Concepcion been of one mind, probably nothing could have resisted them; but such was not the case. One arrayed itself under the banners of Cruz; and a large number, if not all of the other, marched to join Bulnes. General Viel was left a prisoner in the hands of the opposition.

Every disposable man not previously sent to the south, even the President's escort and portions of the police from Santiago and Valparaiso, were hurried off in the same direction—a part by sea, and the remainder through Aconcagua.

A day apparently darker for the prospects of the ministerialists was close at hand. Expresses arrived on the 14th with the startling intelligence that serious revolts had occurred that day both at San Felipe and San Bernardo. San Felipe in arms against them; Valparaiso with a mob ready for plunder of the warehouses at any instant; San Bernardo completely at the mercy of armed men; and the capital without protection, except such as could be afforded by one company of artillery, a few newly recruited Vijilantes, and a company or two of young gentlemen, who had enrolled themselves as a night patrol, and were better acquainted with walking-sticks than with muskets!—most critical seemed their condition, and highly did they appreciate the encouraging beam which came on the following morning to illumine darkness that had almost become despondency.

Leaving a garrison at Serena, Carrera and Arteaga had started for the capital with the remainder of their forces. A battle had taken place near Petorca between them and those of the government, each about 1,000 strong. Petorca is a little town, twenty leagues to the north of San Felipe. The combat lasted for three hours of the 14th, and resulted in the complete rout of the revolutionists, with the loss of a number of officers and men, together with their artillery, ammunition, and baggage. Carrera and Arteaga, and a considerable portion of their little army, dispersed for more rapid flight, retreating towards Coquimbo. As soon as the news was received, a *feu de joie* was fired from Santa Lucia, and military bands were sent to parade the streets with cheerful music. A report of this action from Col. Vidaurre Leal, commanding the government troops, merely states the fact that he had encountered the enemy occupying heights overlooking Petorca; that the resistance had been vigorous; and, briefly referring to the results already mentioned, promises further details hereafter. Capt. Peña y Lillo is somewhat more communicative. The three companies under his command were ordered to dislodge No. 1 of the Coquimbo division, commanded by Arteaga, and posted on the summit of a hill rendered almost impregnable by its steepness. After exhausting their ammunition, his men were led to a charge, and succeeded in putting most of the enemy to flight. He took five officers and many (29) soldiers prisoners, and lost 36 men, three of whom he knew to be dead, and two others wounded. The *official* return, published two days later, enumerated in all of Leal's force five killed and twenty wounded; and a letter from one of his officers, which was printed in the same bulletin, says their opponents lost not less than 364 prisoners and 70 killed, of whom nine or ten were officers. Remembering that Arteaga occupied a hill, could rake the plain by cannon without molestation, that he is admitted to be their best artillery officer, that he is acknowledged to have fought gallantly on this occasion, and that the fight continued three hours, if the statements of losses by the commander and Lillo be true, we are forced to believe that the obstinacy of the struggle was very greatly overrated. I prefer believing that the mortality was under-estimated.

Whilst this was going on, a body of men, sent from Atacama, having approached Serena, an action took place on ground between the city and port, in which the former were defeated; though the Coquimbanos eventually retired within Serena, fortifying the principal entrances to the plaza. How many were *actually* lost in these actions is kept secret, out of compassion, it was said, for the friends of survivors. Respecting the losses, the commandant reports his own to the Minister of War, five killed and four wounded; that of the Coquimbanos, thirty killed, with a like number of wounded and prisoners.

Government having declared the steamer Arauco, which had been seized at Talcahuano, a pirate, and having offered her as a prize to any vessel that would take her, the British admiral despatched the Gorgon for her capture. Nor was there the least difficulty in taking her from under the guns of the fort before hostile purposes could be suspected. As the acting Intendente had no force with which to redress the aggression, his only remedy was a formal protest against violation of neutral rights. A large amount of property in mills is owned by citizens of the United States residing there; and the port is a constant resort of whale-ships. Both of these interests a United States corvette had gone there some days before to look after; and it is understood that a copy of the protest was filed with the commander. As soon as the seizure was known at Santiago and Valparaiso, there was a storm of indignation against the English, and not only was every John Bull bequeathed to the knife as soon as Gen. Cruz should triumph, but another paper was freely hawked about the streets containing details of many not very creditable events in the domestic and personal career of H. B. M. Chargé d'Affaires. Bitter and mortifying it must have been to know that these *truths* were passing about the cities in handbills, without the superadded fact that the policy of the measure which caused their appearance was a subject of argument even among his interested countrymen. The notes that follow contain all the history of the act which the world outside was permitted to read:

SANTIAGO, *October* 25, 1851.

SIR: I have the honor to inform your Excellency that, conformably to orders from the commander in chief of H. M. forces in the Pacific, Commander Paynter, of H. B. M. steamer Gorgon, took possession of a steamer called the Arauco, at Talcahuano, on the 15th of October last.

In the note that I had the honor to receive from your Excellency on the 12th of October, your Excellency enclosed to me a copy of a decree from the President of the republic of Chile, to the effect that this steamer no longer enjoyed the protection of the Chilean flag, nor was considered as a Chilean vessel; and the decree went on to say that the Arauco might be legally captured by any ship, for the protection of the interests of any nation that it might compromise.

The case has occurred. The steamer Arauco has been the instrument by means of which Britannic interests have been prejudiced, by means of which British subjects resident in Chile have been misused and despoiled of their property, and by means of which British insurers may suffer great losses.

However a British agent may lament to see a prosperous and flourishing country, as is the republic of Chile, faithfully allied to Great Britain, blessed until now by peace, with an enlightened government making constant progress and forwarding commercial prosperity, and with a President recently elected by the popular will—however he may lament to see a similar country in the midst of civil war and internal dissensions, it is his duty to preserve a neutral position and leave internal difficulties of the country near which he has been appointed to be regulated by the constituted authorities.

But when there are two contending parties, it is also the duty of the diplomatic agent to take care that one of these two parties does not avail itself of circumstances to injure interests of his compatriots. That one of these parties may be empowered by civil war to overthrow the government of its country, violently and piratically take possession of a steamer under British colors, and make an unlawful use of it for its private ends—that this same party may prejudice British interests, as in the case of the steamer Arauco, cannot be permitted.

It is for this reason that, by order of the commander-in-chief, the Firefly was taken; that indemnity has been twice demanded, and security exacted for the payment of the demand. It is on this account that the same commandant issued the order for the capture of the Arauco. But no unprejudiced person will pretend to discover in these measures an infraction of neutrality.

I avail myself of this occasion to renew to you the assurance of my high consideration.

H. S. SULLIVAN.

His Excellency Don ANTONIO VARAS,
Minister of Foreign Affairs, &c.

REPLY.

SANTIAGO, *November* 7, 1851.

SIR: I have had the honor to receive, and have made known to the President, your note of the 25th of last month, in which you inform me that Commander Paynter, of H. B. M. steamer Gorgon, had taken possession of the steamer Arauco at Talcahuano on the 15th of the same month, in accordance with orders received from the commander-in-chief of H. B. M. naval forces in the Pacific.

You refer for the motive of this to the supreme decree of the 12th of October, in which it is declared that the Arauco no longer enjoys the protection of the Chilean flag, and may be legitimately captured by any vessel in protection of the interests of the nation to which she might belong and that the Arauco might prejudice. You show that the case anticipated in the decree had been verified, and have made an exposition of the principles which, in the present condition of things, should govern the conduct of a British agent desirous, on the one hand, to preserve neutrality, and, on the other, obliged to protect the interests of his country against a party who, in undertaking to overthrow the national government by means of a civil war, violently takes possession of a steamer wearing the English flag, and unduly employs it in prosecution of its own particular ends.

The President, who has perused your note with due attention, coincides entirely in your views, and can do no less than recognise the justice of the principles that you have expressed to me.

I avail myself of this opportunity to renew to you the protestations of my high consideration.

ANTONIO VARAS.

To the CHARGÉ D'AFFAIRES H. B. M.

There being no longer need for their services in Aconcagua, the Buin battalion was ordered to report at the head-quarters of General Bulnes, established at Loncomilla, eight or nine leagues to the south of the Maule, and between that river and the Ñuble. General Cruz had advanced as far as Chillan, within sixty or seventy miles of his adversary. A part of the Buins reached their destination in safety; but the others returned to Valparaiso, after being three weeks at sea. They had failed to reach the mouth of the Maule, less than one hundred and fifty miles distant, and returned for want of water. Such was the excuse, though the troops were landed, and the vessel sailed for Coquimbo, with orders for the return of a government steamer sent there a few days before. What influence on their detention a threatened outbreak by the mob at Valparaiso may have had, or how dangerous the officers found it would prove to trust the old Valdivias before an enemy, are questions not likely to be solved.

On the afternoon of October 27, just as the warehouses were being closed for the day, from three to four hundred of the mob assaulted and obtained possession of the garrison belonging to the 2d battalion of civic troops at Valparaiso. Taking out the arms and ammunition, they proceeded to throw up defences as rapidly as possible at the *Plaza de la Municipalidad*. Everybody was astounded at the result, of which information instantly spread through the town. Whilst the Intendente proceeded to collect troops and arrange a plan of attack, the foreign merchants sent to the ships-of-war for sailors and marines to protect their property, many of them asking an asylum on board for their wives and children. Battalion No. 3, with all the other troops that could be collected within an hour, were marched to put down the mob; and a conflict ensued, during which the firing was incessant for about three quarters of an hour. At the end of this time the insurgents fled, leaving the two pieces of artillery they had taken and some sixty or seventy prisoners in the hands of the government troops. Private accounts state that at least one hundred were killed on the spot; the papers mention only fifteen killed and twenty-five wounded.

As most of those who had been engaged escaped to the hills, the city was kept in alarm all night by discharges of fire-arms; and as the foreign population very generally reside on the heights, it may well be imagined how anxiously the hours were passed by those who remained on shore. During the conflict in the plaza two hundred well equipped marines had been landed on the mole from the American, British, and French ships-of-war; and a part of these continued near the custom-house all night, ready to render assistance in case of pillage, but they were too distant to inspire confidence among the timid. Towards midnight two hundred of the rabble reassembled, made a descent on the house of a French armorer in the Almendral, and thence moved towards the *Plaza de la Victoria*, near which there were stores reputed to contain much money, as well as articles of food and drink. Information of such probable renewal of the struggle having been obtained from some of the prisoners, a body of No. 3 battalion had been sent to the plaza secretly, and the mob was early put to flight. For the purpose of liberating their companions taken during the night, a third party made an assault on the jail just after daylight; but, being received in the same manner as the last, the organization was broken up, and no further attempt was made to disturb the public peace. Confidence among commercial men, however, was slow to return; and days elapsed before their warehouses were freed from their many bolts and bars. No person of note had been recognised among the insurgents at any time. According to the government paper, their only visible leader was a tailor, their only object pillage; but it is stated that blackened and otherwise disguised faces moved wherever work was to be done, and it will hardly be supposed that *rotos* were desirous of concealment.

A similar but more successful outbreak had been made by the miners at Chañarcillo on the very previous evening. So numerous are the laborers, that with any concert of action the *administradores* and *mayordomos* have no chance, although assisted by a guard; and thus, after a shot or two, the picket of soldiers very prudently retreated to the Descubridora mine. Rifling the mining houses of San Francisco and San José, then two of the wealthiest in the mineral district, and destroying their works as far as possible, the mob next went to Juan Godoi, where similar excesses were perpetrated. All the stores were broken open, and the money and goods carried out of doors; and not contented with depriving the owners of as much as they could carry off, oil, turpentine, spirits, and molasses, were emptied over bales of goods and bags of flour. As occurs during every sack, the vilest passions were indulged without restraint; and when these human brutes had glutted their appetites for violation, conscience began the germination of fear, and the larger number absconded with their ill gotten booty in the direction of Huasco and Freirina. At 3 o'clock A. M. news of the outrage reached the city of Copiapó, and twelve hours afterwards a hundred men were on the spot ready to attempt the restoration of order. But they came too late to secure the riotous leaders, and found only those whom partial drunkenness had rendered indifferent to their fate, and honest workmen who had taken no part in the disgraceful proceedings. Indeed, it is probable that most of the robbers had departed before the express left Chañarcillo for the city, and that this fact was made known by him; else what could the Intendente have expected to accomplish with fifty cavalry and a like number of infantry, against ten times that number of the most athletic men in Chile? At Copiapó it was supposed that the departure of the troops for Chañarcillo would be the signal for a rise of the lower orders; but the police ascertained and seized the places where they were to have assembled, made a number prisoners, and published a *bando* ordering all fire-arms to be deposited with the public authorities, prohibiting all collections of more than four persons in one place at a time, and constituting every citizen competent authority to arrest individuals violating either of the preceding commands. At the latest accounts the orderly portion of the inhabitants were in the greatest alarm, not knowing at what moment the five or six thousand rabble surrounding them would be hammering at their doors for wealth, wives, and daughters. None thought of tranquil sleep. Those on the spot *say*, in the newspaper, that the revolt had no political motive; and in the same breath they assert that it was excited by unknown emissaries from the malcontents at Coquimbo, who disappeared two hours after the pillage commenced, satisfied that their malignant views would be fully carried out. Contemporaneous disturbances at Valparaiso, and the tolerably well authenticated fact that, had it not been for timely warning, the city of Copiapó would have suffered in like manner a few hours later, are strong circumstancial evidence of concerted action beyond the means or ability of a mere mob to plan or execute.

At Santiago there was "no peace for the wicked." In bed-rooms and closets, through orchards, over the house-tops, and even through the *acequias*, emissaries of the police ferreted out those suspected of expressing opinions against ministerial policy too strongly, and a forced sojourn in the country for an indefinite period was the mildest castigation for the heresy. It was of little moment that no overt act had been committed; courts were often long in arriving at conclusions, and then not always in the right way, and it was not required to establish so unimportant a fact. It was only necessary for the President to know that any one advocated openly the course of General Cruz, to entitle him to a billet from the chief of police, under the commands of which he was compelled, at every hazard, to quit friends and business within twenty-four hours. Nor was the persecution confined wholly to men; ladies also were included among those ordered to seek air without the pestilential political atmosphere at the capital, the papers on one occasion making merry over their banishment from the charming saloons of Santiago at so unfashionable a period. One more resolute than the rest appealed to the Peruvian Chargé d'Affaires for asylum—a courtesy not often denied by diplomatists to mere political offenders of the ruder sex; but in the present case, extended as it was to one of the most distinguished women of Santiago, the hospitality must have afforded great pleasure to Señor Pardo. It was very generally known that the ability and wealth of this lady gave her powerful influence; and as her brother was one of the leaders of the revolutionists at Coquimbo, the hours necessarily passed over accounts and other business matters of the extensive estate to which she is guardian, were readily believed to be occupied in treasonable correspondence. Money sent to him (if any was sent) was regarded in the light of subsidy in the cause of insurrection; and, indeed, she had full credit for having sent $30,000 to excite an outbreak of the mob at Valparaiso. No wonder, then, the ministers desired to destroy her power by banishment; nor that they should have accepted the voluntary services of the British Chargé to mediate for her expulsion from the house of Señor Pardo. But, to the honor of the latter, the intermeddling gentleman returned "with a flea in his ear;" and his employers were scarcely prepared to violate the sanctity of her asylum. War against women—because they had used their only weapon, the tongue—was a new order of things to us of Northern America; and it was somewhat spicily remarked, "If government will thrash the men, the women will soon be silenced again by their babies."

After a lingering imprisonment, most of those who had been arrested for participation in the affair of 20th April were summarily tried by court-martial and condemned to death; a punishment commuted to banishment in every case, and carried into effect during the latter days of the month. Thus, October terminated gloomily for the republic. There had been *pronunciamientos* in every principal town of the northern provinces: in the bishopric of Coquimbo, the clergy almost to a man had turned against government, the names of many appearing conspicuously on the rebellious handbills; from Chillan to the Indian frontier, the whole South was hostile and in arms; the wheat-fields were greatly neglected, and in some cases destroyed; cattle were consumed and wasted by armies and idle men; mines and miners, from whose products almost the entire foreign dues are paid, were yielding comparatively nothing; in short, the commercial and agricultural industry of the country was in a state of paralyzation, whilst to support it in hostile condition extraordinary resources were indispensable. Not only this: the elements of prosperity which had been taking root through twenty years of peace and order, were now perishing in the atmosphere of blood and rapine, generated by civil war; patriots were fast becoming partisans who thought only of retaliation—thirsted only for revenge; the common welfare and enviable position among nations of the world, attained after so many struggles, were forgotton; and the gulf of anarchy that yawned so threateningly beside the altar of republicanism was wilfully overlooked.

November passed with equally cheerless symptoms. The struggle was apparently as far from conclusion as ever. The movements of General Bulnes not being so rapid as the impatience of the government coveted, or as (at the distance of 200 leagues) its ministers considered expedient, and his opponent showing no disposition to leave the encampment at Chillan, peremptory orders were sent the General to cross the Ñuble and assume the offensive with the least practicable delay. Four leagues from San Carlos, and two from Chillan, where the main road from these towns passes it, the width of the river may be near a quarter of a mile, and its depth, in holes, sufficient to swim a horse. For more than forty miles above the road, its direction is from E. by N., and thence to its source in the great cordilleras is E.S.E. The Cato, a tributary also originating in the Andes, joins it near the road, and sometimes adds greatly to its volume. Horsemen sometimes cross at a ford called *Nahuel-toro*, five or six leagues up the stream, though travellers ordinarily make use of the ferry-boats and balsas on the main line of road. In accordance with instructions, Bulnes made a feint of crossing at the ford on the 14th. Planting a formidable battery, with suitable cavalry protection, to command the opposite side, the main body kept away from the river until ready to cross at Nahueltoro, reaching the south shore without molestation. At a later period, the artillery and dragoons met with like fortune. It was supposed that the passage of the Ñuble would have been disputed, and that the loss to the government army would inevitably be considerable. Such does not appear to have been the policy of General Cruz. He had consumed all the provisions and forage around Chillan: he had no doubt of its loyalty, should he desire to repossess himself of it; and his infantry and artillery were inferior to those of his opponent; yet, whilst he sent a few parks and three or four cavalry squadrons to reciprocate the compliment on the river bank, his army moved quietly to *Los Guindos*, an estate five or six miles E.S.E. from Chillan, better capable of fortification, and affording ampler room for manœuvring superior cavalry.

Three weeks previously, Zuñiga (a half-breed) had been despatched by General Bulnes with a squadron of horse, to raise a force of forest warriors among the Araucanians, for the purpose of attacking General Cruz in the rear. Zuñiga held from government a commission as a *Capitan de Indios*, whose duties are to cultivate the good will of the more than semi-savage race still unsubdued within the republic. Of necessity these appointments are given only to men trusted by the administration. He was accompanied by a brother and two sons. Partially participating in their blood, living among them, and their friend on every occasion, it was supposed he would have a powerful influence. His presence with a horde of untamed Indians in the rear as enemies, could accomplish more towards intimidating the army of Cruz than a greater number of far better armed men. Therefore the Intendente of Concepcion started to intercept him, with such troops as could be spared from the small garrison and as were otherwise hastily collected; but from the results it would appear this had been unnecessary. Cherishing bitter hostility to all the associates of Bulnes, on account of former wrongs, the Araucanians massacred Zuñiga and all his associates, as soon as they set foot within their territory, and nearly 2,000 warriors then proceeded under Catrileo, one of their chiefs, to join the revolutionists. Exclusive of these, the army of Cruz numbered at this time 4,650 men, one third of whom were cavalry; and a letter from him to an intimate friend at Santiago states that they were both better men and better disciplined than those of the government. There was a tone of confidence through the whole letter that could not fail to inspire a similar feeling among his partisans at the capital, by whom authentic intelligence was rarely attainable, and who, in consequence, had begun to despond. From day to day, and every day, news was transmitted from house to house with a rapidity which only Santiago knows; but to those who reflected, it too generally bore on its face evidences of home adulteration, if not of actual domestic manufacture. Both sides wilfully perverted the truth. Even government officials, with no other object than to dishearten adversaries, consented to the publication of reports knowing them to be false. And as connected with the intelligence it was necessary to send by the steamer that took the mail for the United States and England, there will presently be occasion to mention this practice more particularly. For the purpose of effecting similar results, recruits were collected as rapidly as possible, and within a few days of the departure of the steamer several bodies of them, numbering from 100 to 300 each, were marched to Talca, for the formation of an army of reserve in case General Bulnes should be compelled to fall back. A part of these were mere boys, certainly not exceeding sixteen years of age, conveyed from the city by night, and in carts, under escort of a squadron of lancers. Arriving near the Cachapual, they mutinied and dispersed as suited the will of each, the escort having no power to prevent them. But information of the revolt, and of another that took place at Talca about the same time, fortunately arrived too late for the steamer; else the state of the country must have been seen in its true colors.

To return to the principal actors in the domestic tragedy. The army of Cruz, being covered on one side by a *callejon* (lane) protected by a fosse (so says the government paper), and on the other by a palisade, in order to attack him in the rear Bulnes put his troops in motion at dusk of the 18th, passed along the left flank, and took up a position on the heights of Urra at 11 o'clock next morning. Flanking parties, principally of Cruz's cavalry and Indians, were soon dashing among them; and this brought on quite a general engagement between the artillery and cavalry of both sides, which continued with little intermission for more than three hours. His infantry did not participate, nor could they be forced from their entrenchments either that afternoon or next morning; and arriving at the conclusion (Bulnes says) that his adversary did not mean to risk a general action, he considered it advisable to proceed to Chillan, for the purpose of giving rest to his troops. The first information of the action of November 19th was in the following letter from the military secretary:

MONTE DE URRA, *November* 20, 1851.

I am directed by the General to inform you that we reached the camp of the revolutionists, situated in *Los Guindos*, yesterday, and finding it between fosses and palisades, passed his flank to the north, taking possession of the place from which I write. At 3 o'clock a guerilla combat was commenced, that was continued by the cavalry of both armies until 5. The advantage was on our side in every charge, and we learn that the enemy suffered much from loss and dispersion. Ours does not exceed eight dead and thirty wounded. On account of the position of the enemy, the infantry could not be employed, and the action has had no definite result—both armies preserving their positions. This is written to keep you advised of what occurs, and that you may transmit the letter to the authorities at Santiago with practicable promptitude.

ANTONIO GARCIA REYES.

To the GOVERNOR OF SAN CARLOS.

Accompanying it, in the same publication, were three lines from the colonel of cavalry to his wife, telling her "we completely routed nearly the whole of the enemy's cavalry." This information, together with a statement that several of Cruz's best officers and 400 men had been killed, that the Indians had deserted him in a body, and that nearly all of his mounted men had dispersed, was forwarded to Valparaiso in time for the mail of December 1st.

It has just been shown that nothing was to be expected from the silver district of Chañarcillo. Coquimbo, the great copper region, from similar causes, was equally unwrought; and the South, instead of having a surplus of grain for export to California at the beginning of the coming year, it was now certain would need all that the less disturbed central provinces could afford them. In what manner, then, were imports to be paid for four months later? If there were evidences that government was sufficiently powerful to strangle the conspiracy, and that the principal opposing force was tottering, foreign exporters might ship their goods with some degree of confidence, otherwise they would scarcely risk ventures to a bankrupt market. This was well known, and its consequences feared. Without imports there could be no custom-house receipts; hence the desire by government that only favorable accounts should be found in the papers to go by this steamer.

Two days after its departure, the annexed letter, from "head-quarters," was printed; but its publication was neither welcomed by salutes from Santa Lucia nor with martial music:

HEAD-QUARTERS ARMY OF OPERATIONS OF THE SOUTH,
Chillan, November 20, 1851.

In execution of the plan of the campaign, of which I gave you an account in my last letter, I proceeded eastward from San Carlos on the 14th inst., and succeeded in passing the Ñuble by the Machicura ford. - This first obstacle being overcome without opposition from the enemy, I took the road along the foot of the hills in order to pass the Cato, on whose banks he might show himself in force. Nevertheless the enemy had no intention to dispute it, having concentrated his forces at a place called *Los Guindos*, distant a league and a half from this town. On the 19th inst. I undertook a march in his pursuit, and passed his left flank, until, having reached his rear, my camp was established on the heights of Monte Urra at 11 A. M. At 2 P. M. the fire of guerillas began to be active, and afterwards a combat of cavalry and artillery was commenced, which lasted until 5 P. M. During this time, repeated charges and recharges were sustained firmly on both sides; in which our soldiers, as well as officers and leaders, gave marked evidences of courage, and succeeded in breaking up the enemy's squadrons. But their boldness had not the result it merited, because it was impossible to bring the infantry into action on account of the position of the rebels behind fosses and palisades, as I have said; and thus both lines preserved their positions.

This morning I endeavored, by repeated manœuvres, to provoke a general combat; but the enemy has been obstinate in refusing it, and in a manner that convinces me his plans contemplate another class of hostilities. In this belief, and it being proper to rest the troops, I decided to take possession of this place, which was accomplished at 2 P. M.

No other object is proposed in this communication than to give you a general notice of what has transpired, a circumstantial detail of yesterday's engagement being reserved for a future occasion. The course which the campaign will henceforward take depends on the plans shown by the enemy, whom I shall endeavor, by every possible means, to draw out of his position; but if this cannot be done, because of the weakness in which he finds himself by the destruction and dispersion of his cavalry, I must make an effort to overcome the physical obstacles behind which he is sheltered.

God preserve you.

MANUEL BULNES.

To the MINISTER OF WAR.

With this letter there were also published several from officers, giving details of the valor and patriotism of their troops, the dreadful havoc they had caused among the enemy's cavalry, whose loss they rated as high as 400 men in killed and wounded, and his total rout in this arm, of whom a large body had deserted to the north of the Ñuble. But, with the exception of the "eight killed and thirty wounded," mentioned in the letter of Señor Reyes, an ominous silence is preserved by all respecting the casualties on their side. Now what was the truth about this action? *Was* it a drawn battle, as General Bulnes claims? In the first place, it must be mentioned, his own officers acknowledge that the formidable palisades preventing an attack on the infantry of the enemy were only a few stakes, driven in the ground years ago, as a defence against Indians; and that the fosses were only ditches, not exceeding four feet in width or depth, at which his horsemen would not have stopped an instant. Moreover, where was his artillery, acknowledged to be so much more numerous and efficient than that of his adversary? He was undoubtedly seeking an action on ground chosen by his opponent, and in this respect was at a disadvantage, possibly increased by being attacked before completing the disposition of his forces. Most probably he underrated their strength, and, instead of striking terror among them and accomplishing a decisive victory, his squadrons of cavalry were met by foes more numerous, equally disciplined, and better prepared for combat, because of the long rest they had been enjoying. In fact, "he caught a Tartar," and, as the sequel proved, he was glad to escape so easily; for, had his adversary been aware of his actual condition, nothing short of a miracle could have saved his army from destruction.

By the arrival of the U. S. ship St. Mary's at Valparaiso, from Talcahuano, we were favored with the perusal of papers printed by the revolutionist party, which otherwise would scarcely have been permitted to approach the capital. As the semi-official journals reprinted, without contradiction, a part of the letters contained in them, we have a right to suppose them authentic. The first is from General Cruz to his opponent, dated November 19, the day of the action at Los Guindos. He tells him that, being at the head of such an army as assured to him (Cruz) the victory, he earnestly desired to save the blood of their fellow-countrymen, and therefore entreated him to spare, if possible, this terrible resort to arms. Although it was not the time to discuss political questions, he believed that the justice of the cause he espoused must be recognised; and as he was not actuated either by passion or revenge, if General Bulnes would agree to refer national interests (the Presidency) back to the people, he was ready to unite his force for the preservation of public order. He then goes on to say: "Among the forces under my command there is a division of Araucanos, whom it may not be possible to control in the defeat that you may suffer. My first duty is to secure the triumph of the cause I defend. This done, as our enemies have striven only to arouse the Indians against the provinces emancipated from the government you obey, it would be but just to meet you on the same terms. You are authorized to send an aid to examine the number of our troops. This examination will be sufficient to convince you that victory must be on our side. Relying, as we do, on justice and the recovery of public liberty, their moral strength is superior beyond your thought; and it is in this that I have most confidence and security. Whatever be my fate, this proposition will ever be a gratifying recollection to me. A tear shed for our republic is inestimable: a field of battle but a bloody memento of anger and passion, the result of obstinacy and the contempt in which public opinion has been held."

General Bulnes tells him, in reply, that he has not been invested with power to revoke the political act recently effected by the republic, and consecrated according to the forms prescribed by the Constitution, of which himself (Cruz) had long been a zealous defender, and by authority of the National Congress, whose edicts had been respected alike by each. A soldier of the government organised by this competent authority, he could enter into no stipulations which would place in doubt the existence of the administration and throw back on the people a new election—the Constitution requiring of the military chieftains obedience only. Recognising the humanity and patriotism that dictated anxiety to spare the blood of their fellow-countrymen, he reminds him it was not the government that invoked arms for the settlement of a political question which the ballot-box alone should have decided, but that he had received its orders to quell a revolt instigated by a part of the military forces garrisoned in the province of Concepcion. Respecting the employment of Araucanians, he repels the charge made against the government of having attempted to engage these forbidden troops in its support, and asserts that no single instance of such a discreditable measure can be cited, whilst he can show that its influence has been exercised to control and moderate the savages when operated on by other agents; and he laments that at the moment he was about replying to a peaceful overture, this perfidious portion of his opponent's force had made an attack on him, no doubt contrary to orders, but which forced him into a defence, and did not permit the present answer at an earlier hour. This letter also bore date November 19.

Unfortunately, on the person of Zuñiga, whose death has been mentioned, there were found letters from officers on the staff of General Bulnes, and one from *himself*—conclusive tokens that he had left nothing undone to obtain the assistance of these very forbidden troops. In a report to the Intendente of Concepcion, General Cruz claims the action thus brought on as resulting favorably to himself; and, arguing partially from the facts, that General Bulnes retired to Chillan early next morning, that the military secretary was despatched on a secret mission to Santiago on the same day, and that new troops and ammunition were sent to the south immediately, he appears to have had a right to do so. One of the objects of the secretary, it leaked out, was to hasten a supply of ammunition, nearly the whole of that in the possession of the government troops having been damaged in crossing the Ñuble—a secret too important to be committed to writing, infested as were the roads by *montoneros*. These last were small parties of young men, in many cases of good families, whose object was to intercept arms, ammunition, and correspondence. They had predetermined points of re-union, in case of separation, and held themselves in readiness to disperse if attacked by a superior force, and to join the ranks of Cruz whenever they could approach his vicinity. Personal robbery or injury seemed to form no part of their plans. It is probable that they suspected something of the deficiency in their enemy's camp; for an express-rider was robbed of his mail two days afterwards on the very skirts of the city, and within cannon-shot of the palace.

Reliable particulars of this engagement may be written one day, and those interested in military events have an opportunity to learn something of the truth concerning it, as well as of the part borne by the Araucanians, and the terror that their small band inspired among the semi-disciplined troops of government. Usually mounted bare-backed on almost untamed horses, which the powerful bit of Chile enables them to control with the ease of thought, their dark and half-naked bodies painted in colors of many shades, their long hair streaming in the wind as they rush to the fight, waving lances of extraordinary length, and uttering such shrieks as only children of the forest can compass, they are objects that may well terrify. To strike them seems almost impossible. With the left arm clinging to the neck, and one foot only over the horse's back, they lie close along his side, and in this manner ride with such momentum that they will sometimes unhorse a rider and carry him several yards on the ends of their lances. So thoroughly do they seem a part of their animals, that they will pick up small articles form the ground when at rapid speed, and without dismounting.

In Santiago we only knew that such scenes did occur, and endeavored to infer the truth from subsequent results. That General Bulnes was defeated, seemed to admit of little doubt; and being on the south side of the Ñuble, there was no alternative for him but to take possession of the town evacuated by General Cruz, and there make preparations to continue the campaign, or to attempt a retreat, in which the moral effect on his army would cause either revolt or desertion. Both movements followed on the heels of each other.

Except in a southerly and easterly direction, Cruz had denuded the adjoining country. Every blade of grass, or wheat, or barley that could contribute as forage for cavalry had been destroyed, and even its wood had been collected together and burned in piles; so that Bulnes found himself absolutely without resources. He was no sooner quartered in Chillan, than Cruz despatched a battalion to capture the ammunition and three hundred troops left to guard San Carlos, a service that was successfully performed. Perceiving that his communication with the capital was likely to be cut off, and himself prevented from receiving succors, Chillan was hastily abandoned, and Bulnes recrossed the Ñuble with his whole force, though not without much annoyance from the Indians and skirmishers of his opponent. In this retreat four pieces of artillery were abandoned, making, with two taken from them in the action of the 19th, the battery of Cruz superior in number. Better provided with both cavalry and cannon, it is not easy to comprehend why a general battle was not forced at once, instead of permitting the ministerial troops to approach Talca, where a reserve army was forming, known to comprise some 1,500 men. Had Cruz done so, there is no doubt his victory would have been both easy and complete, and his army could have marched to Santiago without further resistance. But he had other policy, and, without event of consequence, the two armies encamped between the Maule and Loncomilla, within half a score of miles of each other—just near enough for the chiefs on both sides to tamper with the loyalty of subordinates, gold being a more favorite and quite as effective a weapon in Spanish-American wars as iron and steel guided by science and courage. Here let us leave them for a time, to glance rapidly at what had transpired in other parts of the republic during the month.

Around Serena government had collected troops immediately after the battle at Petorca, and the siege seemed to be contested more and more obstinately every day. A handful of men apparently set at defiance all who could be spared to send against them. Orders after orders were despatched from Santiago to storm the town, and relieve the ministry from the jests to which it was subjected by the repeated failures of prophecies put forth by their adherents. But the orders were all to no effect. Wearied with the delay, and as the officer in command appeared to be too humane (others said he *knew* himself to be too weak), in order that some one item of good news might go by the next foreign mail, Señor Mujica—an ex-minister who possessed the credit of regarding life with as little sympathy as a famished tiger—was sent in the steamer Cazador to direct the assault in person, and bring back to the President news that legal authority was once more dominant. Some days prior to the time that this was to have taken place an ambush was laid by the besieged, which in such a struggle, though barbarous in its results and subjecting its authors to infamous punishment should they be taken, was rather cleverly conceived.

In accordance with preliminary stipulations for evacuating the city, in order that the besieged might pass out with less obstruction, the besiegers retired from a part of the ground they had gained. A mine was immediately excavated under it by the former, and, there being no symptom of retreat at the time agreed on, the subterfuge to gain time was apparent, and about 200 of the government cavalry unsuspiciously returned to occupy their old lines. The treacherous fate intended was known only to the minority when the mangled remains of their companions came hurtling through the air in all directions within the circuit of half a mile. Such was the story told at Santiago by persons intimately connected with the leaders of the opposition; yet there were so many *cuentos de frayle* current, that one could only give faith to acts in which he had been a personal participant.

A large number of families from Serena had taken refuge at the port. On arriving there, Señor Mujica expressed every confidence in a successful result, and left his friends for the headquarters of the besiegers, promising to come back next morning with tidings that they might return to their houses, the rebels having been exterminated or driven from the vicinity. Learning his arrival, Arteaga sent a well instructed partisan without the trenches, who was to report that the leaders within were quarrelling among themselves, the troops starving and dissatisfied—in short, that anarchy reigned to such an extent, that a large number would welcome the government troops at any instant. Rapid and repeated discharges of fire-arms, and unusual noises in the plaza, distinctly audible at the camp of the besiegers, seemed to confirm the account, and under cover of night two companies, each with a piece of artillery, were placed under guidance of the emissary for safe conduct across the entrenchments. Again treachery awaited them. They were cut down or made prisoners by ambushed parties just within the barricades; and the ex-minister returned to the port, and thence to Valparaiso next day, his only success the destruction of a few houses belonging to members of his own party.

Illapel, Combarbala, and Ovalle—towns to the southward—had been assailed by montoneros, and the government officers kept in constant alarm. Haciendas belonging to ministerialists were laid under contribution to furnish cattle and provisions for the use of the besieged. In fact, the province of Coquimbo was as far as ever from being subdued. Nor was the fire of revolution suffocated in Atacama, Aconcagua, or Valparaiso; indeed, only the most sleepless vigilance and most dictatorial measures by the Intendentes, and the want of responsible and open leaders among the opposition, prevented new outbreaks. There were incipient difficulties at Copiapó, Chañarcillo, and Valparaiso again; and the bulletins were filled with letters telling of the attacks of montoneros in almost every town. But experience had been gained; the populace had few arms, little money, and not a competent man of nerve to direct them; and, of course, they accomplished nothing towards their proposed end.

About this time a part of the reserve army mutinied at Talca, and was only put down after three hours of sharp fighting and considerable loss. From the published accounts, those who took a lead in the revolt had permitted aguardiente to be distributed too freely; so that when their men should have sallied from the cuartel in a body, the intoxicated were so numerous, and so many others were obstinate, that they were penned, like sheep, in its patio, before they understood their danger. Had they been provided, by closing the doors they might have held out here a long time; but they had no provisions, the supply of ammunition was extremely limited, and most of them, raw recruits, were content to obtain favorable terms, after a dozen or two of their reeling companions had been shot down about them.

December 9th was a memorable day at Santiago. By daylight the Serenos were thundering at the doors of the houses in the upper part of the city. A fire had broken out near the plaza, and they wanted admittance to the acequias, for the purpose of turning the streams into the street where it was raging. It had originated in one of the shops of a large house during the night, and was then showing itself through the doorway and part of the roof, and this summons from the Sereno was the only way in which it was made known to the distant public! There was no ringing of bells to alarm the population; no cries of *fire!* to disturb slumbers in the still morning; no rattling of engines or deep bellowing of self-important men, with trumpets understood only by themselves, as in some of our cities; but half the town might have burned down, and the other half have been none the wiser.

Much time passed before any assistance whatever could be obtained; and long before a force was properly organized for work, there had been great losses from the flames, breakage, and the conduct of injudicious persons. At this time of great excitement, the fire-engines could not be taken out without permission from the Intendente, who lived at a distance, and, like every one else, was asleep. Mere squirts as they are when got out, there were none to manage them properly. The citizens may enrol themselves in the fire brigade or National Guard at their option. If in the former, they are nominally exempt from the military duties required of the latter, though really a part of them are constantly on guard at the doors of the engine-rooms, musket in hand; and the whole brigade, even had they been there, having been drilled as soldiers for months if not years before, knew infinitely more about musket-barrels than engine-nozzles. Gentlemen could not condescend to manual labor, and peons were not disposed to do so without pay: so for hours the flames roared and crackled laughingly.

Towards 6 o'clock, when all the immense roofs of the edifice were in flames, and fire, water, and pillage had left little that was worth saving, a body of men were set to work systematically. Obliged to pass within thirty yards of the actual fire at least once an hour, it is extraordinary how the Serenos could have remained unobservant of the smoke which must have issued from the house for several hours before they gave even the alarm mentioned. Luckily for Santiago, there are very rarely strong winds, and the construction of the houses is such as to render most of them nearly fire-proof; otherwise the custom of the population to smoke at all hours and in all places (except church) would keep it in constant jeopardy. The supply of water is ample; but the engines, like most other machinery here, being of French construction, are almost worthless; and as they are supplied from streams in the middle of the streets, where rapid descent causes them to bring much earth and extraneous matter along, it is not remarkable that they are soon choked. Insurance companies were unknown, and there were very few houses in the republic on which the proprietors had taken out policies abroad. Many of the foreign merchants at Valparaiso, and two at Santiago, had recently insured their goods; but no case could be ascertained of a house in the latter city. The probabilities of loss by fire may be estimated from the fact that the city covers more than 2,700 acres, and this was the first fire during three years.

Notwithstanding the very small proportion of combustible materials, at 9 o'clock the fire was still burning rapidly. At each corner of the streets, for several squares around, guards prevented the rabble from going near, and others immediately about the house preserved order, and prevented interference with the gangs working the engines or passing water.

Early in the afternoon a second memorable event occurred. After months of suffering, General Fréire, the oldest surviving officer of the revolution, was gathered to his fathers. His devoted patriotism, courage, and skill, his stern integrity, his liberal sentiments on every political question, and high social position, had especially endeared him to the opposition. Consequently, although the result had been looked for during some days, the intelligence was received with emotions of great sympathy.

Before sunset an express arrived from Talca, bringing letters from the Minister of War, the Intendente, and two others, notifying government that a Colonel Letellier had just come from beyond the Maule, with information that the cavalry and part of the infantry of Cruz had been completely routed. Another portion of the infantry had taken refuge in a house near by, within which it was supposed the leaders were. The Minister of War wrote to the President to prevent his "being surprised by adverse news, as has occurred here;" and his letter, dated 4 P. M. of the preceding day, had been brought eighty leagues in twenty-five hours! At the time his informant left the battle-field, Bulnes had drawn up his infantry without musket range, and was besieging the house, which he expected to destroy in a short time, if it did not surrender previously.

Such intelligence was an unexpected shock to the opposition. Their hopes had risen very high within a few preceding days, and they believed the triumph of their party almost absolutely certain. Of course the news was rapidly conveyed through the city; and among the crowds to be met going towards the palace for verification of the rumors that came to them, there was rarely a countenance that permitted doubt as to the party to which its possessor belonged. How many an aching heart was there! how many among them whose dearest relatives were compromised with one side or the other—whose homes and subsistence depended on the result of this one mortal combat! Alas! how great the horrors of civil war in a country where banishment, breaking up of social ties, and sacrifice of property, are the certain consequences of failure.

But few lingered near the palace, and these were principally rotos and peons. Each of the others, as he learned the tidings authentically, hurried away to offer consolation or felicitation at home; and thus there were gravity and silence, apparently expressive of regard alike for the feelings of those allied to the vanquished, as for those who trembled till they could learn the fate of husbands, fathers, and brothers, on the battle-field. By nightfall the streets were deserted, except by the Serenos and occasional patrols, and the street doors were very generally closed before 11 o'clock. Distress, doubts, want of confidence, perhaps (and, it is to be hoped), inspired each family to commune within its own circle. The wind had blown from S.W. all day more freshly than usual, heaping up over the Andes masses of cumuli, which gradually extended across the plain towards sunset, making the night dark and damp—unlike as possible the serene evenings of summer. As the cool breeze ceased with the decline of the sun, the atmosphere became sultry, and, according to our North American experience, threatened a rainstorm—an event which followed, with thunder and vivid lightning, soon after midnight. A few years ago, rain in December, or thunder and lightning over the city at any time, were phenomena to amaze the wisest. Since our advent, this was the third occasion of atmospheric revolution; and as many of the people of Chile have actually greater terror of lightning than of earthquakes, it is no wonder that the roar and blaze of heaven's artillery at such an hour should have caused more trembling among the multitudes of anxious watchers, than its iron imitators had done to their countrymen on the field of Loncomilla.

There was no public demonstration or other evidence offered during the night that government had routed the main body of the men in hostility to it; but early on the following morning cannon were dragged up Santa Lucia, and a national salvo inspired new courage among doubting and uninformed ministerialists, though it sounded almost like a death-knell to the anticipations of their opponents. As most of the latter supposed that confirmatory intelligence had been received in the night, which was thus announced, the salute was doubly depressing. Immediately afterwards a military band paraded the streets playing the national hymn, halting before the dwellings of one or two prominent members of the opposition, and in one case entering to perform in the court-yard, if possible to mark their exultation more thoroughly. The absence of generous feeling shown by such conduct, and the spirit dictating public rejoicing for an event in which thousands of their own countrymen only (their brothers and neighbors) had lost life, bears little token of humanity. Only vindictiveness and revenge could inspire the cruel mockery, and among those who would participate in like celebrations the finer affections can never exist.

A staff officer belonging to the army of Bulnes arrived towards noon of the 10th. He had left the field of battle late in the afternoon; but he either brought no written account, or its information was of so doubtful a nature that the ministry dared not publish it. As a consequence, the most contradictory reports were circulated as coming from him, respecting the losses and condition of the combatants. All agreed, however, that the action had been long, obstinate, and bloody; that nearly three thousand men, or one third of the entire force engaged, had perished;

that a company of American riflemen in the army of Cruz had "picked off" officers on the government side at incredible distances, causing extraordinary loss of life among them; and that the action was still undecided when he left. Some went so far as to assert that each rifle was furnished with a small telescope, the better to enable these marksmen to select their victims. Nor were they the ignorant of Santiago who believed the story of the rifles, but men among the "upper ten" of the ministerial party, who were loud in denunciations of Yankees intermeddling—forgetful how grateful they had shown themselves for *official* British interference. All the success was attributed to Yankee rifles, whose number was magnified to tenfold, as was known from a report made by the United States consul at Talcahuano. That gentleman notified our minister plenipotentiary, Balie Peyton, Esq., that twenty-one Californians had left a ship which put into Talcahuano for supplies, and joined the revolutionists. To their credit be it told, they were "volunteers without pay, who offered themselves from a hatred of oppression, and spirit of adventure," characteristic of the race. A published decree from the acting Intendente mentions these facts, and very properly compliments whilst it expresses gratitude to the individuals for the service proposed. An English traveller paid the nation the tribute to tell one of the ministerialists, who insisted so earnestly on the presence of at least 200 *malditos rifleros:* "Had there been so many, Cruz would have been in Santiago long ago."

The departure of a large supply of ammunition during the night could not be kept concealed, and the offers of $25 bounty at the several additional rendezvous opened for new recruits was another fact calculated to keep up hope among the revolutionists. At sunset there was a repetition of the salute and music, and the same class of insults were offered to individuals as in the morning by those who controlled the movements of the band. Others—individuals, most probably, influenced as much by personal envy as by party spirit—vented their animosity secretly, and sent cows' tails decorated with flowers to members of the apparently defeated party. Nor was it uncommon, in passing along the street, to hear the word "*cola*" (tail) contemptuously uttered when one of the same unfortunate number came near his rejoicing adversary. As on the preceding night, silence and solitude reigned in the streets from an unusually early hour.

On the 11th, the only event of consequence was the burial of General Fréire with military honors. Persons of the highest rank of both parties, and all foreigners of note, attended his remains to the cemetery. He had ever been a fast friend to the latter, regarding their interests as inseparably connected with the advancement of his country; and they sincerely lamented his loss. The car on which his remains were transported was decorated with his uniform as a captain-general, covered with a wreath of laurel. It was drawn by personal friends, his sons and nearest male relatives walking beside it, and subsequently assisting in conveying the body to the chapel and grave. An account of the procession and ceremonies has already been given in Chapter VI, together with the bold assertion by one orator: "Fréire is dead, and with him Liberty!"

A bulletin was printed during the day. This contained a brief account of the intelligence brought from the field of battle by the staff officer; but there was neither official statement nor other particulars than those previously current, and anxiety to learn something of the truth became manifest even among transient sojourners. Thirty-six hours had now elapsed since the arrival of the first express! Then the main army of Cruz was reported to have been routed, and his cavalry driven into the Loncomilla and drowned by squadrons; and there remained only a few hundred men in a farm-house, whose capture within half an hour was regarded as certain; yet nothing had come from the commander-in-chief opposed to him. Where facts were not attainable, recourse was had to invention; and the city was filled with a thousand rumors contradictory as the diverse desires of their originators could make them. Bulnes was routed; he was dead. He had only defeated Cruz's vanguard, and had himself been vanquished by the main body of revolutionist forces coming upon him when his own men were worn down by a hard day's struggle. Two of Cruz's generals were dead, and a third had lost his reason by the wind of a cannon-ball. Six hundred of his men and twenty officers were prisoners, and the rest cut

42

to pieces or utterly dispersed. Bulnes had achieved prodigies of personal valor and skill, but none had seen Cruz on the field of battle. The montoneros had robbed all the despatches sent by both sides. These were some of the stories circulating in addition to those of the day before, varied and embellished as they passed from one narrator to another, until even the most credulous could but smile at them.

Neither the 12th nor the 13th brought any relief to the anxious. Government claimed to have ascertained that the montoneros had robbed the express bringing the official report from General Bulnes, and refrained from printing verbal reports brought by other officers known to have reached Santiago, until a copy of it could be obtained. When the staff officer arrived, he had mentioned the death of the colonel of a ministerial regiment, and the relatives were desirous to learn the particulars; but it was considered prudent to enjoin silence, and his lips were thereafter closed. The *birlochero* who had brought the same officer from Talca made it known that he had arrived there without hat, shoes, or sword; and to save him further questioning by the curious, he was put under lock and key. Subsequently, a letter from General Bulnes proved (as will be seen) the report of the robbery of his official narrative to have been invented. Many things, however, could not be concealed. More troops were collecting hourly, every detachment that left escorting a large supply of ammunition. An additional number of surgeons were sent to the wounded, for whom vehicles started to convey as many as possible to the capital; and it was conceded that the portion of Cruz's army driven into the houses had made its escape—whether by cutting their way out or by eluding the vigilance of the besiegers, was not told. It was only certain that they were gone—the government pretended not to know whither. There was evidently more confidence among members of the opposition. They claimed to be in receipt of highly gratifying intelligence; and by night of the 13th, the Portal and streets began to exhibit the usual number of gaily dressed purchasers and promenaders. Their three thousand relatives and fellow-countrymen cumbering the field of Loncomilla were already measurably forgotten!

At last—on the 14th—the smoke of the battle began to blow away. A letter came to the President from General Bulnes, very evidently written in reply to one expressing surprise that no official report had been received from him. He says:

"*I have not written to you* [the italics are mine] since the battle of the 8th, as well because I supposed you informed by Borgoño [the staff officer] and the correspondence of friends who accompany me, as because I hoped shortly to have occasion to announce the definite result of the campaign. This has taken place at this moment. The remainder of the enemy's army has rebelled against its leaders; and after a great many soldiers had passed over to my camp, the rest took up their line of march for the south. The chiefs of the Carampangue and Guias [two of Cruz's battalions] go with them in order to prevent disturbances on their march. At this very moment I send Major Urrutia to regulate their march, and my cavalry goes also.

"He who communicates to me the prelude to this result is Cruz himself, in a note, of which I shall forward to you a copy. Since last night Don José A. Alemparte has been in my camp, having come to adjust with me the surrender of the remains of Cruz's army, and the successful result just referred to has occurred here. A thousand congratulations on this conclusion, my friend! In a few days, throughout the whole extent of its territory, the republic will recover its precious peace."

The cannon on Santa Lucia, and bands of music in the streets, uttered their notes of rejoicing—Sunday as it was—as the bulletin containing this letter issued from the press; and along every thoroughfare there were groups listening with earnest attention to one of their number who read the document aloud.

From the best information obtainable at the time, the occurrences at Loncomilla were as follows: On the evening of the 7th, the army of Bulnes was encamped about Cerro Bobadilla, a mile to the south of the Maule; that of Cruz in and around the houses of a hacienda occupied by Señor Urzua, distant nearly two leagues. The surrounding country is a slightly undulating plain, limited on the west by the river Loncomilla, whose stream, scarcely more than a mile distant from the house of Urzua, is bounded by steep and precipitous banks, and at that season is too rapid and deep to be forded without danger. Cruz had lost and left behind to guard the rear nearly a thousand men, including all the Indians except sixty, so that his effective army numbered about 3,500 men. Fifteen hundred of the army of reserve from Talca increased the force of Bulnes to 4,500. These were formed in two parallel lines, with the cavalry on the right, and he marched in pursuit of his adversary on the morning of the 8th. Cruz was prepared to receive him, and the cavalry on both sides were soon engaged. In the first charge, that of Bulnes drove their enemies before them, pursuing them closely. Many were cut down with sabres and lances, others were crushed in their fall over the cliffs, and large numbers were drowned in attempting to cross the Loncomilla, on whose flood a mass of men and horses were soon seen floating. However, this success was only temporary. Penned as they were like rats in a corner, the pursued rallied, and in turn drove their oppenents: a part fled through Talca with tidings of their defeat, and another part were overwhelmed by the waters of the Maule. The result of the cavalry contest was the almost total loss of this arm to both armies.

Whilst this was going on, the infantry and artillery engagement began; the Chacabuco and Chillan regiments belonging to Bulnes being deployed to make an attack on the rear of the houses. After having made them change their uniform for the ordinary dress of civic troops, Cruz had posted his Carampangue regiment here; the Guia and Alcazar in front. The action soon became general, and for five hours a more galling and deadly fire was scarcely ever known. Cannon and muskets were then thrown aside: "hand to hand and steel to steel," knife and bayonet, did the work. Countrymen who had bivouacked by the same camp-fire, who had guarded the same post alternately, who had shared the same ration, who were born from the same womb—aye! father and son—had met in mortal combat with a degree of ferocity belonging to untamed forest tribes—not to those who profess Christianity. Different corps became so intermingled that officers knew not where to find their own men, and were cut off, captured, and recaptured several times during the engagement. After seven hours, Bulnes gathered the handful of men about him, abandoned his wounded, several pieces of artillery, and much ammunition, and returned to his camp at Bobadilla. Undoubtedly he was defeated, and nothing but the want of cavalry prevented his army from falling prisoners to Cruz on the spot. As it was, the field was literally covered with the dead and wounded, the floors of the houses of Urzua drowned in the blood of near 600 victims, and both armies were appalled at the carnage in which they had been participants. Of 8,000 men who filled the ranks in health and vigor at daylight on the 8th, less than 3,000 capable of bearing arms could be found on the morning of the 9th, when neither party was willing to renew the combat. Indeed, it was very generally believed that they *refused* to do so at a later hour of the day.

Considering himself the victor, an envoy was sent by Cruz on the morning of the 10th offering terms to his adversary. In consequence, Señor Tocornal was empowered to arrange preliminaries; but after several hours' discussion, nothing could be agreed on, and he returned to the head-quarters of Bulnes. Other overtures on the following day met with a like result. Meanwhile the government had not been idle with emissaries of another character, armed perhaps with more subtle weapons—arms that never fail to assure victory in Spanish-American revolutions. Fifty thousand dollars, it was said, had been offered a Colonel Zañartu for himself and the famous Carampangue battalion, if they would abandon General Cruz; and the temptation proved irresistible. Principles were but words, golden ounces were *facts;* and though some few refused to transfer their allegiance, Cruz found his noblest regiment deserting him to an alarming extent—individuals joining the ranks of his rival—companies taking up their line of march for home. But there was also cause among them for discontent against himself. He had kept them at the houses of Urzua for several days amid wounded and suffering companions, surrounded by multitudes of graves—both depressing evidences of the conflict. Unfortunately, there was the least possible provision for the maimed; and their lives of inactivity, after days of most intense excitement, were only varied when some comrade was to be added to those already beneath the sands. No wonder they were desirous to get away.

Perceiving, when too late, the treason in his camp, and the certain consequences of continuing longer in his present position, the shattered remains of his army was put in motion on the 12th, and recrossed the Loncomilla. Bulnes started in pursuit on the same day. He had been reinforced by a few small detachments from the vicinity of Talca and other parties of infantry and cavalry dispersed on the 8th, and therefore could again afford to assume the offensive. Of the events of the 13th and 14th near the belligerents, no one at Santiago spoke; nor does it appear that any event of primary consequence transpired. The two parties were convinced that the government, in spite of its unpopularity, had the means to gain ground; *liberalism* was too poor for success.

Two days after, the cannon on Santa Lucia announced, and every good citizen hoped, that this had been the concluding act of the domestic tragedy. The Vijilantes had gone round early on the evening before, directing each housekeeper to display the national flag over his roof-tree, as a treaty of peace was to be thus publicly celebrated. The two military secretaries had finally agreed on the following terms: The revolutionary party to recognise Señor Montt as the legitimate President, and place all the regular troops in their ranks under the orders of Bulnes; Cruz and other officers holding commissions under the republic to retain rank unprejudiced by the parts they had taken, except for offences prior to September 1st; Bulnes to use his influence to obtain a general amnesty which should include those of April as well as civil offenders; and Cruz to endeavor to effect the dispersion of the montoneros, and the cessation of resistance at Coquimbo.

Both parties were rabid enough at the result: ministerialists, because they hoped for and would have gladly witnessed the extermination of their opponents; and revolutionists, because they had spent their money fruitlessly, and compromised themselves, whilst their leaders and friends, not already in exile, were less than ever likely to escape from their places of concealment. No stipulation for civilians had been made in the capitulation, and they had strong reasons to dread the dictatorial and irresponsible powers with which the President remained invested. On the same day that the terms were signed, the camps, as hostile bodies, were broken up. Bulnes set out for the capital via the Maule and Valparaiso, and entered Santiago on the 24th. His friends had prepared a civic escort and banquet for his arrival—the President and ministers joining in the procession to receive him at the outskirts of the city; and the *cortége* passed through the streets amid the firing of cannon and strains of military music. But there was no popular enthusiasm; and if, by chance, a few "Vivas" swelled the noise of vehicles and music, the sequent was a sign of the cross over the forehead, not the name of Bulnes or Montt. Nor would the mass believe that he came otherwise than as a fugitive; for they asked, "Whoever heard of a victorious general coming to Santiago without soldiers; and where are his?"

Cruz returned to his hacienda, near Concepcion, a disappointed and almost ruined man. His letter to the Intendente there plainly exhibits the former, and elicited from those who knew him most painful sympathy. He says:

"The necessity, on the one hand, for terminating civil war, and, on the other, events crowding upon me which it would take long to detail to you, have obliged me to initiate a treaty in which no better condition has been obtained for the republic than before the war. But I was compelled to a treaty, though nominally with sufficient force to continue the war.

"I have not heart to criminate an individual; yet the origin of the results which have so greatly distressed me during the last eight days was in the very bosom of my own camp. On signing the treaty yesterday, and returning to private life, I felt that I was laying down a load whose weight had not been easy to bear. I lacked not disposition to fulfil the promises given. We had already advanced far; but I counted on the co-operation of others who failed me in the hour of need. I counted on the ordinary course of human successes, and have found myself thwarted on every hand; even successes themselves inexplicably reversed, and victories represented as routs.

"I forward to you a copy of the treaty; and having been endowed with authority to negotiate it, I hope you will accept and cause its execution, if not as a benefit obtained, at least as a necessity to which we have been dragged. God preserve you."

This closed the war in the south. The steamer Cazador was sent with news of the fact to Coquimbo, together with a letter from General Cruz to the leaders there. Seeing the hopelessness of attempting to contend against government with their small force and resources, now that its attention was no longer occupied by their chief co-laborer, the Coquimbanos made every effort to secure the most favorable terms of capitulation. Arteaga and Carrera, it will be remembered, having been criminated in the revolts of April, were beyond the pale of the treaty concluded at Purapel; and both, no doubt, earnestly contended for such stipulations as would permit them to return to their families at Santiago. Arteaga, indeed, for participation in the April revolt, was under sentence of death by court-martial; but the commander of the ministerial forces could not or would not make exceptions in their favor, and the besieged troops, unwilling to surrender on any terms, or to believe the account of General Cruz's defeat, mutinied against the leaders, chaffering only for themselves, drove them from Serena, and then marched out, taking the direction of Huasco. Arteaga found refuge on board a French vessel in the harbor; Carrera escaped to the Andes; Coquimbo was taken possession of by the besiegers; a part of the retiring troops fell in a conflict with a detachment sent after them, and the remainder pursued their journey to the north, where their compatriots had successfully raised the revolutionary banner.*

Copiapó, the city of almost improvised wealth, at midnight of December 26, had been seized by less than one hundred resolute men, around whom a thousand others rallied within three days, though the majority of them were more accustomed to the use of crowbars and hammers than muskets. So sudden and unexpected had been the attack, that the Intendente had barely time to strike one hurried blow and retreat to the interior; not, however, until two gallant young men who had flown to his assistance, and several soldiers, had fallen near him mortally wounded. The leader of the revolutionists was at once installed as Intendente, his followers believing that Cruz had been fully triumphant in the south, and that like success had attended the Coquimbanos. Perceiving himself single-handed in the war, when news of the treaty of Purapel was received by the steamer, four days afterwards, the Intendente, as a sensible man should have been, was desirous to repair his error at the earliest moment, and he would gladly have accepted any reasonable terms. He had sought revolution at a time when his party was believed to be in the ascendant throughout the land, as the redress for grievances inflicted by government; and even his opponents have made public acknowledgment that his brief executive career was marked by ability, energy, and determination, quite equal to the emergency. Such order and decorum had never been observed in Copiapó as during these few days.

But the wizard who had called up the whirlwind was not able to control it. Whilst the mass submitted without a murmur when individuals of their own set, detected in robbery, were publicly shot by his order, it was only because they were biding the time when siege and assault, certain to ensue, would license pillage and rapine. Therefore, when troops arrived from Valparaiso and Coquimbo to aid the displaced Intendente, they positively refused to be surrendered. Several days were spent in preparations to march from the city, the government leader meanwhile collecting the dispersed troops of the vicinity, and entrenching himself near Linderos, about a dozen miles from Copiapó, on the line of the railroad. An action took place on the 8th of January. Where the leader on one side was unwilling to fight, and his men, though superior in numbers, were immeasurably inferior in the use of arms, and on the other not only every man was a well-found veteran, but a veteran smarting under the mortification that a

* At Petorca, a white flag with a red cross. This was indicative of their principles, and, at the same time, complimentary to their chief, Cruz (Cross.) I do not know whether it was afterwards displayed.

handful of raw countrymen had, for more than one hundred days, successfully resisted them at Coquimbo, the result of the contest could not be doubtful. Thus the miners, becoming disgusted with weapons they found so difficult to manage, flung them away very soon after the action commenced, and rushed into the combat with only stones and knives—an inequality they fought under for more than two hours, against troops entrenched and barricaded with all the skill a regularly educated soldier could devise. Some fifty were killed; a like number fell wounded or were taken prisoners; and the remainder, perhaps four hundred and fifty, adopting the belief of Falstaff, that

"He who fights and runs away,
May live to fight another day,"

"made tracks" for the city. This was quietly surrendered next day, after exchanging one or two notes, for appearance sake.

There was no subsequent contest at the north. Owing to evidences of still existing disaffection among the populace at Valparaiso for several weeks after, orderly citizens were under constant excitement. Seconded as was the Intendente, the motions of the mob were kept under control, though nothing but the most untiring vigilance prevented open revolt again.

One other part of the republic remained to be heard from—the "*ultima thule*" of the continent, as of its society. Of all its territory, the penal colony at Magellan was the only portion from which the sound of revolutionary voices had not yet been heard. True, except when a new living cargo was to be added to its numbers, few thoughts were given by government to that congregation of felons and political offenders; and perhaps no one anticipated the contemporaneous tragedy enacted there. If the news was somewhat tardy in coming from that isolated quarter, its people had been scarcely less prompt in action than their more favored fellow-countrymen; and thus the distaste to the new incumbent of the Presidential chair was either universally innate, or the opposition had scattered the seeds of discord very widely. A successful revolt had taken place about the middle of November, though intelligence of it was not received at Valparaiso until about two months later. The news was brought by two or three persons who succeeded in escaping to an English mail-steamer, and informed the commander that the leader was a lieutenant of the military guard sent there to aid the governor. Supported by others of the guard, and a few political captives, the lieutenant had made a prisoner of his captain, and took possession of the arms and ammunition. The governor (captain), with five others who rallied to his support, had been obliged to take refuge with the curate.

Five days later the American ship Florida, freighted with political prisoners, arrived from Valparaiso; and the governor, who seems to have suffered no restraint till then, immediately went off to her. But his movements had been too slow. Intelligence of the condition of affairs on shore had already reached the passengers; and these deriving confirmation from musket shots at his boat as it pushed off, took possession of the ship, also turning their arms upon him. Assailed from both sides, there was no alternative but flight; and the mere shallop in which himself and little party had left the shore being wholly unable to contend against the fresh breeze and powerful tide sweeping through the passage, he was driven to the southern side of the straits.

Chilenos report the Fuegians savages tractable only at times; and, as the latter are known to be hostile to the neighbors which government has imposed on them, it is to be inferred that their humors have not always been acceded to during visits to the northern side of the straits. Inhabited by such a race only, the governor did not perceive his approximation of Tierra del Fuego with any great degree of pleasure, more especially when he found that the natives were awaiting the moment he should be forced on shore. We know that a conflict almost immediately ensued, and that his party eventually put to sea again in the same crazy canoe; but nothing of the origin. To have remained longer would have exposed themselves to attacks from irresistible numbers as well as to starvation, and it was preferable to risk the possible charity of misguided countrymen rather than hazard such fate in this land of fire, with the prospective *finale* of being eaten for supper some night. Unfortunate refugees! their kith and kin were *scarcely* less compassionate. On recrossing the straits the whole party were seized, and a portion of them, including the governor and priest, were not only shot, but their bodies were subsequently gibbeted and burned; atrocities scarcely credible when it is recollected that they were inflicted on persons whom the same mutineers had suffered to remain near them nearly a week almost without molestation. The cause of such treatment is only explicable on the supposition that a part of the passengers by the Florida had roused new animosities, and instigated this in retaliation for some of the high-handed measures going on about the capital.

An American barque homeward bound from California, which had a quantity of gold dust on board, was taken possession of by the revolutionists soon after these events. In her passage through the straits she had anchored at Punta Arenas for supplies, but instead of assistance had her treasure rifled and distributed, and her master detained to await the further purposes of the new colonial government. From this time until January 2d the revolutionists were making ready for a voyage, killing the cattle, drying charqui, and gathering other provisions whencesoever they could. Destroying the property at Punta Arenas and Port Bulnes, they made sail for Talcahuano or Lima, in case they could not enter the former port. When the news reached Valparaiso, the small navy of Chile was fully occupied in settling the Coquimbo and Atacama difficulties. The last ship of the United States Pacific squadron had gone to Peru only a few weeks before. With such bands of miscreants free on the ocean, it was impossible to foresee what atrocities might not be committed. Perhaps out of charity to the two nations most interested—Chile and the United States—the British vice-admiral at once despatched a steamer-of-war to examine into the matter, and if possible arrest the pirates. Fortunate in her search, the British steamer brought both vessels in as prizes, and the ring-leaders at Magellanes paid with their lives the penalty of the law.

This closed the revolt of 1851. The treaty of Purapel was, of necessity, ratified by government; yet it surprised us no little to learn that a part of the officers who fought against it in the early days of December, on arriving at Santiago, were restored to posts about the executive departments before the last day of the same month; overweening confidence or magnanimous forgetfulness of the past, one does not know which. The final acts of the drama were sumptuous banquets given to the ministerial chiefs by their partisans; and, before the first month of the new year had passed away, the country had apparently returned to its normal state, the mass of its people having already forgotten the lives lost and treasure wasted. Subsequently, some additional particulars were learned from participants and eye-witnesses of the battle on the field of Loncomilla. These will be found in Chapter XV.

We have seen the results: let us examine for a moment what the revolutionists proposed to accomplish. That both the law of elections and the constitution had been violated in fact as in spirit by those sworn to guard them, does not admit of doubt; and government was rapidly centralizing its powers instead of becoming more democratic, as is the tendency of republics. One evidence of this is nomination by the administration of its candidate for the Presidency. The people, in convention or by other mode, do not select the individuals who are to serve as their representatives, or as electors of President. Names of ministerialists mostly resident at Santiago are forwarded from the Ministry of the Interior to Intendentes of the provinces, and it is the duty of these last officers to cause the return of persons thus named. Electors reside in the provinces for which they are chosen, but are selected in the same manner. Not only are these so called representatives, and those who will nominally determine their Chief Magistrate thus appointed, but even members of the municipal councils are decided upon by the same functionary. Meetings in the open air for the discussion of political questions are prohibited by law; and since the organization of socialist clubs, in the early part of 1851, assemblages in houses for like objects are equally under its ban. As the intendentes, governors, sub-delegates, and officers of the National Guard hold office directly from or at the will of the President, and without the necessity for sanction by even the Council of State, it is fairly inferrible that they are creatures of his commands. Moreover, commandants of battalions and haciendados or their mayordomos take charge of the certificates of qualification when they are issued. If by chance the soldier or tenant be disposed to vote adversely to the will of his superior, the paper is withheld, and he cannot present himself at the polls. Again, the fact was notorious that certificates thus withheld were given to inmates of hospitals and paupers, and that others were openly bought and sold adjoining the polls. Another ground of complaint was, that the whole surplus receipts of the treasury were expended on the provinces of Santiago and Valparaiso, to the neglect of the more necessitous and distant confederates. The capitals of the former were adorned and their roads improved, whilst the thoroughfares and highways about those at a distance remained in the primitive condition of the last century; or, if improved, it had been done by treasure obtained from local resources, not from the national coffers. And the third grievance alleged was, that the powers of the municipal boards had been encroached upon until, in fact, they were but nominal assemblages.

When the term of the late President was drawing to a close, there was doubt, during some months, whom he would name as his successor. The cabinet were divided in opinion, and perhaps opposed to the candidate it was his interest to support. Probably his predilections would have led him to select General Cruz, a relative; but Señor Montt was the favorite of a large number of the wealthiest miners, and some of the haciendados, and from the former of these General Bulnes had borrowed large sums of money. Some maliciously said that the miners threatened to withdraw their funds unless he would support their favorite; and as the money was already embarked in extensive landed and business speculations, it would not have been convenient to pay just then. At this time two ministers known to be in opposition to Señor Montt were dismissed; a third resigned; and others, favorable to his pretensions, were chosen in their places. This settled the question as to the policy of the administration.

Up to this time the candidate of the opposition or democratic party was Señor Errazuriz, a senator who had filled with distinction various posts of honor, and was noted for enlightened and liberal views on all questions of public policy. Unfortunately, he was truly appreciated only by the more intelligent and patriotic of his countrymen; and therefore, when the mass of the party, comprising all who wanted offices, found that the money of the miners was likely to secure the election, they cavalierly dropped him and took up General Cruz, whose military prestige would be of vast weight in case of a battle for the succession. When the latter came from Concepcion for the purpose of remonstrating at head-quarters against the course pursued respecting the troops under his command, he was well aware of the antipathy felt by the majority towards the candidate opposed to him. Desirous to obviate the difficulty he probably foresaw, and to secure some one who would measurably be acceptable to all, it is believed that he proposed to the administration that both Señor Montt and himself should withdraw, and a third person be chosen by government from those who had been prominently mentioned among its citizens. In this he was honest; for up to that time it was well known he had no desire to occupy the Presidential chair.

But the proposition was not acceptable to the Monttistas; they were unwilling to sacrifice personal interests and aspirations on the altar of patriotism; and Cruz returned to Concepcion to be incited to more active opposition by his immediate removal from the post of Intendente. A military man only, somewhat obstinate (according to the account of friends), with no remarkable amount of talent as a statesman, and at best but limited administrative capacity, his nomination was received with great apathy by a large number of those who could have exercised influence, and the preparations for the electioneering campaign were only prosecuted vigorously by the Montt party. Moderate energy might have secured success to the others; but more than one of them remarked to me, "It is useless to attempt it: the government always elects its candidates—by force, if need be; and why shall we risk imprisonment or banishment by openly organizing opposition?" And in this manner they actually suffered the election to go by default, three fourths of the voters either staying away from the polls voluntarily, or by the will of their superiors.

If they chose to be so defeated, they should have remembered that the prominent cause giving character to their country abroad is the order and regularity which had been observed at its changes of rulers, and should not only have been determined to remain quiet themselves, but also have exerted their influence to restrain less prominent partisans. So far as foreign nations could judge, instead of appeals to the sword to decide between aspirants to supreme rule, as under all the other Spanish-American governments, in Chile the moral power and purity of its Constitution remained intact. No doubt there were some of its citizens who would prefer any ruler to the horrors of civil war and domestic losses, with injury to the national reputation; but these were a small minority—not those who craved the archbishopric, a Ministerio, or Intendencia—not those whose relatives had been imprisoned or banished since April, or who still lurked in obscure places under cover of the night. *They* were at work from July collecting money, and insidiously corrupting the troops and lower orders.

At first General Cruz took no part with them. In fact, he had always belonged to the *Pelucon** party, against which the contest would have been fratricidal. But he was not permitted to remain quiet. Those who had nominated him, did so in anticipation of the very emergency which had occurred. They needed a military leader to carry out their schemes, and began by painting in the strongest colors the chains with which the administration was gradually enslaving the nation. Twenty years of peace, they said, had built upon the ashes of liberty a love of spoils. The rights their fathers had fought for, and thought to transmit to them through the Constitution, though nominally existing, had been violated one by one, and now none dare claim them. Such sentiments fell not idly on a man who was smarting under the mortification of dismissal from office, and subsequent defeat through illegal influence of the same party; and the emissaries from Santiago and Coquimbo were not long in bringing about their objects. Whilst the citizens of the capital were enjoying the national festivities, those of Concepcion were celebrating his *pronunciamiento*. This was the only paper made public, in which the causes for an appeal to arms are specified; and the portion of it embracing these reasons is worthy of a place here on that account. It is addressed to the *army*, whom he hails:

"Old Companions! The last political act of the province of Concepcion placed me at the head of a heroic people, who desire to reconquer rights trodden down by a government converted into a faction of party, which intends to annul the republic, and with it justice and the liberty of its citizens. I have merited the confidence of my fellow-countrymen, who have confided to me the honorable charge of defender of their imprescriptible rights—a charge that I can only fulfil aided by the noble abnegation of citizens ready to sacrifice themselves for liberty and the country.

"I have been called by the provinces of Concepcion and Coquimbo, always united in their patriotism and noble tasks. I have been called by hundreds of citizens who, in the other provinces, groan under the weight of the harshest despotism. I have been called by the dolorous clamor of mothers and wives whose sons live in the filth of prisons, or whose husbands beg in a foreign land the bitter bread of the proscribed.

"My feelings, my honor, my convictions have finally imposed on me the duty of accepting a revolution whose spirit is to reconstruct the republic—that republic conquered by the precious blood of our fathers, the heroes of Independence. I have never been able to remain indifferent to the establishment of a dictatorship, in which flattery of the ambition of a man to whom public opinion and the rights of a citizen are of no value must always terminate.

"Accepting the responsibility of such a sacred duty, I have a right to count on the heroic co-operation of my old companions in arms, on their pure patriotism, on their established valor. At the voice of an oppressed country I have recovered the strength debilitated by years of campaigning, that I may consecrate to it the last services of my life. Where is the soldier

* Literally a *big wig*, or one who arrays himself in fantastic dresses. The reader will probably see its origin in misapprehension of the English words *whig* and *wig*.

of the Independence who is not, as I am, ready to die for the country freed by his arm after a hundred glorious battles?

"National Guards of the republic,—you to whom is confided the custody of public security; you who exercise the noble and honorable charge of citizens armed to defend the institutions, order, and tranquillity of the people,—follow the example set by your brothers in Concepcion and Coquimbo; and this unanimous *pronunciamiento* will pull down the despotism of an administration which longs to convert you into a blind instrument of tyranny, ridiculing your noble mission. Listen to the voice of the country claiming her sons, and in a brief time the republic will have been saved without a drop of kindred blood having been shed to darken your glorious triumph.

"Valiants of the Carampangue Battalion and Regiment of Cazadors: to you I should especially direct myself, that we may recollect a sacred duty at moments so precious to the republic. In your ranks I learned to defend liberty, and I have the honor to have been one of your founders. With you I have shared the glories and dangers of war, my grades have been earned fighting beside you, and I have a claim to hope that now you will listen to the call made to us in the name of our country.

"Troops of the Line: your cause is that of the republic; you would be irresistible with the decided support of the people. We mean to destroy tyranny or die honorably fighting it. Wherever I am, I am your old companion and friend,

"JOSÉ MARIA DE LA CRUZ.

"CONCEPCION, *September* 23, 1851."

No one believed at first that Gen. Cruz would lend his name to a revolutionary enterprise; and even after the *pronunciamiento* was circulated in Santiago, none were more obstinate in expressing their disbelief than the foreigners domiciliated in Chile. To a man almost they pronounced the document a forgery. Then his intimates claim that the General said openly, he "had neither desire nor intention to become President, but would call a new election by the people at a successful termination of the campaign, taking care that suffrage should be exercised in accordance with the spirit and letter of the Constitution." This was what the wire-pulling friends of Errazuriz expected; and they counted on the election of their candidate with much confidence. As time passed on, through the influence of officers by whom he was surrounded, the patriotic singleness of purpose which had influenced the military chief yielded to personal ambition; and long before the final battle he spoke openly and authoritatively of the regard which the nation bore to him, and of his claims to its gratitude. With the army at his back, and faithful, small as it was, he might have obtained and maintained absolute power. Carrera also was aiming at supremacy; and had the result of the battle of Loncomilla been different, it would probably have been worse for the republic. The manœuvres about Chillan, the permitting of Bulnes to cross the Ñuble unmolested and recross it without being harassed after he had lost a considerable portion of his force, and the mode of following him in his retreat to Loncomilla, are convincing proofs that Cruz had lost all the energy and decision of character, if not all the knowledge of strategy, absolutely requisite for a military leader. His *pronunciamiento* indicates, and his friends claim for him, that he desired to spare the effusion of blood under a belief that time only was wanted to bring the nation under his banner. Some who proved faithful through everything, more than intimate his feebleness and fickleness, excusing their adherence on the ground that their cause was a righteous one and he their only leader.

Carrera, at first commanding in the north, although a man of intelligence, courage, determination, and promptness, had not received military training, and, wanting this, could not be called on to direct a battle. Patriotism, probably, never for a moment entered his mind. He aspired, as did father and brothers before him, to be chief of the nation; and was so impatient to have the Coquimbanos declare him, that his own party were compelled to displace him from civil authority. It is said that they imprisoned him for a short time; and it is certain he was sent without the city of Serena long before the termination of the siege. Col. Arteaga was left at the head of the military force.

If Cruz had reached Santiago in triumph, the government forces in other portions of the republic would have abandoned the contest at once; and it is more than probable that the revolutionary chiefs on failing to obtain the positions they conceived due to them, as many must have done, would have incorporated themselves with the troops from the north, and have marched against him after a very brief delay. What the end of such a struggle would have been, it is not difficult to foretell: anarchy, loss of public credit, and the reduction of the nation to the level of the rest of Spanish-America. As it is, what did the liberal party gain? Not the concession of a single withheld right, neither freedom nor purity of suffrage, no extension of municipal privileges, no equalization of public receipts and expenditures between North and South; but, on the other hand, it cost their country the lives of 4,000 of its working men, more than $2,000,000 of its capital, effected the banishment of fathers and brothers by hundreds, and, temporarily at least, paralyzed its commerce, agriculture, and mineral resources.

CHAPTER XIV.

A VISIT TO THE COUNTRY.

THE PLAIN OF SANTIAGO: SCENERY; LAKE ACULEO; GEOLOGY AND BOTANY.—BREAKFAST ON THE LAKE SHORE.—ANGOSTURA DE PAYNE.—COUNTRY LIFE: THE LABORERS; MEDICAS; PABLO CUEVAS, THE MEDICO OF CHUAPA; PROBABILITIES OF HEALTH AND LIFE IN THE COUNTRY.—CULTIVATION; IRRIGATION; AGRICULTURAL IMPLEMENTS.—WHEAT CROP; HARVEST; THE TRILLA (THRESHING); HORSES AND RIDERS; WHEAT PRODUCED.—DIFFICULTY OF OBTAINING ACCURATE RESULTS.—BEANS; MAIZE; BARLEY.—ATTEMPT TO INTRODUCE RYE.—THE VINEYARDS; THE VINTAGE; PRODUCT OF THE VINEYARDS IN THE SOUTHERN PROVINCES; MOSTO WINE.—CATTLE, AND THEIR DISEASES; THEIR ENEMIES, THE CONDORS AND LEON (FELIS CONCOLOR); THE RODEO; EQUESTRIAN FEATS; THE MATANZA; PREPARATION OF CHARQUI; PROBABLE NUMBER OF CATTLE KILLED ANNUALLY.—RETURN TO SANTIAGO OVER A LASSO BRIDGE.

The plain or basin in which lies Santiago varies little in aspect as one leaves the immediate vicinity of the city. As the cultivation is more directly confined to its sides, the vicinity of the main thoroughfare leading southward is somewhat desolate. This continues beyond the river Maypu, six leagues from the capital. The stream is traversed by a handsomely constructed lattice bridge, some 80 yards long, in two spans, the materials for which were brought from the United States, notwithstanding the immense forests of fine timber in the southern provinces. Its engineer was also a North American. At the time of this visit a large force was engaged along the road, digging water-drains at the sides, and heaping up the centre—proofs that a new order of things is progressing, and the day is perhaps not distant when the suspension bridges of lassos and canes made by the Araucanians, as well as the quagmires and bridle-paths over which their desperate forays were perpetrated, will remain only on the pages of the historian.

Great as had been the fall of snow the preceding winter (June to August, 1850), and powerful as was the heat at the time (December), the stream was scarcely more imposing than the Mapocho; but its vertical banks were sufficient evidences that winter rain-storms sometimes swell it to a roaring volume, half a mile wide by fifteen to twenty feet in depth. Now, its breadth did not exceed thirty yards, with an average depth of three feet. Both above and below the bridge the main stream is divided into several smaller ones, separated from each other by piles or islands of shingle. These change with every flood; first to one side, next to the other; often in one rapid body, not unfrequently in many; each covering as great a superficial extent. To one accustomed to the broad and placid rivers of America, at a little distance these Chilean streams appear insignificant rivulets; but the volume of water which is daily discharged by the Mapocho exceeds that of the Potomac at Washington. In the aggregate the surfaces of the Mapocho's streams will not measure thirty yards across; the Potomac exceeds a mile; yet such is the effect of rapid inclination in carrying off the melted snows of the cordilleras.

Prof. Domeyko's narrative of a journey to Araucania* distinctly conveys the impression that the Espino is the only indigenous tree found on the plain within fifty or sixty leagues of Santiago; yet the Patagua (*Tricuspidaria dependens*) and several others may be seen a little to the southward of the bridge, and in places wholly destitute of artificial irrigation. Fields of wheat, herds of cattle, and flocks of sheep, scattered about the bases of the distant hills, were picturesque accessories to the scene; those close by, as evidences of the fatness of the land, possess interest of a different character. Three or four leagues farther on, the haciendas are generally

* Araucania y sus Habitantes, por Ignacio Domeyko. Santiago: 1846.

J. Queen. P.S.Duval & Co's Steam lith.Press, Phil[a].

of considerable extent, and are appreciated for the incomes their products afford, as well as for summer residences, when fashion commands its votaries to leave the capital.

There are isolated, abrupt, and rugged hills scattered all over the bottom of the basin. From a miniature base sometimes they rear a lofty peak towards the skies; at others they cover miles with their gracefully curving outlines; and the distance between the Andes and western chain having sensibly widened as the southern rim has been approached, the only perceptible break in its mountain walls is where the Maypu with its increased volume of waters from the Mapocho and Angostura has burst a passage through the Central cordillera. There is no diminution of the glorious grandeur of the Andes, but rather accessions to it in the extinct volcanoes of Tupungato and San José, which are invisible to those residing immediately under the chain at Santiago.

Leaving the main road, twelve or thirteen leagues from the city, a less frequented one strikes across limpid mountain streams running northwestwardly among spurs that spring from the western mountain ranges. Here the face of the country is most beautiful. One finds a rich alluvial soil, covered with profuse vegetation, now in its greatest luxuriance; roads shaded for miles on either side with Lombardy poplars; orchards, vineyards, bright flowers, and sparkling waters—all that nature can contribute to charm the sight! Would that man and his creations might do justice to them; or, at least, that his productions were not in such marked contrast! Pursuing the latter road something more than half a score of miles, the native woods become dense, and we find ourselves surrounded by great trees covered with the thickest foliage, their branches bent towards the earth, so as to render the forest almost impenetrable. Nearly all of them were in flower; but the most attractive was the Patagua, the contrast of whose delicate white bell with the almost olive-color of its evergreen leaves being both striking and graceful. This is the Banyan tree of Chile; for wherever its branches touch the earth they take root, and new plants spring upwards, thus forming myriads of natural vegetable arches.

A rivulet of clear water from the westward is the first intimation one has of a concealed gem in this mountain glen. The hills have gradually approached each other, and on both sides are from three thousand to six thousand feet away over head; whilst to the east and west, mountains of scarcely less elevation close it in. In the early morning light the Cereus quisco is seen on their grey summits, flinging its arms against the sky; and farther down their steep sides the ravines are filled with vegetation of various hues—contrasts relieving an otherwise arid aspect, unpleasant for the eye to dwell long upon. Crossing a slightly elevated promontory, there is spread out below, in pristine placidity, the mountain lake of Aculeo—a type of tranquillity. At early hours of the morning there is not a breath of air to ruffle its polished ice-formed waters; and they are disturbed only by wild fowl, whose ancestors alone possessed it. Before us, to the south and east, and also in one little spot to the westward, the bases of the hills slope off into plains, in some places perhaps a mile or more in width; but at every other point they descend precipitously, forming an elliptic, or, more properly speaking, an hour-glass shaped basin, two leagues in length by one in width at the water surface. Within the oblong bowl thus formed the storms of winter deposit rains, and melted snows trickle from the mountain sides. A part of this water finds outlet in the rivulet last mentioned, until the heats of summer reduce the level of the lake too low for further exit. Its greatest length is from east to west. Two promontories opposite each other divide it into basins of nearly equal superficial extent, connected by a short strait not above half a mile across. The western basin has a chain of islets from a few yards to an acre or two in extent, which are the haunts of vari-colored water-fowl.

The geological formation differs on the two sides of the lake. One is sienitic, the other porphyritic, as are the hills northward of Santiago. As the disintegrated materials have been washed down during rains, the bed of the lake has filled, and there are now dead trees thirty or forty feet within the margin thus extended by the displacing materials. Was such the cause, or is the climate changing, and the retrogression of the shore-line due to an annually increasing quantity of rain? or has an earthquake uplifted its alluvial and less resisting bed, causing its waters to embrace so many Espinos within their bounds? No other tree was found within the lake, though the surrounding shores abound with Pataguas, Quillais (*Quillaja obliqua*), Peumo (*Laurus p.*), and Litres (*L. venenosa*), besides others of growth naturally smaller. The last named, as its botanic designation imports, is poisonous to the touch. In a brief time it transforms the body to a leprous-looking mass; and as we stood beneath the shadow of one admiring its pretty foliage and flowers, our guide, in alarm, called on us to mark our execration by spitting upon its decitful livery. According to popular belief, contact is not necessary for impregnation. Even some who sleep or stand long under its shadow are said to be affected, though others are wholly exempt from its poison. Its wood is of a dark reddish color, close-grained, and admitting of high polish—qualities which cause it to be greatly admired in the manufacture of cabinet furniture.

At a rancho beside one of the paths we had given directions to prepare such a breakfast as may be obtained anywhere in Chile, and spent the two or three hours ensuing after sunrise in examining the landscape pictures presented from various points; approaching as closely as we could to the flocks of black-necked swans (*C. nigricollis*), scarlet-winged flamingos (*P. ignipalliatus*), and white herons (*A. egretta* and *A. candidissima*); rambling along the little patches of beach, to find a few perfect specimens of the only shell we perceived (a Planorbis); and in plucking here and there a cluster of brilliant flowers, until warned by the increasing intensity of the heat, and the cravings of hunger, that it was time to return towards our morning meal. Alternately riding and walking as a cluster of pretty plants seduced us from the horses,—now rambling along turfy sward, now picking a foot-hold among rocks of the mountain cliffs,—we reached the rancho hot and tired. But the ponchos thrown off, and our heads bathed in the cool waters of the lake, new life was imparted, and we sat down to our "*casuela*" with appetites no little sharpened by a six hours' ramble.

Except in Atacama, in every other part of Chile where there are habitations, the hungry traveller may count with great certainty on a substantial soup denominated a "casuela," composed of a fowl or part of a lamb cut in pieces, and simmered with an egg or two and various vegetables. All the ingredients are kept over fire in an earthen olla or pot for two or three hours, and are rendered no little piquant by a dash of *aji* (red Chile pepper), which the cook invariably adds. We had brought bread, a bottle of wine, and freshly-plucked oranges from the hacienda of our friend; and we amazingly enjoyed our breakfast under the trees, scarcely less objects of curiosity to the group of scantily clad children about the rancho door, than of interest to the half-starved dogs that prowled round us, eyeing each mouthful askance. These brutes are among the curses of the land. They infest its streets and highways, fill it with fleas and other vermin, render night hideous by their barkings, and are eyesores by day as well as nuisances at night. There being neither taxes on their owners nor law limiting their numbers even in the large cities, everybody possesses one or more; and as their usual sleeping-places are the sidewalks before the houses, it is difficult to walk without kicking them aside, or taking to the middle of the street. Families who have scarcely bread and no meat for their children, will keep half a dozen ugly curs; and in our ride towards the lake, there was one miserable rancho scarcely large enough to contain the dogs alone, from which there issued, as we approached, no less than thirteen, attended by half a score of children.

After breakfast, we spread the skins forming part of our saddle equipments under the shadow of a cluster of Peumos, and, using the saddles as pillows, enjoyed both shelter and rest during the hottest part of the day. Around us rose a forest of venerable trees, varying little in the colors of their glossy foliage, and only in the form of the white or cream-colored flowers they bore. Farther off there were fantastic shaped rocks, unchanged since the instant when earth and chaos took leave of each other. At our feet there were Mariposas (*Phycella ignea?*), Peregrinas (*Alstrœmeria peregrina*), Calceolarias, and Siempre-vivas (*Triptilion spinosum*), with flowers of crimson, violet, golden, and purple hues,—a multitude not easily embraced at a glance in the flora of a country. And lower down lies the lake, its mirror-like surface sending back to us a duplicate of the gigantic hills and crags on the opposite shores. Verily, a most lovely view is commanded by the little promontory that juts midway across the lake of Aculeo; a panorama of natural scenery difficult to excel, and in all its accessories rarely to be equalled.

About noon the heat of the sun was intense. A gun-barrel exposed to its direct action became so hot in a few minutes that it could not be held in the hand; and though the temperature was charming in the shade, the dryness of the air and reflected heat thoroughly burned the skin of the face and hands. Towards 2 o'clock cumuli began heaving up over the mountains on the south shore, and a few minutes later the first breathings of the southwest monsoon came across the surface of our picture mirror, soon to increase until the whole lake was broken into wavelets and the silver converted into azure. This enabled us to take another ramble along the shores, serving to impress the beauties of the locality more strongly on the memory, but without adding material information to that already given.

Our ride back to the main road was unmarked by incident, except the sight of a large number of condors sweeping in broad circles round the body of a dead horse. The animal had fallen near the base of a conical hill, on which, as I subsequently learned, there had been an Indian fortress in times past; and, in the few hours elapsed since we passed it in the morning, these giants of the feathered race had become apprized of the feast awaiting them. The plain is much narrower here, and within a short distance towards the south the mountains apparently close it entirely. But when we have followed the great highway into the round, bold sweep which the mountains make towards each other from the two sides, within pistol-shot of their steep slopes on the southern line we detect the noise of water bubbling over pebbles, and at the same moment the eye perceives a narrow gorge through the ridge immediately in front. At its centre we find ourselves in a contracted pass, evidently formed, as was the pass through the Blue Ridge at Harper's Ferry, by the bursting of the water through the chain. This aperture, called the *Angostura de Payne*,* is scarcely one hundred yards broad, or more than six hundred yards long. Beyond that distance it rapidly widens into the plain of Rancagua. On both sides the hills are extremely steep, and in some places precipitous, the greater portion of the road between them being filled by a tortuous mountain stream, rumbling to the northwest, with fine trout and other fish within, and wild fowl in abundance upon its waters. Altogether, it is a remarkable pass—attractive to the painter for the landscapes commanded in both valleys, to the geologist from its physical formation and probable origin, and to the military man as a place of defence.

Excursions to these two places of interest were made during a week's sojourn at the hacienda of an accomplished and hospitable friend, whither I had gone for relaxation, after a long series of observations on the planet Venus. Visits to the ranchos of the peons, the vineyards and wheat-fields, the magazine where wines are made and stored, and the flower and fruit gardens, occupied every other hour that the sun permitted us to pass out of doors. These, however, were only portions of the pleasures. Freed from the formal conventionalities of the city and the courtly insincerity too often attendant on its intercourse, nothing is more grateful than the companionship of graceful and intelligent people, such as it had been my good fortune to encounter, and the week passed in the country is fraught with most pleasant memories. Near enough to Santiago to keep up intercourse every day or two, and yet sufficiently far away to have left its formal etiquette, the stranger was admitted to the frankness of friendship, and his comforts and wants consulted with the most delicate and unostentatious kindness.

Unlike our country, there are few families who reside wholly on their haciendas and devote their lives entirely to agricultural pursuits. Divided, as is Chile, into a comparatively small number of estates, the proprietors are generally wealthy, and can well afford handsome city establishments, making visits to their haciendas more or less frequently, as the season may

* Pronounced Pi-ny.

require or distance will permit. Had not the law of entail, so favorable to the aggregation of property, been recently abolished, within a few years the Mayorazgos would have possessed the whole of central Chile, and thus one of the most effectual modes of ameliorating the condition of those emphatically tillers of the soil have been absolutely cut off. Living away from his property during the larger part of the year, holding intercourse with the hired peons or their families only through his mayordomo, essentially if not necessarily influenced by self-interest, there are few proprietors who look forward to elevating the character and condition of their humbler countrymen; and the majority, year after year, regard with careless indifference a class of his fellow-men scarcely more cared for than the beasts in his fields. The unfortunate poor! Most of them literally fulfil the command of scripture, "take no thought for the morrow;" nor would they think of *hereafter* either, but for the annual visit of some ghostly father in search of the few reals saved from their weekly earnings.

It is difficult for one accustomed to the cleanly and comfortable dwellings, tidy-looking children, and other evidences of prosperity surrounding the homes of our small farmers, or even the neat quarters and healthy, well-clad offspring of the negroes in our Southern States, to realize how his kind can descend so nearly to the level of brutes as they have done in Chile. All the shelter the peon possesses is formed with a few stakes driven in the ground, and wattled with reeds or brush, and thatched with flags or rushes. Even this is often in a most dilapidated condition. A rude doorway, closed with rough boards, the cast-aside door of some house in process of renovation, or perhaps a bit of raw hide, permits ingress to the bipeds and quadrupeds who equally occupy its earthen floor. In one corner stands the rough bedstead of the parents, and near it, perhaps, the infant's cradle—an oblong board suspended from the roof by a single cord secured to each of its four corners. All the other members of the family—grown brothers and sisters, uncles and aunts—occupy skins and straw on the floor indiscriminately; and although this constantly results in crime the most shocking to humanity, its publicity scarcely creates comment. Where girls commence at thirteen, and bear annually until fifty, children are almost as numerous as the leaves about them; and were it not for excessive mortality, the population of the country would soon be driven into industrious habits, to migration, or starvation. As it is, marriages are not frequent. Men and women live together during convenience, then take up with other partners, sometimes after the birth of three or four children. In such case, if not dead, the offspring remains with the mother. One whom I asked whether she had ever been married by the priest, was fully persuaded that, in case of offence, a legal husband had a right over her life: and as fidelity (from principle) is not very general among them, she told me frankly that she greatly preferred living as she was; for if "Pepe does not treat me well, I will quit him and go to Pancho, who will." She was very pretty, and evidently well aware of the powers of her bright black eyes and elastic figure. Belief that the husband has the power of life and death is probably inherited from the Araucanians, who exercise it unscrupulously to the present day, and whose blood flows in the veins of many of them. Should the family of the murdered (Araucanian) woman be disposed to resent the outrage, they are recompensed by presents of horses, cattle, or clothing, nearly equivalent to the original chattels paid them for her purchase.

Should the priest arrive, on his annual visit, just subsequent to a new domestic arrangement, and the present partners either possess or are able to obtain the necessary fees, excommunication and the pains of purgatory are preached at the pair until, in payment of the marriage and baptismal fees of the children, the whole earnings are swept into the capacious pocket of the church. From one or the other of them the confessional extorts information on both points, though it is seldom anything can be laid by from their small earnings; and the couples continue to live on without the benediction of the priest over their couch or his holy invocation over their child. Therefore there is no question that the greater number of children born in the country are illegitimate, and some of them incestuous. Under such circumstances parental affection can scarcely exist; and the death of a child, if not actually desired, is regarded with little more than indifference—a new one struggling in the mother's bosom before the last has left her arms. The groups of half-clad or naked little children just able to walk were thus accounted for, and one could then easily comprehend why they were occasionally left to gratify their appetites at will from piles of green fruit.

I must not be understood as asserting that all ranchos and all peons on the haciendas are living in this miserable and criminal condition, but only that such is the general rule. There were many exceptions on the estate of my friend, where walls were neatly plastered, roofs well thatched, and there were clusters of flowers about the doors—external evidences of industry and desire for improvement, not less creditable than the well-ordered and comparatively comfortable arrangements within. These had clean stools to offer us, and a well swept floor took away the fear of vermin which originated on entering so many of the others. In one of these a mother sat busily twirling her spindle beside the primitive cradle of an infant, not then three days old, saying, in reply to the expressions of surprise addressed to her, "My children need clothes, and I cannot afford to lie idly in bed any longer!" Most of her children, she told us, were at the school, established by the liberality of the "patron." Education and the example of such mothers will go far towards reclaiming the race from habits of idleness, improvidence, and beastliness, so encouraged by climate and soil—vices in whose exemplification it may be mentioned that many had refused to build adobe houses for themselves after all the materials had been offered gratis, nor could they be persuaded to whitewash those in which they then lived when the lime was taken to the doors; their excuse being, the pigs would soon soil them again!

Indolence and improvidence render the peons of Chile quite as thoroughly slaves as are the negroes of Cuba or of the Southern States of America. Generations after generations occupy the same spots, without advancing a step in intelligence or worldly wealth, and by their habits have become as unable to move as though bound to the soil by the ties of law. True, they have a legal right to seek new homes and new employers; and this has been taken from the African. But of what avail is the right, if any cause incapacitate from its exercise? Whose condition is best—the one nominally free, who was born in sin, reared in idleness, lives through the Sabbath, and generally the following day too, in the debauchery which a previous week's earnings will produce, and is left to starve or subsist on charity when sickness or old age overtake him; or the slave, born in legitimate wedlock, taught the precepts of the Bible at Sunday school, is well clad, well nurtured, and kindly watched over when infirmities or declining age have rendered him useless?* Yet the picture is not over-contrasted. Indeed, it would be difficult to convey to the mind their uncleanliness and misery, or to impress a more deplorable idea than actually exists. There are some who, by industry and economy, have become possessed of a cart and a yoke or two of oxen, and who cultivate half a score of acres of ground, rented from the proprietor of the hacienda. Their wives, like the one with her distaff, contribute portions from the poultry-yard, and their children are made to gain *medios* (six cents) or *quartillos* (three) in the harvest and vintage seasons. These are thriving in the world; but they seemingly live apart, uninfluencing the rest—the exceptions which confirm the rule.

Laborers on estates are of two classes: *peons* (hired men) and *inquilinos* (tenants)—veritable remnants of the feudal system. The whole time of the former is disposable for the cultivation or benefit of the property. He receives three rations in meals, and from fifteen to eighteen cents per day, paid weekly, in money. A ration for breakfast consists of a pound of bread; for dinner, a pint of beans, mixed with wheat and grease; and for supper, a peck of corn or wheat each week. Usually the food for the peons is cooked at the house, whose mistress, when present, strives to send something extra from her own *dispensa*. Prepared at the kitchen of the residence, it is served to them at the sound of a bell, each one conveying his allowance to his family, if he has one. Perhaps, too, they are permitted to milk a cow or two, and cultivate a little ground immediately round their ranchos, in onions, beans, and potatoes.

* With the consent of the States, most gladly would I witness the departure of *every* descendant of Africa from our shores.

But these are favors, not rights of the peon. The scanty wages supply additional food and clothing for wife and family, and furnish him with chicha and tobacco, to say nothing of gratifying occasionally the unquenched thirst for a game at cards, yet remaining in the few drops of blood inherited from the most thorough gamblers the world ever saw—the early invaders of America!

Inquilinos hold ground by different tenures. They have from one to twenty, or even more acres; for the use of which they bind themselves to keep the fences in repair, the *corrales* and *acequias* clean, to assist at the *rodeos* and *trillas* with their own horses, and, together with a multitude of like services, on payment of small stipulated sums, to travel with letters or messages. Sometimes they become possessors of one or two carts, which they hire out in the neighborhood, and are permitted to use young oxen belonging to the hacienda. In the latter case, they must first break the animals to the yoke. The amount of service rendered depends on the body of land treated for and the privileges granted, things variable according to the liberality of one party and the character and necessities of the other. But the system throughout has all the ear-marks of the old feodal times.

On every estate there is a *bodegon*, or shop belonging to the proprietor, where sugar, mate, candles, aguardiente, chicha, common goods, and such other articles of necessity may be obtained as are in demand. These are generally sold at such moderate advance on the cost as will cover the expense of transportation, loss, and distribution; the object being to remove the necessity of going to a distance to the neglect of work, rather than for profit. At the same time a part of the produce of the estate, its chicha and aguardiente, finds consumers at home; and these no doubt are among the most profitable. Indeed, if the liquors are of special quality, it is soon made known in the neighborhood; and the favored bodegon is thronged on Sundays by peons and guasos, with their sweethearts, from all the surrounding ranchos. This is their *fiesta* (holiday); and they spend it in dancing the *zama-cueca*, gambling, horse-racing, and drinking,—taking Monday to clear away the fumes of the debauch, if blood has not before suddenly obliterated them. Unlike the wines of southern Europe in their effects, chicha, instead of inspiring gayety and innocent mischief, very quickly fires the brain, producing sullen vindictiveness, that calls the knife from its sheath at every fancied grievance. Occasions for quarrels are rarely wanting; jealousy, and disputes about their races or games, are sources prolific enough.

Like the *cachucha*, or any other dance common among the populace, the zama-cueca may be made a spectacle of the most lascivious kind; but, to their credit be it said, the tendency is less frequent among the poor than at its occasional exhibition among their superiors in the social scale. One half the time the words that form part of its slightly varying chaunt are apparently improvised; and on the skill of the singer in this accomplishment depends, in a great measure, the mirth of the company. Some of the *chinas* (girls of the lower class) are famed for their ready wit, and are not slow to exercise it upon the company as well as on the dancers, cutting right and left with satirical recitative, and creating shouts of applause all round. These *chinganas*, short races on horseback, the *bolas*, a sort of game like billiards, elsewhere described, and games with cards, are the only country diversions. The last, however, is positively prohibited, and can be practised only by stealth.

They have no other surgeons for the desperate wounds often resulting from these frolics than *medicas*—countrywomen who have learned the characteristics of the herbs and simples which nature has spread around them. One of these, the *matico*, a plant originally from Peru, is said to be invaluable as a healing styptic; and medicas have the credit of skilfully binding up wounds that heal quite miraculously. An English gentleman, who had been long a resident and had married in the country, told me that on one occasion a peon on his estate had his abdomen ripped from side to side, so that all the entrails hung out in front. These were replaced by a medica who was sent for in haste, the wound sewed up by her with a common needle and thread, and in three weeks the man was at work again. The same doctress had set limbs with compound fractures, which healed immediately; had cured scrofulous eruptions and inflammatory rheumatism that had defied the faculty at Santiago; was equally successful with a multitude of the "ills that flesh is heir to;" and yet was as utterly unable to read, and as ignorant of the received theory of medicine, as an infant. Nor was she singular in these acquirements. Every neighborhood has one such unlettered disciple of Esculapius. But I must tell of a male practitioner in the art, so famous in his time that Padre Guzman devotes an entire chapter to an account of his skill and charity. This was Pablo Cuevas, the medico of Chuapá. Moved wholly by a spirit of philanthropy, Cuevas devoted all his means and time during a long life to the cure of the poor who sought him. Quarters were provided in his own house, and the simple remedies of which he had obtained knowledge were, at first, administered by his own hands; subsequently, when he became old, by his daughters. No compensation was ever asked for their expenditures or services; and though many of the wealthy who had previously lingered under the hands of physicians received relief through his applications, and made him handsome largesses in return, these were invariably applied for the benefit of suffering humanity rather than to the increase of his own wealth, and he died at an advanced age quite poor. Padre Guzman says: "The method by which Cuevas ordinarily cured the sick, considered under all aspects, was the most admirable that can be imagined. He needed no other diagnosis for perfect knowledge of the disease of a patient than observation of the features and examination of the urine, which last he required to be presented in a bottle, and subsequently scattered it in the air. By the latter alone—simple and momentary inspection of the urine—he could tell the state of the patient, the gravity of his disease, and its origin. Remedies that appeared proper were then applied, and with so much certainty that a case was rare where the patient did not remain perfectly healed. This virtuous man appears to have been sent by Heaven for the succor and health of indigent mankind. His cures of diseases of every variety were like miracles; and innumerable were the sick given over by the most learned of the medical faculty, who were restored to health by the simple application of herbs, baths, sudorifics, drinks, and lavations, administered by him."

Not satisfied with curing the physical infirmity only, no sooner was a patient restored whose disease had originated in sensual indulgences, than Cuevas took him aside, pointed out the cause in plain terms, dictated moral no less than physical rules for his guidance thereafter, and ended by warning him that a departure from the counsel given would infallibly render him a victim to the malady. A man so renowned was not permitted to remain quiet in the country altogether, and a part of his time was demanded by the Santiaguinos, who crowded his rooms day and night applying for relief. Those unable to walk sent a vial of urine by a friend. During these visits his home was at the Franciscan convent. On one occasion a vial was brought from a sick man only two or three squares distant, when, after looking at it a moment without asking respecting the character or gravity of the disease, he turned to the person bringing the vial, saying: "Why seek you remedies for one who will probably be dead before you can reach his house?" And the prognostic proved true; for on opening the door, the messenger was met by the relatives with tidings that death had occurred during his absence.

One with such reputation for learning, skill, and benevolence, could not but be of interest to the nation at large. In order to profit by his experience, and to extend the benefits of his knowledge to others, government selected one of its most intelligent and judicious citizens to visit the wise herbalist at Chuapá, and ascertain directly from himself the virtues of the medicinal plants used in different diseases. The commissioner duly passed several days with the medico; but he was then (1835) some 86 years of age, and quite sick himself. It was the end of autumn; the dried herbs shown him were so disfigured by handling, that they were no longer recognisable, and no other Pablo Cuevas has ever appeared in Chile.

One short paragraph more from Padre Guzman, and we must take leave of him, remarking only that eighteen years have not yet elapsed since the date of the subsequent note quoted, and that its writer, now in the prime of life, enjoys among his countrymen a most enviable repuation for intelligence and benevolence. Guzman says: "Although, as has been shown, general opinion credited the curative powers of the doctor of Chuapá as a special gift from God, in reward for ardent charity, there will not be wanting a large number who consider themselves philosophers, and may laugh at our account, attributing the whole to preoccupation and fanaticism." But, in confirmation, let us see what Señor Bustillos says—a gentleman who, from his knowledge and recognised talent, is not one likely to be easily fascinated by vulgar credulity. In a note to the government, dated May 12th, he says: "Notwithstanding the medico of Chuapá was ignorant of the principles of medical science, he made admirable cures; at least, I could not discover any of those principles in Cuevas; and I ridiculed the credulity and superstition of the vulgar. But when I witnessed the prodigies effected in his cures, I could do no less than recognise in him a special gift from Heaven, conceded by God to a truly charitable man in order that he may exercise benevolence towards the poor who are deprived of all human resource." The commissioner afterwards tells government of other peculiar virtues of the memorable medico of Chuapá, and says, that "in this worthy old man he had not perceived one immoral habit; that he was ignorant of selfishness, and lived in the midst of privations, dedicated wholly to the care of the sick poor, aided by the daughters who were constantly occupied in serving them."

When a peon becomes ill, if there be one not too distant, the landlord strives to get him to the hospital at the nearest town; but, as with the poor everywhere, they have a dread of hospitals, and so great is their repugnance that few can be induced to go from the country. In such emergency a friend is sent off to the medica with a vial of urine, in accordance with the practice adopted by Cuevas; from which (it is pretended), and the statement made, she is enabled to judge of the remedy required and the necessity for personal examination. Her knowledge of the properties of medicinal herbs enables her to send back a preparation quite as likely to prove successful as a prescription by the learned faculty; at least, the bills of mortality show that life is equally as safe in the country as in the city. The number of deaths in the whole province during the year 1848 was 6,143, of whom 4,171 were under seven years of age. Without the city, 2,739 died, of whom 1,482 were children. The births numbered 14,097, of whom only 4,559 were born within the city. Very little reliance, however, is to be placed on these data; for the volume (*Repertorio Nacional*) from which they are taken gives the population of the province as 207,434; from which, the deaths being only 6,143, or scarcely three per cent., and the births more than 14,000, one would infer a rapid increase. Yet it is well known that such is not the case, there having been very little visible augmentation of the campestral population in many years.

From the disproportion observed between the two sexes, one of necessity infers that women are healthier, and, by consequence, longer lived than men—a result towards which several causes contribute. Some physicians regard the loss of blood monthly, and in parturition, as especially beneficial to health in this climate, and as the predominating cause; but I am disposed to suggest that uncleanliness, drunkenness, gluttony, and licentious intercourse, characteristic of the lower classes, may be quite as strongly prejudicial as the stated loss of blood is beneficial. It is quite certain that the numbers one meets of old women, and of young ones with robust and healthy figures, attract attention, whereas an old or portly man is rarely seen; and this condition of society is applicable at Santiago as well as in the country. According to the returns, there died in the province during 1848, 74 women and 41 men who were more than 90 years of age. Of these there was one woman of 112, one of 108, one of 104, and eight of 100 years each. One man only attained 111, and two others 100 years each.

The men are usually spare, scarcely of the average height of their Spanish ancestors, and generally have not the muscular development belonging to laboring men of such proportions but rather those of sedentary persons. Indolent, and averse to labor, the little strength given by nature is never improved by exercises or athletic games; the propensities are all animal: to gormandize—to sleep—to gratify lust. During the fruit season, a peon will consume for breakfast a watermelon whose diameter is nine to ten inches, and settle it with a hearty draught of water ; or he will eat half a peck of peaches or pears with like facility. Where they find space to stow so much, has more than once perplexed me. But it was not a matter of surprise that they should seek the shade, and stretch themselves upon the bare earth, face downward, immediately afterwards. And there they often lie after bell-ring, if their siesta is not completed, preferring to lose the value of their morning's labor rather than deprive themselves of the enjoyment. On the other hand, the women are above the average height, with something of the squareness of their Indian ancestors, and, maugre almost incessant nursing of infants, have full, round figures and faces, a spare one being as uncommon as is a portly man. They also seem more active, more intelligent, and better disposed than their partners, and, altogether, create an impression much more favorable.

The extent of cultivated land belonging to each estate will vary with the intelligence of the proprietor in agriculture and his necessities, or both ; and, as there are few who seem to be aware how essential is rest to their fields, and none ever attempt renovation by manures, nothing saves the soil from exhaustion but the rich mineral deposit annually left during irrigation. As the surface has a natural and rapid slope from east to west, streams generated by the melted snows of the mountains fall with impetus towards the ocean, urging along masses of limestone and other rocks that contain mineral manures. By attrition these are converted into a fine powder, which is mingled with the water. Longitudinal canals along the base of the Andes are supplied from the rivers. These, in their turn, are tapped to furnish the different haciendas, and the water finally traverses the fields in ten thousand petty streamlets, or acequias, managed by a special class of experienced laborers, who have no other duty than to attend them, preserve them free from obstruction, and water the several fields at the intervals they require. Wheat-fields ordinarily receive four irrigations between the cessation of the rains in September and the maturity of the grain at the close of November ; on each occasion the fields remaining submerged during one night, and sometimes for twenty-four hours. When the water is deep enough on the ground, the supply is reduced until it equals the absorption and evaporation, thus preventing currents over the growing crops and abrasion of the surface soil. One result from this method of flooding is the mineral deposition referred to, which in some years amounts to a stratum of three fourths of an inch. A few years ago, the plain of Maypu, just south of the city, would not yield the planter five-fold of wheat. The surface was little more than gravel and coarse sand ; but by treating it in this way, large proportions of it now produce from twenty to forty fold. Could proprietors be persuaded to use deep or sub-soil ploughs, and free the land of pebbles somewhat, it is impossible to fix a limit to the probable returns from the rich sandy loam covering the whole surface of the valley. Not an ounce of manure has ever intentionally been placed on any part of it ; and yet the successive floodings have elevated several fields more than half a foot.

The only implement for breaking up large pieces of ground is an almost exact pattern of the old Roman plough. A knee-shaped log of wood, the larger end of which serves as the share, and the smaller as a handle, has a second straight log inserted in it near the joint, intended as a tongue or draught-beam. The angle of the latter with the part forming the share is variable at pleasure by wooden wedges, and the end of the share or mould-board is shod with iron, so as to form a sort of coulter. A yoke of oxen secured to the rude instrument will scarcely open a furrow three inches deep ; and, in fact, rarely penetrates as deep as a careful farmer would harrow. At different times, other implements have been brought from the United States and Europe, and whilst the proprietor stood over the laborer he compelled their use; but such is the force of custom that they have been abandoned, after a trial or two, in despair at failures to instruct in their manipulation. Let them but try deep ploughing, with alternations of rest, *alfalfa* (lucerne), and cereals, and there is no part of Chile between Coquimbo and Valdivivia which would not produce above thirty-fold. In fact, even under the present system of cultivation, sixty-fold is not an uncommon return in the province of Concepcion ; and there are fields which readily return one hundred for one. In the northern and central provinces wheat and barley are the staple products, though each of the larger haciendas has a vineyard more or less extensive.

From one and a half to two bushels of wheat is sown broadcast on each acre, and covered in by dragging brush over it, or sometimes a harrow, whose construction is on a par with that of the plough. This takes place in the autumn, as soon after the rains commence as the lands can be prepared. Hill-side fields, above the reach of artificial irrigation, are first attended to, that they may have time to mature under the influence of late spring rains and a warm sun. About the close of spring, say during November, the crop is liable to be infested by the *polvillo* (rust), and is sometimes attacked by an insect called *capachillo*, after the berry is swollen and full of milk. The insects transform the grain into a shrivelled and inferior quality without wholly destroying it. They are not common, and it appeared difficult to obtain a sight of one; but enough was told to satisfy me that it resembles the wheat midge (*Cecidomia tritici*) so common in England, rather than the Hessian fly. Should rains on misty nights occur during the latter part of November, and be followed by hot and cloudy days, there is scarcely a field which wholly escapes rust, and many that have not a sound stalk left in them, the waving heads very shortly assuming the bright color of rusted iron. As rains heretofore have been very unfrequent during November,* the risk of injury is nothing like so great as in the United States.

Cultivating immense fields as do some farmers, one might suppose they would adopt the most expeditious mode of reaping; but this is not the case, and the old sickle or reaping-hook is still universal. The field is laid off in sections, called *tareas* (tasks), each sixty varas long by forty varas wide. A reaper will take as many as he thinks he can accomplish, at so much per *tarea*. Extra hands are always hired to assist in this work. Instead of making the straw into bundles, it is laid in piles; and as the grain is usually suffered to stand longer than in the United States, the loss by falling out and their mode of handling is quite considerable. A smart reaper will cut a *tarea* in a day, if not served as an Englishman who lived near Santiago told me quite exultingly he had managed with his hands. On bargaining with them he proposed to make *tareas* fifty varas each way, instead of 60 by 40, alleging that he could better accommodate the form of his field. Sixty and forty make a hundred—fifty and fifty no more. Their arithmetical knowledge extended no further, and, of course, no objection was made to cut square *tareas*. Perceiving, after a day or two, that they failed to cut a *tarea* in the usual time, there was no little discussion among the poor fellows; but the only reason they could think of was, that the days had actually become shorter. That they had unwittingly consented to cut one hundred square varas more in each *tarea*, seemed never to enter their minds. The haciendado quieted his scruples upon the ground that they had assented to the change, and therefore there was no cheating on *his part!* Nor were his "fair business transactions" confined to illiterate peons only, a friend and myself having reason to remember his "sharpness" in our attempts to recover an aerolite that had fallen near the house some years previously.

The threshing out of the grain (*trilla*) is one of the annual events of most importance at the hacienda. Proportionate to the amount of ground cultivated in wheat, a spot slightly elevated above the rest is selected, levelled on top, and enclosed by stakes and cords. Sometimes young trees are planted round it, though they are never permitted to attain any great height. As fast as the wheat-stalks are cut on the field they are brought to the *era* (the spot thus prepared) and piled up, until there is not unfrequently formed a hill very respectably sized even for this mountainous country. One may appreciate this from the fact that "La Compania," a single estate formerly belonging to the Jesuits (*Compania de Jesus*), produces annually more than 50,000 bushels of wheat.† As soon as the pile within the *era* is high enough, the *inquilinos* are summoned and their friends invited to the frolic, the *patron* providing a daily feast so long as the work lasts. In this, one, two, even four hundred animals are employed, mares being

* Only eight since 1824, or an average of *2h. 02m.* for that month in thirty years.

† The *trilla* of 1851 yielded 32,000 fanegas, or about 72,000 bushels!

kept for this purpose only and to increase the stock of horses. If the estate does not possess so many, they are either borrowed for the occasion from relations or intimate friends, or are hired in the neighborhood. On the appointed day the mares are divided into two equal droves; each of which is again subdivided, and retained under control of its particular inquilino. A small part of the pile being raked out so as to cover the entire surface of the era, the mares are driven in by squads, each squad followed by its supervisor, well mounted. When all the animals are arranged, at a shout from the mayordomo, stationed on top of the pile, the whole drove is started to a full run. After a given number of turns, the count of which is kept by the mayordomo, or *yeguarizo*, (from *yegua*, a mare), he calls out "*vuelta!*" (wheel!) the race in that direction is arrested, and they turn upon their tracks at a like speed. Away they go, round and round again, dust and straw whirling in clouds among the excited mass, maddened by the shouts and gestures of the drivers and the crowd who throng the stakes or trees of the enclosure. Greatly do the boys love to climb the posts to urge on the half-tamed animals with domestic whips, as if themselves were not sufficiently scare-crows to frighten any ordinary horse. Among so large a number of mares, terrified by shouts and screams and occasional lashes from half a hundred men and boys, half the time buried and blinded by flying straw, it would be wonderful if all retained their footing. Under such circumstances, a stumble is necessarily attended by a piling up of all who follow. Yet such is the mass of straw, and the extraordinary skill of natives as horsemen, that they are rarely injured; but, as the cat is reputed to do in like cases, they are pretty sure to land on their feet. Knowledge of horses and horsemanship begins with *early* boyhood, and often with early *girl*-hood, too, for there are not a few of the gentler sex in Chile who at times manage their steeds with a skill and fearlessness startling to us astronomical sailors. How often have I envied the freedom and ease with which the *guasas* sat when my own beast, no doubt easily divining how much my education had been neglected, was disposed to exhibit airs and graces regardless of the discomfort and instability he occasioned.

But there are no riders more merciless than Chilenos. The poor brutes who carry them so well at the time, are treated with harshness subsequently, with disregard of their necessities, amounting almost to barbarity. Elsewhere the horse is valuable, and interest prompts care of him: not so here; a handsome saddle is often of greater value in the market than the good horse on which it is placed. Until recently, saddles of European make were quite uncommon, and guasos even now adhere to the old-fashioned saddle-tree, piled with blankets and covered with skins to a height that their thighs are completely buried in the long, seemingly silken wool. Were it not so hot, *pellons*, as these are called, would be most comfortable to the rider, but whether so to the animal may very safely be doubted. The stirrups are large triangular blocks of wood, eight or nine inches across at the base, elaborately carved, and generally painted black. They have apertures into which the toes may be inserted, and are extremely comfortable, as well as protectors to the feet when riding through bushes or thorny fields. A Mendoza bridle, made of delicately-cut fibres of raw hide not larger than a broom straw and very handsomely plaited, a bit so powerful that a horse at full speed may be arrested and thrown on his haunches, and a pair of spurs weighing from two to three pounds, with rowells as much as four inches from point to point, complete the equipment. One must not suppose the spurs do execution proportionate to their inordinate length; for, in fact, the rowells are often about the size of goose quills, and very little sharper—ungainly, clanking, and noisy things, that give the most comical appearance to their wearers, who go tip-toeing to and from the horse. Except in the fineness of the skins composing the pellon and the costlinessof the stirrups and bridle, the horse-furniture of the era riders is the same as that of the gentleman guaso—a load of itself, under which one would think the quadruped would swelter in the heat of a January sun. But they go at tip-top speed amid the impeding straw, and perhaps without a mouthful of food or a drop of water from morning until night. As the whole of the cavalcade wanted on the road is sometimes driven from one city to the other without even a handful of alfalfa, and not more than one drink of water, neglect of this kind made the greatest impression on me during journeys to and from Valparaiso shortly after arrival. If the journey occupies parts of two days, as it does most frequently, and the traveller sleeps at Curacavi or Casa Blanca, the animals are allowed food, and from six to eight hours for rest. Otherwise, unless heaviness of the road in winter somewhat lengthens the trip, the journey is accomplished in fourteen hours. The endurance of the horses, however, is scarcely greater in comparison than that of the men who ride them, and who frequently come up one day to Santiago—thirty-two Spanish leagues, return on the following, and so continue coming and going for a week or two in succession. With skill, fearlessness, and prudence, and so habituated to the saddle that they often sleep soundly whilst trotting over the level plains, they are among the very best drivers in the world. Good riders, therefore, are found everywhere. Acquisition of the art is encouraged by the small price of horses, and the very moderate sum—six to ten cents per day—for which one can be maintained. Except for stock purposes, few will purchase mares at any price ; nor will a gentleman mount one, unless it be a rare animal, remarkable for beauty of form and gait. No satisfactory reason is given why they are thus held in disrepute and all the drudgery of the hacienda exacted of them, while horses revel in the clover-fields. Very superior animals are sometimes known to sell for ten to fifteen ounces ($175 to $260), and if broken to harness may command $500 ; yet good ones, capital saddle-horses, are purchased for an ounce ($17.25), and I remember being accosted whilst ascending Santa Lucia one day to know if I did not want a little horse for my saddle? Some years ago a story was current of an officer who talked so much of his horse that he believed in the reality of property purely imaginary, buying a saddle and bridle for the animal when touching at a somewhat celebrated Spanish port on his way home. But here was a guaso most earnestly persuading me to buy his *caballito,* to find use for a saddle which his imagination had previously placed in my stable !

To return to the era, however. After the wheat is threshed out, the next process is to free it from chaff and dirt, a result attained by tossing it in the air with shovels, at some deviation from the vertical. This is repeated until the grain is perfectly clean and ready to be stored, awaiting sale. To considerable extent the freshness of the breeze influences this ; and it often occurs that the trilla continues a fortnight, the participants keeping up their frolic until the very last moment.

One tenth of every product of the hacienda is collected by government. Elsewhere this might afford data for determining the progress of cultivation and improvement ; but it is not so here. Owing to their system of farming the *diezmo* (tythe), it is not possible to ascertain with any degree of truth the quantity of any product in the republic, or even in a single province. The fortunate bidder takes care to conceal how much he receives from the haciendados, lest new competitors attend the auction in the following year. By those most competent to judge, the product of the wheat crop for the year 1850 was estimated at not short of 5,000,000 fanegas, or 11,250,000 bushels. The surplus exported in 1851 amounted to 170,732 bushels of wheat, 366,510 bags of flour of two hundred pounds each, and 7,867,200 pounds of biscuit. The exports of that year were considerably affected by the closing of the port of Concepcion during the revolutionary difficulty. In 1850 there were 405,544 bushels of wheat, 321,798 bags of flour, and 1,874,300 pounds of bread. On the assumption that the population of the country is one and a half millions of souls, if so great an amount was obtained from the harvest, there must have been 400 pounds retained for the consumption of every individual! The reader has been given a proof of the difficulties of obtaining reliable data on page 56.

Greatly more important in one sense, if not in the aggregate so valuable, is the bean crop—a vegetable which at this day constitutes a larger proportion of the food of the laboring classes than the above data indicate. If we look to the number who rarely eat bread, except of the very coarsest kind, it may be doubted whether failure of the wheat or bean crop would be most deplored. It is a favorite dish at all seasons, but is more especially so during the absence of fruits. Sixteen or seventeen varieties are grown, all of them nutritious, valuable, easily cultivated, and yielding an abundant return for the labor bestowed. When the crop is matured, the legume is threshed from the pod in the same manner as wheat. The plants are liable to mildew, at the same time, and from the causes producing the *polvillo* on wheat. Injury to the two crops may proceed *pari passu*.

Maize, or Indian corn, which is less liable to disease, might be cultivated to a far greater extent than it is; and it will be one day, when the *patron* introduces bread made from its meal on his own table. At present, very little more is grown than to supply the consumption when in a green state. The plant does not thrive well in Chile, and seed very greatly degenerate in a few years; so that the ears are small, and the grain has an ungainly, shrivelled look. Inadequate preparation of the land, a hot, dry atmosphere by day, and a temperature 20° colder at night, all conspire to produce these results.

Barley is a staple cultivated for the food of animals quite as generally as for man. It takes the place of oats as winter provender, and of green pasturage in the arid mining districts. As far south as Colchagua, wheat and barley occupy the largest portion of tilled ground. The return is from twenty-five to forty for one sown, and the berry of the former, besides attaining superior size and whiteness, has an average weight exceeding sixty-six pounds to the bushel. Rye-seed were brought from the United States a few years ago by an American gentleman, who intended to distil whiskey from the product. A distillery was imported at the same time, and put up at Colina, near which the grain was duly planted. There the ground is extremely rich, and, with moderate care, one hundred bushels were obtained for every one planted, so that distillation was commenced at once. When the time came to sow again, there had been so little demand for whiskey that it was not deemed advisable, more especially as plants were already growing very freely from the seed scattered at the preceding harvest. Watering these when necessary, no less than forty times the original sowing was obtained at the second crop; and in the third year twenty-fold more was actually reaped, without even a drop of water having been turned on the land in the dry season! But the attempt to make Chilenos drink whiskey instead of aguardiente proved a failure, and it was not worth while to accumulate a useless grain. From that time its culture was abandoned, and now rye cannot be found in the country. This statement was given me by the experimentalist himself, a quiet old gentleman from Rhode Island.

It has been said that there is a vineyard more or less extensive to each of the larger haciendas; though greater attention is given to the vine, or rather they have a greater proportion of their estates in vines, in the southern half of Chile; and, were there competent persons to supervise the process of wine-making, a very superior article could be prepared at low rates. Next after wheat, the product of the vineyard is of most consequence to the haciendado, the consumption of chacoli, chicha, and arguardiente, by the lower orders, demanding immense quantities of grapes for their fabrication. Chacoli is the unfermented juice of the grape only, and in taste is not unlike cider. Chicha is obtained by boiling chacoli or *lagrimilla* (*lagrimas*, tears), as the grape-juice is called, when just expressed. Green fruit seems preferred for making chicha; nor do the manufacturers confine themselves to grapes, but use apples and pears also. Boiling hastens fermentation, before which the liquor is not saleable. Aguardiente is made by distillation of the skins, pulp, and seed left from the chicha, with a portion of the lagrimilla.

As the soil appears to be well suited, and the facilities for irrigation at will prevent vines from suffering during long summer droughts, the yield is not only abundant, but the grapes are of many and fine qualities. A certain demand for them, either as fruit or as one of the beverages mentioned, makes it more profitable to haciendados near the towns to cultivate grapes than wheat. My friend's vineyards are quite extensive. In favorable years they afford him 40,000 gallons of lagrimilla; in unfavorable ones, perhaps not more than half that quantity. His 60,000 plants occupy about eighty acres of ground in parallel rows, six or seven feet apart. They have trenches at the roots, in which water may pass from one to another across the entire enclosure. Each plant in his vineyards is sustained by a pole about four feet high, and they are annually trimmed quite close, in the latter part of August. No especial disease has become common, though there are years when a large portion of the young fruit on each stalk shrivels and falls; and other seasons when the grapes are not only small, but are also acid and watery. This was the case in 1851. Generally his vines yield well, each plant affording two thirds of a gallon of juice. In the province of Aconcagua, vines in thrifty condition produce one and a third gallons on an average, whilst in Maule they scarcely afford one third of a gallon. Aconcagua is famed throughout the land for its aguardiente. In process of time they can no longer properly be called *vines;* for they become rough, gnarled masses, only five feet high, yet exceeding half a foot in diameter, and at most have but two wreathing chaplets about the crown.

As the fruit begins to ripen towards the latter part of March, there are two classes of depredators to be watched and driven off—birds by day, and dogs by night. Aye, dogs!—and they destroy more grapes than their feathered fellow-pilferers. Day and night, from the moment the fruit is edible, the vineyards are perambulated by "*pajareros*" and "*viñateros;*" one body by sunlight—the other after dusk. Both of them are charged to prevent depredations. That they may travel with rapidity across the vineyards, a portion of the pajareros are mounted; while others on foot, to compensate for leisurely motion, repeat shrill cries at intervals. Dogs only attempt thefts at night. Against them the viñateros are armed with lassos to capture, and stones attached to thongs of hide, with which they can produce a noise as loud as the report of a pistol. They also constantly iterate shouts and screams, so unlike the pajareros that a foreigner, if not instructed by the patron, might think some dreadful assault going on quite close at hand.

According to the propitiousness of the season, the vintage begins, in the province of Santiago, between the 1st and 15th of April. Three weeks will be occupied in expressing 40,000 gallons of grape-juice, working from sunrise until 9 or 10 o'clock every night. During this time the peons are allowed grapes *à discretion*, and almost invariably gain flesh under the fruit diet.

"*El lagarejo*," or the tank in which the grapes are thrown to be trodden, occupies one end of the "*bodega*," a large building filled with earthen jars called "*tinajas*," each of which will hold from 200 to 240 gallons. "El lagarejo" is built of brick and cement, is twenty-five to fifty feet square, two feet above the level of the floor, and some twenty-five to thirty inches deep. Between it and the body of the bodega is "*el lagar*," a smaller though similarly constructed vat, nearly on a level with the floor. This, in turn, communicates with a tinaja, usually sunk below the surface. An aperture between "el lagarejo" and "el lagar," for the passage of the must from one to the other, is guarded by wire gauze, filtration also taking place before reaching the tinaja, from which the jars occupying the body of the edifice are filled by portable tubs, or the liquor is at once conveyed to the kettles to be boiled.

A coarse sieve made with strips of raw hide netted across the bottom of a deep frame, and large enough for three men to work at, is placed within the lagarejo, and near an open window, through which the fruit is tumbled as the carts bring it from the vineyards. As the whole force of the estate is employed in cutting from the vines, attending the carts, or in the bodega, those engaged at the sieve in rasping fruit from the stems are kept busily employed. No selection is made of unripe or decayed berries for inferior uses, but all fare alike, and the stems, gathered in bunches, after being rinsed in a tinaja of water by another person, and suffered to drain for a few moments, are thrown aside as of no further use. By night a sufficient quantity of grapes will have been gathered to fill the lagarejo from twelve to eighteen inches deep on a level; the sieve is removed, and the bodega lighted in preparation for the expression of the juice. But its mud walls are so blackened, and its roof is so covered with dust and webs, that the feeble rays of candles scarcely penetrate the gloom, and serve rather to increase than to diminish the wildness of the ensuing scene. In a little while those who have been engaged in the vineyards all day make their appearance at the doorway prepared for the tramp. Their feet have been washed in the running brook close by, and themselves stripped of all clothing except a pair of pantaloons, which fit tightly about the waist, and are rolled up close to the hips. Arranging themselves in two parallel lines within the lagarejo, with arms interlocked, their march is begun across it with slow, stamping, and measured tread, the echo of the heavy footstep resounding from the open-mouthed tinajas throughout the bodega. Instead of turning to retrace their paths when they reach the opposite side, they march backwards; and so cross and return at the same slow, even pace, until the berries have been considerably mashed. Then a chant is commenced, the motions of the two lines are quickened, and a sort of solemn dance is begun, increasing in velocity, until at last the lines are broken and a boisterous romp takes place. Savage enough they look and act; so that one can scarcely convince himself that the light copper-colored race in the dim and flickering light before him, who, with almost naked bodies and long, flying black hair, make uncouth gestures to a monotonous song, can be children of his Holiness Pope Pius, but would rather imagine the scene a ritual of the stock from which they originally sprung. From three to four hours are occupied in the treading out.

It should have been mentioned in its proper place that the floors of the lagarejo and lagar are both slightly inclined towards the apertures, that the must may flow more freely. When it ceases entirely, the skins are raked together, and any remaining juice is forced out under a press. The skins and seeds serve in the distillation, and for coloring and giving flavor to wines, if any be made. If any part of the lagrimilla or must is intended for chacoli, it is not usual to take farther steps with it, but it is suffered to stand in the tinajas uncovered until fermentation takes place. So large is the quantity of fruity substance remaining, that this usually occurs within three or four weeks; but as the liquor is not brandied, it retains its indigenous name even after the vinous fermentation. If to be made into chicha, it is poured into the copper vessels and boiled as fast as they can accomplish the work by unceasing attention night as well as day. Each kettleful of liquor remains over the fire until no more scum rises to the surface. After fermentation, thus hastened by ebullition, the liquor is ready for market; and the new chicha being held in especial estimation, every haciendado endeavors to introduce the first supplies. He must have at least one or two mules loaded with skins containing it despatched to the bodegon in time for the grand fiesta of Easter Sunday. More than one credible person informed me that these skins are stripped from the living goat—the animal being suspended by its horns, and the hide drawn off amidst its screams and struggles. In palliation of the barbarity, they allege that the skin will not come off the dead creature either so easily or so perfectly. In this process, the only apertures made are where the skin is separated from the base of the head and at each hoof. For the sake of humanity, it is greatly to be rejoiced at that sewed bags of hide are now coming into use, and no doubt will eventually supersede the pretext for a practice so revolting.

Both climate and soil eminently fit the country for the production of wines of many varieties in every perfection. All that it wants is persons experienced in the treatment of the must. Prior to 1850 I do not find that any white wine was made for sale or exportation, and then less than a hundred gallons was sold abroad. At the vintage of 1852 more than 30,000 gallons was produced on the estate of a gentleman within a league or two of Santiago. There were three varieties, all light, and with a flavor as delicate as the *alba-flor* of Catalonia or the *orvieta* of southern Tuscany. The period for the acetous fermentation had not arrived when we left Chile; but though they escape under the influence of its equable temperature, like the European wines named, they can never bear transportation except by subjecting them to adulterations which would destroy their characteristics.

It has been mentioned that the southern provinces cultivate the vine to a greater extent than those of the north or centre. There, rains at all seasons of the year enable farmers to grow plants on the hill-sides—a character of land which is wholly uncultivable on the central range of mountains north of Rancagua, for want of water. Once planted, further thought is scarcely given to them until after they begin bearing and their fruit is wanted. Next year, and every subsequent one, they are pruned slightly; but they are neither supported nor tilled, and very generally the weight of the fruit and foliage will keep them on the ground. Quite a large quantity of wine is made from grapes which ripen in this manner, the soil imparting a peculiar though by no means an unpleasant aroma. This *mosto* (literally *must*), as it is called, has a body and flavor between that of port and claret, with more saccharine matter than either—a quality that would render it more easily preserved in wood than is claret. As it is produced at a very low rate, and gains favor with consumers most rapidly, it might be imported to great advantage. In 1848, when California had purchasers for every article of consumption, some 21,000 gallons were shipped from the republic, of which more than one fourth went to that golden land. During the same year Talcahuano, Constitucion, and Valdivia sent 150,000 gallons to other ports of the republic; yet in 1850, whilst they supplied the same ports with double that quantity, the foreign export fell off to less than 2,500 gallons.

This—the month of April—is the most busy period of the year. The squash, bean, potato, and other root crops, are also to be harvested; grapes and squashes are to be hung up for winter use, and the beans are to be threshed out. As rains not unfrequently occur during the latter part of the month, and the inquilinos and many of the peons have also their patches of cultivated ground whose products are of primary consequence to them, all necessarily "make hay while the sun shines;" for a rain on the bean-pods when they lie in heaps ready for threshing is almost certain cause of loss, and a loss to the poor which their ordinarily improvident habits badly qualify them for encountering.

Other sources of profit are immense herds of cattle. These range the mountainous portions of the haciendas where cultivation is impracticable. On one or two of the larger estates as many as 20,000 head are numbered; and as the annual disposable increase is estimated at one fourth, and the average value of each animal will scarcely fall below $12, the income from this item alone will amount to $50,000 after all expenses are paid. Although there are years when the mortality of all ages in the single province of Colchagua has been 15,000 head, at a value exceeding $100,000, yet cattle are regarded as their most valuable source of revenue. Supposing the ratio resulting from the statistics of Maule applicable to the whole country, the horned cattle in Chile will number 1,125,000. This coincides precisely with the ratio existing in the United States at the census of 1850.

The causes of mortality do not appear to be thoroughly comprehended. When rains are very copious during the winter months of some years, and much disease among them follows, these are alleged as the origin. On the other hand, if rains are unusually unfrequent, the pestilence is attributed to the dry weather. The *picada*—an epidemic said to have been introduced with cattle from the pampas of Buenos Ayres—has become quite common. This is easily recognised and is eminently fatal. During its early stage the animal shows indifference to food, its eyes become heavy and languid, and stupor ensues. If remedies be applied promptly, the chances are equal that the beast may be saved; otherwise, within a few hours the evacuations become frequent and bloody, and the animal dies in a little while, its whole interior seeming to have been discharged in this form. As the disease almost always occurs during summer, when the stock are fattest, very poor peons will at times be tempted to eat of the flesh, or may do so in ignorance of the cause of death—an indulgence which invariably prostrates them. In the human subject the malady produces violent fever and frightful swelling of some part of the person. At times only the lips are affected; at others the hands or arms; again only the feet or legs; and, though such instances are rare, sometimes the whole body is dilated. So thoroughly does the poison penetrate the system of cattle, that whoever touches the skin of one under its influence becomes immediately inoculated; the horse over whose back is laid the skin of an animal that has perished under it, soon swells and dies in terrific convulsions. Yet dogs eat of the carcass with impunity. Though men attacked still suffer dreadfully, the disease has become controllable by remedies, and its terrors have measurably departed under knowledge of this fact, and that when once experienced one cannot take it again. Another recognised, though, as yet, incurable malady, is called "*La Araña*" (the spider). It is believed to originate in the poison of a small spider, or other insect, eaten with the herbage. Fever ensues a few hours afterwards, the animal swells rapidly, and death follows during the day. It is not contagious like the *picada,* and is most frequent in dry seasons.

The herds are watched over by a special class—the vaqueros—who, together with certain of the inquilinos, traverse the hills from day to day, looking for the sick and maimed as far as possible, protecting very young calves from attacks of condors, and driving stragglers within the boundaries of the hacienda again. As condors are almost the only enemies to be feared, and their mode of attack is so sudden as to leave little hope of rescue, it is important to be constantly on the alert for them. They never make an attempt singly nor when the cow is near, but, watching for the first moment when she leaves her newly-born calf at a little distance, two or three will pounce upon it suddenly from a mid-heaven flight. One claws out its eyes at a stroke, and, as its mouth is opened in the agony, a second seizes its tongue; and thus its cries are stifled before a single sound could have reached the mother. The sharp eye of the vaquero may have caught a glimpse of the rapid swoop perhaps a mile or more away; yet, what can he do? Long before he could approach sufficiently near, life will be utterly extinct; and the animal being too young for the patron's table, it is scarcely worth his effort to attempt interruption of the dainty banquet. On some estates, and generally during or about the calving season, there is an annual wholesale slaughter of these pests the condors.

Though not an ornithologist, I was desirous to inspect closely a bird so famed, not less than to obtain specimens for the National Gallery at home, where the student of the feathered tribe could examine them at leisure. On expressing a wish to possess a pair of the largest dimensions, my friend quietly replied: "Very well; I will kill a mare, and you shall have a dozen if you wish. They are customers we like to be rid of, and would gladly resign all the '*Buitres*' to the personal inspection of ornithologists." This will afford an idea of the value at which mares are held, and the resort of the haciendado in case no animals happen to die at the time he wishes to destroy condors.

In order to destroy them, usually, a corral or pen is formed of high stakes set in the ground, within which one or more carcasses are placed to entice the birds. Not long afterwards they may be seen flocking from far and near, and they are soon busily engaged pulling the flesh in pieces. Knowing that they habitually cram themselves until unable to move without disgorging a part of the food, and that their great weight will prevent their rising without a long preparatory run, which the corral does not allow room for, the haciendado quietly bides his time. When he thinks this has arrived, peons, armed with clubs and lassos, enter the corral and beat the birds to death. Sometimes this is not accomplished without fierce struggling and occasional bad wounds to the assailants; but it is rare that a condor escapes; for if one manages to clear the ground, he will suddenly find a lasso about his neck or leg, and he comes toppling back again. Five of them—monstrous birds of both sexes—were brought to me late on the evening before my return to Santiago, two of the males measuring each eleven feet ten inches from tip to tip of the wings; but they could not be conveyed in the birlocho with us; and though every effort was made to preserve the skins next day, the heat was so great that when they reached the city, three days later, they could not be saved. Subsequently, however, another pair of equal dimensions was obtained, and these form part of the collection brought home by the Expedition.

Having the sleepy, sluggish, and ungraceful attitude which belongs to nearly all of the vulture tribe, the bird is far from handsome. Except about the wings, back, and neck, the plumage of the male bird is of a bright black color, with occasional greyish tinges. The ends of the wings are of a mottled brown, and the head and neck, as far as the commencement of the breast-bone, wholly bare, the dirty red or brownish skin which covers the latter lying in folds or corrugations. A ruff or circlet of milk-white and downy feathers, about an inch in diameter, surrounded the necks of a part of those brought to me. Those which were without it were smaller birds, most probably of a different species; for not only was their plumage generally of a lighter color, but brown feathers were also perceptible on every part of the body. The circlet is a distinguishing mark of the true condor. Even the very young birds possess it, though the color is then a light blue-black, differing little from that of the rest of the plumage. Its color, and that of the wing and back feathers, changes with age. Two years elapse before the young leave the nest in search of food for themselves, a pair which had been in Santiago more than a year still retaining their downy feathers. Males are distinguished by a thick caruncle, which extends over the head as far as the insertion of the bill. Though strong and thick, the latter is small in proportion to the size of the animal. It is nearly straight on top, with rather a downward curve of the upper mandible where it enters the cranium, the lower extremity being arched in a form indicative of power. The talons are as short and flat almost as those of the barn-door fowl. With an eye lacking fire, or even animation, half drooping wings, often trailing on the ground when it walks, and a crouching head, one would not fear to attack half a dozen of them, unless at a time when hunger had roused the dormant fiend within. And so, after looking at it carefully, I cannot but think that all the stories about children and sheep being carried away by condors, or men and grown cattle being attacked by them, are wholly fabulous. A bald eagle would comb one of them in "no time," and is, altogether, a much more desperate bird to encounter. One of these days fortune may permit me to learn something of their habits from the vaqueros, who are often in the vicinity of their nests; but the present visit was too brief to undertake climbing the mountain crags even to wait upon the condor at his home.

At one time the "*Leon*" (*Felis concolor*) was also a troublesome enemy to the haciendado, the hills about Aculeo being then specially infested by them. No species of animals were exempt from their wary, sudden, and ferocious attacks. Ordinarily, the animal is hunted with dogs of a particular breed, called "*Leoneros*," themselves only courageous when in numbers. They appear to have a particular antipathy to the prey, and special instinct to follow it, driving the creature to a tree or pinnacle of rock, which they are unable to climb. When she has young to care for, the female will at once make desperate battle with the dogs, and, unless overwhelmed by numbers, will put them to flight, lacerated and bleeding; but the male always, and the genus generally, are pusillanimously cowardly, and when thus made prisoners are known to weep and fill the air with piteous moans. A lasso drags one from his perch, and he is soon despatched, the fortunate captor conveying the feet to the haciendado to claim a promised reward. As encouragement to the vaqueros and inquilinos to hunt them, most proprietors offer a bonus of a quarter of an ounce ($4.31) for each foot of the captured animal, and if the hunters are from several estates, they may claim fulfilment from their several patrons. Like the panther, the leon springs on his prey from an elevation, where he patiently and silently awaits the proper moment; then, clinging to the neck, his fangs penetrate the life veins of the throat, the muscular power of his fore limbs rendering it almost impossible to shake him off. They prefer attacking horses to horned cattle, and will not assail an ass unless driven to extremity by hunger; for the last never succumbs without inflicting terrible bruises either by placing his head between his legs and rushing against trees or rocks with his adversary, or, failing in this, by rolling on the ground and crushing him under his weight. When his hunger is satisfied, the leon drags the remainder of the carcass to some retired place, carefully covering it with bushes, that it may serve if a fresher supply is not obtained next day, for he loves not stale meat. Incredible stories are told of their power to drag carcasses of horses and cattle to hiding-places. The condor, however, scents or sees (which is it, naturalists?) a banquet for himself, *though ten leagues away;* but as his approach is watched by the vaquero, the leon's onslaught is discovered, and his hiding-place soon tracked. So effectively have they been persecuted that few now remain, and it was only with difficulty that the specimen described in the report on natural history could be obtained for our collection.

Annually, during the months of August, September, and October, the herds of cattle are driven from the hills into large corrals, where they can be counted. Those intended as draught-oxen, as milch-cows for dairy or family use, or to be fattened for slaughter or the market, are separated from the rest, and the yearlings are branded so as to be recognisable should they stray among the herds of adjoining estates. Moreover, as they are kept together for several days, the tendency to procreation is very greatly increased. This bringing of them together is called the "*rodeo.*" Like the *trilla* it is a country festival; there is sure to be merry-making; and as it is the occasion when horsemanship and skill in the use of the lasso—the two accomplishments on which a guaso most prides himself—can be best displayed, all the neighborhood participate. The number of corrals depends on the extent of the herd and the force that can be collected to drive and retain the cattle under control. As it is a sort of hunt on an immense scale, productive of excitement as well as sport, the patron and his friends also take part in it, and often go to the hills on the evening preceding the day fixed for the gathering of the animals on the plain. Of course, his party are well provided with conveniences and comforts for passing a merry night. The friends of the inquilinos and guasos are also on the heights, scattered along the extent of the pasture ravines, or such numbers of them as will probably embrace as many cattle as can be disposed of during the day. It is a pretty sight of a dark night to see their fires along the mountain sides, and to hear their voices echoing from hill to hill as they send good humored or jesting greetings to one another.

On the occasion more especially referred to, there were five thousand cattle on the estate; to collect which above fifty horsemen gathered, all of them belonging to it as inquilinos or peons. When we went to the fields prior to their last ascent of the hills, they were resting under the shadows of the trees in groups of ten to fifteen, their horses and dogs near by, some browsing, others munching crusts thrown by their masters from the remains of a just concluded dinner. A more picturesque or striking scene it would be difficult to arrange.

I have called the back-ground *hills*, because every one in this Andean country so speaks of them, notwithstanding one of the peaks is more than a thousand feet higher than Mount Washington. They present every form and hue: deep ravines, sharp crags, castellated pinnacles, graceful curves, the colors of snow and plutonic creations, with every shade of green from the pea to the dark olive-leaf. At their bases on the plain, the Maiten (*Maitenus chilensis*), with its slender and willow-shaped leaves; the Boldo (*Prunus fragrans*), with its dark and fragrant foliage; the Canelo (*Drymis chilensis*), the cinnamon-tree of Chile, with its graceful magnolia-like structure; the Maqui (*Aristotelia m.*), with its clusters of purple berries; and a thousand smaller plants, diversify the surface. Not less attractive is the animated portion of our picture. The men are dark and swarthy, with beards and heads uncombed, crowned by coarse, broad-brimmed hats of straw; their costume, heavy ponchos; leggins of hide, laced over the trousers with dangling tassels far up the thighs; spurs of the kind mentioned a page or two back; and shoes with heels above two inches high, to keep the last from touching the ground. Nor are their horses much less remarkable objects; high piles of skins forming the *pellon*, their immense wooden blocks for stirrups, and lassos coiled on the right of the crupper. But the equipment is of the most useful kind. The pellon, saddle-tree, and poncho, form an excellent bed, pillow, and blanket when night comes; and dashing or dragged through trees and thorny bushes, as they constantly are when pursuing refractory animals, their faces and legs would be terribly lacerated but for the leggins, stirrups, and slouched hats.

At the order of the *Capataz* (captain or overseer) the party mounted. In accordance with previous arrangement, they divided into two bodies, to ascend ridges on opposite sides of one of the ravines nearest to us; and as they rode upward the individuals spread themselves to embrace the entire hollow. In a little while the whole body was lost to sight, except when an occasional horseman appeared as he issued on a barren ledge.

If distant from the plain, the party on the crest of the hill begin their descent at dawn, or even before; driving all the cattle before them as they come downward, each flanker of the ravine falling into line in turn. Often an animal becomes frightened, and makes efforts to break the line. Then commences the sport. Regardless of the inclination of the surface or its broken character, a dozen horsemen make after him at the top of their speed, whirling their lassos at the horns or heels of the flying fugitive the moment that they come within reach. Rarely does a skilful guaso miss his aim, and the wild brute, terrified by the presence of so many men and by the pinching of the thongs about his head, will start furiously down the hill, not unfrequently dragging horse and rider at a pace frightful to witness. But no sooner do they reach the plain, where the speed of the horse is greater, than the rider suddenly wheels, and by the quick tightening of the lasso the bull is thrown to his back, thoroughly subdued by the unexpected and violent shock.

An English gentleman, owning an estate here, told me that on one occasion himself and a party of friends were witnesses to a most exciting race of this kind. In order to obtain a good view they took a position near the mouth of a ravine by which the herd must pass, and had not been long there when they saw a solitary guaso coming down the hill at the top of his horse's speed, his lasso fast to a heavy bull some five or six years old. Every leap of the animals made the fire fly, and the loose stones followed behind in a stream. At a hundred yards from the spectators on the plain a large tree stood, with arms growing at right angles to its trunk near the ground, for which, to their horror, the animal made a dash the moment that he saw them. Onward he went desperately, never swerving an inch from a straight line, and it was evident to the lookers-on that the space was too short for the rider to gain the ground necessary to wheel his horse upon. To escape death seemed impossible for him. The heavy, outstretched arms were apparently too near the ground for passage beneath them; and to shouts of "Cut your lasso," they could only gather that his knife had already fallen in an attempt to do so. Intensely thrilling were the few seconds that elapsed after he passed them; but whilst their hearts throbbed painfully, just at the only spot where life could be saved he threw himself along the side of his horse, leaving but the left ankle across the saddle, and holding by the neck with his left arm. In a twinkling more he was careering safely across the plain amid cordial cheers from the whole party, and in less than five minutes the big bull was rolling amid a cloud of dust. When he returned with the captive soon after, it was found that the horse, with the saddle fixtures adjusted, could not stand under the bough beneath which he had passed, and there was sufficient diminution of height to accomplish it only when stretched in a full run! To relate all the feats which it is said an expert rider can perform would fill many pages. I have often seen them pick up their hats while going at a quick gallop, and have no reason to doubt that for a trifle they will permit you to draw a rope across the road suddenly, and whilst they are at a rapid run their horses falling, but themselves alighting on their feet bridle in hand! It is related, too, that the daughter of the late Buenos Ayrean Dictator had no hesitation in attempting this equestrian feat.

Towards four o'clock we were notified that the cattle were coming down, and mounting ready-saddled horses awaiting us, half an hour of sharp riding through the fields brought us to a knoll, from which we could overlook everything near the mouth of the ravine. For some time afterwards we could only distinguish the moving specks by their contrasts in color with the foliage and hill-sides, and scarcely hear shouts echoing from side to side of the ravine when the calm air permitted them to reach the ear. But each moment rendered individuals more definite, and in an hour nearly a thousand heads were hurrying past us. Many of them, for the first time looking on the bipeds by whose will they were controlled, came in disordered groups, startled and terrified by the constant cries of the drivers. Beautiful creatures they were, too; of bright colors all, gracefully formed and not too fat, yet sleek as though each had its groom—fit subjects for pictures! Our horses had been so accustomed to participate in the rodeos, that when the herd came in sight it was difficult to keep them from taking a place in the line, and the air resounded with cheers and shouts from every side as the guasos urged the animals downward.

The separation began at daylight next morning. For this purpose there were four corrals, varying in extent from one to four acres each, and formed by upright poles some seven feet high, set close together, and fixed firmly in the ground. Each had at least two entrances—one opening from the principal grazing field, the other communicating with another corral, or smaller pasture-ground. Mounted guasos guarded every entrance to prevent the escape of any animal not intended, and others similarly provided were stationed round the sides of the main corral, into which a portion of the herd had been driven. Scarcely does the proprietor designate the destination of a quadruped before a lasso reaches its neck; and the horseman who has secured it hurries to the appointed place, others lashing it onward with the ends of their lassoes if resistance be made. In this manner the distribution is both expeditiously and safely effected; the power which their lassoes and the management of their horses give guasos for quickly subduing the most dangerous cattle, inspiring them with the self-confidence essential to prompt action. Yearlings to be marked, and others intended for oxen, are last dealt with, and are led to a corral apart, where either or both operations are subsequently performed with equal celerity. On both sides of the entrance leading to the meadow a line of horsemen is ranged, lassoes in hand; a few others remaining within the corral to prevent the escape of more than one animal at a time, and to drag or drive it out should it hold back. As the cattle cannot see the guasos outside, no sooner do the guards at the entrance withdraw a step, than one makes a dash for it. But he scarcely clears the corral in fancied freedom, before one lasso has secured the fore feet, two others the hinder ones, and the horsemen, starting in opposite directions at the instant of throwing, bring the creature to the ground stretched to the utmost extent of its legs. The *capataz* stands ready with a branding-iron and keen blade; and in less time than one could even tell of it, the young ox, not fairly recovered from the shock of his fall, is freed from the lassoes, and bounds over the plain maddened and smarting under the double wounds inflicted. How guasos manage to loose the lassoes without approaching their victim is not easily comprehended. Such is the fact; and I could but regard it as accomplished by a sleight perhaps more difficult to acquire than the placing of it securely around either horn or limb as you direct, even when both animals are at full speed. This is the closing drama of the rodeo. There are others for the purpose of changing the cattle from one pasturage—or rather from one set of ravines—to another; but in these cases they are rarely driven to the plain, and the occurrence is of no interest beyond the immediate hacienda. As a thousand animals may be thus disposed of in a day, the duration of the rodeo is readily estimated for most haciendas, though there are some in which the formation of the ground greatly facilitates or impedes the operation.

The *mátanza*, or slaughtering of those which have been fattened, takes place in December, January, and February, when there are no rains; and the dry air greatly hastens the preparation of charqui, or dried beef. For this purpose a large open corral is used, on two or more sides of which shambles are formed of brushwood, where the men may work. Instead of bringing the cattle to a ring, and then rendering them senseless by a blow with an axe, they are lassoed head and heels. The four feet are next tied together, and while thus prostrated the butcher uses his knife. When the blood ceases to flow, a pair of oxen drag the carcass to the shambles on a hide, each stall having its occupant or occupants engaged in various processes, from flaying to cutting up. An animal is not suspended to bleed or to be skinned, but is turned from side to side on the ground, as the workmen require. Nor is there any subdivision of labor. Each man, aided by a boy perhaps, takes charge of a carcass, working at it until the bones are left bare, the feet deposited in one place, head in a second, tallow in a third, fat, bones, and offal in as many more. The meat is then sliced, with sharp knives, from lumps into flakes about half an inch thick by a yard or more in length, the operator dividing it uniformly from the outside. When the ox is entirely cut up, the strips of flesh are laid on cane wickers; and in order to make them more tender as well as to hasten the drying, the boys tread them for an hour with their bare feet. A little coarse salt is finally sprinkled over the strips, and they are left in the open air to cure; nor are they taken in or covered until thoroughly deprived of moisture, unless the season is advanced and night-dews are heavy, in which case at sunset they are covered with dry hides. Four days, during summer, will render the charqui fit for packing; and it is then compressed into bundles, of 100 and 200 pounds each, enclosed in net-work made with strips of hide. A dexterous man, assisted by two boys, will earn from four to five reals per day, three reals being paid for the dissection of each carcass. Whilst he slices the lumps of meat, the boys clean the stomach and strip the fat from the entrails and bones. If no one offer to purchase, the heads and hearts become the property of the *matanzeros* (butchers), the liver and part of the entrails seeming to be the only portions not used by man. However, there are a sufficient number of dogs and carrion birds without the corral to dispute with each other these rejected parts. On one side of the enclosure there are large caldrons where the fat and grease are thoroughly boiled, the crushed bones being submitted to the same process. This *grasa* is poured into the cleansed stomachs whilst warm, and, being preserved from contact with air, remains sweet a long time. It is universally used in cooking instead of butter or hogs' lard. Tallow is moulded in large blocks, without external protection. Skins serve for the covering of carts, leather, and a thousand domestic purposes for which manufactories elsewhere have provided substitutes, and are exported. Tallow for candles, and such horns as are not consumed in rude implements of the country, have of late years found their way to Valparaiso for shipment abroad.

The slaughter and preparation of cattle becomes very profitable. If the proprietor purchase for the purpose, the first cost will range from $16 to $20, his subsequent expenses from $4 to $6, and the return is from $30 to $35. Several who have no suitable lands for raising cattle depend wholly on other estates for their supplies. There are many others, who not only have sufficient numbers to kill, but have also large herds from which to supply the markets of the cities. On the estate "La Compania," 2,500 animals are annually converted into charqui. No meat is salted on the haciendas, and at Valparaiso the small quantity put up is exclusively for the use of shipping; so that charqui becomes almost the only meat consumed by the poor and laboring classes. If we suppose one fourth of the estimated number in the country to be killed each year, viz: 281,250 head of cattle, these, at 400 pounds each, would give us 112,500,000 pounds of flesh, of which the exports in 1850 were:

Articles.		Quantity.	Value.
Salt meat	pounds	285,200	$15,518
Charqui	do	356,300	26,643
Tallow and grease	do	63,225	7,367
Dried tongues	No.	10,800	1,442
Tallow candles	pounds	16,375	13,679
Butter	do	17,442	6,538
Hides	No.	57,605	143,395
Hide baskets	do	120	120
Hoofs	do	255,000	1,475
Horns	do	161,000	2,570
Bones	pounds	7,900	316
Total			$219,063

Then if each pound of dried meat represent three in its green state, the hides twenty pounds each, hoofs one, and horns three, the total exports will have been only 3,266,500 pounds; and thus we establish that the home market requires nearly all this product of the haciendas.

It will have been observed that "A Visit to the Country" embraces the occupations of a haciendado's life at very different seasons of the year, of which personal knowledge could have been obtained only at successive epochs. Such was actually the case, though neither of the subsequent visits was so long as the first, and it has been thought better to connect them in the present manner.

After spending a week most charmingly, the recipient of hospitality as cordially extended as it was gratefully received, my host returned with me to Santiago by the old road, passing through

San Bernardo, a town four leagues south of the capital. He was desirous to show me a bridge over the Maypu, constructed with lassoes and branches of trees, after the ancient Indian method. This bridge is some four or five miles lower down the river than the one previously mentioned. As the stream here is on one side of the wide space which is sometimes washed during floods, the bridge has been made only across it, and not from bank to bank; therefore its length is scarcely 200 feet. Two chains, whose ends are firmly secured to the shore, are supported at one third the distances from their extremities by piers of wood some fifteen feet high, imbedded in piles of stone. Between the uprights the chains hang in curves, to which strips of hide of unequal lengths are fastened, supporting stout ropes of the same material drawn tolerably tight from shore to shore. A floor of reeds and brush, of sufficient strength to bear a horseman, being laid across the ropes, is secured to them, and then wattled together. The bridge is safe enough, but the passage of a horseman immediately communicates oscillation not altogether pleasant. Among the aborigines of course there are neither chains nor midway uprights, but only hide ropes between the most elevated natural points; an idea for which engineers of the Old World are indebted to unlettered savages for their airy suspension bridges.

CHAPTER XV.

A VISIT TO THE SOUTHWARD.

ÑOR NICOLAS.—EQUIPMENT FOR THE JOURNEY.—COUNTRY CARTS.—MULE TRAINS.—SAN FERNANDO; POSADAS; BEGGARS ON HORSEBACK.—FROM SAN FERNANDO TO THE CHIMBARONGO.—FROM THE CHIMBARONGO TO THE TENO.—THE POSADA AT QUECHEREGUAS.—REGION OF TUFA.—MOUNTAIN CHAINS.—SNOW LINE.—FROM THE TUFA DISTRICT TO TALCA.—THE CITY OF TALCA; PUBLIC BUILDINGS; ITS PEOPLE; MORTALITY; CLIMATE; HOSPITALS; EDUCATION; HOSPITALITY.—ÑOR NICOLAS AGAIN.—LEAVE TALCA.—THE COUNTRY BETWEEN THE CITY AND LOS PERRALES, ON THE MAULE.—LOS PERRALES.—BOATS ON THE RIVER.—NAVIGATION OF THE MAULE; ITS SCENERY.—ENVIRONS OF CONSTITUCION.—MOUTH OF THE RIVER; ITS POSSIBLE IMPROVEMENT.—CONSTITUCION; SHIP-BUILDING; TRADE; BIRD'S-EYE VIEW FROM CERRO MUTUN; NATURAL HISTORY.—LEAVE THE CITY.—SCENES ON THE RIVER.—PASSAGE UP STREAM.—THE WESTERN CORDILLERAS AND PENINSULA BETWEEN THE CLARO AND MAULE.—GOLD MINES OF CERRO CHIVATO.—THE MAULE AT THE FORD.—FROM THE RIVER TO THE BATTLE-FIELD OF LONCOMILLA.—HEAD-QUARTERS OF GENERAL CRUZ.—ORDER OF BATTLE; INCIDENTS OF THE ACTION; ITS ANOMALOUS RESULT.—RETURN TO TALCA.—HOLY THURSDAY.—GOOD FRIDAY.—MONTE BAEZA.—EASTER SUNDAY.—LEAVE TALCA FOR THE NORTH.—TUFA.—CONDORS.—FROM THE MIDWAY POSADA TO QUECHEREGUAS.—THE RIVER LONTUE, CROSSING A HIDE BRIDGE.—CURICÓ.—CERILLOS DE TENO.—FROM THE CHIMBARONGO TO SAN FERNANDO.—SAN FERNANDO.—THE PLAIN TO THE NORTHWARD.—NATURAL HISTORY.—VALLEY OF COLCHAGUA.—RENGO.—THE COUNTRY TO THE NORTHWARD.—TO THE BATHS OF CAUQUENES.—THE RIVER CLARO AND LAKE CAUQUENES.—SCENERY.—PANORAMIC VIEW FROM THE BATHS.—ACCOMMODATIONS FOR INVALIDS; THE BATHS; LIFE AT A WATERING-PLACE; ELEVATION OF THE PLATEAU; METEOROLOGY.—LEAVE CAUQUENES.—AN AVALANCHE IN 1847.—THE CACHAPUAL.

I left Aguila at noon of the 26th of March (1852), in company with Ñor Nicolás,* an old dependent of the hacienda, selected by my good friend. Nicolás was to be my guide, and was charged with the care of the horses and such personal service as might be needed. He was decidedly a character in his way, and, as my only companion of the road for above two hundred leagues, is worthy of a tributary notice.

He might then have been some 50, or at most 55 years old, was of moderate height, and, except in hair and eyes, quite Indian-like in color and features. The former, or what was left of it—for he was somewhat bald—had a tendency to curl; and the latter were of a positive brownish hue, as though the sun had caught him with them open one day and extracted their original "ivory black." Possibly the disposition of his hair to twist itself upward may only have been apparent; for there was some reason to believe him still in happy ignorance that pretenders to civilization had invented an implement called a comb. Diagonally across the nose there was a broad and whitish scar, which preserved a distinct color from the rest of the face in spite of abstinence from water, as though the skin of dirt that formed over it peeled off every day or two. Whether originating in the solitary life he had led among the hills whilst a vaquero, or from natural disposition, Ñor Nicolás was never garrulous unless when scolding his mules. If by chance seduced into a talk during the preparation of a "casuela" for our meal, in less than two minutes after he had bolted nearly whole potatoes and swallowed a quart of soup, he would be snoring on the already-arranged bed of pellons, and a monosyllabic reply was all that was obtainable from him until the time of our departure on the following morning.

For shoes, his feet were encased in triangular bits of raw hide, laced with thongs of the same material over the top of the foot, and forming a point which curled upward like Turkish slippers. Wide and flowing blue trousers, reaching to the calf of the leg, were held above the hips by a broad band of leather, fancifully colored and fringed. This served at the same time as a purse and to support a long sheath-knife. Cotton drawers of equal width with the trousers

* Ñor and Ña are abbreviations of señor and señora, applied to dependents whose age and good qualities entitle them to this evidence of respect by their employers.

were visible below them, the glory of their pristine color long since departed and forgotten. A calico shirt with a wide collar, turned over the neck of a tight jacket made of faded ticking, its sleeves half-way up his bony wrists, and cut with a sharp peak quite down the back, a blue and red poncho tied diagonally across the shoulders and body like a scarf, and a coarse, dirt-colored straw hat, in the form of a truncated cone, hauled down on a mass of crispy hair, complete his costume. When it became warm, two ends of a red cotton handkerchief were stuck under the hat, the remainder forming a flowing bag behind. At the same time, his poncho was put on properly. It might be inferred such changes would increase the bodily heat; but experience proves the contrary, the motion of the horse converting both handkerchief and poncho into fans, which keep a pleasant circulation of air about the neck and body. For this purpose, and to protect the hair from dust, equestrians, both male and female, have almost universally adopted the fashion of wearing a loose handkerchief about the head. Horsemen elsewhere may, in summer, take a hint from the Chilenos.

Nervous and twitching at all times, the walk of Nicolás certainly was not improved in gracefulness by the use of spurs with rowels three inches from tip to tip, for there were no heels to his sandals, and he could only move on the extremities of his toes. Yet, masses as they were,—a load of iron to be lifted at every step,—he never parted with them until ready for sleep at night. So essential are spurs regarded to a horseman's equipment, that the servants at the posadas, not comprehending how or why a gentleman should ride without, invariably intimated to me at starting that I had forgotten them; and when told that I never wore such things, the bare heels of my boots were looked upon with more curiosity than my light hair and fair skin. More than once they hallooed to companions across the street, "*Mira al caballero que anda sin espuelas*" (look at the gentleman who rides without spurs). But to conclude with Ñor Nicolás. He had a pile of ponchos and sheepskins for the composition of his saddle in bulk quite sufficient to load a mule; yet he managed to arrange them so as to travel on top, though my sympathies were no little interested for the four-legged animal compelled to travel beneath such a sweltering burden day after day.

As a part of the intended journey would be through a country where the best accommodations to be expected are shelter from the night air, bread, a casuela, and perhaps a little mosto, a sumpter mule carried bedding, luggage, a package of tea and sugar, and some few other articles of provision which custom has almost rendered necessities, but which would be asked for in vain at any country inn. The mattress and bedding are placed within a case of raw hide, called an *almofrez*, which laces with leather loops at the centre and sides. Besides these legitimate articles, the almofrez serves to contain a multitude of others, and, being impenetrable by ordinary rains, when packed on top of the trunks, it becomes an efficient protection to them. Except between the capital and Valparaiso, few persons ever travel fifty miles without an almofrez, and previous experimental exercises, with fleas in the bedding of the posadas, rendered it an inestimable pleasure to know that when a day of fatigue on horseback was terminated, it would enable me to rest free from these agile young lobsters. In order that I might change to animals of different gaits from day to day, there were two extra saddle-horses. Nicolás had one, making our number of four-footed animals six in all; of which four were driven in advance along the road, and were secured by his lassoes when crossing the streams.

The scenery and topography of the country between Aguila and Rancagua are described in another place; and therefore I need only mention that we arrived within five hours, and took up the same quarters I had occupied about two years previously. The elevation of Rancagua above the ocean is 1,552 feet.* A walk through a part of the town did not bring to light many changes or improvements about which to talk with the landlord. The distance proposed to be accomplished next day was forty-five miles, and though I had on this occasion abundance of books and papers to occupy the early hours of the evening, it must be acknowledged that the

* By levelling of the engineers of the Santiago and Valparaiso railroad, 1,600 feet.

North American papers of December preceding (the last and latest possible dates), filled, as many of them were, with rhapsodies about Kossuth, were less attractive than bed.

As in passing over a country one is likely to judge erroneously of some things, and omit others of a more important character altogether, only brief notes were taken during the journey *to* the southward. Therefore, although the reader may be subjected to occasional repetitions, I will endeavor to pass over the ground to Talca rapidly, telling him more of events than localities, rather of transient than of permanent objects, and rely on the narrative of the return ride for accurate descriptions. A long dry summer had passed; autumn had consumed nearly one third of its alloted span; the fields of wheat and maize, which form such important and beautiful portions of agricultural scenery, had already been garnered; and there remained only stubble-fields to disfigure the earth. The deciduous trees, too few in number to fascinate the eye by the variant colors of their dying leaves, were already robbed of their charms; and there was little, except the everlasting mountains and a limited number of the feathered tribes, to demand one's particular attention.

March 27.—We made an early start, in order to accomplish a part of the fifteen leagues before breakfast. Crossing the Cachapual about 8 o'clock, so much time was occupied in fording its multitude of little streams and in traversing its wide stony bed, that we did not reach the hacienda of Señor ——— until after 10 A. M. At leaving Aguila, where this gentleman was then making a visit, he had insisted on my stopping at his house for breakfast, instead of going to a posada; and had given me a note for the mayordomo, instructing him to save us all possible detention, and to supply me with another horse, should one be required. As our cavalcade had so far proved perfectly satisfactory, to my mind there was no necessity for this extra tax on his generosity, and the subject was not even alluded to when the mayordomo solicited orders. Judge then of my surprise, at starting, to find another fine animal in the train! Ñor Nicolás, it seems, entertained different views from myself, and, knowing the authority, had notified the mayordomo that I (he) required another horse. Vanity was at the bottom of it. The old man had too much pride to ride a mule, if he could obtain a horse; and though he continued on the long-eared brute that day to keep up pretences, he never mounted her again until the afternoon we returned to the hacienda.

Apart from the quantities of agricultural products coming from the fields, there was very little of interest to note during the day. These, instead of being conveyed in large covered wagons constructed like those to the north of the Maypu, were generally packed in small rudely wattled bodies mounted on solid wheels of wood. I was about terminating the sentence with, "of from two to two and a half feet in diameter;" but this would have implied that they were circular; and as they are of every possible form *except* round, it is necessary to substitute instead the word "across." As the axles are composed wholly of wood, and a guaso would invariably prefer lubricating the inside of his throat to the outside of an axle, no grease is ever used on them, and the creaking of these queer vehicles may usually be heard at the distance of half a mile. Nor do proprietors or drivers seem to regard it as of the least consequence that the holes in the hubs should approximate to the diameter of the axles, but will sometimes make the former two or three times the dimensions of the latter; so that when one wheel chances to be nearly a square, and the other an elongated oval or ellipse—as I once saw—the locomotion would make some of our wheelwrights stare. And yet the driver sat contentedly in his hoppity-go-jump vehicle, puffing a cigarrito and punching the oxen with his long goad, evidently well pleased to be saved the trouble of walking. There were many of these carts loaded with pumpkins, maize, and onions; some going to hamlets not far off the road, others from distant parts of the haciendas to the residences; and at every mile or two groups of them were collected about rude arbors by the roadside where piles of melons were exposed for sale. A water-melon and half a pint of flour made from roasted wheat is a common meal for a peon, and one highly relished by him. Bits of melon are dipped in the flour until sufficient has been eaten from the centre to pour the remainder of the flour into the cavity, when the soft and liquid pulp is converted into paste. If not in strict accordance with the taste of epicures in fruits, as the wheat has been thoroughly cooked in the roasting, it is doubtless a very wholesome repast, and may be pleasant to the palate. What most excites surprise is the facility with which they can stow a melon nearly a foot in diameter under their waistbands.

From the accounts which had been given me, I supposed the country a continuous plain or valley, with a slight though uniform inclination to the southward. Strictly speaking it cannot be so considered, but is rather a succession of basins that communicate with each other through gorges sometimes on the same level, though quite as often with slight intervening eminences, the continuation of spurs abutting the two ranges of mountains. There were just clouds enough overhanging the latter to temper the heat and render the day pleasant; and but for the dust stirred up by the constant mule-trains, the ride would have been charming. Many of these trains were bringing planks and small timber from beyond Talca. From 300 to 400 pounds weight is packed on each animal in such manner that the upper ends project above and in advance, and the lower trail along the ground free of the mule's heels. It is by no means pleasant on a narrow road to encounter caravans thus loaded. Wandering as the animals will in search of melon-rinds left by travelling cartmen, or impelled by the cries of the arrieros from side to side, it is much safer to give them the whole road than risk the legs of a horse among the trailing lumber.

Rengo—a straggling village built on both sides of the main road for more than a mile—is an hour's travel from the hacienda of the Requinua. Some of its houses have decided pretensions to the first rank, and its people a regularity of features especially notable. We made no halt here, but continued our journey over a road that left the town of Curicó two miles to the right. San Fernando—our resting-place—was reached an hour before sunset. Stopping before an untidy-looking house in the northern skirts of the town, the guide told me it was the posada; but its appearance was so uninviting, I concluded that so extensive and populous a place must afford better quarters, and pushed on, thinking to find them nearer the centre. Evidently (in my thought) Nicolás knew nothing, having never departed from the line of the road to the south, and, like the rest of his kind, having never made inquiries beyond the want of the instant, little caring for others if that want was supplied without his aid. But the only other inn to be heard of was at the most distant extremity of the town, on the road to the Tinguiririca ford. Not supposing it could be worse than that before us, as so much would be gained in the direction of the journey, there seemed no risk in seeking it.

When we arrived there, its very decent sign-board, a house large enough to accommodate a score or more of guests, good corridors along its front, and an ample patio, together with a field in the rear supposed to afford good pasturage, were all fair external promises; and when the landlord promised "anything" to eat, the decision to come on seemed a subject of congratulation. "All is not gold that glitters," says the proverb; and so it proved here. The rooms had never been whitewashed; and their bare earthen floors apparently gave repose to the accumulated dust of ages—all but one being as destitute of furniture as on the day that the builders had left them. Within this room there were a pair of tressels, with three or four boards across them, to serve as a bedstead, an equally rude table of unsmoothed planks, and one rush-seat chair—the only one, I believe, within the whole enclosure. True, there *was* an abundance of dry pasturage, though neither a stalk of alfalfa nor other green food for the horses; and as for the "anything" promised as our food, there were small potatoes, a pumpkin, and fowls still pecking about the yard. But the horses had been unsaddled and the cargo-mule relieved of her load, before its impoverished condition was fully ascertained; and as there might be many such accommodating posadas to encounter before returning, it was better to meet the *contretemps* with a smiling face. And thus it was not long before a couple of fowls, knocked over with sticks, were simmering with some vegetables in an *olla,* and a neighbor sold us a small loaf of bread to help out the repast.

Meantime tidings of the arrival of a stranger got wind among the beggars, and we were not destined to be long neglected by some of the most pressing members of the profession belonging to San Fernando. With the earliest of them came a robust and well dressed man on horseback. He was evidently blind of both eyes. The story of "the beggar on horseback" is familiar to every boy; but Chile gives finishing touches to anomalous pictures, and furnishes servants or companions well dressed and well mounted, to lead the horses of sightless equestrian mendicants! As they seemed unwilling to receive "No" in answer, and could not be regarded as objects really needing charity, it was suggested to the companion that he might earn a creditable support for both, if he would sell the horses and rent a bit of ground and till it. To ascertain how much laziness had to do with their pursuit, I proposed to pay the companion a real, if he would bring me meat, bread, and a bottle of mosto from the town; his blind friend to be led away with him, but his own horse to remain as a security that he would return with the value of the money to be given him. In a region where a peon can only earn a real and a half per day, two thirds of that sum for half an hour's walk with a little basket on his arm seemed pretty good pay; but the pair probably regarded the occupation and *walking* as degrading, and marched off in great indignation. While these were talking, two other active and healthy men laid at my feet a hand-barrow containing a paralyzed and deformed old woman, the contortions of whose face, in her efforts to speak, were most painful to behold. Repeating to her bearers the thankless counsel given the blind beggar and his companion, the wretched semblance of humanity was gotten rid of with a bit of silver, and Ñor Nicolás proceeded to bar the entrance to the patio, as a relief from further importunity, the outsiders grumbling loud as well as deep at the "*maldito Gringo*" who would not even listen to them. The entry of my host just afterwards with a black earthen dish (borrowed from the neighbor who had sold the bread), was an intimation that the casuela would soon be ready, and I removed a pile of newspapers from the table, that he might arrange it for the meal; a needless precaution, as this dish and an iron spoon proved to be all the table furniture. The only knife belonging to the premises was a huge weapon used by the cook, that would (and no doubt did) serve to slaughter oxen; and of course there was no fork. Luckily my penknife had a blade stout enough to divide the joints of a fowl, fingers proved capital substitutes for the steel-pronged implement, and hunger made a charmingly conclusive argument in favor of primitive customs.

To the westward there is a range of moderate hills, rendered lofty by their proximity; and whilst discussing the really excellent casuela, the sun had gone down behind them, leaving above their summits masses of cumulo-stratus, tinged with vermillion and gold, as brilliant in their hues as the most glorious inter-tropical exhibition at sunset. These I watched from the corridor, following the changes of each little flocula through a misty veil, of Cuban origin, and listening to the murmuring waters of the Tinguiririca to absolute forgetfulness of the present, until the nearer buzz of mosquitos proved as effectual in recalling the *locale* as if Ñor Nicolás had sounded a trumpet beside me. At half-past seven, although the moon had reached its first quarter, the sky was almost of a black color, and the stars of a brightness rarely equalled, perhaps, even in this extraordinary atmosphere. When the planet Venus sank behind the hill, the sight was an interesting one, as astronomical readers will perceive. It was not an instantaneous immersion of the entire disc, but a rapid and strikingly notable diminishing in the brilliancy of the planet's rays; the final disappearance, however, so pronounced that a keen observer would scarcely have erred one tenth of a second in the time of its occurrence.

March 28.—The morning was sharp, almost frosty, and when we rode out of the posada yard the sun was struggling behind just such a bank of clouds above the Andes as had witnessed his setting yesterday. Immediately after leaving San Fernando, the road leads up the dry bed of the Tinguiririca; and as it is scarcely anything more than stones and gravel, rolled smooth in their rapid journey from elevations of the mountains, there was little opportunity to start the blood by a gallop, though abundant time to admire the lower ranges of mountains terminating the view to the eastward. A viler highway than movable stones at the bottom of a torrent one would not wish to persecute a traveller with; for if the horse stumble, at the very least he is sure to receive bruises as well as a wetting. Yet such is the character of all the fords, except across the Maypu, and at one or two lasso bridges over the deepest parts of other streams. There are two principal branches to the turbid Tinguiririca, both of them rapid; though neither of them is more than fifty feet wide on an average, nor more than two and a half feet deep at the centre. From this stream to the Chimbarongo, fifteen or sixteen miles, there is very little cultivation. The surface of the land is almost wholly sand and pebble stones. At the same time, the ranges of mountains on both sides are sensibly lower than to the northward, and are well covered with foliage almost to the plain.

It was a Sunday in Lent. On arriving at the "posada" of the Chimbarongo, where we expected breakfast, the household—cook and all—had gone to mass, some four or five miles away. As it was not certain that they would return before night-fall, there was no alternative but to ride two leagues farther, where we found Boniface and his wife apparently less devoutly inclined. Here the house was filled with young of both sexes from the neighborhood, who were holding a "chingana." Two or three sang to the accompaniment of a guitar, and a pair were dancing the "Zama Cueca" with the solemn monotony that renders it in appearance quite as much a religious ceremony as some of their church exhibitions, and certainly as little as possible like an inspiration of Terpsichore.

From the Chimbarongo to the Teno the face of the country is now quite a desert, the only cultivated portion being a narrow strip in the vicinity of Curicó. Such is also its character east of the road from Guyquillo creek to the Lontue, the principal affluent of the Mataquito. As a visit to it was intended at returning, we kept the higher ground to the eastward of Curicó, and reached the Lontue by 3 P. M. In the main branch of this stream there is, apparently, a greater volume of water than in either of those to the north; but it must be recollected that few irrigating canals between the ford and the Andes are supplied from it. Like the others, there are two principal torrents. A suspension bridge, formed of sticks not above an inch in diameter, wattled together and supported on twisted ropes of hide elevated upon four crotched trees, has been thrown over the deepest and most rapid of these. As there is abundance of water and level land southward of the Lontue, and for a league or more beyond the hamlet of Quechereguas, Chile recovers its lost character for fertility, and again one meets abundance of fruits and vegetables. Wherever a little moisture had stolen from the acequias near the road, the "flor de perdiz" (*Oxalis lobata*) had thrust its golden-hued petals to the surface; but this was almost the only flower. There are very few on any part of the plain, except during the spring months, when the rains of winter have had time to call the bulbs into life again.

The surrounding country is divided into small farms, as in Aconcagua. Beans and corn are its staples of cultivation, wheat and grapes not being raised in greater quantity than the neighborhood will consume. Here the valley is thirty miles wide; and from the barren hills about the river Teno, to the southward, only one small hill interrupts its seemingly level surface. Before crossing the latter stream, indeed soon after leaving San Fernando, the form of a lofty mountain in the Andes chain induced me to believe it the famed Descabezado. And so it eventually proved to be, though neither Ñor Nicolás, nor any of the travellers we met, had sufficient knowledge to satisfy my curiosity. From near the same point one may also see the peak of San Francisco to the northwest of Tupungato; indeed, but for the winds that load the atmosphere with sand, vision in Chile seems bounded only by the care that one has given to the inestimable organs of sight.

Heat, the hilly surface of a portion of the ground, and the pebbly beds of a considerable number of streams over which the road passes, compelled me to travel slowly all day, and we reached Quechereguas at 4½ P. M., having ridden eighteen leagues in nine hours. A number of travellers came into the posada shortly afterwards—some from Curicó, others from Talca; and in a little while its patio presented a bustling scene, with arrieros unloading packs, servants spreading their pellons beneath the corridors, and others carrying dishes of food, their long spurs clanking at every step like so many chains on the hard ground. The posada was really a good one; its rooms clean, and the hosts actually able to supply any reasonable want cheerfully, and at very small cost. No little comfort was it to obtain a wash-hand basin and clean water, instead of the greasy dish in which the "casuela" had been served the night before, and muddy water from an acequia.

March 29.—Nearly the whole of the fifteen leagues remaining to be travelled being over a road wholly unprotected from the rays of the sun, Ñor Nicolás was desirous to accomplish half of it before breakfast, and was knocking at my door by daylight, impatient to be off. A similar spirit seemed to actuate all my neighbors of the adjoining rooms, and the bustle was even greater than on the previous evening. We were the last to move, the sun just peeping over the Andes as we started.

For more than a mile, a tall row of poplars bounds both sides of the road. Beyond them the fields teem with the most luxuriant vegetation, exhibiting a fertility of soil fully comparable with the best districts between the Mapocho and Cachapual. A heavy dew, deposited during the night, thoroughly laid the deep dust of the road; and glittering drops still hung from outspread branches, as though a recent shower had passed over the avenue. Within a league is Villa Molina, a clean little town, with nearly 2,000 inhabitants, built along the main road for half a mile. It has only one indifferent-looking church. A broken plain that extends to Talca, and which is almost utterly barren, commences at a very short distance south of the town. Dwarf espinos, and occasional clusters of peumos in the ravines, are the only growth. Nor can a large portion of it ever be easily reclaimed, the rolling nature of its surface rendering irrigation impossible, except at enormous expense. There is a change observable in the western range of mountains, too. They have become little more than bleak and arid hills, with scarcely a visible shrub upon them. Where the river Claro crosses the plain diagonally, the latter may be forty miles wide, with a narrow cultivated strip on either bank of the stream; but from these to the limit of vision there is the same aspect of desolation. In this region a stratum of *tosca* (tufa), immediately below the surface, prevents the penetration of water or roots of plants that strike deeply, and scarcely anything grows. As the distance of this stratum from the surface varies from six inches to three feet, and it lies nearly parallel with it, they tell me that portions are at times cultivated in wheat, which of necessity depends on natural irrigation; but I saw no stubble for leagues, nor any other evidence of the husbandman's labors. The material mentioned is of two colors—one that of slate, the other a greyish white. Its specific gravity is very little greater than that of pine wood, and it is so soft that it may be readily chopped into any form with a stout knife. On the latter account, and because of its abundance and durability, it is extensively used for fencing, the faces being trimmed smooth when the walls are of the required height.

Soon after passing through Villa Molina we encountered a straggling train of women and children, the wives and offspring of a battalion of Cazadores who had served in the late revolutionary struggle. They were now on their way to Curicó, whose vicinity was not considered as tranquil as lovers of order desired. Some of the women were mounted, others on foot, and nearly all slovenly and dirty, as camp followers usually are. A short distance in their rear came burden mules with the officers' luggage; these were closely followed by troops; and two or three ladies, surrounded by officers, brought up the rear of the column. We passed each other in crossing the limpid waters of the Claro, here a narrow stream not above twenty yards wide, between steep and high banks.

By this time the mists of the morning had been dissipated, the southerly wind had commenced, and the atmosphere was extremely serene, exhibiting the mountains with great distinctness. Among the Andes, composed of many separate ranges, the Descabezado* (truncated) is in the fourth, and is the highest visible from this plain. To the northward, Cauquenes is quite clear; thence, following along the most elevated line, Peteroa, Descabezado, Cerro Azul, and

* Literally, *headless*.

Chillan, embrace nearly a hundred miles of latitude. Though none of the others are so lofty, there are several peaks in the vicinity of the Descabezado. Some are covered with snow to their summits; but others are entirely bare about the crests, although three or four thousand feet above the line of perpetual congelation. This peculiarity has induced one or more writers to infer that the Andes of Chile generally are not as high as the snow-line; when the fact is, that nearly the whole of the higher range, to the southward of the 30th parallel, is covered with snow through the upper third or fourth part of their elevation. Subject as are these summits to strong winds from the southward, if, by chance, snow is deposited on them during a calm, it is of so light and dry a nature that the first winds of the morning drive it into the ravines, creating deep beds in some places, and, owing to the formation, leaving others entirely denuded, or at most with lines of blackened rock, like radii drawn on a white cloth. More than once we have witnessed the drift over the steep face of San Francisco and the lofty ovals to the southeast of it—its peak and the summits remaining black and bare, whilst the bottom of the snow-line was at least eight thousand feet below.

There is a posada in the tufa region, midway between Quechereguas and Talca, where we halted for an hour. Every step of the road after leaving it was more and more desert-like, until we approached the Lircay, within two leagues of Talca. During the whole day scarcely a mule-train was met. Two small droves of half-starved cattle coming to the northward, and a solitary horseman with face and head muffled from the fierce reflected heat, were the only living creatures from the banks of the Claro; and this absence of animal life tended no little to increase the apparent desolation. Approaching the banks of the Lircay, the soil becomes better. One has got across the tufa stratum, and the first evidence of it is in the greater numbers and luxuriance of the espinos. Thence there are more passers. One meets venders of fruits and vegetables, with hide panniers, going or returning between the town and the cultivated tongue of land between the Lircay and Claro; and a new specimen of the ox-cart, whose proportions have been reduced much below those last mentioned. Clumsiness and weight are here compressed in all their perfection, lest the poor oxen should not have enough to drag. The prongs of a tongue not unlike a tuning-fork in shape, and some five inches in diameter, are fitted into the axle, and with it serve to support a rough flooring and sides of sticks laced over them. A bit of hide is their only head or tail board. They are from seven to eight feet long in the body, have wheels two feet *across*, and their sides are three or three and a half feet high above the axle. Many of them were being loaded with rounded stones at the Lircay ford, to be used in paving the streets of the city; and others toddled along with full cargoes, on top of which the drivers reclined in the full enjoyment of indolence.

A league S.W. of the ford the Lircay falls into the Claro, the course of the latter remaining unchanged by the additional volume. Across the stream (Lircay) there is no variation in the aspect of the land; at the distance of a few hundred yards it becomes as barren as that to the northward, and thus the approach to the city is by no means prepossessing, or at least it is not so at this season of the year. The first houses are at two miles from the principal population, and less than a mile to the E.S.E. of the Claro. Talca is five miles from the ford. Owing to the cultivation, perhaps, it can scarcely be considered to have any northern suburbs, and one at once enters the city on that side by a pretty alameda. Five minutes' ride enables you to reach the posada near the plaza and its centre at the same time.

The base of the Andes is more than twenty-five miles distant from the city. Its higher peaks, the Descabezado, Longavi, Cerro Azul, and Chillan, as well as parts of the ranges on each side of them, are covered with snow to within 9,000 feet of the plain, and from one third to one half of their heights from the summits downward. I am not aware that the height of the Descabezado has ever been measured; but comparing it with other elevations known to me, I should think it under rather than over 14,500 feet. Owing to the increased amount of moisture in the air, and to the fact that the atmosphere during the day was constantly loaded with fine sand driven along by the prevailing S.S.W. wind, the different ranges composing the chain were not clearly distinguishable, as at Santiago, or as I had seen them on the preceding morning. But there is a marked contrast between them and the western range, whose summits are here scarcely a league distant in an air line; the former being thickly covered with trees, and the latter having on it scarcely wood enough within the whole range of vision to kindle a watch-fire.

The city was founded in 1742. Its latitude is 35° 14′ S.; longitude 71° 57′ W.; and from a mean of six barometrical observations on four different days, it is 620 feet above the level of the sea. Prof. Domeyko makes it only 114 varas, about 317 feet; but I apprehend there must have been some misreading of the barometer, as I had the same instrument, and all the observations agree. The city is built on undulating ground, falling towards its centre from three directions; and its plan differs in no respect from that of other Spanish-American towns, viz: rectangular streets, with an open plaza near the centre, on which its principal public edifices front, and an alameda. From one extremity to the other of its longest streets the distance is about a mile, although in compactly built houses Talca probably does not cover more than half a mile square. A small stream flows along its southern suburb in a northwest direction; from which, and a number of springs to the northeast, a supply of water is obtained for drinking purposes, as well as for cleaning the town. There are no public water-carriers. Each family has its little hand-cart and barrel, with which a servant brings a daily supply of potable water. The streets are quite wide, well paved, and most of them have sidewalks of a sandstone found in the vicinity. As they are kept in good repair as well as clean, the city fathers and police are probably faithful also in other obligations to the public.

In their architecture, the houses resemble those of other national towns, some few attaining the respectable height of two stories, the upper one having balconies on the streets. All are well whitewashed; and as there is no illumination at the general expense on dark nights, each proprietor is required to suspend at his front door a lantern with a light. The style of the churches is in better taste than those even of the metropolis. Indeed, its cathedral, when completed, will be an extremely handsome building. Only a part of it has been roofed, and its towers are wanting, so that one can scarcely appreciate its future appearance; but the limited population of the city, and the multitude of other religious edifices claiming alms, will probably prevent such a result for many years. Within three squares of this (the plaza) the Franciscans, Dominicans, Mercedarios, and Augustins, have each large churches attached to their convents; the last order, as well as a body of nuns, having extensive new establishments in course of construction. There is very little within the churches to attract attention. They are poor, and are note-worthy only for their outward architecture. Though occupying space enough for several hundred cells, according to published returns the convents have only thirteen occupants in all of the several orders—a statement which, if reliable, shows them to possess a power that would sometimes be invaluable to the commander of an army; for I certainly never saw so few men appear so numerous in any other streets.

There is nothing to remark in the other public buildings. The cabildo, prison, and intendencia, are all on the plaza; though the last, occupied by the chief of the province, is only private property. No public mansion has been provided, as in some other parts of the republic. In the ordinary acceptation of the word factory, there is no such establishment, except one or two small flour-mills. In various parts of the surrounding country, as well as in the city, there are hand-looms employed in making blankets, ponchos, and coarse cloths of wool; and some of the blankets are subsequently embroidered by hand with much elaborateness and taste. The ponchos wrought are quite famous for their evenness of texture, the excellent quality of the material, and the tenacity of the interwoven colors. So abundant is good wool that it may be purchased at $4 per hundred pounds, and it is a matter of surprise that a manufactory has not been erected long since. There is ample water-power at command for a dozen. All goods made from wool fetch high prices, labor is cheap, provisions of native growth at scarcely half the Santiago rates, and the Maule affords an economical line of communication with a port from which to ship the surplus of the factory. Enterprise alone seems wanting to carry into operation an undertaking which could not fail to be lucrative to its projectors.

The only perceptible difference in the mass of the population from their countrymen farther north is in their dresses. Closer fitting garments here take the place of the wide and flowing trowsers worn there, and straw hats are superseded by sharp cones of felt pulled closely over the ears. One occasionally meets a full-blooded Indian, too; but the mass belong to the mixed race propagated through generations. According to the last census, (five years ago,) the population was 14,391, and its best informed citizens do not now suppose it to contain more than 15,000 souls. Some years its increase at all appears extremely problematic, the returns made to the curate for 1850 and 1851 showing that the number of deaths actually exceeded the number of births.* To account in some manner for the apparent decrease, it is supposed that a part of the illegitimate births were not registered, the mothers probably being too poor to pay the baptismal fees. But if it be true that the population is falling off, it must be attributable to the notorious neglect of young children, rather than to any local cause—the situation of the city and its climate being eminently healthy. I could not find any meteorological register from which to learn accurately its atmospheric changes; yet the fact that it is near an abundant supply of fuel, and that even the houses of the wealthy are without fire-places, is a proof that the winters cannot be very rigorous. During the three days of my visit, the mean height of the barometer at 9 A. M. was 29.472 inches, at 3 P. M. 29.378 inches, and its range 0.201 inch; the temperature of the air for the same hours was 64°.4 and 74°.0, the extremes differing 20°.8. The barometric heights are not reduced for temperature of the attached thermometer. Throughout the winter season rains are more frequent and copious than at Santiago, and they are often accompanied by more violent N.W. winds. In summer the heat is not so excessive. Moderate elevation of the plain above the ocean affords it nearly 1,400 additional feet of the denser strata of the atmosphere to temper the sun's rays. The latter fact, and also its geographical position, preserves to it a more humid climate all the year.

The diseases most common are such as arise from excesses, and prevail equally elsewhere—dysentery and venereal. Goitre, though known, is not so prevalent as farther to the north; and it may be remarked, that the waters of the neighboring streams are quite limpid, instead of possessing the milky turbidness of the Mapocho below the junction of the Maypu canal. There is a charity hospital supported at the expense of the municipality; and subsequent to the battle on the plain of Loncomilla, a large building, erected for religious penance, was temporarily converted into a military hospital. Of more than 600 wounded conveyed to it, only about 80 died; whilst of those taken to San Juan de Dios, in Santiago, after the *émeute* of April 20, 1851, quite two thirds left it only when conveyed to the cemetery. As physicians came from the capital to attend at Talca the unfortunate victims of the fratricidal battle, the relative proportions of deaths at the two places is the best argument which could be adduced in favor of the more salubrious atmosphere of the latter. In this connection, it would be unjust not to mention that the ladies of the city attended their suffering fellow-countrymen in the military hospital day and night, and in some cases either took individuals to their own houses, or provided them quarters where they would have more airy rooms and more careful attendance than its crowded wards could afford. At the same time, scores of the benevolent at Santiago passed hours in preparing lint, bandages, and delicacies to be sent to Talca—acts of charity for which the recording angel will blot out many a sin.

There is an institution for the education of males supported at the expense of the general government, those only who live within its walls paying a monthly sum for board. After completion of the course here, young men were formerly sent to the parent establishment at Santiago to study medicine, law, mineralogical chemistry, or surveying, as might be elected; but a recent

* In 1850 there were 858 deaths, and 814 births: in 1851, including those who died in the hospital from the effect of wounds, the deaths were 834; the births, 815. Of the 834 deaths, 537 were under seven years of age. The illegitimate births registered more than twenty-five per cent. of the whole number.

re-organization of the latter, requiring among other things the dismissal of all boarders above sixteen years old, has effectually excluded those whose parents reside in the provinces from participation in its benefits. There are also several private schools for the education of both sexes, at which the attendance is quite good.

From what had been experienced elsewhere of the provision made for travellers, a commodious inn was not looked for, and consequently there was no disappointment. There are, however, two houses that offer entertainment—one possessing an abundance of everything except lodging-rooms; the other a multitude of apartments, though very little of anything else. In fact, the first is a restaurant, with a single spare room, where one's "almofrez" may be spread; and the chambers of the latter, though cleaner in their equipments, are only one step in advance of the San Fernando posada. Happily I was not destined to try the merits of the first very long. Friends had provided me with letters to several persons; and within an hour after most of them had been sent to their respective addresses, invitations were extended to me in the kindest and most considerate manner. Two notes awaited my return from a short walk; and as I sat hesitating which to accept, the secretary of the Intendente came again, with three soldiers, saying good-naturedly: "I have *orders* to take you to the Intendencia. These are the troops to aid me if you resist; if you submit quietly, they will only convey your luggage." And so I was marched off a voluntary prisoner to one of the most accomplished and hospitable young men whom it has been my fortune to meet anywhere.

March 30.—As the season had arrived when rain might be expected almost any day, it was concluded safer to make the proposed excursion down the river Maule at once, deferring visits in the vicinity until after my return; and therefore I determined to leave Talca on the day following my arrival. When Nicolás presented himself to pack the mule, he had so far conformed to the dominant fashion as to exchange his greasy-looking straw hat for one of the fancy-colored cones, and the rest of his outward man had also evidently been renovated; but there was something gnawing at the old man's mind, and he hung about fidgeting over the almofrez and trunk with a face betraying all the mental struggle his features were capable of expressing. As the cause was apparently connected with the proposed journey, I resolved to remain both blind and silent, to test whether he would initiate a conversation. Time pressed, and he at length spoke out.

One of the kind and attentive friends whom the letters of introduction had obtained for me, finding I would not permit him to undertake so comfortless a journey only to accompany me, had sent a well dressed and sprightly young servant to act as a guide to the landing; and Nicolás feared he would be taken down the river instead of himself. At first vanity suggested that the old "vaquero" was jealous; but it subsequently proved that, instead of regard for my good company, he was thinking of the donkeys at home. Nicolás owned half a dozen mules at Aguila, and desired an opportunity to traffic a little in sheepskins with which to repair pack-saddles! No one was really needed after my equipage was placed in the boat, and I had no thought to avail myself of the generous offer of my friend and take away his servant; but I was quite willing to oblige the old guide, and when told he might take charge of the luggage if he chose, in the hurry of his motions there was such an incessant clattering with spurs that every one was rejoiced when he left the patio.

We left Talca at 5 P. M. by a road to the westward, towards a gorge of the near cordilleras, through which pass the united waters of the Claro; its affluent, the Lircay, from the northeast; the Maule, from nearly east; and the Loncomilla, with its many tributaries, from the south. The Claro washes the base of these mountains from the immediate vicinity of the ford mentioned a page or two back, and both it and the Loncomilla fall into the Maule within six leagues of Talca. For two leagues the road lies through some of the best-cultivated lands in the country. At three miles from the city, and even where the supply of water for irrigation is insufficient, farms are worth $50 per acre. Like the land near the banks of the more northern streams, it has a shingle substratum, with a soil of vegetable and mineral detritus that yields almost incalculably; and, as it is divided into small estates, every portion is under cultivation. Colin, a settlement like Renca, near Santiago, is at the distance first named, and scattered over a mile or two in each direction about the road. Within that space is embraced a population of nearly 4,000 souls, famed for their honesty in the neighborhood of a district somewhat proverbial in the northern part of Chile—the *Maulino* being the type of all that is finished in knavery. Beside the road there are but two dwellings of persons probably wealthy; the rest are a better class of ranchos surrounded by a few acres of ground. From the "chacras" of Colin the finest fruits and vegetables are carried to Talca, the white strawberries having especial recommendation.

Passing by occasional trees and a mile of shrubby bushes near the south bank of the Lircay, the road turns to the south for a short distance, and ascends a slightly rising hill, in reality a part of the western cordilleras intercepted between that river and the Maule. Here night overtook us; and sterility, the dominant characteristic of the surface of this range, needed darkness to soften its desolate aspect. For miles the ground is so indurated that loaded carts, though constantly passing, fail to cut tracks; and there are so few rocks to serve as guides, that even with bright moonlight one may easily be lost on its monotonous waste. By riding in advance of the guide I once or twice got astray, and nothing but the sound of horses' feet on the hard surface enabled me to regain the road. It was just such an evening as that at San Fernando, when all space above was seemingly deprived of atmosphere, and the stars almost within one's grasp. As I stopped for a few moments on one occasion to detect the direction from which the sounds came, there was an instant when I thought the Descabezado again an active crater after its ages of repose; but the light which glimmered about its black and flattened summit was that of Jupiter just coming to replace the bright rays of Venus, then disappearing behind the cordilleras to the northwest.

Soon after eight o'clock we reached the bodega, a store-house on the banks of the Maule for goods in transit. Its distance from Talca is said to be seven leagues, and here passengers await the departure of the launches or the arrival of conveyances from Talca. When we left town it was supposed that there would be a boat ready to start at daylight, but we had been misinformed. The agent told us one would be despatched some time during the day, if the remainder of the intended cargo arrived; though as the river was very low, he thought it might be the better part of two days in reaching Constitucion. A rather discouraging prospect this! Usually travellers pass the night in the bodega, so as to be ready for an early departure, and make all the voyage during daylight. At this time it was half filled with new cheese, whose odors, if not sweet, were certainly strong enough; and during the first five minutes I sat within it I received proofs that a multitude of its inhabitants would highly appreciate company. Having, unfortunately, neither taste to enjoy the fragrance, nor generosity to gratify the desire one moment longer than the usual hour of leaving, if it should be possible to get away, a bargain was struck by which, in consideration of six dollars, the launch was to start at daylight with the half freight it would be possible to put on board during the night.

After a night passed in combating the insinuating solicitations of my co-occupants of the dark and odorous domicil, it was no little gratification to learn from Ñor Nicolás that the day was at last breaking. But instead of being able to commence our journey at once, as had been agreed on, not a man of the crew had come, and the bags of barley intended for cargo were still lying on shore. Even the agent, or owner, with whom the contract had been made, had gone, the Lord only knew where. As there was no chance to get away for hours, I availed myself of the stream to drop some of the young lobsters of the bodega into it, whilst Nicolás superintended the preparation of a casuela for our breakfast in a rancho near by. About nine o'clock, and when the very estimable gentleman knew that I had just commenced the meal, he bustled to the bodega, and had the assurance to complain that *I* was detaining the boat. This was spoken in such a tone of injured innocence and outraged rights that Nicolás, I verily believe, bolted potatoes and chicken legs whole in his hurry and fright. Too glad to get away even at this hour of the day, as nothing was to be gained by altercation, (he had shrewdly secured the passage-money the night before,) his charge was submitted to with the utmost humility, and we posted to the boat like real culprits. Luckily he took care not to follow, else Nicolás had assuredly been offered a bribe to horsewhip him soundly; for a large part of the cargo still lay on the shore, and the crew were dividing their time pretty equally between its disposition and two or three dark-skinned damsels who came to see them off. There was ample time for us to have administered this act of strict justice, whilst our patience and forbearance oozed out under the beams of a hot sun. When all were on board the boat was *full;* in fact, instead of having accommodated me, he had quietly swindled me out of four dollars: so much for the special letter of recommendation carried to him.

March 31.—After the first heavy rains, and until the middle of summer, the rivers are high, and launches may ascend the Claro to within a league or less of the city. During the rest of the year this (*Los Perales*) is the nearest place of embarcation. Having more water for ten miles above its mouth, the Loncomilla is navigable all the year by boats carrying forty tons. More than a hundred launches find constant employment in conveying produce of the surrounding country to Constitucion, each hundred-weight carried about seventy miles down stream paying one real. Besides these there are smaller boats regularly occupied in the conveyance of fruits and vegetables for the market of Constitucion, and shipment to Copiapó and other northern districts where nature has been less bountiful in its supply of water. Wheat, flour, beans, cheese, charqui, wines, and wool, are the principal exports; the province of Maule also sending its surplus produce by this route. Ordinarily the launches return empty; and if, by chance, a freight is obtained, unless specially agreed on, the freight-money belongs to the crew. The largest of them will carry from forty to forty-five tons. Each has five or six men, one of whom is dignified with the title of *Piloto,* and is really the navigator of the shallow craft. He receives $3, the others $1.50, for the round trip; and each is furnished by the owner with a peck and a half of flour made from toasted wheat, and water from the river *à discretion.* During summer, when the river is at its mean height, the voyage down is made in from eight to twelve hours, depending on the boat and crew; the return trip in from two to four days. With a cargo, the latter is often extended to six or eight days. When descending the stream, a velocity of two miles per hour is maintained with the oars; and where the rapids make it necessary to have the boat well under control, even double that speed is kept up for a time: but in coming back they are obliged to track the launch nearly every step of the distance, and rarely use their oars except when necessary to shoot the river to obtain a better beach, or to take advantage of an eddy. Sometimes they are aided by the prevailing southwest winds, though the hills are so high and steep that they more frequently sweep above the surface of the water from ravine to ravine of opposite shores. It is hard work dragging a heavy boat against such a current all day; and though excessively annoying to lie by when the night was bright and the wind favorable, I was subsequently obliged to confess that the crew had fairly earned a right to rest. As soon as the current becomes greater than the velocity attained by the aid of oars and wind, all hands strip to their shirts and jump overboard with a tow rope over their shoulders, ranging themselves at equal distances from each other. Walking barefoot as they do over the shingle, with bodies thrown forward the better to overcome the resistance, their feet become thick and hardened, and their legs attain surprising muscular development. The soles of the feet of those in the launch with me seemed quite double the thickness of those of ordinary men. But the chronological order of the story has been somewhat anticipated.

As has been said, it was a bright and warm day, without a breath of air to temper the heat. At 9 A. M. the barometer at the level of the river, reduced to 32° Fahrenheit, was 29.485 inches; and the temperature of the water at the junction of the Claro, a few hundred yards below the landing-place, was 60°.8. Near Constitucion, where the ocean influenced it, the temperature was 4°.5 warmer. At the place of embarcation the river is fifty yards wide and from two to three feet deep in the centre, with a current varying from three to four miles per hour, according to its depth and width. In the strongest rapids it possibly attains to seven miles, and the noise of the water over the shingly bottom may be heard for a long distance. During the first thirty miles it is often divided into two or more branches, though invariably one is much greater than all the others would be in a combined volume. Within this distance, also, there are occasional snags, the remains of trees brought down by heavy freshets. At such times the water rises between six and seven feet above its present level, and entirely submerges the flats that form the shores for more than fifty miles, sometimes on one side and sometimes on the other. Along the first five leagues, except clumps of shrubs with small trees here and there, the hills back from the river are destitute of herbagė; and such continues to be the character of the *southern* shore full ten miles lower down. Both become more and more densely clad as you approach the ocean, until, from the edge of the stream to the summits of the hills, there is a forest of trees so entwined with climbing plants as to be almost impenetrable without an axe. Solitary sentinels on opposite sides, and not far below Los Perales, are two of the coco-palms (*Jubæ spectabilis*) so common near Valparaiso. That on the south shore is growing on a shingle flat, evidently overflowed at every freshet; but Robles, Peumos, Boldos, Canelos, Litres, Quillays, and Maytens, form a forest comparable in its density to those of North America. The birds most common on the river are Garzas (*Ardea egretta* and *candidissima*), Cuervos (*Ibis falcinellus*), and several varieties of ducks. There was also a flock of Flamingos (*Phœnicopterus ignipalliatus*), with their long and graceful necks, one of Bandurrias (*Ibis melanopis*), and a few gulls, tempted from their ordinary haunts about the sea-side.

By noon the heat of the sun and the glare reflected from the water became so oppressive that they could no longer be borne without suffering to the eyes. Although an awning had been included in the bargain, it was discovered after we had started that there was nothing in the boat with which to make one, except the large lug-sail, and this was too unwieldy. The launch was therefore run ashore, some fragrant branches were cut from a Boldo, and a poncho hung over them afforded shade and refreshing odor at the same time. Ordinarily, when there are passengers, three or four willow branches are bent over and across the stern, and a bit of old canvass or cotton cloth spread over them makes quite a comfortable cabin for inland Chile travel.

Half-way down the river begin the districts in which timber is cut; and on both shores there are spots on the hill-sides worn bare by logs which are constantly being tumbled down to the water. These are most frequent on the south side; as are also patches of ground from which the undergrowth has been burned, and where only trees with blackened trunks and denuded arms remain, sad monuments of the power of the devouring element. From this portion of the river the rapids become less frequent, and there are fewer separations of its stream by pebbly islands. At ten miles above Constitucion, the hills rise from the water at angles of 35° to heights ranging from 200 to 300 feet. In some places the formation is entirely concealed by a reddish clay, like that of the hills back of Valparaiso; and in others black and irregular strata of porphyritic rock form walls whose bases are laved by the stream. Within this distance one never finds more than a single beach, and that continues on the same side only for short spaces, interrupted by spurs that project into the river. Here, too, the latter begins to widen, and thence continues to do so almost insensibly, until opposite the town it is three fourths of a mile across. Here, for the last time, it is divided by a low, sandy island partially covered with shrubbery. In the direction of the stream the island is about five sixths of a mile long, with a breadth of nearly 300 yards. A steam saw-mill is in course of erection upon it, and many rafts of timber are already moored along its shores awaiting final preparation for market.

During the last league the southern shore of the Maule has again become barren; and at the distance of a mile and a half from the sea the hills bend away from it, enclosing a semicircular basin, the lowest portion of whose rim is opposite the island. This range terminates in a steep granitic eminence, much resembling in form the rock of Gibraltar, or a huge grave, though it scarcely attains half the height of the European promontory. It is covered with shrubby bushes and verdure, has a signal-staff on its most elevated point, and on a small plateau near its northern extremity is the old and unenclosed cemetery of Constitucion, for whose tenants the ocean, full 500 feet below, beats an eternal requiem against its vertical face. Though more broken by ravines the northern shore continues of nearly the same height, and is quite as densely covered with trees as far as the flat sand-spit at the mouth of the river. Here the beach is not above half a mile wide, but it stretches away to the northward for six or seven leagues, with more than twice that average breadth—probably the most extensive flat boundary to the Pacific in all Chile. Below the island the river again narrows rapidly, and in less than a mile has so diminished that its width, at low water, is less than three hundred yards, between the extremity of Cerro Mutün (the hill referred to) and the sandy point that terminates the northern shore. Seaward from Cerro Mutün, but quite close to it, are two high pyramidal masses of rock, named *Las Ventanas* and *Piedra Lobos;* from the former having apertures through it like windows, and the latter being resorted to by large numbers of seals (lobos). Half a mile to the southward another somewhat similar elevation, the most imposing from its size and gothic outlines, is known as *La Iglesia* (the church), a door in keeping with its natural architecture contributing no little to the resemblance. All these rocks are frequented by flocks of penguins, gulls, and other sea-fowl.

Just beyond the "Piedra Lobos" a bar is formed, where the current of the river and the impulsive force of the waves neutralize each other, and deposite the sands each had previously carried along. This forms a line on which the waters break, extending in a northeasterly direction, and varying in magnitude with the strength of the wind and set of the sea. Of course, as the same agent gives varying momentum to the volume of sea water, the bar and its channel are constantly changing, and they rarely remain in the same place through an entire winter. As will be seen from the map, vessels drawing more than 15 feet water can never enter; and even those of 300 to 350 tons are almost always delayed some days, waiting a smooth time. The difficulty they experience arises from the fact that the prevailing southerly wind is lost on approaching the Piedra Lobos, where they encounter the current of the river at the moment of losing their headway, and thus are thrown on the northern spit of the bar. In such a case, unless the wind at the time be very light, the sea in consequence smooth, and relief soon come from the town, the vessel is almost certain to become a total loss. So secure is the anchorage when once attained, and so important is the port becoming from the annually increasing produce sent to it from the interior, that government has been repeatedly and earnestly urged to apply some remedy. To this end two propositions have been presented—one of which, coming from a commission of the government, is somewhat remarkable. They propose no less than to empty the whole of the river Lontue into the Claro by means of a canal, and, by the increased volume of water given to the Maule, to drive the bar farther out to sea. But they evidently forgot that an increased amount of detritus would inevitably be brought with the water; and the equally certain consequence, that the first freshet occurring at high tide would wash out the amphitheatral basin, and leave it as bare of human habitations as when nature desisted from her tasks here about. During floods, even with the Maule alone, if the tide rise more than its usual height of five to six feet, the people of the town are not unfrequently in trepidation for their property. The other proposition seems much more rational. It is, to build a sea-wall between the Ventanas and Piedra Lobos, of which they would form a part. By using the admirably suited rock of which they are composed, they would be cut down so as not to impede the winds greatly; and at the same time the sweep of the sea between them would be interrupted. Once clearly within the bar, and under the action of the river current only, and there is no danger. The proposition is certainly practicable, and would not be attended with very great expense. Meantime a good steam-tug would find ample employment and recompense; as would also one of lighter draft for the navigation of the river. A little while ago government gave an exclusive privilege to use steam tow-boats on the river, and it is understood that a vessel was constructed in the United States for this purpose; but she was lost on the way out, and the period within which the privilege might take effect has expired.

U. S. N. Astr. Expedn.

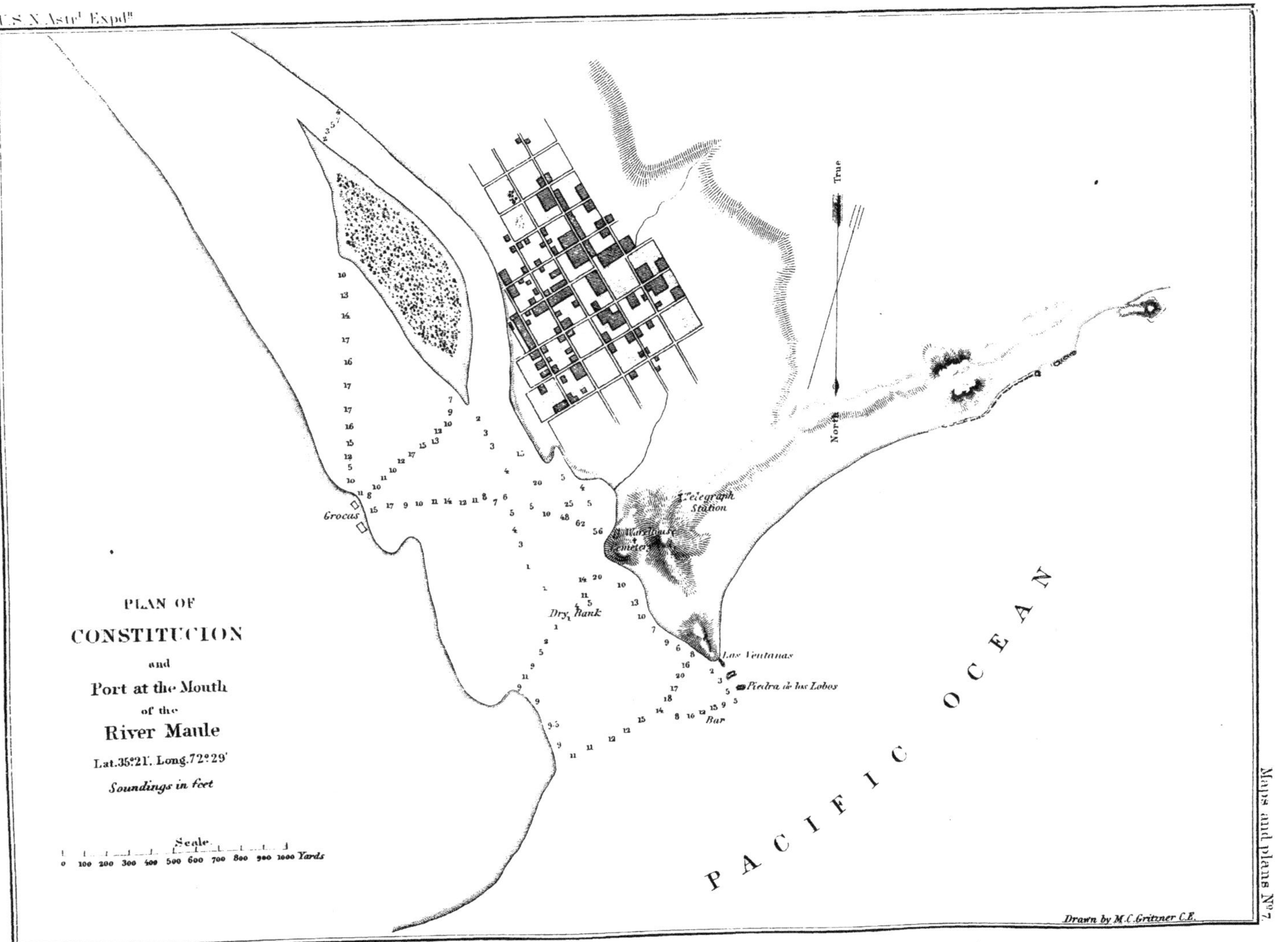

At the bottom of the amphitheatral basin, and some ten feet above the water of the river, is the city of Constitucion,—named by its sponsors *Nuevo Bilbao*, rebaptized under its present legal cognomen after the revolution, and by natives of the province more generally called *Maule*. A lucky town that with *three* titles! Thirteen years ago its population, then less than 2,000 in number, were scattered over nearly the same extent of ground as at the present day—that is, about half a square mile; and an acre of land was bought for less than twenty dollars. Now, as the population has more than doubled, and the new houses necessary for the accommodation of the increased number have all been erected within the old limits, the same lot is worth nearer $2,000. Thus it is beginning to assume the appearance of a compact and well ordered town, in which its foreign residents have inspired some of the life and activity visible at Valparaiso. Though there are several residences expensively finished, which have also pretty gardens about them, the larger portion of its one-storied houses are quite provincial. Its streets are parallel, and at right angles to each other; they are of good width, but not paved. It has a plaza near the centre. On this front the church, barracks, and prison—public establishments whose external appearance is sufficiently humble to secure pardon for omission of the details of their poverty. When it becomes a great town, as it one day will, its municipal authorities will no doubt ornament the one, and substitute others more becoming. As very few wells have been dug, there is a scarcity of water for domestic purposes. That which is principally used is obtained from a rivulet that flows from the hills back of the town. Although dependent on the interior for provisions, as has been stated, so productive is the upper country that every necessary of life is sold at reasonable prices; and the ocean furnishes so many and such varieties of fine fish that it has no small influence on the sale of the offerings of the earth.

Abundance of timber along the river, a good harbor at its mouth, and a sloping beach for launching ways, offer inducements to ship-building, of which advantage has been taken to some extent, and a large number of the vessels of Chile have first floated on the waters of the Maule. During four years, ending with 1852, there were launched one ship of 500 tons; nine brigantines, having an aggregate tonnage of 1,450; fourteen schooners, measuring 1,132 tons; and launches and other boats, 1,802 tons. These gave employment to about 150 carpenters and caulkers: the first of whom receive from four to eight reals per day; ordinary wood cleavers, from two and a half to three reals each. At the time of my visit there were only three or four launches, of about 40 tons each, on the stocks. This was the only kind of manufacture in the town, of which our brief sojourn enabled me to obtain intelligence. Its people are almost exclusively occupied in sawing into boards or otherwise preparing the timber, which arrives in rafts by the river or from the back country on little carts like those about Talca, and in the transhipment of produce. There is only a nominal foreign trade. The whole amount of duties collected since 1844 does not exceed an average of $500 per year. According to their value, the articles of produce with which it furnishes other ports of the republic are, flour, beans, timber, barley, wine, tallow, and charqui. After the commencement of the Copiapó railroad, an impulse was given to the timber trade which placed it second if not first in rank in export of this material—a position it will probably retain because of the increased facilities in bringing it to market. The value of its commerce during eight years, terminating with 1851, was as follows:

	1844.	1845.	1846.	1847.	1848.	1849.	1850.	1851.
To other ports . . .	$190,010	$172,695	$206,870	$186,322	$138,972	$46,367	$479,019	$251,835
From other ports . .	174,221	182,274	185,453	167,373	28,309	27,840	75,869	7,657

No reason could be ascertained to explain why the trade diminished to such extent during the years 1848 and 1849. The same fact was observable to a greater or less extent in all the ports of the republic; and in 1850, the total coasting trade, which had previously averaged six millions of dollars, fell off to three millions and a half. In 1851, revolutionary difficulties, whose closing struggles were in the vicinity of the Maule, afford satisfactory explanations. After the commencement of the Copiapó and Caldera railroad, there were usually from twelve to fifteen vessels off the town awaiting or discharging cargoes; but at this time there were only half that number. That it is destined to increase rapidly, and to become a prosperous city, none can doubt who examine its natural advantages; and though in the amount of its foreign trade it can never rival Valparaiso, the day is not very distant when goods needed for the provinces of Colchagua, Talca, Maule, and Ñuble, will find their way direct to Constitucion, instead of paying tribute, as now, to the merchants of the former port.

We reached the landing soon after 7 P. M.; and as friends, both at Talca and Santiago, persisted that the posada would be uninhabitable, I was soon enjoying the hospitality of a German gentleman to whom I had been commended. They had reasoned analogically, forgetting that the advent of foreigners, ever on the watch to avail themselves of increasing trade, would measurably compel the introduction of customs and conveniences of their own countries; and the "*café*," as it is called, has, in fact, become quite a respectable place.

The following day was passed in visits to the island, Cerro Mutün, and the Piedra Iglesia; and by night I was ready to take advantage of the first ascending launch to commence my return. From Cerro Mutün—commanding, as it does, a view of all the landscape and the vast Pacific ocean, rolling in stately majesty from beyond the bounds of vision—the prospect is extremely beautiful. Hence, too, the topographical position of the town is more fully appreciated; and could the slopes of its semi-surrounding hills be clothed with verdure, nothing would be wanting to render its location one of the most picturesque in the country. When its increasing population spread their dwellings up the gentle inclinations, and extract from the bosom of the earth limpid streams for their bodily wants, the surplus will fructify its surface, and sterility disappear. Then, with a climate unsurpassed for genial salubrity, a perfectly secure harbor, and a river with bold and beautiful scenery, which affords facile communication with the great plain at the base of the Andes, Constitucion will be one of the most attractive cities in Chile.

The season was so far advanced that very few flowers were found. Calceolarias, portulaccas, and a parasite on the arborescent cactus, were the most common. In the quebradas, east of the town, the Copigue, with its superb coral-colored and wax-like flowers, is found climbing from tree to tree, and the flowers of the Chupon, mentioned by Dr. Darwin as also common in Chilóe, are quite ornamental. They are of a dark red. Its common name is evidently derived from the verb *chupar*, to suck; its seed-lobes containing a sweet, aromatic, and edible substance, which is thus expressed. Its seed-pods ripen in April; but the flowers were not seen. There is a white Copigue, also; and, by common rumor, one in which the white and coral colors are blended; though no one tells me he has ever seen it. After much care and trouble, a plant has been safely conveyed to the green-house at Washington, where its flowers cannot fail to be among the most admired for their color, graceful form, and velvet-like petals. Though looked for carefully, there were no fossils perceptible in any of the cliffs; and the constant beating of the sea appears to destroy marine shells as fast as they are thrown up. On the island, and in the little rivulet back of the town, a *Nerita* and *Mytilus* were the only fresh-water shells, and a small crab the only crustacea. There is also a crayfish (*astacus*), of which specimens were subsequently obtained, though none were seen at the time of my visit. Each of these is appropriately mentioned by Mr. Charles Girard, to whom the specimens were referred.

April 2.—The day was overcast and raw, threatening rain all the morning. Most of the launches bound up the river were deeply laden with machinery for an extensive flour-mill erecting on the Loncomilla; and, as there was little probability that the voyage to Perales, by which they must pass, would be made short of five days, it seemed preferable to risk waiting for another arrival from above. However, shortly after noon Ñor Nicolás, who was on the look-out, came with intelligence that a fine new boat was about to leave, and if I would hurry to engage passage, the Pilòto would wait until the luggage could be gòt down. Hasty leave was taken of the several gentlemen who had omitted nothing to render my sojourn pleasant; and by 2 P. M. we were gliding up stream before a light westerly wind—the lancheros invoking San Antonio to freshen it, and whistling with all their might. But as it soon died away altogether, their patron saint either regarded them as reprobates unworthy heed, or had "other fish to fry" just then. It was dead low water, and the crew had only got fairly underway with the oars to stem the current, met at two miles above the town, when our attention was called to a horseman riding after us as if for life, and waving a handkerchief like one demented. The boat was at once put on shore. A moment afterward, the owner rode up, furious with passion that the Piloto should have departed without directions—giving vent to his anger with a volubility and selection of language which might grace the annals of Billingsgate, but not my pages. Having received what himself and crew considered proper "sailing orders," under unmerited abuse, the Piloto was equally roused; and, as obedience to the order to return forthwith would cost them the passage-money of six guasos, besides Ñicolás and myself, after tempests of words, the owner was told they would obey, but he might whistle for another crew from the moment they touched the landing, as they would influence every *marinero* in Constitucion against him. How the squabble ended was not learned. Halfway back we met another launch bound up; and making a rapid bargain with the Piloto, my chattels were shifted, and in a few moments more we were again with our faces to the eastward, our craft aided some little by a young flood tide. There is a ferry rather more than two miles above the town, across which a drove of mules were swimming as we passed, the arrieros, with the packs, following in the boat to urge them over, whilst a man on the opposite side constantly tinkled the madrina's bell.

As the afternoon advanced the clouds broke away, and the sun shone through their midst, sending a flood of golden light down the deep quebradas. As the wind freshened we glided before it, the ripple of the water about the bow the only sound disturbing the solitude of nature. A "boatman's song," which such a scene and such freedom from exertion would have inspired among any other people, is perhaps a proof of cultivation unknown to the mariners of the Maule; indeed the only chant heard from the lower classes is the doggerel, Zama-Cueca, so often mentioned. Near sunset, when the shadows fell across the multitudes of ravines, the river views became even finer. The best picture is on the north shore, and some ten miles up stream, where there is an eminence between two quebradas, which terminates abruptly in a semi-elliptical cliff, with a narrow and level plateau at its base, some twelve or fifteen feet above the river. Several plateaus or shelves even more extensive, though without the back landscape, form portions of the margin. Some of them are planted with vines and vegetables; and though the surfaces are mostly covered with loose sand, they produce thriving trees and shrubby plants. Rains here are said to be sufficiently frequent to mature good wheat crops—the initiatory step for which is to fire portions of the forest, as was remarked in descending the river. Even about Constitucion it would be impossible to irrigate artificially to any extent; and at this distance from the sea, the hills rise in altitude at every few hundred yards.

Although it was a bright moonlight night, and the wind was not only fair but also quite strong, we stopped, soon after sunset, at the foot of the Piedra Santa (Holy Rock), some twelve miles above Constitucion; nor could promises of increased passage-money induce the *lancheros* to go on. They say, and say truly, Our work is hard all day; when night comes we must have rest. They therefore moored the boat for the night, and made me a very excellent cabin with willow-branches and canvass. The night having become raw and cold as soon as the sun disappeared, in a little while they had a huge fire burning on the sand bank, its light and flames penetrating to the opposite side of the stream, imparting a more aboriginal character to the scenery and features of the group assembled around it. Finding they had only coarse bread and toasted flour, I gave them two or three pounds of beef, in the hope that the luxury might enliven them, after they had eaten the broth made of it; but the animal appetite satisfied, a pile of sticks was heaped on the fire, each spread a sheep-skin on the sand near it, and was soon asleep, his head and shoulders enveloped in a poncho. Songs or tales form no part of their unintellectual lives. Work, eat, and sleep—they live for nothing else. Ñor Nicolás had opened my almofrez in the little cabin, and composed himself under the thwarts of the boat outside the screen. Passengers and crew alike had forgotten the world, so that there was no prospect to hear marvels of even Santos or Medicos; and as there was no other light than that of the moon and fire, I was glad to follow their example before darkness should render footsteps insecure descending the bank, and a plunge in the Maule terminate journey and life at the same time.

April 3.—A hazy atmosphere without clouds obscured the sun until nine o'clock, after which we had the full power of his rays during the remainder of the day. As we did not leave the Piedra Santa until the sun was well up, I clambered up the bank again in the hope that a copigue might be found with a pod of ripe seed; but there was not one seen, and the only plant in flower was the Jamestown weed (*Datura stramonium*), which grows in abundance in the whole district from Talca to the coast. I never saw it to the northward. Dripping with heavy dew in the early morning, the foliage of the trees was beautiful; but the forest wanted the matins of birds to give it life, or at least an occasional breath of air to send its crystal visitants sparkling to the ground. Utterly silent and motionless as it was, every leaf appeared to have been touched by the icy hand of death. Animation, mobility, are the great desiderata in all the scenery of Chile.

A light breeze sprang up after we got off; but, as it was adverse, and the current had become too strong to be stemmed, the crew took to the shore, and tracked the boat all day without cessation. So strong are some of the rapids that the launch can only be moved by impulses, and, if loaded, the crews of several boats are often necessary to drag and push a single one up the ascent. On these occasions even the man at the steering-oar quits his post to push, managing at the same time to keep the head of the boat in the proper direction. Once or twice he looked at me, as though desiring me to imitate the guaso passengers, and walk round the rapids; but the shingly beaches were too rugged and uninviting to tempt me into imitation of the chap who worked his passage by the canal-boat.

Æolus was more kindly disposed to us as the sun declined, and we glided along with a fresh westerly wind unaided either by oars or drag-rope. Yet, as soon as evening came, a lodging-place was sought, although it was remarkably clear, the wind strong, Los Perales within three leagues, and the morning certain to be calm if the wind should not be adverse. Neither the prospect of double labor next day, nor the promise of an extra dollar for chicha with which to wash down the supper my basket would afford, could tempt them to depart for once from the customs of their forefathers on the river. As the moon was within one day of the full, and the wind would have aided us through the water at the rate of at least four miles an hour, we might easily have reached the landing before ten P. M.; but we passed the night in the same manner as the preceding one.

April 4.—A light breeze from the westward started Nicolás before the dawn; and he was determined the lancheros should sleep no more, even if they did not go onward. No doubt he was as tired as myself of moving at the rate of a mile an hour, and longed to be on horseback once more. Simple, credulous, good creature, in his way, he had been quizzed into the belief that he had been most fortunate in escaping sea-sickness, and greedily swallowed all the stories invented by the piloto and crew to impose on him. This morning they were determined to have revenge for unreasonable interruption of their slumbers as well as to free the boat permanently from his weight; and under their influence, he actually started to walk the remainder of the distance, lest he should at last be compelled to render tribute to Neptune. No doubt he would have completed the walk, had I not compelled him to return on board when toiling so hard among the loose stones. Leaving at 6 A. M., by the most strenuous exertions we accomplished the nine miles in seven hours, passing on the way loaded launches which had left Constitucion on the day before my arrival. Fifteen men were dragging one up a rapid, their own boats left below, to be returned for afterwards by the same united parties. The velocity of the water was not so observable when descending; but now a difference of elevation amounting to more than a foot in twenty or thirty yards was plainly notable. Both ascending and descending the wind was invariably fresher over these spots.

In expectation of our return, the obliging friend who had furnished the guide for Los Perales had sent horses to await us early in the morning; and, as soon as the heat was somewhat moderated, we started for his country residence near Talca. Seen from the hill above the bodega, the valley of the Claro, at its junction with the Maule, is about a mile wide, and for several miles in a northeast direction scarcely changes its breadth. The stream is but a narrow rivulet, with very few native trees near it; and as the banks are steep, and the supply of water limited, no great number of fruit-trees are cultivated. All the land is evidently under the rude tillage of the country; though, from the greater admixture of sand in the soil, and the absence of fertilization which lime and other mineral manures afford in the process of irrigation there, it is not so productive as further east, where water for the fields is drawn from the Maule. The range of hills bounding the western side of the valley rises to a height of seven hundred feet. They are undulating, not much broken by ravines, and are covered with moderate-sized trees to a distance of three or four miles from the river; north of that they are barren. The extremity of the peninsula between the Claro and the Maule, composed to the very base of sand and water-worn stones, is not more than one hundred and fifty feet higher than the streams. There is very little to add to what has already been said respecting the country between the river and Talca. The barren portion is as uninteresting as possible, its only inhabitants being field-rats (*M. longipilis*), a few carrion-birds, the traro (*Caracara vulgaris*), and tieuke (*C. chimanga*), the latter enjoying such exemption from molestation that they scarcely deign to move out of a horseman's way. We reached the chacra of Don ——— soon after sunset, where the two ensuing days were passed; and the hours of agreeable conversation with himself and wife will always prove as pleasant a subject for retrospect as their kind and courteous hospitality forms one for grateful remembrance.

April 7.—Leaving Talca by the main road to the southward, the soil is composed of rolled pebbles, sand, and mineral detritus, producing abundantly whenever water can be brought upon it. It is planted with vines, fruit trees, and garden stuff, intended principally for consumption in the city. After rather more than a league its character changes; there has been no artificial irrigation to supply the fertilizing mineral constituent, and it becomes similar to the tract immediately north of the city. Only a growth of espinos is to be found upon it. Population becomes more sparse, and one only occasionally finds a rancho with its small patch of beans and pumpkins. Two leagues S.S.W. is Cerro Chivato, a semi-elliptic spur from the western range, its most elevated portions attaining a height of three to four hundred feet above the plain. A few shrubby plants, and the arborescent cactus, are the only vegetable specimens on its surface. The concavity is towards the Andes. Rains have not worn many gullies; but where the soil has been thus exposed, it is of a reddish-ochry cast. Along its base, on the whole of the east and southeast sides, there are erratic granite boulders, in many cases of great diameter. The gold mines of Chivato and Chuchunco are on the summit. Both of them have occasionally yielded rich ores, though at this time not more than one dollar of gold is obtained from each hundred pounds of metal extracted. The matrix is composed of quartz, soapstone, pyrites, and other equally valueless substances. These mines have been worked for nearly a hundred years; and as the whole hill is said to be similarly constituted, the supply is inexhaustible. Few persons, however, are willing to risk working mines where the chances of rich deposits are so slender. After heavy rains in winter the poor of the vicinity resort to the ravines through which the largest bodies of water have flowed, where their search is usually rewarded with grains of pure gold. An establishment for separating the metal from its matrix has been erected on the bank of the Maule. After pulverization in the same manner as the silver ores of Atacama, the earthy portions, being lighter, are washed from the trough by constant additions of water; and finally the remaining ground mass, thoroughly mixed with water, is poured down an inclined trough through a species of sieve made of bunches of loose wool. Two or three such washings effectually liberate the gold from its worthless adjuncts. Specimens from these mines form part of the collection brought home by the Expedition.

The Chivato spur, probably a league and a half in length, continues to the Maule. To the eastward the valley appears covered with verdure; and there, the haciendas being supplied with abundance of water, the proprietors are enabled to raise large surplus crops of wheat, which has hitherto either been ground at Talca or sent down the river for shipment to the north. Like the other water-courses which have been mentioned, the Maule above Perales is composed of several small streams, spreading over a bed a mile wide. Its north shore, like that of the Cachapual, is much the higher; the southern being very little above the surface of the water. Thence the plain again gradually rises until, at the distance of ten miles, it is traversed in a northwest direction by the Loncomilla,* bounded by steep banks some thirty feet high. Though too deep to ford even at this season of the year, the main stream of the Maule is not more than thirty-five yards wide; then follow, for the space already mentioned, islands of shingle, with small trees and bushes, and other intersecting rivulets. During winter rains, and in summer when the snow melts rapidly on the lower ranges of the Andes, the islands are sometimes entirely submerged; and for days it is wholly impassable, the launch kept at the ferry not daring to venture on so wild a torrent. Near both shores there are a number of poor ranchos, whose occupants are frequently on the very verge of starvation, their whole winter dependence being the savings from their chacras in autumn, over which the floods may bring destruction.

Immediately after leaving the river the character of the surface soil again changes, and is light sand, so deep that a horse sinks to the fetlocks, though I am credibly informed there is sufficient mould beneath it to produce excellent pasturage (alfalfa) as soon as irrigation is applied. A little further on is Cerro Bobadilla, an eminence east of the road, not above a mile long, and whose greatest height may be 200 feet. More than once it has been of especial interest in the history of the nation: first when fortifications were hastily erected on its summit during the revolution of independence, and more recently as the ground on which General Bulnes posted his army when retreating from the Ñuble. As the highest ground near the main road through the great plain, and commanding the passage of the Maule, it will always be regarded as important by military men seeking advantages. From this to the Loncomilla—three leagues by the road—there is a slightly undulating plain, covered with loose sand, and which has a moderate acclivity from northwest to southeast. Except where irrigated, dwarf bushes are the only species of vegetation. Of these the pichi (*Fabiana imbricata*) is the most abundant. Señor Pissis tells me the same plant thrives in the province of Santiago, though at an elevation of 2,000 feet above the plain. Notwithstanding its actual desolation, and the considerable cost of conveying an adequate supply of water to it, as the land may be made productive, tracts have recently been sold for more than $50 per quadra of about four acres. It is in contemplation to build a town two leagues from the ferry, its lower portion to be bounded by the Loncomilla. The spot thus designated was a part of the field of battle—the scene of a strife whose results have probably no counterpart in history. Along the line of the road and within the triangle enclosed between it, the Maule, and the Loncomilla, houses are extremely frequent. Towards the southern angle the ground is much more broken, still further subdivided, and under more extensive cultivation; indeed, perhaps no part of the province is better attended to.

Two thirds across the plain, by the road, and to the east of the latter, are the houses of Reyes or Urzua, as they have been indiscriminately called, in which Gen. Cruz established his head-quarters when in pursuit of the troops commanded by Gen. Bulnes. They enclose a space 120 yards in a north and south direction, facing the road by rather more than 90 yards from east to west. A corral forms a very large portion of the ground included. Except a single door for the admission of cattle into the corral at the back of the enclosure, the only doors or

* In the Araucanian language *lonco* signifies "head," *milla* "gold."

windows are on the front facing the road. There also, and not fifty yards distant from the road, is an open corridor. Three sides have dwellings and store-rooms; the fourth is an adobe wall, some nine feet high. At the same distance to the west of the road as the houses are to the east, the ground is rather higher than to the north or south; in a line parallel with it, but within short cannon range to the east, and in the direction of Bobadilla, there is a small table-range on the same level. From this to the houses the road is bounded on both sides by close lines of young poplars; so that the occupants of the two ridges are not visible to each other. A couple of miles N.W. of the houses two deep gullies, half a mile apart, cross the triangle in a direction nearly perpendicular to the course of the Loncomilla; of which the nearest bend is perhaps two miles off. All the river-bank traversed by the combatants is vertical; and though there is but little current at the present time, few whom the fears of battle drove to the risk passed safely across its torrent in December.

Eastward and southward of the houses, there are enclosed gardens and vineyards, from ten to one hundred acres in extent, separated from each other by adobe walls. In the same direction, and within cannon range, is the Cerro de Reyes, quite a long and elevated hill; from which, at a late hour of the conflict, both shot and shells were thrown with considerable effect. If one may judge from the resultant mortality, the severest part of the combat took place between the houses and the Cerro de Reyes. There it was that squads of men, separated from their officers, resorted to Indian modes of warfare; and it is asserted that those of Bulnes, in many cases, shot down their own companions. Charity urges one to believe that among the foliage they were unable to distinguish friends from foes; yet those who were eye-witnesses of the struggle discourage the idea. They say that a thirst for blood and pillage raged, and the troops cared not whether it was antagonist or companion who presented himself to quench it.*

At the commencement of the action, the army of Bulnes was posted as follows: on the eminence north of the houses, and his extreme left, two pieces of artillery, supported by three battalions of infantry and a squadron of mounted lancers; to the right of the road eight pieces of artillery, sustained by three battalions of infantry, drawn up in the same line as the last; and in their rear the main body of cavalry, with horses vastly superior to those of his opponent. The reserve consisted of two battalions of infantry. Cruz had two cannon before the north wall, three others in the road, and two on the little eminence to the westward. His extreme right consisted of a battalion of infantry; other two supported the parks last mentioned; a small body of cavalry occupied the Cerro de Reyes; and the main corps was thrown in advance to the left between the gullies and the river. Parts of three infantry battalions occupied positions on the walls and roofs of the houses, or were held in reserve. Such was the disposition of the two armies; and it is quite probable that their numbers were not greatly disproportioned—say about 4,000 men each.

Cruz remained on the roof of the houses until a part of the forces of his opponent, having attained a position in the rear, exposed him to a cross-fire, when he was induced to descend only by the earnest solicitations of his aids. The head-quarters of Bulnes were on the road near the centre of his extended line. There was no eminence near from which to overlook the field and learn how the fate of the day was going—an advantage, though a perilous one, enjoyed by his rival; and it is admitted, that after the order to commence the attack, each body of the government troops fought on its own account.

At the first charge Cruz's cavalry broke in disorder, whether from terror, or because deserted by their officers, cannot be said with certainty; but they made no important subsequent rally; and whilst almost every individual officer has "lived to fight another day," the bodies of four hundred privates were gathered from the sands and pebbles of the Loncomilla. The three pieces of artillery in the road were commanded by a young North American, who had served

*The Administrador of the Casas de Reyes told me he had interred more than 1,200 bodies. If to these be added 400 of Cruz's cavalry drowned, 100 buried by others on the field, and 80 who died in the hospital at Talca, we shall have pretty nearly the loss of life by the battle—1,800 men!

49

unscathed through most of the late war with Mexico, and in this one battle received no less than three wounds, one of which cost him his right arm. He claims to be of good family in Connecticut; to have been educated at West Point; resigned; commanded a volunteer company during the Mexican war; went to California gold-hunting, where his health broke down; and, having taken passage for Concepcion to re-establish it, his countrymen there, then all excitement about the revolution, persuaded him to volunteer in the struggle. As a strongly supported body of cavalry advanced to charge his position, the Chilenos, constituting half his company became excited and impatient, constantly soliciting orders to open their fire, and it was with great difficulty he could restrain them. He "wanted to see the whites of their eyes," (as he told me), and to this end held on until the closed column was within 300 yards. Then he opened his battery with an effect that cost Bulnes some of his best officers, and threw the column into complete disorder. A part of them never drew rein until they were 70 miles from the field of battle, and the Maule between them and cannon-balls. All his company had not his cool, unflinching courage. They were driven from their posts; he was captured soon after; was liberated in an hour or two; and when made prisoner for the second time, was robbed of everything except shirt and pantaloons; in which destitute condition he was left to the skill of such surgeons as could be improvised, and the mercies of a people no little exasperated against North Americans, from the fabulous stories invented against them during the combat. The artillery west of the road was also commanded by an American, of whom his brother in arms speaks in not very flattering terms. The colonel of the battalion facing this last battery told me, that, entertaining some doubt of the fidelity of his men to the government cause, he went to their front, hoping their personal attachment would prevent treachery. He was ordered to storm the guns, and his regiment—drawn up in two lines—followed him briskly, until a discharge of grape broke the front line. This deployed right and left, and for full fifteen minutes he was exposed not only to the grape and canister of the enemy, but also to incessant discharges of musketry from his own rear line. How he had escaped uninjured remained inexplicable. Poor fellow! he soon met an equally sudden, if not so honorable a death!

In a little while the battle was raging from the shores of the Loncomilla to the eastern extremity of Cerro de Reyes—men without officers, officers without troops; for orders were never given from Bulnes's head-quarters, or, if given, could not be delivered to the detachments for whom they were intended. Pillage followed the fall of every individual, until the combat seemed rather for plunder than for the decision of a political question. More than once, wounded officers were murdered for the money and valuables supposed to be about their persons; and even a woman, whilst giving a drink of water to a disabled officer, was deliberately shot in the back by two soldiers. She was known to have obtained several watches and some money during the day, and the savages coveted her spoils. Of course the unfortunate victim whom she was tending shared a like merciless fate.

It was a sweltering day near midsummer. Besides having marched from Bobadilla through the sand after daylight, the army of Bulnes had fought from 7 A. M. until near 3 P. M. A part had fled across the Maule, carrying tidings of his defeat through Talca. Wherever his aids penetrated, hundreds cumbered the field to rise no more; multitudes were gone, none could tell where; and only broken skeletons of regiments could be found maintaining the unholy butchery. Though he had succeeded in firing the houses where his adversary was posted, the flames were immediately extinguished with wine from the jars of Señor Urzua, no water being at hand; and he was well aware that Cruz had too large and too well appointed a reserve under cover to think of surrender. His own reserve had long since been ordered into action, and the only chance for safety was by abandoning his position. Ordering a retreat, he became sensible of his very critical condition by the smallness of the force that assembled at the call; and he pushed back to Bobadilla with less than a thousand men, haste compelling him to abandon the wounded of the hospital established in the rear of head-quarters. A part of Cruz's force followed in pursuit as far as the hospital, of which they took possession. But Bulnes had too much the start; there was not a mounted man among them; and it is quite reasonable to suppose that they also were suffering from the fatigues of such a day. Thus closed the conflict of the 8th of December. During the night, excepting the cavalry of Cruz, and that portion belonging to the army of Bulnes which had crossed the Maule, the dispersed of both sides again collected about their respective standards; and on the morning following the action the revolutionary party was decidedly the strongest.

These are unvarnished facts, derived from eye-witnesses and participants—men whose regard for truth is more powerful than mere party predilections. To this day neither detail nor official account of the battle has been published by government; and how it came about that the general who was pursued from the field became victor without firing another shot, probably will only be known to those who contributed to give so anomalous a result to the revolutionary struggle. The manner in which it was effected is delicately, though unmistakably, insinuated in the letter from Gen. Cruz to the Intendente of Concepcion; and partisans who reside in this vicinity openly charge some of his leading officers with treachery, asserting that the contents of his military chest (some $40,000) was their reward. It is further said that Bulnes would have continued his retreat across the Maule, but that the launches prepared for such emergency had been stolen during the preceding night by a party who came expressly from Talca, confident of his defeat, and desirous to leave no possible chance for his escape. He was among people comparatively hostile; and not only were his men disaffected and deserting every hour, but it is known that his subordinates, having become thoroughly dissatisfied, had assembled in caucus at Chillan, and actually proposed to invest with supremacy the second in command. The officer to whom the offer was made promptly and properly declined the mutinous proposition. An impartial gentleman, who had the very best means of knowing, assured me that, had Bulnes postponed an engagement one week longer, he would not have had three whole regiments to fight with. On the other hand, nearly the entire populace of the country was friendly to Cruz. He purchased every article of provisions needed by the troops, and paid faithfully even for cattle consumed at the Casas de Reyes, though they belonged to the colonel of a regiment then marching against him. The money thus left in the track of his army helped no little to secure the good will felt towards him. Aware of this and of the discontent among the government troops, he was opposed to a conflict; counselling a "masterly inactivity," and a line of march towards the capital, which would enable him to cross the Maule near the Andes. Once to the northward of the river, he was confident resistance would cease, and the triumph of his cause be assured without sacrificing the lives of his fellow-countrymen. For the same reason, when overruled in council respecting the line of march to be followed, instead of forcing Bulnes to a battle, as he might have done anywhere between Chillan and the Loncomilla, he only dogged him from day to day, keeping just far enough behind to prevent an engagement. It may be said that the man who holds certain victory in his hands, yet hesitates about a few lives from humane or patriotic motives, is not competent to the command of an army; and such was probably the fact. Whether the actual result is to be for the advantage of the nation, is a question time is yet to decide.

In anticipation of the visit, Señor ——, the lessee of the Casas de Reyes, had given directions to his administrador to provide for me; and, on returning to the houses after a long day in the saddle, every possible disposition was manifested to supply my wants, as well as to give me information of the prominent events of which they had been the scene. Don —— had jestingly warned me, that the guasos of the neighborhood still looked with dread on the entire range of buildings, because of the arms and legs and heads that came at midnight to the chamber I would occupy seeking bodies to which they had belonged, and that I must be prepared to witness many strange sights and encounter numberless adventures. And there is no doubt that the chamber was haunted! not by remnants of humanity, however, but by multitudes of hungry avengers, impatient for another banquet of blood. Every drop shed on the field seemed to have become a flea, thirsting for retaliation. Nervous from being so long in the sun without food, or even water, bed proved no place of repose, and I was heartily glad when dawn permitted me to surrender it to the tormentors.

April 8.—I returned to Talca from Loncomilla on (this) Thursday of holy week, when all the stores were closed and its population as though dead. Even the vigilantes were not visible, until near the plaza; so that I passed on horseback without question direct to the Intendencia. As no one but the police, the curate, or the doctor is permitted to enter a city, except on foot, from Wednesday morning till Saturday noon, no little surprise was manifested that I should have escaped arrest for violation of a custom universal in towns of the republic. Fortunately, my accomplished host was omnipotent had the reverse been the case, and, I doubt not, would have exhibited the generosity and courtesy with which he untiringly distinguished his stranger guest.*

A like silence and solitude were observed in the streets throughout the day, and it was dark before evidence of animation appeared; and then such life! Bells being prohibited, as soon as the men with their matracas began their clatter on the church tops, groups of two or three, and sometimes a dozen, issued from each house, uttering aves in loud tones as they passed from church to church. Soon the city was like a swarming hive; and, it being the fashion, we visited the churches of most note, though, it must be confessed, our party were not so much influenced by religious feelings as by desire to see the illuminations. To increase the perspective effect, screens were arranged before the altar of one as before the scenery on the stage of a theatre. Its altar and back-ground were crowded with images dressed in the usual style, and brilliantly lighted up. Another had a pyramid of lights also arranged for pomp not less than pretty effect. All were filled with audibly praying multitudes, and each had at least a pair of extravagantly equipped Saints near the door, at whose feet sat boys with salvers asking alms from every passer-by—"*para Maria Santissima, nuestra madre*," or "*San Francisco*," or other, as the case might be. In front of the door, there were prisoners under charge of armed guards, who besought "*una limosnita por el amor de Dios*," (a little alms for the love of God,) clanking their chains to influence more powerfully the compassion of the superstitious crowds who passed to their estaciones. According to custom, the military band came to the Intendencia at 9 o'clock, for nearly an hour entertaining the friends assembled there with well played music, and afterwards diverting the populace in the plaza for a longer time. Among the performers was a drummer who had served during the revolutionary campaign, and whose stature certainly was not more than twice that of the instrument he bore. On the field of Loncomilla he was humanely placed, with a companion very little older than himself, in a rancho, beyond the reach of balls—an arrangement to him by no means satisfactory. He was anxious to accompany his battalion in their fratricidal conflict, and actually stole out to do so, contrary to the orders of his colonel. Many of them, poor fellows, lived not to hear the retreat he helped to sound that afternoon, or to wonder at his premature gravity and thoughtfulness. Though scarcely eight years old, he is never known to smile or participate in the plays of boyhood, but constantly maintains a reserved and military deportment that would well become an old guardsman.

April 9.—Until towards noon, Friday was equally death-like in the town. So rigidly do Talquinos mortify the flesh by fasting during passion week, that even the market people had few purchasers for their commodities. At noon, sermons in the churches drew many out again; and, at a later hour, large numbers visited a cross erected a year or two ago by a Jesuit missionary, near the northern entrance to the city. He had been refused permission to put it up by the Intendente of Copiapó and one or two other chiefs of provinces,—men who knew the tendencies of the populace, and were unwilling to contribute to superstitious idolatry,—and had brought it along with him through the country until successful through a late Intendente

* Most sincerely do I lament that he has not lived to peruse these lines. Coming to the capital in the following month, he was taken ill suddenly at the baths of Colina, and died before medical aid could reach him. A finished scholar, an ardent lover of his country, brave to a fault, yet modest and retiring as a woman—Chile could ill afford to lose so courteous and accomplished a gentleman.

here. Of course, a box is left at its foot; and there the faithful may leave donations, with which many hope to pay their way to heaven. Inviting as is the alameda, and charming as was the afternoon, none were tempted to promenade its shady walks, and almost the only persons to be seen abroad were those going to or returning from the Jesuit's cross. A procession, to be followed by a sermon in the plaza, was promised for the night, and multitudes flocked to San Francisco at sunset to witness the display; but the Padre had had the misfortune to lose his sermon by fire only a day or two before, and as there was not time to write another for so important an occasion, the crowd was disappointed. Music, as last night, closed the festivals for the day.

April 10.—As early as 10 o'clock, the ringing of bells announced to the public that the days of tribulation were passed, the hour for rejoicing had come; and scarcely were the first peals struck than guasos and peons, like condors towards their prey, were to be seen flocking from all directions. To get beyond the bell-clattering and noises of exploding fire-works near every church in town, I rambled to Monte Baeza (Baeza woods), a low semicircular basin of slight depression just without the N.E. suburbs. Here water oozes from the earth on all sides of the amphitheatre, and forms several small rivulets, which are finally collected into one and brought into the city. The entire basin is covered with a growth of fine trees and vines, whose foliage is so dense that the sun rarely penetrates many portions. A retreat so cool and charmingly pleasant might be rendered an attractive public resort at very small cost. There are singing birds in numbers, and multitudes of crayfish, but no other varieties of animal life in the small portion it was prudent to penetrate without a guide.

Easter Sunday.—At 7 o'clock in the morning there was a procession from the church of San Francisco to the plaza, composed of the clergy, the friars, the specially devout laity, all with wax candles, and a company of the civic battalion, with their military band. During the preceding night a triumphal arch, flanked by trees and decorated with flags, had been erected near the centre of the plaza; and as an image of "Christ risen" approached from the westward, other representations of the Virgin and Mary Magdalen were brought from the two opposite directions to receive him under the trophies of rejoicing. The meeting was well-timed—the effect pretty; and were it possible to divest one's self of the knowledge that the object of these displays is but to bind more strongly the fetters of superstition, the pageant might be applauded. Justice to the ladies or others at Talca, who have the decoration and attitudes of the saintly images to arrange, requires the acknowledgment that they exhibit much better taste and more grace than similar representations at Santiago. Christ was represented in a mass of clouds; the Virgin amid angels; and Mary Magdalen just leaving her house, placed in a garden of miniature trees and flowers. True, the clouds were but folds of muslin, the angels were clad in robes whose curtness would have shocked Taglioni or Ellsler, and the domicil of the Magdalen was more like the temple of Vesta, at Tivoli, than the one we would suppose occupied by the sinning Galilean; but these are liberties the church allows, or its ministers take, as novel writers do with chronology. After a march through two or three streets, the procession again came to the plaza, where another image, dressed in scarlet, representing Judas, and loaded with pyrotechnics, was set fire to, greatly to the edification of the children and rabble. This was the last of the ceremonies it was permitted me to witness in Talca. A few friends, made in the brief visit, were at the door of the Intendencia to wish me "God speed;" my horses had been in waiting for an hour; and before 9 o'clock I had crossed its plaza for the last time.

Reached the Lircay ford at 9½ o'clock, and the Pangui at 10½. The country, as far as the region of the tufa, has been more cultivated than was supposed when first passed over; and there are several small tracts of ground ploughed for wheat, to be matured by rains. It is rare that the tufa is found more than two feet thick. Its stratum sometimes crops out, and at others lies as much as three feet below the surface. Invariably there is vegetable soil below it.

Not far from the midway "posada," a flock of condors, gorging themselves on the body of an unfortunate mule that had died near the road side, were so intently occupied in the repast that they scarcely moved at our approach. Others were sweeping in gradually diminishing circles round the spot; and yet there were numbers at loftier elevations, evidently seeking the object to which their powers of scent (vision?) directed them, though the faculty of vision (scent?) had not yet enabled them to detect the precise spot where lay the prey. Some could not have measured less than twelve feet from tip to tip of the wings, and there were more full grown, old birds than I had ever seen collected together.

The posada was reached in four hours from Talca; and as the rate of travel had not exceeded an average of five and a half miles per hour, the distance is about twenty-two miles. By a mean of three barometrical measurements on two days, the elevation of the table-land on which it is built is 1,030 feet above the sea, or a rise of nearly nineteen feet per mile. Thence northward, as far as the banks of the Claro, the impression of absolute sterility, formed when passing over the ground before, is not wholly true. As it is to the southward, here also are small tracts sown in wheat, similarly dependent on natural irrigation; but, as has been said, the surface of the greater portion is indurated sand, resting on tufa, and destitute of herbage. Between the posada and the ford of the Claro two or three ravines cross the plain, perhaps thirty feet deep below the general level. Minute ribands of water flow westward through these; but where the road traverses them, the only habitations are ranchos of the most wretched description, that have very limited amounts of cultivated land in their immediate vicinity. To the Claro ford the distance is fourteen miles. After so much barren country, the approach to it is rendered more notable from a line of poplars extending more than a mile from east to west, while to the eastward there is a spot at the angle of a glen, formed by two spurs from the chain of the Andes, wonderfully resembling a distant city. From the Claro to Quechereguas, five miles, there being a superabundance of water from the Lontue, a perfect garden spot might be made. It is tolerably well cultivated; and a part of its fields, between which lies the highway, are bounded by rows of immense poplars from the northern entrance of Villa Molina to the Rio Seco, an arm of the Lontue, nearly a league distant. From these autumn had already stripped more than half the foliage. Three barometrical observations at the inn here on two days, give the height of the plain as 1,170 feet.

As it is by far the best found south of Rancagua, one word about the posada of Quechereguas, for the benefit of some future traveller. Its proprietor, an old, wheezy, and asthmatic Spaniard, though very courteous and civil, leaves most of the talking to his more attentive and energetic wife. In addition to the never-failing casuela, one may really obtain most of the wants of life—a cup of good tea, a bottle of sound wine, and no doubt a bed, if desired. The servants, too, have been well trained, and are kept in good discipline by the old lady, who nightly assembles all hands at prayers, of which, if the quality be not edifying, the quantity is sufficient, as I can vouch.

April 12.—Nicolás had packed the mule before sunrise, and at the first peep of the god of day over the Andes we rode out of the posada. A more delicious morning is rarely seen; its clear fresh air, loaded with the balmy odor of wild mint flowers that literally covered a part of the plain. The black outlines of the mountains had lost none of their sharpness of definition, as they do at a later hour of the day under the heat of the sun; while the Descabezado, now a little to the south of east, and the ragged peaks of Cauquenes, northward of San Fernando, all rose grandly against the sky. Away to the N.W., where the Mataquito passes through the Western cordilleras, clouds were pouring into the valley in a thin sheet, so purely white in the reflected light that it was difficult to believe unexpected winter had not enveloped them to the plain in a mantle of snow. As the sun gained power, the dew evaporated, settling in strata of filmy vapor against the mountain sides on either hand; and the volume from the coast, meeting the heated rays, broke into cumuli tinged with almost every color.

There are five streams forming the Lontue where the road passes it. Of these the first and smallest is within a league of Quechereguas; the other four all within two miles of the first. Each discharges a considerable volume of water. The third, or central, is the deepest and most rapid, and is so rarely fordable that a suspension bridge has been thrown across it. I was doubtful for a moment whether to risk the bridge or try the ford somewhat lower down. Ñor Nicolás had got out of hearing ahead, the shingle beach afforded no indication where the ford was, and there was no way to test the depth of the stream but by actual experiment, whilst the rickety condition and vibratory propensity of the bridge were by no means inviting. Recollecting that a very small strip of raw hide will bear a considerable weight, as there was no time for much deliberation, it seemed better to try the bridge than risk a cold bath in an unknown stream with one's boots and poncho on. But, in order to distribute the weight as much as possible, and at the same time endeavor to check the oscillation, I dismounted, took the extremity of the bridle, and started to lead my horse over the foaming torrent. As soon as the vibration began, he resisted, and in an instant more stood still from terror. Nor could he be induced to move until the motion had entirely ceased. When over the very deepest part of the roaring waters, and the swinging had again commenced, his foot caught among the badly tied sticks. Here was a fix! To await the chance of a passing guaso, *au fait* in such difficulties, was out of the question. The animal was too restless and alarmed, and would inevitably have kicked all his legs through in two minutes, even if he did not knock away the whole portion we stood upon. There was no alternative but to approach and liberate him promptly. Quickly laying boots and poncho aside, the better to be ready for a swim in case of necessity, the bridle was gathered in at each inch of my advance; and no one ever tried harder to imitate the soothing and coaxing terms of the guaso than I did. I fancied myself quite successful; for after extricating him, although the bridge swung more violently than ever during the rest of our transit, he went over beside me without hesitation, actually standing perfectly quiet while my clothing was donned again. It would be difficult to say which was most rejoiced to set foot on terra firma—horse or rider.

Beyond the Lontue the valley becomes narrower, and its acclivity is plainly perceptible. To Curicó, twelve miles N.N.E. from Quechereguas, the country is tolerably well populated. The land is good, and apparently it produces well. The town lies at the base of a little isolated hill, four or five leagues distant from the western range; and the white tower of one of its churches is perceptible to the southward of the hill as you approach it from either north or south: but as the body of the population is on the southwest side, and its low houses are completely embowered in trees, one is in its streets before it can be fairly seen. It contains 7,000 inhabitants; is regularly built; has three churches, paved streets, a good supply of water from a clear little stream flowing from the Andes, and a handsome alameda; though there is not a single attractive building in all its limits. The Lancers, whom we passed when crossing the Claro, were lounging in its alameda; and at this early hour of the morning, a number of citizens in its streets gave to it quite a lively appearance. Near the summit of the hill a cross marks the position of its cemetery, to which there is an ascent by a tedious zigzag road on the west side. Just below it is the only house claiming to be a posada. This possesses one small room with a single bedstead. Usually one may obtain a casuela within an hour; but here more than two elapsed before it could be got ready, and then it was made badly enough. The poor landlady was sufficiently humble in her exculpatory apologies: "The patron was in a hurry—in trying to catch the chickens quickly, they had been frightened into the vineyard—she could only find these poor bits of mutton at the plaza—there was nothing but small sticks of firewood, and these would hardly make the olla boil—so the patron must give her another opportunity to show what she could do." And thus the sun had passed the meridian when Nicolás came to say our horses were ready again. An old gentleman who had the kindness to serve as guide to the posada, and with whom I walked through the town whilst breakfast was preparing, told me that it was customary for travellers to stop at the first house whose appearance they liked, and ask hospitality—a request rarely, if ever, declined. As it is a national practice that has existed from time immemorial, and there are very few strangers travelling in the country, public houses cannot very well prosper.

There are two schools in Curicó. One for boys, in which Latin and French as well as the ordinary branches of education are taught, had 45 scholars. The number of pupils in that for girls could not be learned. Both these are at the cost of the municipality, who also support teachers for two primary schools, at which the attendance is small and very irregular.

At 10 A. M. the barometer stood at 28.854 inches, corresponding to an elevation of 1,070 feet.

After leaving Curicó, the first five miles are over a slightly elevated road, with good soil, plenty of water, and cultivation on both sides, according to the mode known here. Then follow two miles of barren and hilly country like that to be mentioned directly. On the border of the Teno—a clear stream flowing into the Mataquito four leagues below—there is some vegetation. Immediately after crossing it, however, the land rises quite rapidly; and from one range of mountains to the other, it is broken into an infinity of hillocks of every imaginable form, though none of them rise more than 20 or 30 feet above the general surface. For twelve miles in the direction of the road, the entire valley, from chain to chain, is a complete desert—the surface of the ground being covered with broken rocks and pebbles which do not seem to have undergone much attrition. One huge boulder stands off to the east of the road, a monument in the midst of desolation. Two or three pretty flowers clinging to the ground find sustenance even on this arid surface; and the little snipe-shaped bird (Certhilauda?), common on the sands between Caldera and the city of Copiapó, also finds a home here. The tract is called "*Los Cerrillos de Teno,*" and is, apparently, a uniform and regular dike, upheaved to a height of one hundred feet from the Andes to the Western cordilleras, on whose surface these hillocks lie.

Descending from them to the plain across which the Chimbarongo creek flows, abundant vegetation is again met with; the distance between the two mountain chains begins to diminish, and continues to do so with rapidity as we proceed north, until they are not more than nine miles apart. Indeed, an oval hill between them, and a little to the south of the Tinguiririca, makes them seem still closer to each other than they really are. It was hoped something might be had for ourselves as well as our horses at the posada of Chimbarongo; but, as when we passed previously, its proprietors and servants were away, and there were only two or three half-naked childen, who were amusing themselves turning somersaults in a pile of straw. It was already five o'clock; and the western sky was covered with clouds, boding no good to the equestrian traveller at this advanced season. The Tinguiririca had to be crossed; and as there was no ascertaining when our necessities might be supplied, it became of primary importance to push on, rather than risk rain in such a den next day. Yet a little later, and when the proximity of the road to the western range caused the disappearance of the sun to us long before it set, it was no little gratifying to see the masses of leaden-colored clouds converted into a crimson canopy, and the distant snow-covered summits of the Andes illuminated with rosy-orange tints. During the last ten miles, the valley is scarcely that many in width, but evidences the advantages which irrigation from the river produces. It supports a larger population, and, in consequence, there is much more animation than in the vicinity of Curicó. From neglect to drain it properly, a part of the land has become swampy. On this, flocks of that pretty ibis, *Fallicinellus*, with its changeable hues of green; garzas (*Ardea egretta*); and taguas (*Gallinula crassirostris*), were feeding quietly, utterly indifferent to the passer-by. As it was night when we reached the ford, Ñor Nicolás took the lead across the pebbly bed; and so slowly were we obliged to proceed through the two milky torrents in the dark, that it was half-past 7 o'clock when we reached the posada at the northern entrance of San Fernando.

The town is nearly a league from the Tinguiririca, and about the same distance from the base of the Western cordilleras. Its compactly built houses cover half a mile square; its location, below the winter floods of the Tinguiririca and Antinero creek, being most unfortunate. Though larger than Curicó, like it the houses and streets are rude and wretched to appearance—the latter, in many cases, being only paved on one side, and the former, low and incommodious. Including the suburbs, its population is estimated at 12,000 souls, for whom, strange to relate, there are only two churches, and these are far worse looking than many in the hamlets of the country. The suburbs extend more than half a mile in each direction from the closely built portion of the town—each house having an enclosed field and garden. From a mean of three barometrical observations on as many days, the height of San Fernando above the ocean is 1,410 feet.

There are three principal establishments for education here—two for boys, and one for girls—all at the expense of the public. The "Literary Lyceum," established by government, seems to have been unpopular from the time of its creation, and has never attracted many scholars to its halls of gratuitous learning. The other school for boys, called "Union College," has been recently established; and as it is directed by a competent person, it is to be hoped that he will prove more successful. The school statistics of San Fernando, published during our residence in Chile, show a much smaller number of pupils attending them than is proper for even a Hispano-American population. It was complained of at the time by government, whose editor believed that it was owing either to reprehensible negligence, or the desire of parents to send their children to the more perfect schools at Santiago. In these schools, the Intendente says, the "pupils who ordinarily attend" number 100; but it is very certain that the number was scarcely more than half as great in 1852.

Just without the town to the north is Tambo creek, now nearly dry. It penetrates the Western cordilleras, leaving bold promontories close to each other on either side; and a hill properly belonging to that chain is thus within the plain. There is also a spur which extends in a southwest direction from the Andes towards the hill of Tambo, or Minas, as some of the guasos called it; so that at five leagues from San Fernando the two ranges are not a hundred yards apart. A little streamlet winds closely along the southeast base of the Andean spur, and passes through the Angostura Requelemu to the northward. In the dry season its waters are wholly lost in the pebbly bed of the pass or gorge; but the abundance of verdure to the southwest on the northern side of the hill separated from the western cordillera, is evidence of its reappearance within a short distance, and use for irrigation. Passing the Requelemu, one is again enclosed by hills to the north scarcely a league distant, through which there is a somewhat similar pass into the plain or basin of Rengo.

The luxuriant growth of espinos, with which the upper extremity of the plain of San Fernando is covered, was fairly alive with birds, apparently rejoicing in the absence of the sun or envious of each other, from the shrillness with which their several notes were whistled. Loicas (*Sturnella militaris*), tordas (*Agelaius curæus*), trencas (*Mimus thenca*), loros (*Cornurus cyanalysios*), even the discordant queltregue (*Vanellus cayennensis*), each seemed striving to make the greatest clatter among the undergrowth of thistles where they were seeking food. And along the fences here, and very frequently elsewhere in Chile, formed from branches of espinos piled against posts, there were multitudes of field-rats (*M. longipilis*), not unlike squirrels, with their long, curled, and somewhat bushy tails and erect posture. Dozens of them sit inquisitively in the road, with quite the grey squirrel's attitude, until the traveller is near, when they scud to their holes beneath the brushwood.

Dense volumes of clouds concealed the summits of all the mountains, and in some directions extended so far into the ravines as to prevent a satisfactory view of the valley to the northward of the hill cut off by the Tambo. Coming into that of Colchagua, or as it was called above, Rengo, the pass is over a road elevated some fifty feet above the plain, and is extremely short. Beyond it, within a brief half hour's travel of a tired horse, the cordillera due west is twenty miles away; and though the near range of the Andes is closer, one sees, at every step to the northward, how the valley widens. It was no little grateful to the eye to come amid verdure again; not verdant belts and patches by the river banks, but a broad plain and the mountain sides, as far up as the clouds permitted them to be visible, profusely covered with vegetation. In every direction the laborers and inquilinos were gathering their small harvests; and every rancho had its pile of red peppers spread on the earth to dry, most of their denizens being busily engaged in threshing or treading out the bean-crops.

Within a mile of the pass, and between deep banks, is an arm of another Claro, a small stream that originates in the eastern ranges of the Andes, crosses the plain in a W.N.W. direction, and unites its waters with the Rapel near the Western cordilleras. A little farther to the northward is the principal volume, even at this season not more than forty feet across. On its border lies the village of Rengo. This has but one irregular and unpaved street; though, as has been already remarked, many of its houses have more than ordinary claims to elegance, and its single thoroughfare exhibits more of life and animation than any town southward of Santiago, Constitucion not excepted. The population numbers about two thousand, for whose spiritual welfare there is one well constructed church near its centre. But what most elicits the attention of the passer is the handsome features of the women, an ugly one being rare in the street. True, most of those seen belonged to the humbler classes—wives and daughters of mechanics and laborers—among even the aged of whom there was a degree of beauty still preserved. Doñas of "sangre azul" might not have cared to appear in sunlight when travellers would be passing through the town. This physical advantage had attracted attention when riding through previously. Then it was thought that the individuals seen were possibly exceptions to the mass, not a peculiarity of the mass itself; but as it now became necessary to remain for an hour whilst dinner was preparing, there was ample time to become convinced that pretty faces were decidedly in the majority. Its posadas are by no means recommendable. The one having the most attractive sign-board was first applied to; but it possessed only the fowls pecking about the yard. There was no fire; neither vegetables nor a bottle of chicha, strange to say for a country teeming with productions; and its proprietor was sick in its only room. However, instead of keeping me waiting for the real or two he might have gained, the poor man had the honesty to recommend a neighbor across the way; and though the supplies there were not much more abundant, no one could have made greater exertions to expedite my journey than did its hostess, her servant coming in search of me before a ramble through the town could be completed. Finding, shortly afterwards, a reptile in the garden which would have been an interesting addition to our collection, it was taken to the house in the hope that a suitable bottle might be obtained for its preservation. Had I been the "imp of darkness," with the symbol of eternal punishment in hand, greater terror could not have been displayed by the hostess and one or two friends who had dropped in, all of whom ran shrieking to the streets. Nor would they return until satisfied that death had rendered the serpent perfectly harmless. As there were only wine bottles about the premises, and there was no mode of carrying such bulk many miles, each of the party went in search of a suitable receptacle for the prize with as much earnestness as though devoted students of natural history. Unfortunately their mission proved fruitless. A number were brought, but those whose necks would admit the prize were too large for any pocket; the holsters were already crammed; Ñor Nicolás had gone ahead with the luggage; and herpetologists have lost a treasure.

By night-fall I reached the hacienda of a friend, where the following day was passed in the enjoyment of rest and courteous hospitality. Situated, as is his residence, near the high road, one sees quite as much of life as in the populous city—mule-trains, ox-carts, and horsemen, passing in a continual stream from morning till night. Pedestrians only are wanting; but the poor guaso, even, is too indolent and too proud to walk, and must have out his horse if the journey be only for a mile. Wife and children are often piled on the same animal; and as his saddle may be composed of twenty skins, each of which lies in its particular place, not unfrequently as much time is consumed in equipping the horse as in making the journey afterwards. The tinkle of the madrina's bells, the loud cries of arrieros as some hungry animal steps aside to crop a mouthful of herbage or a bite of melon-rind, the creak of cart-wheels as the cumbrous vehicles drag slowly along, and the various costumes of their attendants, afford no little of distraction in country-life. These are not all however.

The district from the Cachapual to the Claro last named is one of the best irrigated in all the republic; and though pebbles and sand to an extraordinary extent have been disseminated through the soil by successive floods, one cannot fail to take pleasure in witnessing the fecundity of every foot of ground, and appreciate the beneficence of nature in affording natural means for its annual renovation. In the south, or rather in the vicinity of Talca, land must be left fallow for a year or two, that it may recover from the exhaustion of a crop. Here, as in the valley of the Maypu, the mineral manure deposited each season is precisely suited to the sandy and porous soil, and fully compensates for what the crop of wheat or corn may absorb. A few years ago all the space between lines along the centres of the Andes and Western cordilleras, the Cachapual and Claro, belonged to one proprietor! Recently a part was sold, and other portions rented to various individuals. That in possession of the friend mentioned contained sixteen thousand acres, the whole of which lies in the plain; and nearly all of it is cultivated in wheat, corn, and alfalfa, as pasture-lands to fatten cattle for market, and as small chacras apportioned to the inquilinos and other laborers on the estate. On the original tract its proprietor established a residence near the centre, building a chapel there at a cost of some thirty thousand dollars. A curate is still supported at his expense, and the more than thousand souls remaining within his principality have no need to seek spiritual counsel elsewhere. The chapel is in good taste, both within and externally; and its altar, pulpit, and decorations are in a style superior to a very large number erected from the public purse. A few leagues east of Santiago the same gentleman has erected a second church at scarcely less cost, and there also supports a curate.

April 15.—On the previous evening Ñor Nicolás was despatched across the Cachapual, to ascertain whether the friends who contemplated a visit to the baths of Cauquenes had passed up the river; in which case he was directed to return with the mules as far as the ford. A visitor to these springs must go well provided, be sure he has a friend there ready to see to him, or expect to adopt the plan bears are said to do when hungry and have not wherewithal to satisfy appetite. At least such was the account given to me, and hence the apparent importance of the information Nicolás was to obtain.

So dense a fog poured over the Central cordilleras into the valley before sunrise, that vision only extended a rod or two on each side of the road, and brisk riding accumulated moisture so rapidly on the eyelids as to become annoying. Of course no proper estimate could be formed of the landscape until the sun had risen high enough to drive the mist to the upper regions of the air in gradually dispersing cumuli. By this time I had reached Rio Seco—a former bed, though now only a small branch, of the Cachapual, distant two miles from the principal stream. The old bed is three hundred yards wide; the stream itself scarcely thirty feet, with a depth of two feet at the centre of the ford, and a current of two miles per hour, or about half that of the principal volume. As the old guíde was not at the posada here, it was supposed that the visit proposed by my friends had been deferred; and the saddle-girths were tightened preparatory to stemming the streams at the several fords. But they had gone nevertheless, and Nicolás, mindful of the journey before us, had halted on the dry bed of the river nearest where we must begin its ascent, and where I would of necessity pass. His thoughtfulness saved at least two leagues to the animals with him, and they of the worst character of shingle road.

Two miles above the ford nearest Rancagua, the path temporarily leaves the river, and passes up and along the face of a steep hill bounding the southern shore, and against which nearly the whole volume of water is here forced. Had I been pre-advised that it was necessary to cross an eminence six or seven hundred feet high, whose surface was mainly small loose fragments of metamorphic porphyry,—sometimes in a path scarce two hands in width, and on the edge of a vertical cliff with a torrent of rushing water three hundred feet below; at others ascending at angles of 40°, each step of the horse starting the sliding mass of fragments into the boiling stream,—doubtful as appeared to be the footing of my horse, I would have encountered a longer journey by a road more directly across the plain. But we had already crossed several deep and rapid canals for supplying water to the estates; Nicolás, accustomed from childhood to gallop headlong up or down mountains, insisted there was no danger; and, as he promised a first-rate *road* as soon as we passed one other hill, there was no alternative but to follow him. Moreover, he had no acquaintance with the other road, and to turn back now was to risk passing the night in the mountains with only a rock or tree for a shelter.

From the ford to the baths the distance is rather more than seven leagues. The first two and a half are of the character just described, varied by an occasional descent to the river-bed, along which the horse must pick his way among loose stones and sand-knolls, thrown up by occasional changes of the course of the stream during freshets. Scanty natural vegetation may be found on all these knolls, and the hill-sides abound with dwarf palqui (*cestrum p?*) bushes and arborescent cacti; the latter beautiful only from their forms, and the clusters of scarlet quintral blossoms crowning their highest arms. Here the river is departed from; its course is more from the northward; that of the good bridle-road now entered on, southeasterly, until passing the houses of the estate to which the baths belong. A narrow stream of limpid water, flowing from the latter direction, and called the Rio Cauquenes, serves to irrigate a portion of the table-land on its banks, its surplus falling into the Cachapual at this place. Within another mile the road winds up and around the southern base of an arid hill, and one is wholly within the Andes. Distance has already softened the hues of the hills near the ford; the noise of the river can no longer be heard; before you stand forests whose ever-vital foliage is more obscure than the olive-leaf in color; and away to the eastward, above the summits of mountains thus clad, tower the barren and ragged snow-cliffs. Though traversable only on foot or by equestrians, the last five leagues of the road are perfectly safe and comparatively good. Exquisite mountain-views are constantly afforded: sometimes of small verdant terraces at the base of lofty hills, yet high above the surface of the river; at others of bold headlands round which the stream sweeps in a graceful curve, a mass of foam marking every obstacle to its impetuosity; and again of deep ravines strewn with enormous fragments tumbled from the surrounding rocky hills by the mighty internal power that so often shakes this quarter of the globe. Within the second of the last five leagues we again approach the river; and thence to the end of the journey the path never departs so far that its voice may not be heard amid the forests of boldo, litre, quillay, and peumo, adorning the hill-sides. Each of these trees is of note: the first, from the aromatic odor of its leaves, and their extremely dark hue; the litre, from the silvery clusters of berries pendent amid its glossy foliage; the quillay, from the excellent qualities of its bark; and the peumo, from the crimson hue of its now just ripening fruit.

The third Claro that I have named, a small silvery stream from the southeast, unites its waters with the turbid torrent from the Andes, within a league of the baths. It is a very short, though not very rapid stream, originating within the outer range of the Andes. Some of the guasos told me that it was supplied from the surplus of Lake Cauquenes; though M. Gay places this small mountain deposit some distance to the westward, with a range of mountains between it and the head-waters of the Claro. The lake is smaller than that of Aculeo, but, like it, abounds in fine fish and wild fowl of the same varieties: truchas (*Perca trucha*), vagres (*Trychomycterus maculatus*), and pejereys (*Basilichthys microlepidotus*), being the greatest table favorites among the finny tribe; swans, an infinite variety of ducks, flamingos, planetas (*Platalea ajaja*), pillos (*Ciconia pillus*), and cuervos, forming a portion, and the most conspicuous, among the feathered race. A like origin is assigned by the guasos to the river Cauquenes.

Above the Claro the ground is more broken, and the hills smaller and closer together. As the road along their northern slopes becomes more undulating, every few moments of travel brings new and more picturesque scenes to view, eliciting admiration and astonishment. One of the most remarkable eminences is on the same side, and just beyond the Claro. It is a mountain with a summit a thousand feet above the stream, whose northern face is strewn with untold millions of blocks of metamorphic porphyry broken from its crest, and leaving it for more than half a mile a vertical blackened wall resembling a great battlement that had encountered the fire of artillery during ages. As the upper and lower lines of the vertical palisades are nearly parallel, and there are occasional breaks in them, not unlike embrazures in the twilight, it might very readily be supposed a fortress. On the south bank, also, and within sight of the baths, there are immense granite boulders, one of them containing more than 2,000 cubic feet. They lie on a narrow terrace more than 150 feet above the river, and there is no granite cropping out of any of the surrounding hills. Whence came these great blocks?*

Whilst I halted beneath the peumos, near the Claro, and made a breakfast of bread supplied from the alforjas (saddle-bags) of Ñor Nicolás, and a horn of water from its clear stream, he had pushed on to the houses at the baths, and sought the apartments of my friends, so that they were awaiting me with no little impatience as the tired horse plodded over the last portion of the journey.

On a triangular terrace, or plateau, at the immediate base of a hill that rises nearly a thousand feet above it, and which terminates in a vertical cliff over the river, the mineral waters of Cauquenes are found; and here houses have been built for the use of invalids. The plateau will measure about three acres. Within a few hundred yards, up the stream, a somewhat similar hill to the one back of the springs rises to nearly the same height; and between the two there is a deep quebrada with a rivulet of clear snow-water. Opposite the up-stream hill, on the other side of the river, there are other small terraces, behind which rise series of steep mountains, also covered with perennial verdure. Between the two hills last mentioned, and whose bases are scarcely 150 yards apart, is the gorge through which the river flows, exhibiting other mountain buttresses close at hand. Their summits are widely enough separated to permit a view of the dreary peaks of the loftiest, and still far off, Andes. Hill beyond hill, as they are arranged, the perspective is so foreshortened that the snow-cliffs seem almost at hand; and about sunset so distinctly are the shadows marked, that one thinks them accessible in a walk of an hour or two; yet an active horseman will be two long days climbing to their crests.

The terraces are now 150 feet higher than the surface of the river, their faces broken down vertically by its furious and muddy torrent. Just above the baths the latter is separated into two streams by a pyramidal mass of rock. This has nearly the same height as the plateau, and is connected with the terrace of the springs above the water-line. There is a like pile of rock between it and the north shore, so that the entire volume of water is again collected in a stream not more than ten yards wide. At night, when everything is still, the roar of the waters through this narrow pass is equal to that of the ocean breaking on a lonely beach. So rapid is it that no one has as yet been able to ascertain its depth at this point. Along the bed there are large boulders of granite and limestone, over which the water is forced by its descending momentum, presenting to the sight a surface broken like a miniature sea. Within an oval panorama, scarce a league in its longer diameter, the eye embraces blackened masses of rock, on which fire seems to have exercised its influence but yesterday, tumbled in every possible direction—sometimes in the streams, sometimes in broad patches of the hills as though injected through the broken up surface; now with columnar faces, like basalt where the mountain tops had been convulsed; again of the size and form of habitations without their concomitants of human life. In one place there is a dense forest; in another a solitary tree, an arborescent cactus, or a Chaüar, (Molina, *Puya*), with its gigantic spike of flowerets conspicuous against the blue sky. On one side we see a patch of wild pasture, golden in its decay; opposite, a level and narrow glen covered with foliage variant only in its hues of green; above and around there are mountains whose slopes and heights are of every graceful curve and inequality; and

* "This second fact is yet more remarkable, and M. Gay has known how to appreciate all its importance.

"On the hacienda of Cauquenes he observed it with all its developments. The valleys of this district are, as we have just described, formed with steep walls composed only of basalt or analogous rocks. No other rocks are seen, says M. Gay, for twenty leagues round.

"There is not known, either in the valleys, or at their origin within this limit, any bed, peak, or mass of granite in situ; yet the valleys are full, cumbered to the third of their height, and obstructed by an immense accumulation of pebbles and blocks of granite—an accumulation which one may assert to be prodigious and inconceivable, notwithstanding all that we know, and all that has been observed in other countries respecting pebbles or blocks foreign to the soil they cover." *Rapport fait à l'Académie Royal des Sciences sur les travaux géologiques de M. Gay. Annales des Sciences Naturelles, tome XXVIII.*

The *basalt* is the same dark porphyritic rock of which Santa Lucia and so large a portion of the Andes are constituted. Such accumulations of granitic fragments may exist higher up the Cachapual than my journey.

beneath, a milky stream foaming resistlessly through a contracted stony gorge. A landscape, combining more of wild grandeur and picturesque loveliness at the same time, can scarcely be imagined. How awful must have been the commotion when the power of the internal fires thrust towards mid-heaven the infinity of separated hills within the compass of vision, and the consternation with which the rush of the pent-up waters would have been beheld, sweeping before them huge rocks that nothing but earthquakes could have moved from their resting places!

The cabins, thirty in number, are in four ranges, enclosing a small square. They are rudely built of adobes, thatched, whitewashed inside and out, and have corridors facing on the square. As the invalids and other visitors appear to have had few diversions, the whitewash has almost entirely disappeared under doggerel verses and other mementos scribbled with charcoal. Their floors are the bare earth; and for furniture each room is supplied with two rush-seat chairs, a table of rough boards, and two tressels, across which planks are laid to form a bedstead. Yet, for the largest of these—perhaps twenty feet square—the charge is nine reals per day; and there are none at a lesser price than four reals. Besides these buildings there is a small chapel; though neither it nor any room on the premises has a window or a pane of glass to admit light or air, when its doors are closed. Luckily the latter have crevices enough to permit a tolerably free circulation, without the necessity of keeping them open at night. It has already been intimated that provisions are not easily obtainable, and one must come provided with every requisite—even a cook, for whom a sanctum is formed with branches of trees at the back door.

The baths, five in number, are on a narrow shelf of land, twenty feet below, and between the houses and river. They are oblong boxes, with tiled bottoms, enclosed in small thatched cabins; greatly more commodious and sheltered than those of Colina. The water which supplies them flows through a conglomerate of lime, sand, and pebbles, whose surface is encrusted with a portion of the mineral substances held in solution; their temperatures varying according to the size of the stream. None are more than half an inch in diameter, and one is but little larger than a quill. The latter, of course, requires several hours to fill the bath into which it empties; and its temperature becomes greatly reduced from the heat carried off by the earth. They are situated along the shelf for a hundred yards, and have names in accordance with their temperature or position, thus: Tibia (tepid), Corrimiento (flowing), Solitario (alone), Pelambrillo (warm), Pelambre (hot), whose temperatures range from 79.2° to 120.5°. Prof. Domeyko tells me that the lowest temperature he found was 98.6°, and the highest 121.4°. This was in the month of January. A single degree of difference in the heat of the warmest bath is explicable by errors of the thermometers; but 20° between the temperature of the coldest now and at his visit only a year or two ago, is not so easily accounted for. There is no difference between the temperatures at noon and midnight, as some have asserted; and Molina's account, like a very large portion of his work, is sheer fable. It is charitable to believe that the Abbé received as gospel whatever was told him, and with equal confidence presented to the world accounts of many things of which he certainly had no personal information. Gas, presumed to be azote, escapes freely in two of the baths; the others are filled by streams flowing from the vertical face of the cliff; thus, perhaps, preventing it from being seen in them, for, when at the same temperature, there is no perceptible difference in the taste of the several waters.

Invalids, who can afford it, are carried from their cabins in a sort of hand-barrow, without feet, called a *langarillo,* which is formed of four sticks, with a raw hide laced over them. Returning in the same vehicle, though now enveloped under a pile of blankets and clothing, one may well conceive them corpses; and the usual remark, when they cross the patio, is, "*Aqui viene otro cadavre*" (Here comes another corpse). The bearers deposit the langarillo within the cabin, where the friend or companion heaps on more cover; and the patient remains so wrapped up until perspiration, induced by the bath, begins to decrease. Quantities of the water are also drunk, and, as might be anticipated from imbibing any heated water to excess, it produces vomiting; but its mineral constituents indicate that it must be almost tasteless, and experimentally it is so nearly so, that I followed the custom of the place, well knowing that if it did no good it could do no harm. From September until June is the season when they are most frequented: persons coming from Copiapó and Valdivia—the extremities of the republic—many of whom are conveyed on a langarillo, or are held on horses during the last five or six leagues of the journey. Nine days is the period designated as sufficient for the waters to prove their efficacy; and so extraordinary are some of the cures reputed to have been effected within that time, that they have more fame than any other mineral springs,—yet they differ from those at Colina only in their temperatures. Cutaneous, rheumatic, and diseases originating in criminal intercourse, are those for which Cauquenes is most resorted to. At this time nearly all the rooms are occupied, some of them containing families of five or six persons, so that there is quite a populous colony. Among them is an old friar of La Merced, who rouses the (female portion of the) visitors to attend mass before daylight in the morning, that he may not be interrupted afterwards whilst administering to his own physical necessities. He is decidedly the most popular person, and never opens his door that a bevy of women do not flock to it.

Mass is the only public distraction. A common room in which all might assemble—except the chapel—is an advance in civilization of which the merits are yet to be appreciated. Even the regular posadas do not always possess one, but each traveller eats in his bed-room. And thus life at a Chilean watering-place is by no means a gay one. A bath at sunrise; breakfast; a lounge; another bath; dawdle again, or gossip with a neighbor, if you can catch one with a door open; dine towards sundown; a mate or two; bed. You may vary this with two or three walks or horseback rides, but the latter require prevision. For want of pasturage the horses are kept ten miles off; and if you would walk, you must be content to wade through the dust ankle-deep of the bridle-path, or climb steep hill-sides, keeping a sharp lookout the while, that a branch of litre venenosa does not strike and poison your face. Such a routine is the lot of most who go; and perhaps the sort of animal existence to which they are accustomed makes them content with it. At Colina, dancing under impromptu arbors has more than once varied the Chinese-like uniformity, but no one had ever heard of such departure from staid custom here; and the multitude who encounter the privations of a journey are *real* invalids, not seekers of fashionable diversions. Our party was of a gayer stamp. We climbed the hills, and, spite the sea of dust, rambled along paths by the south shore of the river, sometimes visiting the ravine in which flows the snow-water supplying our kitchen, and at others crept along the pebbly bed and up the pyramidal rocks in the stream, where none but goats had ever been before, enjoying the infinite variety of picturesque views presented within every hundred yards we moved. Then we had agreeable books; one member of the party was an accomplished musician; there were cargoes of provisions and fruits from kind friends to our fair companion often twice each day, and we were made the dispensers of her bounty among the poor and unprovided invalids. More than all, we were in the enjoyment of robust health; prepared to appreciate nature, and to laugh at the substitutes we were obliged to introduce for accustomed conveniences of domestic life.

Originally my plans did not contemplate a sojourn of more than one day beyond that on which I arrived; but there were many views to be seen, and the solicitations of my two friends to commiserate their isolation were urged so earnestly, that it would have been ungrateful to refuse; and two other days were most agreeably passed here, the last probably that I shall ever spend at a Chilean watering-place.

From a mean of eleven barometrical observations during the four days, the height of the plateau on which the baths are situated is 2,790 feet above the sea. During the same period the greatest range of the mercurial column was .130 inch, and the extremes of temperature for the same hours (9 A. M. and 3 P. M.) were 61.8° and 77.0°. Of necessity, in summer the climate must be subject to great changes of temperature, caused by reflection and radiation in the ravine by day, and the cold air which invariably pours down it from the Andes by night. Doubtless the S.W. wind prevailing by day at that season somewhat tempers the heat; but the decreasing width of the gorge as it ascends converts it into a sort of funnel, and the breeze of the plain often drives by the baths so furiously that it is quite as unpleasant as heat.

April 19.—Ñor Nicolás was despatched with the cargo mule some hours in advance, and I made the descent to a ford near the little island of Gorocoipo in two hours and a half. As the island is approached from the eastward the profile resembles that of a mammoth tortoise with its head to the S.S.W.—a depression of its rocky extremity representing the neck, and a short line of boulders forming a tail; feet only are wanting, or one might almost fancy it moving—its shrubby trees and broken rocks mistaken for huge barnacles, the growth of ages. Half a mile above, the river is divided into three streams—two of them comparatively insignificant, the third spread over a width of forty yards or more. Although the water for about two thirds of this breadth scarcely touched the horse's belly, and the other third was shallower, yet, as the current is from four and a half to five miles per hour, its passage is of necessity slow. It is not safe to urge a horse over loose rounded stones scarcely larger than his feet, and among which the water is rushing with a momentum nearly if not quite equal to their own gravity; for a cold bath and subsequent colder ride are the lighter penalties of a stumble.

Five years ago, when the snow broke up in the Andes, after an unusually severe and prolonged winter, immense glaciers were brought down by the torrent. These blocked up the ravine about the baths as high as the level of the plateaus, and the water overflowed the houses in the vicinity, spreading consternation among the people at a copper-smelting establishment a league or two above. So sudden was it that the peons rushed to the house of the proprietor with intelligence that the day of final retribution had come. The Andes, they said, were moving; and the mayordomo had scarcely gotten clear of the premises, before the floors were submerged by the rapid flood. The rise of the water ceased almost as quickly as it had commenced; but some days elapsed before the mass of ice and snow accumulated at the narrow gorge was undermined and carried down stream. Until that time the main volume of the river had flowed from Gorocoipo island through the dry bed, now called Rio Seco; but the debris of rocks and trees partially dammed the channel, destroyed the irrigating canals originating here, swept thousands of tons of shingle over the low cultivated fields on their banks, and the mass of water wore a new channel for itself in its present position. It is a rare year, however, that some part of the channel does not suffer a change. This, as well as the other mountain streams, are highest in December and January, when the power of the sun is most effective in melting snow on the lower portions of the Andes; and there is never a year that the haciendados along its banks have not to lament the loss of servants or animals in their attempts to pass the fords. During heavy and continued rains in winter there are times when the floods are deeper; but they are not lasting, for the streams subside to near their autumn level as soon as the rains cease—a few hours being quite sufficient for the water to run off. It was supposed that the Cachapual had its origin in a lake of the Andes; and as the belief obtained a greater semblance of probability after the avalanche mentioned, government sent a competent engineer to explore its source. He travelled within the mountains beyond Cauquenes for four days, and was obliged to return for want of sustenance without having reached it; but I am assured by one who has crossed to Mendoza by this route, that the waters of the lake here flow to the eastward, and not to the Pacific. Above the baths, accounts conflict somewhat, though it is certain that there are at least three principal sources from which the river is supplied. Below, there are only the two small ones, already mentioned as probably originating in Lake Cauquenes.

Within an hour after crossing the ford, Rancagua was reached; and before 8 P. M. I was once more with my hospitable friends at Aguila, well gratified with the 600 miles journey.

PART II. NARRATIVE.

CHAPTER I.

NEW YORK TO PANAMA.

EMBARK ON BOARD THE EMPIRE CITY WITH 200 PASSENGERS BOUND TO CALIFORNIA.—GRAND MASS MEETING.—CHAGRES.—CANOES.—THE RIVER.—SCENERY ASCENDING THE STREAM.—RAIN.—SAN PABLO.—THE CHAGRES AND ITS BOATMEN.—CRUCES.—FROM CRUCES TO PANAMA.

At 3 P. M. of the 16th of August, 1849, the steamer Empire City left New York with more than two hundred passengers bound for California *via* Panama. Her agents promised, and I hoped to reach the latter city in time for the British mail steamship appointed to leave for Valparaiso at noon of the 27th. At so late a date the daily detail of a voyage since performed by so many would scarcely interest any one; but a general outline of our associates, their habits and occupations, may give the reader an insight into the sea-life of outward-bound Californians.

At starting, much was "*couleur de rose.*" Both the ship and passengers were in holiday attire; even nature, though somewhat ardent, put on a smiling face, and, save the heat, a more lovely night one could not desire. As the ocean was quite tranquil, the greenest of the embryo gold hunters boldly promenaded the deck. Groups of singers had collected in all directions, and the glories of the "Sacramento," and "Uncle Ned," with an occasional stave about "sweet home," resounded from every quarter. However, "California," more than any other subject, proved the burthen of the song. Morning brought no change of weather; but the fine dresses had partially disappeared, and the men began to appear in their true characters; a majority of the two hundred and twelve being adventurers whom the eastern portion of the United States could well spare! True, there were gentlemen among them—that is, men whose *consciences* control their physical acts; but the larger number either were, or pretended to be, uncleanly as well as unmannerly. Luckily, at that era of California travelling, at table one was not forced into intimacy with them.

Fine weather and smooth water continued up to bed-time of Saturday night; but on Sunday old Neptune seemed purposely to come to aid the steward, and prevent desecration of his turtle by such a gang. An old-fashioned smoky southeaster brought a heavy sea, the number at the dinner-table was suddenly reduced below forty, and until the 24th the decks were crowded by those from whom the sea-god mercilessly exacted the penalties of initiation. Whether or not there be similarity in constitutions subject to the most violent attacks, has probably not been a subject of investigation by physiological inquirers; but we know that love and sea-sickness find no commiserators, and therefore the gold hunters received little sympathy. The sea had become "very ugly," as sailors term it; and it was as much as one could do to hold on to his plate. With the air-ports of the vessel closed in, and the thermometer never under 83° for five days and nights, the atmosphere below was quite equal to that of a steam-bath. On deck woe-begone faces were predominant; and cheerfulness remained only with the "old salts," whose ingenuity was taxed to find new tortures for their despondent messmates.

The Spaniards have a proverb, "*Viento y ventura poco dura*" (wind and good luck never last long); and as we drew into the Caribbean sea, fair skies and smooth water awaited us. Its continuance brought out many writers, and the world seemed threatened with a deluge of "First Voyage of a Gold-hunter," "Notes from a Californian," or perhaps "Letters from our Special Correspondent." Such a variety of note-books and journals was scarcely ever before displayed in one apartment, and our steward soon found it difficult to obtain accommodations for the patients to whom he had been administering gruel and weak tea during the preceding week. Revolvers and bowie-knives also came in for a large share of attention and comparison; the owner of each doffing the habiliments of city life, to make his appearance in the garb of a hunter (of gold), fully prepared to defend the treasure he expected to extract from the earth.

By this time it had become evident that we could not arrive at Chagres in time to reach Panama for the Valparaiso steamer. In the estimation of us heretics—the passengers—the boat was a "slow coach," positively a failure, if speed was to be any criterion; though the captain and others of the household found reasons "plenty as blackberries" why she did not go faster. The coal was bad, boat too deep, engines too new, boilers leaked last time, &c., &c. On the evening of the 25th, immediately after supper, the steward gave notice that the passengers were desirous to hold a meeting on deck, for the purpose of expressing to the captain and officers their sense of his high qualities as a seaman, gratitude for kind attentions, &c. Supposing my name unknown to all but the captain, I was no little surprised to hear it read out as one of the vice-presidents, and to receive escort to one of the seats provided for us dignitaries of the convention. Everything appeared to have been "cut and dried," as is usual; and the meeting was going on famously, with a probability of speedily transacting all its business. But some one, perhaps disappointed that his merits had been overlooked, and convinced that his name ought to appear in the papers to which our proceedings might be sent, had the ill will to suggest a committee to draught proper resolutions instead of those our president extracted from his pocket. This was a poser to the getters up; but the majority were so unreasonable as to desire additional trouble, and of course they could not object. Thus, as the mal-contents managed to have most of their own party on the committee, the resolutions brought back had very little semblance to those read at first. When their report was made, a new faction sprang up. The steerage passengers—the real democracy—declared that they had had no voice in the committee; a claim which brought out representatives from the "sunny south," who insisted that each State should have had its delegate. A hot discussion ensued; and as many had been keeping their "spirits up" all day, from the want of proper restraining centrifugal power in our chief, we presiding officers were likely to be smashed up. Perceiving that one of the tropical showers to which we had been subject for two or three days was rapidly approaching, my post was incontinently deserted without warning to my neighbors, and I had scarcely reached the saloon when the drops were pattering thick and fast. Before the mass of our companions could descend the ladders in the dark, most of them were drenched to the skin, the ardor for discussion extinguished as suddenly as the shower had come upon them, and the tumult quenched at a dash. But it had the effect to restore good humor, and set all hands laughing; an object of greater consequence than all the resolutions they could have draughted between New York and Chagres, for another half hour would probably have made us witnesses to bloodshed by some of the rougher ones.

One of the resolutions originally prepared declared that we had found the ship "unsurpassed for speed by any steamer on the ocean," and ended by a disinterested though "earnest recommendation of it to government for the transmission of the mails!" Luckily the question was not taken. Owing to the incorrect information given about this very quality, before me was the prospect, amounting almost to a certainty, of a month's detention on the Isthmus; and every moment of that month was needed at a point more than three thousand miles distant. If the rain-squall did not cool my ire, it saved me from proving traitor to the party that placed me in power.

August 27.—About 9 P. M. we dropped anchor off the bar at the mouth of the river Chagres, indicated to us by lights displayed on board the British mail-steamer then lying there. Soon afterwards the captain of the Orus, a small steamer brought out for navigating of the river, came off to us; and, as is usual when people are about landing in a strange country, much anxiety was evinced by the passengers to learn all that was possible respecting the route they were to travel, its conveniences, privations, dangers, and costs. Nor did they forget to inquire whether the latest intelligence from the golden region of their aspirations was favorable, or themselves likely to be detained at Panama, because of the number of persons already there awaiting passage. Had the skipper charged for each question propounded him, his fortune would soon have been greater than that of most of those he will probably greet on their return. But there were business matters to be attended to, and our captain suddenly abducted their prize, leaving the multitude to digest the few grains of knowledge precociously obtained.

Hoping that something might have occurred to detain the Valparaiso steamer, and in accordance with previous arrangements, Mr. R. and myself went on shore, for the purpose of proceeding up the river immediately. Landing, as we did, in the night, it was scarcely possible to distinguish more than an outline of the river landscape, or to perceive either the structure of the houses or the costumes of the people of Chagres. The town lies on the southeastern bank of the river, and consists of about 150 huts or cabins, made of canes, thatched with leaves of the palm-tree. The canes stand from 15 to 20 feet in height, and are wattled together with cords of cocoa-nut bark, forming houses 30 or 40 feet long. They have steep pyramidal roofs, that project five or six feet beyond the walls, and protect the doors and windows from driving rains. Very few are plastered, even on the outside, the free air of Heaven penetrating where it lists; and I greatly doubt whether there is a pane of glass in all the town. Partitions are made with canes or bamboos, wattled, in the same manner as the outer walls, and the doors are of cotton cloth, or perhaps some heavier vegetable material. Of course, there can be no great privacy in a town so constructed. But this lattice-work structure is quite necessary; for a high bluff cuts off most of the northeast trade winds that reach so near to the equator.

The streets of the old town were paved, and when Carthagena and Porto Bello flourished, Chagres was probably a place of comparative comfort; but its thorougfares are now little better than quagmires, which only the hogs seem to enjoy. The canoemen told me that a few of the houses are built with plank floors; though most of them, and all that we saw, had only the bare earth raised a few inches above the level of the street outside. Quadrupeds as well as bipeds of the family occupied them. One who had never visited a hot climate would have found much to wonder at in the toilet and manners of the people. A white shirt and cotton pantaloons, or a chemise, *at most*, composed their costume. Some sat near a little table, with a tallow candle and greasy pack of cards, playing at *monte*. Others lolled in grass hammocks, perhaps half their persons exposed. Few seemed to have sufficient energy for locomotion. All chattered in a musical tongue, men, women, and children smoking cigars. The Spaniards are musical, and their full-blooded descendants of the new world inherit the taste; but the national instrument here was that squeaking thing called "harmonicon" or "æolino," an ear-mark, I fear, of their recent associations. The tramp of boots as we passed along startled them from apathetic drowsiness, and even momentarily from their passion as gamblers; and whilst some simply muttered "Americanos," others, more full of fun, displayed their acquisition of English since January, by a full stave from—

"O Susannah, don't you cry for me;
I'm bound for California,
The gold mines for to see."

Though necessarily brief, our stay in a town with a reputation so fearful was quite as long as either of us cared for. In half an hour we had concluded a bargain with the owner of a canoe, and were on board the Orus, on the opposite side of the river. Our stipulations were, that he should come to the Orus for us by midnight, the canoe to have four young men for its propulsion, besides himself; and that he should land us at Cruces, 49 miles above, in 28 hours. We were to travel all of both nights, and to pay $80 if we arrived at the time agreed upon; $5 per hour less for every hour that he exceeded twenty-eight. Punctual to the time, the "dug-out" came alongside. It was 35 feet long, nearly 4 feet wide, and made from a single log, resembling mahogany in texture, though scarcely of half its weight. About twelve feet of it was covered with an arched thatch roof, barely high enough to crawl under, yet affording good protection from the sun and rain. Under this our luggage, provisions, and bed, were arranged. Having crossed the Isthmus twice before, my companion was provided with a pallet, made by sewing a "comfortable" together, and a pair of blankets, as well as several minor articles experience had taught him the utility of. Spread on strips of bark overlying a ballast of cocoanuts in the bottom of the canoe, the comfortable and blankets made us a very excellent bed, its only objection being the proximity of the canopy to our nasal extremities.

Lighting the lantern, and bidding good-bye to the captain of the Orus, we crept to our resting-place, and with carpet-bags as pillows, disposed for sleep—our light-hearted boatmen starting cheerily with their paddles. These canoes afforded the only means of travel between Chagres and the hamlets on the upper waters of the river, until the arrival of the Orus and General Herran (another small steamer), sent out by the Pacific Mail Company since January. Some of them are nearly 50 feet in length, and as much as five feet wide. The bow and stern are curved upwards, so that a section in the direction of the length somewhat resembles a crescent. They are light, flexible, and strong, and are managed with incomparable skill. Of course, the boatmen look with jealousy on the intruding steamers, foreseeing the loss of their own occupation at no distant day; and when one of them ran aground only a little while before, they positively refused to convey coal to her on any terms. No doubt they hoped the heavy freshets of the river would soon break her in pieces.

Sleep was out of the question. The novel mode of locomotion; the shrill songs of our boatmen as they dashed their paddles into the stream, or their gay salutations as we passed descending canoes; the rush of waters within an inch of my ear; and a knowledge that a capsize would prove inevitable death, long prevented even drowsiness. Memory had just parted with consciousness when we stopped at Gatun, a little hamlet some seven miles above Chagres; the crew reminding us that we had promised to obtain a bottle of "strong waters" here wherewith to keep their spirits up. This was a famous stopping-place with all boatmen; and some of our countrymen whom we found there seemed to think it quite funny that we should expect ours to return before daylight. They had come from New Orleans in a schooner, and had left Chagres ten hours before us; stopped here at sunset on the same plea as ourselves; and once landed, their crew told them it was not customary to travel at night. Ours did *not* deceive us, and in a few minutes we were again *en route*.

The earliest beams of the morning caught us both napping; and it was not until his solar majesty had attained an elevation of some 15° that we looked abroad on the new creation, or critically examined the arrangements of our bark. At home, but little additional information was obtainable. Before us stood four dusky-hued, small, but athletic men—their only garments a hat and narrow cloth about the loins—wielding, with quick and regular strokes, broad-bladed paddles of moderate length. The *patron* sat at the stern occasionally plying a similar paddle, but more frequently using it as a rudder. He had a whole shirt. But abroad! one could scarcely imagine scenery more picturesque or beautiful; indeed, so extraordinary had been the changes of twenty-four hours, that little more was required to impress at least momentary belief that the whole was a curious dream. We were dashing through the waters of a stream not more than 80 yards wide at the rate of nearly nine miles per hour. More tortuous in its course than a serpent, each instant brought new objects into view; and before they had been fully seen, an intervening point obstructed the vision. Where we first saw them, the river banks generally were rolling—varying from 10 to 30 feet above its surface, and carpeted to the very edge of the waters with dense verdure. Here and there a pebbly beach bounded an evergreen savannah, and farther back the elevation gradually increased to heights of several hundred feet. And their productions!—towering cocoas, with tufts of leaves and clusters of nuts; palms, with graceful leaf-stalks and brilliant masses of pendent flowers; palmettos—emblem of our chivalric State; broad-leaved plantains and bananas, with massive bunches of fruit in every stage from green to gold; wide-spreading caobas, with intensely dark green foliage; tall canes and bamboos, and multitudes of other unknown varieties—some matted over by vines of different hues—others solitary monarchs of little knolls,—all telling of a vertical sun and copious rains—of the almost cotemporaneous birth and decay of vegetable productions. From the mutilated extremities of many vines, evidently cut away to facilitate navigation, long crimson fibres stole earthward in search of foothold again—the mass of the plant sustained meanwhile through the tendrils about the tree to which it clung. No colors could be more exquisite than the shades reflected in the morning sunlight from stout waving masses of these fibres contrasted with a verdant back-ground. What a scene! Rank tropical vegetation found its way into the bubbling stream, and the forests—a tangled and matted mass, which man had never penetrated—charmed the sight with their gigantic, graceful, or gorgeous productions. Both of us remarked the absence of flowers: a few varieties of the convolvulus tribe, and one or two of a scarlet color, at some distance from the river bank, were all that we saw; nor could an infinite variety of parasitic plants made up for the deficiency. Parrots and parroquets in flocks, numberless swallows, an occasional heron, a few iguanas, lizards everywhere, and some not very attractive butterflies, were all the specimens of animated nature within our changing panorama. Smaller species of the feathered tribe often darted across the stream or among the trees, but we were not sufficiently versed in ornithology to recognise them at a passing glance.

August 28.—At 9 A. M. stopped at a settlement on the north bank of the river called *Dos Hermanos*. It is perhaps fifteen miles from Chagres, and is ordinarily a place for breathing the crew, and obtaining something to eat. There are three reed-houses here whose proprietors have an abundant supply of fowls, rice, and tropical fruits in their season, and know how to brew very tolerable coffee. Whilst our men refreshed themselves in the running-stream fearless of alligators, we were contented with spring-water and a big calabash as a substitute for a basin. All hands having done ample justice to the provisions brought from the Empire City, as well as to the old lady's coffee, ten o'clock found us under way again, our people paddling against a current running from three to four miles the hour.

As we ascended, the country gradually became more elevated, sometimes rising into alluvial knolls of considerable height, some of them perhaps of very recent origin; in fact, there are many places on the immediate banks of the river where a stratum of earth from ten to fifteen feet in thickness overlies another of still undecayed leaves. In one or two places there are distinct traces of where the river-bed had previously been; but we saw neither boulders nor out-cropping rock strata during this day.

Winding along with nearly uniform width above Gatun, the Chagres rarely proceeds in a straight line for more than half a mile; and as the current gradually increases from the mouth towards its source, every advantage is taken of eddies by the boatmen, and with every new reach you cross the stream. Though so narrow, it must be very deep in the middle; for poles ten feet long would barely touch bottom within a few feet of the shore, and most of the time one side or the other of our canoe was brushing the bamboos or vines on its banks. You are rarely in mid-stream, or beyond the shade of overhanging trees; indeed, branches stretch far towards the centre, forming a perfect fairy scene.

The morning passed without notable incident. Two or three parties with their treasures from California were met descending; to whom, if we could judge by their hurrahs and cheers long after they had turned the reach below, the tidings that the Empire City awaited them below was not less welcome than was the first lump of glittering metal to their sight. Not far from two o'clock we had got well among the highlands, when the gathering of cumuli and distant rumblings warned us of an approaching storm. Our crew being already stripped, they had no preparation to make; but to render ourselves more secure, a large India-rubber cloth was spread over the thatched roof. Here, nature commands the attention of the uninitiated to her atmospheric phenomena, as well as to her vegetable productions. For about three quarters of an hour the rain descended vertically in drops that raised bubbles on the water as large as half a walnut, and so rapidly that the cocoa-nuts in the bottom of the canoe were covered in less than half that time. I have witnessed as vivid lightning elsewhere, but the crash of the thunder among those old hills actually made my ears ache. Though more moderately, rain continued falling until near four o'clock, at which time we stopped for a few moments to obtain spring-water, and give the men something to eat. Adding a little grog and a cigar to their ample.rations of salt-beef and bread (great luxuries to them), at the end of fifteen minutes they dashed at their work seemingly as fresh as ever.

The evening wore on most beautifully. Myriads of fire-flies, and also the audible chirps of other novel insects flitting among the foliage on shore, afforded interest to us. But the river was rising rapidly, and its waters fairly roared through the branches of fallen trees. Since dinner our men had laid aside their paddles for slender but elastic and tough poles ten feet long, and by midnight we had reached within nine miles of Gorgona. Three different trials did they make to reach the eddy of the opposite shore, only to be swept half a mile down stream by the furious current. The river had risen ten feet since the rain, the moon had gone down, we were left in pitchy darkness, and out of the eddies the strength of our men was exerted in vain. After the third failure, they told us frankly, that to persevere in attempts until daylight returned, or the river subsided, would greatly peril all our lives, and they were unwilling to incur such risks. "The merciful man is merciful to his beast." We had no right to constitute ourselves judges of danger in navigating a strange river. There was no adequate return for the enormous expenditure of muscular exertion we had witnessed during an hour; and so, releasing them from the forfeit for non-arrival within twenty-eight hours, we turned back a few rods to obtain shelter under the bluff on which stands a single house, called *San Pablo.* How these poor fellows could have labored twenty-two and a half hours of the twenty-four preceding, apparently straining every muscle of their shoulders, arms, and thighs, and then, as soon as the canoe was secure, spring ashore with alacrity, ready for a frolic, is a phenomenon in physical endurance utterly beyond my comprehension.

August 29.—Mr. R. and myself were roused at daybreak by the chattering of flocks of parrots and parroquets just leaving their nests. There were several canoes in-shore of us, and these the fall of the river had left high and dry. The violent rains often raise the surface of the river twenty feet within a few hours, the flood subsiding as quickly after they have ceased. No doubt new channels originate in the overflowings of the banks at such times, and the velocity of the current is proportionately increased. Making a lavatory of the running-stream, we roused our faithful workers, and went to the house on the bluff to purchase a cup of coffee. Although this belongs to the padre (priest) of the parish, as everybody does a little trade since the Yankees began to cross the Isthmus, the piloto assured us *el clerigo* always kept an ample supply of the berry. His solitary house is quite elevated above the ground, and occupies the top of the hill, about which the scene is really sylvan. There are clusters of tropical trees around it, and goodly numbers of the several farm-yard denizens. Away to the west, the eminence slopes into a broad and grassy plateau, over which a herd of sleek, fawn-colored cattle were feeding close to the serpentine river.

The padre was not at home, but his *sobrina* was, a comely colored damsel some 17 to 20 years of age. She soon put on an iron oven and boiled a gallon or two of the desired beverage, scarcely removing the cigar from her lips even to answer the joking questions of our boatmen. It is quite a common occurrence to find *sobrinas* (nieces) in the houses of country curates, the world being sufficiently ungenerous to say that the asserted consanguinity is only a cloak for more intimate relationship. In this hot climate the church has probably found it expedient to sanction such housekeepers, as well as moderate recreation at the cock-pit and *monte* table.

Leaving San Pablo about 8 o'clock, we promised the crew an extra dollar if they would land us at Cruces by 1 P. M. The distance was thirteen miles, and the current against us full six miles per hour, making about 43 miles of water through which the canoe was to be pushed by poles in five hours. Gratitude for kind treatment was probably an additional incentive; for they struggled every inch of the way, and actually landed us at half-past 12. Above San Pablo the river banks change character. Pebbly beaches, vertical earth-walls 20 to 30 feet above the stream, and strata of rocks occasionally show themselves, and the number of trees and tall canes growing at the water's edge constantly increases. Seven miles above is Gorgona, a village rather larger than Chagres, and better built, though of similar materials. As we made no stop, we could only admire the beautiful pebbly beaches above and below the town, and its picturesque appearance amid cocoas, palms, and plantain-trees. The washerwomen were busy on the beaches, and a party of Americans were fully occupied with open trunks and clothing at the landing-place.

The river varies very little in width from the point near Gatun, where we first saw it, to Cruces. There are occasional places, as the mouths of tributaries, or where it temporarily occupies an old bed, at which it spreads out to double or even treble seventy yards; but these are far apart. Its course is extremely sinuous. Above Gatun there is no straight reach exceeding a mile in length, and it occurs more than once after turning a point that your direction is almost back to the bend last left. The velocity of its current increases with the volume of the stream and the approach to its head-waters. When we left Chagres it was not more than three miles per hour; at Cruces we found it very little, if at all, less than six miles—a speed which only the most dexterous management and exertion would enable the boatmen to overcome. It would be impossible for them to keep a canoe in mid-stream and make the voyage of near fifty miles in 28 hours against an average current of 4½ miles. They therefore take advantage of the eddies under the points, hug the shore closely to the bend of a new reach, and necessarily "shoot" the stream to take advantage of it. The canoes, being sharp and light, are well calculated for the navigation; and they are handled by small, active men, whose wiry muscles seem capable of almost unlimited endurance. Frugal in their habits, mild and respectful in their deportment, thankful for the least favor or a kind word, and ready to bandy jests with every crew they meet, they cannot fail to make a favorable impression on all who deal fairly by them. But it is a source of no little mortification to see some of the "citizens of the United States" stalk among these timid people with dirks, bowie-knives, and revolvers enough to equip a small company, threatening death or mutilage if their impossible wants are not immediately gratified. Such weapons may do well enough for California or the Southwest, but are of no service here except to bring discredit on our country.

Looking back on the journey between Chagres and Cruces, I cannot but consider myself amply repaid for the privations and fatigue. With boats somewhat differently constructed, a pleasant companion or two, and ample time to enjoy its many and multiform beauties of landscape, I could not point out to a lover of nature from an extra-tropical climate an excursion that would afford him more enjoyment than the ascent of the river Chagres. There are those who grumble at everything—even the luxurious coaches of the English railways, the sumptuous fare at our best hotels, and beds of eider-down. Such persons will find no comfort here, and had better remain where they have a right to vent ill humor or bad manners; but to the traveller who journeys for information, bringing with him cheerfulness and a determination to overlook trifles for the benefit he is to derive, there is nothing to prevent its being a most gratifying and instructing voyage, even with all its present *désagreménts*.

Cruces is situated on an eminence of the left bank of the river, which here rises gradually from the water, and is almost destitute of vegetation. It has nearly two hundred houses, disposed in regular order; each standing apart from its neighbors for greater circulation of air.

One or two are of adobes, and a few have received coatings of plaster over the canes; but most of them are only of bamboos, with thatched roofs. One of the most conspicuous is the church, occupying the summit of the hill. Every house appears to be full of people, of whom quite one half are of unadulterated African blood; three fourths of the remainder various combinations of Spanish, Indian, and African; and one eighth descendants of the early Spaniards, without recent admixture, and Europeans. Women are more numerous than men. They appear an idle, slip-shod race, lounging about the doors on stools that elevate their knees nearly to the level of their chins, and spread them at an angle of more than 90°. Such as they are, Cruces numbers two or three hotels, and sundry livery-stables, where animals may be hired. As our basket contained an abundant supply, we had no need of the services of mine host. Packing something to eat on the road to Panama, the remainder was given to our boatmen, who took their leave with multitudes of compliments and good wishes for our speedy and pleasant ride.

On leaving Chagres a resident acquaintance had given my fellow-traveller a letter to a Monsieur P., whom we supposed to be an especial friend; its object being to facilitate our departure and travel over the road. This, it was stated, could not be done so well by any one as by Monsieur P. We found him without trouble. To estimate him according to his own claims, he is one of the great self-martyrs of the world. He has sacrificed the comforts and elegancies of the "*belle ville*" for the sake of being permitted to forward Americans and their luggage between Cruces and Panama—for a consideration. But he makes no mention of the last until you descend to particulars; and prefers leaving one to infer that philanthropic zeal for the Yankee race induced him to this great sacrifice. Monsieur P. is a French Jew; and when we came to treat for mules, he was more eloquent about "hard times" than he had been on the subject of self-sacrifice. Nevertheless he furnished good saddle-mules for $14 each, and agreed to forward our trunks at $12 per mule-load; and his beasts were certainly ready some time before we were.

As the trunks would not reach Panama until the following afternoon, a change of clothing and a few necessary articles were packed in an India-rubber bag and strapped to the shoulders of the guide who was to accompany us, as was also a small lantern, in case we should be compelled to stop at any of the ranchos, where candles are almost unknown. We had evidence in the condition of the streets, and a heavy shower, which had lasted from the time that our trunks were under cover to the moment of departure, about 3 P. M., that the rainy season had fully set in; but whilst quite reconciled to a thorough drenching during the ride, due preparations were made to ward off as much water as possible, and by the use of cloth clothing to guard against the injurious effects of the rest.

It was not without consciencious qualms that I could mount the small, skinny, and half-starved beast brought to me; for she seemed tired, and altogether unfitted to carry my weight a journey of twenty-one miles, and twenty-one *such* miles as I had reason to believe them! But the whole troop in front of the house were alike, and there was no alternative. Similar animals could scarcely have been sold in the United States at any price; yet so great has been the demand since the commencement of the emigration to California, that their value here is from $80 to $100 each.

Passing across the hill by the church, a sample of the road we were to travel over was at once presented; or rather a sample of the path was, for the places where it is wide enough to be dignified as a *road* are extremely few and far between. For the greater portion of the distance it is only a succession of gullies worn in the rock by the action of water and the feet of animals, just wide enough through the principal length of each for a single traveller, and even he must be watchful to prevent his feet or legs from being torn by the rocks beside him. In other places there are remains of an old paved road, said to have been made in the time of the buccaneers, now torn stone from stone by mountain torrents. The *débris* lie in patches distinct from each other, each interval a foot or more deep in mud and slime. And again in other parts there are quagmires for more than a hundred yards on a stretch, with rocks and roots of trees immersed half saddle-girth deep in water not of the sweetest odor. Indeed, except where the government troops have recently paved a few rods in the vicinity of *Cruz de Hierro*, there is not a quarter of a mile in the first eighteen from Cruces that would be regarded as a moderately good road in the very worst sections of Maryland or Virginia. Abrupt gullies like flights of steps, filled with huge pebble-stones, and shaded by overhanging vines that momentarily threaten you with the fate of Absalom, now forcing you to lie almost on your face as the mule climbs the steep, anon requiring similar precaution to prevent mutual overthrow as the frail beast picks her way down a steep declivity, and pools from which the mire and water are dashed to your very eyelids—such is the character of the Cruces and Panama road *before* the height of the rainy season. The last three miles are in better condition, and in winter doubtless afford a pleasant ride. At that season, as the country through which it passes is more level, though six miles longer, the Gorgona road is considered preferable.

Though on foot, by taking advantage of short cuts directly across the hills, our guide was enabled to keep a little in advance of us and give timely warning of the approach of other travellers, that either we or they might halt and avoid meeting in gorges so narrow that neither could turn to retreat. With cargo-mules this is a difficult if not impossible task, and serious loss may result from the guide's want of care. Custom sharpens his organ of hearing, and on approaching these places he utters a shrill and peculiar cry, which may be heard for a long distance in the stillness of the forest. If no response comes, one may proceed.

The sun had gone down by the time we reached Cruz de Hierro, and in this latitude, with the shadows under foot at noon, a very brief period intervenes between sunset and dark. Our guide was at least fifty years of age, and *seemed* to be tiring for the last mile; rather an unpromising prospect, as there were still fifteen miles to accomplish. Contrary to orders he had lagged behind, and was evidently desirous to pass the night in the comparatively comfortable quarters here; telling us only a little while before that it was impossible for him to travel so fast, and unless we were armed and would remain near, some of the many *picarones* in the neighborhood would not hesitate to draw their knives across his throat for the sake of the bag on his back. The same story, increased by the terrors of awfully bad roads, and the impossibility of travelling through to Panama by night, was repeated by the proprietors of the groggeries at Cruz de Hierro. No doubt they hoped we would tarry and might leave something at the *monte* table, as well as a dollar or two for hotel accommodations; but it was our intention to go on, and showing the old man our means for defending him, we gave him to understand he would be kept between us until we were at the gates of Panama.

A more lovely night was never beheld, and a twenty miles' ride over a rolling country and good road, with an agreeable companion, under such moonlight, would be most keenly relished at any time. Here, however, there were serious drawbacks to enjoyment. Though a nearly vertical moon poured a flood of radiance on forest and mossy rocks at the summits of the hills, and dew and rain-drops sparkled as gems around us, there were narrow gorges and ravines in the midst of impenetrable masses of evergreens, through which scarce a beam could find way, and we entered them ignorant of what was before us. Nothing could have been more deceptive than the effects of the moonlight in some of these confines of Erebus. The few pencils of light that found crevices in the dense foliage, brightening as many points, seemed huge self-luminous insects beside the path; and on emerging from the dark caverns, when the moon had declined somewhat, patches of light served but to mislead one as to the direction of the highway. When the descent was steep, these were fearful places for a stranger to enter. No faculty of one's own was of the least service towards self-preservation. There are few who can give experience of the "blackness of darkness," and at such times one must rely wholly on the reason, or, as the world is pleased to call it, the *instinct* of his beast. At first I knew not how to manage her, but kept a tight rein, and consequently was in constant apprehension of broken limbs, by the stumbling of the poor brute as she picked her way among stones and gnarled roots; but as soon as the bridle was loose, the faltering gait ceased, and she pushed along confidently through places in absolute darkness to me, apparently knowing every rock and mud-hole on the route. After that, we got along famously; and I am quite convinced a mule has vastly more sense in travelling over a bad road than the two-legged animal bestriding her.

Half way between Cruces and Panama we stopped at a rancho to obtain a glass of water for ourselves, and something more potent for the guide. It was but a thatched roof, supported on a few poles. The family were all asleep on raw hides spread on the floor that nature provided, but got up cheerfully to sell a *tortilla* (a coarse corn-cake) and some country rum for the old man. Both the proprietor and his son were chatty, good-natured fellows; and *la Señora* also occasionally joined in the talk, as we sat enjoying the supper our saddle-bags provided: but being probably in her night-dress, she modestly kept her charms in the obscurity. Greatly refreshed, we started on the second half of our journey at half-past eight, amazingly strengthened in body and spirits by the repast; Mr. R. cheerily singing "O Susannah," and the guide and myself indulging in a bit of scandal between the whiffs of our cigars. And it was well that something had imbued us with fresh valor, for the path during the next mile was the blackest, and most tortuous and abrupt in its descent, of any we had yet passed over. Down! down!! down!!! we went, until I could almost have sworn the kingdom of Pluto was at hand, and have felt little surprise at meeting old Charon on the bank of the stream whose waters could be heard. Multitudes of bats and other night-birds dashed whizzingly by us; and myriads of fire-flies, though rendering the "darkness more visible," yet served to connect us with animated creation. Otherwise the stillness of that lonesome glen would have been irksome. How the mule picked her way round salient points of the rocks remains to me a mystery. I knew her nose was close to the ground, because of the small portion of the bridle remaining in my hand, and I could feel that the security of each spot was thoroughly explored before the fore foot was suffered to rest firmly on it; but there surmise of the probable guiding faculties ended.

Emerging from this, we entered a moonlit valley, watered by one of the tributaries to the Rio Grande—the first stream on the route whose waters flow to the Pacific. Its depth was not above a foot, nor its width more than a few yards; but its fall is so rapid that it makes quite a rumbling noise in its progress amid the rocks and pebbles of its shores. The country is more open henceforward. Looking back at the hills we had crossed, as well as to those yet before us, there was a mistiness about the upper foliage of the old forest monarchs rendering it difficult to distinguish them from dark azure clouds; and indeed it was only after tracing them from their firm buttressed trunks to the broad overhanging foliage, that the mind could properly appreciate the reality and semblance to which night gave birth. Here trees attain great size and height. Some of the older ones, whose bark resembles the beech, have radial laminæ at regular intervals, like buttresses to the main stalk. They extend from the ground upwards through fifteen or twenty feet, the height depending on the size (or age) of the tree, the inclination of its trunk, and the slope of the ground. Whether a provision of nature against hurricanes, little tenacity of the wood, or other peculiarity of the species, I know not; but I did not observe these adjuncts on young trees of the same species, and they were widest on the side that apparently required most support.

The earliest evidence of approach to the vicinity of civilization is an old though ruined stone church, on the left of the road, two miles distant from Panama. A bridge near by, of similar materials, supports part of the paved highway before alluded to. From thence a macadamized road winds over a gently undulating savannah, in sight of the great southern ocean, both its sides lined with bamboo houses with sharp pyramidal roofs. Massive stone bridges with seats ranged in a semicircular form on each side, and obelisks of masonry with crosses and saintly images, occur at every few hundred yards. The wealthy founders of the city sought to turn the thoughts of the pedestrian heavenward as he rested at these monuments of their opulence.

A little farther on, edifices of stone with balconies and tiled roofs, and the ruins of old garden walls, denote the suburbs proper, which cover a greater extent than is enclosed by the walls.

Walking our animals slowly during the last three miles, for the convenience of the guide, we reached the city at not far from 2 A. M. of August 30, without having dismounted during the ride. Wearied and stiff, from the necessity of sitting so long in one position, lest by unfortunate preponderance the small lank beasts should capsize (as often occurs), spattered with mud from the crowns of our heads to the toes of our boots, and, thoroughly wet from the hips downward during the last seven hours, we were heartily rejoiced to reach the portal of the French hotel, just inside the western gate. A good scouring with water, and final rubbing with strong brandy, to prevent taking cold, and 3 o'clock found me on one of the very best beds in Panama—a cot, with one small pillow and two thin sheets!

CHAPTER II.

THE CITY OF PANAMA.

EXTENT.—POPULATION.—FORTIFICATIONS.—HOUSES.—CHURCHES; THEIR RUINOUS CONDITION; EVENING SERVICE, ENDING WITH A DISPLAY OF FIREWORKS.—SUNDAY OCCUPATIONS.—BELLS.—OTHER PUBLIC BUILDINGS.—VIEW FROM THE SEA BASTION.—BATHS.—THE PEOPLE.—CONDUCT OF AMERICANS THERE.—ANIMALS.—BIRDS.—FISH.—CLIMATE.—GEOGRAPHICAL POSITION.—DESTRUCTION OF OLD PANAMA BY MORGAN.

A peninsula jutting from the base of Mount Anson towards the east, rather less than half a mile long by one fifth of a mile wide, was selected as the site of the new, when the old city of Panama was destroyed by Morgan and his buccaneer companions about the close of January, 1670. The ground enclosed by the fortifications subsequently built is only a third of a mile in length by the breadth of the peninsula; and here there is a population not varying greatly in number from 3,500 souls. A part of the suburbs is built up quite as compactly as the city proper, and a like population is said to reside without the walls. A deep and wide moat separates the city from its suburbs. On the other sides the walls are washed by the sea at every tide; but as the ledges of volcanic rock on which they are built have a very slight inclination, and the vertical rise of spring tides is twenty-two feet, there is visible at low water, beyond the fortifications, a mass of blackened rocks more than a quarter of a mile wide. At the gateway on the landward side there are guard-houses, flanking towers, loopholes, and many other resources for defence, with whose names or immediate purposes I have no sort of acquaintance. From thence the walls have an average height of thirty feet above high-water mark, and broad parapets perhaps ten feet higher than the level of the streets. They were most substantially built; but the action of the atmosphere since 1720 (the date I found), and the beating of the waves disregarded by the indolent race which has succeeded the original proprietors, have given to every portion the most dilapidated and tumble-down look. Indeed the sea-walls have been breached in many places; and the tooth of old Neptune nibbles out bits of masonry, whilst worms and moisture have wholly destroyed two of the four gates. At present there are only three or four heavy brass guns mounted, and it is somewhat doubtful whether they will not take leave of their carriages at the first discharge.

Within the walls the streets cross each other at right angles, in the directions of the four cardinal points. They are generally thirty feet wide, paved with round pebbles, and have narrow elevated footways at the side. As the platform adjoining the parapet walls and the beaches are made receptacles for offal, the thoroughfares are quite clean; and one might enjoy walking, but for the danger of much exposure to the sun in this hot and steamy atmosphere. The houses, two and three stories high, are of sandstone, whitewashed, and extensive enough to accommodate several families; all of whom have a common entrance and stairway. There are balconies to each story along the entire length of the front and rear, the lower one extending over the footway of the street. Every room has access to the balcony by a double door, the upper panels of which are hinged and serve as windows. None others are known in Panama, and the number of those that have enjoyed the distinction of glazing certainly does not exceed a dozen. Floors are made of planks or tiles. If of the former, the boards are wide and rudely fitted; and in neither case is the ceiling of the under-room plastered, so that dirt readily sifts through. A greater annoyance, however, is from the continuous deposition of a small insect existing in the bamboos that support the tiled roofs. Partitions between rooms are also of rough boards, whitewashed, not unfrequently with crevices so wide as to permit knowledge of your neighbor's actions without very close prying. As in every Spanish town, there is a public square near the centre, ordinarily a market-place; but here country produce is offered for sale in a *plaza* without the walls; and if brought in canoes from the islands, there is a market-place at the southwest gate, where a sort of wharf has been built for commercial purposes.

Of the seven churches once flourishing within the walls, all five that remain are in the most ruinous condition. One, it is said, was burned, though there are no visible traces of fire; the other has of necessity fallen into decay with the fortunes of the city. All of them were built of the most substantial and durable materials of the country; yet so rapid is the action of the atmosphere on the porous stone, and the ravages of an insect or boring-worm on woodwork, that the decreasing prosperity of the church permits no repairs to its edifices. Constant moisture of high temperature rapidly germinates seed deposited by the wind in crevices of the roofs or towers of the sanctuaries, and in a brief period they are covered with a vegetation whose roots dislodge masses of the walls piece by piece. The cathedral occupies one half of the west side of the plaza. Its style of architecture, both external and internal, is of an imposing and costly character; and, from the great wealth of the builders of Panama, its service and equipments were doubtless of the richest and most valuable kind. Now, in the semi-twilight ever lingering beneath its arches and columns, the poverty of its altar adornments is scarcely concealed, and the crumbling pilasters and tumbling grated windows of its majestic front are painful tokens of its declining fortunes.

The edifice reputed to have been burned was near the eastern gate. Its still erect walls, elliptic and shell-shaped arches and niches, mantled with evergreen, render it attractive. Formerly its adjoining corridors enclosed a handsome garden, around which the cells of a monastery were probably arranged; but everything has disappeared, except the pedestals to the pillars that supported the roof of the corridor.

Near the western gate, and facing its entrance, is the little chapel of *La Merced*, connected with the adjoining church of the same name. That the multitude who daily enter the city from the country may at once implore the intervention of Our Lady of Mercy, it stands open all day. At the time of our arrival a *novena* (nine days' service) was in progress, during which, and until its termination on "nativity day," the chapel was very generally attended by the humbler classes morning and evening. The early mass was before sunrise, and the evening solemnization at 7 o'clock. On the last day of the festival the pavement in front was covered with old sails and mats, so as to accommodate about a hundred persons in addition to the thirty who could be packed in the chapel, and awnings were suspended over these from temporary poles. The building was decorated fancifully with pennons, evergreens, and an extra number of wax candles; and quite a number of church dignitaries were present during a portion of the evening ceremonies. Auditors, as well as worshippers, were almost wholly females; and as the Panameñas are ordinarily dressed in white, with a simple kerchief over the head that permits only a braid of their intensely black hair to be seen on each side, their straight figures, in kneeling posture, illuminated in the darkness by a blaze of light from the altar, might well inspire respect for their faith. The feeling of reverence grows stronger as one hears the melody of their responsive chants beneath the vault of heaven, or under the gothic arches of sombre aisles; but distance only permits the sensation,—the sound of violins and flutes soon puts to flight all thoughts of eternity and omnipresence not previously dissipated by the nasal twang of the choristers, or the sing-song recitations of the officiating priest. From the simplicity of their phraseology and melody, many of their hymn-tunes are of such marked beauty that they often haunted me for hours afterwards. During "nativity day," and to the commencement of evening service, musicians with drums and fifes kept up a succession of tunes in front of the chapel, frequently attracting the attention of our countrymen by "Yankee Doodle," "Sailor's Hornpipe," "Nancy Dawson," and other airs equally appropriate for religious ceremonies. Interludes to the anthems played within the building during service were of like character. Another grand celebration came off on "Lady day" very shortly afterwards. This was terminated by a display of fire-works at the church door, at the close of which men covered with bulls' hides, loaded with pyrotechnics, rushed among the crowd. Formerly *bona fide* bulls were employed; but the brutes were often maddened by the burning fuses and explosions, and in their agony destroyed many lives. Human monsters are now decorated in their stead.

On the Sunday morning following our arrival, we were roused by the approach of vocal and instrumental music. It proved to be a priest followed by flute and violin players, and a crowd of women going to early mass. The priest knocks at the doors of his congregation at three o'clock every Sabbath morning, and the females accompany him; a custom, I believe, peculiar to Panama. The hymn they sing in their march is sweet and plaintive; and in the calm silence of the night the multitude of voices should make one think of a better world. But whilst the priest has sufficient influence with certain classes to bring them out at these unseasonable hours, neither do their precepts inculcate nor their examples inspire reverence for the holy day; and all Sunday morning one may find shops open and women sewing at doors adjoining the cathedral itself. They tell me "the day sanctifies the work;" and thus one's clothes so carefully ironed on Sunday, in their sight should possess especial purity. It is greatly to be regretted that the ministers of the gospel here do not all possess characters without reproach. More than one notoriously frequented the public gambling table, at a restaurant, on Sunday; and I have seen another enter the cock-pit on the same day, his bird having remained tied by the leg at the church door until the conclusion of morning mass. Moreover, my landlady, who is of good family and well educated, tells me her uncle, a canon, has two children, one of whom is in the house with us, and that the *padre* at Taboga is reputed to have been instrumental in adding *fourteen* to its population last year! The number is probably exaggerated; but there is no doubt that he has many "responsibilities" around his church, nor that a sister who lived under the same roof was notoriously immoral. Therefore, so far as its influence over the better class is concerned, priesthood is probably on the decline here; and the church derives its principal support from the revenues obtained from property accumulated in its earlier and purer days.

The number of bells to the churches is very great, many having no less than eight, arranged permanently in the arched windows of their two turrets. As few of them possess clappers, and nearly all have been cracked, they are beaten with mallets, and the sounds emitted are far from musical. Such a clatter as is made two or three times a day, probably cannot be equalled in any similar space of christendom. One or two are yet unbroken, and have mellow tones, that belonging to the burned church being of the number. On one occasion when some of the earlier emigrants were visiting the ruins, they were so rejoiced at finding a musical bell with a clapper, that they rang a good hearty peal to the great amazement and horror of the guardians to the (so regarded) sacred relics; and now, before a Yankee is permitted to enter, a promise is exacted that the bell will not be touched.

A custom-house, a court-house, and an adjoining prison, unless I include the convent with its two remaining vestals, and an immense college commenced by the Jesuits, but never completed, are the only other public buildings pointed out to me at Panama. A decree of the central government to abolish all duties in the port from the first of January next, will soon break up the first. The tenants of the second, principally Indians and negroes, may be seen daily at some lazy work about the city, a heavy iron chain fast to the body and leg, and a sentinel with loaded musket near, to prevent escape. The angel of death will soon violate the sanctuary of the sisterhood, and their portals be no more closed to the world.

The barracks for the soldiers not on post are near the southeast extremity of the peninsula; and here, above the casemates, there is a promenade overlooking the shores and islands of the great bay. If any breeze be stirring, one is sure to perceive it at this place. In a climate where the thermometer is rarely below 78°, this should be inducement sufficient for frequent visits; yet, with all the beautiful panorama it commands, few resort to it. The broad waters of the Pacific roll sullenly towards the ramparts, and break in foamy spray over the reefs. At different distances, and in varied directions, there are scores of beauteous islands and rocky islets adorning a surface made placid by distance—the same cause changing their color through every hue from emerald to sapphire. An abrupt and solitary mountain occupies the immediate background. Its southeast and southwest sides slope off into undulating hills, which, as the eye traces along, suddenly change into mountains, beneath whose summits float vapory clouds. On the land side, every variety of tropical vegetation comes in as accessory to the picture. I loved to sit alone on the old walls at night, and watch the stars as they moved slowly over the dark blue vault; for the familiar gems of the firmament were still before me, and were soon, as the treasures of my homestead already were, to be hidden from sight during years. How noiselessly move the wheels of time, and how slight the record of his passage, when surrounded by loved ones! When alone, without a familiar face to look upon, every flap of his pinions as he creeps vibrates a heart-string that marks each passing hour!

What change the discovery of gold in California is destined to effect in Panama and the appearance of its bay, is yet to be developed. A few short years hence, and fleets may crowd here from every part of the vast Asiatic continent, Oceanica, and the western shores of our own land, laden with wealth for transport; and the city may resound with the noises of commerce and the trades far more than during its previous palmy days. In fact, it can no longer be doubted that American industry and American capital will be largely employed here within five years.

For a city in whose erection so much money was expended, it is surprising how little thought appears to have been given to the comforts or even the conveniences of life; and this, too, in a climate where baths and other essentials to families must be of the last consequence. There are numbers of wells from which bathers could have been supplied, and it is possible that the water may have been drinkable at that period; but now all that is drunk is brought from a stream outside on the backs of mules. Every animal carries two kegs holding six or seven gallons each—a load being valued at twenty-five cents. The only baths are small bamboo sheds with roughly tiled floors, in which, for a *real* ($12\frac{1}{2}$ cents), you are supplied with a towel and a bit of soap, and with half a calabash have the privilege of pouring water over yourself from a large jar placed within the shed. Access to an ample supply of water is pleasant enough in its way; yet I greatly marvel that some Yankee, on whose hands time hung heavily as he awaited a departing vessel, has not manufactured shower-baths from the bamboos and calabashes so abundant, and thus filled his pockets with dimes to help him towards the land of his aspirations—California. Their drinking-water is kept in large earthen jars, called *tinajas*, each of which will hold from 15 to 18 gallons. These are placed in the open air of the balconies; and as they are somewhat porous, constant evaporation is kept up on the outside, tending to cool the water, and somewhat remedy the want of ice.

I have said what number of people probably dwell within and about the city. How many of these are permanently occupied in trades it would be difficult to ascertain; yet there is no doubt that the influx of Americans sensibly increases the demand for domestic products; and carpenters, tailors, shoemakers, hatters, &c., have each a few representatives, who both ask and exact quite a hundred per cent. more for their fabrics than the same class of articles cost in the United States. One principal cause of this is the absolute indolence of negro laborers. These compose a large proportion of the working class, and are unwilling to work one moment after they have obtained sufficient to gratify their appetites during two or three days. On this account intoxicating liquors are sold in every third or fourth house, and these shops receive more than half the earnings of mechanics. A little rice, yams or yuccas, and native fruits, are all the food they require. With plenty of such cheap sustenance, a bottle of country rum or brandy, and a bundle of cigars, they loll about the floors or in hammocks until the supply of money is gone, and hunger forces them to work again. Even then, if they can obtain loads to carry on their shoulders, which ordinarily requires brief labor and brings prompt as well as large recompense, they will not go to their trades. Apparently, the women are more inclined to be industrious; but, under the influence of an enervating climate, a very large number of them fully appreciate the "*dolce far niente.*" With a tunic of some white or fancy colored muslin, having a broad fringed ruffle extending from the neck half to the elbows, a skirt of similar though different colored material, with wide flounces from the knees downward, and their toes stuck in slippers, they lounge all day about the doors or balconies in hammocks or deep-seated chairs. Like all Spanish women, they arrange their hair with taste, and when walking in the sun wear Guayaquil hats very jauntily. Until six or seven years of age nature supplies all the clothing of both sexes.

These remarks must not be understood to include citizens of the better classes. They probably possess greater energy and self-respect; but it was not my good fortune to be associated with them, and I have only their dignified deportment as they passed through the streets to sustain me in the belief. Such had been the conduct of emigrants, that ladies have been compelled to withdraw wholly from the streets, and in a great measure from their churches; and I could not but feel mortified in acknowledging as countrymen the drunken vagabonds daily encountered. Their behavior, of course, influences the reception of all Americans; and so strong had already become the aversion of some Panameños to us, that the name of the nation to which we belonged was quite sufficient to exclude one from rooms the proprietor would gladly have rented. And there is no remedy for this. They are (*soi-disant*) free and independent citizens of the United States—a fact which they conceive gives them the right to trample on any weaker unresisting creature; and when about to leave, may, if they please, commit nuisances of every description in the rented apartments of unsuspecting people; because, forsooth, the agents of the New York steamboat company fail to despatch them to the (accursed) golden country on the appointed day! However disgraceful, these traits are not the only tokens of brutalization generated by the unhallowed thirst, as the following will show.

On the third day after our arrival, and when some forty or fifty of the passengers by the Empire City had got over, a report was current that a man wrapped in an American blanket, and lying within twenty feet of the road, had been passed by two or three of the parties. Only one of them went near enough to satisfy himself that the body before him was that of a dead American: no one had dismounted! Who or whence he was, it mattered not to them—nor whether he should be food for buzzards or worms. They *feared* he might have died suddenly of cholera or other infectious disease, and left him unknown and unsepultured, without examining for a word which would have served to relieve the agonizing suspense of loving kindred in his distant home! As soon as we had obtained facts that would enable us to find the body, Mr. R. and myself at once made arrangements to go and bury him; but just as we were without the city other passengers came in who had seen a newly made grave at the very spot, and we found the man who had started from Cruces with him some fifteen days previously. The natives had shown more humanity than his fellow-countrymen! Shocking accounts have been given me, by those returning from California, of the utterly brutalized wretches who compose a large number of the gold-diggers. They assure me that there are many who would not turn aside to give a dying brother a drink of water; and as to burying dead men, it was regarded as waste of time.

The only wild animals seen were a species of catamount and several wild boars, all of which had been shot in the woods just without the city. It is not very uncommon to destroy the former in some of the gardens within the walls, and the latter are never difficult to find by hunters. The domestic horned-cattle are small, and, though well conditioned, the meat is neither tender nor juicy. They are inclined to be of a uniform dun color. For the number of cows to be seen without the enclosures, milk is scarce, and, indeed, that of the cow is of so little repute that the main reliance is on goats. It is offered with tea and coffee at most gentlemen's houses, but its bluish appearance is not very inviting. One of the vilest-looking animals encountered is a hairless dog, belonging (they tell me) to a Chinese breed. The beasts are as smooth as newly-shaven pigs, (glossy, fat, and lazy,) yet are peculiar pets: the fatter and more glossy the skin appears, the greater the admiration of the mistress. One usually admires contrasts with one's self; and the Panameñas are so nearly naked, I should rather have thought they would give preference to well clad curs.

The most numerous of the feathered tribe are the buzzards. Look where you will, from house-top to garden-wall or public thoroughfare, there the creature may be seen scratching fleshy morsels from the offal, or devouring some choice bit of a decaying carcass unmolested by the passer by, because protected in his enjoyments by the laws of the land. In some cities of South America, the fine for killing one of these public scavengers is twenty dollars. Though not so large as his relative with us, he is a more horrid and filthy-looking wretch, whose exterior brought many a one to sudden end by Yankee bullets, fines to the contrary notwithstanding. Next them in number are brown-backed pelicans, oceanic vultures, that frequent the beaches in very large numbers, and in great apparent delight dash beneath the breaking surf to seize their prey. Curlew plovers, several varieties of snipes, and sand-birds, are also quite numerous, and would be an acquisition to the tables of Panama if there were energy enough among its lazy people to shoot them. Swallows and wrens also frequent the habitations of man, their plumage and habits closely resembling those of our northern birds, though the song of the latter differs through one half its notes. Several varieties of parrots and parroquets have been found in the neighborhood, and, as usual, are great pets with the old ladies when they can be caught.

Twice each day an abundance of good fish are taken from the bay with hook and line. Those caught in the morning are considered unfit for use by dinner-hour. An edible oyster and another very excellent shell-fish resembling in form the Choro (*mytilus*) are supplied from the same source. Occasionally, moderate-sized alligators so far forget their proper cruising-ground in the Rio Grande as to be caught napping on the volcanic ledges under the batteries, and in consequence are apt to be inspected in the plaza. One measuring twelve feet was killed very shortly after our arrival, and brought up for the Yankees to wonder at. On the spot where the boys subsequently tore it in pieces, there were patches of phosphorescent light for several evenings afterwards. Sharks abound in the bay, rendering its waters dangerous to bathers. Pirate-crabs may be found on every part of the beach, and often among the garden-plants and shrubbery within the walls. I have sometimes thought them seeking some of the smaller lizards, for whose capture their peculiar habitations and short, strong claw so well fit them; but such an encounter was never witnessed. Lizards there are of all sizes from an inch to more than a foot in length, and of all colors from light green and blue, through speckled browns, to black. They are graceful little creatures, and many of them will sit and watch you, whisking their tails from side to side, or run to holes of the wall as you approach, and instantly poke out their heads again, as though inviting a game at romps. No one molests them even in the houses.

The British steamer had gone when I arrived, and it was no easy matter to pass four weeks without society, and almost without books, in such a place as Panama. In anticipation of passing direct through to Valparaiso, only an aneroid barometer and one thermometer, together with three or four volumes, had been retained. The record of the aneroid, which had been kept at sea for the purpose of testing its usefulness as a marine instrument, was continued here. The observations at length will be found in Appendix C. From its indications, there is a region commencing just south of San Domingo (latitude 17° N.), and terminating near latitude 1° N. on the west coast of South America, where the atmospheric pressure rarely exceeded 29.85 inches; and in that whole distance, occupying me from August 24th to October 2d, it was only once so great as 29.90 inches. A mean of the observations at Panama, made regularly at 9 A. M., 3 P. M., and 9 P. M., gave 29.795 inches, with a mean diurnal fall from the first to the second hour of .08 inch. The mean temperature for the same hours was 81°, with a mean range of only 2°.9. Though rain fell no more frequently than often occurs during the same season in the United States, the atmosphere was so nearly saturated with moisture that clothing could only be dried by exposure to the direct action of the sun or fire, and any damp articles left in the shade became mouldy in forty-eight hours. The light wind experienced during the day was almost constantly from the northward and westward; at night it was variable. Meteorological observations from March to May of the same year, by Col. Emory, U. S. A., published in the Mem. Amer. Academy, Vol. V, New Series, show a greater mean pressure, a temperature nearly 2° less, and the same prevailing light winds. This officer found the latitude of the northwest bastion of the fortification to be 8° 57′ 12″ N., its longitude 79° 29′ 24″ W.

I will close this account of the Isthmus by a free translation of a few extracts from a work entitled *Piratas de la America, y luz en la defensa de las costas de las Indias occidentales. Segunda impression. En Colonia Agrippina*, 1687. "On the 18th January, 1670, Morgan set out from the castle of Chagres with 1,200 men, five boats with artillery, and thirty-two canoes filled with these people, directing his course up the stream for the city of Panama."

After many difficulties, on the seventh day they arrived at a point on the river called "Cruces, a village in latitude 9° 02′ N., sixteen Spanish leagues distant from the mouth of the river Chagres, and eight leagues from Panama. This is the highest place to which one may travel in boats; for which reason storehouses have been erected here, where goods may be preserved until they come from Panama to seek them with troops of mules." There Morgan was obliged to leave his canoes, and place them under the protection of a proper guard, in order that his return down the river might be perfectly secured.

On the ninth day they saw Panama and the islands from a high mountain, and, as is customary with freebooters when the object of their wishes is in sight, they stole every animal from the harmless people around them, and gorged themselves with eating and drinking.

"The tenth day all the men were placed in order, and, to the sound of drums, they pursued their march directly for the city. But one of the guides advised Morgan not to take the great road, because he believed they would find much resistance from parties in ambush; he therefore selected another route that penetrated the forest, and was very difficult and toilsome. Then the Spaniards, seeing that the pirates did not pursue the road they expected, were obliged to leave their fortresses and come to the encounter of their enemies. The Spanish General placed his troops in order, consisting in squadrons, four battalions of infantry, and a very large number of fierce bulls that many Indians, with some negroes and others, had brought to this end.

"The pirates found themselves on a hill, from whence they could see to a long distance; and discovering the extent of the forces from Panama, they feared them so much that every one wished himself free from the obligation to fight or die. But now they were obliged to make a virtue of necessity, and they resolved to die on the field of battle, knowing that there would be no quarter shown them; and thus they resolved to shed the last drops of their blood. They afterwards divided into three battalions, sending in advance 200 buccaneers, who are very dexterous with fire-arms. The pirates left the hill, and, descending, marched straight against the Spaniards, who were posted on a good field, awaiting their opportune arrival. When the enemy got near, they shouted '*Viva el rey!*' and immediately made a charge against the pirates; but, as there are many swampy places in the country, they could not skirmish as they wished. The 200 buccaneers knelt down and fired on them, whereupon a great battle commenced, on which occasion they defended themselves valiantly, doing their best to throw the pirates into disorder. And thus the infantry had to follow to second the cavalry, but the enemy made them separate; so that, seeing the impossibility, they endeavored to drive the bulls behind the pirates; but the greater part of them ran away, and those which passed through their lines did no other harm than tear some English banners, and the pirates, shooting them, did not permit one to remain alive.

"Two hours passed in the combat, the larger portion of the Spanish cavalry being destroyed, and almost all dead, the rest escaped. The infantry, seeing this, and that there was no chance to conquer, discharged their muskets, threw them away, and every man took to flight, the best that he could. It was impossible for the pirates to follow them, because they were tired after the long journey they had just made. Many who were wounded hid themselves among the thick bushes that are on the shores of the river; but they were very unfortunate, because the pirates, finding them very soon, killed them without showing quarter to a single person, just as if they were so many beasts of the field. They brought a large number of friars (*religiosos*) to the presence of Morgan, who, without caring to hear their prayers and supplications, caused them to be put to death with pistols. They afterward conducted to him a captain who had been wounded in the combat, and Morgan examined him about a diversity of things, asking him what the forces of Panama consisted of; to which he replied that his hopes were based on 400 cavalry, 24 companies of infantry of 100 men or Indians each, and some negroes, who managed 2,000 bulls, that were to be driven on the pirates and totally ruin them. He also discovered that they had made trenches in divers parts of the city, in all of which they had planted artillery, and that at the entrance of the road they had built a fortress, where there were planted eight brass guns, with fifty men.

"Morgan immediately gave orders to take another road, and made a review of his men, of whom the dead and wounded were a considerable number, and more than he had thought. Of the Spaniards they counted more than 600 dead on the field, besides wounded and prisoners. Although they saw themselves less numerous, the pirates were not disheartened, but rather, considering the great advantage they had gained over their enemies, they were full of pride; and as soon as they had reposed a little, prepared to march on the city, swearing to fight until the last one of them should perish; and so they started vigorously to the conquest, taking all the prisoners with them.

"They found great difficulty in reaching the city, because they had placed heavy artillery in divers quartels within it—some loaded with pieces of iron, and others with musket-balls—with all which they saluted the pirates, killing many of them. But they did not stop advancing even in the face of these manifest dangers; and although the Spaniards fired opportunely, they found themselves forced to surrender the city after a combat of three hours, the pirates becoming possessors, killing and destroying all who defended themselves. The inhabitants had already caused all of their most valuable property to be transported to the most occult places. Nevertheless, the warehouses were well filled with all sorts of merchandise, as well silks and cloths as linens, and other things of importance. When the first rush was over, Morgan ordered that all his troops should meet at a certain spot named by him; and there he commanded that no one should dare to drink or taste of wine under the gravest penalties, because the Spaniards had poisoned it; but we should believe that this prudent order was to prevent his companions from becoming drunk, fearing that the Spaniards would rally a sufficient number of persons and fall upon them.

"Thus Morgan having garrisoned the quartels that he found in and without the city, he sent twenty-five men to take a vessel that had remained for want of water, because the tide, which was very low in the port at that time, left it all muddy. Then (already near noon) he caused fire to be communicated to many edifices of the city, in such manner that it could not be certain he had been the incendiary; but so rapidly did it burn, that before night almost all Panama was in flames. Morgan intended to make the public believe that the Spaniards had caused it; and such a rumor was urgently spread among his own people. Many of the conquered and some others endeavored to stop the fire by blowing up some houses with powder in order to make spaces between them; but their labor was useless, for in less than half an hour one entire street was enveloped. All the buildings were of cedar, well and curiously wrought and richly adorned within, principally with magnificent pictures and paintings; of which a part of the jewels were removed, and others perished in the devouring flames.

"Eight convents decorated this episcopal city; seven houses belonging to other religious persons, and one of nuns; as also two sumptuous churches, magnificently adorned with portraits and very fine paintings; much gold and silver, all of which the ecclesiastics had concealed; and a hospital, where the poor and sick found the charity of its founders very exactly administered. More than this, it was beautified by 200 houses of prodigious structure, habited by the richest merchants, to say nothing of 500 others, more or less valuable, for the rest of the inhabitants. It had many stables for the horses that ordinarily carried the silver to the northern coast. In its environs and neighborhood there were many rich plantations and fruitful gardens, making delicious perspectives all the year.

"The Genoese had a magnificent house that served as a counting-house in the commerce that they made of negroes; which was also ordered by Morgan to be fired, as was done. This, with others amounting to the number of 200 magazines, were burned to the very ground, together with a large number of slaves who had concealed themselves in them, and an infinite number of sacks of flour, which continued burning for four weeks after the fire commenced. The greater part of the pirates were some time without the city and became timid, believing that the Spaniards would come to renew the combat with them, knowing that they had incomparably more troops than themselves; and so they retired to unite their forces, which were much diminished by the preceding losses and because there were many wounded, whom they conveyed to a church, the only one remaining standing; and, moreover, Morgan had sent a convoy of 150 men to the castle of Chagres to announce the victory obtained at Panama."

And so fell Panama *the old;* twelve hundred vagabonds against the population of a city needing 5,200, or, as others have it, 7,000 houses for their accommodation!

CHAPTER III.

FROM PANAMA TO LIMA.

EMBARK ON BOARD STEAMER NEW GRENADA.—RAIN.—BUENAVENTURA.—THE ANDES.—CROSS THE EQUATOR.—REFUSED PERMISSION TO LAND IN ECUADOR.—ANCHOR AT PAYTA.—POSITION OF THE TOWN AMID STERILITY.—MARINE FOSSILS.—HOUSES.—PEOPLE.—NO FRESH WATER.—SHIP-BUILDING.— A BALSA.—VEGETABLES AND FRUITS FROM THE VALLEY OF PIURA; CHERIMOYA; ALLIGATOR PEAR; GRANADILLA; PEPINO.—WHALERS.—LAMBAYEQUE.—HUANCHACO AND TRUJILLO.—BALSAS AGAIN.—STRIKE ON A ROCK OFF CASMA BAY.—CALLAO.

September 27, 1849.—Embarked on board the iron steamer New Grenada at noon, and left for Callao at 1 P. M. Air nearly calm, with occasional showers of rain and severe thunder and lightning. Passed the Pearl islands about sunset, though at too great a distance to see them distinctly. Many porpoises and flying-fish about the ship during the afternoon.

September 28.—Very heavy rain from midnight until 1 A. M.; and the early morning being overcast and murky, with very little wind, was rather unpropitious. So smooth was the sea, that of our twenty-three passengers there was only one incommoded by the motion. During the forenoon the S.W. wind gradually grew stronger, and we had a remarkably fine day, our ship running on a S.E. by S. course, about eight miles per hour.

Two or three land-birds took refuge on board, and were so wearied that they made no effort to escape capture. One, a small crow-shaped species, had a dove-colored head, with white stripes round the eyes, and long mandibles. The rest of the body was dark, and its toes webbed. Innumerable schools of porpoises and bonitas jumping near our track. Latitude at noon 6° 26′ N., the land distant to the eastward 40 miles.

September 29.—A violent rain-storm, with thunder and lightning, lasted, almost without intermission, from 2 to 8 A. M. At sunset entered the mouth of the river Buenaventura, and at 7½ P. M. dropped anchor off a town of the same name, situated on its left bank. The distance across the mouth of the river is about a mile, and its shores are apparently quite bold. This is the nearest port for passengers and the mail to and from Bogota. Darkness and our distance from the shore prevented anything more than the lights of the town from being seen, as we were not permitted to land. People who reside in countries rarely free from yellow fever, and other similarly harmless tropical infirmities, probably consider themselves favored with climates especially healthy. *We*, having come from a place where the cholera had prevailed some month or two previously, still bore pestilence about us, and passengers, freight, mail, all were declared in quarantine! So excellent a joke did it appear to the Spanish passengers on board, that the health officers and boatmen who came off were most unmercifully burlesqued and laughed at during the hour we remained at anchor. Maugre the bad character the officials endeavored to fasten on us, it did not prevent several persons coming on board to accompany us down the coast; and by 9 o'clock we were again outside, in a torrent of rain, which never ceased during the remainder of the day.

September 30.—The thermometer fell below 80° during the preceding night, throughout which, and up to 8 A. M., there was incessant rain. At noon we were a mile to the southwest of Gorgona, steering a S.S.W. course, against a head wind and moderate sea. The island is small, though covered with vegetation, and is extremely picturesque and beautiful. It has a good bay on its southwest side, with abundance of water, and is reputed to possess a valuable gold mine, as well as a pearl fishery of great extent in the adjoining waters. Difficulty of access and venomous reptiles prevent the former from being worked, and multitudes of sharks keep watch over the latter, ready to devour all divers who may seek their gems. At least such is the story told on board. Twenty-five leagues farther south is the less inviting island of Gallo, where Pizarro made his famous stand, bidding all who sought Peru, fame, fortune, and pleasure, to follow him across a line traced in the sand with the point of his sword; those who preferred Panama, disgrace, and poverty, to remain beyond it. The thirteen from whom famine, disease, and perpetual rains, had not driven every spark of enterprise, have been immortalized in history. Shortly after their decision, Pizarro removed with his little band to Gorgona, where they were able to obtain something of shelter beneath the trees, and a scanty supply of food from the game found on the island. During the latter part of the day the wind gradually decreased and the weather brightened, so as to give us an occasional gleam of sunshine. Night pleasant, and without rain.

October 1.—Towards daylight the S.S.W. wind sprang up again, bringing with it a heavy ground-swell, and weather so thick that the coast could not be seen, though only thirty miles distant. During the morning, grampuses, flying-fish of large size, and many varieties of sea-birds, were quite numerous. Latitude at noon 1° north.

October 2.—The frequent and violent rains to which we had been subject between Panama and 2° north latitude have ceased; and though there are dense masses of cumulo-stratus constantly over portions of the neighboring coast, no rain fell on our decks south of Gallo island. Not less striking was the change in the appearance of the land in these few hundred miles. On Gorgona at noon of September 30, there was dense tropical vegetation. When the sun rose brightly, October 2, we were near yellowish and rocky cliffs, on which there were but a few half-burnt plants. At noon we were within less than a mile of Cape San Lorenzo, to the southward of which a little village lies sheltered in a secluded valley. Off the cape there are two rocks, each of them somewhat remarkable—one for its regular obelisk form of great elevation; the other for its flat summit and trees, and sides striped alternately white and brown. The former color is probably due to the sea-birds that make its crags their homestead. Doubling San Lorenzo, the Andes become a more prominent feature of the landscape. Monte Cristo, the most northern summit visible, rears its dark head above the arid cliffs; the distant ranges to the southward lose their peaks amid the clouds; and solitary detached, intermediate elevations give a graceful finish to the picture.

The barometer at last rose above 30 inches, and the extraordinarily saturated atmosphere of the region near Panama seemed to have been passed through. Overhead there were light cirro-cumuli, betokening fair weather; and a fall of the thermometric column below summer-heat was an event just south of the equator most gratefully chronicled. And so in the calm and silent watches of the night we slept from autumn to spring without knowledge of the storms of winter.

October 3.—A dark, hazy morning, and the atmosphere unusually calm. At 7 o'clock the ship was just within Point St. Elena, on the north shore of the Gulf of Guayaquil. This last is low and possesses little variety of outline. Here and there, evergreens may be seen; but most of the vegetation seems burnt, and gives to the land an arid and especially uninteresting look. We found many small whales and black-fish (grampus) playing about the mouth of the gulf, and multitudes of dark-backed pelicans floating near the lazy monsters. Occasionally some of the birds, flying at considerable elevation above the water, would press their wings close to their sides and dive after their finny food beneath the surface with the velocity of an arrow.

Thirty miles from the ocean we were hailed by the commander of a small government steamer, sent there to await our arrival and forbid a nearer approach to the city. Fear that we might introduce the cholera had thus seriously infected the authorities of this noisome and pestilential town. Besides the mail, there were nearly a dozen passengers and some freight on board for Ecuador—all of which, except the letters, we were commanded to keep on board. Among the passengers was a United States Chargé d'Affaires accredited to the government of Ecuador, in whose behalf remonstrance was earnestly made by the captain of our steamer; but he was piously told, "If you had Jesus Christ himself on board, I would fire into you if you attempted to land him." Nor was the personal application of the Chargé more successful, if more respectful. Although those on board who had business here would be put to great inconvenience and expense by being carried on to the next port where the steamer would anchor, all recognised the sanctity of the quarantine laws, and submitted with what grace they might. Some begged to be landed on Punta Arena as we passed down, because they claim, that in making a quarantine law it is the duty of Ecuador to provide a lazaretto; but they were not gratified.

Finding that the meek and Christian-like officer of the navy of Ecuador was inexorable, the mail-bag was passed to him *through the water*, and we started down the gulf at 2 P. M. Abreast of our temporary anchorage there were a few houses on the shore, of the same general structure as those at Chagres, and differing only by being built on strong posts that elevate them some ten or twelve feet above the earth. This is, no doubt, intended to protect the inhabitants somewhat from insects and reptiles. Their balconies or verandahs are nearly close, and seem made of canes wattled together. Cattle stood under the houses, out of the sunlight, but not a single biped could be detected even with the aid of a spy-glass.

Between sunrise and 3 P. M. the temperature gradually increased from 71° to 80°; but as we drew near to the mouth of the gulf, and recovered the S.W. wind, it became cooler again, and the night proved very pleasant.

October 4.—Sunrise was visible through a misty haze, overhanging the arid and wretchedly sterile coast of Peru, just to the northward of Cape Blanco. As the day advanced, the mist rolled into cirro-cumuli over portions of the heavens, permitting the sun to give us the full power of his rays; but such is the effect of the S.W. wind, that the temperature constantly decreased, and at 3 P. M. the thermometer showed only 65½°. We closely coasted the shore all day without seeing a plant or a shrub, and only a long and almost unvaried line of yellow sand-hills. A few fishermen, and a flock or two of "ice" birds, off Cape Blanco, were the only animated objects passed. Just at sunset the ship anchored amid half a dozen American whalers in the harbor of Payta. They were here for repairs, or supplies of vegetables. Three others left the port as we entered, bound home, or perhaps to pursue the perilous employment that had brought them to the South Pacific.

The health officer (who, by-the-by, was a Yankee) was alongside by the time the anchor was down; and, with some brief questions, came on board, he said, "to examine our sick." Finding no such unfortunates, we were at once admitted to all the privileges of the renowned city of the whalers; for they have probably contributed more to its commerce and prosperity than any other portion of the trading world. So much for a grain or two of plain, practical sense, and reasonable discretionary powers intrusted to a descendant of the Anglo-Saxons. A Peruvian would probably have refused us *pratique* on learning the treatment at Buenaventura and Guayaquil, and would assuredly have entailed quarantine at all the other ports on the coast, simply because their health-officers had been so absurd.

As the customs of the country exact no extraordinary amount of care on the toilet, but few moments sufficed to prepare a large number of the passengers to avail themselves of the liberty denied at the other two ports, and we were soon on shore. And such a shore as it proved to be! But, as darkness probably prevented objects from being correctly seen, it would be unfair to detail first impressions of Payta. Whilst the ship would be receiving coal next day, a better opportunity would be afforded; and I returned on board to enjoy, with my companions, a basket of cherimoyas and aguacates from the valley of Piura. The evening passed pleasantly. Stars shone out in glorious brilliancy overhead, and the temperature was down to Autumn heat of our central States.

October 5.—Payta is at the bottom of a shallow bay of the same name, in latitude 5° 02′ S. Its shores, which are quite precipitous, are composed of silicious and clayey deposits, with occasional masses of soft and light-colored sandstone, and are elevated more than two hundred feet above the sea level. Multitudes of marine shells in the upper strata of the hills north of the town show that they were submerged at some previous epoch. Foliage of any description, or even blades of grass, except those that thrive in the ocean, are not to be seen in any direction from the eminences, unless we look at the windows of the ladies.

The houses are built entirely of split canes or bamboos brought from Guayaquil, and wattled together, with occasional strengthening studding of wood for support of the roof. Many are plastered with mud and whitewashed, though the larger number permit a free circulation of air. They have high-peaked roofs thatched with palm or cocoa leaves, and wide projecting eaves to shelter street passengers from the great glare of the sun. A more miserable collection of dwellings one could not easily find in a place through which so much wealth had passed; and yet one of them, by no means very extensive, is said to have cost more than $40,000. The carpenters of the United States would gladly furnish one more extensive and better suited to the climate for half the money. There are two or three churches partaking of the same character of structure as the private buildings. On one of them, not yet completed, a huge image of the rising sun has been wrought, perhaps to remind the people of the worship of their forefathers; but, although we awaited the coming of the *padre*, apparently indicated by the crouching groups of women near the door, it was not our good fortune to gain admittance within the edifice. After seeing us, the prelate started in another direction, and we continued our ramble.

The population, estimated at 1,500 souls, appear in keeping with their country and the structures they inhabit. They are generally short, dark-colored Indians, slatternly in dress, as the worst of such nations usually are. Thoughts of cleanliness or modesty do not find resting-places in their minds; they are contented to crouch about the floors or sand under the shadow of the eaves, and to swing in a grass hammock seems luxury. Yet there are interesting faces among the women, with their long, dark, and flowing hair, and quiet, submissive casts of features. The descendants of Spaniards are not numerous. All the water they consume is brought on the backs of mules from a distance of twenty-five miles. It is sold at two cents per gallon. Ship-carpenters receive a dollar and a quarter per day; the commonest laborers not less than sixty or seventy cents. How the disparity is occasioned I cannot comprehend; but it is somewhat anomalous that the water-carrier will employ two days of his own time, and that of a mule, for a smaller remuneration than the most common laborer obtains alone, unless each *arriero* (muleteer) has many animals under his charge, and their hire is of comparatively trifling value.

The Indians have built two or three good-looking schooners, and there were others of small burden on the stocks. Their models are similar to those of the nation whose representatives are most frequent here; and it is not unlikely their knowledge of navigation has been derived from the same race. All the timber used is brought from the vicinity of Guayaquil. Boats for *ordinary* purposes on the coast are unknown, the navigation being by means of a sort of raft called *balsa*, perhaps from the wood of the same name which is the material of its construction. They are formed of three or more logs secured by cross-pieces, each log a foot or more in diameter, and from twenty to thirty feet in length. A platform is erected in the centre for freight and passengers; a single squaresail propels the craft, and it is steered with a broad-bladed paddle. With a fair wind, their huge mast and sail enables them to make very fair speed; but in working to windward, their progress is quite slow. It is, of course, difficult to capsize them, and they will pass safely through surf on the open coast, in which no ordinary boat could possibly live.

Payta is subject to long and, indeed, almost perpetual drought. No rain had fallen since 1845; and prior to that, seven years had intervened; but the "oldest inhabitants" thought "the signs of the times indicated an abundance this year." Under existing atmospheric conditions, the immense beds of nearly decomposed shells are absolutely valueless; rain would render the shores productive beyond calculation. As nothing whatever is grown here, every article of consumption is brought from the valley of Piura, the nearest gardens of which are from fifteen to twenty miles distant. An abundant supply of fruits and vegetables is brought on the backs of mules or Indians, and, in spite of intervening barriers, is sold at reasonable prices. Potatoes (Irish and sweet), pumpkins, cabbages, yuccas (a long fusiform root), beans in profusion, and many other garden vegetables, are of excellent flavor and of good size. The principal fruits are plantains, cherimoyas, oranges, lemons (sweet and sour), melons, paltas, pomegranates, granadillas, and many others of inter-tropical growth, besides apples, peaches, pears, &c.

The potatoes of Peru are of a remarkably fine quality, and a yellow variety that is grown in the mountain regions are far superior to anything produced in Nova Scotia or the Emerald isle. Every effort to introduce them elsewhere has proved abortive, as they degenerate after the first crop. The sweet potatoes, called *camotes*, are also of two colors—white and purple-skinned. Preference is given to the former. They have more saccharine matter than the yellow variety of the United States, but are not so mealy. When properly cooked, yuccas are valuable substitutes for the Irish potato, to which they are not wholly dissimilar in taste. They are often a foot or more in length, and two or three inches in diameter. The Lima beans are famed throughout the world. Few eat of the cherimoya without declaring it the most exquisite of all fruits. It is the product of a delicate tree (*Anona cherimolia*), that attains to a height of fifteen to twenty feet, and is almost as many years in coming to perfection. The leaves are oval and pointed at both ends; its flowers, small, of white color, and very fragrant, are solitary; and the fruit, of a heart-shape, grows from two to five inches in diameter. When ripe, externally it is of a brownish green, covered with small knobs and scales, and often has black lines like network spread over it. The skin is tough, but not very thick. Internally the pulp is of a creamy white, with a number of dark brown or black seeds ranged round a small central core. Some have likened the exquisitely luscious flavor of the pulp to that of strawberries and cream, but it is comparable with nothing else. There are two or three varieties of the tree, differing in their magnitude, the size of the fruit, and number of seeds. Those of Huanuco and the valley of Azapa are considered better than those of Piura.

The palta, sometimes called *aguacate*, and by foreigners "alligator pear," is the fruit of the *Persea gatissima*, Gärt.—a slender and very tall tree, sometimes fifty feet in height. It is nearly as large as the egg of a goose, but pear-shaped. The rind is tough, but not thick, and of a brownish-green color. In the centre is a heart-shaped stone or kernel about an inch in diameter, between which and the rind there is a greenish saffron-colored pulp that dissolves on the tongue like marrow. Its taste is peculiar, and at first is not generally agreeable to a foreigner; but, with a little pepper and salt, it acquires favor with great rapidity, and many prefer it to the cherimoya. Sometimes it is dressed as a salad, with oil and vinegar; and as it is a most nutritious and wholesome fruit, that does not deteriorate for some days, it is much sought after by passengers in the steamers. The kernel is very astringent and bitter; and, on being cut, a juice flows which is said to leave an indelible stain.

The granadilla is the fruit of the *Passiflora quadrangularis*, and is somewhat egg-shaped, with a hard and rather thick reddish-yellow skin. Internally it is lined with a soft membrane, containing a gray gelatinous pulp of an agreeable sub-acid taste. Its seeds are dark-colored and very numerous. The pepino (a *Cucurbitacea*) is a more common fruit, growing in great abundance on plants about a foot and a half high. It is a rather pointed oval, from three to five inches long, having a yellowish green rind with purplish stripes. The edible portion is solid, though juicy and well-flavored; but it is not considered so wholesome as many other fruits, and is not a favorite where there are so many better to select from.

The Bay of Payta was discovered by Pizarro, and is the best harbor on the coast of Peru. Small quantities of silver, cinchona bark, ratana, and wool being sent here for shipment, it is more frequented than any other port except Callao. But American whalers, as has been said, are its great frequenters—its tranquil waters permitting repairs and coopering of their oil-casks; whilst the valley furnishes them supplies, and they can drive a little trade with the people on shore. San Miguel de Piura, of which it is the port, was the first town founded by Pizarro. It lies upon a small stream of the same name, that fertilizes a valley celebrated in Peru for the salubrity of its climate, and which is said to contain a population of 75,000. The town has only 5,000 or 6,000 inhabitants.

The requisite supply of coal being on board, our diplomatic and several other passengers went ashore, and we left Payta at 3 P. M., with quite a number of Peruvians in place of the departing messmates. Afternoon and night proved particularly fine, with a clear starlight and cool atmosphere.

October 6.—Morning dawned cold, damp, and cloudy, native passengers shivering under thick clothing and overcoats. Immediately on the coast the land was too low to be seen through the hazy atmosphere; but we caught occasional glimpses of the glittering snow-peaks of the cordilleras far above the vapory stratum. There were considerable numbers of cape pigeons (the spotted variety) about the ship all day, but no fish of any description.

Anchored off Lambayeque (latitude 6° 47′ S.) at 2 P. M., and remained two hours to land and receive freight, mail, and passengers, all which were transported on *balsas*. This is a perfectly open roadstead, where the sea breaks eternally along the beach. Ships anchor nearest to a little town called San José, containing three or four hundred people. Lambayeque, with as many thousands, lies five or six miles to the northward. A spirited account of a visit here, and of the *huacas* (Indian mounds) in the vicinity, may be found in "Three Years in the Pacific." To the north of San José, the hills produce scattered and scrubby vegetation for nearly a mile; but southward again the soil resumes its arid and desolate aspect.

October 7.—At 8 A. M. anchored off Huanchaco, in latitude 8° 04′ S., a perfectly open roadstead, where the sea breaks heavily on the beach at all times. It is a village of some five or six hundred people, immediately on the beach, with a back-ground of the most abrupt possible volcanic mountains, against which a white church stands in distinct relief. It would be difficult to imagine more wild and picturesque clusters of peaks than are arranged about Huanchaco, or a more dreamy landscape than they present in the declining sunlight, with misty scrolls floating among them. The city of Trujillo, of which this is the port, was founded by Pizarro soon after Lima. It is on a sandy plain, watered by a small stream, two leagues distant from Huanchaco, though not more than three miles from the sea.

As there is always a heavy swell in the roadstead, and the surf breaks in much fury on the shore, it is difficult, as well as tedious, to ship or discharge cargoes; yet the valley about Trujillo is so fertile that several vessels are constantly employed in transporting wheat, sugar, maize, a small amount of cotton, and bars of silver brought from mines in the vicinity. Passengers and freight were brought off in stout launches made sharp at both extremities, the better to encounter breakers; and at a later hour the mail came by a courier mounted on a little balsa called a *caballito*. This last consists of two conical bundles of rushes or straw lashed firmly together, and the sharp points turned up like the toe of a Turkish slipper. Its length does not exceed ten or twelve feet, and, as it is very light, the *balsero* may carry it out of the reach of the breakers as soon as he touches terra firma. He sits astride his "pony," and, with a split bamboo for a paddle, rides over the seas far more rapidly than the launches can be moved. I never saw the caballito at any other port on the coast; but there is a third kind of balsa common from Panama to Valdivia. This consists of two seal-skins made air-tight, and inflated like bladders. These are lashed side by side, and have a small platform of cane or rushes in the hollow between them. The balsero occupies the platform, propelling his craft with a double-bladed paddle, and will venture to sea when no ordinary boat could possibly live. Some of the balsas are large enough to carry two or three persons, and may occasionally be seen with a sail made of ponchos tied together. Smaller ones are universally used by fishermen on the coast.

Leaving the anchorage at 3 P. M., we soon opened Trujillo, four or five miles distant from us; its cathedral, towers, and whitewashed walls, amid the dark verdure of the valley, making one long for a ramble by the side of its fertilizing river. The ruins of the ancient town of Chimu are between Trujillo and the sea; and the huacas of the vicinity have yielded many treasures and curious antiquities, deposited by the wealthy idolaters prior to their subjection by the Inca Yupanqui. As we coasted upwards during the afternoon an occasional glimpse was caught of the distant snow-peaks: but they were only momentary, for clouds hung perpetually over the ridges; and even when immovable, our change of locality would soon interpose them between us and visible objects. The night was cold and damp, accompanied by a sort of fog-cloud that shut us out from the heavens.

October 8.—Close to the northern entrance of Casma bay, latitude 9° 28′ S., I was startled from slumber about 3 A. M. by a shock that nearly threw me out of the berth. Hastening on deck, the captain told me we had struck a whale; though, as I passed to the opposite side to look at the land we were approaching, the officer of the watch whispered, "More barnacles than blubber on that chap's back, anyhow." Whether rock or whale, the ship was not detained an instant, nor did she leak any more afterward; but passed rapidly to an anchorage, pitchy dark as it was, and speeded on her voyage an hour or two later, when daylight would have assisted investigation of a matter so important to navigators. Subsequently the surmise of the chief officer proved correct: a dangerous rock was found here.

The weather was charming from 10 A. M. until sunset, after which there was a foggy mist and low temperature. We coasted within a mile of the land all day, the ocean almost as smooth as a lake.

October 9.—Anchored quite near to the mole in Callao bay at 8 A. M., some sixty vessels of other nations imparting an air of maritime importance to the little town on the beach. This, one of the largest and best sheltered anchorages on the west coast of South America, is protected on the south and west by a long, narrow point, and two islands, of which San Lorenzo is the principal. In a part of the space between San Lorenzo and the point the water is shoal, though there is a passage at all times for the largest ships. The distance from the point to the island is about a mile and a half, with a bank near midway on which the sea breaks very constantly. San Lorenzo is only a mile wide, and fifteen in circumference, its sterile and sharp-crested hills rising to a height of nearly 1,500 feet. Its northeast declivity is much less steep than the opposite side, on whose almost vertical face seals and multitudes of sea-birds take up their abode. Vessels to be quarantined, and ships of war refitting, find berths at the island; but their crews or passengers have no sources of recreation unless in the study of its geology. It is a barren spot, absolutely without verdure except during a few weeks of the winter season.

The river Rimac, flowing from the eastward, empties into the bay a mile to the northward of Callao; and six miles farther in the same direction the Carabaillo discharges itself. Between these streams there is a gently sloping plain to the eastward, whose fertile fields are covered with trees and shrubbery, patches of wheat, and maize; but to the south and southeast, bare rock and sand alone greet the eye. Callao itself adds nothing to the charm of the view from the water. Fortifications, barracks, and the custom-house, conceal more than half the dwellings. The former consist of two castles built by the Spaniards, and capable of mounting nearly four hundred pieces of ordnance. At present only sixty guns are serviceable. The principal, now named *La Independencia,* has two round towers connected by a curtain, spacious court-yards, and low, thick walls, surrounded by a ditch that can be filled from the sea. The other, on the point that stretches towards San Lorenzo, is called *El Sol.* General Rodil threw himself into the former during the revolution of independence; and for a year and a half after Lima had surrendered to the patriots he withstood all the privations and sufferings incident to a siege both by sea and land. With the fall of *Real Felipe,* as the castle was then called, fell the power of the mother country in Peru.

The Callao built during the reign of Philip IV. stood farther out on the point than the present town. It was swallowed by an earthquake and the sea in 1746, at which time 4,000 people are said to have perished, and a part of the vessels at anchor in the bay were transported far inland. Some of the ruins are still visible. The present town contains about 750 numbered houses, spread over three or four streets parallel with the low shingle beach, and others at right angles to them. They are flat-roofed, constructed of canes or wicker-work plastered, and are of no great pretensions either in point of size or architecture. The frequency of earthquakes and the rare occurrence of rains render structures of this character essential and commodious, and the mildness of the climate obviates the necessity for glazed windows. We found its unpaved streets suffocatingly filled with dust; in winter, rainless as are the clouds, sufficient mist is deposited to convert them into mud. Altogether it is a dirty, uninviting place, from which one escapes to the capital at the earliest moment.

A fine wharf or mole encloses a small basin, within which boats may land cargoes at all times. Its foundation is the hulks of old vessels driven round with piles, and filled in with stone quarried on San Lorenzo. Cargoes are discharged from vessels into lighters, and transported to the mole, where there are convenient landing-slips and tackles for hoisting them out. For want of warehouses, great piles of wheat from Chile, and bales of goods from other parts of the world, remain uncovered on the mole for weeks, ample evidences of the dryness of the climate. Although the railroad to Lima had been for some months traversed by passenger cars when we returned in 1852, freight for the city was still wholly transported on mules or in ordinary carts. Hence the delay in removing goods, and the necessity of guards to keep off pilferers. One might steer clear of bales and boxes, stacks of grain, sailors, and boatmen, but that the venders of fruits and *dulces* perch themselves on every unoccupied spot; and it is only by extraordinarily good management, aided by admirable luck, that one escapes running foul of a tatterdemalion negress or Indian before reaching the custom-house at the end of the wharf.

CHAPTER IV.

LIMA.

TRAVELLING AND SMOKERS.—FOUNDATION OF THE CITY.—ITS PLAN AND STREETS.—BUILDINGS.—FOUNTAIN IN THE PLAZA.—THE CATHEDRAL.—CHURCHES.—REMAINS OF PIZARRO.—CHURCH ERECTED BY THE CONQUEROR.—CHARITABLE INSTITUTIONS.—PALACE.—CHAMBER OF DEPUTIES.—SENATE.—EDUCATION.—AMUSEMENTS.—THEATRE.—BULL-FIGHTS.—SAYO Y MANTO.—BRIDGE OVER THE RIMAC.—ALAMEDA.—MARKET.—POPULATION.—CLIMATE.—EARTHQUAKES.—MANUFACTURES.

In 1849 omnibuses travelled every hour between Callao and Lima, each passenger paying a dollar for his conveyance, a little more than six miles. The road is nearly a straight line, and, apparently, is almost level; but, in fact, the rise is more than 90 feet to the mile. It was constructed at the close of the last century at an expense of $341,000, its plan embracing a central elevated track, guarded by low parapets, or curbs, and a lower one on each side for carriages. The last mile, near Lima, is well paved, and shaded by rows of closely planted trees, that include convenient foot-walks and occasional stone benches for weary pedestrians; but most of the remainder is over pebble-stones that have been torn from their places, and loose sand, part of which a moving crowd keeps constantly in the atmosphere. Until one reaches the last half league of the journey there is very little of interest to be seen. The half-deserted village of Bellavista, founded after the destruction of Callao at the middle of the last century, and abandoned for the present location of that town when the terror of earthquakes had passed away; a few mounds, supposed to be burial places of Indians; a wretched church, and a low *pulperia* half way—these are all. Immediately away from artificial irrigation, as all this tract is, the soil seems parched, and there are few varieties of flowers or birds to render the rest attractive; so that one longs to escape at the earliest moment from the twelve or fifteen smokers by whom he is surrounded. Neither sex nor social position seems to have influence to prevent this use of tobacco. Apparently, the custom is almost universal; and I sometimes fancied that the gentler sex, who were most expensively dressed, and showed most jewellery in public, not only consumed the largest, but also the greatest number of cigars. Whether those of *sangre azul* would permit a *Gringo* to see them thus indulge, I doubt; but no one else does doubt that, in secret, their pretty lips blow many "a cloud." At that time I felt it somewhat novel to be seated between graceful, courteous, and elegantly dressed women, each of whom puffed away a pair of stout cigars in the two leagues ride—aye, and evidently enjoyed them too.

Subsequently, a railroad was built between the two cities at a cost of more than $700,000. As there was very little grading to be done, it is a mystery to all who have seen the inefficient returns from it, how the English engineers could have expended so much money. So slightly is the track constructed, that the company fear to transport freight over it, though passengers are permitted to take luggage on the train with them at an extra charge of one cent per pound.

Lima was founded by Pizarro on the 18th of January, 1535. The province of which it is the capital occupies the centre of a department also called Lima, which has a length of fourteen leagues from north to south, and ten leagues in its greatest breadth from east to west. In commemoration of the day of its foundation (Epiphany) it was called "*La cuidad de los Reyes*" (the city of the kings); two years later Charles V. made it a royal city, assigning as part of its coat of arms three crowns and the star of the magi; and after the revolution it was styled "the city of the free." It seems to be admitted that the name by which it is usually designated, "Lima," is but a corruption of "Rimac," originating in the habit of substituting

L for R in pronunciation at that epoch. The city lies in an amphitheatre of hills on both banks of the river Rimac, latitude 12° 02′ 34″ S. These hills appear to have been broken through by the waters of that stream. From the summits of San Cristoval and Amancaes, two of the nearest to the northwest, a bird's-eye view is commanded of the valley of the river far to the eastward; of its ornamental gardens and productive haciendas; of the city at one's feet—its grand cathedral and multitude of churches—its huge circus for bull-fights—its alamedas, gardens, and picturesque bridge; and of the distant ocean and harbor, dotted with sterile islands and ships. A gleam of sunlight to illumine a spot or two, and the picture would have been perfect; but both my visits chanced to be at periods when sunbeams are rare, and I was not so favored.

The river divides the city into two unequal parts. That on the southern side is the most extensive, and is of a triangular form, the Rimac constituting the base. Perpendicular thereto, the breadth is rather less than a mile. All this portion was enclosed by walls erected towards the close of the 17th century, for defence against the buccaneers. A considerable portion of these fancied safeguards having fallen into ruins, they were rebuilt in 1807. The smaller portion of the town, consisting of the suburb of San Lazaro, has its greatest extent perpendicular to the course of the river; but the utmost circumference of compact population will not exceed ten miles. It was originally intended that all the streets should be in two directions perpendicular to each other, and also that the houses should afford the greatest amount of shade; but this was only carried out to a certain extent in the vicinity of the great square. They are of tolerable width (12 varas), suitably paved in the more populous portions, and have sidewalks of broad flag-stones. The last, however, are rarely elevated above the general level, and foot-passengers instinctively shrink to the wall whenever a carriage or other vehicle approaches drawn by animals. A stream of water flows constantly through the centre of each east and west thoroughfare. As the site has a decided slope towards the ocean, offal and garbage thrown into the rivulets, and not immediately rescued by the flocks of buzzards that frequent them with the confidence of domestic fowls, are carried rapidly away, and consequently the streets are quite clean.

Climate, and the apprehension of earthquakes, compel the people to build low houses. If the latter are of more than one story, the upper one is of wicker-work, plastered with mud and white-washed or painted in fresco. The lower story is of adobes similarly finished. Of necessity they cover much ground, and for ventilation and convenience are ordinarily built round one or more quadrangular courts, that have a common entrance from the street. Over this great door-way, usually large enough for a carriage, there are closed lattice-work balconies, where ladies are accustomed to sit and watch the passers-by—themselves unseen. Most of the walls on the streets have neither balustrade, cornice, nor finish of any kind, but terminate abruptly, and support roofs that are flat or very nearly so. The portals, ceilings, walls of the patios, and apartments of the better-class houses are handsomely painted with fresco colors in rich groups or landscapes, that gives them a most charming and airy look; and this is often increased as one passes, by the perspective obtained of gracefully twining flowers about the rear balcony. Some few have ornamented fronts; but as the great majority have only windowless dead walls, the royal city by no means favorably impresses a stranger.

The great plaza, near the centre of the business part of the city, is more than 500 feet square. There is an ornamental fountain at its centre, which is supplied with water from the Rimac, and is resorted to by water-venders, with donkeys and kegs, from many surrounding squares. As some of the fraternity possess wit of no mean order, this is a scene of constant noise and humor. The fountain is composed of a reservoir, 24 feet in diameter, and two basins. Four lions in the former eject water from their mouths, and its rim is externally adorned with flowers in semi-relief. The lower basin rests on a pedestal, perhaps fifteen feet high, and the upper one, supported on a column of nearly half that altitude, itself sustains a shaft surmounted by a ball on which stands a figure of Fame. The pillars, basins, and figures are of bronze, and were cast by Antonio Rivas in 1650. Half a mile to the eastward there is another, though irregular shaped and smaller public square, at one time used as the market place; and several of lesser size, in different parts of the city. Most of them have rude fountains, with ample supplies of water for their several precincts. And, in connection with these aqueous reservoirs, it may be mentioned that the city authorities require the water-carriers to slay and bring to the plaza, every morning, a certain number of dogs. There they must remain until counted by the official whose duty it is to inspect and remove them; and as the buzzards commence their feast meanwhile, the sight is by no means attractive. Though a little "hard," the water of the Rimac is limpid, cool, and good. It is certainly melted snow, but I do not recollect to have seen more than one or two cases of goitre.

The cathedral and archbishop's palace occupy the whole of the eastern side of the great plaza; the south has private dwellings, with balconies overlooking it; the western is somewhat similar to the last, except that the Senate chamber and Cabildo are numbered among its edifices; and on the north is the government palace. There are wide colonnades beneath the balconies both on the south and west sides, and these are lined with shops for the sale of goods and wares of every class. One is called the *Portal de los Escribanos;* the other, *Portal de los Botineros;* and both are constantly filled by a sauntering crowd of promenaders or purchasers.

The churches have received the lauds of many for the intrinsic value of their decorations and ornaments, and they doubtless merit all that has been said of them. Gliding rapidly from place to place, as brief time compelled me to do, and sometimes arriving at the doors of an edifice just as they were being closed, there remains on my memory only a confused impression of moderately good taste, much wealth in silver-plate and ornaments, and generally very indifferent paintings. Pre-eminent among them is the cathedral, a truly noble structure in its internal proportions; its groined roof; its altar, with massive columns of richly carved silver; its superbly finished chapels and crimson-velvet hangings. It is of colossal dimensions (180 feet front by 320 feet deep), but has scarcely pretension to external architectural elegance, and would not arrest attention more than a moment unless one of its several mellow-toned bells chanced to be tolled at the time of passing. Dr. Ruschenberger, U. S. N., says that the largest bell weighs 31,000 pounds; a second, 15,500; and a third, 5,500. Softer, more liquid, or more sadly sweet notes never thrilled the heart of man than are uttered by *la cantabria*, the first of these old instruments.

Off in an eastern corner of the edifice one may read the following inscription: "*Del illmo. S. D. D. Gonzalo de Ocampo dignissimo IV Arzobispo de esta santa Yglesia celebró la consagracion de este templo en* 19 *de Octubre de* 1625, *con la solemnidad correspondiente á tan augusta ceremonia. Comenso la funsion á la* ——— *mañana, y termino á las cinco de la tarde. Este quartro de Ernero* 1844."

There is no reason to doubt that a cathedral was consecrated on this spot by the illustrious and most worthy Gonzales de Ocampo, fourth archbishop of that holy church, just two hundred and twenty-five years ago; but I could not believe that the present edifice was completed at that time. The hour at which the ceremony commenced has been partially obliterated, and is no longer legible after only six years; but Dr. Von Tschudi says: "Such was the pomp observed at this ceremony, that, though mass commenced at six in the morning, it was five o'clock in the afternoon before the host was raised."* His information was doubtless from some better record; but with only the data preserved to us in the cathedral, his Reverence must have been a tolerably long-winded gentleman under even the five remaining hours preserved to us. The embroidered and jewelled robes worn by the dignitaries on high occasions correspond with the internal magnificence of the cathedral; and its splendor at these times probably exceeds that of most European churches.

Among the riches and relics the curious visitor is sometimes permitted to see are the mortal remains of Francisco Pizarro. It is not often that the Dean and Sacristan can be found at the same time, and several efforts to obtain access failed. The former has charge of the key,

* Travels in Peru during the years 1838, 1842: George Putnam, New York, 1849.

and the duties of the latter require him to accompany persons to the vault, beneath the high altar, where lies the so-called body of the renowned captain. But in strange lands one listens to legendary narrative with willing ear, and I was not to be thwarted. Two or three Limeños accompanied the party, whom it was considered expedient to admit rather than contend longer for the dollar demanded for each wax light necessary. The Sacristan led the way. There are many cases, containing the remains of archbishops and other great men of the church, spread over the vault, each labelled with the name and rank enjoyed in life; and in an open niche on one side there is a perfect skeleton, without such evidence of identity, but which the Sacristan assured us the chronicles of the cathedral assert to be the remains of the conqueror of Peru. Perhaps, like the traveller already referred to, who talked of his horse, the worthy Sacristan has so often said, "There lies Pizarro," that he really thinks so. The flesh is entirely gone from the nose and cheek-bones, though a portion, dried, as on mummies, remains on other parts of the body. A finely plaited shirt, buttoned closely to the throat, envelopes his full round chest—for I sacrilegiously examined to the very sternum—and over this a doublet of dark-colored serge. The body lies on its back. A part of the clothing, consisting of strong, coarse, blue linen, resisted my effort to tear it; but that about the extremities—a cotton fabric—is much more decayed, moulders at the touch, and lies in heaps. One shoe remains on the foot; the other lies on the body.

After searching a whole morning on the north side of the bridge thrown over the Rimac, and making fruitless inquiries of a Sacristan within a hundred yards of the very spot, I finally found the little church which I supposed to have been erected by Pizarro. I had taken this long walk only to stand on the spot where he and his grim warriors had knelt to be shriven. Its appearance was strictly consonant with what one would expect of the sixteenth century, and the location fully corresponded with the landmarks given me by an American some years a resident of Lima: a primitive uncouth building, without exterior ornament or decoration, whose venerable bell was then summoning the congregation to worship. I was satisfied with the identity, and found it no hardship to pass an hour within its walls, the handful of heroes of the past, and the awe-inspired followers of the Inca, my only companions. But alas! when the termination of the services permitted examination of the edifice, my mental creations and philosophic reflections proved to have been wholly mistimed, an inscription on the wall informing me that the miserable flea-hole wherein I had suffered bodily torture during sixty mortal minutes, and therein denominated "Esta sumtuosa Yglesia," was only erected in 1724, or thereabout! The church really erected under Pizarro's auspices is a small building on the same side of the river, but much nearer to the bridge. As it is no larger than the dwellings now in contact with it, and differs from them externally only in the pilasters on each side of its door, and in having two small square turrets, it readily escapes observation. Its doors were closed on the only occasion when I could return to this portion of the city, and its interior was not seen.

Another church that attracts much attention is Santo Domingo. At the time of our visit it was decorated with flowers, and myriads of many-hued ribbons and wax candles, preparatory to a great celebration to come off on the 14th. It has a front of 80 feet, depth 300 feet, the highest steeple in the city, and a profusely ornamented arched ceiling. There is an altar dedicated to Santa Rosa, whose relics are preserved here near the chapel pertaining to the titular saint, and one to Our Lady of the Rosary, besides many chapels ornamented with figures illustrating passages of Scripture. The convent to which it belongs occupies a whole square; and its inmates still enjoy a handsome yearly income, though the neglected pictures of its cloisters seem tokens of declining fortune. On the evening of October 13 the church was very brilliantly lighted, the services closing with a display of fireworks on the *plazuela* before it. How pyrotechnics and religion come to be affiliated we heretics are not permitted to know; but doubtlessly the church is able to explain satisfactorily, and the people evidently enjoy the former quite as much as the latter.

The church of *San Lazaro*, in the parish of that name, is among the most remarkable for the architectural taste displayed in its construction, and the unexceptionable arrangement of its internal ornaments. *San Francisco*, one of the oldest as well as one of the largest of the monasteries, is near the Rimac, and not far from the plaza. Its church, gardens, and cloisters cover two squares of ground; and the order is still wealthy. The church has three naves, traversed by aisles forming a double cross; with many chapels, paintings, sculpture, and plate, that rival portions of the cathedral. Its spacious gardens are well arranged, and are adorned with fountains.

Since the expulsion of the Jesuits in 1773, *San Pedro* has been occupied only by a very small number of priests, and as a hospital for poor members of the clergy who are supported from the revenues of estates that escaped the general confiscation. Its great extent, and the known wealth of the order that founded it, must have made it, under their rule, the principal monastic establishment of the vice-royalty. At that time the poor were furnished with medical advice and medicines from their dispensary. Its church is not so large as that of San Francisco; but it is prettily fitted up, and on one or two of the annual religious festivals is a scene of much pomp. *La Merced* and *San Augustin*, two other convents, are in its rear. The former is spacious, but suffered much during the revolution; and as it is not largely endowed, it makes rather a poor display among its wealthier brethren. The latter is one of the old and opulent institutions, though its fortunes are rapidly on the wane; and there are few tenants in its cells to mourn its neglected corridors and gardens. Its church has an elaborately carved front, whose profusion of figures have little elegance of design or artistic execution to recommend them. Internally, it scarcely differs from several others already named.

Prior to the revolution there were forty-six convents of monks and nuns, some of which have been abandoned or broken up. There are still several besides those named, and fifteen or sixteen nunneries, each of which has its open chapel or oratory. Moreover, there are nearly sixty parish churches! Amongst the nunneries, *La Concepcion*, *Santa Clara*, and *La Encarnacion* are the best endowed; the *Capuchinas*, *Nazarenas*, and *Trinitarias* are the most rigorous in their conventual rules. The former have not been famed for the piety of their secluded lives. The *Refugio de San José* is a house to which married women may retire who desire to withdraw from the ill-treatment of bad husbands; and to which—by permission of the archbishop—husbands may temporarily send their wives, if they think a little seclusion and quiet meditation likely to improve their manners. There is also a house of refuge for indigent females, and others who "loved not wisely, but too well," which was established in 1670 by the reigning viceroy. Nearly a century before, a legacy had been bequeathed for that object by some charitable person, the accumulated value of which enabled him to provide properly for these unfortunates. There were but few inmates in 1849.

The principal hospitals are *San Andres* for males, and *Santa Ana* for women. The former was founded in 1552, and has subsequently been added to until it can accommodate 400 patients. One portion of the building is appropriated to the poor, who receive gratuitous assistance; and another is set apart for insane persons. It is quite customary for the public to visit the hospital on St. Andrew's day, at which time the lunatics are objects of most curiosity and remark. *Santa Ana* was founded three years previously. It has now thirteen wards, containing about 300 beds. *San Bartolomé*, a military hospital, has eleven wards and 220 beds. A hospital originally intended for leprous patients was founded in 1669. Now, persons are sent there who may be afflicted with cutaneous maladies of any kind, but more especially with those of a contagious character. The foundling hospital, instituted at the commencement of the seventeenth century, has only about 100 children under its charge.

The palace occupied by Pizarro was opposite to that subsequently erected for the viceroys on the north side of the plaza, and now tenanted by the President of the republic. The latter covers a whole square, and is a mean-looking building, which one would suppose the property of peddlers rather than the dwelling of a nation's chief magistrate. Both fronting the plaza and

55

on the west side, rows of sixpenny shops usurp the ground-floor, the occupants securing their trashy goods from the action of the sun by awnings in keeping with their assortments. Well do these box-like tenements deserve their name—"cajones." Above them, on both sides, there are open balconies; but the whole pile is destitute of architectural taste or execution both externally and within. Formerly the walls of a very large room, where the government now gives occasional entertainments, were ornamented with portraits of the viceroys from Pizarro to Pezuela—forty-four in all; whence it was called *La sala de los Vireyes.* After the triumph of the patriots, these pictures were removed to the museum, where they still form a most attractive collection for the student of physiognomy.

On one side of the old *Plaza de la Inquisicion,* in the northeast part of the city, is the Chamber of Deputies, built—like most other houses—round a quadrangular court. The walls of its colonnade contain roughly executed allegorical fresco paintings of the sciences, arts, and virtues. Rooms for the secretary and other officers occupy three sides of the quadrangle; the Representatives' hall nearly all of the fourth. The latter is an oblong room, tastefully ornamented with carved seats, paintings, and hangings. About one half of it is appropriated to spectators. As in the English House of Peers, there is a long table at one end mid-way between the side walls of that portion of the room. The presiding officer occupies a seat at the farther extremity of the table, the secretary a chair on his left, and the deputies—apparently arranged in parties—have high-backed chairs placed in two rows along the walls. About fifty were present on the occasion of my visit, all of whom, except two or three priests, were men from twenty-eight to thirty-five years of age. Speeches were made from two tribunes; that to the left of the President being considerably more elevated, and more costly in material and elaborate carving, than its lowly *vis à vis.* Three brief speeches were delivered on a question of some consequence; two by members of the opposition, and one in reply by a minister (I supposed), who ascended the left and higher tribune. Neither of them evinced much oratorical power. Male spectators occupy benches on the same level with the deputies, from whom they are separated only by a railing. Ladies are provided with massive and carved chairs of the same style as the left tribune, arranged in a handsomely wrought gallery elevated above the floor. The sitting was conducted with great decorum as well on the part of the deputies as by the limited audience, and might serve as an example to other legislative bodies. Armed sentinels are stationed on each side of the doors of entrance, and at the secretary's office. They offer military honors to each passing deputy.

Externally, there is nothing to designate the Senate chamber amid the range of buildings of which it forms a part; and as its honorable body was not in session on either occasion when it was possible to visit it, there was no opportunity to examine its interior arrangement. But, if one may judge from an hour's lounge in the outer court-yard, the "lobbying system" has found its way from northern lands, both here and at the other chamber. True, the gentler sex only conceal their persons in Lima, and no one invites a legislator from his seat; but each expectant suitor waylays his intended advocate *en route* through the court, forgetting not the courtly blandishments so elegantly expressive in the language of Castile.

A national library, established in 1824, is near the convent of San Pedro. It contains about 29,000 volumes, of which 450 are MSS.; and is increased by the proceeds of a duty of six per cent. on all imported books; from which sum the salaries of librarian, &c., are first to be paid. The revenue thus collected varies little from $3,000 per annum; and as the expenses amount to $2,500, few additions can be made. It is open to the public from 10 A. M. to 3 P. M., except on Sundays and feast-days.

There is a museum of natural history in the same building, also open to the public. Its riches are the suite of portraits before alluded to; native mummies, with ornaments of the precious metals, and earthenware exhumed in various parts of the republic; and a collection of minerals. Government pays its director a moderate salary; but the allowance for preserving the collection already obtained is miserly, and the establishment reflects little credit on the country.

Government appropriates other two rooms in the same edifice to an academy of drawing, paying the director $600 per annum to instruct pupils gratuitously on four evenings of each week. A collection of lithographed and engraved sketches and models has been obtained for their use.

A university, chartered by decree about the middle of the sixteenth century, was endowed by Pope Pius V. with all the privileges enjoyed by the renowned institution at Salamanca. At one time its professors were the ablest and most assiduous in all South America; but, as with all ecclesiastic instructors, more attention was given ethical and scholastic than more immediately utilitarian subjects. Now, their chairs are only nominal, and the corporation confers degrees earned by students at the colleges of Santo Toribio and San Carlos. The former is exclusively appropriated to theological students; geography, physics, mathematics, drawing, music, modern languages, and law, are taught at the latter. Santo Toribio has the greater number of graduates; there are few students at San Carlos. Santo Tomas, a normal school on the Lancasterian system, and the high school of San Lazaro, have about 250, and the primary schools 2,600 pupils of both sexes.

A mèdical college was founded in 1810, with seven professors. In 1834 Dr. Ruschenberger thought it in a languishing state; though from being attached to extensive hospitals, and no prejudices existing against dissections, it might in other hands have become a flourishing school. Seven years later, Dr. Von Tschudi says it well deserved the name *Colejio de la Medecina de la Independencia*, which had been conferred on it in 1826; for, certainly, medicine was taught there with a singular independence of all rules and systems. He thought the professors had never received any regular instruction, and their scanty share of knowledge was communicated to the students in a very imperfect manner. A school of obstetrics for females has 18 pupils; a like number having passed satisfactory examinations during the seventeen years that it has been in operation. A lying-in hospital is connected with this, where the poor are assisted gratuitously, and subsequently afforded succor during ten days. The number of births at the latter institution in the year ending September 30, 1851, was 245; death from parturition, 1; abortions, 33. Twins were born in February, March, and May.

From the number of placards about the plaza one might infer that there is a succession of public amusements in which the stranger at Lima may participate. Such, however, is not the fact; closer inspection of the notices proving that the majority of them refer to religious rather than to secular affairs. The theatre is open only a part of the year; the arena for bull-fights only once a week during a part of the summer. Cock-fights and lotteries alone are perennial. In 1835 the foreign merchants established a board of commerce, and have now a library connected with their rooms, where American, English, and other foreign books and periodicals are regularly received on the arrival of the steamer from the north. This is open every day, and the transient resident, readily obtaining access through one of the directors, finds it the most reliable source of recreation.

The theatre building, in the rear of the convent of San Augustin, is not remarkable among the houses about it; nor is its interior especially elegant or commodious. It has three tiers of seatless boxes, those of each tier separated from the others by close partitions. Each lessee for the season conveys the number of chairs he stipulates for. The benches of the pit are divided into stalls, each of which is numbered, and they are more comfortable than the boxes. One large double box in the centre of the first tier is retained by the municipal authorities, and another (a stage-box) by the President. The stage is small, the scenery indifferent, and the house is rarely more than half lighted. Its orchestra is usually good; and when some of the best second-rate opera-singers make visits to the capitals along the west coast, as they do occasionally, all the beauty and fashion of Lima crowd to hear them. Generally, however, the actors of comedies and tragedies attract small audiences; and to sit out their performances, under the persecutions of the insects that swarm about all long-closed houses, the foreigner at least needs the hide of a rhinoceros.

The building for bull-fights, called *La Plaza Firme de Acho,* is an amphitheatre near the northeast quarter of San Lazaro, capable of seating more than ten thousand persons. Its arena is four hundred feet in diameter, above and receding from which the boxes and benches rise step by step. These are supported on brick pillars, the lowest eight feet above the floor of the arena. Each tier is accessible by a stairway on the outside. In former times the exhibitions here were of greater interest than any other public diversion. For days in advance nothing else was talked of, and hours before the appointed time thousands thronged the thoroughfare leading to the spectacle. All Lima was in holiday attire. Even ladies the most elegant and refined of the age, and dressed in the most costly style, took equal pleasure with the ruder sex in the barbarous show, loudly applauding when an infuriated animal, which had perhaps torn the bowels from three or four horses and maimed for life two or three less experienced combatants, was at last dexterously slain. Of late years public sentiment is somewhat changed, and few ladies care to acknowledge openly their admiration of such inhuman sport. Those who do attend disguise themselves in the *saya y manto,* a costume that effectually prevents recognition by their own husbands or brothers. Formerly, when such costume was fashionable, it may well be conceived how tantalizing it was to remain near a Limeña—all of whom were notoriously famed for exquisitely formed persons, small feet, and graceful carriage, so well displayed by the *saya*—and to feel that one eye was bent on you through the *manto,* whilst the features by which it was surrounded remained an unseen picture. European fashions having driven them out of vogue; the dress is now rarely seen, except on feast days and Sundays (I am told). It is regarded rather as a screen to a somewhat tarnished reputation than the garb of modest women.

Just to the northward of the palace, a substantial stone bridge over the Rimac unites the two portions of the city. Its roadway—nearly forty feet above the three or four babbling rivulets composing the river—is more than 500 feet long, and is supported on six strong arches which have resisted earthquakes during more than two centuries, although almost everything else has been twice overthrown. There are elevated footways for pedestrians, and benches with parapets for the weary. In the afternoons and evenings of summer it is a scene of much gayety, as all passing to enjoy a ride or promenade in the Alameda, or to partake of the cool and refreshing air that descends with the current of the river, must pass over the bridge. Neither the plaza nor the smaller public squares have been planted; and except the arcades on two sides of the former, they are not resorted to as places of promenade. All the fashionables may be found about sunset in the Alameda, a long and shaded walk extending from the northeast quarter of the city along the banks of the river, from which streamlets have been led to water its rows of orange and willow trees. There are frequent ranges of seats its entire length, and it is quite customary for ladies to leave their elegant carriages to pass an hour in the cool and pleasant fragrance of this charming walk.

In 1849, market was held in the square near the Chamber of Deputies; subsequently it was removed to an ill-contrived building three or four squares to the south. Here one may find Indians from the interior with fruits, vegetables, and flowers; Indians from the coast with fish; Indians from the city with butcher's meat, bread, and manufactured goods; and Indian servants as purchasers. Creole Spaniards frequent the place in no capacity; and though negroes and their admixtures form a numerous portion of the denizens about the market, the mass are unmistakably "Children of the Sun." They are a short, stout-built race, with many of the prominent physiognomic characteristics of the North American tribes; and the idols belonging to their ancestors, that are still occasionally disinterred, prove that the lapse of centuries has wrought little change in the national cast of features.

The supply of vegetables and fruits is extensive and of excellent quality. Fine potatoes (both sweet and Irish), cauliflowers, beets, pumpkins, radishes, beans, pine-apples, cherimoyas, peaches, paltas, pepinos, mangos, oranges, lemons, &c., are very abundant. As all the pine-apples for sale had been shorn of their leaves, it is probable that they had been brought from a more northern port. Those from Guayaquil are usually regarded as the best both in size and flavor. Some are grown in the interior valleys, but cannot be brought to market in as good condition as those by sea. Although the supply of flowers is large, both in color and perfection of form they are greatly inferior to the productions of similar plants found in gardens of the United States, unless perhaps the tuberose and a marigold may be excepted. Roses, single dahlias, two or three varieties of scabius, pinks, larkspurs, sweet marjoram, and several kinds of marigolds, are among the most numerous; but there are also annuals of great beauty that I never saw in the United States. Wherever there is the least moisture by the roadsides, yellow and scarlet nasturtiums and Scotch thistles grow profusely; and about crevices on the rocky hills at the back of the city I found a very pretty oxalis, an ice-plant, a long and tapering cactus in flower, and several other species unknown to me. The castor-oil plant (*Ricinus communis*) seems to thrive everywhere. Among the indigenous plants superior to those of the same varieties cultivated by our florists are a scarlet convolvulus and the white garden jasmin. The *Amancaes*, a beautiful yellow lilly, is already a favorite amongst us. They flower after the winter mists have commenced, usually by the 20th of June; and the anniversary of St. John—the 24th—is the festival of Amancaes, when half the populace leave Lima to spend the day in merry-making on the hill of that name.

Nor does ocean yield her treasures for the wants of man less liberally, but amply rewards the fisherman for his exercise of the patient craft, and the market exhibits many species of the finny tribe. Corvinas (*Pristipomas*), bonitos (*Pêlamys*), pejereys (*Atherinas*), sardines, shrimps, and two or three kinds of mytilus, are all most valuable accessions to the table. Were animals properly slaughtered, and the meats appropriately dressed and exhibited, they would doubtless look as well as they taste when subsequently cooked. But they are abominably hacked and mutilated, then placed on dirty benches in ugly lumps, and disposed of by slouchy and unclean Indian or negro women. Therefore, even after one duly obtains insurance against being eaten alive by dogs and fleas, if he have delicate digestive organs a walk through the meat market before breakfast is scarcely commendable. Mutton and beef are most abundant; pork is rare; veal, lamb, and young pigs are prohibited. The daily demand is from forty to fifty head of neat cattle, and two hundred and fifty sheep; portions of each of which are sold at smaller markets in other quarters of the city.

In so brief a visit it would be difficult to obtain accurate knowledge on all the subjects it is desirable to examine; or, indeed, to obtain any information at all on some of them, except such as vision and a habit of memorial classification will permit one to accumulate. Among such subjects may be mentioned population, in its various classes and their industrial resources, data essential to a proper estimate of a city's progress. Inquiries respecting the aggregate number within the city limits in October, 1849, obtained pretty uniform replies—60,000 souls; but as to the relative proportions of natives (Indians), creole whites, and negroes, and the several castes arising from the three races, there was but one response to my query—*quien sabe?* and who indeed does know? Indians of unmixed blood are numerous, and are unmistakable with their nearly universal short and stout frames, high cheek-bones, and straight black hair. Spanish lineage, also, is ordinarily well marked; but intermarriage with descendants of their Norman neighbors, and crossings with Indian blood, have rendered their class less distinctive, both in color and physiognomy. Foreigners may be readily detected by their accent; and even though the color of the skin might place them among offspring of original white or copper-colored parents, negroes are betrayed by their hair and lips. Yet how many there are of each it seemed impossible to make any estimate of, with probable approximation to truth. Dr. Von Tschudi enumerates no less than twenty-two half-castes, and says there are many others not distinguished by particular names, because they do not differ materially in color from those he has specified.

The census of 1790, and the tax register drawn up in 1836, gave the following returns for the city proper:

Population of Lima.

Classes.	1790.			1836.		
	Male.	Female.	Total.	Male.	Female.	Total.
Spaniards and white creoles . . .	8,335	8,880	17,215	9,423	10,170	19,593
Ecclesiastics (lay and monastic) . .	2,555	2,276	4,831	475	350	825
Indians	2,190	1,722	3,912	2,561	2,731	5,292
Negroes and castes	12,657	14,012	26,669	11,771	12,355	24,126
Slaves				2,186	3,606	4,792
Totals	25,737	26,890	52,627	26,416	29,212	54,628

In 1851 an official publication states that the province was estimated (in that year) to contain 85,116 persons, of whom about one third were whites; one seventh native Indians, without admixture of blood; rather more than one half half-castes; the remainder foreigners. Of the half-castes one fourth were slaves. From 1600 until 1746 the increase was steady and quite rapid. In the latter year epidemic diseases, following the great earthquake, swept off above 6,000 people; and it was not until 1781 that the census again showed 60,000. By 1810 the number had augmented to 87,000; since which time epidemics, revolutions, and banishments have caused great fluctuations, and the tendency still continues rather to diminution than increase. At the commencement both of summer and winter, putrid fevers, consumption, dysentery, and diseases of the liver, prevail to much extent, and make rapid progress with the invalid. These disorders the physicians attribute to debilitation of the nervous system, arising from the absence of electricity in an atmosphere which storms never and high winds rarely disturb. Thunder and lightning are never known. Without such currents to renovate and purify the air, dense and loaded as it is with moisture during successive months, a mortality exists greatly disproportioned to the number of inhabitants.

Near as is Lima to the equator, the temperature is pleasant, its range being from 61° to 85° Fahrenheit, with a mean of 77° during the summer months, and 63°.5 during those of winter. The prevalent winds are from south and southeast, though they sometimes blow from east and north; the former is a cold, and the latter an exceedingly sultry wind, if of several hours' duration. From April to October a heavy and damp mist hangs almost perpetually over the city, and this is the only deposition of moisture. At times it is so dense that puddles of water collect in little hollows of the roofs and streets, though never in sufficient quantity to penetrate through the stratum of clay covering the former. By nine or ten o'clock the deposition ceases, and everything dries; and the sun becomes indistinctly visible through the warmer hours of the day. At night the curtain again descends near the surface. The vicinity of the cordilleras and ocean sensibly modify the temperature; and in summer, though there is much clear weather, it is rarely very oppressive. A flood in the Rimac at this season is not unfrequently preceded some hours by the heaviest drizzling mists ever known.

Earthquakes are very frequent, though no disastrous shock has taken place for more than a century. The most remarkable occurred in 1582, 1586, 1609, 1630, 1655, 1678, 1687, 1690, 1697, 1699, 1716, 1725, 1734, 1743, 1746, 1806, 1828. That of 1746, destroying Callao and a large part of Lima, has already been referred to. Next to it, the most considerable were those of 1586, 1630, 1687, 1716, and 1806.

Within a few years manufactories of cotton, wool, and glass have been established in the suburbs of the city; to protect which, government imposed enormous duties on similar articles of foreign production. But they had all languished to the date of my visits, owing to importation by the foreign merchants, before the law went into effect, of a quantity of goods sufficient to last six or seven years. Thus they were still able to undersell the domestic manufacturer; and it was believed that the whole of the companies would fail prior to the time when the foreign stocks would be exhausted. Silk laces, fringes, and gold and silver embroidery, are wrought by hand to a very considerable extent; though, as the ladies, military, and priests, vie with each other in displaying these several fabrics, demand for home consumption keeps pace with the supply. Utensils and ornaments of silver and gold, both solid and fillagree, furnish employment to quite a number of artisans; but there are few domestic manufactures of any kind to attract wealth from abroad.

I was sorry to leave that quaint old "City of the Kings." There is a witchery in one's surroundings here; commencing with the almost fabulous history of the past, yet linked to the fanciful present by numberless little romances that divest life of the prosiness which renders it at home but a tedious melo-drama. Short, and occupied in the business of sight-seeing, as the visit was, their influences had made me think this came nearer to terrestrial paradise than any other portion of our beautiful world; and I could but regret that fate had not cast my lot in so pleasant a spot. Its climate, fruits, and flowers; its solemn old temples with their musical bells; the eternal pageantry of streets, where costumes vie in varieties with the color of the skin, from the snows of Caucasus to the ebony of Africa; the wonders of its history; its chambers piled with gold for royal ransom, and streets paved with silver to honor vice-regal advent; the calm, uncomplaining magnanimity of its last Inca, whose simple followers—

> "Religious in their ignorance, adored
> The sun that looks upon his worshippers,
> But knows of them no more!"

the immolation of hecatombs by command of that secret and irresponsible tribunal, the mysteries of whose court, or its implements for rending life-strings one by one, none who escaped dare tell of; the more than royal tyranny and extortions of a long succession of vice-kings; the contests when the oppressed had resolved to shake off their task-masters, or yield up lives no longer worth preserving; and the final epithalamium when a new star was added to the galaxy of republics;—all these extend their inviting arms to the traveller, and insensible is he who can voluntarily resist such solicitations. Why, the very beggar here sits in the sun smiling from excess of contentment; and though one may see women bending under burdens borne on their heads, wreaths of flowers adorn their hair; and if the face be an index to the heart, a brighter chaplet circles it. Ascending the social ladder, there are graces of person and carriage, with all the queenly dames one meets in the balmy atmosphere of its Alameda; a winsome music in their language, to perfect charms and conquest which their eyes rarely leave imperfect; and one sits beneath the branches of its pendulous willows listening to the songs of birds in their green homes, and the murmurs of the impetuous Rimac fretting at the obstacles in its way, forgetful of the hours that Time is inscribing in his golden volume.

CHAPTER V.

FROM LIMA TO VALPARAISO.

LEAVE CALLAO.—CHINCHA ISLANDS.—OTHER HUANO ISLANDS ON THE COASTS OF PERU AND CHILE.—PISCO; REMARKABLE CROSS ON THE SHORES OF ITS BAY.—AT SEA.—METEOROLOGICAL.—SALT PATCHES ON THE STERILE COAST.—YSLAY.—ARICA.—ANCIENT GRAVES NEAR THE CITY.—INDIAN ANTIQUITIES.—VALLEYS OF AZAPA AND OCUMBA.—TRADE ALONG THE COAST.—IQUIQUE; SALTPETRE MINES NEAR IT.—MARINE PRODUCTS.—COBIJA.—SCARCITY OF WATER AND FOOD.—TRADE.—PORT OF COPIAPÓ.—HUASCO.—COQUIMBO BAY.—WANT OF GEOGRAPHICAL INFORMATION.—ARRIVE AT VALPARAISO, AND LEAVE FOR SANTIAGO.

The hour of departure being fixed for 1 P. M., I returned to the steamer New Grenada shortly after noon of October 14. As is usual among Spanish and French people, there was much unnecessary noise and vociferation by the embarking passengers and their friends, making it difficult for the officers of the vessel to ascertain what they were in need of; and, indeed, it might reasonably have been doubted whether they knew themselves. Something like order was restored towards 2 P. M.; the decks were cleared of luggage, friends had departed, and we awaited with what patience we might for liberty to get under way. So far as depended on the company, the ship was ready to sail at the hour appointed; but the supreme government invariably has despatches to forward, and also invariably these are never delivered in less than from one to five hours after the time named. As they are brought on board by the captain of the port, whose signature is essential to the clearance-papers, there is no alternative but to await his pleasure; and he, as well as his masters, much need a lesson in punctuality.

Finally, at 3 P. M., we steamed out of the port with forty-five passengers bound to various ports between Callao and Valparaiso. Passing through the Boqueron channel, between the island of San Lorenzo and the main land, in an hour we were again climbing the long swells of the Pacific. The afternoon and remainder of the day proved fine, and at night the stars shone brilliantly overhead; but there was a fog-like bank hanging about the land, occasionally illumined by flashes of silent lightning.

October 15.—We passed at 6 A. M. the Chinchas, a cluster of three islands valuable only for the deposits of guano on them. Their whole superficial extent is about seven square miles; yet, from actual survey, it has been estimated that ships may take 50,000 tons annually for a thousand years without exhausting the supply. The deposit on the northern islet, where ships now load, is above eighty feet thick in the centre, diminishing gradually towards the shore-lines. *Guano*, or more properly *huano*, is the excrement of marine birds which frequent the uninhabited islets and desolate promontories on several parts of this and other coasts in innumerable flocks. Eight species are enumerated as contributing to form these almost incredible layers, among the most important of which are pelicans, cormorants, and a kind of petrel, the *Sula variegata* (Tschudi), perhaps the Potayunka of the natives. At first the excrement is of a light color, and is called by Peruvians *huano blanco*. It is the most valuable in this state, and the market-price is nearly double. At the end of a year it becomes of a greyish brown; and as subsequent deposits are made, the inferior change gradually to brownish red. These last, by evaporation of their watery particles in an atmosphere of perpetual drought and under pressure, become more solid. Birds' eggs and skeletons are frequently found in excavating the layers. Its value as a fertilizer has certainly been known to the natives as long ago as the time of the Incas, and large quantities are annually consumed in all the cultivable valleys of the coast. Without it the crops of maize, beans, and potatoes, all essentials in the domestic economy of the country, would be diminished one half; and, large as the supply seems to be, Peru would act judiciously if less disposition was shown to reap immediate benefits by the sale of it to foreigners. After the Chincha islands, the most extensive and chemically valuable collections are at the Lobos islands, in latitude 6° 57′ S.; the Hormigas, latitude 11° 58′; the islands near Yslay, latitude 17°; Punta de Hormillos, &c. There were about thirty vessels at anchor at the northern Chincha as we passed.

Within two hours we came-to off Pisco, a pretty little town in latitude 13° 43′, some ten miles E.S.E. from the Chinchas. The town is about a mile from the beach, its pagoda-like churches giving to it, at this distance, quite an oriental aspect. As the mere port of Ica, a large town some fourteen leagues distant in the interior, Pisco stood still until the increase of the huano trade created a demand for additional population. Now, it contains above three thousand souls. A valley extending to the north and east, and watered by a small river of the same name as the town, teems with vegetation, whose surplus is sent to less favored portions of the coast, the huano ships, &c. Sugar, olives, dates, wine, spirits, and fresh fruits are its principal exports. Large quantities of rum and brandy from sugar and grapes are sent annually to the markets of Callao and Chile. Here, also, they distil a very pure spirit of aromatic odor and flavor from the Italian grape, which thence is called *Italia de Pisco*. It is put up in conical earthen jars, with narrow necks, each holding about three gallons, and is highly esteemed by *connoisseur* drinkers of *liqueur*. A *pisquito* (the jar is so called) of the best quality will cost $8 on the spot.

We remained at the anchorage very little more than an hour. There was scarcely any cargo to discharge; and the quantities of wine, italia, and fruits brought off were taken rapidly on board. Baskets of fine cherimoyas, oranges, and sweet potatoes were offered at very reasonable prices to the passengers; and several laid in a stock for themselves, or as presents for friends in Chile. Sweet potatoes form a very regular portion of the freight sent to Valparaiso.

As we sailed to the southward out of the bay, a remarkable object claimed attention on the sloping face of the high land. As nearly as it could be sketched, when passing at the distance of two or three miles, it is of the annexed form; and is apparently made of white or light-colored stones set in the face of the rock.

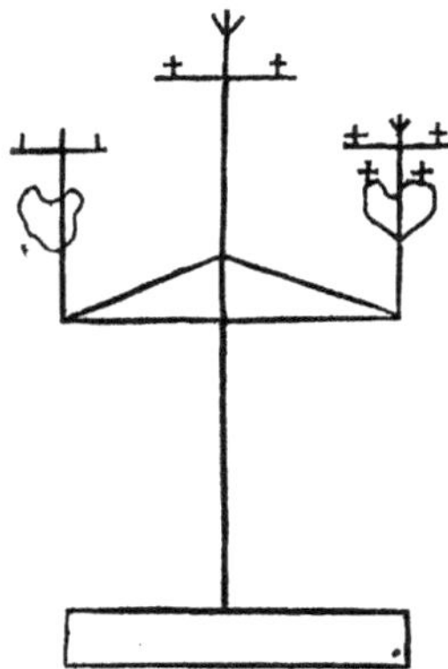

From the base to the top of the central cross the height must be greatly more than two hundred feet; but the absence of shrubbery, or other objects of comparison, rendered accurate estimate impossible at such a distance. The proportions between the several parts are pretty well preserved in the sketch. The shadows indicate that each line has been excavated, and that the multitudes of blocks are inserted below the level of the surface. By whom, or for what special object this huge emblem of the Christian faith was constructed on so desolate a shore, there was no one on board who could tell satisfactorily; and I do not find it mentioned by either of the writers whose volumes are accessible to me. A father of the church, on board, assured me that Christ himself wrought it in a single night, during the rule of Pizarro, and as a warning to the sun worshippers, whose country he was empowered to take possession of; but, as I afterwards saw the reverend gentleman gambling with other passengers at *monte*, it occurred to me that his assertion was possibly made under the influence of a little too much wine with the water he had imbibed for breakfast. Annually the devoutly inclined come with the priests from Pisco to the cross, and a great ceremony is performed there—its conclusion smacking more of "earth, earthly," than of "heaven, heavenly."

At the southern entrance of the bay the wind increased to freshness from the southeast, and gave us the first wholly clear sky that had been witnessed in many days. To myself its temperature felt wholesome and invigorating; but the multitude of sea-sick passengers, who had been tempted on deck by smooth water near the anchorage, hurried shivering to their berths again,—the sea that it created bringing the landsman's pestilence to them with greater force than before. Towards night there was some decrease in its strength, and by 10 o'clock the heavens were entirely obscured; but there was no diminution of the swell, and the ship could only make five miles and a half per hour against them.

October 16.—During the night the southeast wind lulled, the swell subsided to a considerable extent, and at sunrise the ship was again making fair progress. But with the sun's elevation the wind rose; and before noon we had a breeze as fierce and sea as heavy as on the preceding day—a condition of affairs altogether irreconcilable with the idea of a Pacific ocean. All the morning we were steaming very close to land most abrupt, broken, sterile, and desolate in its aspect; with multitudes of penguins, cape pigeons, cormorants, loons, and ice-birds, about the ship. The afternoon brought with it an accession both of wind and sea, with a temperature varying little from 62° in the open air, so that the passengers huddled about the smoke and steam pipes to keep warm. The night was more moderate, but densely overcast.

October 17.—Our captain says, from the commencement of August until the end of October the southeast trade winds on the coast, for 200 miles to the southward of Pisco, are much more violent than during the other nine months of the year, and often make a difference of eight to ten hours in the length of the voyage between that place and Yslay. The distance between the two is 333 miles. By daylight the wind had wholly subsided, though a long swell continued to set from the southward. The shore along which we were steaming—scarcely five miles distant—was much varied in outline; and after passing the quebrada of Ocoña, at 9 o'clock, gradually became quite densely covered with cactus, which somewhat relieved the arid appearance so long offered to us. There were only a few cape pigeons about the ship during the morning. Later in the day considerable numbers of whales were encountered, principally of the *fin-back* species, and the sea-fowl returned in countless flocks. The dark, fawn-colored rocks of the shore were diversified by white patches hundreds of feet in extent, and in hollows, or sheltered places, several inches thick. A difference of opinion exists respecting the origin of this substance, which is as consistent as flour that has been damped and suffered to dry in a damaged barrel. The people of the neighborhood assert that it was thrown out of the volcano of Arequipa many years ago; to which view Capt. Basil Hall inclines. But the more rational supposition is, that it is a crust of common salt and stratified saliferous alluvium, deposited as the land slowly rose above the sea-level—similar in every respect to the depositions found by Dr. Darwin between Iquique and the saltpetre mines fourteen leagues distant. He found "the appearance of this superficial mass very closely resembled that of a country after snow before the last dirty patches are thawed."

Anchored in the port of Yslay just after dark, and were excessively annoyed all night by the effluvia emitted by whales sporting in the waters around us.

October 18.—Yslay, in latitude 17° S., a collection of less than two hundred wretched houses perched on the brow of a gradually sloping bluff, without a tree or even a blade of grass to relieve its barren look, is at the bottom of a little bay formed by the main coast and a cluster of volcanic islets tossed up from ocean's abyss. A bold, precipitous, and beachless shore, and a constant swell rolling in from the Pacific, render landing difficult at all times. Here it rarely blows home, and ships ride in comparative safety; but the volume of the rollers in the bay is augmented with every accession to the strength of the wind at sea. However, by the aid of a little pier, "man ropes," a rope ladder, and watching for *the smooth time*, landing may be effected without danger. The gentler sex are of necessity hoisted out in an arm-chair suspended from a revolving crane; and cargoes are shipped into and from launches by the same implement.

Its population is estimated at 1,000 souls, most of whom are employed by the merchants of Arequipa, a town of 30,000 inhabitants, thirty leagues distant to the northward. Their houses are principally of poles, driven closely together in the earth, and lined with mats. Some few are of planks, as is the custom-house, the residence of the British consul, &c.; but the location of the multitude, and the construction of the individual tenements, excite the wonder of every foreigner who comes here. Water is obtained from rocks to the north of the town, which rise to a height of nearly 3,000 feet. It is the deposit of winter mists and drizzles that filter through crevices and collect in natural basins. Recently the governor directed the laying down of pipes, through which the stream is to be brought into the plaza. On the same hill-tops a short, sweet grass is obtained, partially supplying the troops of mules used in transporting goods to and from the capital—Arequipa. Fruits, vegetables, and provisions of every kind for man, are brought from a distance.

Quite large quantities of alpaca and other wools, cinchona bark, rice, and bullion, are annually shipped from the port; English and French vessels obtaining nearly all of them in return for manufactures of their own countries. The amount received by the New Grenada for freight from Callao exceeded $400; and the freight-bills for Chile peppers and salt, received to be delivered at other ports to the southward, nearly half that sum. Usually the freight-bill from Callao amounts to $1,000.

There was a driving mist from the southeast all the morning, and we did not leave port until afternoon. Towards sunset the mist and wind ceased, and the western sky soon mottled with clouds tinged with brilliant colors, whilst to the eastward the mountain summits were bathed in crimson light, with a line of fleecy cumuli floating at a short distance beneath. At night the sky was clouded again, and moderate breezes came from the land, in whose direction also there were occasional flashes of lightning.

October 19.—As the clouds were in more broken masses than had been seen during many mornings, and the thermometer rose with the subsidence of the southeasterly wind, our day commenced auspiciously for the west coast of Peru. At 8 o'clock there was still sufficient breeze to ruffle the water, and mark the contrast between its color and the sky, over which the vision passed to their apparent junction in the west. Close on the left the great Andes rose, a serrated chain above the line of perpetual snow, and, barely perceptible, on the verdant background ahead peeped out the turrets and white walls of Arica. By 10 o'clock we were at anchor, quite near the shore.

The town of Arica, in latitude 18° 28′ S., is built close to the beach, in a small bay formed by a precipitous bluff and a low rocky islet on the right as you enter. The height of the bluff, or *morro*, as it is called, is more than 600 feet above the sea, and from the anchorage appears to continue at the same level as far as can be seen. The town lies at its northern base. It has experienced many vicissitudes, having been sacked by Sir Francis Drake, in 1579; almost entirely buried by the earthquake of 1608; attacked twice by the buccaneers; again nearly shaken down by an earthquake; and finally has almost been desolated by revolutionary struggles. Portions of the entombed city have recently been disinterred, the lines of its streets traced out, and human bodies, golden idols, crosses, and arrow-heads of translucent flint have been brought to light.

The town built since the earthquake is regularly laid out, has its plaza, custom-house, two or three churches, and a sufficient number of houses to cover half a mile square. As the ground is sloping, and the churches occupy the higher portion, its appearance from the bay is quite imposing; but on nearer inspection there is nothing attractive about either of them, and one is soon willing to escape from the glare of whitened walls along its narrow and hot streets. I should suppose its population less than 1,500 souls, mostly Indians and half-castes, employed in the conveyance of goods and provisions as far as the interior of Bolivia, 300 leagues distant. Several large foreign commercial houses have agencies here, and there are a few Spanish creole merchants connected with establishments at Tacna—a city of 9,000 people, 36 miles distant in a N.N.E. direction. Recently a railroad has been projected between the two places, and the contracts for its construction entered into await execution only until the country shall again become tranquil. To render the bay more secure, and obtain smoother water for landing goods, they have commenced filling in between the *morro* and islet, using for the purpose masses of rock blasted from the bluff, to be filled in with the sand now lying over the old town. There is already a convenient mole near the custom-house, where launches may discharge, unless the wind blow freshly. Eight English and French vessels were lying in the bay with goods, and awaiting cargoes. The exports consist of large quantities of Peruvian bark, alpaca and other wool, and copper and silver, both in ores and bars, sent from Bolivia.

A mile to the south of the *morro* is a burial-place of the ancient Peruvians, whose graves have been so perseveringly violated by foreigners, notwithstanding the prohibition against it, that there are few if any bodies left. Numbers were carried off by the officers of a French ship-of-war some years since. Following universal custom, a friend endeavored to obtain one of the mummies for me, and succeeded in finding a tomb of masonry containing five bodies—a man, a woman, two children, and a dog; but they all fell to pieces on exposure to the air, and he could only send me the earthen and wooden vessels, household implements, provisions, &c., interred with them. Of these an interesting account will be found in the report of Thomas Ewbank, Esq., Appendix E. All the bodies found in these tombs are in a sitting posture with the knees close to the chin, the elbows at the sides, and hands near the face. They are wrapped with many folds of coarse woollen or cotton cloth, and, though dark-colored and shrunken, are usually in good preservation. The nitre contained in the earth is supposed to contribute to this. A tradition still remains among the Indians of the vicinity, that some families caused themselves to be buried alive rather than submit to the rule of Atahualpa. Some ten miles from the city there is another place supposed to have been used for interments; and as this has never been disturbed, we shall probably learn of interesting ethnological researches before the completion of the Tacna road. Soon after my visit, an accomplished friend wrote me: "After my next campaign to Peru, I shall be able to present you something of interest, as I know of an extensive burial-ground near Tacna entirely occupied by Indians who were interred long before the conquest. On the bare face of the sloping mountain at whose base these tombs are, I noticed huge characters traced in the sand. They can be perceived with great distinctness, and could be read with the unassisted eye—if one understood them—at the distance of ten to fifteen miles. The whole side of the mountain, or hill, as they call it in this country of colossal cordilleras, is covered with them. They appear to be written as are Chinese characters, in vertical lines. Some of them must be ten or twelve hundred feet in length—I mean each character is of that size, and it looks as fresh as if just made. When first seen, I thought them windings and zigzags made by mules traversing the inclined face of the hill; but the mistake was discovered before inquiring of any one. Every person in Tacna from whom information was sought, assured me that they were ancient Indian records." None of the travellers known to me make mention of this gigantic specimen of picture-writing.

There is another object of interest more immediately in the vicinity of Arica. It is a cave whose extremity no one now living has ever seen; and the Indians say that fish were conveyed through it for the Incas all the way to Cuzco. A few years since an old Spaniard came to Arica who had been somewhat famed for appropriating other people's goods to himself on the high sea. Making known to an American in business here that much riches had been deposited in the cave, the adventurous spirit of the latter tempted him to consent to an exploration. They were seventy hours under ground, and only relinquished the search when accident, fatigue, and want of lights drove them out. As they were proceeding through one of the passages, the old freebooter, who was ahead, suddenly disappeared. He had stepped into a chasm twenty-five feet deep, and was lucky in being able to crawl out much bruised. At this place, the air was so foul that their candles would scarcely burn; they had been on the move nearly all the time since entering, and they returned disgusted as well as fatigued with the results of the exploration. No one has since attempted to penetrate more than a hundred yards.

In the direction of Tacna is the sloping and fertile valley of Azapa, with its palms and evergreens, filling a large portion of the broad interval between the ocean and cordilleras. Cotton, sugar-cane, tropical fruits, and vegetables, thrive most luxuriantly wherever huano is used and water can be obtained. Another valley, whose name is Ocumba (or Locumbo, for it was badly pronounced to me), is famed for its extensive vineyards, as well as for the other products named. The cotton is a perennial, not an annual plant, and is not grown to a greater extent than will supply local demands. Nor is there much sugar for exportation, most of it being consumed in sweetmeats, or as chancaca—cakes of crystallized brown sugar, from which the molasses has been drained. A portion of the life-stream from the valley of Azapa supplies the inhabitants of Arica and the shipping with excellent drinking-water, and irrigates several gardens on the northern skirts of the town. In one of these there were ripe fruit and blossoms at the same time (in October) on a peach-tree destitute of leaves.

Besides the exports mentioned, much fresh meat, vegetables, and fruits, are sent to Iquique, Cobija, and even Copiapó, all lying in absolutely sterile districts. Even flowers are regularly conveyed by the vegetable dealers, carefully enveloped in plantain leaves to preserve moisture about them. These dealers are mostly women—bustling and active—who leave their husbands at home (if they have any), to take care of the babies probably, come down to Arica by the steamer bound north, and have their supplies of meats, maize, potatoes, cabbages, onions, sugar-cane, and fruits, ready to embark a fortnight afterwards. With us it would be remarkable to find a trafficker in such commodities with several hundred dollars' worth of rings on her fingers, silk stockings, and embroidered satin slippers on her feet; yet such is actually the sea costume of a sprightly young half-breed, who is a regular passenger between Cobija and Arica, and purchases most largely. More than 300 packages of freight were taken on board in addition to the provisions for Iquique and southern ports, and at 3 P. M. our journey was resumed.

For the first time night brought with it a clear atmosphere, and for an hour or two permitted a view of the southern firmament; but just as I was hoping to be able to contrast the brightness of Canopus and Sirius, the almost eternal misty veil of the coast fell over us. Ocean, as if in recompense, presented millions of animalculæ glittering under the darkened canopy wherever its surface was agitated. This brilliant phosphorescent exhibition extended over the whole belt of ocean we traversed during the night, and the atmosphere was charged with an odor similar to that near beaches, where much sea-weed is deposited.

The lights of the steamer Ecuador were seen approaching from the south shortly after 10 P. M., and by a somewhat unwise manœuvre on board that vessel, when we were within speaking distance the two ships came in contact. Fortunately, the engine of the New Grenada had been stopped some minutes previously, or the damage would have been very serious. As it was, she escaped with loss of boat and crushed rails—we, with displaced figure-head and a bent cutwater.

October 20.—Iquique, a town containing about 1,000 souls, mostly Indians and mestizos, is at the bottom of a little open bay, formed by an indentation of the coast and a cluster of rocky islets. Its latitude is 20° 12′ S. Its cluster of wretched houses is on a little plain at the foot of a bare rocky wall more than 2,000 feet high, desolate as Sahara. Sea-weed excepted, there is not a blade of grass in sight, nor a drop of drinkable water within more than thirty miles;

and unless the mist at the summit of the high cliffs back of it may be so termed, it never rains. The only food, then, obtainable, is drawn from the sea, and of this the supply is both good and abundant; but with no other alimentary resource near, it passes my powers to divine what a settlement should ever have been made here for. Drinking-water is either distilled from the sea-water or brought in boats from the river Pisagua, 40 miles to the northward—the stream laid down as near this place on two or three maps in my possession, having no existence whatever. A grinding-mill, to be driven by steam, was erected two or three years ago, and there are now two in operation. Some are ill-natured enough to say that the last machinery was brought to grind silver ores; but as none could be found after it arrived, its principal use is in the distillation of sea-water.

The only export of much value is saltpetre, brought from mines in the mountains at a distance of twelve leagues. A much larger quantity is shipped from Mexillones and Pisagua—the former 20, and the latter 45 miles distant. The vein from which it is extracted is between two and three feet thick, and follows the margin of a grand basin or plain for one hundred and fifty miles. The nitrate is mixed with a little sulphate of soda and a good deal of common salt. Between the mines and the cordilleras there are two or three small villages, and a small supply of water for irrigation from the melted snows. The fields here situated supply the population on the coast with a part, and animals with all their food. An English merchant largely engaged in the trade told me that the mules employed in bringing saltpetre to the port have neither food nor drink from the time they leave the mines until their return on the third day. We saw troops of the poor beasts just relieved from their loads, first throw themselves on the sand with protruded tongues, then rush into the sea to allay their agony of thirst by absorption of moisture through the pores of the skin.

An American brig and one English barque were the only vessels loading. Their cargoes were put up in sacks weighing from two hundred and fifty to three hundred pounds each, which are conveyed from the shore to launches in deeper water by balsas, five sacks being the freight of a balsa. A mule-load is two smaller bags weighing from seventy to one hundred pounds each, and the cost of conveyance from the mines is half a dollar per hundred weight.

We found the atmosphere strongly charged with the odor of sea-weed, which clings in extensive masses to the igneous rocks bounding the shore. It is said that lime, of a superior quality to that obtained from shells, is prepared from it. The latter lie in great quantities on the beach; the *Trochus ater*, *Mytilus orbignyanus*, *Venus Peruviana*, and a *Mesodesma*, being among the most numerous. *Chitons* and a large edible barnacle (*Balanus*), called "pico," from its peculiar projecting beak, are also found on the rocks, and are greatly esteemed as articles of food. But the supply of many most excellent kinds of fish is so abundant, that no one values them much. A solitary exception is an old fisherman, whose hut was shown us near the sandy beach to the south of the town; his food being almost wholly of marine productions, the mass of skeletons accumulated is quite extraordinary. He has passed forty years alone on the spot, during the latter half of which he has never been known to visit Iquique. The small supplies of bread, water, and clothing, required by him, are conveyed regularly by those who purchase his fish.

Left the port shortly after 1 P. M., and sailed along within a mile or two of the coast as nearly as straight lines from point to point would permit. Throughout the afternoon the sky was obscured by cirro-stratus, apparently essential to human life on this arid coast; the night, until after ten o'clock clear and calm, permitting an excellent view of the stars that had risen higher than the Andes. The sea was not luminous, as on the preceding evening.

October 21.—Until 2 P. M. the day was wholly overcast, and the air calm, with a smooth and almost placid sea. So little regard is exhibited for the observance of the Sabbath in this part of the world, that one soon ceases to recognise the days of the week, unless marked by other events; and consequently, until reference was had to the date, I could scarcely believe that the day appointed for man's rest had again come round.

Shortly before 10 o'clock anchor was cast in the Bay of Cobija, the only port possessed by Bolivia. Its latitude is 22° 34′ S. Scattered for about half a mile along a beach at the base of a lofty range of hills, part of its houses of stone and others of planks, the town presents the most neat and tidy appearance of any place yet visited on the coast. Because of its bold and almost overhanging cliff, and the contrast of white walls with the verdure of the valley, Arica is more picturesque from the sea; but once landed, the superiority in cleanliness must be awarded to the Bolivian town. As there is neither breakwater nor wharf, everything is necessarily carried through the surf on the backs of *cargadores*. Some of these exhibit great strength and skill in transhipments.

Cobija has but one street, a custom-house, a church, and 1,500 inhabitants, for whose protection there is a fortification mounting five guns. The last is on a rocky point forming the southern shore of the open bay, and there is a company of soldiers quartered in rude barracks at the opposite extremity of the town. Forty officers were on duty, and indeed men in uniform appeared more numerous than those in plain dresses. The revolutionary disposition which has so long proved the curse of South American States, is doubtless fostered by such disproportioned military collections; and the disaffection of a crafty junior or subordinate, who manages to gain the confidence of the troops, is always sufficient cause to bring about a change of rulers, generally of a summary and violent kind. Only four or five months before, a governor was shot in his office here in broad daylight; the only charge against him was, he desired a change of the supreme government.

Situated within the desert district of Atacama, and sixty miles from its northern limit, there is no terrestrial vegetation, and it was a matter of no little interest to witness the avidity of the population on landing the garden-stuff brought from Arica. Probably within ten minutes after the first boat-load of bags had been landed, all over town Indians, including soldiers, might have been seen stripping the rind from green sugar-cane, and grinding out its saccharine juice with their teeth; the housekeepers bearing away piles of ears of maize, sweet potatoes, and other substantial productions; whilst a few damsels, more fair-skinned than their neighbors, were enjoying the odors of Peruvian bouquets. An hour later, the beach—which had served as the impromptu market-place—was again bare; the dealers had disposed of every article! Nor is the privation of provisions their only hardship. The supply of water is exceedingly scanty, and brackish besides; it is collected on the hills in the rear, and conveyed through pipes to two places kept under lock and key by the town authorities, who daily deliver its quota to each family. As soon as the distribution is completed, the little streams (not larger than one's finger) are shut off. If more is wanted, it must be purchased from carriers, who bring it from a lagoon in the interior. Cattle are driven from the pampas of Buenos Ayres to the vicinity of Calama, forty leagues distant, and are subsisted until wanted on a species of rushes found near the latter place. Sheep and goats may browse on a narrow belt of verdure found where the cirro-stratus clouds hang, two thirds the distance up the sea range of hills; but so scarce are water and herbage, that burden-mules neither eat nor drink from the time they leave Calama until returning to it. Neither are fish so abundant as at Iquique. As I stood on the beach a fisherman landed from his balsa, having been out the whole preceding night without taking any fish. It was the worst luck, he said, that he had ever had.

There are valuable copper mines in the vicinity, whose products are shipped principally from Catica, six miles, and Algodones, 28 miles to the northward. The mines are owned by English companies, who import every article of necessity, and ship the larger part of their ores to Swansea. It is essential for government to have a port of entry, through which its silver, tin, copper, and cotton may be exported when the ports of Iquique and Arica are closed to it; and every effort has been made to attract trade by declaring Cobija a free port. But the country between it and the populous portions of the republic affords too few resources, and the distances are too great for competition with the routes through Tacna and Tarapaca. Nevertheless, its exports in the preceding year amounted to about a million and a half of dollars; and the dues collected in the same time were $120,000. We found no vessels in port; but the tone of the bells to the time-keepers told very plainly that Yankeedom has had its Sam Slick here, with clocks and probably other "notions" to exchange for tin and silver.

Sailed from the port shortly after 12 o'clock, and soon ran from beneath the cirro-stratus into a clear atmosphere. This we greatly enjoyed, until the departure of the sun again permitted clouds to accumulate. Though there was a long and regular swell setting from the southward and westward all day, the surface of the sea remained almost unruffled.

October 22.—Except a diminution of heat, no change took place in the weather until after nine o'clock; every feature presenting an aspect unvaried from that detailed on several successive mornings. We were farther off-shore than usual, and encountered only a few albatrosses and cape pigeons, with occasional patches of long and coarse sea-weed. Altogether, it was the most uninteresting day we had spent.

October 23.—When day dawned we were steaming along the comparatively low and sandy strip of Atacama, which lies to the north of Caldera, and between the sea and the mountains. At 8 o'clock we had anchored in the roadstead of Copiapó, latitude 27° 20′, (then) the port of its wealthy mining district. A worse place for ships to enter or lie in can scarcely be found on the whole west coast. More than one has been driven on shore from its anchors by rollers setting suddenly in; and the landing is more difficult than in any port to the southward, because of the constant swell from the S.W. We found but one ship here.

The formation at the sea-line is of igneous rock, with a superstratum of sandstone in nearly horizontal layers, that attain an elevation of forty or fifty feet. A few rods inland the sandstone has been penetrated by black and ragged volcanic masses, which seem to have burst through the surface and cooled suddenly. According to Arrowsmith's map, a river should empty into the northern portion of the bay; but, as has been stated in Chapter X, PART I, all the water of the Copiapó is absorbed long before it reaches the ocean, and there is only a dry bed, showing where a stream flowed within a moderate geological period. The face of the country, then, is sand, mixed with shells and gravel; utterly destitute of vegetation, except when a slight shower falls once in two or three years. Though more than a degree to the south of the limit assigned by geographers to the desert of Atacama, for all that the soil yields to support life, it is absolutely a part of it. Such are the charges for transportation, and the depreciation of money where the heavens prohibit all other products than gold, silver, and copper to the earth, that beef is sold at four *reals* the pound; whilst at Santiago, only 400 miles distant, the market price is from a half to three fourths of a *real*. However, all these matters have been mentioned more in detail in the chapter referred to.

Having received on board thirty-five passengers, 40,000 marks of silver, and 2,000 ounces of gold in bars, we left the port at 11 o'clock. At sea, the remainder of the day proved overcast and cool; but in some of the valleys on shore there was bright sunshine, strangely contrasting, at times, with the unilluminated summits and opposite declivities of the same range of hills. Views of the distant Andes, with their snow-peaks, were also obtained at times; and as more than half the hills were dark, as with verdure, the eye finds much to compare pleasantly with the desolation of Peru and northern Chile.

Shortly after dark we stopped for an hour in the mining part of Huasco, latitude 28° 27′ S. There are about 25 or 30 plank and adobe houses here, a custom-house, church, and 250 inhabitants; but, if possible, the country around presents a more miserable aspect than any part even of this desolate coast. Dr. Darwin states that there is no fresh water in the immediate vicinity; the little river of the same name that flows through the valley being at some miles to the north. Commencing at the sea margin, there is a similar natural feature here to that existing at Coquimbo. "The phenomenon of the parallel terraces is very strikingly seen; no less than seven perfectly level but unequally broad plains, ascending by steps, occur on one or both sides of the valley. So remarkable is the contrast of the successive horizontal lines, corresponding on each side with the irregular outline of the surrounding mountains, that it attracts the attention of even those who feel no interest regarding the causes which have modelled the surface of the land."* But for these, more land might be cultivated, small as is the stream and unfrequent as are rains.

Though the anchorage is much exposed during northerly winds, and the sea is then violent, these are quite as uncommon as heavy rain-storms; and ships lie here in all confidence. It is frequented mostly by the English, who are proprietors of several valuable copper mines in the neighborhood. Their ships bring out coal, and such necessities as miners purchase, and take home freights of copper bars and ores. For a long time the Huasco mines were considered the richest in Chile; Carrisal, San Juan, La Higuera, and the Camerones yielding purer metal and more abundantly than any others. Its silver veins have never rivalled those either of the valley of the Copiapó or the Coquimbo; but as there is a supply of water, mills for reducing such ores by amalgamation were established many years ago. As has been alluded to, the richest ores of silver brought to these establishments are those stolen by laborers at Chañarcillo and other nearer mines, and sold to persons who make a business of such traffic. It is well known at the reducing mills that most of these have no property in mines; but it would be impertinent to inquire too closely respecting the affairs of one's neighbor. Four bars of silver, each of 400 marks, were brought on board here; and so completely does pilfering appear to be systematized and acquiesced in by proprietors, that the shipment from Copiapó is quite a sure index of the sum that will be despatched from Huasco.

October 24.—Very soon after midnight an old-fashioned rain began falling, the first experienced since the close of September, when we were more than 2,000 miles north of this. As a proper sequel to such notable commencement of the day, the morning was very like a New England autumn day—cold and murky—and the passengers on deck clustered about the smoke-pipe, wrapped in cloaks and ponchos. From the darkness of the night it was considered most prudent to go outside of the *Pajaros* and *Choros* islands; the former consisting of two, and the latter of three rocky islets, the largest of which is about two miles long. The outermost of the Choros, in latitude 29° 16′, is about three miles from the main land; the Pajaros are twenty miles farther south, and twelve from the coast. With its castellated crags, and alternate patches of white and dark shaded rocks, at a little distance the northern Pajaro resembles a compactly built city. We passed it at 9 A. M., and as we drew towards the land the first object made out through the misty atmosphere was the city of La Serena. Shortly afterwards the high lands to its right and left became discernible; then the table-land at whose base it is located; and finally the valley of the Coquimbo river greeted the sight, with its gardens, roads, and white embowered dwellings. Situated near the outlet of a fertile valley, with a verdant terrace in its rear, clusters of trees amid its bright-looking houses and steeples, rows of tall poplars bounding the roads and walls of country seats, the city has a most picturesque appearance from the bay; but, as it is more than two leagues distant from the anchorage, and the steamer intended to delay but one hour, it was only possible to obtain this sea view of it.

Coquimbo, a straggling collection of plastered stone and adobe houses, is in the S.W. angle of the bay. Most of the copper of the province is shipped from here; the largest smelting furnaces belonging to a passenger on board, who a few years previously is said to have kept a *pulperia* in Valparaiso. Subsequently he became possessed of copper mines at points along the coast from Valparaiso to Huasco, a distance of nearly three hundred miles, and his wealth is now incalculable. So extensive have his operations become, that he found it economical to possess a steamer for the conveyance of operatives and implements from point to point. Other smelting establishments at Herradura and La Compania have been mentioned in Chapter X.

There were six vessels at anchor: one laden, another discharging a cargo of salt, and the others taking in or awaiting freights of copper. At Herradura bay there were but two.

After we left the port a foggy mist hung about the land, and a raw southerly breeze swept over the ocean, with very slight changes throughout the day. Whenever the sun penetrated

* Darwin: Journal, &c.

the cloud bank and lit up any portion of the hills, as the ship drew southward we could perceive the increase of vegetation, and that there was a greater irregularity of landscape outline than on the northern coasts.

The coasting voyage being now so nearly concluded, it may be remarked that the map compiled by Arrowsmith,* principally from information given him by a former British Consul General, can scarcely be considered a moderately good guide for the west coast. One town is a whole degree of latitude out of place; the positions of two others are reversed; some rivers are laid down which certainly have had no existence in modern times, and others look quite imposing that are mere streamlets, which the sands absorb before they reach the ocean. But this must not be wondered at. The most wealthy and best informed persons of the country have little correct geographical information of their own provinces. All the published text in Chile relating to it is embraced in twenty-five small octavo pages, and these abound with inaccuracies. No wonder, then, that no two of those from whom I inquired on board agreed in the distance or elevation of the Andes, as seen from Santiago.

October 25.—Morning dawned on us dark, damp, and cold. Though only three or four miles distant, the land was too indistinct to permit a proper appreciation of its characteristics. Without much change of weather for the better during the day, anchor was dropped in the bay of Valparaiso towards 5 o'clock, just seventy days having elapsed since I left New York. It was feared that the ship Louis Philippe, which had sailed from Baltimore on the 12th of July, would arrive before me, and the assistants and equipment embarked on board of her be greatly inconvenienced by my detention; but a glance at the multitude of anchored vessels assured me she was not among them, and the consignees thought it might be a week or more before she would come in. Delivering to the Intendente the despatches sent by the Chilean minister at Washington for his government, and speedily arranging with the United States consul for landing and storing the instruments in case of arrival during my absence, in less than four hours after the New Grenada anchored I was seated in a birlocho, on the summit of the hills back of Valparaiso, on my way to the capital.

* La Plata, the Banda Oriental, and Chile. London, February 15, 1834.

CHAPTER VI.

FIRST EXPERIENCES IN CHILE.

TRAVELLING TO SANTIAGO.—HALT AT CASA-BLANCA.—SCENES BY THE ROAD.—CUESTA ZAPATA.—PANORAMIC VIEW FROM THE CUESTA PRADO.—ACTION OF THE GOVERNMENT.—CHOICE OF A LOCALITY FOR THE OBSERVATORY.—ARRIVAL OF THE INSTRUMENTS.—PREPARATION OF SITES ON SANTA LUCIA.—WHAT PEOPLE THOUGHT OF US.—THEIR INTEREST IN THE STARRY HEAVENS.—SLOW PROGRESS WITH WORK ON THE SECOND OBSERVATORY.—NOVELTIES IN THE STREETS.—STREET SCENES IN THE MORNING.—NOVELTIES OF CLIMATE.

There are but two modes of expeditious travelling here—on horseback or in a *birlocho*. The vehicle so called is a gig whose springs are of extra strength, its shafts secured with longitudinal plates of wrought-iron, and its wheels guarded with tires of nearly double the thickness used in the United States. The postilion's horse assists in drawing the carriage by a strong cord of twisted hide secured to the left shaft. The cord has an iron hook in its extremity, that he may the more readily fasten it to the ring of his surcingle. A third horse is attached to the right shaft in the same manner whenever a hill is about to be ascended. The traveller has only to make himself as comfortable as possible. Ordinarily he makes an agreement with the birlochero on the day previous to departure, and receives a dollar from the latter as a security for punctual fulfilment of the contract. There is no fixed price. If there be great demand, as at the time of the national festivals, or when families are leaving the capital to pass the summer at the port, forty dollars may be demanded for the journey; if there be an excess of vehicles at either end, they will gladly hire one for twelve. As the carriage holds two persons comfortably, at the latter rate the price for each is about seven and a half cents per mile. If the birlochero gives satisfaction, it is customary to pay for his supper or breakfast on the road; but it is no part of the obligation, and a threat to withhold it often makes the delinquent obedient. Not that he would go without such a meal, for that the owner of the vehicle provides at a fixed rate; but when the traveller foots the bill, the sum allowed is a perquisite, and he has the additional comfort of a more abundant feast. Most natives prefer starting late in the afternoon, and making one third of the journey by seven or eight o'clock, resuming it by three in the morning at latest. This is probably the wisest arrangement; because the hottest part of the day and dust are avoided, and the horses have reasonable rest. Post-houses have never been established; and want of confidence in their subordinates prevents proprietors from having relays on the road, so that all twelve of the horses usually employed in the journey are driven through from city to city, and are changed on the road as required. To take care of the loose herd, there are two other persons besides the birlochero, one of whom is a boy often not larger than an ape, yet who will ride as boldly and throw his lasso as confidently as a more matured individual.

With my head protected by an old slouched hat, and my person comfortably wrapped in a cloak, I started on the journey without a companion. In an hour and a half of pretty steady climbing over a zigzag road, with three horses abreast, we reached the summit of the hills immediately back of the city, and some 1,350 feet above it. Here, a cold and driving mist was encountered. To one unacquainted with the road this rendered objects and distances uncertain; and the fog continuing all night, it obstructed the views that moonlight would have made pleasant. From the highest portion of the hills to a cluster of huts on the eastern side—some three miles—the average descent is only about one hundred feet per mile, though there is a small portion of the road with quite five times that inclination. Then succeeds eight or ten miles of nearly level road across indurated sand destitute of trees; and afterwards—to Casa-blanca, a village thirty miles from Valparaiso—the country is rolling and tolerably well wooded. Casa-blanca is about eight hundred feet above the sea. Here the birlochero claimed an hour's delay, to enable him to collect his horses in the vicinity; an indulgence which four hours and a half in a cramped position, with alternate showers of mist and dust in my eyes, induced me to yield very readily.

October 26.—One, two, three! hours had passed, and still there was no sound of approaching horses' feet to relieve the impatience each moment rendered more irksome. Tired with alternately pacing the short paved *trottoir* in front of the posada, and lingering over the old newspapers on its tables, as day began to lighten the dense fog, a start was made with the same animals that had brought us from Valparaiso; I, in ignorance, hoping we should be able to hire fresh horses by the way; the birlochero expecting that his own herd would overtake us before we could reach the first considerable eminence on the plain. Many a time did he look back as he thwacked the tired beasts into a moderate trot, muttering oaths "not loud but deep," and shaking his clenched fist earnestly towards invisible delinquents.

Broad daylight found us still trotting over the slightly rolling plain between hedges made musical by the matins of many birds in their (spring) gala robes, and charming to the sight by flowers of various colors. The air was loaded with the perfume of *Acacia cavenia* flowers, which are in such profusion that the trees are cut down to repair hedges. By the roadside, the dwellings of the peasantry are of the most comfortless description; mostly a few wattled canes or sticks, thatched with straw, and sometimes plastered with mud, though rarely whitewashed. The occupants are in keeping with them—a swarthy and unwashed race, whose every feature and motion betray want of energy and intelligence. Of moderate height, well formed though small limbs, tolerably prominent cheek-bones, and straight black hair, their origin cannot be mistaken; but these characteristics are not so distinctly marked as among the Peruvian Indians. Huge wagons containing merchandise from the port, or sacks of flour from the mills of the city, were met every mile or two. They were, ordinarily, in trains of four or five wagons, each having an arched thatch roof, covered neatly with raw hide, and being drawn by four or six yoke of well-conditioned oxen. They are kept in tidy and serviceable condition, and the carreteros are neat, well behaved, and good-natured fellows.

Within a little more than three leagues of Casa-blanca begins the ascent of the Cuesta Zapata, the first considerable eminence to be crossed. The road is cut in a winding line in the faces of the hill to an elevation of 1,850 feet above the sea, and its ascent is tedious from either side. Fortunately, near the western base we obtained assistance from a traveller on horseback; and relieving the vehicle from my weight, it was drawn up without much difficulty. At the summit a fresh southwest wind was driving clouds close to the face of the mountain into the eastern valley, and entirely obscuring everything more than a rod or two distant. Of course the birlochero was unable to see whether his reliefs were coming across the plain we had just left. Pushing rapidly down, and then slowly over a rolling country (for our tired beasts could scarcely move), we reached the village of Curacavi to early breakfast. Its distance from Casa-blanca is 25 miles, from Santiago 28; and the elevation above the sea is 550 feet. Within half an hour our cavalcade overtook us.

Fast and furiously drove the birlochero over the next four leagues, starting multitudes of field-rats and carrion hawks (*Caracaras*) from their enjoyments by the roadside. Nor did he cease the pace until we had partially ascended the Cuesta Prado, a mountain belonging to the range that bounds the great valley of Chile on the west. The ascent to be overcome from the west side is about 1,700 feet; and, as the slope of the mountain is more rapid than Zapata, the zigzags are shorter and steeper. Alighting, to relieve the horses from my weight and to admire more closely the novel flowers by the roadside, I was amply repaid for the fatigue it occasioned: the sun was gaining power, and as his beams touched the ascending volumes of misty vapor they were converted into cumuli, between whose interstices flashed stray pencils of light, that curiously illuminated the dark verdant slope of the opposite ravine.

Taking advantage of a by-path followed by equestrians and cattle, I was able to reach the summit crossed by the road some time before the carriage. The gradually dispersing mist-wreaths had permitted me to anticipate a satisfactory bird's-eye view of the valley we had just traversed; but I was wholly unprepared for the magnificent panorama suddenly unfolded, and for a time could scarcely believe the scene real. Loss of sleep and regular diet had imparted something of nervous excitement to the brain, and the picture offered to it by the retina resembled rather the creation of an artist's fervent imagination, or one of the scenes fitfully offered in the half-waking dreams of a summer morning, than a portion of our matter of fact globe. How majestic, yet how charming, was the view from this elevation of 2,400 feet!

The great Andes, with eternal snow-clad peaks extending as far as the eye could reach, rose to the eastward as a wall before me. Seemingly upheaved at almost regular intervals below the broken and jagged eminences, and as abutments to their grisly sides, there were countless spurs with intermediate dark glens and ravines. Under foot, and winding to the north and south, so as very nearly to meet some of the Andean spurs, was the Western cordillera—its gently swelling curves and verdant sides alternately in light and shadow, as openings of the overhanging cumuli permitted. Between these chains, and bathed in sunlight, lay a broad and fertile plain exquisitely diversified. Isolated and multiform eminences; the river Maypu and its tributaries, like ribands of silver; rows of tall poplars surrounding the white walls of country seats; groups of peasant travellers enjoying their morning repast beneath the thatched roofs of open road-side huts, near the foot of the Cuesta; horsemen, visible as pigmies, in the distance mid clouds of dust; herds of cattle and sheep quietly browsing the near mountain sides; and in its midst, just perceptible to the unassisted eye, within long shady groves, the great centre of Chilean life, Santiago—all adorn it.

Looking towards the coast, the angular road that descends the almost vertical face of the hill extends in an arrow-like line across a semi-cultivated plain, bounded by analogous ranges of eminences. Caravans of ark-like wagons, with bovine teams, seem scarcely to move along its surface; and were it not for the thin pencils of smoke ascending from scattered cottages, one might fancy it a land of desolation. Nearer at hand the vision is captivated by tall candelabra-like cacti, Chaüars (*Puyas coarctata*), with long drooping leaf-stalks and great spikes of pale-green blossoms; multitudes of evergreens and flowers of every tint, now in the glory of spring luxuriance; and the ear is charmed by the notes of many beauteous feathered songsters:

"All, save the spirit of man, is divine."

I had rambled out of sight of the road; and the birlochero, unable to comprehend any reason for it, was shouting at the very top of his voice for my return. Apparently, his patience was as much exhausted as mine had been at Casa-blanca; and as he could scarcely take the liberty to vent his anger upon me, the poor and unoffending horses were made victims. In spite of remonstrances, they were lashed into a full run, although we were descending at angles of scarcely less than 15° in sharply turning zigzags. Erect in the stirrups, with poncho and a handkerchief covering his hair flying behind, and his whip-lash whirling overhead, he thundered Jehu-like down the steep at a pace in which a falter or stumble of either horse might have projected us over the precipice at a speed sufficient, perhaps, to keep us revolving as new satellites about the earth, provided the old snow-peaks on the other side of the valley did not arrest us in the first gyration.

There is little to note in the approach to Santiago from the westward. As the supply of water for irrigation is scanty, few country-seats on this side betoken the wealth of its citizens. Midway between the summit of the Cuesta and the city the road crosses the Pudaüel, quite a body of water formed by the junction of the Mapocho and Colina, the united column falling into the Maypu a few leagues to the southwest. Farther on, the plain is very slightly cultivated, and the road dusty, until we enter the suburbs of the capital between rows of the quick-growing poplar and comfortless hovels of adobes.

Resting for an hour or two, during which the official letters relating to the expedition, as well as those not merely introductory, were despatched, I started for Santa Lucia, the little rocky hill in the eastern portion of the city which had been indicated by the ambassador at Washington as suitable for our purposes. Though it commanded a most charming panorama, the result of the inspection was far from favorable, because of the vicinity of the Andes, of its somewhat precipitous ascent, and the inevitably tedious and expensive labor required to level sufficient space near its rugged summit. A visit to Cerro Blanco, just on the northern skirts, and another to the plain south of the city, resulted somewhat similarly. There were no suitable accommodations for the officers near enough to either of the latter; and as the last was reputed to be excessively wet during winter, it was wholly unfitted for our purposes. So discouraging appeared to be the prospect of a location at Santiago, that arrangements were made to visit Talca as soon as the government should signify its approbation to our establishment in Chile. But both intelligent natives and resident foreigners well acquainted with the country advised against this, assuring me that while Talca possessed no advantage, so far as distance from the mountains could be considered, it would be impossible to obtain there the facilities which the capital afforded for erecting instruments, or their repair in case of necessity. The last difficulty was of vital moment. Moreover, the foundation of a permanent observatory on the southern portion of the continent was a great desideratum, which could only be obtained, they said, by enlisting influential persons in its behalf. This might require the intervention of two distinct classes—scientific men who would appreciate its utility, and political men to vote the necessary outlay. These could nowhere be found so well as at Santiago, about its university and government.

The action of the Minister for Foreign Affairs was prompt, liberal, and kind. Government recognised the importance and utility of the work we came to perform, and volunteered every facility within its control, viz: a portion of San Lucia should be levelled for our use, if that hill was selected; rooms in the castle should be placed at our control; a guard should be stationed at the observatories for their and our protection; and everything intended for us should be admitted free of duty. These evidences of the strongest good will and most liberal intentions towards us coming in aid of the reasons indicated, there was hesitation no longer; and having decided on making the city our head-quarters, within an hour or two after communicating such intention to the government, intelligence reached me of the arrival of the Louis Philippe at Valparaiso. Luckily for me, the United States had no minister in Chile at the time, and my business could be transacted with the Minister for Foreign Affairs without the formal, tedious, and unnecessarily prosy intervention required by diplomatic etiquette.

Returning to the port immediately, everything was carefully packed for transportation in and on eight of the great wagons of the country; and on the morning of the 9th of November our caravan delivered its assorted cargo at the foot of Santa Lucia, almost uninjured by rough handling and the last eighty miles' journey. Chronometers, barometers, and other delicate instruments, were suspended from the roofs by thongs of hide, guides of cord preventing their lateral motion; and they all arrived safely. The assistants had preceded me some days. Meantime the task of levelling a part of the hill had been placed under charge of the chief of police, who had a large gang at work on the tough porphyritic blocks. Situated in a populous portion of the city, blasting was absolutely prohibited, and the seemingly basaltic masses could only be broken down by building fires and suddenly pouring water on the heated rock, or with iron mauls and wedges—both processes necessarily tedious. But the work was progressing quite "as well as could be expected."

In order to form a terrace of sufficient width for the smaller and rotary observatory, it was necessary to build a wall across a short and steep ravine, and fill between the artificial and natural walls with rocks and earth. But as such a foundation would have been unstable for even the outer edge of a wooden tenement fifteen feet in diameter, the fire-engines were called in requisition to throw up water, for the purpose of settling the soil among the rocks. As it was necessary to wait until Sunday morning for the services of the only persons drilled to their use, this was attended with some difficulty and delay. The engines belong to government, and are manned by citizens who choose to serve in this capacity rather than in the National Guard; and Sunday morning is their regular period for exercise. But the machines proved insufficient, and the chief of police subsequently caused a supply to be carried as far as the castle on mules, and thence in goat-skins on the backs of peons. Each skin holds from five to six gallons. The first ascent was by a ladder, and thence the vertical height to be overcome is sixty or seventy feet, over an irregular surface of rock, inclined about forty degrees. As the sun was glaringly hot, the labor proved very severe. Stripped as they were, with only pantaloons, hat, and sandals, when the poor fellows deposited their loads beside the excavated trench every muscle of their bodies trembled, and their hearts could be seen throbbing as though they would burst. But the task was accomplished without accident. The little building originally constructed at Washington, and then packed for shipment, was again put together, and on the 6th of December I had the satisfaction to obtain a first look through the telescope erected on its pier.

As the buildings advanced, the curiosity of the people increased, and there were stories of all kinds circulated respecting them. One was that government had imported a new kind of flour-mill from America, and these were the two houses—we the millers. Nor was this at all implausible to those who were unable to ascend the hill; for the smaller observatory (as has been said) is circular, and has a conical roof, whose apex is of tin. The latter opens upward, on a hinge at one side, and has also a roof-door, extending from the eaves to the junction with the tin, which opens to something more than a right-angle. As the whole house revolves on balls that move between grooved rails of cast-iron under its sill, when it is whirling round with the doors open, it might readily be thought a mill. Moreover, our stone-mason (something of a wag in his way) assured many good Chilenos that the broad flat stones he was conveying to the summit were to grind flour with! It was rare sport for the boys when permitted to turn the house, and curious enough to see how many *grown up* boys (and girls too) were desirous to take a fancied ride within it. The flooring on which they stood was permanent; but the illusion was so perfect, that the motion of the house produced giddiness to those within, and in one or two instances, among the ladies, nausea like sea-sickness. Will some M. D. expound the sympathies of the eyes and esophagus?

With the erection of the telescope a new era commenced. The planet Saturn presented a never failing source of admiration and interest to the crowd that assembled every evening about our doors. Where there were so many spectators, all eager to look through the instrument, it was necessary to restrict their view to one object, and close the doors at the hour fixed for the commencement of work. Yet numbers returned several successive evenings to wonder at the new world and its gorgeous system of rings and satellites displayed to them for the first time by us; and for nearly three hours of every evening, during three months, either Lieut. MacRae or myself attended the pleasure of all who came. Rich and poor, old and young, were alike treated with attention; and when all others had had their turn, the sentinel, who stood patiently by the door, was never forgotten. Soon the younger portion of the visitors were desirous to know when the class would be formed and lectures commence;* the older to speculate about the cost of such a beautiful machine: both good symptoms, if the sparks thus elicited could only be nursed into flame. As one of the fruits of our expedition here, I hoped to make it burn brightly, and that we might boast that Santiago through our influence established the first national observatory of South America.

Slow progress was made in obtaining piers for the meridian circle. The instrument required blocks six feet eight inches long, two feet square at the base, and one foot square at top; but, from the imperfect knowledge of blasting possessed by our workmen, it would have been exceedingly difficult to obtain single masses of such dimensions, even had it been possible to elevate

* The ambassador at Washington had advised his government to place some of the best and most advanced students of the National Institute under my direction, that they might learn the use of instruments, and become familiar with astronomical computations. His letter had been printed in the journals of the day, and those who read it doubtless understood my position; but the mass supposed that, like every other foreigner, I had come to make money, and to this end was about to teach astronomy.

them to the observatory with the means at command in Santiago, and I found it necessary to construct them of three blocks each. These were drawn on a sled, by two yokes of oxen. They could drag but one at a time, and then only as far as the castle. From thence they were hauled up to the observatory by men, with ropes and boards—what sailors call "par-buckled;" a job that would have been accomplished easily, if the power could all have been applied in the line of motion; but, unfortunately, the broken surface of the hill scarcely permitted two men to stand in the same plane. In illustration of the difficulties encountered, it may be mentioned, that although fifty per cent. was added to the original contract price, in order to hasten its execution, more than two weeks were spent in efforts to blast a block as large as ten cubic feet; and when deposited on the terrace, near the castle, thirty men were more than three hours in raising it to the observatory.

In the midst of erecting the piers, one of the many "feast days" observed in Catholic countries occurred, when, for the day, their church places a ban on labor. To us, who acknowledge no days of rest but the Sabbath and our national holiday, or at most Christmas and Good Friday included, the frequent recurrence of interdicted periods, when much was to be accomplished, was extremely annoying; and so public sentiment begins to regard it here. Yet, as government supports the pretensions of the church and its infliction of fines for violation of the appointed times, of necessity the lower orders obey; and while this continues, and the well fed and well clad friars are encouraged to indolence, Chile can never advance to the eminence to which it is entitled to aspire.

Though the carpenters did not complete the last one until the meridian circle to be mounted in it had arrived from Germany, both buildings were finally ready about the 1st of January. Indeed, the mechanics had been longer reconstructing houses that required only putting each marked portion in its place, and inserting the screws, than it had originally taken to build them in the United States. Even the Yankee master-workman employed had lost all idea of the value of time, and by procrastination tired my patience beyond measure. True, there was ample work for the small party with the instruments already arranged, and there were few hours of rest even by daylight. Night after night—eighty-seven out of ninety in succession—did the planet Mars command use of the equatorial; and the days and hours pre-arranged for the magnetical and meteorological observations required the constant presence of one assistant at our residence near the foot of the hill.

We were domiciliated under one roof, and were gradually becoming accustomed to the novelties of Santiago life. Ordinarily, my earliest consciousness was of the cry of the *aguador* (water-carrier) who supplied our household, and heralded his entrance to the patio by drawling in a crescendo tone, "A-gua-ti-ro," lengthening each syllable to the duration of a respectable word. He is one of a privileged class who spend their days, from early dawn till nightfall, conveying that essential of life from the two or three fountains through the streets of the city. With a keg strapped on each side of his horse, and a can with which to fill them, his whole life is passed in perambulating a few thoroughfares. He wears cotton drawers and a shirt that are rarely made acquainted with the element in which he deals, a poncho, a high peaked hat of rushes, and sandals of raw hide, or coarse shoes. For seven eighths of a dollar per month he supplies all the water we need for every purpose; but as it is quite turbid, from the admixture of river earths in its passage to the reservoirs or fountains, we are obliged to filter before using it. Soon the streets resound with the cries of venders who have "big, fat fowls and chickens;" "potatoes by the peck;" "onions by the dozen;" "pork, fat pork;" "pejereys from Aculeo;" "corn, green corn;" and a host of other edibles that form part of the substantial Spanish breakfast. Each has his peculiar cry and intonation, interpretable at times only by his class or immediate customers, and defying the philological acumen of most of his own countrymen. With the momentary succession of new candidates for the favors of housekeepers, each screaming at the top of his voice, and the tramp of horses and mules within a few feet of one's ear, sleep is no longer possible. By eight o'clock the streets are thronged. Huge carts are passing to their several destinations with merchandise from the port, and wood, charcoal, or watermelons from the country. Here you encounter a cavalcade of mules, carrying long pieces of scantling crossed above their heads, and trailing the ground at several feet from their hinder legs on each side. Probably they have been thus dragged for three hundred miles! Woe to your shins if they come in contact with them. A little farther on is another troop, loaded with wheat in sacks of hide. Yet a third conveys the beds of a family in similar coverings, and their apparel in trunks, also protected by cases of the same material. In another place a train of long-eared donkeys stagger under loads of sand or pebble-stones for paving. They nibble, as they pass, at rinds of melons cast aside by the chain-gangs at work on the streets under guards of soldiers. Here comes the baker on an ambling mule, with two neatly finished and trunk-like panniers. He occupies nearly one third the width of the street. He utters no cry, and looks moderately tidy. Silently, also, the milk-woman comes next, with tin vessels similarly suspended; her costume too often resembling the aguador's. There are countrymen on foot driving flocks of turkeys, or with baskets piled up with grapes or figs; and others riding between panniers packed high with radishes larger than one's arm, onions, salads, all other vegetables not requiring a cart to carry them, and every fruit in its season. Each has its recommendatory song, and the combination of sounds renders Santiago a perfect Bedlam. But hark! there are short and rapid strokes from one of the bells of the cathedral; and, with an instant's intermission, from the campanile comes a single solemn vibration through the air. Behold! the life-current is apparently paralyzed. Riders dismount; pedestrians fall to their knees; all bareheaded, bowed, and silent, are motionless as the grave till the third stroke releases them from the act of humiliation, and they rise, crossing themselves. Probably nothing makes greater impression on one arriving in a Catholic country, who knows not the cause of an act apparently so solemn, nor has had opportunity to ascertain the amount of religious intelligence possessed by the community surrounding him. The unseen cause of this remarkable custom is the elevation of the Host in the cathedral at that instant, a ceremony repeated with clock-like regularity each day. Mass over, the friars seem to be let loose. One takes with him a puppet fantastically dressed, borne by a lay brother; himself charged only with a plate on which to receive contributions from the pious, who have the privilege of kissing the doll, or it may be a bit of the fustian of his own garment offered for salutes. Another, and a more humble mendicant brother, presents with one hand a box containing a small wax image amid tinsel ornaments, with the other a tin box in which to receive your oblations.

Soon the days became extremely warm, and at times oppressive before noon. Once in these early weeks the clouds banked heavily over the Andes, and towards 4 P. M. we heard the first thunder since leaving the region of the equator. There was evidently a violent thunder-storm on the peaks thirty miles to the eastward; and when the clouds rolled away, so that we could perceive the mountains again, the snow-mantle had descended half way down their rugged sides. Snow and thunder-storms! But if we had no near displays of thunder and lightning, the muttering precursors of earthquakes sufficiently resemble the rumbling of heaven's artillery to keep up our recollection of the phenomenon; and though we had not the warning of the sharp and vivid flash in the cloud, there inevitably followed short, quick pulsations of the earth, more startling because invisible and inevitable. Lightning is a monitor—seen, and one is safe; the murmur of the coming earth-storm may warn without preserving from annihilation.

CHAPTER VII.*

EXPERIENCES—CONTINUED.

ADVANCE OF AUTUMN.—SUNDAY AT SANTIAGO.—ANNOYANCES.—SEARCH FOR A DESAGUADOR OF THE MAPOCHO.—SUNDAY OCCUPATIONS.—A RAIN-STORM.—THE SALTO DE AGUA.—ICE.—AN EARTHQUAKE.—A FLOOD IN THE RIVER.—LEAVE FOR VALPARAISO.—RAIN-STORM ON THE ROAD.—APPARENT DESOLATION IN THE COUNTRY.—CURACAVI.—NARROW ESCAPE.—CASA-BLANCA.—APPEARANCE OF VALPARAISO AND ITS ENVIRONS FROM THE HILLS.—RETURN TO THE CAPITAL.—ANOTHER FLOOD IN THE MAPOCHO.—CLERK OF THE WEATHER.—AGRICULTURAL.—BIRDS.—THE COUNTRY NEAR THE SALTO DE AGUA.—CARNE CON CUERO.—CHRISTMAS; CHRISTMAS-EVE AT THE MARKET-HOUSE; SERVICE IN THE CATHEDRAL.—NACIMIENTOS.

May 1.—We had had a whole week of cloudy and uncomfortable weather, terminating in rain about the close of April, and clearing away partially after sunset, so that our observations could be resumed. The morning of this day was bright and clear, with a freshness in the atmosphere most invigorating. Our rain had been snow on the mountains, and they presented a most picturesque sight, clothed as they were in winter mantles, perhaps one third of the distance from the summit of the nearer range towards the valley. Returning from my usual walk along the bank of the river, I was struck with the change which a week had wrought in the long rows of poplars intersecting the plain in every direction. A few days ago their dark green foliage was a grateful relief to the eye in the sun's bright glare; now, in the morning's breeze, leaves were falling in golden millions, and the higher branches of many were already stripped—evidence of the repose which nature demands for some classes of vegetable life.

It was Sunday; but there were no outward tokens of "the day of rest" for man. True, the church doors were open; and women, gracefully wrapped in *mantos*, with rugs hanging over the arm, or borne by a following servant, were encountered at every step, going to or returning from their devotions: but these are constant occurrences, and therefore served not to designate the day. On the other hand, multitudes of *guasos* thronged the streets with droves of turkeys, baskets of fowls, and autumnal fruits, rendering the thoroughfares a nuisance with their cries respecting the various articles for sale. I was no great hand at keeping the Sabbath at home as the strict fathers of the Protestant church would have had me; but it was always a day grateful for the quiet it brought, and in this sad Bedlam memory turned with a feeling of veneration to the customs of our Puritan land. "Sad Bedlam!" one may regard as contradictory words in juxtaposition; but the designation is approximatively true of Santiago. The absence of activity and evidences of commercial life and thrift during ordinary business hours, of crowded streets, and of the hum that ever pervades large cities in all other parts of the world, most emphatically impress one that it is sad, whilst almost eternal cries and the clatter of bells fully entitle it to be classed as a second Bedlam. Even the observatory was no place of refuge; for the noises came up on all sides of Santa Lucia, and the cordilleras sent back the echoes.

On arriving at Santiago, if not more than half inclined to side with the Catholic faith, I was by no means willing to remain silent when their mode of worship was contemned. But there is quite "too much of a good thing" in an exclusively Catholic country; and when, at night, the churches began firing their squibs and ringing bells, sometimes I almost wished bells and friars at the bottom of the ocean. In any but a Catholic country one can form no idea of the senseless and intolerable clatter they frequently keep up during an hour or more. This starts into concert scores of worthless curs, about the base of Santa Lucia, utterly masking the beat

* In this and the following chapters chronological order has been disregarded for the purpose of grouping analogous subjects.

of our clock, and sorely trying one's temper when clusters of stars came rapidly into the field of the telescope, as was sometimes the case. Had they been mellow-toned bells rung harmoniously, or the sharp and angry barks of faithful watch-dogs, one might have abided the infliction amiably; but all Santiago does not boast a sweet-lipped bell, and the little clappers fly as though suspended from the necks of running cows; whilst the villanous dogs do nothing but cumber the sidewalks, and foot-passengers—fearful of disturbing their slumbers—must take the outside of them. It being quite certain that there is, on an average, one dog for every house in Santiago, we are astonished that the city government permits such a wholly worthless multitude. It would be a different matter were revenue derived from their retention; but the city imposes no taxes, except a very moderate one on every house, with which to pay for police and lighting the streets. This amounts to nearly three fourths of one per cent. of what the house rents for, and is collected from the occupant. House, furniture, and all other personal property are exempted. Of course things work badly, and the means for repairs or improvements derived from privileges to sell snow, kill cattle, &c., are wholly insufficient for the wants of so extended a city.

May.—In company with Mr. P. and Prof. Domeyko, an early start was made one Sunday morning, to examine two localities a few leagues distant. At one of these, the waters of the Mapocho were said to disappear; at the other, they re-issue from their subterranean filtration thoroughly limpid. Striking the stream within half a league of the city, we continued between its banks, fording and re-fording as often as it became necessary in pursuing our way among the water-worn pebbles and sand. There is little change in the width or character of the bed for four miles. It has an average breadth of one hundred and fifty yards, and is wholly composed of the materials just mentioned. At this time the water in places was separated into two or three rapid rivulets; farther down, it was united into one stream perhaps ten or twelve yards wide, and it is only during heavy and continued rains of winter that the volume is increased to fill the wide space between the banks. That floods do so fill it, there are abundant traces to show in the recent washings on either side of the low gravel-formed shores. At a league and a half from Santiago the nature of the surface-soil somewhat changes, and the distance between the banks is diminished to less than thirty yards, with a considerable but not proportionate increase in the depth of the water-way. As there are no indications of overflows, it is evident that a large body must percolate the pebbly reach just above; and it was here, if anywhere, that we expected to lose the stream. This was the place indicated; but we found only such a diminution in the volume as could readily be accounted for in the multitude of irrigating channels, and the ordinary operations of absorption and evaporation. Inquiry of guasos afforded little satisfaction. The general opinion among them was, that the water only disappeared during a portion of the summer, when they most needed it; and that as soon as the rains began, there was always abundance. However, they all asserted (and inquiry addressed to other creditable persons on our return went to show) that there is such a locality as we were in search of some eight or ten leagues farther to the southwestward. Recollecting the difficulty of obtaining correct information from countrymen even in lands where there is more intelligence among them, the rivulets were followed a league farther, but without success; and we were only partially rewarded for the task of tracing its abominable paths by seeing the plants of its peculiar botany and a few novel specimens of birds.

On our return, leaving the river to the right, we struck into a main road that passes through a village at the base of the Cuesta Renca. Dividing there, one branch of the road extends westward; the other passes over a *portezuelo* to the northern side of the hill, and thence along a shallow lake formed by unconsumed water of the irrigating channels to the eastward. On either side of the portezuelo the ground has been thoroughly perforated by field-rats, whose principal sustenance is the bulbs of plants. So abundant is the *Oxalis lobata* there, that the flowers which had matured under the rains of the few preceding days literally made patches of earth appear at a little distance as though covered with cloths of gold. The summit of Renca is rather more than 1,100 feet above the plain. Its general geological structure is similar to that of Santa Lucia, though disintegration has covered large portions of its surface with a rich soil producing pasturage for multitudes of sheep and cattle, until the droughts of summer burn up all vegetation that has only superficial roots. On the northern side, a small canal winds close to its base. Well up the slopes there were fields of grain dependent on natural irrigation; and still higher, the Acacia cavenia and arborescent cactus throw out their arms towards the sky amid outcropping prismatic rocks on whose surfaces rain can scarcely be known for six months at a time. Except a marshy plain near the southeast border of the lake, all the surrounding valley presents that abundance of vegetable life with which so benignant a climate blesses Chile. Here the finest strawberries are grown; and, in their season, pleasure parties come frequently from the capital to enjoy freshly gathered fruit.

Guasos and peons were collected at Renca, the village mentioned, for their usual Sunday dissipations and diversions—new chicha (like new cider in two respects, cheapness and agreeable flavor) tempting many to debauchery, which often terminates in murder. Unlike cider, it quickly inflames the brain; and under its influence, they resort to the knife for redress of real or imaginary grievances. One ragged vagabond, whose nose, like Bardolph's, was an index of the strong waters he had imbibed, chased us nearly two miles, unsuccessfully begging means to obtain a drink of his favorite beverage. His only reward was advice to soak his proboscis in water—perhaps that would afford him a liquor sufficiently potent. He had left many companions playing at *bolas* at the *pulperias*—a favorite game, which tradition claims to have been transmitted from the time of the conquest. It is a sort of billiards, in which the earth forms the table, and an iron ring the pocket; the balls are of hard wood four and a half or five inches in diameter, and flat pieces of board some two inches wide serve instead of cues, or rather maces. The earth is made perfectly level and smooth for a space one half larger than the ordinary billiard-table, and has guards to prevent the balls from passing beyond its limits. There are three balls. These are not struck, as in playing billiards, but receive their impetus by being scraped along under accelerated motion of the flat pieces of board. The great stroke of the game is to make a cannon from the third ball to that of your adversary, driving the latter though the ring. Other parties had withdrawn from the roadside, and were earnestly occupied with cards; the use of which being prohibited, every peon covets a pack, and will gamble away his last real at *monte*.

May 13.—A storm of wind and rain from the northward commenced early in the morning, at times blowing with much violence; and though the rain did not fall as heavily as during short periods on two or three previous occasions, it was absolutely without cessation for about thirteen hours, and the amount deposited exceeded three and a half inches! Towards sunset there was a narrow streak of clear sky to the westward, and by eight o'clock the heavens were cloudless. Still the wind blew as freshly as during the day, and a nebulous haze surrounded all the more brilliant stars. By midnight the temperature had fallen to 40°, evidencing the deposition of a large body of snow on the Andes, which the starlight partially and the dawn of the following morning wholly revealed. Far as the eye could trace the ranges, they were enveloped full two thirds from the crests downward; and there were also patches about the more elevated summits and table-lands of the Western cordilleras. The following day proved calm and cloudless; and the sharp, cool air that poured down from the mountain-sides, modulated by a bright sun, was most refreshing and invigorating. But it was torture to the poor peons, whose cotton garments, threadbare ponchos, and perhaps bare feet, kept them shivering as they crept along the sunny side of the streets.

May 21.—Starting shortly before noon on one of the Indian summer like mornings with which we had occasionally been favored, a gay cavalcade of us rode to the *Salto de Agua*. For he first two or three miles the road follows near the south bank of the river, between *quintas* (country seats) of the more wealthy citizens and quite large orchards of figs, oranges, olives, and nut-trees, with ornamental cypress and flowering trees interspersed. Rows of poplars bound the road on either side. It rises rapidly as we wind the base of San Cristoval in following a bend of the river, each moment bringing more grandly into view the masses of mountains hidden from the city. Here, the muddy streams seen within the city walls are limpid, and sparkle as they gurgle over bending water-lilies profusely growing within the river banks. Once in the country, and the main highway deserted, the effects of late rains became strikingly apparent. Whilst nature was starting some forms of vegetable life into visible existence, others were paying their autumnal tribute, and waved their leafless arms across the blue sky. Brilliant flowers and verdure clad the earth in all directions. In one place a broad hill-side is wholly hidden by the little *flor de perdiz;* in another, the parasite *quintral* displays, as if in mockery, its bunches of brilliant scarlet flowers on denuded limbs of the tall poplar, or amid the dark evergreen foliage of the olive.

Though no broader, at four miles from the city the river is more rapid, and has a slightly greater volume. Its southern bank is quite twenty feet above the water surface; that to the north, when the bed is full, is the base of San Cristoval. A bridle path leads across its pebbly bottom, now, in a great measure, overgrown with shrubs; thence the path continues up to a depression in the spur, perhaps a hundred yards above the level of the stream. Here, a small sheet of water precipitates itself to a depth of forty or fifty feet, amid reeds and shrubbery, and thence dashes along in a line of foam through more than three hundred, till it reaches the great plain. Water is taken from the Mapocho at a point of the river above this level, and led in a canal along the southeastern slope of the spur, for the purpose of irrigating some of the estates lying north of Santiago. A surplus from this canal makes the "*Salto;*" and the water thus wasted has converted a hollow of the plain into a marshy swamp, which in a few years will be irrecoverably grown with rushes. The remainder of the water is distributed into two or three smaller canals that follow the involutions of the sloping hill-sides to the northward, until the whole is finally absorbed for the purposes of man. Tradition alleges that all of these channels were cut by the Mapochos long before the arrival of the Spaniards; and as we know that the Peruvians resorted to this portion of the country to receive an annual tribute, it is not at all improbable. Indeed, none but the hardy and inoffensive race inhabiting nearly all of South America north of the thirty-sixth parallel would ever have had the patience to execute such a task. The Spaniards might have commanded and supervised, but had not the numbers to execute the work; and we have a right to believe that they found it completed, because *they* would have thrown aqueducts across narrow ravines rather than follow the hill-sides so many additional miles. Beyond a doubt these canals are many scores of times longer than the fields they benefit.

A small monument of red porphyry has been erected near the precipice from which the water makes its spring, and the view of the plain from that point is very lovely. The southwestern sugar-loaf of San Cristoval conceals the city; but Cerro Blanco and Renca remain in sight, with all the country-seats near its northern skirts, and the dwellings of the haciendas as far as the Western cordilleras.

June 4.—As had been the case on several preceding mornings, there was a dense fog until 11 A. M., which on this day was followed by a brightly clear night and pellicles of ice on little pools near the river.

June 19.—Shortly after midnight there was a brief though somewhat violent earthquake, in one respect unlike any of which we had been observers. All but one of our little party were seated round a handful of fire in an open stove discussing the affairs of the day, and that most interesting topic to some of us at all times, the arrival of the monthly mail. Of a sudden two of us were flying towards the door leading to the head of the stairs, and one had got half way down when the full tremor of an earthquake was upon us. On my part the flight was wholly involuntary; and at the instant of consciousness that it was a subterranean disturbance I turned in the opposite direction to watch the oscillations of the barometer. The shock was not preceded by the usual rumbling noise, but was accompanied by it, and the whole, except the receding echoes from the hills, did not occupy more than four seconds. Short as it was, people rushed to the streets, utterly regardless of scanty toilets.

It is not easy to comprehend why we attempted to fly from danger. Had there been the customary warning to influence, it might have been explicable; but there was no such precursor,—nothing to tell of the coming shock,—and thus the mind was absolutely dormant, whilst the body was sensible. Experience had taught me that life was in no great jeopardy at such a distance from the focus of these convulsions; nor, indeed, was property, unless nature meant to change the order she had followed for two centuries. Therefore one ordinarily cool and reflecting usually has time to take out a watch, and prepare himself, before the tremor is under foot, to seize as many of the concomitants as their brief duration will permit. These can be noted more satisfactorily at the second shock than at the first, because the little flurry of the moment will have subsided in the short period of time between them. But all are not thus calm; intuitive apprehension of danger sends half the population flying to the patios and streets, scarcely cognizant of the cause.

June 24.—St. John's day. A heavy rain having fallen almost continuously for forty-eight hours, the broad and pebbly bottom of the Mapocho was filled with a wild and muddy torrent, attracting people from far and near to witness it. Notwithstanding the inclemency of the weather, the river-bank and bridges were crowded with the gazing multitude, many of whom had come in carriages. By the afternoon the foundations of the upper bridge must have been seriously undermined; yet, in spite of the warning of an uprooted tree that had grown beside one of the piers, the crowd continued to collect upon it in numbers. Suddenly a hand-rail gave way under the pressure of human weight, and many were precipitated amid the foaming waters. Within a stream so furious, one would have thought the chance of life scarcely worth struggling for, and a rescue from death by others next to impossible; but two of the bystanders actually plunged headlong into the roaring volume to save their unfortunate countrymen; and, stranger still, only one was drowned. Afterwards the lookers-on were said to have a horror of water, amounting almost to hydrophobia. When the mischief was done, the police received instructions to exclude persons from the bridge; and they went so far as to prevent even those from going upon it who were desirous to obtain a view at some risk to life.

Disagreeable as was the day, the namesakes of the holy Baptist confidently awaited visits of gratulation; and woe to the *soi-disant* friends who forgot to present themselves in person or by billet to all the Juans and Juanas of their visiting circle.

June 28.—Forty-eight hours' cessation of the rain giving reasonable hope that the roads would be in tolerably passable condition, I left the capital before daylight on a brief visit to Valparaiso. The morning was overcast and raw; but the clouds were evidently high, and ranged in strata, which are ordinarily precursors of fair weather. As the birlocho was new, and the owner promised eighteen fine horses to start with, there was no doubt that plenty of wrappings would protect me from the cold of the mountains and gorges, and I anticipated a pleasant ride.

Rain began to drop again as we crossed Pudaüel; and by the time we had ascended to the pass of the Prado, three hours after leaving the city, it descended furiously, an easterly wind driving it over the face of the mountain behind us. Diminished temperature, consequent on height, converted it into snow on the higher portions of the chain to the right and left; and the cold wind from the Andes pouring through the gorge was the first discomfort of the journey. On every side nature was in her most velvety and brilliant livery: not ornamented with flowers, as in early spring, it is true; but the valleys and ravines, and mountain sides—to the very snow-line—presented verdant hues that varied in tints with the character of the vegetation. Of flowers there were only one or two—the little flor de perdiz, and one other small pinkish oxalis, whose season had almost gone by; but the shrubbery was in full foliage, with clusters of swelling buds, which a few warm days would expand into flowers. By the time we had descended the mountain, its rapidly shelving sides saturated by preceding showers—having thrown off the water as fast as it fell—had swollen the streamlets considerably. Thus, beds which are nearly dry during so long a portion of the year were now rapid brooks, some of them whirling across the road with much violence.

Faster and heavier fell the rain-drops as the day wore on; and the drivers—both now constantly aiding the shaft-horse on account of the increasing heaviness of the road—spurred and lashed their beasts more energetically with the augmentation of the storm, and a disk of water steadily accompanied the wheels. Knowledge of the inconveniences of these vehicles, and the difficulties of crossing streams after a few hours of heavy rain, had prevented any traveller from starting towards the capital. Even the heavy freight wagons had been stopped at the ranchos; and the drivers, half suffocated in smoke, whose only egress was by the door or through the straw thatch of the roof, were huddled comfortless about little fires built on the earthen floors. How cheerless looked the country! During the last days of spring, when the earth is covered with flowers and the air redolent with their perfume; when long trains of wagons wind across the plains, or are picturesquely projected in the zigzags up the mountain sides; when greetings from strangely costumed peasants, and hasty though courteous nods from passing travellers constantly attract attention; and when the gay warbling of birds prevents the mind from "preying on itself," the absence of dwellings for the better classes, and of evidences of civilization, prosperity, and wealth, is not so apparent to the eye. But now, when the road was deprived of its fair-weather occupants, and the earth of its gems, its solitariness and comparative desolation appeared striking. There may be country-seats and cultivated farms at a distance not visible to the traveller over the great thoroughfare; but in the more than eighty miles to Valparaiso only three or four are to be seen. Want of water for irrigation is the great drawback; and perhaps the still existing law of entail has some influence. The latter, by preserving immense estates in the possession of individuals who have almost a Chinese amount of aversion to depart from the customs of their ancestors, necessarily produces large tracts of uncultivated land. Then, too, in accordance with the example set by large numbers of their employers, the peons who cultivate the soil are indolent in the extreme, and utterly improvident. If they can obtain sufficient to gratify present appetites, there is no thought for the morrow; and it may be doubted whether there exist ten individuals of the class in Chile into whose minds ever entered the idea of purchasing homesteads for themselves. A lazy, careless race, given to ebriety and sensuality whenever occasions are presented.

Curacavi was reached near 2 P. M.; and though there was no moderation in the violence with which the rain descended, the temperature of the valley was far more pleasant. Here the corridors were occupied by a group of peons and barn-yard fowls, both seeking shelter from the storm, though the latter were no little persecuted by a brace of bare-legged and bare-headed boys, who chased them from point to point, practising early lessons with twine lassoes. Greatly to the annoyance of his less dexterous companion, and doubtless no less so to the feathered tribe, one of the little fellows rarely failed to noose his bird; and in the excitement of the sport utterly disregarded wet and mud, although the water streamed from his long, fair hair, and his legs were fairly purple from cold. An old peon, whose round, good-humored face betokened frequent acquaintance with the chicha-cup, entered into their amusement with much earnestness, and was himself no uninteresting figure in the picture. Although he had but a cotton shirt, drawers, and a tattered poncho—just clothing sufficient for a summer temperature, as we should estimate it in a similar parallel north of the line; for shoes, bits of untanned hide laced with twine at the heel and over the instep; and for a hat, a conical pile of woven rushes—there pervaded his features an expression of profound satisfaction, and he moved from his seat to render homage, as I alighted, with the dignity and grace of a courtier of the old school.

Night overtook us still on the road. In many flat places the ground was completely submerged, and it became necessary to change the three horses every hour instead of every two, as is customary. At starting there was a hope that the journey to Valparaiso would have been practicable without stopping; but as the darkness came on, and the roar of the mountain-torrents made itself heard, prudence dictated otherwise. Indeed, the multitude of deep ruts that required no ordinary skill to avoid, even with daylight, had rendered progress extremely slow for the hour or two about sunset. At half a league from Casa-blanca a brook crosses the road, which the rains had swollen to a wild and angry torrent, whose rumbling was audible a hundred yards or more before reaching it. Ordinarily, in summer the stream is not more than a few inches deep; in winter, perhaps two feet. Now, in the darkness, the drivers appeared doubtful of its depth; and as the horses plunged in, I was rather startled to hear the capataz say: "Cuidado, patron!" (Take care, patron!) I had two of the best, the boldest, and most skilful drivers in the world, and was morally confident that, if the vehicle could be conducted safely across, they were the men to do it; but so unexpected was the warning, that my cloak was thrown off, and overcoat instantly unbuttoned, to be ready, if need be, for a struggle with the waters. Whilst in mid-stream, and the torrent poured across the bottom of the birlocho, the shaft-horse stumbled and fell, momentarily impeding the others, and placing our safety in great jeopardy. It was pitch dark: one horse was floundering; the other two, scarcely possessing power to sustain the vehicle against the stream, only kept their footholds through the weight of their riders; and thus there was an instant of thrilling anxiety. It is difficult to say what I should have done on detecting that the carriage was drifting; but probably no one ever divested himself of coats with greater celerity, and I well remember how my heart throbbed for some minutes afterwards. Nothing but the wonderful dexterity and good management of the men prevented the whole of us from being swept away by the current. Had any lingering longings to go on remained, this adventure would have dispelled them, especially as there was another such place a like distance beyond Casa-blanca; and I sat me down contentedly over the dry air of a brasero in its *auberge*.

One may ask, Why was such risk incurred; why not have turned back even as far as Curacavi? and be surprised at the seemingly useless hazard of life. But the truth is, my first knowledge of risk was the warning as the drivers dashed in, and there was no time for remonstrance. They knew that the streams in our rear were equally dangerous; the mountain between us and Curacavi not less so; and they must either push across to a hot supper and comfortable quarters, or sit all night in the pitiless storm. The landlord regarded our escape as no little surprising, soundly rating the drivers for crossing the branch after such a day of rain as we had had; but they defended themselves on the plea that they dared not attempt repassing the Cuesta Zapata with their tired horses, even had they succeeded in getting so far, and there was no place nearer than Curacavi where I could have been decently lodged. An hour later the mail from Santiago was transported across the same stream on a rope, horse and rider swimming over, aided by cords leading from the shore!

The creek beyond Casa-blanca is more difficult of transit, because of its steeper sides and bed of loose rocks. At the moment of our arrival in the village, it could only be passed in the manner just indicated. Indeed, though the rain ceased by 8 P. M., and the inclination of the bed is such as to create a current during freshets of at least ten miles per hour, we found some difficulty in crossing at 8 o'clock on the following morning. One of our best horses was completely lamed in the attempt.

It is a matter of surprise that government has not thrown bridges across these places, and at Pudaüel. Every public improvement is at its expense and under its control, and the people who pay tolls for travelling over this great highway have the right to require that it shall be kept in safe transitable condition. Such is not the case in winter; and though an engineer and laborers are constantly engaged in repairing bad places, as most of the road surface is concave instead of convex, heavily-laden carts soon work it into sloughs again. Usually their repairs consist in removing the mud, which is carried off in hand-barrows, and replacing it with an equal quantity of clay. At the same time there is often excellent gravel within a few hundred yards, and always an abundance of stone close by suitable for macadamizing. As the wrecks of many loaded carts surrounded by their dismayed drivers and solemn-looking beasts amply testified, the most unsafe part of the road is that over the last cuesta, near Valparaiso. Other carts were hard and fast in mire, from which the united strength of ten yokes of oxen, goaded and urged by the shouts of the drivers to each pair, was barely sufficient to extricate them. Once or twice I thought it absolutely impossible to pass the immense ruts and quagmires without capsizing, and stopped the birlocheros for the purpose of alighting; but they knew better, and moved on regardless of remonstrance or question. The fact is, they do not require more than a quarter of an inch on each side of their wheel-hubs, and can measure the depth of a hole to a shadow. They have lived on horseback full one half of their lives, and can manage their beasts as though part of the same animal.

On a clear day the view from the summit of the hill called Alto del Puerto is very fine. Its sides are divided by ravines, which are filled with the most verdant and luxuriant foliage, and slope on the west to the shores of a shallow bay now swarming with ships from all parts of the world, for a moment arrested in their race to the Pactolian stream of the northern hemisphere. Palms, huge cacti, oranges, lemons, and myrtles, lend an air of semi-tropical beauty to the sheltered glens that surround the bay; whilst the horizon is bounded by the snow-crests of the Coast range of cordilleras to the eastward, and the dark blue waters of the Pacific on the west. From the shores of the bay the hills rise quite precipitously, leaving only a narrow strip of beach at their bases, and long and steep tongues of land between converging ravines. On this narrow beach and these tongues Valparaiso has been built; the houses that occupy the former being devoted mainly to business purposes, and those on the eminences to habitations. Thus, the houses between the face of the cliffs and the ocean are necessarily crowded, and built with European elevation, notwithstanding the dangers and terrors of earthquakes; and it is to be feared that one day, in the return-wave that follows the billow of the earth, old ocean will claim back her own grasped by the cupidity of man, and Valparaiso, like Baiæ, will slumber beneath its purple waters. Spread round the amphitheatre above, and overlooking the bay from an elevation of two hundred feet, are the dwellings of the wealthy merchants, amid gardens filled with choice, sweet, and exotic plants, many of them at the time of our arrival in full bloom. Moss-roses, heliotropes, callas, floripondias, pinks, and violets, together with a score or more of native plants, flowering in the open air at the close of December, would be rare sights in 33° north latitude; yet here they were in profusion, together with a host of floral treasures, for whose selection and cultivation Chilenas almost universally possess exquisite taste and passionate love. So far as temperature is concerned, one absolutely forgets the lapse of seasons. Except in the cessation of rains between September and May, when gardens are artificially irrigated, there reigns almost perpetual spring, and thus the foliage of nearly all plants is perennial. Almost all foreign trees, as apples, peaches, pears, walnuts, figs, and grapes, are deciduous, as is also the Lombardy poplar, and one or two other ornamental trees introduced into the country; but native fruits, together with the roses and jasmins, and a very extensive variety of indigenous shrubs, are evergreens, many of the second class ever-flowering also.

Valparaiso and its people have already been spoken of at length; and I need only add here, that after enjoying generous hospitality—cessation of rain in the interval having rendered the roads more passable—I returned to the capital on the sixth day, without incident worthy of note.

July 15.—There was quite a heavy rain (more than an inch and a half on a level) between midnight and 8 A. M. of the 13th, succeeded by light showers throughout the following day. Shortly after 9 o'clock P. M. of the 14th these showers became frequent and heavy, and by daylight of the 15th the bed of the river was again full. Its roar was heard over all the noises of the city; and the dark, muddy torrent rushed along with such impetuosity that the impact of stones and rocks whirled in its mad course was distinctly audible from the parapet of the tajamar.

As usual, the river banks were crowded with spectators; vijilantes moving everywhere among them to prevent the collection of too many at any one spot. The accident of the preceding flood rendered them unnecessarily cautious, for they even dispersed gatherings along the walls erected to prevent overflows. Perhaps there were other operating causes than fear of accidents by water; and the approach of the presidential election may have had influence here, as well as in the regulations then recently adopted for the prevention of meetings at night. Yet it was well to have the police among the rabble, even had they no other occupation than laughter at the unsuccessful efforts of those who endeavored with their lassoes to rescue logs and brushwood from the wild stream. True, so accurately did they throw, this did not often occur; but there were occasions when the tumultuous waters snatched away the prizes after they were fairly within the noose, and then the mirth was more vociferous.

About this period a belief was current that we were at least cognizant of what was to take place in the atmosphere, and had given timely notice to the government—if we had not actually been instrumental in producing so unusual a quantity of rain during the winter. Nor was it among the lower classes only that such belief was prevalent. Our friends heard it in every circle, and in turn questioned us as to its credibility. That the uneducated should be amazed at the wonders our instruments unfolded, and believe us possessed of the faculty to see into the future, if not directly to exercise some controlling influence over events, is not a matter of great surprise; but that any with pretensions to intelligence should for a moment suppose another capable of foretelling atmospheric changes for weeks and months in advance, betrayed an amount of credulity scarcely consistent with absolute knowledge. Nevertheless, so thoroughly grounded was the opinion, that if not "*the* clerk of the weather" himself, his mantle at least had been temporarily thrown over my shoulders, that I almost determined to combat the impression no longer.

August 6.—An excursion in search of specimens of natural history afforded an opportunity to observe five or six leagues of the plain lying to the southward of the city, of whose increasing fertility with the distance in that direction so much had been told to us. We found a gradual depression, and also a slight declination from east to west, as we receded from Santiago, though the inclinations were not notable until after several miles of travel. These slopes render irrigation practicable throughout the valley. Streams that originate in the melted snows far up the mountain sides, increasing as they descend, bring down an immense amount of soil formed by the disintegration of surface-rocks and the attrition of others hurried along by the torrent. This the irrigating canals spread over the valley to the thickness of nearly half an inch per year. Composed, to a depth of many feet, almost wholly of pebble-stones, whose interstices are filled with loose sand and soil, only a few years since a large portion of this basin was considered unfit for cultivation; but since its proprietors have begun to flood it with water from the Maypu, the annual deposits of mineral silt have rendered it valuable, and now there is scarcely an acre, on which water can be introduced, that is not highly productive. Except that dropped by herds temporarily there, the use of manures on lands is wholly unknown. The products of the stables in town are daily collected by offal carts and emptied into the river, so that nature is everywhere left to renovate herself. Yet there is scarcely a better soil in the world; and its productiveness, even under the wretched system of cultivation practised, is greater than that of the majority of the best lands in the United States.

On some fields the wheat was already an inch or two high. On others, they were just at work scratching the surface with their primitively constructed ploughs. Plough it, in our acceptation of the word, they certainly do not, because the furrows are not as deep as harrows will make in a light soil, and they rarely exceed one or two inches. But improved implements of husbandry meet with no favor among Chilean peons; those bought by enterprising farmers have been thrown aside after a single trial, and are again resorted to only when the master stands by to watch them. Broad fields, extending almost as far as the eye could reach, without a dividing fence, were being traversed by more than a hundred yokes of oxen; and others waited their turn for employment, a little on one side. With the irremediable indolence of the peons, it is well, perhaps, that these ploughs are retained; for the sub-soil implement of the northern hemisphere would be arrested every moment by the pebbles that constitute so large a portion of the stratum, and by the roots of espinos which have been cut down. Although charcoal made from the last will readily sell for half a dollar the bushel, an English gentleman domiciliated here told me he had vainly endeavored to get rid of them on his estate by offering them as gifts to the peons. And thus roots and round stones—both great nuisances—remain in the soil, every now and then compelling the ploughmen to make a *détour*, or, as is more generally done, the two sticks are lifted and set down again on the other side, the furrow being continued in the same line. A wall entirely of adobes, or of round pebble-stones and mud, separates cultivated fields from the highways; and occasional fences of the same description divide pasturage and grain-fields. Flocks of sheep and herds of neat cattle are quite numerous, though not as extensive as on the haciendas lying about the base of the mountains farther south, where cows and horses are numbered by the thousand, and a good sheep may be bought for seventy-five cents.

Except the orange, with its ever present foliage, flowers, and fruit, and the almond (*Amigdalus communis*), cypress, and other evergreens in the gardens, there were no trees in foliage on the plain. Neither the poplar nor the varieties of willow had yet put forth their leaves. It is believed there never have been (in modern times) any native trees on the plain north of the Maypu, except Espinos; and the only specimens of other kinds to be found are on the hills and mountain sides. But of herbage with delicate flowers, and extensive patches of the luxuriant Carda (*Dipsacus fullonum*), wherever the eye turned there was a profusion. Even the top of the mud walls presented a verdant band, amid which gay-colored birds were carolling their spring chants.

The porous character of the surface permits rain to pass off from the roads without great detriment; and, except where the soil was more clayey than sandy, they were in tolerable condition, so that the party I had joined reached their hunting-ground after a drive of two hours. They had selected the base of a hill between the Andes and western range, pretty well clad with shrubbery. The three speeded forthwith on their errand of destruction, returning near sundown with about as many birds as one member of the party could eat on the following day. Not that there were not wild pigeons (*Columba araucana*) enough, with occasional glimpses of partridges (*Nothura perdicaria*), an abundance of doves (*C. aurita*), loycas (*Sturnella militaris*), robins (*Turdus falklandica*), horned plovers (*Vanellus cayannensis*), hawks, an eagle (*Pontoactus melanoleucus*) or two, and a huge condor; but the pigeons and partridges were the only true game, and they were too wary to be caught napping. We were desirous to obtain his majesty of the Andes, the condor; but as our supply of ammunition was small, we concluded to salute him in a body; and as this was not agreeable, he gave us wing bail before we had approached within telling distance. Eagles, too, are not every-day birds; and next to the feat of shooting a condor, that of shooting an eagle would have been the most to boast of. At each individual there were fair chances, and one of the party claims that his bird was struck and alighted on the hills mortally wounded; for myself, I confess to having fired two barrels very deliberately at another, which flew away without so much as winking at the storm of impotent pellets sent after him. With other varieties, however, there was greater success, and I succeeded in bagging a pair of each as specimens.

The pigeon is quite one third if not one half larger than the North American bird, and its flesh when young is very tender. Its plumage is darker and somewhat differently marked from its relative, having a delicate white ring around the neck of the male bird. They go in large flocks, are not easily approached by hunters as inexperienced as ourselves, and in flying from hill to hill were generally beyond the range of our guns. The natives take them in such numbers that four of them may often be purchased in market for a real. The dove, in form, size, and color, is almost precisely the pigeon of Carolina; and the loyca is our meadow-lark in form and action, with red substituted for yellow on the breast, and dark or blackish brown for light brown on the back and wings. Our robin is a more sprightly bird, and his breast is more decidedly marked with red than that of his Chilean relative, which appears to have inherited the characteristic of greater bipeds, and takes things easily. He will permit himself to be driven between hedges of brush six or seven feet high that incline towards each other, and to be knocked on the head with a stick rather than attempt to fly over such barriers. The horned plover, or, as it is called by the natives, *Keltehue*, takes his English appellation from a horny projection half an inch long, that extends from the middle joint of each wing, and with which he makes war most effectually. His colors—dark brown, white, and golden-green, combined most prettily—are still in strong contrast.

Rambling among the laurels, myrtles, and arborescent cacti, that thrive on the southwest side of Cerro Negro, with Tupungato towering above the plain in the northeast and the summit of San José to the eastward, the day rolled away rapidly, and we were warned by the declining sun only in time to reach the city after his departure.

October 8.—A storm of wind and rain, unparalleled for the season, continued almost without intermission from 2½ A. M. until 7 o'clock of the evening. Very nearly four inches of water were deposited on a level. As the accompanying wind was cold, that which fell on the cordilleras was converted into snow to within one thousand or fifteen hundred feet of the valley; else we might have had something of a flood in the river again.

November 4.—Made another excursion to the *Salto de Agua*, in the rear of San Cristoval. On this occasion we followed the route along which we had returned at the previous visit. The road hugs the northern base of the hill very closely; and as it bends to the northeast after leaving the suburbs, the ridge of the spur where traversed by the water is evidently much narrower than the southern terminus of the hill. Nothing could have been more beautiful than the appearance of the country. From the unusually late rains, the hills which at this time of the preceding year presented a scorched and desolate appearance were now covered with flowers and verdure. As far up the sides as the artificial supply can be led from the principal stream, there were fields of beans and maize—the former already bearing their long edible pods, and the latter beginning to tassel. In the valley, the dark foliage of the fig and olive; the dense groves of peach and cherry trees bending under loads of green fruit; the walnuts and poplars, with the odor of the full-blown new leaves; and the delicious perfume from that ugly touch-me-not—the *Acacia cavenia*—were charms an admirer of the vegetable kingdom would not easily tire of.

A most lovely picture there was from one spot. Almost over our heads were craggy peaks sharply defined against the sky, bold and picturesquely grouped as nature had cast them at the creation. A few yards lower, where time with his disintegrating tooth had deposited the nibblings of ages to form a foot-stool for Flora, the broad arms of quiscos sheltered the first patches of verdure from the scorching rays of the sun. From herbage, as the eye descended it encountered shrubs with yellow flowers, myrtles, lilies, calceolarias, tropæolums, fumarias, alstrœmerias, calandrinias, with a host of other flowers, whose species even it would require a skilled botanist to name; whilst here and there a rocky mass peeped from the foliage, as though to witness how his dominion had been overrun. A half-grown herd-boy stood on one of the latter, over whose face a miniature cascade tumbled gracefully, the foamy stream plashing over the lad's feet, and his sleek-looking cattle browsing within reach of his voice. Farther down, and as far as the road-side, were patches of garden vegetables, with laborers busily at work among them; and beyond this—stretching away to the Western cordilleras—a broad sea-like plain, interspersed with evidences of civilized life to adorn the handiwork of nature.

Our party was but a small one, composed exclusively of Americans, desirous to inhale the fresh country air as we enjoyed the prospect commanded by an elevated position on the mountain spur. We had therefore made preparations to pass the day at a spot near the *Salto*, whence we could climb cliffs and explore the ravines at leisure; but after scaling the face of the hill, and following for half a mile the canal cut by the Indians along its western slope, the sun was found to have so much power that the ladies voted a return, and carried their proposition by influence, if not by numbers. It must be acknowledged that the effort to descend the rugged and, in many places, previously untrodden ground, rendered the shade and cool breeze at our rendezvous most grateful to the sturdiest lover of nature among us. We were permitted to occupy a spot which had been chosen for the mansion of a gallant son of the Emerald isle, who bore no undistinguished part in the war of the revolution. A portion of its walls had been erected some 600 feet above the plain, with only columns on the front overlooking the latter; and here the proprietor had recently made a banquet, to which were bidden most of his *confrères* of the war, and such others as he knew sympathized in love for his adopted country. The "*carne con cuero*"* was capital, the champagne cooled to a charm, and wine and wit circulated fast and frequently, until the old adage was fully realized—one ran out as the other was poured in. How a number of the chosen ones got back to town at all they never learned; and few could tell the hour of their arrival. Independently of the wisdom nearly half a century had given to the youngest of them, one would have thought that the necessity of descending such a bridle-path would have warned them to keep the serpent out of their mouths; but as no neck was broken, we may probably agree that "all's well that ends well," and that they did right to enjoy the festivity of the hour.

The covering of boughs and matting over the walls and table, as well as the matting on the high settees along each side, which had been prepared for the earlier feast, were retained for our accommodation, so that few picnic parties find themselves better provided for than we were. But that which claimed attention on first entering to deposit the basket of edibles, was a tablet of white marble inserted in the south wall. Beneath the gilded outline of an engraved heart there is inscribed in gilt letters: "*Here lies the heart of Gen. O'Brien, que nada preferia á la libertad de Chile. Chacabuco, Maypu:*" (who preferred nothing to the liberty of Chile.) The old soldier has his excentricities, and has probably placed this where he may be constantly warned of the uncertainty of life; but many a fervent wish daily goes forth that the heart may long throb its pulsations of frankness, generosity, and hospitality—characteristics of his nation—ere it be placed to moulder on the hill-side of San Cristoval.

December 25.—There is nothing to remind one of the merry-makings of our northern homes on this peculiarly social festival; no legends of Santa Claus, with his sled-loads of rewards, by which to enslave the attention or awe the mirth of children; no hanging of stockings, or quiet creeping to the chimney-side in the dim grey of the morning; no joyous exclamations at unexpected results; no messages or visits from friends to invoke a merry or a happy day; no annual assembling of the family at the old homestead to partake of the time-honored turkey and mince pie; no pleasant games in the evening, or narrative of the olden time to interest the younger members;—in short, there is no Christmas in Chile as Anglo-Saxons know it.

On the evening of the 24th—*la noche buena*—the market-house is swept clean, its quadrangular walks covered with pieces of carpet or matting, and tables are set out with ices and confectionery, as well as more substantial roasts and salads, not forgetting a due proportion of drinkables. In some instances they were ornamented with silver candelabras, mate cups, fine flowers, and little banners; and each was surrounded by a dozen or more chairs for the accommodation of visitors. In the portion of the building occupied by the butchers, gardeners, and fishermen, the supply of meats, vegetables, and fish was greatly more abundant and of far better quality than on other days, every effort being made for display, though it was principally in fruits and flowers that the greatest exertions were manifested. All the gardeners think it of the greatest consequence to present the earliest specimens at this festival. The show is really very fine. Usually there are very superb flowers of the magnolia grandiflora, dahlias and jasmins of

* A common preparation in the Argentine provinces. The meat (usually a calf) is wrapped in the fresh skin and baked in a hole previously heated. All acknowledge that the richness and juices of meat are better preserved in this than in any other mode of cooking. Try it.

half a dozen kinds, with piles of oranges, lemons, figs, plums, strawberries, cherries, pears, medlars, and water-melons—the last undoubtedly green, as it is probable that a proportion of the others are. Then as to vegetables, there are small mountains of green corn, potatoes, beans, squashes, cabbages, and onions. The flowers most in demand are clusters of spicy pinks of every color and size, the poorer classes delighting also in bunches of marjoram and sweet basil.

At nightfall multitudes of candles and lanterns about the tables and stalls of the venders are lighted, and for a little while the scene is strikingly gay; but the ladies begin flocking to make their visits before sundown, and a crowd soon obstructs visions of the illuminated *coup d'œil.* As it is fashionable to visit the market on *la noche buena*, unpleasant as are the odors and sights of butchered meats, and obscene as is the language of the crowds of half-drunken loafers who revel there, the most refined and delicate occasionally resort to it until long after midnight. Scalding mate, green fruits, and water-ices to excess under the open sky at such hours! No wonder that the priests are kept busy during the ensuing three days in carrying round the Host. In order to avoid the disagreeable objects just mentioned, or a part of them at least, the ladies whom I accompanied deemed it prudent to go just before sunset, when we would be able to see every production to the greatest advantage. But the world of Santiago had not then assembled; and as we left after a turn or two though the vacant walks lined with flowers and fruits, my curiosity was unsatisfied. Later at night, or rather at half-past 1 A. M., finding the service at the cathedral very monotonous, I made a second visit alone. All the choice specimens were gone; and though the number of fashionable people about the tables was quite large, and the night most lovely, I was glad to escape at the very first door.

Though destitute of special interest to me, there was service at the cathedral from about half-past 11 until 3 A. M. There was a procession through the aisles by priests with lighted candles; any amount of Latin very badly recited and worse chanted; the old story of using the archbishop every five minutes as a sort of tailor's block for the trial of new garments; only tolerably good music for the very first time; and the reading of a special bull from Pope Pius IX, who was formerly secretary to a nuncio at Santiago—*voilà tout.* At three o'clock in the morning, as I went towards home, the venders of ice-creams, cakes, and fancy bread were still about the plaza, and the streets were gay with promenaders going to or coming from the market-place.

Returning to it after breakfast, a miserable wreck was presented. Its ornaments were gone, the tables in many places were overturned, and the venders slept on the bare ground beneath the benches, amid remnants of confectioners' freezers, broken fruits, and flowers. The day being a festival, the church closes the doors of the shops; and as there were neither visits of congratulation nor ceremony, and no animation among the juveniles, the streets were unusually quiet.

One of the customs in a number of private residences is to make a display during the Christmas holidays of elaborately dressed images, the groups representing eras in the infancy of the Saviour. Much taste is frequently displayed in the combinations and arrangements of the children's dolls and playthings, of which these exhibitions (called *nacimientos*) are composed. One side or end of a room is fitted up with broad shelves, every portion of them filled with groups or isolated figures symbolical of every age, clime, and occupation. The infant Saviour occupies the centre, under a gilded canopy, "clothed in purple and fine linen," with jewels and ornaments in profusion about his couch. Near by is Herod on his throne, surrounded by guards, who await the order to slay. In front ride *three* kings, as they persist in fixing their number, one of them invariably a negro; and on the side opposite Herod we have the shepherds with their flocks. In another house I saw the "Annunciation," the "expulsion from the garden of Eden," the "gathering into the ark," and the "deluge," together with any number of military horse and foot companions, husbandmen, tradesmen, robbers, and priests, the last with miniature garments of existing orders at Santiago. Well arranged and lighted, the effect is rather pretty, and especially interesting to the crowds of children, for whose entertainment one would suppose they were more particularly gotten up; yet the crowd of grown persons, unaccompanied by children, who may be met in the street near one of these displays, is an evidence that even age receives gratification at the sight. Of course the dolls, fancy ornaments, and toys belonging to the children of friends and neighbors far and wide, are laid under contribution to furnish materials for an exhibition very benevolently thrown open to the public until the festival of the "adoration of the kings."

CHAPTER VIII.

A VISIT TO THE CACHAPUAL.

ARRIVE AT THE HACIENDA OF A FRIEND.—THE PLAIN OF RANCAGUA.—A CURIOUS HILL.—RANCAGUA.—THE CACHAPUAL.—THE POSADA AT THE DEPARTMENTAL CAPITAL.—TRIALS OF A NIGHT.—RETURN TO THE HACIENDA.—TRAVELLING CHILE FASHION.

April 3.—Left Santiago in company with the engineer of the Copiapó railroad, to visit the river Cachapual, separating the department of Rancagua from the province of Colchagua, at the distance of twenty-two leagues from the capital. During the preceding week the weather had been unusually cool for the season, and greatly more overcast than in the corresponding period of the preceding year, rendering it probable we might anticipate an agreeable temperature by day, even if half stifled with dust on the road. Starting from the city with a relay of five horses, we reached the Maypu near sundown, Mr. C. desiring to examine the newly constructed bridge with a view to its future use for railroad purposes. The stream was lower than when I crossed it in December, presenting, however, the same rapid, muddy, and torrent-like brook as then. A part of the high banks bounding its waters during floods had been thrown down by the earthquake of the preceding morning, and the walls of the neighboring houses had also been injured to some extent; but the strong stone abutments and piers had not experienced the least damage, and the lattice-framed superstructure of wood had proved too flexible to be strained by the undulations of the earth. Indeed, from the accounts of the toll-receivers, and the visible effects of the phenomenon, it was concluded that we were without the eastern line of maximum disturbance—a fact of which the diminishing number and extent of broken walls, as we had drawn nearer the Andes, had duly warned me.

We were most kindly and hospitably welcomed at the hacienda of the friend with whom a week had been passed so pleasantly in December; and being the first persons whom they had seen from the city since the earthquake, we were soon busy answering the thousand questions which the vivid memories of its violence suggested. The mansion had been terribly shaken; its walls broken; and one of the ladies—a visitor—in her efforts to escape impending danger, was very considerably injured by a fall. As the results of this earthquake have been detailed in Chapter IV, Part I, no further mention need be made of it here than to say, that the ladies continued so alarmed that they slept with doors partially open, and every preparation for instant flight. True, there were still shocks every hour or two; and at the commencement some of them were sufficiently violent to cause the most serious apprehension. Instead of decreasing with the frequency of their repetition, the terror they inspire augments in rapid ratio: one cannot become "used to them."

Soon after daylight next morning we were off again in the birlocho, and at sunrise had reached the Angostura de Payne. The first beams were just illuminating the snow-peaks of the cordillera del Diamante and the cliffs that towered on either hand beside us, whilst the limpid stream of the gorge was rendered more darkly blue by reflection from a vertical sky wholly unclouded. The plain extends rapidly to the east and west soon after clearing the defile, presenting the same general characteristics that mark the basin to the northward; though the eye does not fail to detect its more general cultivation, as well as a change in the number and variety of the trees. For the first league the gently rising road winds along the base of the western range, frequently crossing the narrow stream. Of a sudden the mountain chain bends away to the southwest, the current flows more from the direction of the Andes, and the highway continues direct towards the south, over a surface soon again declining in the same line. There are neither towns nor villages along it until Rancagua is reached, and not a great many dwellings, except those of the poorer classes; but surrounded by such scenery, the large number of travellers, of carts loaded with agricultural products, and of mule-trains going to and returning from Santiago (apart from their dust), rendered the route pleasant and attractive. Attractive it was, even with the inconvenience of dust; for the land is surprisingly productive, and its fields of maize and melons of different kinds, not less than the equipages and costumes of the motley travellers passing over it, could not fail to claim attention. Midway between the Angostura and Rancagua there is a hemispherical hill to the left of the road, of a strikingly regular form. It rises from the plain to a height of between 300 and 400 feet suddenly and almost without slope, its surface covered at intervals of a few feet with a net-work of lines intersecting each other diagonally. It is not on one side of the hill only that these lines are visible, but the whole surface is traced with them; and from the road they are not unlike paths made by goats or other small animals by constant use. The regularity of their intersection, however, would forbid such a supposition, even were there such a multitude of these animals hereabout.

Halting only to obtain breakfast at a wayside posada, Rancagua was reached about half-past ten in the morning. This town is very prettily situated nearly midway between the Andes and Western cordilleras, on an elevated portion of the plain, a mile or perhaps half a league to the north of the river Cachapual. At a little distance it appears to be quite a charming village, with steeples and an alameda on the outskirts; but when one comes to drive through its streets, solitude, poverty, and dirt dispel the pictures imagination had drawn. There are four or five streets, half a mile long, from north to south, intersected by others at right angles, and dividing the town into squares of about 150 yards each way. Only the central north and south streets are closely built up. Here are the public square and two churches. In one of the latter the patriot army under O'Higgins took shelter from an assault by the royalists; and the holes made by the balls of the attacking party are preserved as patriotic *souvenirs*. A force numbering, at the outset, more than four to one, had finally driven the patriots to the buildings about the plaza, cut off their supply of water, and reduced their number to 250 men capable of bearing arms. After a resistance of thirty-six hours, their leader finding himself wounded, and that it would be impossible to contend longer, the little band cut through their enemies and escaped to the capital unpursued.

There are also a prison and a military guard-house on the plaza, a vijilante or two about the streets during the day, and at night some pretensions to lighting and serenos. Some of the houses are of good size, and apparently are as well built as those at Santiago; but in the whole town there was not one that had glazed windows, or, if so, it eluded a special search for it made by Mr. C. and myself. There were quite a number of stores in the principal street, with a due quota of shops occupied by artisans; but silence and inactivity seem to mark the population more than at the capital. Even at sunset its pretty alameda—the two extremities appropriately terminated with the Araucanian pine and native palm—attracted only ourselves and two dirty-faced boys, whom we found dabbling in the acequia by which its trees are watered. We had been warned that but little could be expected at the inn, and hoped to obtain more comfortable quarters. To this end letters had been supplied us for the governor, from whom a kind invitation had been extended to me some months previously; and it was unfortunate for us that he had gone north several days before. This proved the more vexatious because we had been advised to depend on him for the horses and guide we should need in visiting the river, and there were no animals to be hired. Here was a predicament! It seemed incredible to be in a town of Chile having nearly 3,000 inhabitants, almost every *man* of whom owned a horse, and yet there be none to hire. Yet such was the result of our inquiry; and there was no alternative but to use the tired beasts of the birlocho. After no little perseverance and much patience a pair of saddles were hired, for the remainder of the day, at a dollar each, and with our driver as guide, a start was made.

Like the Mapocho and Maypu in the dry season, the Cachapual is only a mountain brook formed by melting snows. After the ground has become saturated by winter rains, it rises and widens to a mile where the main road intersects it. As there are no bridges, it is of course impassable at the latter stage of the water. For a league above and below Rancagua (the limits of our ride), the north shore is a high and perpendicular bank, on which various lines show the heights attained by freshets. The southern boundary is so low that extraordinary floods often change the shore-line half a mile or more, threatening the valley in that direction with overflow. Its bed is a mass of sand and gravel rolled from elevations of the Andes. Half a league above the town, a rounded porphyritic hill rises from the river to a height of quite 200 feet. Originally this appears to have formed a part of the Andean spur, now terminating 300 yards to the south, and from which it has been separated by the action of water. The main volume at the time of our visit passed between them, though there had evidently been a large stream north of the hill within quite a few weeks. Above and below the little islet—for such it really is—the sand formed by attrition of the rock is deposited in lines covered with vegetation of various characters, a part of it of several years' growth proving that the freshets are not uniformly violent. There is a beautiful view in every direction over the plain from the top of Gorocoipo—the islet. It extends from the snow-tipped cordilleras of Rancagua, along the course of the stream by the baths of Cauquenes, to the gradually sloping ridges of the western range, through which it penetrates to the ocean, and from the Angostura de Payne in the north to the limit of vision across the plain to the S.S.W. In its tall cacti and innumerable Chaüars, with their towering spikes of pale-green flowers, the islet itself is not without interest; yet, as in almost all the scenery of Chile, the picture wants life and animation. As I looked upon it, I could but hope that with the thunder of the locomotive across this noble valley, there will come into existence a race more imbued with enterprise and energy—a people more competent to the development of its vast and incomparable agricultural wealth.

After picking our way along the stony paths for four or five hours, traversing the noisy stream at every hundred yards or so, miserable as it was in appearance, and inattentive as its proprietor had proved at our arrival, we were glad to get back to the posada. Such were the effects of heat and dust and fatigue in reconciling one to discomforts. Before leaving the village in the morning, dinner had been ordered for the hour at which we expected to return; but on ascertaining that Mr. C.'s examination would be completed earlier, the guide was sent back in the hope that his warning would expedite the repast. However, we had literally "reckoned without our host," as we were duly notified on requesting the meal to be served. There had been too many trials of patience during the day to permit a trifle to vex us; and as there was abundance of cool water to refresh the outward man, and a glass of fragrant Italia to comfort the inner, we awaited the pleasure of our landlord's cook with becoming equanimity. Afterwards, ten minutes or less of walking enabled us to pass from one extremity of the principal street to the other; and the alameda was perambulated in a like period, bringing us back towards the posada as the bell was being rung for vespers at the church on the plaza. There was nothing to do—not even a paper to read—and we fell into the stream of women going towards the church, hoping there would be an opportunity to see some of the beauties and fashionables of Rancagua. In this, too, we were disappointed. The little edifice was only relieved from almost cimmerian darkness by a wax taper or two; and in order to make room for new-comers, a snappish and growling priest pushed the women towards the altar, whilst their terror of earthquakes induced them to prefer remaining near the door. Even the music was execrable; and to encounter the odors and risks from contact with our own sex around, were rather heavy demands for the probable religious benefits we should derive from remaining long under the voice of so unamiable a curate.

Though there was not a pane of glass belonging to the inn, nor other apertures in either dining-room or chambers than the doors of entrance, it boasted quite a respectable billiard-table; and as the game is a favorite amusement in all Spanish countries, we fully calculated on seeing something of the younger part of society at least, if not to divert ourselves during the early part of the evening. In this, too, we were destined to be deceived; and as there were few answers to be obtained to questions, except *quien sabe?* there was the less hesitation to court "nature's sweet restorer" at the earliest reputable hour. Alas! for man's good intentions. Our beds were in the same little room, and had only occupied attention when a servant asked if they should be prepared for us; a question not so superfluous as one who does not know Chile might suppose. Nine of every ten persons convey beds and bedding, put up in an almofrez, whenever they travel off the road between Valparaiso and the capital; and probably the larger number of travellers, to avoid heat and dust, start on their journeys about nightfall.

It was only when the light had been extinguished that we became aware the bedsteads had not been made for six-footers; but as we had seen that they were apparently clean, and meant to be up and off in six or seven hours, it was not a matter worth complaining of or trying to change. Mine was of iron, with narrow bars across it only at every twelve or fifteen inches—somewhat like a mammoth gridiron; and as the mattress was evidently no thicker than a stout board, every bar left its impression across the body. If I attempted to lie doubled, the hip-bone was in a most uncomfortable position over a bar, or my feet thrust the end of the mattress between the last bar and the bottom of the bedstead, leaving an aperture a foot wide; and so I finally accommodated myself diagonally—pushing my head through a space in the ornamental work of the top, and my feet through another at the bottom. Not the most eligible position from which to make a sudden escape in an earthquake, though it was by no means despicable to a man who had not slept a moment during the preceding night, and whose companion on the opposite side of the room—already in the land of forgetfulness—inspired the most lively envy to imitate so good an example. But I was soon made sensible that there were other occupants of the bed; and as my nimble companions sprang from point to point for a fresh vein to tap, it soon became a serious matter how to move quick enough in efforts to secure them, and yet not scrape the skin off forehead and feet. What a predicament!

An hour or two of this exercise in the darkness was sufficient, and a light was struck to facilitate the hunt, when the game appeared so numerous and agile that my only apparent chance of running them down was to take each article to the door and shake it in the patio. Although others soon found me, I was completely wearied out; but towards 2 A. M., just as memory was reeling, there came trembling on the air the first vibrations of the unmistakable rumble which precedes an earthquake, and I was startled to full sensibility again. As the earliest and alarming spasmodic shiver was beneath us, Mr. C. and myself simultaneously sprang for the lucifer matches, not knowing whether the walls were to be heaped over us or not. The shock was short, and as the murmur of its agitating voice died in the distance we again composed ourselves for a nap, my bedfellows being enabled to return to their feast with appetite sharpened by the respite they had had. It was probably three o'clock. Nature would no longer be cheated of her due. Alternate instants of sleep and wakefulness satisfied me that slumber was fast obtaining the mastery, when, in one of the latter intervals, there was a sudden and heavy crash, inducing belief that the house had been destroyed by an earthquake. We again sprang from bed, and by the time a light was obtained there was a vivid and blinding flash, quickly followed by a repetition of the peal, telling that a thunder-storm was raging near us. Rain followed in a little while, and fell with great violence.

Sleep and disposition to slumber were gone. The beating of the heavy drops on the tiled roofs, instead of soothing, tended only to excite nervousness, and we talked through the other hours of darkness. When daylight came—determined though we were to risk many discomforts on the road for the sake of getting away—there was no prospect of relief from the scene of trials. Rain fell in torrents, and the clouds were drifting low down in the valleys; nor was there such a cessation in the storm as justified our starting until near noon. Even then, for several hours, we were twice driven under shelter by the road-side, and did not finally reach my friend's hacienda until after sundown. A warm welcome and dry clothes soon dispelled the thoughts of previous discomfort; and though occasionally startled by still recurring earthquakes, they were quite as frequently stimulants to sprightly conversation as sources of terror. The injury to my eye required abstinence from labor of every kind in order to restore it, and nearly two weeks were passed in rambling about the vineyards and woods near the mansion—riding occasionally to admire anew the wonder of the Angostura, and to become more fully impressed with the amazing productiveness of the soil.

Whilst there, the ladies of the family went in their cart—Chile fashion—to pass the evening with one of the neighbors. These carts are four and a half or five feet broad by twelve or thirteen feet long, and are covered with strong rushes or flags neatly woven together. As the arched roof is high enough for a woman to stand under and is water-tight, is closed by curtains at the two extremities, and there are barred windows in the sides, they are not altogether uncomfortable portable houses. They have but two huge wheels and wooden axles; and as neither tallow nor tar is used on them, they make a screeching noise by no means agreeable to the nerves of every stranger. Most families travel to and from the city and their country-seats in these vehicles. Their beds are spread on the floor, where the travellers lounge and sleep with great satisfaction, they say, because the motion of the cart and the noise of the wheels produce irresistible drowsiness. The floor is large enough for four single beds; and on an excursion a dozen will find seats—the party jogging along, behind the two yokes of oxen that draw them, at a pace which would astonish our railroad and steamboat people. When starting on a journey of any length, as they often do in trains of two or three carts, they carry provisions with them; and if there are young people, they usually have a guitar, and their monotonous songs may be heard as they creep over the road. The oxen are always fine, large animals: the first pair are secured to a heavy wooden tongue by a yoke lashed on the back of their necks with thongs of raw hide; and the second pair are attached to the yoke of the first by a stout rope of similar material. The driver (or, as he would be more properly named, the leader) marches in front, with a pole fifteen feet long, armed at one end with a bit of pointed iron. This pole is carried on his shoulder, with one extremity resting on the yoke of the oxen nearest him. When he turns they follow; and it is only as they are perverse, or he desires to quicken their speed, that he uses the goad to them. His head, loosely enveloped in a kerchief to keep dust from the hair and promote circulation of the air about it, is surmounted by a ribbonless, conical straw hat; his body concealed under a poncho, with gay stripes along the borders and centre; his nether extremities in flowing trousers of white cotton that reach little below the calf; and his feet are inserted in curiously constructed shoes, with heels almost high enough to trip him over: altogether, the *carretero* is not the least unique part of the travelling equipage.

CHAPTER IX.

PUNISHMENT OF CRIMINALS.

A MURDER.—PREPARATIONS FOR EXECUTING THE CRIMINAL; HE IS SHOT.—CRIME OF THEFT.—THE EGUALISTAS: THEIR PLANS; ARREST OF THE LEADERS.—REVOLUTIONARY PLOT CRUSHED.

August 22.—A concourse assembled in the plaza, near the prison doors, indicated that something unusual was about to occur; and it proved, on inquiry, that a criminal was to be publicly executed at high noon. He had committed murder deliberately, the only crime for which the law *exacts* so heavy a penalty. On the preceding Good Friday, and the fourth day after discharge from an incarceration of ten years, he, with others, had gone into a shop where chicha and liquors were kept for sale. Its proprietor was one of the Brothers of St. Sepulchre, familiarly called "Cucurúchos," who are privileged to wear a peculiar dress mentioned in the incidents of Holy Week. Having turned his back on demand of drink by the new comer, he was stabbed repeatedly and died almost instantly. Although intelligence of most events is disseminated through the city with a velocity elsewhere known only in gossiping villages, the murder of one of the *canaille* was too unimportant to be talked of among the "upper ten;" and as the papers chronicle neither "horrible casualties" nor "dreadful accidents," our first intimation of the atrocious act was the preparation for executing the criminal.

By 11 o'clock, hundreds of rotos and peons thronged towards the place selected for the execution; and at the instant the culprit was brought from the prison to the cart, those who had filled the plaza poured in a compact mass in the same direction. Thinking that the dry bed of the river would be chosen, as was currently reported, a stand was obtained on the tajamar, within a hundred yards of where the great crowd had gathered. This commanded a view of the pebbly plain for a mile or two, and it was presumed would permit distinct vision of a method of capital punishment not previously witnessed. But it proved otherwise.

Just before noon the cart containing the condemned, and its escort, made their appearance at the opening of one of the streets a square or two below us; and there was a short delay whilst the guards shifted him from the vehicle to a hurdle of raw hide dragged by oxen. As the most ignominous addition that could be made to it, the sentence of the law was, "that he be drawn to the place of execution on a hurdle;" but the officers charged with its fulfilment extended some mercy in his last hours, and instead of causing the wretched man to be dragged over pebble-stones for a mile, only carried that portion of the command into effect during the last two or three squares—perhaps three hundred yards. The *cortége* was preceded by a deputation from the Brothèrs of St. Sepulchre, bearing cross and banner, and many friars of the order of *la Merced.* Its rear was guarded by a file of soldiers with loaded muskets. These were to be the executioners. Two friars were seated on the hide with the prisoner, urging spiritual consolation,—if it was possible to utter other than disjointed words in such a conveyance,—and a battalion of the civic troops formed a hollow square round them to keep off the crowd, their mounted officers in advance opening a path for the procession through the masses. Although the hurdle passed within twenty feet, and my eye was at least ten feet above the road, the crowd was packed so closely that it was impossible to obtain a glimpse of the prisoner. Subsequently I learned there was so little malevolence indicated by his features, that they set the laws of physiognomy at defiance, and the habit of a Mercedarío in which he was outwardly clad was removed before execution. Two or three women were among the spectators.

Even the trees and house-tops of the vicinity were crowded, and the ocean of uncovered heads was immense. But it was extremely creditable to the population of Santiago to say, there was not a person of the better class, man or woman, in the whole multitude: the straw-hatted, ponchoed gentry and their "*compañeras*" were the only spectators of the sad scene.

A seat had been prepared near the wall and firmly secured to a stake driven in the earth. To this the culprit was bound, the crowd pressing as closely as the civic troops would permit, and absolutely tainting the air so soon to be breathed by him no more. Short respite was there afterwards. Whilst I looked to see the procession file into the bed of the river, the sharp-ringing reports of three muskets told that the mandate of law had been executed, and in an instant every lip murmured a prayer for the soul of the departed. But the soldiers had proved inefficient marksmen, although stationed within ten feet of the victim, and the writhings of his body two minutes later brought another round, followed by yet a third single discharge three or four minutes afterwards. Terrible barbarity this, and a butchery that our populace would not quietly witness a second time, though perhaps no greater retribution than the crime merited. If government considers it most expedient to effect capital punishment by shooting, better drilled soldiers should be detailed for the purpose, or a single one be selected to place the muzzle of his weapon on some vital spot, and not hazard the continued existence of the poor wretch during the moments in which executioners reload their muskets before him.

One of the attendant friars preached a sermon over the remains immediately afterwards, and the body continued exposed to the gaze of the curious for four hours. However, neither the counsels of the holy man nor the tragic fate of the law's victim appeared to have weight with the spectators, the light-fingered gentry availing themselves of the occasion to inspect the pockets of several acquaintances (foreigners) whom curiosity had tempted to the spot. At night, and on several subsequent evenings, lighted candles were placed round the stake, each passer-by whispering an *ave* for the soul that had thence taken flight.

The lower orders are extremely prone to the commission of theft; and if the opinions of their own countrymen and countrywomen are to be fully received, the crime is almost universal among them. The rigidly honest are exceptions among the mass. Caution respecting servants was given us by every one, on our arrival in Chile; even the proprietor of the hotel warning us that everything not under lock and key would be unsafe. We, however, were exceedingly fortunate, having obtained honest and faithful servitors, who, if anything, were over-careful in the preservation of property; and therefore we had little personal experience of their propensities as a body. But I have no right to doubt the testimony of so many unbiassed witnesses that generally they are petty thieves. Burglary, of necessity, is a rarer crime. The serenos perambulate the streets at intervals so short, that entrance cannot easily be effected within the castle-like houses. Sometimes admission is obtained through the acequia; and once within, the houses cover so much ground that depredators proceed fearlessly in their operations until ready to retreat by the same channel. As was just said, the papers publish none of these incidents; and when heard of, their occurrences are coupled with so many fanciful circumstances, that the truth is not easily sifted even from the columns of the law journal specially devoted to condensed statements of the suits tried in the several courts.

September 14.—Rain fell heavily over the city during the preceding night. Its drops were converted into snow-flakes on the cordilleras; and as the bank descended to within a few hundred feet of the level of the plain, the contrast of verdure and virgin whiteness was no less singular than beautiful. Until the heat of the sun drove the lower limit some thousands of feet higher, we had winter temperature back again.

For a month or two previous, a club composed of mechanics and loafers, headed by a few individuals of the better class, had assembled nightly in one of the largest halls of the city, nominally discussing equality of rights—socialism, and really taking measures to overthrow the legal government at the approaching celebration of its independence. On one occasion of alleged disturbance within their room, the police took occasion to enter, breaking a few bones in the contest that ensued, bruising a larger number, and capturing several for conveyance to prison. Government was evidently fully informed of their designs, and had followed them from step to step. All the officers of the National Guard known to belong to the club had been removed; the number of the mounted serenos had been increased; a sufficient body of the troops recently returned from the south, to furnish sentinels along the principal paths up Santa Lucia, had been stationed at the castle; and an old decree respecting the carrying of arms was republished. All these measures were executed without ostentation or exciting the suspicions of those not in the secret of the intended movement, and were generally regarded only as precautions for the approaching holidays, always more or less attended by drunkenness and disorders among the rabble.

The leaders among the "*Egualistas*" (socialists) were men related to families of the highest standing, and their connections so extended as to embrace a very considerable portion of the influential population. Undoubtedly their desire was to obtain possession of the government, by holding out to the mass a division of the spoils not less certainly to be obtained on sacking the houses of the wealthy; but which of their number was to have been elevated to supreme power seems not to have been decided. Until the 13th, as they supposed, things were going on swimmingly. Emissaries had been sent to sow disaffection in the nearer provinces, one of which, to the north, had been noted for the insurrectionary spirit of its population; and the better to mask their designs, the governor of that province (Aconcagua) was accused of treason by a member of the Chamber of Deputies, also a leader of the club. The charges were deemed of sufficient gravity and semblance to truth to warrant the arrest of the governor, and his trial by the Senate; but, as was foreseen by his friends belonging to the government party, his acquittal was almost unanimous. Meanwhile ball-cartridges and arms were being collected for an outbreak; and on the very day that the governor was set at liberty a gig-load of the former was despatched to San Felipe. Government being apprized of the movement, a number of trusty soldiers, disguised as police, followed the vehicle; and at the very first halt the driver was arrested, and himself and munitions brought back as witnesses. The information thus elicited authorized the arrest of eight or ten prominent individuals, and created much alarm in their ranks; though, as the evidence against their most dangerous man was by no means conclusive, the club were not hopelessly cast down. The same day, being the anniversary of the saint (Carmen) selected as "*Patrona*" of the Chilean army, a new flag was to be presented to one of the regiments at Santiago; and as they cannot fight under colors not blessed by the priest, a great show was to come off at one of the churches about 2 P. M. Previously the Egualistas had bribed four disaffected sergeants of the Valdivia regiment, then recently returned from the south, and quartered in the same building as the battalion for whom the flag was intended. As the ceremony would call off other troops and a large concourse of citizens, the time would be favorable for commencing the outbreak, and the subsidized "Valdivias" agreed to deliver the quartel and its arms at that instant. There are collateral circumstances to prove that pillage—*equalizing worldly goods*, as they expressed it—would have been one of their first attempts. Almost in the same hour when the driver with the ammunition and the members of the club were arrested, a leader of the opposition at Valparaiso and all the sergeants also found themselves in durance; whilst a colonel of artillery (the member of the Chamber of Deputies just referred to), having been somewhat too open in his predilections, was notified by the Minister of War that an application for frontier service would be immediately granted. In less than twenty-four hours the latter found himself separated from his regiment, and *en route* to execute duties improvised for the occasion. This was on Saturday.

Sunday noon came, and instead of the active struggle in which the Egualistas hoped to find themselves, they stood in groups about the plaza, with countenances sufficiently indicating how disheartened they were. At night the number of mounted police was doubled, and those on foot were early in their examinations of the fastenings of shop doors and windows. The multitude of ladies who ordinarily promenade the Cañada on Sunday, and visit from house to house of their friends at that hour, had almost entirely disappeared; and by 10 o'clock, except serenos and mounted police, who were moving between the guard-house and various parts of the city with the utmost celerity, there was not a living soul encountered in a walk of nearly a mile along the streets! On Santa Lucia the guards challenged every one; and, although my keys and books were passports for myself, they strongly objected to my servant following, only consenting on my pledge to bring him as low as the castle again. Though there were intimations that the main blow was to be struck during the review that was soon to take place on the plain south of the city, so sudden and effectual had been the government preventives that the plot was crushed at the moment of the arrests. That the then President, and a majority of his cabinet, were not only unpopular with the people, but also in a decided minority in Congress, there could be no doubt; yet, it is honestly believed there were few in Chile who had the power to control affairs as well. Nominally a republic, the government is in reality a military dictatorship—probably the only form which could last six months with a race too proud and apathetic for labor, and who plot revolution in the hope that themselves and friends may obtain offices and incomes. •Apparently, a craving for office is the only reason for constant agitations throughout Spanish America. If the success of principles were sought, at its consummation those who had striven for the elevation of their party would be satisfied. Such is not the case in any of the governments under the control of Spanish populations; and no sooner is one chief elevated to supreme authority than a new one begins undermining him. Undoubtedly Chile is the most stable of them all; but she can never remain long truly republican with the incubus of any exclusive religion about the necks of her people.

All of these revolutionary leaders eventually "left their country for their country's good."

CHAPTER X.

THE NATIONAL HOLIDAYS.

CELEBRATIONS ON SEPTEMBER 17th.—ON THE 18th: PROCESSION TO THE CATHEDRAL; HIGH MASS; VISIT TO THE PRESIDENT; TO THE ESCUELA DE ARTES Y OFICIOS; ILLUMINATIONS.—ON THE 19th: THE MOVING CROWDS; THE PAMPILLA AND ITS SCENES; DISPLAY ON THE CAÑADA.—ON THE 20th: ENCOURAGEMENT AND REWARDS OF MERIT; DIVERSIONS ON THE PAMPILLA; CONCLUDING AMUSEMENTS FOR THE POPULACE.

Though the 18th of September is the anniversary of the independence of Chile, government ordains that the 17th and 19th shall also be national holidays, and the masses continue their frolics and carousals until near the commencement of October. In the year 1850, the celebrations began at noon of the 17th by a national salute fired at the castle, a general ringing of the bells, a display of the Chilean flag from every house, and bands of the several regiments parading through the streets playing the national hymn. By 1 P. M. the musicians had all collected in front of the Mint (President's quarters); but as there had been a heavy snow-storm on the mountains (rain in the city) on the preceding day, the air was raw and comfortless for Santiago, and scarcely more than a thousand persons assembled in the square. For the same reason it was found necessary to postpone a portion of the ceremonies until the 20th; and, outwardly, the day closed with more music, another military salute, and a partial illumination of the houses at night. Next year the celebrations began at sunrise, and though essentially the same, the order of ceremonies for the several days was somewhat varied. It was an epoch of much anxiety and excitement. There were more salutes fired, more flags displayed, and more general illuminations at night (by order of the municipal chief); but previously, the police were specially particular to notify the head of each household that the new Intendente was resolved to enforce all fines for non-compliance with these patriotic ordinances, as well as for omitting the preparatory annual whitewashing. As the fines range from $4 to $20, at his discretion, in order to save the mulct, every one runs up a piece of bunting, and manages to place a few tallow candles along the blank walls. A stranger in Santiago, without this explanation, would imagine himself among a people enthusiastically patriotic. Of course our contribution to the display could not be very great, but our own bright flag was run up (and a superb one it was); and at night, as there was too much wind to expose it on the observatory, a star-shaped frame crowded with lights was erected on the front of our house. The latter needed distance and elevation to give it effect, and when appropriately placed on subsequent nights it attracted much attention.

By direction of the President, an invitation was sent to us from the governor to meet the public authorities and foreign ministers in the Senate chamber at 10 A. M. of the 18th, thence to proceed to the cathedral and participate in rendering thanks to the Almighty for his blessings on the nation. It having been arranged that we should proceed in the carriage with Mr. Peyton, our party repaired to the United States legation in full dress shortly prior to the appointed time. Besides himself, the only foreign representatives present were the Chargés from France and Brazil: the English gentleman pleaded indisposition, the Peruvian actually was ill and at Valparaiso, and the Spaniard could not thank God for having deprived his country of one of her fairest colonies. We found there a number of officers in superbly embroidered uniforms; no inconsiderable proportion of church dignitaries; and all the cabinet ministers, municipal authorities, and members of the University. The procession was formed as soon as the President appeared, and marched from the Senate chamber to the cathedral—two squares distant—preceded and followed by squadrons of lancers. The head of the column consisted of distinguished officers;

next came the ecclesiastical corporations; then the faculties of the university and national institute; fourth, the governor and municipal authorities, with our party in their midst; fifth, the foreign ministers; and finally the President and his cabinet, himself in a richly embroidered uniform as general, with the insignia of his civil office—a broad tri-colored band, and similar tinted plumes in his chapeau.

On either side of the streets leading to the cathedral, and around the four sides of the great square, the National Guard were drawn up to the number of 6,000 men; their several bands commencing the national hymn as the head of the column drew near. Except where the lancers kept an open lane for us, the streets and plaza were occupied by a compact living mass; but there were neither "*vivas*" nor outward evidences of enthusiasm—scarcely animation; simply passive curiosity, from the high-born dames who occupied the balconies overhead, to the unwashed loafers of the thoroughfares. We were received between lines of priests at the door of the cathedral. The body of the edifice was already occupied by spectators. All the chandeliers over the choir, and the candelabras of the altars in the aisles, besides candles in infinite number over and about the high altar, were lighted, producing a brilliant effect. On both sides of the nave, from the centre of the church towards the choir, arm-chairs of crimson velvet had been substituted for the benches usually there, each chair having before it a cushion of down, covered also with silk velvet. These seats were occupied by the members of the procession, that of the President being midway between our two lines and farthest from the altar. Closing immediately in the rear of the procession was the company of cadets from the Military Academy, who entered the cathedral, posting two guards on each side of his Excellency, and one on either side of the chair nearest to the body of the church. As they were required to remain immovable on post, it was necessary to relieve them every fifteen minutes; and the sharp clang of the bayoneted musket in the midst of the rites, was no uninstructive subject of reflection on the religion of a country claiming republicanism. The remainder of the company remained just at the door until wanted; but the side aisles and a portion of the nave beyond the special guests and officials were filled with officers of the line and regiments of civic troops; so that the assemblage was extremely showy. Nor was beauty wanting to lend its charm. Many of the most superb women of Santiago were present, probably deeming it of vital consequence to attend at the high mass of this morning. Custom forbids the entrance of females into church with bonnets, or any other than black dresses; so that they are wholly dependent on their own charms; but during the national holidays they substitute costly black lace for the thick mantle usually worn, and exhibit no little taste as well as display in their splendid missal—a ring or bracelet being sometimes permitted to be seen in even that sacred place.

To describe the service of high mass may not easily be done by one uninitiated; and I confess myself wholly unable to speak of it with the reverence that it perhaps merits. A multitude of priests in vari-formed and parti-colored robes, amid clouds of incense swelling from silver censers, were in constant genuflexion as they passed with missals and vessels before the altar to the archbishop or desks. Some of them wore a species of short gown of white muslin over a black robe, for all the world like those so common in *déshabille* among the ladies of the United States. These priests seemed to have little other employment than the conveyance of different articles of dress, one by one, to and from the archbishop and altar. The vestments were borne on broad silver salvers, were received by two old gentlemen in yellow silk embroidered robes, and occupied in putting on and taking off from his right reverence quite as much time as either of the other portions of the service. At one time I began to think the head of the church would be enveloped to such an extent as to exclude a view of the altar, and was only relieved from apprehension when they began stripping him again. This, with a few words of half-sung, half-drawled Latin, a sermon from a toothless old canonigo which no one near us could hear a word of, and an abundance of good music from two organs, made up the whole ceremony. At four different times a deputation of priests, preceded by their usher, came from the altar to perform a portion of the rites over the President. First, to bless him; and judging from the closed hands kept before him, I presumed it a proxy sent by the archbishop. At the second visit they perfumed him with incense; next, they brought a book for him to kiss—perhaps the New Testament; and lastly, a silver crucifix was in like manner offered for the salutation of himself, and subsequently to each of *us*. It was borne on a richly embroidered napkin; and a smile possibly crept over my face as I watched the progress of the priest towards our minister plenipotentiary; for the gentleman beside me, properly estimating how we would regard such "lip-service," appealed to me in a serio-comic manner, "Don't laugh, but follow the example of others." Watching our file-leader—the President—and following his motions, we had been on our knees it would be difficult to say how many times; and I would have kissed a bit of the arch-enemy himself had it been presented,—though I rather think my companion would have preferred the ruddy lips of a dark-eyed Chilena just before us: so I put on the gravest face, and saluted the emblem in all humility, well knowing that if it did me no good, it would do me no harm.

Except a *Te Deum*—such as only a grand organ like the new one here could do justice to—this was the closing part of the ceremonies; and we filed out of church in the order we had entered, proceeding to take leave of his Excellency at the place of assembling. The whole had occupied three hours, and we were tired enough. But the day was not yet over. We had embarked to render all honor to the nation, and resolved to leave no courtesy unextended. The next step was an official visit to the President at the palace.

Crowds returning from the plaza, dressed in their gayest apparel, thronged the streets; and the troops marching to sprightly music, with banners flying from the portals of the low-walled houses, produced a scene highly animating. All evidences of the preceding storm had passed away, leaving, under a sunlight tempered by fleecy clouds, a balmy air exceedingly delicious to inhale. Neighboring hills robed in the richest verdure; Santa Lucia, with its castellated and seemingly basaltic crags, surmounted by our eyrie; the snow-capped Andes in the back-ground to the east; the Central cordilleras on the west,—all were enveloped in a bluish haze, not unlike the atmosphere of our Indian summer.

We were the first strangers to reach the palace, finding there only his Excellency, the "*Presidenta*" with her children, and three sisters; himself portly, gracious, and obliging as ever; they, courteous and kind-hearted. In addition to the cabinet ministers, I doubt whether more than fifteen persons subsequently presented themselves. Among them the Chargé d'Affaires from France was the only other diplomat, and General O'B. the most conspicuous among the military men. The latter stands something more than six feet two in his stockings; is a well formed, graceful native of the Emerald Isle, who lost the use of a hand in the service of Chile, and his breast was literally covered with medals and decorations the rewards for gallant services. Having been early invited to accompany his Excellency to the National School for Mechanic Arts in Yungai, an hour was passed in conversation with the ministers and officers of the revolution who came to make their respects to the Chief Magistrate; though I confess that the mother and her group of children were more attractive to me. A lunch of hams, turkeys, fruits (Chile boasts the last all the year), pastry, ices, wines, and flowers of the most exquisite beauty and perfume, stole away nearly another hour, so that it was almost four o'clock when our *cortége* started from the palace. As the French Chargé had married a Santaguina, it is presumed he thought it would never answer to have the American Ambassador and his countrymen more attentive to the President than himself, and therefore joined the party; so that there were three carriages, enclosed within a troop of lancers, that of his Excellency taking the lead. All the windows and doors were crowded to see the cavalcade as it dashed by; but there was no cheering, nor a handkerchief waved in honor of the chief who had fought their battles, and had been called to the helm of state. Why? There was no one present to tell us; and we could not help thinking how unlike the receptions our own late President experienced whenever he appeared in public.

Yungai being but a suburb of the capital, named after the battle-field on which this very President was the hero, the distance of the School of Arts is less than two miles from the palace.

The pupils—sons of artisans, and some fifty in number—with the director, a Frenchman, awaited us in two lines at the door, the latter prepared with a preliminary harangue. The institution being wholly at the expense of the government, the young men were clad in a neat though plain uniform, and their quarters were clean and comfortable. Its origin being recent, and the engine the first erected in central if not in all Chile, the carpenters' and blacksmiths' shops and steam-engine were the only objects for inspection. A speech was made over the boiler, one of the ministers whispering to me, "What a chance for the revolutionists to send us up among your stars." An examination of the mechanical drawings followed, some questions as to the mathematical proficiency of the pupils came next, and the show was over; though not until I strongly suspected his Excellency was nodding during the algebraic solution of a problem about two eggs. As an instrument for implanting and cultivating practical as well as theoretical knowledge—in which natives are usually too ignorant—the institution reflects the highest honor on the patriotism and liberal policy of the government; a policy most worthy of admiration and success.

Our party broke up here. Each carriage wended its way homeward as inclination dictated, no small number of friends claiming the right to exercise hospitality towards us. But the sun was lending his last rosy beams to the summits of the Andes; we had our illuminations to see after as soon as a hasty dinner could be obtained; and there was no time to be lost. At an early hour the old palace fronting on the plaza, that now occupied by government (the Mint), and nearly all the churches and private buildings, were lighted, the first two very brilliantly, and the others as well as their construction will permit. It must be recollected that there are not as many windows on the streets as in our houses, and the art of transparencies had never been introduced until those suggested to the United States legation by ourselves. In one of the windows the Chilean, and in the other the American coat of arms was represented, with the flags of the two nations blended, and the words "Libertad" and "Union" inscribed. They were well executed, and very greatly admired for their novelty. But the "Star of the South" on the observatory was a gem, emblematic of our pursuits as well as complimentary to the nation whose flag bears a single one in its folds, and under whose protection we were. It was visible from the great plaza where the mass of people had assembled to witness fireworks; from that in front of the mint; from the opera-house—in short, from no place of resort could the eye be turned eastward without beholding its sparkling rays as of a mass of brilliants above the snow-crests; for darkness and the lead color of the house utterly concealed the object that sustained it. It thus commanded universal attention and admiration. Bands of music were stationed in the plaza and at every two or three squares' distance along the Cañada, and the night was such as should have tempted the population abroad long after the display of pyrotechnics terminated; but as the movements of the revolutionary Egualistas had impaired public confidence, the streets were soon after deserted, and the musicians were without auditors.

On the 19th the military salutes and music which heralded the advent of a new day, and the commencement of its festivities, rendered the neighborhood of Santa Lucia far from quiet. At 10 A. M. there was a great parade in the Cañada by detached battalions of the National Guard, who subsequently moved to the broad plain south of the city, and generally called *La Pampilla,* though not unfrequently *Campo de Marte.* At a later hour all the troops (regulars and civil) were to be reviewed there by the President. This was to be *the* event of the day: and it was invested with more interest to the young bloods, because the Chief Magistrate had signified his determination to manœuvre the troops himself; and it had been asserted that the conspirators would embrace the opportunity to rally known disaffected regiments, and seize his person. No President had ever availed himself of the constitutional privilege to direct the evolutions; and it was said that ineffectual attempts were made to dissuade General Bulnes, because he would be exposed to far greater danger. Every soldier had it in his power to drop a ball in his musket when the order should be given to load, and might shoot down a passing officer almost without risk of detection; but the General probably despised the exhibition of fear, and rightly judged that he would be in the position above all others which would immediately enable him to rally the loyal to government.

The day was sufficiently overcast to make it pleasant when the sun shone brightly for a few minutes at a time, yet not so much obscured as to render it chilly. From an early hour the streets were alive with people, all in holiday dress; many hundreds, if not thousands, having saved their profits for months in order to make a display on the Campo de Marte. Wending towards it from every quarter were carriages which only make their appearance on this one day of the year. In many cases they were venerable relics handed down from the revolution; in others, tall spectral-looking vehicles covered with a profusion of ornamental gilding, and perched in mid-heaven; in others again, superb specimens of French or English workmanship, with all the accompaniments of modern luxury. The occupants of nearly all were dressed with that taste and elegance especially characteristic of Chilenas in public. Intermixed among them, and following guides whose high-peaked straw hats, broad-legged cotton drawers, poncho, and fifteen-feet goads made them notable, sleek oxen slowly dragged huge wagons, whilst from the interiors of the carts came notes of guitars and voices, not always of the sweetest or most melodious kind. Nevertheless, if one might judge from the mingled music and laughter, their occupants were merry parties. A little farther on were crowds of horsemen mounted on every variety of steed, from the high-blooded courser to the humble donkey; slashing *caballeros* with bridle and saddle mountings worth a score of golden ounces, and greasy *guasos* with a single sheepskin and bridle of hide; high-born *donzellas* with costly habits floating in the wind as they sped gracefully along, and dark-skinned *guasitas* with eyes like living diamonds, sitting their wild steeds with instinctive grace, and dashing over the ground with a recklessness fearful to behold. This was evidently the favorite mode of locomotion: it rendered one free; but ladies generally are afraid to attempt it, because of the racing and jostling invariably practised at this festival, and the consequent risk in such a crowd. Yet there were many of the "upper ten" among the moving mass of men; for the whole nation appear to ride well, as if intuitively.

Families were collected at the doors of the houses, watching the passing crowds; the pulperias and confectionery-shops, so numerous in every street, were filled with numbers of the ever-thirsty and ever-hungry race; and other groups surrounded the ambulant venders who were travelling towards the pampilla with fruits, ices, and cakes. On the house-tops and doorways, on moving wagons, and even on the trees, fluttered flags and pennons of every variety. Indeed, the head of one of our horses was decorated with a miniature Chile banner; the other with the stars and stripes of our own country. A cheerful and animated scene it was, notwithstanding it led through mud and among wretched hovels between the centre of population and the outskirts. From these very ranchos issued many of its gaily dressed participators.

Our party comprised three young ladies and myself in a close carriage, two gentlemen in a birlocho, and four others on horseback. Those mounted were to scour the field and serve as pilots to such portions of it as were offering scenes of interest approachable by the carriages. Already some six or seven thousand troops had assembled when we arrived, shortly after noon; artillery, infantry, lancers, and dragoons stretching over the plain for more than a mile, and kept by pickets of mounted municipal police within lines which visitors were not permitted to traverse. Beyond the square thus formed by the military, and within which it was intended to manœuvre them, carts were drawn up with booths and tents at every few paces, hastily erected, so as to form a sort of street, through which the carriages and equestrians paraded. Outside the booths, in deeply-dug trenches, cooks were busy roasting whole sheep and great pieces of beef, on spits of wood lying across earthen walls. And beyond all these were tethered the oxen or mules that had transported the population of the capital to the festival, their piles of edibles, and the barrels of drink necessary for more than twenty thousand souls.

Stopping, as they often did, to witness various scenes, or to interchange salutations with friends, the multitude of carriages and mounted riders moved with difficulty within the busy mass, and at times were actually at a stand in the almost inextricable confusion necessarily consequent on a self-controlling assemblage of so many thousands. Finally, towards 2 P. M., came the President, his aids and suite, and the exercises of the troops commenced. No doubt the latter were well executed, imposing, and interesting enough to those who saw them; but every moment our carriage was hurried from place to place by the marchings and countermarchings of different battalions towards us, and the close firing of artillery was by no means pleasant, shut up as we were, and at the mercy of prancing horses. Occasionally a glimpse would be caught of the colossal President galloping from side to side, surrounded by his suite, or of aids hurrying from point to point with orders. Yet those who received most of my sympathy were the wife and two little ones, occupying the state carriage, which ever kept as near the husband and father as the bodies of troops would permit. I may have been mistaken in supposing an expression of anxiety on *her* face, for which there was ample cause, though he most certainly betrayed no such care. The feeling of the warrior and recollection of actual combats more probably absorbed every sentiment connected with personal risk, and, dressed in his superbly embroidered uniform, he rode his strong charger as free and unconstrainedly as though treason had never been whispered.

All the fashionables returned to the city towards 3 P. M., to obtain suitable stands from which to observe the several regiments as they marched up the centre of the Cañada, on their return from the pampilla; and the concourse here was most brilliant. Indeed, so great is the passion for costly dresses, the taste of Santiaguinas, and the efforts all classes make for display on this particular occasion, that it may well be doubted whether a like scene could be presented by any city in the world of equal population. The beautiful promenade where this annual display takes place has already been described; but, at the risk of repetition, I will mention that it passes from east to west nearly through the centre of the city. A weeping willow, with the snow-capped summits of the Andes, bound the view in the first, and a church, overtopped by the Western cordilleras, limits it in the second direction. The space between the houses on either side exceeds five hundred feet in width, and is very nearly two miles in a straight line. Longitudinally, this is divided into two paved carriage roads, with three wide intermediate walks for pedestrians, separated by rows of poplars and never failing streams of water from the Mapocho. The central walk is from twenty to thirty yards wide, and furnished on both sides, its whole length, with stone benches, at intervals of eight or ten feet from each other. The other walks are narrower, probably half that width. All the seats were occupied by ladies when we reached it; the central walk was crowded with promenaders, and it was with difficulty that a good stand could be found among the equipages lining the sides of the paved roads. After the arrival of the President, and when the regiments of dragoons and lancers appeared, filing in far down the Cañada, the promenaders moved to the outer walks. Each battalion passed quickly along to the music of its own band, and after saluting his Excellency proceeded to its quarters. By the time half of them had filed past, the concourse had poured from the pampilla and from the suburbs of the city, so that wherever the eye turned there was a sea of heads. But there was neither riotous conduct, noise, nor insolence, even to the numbers of unprotected females, although there were many scores of men evidently excited by drink. True, there was racing and jockeying even among others than guasos, many a one endeavoring to upset a neighbor as he rode along. Still, it was for the fun of the thing, and in the knowledge that, like a cat, the Chileno rider falls on his feet, whether dismounting voluntarily or by casualty.

Thus terminated the public events of the third day. The illumination was repeated at night, and the opera and many private parties rendered the city somewhat gay; but there was no enthusiasm or even occasional patriotic huzzas by the people, over whom there seemed an incubus which the bands of the Cañada and plaza with all their cheerful music could not shake off.

The morning of the 20th was celebrated in the same manner as those of the two preceding days—music and military salutes; though the show was evidently beginning to lose its interest even for the lower classes, and, as if in keeping, the flags on many houses had drooped to half-mast. Not a little remarkable are these same "banners on the outward wall." Whilst the red, blue, and white colors are preserved, they are often combined to make Chilean, Dutch, French, Russian, and non-descript flags, ranging through the various dimensions and materials that wealth and ostentation, pride and poverty, can obtain; many hoisted as signals of distress, union down; others in mourning, at half-mast; while the national emblem properly elevated was a rare sight. At 1 P. M. the great flag of the nation was taken from the old palace by the governor of the city, supported by the aldermen and other members of the municipal board. They were preceded by a troop of mounted artillery, the pupils from the School of Mechanic Arts, the interns from the National Institute, and the corps of civic officials. The corps of cadets formed a guard of honor, and the rear was brought up by pupils from the schools of music and painting and a military band. Proceeding to the residence of the President, the procession was joined by himself and aids, the cabinet ministers, and officers of the line and National Guard; and it returned to the plaza, where a platform, tastefully ornamented with flags and festoons of evergreens, had been erected in front of the chambers of the municipality. The stage was large enough to accommodate the distinguished people and most of the pupils, but the larger number were compelled to remain members of the crowd in the plaza. As the procession "changed front" in returning, the pupils of the School of Music reached the platform first; and at the moment of the President's arrival they commenced singing the National Hymn, part of which is most sweet and plaintive. Then succeeded the recitation by the authors of poems offered for prizes; discourses; distributions of premiums, &c.; during the intervals of which the pupils sang the "Prayer" from Rossini's opera of Moses, and other simple choice selections, with very considerable effect and credit to themselves. One of the poems offered for a prize, entitled "*La Fé sobre los Montes*" (the Religion of the Mountains), was based on the popular delusion respecting Santa Eusebia, current some months previous, and of which some mention has been made. I make a free translation of the two first stanzas, to show the author's style and his allusion to ourselves:

"Mountain of Lucia! Ancient home of the Araucanian condor; then, stronghold of the proud Castilian; now, habitation of science! Glory and ornament of my country! Why on thy heights do learned and simple so seek God? Whilst on thy summit the sage American, in observation of gem-like stars, seeks of our Creator the luminous foot-prints, a reverent nation climb silently thy venerable sides; and, as they upward bear the cross with hearts of faith, mysterious hands enkindle suddenly a thousand torches on thy brow! Luminous symbols with which a people write their faith and holy superstition upon high mountain crests; religious sentences they lovingly accede to."

At the end of about an hour the names of the individuals most entitled to the gratitude of Chile, whether for efforts to effect moral or physical advancement, commerce, agriculture, or the mechanic arts, were publicly announced. Among the number was our countryman, William Wheelwright, Esq., to whom was presented a gold medal, bearing on one side the coat of arms of the republic, and on the obverse a steamship, with the inscription, "The Government of Chile to William Wheelwright: a token of gratitude for the introduction of steam navigation and railroads." And no man more richly deserved so public an acknowledgment.

Medals were also presented to others (all foreigners except one), for the introduction of honey-bees, new breeds of cattle, new methods of smelting copper ores; diplomas for specimens of cabinet-work, silver-ware, gilding, engraving and carving in wood; and rewards of money to the manufacturers of a handsome piece of carpeting, similar to the imperial, and a tapestry coverlet wrought by a lady. At first the names were read from the rear of the platform, where his Excellency was seated; but as they could not be heard beyond his precincts, the well known leader of a charitable society (Brothers of the Holy Sepulchre) came out to the edge and announced the honored individuals in loud tones. This was good policy. Several of those rewarded or honorably mentioned for moral conduct during the year were but journeymen mechanics, and the reading of their names in this manner might inspire emulation. Nor must I omit to mention that the only premium by the University, or rather by its advice, was announced: "For morality. Presented by the University of Chile, to Presbyter Don José Santiago Rabanal."* A very anomalous condition of Christianity, when it becomes expedient to reward the clergy for leading *moral* lives!

In the apartments of the municipality the various specimens of the mechanic arts, painting, engraving, &c., were arranged for examination. These embraced portraits of Columbus and Valdivia, painted for the National Gallery by the professor of the academy, and whose performances are about of the same comparative merit as those of his countryman in marble which disfigure the eastern portico of the Capitol at Washington; one or two smaller paintings copied by Chilenos, and with considerable skill, from galleries at Rome; and quite a large number of old paintings borrowed from the monasteries and private collections, for the purpose of filling the walls. Let us hope, too, the committee desired thus delicately to show the professor how artists had worked. There was a model of a church very prettily made of pasteboard, a French bedstead or two, the carpet and coverlet alluded to, and probably fifty, or at most sixty smaller articles, comprising shoes, leather, silver-ware, and embroidery. This was the whole national exhibition of domestic products; and, as the names of the exhibitors proved, nearly every article came from the shop of a domiciliated foreigner.

The 20th is more emphatically the people's day. Horse-racing, for which government provides the purses; trials of skill at various games, when its officers or agents are the umpires; and free permission to gratify the universal passion for gambling, are great attractions to the mass. Then the booths and carts are arranged much in the same way as on the preceding day, but on a part of the pampilla just without the city; and as the thousand and one impulsive characteristics accompanying national games can only be properly witnessed on foot, I walked to the scene. By 2 o'clock thousands, on horseback and on foot, were moving between the lines and crowding every resort of amusement, mirth and good humor predominant everywhere. Perhaps the display of fancifully decorated carts, filled with well dressed women with their guitars, was greater than on the preceding day, and the number of the *people* was certainly not less; the opportunity to feast and dance, gamble and jockey, without hindrance, being paramount to every other consideration with them. On these occasions their only dance is the "*Zama cueca,*" in which only two persons take part. Each holds a handkerchief in the right hand, which is alternately waved by one over the head of the other as they turn after a few steps backward and forward, the body being occasionally inclined during these steps—often gracefully, sometimes lasciviously. The step is by no means elegant; but is slow, monotonous, and as destitute of animation as the sing-song music by which it is accompanied. Besides guitars, a large number of the booths had rudely made harps, whose bases rest on feet, so that the players remain seated. There were also small tables, with tops composed of five or six slats of brass or hard wood, that produced, when beaten with the palms of the hands, a rattling noise not unlike castanets. The instrumental is but an accompaniment to the vocal performance; but the only words I was able to distinguish above the din and peals of laughter were, "*Adios, mi querido amante*" (Farewell, my dear lover).

In one place there were masks fixed on poles between lists, and bundles of lances, for mounted tilters: in another, a stiff revolving horizontal bar resting in axles made slippery with tallow. It had supporting cords at arm's length on each side, and a piece of money placed as a prize for the successful promenader to the far end of the bar. He who walks the bar without overturning, gains the reward; but, as the name of the diversion, "*rota cabeza,*" implies, there are more broken heads than prizes gained. Few experimentalize without having their "knowledge boxes" sounded. Here, a group surrounds a board marked with six numbers, whose proprietor decides the fate of stakes placed on them by a twirl of his tee-totum. There, we find a circular table having eight equi-distant numbers, with intermediate spots of red and blue, and a re-

* See Araucano, No. 1137.

volving arrow of iron fitted over the centre. After being whirled by hand, if the arrow rests over a number on which a bet has been made, the owner of the table pays eight-fold; if the stake be on a colored spot, and the index comes to a stand over one of the four of that tint, an equivalent only is gained. A little farther and *monte* (a game with cards) has its votaries; whilst no small number are engaged at a sort of "*thimble-rig*," in which the victim feels sure he is able to follow the rapid changes of one of three cards from hand to hand. Tee-totum, however, was by long odds the favorite, and there were dozens of them on various parts of the field.

With the music from countless *chinganas;* amid clusters of carts whose curtains and pennons fluttered in the breeze; venders of every imaginable edible crying their comestibles with such voices as only Santiaguinos can use; cavalcades of gaily dressed guasas on prancing horses; groups of peasants or laborers with conical straw hats, slouching ponchos, and flowing white trousers; elegant carriages filled with the *élite* of the province; and the omnipresent mounted police, with sabres and escopettes for the preservation of order,—it is a scene of rare excitement, heightened no little by the grandeur of the surrounding landscape: such a one as only Chile can exhibit.

Though they were continued two days longer, this closed what I saw of the amusements. Horse and foot racing, kite-flying, and a repetition of a part of the games of the preceding day, were indulged in; in short, the government offered every opportunity to divert the minds of the populace, whilst, for more general entertainment, military bands tempted promenaders to the cañada night after night.

CHAPTER XI.

POLITICAL TROUBLES.

NEWS OF THE OUTBREAK AT SAN FELIPE.—GOVERNMENT MEASURES.—OPPOSITION ACCOUNT OF THE DIFFICULTY.—ITS FRUITLESS RESULT.—NEWS OF THE INSURRECTION AT SANTIAGO, APRIL 20, 1851.—COLONEL URRIOLA IN THE PLAZA.—DELIBERATIONS AT THE PALACE.—THE INSURGENT LEADER TAKES UP A NEW POSITION.—THE LOCALITY OF THE CONFLICT.—PREPARATIONS FOR ACTION.—THE STRUGGLE.—FALL OF URRIOLA.—CAPTURE OF CANNON BY THE INSURGENTS.—CESSATION OF THE CONTEST.—THE KILLED AND WOUNDED.—FORCE ENGAGED ON EACH SIDE.—THOSE INTERESTED.—THE VICTORS VANQUISHED.—FATE OF THE INSURGENTS.—CAUSES OF REVOLUTIONARY TURMOILS.

November 6.—At early daylight an express came in to the government, and the city was soon filled with rumors of a revolutionary outbreak at San Felipe. It appeared that a Socialist club, similar to the one at the capital, had been some time in existence, its leaders preaching doctrines subversive of morality and good order, but taking care, like their fellows in Santiago, to commit no direct infraction which would subject them to the penalties of the law. At last two of them were arrested and thrown into prison for some real or nominal offence. One of them was the gentleman who a few months before had charged the Intendente with treason, and both were connected with the highest blood in Chile. A meeting of the club was called as soon as the incarceration was known, and a banner was hung from the windows of the club-room inscribed "Death to tyrants." This having been ordered to be taken down, and the assembling of the members forbidden, as both commands were resisted, the governor proceeded to the spot to enforce obedience in person. Promptly resisting him, the mob overpowered the few troops that remained faithful, seized the provincial acting chief magistrate, and in a body proceeded to set their leaders at liberty. Not contented with this, the legally constituted public authorities were thrown into prison manacled, felons were turned loose with arms in their hands, and new rulers were chosen. According to the several versions, the revolutionists numbered from 500 to 800 men, who had appointed one of the leaders of the Egualistas as their chief.

On the arrival of the express, the cabinet and Council of State were summoned forthwith; and before sunrise Gen. Aldunate had marched at the head of a body of troops destined to put down the insurgents. As a body of these last were reported to have started for Valparaiso, the Intendente of that province, temporarily on a visit to the capital, was instructed to leave without delay, and after placing himself at the head of the Valdivia regiment, which he would meet on the way, either turn off to intercept the rebels, or continue on to the relief of San Felipe. Not a moment was lost in placing the troops at the different barracks under arms, and making such other dispositions as would prevent surprise, should the Egualistas and opposition party be inclined to play a similar game at Santiago. However, no such intention manifested itself, unless small groups of rotos talking earnestly in the thoroughfares, and the excited countenances of those who were known to be authoritative, might have been so regarded, and the day passed quietly off.

November 7.—The "Araucano" announced that "The bloody revolution, provoked by a number of disorganizers in San Felipe, has spread consternation among all good Chilenos. Blood has been shed by the hand of an assassin armed to overthrow the authority of the republic—by one Ramon Lara. This is the individual who, in September, brought charges against Señor Novoa,* and shortly afterwards established and presided over the society of Egualistas at San Felipe, a branch of that existing amongst us, with the same name and like tendencies

* The Intendente whose trial and acquittal is referred to on a preceding page.

to disorganization and criminal ends. The object of each association is the same; they inculcate the same tenets, have the same revolutionary views, the same means of action—demoralization and crime.

"In Santiago a ridiculous symbol* is borne before their processions; in Aconcagua, a banner covered with insulting and sanguinary mottoes. Here they counsel disobedience of the soldier to his chief, of the citizen to the lawful magistrate; there they make insurrectionists of the incautious, open the prison doors, and give to the criminals liberty and arms. In Santiago a cowardly and infamous member of the club† spat in the face of the Intendente of the province; in Aconcagua its governor is vilely and treacherously assassinated by the president of the society. We have thus before us the objects of these secret and mysterious gatherings. An insurrectionary movement has been contemplated for some time; hence the accusations against the Intendente, and the despatch of ball cartridges which were detected about the middle of September. At Santiago the club has contented itself with threats, because it saw the impotence of a struggle with the more extended elements of order and intelligence, which, creating healthy opinions, control the disorders desired by disorganizers. For want of those elements the resistance was less at San Felipe, and on this account the revolutionists have long had that city in view. The movement so prepared there has burst out at last; but, happily for the republic, its consequences will not be what the outlaws hope for. Public opinion is emphatically and energetically opposed to the insurrection; patriots of all parties will unite to save the republic from anarchy, and—though called on to mourn the blood of Señor Mardones shed by an assassin—the lesson will be invaluable to the future."

Such was the bulletin, and such the sentiments of government. During the day, a report reached town that the insurgent troops were on their way from Aconcagua; and it was also quite current that the Egualistas meant to strike a blow that night on their own account. All day long the Council of State were in conclave. As a consequence of their deliberations, just before sunset a body of military, preceded by trumpeters, paraded in the plaza, publishing a bando

* Liberty.

† Señor Sanfuentes, the member of Congress from Valdivia. This grew out of an obnoxious "*Bando*" just published, and which was as follows. He was instantly handcuffed and imprisoned.

"It is determined and decreed:

"ART. 1. No society or club, whatever may be the number of persons composing it, shall be permitted to present themselves in the streets or public squares as a body, or to make exhibitions in said places of any description whatever.

"ART. 2. In the act of issuing from the place in which the society or club may have held its meeting, the members shall disperse.

"ART. 3. The meetings of the society called 'La Egualdad,' or those of any other of the same character, shall be announced at the Intendente's office, by those who control it, at least one day in advance, designating the place, day, and hour of assembling, in order that police may be sent to preserve order should it be deemed necessary.

"ART. 4. The meetings of the society of 'La Egualdad,' or any other of the same character, shall be public, without hindrance of admission to any who may desire to attend, even if they are not members. As at every public re-union, the police will take care that no disorder is committed. They will also prevent the crowding of persons about the doors of the locality, under the pretext that they cannot enter; as also, that there be no hindrance to the entry of those who desire, should there be sufficient room.

"ART. 5. The name of the proprietor or landlord of the house in which the society, or any part of it, may meet, shall be made known at the office of the Intendente, together with those of the directors, presidents, or any other officers, in order that the police may know the persons who assume the responsibility of giving a legal direction to these assemblages, and to prevent the infractions of law.

"ART. 6. An authentic copy of this decree shall be affixed in such position at the entrance to the rooms of the society of 'La Egualdad,' and every other of the same character, that those who assemble there shall see it. The said copy shall at least comprise the whole of the dispositive portion.

"ART. 7. Infraction of the terms of this decree shall be punished, according to the circumstances of the case, by fines or imprisonment; which, conformably with Article 127 of the laws for internal government, may be adjudged by this Intendencia without appeal by those who may be found guilty.

"Publish it, make it known to the directors of the society of 'La Egualdad' by the sergeant major of the corps of Vijilantes and file it.

"EVARISTO DEL CAMPO, *Secretary*.

"OVALLE."

declaring the provinces of Santiago and Aconcagua under martial law for the space of seventy days. Government deemed it expedient to have a more prompt, certain, and desperate remedy for offences than the procrastinations and vacillations of common law afforded. The bando was signed by a new Intendente, Señor Ovalle being considered too inefficient in the crisis.

At the same time, the Egualistas were absolutely prohibited from assembling; the printing offices of "El Progreso" and "La Barra"—both liberals—were closed; and the few opposition papers printed elsewhere in the republic were directed to be excluded from the mails coming within the infected districts. Simultaneously the police were started in pursuit of political offenders, whose numbers it was whispered amounted to more than forty, including members of Congress, editors, lawyers, and the prominent men of the club, who had been guilty of speaking or writing doctrines repugnant to the rulers of the nation. There had been no overt act of treason, nor could one be directly alleged; although it was charged, and probably believed by many partisans of the ministry, that papers had fallen into the possession of the latter which proved a deeply laid scheme for the overthrow of the administration, and specified the names of the persons who were to succeed. These gentlemen were, of course, to be among the first secured; and as few of them anticipated such an event, they were arrested and conveyed to prison before learning the nature of the offence charged. However, as there is a sort of vocal telegraph in the society of Santiago, notice of the intentions of the government was given to a portion of the proscribed, and they were not found by the police. One effected his escape by flight over the tiled roofs while it was still daylight. Panic spread through all the opposition ranks, and there was not a man bold enough to strike a blow for the relief of their leaders. Deserted by those who should have rallied for their support, the artisans and laborers who had been seduced from loyalty under the promise of amended fortunes now crept cowed to their abodes of improvidence and idleness. Not a voice was raised in encouragement; not a dollar laid on their so-called altar of liberty and equality; not an arm raised to arrest the oppression against which they had made such outcries. "*Sauve qui peut*" was the watchword; and though some of them were among the highest born, they were begging shelter and concealment at the hands of those whose houses were least liable to search, no matter how humble. Greater treachery to avowed principles or to a party never was exhibited.

Even among the better classes throughout the city the utmost consternation prevailed. A ball given by the American minister was deprived of three fourths of its intended guests, who feared going out, or from distress because of the incarceration of friends. Safe as they were likely to be under the protection of the "stars and stripes," should an outbreak really occur, the few who had assembled were not unfrequently in whispering trepidation. Dearly as the Chilenas love dancing, and gaily as sounded the good music, life and spirit could not be roused, even with the aid of champagne; and the timid groups, startled at every external noise, returned to their homes long before midnight.

November 8.—The government bulletin announced: "Not a drop of fraternal blood has been shed. Praised be God. Favored by Heaven, the criminals have concealed their shame by flight. From to-day the tranquillity of Chile is more stable. Notwithstanding there were names in its support which authorized revolution, anarchy has proved impotent."

As none of the liberal papers were permitted to circulate openly in the capital during the state of siege, we had only one-sided versions of the difficulty; and these were not always destitute of embellishments. An account was subsequently published by those most interested, which was essentially as follows:

On the regular day for the meeting of the Egualistas at San Felipe, according to custom, the national flag was hoisted over the house. This flag bore the inscription: "*Viva la republica democratica; viva la Sociedad de la Igualdad; valor contra la tirania*" (Huzza for the democratic republic; huzza for the Socialist society; war against tyranny). An hour before the time of meeting, the acting governor of the province sent the commandant of police to remove it, and, without waiting for the owner of the house or giving him notice, it was violently torn down, and taken to the Intendente. A number of citizens went to the meeting of the society on the same evening, though without other object than to pacify the artisans, whose excitement and anger had been strongly roused by the act just mentioned. It was pointed out to them that the public authorities could legally prohibit the display of a banner on private houses, but that on the following day it would be quietly reclaimed as individual property. Persuasive speeches apparently quieted the greatly agitated mass. It was shown to them that the authorities were eminently interested in fomenting disorder, that they might have a pretext for securing the most patriotic and influential citizens: not a difficult task in an unarmed population whose only wishes were to protect themselves from corrupt legislation.

On the following morning Señor Lara went to the Intendencia, when, without cause—unless his previous energy in defence of liberty might be regarded as sufficient—and before he had opened his lips, the Intendente ordered him to prison. Appointing Señor Caldera his counsel, and advising him of the unexpected oppression he was suffering, the latter proceeded to the Intendencia forthwith, and requested to be informed of the charges against his client. The only satisfaction obtained was, that the accusation would soon be sent to the judge under whose jurisdiction it came, and there the information might be learned. Knowing the judge to be a personal enemy of Lara, and that the latter had a previous indictment against him in the same court, to prevent influence on the new cause the attorney drew up a paper consenting to pay all the fine demanded by the old accusation. It was necessary for Lara to sign this, and, as he was incommunicated, Caldera entreated the judge for permission to enter the prison under any restrictions he might consider essential; but the privilege was obstinately refused. Señor Caldera returned to the Intendencia, seeking the charges promised, and was assured that they would be forwarded within half an hour, before which time the judge should not leave the court, and an officer was sent to the latter requesting him to remain. Perfectly satisfied with the conduct of the Intendente, Señor Caldera went home, where he found many respectable citizens much alarmed from the fact that the populace would not leave the house in which the Egualistas met, having gone there with a determination to take Lara from prison by force if he could not be liberated otherwise. Many had attempted to dissuade them from so rash an attempt; but the resolution remained unchanged, and, as a last resort, all who were at Caldera's house proceeded in a body to intercede with the mass. This resulted in the dispersal of the crowd.

Grieved more at the excitement which was again springing up among the people than because of the imprisonment of his friend, the counsel of Señor Lara went a third time to the court of the judge. Not finding him, and the clerk assuring him that the indictment had not yet been received, his steps were again turned to the Intendente's. Appealing to this officer, by all their previous friendly relations, that he would communicate his charges, he was haughtily told, "I will do so when it suits me." Distressed with the memory of the scene he had just witnessed, Caldera then said to the Intendente: "Señor Don Blas, the people are aroused, and it has cost much to restrain them. Do not force them into a painful conflict. I promised that I would not rest in my efforts until the liberty of Señor Lara was legally obtained." Losing all dignity, and forgetting the language held but a little while previously, without further provocation the Intendente heaped unbecoming terms on the advocate; and as his anger increased with the expression of his own words, he actually ended by sending Caldera to jail.

A few minutes afterwards a bando was published against all patriotic societies, prohibiting, under penalty of imprisonment, all who might be suspected by the police, or whose political sentiments were known, from assembling in numbers of more than six persons. On hearing so scandalous an outrage of national rights, and witnessing the privilege of association torn from them—the only privilege or right through which a people can arrest despotism—indignation pervaded every breast, and from all directions the people flocked spontaneously to the plaza, in their anger thrusting aside the moderate men who wished to control them or to beg the liberty of the prisoners. All the most respectable citizens hastened to the Intendente, earnestly entreating him that, for the sake of the country, their children, and families, he would allay the tumult by discharging the prisoners under recognizances. But he refused them all; defied the people with provoking and abusive words, offering them the heads of the prisoners; and as his fury rose momentarily, orders were given to the guard to fire on the crowd—an impotent command that none obeyed, and which only served to impel the populace on the cuartel. That was taken without resistance. At this time a younger brother of Señor Caldera most generously interposed between the Intendente and the infuriated crowd, succeeding at the risk of his life in securing liberty to one then seeking the head of his brother, and subsequently escorting him to the mayoralty, whose door he resolutely guarded to prevent the people from penetrating and putting him to death.

The people armed themselves forthwith, and named a military chief to lead them. On the other hand, the principal citizens, alarmed at these unexpected results, met at the municipality, and appointed a council for the preservation of public order. The military leader promptly submitted to the orders of that authority, as he might do without disobedience to the orders of the supreme government, or any other authority the latter might send into the province. A record of their proceedings was prepared and signed by the Cabildo and principal citizens.

As soon as this was done the chief of the council informed the President of the republic of the occurrences, and placed himself at his orders, notifying the minister at the same time that as tranquillity was restored, and the Intendente (not the *acting* chief Mardones, heretofore mentioned) was known to be in the province, he had written to him to come and resume his authority. Both communications were despatched at 1 A. M.—that to the President by express, the other by a well known gentleman of the province, who was accompanied by the public notary. A few hours later two officers arrived, bringing word from the Intendente, pledging his honor that, if the people would be orderly and peaceable, no one should be molested, nor should the least charge be brought against any individual for participation in the events of the preceding day. The excitement of the moment having passed over, the citizens were well satisfied with the conditions, and caused them to be written out and signed by the officers and authority selected by themselves. Perceiving how easily they were controlled, the Intendente endeavored to mystify the affair, giving greater consequence than it merited to the successful termination of a difficulty which may almost literally be said to have been stifled in its birth. Noticing the delay, and suspecting a political plan to give importance to a momentary tumult resulting rather from the action of the authorities than from the people, the citizens referred to their council to learn the manner in which their anxiety would be appeased, and the latter sent two of their number to the Intendente. Wilfully forgetful of the pledges and terms signed on the same day by his commissioners, this gentleman sent a letter conceding pardon, couched in language almost such as Roman emperors directed to plebeians; without doubt mentally reserving the patriots who had served in the cause of liberty to be used as warnings for the nation when disposed to resent the encroachments of tyranny.

Such being the case, it was not until after two hours' entreaty that the citizens induced the troops to lay down their arms; but by 1 A. M. they issued quietly from the cuartel, and law and order reigned again.

This is what some persons designate a *revolution*, probably with the sinister hope of involving in revolutionary processes at law our most pacific citizens and earnest friends of order. The acting Intendente was the whole and sole cause of the difficulty; but the desire to declare martial law in the province of Santiago needed support in ideal crimes he claimed to have found in Aconcagua. These are the sole acts for which our citizens have been imprisoned, more than forty of whom, of the most respectable standing, have been incarcerated to satisfy the exigencies of a wretched policy and the revenge of the acting Intendente, inspired by the antipathy they had always shown for him. This is the reward of moderation to those who desired the preservation of harmony and order at every risk, and to whom there have been given such repeated causes for complaint.

The preceding version, embodied in the "Comercio" of Valparaiso, was very generally admitted by the more impartial of the ministerial party to be a very fair *ex parte* statement, which it doubtless is. Subsequently arrests went on in the two provinces, until a sufficient number of deputies were secured to give the government a preponderance in the Chambers; and the prisoners were banished and prohibited, under heavy penalties, from returning to Chile within a given time. Thus, at the end of forty days the President found himself strong enough to convoke Congress, at the assembling of which martial law ceased by provision of the Constitution.

And after so much talk; such stringent, and in some cases cruel, measures by government; such harangues and processions; so many intimations of bloody deeds, and of the conquerors' distribution of the coveted offices by Egualistas—*on paper*—what came of it? In the hope and under the promise of sharing better things, artisans were inveigled from honest employments to idleness and criminal covetousness, by men too pusillanimous to assume responsibility, when only personal risk would avail—men who were cowardly beyond contempt, and who deserted them at the first crisis. This was infinitely better for the country and humanity, provided the result did not so far encourage despotism as to induce another blow at the advance of knowledge and liberty—an event which in a country like Chile, laboring under the incubus which every exclusive church would throw over the intellect, is more greatly to be dreaded than in one where liberty of conscience is an acknowledged right. But "the snake was scotched, not killed," as the following occurrence, six months later, will show:

April 20, 1851.—I had injured my right eye by over-work; and finding the weather did not promise well for observations, and that it would be advisable to avoid tasking it during another week, even should the nights prove favorable, a seat was accepted in the birlocho of a friend, and I went to Valparaiso to receive a son expected to arrive in the monthly steamer from Panama.

From the effects of the earthquake nearly three weeks before, the appearance of the villages and ranchos along the road was still deplorable. Many of the inhabitants continued to occupy the temporary shelters thrown up after the great shock, though the injuries to dwellings had already been partially remedied, and most of the crevices in the earth were obliterated. There remained only broken walls and one or two rents to show how severe the convulsion had been. We reached the port on the evening of the 19th, and I was welcomed by my intelligent and hospitable friend ——.

On returning to the parlor from dinner next day, we learned that a traveller had just got in from the capital, bringing tidings that the whole military force was in revolt against the government, and that, as every street leading out of the city was guarded, he had found great difficulty in making his escape. Of course, such intelligence startled us not a little. One fellow-guest, who had arrived by the steamer, had long been a resident of Santiago, and his family and property were there. The merchants at the port were almost equally interested; for if the mob obtained the ascendancy, the coffers of their agents at Santiago, and their warehouses at Valparaiso, would be the first to be rifled. Being one of the most largely concerned parties, our host could not be satisfied until he had conversed with the traveller and had visited the Intendente to learn whether official intelligence had been received from Santiago. But no more satisfactory information had arrived; nor was it until midnight that an express came to the Intendente, notifying him that the government had triumphed, and order had been restored again. Nearly at the same time an order arrived from the leader of the insurgents to the commandant of artillery, directing him to recognise no other authority than his own; and such had been the influence of the insurgent party along the road, that the express-rider to the Intendente had been detained several hours.

Experience having taught how dangerous is power in the hands of such a mob as can be congregated by the lower classes of Spanish-Americans, even this intelligence afforded great relief, and every one slept the sounder for it. Few felt more grateful than Mr. —— and myself: he, because wife, children, property, and home, had been in jeopardy; I, because the unenviable reputation we enjoyed gave reason to fear that the instruments and observatories might be destroyed in their first moments of leisure, to take away the means of prognosticating earthquakes we refused to warn them of, and to prevent further visitations of rains on them in summer. They knew that we were nearly all broken down by incessant clear nights in the summer and autumn (winter and spring) of 1850, and believed we had caused these unheard-of summer rains to obtain a respite from labor.

Morning brought the particulars. The larger part of the Valdivia regiment, commanded by a Colonel Urriola, who had figured conspicuously in preceding revolutions, had marched to the plaza about 3 A. M. A few troops belonging to the same regiment who were guarding the prison, and such of the fire brigade, occupying the western extremity of the same building, as offered resistance, were overpowered, and a summons despatched to the cuartel of the Chacabuco regiment to come and join them. After liberating and arming the prisoners and a portion of the Egualistas who had collected, Urriola, a Señor Ugarte, and some others, made harangues to them, endeavoring to impress upon the multitude who soon flocked to the square that the ministers were tyrannical and ought to be dismissed, themselves oppressed beyond further endurance, and General Cruz was the only man who could release them from their burdens or restore their rights. But it seems to be admitted that the arguments of the orators made few converts; and of the thousands of idlers and curious who had hastened there on the first rumors of disturbance, multitudes were quite as desirous to get out of the way when they comprehended that revolution was contemplated. The people's cause as there proclaimed was not the popular one; or, if so, the fear of consequences by participation was more powerful than the sense of injury.

For the purpose of protecting the arms of the battalion and for instruction in military life, a portion of the civic troops always remain on duty at their respective garrisons. Finding there were few volunteer accessions, a detachment was sent to take possession of the cuartel adjoining the university building, and belonging to the third battalion of National Guards. It is supposed that the object was to gain possession of the munitions, and then beat to arms, for the purpose of inducing belief that the civic troops had united with them. The move proved unfortunate; for two of the sergeants despatched there deserted with their piquets, one of them deliberately shooting the lieutenant in command as they filed off to the palace in support of the President. The remainder encountered a strong resistance by the guard at the cuartel. No greater success attended overtures to the Chacabuco regiment. The messenger to the colonel was arrested; and though individual members both of that corps and the artillery joined the standard of revolt, notwithstanding the assurance that the whole population would at once place themselves under his orders, Urriola found himself with less than six hundred men, including soldiers, Egualistas, and loafers. Three or four hours passed. He had struck no blow, gained no advantage, had scarcely added a man to his numbers, whilst his force of regular troops was diminishing; at the same time government was by each instant of delay gaining confidence and (what was of equal consequence) numerical strength. That the latter felt its weakness was apparent; for, when a demand was sent to the President to dismiss his ministers, instead of arresting the envoy, and commanding immediate and unconditional surrender of the insurgents on penalty of death, there was temporizing and a parley. There was probably no personal timidity, but apparently doubts of their own judgment in the crisis—dread of the responsibility in case revolution should ensue. At least their hesitation to act suggests this, and scarcely admits of other interpretation. They had cause for it, too. Of five battalions of National Guards, the Chacabucos, the artillery, the fire brigade, the cavalry, and the faithful of the Valdivias—in all numbering not less than five thousand men—scarcely one in six had assembled at the palace.

As the President was about to leave it at the head of the troops who had collected, Señor Montt, then chief judge of the supreme court and the government candidate for the presidency, suggested to General Bulnes to spare the effusion of blood to the last moment, so as to give the misguided men the utmost opportunity to acknowledge their error and return to duty. Probably nothing is more painful to a really brave man than the necessity for sacrificing life, and

General Bulnes, if not born "insensible to fear," has that written on his rough countenance which might easily be so interpreted. Of course he would be glad of any excuse for delay in firing on his countrymen, and thus orders were issued to the cavalry to neither draw sword nor fire a shot under any circumstances. Conformably with this command, it is said that the squadron composing the body-guard of his excellency, their swords in scabbard and carbines pendent, traversed various parts of the city without once returning the shots occasionally directed at them, or exhibiting anger when assailed by the mob with volleys of stones. It was also known that the President gave an example of confidence by riding unarmed through some of the streets attended by only three of his usual escort.

When the conversation with Señor Montt took place, there was also present Don Anjel Prieto, a son-in-law of Urriola, who was entreated to use his influence that things should go no farther. At the same time, the first named gentleman promised the weight of himself and friends to obtain the utmost possible mitigation of the severities of the law, if the insurgents would disperse. "It must be evident to you," added Señor Montt, "that the revolt will be quelled, because the populace prove their disposition in the presence of the National Guard." A greatly over-wrought cause of gratulation, by-the-by; for, as has been said, there was not one in six of them present. However, after expressing great doubt as to whether he possessed sufficient influence to change the purposes of his father-in-law, Señor Prieto finally acceded to the wishes of two of the ex-ministers,* and left the palace in their company. Half way to the plaza his doubts returned, and he dissuaded them from proceeding, assuring them that the determination of his relative was probably unchangeable; and if he could not effect it alone, the presence of conservatives like themselves would perhaps do more harm than good. Persisting in this, the mission was completed alone; but instead of listening to the benevolent suggestions of friends, and dispersing his force, it was soon apparent that Urriola was about to take a further step.

Nothing was to be gained by remaining longer in the plaza. The Chief Magistrate had not come to them and surrendered; and at best, under inactivity, the populace around were lukewarm. Therefore there was no alternative but to take him, and dictate terms, or sneak back to the cuartel, to be afterwards dragged out and shot seriatim. Yet, how accomplish this? The palace was some squares distant, and strong; and they possessed neither cavalry for a charge, nor artillery for battering. Moreover, if they remained at their present position—the plaza being hemmed in by four high walls—they could be mowed down like reeds, from the streets that open at each of the corners. True, there were the buildings surrounding the plaza, within which they could take refuge, and, with ammunition, defy all the force that might be brought to dislodge them; but they had too little powder and ball to risk this; and without provisions, they must soon have been starved into terms. Therefore, towards 7 A. M. Urriola moved his force through the Calle de Estado to the Cañada; and on arriving in front of the convent of San Francisco, soon got up quite an excitement, the troops hurrahing for "*el pueblo y libertad*," and the Egualistas and rotos reciprocating the compliment with cheers for "*la linea*" (the regulars). A few moments served to show that a favorable effect was produced for the cause of revolt, an under-current working for it that was probably set in motion by other and more tangible causes than *vivas*. As its ranks began to swell, such arms as could be obtained were distributed among them, though not a few had only clubs or paving-stones. About the same time Col. Videla, with two pieces of artillery under charge of nearly a hundred men of his own battalion, the Chacabucos, crossed the lower part of the Cañada, on his way to protect the palace. There he found the President at the head of about 700 men, consisting of his escort (200 cavalry personally attached to him), quite 400 of the National Guards, and perhaps 100 from other corps, who were disposed to strike a blow for the preservation of order and existing law, rather than risk confusion and anarchy.

Two or three hours more were frittered away by each party, Urriola making the most delib-

* The two opposed to the nomination of Mr. Montt; referred to on page 315.

erate preparations to attack the artillery cuartel—the government not yet strong enough to assume the offensive. If the coolness of the people had at first mortified the former, they were now making amends; and he had a right to believe there wanted but a trifling success to bring under his banners a very large proportion of the tens of thousands who filled every avenue leading to the probable scene of conflict. The cuartel, at which he was aiming, lies at the base of, and on the southwest side of Santa Lucia; the Cañada, its south front; and Calles Recojidas and Breton flanking it—the former on the west. Two squares being united in one, as occurs in several other parts of the city also, there is no street in the rear proper. It walls are of adobes, with the principal entrance on the south front. There is a second and smaller door in the rear, in Calle Recojidas, and a number of windows on each of the streets, all protected by strong gratings of iron. Within, there are suites of rooms around open courts; but to guard all this space of more than four hundred feet square, enclosing above twenty field-pieces of different calibers, howitzers, small-arms, and munitions for an army, besides sufficient powder to have shaken the earth *almost* as did nature on the morning of the 2d of the same month, ordinarily there were only some thirty or forty soldiers. Strange to say, instead of putting others into it within the preceding four hours, two howitzers with their due quota of men had been ordered out.

It has been mentioned, in the description of the prominent objects of the city, that there are two forts on the angular ridges of Santa Lucia: one on the northern slope, with a battery of six field-pieces; and the other on the southern, still incomplete and without armament. There is, however, a breastwork at the latter; and as it overlooks and is within short musket-range of the cuartel, a single piece of artillery would have been quite sufficient to drive out any force protected only by tiles and reed roofs. Why Urriola did not send a corporal's guard to take possession of the north castle and its battery is incomprehensible, though scarcely more so than his trifling away so many hours in the plaza and Cañada. A single company at an early hour could have made themselves masters of the artillery and its rich stores with very little effort, and the city would have surrendered without a blow. The conduct of both parties was most extraordinary, and is most difficult of explanation. On the part of Urriola we must assume his confident belief that he had but to present himself, and the whole regular and militia force would take sides with him. So far as the artillery regiment was concerned there was certainly good ground for it, because the old colonel (Arteaga), now second in command of the insurgents, had always been personally popular with the soldiers, and the new one (Maturana) was not. But Maturana and his handful of men, like too many others for his purposes, were faithful, and the doors of the cuartel were coldly closed on the ancient leader and his comrades.

It could no longer be concealed that a fight must take place; and in order to protect his men as much as possible, a lumber store close by was broken open, with whose contents, and some sacks abstracted from neighboring shops and paving-stones, Urriola caused a low barricade to be thrown diagonally across the Cañada, and within short musket-shot of the cuartel. Then giving his men a breakfast from the panniers of the passing venders of bread, milk, and fruits, they were ready to begin their work. It is said, and greatly to his credit, that whilst he forcibly took loads of provisions they were liberally paid for in every case. Indeed, as ounces of gold were found in the shoes of several who were killed in the subsequent conflict, there seems to have been no lack of money.

"Round-shot, canister, and musket-balls flying along the Cañada too rapidly for comfort," as Lieut. MacRae wrote to me, it was not prudent for the assistants to continue near spectators after the firing began; and information of the remainder of the morning's events has been derived from the government paper—an account which was said to be reliable so far as it went. For some time Santa Lucia was crowded with spectators, who were indifferent to occasional shrill sounds as bullets whistled over them, and would probably have remained mere lookers-on until the end; but one or the other party, perhaps remembering that "those who are not for us are against us," sent a volley towards its craggy peaks, which brought them from their look-out pell-mell. I quote now from the bulletin mentioned, omitting such portions as do not specially interest the general reader. It was near 10 o'clock.

"The insurgents numbered three hundred and fifty men of the Valdivia regiment, twenty-three of the Chacabuco, about thirty firemen, and some reckless young men and rabble to the number of four hundred more. Urriola demanded the surrender of the artillery, stating that the whole of the troops were under his control; but was answered by Col. Maturana that he should only deliver it to the government. When the former approached the cuartel with so large a force, there were only thirty men within it under the command of the gallant Maturana; and on the instant a desperate conflict must have commenced, had not the Chacabuco regiment appeared on two separate points of Santa Lucia. These diverting the attention of the enemy, saved Col. Maturana, and the handful of brave men he commanded, the necessity of displaying their courage and devotion in vain. A part of the force of the besiegers moved to dislodge Lieut. Col. Videla (of the Chacabucos); but he, passing along the hill, descended by the south fort, and succeeded in entering the cuartel door before they could re-occupy their position in the Cañada. With this reinforcement, arrived at a moment so decisive, the defence could count a hundred men; and the two chiefs, agreeing to spare the effusion of blood to the last extremity, kept the doors and windows closed and withheld their fire. The delay emboldened the attacking party, who having taken their chosen positions, detached a body of rabble to assault the doors and windows with stones. These they also threw upon the roof, and in a very little time there were apertures in the walls beside the principal door, as well as below that in Calle Recojidas. Balls penetrated the shutters on the two streets, and soon the position within was as unsafe as without the cuartel. Things having reached this extreme, a piece of artillery was dragged into the street, and a dreadful fire of cannon and small-arms ensued, alarming the whole city. In the midst of it Col. Garcia appeared in Calle de las Augustinas with about 400 of the National Guards in close columns. Col. Urriola was not discouraged by the arrival of a reinforcement that made his adversaries in number equal, and in power—by reason of their artillery—superior to his own, but despatched a strong division of the Valdivias to follow in their rear; and the National Guards soon found themselves between two fires, in a street only 23 feet wide. The destruction of life was terrible. The commandant of battalion No. 1, Don Ignacio Ortuzar, Maj. Navarro, serving as volunteer aid to Col. Garcia, and Lieut. Hurtado, together with Captains Castro, Aspillaga, Soto, and Lieut. Torres of No. 2, fell wounded. Hurtado died in a few minutes, and Navarro last night; indeed the street was covered with bodies of the wounded.

"A moment of frightful confusion succeeded the surprise of this attack, more impressive on the National Guards, no matter how intrepid or what disposition they possess. As the commandant of the gun placed in that street required that his front should be opened, the civic troops entered the cuartel by the door of Calle Recojidas, which was the object Col. Garcia had in view.

"Col. Urriola continued pouring a galling fire on the National Guards—on the very mass in whose name he pretended to have taken up arms; but Divine justice willed that the transgression should be punished by those against whose laws he had rebelled. A ball reached him and he fell from his horse, saying, in accents of indignation, '*Me han engañado*' (They have deceived me). He had asserted that there would be no resistance, that it would be but a military show, that the legitimate executors of the laws had sold themselves, and that the National Guards were on his side. The unfortunate man fell at a short distance from the bodies of the very National Guards whom he had sacrificed.

"The division of the Valdivias abandoned its position and returned to incorporate itself with the main body in the Cañada. Col. Arteaga—the second in command of the insurgents—mounted behind a servant and escaped to the house of the North American envoy, where he still finds asylum. Then began one of the bloodiest combats of armies ever noted. The insurgents succeeded in placing a ladder against the corner of the cuartel, and, by means of shirts dipped in turpentine, twice set fire to the eaves, though at the loss of two men. The magnitude of the crime committed can only be judged of when it is known that this is the storehouse of an immense amount of munitions of war and a large quantity of gunpowder. To have burned it must have blown the whole neighborhood in pieces, and made thousands of victims. This was known to the insurgents; for they spoke of it, and securely counted on such a result. The main force of the Valdivias had taken up a position on the corner of Calle Recojidas and the Cañada, some twenty yards from the main door of the cuartel; and another portion established themselves at the entrance of 'Calle San Isidro,' just opposite. At this decisive moment, and when the roof was already smoking, Col. Maturana ordered out two field-pieces, under charge of Capt. Gonzales; but the shower of balls wounded so many artillerists that it was almost impossible to work the guns, and their operations were delayed. Capt. Gonzales was wounded; and Capt. Escala, who went out to replace him, was rendered *hors du combat* after a few rounds. Then the old Colonel sent his own son, Lieut. Maturana, to the slaughter-house. He had just left the Military Academy, and proved himself a worthy scion from such a stock. The youth also was wounded; and the father, taking his place, fought until every artilleryman was killed or wounded, when he abandoned the guns; and the enemy rushing instantly upon them, they were dragged to the opposite side of the Cañada. For a moment the insurgents shouted victory; they had obtained those anxiously coveted cannon from whose possession they had augured so much. They then changed position, reinforcing the party in front in order to command the door of the cuartel, and drawing in on all sides the circle of troops thrown around it. But this proved only a change of the *dramatis personæ* of the contest; for the door of the cuartel was again thrown open, and the National Guards poured out a torrent of balls of the same width, thus showing the rebels who had captured the artillery that their condition was in no respect bettered.

"The action continued with renewed fury, and the National Guards revenged themselves for what they had suffered when attacked in the rear. It would have continued without termination if an incident had not occurred to show the sentiments of the Valdivias—sentiments stifled during the ardor of the struggle by the desire to conquer. A sub-lieutenant of the Chacabucos had been made prisoner at the principal guard-house, and was retained in the rear of the column of the insurgents. During the combat he managed to approach the corner of Calle Recojidas, and the moment he could do so he ran to join the commandant of his corps, who was opportunely guarding the side-door; having agreed with Col. Maturana to go to and fro, in order that they might inform themselves of all that passed in the difficult defence of a place so reduced. This incident induced twelve men of the Chacabucos to follow the example of their officer; and one by one the Valdivias also availed themselves of the door of salvation, until about 150 of them were united in the cuartel. The firing slackened in front; and by being open, the principal door soon invited other groups to abandon a useless conflict—a conflict in which all had shown the bravery of Chilenos. In this manner terminated the defence of the cuartel; its walls then enclosing the artillery, Valdivias, Chacabucos, and four battalions of the civic guard. Stupor had succeeded those three hours of terrible combat. The streets were covered with the dead; the interior of the cuartel was crowded with the wounded; and the mob associated in the revolt entered without knowing precisely what was going on, many felicitating themselves on the triumph they thought they had achieved.

"The glory of the day belongs to each of the battalions who successively entered that confined space. The artillerists, the 70 men of the Chacabucos who had surpassed what it was reasonable to expect from human energy, and the National Guards, sustaining the end of the action, secured the triumph of law and that continuation of order which makes Chile the honorable exception of Spanish America. A notable fact is, that the measures taken by the President secured the salvation of the country; that is, the appearance of the Chacabucos on Santa Lucia prevented an attack on the cuartel by an infinitely superior force, and the arrival of the National Guards was at the most opportune moment."

So far the publication issued is explicit, and to near the close it seems fair; but there are several reasons to think that golden spectacles had been furnished the writer whilst inditing the rest. Most truly does he say the fight was desperate, and the shower of balls that left their marks in the Cañada and along the walls of the streets were alone ample proofs for him of the violence of the storm of lead and iron. But we had other and more painful evidences. More than two hundred bodies were buried from the effects of that forty minutes' fight, and nearly a like number will long suffer from their wounds; results too significant to go abroad, and which were consequently withheld from the public prints. The numbers specified by the papers were "from forty to fifty killed, and twice that many wounded." A week afterwards, although a heavy rain had fallen in the mean time, the streets round the cuartel still exhibited black patches where life-blood had been poured out. Nor does the writer admit the fact that the cuartel had surrendered and the insurgents *were* victorious; he only acknowledges that the firing had ceased, and many of the mob who entered felicitated themselves on the victory they *thought* they had achieved. Most fortunate was it for government that there was no leader to confirm them in this thought and conduct them to realize what they had striven for.

Had the opposition newspapers been suffered to appear, we should, beyond doubt, have been able to sift out the whole truth, and perhaps have learned something of the motives of those instigating the revolt; but their offices were closed on the same day, and we could obtain information from members of that party only in conversations which were hazardous to natives, during a period of so much suspicion. Moreover, those who took such part as warranted inference that they were permitted to know the *animus*, valued their lives too highly to remain after Arteaga's cowardly desertion, and forthwith took themselves to parts unknown; so that the versions circulated by subordinates and in the gossiping circles of the capital became as contradictory as possible. It was pretty generally agreed, however, that the courage of Arteaga failed before Urriola left the plaza, and he was forced to participate personally only at the muzzle of a pistol, in the hands of his own party. No wonder he seized the first instant to place his dear person out of harm's way; though whether he had perused during his travels in Europe, some years previously, that sensible maxim of Falstaff, about "the man who fights," does not appear; yet one cannot help thinking so.

But the writer of the official account makes omissions which it may be as well to supply authentically, in order that due credit and reprehension may fall where they belong. So rapidly does information circulate in the city, that direct news of what was going on in the plaza had reached the cuartel as early as 4 o'clock. The Colonel immediately ordered out four mountain howitzers and two four-pounders, determining, as he said, to fight to the last moment in its defence. And when Urriola sent an officer to ask him, "*Que hacia que no salia, que el pueblo estaba con el*," (What was he doing that he did not come out, for all the people were on his side), the gallant old veteran replied, "Tell him to go and ask the President." Subsequently, two mountain howitzers, with their due complement of gunners, were sent to join the Chacabucos, who, to the number of 120 men, came to reinforce the cuartel, and effected their entrance before 8 o'clock. Including the brigade of police—Vijilantes—the total military force collected at the palace amounted to nine hundred men: one hundred and fifty of whom, together with the Vijilantes, were left to guard it; whilst to the mounted grenadiers was assigned the special duty of protecting the person of the President. His Excellency accompanied the troops to the scene of action; but it was asserted, and many believed, that the horses of his escort loved the smell of alfalfa better than that of gunpowder, and so showed clean heels at the first snuff of it, making tracks for the palace again. Some were malicious enough to say that their riders had rather sniff chicha than vile brimstone, and were sufficiently wicked to discuss their cowardice quite openly. On the other hand, the Valdivias fought like tigers, setting an example to their Egualista companions which the latter were not slow to imitate; and when the defeated regiment set out for Valparaiso two days later, so hotly did the taunts flow whilst they were within hearing of each other, that it was difficult to prevent contests between them and the armed police.

There were many most anxious spectators of the struggle: not only the timid and peaceful citizens, who knew not at what moment robbery and pillage would begin; the patriots, who grieved at the evidence of insubordination and incapacity for self-government their countrymen were giving to the world; those whose blood tingled with the excitement to which it had given birth, and who thirsted to mix in the strife; but those, also, who had secretly incited, and had spent their breath and treasure—willing to obtain power, even if the path to it led fathom-deep through the blood of their countrymen. As Lieutenant MacRae wrote me: "There were leading men of the Egualistas very quiet at first, but who rushed in shouting when the men from the barricades took possession of the artillery—a feat that will probably cost them their heads." The apparent triumph of their friends was too severe a trial to their assumed philosophical indifference; the grim iron captives they had brought to the other side of the Cañada were messengers bringing "tidings of great joy;" and the screen concealing their secret and unholy alliance was torn away by the first false sounds that wafted "Victory!" Alas, poor Egualistas! The active head that planned was now pillowed on the earth; the stout heart that cheered you on had nearly welled out its last drops; the mantle of valor, which at least should have fallen on his successor, fitted no such ignoble shoulders, and passed only among his old though humble associates. These—missing the voice that animated and the well known form to follow, disheartened for want of example, bewildered by recognising none to obey, and called by old companions within the cuartel—one by one dropped away until the larger half were gone, absolutely ignorant whether as victors or as vanquished. In the hands of the mob that remained, guns captured, without ammunition, were at best but unstrung harps, serving not an instant to prolong the jubilant.

The struggle was over. The chief men interested among the Egualistas, who had betrayed themselves but a brief while before, were now deserted, and they looked wildly round for a direction in which to escape, each hoping that his participation had been unmarked. Their motto was "*Sauve qui peut;*" and in less than three hours after the artillery fell into the hands of the insurgents, one of them was seen thirty-five miles south of Santiago! But the government had been argus-eyed, and every man of them was registered; some being promptly arrested and thrown into prison, to be banished subsequently, whilst others succeeded in going into voluntary exile. Such of the troops as did not join their fellows in the cuartel marched to the palace and gave themselves up, the Egualistas and rabble dispersing in all directions. Indeed, it was said that a part of the club forthwith ranged themselves on the government side; so that by 1 P. M., instead of hostile battalions contending in the streets, there were only patrols of government troops picking up prisoners. And thus the timid were reassured that order was restored. Confidence they could not inspire. It had been too evident that the mass would not array themselves under the banners of the ministry, if such connexion would involve them in conflict. The civic troops were alike in opposition, or at best indifferent. The disaffected regulars were in a decided majority, and there was a rumor that the Valdivias continued so excited, that they might again rise at any moment. Added to this, there was a doubt as to what General Cruz would do when the news reached him; whether he would march instantly to the capital, with the army and people of the South at his back, to avenge those who had proclaimed him in the plaza and fallen; or whether he would act as became a patriot, and rally to the aid of the legally constituted authorities of his country, irrespective of self. The Presidential election was near at hand too, the friends of Cruz at Santiago claiming 9,000 voters, or more than a majority. From these causes there was distrust and restraint on intercourse at the capital during several weeks.

Within a few days after the revolt a military court arraigned and sentenced twenty-seven of the Valdivias to be shot, one of whom paid the penalty of his crime. The sentences of the rest were commuted to service in the penal colony, and the name of the regiment was blotted out. Arteaga, who had taken an active part in firing the cuartel of his old battalion, was demanded by the Minister for Foreign Affairs; or rather the United States minister was notified of this civil crime, and requested to permit his arrest at the legation: a request declined, probably not from any personal merit of the accused, or because of any claim he had on the representative of the United States, but solely because it has (most unfortunately) been the custom for foreign ministers to shelter political criminals under like circumstances—a custom the most reprehensible tolerated among civilized nations, and one which the well being of society demands should be abolished. The enormity of this man's crime will be better understood when it is known that he owed military elevation and position in life to the then President of Chile, but had become opposed to him a year or two before, when the latter, for reasons of state or other causes, had thought proper to designate a brother officer instead of himself for the post of Minister of War. He, too, was condemned by the court-martial; but the decision was overruled in the Supreme Court, on the ground of informality: Arteaga, being a member of Congress as well as a colonel of artillery, in accordance with the Constitution, could only become amenable to military law after indictment by the Council of State and the Chamber of Deputies, to which he belonged, trial by the Senate, and deprivation of his first-named office. Yet, such is the influence of rank and wealth, it may well be doubted whether the sentence would not have been commuted had there been no such informality of proceeding. Strange enough, the grave warriors who rendered the verdict, gastronomes as some of them were, had wholly forgotten one essential appositely alluded to by a favorite writer—"*first* catch your hare," &c.

Of the Egualistas there were twenty-odd proscribed. These embraced the same members of the opposition in Congress who had been exiled during the Aconcagua difficulty, and who were sharply sought by the police at the time, but were too wily to be taken. All that could be laid hold of were sent out of the country under heavy penalties if they returned within a given time; the provinces of Santiago and Valparaiso were declared under martial law, and the printing offices of the opposition papers closed. Such was the *finale* of the revolt. Let us look for an instant at its probable origin.

Pride, indolence, and poverty—two inherited; the third, partially consequent to the second, and partially arising from the absence of the higher mechanic arts and industrial resources: these are the causes of the turmoils which have continued to agitate all Spanish America since separation from the mother country. The fortunes of ancestors gathered after the conquests by grants or mining and commerce (not at all times the most legitimate or honorable), were sometimes seized for purposes of state; sometimes tempted the cupidity of inquisitors; or if by good luck they escaped both Scylla and Charybdis, they have subsequently been divided and subdivided until in many cases little else has descended to the males of families during the last quarter of a century than the pride of blood, and enough only to keep actual starvation from the door. Climate and the absence of employment induce an apathetic temperament, and produce a race eminently prolific; and were it not that the same causes bring about indifference to their offspring—with neglect and great mortality among them—the continent must have been overrun long ago. But of those who do grow to manhood there are more than enough to have supplied the professions of law and medicine, the army, and all public offices.* Monas-

* In 1850 there were three hundred and twenty-five lawyers and forty-six doctors in Chile, of whom one hundred and one of the former held offices of some kind under the government. The number of the latter is extraordinarily small for a population of nearly a million and a half; but it will appear more remarkable when it is known that twenty-nine of these reside in Santiago. There are five in Valparaiso, three each in Coquimbo and Talca, and one each in Copiapó, Rancagua, San Fernando, Concepcion, Chillan, and Ancud; not one in the country. There, *medicas*, as the women who administer simples are called, and *haciendados*, alone administer to infirmities. Nor could a physician be supported by his practice outside of the towns. The estates are too extensive for him to attend the families on several, even if they tenanted them all the year, and *peons* are too miserably poor to pay. Even at the capital it is not considered necessary to have a family physician; and it is not unfrequent that a new one is called to each case of sickness. From these or other causes none pursue medicine as a profession one moment longer than they can accumulate sufficient to purchase an estate or a share in a mine, and probably there is not a first class physician in all the republic—certainly not at the capital. At the same time there is no city where talent would be more amply and speedily rewarded, or the student have a nobler field. The result of the system has been, that the municipal authorities find themselves obliged to publish weekly lists of the physicians and apothecaries who *must* serve the sick when called on at night, or pay a fine!

The army is composed of seven regiments numbering a few more than three thousand rank and file, with twelve generals, fourteen colonels, twenty-six lieutenant colonels, forty majors, and ninety-nine captains. Of course, a very considerable proportion of these must be out of active employment and not in the receipt of full pay.

teries only offer inducements to those who can bring something to the general stock, and church preferment requires as much influence as to rise in any other profession.

Destitute of manufactories to require engines and machinery; without ports where ships can be built to any extent; possessing neither navigable rivers needing steamboats, nor railroads, whose fiery steeds might startle them into energy; their products exchanged for goods wrought by foreign hands from foreign materials, and taken away in foreign ships; and their only commerce a few vessels (almost unworthy of the dignified epithet) trading in their own waters,—where shall those find subsistence who annually arrive at the age of manhood? The counting-rooms of merchants, most of whom, or at least a very large number of the most extensive of whom, are foreigners, afford places to some, and a few others fill vacancies that occur in the several offices of government; but there are large numbers who are unable to find such employment as their pride of blood will permit them to undertake. They regard manual labor of any kind as a disgrace, and their pride forbids it; indolence is encouraged, and poverty is a necessary consequence. If the first could be controlled, the others would disappear. "Idleness is the root of all evil," was a favorite aphorism set me to copy by a pedagogue of my earlier years; and the impression of its truth has continued through life. Here, I fear it will not be found among the *excerpts* for youths. Weeks, months, and years pass on; the young man has wearied out his own patience and that of his friends; and as he broods over the partiality with which nature's goods have been apportioned, he learns to violate the tenth article of the decalogue. Why should he not have office instead of A B, who has not half his talent? In short, the outs want to get in; there lies the whole secret. Patriotism, oppression, public wrongs, malevolent rulers, violation of the Constitution, are all in themselves very good *pretexts;* but was there ever an instance when the successful party did not proceed in the very same, or perhaps even more arbitrary paths than those whom they had ousted?

In the individual case under consideration I have not been able to trace out different motives of action; in fact, the association of soldiers and civilians seems almost to proclaim that there was none. Had there been a desire by the nation to remove an obnoxious President, the day for the election of a new one was just two months distant, and the people who had borne with the incumbent for nine years and ten months without complaining could surely have waited so brief a time. If his ministers were objectionable, the Chambers were to assemble within forty days, and it would be easy to arraign them. But there were no such avowals. True, Urriola went through the form of demanding a removal of the ministers: but that is the stereotyped pretext for commencing insurrection; and had his demands been submitted to, we may be sure the Egualistas would never have consented to look for successors beyond their own club.

Less than two years before, a beardless youth, at best of *mediocre* talents, returned from Paris after having had the misfortune to witness some of the scenes of February, 1848; his pockets empty, but his head abundantly crammed with ideas of "Liberty, Equality, Fraternity," popular clubs, sections, and barricades. Having nothing to do and no income, of course all these notions were to be disseminated for the benefit of his oppressed countrymen: "Something may turn up," as Mr. Micawber says. With a tongue as smooth as his face, rotos and artisans were soon made to believe that the rich were their natural enemies, who hoarded wealth that all had a like right to; and his doctrines, finding willing listeners among a class ignorant, improvident, and impoverished, in a little while gave origin to the "Sociedad de la Igualdad." Others, men of birth and rank, disaffected from similar reasons, or because riches did not flow to them as rapidly as their necessities or covetous hearts craved, or as they thought to obtain by pillage in office, saw in the society the means of gaining popularity and elevating themselves. They also, to the number of more than twenty, from the most respectable families in Chile, were known as leaders and orators in the club. The good will of their companions with straw-hats and tattered ponchos was forthwith obtained; for the nightly discourses that sapped their loyalty were abundantly seasoned with lessons in reading and writing, to say nothing of occasional distributions of small sums of money. Every one was taught to believe he should have a place after the mint and the coffers of the rich had been equally divided; and the employment would give them good wages with little work. These ideas were actually imparted to some. To how many it cannot be said, though it is well known that like instructions were not confined to Santiago, the members of the Aconcagua association having received equally liberal views of equality and fraternity. They had made such progress by November, 1850, that they were probably almost ready to strike the first blow, when their ammunition was stopped on its way to San Felipe, and the clubs broken up, at least so far as prohibition to their public assembling could go. Then the leaders found that a military man was requisite to conduct the mass. They needed the necessary instruction; or perhaps their nerves were too delicate to bear the smell of gunpowder, and themselves no doubt better fitted to occupy positions of state.

When the periods expired for which the chiefs were banished in November, they returned to the capital one by one, devoting themselves to re-inspiring their former partisans, and to raising money for a new outbreak. With this Colonel Urriola and the larger part of his regiment were bought, he having received $15,000 to take the command, and his men proportionately liberal amounts. He was also assured, at the same time, that the Chacabuco regiment and from three to five thousand others would join him in the plaza; and consequently his troops were marched there in every confidence that it would prove a bloodless display. But it is doubted by those who best knew his character whether in success he would have placed his friends in the power they coveted. They rather believe he would have made himself Dictator without any ceremony whatever, although he had proclaimed for General Cruz. Reports were rife, too, that the colonel of another regiment received purchase-money, and then remained faithful to government—a course not ordinarily permitting one to retain position in the social circle; but as it did not so affect him, the rumor may not have been true. That the affair was lamentably conducted on both sides is quite apparent. The government claims (officially) to have been cognizant of the contemplated insurrection for several days in advance; and some of those assembled at Urriola's parlors on the preceding Saturday evening, when speaking of the coming Easter morning, sacrilegiously said, "There will be a resurrection to-morrow as important to Chile as was that of the Saviour." Thus both parties became criminally responsible for the sacrifice of human life—the ministry for not having arrested the leaders and put a stop to the revolt on the spot, and Urriola for not at once taking possession of the points which must have insured him a bloodless victory. Either might have triumphed without the loss of a man. *Neither* proved the conquerors; and consequently the country was left to feel the evil effects of a minority government with military and official strength to perpetuate men and measures, or men at least distasteful to the mass of Santiaguinos, who form a majority of the educated natives. Far better would it have been for the peace and stability of its domestic policy had one or other party obtained unmistakable ascendancy. Then Chile would have been spared the scenes detailed in PART I, Chapter XIII.

CHAPTER XII.

A BRIEF ACCOUNT OF OUR WORK.

ASTRONOMY.—MAGNETISM AND METEOROLOGY.—EARTHQUAKES.—ORIGIN OF THE NATIONAL OBSERVATORY IN CHILE.—CONCLUSION OF OUR OBSERVATIONS.—TAKE LEAVE OF THE GOVERNMENT.—EXPEDITION OF LIEUTENANT MAC-RAE.—RETURN HOME.—APOLOGETIC CONCLUSION.

During the summer and autumn months succeeding our arrival, there was almost uninterrupted fine weather. From the 10th of December, when the equatorial was ready for use, night followed night unrivalled in serenity; and to the close of the first series of observations on the planet Mars—January 31—there were but four unsuited to work. Labor so continuous in a climate as dry almost as an oven, told severely on unacclimated constitutions; and it was soon perceived that the principal assistant must be temporarily released, or be broken down, perhaps permanently. The opportunity to send him to Valparaiso for the meridian circle was, therefore, a welcome one; and Messrs. Hunter and Smith recorded for me on alternate nights, until the former was disabled by being thrown from a horse. All the aid then was from Mr. Smith; besides which duty, he became wholly charged with the meteorological observations for every third hour between 6 A. M. and midnight. Within the forty-eight working nights embraced between the above dates, nearly 1,400 observations of the planet were accumulated; and by the time that this series terminated, the piers for the meridian circle were finally completed, the health of Lieutenant MacRae re-established, and we were able to give undivided attention to its erection and adjustment; so that the instrument was ready for use about the middle of February.

But it must not be inferred that our nights from the 31st of January were passed idly. Observations for approximate place of the circle had commenced some days before, and extra hours of every night were spent in becoming familiar with the details of the superb instrument that Messrs. Pistor & Martins had sent us from Berlin; and thus, by the time its adjustments were perfected, both of us were expert in its manipulation. Beginning within 5° of the south pole, a systematic sweep of the heavens was then commenced in zones or belts 24′ wide. Working steadily towards the zenith on successive nights until compelled to return below again to connect in Right Ascension, the place of every celestial body that passed across the field of the telescope, to stars of the tenth magnitude, was carefully noted down. The space immediately surrounding the south pole was swept in one belt of 5° by moving the circle, and each zone overlaps those adjoining both in Right Ascension and Declination. Above the polar belt there are forty-eight others—making in all 24° 12′ of Declination; within which we obtained 33,600 observations of some 23,000 stars, more than 20,000 of them never previously tabulated. In these determinations, and others for instrumental errors, longitude, &c., until the arrival of Mr. S. L. Phelps, in September, 1850, to replace Passed Midshipman Hunter, who never became available, Lieutenant MacRae and myself alternately passed from six to seven hours of every night. From October, 1850, Messrs. MacRae and Phelps had the entire charge of the instrument for zone observations. When an accident to one of its screws compelled the services of both at the same time, until a new one was received from Berlin, I devoted every other night to the examination of stars in the catalogue of Lacaille, and between the zenith and our upper zone, which had never been re-observed. These, together with observations of the moon, planets, stars selected from the Nautical Almanac, &c., number about 9,000 measures. As may be supposed, the discrepancies between our estimations of the magnitudes of stars and those of preceding observers were very considerable in a multitude of cases; but we endeavored to preserve a uniform system, and will reconcile discordances if we can. There were many errors in Lacaille's work, at the Cape of Good Hope, and quite a number of his stars certainly do not exist in the reduced places of the British Association publication; but we were only amazed that he should have been able to accomplish so much and so well with a telescope only half an inch in diameter, and in the brief space of ten months.

It was a great satisfaction to work with an instrument like ours, but there was almost too much of it. Out of 132 consecutive nights after the equatorial was mounted, there were only seven cloudy ones! Of necessity, to afford so large a proportion, the air must be exceedingly destitute of moisture—a condition of things favorable to telescopic vision, but not so to eyes employed during prolonged observations. To persons accustomed, as we had been, to heat and moisture combined, the change proved, as has been intimated, exceedingly trying; but with such instruments, and under such a sky, who that possessed the least particle of astronomical enthusiasm would not have battled against the approach of human infirmities, though hard to bear except when surrounded by friends eager to serve and soothe.

"Out of sight, out of mind," runs the proverb. We were on the farther extremity of the continent, and so distant that the words of my earnest appeals for help grew cold before they reached home; unmistakably convincing me before the close of the first autumn that one of the objects of the expedition could only be partially accomplished. I had hoped the day was not distant when astronomers would say, the American navy has mapped the whole heavens. The Observatory at Washington had commenced a catalogue intended to embrace all the stars that appear at a sufficient height above its horizon. With sufficient force we could easily have tabulated the remainder, and the noble work would have been a monument to the service for all time. But it was not to be. There is a limit to physical exertion under every clime, and we were not less human than our kind. I had only half the requisite number of assistants for an undertaking so laborious; and, fixing that limit at the utmost bound consonant with the preservation of health and vision, when my own time was occupied in observations of Mars or Venus, until the meridian circle was again in complete order, it was necessarily unused on alternate nights.

The first winter, with its frequent clouds, afforded great relief; though the extraordinary continuance of similarly unfavorable weather in the spring, summer, and autumn months became a trial of patience as great as had proved the almost eternal clear atmosphere. At the commencement of 1851—midsummer—we began to think that the bright evenings enjoyed in the preceding year were to have no counterpart; and as such a season had never occurred in the memory of man, it of course was a constant subject of remark among all classes. That we had been instrumental in such result, and had publicly prognosticated it, was as religiously believed as—their Bible, I was about to say; but they are not permitted to read "the good book," and I more appropriately substitute—their priests. Through the following and last summer we were again favored. Between the 15th of December and 15th of March I had observations of Mars on seventy-eight nights! and out of one hundred and fifty-two, between November 10th and April 10th, there were observations with the meridian circle also on one hundred and twenty nights! Thus we had the satisfaction to accumulate from a previously unexplored, or almost unexplored field, an amount of astronomical data which has probably never been equalled within a similar period of time.

Astronomy was one of the branches of science for whose advancement we collected materials; magnetism and meteorology two others. For both the latter we were also supplied with good instruments; those for meteorological investigations remaining constantly at our residence near the base of Santa Lucia, arranged in the most appropriate places to afford correct indications. Patiently and perseveringly did Mr. E. R. Smith record their fluctuations tri-hourly during nearly three years, devoting one day (the 21st) of each month to hourly observations. When illness incapacitated him on one occasion, the additional duty was distributed amongst us, each cheerfully assuming certain hours of the twenty-four, in order to preserve the continuity of the journal. The magnetical observations were less frequent, but much more laborious; occupying nearly four hours of two, and sometimes three persons, on the 1st, 11th, and *term-day** of each month, when all the elements necessary for determining the direction and total force of the earth's magnetism were carefully observed. Other observations for changes of the Declination—or Variation, as it is generally called—were made at brief intervals throughout the term-day and on the 1st of each month, during a pre-appointed hour, for the purpose of determining how nearly synchronous might be disturbances in the northern and southern hemispheres. Those of the northern hemisphere were conducted under the direction of the United States Coast Survey. As the iron bars protecting the windows of all houses in Chile made it necessary to leave our residence, when observing for absolute elements, we were kindly permitted to use a large garden in the neighborhood, where arbors and shade-trees afforded suitable protection from the sun.

There was yet one other subject for whose intelligent discussion it was hoped we might collect interesting materials, and for which a rude instrument had been brought to assist us; I mean that startling terrestrial phenomenon of whose coming no man knoweth—the earthquake. With friends this was talked of as one of the physical wonders of Chile; one that invested it with rare interest for the geologist—with constantly recurring terrors for the inhabitants. Nor was our curiosity to experience a shock long ungratified, for within a week there was a tremor that hurried the population to the streets. But we were novices, and moved not. To us it was merely a spasmodic thrill, followed by a subterranean rumble whose moral influence lasted but the moment. The seismometer, erected forthwith, soon had its powers tried; but it could not be rendered sufficiently sensitive, and made no record of the slight agitations which the earth's crust almost daily underwent. This only increased our longing for information, and we earnestly desired repetitions, straining every sense at each to gather facts that might become available. Nor was it until the convulsion of December 6, 1850, that we could comprehend the constant dread shown of the power beneath us, the alarm which each tremor flashed through the population. When that of April 2d took place, and the earth, rocking to its very centre, stifled all human sounds with its groans of agony, we were thoroughly converted to the custom of the country—to flee at every coming murmur; and though thirsting for knowledge still, we no longer cared to acquire it under circumstances so shocking. What it was possible for the mind to grasp in moments so trying and brief, has been detailed in Chapter IV, Part I, and in Appendix A, where the reader may find facts of interest. All the other observations mentioned are in process of reduction, and will be published in the several volumes as rapidly as practicable.

We had scarcely organized work systematically before it was intimated to me, from the University, that the government would probably establish a national observatory at our departure, and to this end was desirous to have one of the professors of mathematics, and two of the most advanced and promising students of the National Institute, acquire a practical knowledge of instruments. The utility of such an establishment, and the honor it would reflect on the country, had been urged by the Chilean ambassador at Washington prior to our departure from the United States; and it was a source of no little gratification to me to witness the incipient step promptly taken towards the realization of an object so noble. Of course assurance was immediately given that no effort of mine or my companions, nor any facilities we could afford, should be wanting for the accomplishment of any object the government might have in view. When officially notified by the Minister for Foreign Affairs that three gentlemen had been designated whom his government desired to place under my instruction, occasion was taken to express to him how greatly gratified astronomers of the northern hemisphere would be at this evidence of Chilean advance to the rank of enlightened and liberal nations. Very shortly afterwards the students were presented by the rector of the University; books, from which to obtain

* A pre-selected day, on which all magnetical observers note the changes of the elements at brief intervals. These days commence at 10 P. M., mean time Göttingen, on the Fridays preceding the last Saturdays of February, May, August, and November, and on the Wednesdays nearest the 21st of each of the other months.

theoretical knowledge of the structure and use of instruments, were placed in their hands; and a month or two later I loaned them a five-feet equatorial, for whose accommodation they erected a small building in the castle-yard. The health of one of them proved delicate, and as he could rarely avail himself of the opportunities offered, he resigned; the others prosecuted their studies until the close of our stay, rendering us assistance on the magnetical term-days whenever it was asked.

Throughout nearly the three years of our residence at Santiago, the government evinced the most earnest disposition to forward the objects of the Expedition, and to extend every possible consideration to its members officially and personally. To its liberal and enlightened policy on all questions of science, literature, or art, the world is indebted for more than one valuable contribution. Its schools of arts, music, painting, and botany, the elaborate work on its natural and political history, and its geological and topographical survey, are all evidences of its generous patronage. The culminating step was yet to be taken; and there was a time when we had looked forward to this—the establishment of a national observatory—at our departure, with something approaching to certainty. Indeed, within the first year the subject was frankly discussed by more than one member of the Cabinet. But the last year had been disastrous. Domestic troubles had swallowed very nearly if not quite all the surplus accumulated in the treasury through years of tranquillity; commerce, from this and other causes, had somewhat declined; clipper-ships, with their thousands of passengers for California, dashed by the ports, no longer leaving their treasure in payment for refreshments; the mines had materially fallen off in their product: added to this, the government had not only just before assumed the lion's share of a gigantic undertaking—the railroad from Santiago to Valparaiso—but had also commenced erecting extensive bonded warehouses in the latter city; payments towards which demanded a retrenchment rather than an increase of its expenses. Comparatively small as would be the outlay, under such circumstances hope expired. No little gratifying, then, was the intelligence that the project had not been abandoned, but that Chile was still resolved to prove her interest in the noblest of all sciences, and to found on the southern half of this continent the first institution to promote it.

Learning that my observations would cease about the middle of September, Prof. Domeyko—then Rector of the National Institute—was authorized to say that the government would be glad to purchase our observatories as they stood, and we arranged the unofficial preliminaries by conference. Dr. Charles Moesta, a graduate of the University of Marburg, was forthwith appointed Director, and was placed in communication with me, so that he could become familiar with his instruments by the time we were ready to surrender them; and when this took place, on the 15th of September, everything was transferred at the cost paid to the artists, without the subsequent charges for freight, the massive piers, &c., &c.

Our work in Chile was done. The manuscript volumes of observations had been packed in two cases—one copy to be sent round Cape Horn, the other to be retained with me; the assistants had been ordered home; our household had been broken up, and there remained only to take formal leave of the government. Our equipment and every subsequent object for public or personal use had been admitted free of duty, a site had been prepared for our observatories, a guard had been stationed there to protect them, every necessity had been promptly supplied when sought, in short we had been the recipients of its courtesy and co-operation from the moment of arrival at the capital; and it was especially grateful to me to fulfil the instructions from the honorable Secretary of the Navy, expressing the acknowledgments and satisfaction of the United States government for the facilities afforded us, and to assure the Minister for Foreign Affairs that our country would consider itself favored when permitted to reciprocate these acts of good will. I notified him, at the same time, that Lieut. MacRae had been instructed to make a series of magnetical observations and other scientific investigations ascending and descending the Andes and across the pampas of Buenos Ayres, and asked for him such a passport to the frontier as would prevent obstruction in his mission. The reply was as follows:

"I have had the honor to receive, and have placed before his Excellency the President, your letter of the 8th instant, advising me that the series of observations in the southern hemisphere with which you had been charged by the government of the United States will terminate in Chile on the 14th instant, and that you propose to embark from Valparaiso with two of the assistants of the astronomical expedition immediately afterwards.

"The sentiments expressed by you on this occasion, in the name of the honorable Secretary of the Navy and government of the United States, have afforded much satisfaction to the President. The assistance which this government has rendered the Expedition has been superabundantly compensated by the benefits which your residence in Chile has conferred on the cultivation of science here; and if, as is hoped, the newly created astronomical establishment prospers—an object to which this government will devote special attention—it will be for yourself and for the United States an honorable monument, serving as a new bond of friendship between the two countries.

"I shall take great pleasure in furnishing Lieut. MacRae with a passport that will insure him due attention from the Chilean authorities in his transit to the Argentine territory, and will also prepare for him a letter of introduction to the governor of Mendoza, promising myself that the former gentleman will have the goodness to notify me of the epoch of his intended departure.

"The President hopes that you may arrive in all happiness at your home, and that from there you will favor him with communications, especially such as relate to the promotion of science in this country, where you leave such grateful remembrances. Uniting my personal wishes with those of his Excellency, I have the honor to subscribe myself, with sentiments of cordial esteem," &c.

I must add, these were not mere words of compliment to the parting guests; for through the University I have twice since availed myself of the invitation from his Excellency—once to recommend for the Observatorio Nacional the purchase of a new clock fitted with an electro-magnetic register; and subsequently, that an astronomical expedition be sent to Peru to observe the total solar eclipse of November 30, 1853: both of which measures were immediately considered and successfully carried into effect.

The expedition of Lieut. MacRae had long been a subject of thought. To determine whether magnetic intensity sensibly varies with distance from the centre of the earth; the measurement of zenith distances exceeding 90°, to assist Baron Lindenau in his investigations of atmospheric refraction; the geography and meteorology of the Andes and Pampas,—these were all most interesting questions, for the attempted solution of which there was but one obstacle opposing him—want of funds. Of the small sum granted by Congress there remained $4,160 when I left the United States, out of which all expenses were to be paid; and this, too, in a country where the wages of ordinary mechanics are more than double those of artisans in the United States. Although it was strictly enjoined that the department would in no event sanction an expenditure beyond the amount appropriated by Congress, notwithstanding the most rigid economy every dollar of it was gone before the observations terminated, and, of necessity, current expenses were defrayed from my own slender means. With the purchase of the observatory all difficulty disappeared, and Lieut. MacRae was left in Santiago with the necessary instruments, to prosecute his laborious journey as soon as the snow should be sufficiently melted from the passes of the Andes. The results of his travels are given in Vol. II. Our last observations in Chile—he being in Santiago, and I at Valparaiso—were to determine the difference of longitude between the two cities by means of the magneto-electric telegraph, for which purpose the directors had very kindly placed the line at my disposal. This executed, we took leave of the considerate friends of our foreign home. Mr. Phelps and myself embarked October 1st on board of the steamer Bolivia, for Panama, and reached New York without special incident, just three years and a quarter after I had left home.

A word more, and I have done. Many things may have been told in the preceding pages apparently ungracious from one who acknowledges so many attentions, so many acts of courtesy, and such valuable assistance; but I claim justification and pardon. These very acts would have inspired lasting regard for the people even had not nature invested their country with elements to create the strongest interest in its and their welfare. And first, it is more than difficult for a foreigner to comprehend fully or to appreciate properly the customs and motives for thought and action of the nation in whose midst he tarries. He brings the standards of his own land by which to measure them; and though long residence may somewhat soften the home character of his criticism, the impressions of childhood will not be effaced, but, like magic ink, will appear plainly whenever subjected to certain ordeals. Constant occupations prevented much of the intercourse that would have imparted some of these softening influences; and it may be that I continue scarcely more competent to truly estimate Chile and Chilenos than in 1849. Faithfully, however, has the motto been kept before me, "Nothing extenuate, nor aught set down in malice." More than this: next to my own, there is neither land nor people for whose prosperity and happiness I feel such earnest desire—none whose advancement I would make such efforts to promote. Will these sentiments give me a right to indicate faults; not as a censor regardless of the pain he inflicts, but as the friend who details errors that they may be the better corrected—the admirer who desires to perfect the object of his esteem? On these grounds I ask the indulgence of friends in Chile, praying they will ever believe me grateful for their untiring kindness and hospitality.

APPENDIX A.

OBSERVATIONS

OF

EARTHQUAKES AT SANTIAGO AND LA SERENA,

FROM NOVEMBER, 1849, TILL SEPTEMBER 13, 1852;

ACCOUNTS

OF THE

EARTHQUAKES IN APRIL AND MAY, 1851.

TRANSLATED FROM THE CHILE NEWSPAPERS.

The tabular observations are given in mean time at Santiago. The *mean* height of the barometer and thermometer is that of the observation hour in that month nearest to the hour at which the shock took place. The barometric observations are not corrected for temperature.

EARTHQUAKES IN CHILE.

Earthquakes at Santiago.

Year, month and day.	Hour.	State of sky.	Barometer at shock.	Mean barometer.	Thermom. at shock.	Mean temperature.	Direction of wave.	Remarks.
1849.	*h. m. s.*		*Inches.*	*Inches.*	°	°		
Nov. 2	5¼	Clear . .	28.000	28.147		61.9		Prof. Domeyko's observations.
18	6 16 —		.170	.148	68.0	61.9		Severe; felt at Coquimbo and Valparaiso. See details, p. 104.
24	21 19		.134	.172	73.2	67.9	S.W. to N.E. . .	Two undulatory shocks, with an interval of 5s., accompanied by noise.
Dec. 22	16 02 35		.126	.150	74.4	77.4	W.S.W. to E.N.E.	Two shocks, accompanied by noise; the second most violent.
26	1 09 —		.002	.140	69.5	67.8		Accompanied by the usual rumbling noise.
1850.								
Jan. 20	22 48 —		.058	.100	66.0	72.5	S.W. to N.E. . .	Two shocks, accompanied by noise; the second sharpest.
Feb. 10	15 30 —	K. 5 . . .	.152	.104	81.0	79.0		Very slight.
18	1 22 08	Clouds . .	.180	.118	68.0	69.2	Westward . . .	Noise preceded; duration of tremor 20s.; clouded afterwards.
19	7 25 —	K. 5 . . .	.219	.124	64.0	65.8		Without noise; short and not severe.
June 18	12 24 34	Clouds . .	.140	.188	54 5	52.9	Eastward . . .	Short and violent; noise accompanied, but did not precede.
27	22 55 50	do . .	.246	.204	45.0	45.5		Short and quick vibration; noise followed 1s. after.
July 22	2 23 30	Clear . .	.360	.166	34.0	43.7		*Three* shocks within 30s., but no noise.
23	23 46 17	K. 3 . . .	.103	.176	39.0	44 9		Slight; no noise.
23	23 46 32	do . . .	.103	.176	39.0	44.9		More severe; duration 10s., with noise.
26	12 53 40	Clear . .	.315	.174	52.0	50.2	S.W.	Two shocks, of which the second was most severe; noise accompanied.
Aug. 1	20 35 —	Clouds . .	.068	.220	50.8	50.8	S. to N.	Slight; clouded immediately after.
25	14 13 —	Clear . .	.180	.186	64.5	60.5	S.E. to N.W. . .	Slight.
Sept. 26	0 25 45	Clouds . .	.190	.186	48.8	49.7		Tremor for 2s.
30	2 — —							Quite a sharp shock.
Oct. 7	11 11 54	Clouds . .	.120	.199	56.0	63.0		Light; continued 2s.
Dec. 6	6 40 03	do . .	.133	.152	56.0	60.3		With noise and premonitory shock. See details, page 105.
6	8 08 33	do . .	.134	.158	68.0	68.3		Do do do.
19	17 07 15	do . .	.162	.138	69.3	73.1		Slight.
20	3 — —	do . .						Do.
20	6 30 —	do . .	.232	.151	72.0	60.3		Do.
26	5 — —	do . .	.096	.151	65.0	60.3		Do.
29	20 10 30	K. 5 . . .	.146	.158	64.2	64.6		Quite severe.
1851.								
Jan. 6	18 36 30	K. 4 . . .	.232	.126	74.0	76.1		Two slight shocks, without noise.
17	18 28 45	Clear . .	.076	.126	78.0	76.1		
19	18 06 —	do . .	.050	.126	75.8	76.1		Two slight shocks.
22	20 01 30	do . .	.040	.143	74.0	66.6		
28	19 30 —	do . .	.146	.134	73.0	71.8		Tremor, preceded by noise several seconds.
Feb. 5	14 59 —	K. 5 . . .	.233	.148	79.2	80.5		Quite a heavy shock.
Mar. 4	8 55 —	Clouds . .	.086	.152	55.8	63.9	N. to S.	Quite severe, with accompanying noise; rain followed.
24	0 14 —	Clear . .	.174	.140	55.6	59.5	N. to S.	Motion undulatory; noise audible 5s. before, and with shock.
24	6 — —	do . .						Light shock.
26	8 18 —	K. 5 . . .	.124	.152	64.8	63.9		Do.
April 2	6 48 10	Clouds . .	28.172	28.206		58.5	N. to S.	The great shock. See details, page 108.
2	7 06 12	do . .						Continued 2s.
2	7 06 52	do . .						Do 20s.
2	7 12 36	do . .						Do 2s.

Earthquakes at Santiago—Continued.

Year, month and day.	Hour.	State of sky.	Barometer at shock.	Mean barometer.	Thermom. at shock.	Mean temperature.	Direction of wave.	Remarks.
1851.	*h. m. s.*		*Inches.*	*Inches.*	°	°		
April 2	7 33 36	Clouds . .						Two distinct shocks as though sudden blows had been struck within the crust of the earth.
2	7 33 38	do . .						
2	8 06 —	do . .	28.190	28.185				Slight shock.
2	10 20 —	do . .						Do.
2	11 34 36	do . .	.204	.178				Moderate; continued 7*s*.
2	12 08 31	do . .			65.0	62.8		Moderate; continued only 1*s*.
2	12 08 34	do . .			65.0	62.8		Tremor during 5*s*.
2	15 06 00	do . .			69.8	65.7		Short and quick vibration, with noise.
2	16 24 —	do . .						Slight shock.
2	17 55 —	do . .						Do.
2	18 29 —	do . .	.214	.168	63.0	60.2		Do.
2	19 01 22	K. 7 . . .					Probably S.W. .	Quite severe; noise heard 15*s*. before to the northward and eastward; there was also a premonitory shock.
2	22 34 03	Clear . .						Slight tremor, with accompanying noise.
2	23 27 15	do . .			50.6	52.8		Slight and without noise.
3	0 00 05	do . .	.236	.174	50.5	52.8		Do do.
3	20 59 06	do . .	.124	.178	59.0	55.2		This was premonitory to the following and accompanied by noise.
3	20 59 12	do . .	.124	.178	59.0	55.2		Smart shock without noise.
3	21 18 —	do . .	.124	.178	58.6	55.2		The premonitory shock.
3	21 18 10	do . .	.126	.178	58.6	55.2		Quite sharp; vibration for 14*s*.
4	21 01 30	Clouds . .	.194	.178	60.8	55.2		A slight shock.
5								There were two or three during this day, but no times noted.
6	0 14 30	do . .	.204	.174	50.0	52.8		A warning shock; rain falling; no noise.
6	0 14 39	do . .	.204	.174	50.0	52.8		More severe, still no noise; continued 15*s*.
7	13 51 30	K. 3 . . .	.180	.170	64.0	65.7		This shock continued 2*s*. See details, page 115.
8	20 34 14	Clouds . .	.192	.178	56.0	55.2		A slight shock premonitory.
8	20 34 22	do . .	.192	.178	56.0	55.2		More severe; lasted 7*s*.; there were two or three others, whose times were not noted.
9	0 20 00	do . .	.182	.174	53.2	52.8		A smart shock, preceded by noise. See details, page 116.
9	20 10 —	do . .			54.5	55.2		A smart shock, preceded by noise; continued several secs.
10								There were several during the day, whose times were not noted.
13	15 41 40	Clear . .	.108	.166	68.0	65.7		This premonitory shock lasted 7*s*.
13	15 41 53	do . .	.108	.166	68.0	65.7		As usual: more severe, but continued only 5*s*. See details, page 116.
15	7 36 15	Fog . . .	.138	.168	51.6	52.0		A shock.
16	21 51 00	Clear . .	.206	.178	54.2	55.2		Slight tremor, with noise.
19	3 43 00	do . .	.250	.164	50.0	48.3		Two smart shocks at short intervals, but no noise.
25	15 28 —	Clouds . .	.130	.166	66.0	65.7	E. to W. . . .	Continued 30*s*., accompanied by noise. See details, page 116.
May 11	18 13 50	do . .	.270	.149	56.0	57.5		A slight shock, with noise lasting 10*s*.; two others late at night.
26	12 14 10	K. 5 . . .	.360	.155	54.4	62.0		Moderate shock, with much motion during 10*s*.
June 2	18 04 14	Clouds . .	27.990	.183	47.8	51.8		A long shock (30*s*.) preceded by noise; most violent at 18*h*. 4*m*. 30*s*.
20	19 31 15	do . .	28.236	.183	51.5	49.8		Quick tremor.
23	19 27 15	Clear . .	.326	.183	49.0	49.8		Momentary though sharp shock.
23	19 27 20	do . .	.326	.183	49.0	49.8		More moderate, with noise; it continued 5*s*.
27	12 51 50	do . .	.210	.186	59.0	56.1		Slight tremor, without noise.
27	15 39 45	do . .	.190	.172	60.4	57.7		Slight, with great noise; it lasted 10*s*.
30	20 14 08	Clouds . .	.238	.183	51.3	47.8		A long, slow tremor for 42*s*., with but little noise.
30	20 14 55	do . .	.238	.183	51.3	47.8		Continued only 8*s*.; there was little noise.
July 6	18 42 17	Rain . . .	27.958	.130	49.8	49.3		A slight shock, which lasted 3*s*.
Aug. 12	17 46 30	K. 6 . . .	28.158	.199	54.4	55.5		Slight.
29	1 30 —	Clear . .	.222	.197	52.0	48.4		Do.
29	6 — —	K. 3 . . .	.200	.186	46.6	45.8		Moderate for more than 10*s*.
Sept. 3	7 45 —	Clouds . .	.250	.199	47.5	50.4		Do do.
6	5 50 —	do . .	.104	.190	40.9	47.2		Slight.
7	13 22 —	do . .	.162	.178	68.0	61.8		Do.
7	13 28 —	do . .	.162	.178	68.0	61.8		Do. Rain fell soon after.
11	0 55 —	do . .	28.177	28.178	45.0	49.7		Do.

Earthquakes at Santiago—Continued.

Year, month and day.	Hour.	State of sky.	Barometer at shock.	Mean barometer.	Thermom. at shock.	Mean temperature.	Direction of wave.	Remarks.
1851.	*h. m. s.*		*Inches.*	*Inches*	°	°		
Sept. 11	17 00 55	Clear . .	28.206	28.177	58.0	57.8		Moderate shock.
19	20 18 —	Clouds . .	.152	.193	51.5	52.5		Do.
19	21 28 15	do . .	.140	.193	51.5	52.5		Do.
19	21 28 27	do . .	.140	.193	51.5	52.5		Do. It lasted 5*s*.
Oct. 26	19 16 —	Clear . .	.182	.190	58.0	61.2		Sharp, with much noise; clouded over within an hour.
Nov. 13	11 09 17	K. 3 . . .	.166	.138	67.0	71.9		Moderate shock.
15	1 19 35	Clear . .	.120	.136	55.5	56.1	N. to S.	Slight during 7*s*.; observed with telescope. See details, page 118.
28	15 21 37	do . .	.120	.118	76.0	73.9		Slight shock.
Dec. 10	13 53 45	Clouds . .	.150	.154	78.0	78.1		Short and quick shock.
11	0 07 00	do . .	.141	.164	57.8	58.3		Sharp and quick, without noise.
18	4 — —	Clear . .	.200	.160	58.0	58.9		Slight shock; clouded over soon afterward.
21	20 08 —	do . .	.240	.179	59.0	62.5		Two violent shocks, with loud noise; they lasted 30*s*.
1852.								
Jan. 11	0 29 50	do . .	.160	.151	60.0	59.6		A slight shock, with noise.
11	0 30 07	do . .	.160	.151	60.0	59.6		Do do.
28	16 24 10	do . .	.128	.148	85.0	80.3		Sudden and violent, but without noise.
31	18 09 08	do . .	.186	.142	77.6	74.4		There were two shocks; noise audible after the second.
Feb. 19	11 41 44	do . .	.134	.121	74.0	78.5	N.E. to S.W. . .	Very slight.
19	11 41 52	do . .	.134	.121	74.0	78.5		Do.
Mar. 5	15 — —	Clouds . .	.080	.143	79.8	79.8		Quick and violent; the noise preceded it nearly 10*s*.
April 7	16 34 45	Clear . .	.062	.128	78.2	63.1		Moderate shock.
23	11 37 53	Clouds . .	.090	.133	61.6	67.9		Moderate shock, 35 miles to south; there was loud noise during 20*s*., but no tremor.
May 6	23 46 30	Clear . .	.128	.155	47.0	47.2		A sudden and smart shock, with noise.
31	11 30 —	Clouds . .	.122	.160	48.6	59.7		Quite severe; felt at Valparaiso also.
June 10	11 42 15	Rain . . .	.132	.198	53.0	54.6		Two moderate shocks, without noise.
27	1 48 —	Fog . . .	.154	.200	42.5	44.7	N.W. to S.E. . .	Two long and heavy shocks, with great noise.
July 5	12 41 —	Clouds . .	.267	.190	45.8	52.3	N.N.W. to S.S.E.	Continuous tremors during 35*s*. See details, page 118.
12	0 40 —	Fog . . .	.176	.208	42 0	41.4	North'd to south'd.	Light, with much noise.
Aug. 6	0 10 20	Clear . .	.237	.221	38.2	45.0		Slight, wihout noise; motion during 15*s*.
12	11 58 32	Rain . . .	.325	.207	49.3	56.1	N.W. to S.E. . .	See details, page 118.
Sept. 10	16 38 —	Clear . .	.120	.198	63.2	55.2		Slight shock.
12	16 06 —	K. 3 . . .	28.100	28.198	56.7	59.0		Do.

Earthquakes at La Serena.

Year, month and day.	Hour.	State of sky.	Barometer at shock.	Mean barometer.	Thermom. at shock.	Mean temperature.	Direction of wave.	Remarks.
1849.								
Nov. 8	22 07	Clouds . .	30.016	30.103	60.8	62.6		Noise preceded briefly a slight shock.
12	5 07	do . .	.016	.114	62.8	66.4		Prolonged and frightful noise preceded slow tremor.
13	6 17	do . .	.020	.114	58.0	66.4		Noise and shock each during 22*s*.; former preceded.
14	17 42	do . .	.008	.099	63.0	70.5		Slow and sustained during 32*s*.
16	5 37	do . .	.040	.114	59.2	66.4		Short and distinct shock, preceded by noise.
18	6 12	do . .	.032	.114	59.4	66.4	N.E. to S.W. . .	Short, terrifying noise, followed by excessive motion. See details, page 104.
18	7 27	do . .	.034	.114	59.4	66.4		Short and slight shock.
18	11 12		.040	.114	65.2	66.4		Moderate and brief.
18	13 57		.039	.099	68.0	70.5		Similar to two preceding.
18	14 27		.028	.099	66·6	70.5		Same as the last.
18	14 37		.028	.099	66.6	70.5		Same as the last.
19	1 to 5		.035	.114	61.4	62.6		Five short tremors between these hours.
19	13½ to 18		.035	.099				Two similar to the last.
20	2 32	Clear . .	.040	.103	63.2	62.6		Severe shock, preceded by loud noise.
20	3 02		.040	.103				Do do do.
20	13 32		.048	.099				Neither violence nor duration specified.
20	22 02		.048	.103				Do do do.
21	16 32							A slight shock.
21	23 02		30.016	30.103	56.0	62.6		A slight shock, with much noise.

Earthquakes at La Serena—Continued.

Year, month and day.	Hour.	State of sky.	Barometer at shock.	Mean barometer.	Thermom. at shock.	Mean temperature.	Direction of wave.	Remarks.
1849.	*h. m.*		*Inches.*	*Inches.*	°	°		
Nov. 23	14 26		29.989	30.099	66.2	70.5		Quite violent.
23	23 32		.997	.103		62.6		Not so severe as the last.
26								There were five slight shocks between the 24th and 26th.
27	6 52		30.040	.114	66.2	66.4		A strong shock, preceded by noise.
28	7 32	Clouds . .	.035	.114	63.0	66.4		A slight shock, without noise.
28	18 02	Clear . .	.020	.099	66.8	70.5		Do. do.
30	18 17	do . .	.008	.099	68.0	70.5		Short.
Dec. 1	14 36	Light clouds	.020	.064	66.8	73.8		Strong shock, preceded by noise.
2	20 32	Clouds . .	.016	.060	58.6	64.6		Short.
4	6 17	do . .	.020	.087	60.8	68.0		Quick and short tremor.
5	13 47	Clear . .	.008	.064	70.4	73.8		Brief noise and shock.
6	3 02	do . .						Slight shock.
6	5 07	do . .	29.973	.089	60.8	68.0		Violent, with noise at same instant; continued 35*s*.
7	0 27	do . .	.981	.103	57.2	64.6		Quick and momentary.
12	23 17	do . .	.894	.103	59.2	64.6		Slight shock.
13	20 17	do . .	.917	.103	61.3	64.6		Do.
14	18 17	do . .	.949	.064	70.6	73.8		Short and slight.
16	15 47	do . .	.965	.064	72.2	73.8		Same as last.
—	12 22	do . .	.958	.064	72.0	73.8	E. to W. . . .	Do.
1850.								
Jan. 1	4 54	Clear . .	29.996	.087	64.0	70.6		Excessive noise, followed by slight shock.
2	18 17	Light clouds	.913	.064	72.5	74.6		Severe noise and shock.
3	8 02	Mist . .	.989	.087	63.8	70.6		Slight shock, without noise.
7	5 54	Clouds . .	30.000	.087	62.6	70.6		Three shocks at intervals of 20*s*.
7	23 52	Clear . .	.083	.060	60.8	66.2		Quick, momentary shock, with noise.
16	23 17	do . .	29.921	.060	65.5	66.2		Slight shock.
18	0 12	Clouds . .	.910	29.933	64.8	61.8		Slight shock, preceded by noise.
20	14 12	Clear . .	.902	.937	73.6	72.2		Slight shock.
27	17 32	do . .	.889	.937	71.0	72.2		Slight and slow, preceded by noise.
30	17 17	do . .	.952	.937	71.2	72.2		Slight, without noise.
31	12 57	do . .	.969	.960	73.6	66.8		Slow tremor, immediately preceded by noise.
Feb. 8	8 50	Clouds . .	.941	.985	66.4	68.4		Noise and rapid tremor simultaneous.
9	14 19	Clear .	.969	.977	73.8	72.2		Tremor and noise together; the latter most prolonged.
16	17 49	Light clouds	30.008	.977	76.0	72.2		Two shocks, with noise, all within 18*s*.
Mar. 2	19 02	Clear . .	29.969	.977	62.6	61.4		Slight, preceded by noise.
9	19 05	Clouds . .	.969	.977	61.2	61.4		Sharp and quick, without noise.
21	11 57	do . .	.968	.993	68.8	65.4		Excessive noise, followed by slow tremor.
22	16 57	Clear . .	.961	.977	69.4	70.4		Heavy, and sustained noise and shock.
29	23 47	Clouds . .	.969	.977	63.6	61.4		Prolonged noise, and shock after its conclusion.
April 17	1 49	do . .	.843	30.052	55.4	58.4		Tremor for 15*s*., without noise.
17	1 51	do . .	.843	.052	55.4	58.4		Lighter, but with great noise.
17	2 06	do . .	.843	.052	55.4	58.4		Great noise, but no shock.
18	9 40	do . .	.898	.068	60.6	60.4		Prolonged noise, followed by slight shock.
19	23 52	do . .	.980	.052	59.0	58.4		Great noise, followed by momentary shock.
22	19 47	Clear . .	.969	.052	56.4	58.4		Slight noise, followed by slow tremor.
25	6 42	Clouds . .	30.071	.068	60.4	60.4		Excessive noise for 22*s*., after smart shock.
May 8	3 17	do . .	.016	.072	56.6	54.6	N.W. to S.E. . .	Great noise for 5*s*.; strong shock before it ceased.
20	15 22	Light clouds	.031	.044	62.4	60.0		Quick vibration, preceded by noise.
23	23 57	Clouds . .	.016	.072	53.4	54.6		Frightful noise for 10*s*., with strong, quick shock before it ceased.
27	17 17	do . .	.008	.044	57.8	60.0		Slow shock during 35*s*., without noise.
June 1	22 52	Clear . .	.012	.083	50.2	51.2		Slow tremor, without noise.
4	6 17	do . .	.068	.095	48.2	51.4		Moderate shock for 65*s*., with noise; clouded 15*m*. after.
14	0 42	Light clouds	.024	.083	48.6	51.2		Frightful noise for 15*s*.; short shock 7*s*. after commencement.
21	2 07	Clear . .	29.996	.095	56.5	51.4		Quick and momentary shock, without noise.
21	2 17	do . .	.996	.095	56.5	51.4		Same as preceding.
July 5	20 47	Clouds . .	.910	.004	53.8	52.2		Slight noise, followed by short shock.
8	11 47	do . .	30.028	30.031	56.8	52.2		Great and sustained noise, followed by slow shock; cleared two hours after.

Earthquakes at La Serena—Continued.

Year, month and day.	Hour.	State of sky.	Barometer at shock.	Mean barometer.	Thermom. at shock.	Mean temperature.	Direction of wave.	Remarks.
1850.	*h. m.*		*Inches.*	*Inches.*	°	°		
July 15	11 42	Clear . .	30.016	30.031	64.2	52.2		Moderate noise, followed by slight shock.
Aug. 1	12 37	Clouds . .	29.952	.134	56.6	59.8		Great noise and motion at same time.
1	18 35		.933	.134	56.2	59.8		Noise greater in comparison than shock.
1	22 17		.933	.118	56.2	52.8		Do. do.
12	5 17	Clear . .	30.000	.118	49.6	54.6		Noise, with sharp, short shock; clouded an hour after.
29	23 —	Clouds . .	29.996	.118	58.0	52.8		Noise, with slight shock.
31	7 42	do . .	30.020	.118	58.2	54.6		Slight shock, without noise.
Sept. 15	4 47	Clear . .	.020	.079	49.8	57.8		Excessive noise and shock: former 45*s*.; latter 30*s*.: clouded 1*h*. 15*m*. after.
19	5 12	do . .	29.996	.079	52.0	57.8		Noise excessive for more than 1*m*., during which there were two slight shocks; clouded five hours after.
Oct. 2	23 08	do . .	30.020	.064	49.8	54.8		Noise first; shock 5*s*. after; the former continued 10*s*.
3	4 17	do . .	.031	.083	48.2	59.0		Noise preceded slight shock.
8	3 32	do . .	.114	.083	65.0	59.0		Slight shock, without noise.
8	12 42	Mist . .	.225	.060	50.4	63.8		Slow tremor during 95*s*.
14	23 17	Clear . .	.031	.064	53.2	54.8	S.E. to N.W. . .	Excessive momentaneous noise, followed by slight shock.
Nov. 19	7 47	Clouds . .	.028	.035	59.2	60.6	do . .	Noise, with quick, violent shock; another soon after.
19	17 32	Light clouds	29.969	.031	62.8	62.0	do . .	Same as the last.
22	7 17	Clouds . .	.965	.035	57.2	60.6	E. to W. . . .	Slight shock.
22	21 42	do . .	30.000	.028	57.8	63.2	S.E. to N.W. . .	Slight, and without noise.
Dec. 6	6 42	Clear . .	.016	.020	62.8	66.6	S. to N. . . .	Slight, without noise; a great shock at Santiago.
6	23 37	do . .	.008	.004	58.0	61.6	do . . .	Slight, with noise.
24	2 32	Clouds . .	29.985	.020	61.0	66.6	E. to W. . . .	Awful noise, apparently atmospheric; slight shock.
28	1 50	Clear . .	30.004	.020		66.6		Awful noise for 4*s*., followed by violent shock.
1851.								
Jan. 2	3 32	do . .	.012	.020	64.4	67.6	Vertical	Noise preceded heavy and quick shock.
6	23 02	do . .	.064	.004	60.8	63.0	S.E. to N. W. . .	Slight shock.
21	16 57	do . .	29.929	.000	71.6	73.2	Vertical	Frightful noise and rapid shock.
Feb. 4	7 02	Clouds . .	30.000	.040	70.4	71.0	E. to W. . . .	Strong tremor.
23	19 02	Clear . .	29.996	.024	64.6	66.2		Four shocks at intervals of 10*m*.; first three vertical; fourth from east.
M 14	7 02	Clouds . .	30.048	.064	62.8	66.6	E. to W. . . .	Slight shock.
18	23 02	Clear . .	.000	.040	58.4	61.8	S.W. to N.E. . .	Four light tremors, without noise, at intervals of 5*m*.; all from S.W.
								Observer absent during April and May.
June 4	20 23	Clouds . .	29.838	.060	61.4	54.2	Vertical	Slow concussions for 35*s*.
17	13 07	do . .	.992	.040	59.8	60.0	N.W. to S.E. . .	Great noise and motion together; continued 65*s*.
30	9 42	Clear . .	30.232	.091	57.4	55.2	Vertical . . .	Noise for 10*s*., then quick shock, and both lasted 10*s*. longer.
July 10	16 02	do . .	29.989	.024	56.6	58.4	N. to S. . . .	Two shocks at short intervals; only the last noted.
17	8 02	do . .	.921	.052	46.2	52.6	E. to W. . . .	Slight and without noise.
26	8 32	Rain . . .	.981	.052	58.2	52.6	do . . .	Great noise, followed by short severe shock.
Aug. 2	7 52	Clouds . .	.969	.095	57.0	57.6	do . . .	Slight.
Sept. 2	11 38	do . .	30.099	.098	59.2	58.0		Great noise, followed by short shock.
3	23 —	Clear . .	.118	.083	51.8	55.2	E. to W. . . .	Slight shock, preceded by noise.
10	3 02	do . .	29.996	.063	50.0	55.2	do . . .	Short shock, with much noise.
Oct. 10	17 32	do . .	30.040	.079	60.0	65.4		Slow tremor.
10	17 42	do . .	.040	.079	60.0	65.4	Vertical . . .	Severe, without noise during 10*s*.; clouded 1½ hours after.
20	17 02	do . .	.110	.079	64.4	65.4	S.W. to N.E. . .	Slight shock.
23	8 17	Clouds . .	.122	.130	60.0	59.4	E. to W. . . .	Sharp, quick, and noiseless; two atmospheric changes in an hour.
25	11 07	do . .	.142	.130	59.0	59.4	Vertical	Wholly vertical and noiseless for 45*s*.
								The observations of Nov. and Dec. are not yet published.
1852.								
Jan. 8	8 02	Clouds . .	.099	.083	61.3	63.2	E. to W. . . .	Noise in the air for 15*s*., with slight shock.
14	11 —	Clear . .	29.977	.083	68.4	63.2	do . . .	Slight, and preceded by noise.
16	7 —	Clouds . .	30.035	.083	60.4	63.2	do . . .	Loud, prolonged noise, followed by slight tremor during 20*s*.
17	14 —		29.996	.019	68.6	70.4		Longer noise than the last, but no shock.
18	12 12	do . .	30.031	.019	67.2	70.4	N.E. to S.W. . .	Slow tremor for 28*s*.
18	15 —	Light clouds	29.973	30.019	67.8	70.4	Vertical . . .	Two frightful noises closely following each other; the latter most sonorous; shock succeeded.

Earthquakes at La Serena—Continued.

Year, month and day.	Hour.	State of sky.	Barometer at shock.	Mean barometer.	Thermom. at shock.	Mean temperature.	Direction of wave.	Remarks.
1852.	*h. m.*		*Inches.*	*Inches.*	°	°		
Feb. 1	21 —	Clear . .	29.981	29.969	61.0	61.7	N.W. to S.E. . .	Two shocks, without noise.
16	17 32	do . .	.952	.969	70.8	71.6	E. to W. . . .	Slight shock, preceded by much noise.
23	20 27	do . .	.985	.969	62.4	61.7	N.W. to S.E. . .	Great noise, apparently atmospheric discharge; slight shock.
Mar. 1	16 32	Clear . .	.952	30.004	68.0	66.4	E. to W. . . .	Two shocks.
5	6 —	Clouds . .	.969	.052	62.8	61.7	Vertical . . .	Two noises at short intervals; shock with latter during 10s.
6	21 32	Clear . .	.913	.001	58.8	58.6		Noise, apparently overhead; short, slight shock.
9	21 07	do . .	.956	.001	58.6	58.6	E. to W. . . .	Two slight shocks; mist one hour after.
9	21 11	do . .	.956	.001	58.6	58.6	N.E. to S. W. . .	Same as the last.
12	6 17	Clouds . .	.996	.052	60.8	61.7	do . .	Same as the last.
12	10 22	Light clouds	.996	.052	66.6	61.7	Vertical . . .	Great noise; severe shock before its conclusion.
22	12 07	Clouds . .	30.068	.004	63.4	66.4	E. to W. . . .	Slight tremor, without noise.
30	21 —	do . .	29.941	.001	58.0	58.6	Vertical . . .	Two noises; a shock with the last.
April 2	12 07	Clear . .	.961	29.973	57.0	61.8	E. to W. . . .	Slight shock.

[From "El Progreso" of April 2.]

EARTHQUAKE OF APRIL 2, 1851.

At ten minutes before seven this morning there occurred the most severe and prolonged earthquake of which we have any memory. Houses oscillated as pendulums moved by a powerful machine, the earth throbbed (vibrada) as does the heart when overwhelmed by terror, and the dust which the violence of the shock threw up deprived the atmosphere of its transparency. The duration of the earthquake was twenty-three seconds, and it is believed that its movement was from the southwest.

Nearly all the *mojinetes* in the city (a sort of niches constructed during the colonial epoch principally for the family coats of arms), either fell to the ground, or have been very severely injured. The greater part of the arches of the church of La Compania have been sprung, for which reason the temple has been ordered to be closed. No doubt they were much weakened by the fire which occurred before the last repairs. The loss is important, as it was the best constructed of all the churches. The cathedral has scarcely suffered less, many of its arches also having been sprung, the stones settling at least two inches, and some of the pieces that fell being more than one third of a vara in length. The ornaments fell from over the door of (the church of) San Francisco, causing the death of one woman, and horribly wounding another, who is probably now dead. One of the arches of the brick bridge across the river also has settled. The palace of the tribunals of justice is considerably injured, there being a notable rent at the doorway. The old government palace is almost completely ruined. Two arches of the fine house building under the direction of Mr. De Baines for Señor Cousiño, though broken, will be easily repaired. Among private houses none appears to have suffered so much as that of Señor Aristea, the whole parapet which was not thrown down being completely ruined. Perhaps there is no house which has not suffered in its roof, partition walls, plastering, or outer walls. Yet we have escaped from the violence and duration of the shocks with less injury than might have been expected; and we trust that no greater injuries have been occasioned at Valparaiso and the South, for nearly every severe earthquake felt at Santiago has occasioned greater damages elsewhere. The strata of gravel on which the city is erected diminishes the risk of injuries by earthquakes.

Architects in our country should take into account the many shakings to which its buildings are inevitably to be subjected; and its architecture must necessarily be national, for it would be difficult to adopt known great systems without much risk. Without this we shall not advance by founding a school of architecture.

It would be well if the faculty of mathematics would offer premiums during five or six years for the best essays on this subject, for thus civilization enriches a country.

Three slight shocks have been felt since the great earthquake.

The streets were obstructed by the destroyed materials encountered in every direction; and the population are moving about, examining them, with a mixture of curiosity and fear visible on every face.

[From "El Progreso" of April 3.]

Yesterday we published such an account as could be gathered in the confusion of the first moments, and which will have given to our readers distant from Santiago a sufficiently distinct idea of the power of the earthquake and the injuries it caused. It would be grateful had we terminated an account of its effects, but new facts demand relation—a sorrowful duty which journalists fulfil in like cases.

The destruction was greater without the city, in the surrounding country; and beyond a doubt, by reason of their isolation, the country houses have doubly suffered. The superb mansions on the estate of Don J. M. Solar, at Colina, are almost completely destroyed. The same may be said of those belonging to Señores Tagle, Bruno Larrain, J. M. Bascuñan, the younger Izquierdos, the property of Apoquindo (belonging to the Dominican friars), and perhaps to many others whom we do not know. In cases like the present, one receives notice only of the misfortunes occurring to those with whom intercourse exists. It scarcely appears necessary to say that the enclosures of all these estates have suffered considerably, it having been impossible for them to resist after the houses had fallen.

At Renca, and about the lake of Pudaüel, a phenomenon occurred which is seen only during great commotions like that of yesterday: the earth opened, pouring out streams of water from rents in several places.

Earthquakes may be the effects of electricity, subterranean fires, and of gases (vapores) heated by these fires. These causes operate alone or combined, and have power in each locality according to the physical formation of the country.

Humboldt says, in Mexico it is observed that earthquakes are more frequent in rainy years, it thus appearing natural to believe that heated steam occasions the phenomenon there. In Chile, as the earthquakes usually occur when the stars are extraordinarily brilliant, it may be supposed that electricity engenders them. There is no part of the republic where the electric power is so great as in Copiapó, nor is there any place where earthquakes are so frequently repeated.

If we were permitted to venture an opinion upon a question comprehended by us very imperfectly, we should say that the circumstance of the earth having opened at two points, considerably distant from each other, would authorize us to presume that the earthquake of yesterday was produced by a combination of electricity with the subterranean fires. These questions, so interesting to science, will surely be illustrated by the superior capacity of the chief of the astronomical observatory, the modest and profound sabio, Mr. Gilliss.

Meanwhile we will pursue the painful task undertaken by us. Among the misfortunes occasioned, certainly the most affecting are those which bring tears among families for the loss of parent, child, or friend. To those announced yesterday fortunately we have little to add.

Señor Serrano, judge of the criminal court, had the misfortune to lose a lovely daughter by the falling of a tile; and it is stated that his wife also was very gravely injured. We grieve for his misfortune.

A young and beautiful lady, whom her mother had left shut up in the second story of a house, threw herself from the balcony, and was crushed. These are the only personal accidents of which notice has been given to us.

[From "El Progreso."]

EARTHQUAKE OF APRIL 2, 1851.

Since yesterday slight shocks have been felt from time to time, occasioning the greatest alarm. It is said that not less than eleven have occurred; but, as we have not felt so many, there is possibly an exaggeration of the number.

A passenger coming from Valparaiso assures us that Casa-blanca is almost entirely in ruins, the posada being the only house which has not suffered.

Among the public edifices, the churches have received the greatest damage; but, notwithstanding this, there was service in them all last night. At the cathedral and La Merced there were dangerous injuries, and it was really imprudent to have opened them until they had been examined. Souls may be saved whilst forwarding the objects of missions; but bodies may perish by the excessive zeal of ecclesiastical prelates.

[From "El Mercurio," of Valparaiso.]

GREAT EARTHQUAKE.

Another misfortune has afflicted the provinces of Santiago and Valparaiso during the present month. On the 2d instant, at 6*h*. 41*m*. A. M., the earth was violently shaken for the space of fifteen seconds, the terrible shock being prolonged with irregular oscillations through two minutes. Since the earthquake of 1822, in which Valparaiso was laid in ruins, none has occurred in any degree so frightful as this.

The houses were moved like ships upon a troubled sea; articles of furniture were thrown from their ordinary places; book-shelves fell to the ground; the papering of the walls was torn with loud reports; the plastering fell; some walls split and opened; some were inclined; others were laid in ruins; many tiles were thrown from the roofs; windows were smashed, the sashes broken and twisted; and families in consternation rushed to the streets, in the midst of the tremendous confusion and overthrow.

The direction of the movement, according to some, was from the north to the south, and according to others from southwest to northeast; which course appears to us the most probable, keeping in view the fact that the provinces to the north and south have not suffered any damage whatever, all the destruction being in those of Valparaiso and Santiago—from the sea to the cordillera.

Vessels felt the shocks distinctly at a distance of forty miles from the coast, experiencing a sensation on board similar to that of striking upon a reef of rocks. The lead which was thrown from the American frigate Raritan immediately buried itself three or four feet in the sand from the effects of the movement, and it was difficult to pull it out.

The air was heavy in the morning, but the thermometer denoted no change in the temperature of the atmosphere.

The shaking of the earth produced very different effects in the two wards into which the city of Valparaiso is divided. In that of the port, which is occupied by commercial establishments and offices, the houses have suffered nothing, no doubt because of the solid foundation upon which they are built; but in the Almendral, where the ground is a stratum of light sand, the greater part of the houses gave way. Nevertheless, we have seen no house there entirely razed; though parts of the walls were bulged out, and the roofs of many were displaced, a hundred remaining uninhabitable, and a great number in want of repairs, which were commenced at once, the neighborhood being urged to it by want of habitations.

All the churches, the barracks, of old and heavy construction, and the older edifices in general, suffered more or less. Brick and mortar walls and cornices split (*le trizaron*) in the shock, but buildings, bound together by numerous wooden braces and ties, remained uninjured.

Providence in this calamity has not failed to favor Valparaiso, for there was no one killed; even a child having been saved who had fallen from a hill amidst the ruins of the house in which he was asleep.

The trembling of the earth continued for several days, the shocks being repeated with great frequency during the first, and gradually diminishing during the last, until the oscillations completely ceased.

Many families—some because they were without houses, others intimidated by the frightful phenomena—took refuge in tents which they set up in the plaza and among the hills.

Among the effects of the earthquake, some peculiarly capricious were noted. The motion appeared to be in ramified veins with different directions: for this reason very ancient and ruinous houses were seen uninjured by the side of new ones in ruins. In the same house all the things of one room fell and were broken, while in the adjoining room nothing was moved. Iron grates were thrown out by the pressure in some houses, while the fragile glass of windows resisted it. Some articles of furniture were seen falling from the south towards the north, and others from east to west. In view of the effects, it would be difficult to account for action producing results so contradictory.

With respect to property, Santiago suffered less than Valparaiso; but it had the misfortune to enumerate three victims who had sheltered themselves beneath the arch of a church. The mint, in which are the government offices and residences, and other public edifices, suffered injuries, as also some of the private residences.

Various villages in the departments of the two provinces, as Quillota, Casa-blanca, Renca, and houses of some estates, shared in the ruin.

On the 4th rain fell unexpectedly, and completed the destruction of the furniture in houses the roofs of which the earthquake had opened or injured.

The loss in houses and furniture in the two provinces may be estimated at one million dollars; though there are not wanting persons who put it down at a larger sum, which we deem an exaggeration.

This loss has fallen entirely upon proprietors or families, and in no degree upon trade.

The pay of mechanics and the cost of building materials immediately rose on account of the haste all made to repair the injuries done to their houses.

The greatest activity in repairs and reconstruction succeeded the panic of the first moments; and within a month there will disappear from this city all the vestiges that now sadden the streets. Meanwhile, a conviction is forced upon the people of Valparaiso that well constructed houses upon solid foundations, and with stout wooden braces and ties, are able to resist the most violent convulsions of earthquakes.

[From the "Comercio de Valparaiso" of April 2.]

The custom-house clock still marks eighteen minutes to seven, a moment when the city was profoundly alarmed by one of the most severe earthquakes. The oldest residents of Valparaiso do not recollect to have felt one more violent or of greater duration since that which occurred in 1822. The motion of the earth continued nearly seventy seconds, and was succeeded by other less severe shocks at intervals of some minutes, the phenomenon continuing to threaten us during the whole day.

There have been many losses and some misfortunes of moment. In the Port, all the houses have suffered more or less: walls have opened; tiles have fallen from the roofs; some old and heavy roofs have fallen; and it is said that a few small houses in the ravines (quebradas) have been destroyed.

In the Anayan two houses supported on piles of wood fell to the earth, one of them covering a child five or six years old. Near to the Matriz, on the side of Cajilla, the roof of a room fell through; by accident its occupants were saved. In Meados street a wall fell in the interior of an edifice. The cross fell from La Matriz, killing a passing dog. Almost every house has suffered immensely in its tiles. The shops and corner stores have lost crockery, glass, bottles, and wine, and oil and liquors have flowed in an extraordinary manner. In the apothecary store of Señor Leighton, the acids and aquafortis took fire; and in others the alcoholic compositions smoked. The earth has opened in many places.

In the Almendral the injuries have been greater. It appears that earthquakes are felt with greater violence there, and by the damages they cause merit the name of earthshakes. All the houses and walls have been moved from their places; many roofs have been destroyed or the tiles thrown into the street. Families this morning found themselves in the street without homes, and without knowing where to seek new lodgings. It is calculated that five hundred persons are without habitations, or fear to return to their houses on account of the condition of the walls and roofs.

A commission of citizens have been instructed to examine the injury done, and to aid the most necessitous families. This zeal is highly meritorious, and the good work should not cease until every family is tranquilized.

It is thought that this frightful shock was felt throughout a large portion of the republic; and it is to be feared that the injuries will have been greater at Santiago because of the thickness of the walls and the antiquity of its houses. The new custom-house of this city is in imminent danger; its roofs appear sunk, and the parapet and pilasters have fallen into the street.

This earthquake will be beneficial to the future: old and ruinous houses will disappear, and in constructing others we shall see the necessity of not using materials so heavy and of such slight elasticity as are bricks and tiles. Experience has shown that the houses least liable to fall during earthquakes are the lightly built ones of the Port, composed of adobes and wood, with roofs of shingles. This earthquake, as did that of 1822, came from the south. It is said that on the near hills the earth has opened, and that new crevices have shown themselves in various places.

[From "El Comercio" of April 3.]

EARTHQUAKE OF APRIL 2, 1851.

The effects of the earthquake have been greater and more unfortunate than we at first believed. Almost all the houses of the Almendral need repairs or entire rebuilding. The sorrowful aspect of the ruins kept up the alarm all yesterday, to which the constant repetition of shocks until a very advanced hour of the night contributed no little. Many families took shelter on the surrounding hills. Others, it is said, went to the Playa; and on Hospital Hill there were about three hundred persons. In the plaza De la Victoria many tents were erected yesterday, and a small wooden house was put up at the last hours. Persons have taken refuge there who fear returning to their own houses, or who are without dwellings.

We were assured yesterday that two women perished under the ruins of the Casa de Ejercicios. During the evening there were many rumors circulating, originated by fear and superstition no doubt. Some feared an invasion of the sea, because it had been prophesied by a priest; and others believed another earthquake certain, because the barometer announced bad weather. Thus few had much desire to pass the night within the city.

Nothing has occurred; nor have we new misfortunes to deplore. There result only some discomforts to those who have adopted a sort of Bedouin life; but the effects of terror will soon have passed, and they will tire of sacrificing the conveniences of civilization for the apparent necessity of living in tents, or "*a la luna de Valencia.*"

The shocks still continue at long intervals, and it is probable that they will be felt for many consecutive days, as occurred in 1822 also.

The captain of a ship which anchored in the bay yesterday supposed that his vessel had touched on a rock until, on arrival here, he learned that a heavy earthquake had taken place.

Man, as every other animal, loses his presence of mind at the sight of this slow and silent renovation of nature; but, being endowed with reason, he may anticipate the peril, and explain the causes and natural effects of earthquakes. Terror was manifested yesterday among the animals of the city and bay. Some of the vessels in the port have many rats on board; and, as is well known, these animals have great instincts respecting the voyages, often taking to the water before a ship leaves port. When the earthquake was felt, they were seen running from their hiding-places, and the crews observed them in great fright about the decks.

The custom-house building has actually suffered nothing in itsef or apartments. The balustrade and cornice only were thrown down by the impulse of the earthquake. Its tower has been weakened somewhat, but remains upright, and, if strengthened a little, will be perfectly secure.

Among those who abandoned their lodgings last night on account of the repetition of the earthquakes, the foreigners figured most extensively, having taken refuge on board the ships in the harbor.

In Viña la Mar the earth opened and water gushed out. There were also some enormous rocks dislodged from the hills.

Earthquakes.—At 2 A. M.; 5*h.*; 8*h.* 30*m.*; 8*h.* 40*m.*; 8*h.* 55*m.*; 9*h.* 32*m.*; 9*h.* 37*m.*; and since the first night five others have been felt.

At Quillota the earthquake was not of the same alarming character, and, according to our information, passed as one of the many shocks occurring in the republic so frequently.

Information from trustworthy persons arrived yesterday advises us that the earthquake caused great damage in Casa-blanca. It is said that the English hotel is the only house standing, the other edifices forming a vast ruin. All the people have abandoned their dwellings, some being in dangerous condition, and the others completely destroyed. Letters from there say that tents and temporary shelters of branches have been formed until their houses can be made fit to use again.

The occasion has occurred, we think, when an appeal should be made to a beneficent public in favor of the families least provided for. The government, as well as individuals, is called on to remedy so great a calamity, and to lend a friendly hand to the sufferers.

A reliable person writing us from Santiago informs us that the earthquake began at 6*h.* 48*m.* 10*s.* A. M., and continued about a minute and a half. This calculation corroborates ours more or less, as we believed that it lasted nearly seventy seconds in Valparaiso. The difference of time between the two cities may serve as data for verifying the direction which it took, and the great extent of territory in the republic traversed by it. The little settlement of Renca has been ruined by the earthquake, a misfortune the more deplorable as the greater part of its inhabitants are poor. The houses on the estate of Don Diego Barros have also been left leaning. May we have no more misfortunes to relate.

In the "Barra" we find the following incidents: Among the notable results we place the varied expressions presented in the faces of the citizens who, without having accordance with each other, think only of flight. If the houses had fallen, we should have been in the primitive condition of society—living as did Adam and Eve in Paradise. The number of those wounded was great: broken legs, cracked heads, &c. In the house of Señor Serrano there are no less than four. One was killed in the plaza by the fall of mouldings from the edifices. At the residence of Señor Chacon, in the Calle San Diego, a poor man who had gone to ask alms was killed by the fall of a tile. In the cathedral a heavy tie-beam fell, the stone of which the edifice is built is much splintered, and that composing the arches settled. Two arches of the portal have been broken, and the eastern parapet thrown to the ground. The house opposite has had its roof settled and walls broken.

[From "El Mercurio."]

A LETTER FROM THE EDITOR.

SANTIAGO, *April* 2, 1851.

To-day there has been felt the most severe and prolonged earthquake experienced since that of 1822. This phenomenon, which is the most terrible of nature, and which most depresses the spirit by its mysterious magnitude, has left the population tremulous and excited, and the air still appears filled with the murmur of a stroke as occurs with a cord that is violently vibrated, and that prolongs its sound in proportion to the tension.

The first shock, which was oscillatory, was felt at 6*h.* 48*m.* 10*s.* A. M. mean time at Santiago, as given by the Astronomical Observatory at Santa Lucia, which has for the base of its calculations a time-keeper regulated to the meridian of Greenwich. The greatest strength was felt from 6*h.* 48*m.* 28*s.* to 6*h.* 48*m.* 53*s.*, and it terminated at 6*h.* 49*m.* 38*s.* Thus it was prolonged nearly a minute and a half.

The great shock, which took place at 6*h.* 48*m.* 28*s.*, startled every one in terror from the beds in which they slumbered tranquilly, but without any accident occurring. Others more matutinal, who had roused themselves with the dawn, and were at the time making their orisons to God at church, were victims to their devotion—sealing their martyrdom with blood. At the church of San Francisco, injured severely by the last earthquake, the fatality occurred. The faithful who at that moment found themselves imploring the mercy of God, flew from its altars before his anger, endeavoring to escape from one of its side doors. At the instant that the motion of the earth had attained its maximum violence, a moulding broken from the arch over the doorway fell upon the heads of three women who were passing the lintel; one was killed on the spot, and the others gravely wounded.

Up to the moment of the mail leaving, no other misfortunes of a personal nature have been heard of.

All the houses of Santiago were sensibly moved, even to their very foundations; the tiles have been started, and there is no street in which fragments are not seen, thrown down by the pulsations of the invisible power agitating the bowels of the earth. In the cathedral one of the great beams crossing the roof has fallen from its place. At the old University and in the Palace of Justice many arches have opened. At the Academy of Painting there may be seen the fragments of a large part of the plaster models recently brought from France. The busts have particularly suffered; and it is a painful spectacle to see the fragments of Diana's head upon the floor; the hair of Cleopatra filled with the dust of crushed models, and by her side the beautiful bust of Antinous, which, in its destruction, appears the frozen fragment of a corpse. A large part of the parapets of the portal have come to the ground, and from the walls of the cathedral many stones have been started.

Every moment news reaches us from the country that the destruction has been great. At the south it was felt with more force, and, judging from the injury to isolated buildings, it is much feared that entire populations have been thrown out of doors. The church of Curacavi is down, and all the hills have rolled down immense stones.

Since the great shock, the earth has been trembling at intervals; and as if fatigued by its effort, it continues to move the surface in its tempestuous exhausted respirations. In less than six hours, besides the principal one, there have been no less than ten successive earthquakes.

The first after the great disturbance of which I have given you an account took place at 7*h.* 6*m.* 12*s.*; this was slight, and lasted just two seconds. At 7*h.* 6*m.* 52*s.* there was another, which also continued two seconds. The third was at 7*h.* 12*m.* 36*s.*, continuing about the same time. To these two succeeded two other shocks that appeared the result of a force issuing from the centre of the earth like two blows given by the arm of a giant to open a path to the outer world. These occurred at 7*h.* 33*m.* 36*s.* and 7*h.* 33*m.* 38*s.*; that is, there was an interval of two seconds between them. At 8*h.* 6*m.* and 10*h.* 20*m.* there were other light shocks. At 11*h.* 34*m.* 36*s.* another was felt, which continued for seven seconds. This renewed the alarm among the people, and the churches at that time filled were depopulated in an instant. There are periods when one seeks refuge at the foot of the altar; and others, as on the present occasion, in which one flies from it as though the Divinity exhibited his anger at the tabernacle erected in which to render him the tribute of worship.

At 12*h.* 8*m.* 31*s.* the last shock was felt; it continued for the space of nine seconds. Since then the earth appears as though slumbering, and may God so preserve it for a long while!

There are contradictory opinions respecting the direction of the movement. Some think it came from the north, others that it was from the south; but it is positive that the line traversed was north, a quarter east; that is to say, in the direction from Copiapó to Concepcion, or vice versa.

APRIL 4.—The shocks continue with some violence. Last night there were two quite alarming ones, and within a short interval of each other. The first was felt at nine o'clock precisely, and the second eighteen minutes afterwards. Both were quite similar, lasting about ten seconds, and the oscillation of the earth was in three distinct successive movements. Other slight oscillations of short duration occurred afterwards at brief intervals. The remainder of the night was also marked by successive shocks.

[From the Santiago Correspondent, dated April 3, 1851.]

The post from Valparaiso was expected with anxiety to learn the effects produced in your city, where it was feared the injuries had been greater than here. Finally it arrived, and the office was surrounded by more than a hundred persons. The first newspapers received from the mail carriage were devoured, and all the details communicated by the "Comercio" and "Mercurio" were in a few moments the subjects of conversations. To this was added the information contained in two hundred and thirty private letters brought by the post—an extraordinary number of letters, contributing no little to augment the excitement.

Though of less duration, the earthquake appears to have been stronger at Valparaiso than at Santiago; at least it was so if one may judge from the newspaper accounts.

Here, people are somewhat calmed; and although light quiverings are felt from time to time, we know that they are the last convulsions of the earthquake. Every one is now occupied in repairing damages, which are not a few; for there is not an edifice in Santiago which has not suffered either in its walls or roof. The latter appear as though the plough had passed over them, and there is no parapet wall, no matter how solid it may have been, that has not been very severely disturbed. Besides the old and ruinous houses which the earthquakes have left standing in equilibrium, there are now more than one hundred and twenty new brick houses in progress, as if the proprietors were insured against earthquakes. * * * * *

By the news which arrived from various points in the country it seems that the shock has caused greater damages there than in the city. There is no house which was not left in a ruinous condition or thrown wholly to the ground, even those of the poor constructed of the lightest materials. This is contrary to the opinion of those who believe that flexible materials are the most suitable for resisting earthquakes.

In Santiago the only houses which have withstood all the great shocks since the past century are those built of brick and mortar and supported by arches. Although the mint has suffered much this time, it is not strange, for the repairs recently made to the edifice have contributed to take from its solidity, and it is in the mended portion that the injuries have been the greatest. It is not in Chile alone that the earth trembles; few are the parts of the earth where the phenomenon is not known ; and it was not because of earthquakes that a flexible style of architecture was adopted, for it is a well known fact that the more solid a house is, the greater is its resistance to them. A proof of it is at Arequipa, where there are constant shocks, and there all the houses are of heavy materials.

The devil himself would scarcely have proposed houses of adobes, as some have done, recommending them for their flexibility, as if flexibility were not the cause of ruin to the roofs, which are broken with the slightest shock, whilst they would remain intact on solidly built walls.

[From the "Comercio" of April 5, 1851.]

Alarm still continues, as is very natural. Yesterday there were slight shocks, which were repeated with greater force at two o'clock this morning. Last night a mist began about half-past eleven ; at one it was converted into a storm, and rain fell copiously, accompanied with thunder and lightning. This morning it began to rain again, and still continues.

Families who took refuge on the adjacent hills must have suffered considerably from the storm. They were not prepared for the new event, and will have confided too much in the benignity of the climate or the regularity of the rainy season, thus anticipated, perhaps, by effect of the earthquake. The plaza Victoria was yesterday filled with tents containing a multitude of people. Some had been fitted with furniture and carpets, increasing the inconveniences when it became necessary to seek other shelter from the wind and rain. There was one tent that sheltered thirty persons, who immediately sought refuge in the theatre and the neighboring houses.

Besides these misfortunes the roofs of many houses in the Port allow entrance to the water, and most of the warehouses have experienced great injury by wetting of the goods they contain. The same has occurred at the custom-house. Stored goods have been exposed to water dripping from the roofs injured by the earthquakes.

* * * * * * * * *

See also some papers for an account of earthquakes in the eighteenth and nineteenth centuries.

[From "El Faro del Maule," Talca, of April 2.]

At three quarters past six this morning we experienced a strong and prolonged earthquake. A few walls were cracked, but no building was thrown down by the shock.

[From "El Talquino," Talca.]

On the second instant, at twenty-five minutes past six in the morning, we experienced a severe movement of the earth, whose duration was not less than forty seconds. There are no misfortunes to deplore in town; but, in our opinion, there has been destruction elsewhere. The character of the motion, increasing as it did gradually, without being preceded by noise, and the continuous agitation in which we have been kept for two days by many slight shocks, remind us of the earthquake of 1835, so fatal in our southern provinces.

We learn that in the Parral it was of little importance; and if we could say as much of the North, it would only be an inconsequent fright we have had; but perhaps Santiago and Valparaiso are suffering actually from the effects of these disturbances, which have so often been disastrous elsewhere in our country.

The Coquimbo and Copiapó papers make no mention of it whatever, so that it could scarcely have been felt in those cities.

[From "El Araucano," Santiago.]

CASA BLANCA, *April* 2, 1851.

SEÑOR INTENDENTE: At about 7 o'clock this morning this town was completely ruined by a severe earthquake, coming from south to north, and which continued in all its force more than a minute. The earth has been trembling all day, at intervals of a quarter of an hour, more or less, although not so severely. Only two or three houses remain in good condition, either of this locality, or on all of the neighboring haciendas; so that, the houses being fallen or completely ruinous, families have no other refuge than under arbors. It is the more lamentable because many will not, perhaps, be able to complete even ranchos in which to live, and the poor must continue in complete desolation. God preserve you, &c., &c.

To the INTENDENTE OF THE PROVINCE.

[From "El Araucano."]

SAN FELIPE, *April* 4, 1852.

SEÑOR MINISTRO: * * * In this department, and probably in all the others, there were no misfortunes or lamentable accidents, notwithstanding that the temblor experienced here at 6¾ A. M. lasted about the space of a minute, and shook the earth with an extraordinarily quick movement. Only the Matriz church of Los Andes, according to a communication from the governor, has had its walls thrown from the perpendicular, and the towers, with the entire edifice, which are cracked in all directions, threaten speedy and inevitable ruin. It has been ordered to be closed, and I have to-day sent detailed information to the minister (of worship), asking funds for pulling it down, &c., &c.

To the MINISTER OF THE INTERIOR.

[From "El Copiapino," Copiapó.]

EARTHQUAKE OF MAY 26, 1851.

EARTHQUAKE.—A great earthquake occurred yesterday at about quarter past one in the afternoon, and which still keeps the population alarmed. The misfortunes of which notice has reached us are various; houses, dividing-walls, and parapets thrown down, though there was no death, perhaps on account of the hour. There were, however, some wounds.

Other more severe earthquakes may have been felt in times past, though none so long, its duration being estimated at two minutes. In shops of every character there were shelves overthrown and glass or crockery broken; but the fright was greater than the reality. Perhaps from two to four thousand dollars have been lost on the whole.

It is generally believed that the shock came from the cordillera, because La Chimba has suffered less than the city; but this is more rationally explained by the distinct character of the soil. In the city, water is found at two varas. In La Chimba there are places where one is compelled to go to eighteen or twenty. The houses between the hills, others say, are those which have suffered most, which indicates motion in the same way. It was accompanied by a great noise, heard also at some of the lesser shocks, though every time more lightly.

The same paper of the 30th says:

After having written our article on Tuesday respecting the earthquake, Wednesday morning passed tranquilly, and alarm was beginning to disappear, when the return of slight shocks at night again created violent excitement. We believe that it is time for quiet again. The phenomenon was repeated yesterday (Thursday), but every time it was with less force; and it would be very remarkable if we should again experience what occurred at first. The last example at Valparaiso is a case in point, and there are an infinity of others it would be useless to mention. Great earthquakes almost always end so, ceasing as it were by degrees.

As to losses, some have been experienced, but it is not becoming to exaggerate them. We insist in saying that the crockery and glass ware broken in the stores will not exceed from two to four thousand dollars. If to this be added the injury to walls, fences, and houses it will be necessary to rebuild, we do not deny that the cost may amount to all that present wealth has gained over poverty of the past.

On the other hand, many of the adobe walls thrown down by the earthquake should have been down a year ago, and would have been if the decree specifying them as ruinous had been complied with.

[From "El Pueblo" of Copiapó, 27th May.]

At twenty minutes past one o'clock this afternoon we experienced an earthquake even more terrible than that of April 2d at Valparaiso. Its duration—a little more or less than two minutes—was accompanied by strong horizontal shocks from north to south. The population is still alarmed by the slighter tremors that have taken place from minute to minute up to eight o'clock at night, the hour at which we are writing. The destruction has been quite of moment. More than a dozen houses are entirely down, and there is not a single one which has not somewhat suffered. All the parapet and enclosing walls have come to the ground. In Calle del Commercio there is not a store which has not suffered considerable loss. The café de Meneli has been nearly all prostrated, as has a part of the interior of the apothecary's shop in the Calle del Commercio. Messrs. Langlie's crockery and glass-ware establishment has experienced no little loss, which has also occurred to Señor Gomez and the Señores Felin.

The fact of its taking place at noonday saved greater destruction. Meanwhile we recommend to the police, that, for the security of passers-by, they cause every ruinous wall to be pulled down. There are other details which we shall give in the next number. The earthquake was not preceded by any noise, and the day was clear and serene.

The same journal on the 28th says:

Between half-past one of the afternoon of the 26th and midnight of the 27th there were more than a hundred earthquakes; indeed, it may be said that we experienced a continuous though gentle oscillation, interrupted from time to time by strong shocks. * * * The atmosphere has continued clear, serene, and of an unexpected stillness.

It is feared that this earthquake came from the south, because it was felt with somewhat greater force at Chañarcillo and lighter at Tres Puntas, although in both mineral districts much damage has been done. By an express from Cerillos yesterday, we learned the destruction of the houses there. Although no one was killed, nor a single person wounded, very great injury was done in the houses used for mining purposes at Chañarcillo.

In the city, a crack opened in the earth about fifty yards long and a quarter of a vara wide, from which water issued. It was in La Vega, on the side next to the grave-yard. * * * *

It may be calculated that the injuries to houses, machinery, and in the mines, will amount to one hundred thousand dollars.

It is now half-past one o'clock, and forty-eight hours have passed by since the first terrible shock. The phenomenon has not yet ceased, there being tremors every ten minutes or so, some of them quite strong, and lasting eight or ten seconds. Anxiety and fright still prevail among the population. Last night the earth moved uninteruptedly. The people have passed two nights watching, and are filled with the greatest consternation.

We beg our subscribers will pardon us for omission of "El Pueblo" yesterday. It will be with difficulty if we manage to print it to-day, the earthquake not having disdained to stir up our establishment also.

On the 31st the same journal says:

We have arrived at the sixth day of the earth-storm, and still the shocks cease not. Last night and this morning we have had at least six, two or three of which were of some duration and violence. Nevertheless we are becoming familiarized with these curious caprices of creation, and the anxiety which governed the people during the first days is gradually disappearing. We are not aware of any injury occasioned since the 26th.

A letter which was published in the "Copiapino" of May 30, gives the following brief account:

PUERTO HUASCO, *May* 26, 1851.

At seven minutes past one this afternoon we experienced a very severe earthquake at this port, ruining various houses in lower Guasco, destroying the church, and throwing down in its transit all the "tapias" it encountered. After the principal shock there was seen, with great alarm, one of the phenomena observed only in a century, viz: the sea retired from the beach with incredible velocity for more than a hundred and fifty yards, the rush of the water being so impetuous that vessels in the bay dragged their anchors. Of a sudden it returned with great violence, in a wave more than ten feet higher than the highest tides, inundating the patio of the custom-house, and washing out the cargoes deposited there. Thanks to the promptitude and boldness of the peons working on the mole, everything was saved without much loss to the owners. The phenomenon could be observed about half a league out at sea, repeating itself many times at short intervals.

It is 8 o'clock at night, and the earthquakes still continue. They come from southwest and move to northeast, so that Copiapó will escape. The people of lower Guasco have gone to the hills, fearing a new sea wave.

MAY 27, 3 P. M.—The earthquakes still continue. In Ballanar* many houses have been ruined, and it is feared that the whole of its buildings will come to the ground at the first strong shock. The people there were all in such alarm that they were encamped outside of the houses. The atmosphere was clear; but last night about dark there was a dense fog with a very distinctly sulphurous odor.

Many people in lower Guasco say that the earth opened, and water came out abundantly. The earthquake lasted from a minute and a half to two minutes.

3 A. M.—The earthquakes continue, but not so frequently; the subterranean noise being uninterrupted and very loud. All the women are imploring the pity of God, and making vows to all the saints in heaven.

Yours, &c.

In a letter from Freirina, received by a gentleman at Santiago, the writer states that the shock was so violent, it was thought that the earth would open beneath their feet; and that

* Vallenar? If so, it is fifty miles E.S.E. of Huasco.

between half-past one of the 26th, when the great convulsion occurred, and eight o'clock of the morning of the 27th, no less than one hundred and twenty-seven earthquakes were numbered without embracing the multitude of noises when no tremors were felt. This condition of things continued at longer and longer intervals up to the 1st of June. He also states that there was a rain of ordinary character about twenty days before the earthquake; and "we think the year will be a very fine one, for the fields are already so green, and the pasturage has grown so rapidly, that the cattle are already eating it—a fact which somewhat consoles us in the midst of loss and other troubles."

INTENDENCIA OF ATACAMA.

COPIAPÓ, *June* 2, 1851.

SEÑOR MINISTRO: I write to make known to you that on the 26th of May last, at a quarter past 1 P. M. an earthquake was felt at this city, which, in the two minutes of its continuance, threatened to overwhelm the entire population. For forty years the people of Copiapó have not experienced so prolonged and terrifying a shock.

Although the phenomenon is repeated so frequently, the earthquake of the 26th threw the whole city into consternation; and as the shocks continued to the 1st instant at intervals of a few minutes, or at most quarters of an hour, the alarm has been still more augmented.

The damages caused are of some importance, although most of the houses are of wood, and all have been built to resist earthquakes. Six or eight have fallen, and many others are much injured. The little village of San Antonio, where there is a mine of the same name, is completely ruined: that of Juan Godoi, at the foot of the mines at Chañarcillo, has suffered considerably; and the houses belonging to the mines which have not fallen, threaten to do so.

As soon as the strength of the first disturbance ceased, a commission of two architects was named, who examined for dangerous buildings. The number which have been ordered to be pulled down in conformity with the report of this commission is twenty-five, without counting a great many whose repairs have been ordered.

The Matriz, Merced, and San Francisco churches have not suffered. Neither have the other public buildings—the theatre, City Hall, and jail. At the hospital and cemetery only some of the internal walls have fallen. The principal one of these edifices received no injury whatever. The earthquake was felt in the departments of Vallenar and Freirina at the same hour; but its damages were not so great, as you may judge from the original notes of the governors, which I have the honor to transmit.

I beg you will make known this deplorable event to his Excellency.

God preserve you.

JOSÉ B. QUEZADA.

To the MINISTER OF THE INTERIOR.

INTENDENCIA OF COQUIMBO.

SERENA, *June* 3, 1851.

SEÑOR MINISTRO: On the 26th of May last, at seventeen minutes past one in the afternoon, an earthquake was felt here which was so severe and prolonged that all the population were forced to rush into the streets and plazas. Its duration was about a minute and a half, and its direction was from north to south. No damage was occasioned here nor in any other department of the province. But such has not been the case in those of Atacama, especially in Freirina, where, according to notices received, there has been considerable injury, of which I advise your Excellency (U. S.)

God preserve you.

JUAN MELGAREJO.

To the MINISTER OF THE INTERIOR.

APPENDIX B.

METEOROLOGICAL OBSERVATIONS

IN THE

PROVINCE OF ATACAMA.

METEOROLOGICAL OBSERVATIONS

IN

THE PROVINCE OF ATACAMA.

Place.	Year, month and day.	Hour.	Barometer.	Thermometers. Attached.	Air.	Wet.	Wind.	Weather.	Remarks.
	1851.		*Inches.*	°	°	°			
Copiapó	July 1	Noon	28.625	60.8	72.2	53.7	W.N.W. 5	Clear	JULY 9.—At noon the temperature of water in a closed well, 14 feet deep, near the plaza, was 67°.7; the temperature of the air at the same time being 74°2.
		3 P. M.	.610	67.8	70.5	57.6	do 2	do	
		6 P. M.	.654	66.0	62.2	54.5	do 2	do	
		9 P. M.	.700	63.2	55.0	52.0	Calm	do	JULY 11, 5*h.* 15*m.* A. M.—Quite a severe earthquake. As near as could be distinguished, the wave moved from the northward, continuing unusually long. Some ten minutes afterward it was followed by a second shock much less violent. The first was almost without noise; but the second was preceded for a long interval by a sound not unlike the noise of wind in an open forest. There was another shock at 0*h.* 23*m.* P. M.
	2	9 A. M.	.680	58.0	65.1	53.1	W.N.W 2	do	
		Noon	.630	64.5	69.7	54.5	do	do	
		3 P. M.	.575	69.1	77.2	60.1	do	do	
		6 P. M.	.612	68.5	62.2	54.5	do	do	
		9 P. M.	.635	65.5	58.5	54.2	do 1	do	
		Midnight.	.650	61.0	53.2	49.2	do	do	
	3	9 A. M.	.670	59.3	64.6	53.5	Airs	C. 3	
	8	3 P. M.	.460	66.0	65.7	53.9	S.W. 3	C. 4	
		6 P. M.	.530	64.0	58.5	53 0	do 2	K. 4	At leaving Valparaiso the Aneroid barometer with which these observations were made was 0.01 inch lower than Mr. Mowatt's standard, and on returning there it was 0,175 lower. The change appears to have been caused by the jolting in going to the mines, and the observations after the 3d of July need a correction of + 0.176.
		Midnight.	.575	62.5	54.7	52.1	Airs	K. 8	
	9	9 A. M.	.570	60.0	55.3	49,3	Airs	Clear	
		6 P. M.	.500	65.0	55.7	49.5	East 2	C. S. 3	
		9 P. M.	.510	65.0	53.8	48.2	do	Clear	
		Midnight	.476	61.0	47.2	44.2	do	do	
	10	9 A. M.	.430	56.5	53.2	45.0	Northward 1	Clear	
		Noon	.400	62.8	71.6	53.0	W.S.W. 2	do	
		6 P. M.	.368	65.8	59.5	50.5	Northward 2	C. S. 3	
		Midnight.	.352	60.8	50.5	40.0	Airs	do 9	
	11	9 A. M.	.375	57.3	57.7	47.5	Eastward 1	Clear	
		Noon	.412	64.0	66.5	53.1	W.S.W. 6	do	
		3 P. M.	.420	66.8	65.0	54.7	do 3	do	
		6 P. M.	.450	65.0	57.3	51.2	East 3	do	
		Midnight.	.500	60.7	50.7	47.1	do 2	do	
Totoralillo	4	5 A. M.	27.800	50.0					
	7	8 P. M.	.760	61.0					
	8	7 A. M.	.750	59.2					A white frost on the roofs.
At foot of El Volaco	7	4 P. M.	26.610	63.0			3,294 feet above the ocean.		
At the mine La Candelaria, Chañarcillo.	4	Noon	.050	70.2	66.0	47.5			
		6 P. M.	.050	68.7	63.6	48.7			
		9 P. M.	.065	68.0	64.6	45.4			
	5	9 A. M.	.033	64.8	66.0	46.1			JULY 5.—There was a fall of snow last night on a mountain bearing 55° 15′ east of magnetic south.
		Noon	.042	66.7	65.0	46.1			
		6 P. M.	.055	68.2	61.6	46.7	S.E. 2		

Meteorological Observations—Continued.

Place.	Year, month and day.	Hour.	Barometer.	Thermometers. Attached.	Thermometers. Air.	Thermometers. Wet.	Wind.	Weather.	Remarks.
	1851.		*Inches.*	°	°	°			
At the mine La Candelaria, Chañarcillo.	July 5	9 P. M.	26.050	68.0	61.1	44.0	S.E. 2		
		Midnight	.020	66.0	59.5	45.0	do		
	6	9 A. M.	.020		63.6	47.2	S.E. airs		JULY 6.—Lunar halo. Valley entirely obscured by clouds.
		3 P. M.			63.0	50.0	Airs	C. 8	
		6 P. M.	.015	64.5	51.7	45.7			
		9 P. M.	.015	63.0	53.2	42.5			About 3,698 feet above the ocean.
	7	9 A. M.	25.974	60.0	57.5	43.5	Calm	C and K.	JULY 7.—Cumuli overhead, and a strata of clouds concealing the entire valley.
		Noon	.945	62.3	60.0		do		
Cuesta de Chañarcillo.	7	6 P. M.	.375	60.0			4,597 feet above the ocean		S.E. side at base.
			.140	59.0			4,850 do	do do	Highest point of the old road.
			.540	57.3			4,412 do	do do	N.W. side at the base.
Caldera	13	Noon	29.670	61.7	62.3	57.5	Northward 2	Clear	
		9 P. M.	.700	64.8	59.6	53.8	S.E. 1	K. S. 10	
		Midnight	.710	63.8	62.5	56.2	Northward 1	do	
	14	Noon	.750	67.0	66.0	58.6	Northward 2	K. 1	
		3 P. M.	.720	71.5			do		
		6 P. M.	.710	69.2	63.7	54.8	do	K. 4	
		9 P. M.	.720	66.8	55.1	51.7	do	K. and C. S. 8	
		Midnight	.700	63.7	53.6	49.2	do	do 5	
	15	9 A. M.	.720	59.0	59.2	54.5	East 2	K and C. S. 10	
		Noon	.750	62.8	61.5	58.5	N.N.W. 4	do 9	
		3 P. M.	.765	65.0	61.2	57.4	do	do 10	
		9 P. M.	.787	63.7	59.0	55.8	do	K. 5	
		Midnight	.790	64.5	58.5	56.1	do	K. 6	
	16	9 A. M.	.940	64.0	63.3	58.5	N.N.W. 4	K. 10	JULY 16.—At 9*h.* 30*m.* A. M., the wind shifted suddenly to S.W., and rain followed almost instantly.
		Noon	30.000	64.5	60.5	59.0	Northward 1	Mist	
		3 P. M.	29.980	65.8	63.5	60.0	Airs	K. and C. S. 10	The zodiacal light very bright until after 8 P. M.; the apex of the pyramid being between Jupiter and the constellation Hyd. et Crat.
		9 P. M.	.925	64.0	55.2	53.3	North 2	Clear	
		Midnight	.900	63.0	50.5	49.5	do 4	do	
	17	9 A. M.	.920	57.5	59.5	55.3	South 2	do	
		Noon	.920	63.0	62.0	57.0	do 4	C. 8	
		9 P. M.	.880	64.0	52.1	51.0	do 3	Clear	

SYMBOLS.

C, cirrus; K, cumuli; S, stratus.

0, calm; 1, light air; 10, strong gale.

0, clear; 10, entirely clouded over.

APPENDIX C.

METEOROLOGICAL OBSERVATIONS

BETWEEN

NEW YORK AND VALPARAISO, VIA PANAMA.

METEOROLOGICAL OBSERVATIONS

BETWEEN

NEW YORK AND VALPARAISO, VIA PANAMA.

Place.	Year, month and day.	Hour.	Barometer.	Thermometers.		Latitude at noon.	Longitude at noon.	Remarks.
				Att'd.	Air.			
	1849.		*Inches.*	°	°	° ′	° ′	
At sea . . .	Aug. 17	9 A. M.	30.127	76.0	76.3	37 59		Light westerly winds, cirro cumuli to north; barometer in state-room eight feet above sea-level.
		3 P. M.	.127	76.0	79.2			Almost calm; light cirri.
		9 P. M.	.156	81.0	81.3			
	18	9 A. M.	.102	78.8	79.4			Wind S.W., moderate; cumuli and cum. strat. 10.
		9 P. M.	.103	80.5	82.0	34 58	72 46	Calm; atmosphere steamy and wholly obscured; much gulf weed and flying-fish about the ship.
	19	9 A. M.	29.952	79.0	79.3			Wind S.W.; weather murky; heavy rain, thunder and lightning since 2 A. M.
		Noon .	.950	79.0		32 41	72 45	Wind fresh; clouds breaking to windward.
		9 P. M.	30.025	80.5				Wind strong; masses of flying cumuli.
	20	9 A. M.	.052	82.0	83.0			Wind S.; clear; flying-fish numerous.
		Noon .	.100	82.6	84.5	29 46	72 40	Wind S. and very light; cumuli to S.E.
		9 P. M.	.152	83.0	82.8			Wind S.S.E., fresh, with rain squalls.
	21	9 A. M.	.201	83.7	84.1			Wind S.S.E., light; cumuli floating from S.S.E.; the gulf weed in streams or lines.
		Noon .	.226	84.3	84.9	26 47	72 20	Wind S.S.E., light; cumuli floating.
		9 P. M.	.210	82.6	82.5			Trade winds; changed to east, and very light at 5 P. M.; now E N.E. and moderate.
	22	9 A. M.	.165	83.8	83.9			Wind moderate from east; masses of cumuli; no gulf weed.
		Noon .	.148	83.0	83.2	23 28	72 40	Wind fresh from east; masses of cumuli.
		9 P. M.	.125	83.0	83.3			Wind fresh from N.E.; dense masses of cumuli; lay to all night.
	23	9 A. M.	.063	83.3	82.9			Wind fresh from E.N.E.; dense masses of cumuli, with occasional showers of rain.
Off Inagua . .		Noon .	.037	82.5	82.3			Wind fresh from E.N.E.; no weed or fish near the ship.
		9 P. M.	.030	82.0	81.9			Wind fresh from E.N.E.; cumulo stratus; frequent lightning over the land.
	24	9 A. M.	29.980	83.3	84.2			Wind very light from E.N.E.; a few cirro cumuli; the water quite green.
Off Cape Tiburon		9 P. M.	.827	83.2	82.6			Wind very light from E.N.E.; a few cirro cumuli.
	25	9 A. M.	.910	83.8	83.9			Wind moderate from east, and trade clouds visible.
		11 P. M.	.878	83.8	82.6	15 38	76 10	Wind moderate from E.N E.; trade clouds; frequent showers.
	26	9 A. M.	.905	83.0	83.6			Wind moderate from E.N.E.; occasional patches of weed; westerly current one mile per hour.
		9 P. M.	.860	82.8	82.2	12 46	78 12	Wind moderate from E.N.E.
	27	9 A. M.	.862	83.8	82.8			Very light airs from S.E.; weather variable; clouds and showers.
60 miles north of Chagres.		3 P. M.	29.850	79.8	80.5			Very light airs from S.E.; weather variable; anchored at Chagres at 9 P. M.

Meteorological Observations—Continued.

Place.	Year, month and day.	Hour.	Barometer.	Thermometers.		Wind.		Remarks.
				Att'd.	Air.	Direction.	Force.	
	1849.		*Inches.*	°	°			
At Panama	Aug. 31	3 P. M.	29.778	81.0	82.2	W. by N.	Airs	Cumuli about the horizon and overhead; barometer 50 feet above low water mark.
	Sept. 1	9 A. M.	.862	79.3	80.5	West	do	Clear to the eastward.
		3 P. M.	.728	78.5	78.8	W.N.W.	do	Cir. strat. and cum. 10.
		9 P. M.	.740	78.8	78.3	Variable	do	Dense cumuli to north, and light cir. strat. to east.
	2	9 A. M.	.778	78.1	78.8	W.N.W.	do	Cum. strat. 10.
		3 P. M.	.750	80.0	80.5	do	Light	Dense cum. E.N.E.; cir. strat. overhead; cum. strat. from west to south.
		9 P. M.	.840	78.0	78.0	N.W. by W.	Moderate	Cirri about horizon; clear overhead; misty rain at 1 P. M.
	3	9 A. M.	.870	79.5	79.5	do	Light	Cumuli about western horizon.
		3 P. M.	.772	81.3	81.5	do	do	Cumuli 7.
		9 P. M.	.860	78.8	78.7	do	Moderate	Light cirri.
	4	9 A. M.	.870	77.3	78.5	Calm		Heavy cum. strat. 10.
		3 P. M.	.762	81.7	82.3	W.N.W.	Airs	Cum. strat. 10; light rain from 11 A. M. to 12¼ P. M.
		9 P. M.	.840	80.0	79.6	Calm		Cum. and cir. strat. 10.
	5	9 A. M.	.852	78.7	79.5	Variable	Airs	Cum. and cum. strat. 10.
		3 P. M.	.734	81.3	81.6	W.N.W.	Moderate	Masses of cumuli 9; rain from 2*h.* to 2*h.* 45*m.* P. M.
		9 P. M.	.810	7c.5	78.2	N.W.	Light	Light cirri about horizon.
	6	9 A. M.	.800	78.0	79.4	N.W. by W.	Moderate	Cumuli.
		3 P. M.	.718	82.8	33.0	Variable	Airs	Cum. and cum. strat. 10.; barometer 40 feet above low water mark.
		9 P. M.	.775	80.0	81.2	N. by W.	Light	Clear except a few cirrus clouds about south horizon.
	7	9 A. M.	.802	81.9	81.9	N.W.	do	Cumuli 7.
		3 P. M.	.750	79.0	79.7	do	do	Raining moderately since 2*h.* 15*m.* P. M.; heavy thunder and lightning to N.W. since 9 A. M.
		9 P. M.	.800	77.8	78.7	do	do	Cir. strat. about horizon; rain ceased at 4*h.* 30*m.* P. M.
	8	9 A. M.	.750	79.4	79.7	do	do	Cum. strat. to S.E.; cum. about horizon; cir. cum. overhead.
		3 P. M.	.762	82.5	82.5	Northward	Airs	Dense cum. from W. to N.E.; cir. cum. overhead.
		9 P. M.	.832	78.6	79.5	W.N.W.	Light	Cir. strat. about horizon; summer lightning to N.W.
	9	9 A. M.	.878	80.2	80.4	N.W. by W.	Moderate	Cum. and cir. cum. 3.
		3 P. M.	.787	82.0	82.2	do	do	Cum. and cum. strat. 7.
		9 P. M.	.725	80.0	80.6	do	Light	Cum. strat. to westward; moderate rain from 5*h.* 45*m.* to 7*h.* 30*m.* P. M., with thunder and lightning.
	10	9 A. M.	.888	80.0	80.3	N'd and W'd	do	Misty rain; sky completely obscured.
		3 P. M.	.740	81.0	81.4	S'd and E'd	Airs	Cir. cum. and cir. strat. 7; rain ceased at 11 A. M.
		9 P. M.	.725	79.3	80.1	N'd and W'd	do	Cir. strat. 3.
	11	9 A. M.	.810	80.4	80.8	S'd and E'd	do	Cum. to westward; cum. strat. to eastward; clear above.
		3 P. M.	.762	83.2	83.2	S'd and W'd	Light	Dense cum. and cum. strat. to westward.
		9 P. M.	.810	80.8	81.3	N'd and W'd	Airs	Cir. strat. to eastward; clear elsewhere.
	12	9 A. M.	.840	82.1	82.5	E S.E.	Moderate	Cum. about horizon; light cirri overhead.
		3 P. M.	.725	84.0	84.3	S.E. by S.	do	Do do do.
		9 P. M.	.800	81.6	82.1	Variable	Airs	Do do do.
	13	9 A. M.	.858	81.6	82.1	Southward	do	Cum. and cir. strat. about horizon; clear overhead.
		3 P. M.	.750	85.2	85.3	S.S E.	Light	Cum. strat. 8.
		9 P. M.	.800	80.8	81.4	N.W.	do	Perfectly clear.
	14	9 A. M.	.834	82.6	82.7	Southward	Airs	Light cumuli near horizon.
		3 P. M.	.840	86.0	86.0	N.W.	Light	Dense cum. strat. 8; thermom. in sun at 2 P. M. 118°.
		9 P. M.	.818	82.0	83.7	do	do	Heavy cumuli to south; light rain from 5 to 6 P. M.
	15	9 A. M.	.822	82.7	83.1	Variable	Airs	Cir. strat. 8.
		3 P. M.	.725	85.7	85.7	Westward	do	Cum. and cum. strat. 10.
		9 P. M.	.790	82.5	83.1	N.W.	Light	Cir. strat. 4; thunder and lightning to north.
	16	9 A. M.	.848	82.0	82.5	Variable	Airs	Cir. cum. and cir. strat. 8.
		3 P. M.	.740	84.2	84.7	N'd and W'd	do	Cir. cum. and cum. strat. 8; thunder and lightning.
		9 P. M.	.810	81.5	82.2	do	do	Cir. strat. 3.
	17	9 A. M.	.832	82.6	83.2	do	do	Do 7.
		3 P. M.	.750	85.6	86.1	do	Light	Cum. strat. 8; light shower.
		9 P. M.	.825	81.9	82.3	do	do	Do 10; thunder and lightning during night.
	18	9 A. M.	.838	83.3	83.7	do	Airs	Cir. strat. 6.
		3 P. M.	.768	85.0	85.3	S.E.	Moderate	Heavy rain, with thunder and lightning since 2½ P. M.
		9 P. M.	.824	82.0	82.7	N'd and W'd	Airs	Cir. strat. about horizon; clear overhead.
	19	9 A. M.	29.828	80.8	81.3	Eastward	Light	Entirely overcast; heavy rain, thunder and lightning at 8.

Meteorological Observations—Continued.

Place.	Year, month and day.	Hour.	Barometer.	Thermometers.		Wind.		Remarks.
				Att'd.	Air.	Direction.	Force.	
	1849.		*Inches.*	°	°			
At Panama . .	Sept. 19	3 P. M.	29.735	85.4	85.6	N'd and W'd .	Moderate .	Cum. strat. 9; thunder to northward.
		3 P. M.	.795	78.2	74.7	do .	do .	Entirely obscured; lightning to southward; a very heavy rain, with thunder and lightning from 4*h*. to 5*h*. 15*m*.
	20	9 A. M.	.820	81.2	81.6	Northward .	Airs . .	Entirely overcast.
		3 P. M.	.725	80.0	81.0	do .	do . .	Cum. and cum. strat. 8.
		9 P. M.	.798	80.0	80.2	N.W. . . .	Moderate .	Do do 8.
	21	9 A. M.	.738	80.3	80.6	N'd and W'd .	Light . .	Cum. and cir. strat. 9.
		3 P. M.	.750	82.0	82.3	do .	do . .	Cum. strat. 10; heavy rain from 2¼ to 2¾ P. M.
		9 P. M.	.810	81.1	80.8	do .	Airs . .	Do 10; thunder and lightning.
	22	9 A. M.	.898	80.8	81.2	do .	Light . .	Cum. and cum. strat. 10; rain last night.
		3 P. M.	.780	81.0	81.6	do .	do . .	Do do 10; showery.
		9 P. M.	.875	78.4	79.5	do .	Moderate .	Cir. strat. 7.
	23	9 A. M.	.898	78.5	79.0	do .	do .	Cumuli and cirri 3.
		3 P. M.	.720	82.8	82.8	do .	do .	Do 9; heavy thunder and lightning.
		9 P. M.	.780	80.0	81.0	do .	Light . .	Light cirri 5; a lunar halo.
	24	9 A. M.	.900	81.9	81.8	do .	Moderate .	Cum. and cum. strat. 8.
		3 P. M.	.805	83.3	83.3	W.N.W. . .	Light . .	Do do 10.
		9 P. M.	.837	78.7	79.8	N.W. . . .	do . .	Cir. strat. 10.
	25	9 A. M.	.725	80.2	80.4	do . . .	Moderate .	Cumuli and cir. strat. 6.
		3 P. M.	.762	79.0	80.2	do . . .	Light . .	Rain since 1½, with heavy thunder and lightning.
		9 P. M.						Showers all the evening.
	26	9 A. M.	.737	80.7	81.0	do . . .	Moderate .	Cum. and cum. strat. 7.
		3 P. M.	.737	80.5	80.8	do . . .	do .	Do do 10.
		9 P. M.	.790	79.8	80.2	N.N.W. . .	Airs . .	Cir. and cir. strat. 5.
	27	9 A. M.	.825	80.0	81.3	N.W. . . .	Light . .	Cum. and cir. strat. 8. Embarked on board the steamer New Grenada.
At sea . . .		3 P. M.	.746	85.8	84.7	Variable . .	Airs . .	Cum. and cum. strat. 9. Standing down Bay of Panama.
		9 P. M.	.837	81.8	81.4	Eastward . .	Light . .	Cir. strat. 10. Heavy rain, with lightning during night.
	28	9 A. M.	.874	80.8	80.8	Calm . . .		Cir. and cir. cum. 7.
		3 P. M.	.773	83.0	83.1	S.W. . . .	do . .	Cir. cum. 4. Lat at noon 6° 26′ N.; land 40 miles distant.
		9 P. M.	.780	82.0	82.1	do . . .	do . .	Do 8.
	29	9 A. M.	.937	78.4	78.3	S.S.W. . .	Moderate .	Rain. Has rained very heavy since 2 A. M. Average speed of steamer 8 miles per hour.
		3 P. M.	.780	80.0	81.0	S.S.E. . . .	Light . .	Cum. and cum. strat. 8. At noon mouth of Buenaventura river bore S.E., distant 20 miles.
		9 P. M.	.890	80.4	80.7	South . . .	Moderate .	Rain; continued till midnight.
	30	9 A. M.	.888	78.0	78.5	S.W. . . .	do .	Cum. strat.; rain just ceased.
		3 P. M.	.778	79.9	80.2	S.S.W. . .	do .	Cum. strat. 10. Passed the island of Gorgona at noon.
		9 P. M.	.890	80.0	79.8	do . .	Light . .	Do 10.
	Oct. 1	9 A. M.	.944	78.7	79.2	do . .	do . .	Cum. and cum. strat. 9.
		3 P. M.	.825	78.3	79.5	do . .	do . .	Cum. and cum. strat. 10. Lat. at noon 1° N., 30 miles from land.
		9 P. M.	.950	76.3	76.4	do . .	Moderate .	Cum. and cum. strat. 8. Black-fish (grampus) and flying-fish numerous.
	2	9 A. M.	30.012	76.2	75.9	South . . .	Light . .	Cum. and cum. strat. 1.
		3 P. M.	29.887	74.7	74.9	S.S.W. . .	do . .	Cir cum. overhead; cir. strat. near horizon. At noon off Cape San Lorenzo, one mile distant.
		9 P. M.	30.010	72.8	71.5	S W. . . .	do . .	Cir. cum. overhead. No rain since night before last.
	3	9 A. M.	.014	74.0	74.0	Airs . . .	Variable .	Cum. and cum. strat. 9. Standing up Gulf of Guayaquil.
		3 P. M.	29.846	79.3	80.1	East . . .	Airs . .	Cir. cum. and cum. strat. 8. Standing down Gulf of Guayaquil.
		9 P. M.	30.024	74.0	73.3	S.W. . . .	Moderate .	Cum. and cir. strat. about horizon.
	4	9 A. M.	29.987	69.5	69.5	do . . .	do .	Cum. and cir. strat. 10. Off Cape Blanco.
		3 P. M.	.882	67.0	65.5	do . . .	do .	Cir. strat. about horizon; clear overhead.
Payta		10 P. M.	30.010	68.0	67.3	S.S.E. . . .	Light . .	Cir. strat. about horizon; clear overhead. Anchored at Payta.
	5	9 A. M.	29.987	67.8	68.3	do . . .	do . .	Cir. strat. and cum. 10.
At sea . . .		3 P. M.	.820	71.8	72.0	S.W. . . .	Moderate .	Cir. strat. and cum. Standing out from Payta.
		9 P. M.	.924	65.3	64.0	do . . .	do .	Clear.
	6	9 A. M.	.975	65.0	64.7	do . . .	Light . .	Cir. strat. 10.
		3 P. M.	830	66.0	67.2	do . . .	Airs . .	Do 5. At anchor off Lambayeque.
		9 P. M.	.940	65.0	63.5	do . . .	Light . .	Do 10.
	7	9 A. M.	29.987	65.0	64.6	S.E. . . .	do .	Do 9. Standing in for Huanchaco.

Meteorological Observations—Continued.

Place.	Year, month and day.	Hour.	Barometer.	Thermometers.		Wind.		Remarks.
				Att'd.	Air.	Direction.	Force.	
	1849.		*Inches*	°	°			
At sea . .	Oct. 7	3 P. M.	29.875	66.8	67.5	S.E. . . .	Moderate .	Cir. cum. 3. Standing out from Huanchacho.
		9 P. M.	.950	64.0	62.4	S.S.E. . . .	do .	Cum. strat. 9.
	8	9 A. M.	.988	65.4	66.2	S.E. by S. .	Airs . .	Cum. and cir. strat. 10. Off Alligata head.
		3 P. M.	.882	65.8	66.7	do . .	Moderate .	Cir. cum. 4.
		9 P. M.	.950	64.7	64.2	do . .	Light . .	Cum. and cir. strat. 8.
	9	9 A. M.	.970	65.0	65.0	S'd and E'd .	Airs . .	Cir. strat. 10. At anchor, Callao bay.
Lima		9 P. M.	.375	68.0	68.4	Airs . . .	do . .	Barometer 20 feet above the plaza; misty.
	10	9 A. M.	.390	69.0	70.4	do . . .	do . .	Foggy mist.
		3 P. M.	.312	70.7	72.2	do . . .	do . .	Cumuli 10.
		9 P. M.	.375	71.7	73.3	S'd and E'd .	Light . .	Cum. strat. 10.
	11	9 A. M.	.378	70.0	71.2	Airs . . .	Airs . .	Cum. and cir. strat. 10.
		3 P. M.	.308	72.2	73.7	SW. . . .	do . .	Do do.
		9 P. M.	.374	71.7	72.8	do . . .	do . .	Do do.
	12	9 A. M.	.278	71.5	73.0	Southward .	do . .	Cir. strat. 10.
		3 P. M.	.310	73.4	74.2	S.W. . . .	do . .	Cirrus, 5.
		9 P. M.	.410	69.8	71.2	do . . .	do . .	Cir. strat. 10.
	13	9 A. M.	.396	70.3	71.5	do . . .	Light . .	Do.
		3 P. M.	.308	70.5	71.8	do . . .	do . .	Do.
		9 P. M.	.375	69.8	70.8	do . . .	do . .	Do.
	14	9 A. M.	.408	71.2	73.1	do . . .	do . .	Do.
At sea . . .		3 P. M.	.904	67.5	68.7	do . . .	Moderate .	Cir. strat. Going out from Callao bay.
		9 P. M.	.975	63.5	64.1	do . . .	do	Clear overhead; cir. strat. over land, with lightning.
	15	9 A. M.	.975	65.8	66.1	do . . .	Airs . .	Cumuli and cum. strat. At anchor, Pisco.
		3 P. M.	.872	63.6	63.4	S.E. . . .	Fresh . .	Cirrus 1.
		9 P. M.	.984	65.0	63.0	do . . .	Moderate .	Clear.
	16	9 A. M.	.962	64.5	64.0	S.S.E. . . .	Fresh . .	Cumuli and cum. strat. 8.
		3 P. M.	.848	62.4	62.3	S.E. . . .	do . .	Cumuli and cir. strat. 5. Off Lomas point.
		9 P. M.	.917	61.7	62.0	do . . .	Moderate .	Cum. strat. 10.
	17	9 A. M.	.906	63.5	63.2	S'd and E'd .	Airs . .	Cum. strat. 10. Off Ocoña.
		3 P. M.	.870	65.2	65.5	S.S.W. . .	do . .	Cum. strat. 18 miles W.N.W. Yslay.
		9 P. M.	.940	62.0	62.8	S'd and E'd .	do . .	Cir. strat. 10. At anchor, Yslay.
	18	9 A. M.	.908	65.0	64.5	S.E. . . .	Light . .	Cum. strat. 10. Yslay.
		3 P. M.	.932	65.5	65.8	do . . .	do . .	Mist; at sea.
		9 P. M.	.984	63.2	63.2	do . . .	Moderate .	Cum. strat. 9.
	19	9 A. M.	.962	65.8	65.0	S'd and E'd .	Light .	Cum and cir. cum. 8. Off Arica.
		3 P. M.	.898	66.8	67.8	S.E. . . .	Moderate .	Cir. cum. 3; Arica. Left at 3¼ P. M.
		9 P. M.	.998	62.5	63.5	Calm . . .		Clear. Sea very phosphorescent.
	20	9 A. M.	.987	65.0	64.7	S.S.W. . .	Airs . .	Cir. strat. and cum. strat. 10. Iquique.
		3 P. M.	.912	65.5	65.5	S.E. . . .	do . .	Do do 9. Left Iquique at 1¼.
		9 P. M.	.937	62.1	62.9	Calm . . .		Clear, except a cir. strat. bank over S.W. horizon.
	21	9 A. M.	.912	62.8	63.0	Southward .	Light . .	Cir. strat. and cum. strat. 10. Just off Cobija.
		3 P. M.	.898	65.4	66.4	do. . . .	Airs . .	Clear; just north of Morro de Mexillones.
		9 P. M.	.962	62.5	62.7	do . . .	do .	Cir. strat. and cum. strat. 10.
	22	9 A. M.	30.006	62.2	62.6	S.S.W. . .	do . .	Cir. strat. and cum. strat. 9. Off Paposo.
		3 P. M.	29.962	64.5	65.5	do . . .	do . .	Cumuli 1.
		9 P. M.	.978	66.2	61.4	South . . .	Light .	Cum. strat. 10.
	23	9 A. M.	30.037	61.5	61.7	S.S.W. . .	Airs . .	Cum. and cir. strat. 10. Anchored at Copiapó at 8 A. M.
		3 P. M.	29.968	62.2	63.0	do . . .	Moderate .	Cum. strat. 7. Left Copiapó at 11 A. M.
		9 P. M.	.988	60.5	60.2	do . . .	Airs . .	Do 10. At anchor at Huasco.
	24	9 A. M.	30.090	60.5	60.5	do . . .	do . .	Cir. strat. and cum. strat. 10. Off Pajaros islands.
		3 P. M.	.050	63.5	64.1	do . . .	do . .	Do do 9. South of Herradura 8 miles.
		9 P. M.	.048	61.0	58.5	do . . .	Light . .	Do do 10.
	25	9 A. M.	.070	60.3	60.2	Calm . . .		Do do 10. Off Vallenar.
		3 P. M.	30.050	61.5	62.0	S.S.W. . .	Airs . .	Do do 10. Valparaiso.
	1852.							
Between Cobija and the Bay of Panama.	Oct. 5	9 A. M.	30.070		64.5	Southward .	Airs . .	Cirrus and cumuli 9.
		3 P. M.	.000		65.8	S.W. . . .	Moderate .	Cirrus 3. Just north of Cobija.
		9 P. M.	.100			Eastward . .	Airs . .	Do 4. Just south of Iquique.
	6	9 A. M.	.065		69.1	S.W. by S. .	do . .	Cir. strat. 10. 30 miles south of Arica.
		3 P. M.	29.960		66.5	do .	do . .	Clea. At anchor at Arica.

Meteorological Observations—Continued.

Place.	Year, month and day.	Hour.	Barometer.	Thermometers.		Wind.		Remarks.
				Att'd.	Air.	Direction.	Force.	
	1852.		*Inches.*	°	°			
Between Cobija and the Bay of Panama.	Oct. 6	9 P. M.	30.110		65.7	S.W. . . .	Moderate .	Cir. strat. 10. 30 miles north of Arica.
	7	9 A. M.	.060		66.0	W.S.W. . .	Light . .	Cumuli 7. Islay.
		3 P. M.	29.975		67.0	do . .	do . .	Do 10. Islay.
		9 P. M.	30.020		65.4	S.W. . . .	Moderate .	Cum. strat. 10. At sea.
	8	9 A. M.	29.980		66.2	South . . .	do .	Cumuli 5. Lat. 16° south.
		3 P. M.	.870		61.0	S.S.W. . .	Fresh . .	Cir. strat. 1. Around horizon only.
		9 P. M.	.960		61.5	South . . .	do . .	Clear. Independence bay.
	9	9 A. M.	30.000		64.6	S.W. . . .	Light . .	Cum. strat. and cir. strat. 10. 18 miles north of Pisco.
		3 P. M.	29.950		64.6	do . . .	do . .	Do do 9. 20 miles south of Callao.
	10	9 A. M.	.910		69.5	Calm . . .		Do do 10. Callao.
	12	9 P. M.	.862		67.3	South . .	Moderate .	Cum. and cum. strat. 9. Left Callao at 6½ P. M.
	13	9 A. M.	.860		66.9	do . . .	do .	Do do 10.
		3 P. M.	.890		67.8	do . . .	do .	Do do 10.
		9 P. M.	.950		66.5	do . . .	do .	Do do 10. Off Lobos islands.
	14	9 A. M.	.950		67.1	S.S.W. . .	Light . .	Do do 8. Left Lobos at 0*h*. 30*m*. P. M.
		3 P. M.	.875		68.5	do . .	do . .	Do do 8.
		9 P. M.	.950		67.7	do . .	do . .	
	15	9 A. M.	.975		67.7	S.E. . . .	do . .	Cirrus 8. At anchor, Payta.
		3 P. M.	.837		66.7	S.S.W. . .	Fresh . .	Clear. Left Payta at 1 P. M.
		9 P. M.	.875		70.8	do . .	do . .	Do.
	16	9 A. M.	.960		73.2	South . .	Moderate .	Cum. and cum. strat. 10.
		3 P. M.	.820		76.1	do . . .	Light . .	Do do 10. East of Isla de la Plata.
		9 P. M.	.900		77.2	do . . .	do . .	Do do 10.
	17	9 A. M.	.875		80.2	do . . .	Moderate .	Do do 9. Lat. 1° 01′ N.; rain showers frequent.
		3 P. M.	.750		82.3	S.W. . . .	Fresh . .	Do do 7. Lat. 1° 50′ N.
		9 P. M.	.805		82.2	S.W. by W. .	do . .	Cumuli 1.
	18	9 A. M.	.870		84.2	S.S.W. . .	do . .	Cum. and cum. strat. 10.
		3 P. M.	.712		82.5	South . . .	Moderate .	Do do 9. Lat. at noon 5° 30′ N.
		9 P. M.	.770		81.0	West . . .	do .	Do do 10.
	19	9 A. M.	29.770		89.7	do . . .	do .	Do do 6. Bay of Panama.

INDEX.

D.

E.

N.

O.

P.

www.ingramcontent.com/pod-product-compliance
Lightning Source LLC
LaVergne TN
LVHW021218110826
845150LV00002B/198